GUNFIGHTER NATION

Books by Richard Slotkin

FICTION

The Return of Henry Starr (1988)

The Crater (1980)

NONFICTION

Gunfighter Nation: The Myth of the Frontier in 20th-Century America (1992)

The Fatal Environment: The Myth of the Frontier in the Age of Industrialization, 1800–1890 (1985)

So Dreadfull a Judgment: Puritan Responses to King Philip's War, 1675–1677 (with James K. Folsom; 1978)

Regeneration Through Violence: The Mythology of the American Frontier 1600–1860 (1973)

GUNFIGHTER NATION

The Myth of the Frontier in Twentieth-Century America

RICHARD SLOTKIN

HarperPerennial
A Division of HarperCollins*Publishers*

A hardcover edition of this book was published in 1992 by Atheneum, a division of Macmillan Publishing Company. It is reprinted by arrangement with Macmillan Publishing Company.

First HarperPerennial edition published 1993.

Designed by Jennifer Dossin

Library of Congress Cataloging-in-Publication Data

Slotkin, Richard, 1942–
Gunfighter nation : the myth of the frontier in twentieth-century America / Richard Slotkin.
p. cm.
Includes bibliographical reference and index.
ISBN 0-06-097575-X (pbk.)
1. Popular culture—United States—History—20th century. 2. Frontier and pioneer life—United States. 3. Frontier thesis. I. Title.
E169.12.S57 1992b
973.9 — dc20 93-14220

---

93 94 95 96 97 CW 10 9 8 7 6 5 4 3 2 1

Democratic nations care but little for what has been, but they are haunted by visions of what will be; in this direction their unbounded imagination grows and dilates beyond all measure. . . . Their eyes are fixed upon . . . [their] own march across these wilds, draining swamps, turning the course of rivers, peopling solitudes, and subduing nature. This magnificent image of themselves does not meet the gaze of Americans at intervals only; it may be said to haunt every one of them in his least as well as his most important actions and to be always flitting before his mind.

ALEXIS DE TOCQUEVILLE
Democracy in America (1835)

You couldn't find two people who agreed about when it began, how could you say when it began going off? . . . Anyway, you couldn't use standard methods to date the doom; might as well say that Vietnam was where the Trail of Tears was headed all along, the turnaround point where it would touch and come back to form a containing perimeter . . . .

MICHAEL HERR
Dispatches

It's time to see the frontiers as they
are, Fiction, but a fiction meaning
blood . . .

JOHN BERRYMAN
"The Dangerous Year" (1942)

Acknowledgments

I began researching this book more than twenty years ago, and over the years have benefited from the advice and criticism of more colleagues, friends, and students than I can readily list. I want particularly to thank the Trustees of Wesleyan University, and former President Colin G. Campbell, for their consistent support of my research through the university's sabbatical and research grant programs; and for helping to create and maintain an academic environment in which undergraduate teaching and research are mutually reinforcing. Parts of this study were completed with the aid of grants from the Rockefeller Foundation and a Summer Stipend from the National Endowment for the Humanities. Thanks also to Jim Belson, who invited me to participate in the NEH Symposium on "The Western" at Sun Valley, 1976.

I am indebted, in ways that footnotes don't quite cover, to the ideas and suggestions of: Jeanine Basinger, Sacvan Bercovitch, Hazel Carby, Mark Cooper, Michael Denning, Eric Greene, Joan Hedrick, David Konstan, Lary May, Richard Ohmann, Robert O'Meally, Joseph Reed, Michael Rogin, Mark Slobin, William Stowe, Alan Trachtenberg, Elizabeth Traube, Duffield White and Christina Zwarg. I am grateful to Iris Slotkin for the understanding and support she has given me, for *years* of good conversation about the ideas in this book, and for introducing me to "systems" theories of psychological, familial, and social interaction. Thanks also to Joel Slotkin, for helping with the bibliography and setting up my computer.

Contents

Part II: Populists and Progressives: Literary Myth and Ideological Style, 1872–1940

Part III: Colonizing a Mythic Landscape: Movie Westerns, 1903–1948

Part V: Gunfighter Nation: Myth, Ideology, and Violence on the New Frontier, 1960–1970

Introduction

The Significance of the Frontier Myth in American History

On July 16, 1960, John F. Kennedy came to the podium of the Los Angeles Coliseum to accept the Democratic Party's nomination as candidate for President. It was a tradition of American political oratory that the acceptance speech provide a phrase or slogan that would define the themes of the upcoming campaign and mark them with the candidate's personal signature—an indication of the style of thought and action that would characterize the future administration. A successful performance on this occasion was particularly important for Kennedy, for despite his personal appeal and strong performance in the primaries his candidacy had several apparent liabilities: his youth and lack of executive experience, his Roman Catholic religion; the internal divisions of his party, exacerbated by his hard-nosed primary campaigns; and above all his need to challenge an incumbent administration headed by Dwight Eisenhower, one of the most popular Presidents in the nation's history.

Franklin Roosevelt had ended a dozen years of Republican incumbency by demanding "a New Deal for the American People," while Truman had won against the odds in 1948 by echoing that slogan in his call for a "Fair Deal." But these venerated party cries had succeeded under a set of political circumstances that no longer existed, and they symbolized a commitment to social and economic reform that Kennedy did not share. They had won broad public acceptance during two decades of extraordinary crisis that began with the Great Depression, culminated in a World War, and ended with the beginning of the Cold War against "world Communism."

Kennedy and his advisers believed that eight years of "stagnation" under Eisenhower had indeed created a crisis in American affairs, but one whose effects were potential rather than immediate. They believed that the administration's conservatism had prevented its making full and effective use of the economic and military power that the federal government had acquired through the New Deal and wartime mobilizations. In this default of action the economy had failed to realize its potential, and Communism had been able to make significant gains in the Third World. Unless checked by a revival of American economic and political dynamism, these trends pointed to a weakening of the nation's ability to sustain its Great Power role. But to make this case against the Eisenhower administration Kennedy would have to engage the public in an unusually sophisticated response to political events, based on an appreciation of threats to peace and prosperity that had not yet become palpable.[1]

The signature Kennedy and his advisers settled on was "The New Frontier." The choice seems an odd one for a candidate identified with the culture, politics, and ideological concerns of the urban centers of the eastern seaboard. Wild West metaphors invoked traditions that seem better suited to Eisenhower, known as a fan of pulp Westerns, and to the Republican Party, which identified itself with the "rugged individualism" associated with the Frontier. Yet Kennedy was able to make "New Frontier" seem an appropriate and credible way of describing the spirit of his campaign and the style of the administration that followed it.

On that first night, Kennedy asked his audience to see him as a new kind of frontiersman confronting a different sort of wilderness:

> I stand tonight facing west on what was once the last frontier. From the lands that stretch 3000 miles behind me, the pioneers of old gave up their safety, their comfort and sometimes their lives to build a new world here in the West. . . . [But] the problems are not all solved and the battles are not all won, and we stand today on the edge of a new frontier—the frontier of the 1960s, a frontier of unknown opportunities and paths, a frontier of unfulfilled hopes and threats. . . . For the harsh facts of the matter are that we stand on this frontier at a turning point in history.[2]

Kennedy's use of "New Frontier" tapped a vein of latent ideological power. While he and his advisers could not have predicted just how effective the symbolism would be, they certainly understood that they were invoking what was a venerable tradition in American political rhetoric. They knew from their own experience of American culture that figures of speech referring to this tradition would be intelligible to the widest possible audience—to Brooklyn and Cambridge as well as Abilene and Los Angeles. They had grounds for knowing—or at least intuiting—that this set of symbols was also an appropriate language for explaining and justifying the use of political power.

The exchange of an old, domestic, agrarian frontier for a new frontier of world power and industrial development had been a central trope in American political and historiographical debates since the 1890s. Sixty-seven years (almost to the day) before Kennedy's address, Frederick Jackson Turner had delivered his epoch-making address on "The Significance of the Frontier in American History," in which he asserted that the contemporary crisis of American development had arisen from the closing of the "old frontier" and the delay in finding a new one. His "Frontier Thesis" would become the basis of the dominant school of American historical interpretation and would provide the historiographic rationale for the ideologies of both Republican progressives and Democratic liberals for much of the ensuing century.

For Kennedy and his advisers, the choice of the Frontier as symbol was not simply a device for trade-marking the candidate. It was an authentic metaphor, descriptive of the way in which they hoped to use political power and the kinds of struggle in which they wished to engage. The "Frontier" was for them a complexly resonant symbol, a vivid and memorable set of hero-tales—each a model of successful and morally justifying action on the stage of historical conflict.

Those who were persuaded to identify with Kennedy's heroic political scenario found that it entailed more than simple affiliation with the campaign or the administration. Its central purpose was to summon the nation as a whole to undertake (or at least support) a *heroic* engagement in the "long twilight struggle" against Communism and the social and economic injustices that foster it. The symbolism of a "New Frontier" set the terms in which the administration would seek public consent to and participation in its counterinsurgency "mission" in Southeast Asia and the Caribbean. And it shaped the language through which the resultant wars would be understood by those who commanded and fought them. Seven years after Kennedy's nomination, American troops would be describing Vietnam as "Indian country" and search-and-destroy missions as a game of "Cowboys and Indians"; and Kennedy's ambassador to Vietnam would justify a massive military escalation by citing the necessity of moving the "Indians" away from the "fort" so that the "settlers" could plant "corn."[3] But the provenance and utility of the Frontier symbol did not end with the Kennedy/Johnson administrations: twenty years after Kennedy's acceptance speech the same symbolism—expressed in talismanic invocations of the images of movie-cowboys John Wayne and Clint Eastwood—would serve the successful campaigns of a Republican arch-conservative and former Hollywood actor identified (perhaps unfairly) with Western roles.[4]

The object of *Gunfighter Nation* is to trace the development of the system of mythic and ideological formulations that constitute the Myth of the Frontier, to offer a critical interpretation of its meanings, and to assess its power in shaping the life, thought, and politics of the nation. By giving a historical account of the use and periodic revision of the symbolic language of the Myth I hope to explain the broad appeal and persuasive power of a set of symbols that is apparently simple yet capable of varied and complex uses; that serves with equal facility the requirements of progressives and conservatives, of political managers and movie scriptwriters, of academic historiography and bureaucratic apologetics, of warfare and child's play; that is rooted in history but capable of transcending the limitations of a specific temporality, to speak with comparable authority and intelligibility to the citizens of eighteenth-century colonies, a nineteenth-century agrarian republic, and a modern industrial world power; that originated in tales told by, for, and about rural White "Anglo-Saxon" Protestant heroes, which nonetheless became the preferred entertainment of the audience of the ethnically heterodox population of the twentieth-century "megalopolis."

Gunfighter Nation is the last of three volumes that follow the historical development of the Myth of the Frontier in American literary, popular, and political culture from the colonial period to the present. *Regeneration Through Violence* (1973) showed how the experience of life and warfare on the colonial and early national frontiers (1600–1820) was transformed into a body of narrative lore, which in its turn was codified as a language of myth and symbol by several generations of historians and fiction writers. *The Fatal Environment* (1985) showed how that mythological system was adapted to suit the ideological needs of a nation in the process of transformation from an agrarian republic to a fully developed industrial nation-state. *Gunfighter Nation* begins in 1890, at the moment when the landed frontier of the United States was officially declared "closed," the moment when "Frontier" became primarily a term of ideological rather than geographical reference.

Before we take up the substance of this history, it may be useful to summarize the theoretical premises on which the study is based and define the terms of analysis that will be used. For those who are interested, the two earlier volumes contain a more detailed discussion of the theory, its philosophical status, and its various sources.[5]

Myth and Historical Memory

Gunfighter Nation belongs to the field of cultural history, which is concerned with describing the ways in which human cultures develop over time—or, more precisely, with giving a historical account of the activities and processes through which human societies produce the systems of value and meaning by which they live and through which they explain and interpret the world and themselves. The cultural historian tries to construct a historical account of the development of *meaning* and to show how the activities of symbol-making, interpretation, and imaginative projection continuously interlock with the political and material processes of social existence.

The concepts of *ideology*, *myth*, and *genre* highlight three different but closely related aspects of the culture-making process. *Ideology* is the basic system of concepts, beliefs, and values that defines a society's way of interpreting its place in the cosmos and the meaning of its history. As used by anthropologists and social historians, the term refers to the dominant conceptual categories that inform the society's words and practices, abstracted by analysis as a set of propositions, formulas, or rules. In any given society certain expressive forms or *genres*—like the *credo*, sermon, or manifesto—provide ways of articulating ideological concepts directly and explicitly. But most of the time the assumptions of value inherent in a culture's ideology are tacitly accepted as "givens." Their meaning is expressed in the symbolic narratives of *mythology* and is transmitted to the society through various genres of mythic expression. It is the mythic expression of ideology that will be our primary concern.[6]

Myths are stories drawn from a society's history that have acquired through persistent usage the power of symbolizing that society's ideology and of dramatizing its moral consciousness—with all the complexities and contradictions that consciousness may contain. Over time, through frequent retellings and deployments as a source of interpretive metaphors, the original mythic story is increasingly conventionalized and abstracted until it is reduced to a deeply encoded and resonant set of symbols, "icons," "keywords," or historical clichés. In this form, myth becomes a basic constituent of linguistic meaning and of the processes of both personal and social "remembering."

Each of these mythic icons is in effect a poetic construction of tremendous economy and compression and a mnemonic device capable of evoking a complex system of historical associations by a single image or phase. For an American, allusions to "the Frontier," or to events like "Pearl Harbor," "The Alamo," or "Custer's Last Stand" evoke an implicit understanding of the entire historical scenario that belongs to the event and of the complex interpretive tradition that has developed around it.[7]

Myth expresses ideology in a narrative, rather than discursive or argumentative, structure. Its language is metaphorical and suggestive rather than logical and analytical. The movement of a mythic narrative, like that of any story, implies a theory of cause-and-effect and therefore a theory of history (or even of cosmology); but these ideas are offered in a form that disarms critical analysis by its appeal to the structures and traditions of story-telling and the clichés of historical memory. Although myths are the product of human thought and labor, their identification with venerable tradition makes them appear to be products of "nature" rather than history—expressions of a trans-historical consciousness or of some form of "natural law."[8]

Myths are formulated as ways of explaining problems that arise in the course of historical experience. The most important and longest-lived of these formulations develop around areas of concern that persist over long periods of time. But no myth/ideological system, however internally consistent and harmonious, is proof against all historical contingencies. Sooner or later the bad harvest, the plague, defeat in war, changes in modes of production, internal imbalance in the distribution of wealth and power produce a crisis that cannot be fully explained or controlled by invoking the received wisdom embodied in myth. At such moments of cognitive dissonance or "discontent," the identification of ideological principles with the narratives of myth may be disrupted and a more or less deliberate and systematic attempt may be made to analyze and revise the intellectual/moral content of the underlying ideology. But in the end, as the historical experience of crisis is memorialized and abstracted, the revised ideology acquires its own mythology, typically blending old formulas with new ideas or concerns.[9]

The sources of myth-making lie in our capacity to make and use metaphors, by which we attempt to interpret a new and surprising experience or phenomenon by noting its resemblance to some remembered thing or happening. If the metaphor proves apt, we will be inclined to treat the new phenomenon as a recurrence of the old;

to the extent that the new phenomenon differs from the remembered one, our sense of the possibilities of experience will be extended. If symbol and experience match closely enough, our belief in the validity and usefulness of the symbol will be confirmed; if the match is disappointing, we will be forced to choose between denying the importance of the new experience and revising our symbolic vocabulary.[10]

A similar process informs the use of myth by a culturally defined social group. A culture has its heritage of "lore," which is preserved for use by designated lore-masters, story-tellers, or historians and is transmitted by them to the "public" in one or more of the genres (oral or literary). The continued use of cultural lore for social teaching and learning tests "the states and processes [of our most favored] symbolic models against the states and processes of the wider [*i.e.*, material] world." As the course of experience confirms or discredits the symbolism, the structure is continuously confirmed or subjected to revision. The most concise description of this process is provided by the anthropologist Marshall Sahlins, in *Historical Metaphors and Mythical Realities.*

> People act upon circumstances according to their own cultural presuppositions, the socially given categories of persons and things. . . . [But] the worldly circumstances of human action are under no inevitable obligation to conform to [these] categories. . . . In the event they do not, the received categories are potentially revalued in practice, functionally redefined. According to the place of the received category in the cultural system as constituted, and the interests that have been affected, the system itself is more or less altered. At the extreme, what began as reproduction ends as transformation.[11]

While the play of continuity and revision in the grand structure of a myth/ideological system cannot be described in its totality, indications of the balance of change and continuity in the system can nevertheless be followed by examining developments within particular forms or genres of expression. The historical development of the culture's repertoire of genres is driven not only by social and cultural change but by the specialized discourses of artists and producers who work in that form and by the institutions that control the production and distribution of their artifacts. The relation between this "internal" discourse and the larger patterns of social and cultural change is often obscure or problematic. This has suggested to some critics and anthropologists that the forms of cultural expression develop from an autonomous (or semi-autonomous) mental activity in which a linguistic or psychological program of some sort—a "collective unconscious" or a "grammar" of tropes or archetypes—determines the essential structure of all myth/ideological expression.[12] But such approaches tend to obscure the importance of historical experience and change in the shaping of specific myth/ideological systems and in the social life of the communities the systems serve. We will therefore be considering both myth and genre as phenomena shaped by historical contingency, rather than as archetypes generated either by "the nature of things" or "the nature of language."

The Politics of Myth

Among the many historical contingencies that shape mythic expression, the one that will concern us most is the state of social politics. The work of myth-making exists "for the culture" that it serves, and we therefore speak of it as if it were somehow the property or production of the culture as a whole. But the actual work of making and transmitting myths is done by particular classes of persons; myth-making processes are therefore responsive to the politics of class difference.

In modern society the mass media provide the broadest-based and most pervasive means for canvassing the world of events and the spectrum of public concerns, for recalling historical precedents, and for translating them into the various story-genres that constitute a public mythology. Since the concern of commercial media is to exploit as wide an audience as possible, their repertoire of genres in any period tends to be broad and various, covering a wide (though not all-inclusive) range of themes, subjects, and public concerns. Within the structured marketplace of myths, the continuity and persistence of particular genres may be seen as keys to identifying the culture's deepest and most persistent concerns. Likewise, major breaks in the development of important genres may signal the presence of a significant crisis of cultural values and organization. The development of new genres, or the substantial modification of existing ones, can be read as a signal of active ideological concern in which both the producers and consumers of mass media participate—producers as exploitative promulgators and "proprietors" of their mythic formulations, consumers as respondents capable of dismissing a given mythic formulation or of affiliating with it.[13]

But we should not assume that the mythologies of mass media are a kind of modern "folklore," or that they constitute the totality of "American culture." The productions of the cultural industries are indeed varied and ubiquitous—from the newspapers and mass entertainment to the textbooks that teach our children the authorized versions of American history and literature—but the authority of these "mass culture" productions has been and is offset by the influence of other forms of culture and expression that are genuinely "popular": produced by and for specific cultural communities like the ethnic group, the family-clan, a town, neighborhood, or region, the workplace, or the street corner. Although few of these subcultural entities are now isolated from the influence of mass media, they are still capable of generating their own myths and their own unique ways of interpreting the productions of the media. A Harlem or a Little Italy, an Appalachian or Mississippi Delta county, a Hasidic or Mennonite community, a rust-belt milltown or a mining town, have been and in many cases continue to be centers of exception or resistance to the formulations of the commercial culture industries, and their productions (particularly in music) affect the development of mass culture. Nonetheless, the symbols and values generated by mass culture have steadily infiltrated, transformed, and compromised the autonomy of "local" cultures. For that reason, I think it is useful to speak not only of "mass culture" but of the development of an "industrial popular culture," whose artifacts are produced primarily by a commercial culture industry but whose symbols become active constituents of a *popular* culture—that is, the belief and value structures of a national audience or public.[14]

The mythology produced by mass or commercial media has a particular role and function in a cultural system that remains complex and heterodox. It is the form of cultural production that addresses most directly the concerns of Americans as citizens of a nation-state.[15] The history of the development of the forms and institutions of commercial or mass popular culture is directly related to the development of a political ideology of American nationality and to the creation of nationwide networks of production and distribution. The basic structure of this commercialized national culture were developed between the Revolution and the Civil War with the emergence of national parties and the development of a nationwide trade in books, magazines, and newspapers utilizing an ever-expanding transportation network. Between the Civil War and the Great War the nascent "culture industries" took advantage of new technologies to meet the demands of an ever-growing and increasingly polyglot culture with varied and complex needs and tastes. By the 1920s this form of cultural production was fully industrialized and had become so ubiquitous that it is fair to characterize it as the clearest expression of our "national culture": when we look beyond the family, ethnic community, or workplace for symbols expressive of our "American" identity, we find the mythologies of the popular culture industry.[16]

Since I am concerned with tracing the historical development of a *national* myth/ideology, I will approach the producer/audience dialectic from the producers' side. This approach has the disadvantage of underemphasizing the complex and various ways in which different audiences receive the production of the culture industries. Audience response can be inferred from the modifications producers make in response to shifts in circulation or box-office receipts; but these readings of audience response are always distorted by the traditional biases and institutional biases of the industry. Nonetheless, by focusing on the producers we can study more closely the dynamics of myth-production in the particular cultural site that has acquired the power to address us *as if* it spoke for an "American" national culture.

Regeneration Through Violence: The Language of the Myth

The Myth of the Frontier is our oldest and most characteristic myth, expressed in a body of literature, folklore, ritual, historiography, and polemics produced over a period of three centuries. According to this myth-historiography, the conquest of the wilderness and the subjugation or displacement of the Native Americans who originally inhabited it have been the means to our achievement of a national identity, a democratic polity, an ever-expanding economy, and a phenomenally dynamic and "progressive" civilization. The original ideological task of the Myth was to explain and justify the establishment of the American colonies; but as the colonies expanded and developed, the Myth was called on to account for our rapid economic growth, our emergence as a powerful nation-state, and our distinctively American approach to the socially and culturally disruptive processes of modernization.

The peculiarities of the American version of this myth/ideology derived from our original condition as a settler-state, a colonial outpost of the European "metropolis." In America, all the political, social, and economic transformations attendant on modernization began with outward movement, physical separation from the originating "metropolis." The achievement of "progress" was therefore inevitably associated with territorial expansion and colored by the experience, the politics, and the peculiar psychology of emigration.[17]

Euro-American history begins with the self-selection and abstraction of particular European communities from their metropolitan culture, and their transplantation to a wilderness on the other side of the ocean where conditions were generally more primitive than those at home.[18] These colonies in turn would expand by reproducing themselves in subcolonial settlements, projected at some distance from the colonial metropolis into a further and more primitive wilderness. Thus the processes of American development in the colonies were linked from the beginning to a historical narrative in which repeated cycles of *separation* and *regression* were necessary preludes to an improvement in life and fortune.

Conflict was also a central and peculiar feature of the process. To establish a colony or settlement, the Europeans had to struggle against an unfamiliar natural environment and against the non-European, non-White natives for whom the wilderness was home. Violence is central to both the historical development of the Frontier and its mythic representation. The Anglo-American colonies grew by displacing Amerindian societies and enslaving Africans to advance the fortunes of White colonists. As a result, the "savage war" became a characteristic episode of each phase of westward expansion.

Conflict with the Indians defined one boundary of American identity: though we were a people of "the wilderness," we were *not* savages. The other boundary was defined by the emergence of conflicts between the colonies and the "mother country," and (later) between the regional concerns of the "borderers" and those of American metropolitan regimes. The compleat "American" of the Myth was one who had defeated and freed himself from both the "savage" of the western wilderness and the metropolitan regime of authoritarian politics and class privilege.[19]

In each stage of its development, the Myth of the Frontier relates the achievement of "progress" to a particular form or scenario of violent action. "Progress" itself was defined in different ways: the Puritan colonists emphasized the achievement of spiritual regeneration through frontier adventure; Jeffersonians (and later, the disciples of Turner's "Frontier Thesis") saw the frontier settlement as a re-enactment and democratic renewal of the original "social contract"; while Jacksonian Americans saw the conquest of the Frontier as a means to the regeneration of personal fortunes and/or of patriotic vigor and virtue. But in each case, the Myth represented the redemption of American spirit or fortune as something to be achieved by playing through a scenario of separation, temporary regression to a more primitive or "natural" state, and *regeneration through violence.*

At the core of that scenario is the symbol of "savage war," which was both a mythic trope and an operative category of military doctrine. The premise of "savage war" is that ineluctable political and social differences—rooted in some combination of "blood" and culture—make coexistence between primitive natives and civilized Europeans impossible on any basis other than that of subjugation. Native resistance to European settlement therefore takes the form of a fight for survival; and because of the "savage" and bloodthirsty propensity of the natives, such struggles inevitably become "wars of extermination" in which one side or the other attempts to destroy its enemy root and branch. The seventeenth-century Puritans envisioned this struggle in biblical terms—"Two Nations [are in] the Womb and will be striving"—and urged their soldiers to exterminate the Wampanoags as God commanded Israel to wipe out the Amalekites. But similar ideas informed the military thinking of soldiers in the Age of Reason, like Colonel Henry Bouquet, who described an "American war" as "a rigid contest where all is at stake and mutual destruction the object . . . [where] everything is terrible; the face of the country, the climate, the enemy . . . [where] victories are not decisive but defeats are ruinous; and simple death is the least misfortune that can happen." Military folklore from King Philip's War to Braddock's Defeat to Custer's Last Stand held that in battle against a savage enemy you always saved the last bullet for yourself; for in savage war one side or the other must perish, whether by limitless murder or by the degrading experience of subjugation and torture.[20]

In its most typical formulations, the myth of "savage war" blames Native Americans as instigators of a war of extermination. Indians were certainly aggressors in particular cases, and they often asserted the right to exclude settlers from particular regions. But with the possible exception of Tecumseh's abortive attempt at a confederacy of western tribes, after 1700 no tribe or group of tribes pursued (or was capable of pursuing) a general "policy" of exterminating or removing White settlements on a large-scale basis. The accusation is better understood as an act of psychological projection that made the Indians scapegoats for the morally troubling side of American expansion: the myth of "savage war" became a basic ideological convention of a culture that was itself increasingly devoted to the extermination or expropriation of the Indians and the kidnaping and enslavement of black Africans.[21]

In American mythology, the Indian war also provides a symbolic surrogate for a range of domestic social and political conflicts. By projecting the "fury" of class resentment outward against the Indian, the American expands his nation's resources and thereby renders class struggle unnecessary. All the antipathies that make for Revolutionary Terror and/or dictatorial oppression in Europe are projected onto the American savage, who becomes the only obstacle to the creation of a perfect republic. But this historical myth and its hopeful political scenario can only be realized so long as a frontier exists: a reservoir of natural resources sufficient to requite the ambitions of all classes without prejudice to the interests of any.[22]

In analyzing the structure and meaning of this mythology of violence, it is vital that we not confuse mythic representation with political reality. The mythic tales and polemics we will be examining are rife with visions of border wars that turn overnight into preludes to Armageddon and with proposals for genocide and wars of extermination. And there has been enough actual violence along these lines—the Indian wars, the slave trade, "lynch law" and race riots, the labor/management violence of 1880–1920, and our currently high levels of domestic and criminal violence—to support the belief that America has been a peculiarly violent nation. However, most of these apparently distinctive forms of political and social violence have also figured with comparable prominence in the histories of other settler-states, and of Europe. Neither the slave trade nor the subjugation/extermination of natives by colonists was an exclusively Anglo-American enterprise. The mass genocides of modern times belong not to the history of the Americas, but to Europe, Asia, and Africa.[23] What is distinctively "American" is not necessarily the amount or kind of violence that characterizes our history but the mythic significance we have assigned to the kinds of violence we have actually experienced, the forms of symbolic violence we imagine or invent, and the political uses to which we put that symbolism.

When history is translated into myth, the complexities of social and historical experiences are simplified and compressed into the action of representative individuals or "heroes." The narrative of the hero's action exemplifies and tests the political and/or moral validity of a particular approach to the use of human powers in the material world. The hero's inner life—his or her code of values, moral or psychic ambivalence, mixtures of motive—reduces to personal motive the complex and contradictory mixture of ideological imperatives that shape a society's response to a crucial event. But complexity and contradiction are focused rather than merely elided in the symbolizing process. The heroes of myth embody something like the full range of ideological contradictions around which the life of the culture revolves, and their adventures suggest the range of possible resolutions that the culture's lore provides.

The moral landscape of the Frontier Myth is divided by significant borders, of which the wilderness/civilization, Indian/White border is the most basic. The American must cross the border into "Indian country" and experience a "regression" to a more primitive and natural condition of life so that the false values of the "metropolis" can be purged and a new, purified social contract enacted. Although the Indian and the Wilderness are the settler's enemy, they also provide him with the new consciousness through which he will transform the world. The heroes of this myth-historical quest must therefore be "men (or women) who know Indians"—characters whose experiences, sympathies, and even allegiances fall on both sides of the Frontier. Because the border between savagery and civilization runs through their moral center, the Indian wars are, for these heroes, a spiritual or psychological struggle which they win by learning to discipline or suppress the savage or "dark" side of their own human nature. Thus they are mediators of a double kind who can teach civilized men how to defeat savagery on its native grounds—the natural wilderness, and the wilderness of the human soul.

The myths of regeneration through violence were developed during the initial stages of colonial experience, in two genres of personal narrative, which first appeared in New England in the aftermath of King Philip's War (1675–77). The first was the "captivity narrative," modeled on the popular personal account of Mary Rowlandson (1682). Through the captivity-myth, the structures of Protestant-Christian mythology which the settlers had brought from Europe were applied to the secular experiences of colonization. Captivity narratives (both historical and fictional) were among the most popular and prevalent form of American adventure story for most of the eighteenth century. The hero of the captivity narrative is a White woman (or minister) captured by Indians during a "savage war." The captive symbolizes the values of Christianity and civilization that are imperiled in the wilderness war. Her captivity is figuratively a descent into Hell and a spiritual darkness which is akin to "madness." By resisting the physical threats and spiritual temptations of the Indians, the captive vindicates both her own moral character and the power of the values she symbolizes. But the scenario of historical action developed by the captivity narrative is a passive one that emphasizes the weakness of colonial power and ends not with a victorious conquest but with a grateful and somewhat chastened return home.[24]

In the early decades of the eighteenth century a second type of narrative was developed which celebrated the deeds of Indian fighters and (later) wilderness hunters. The earliest exemplar of the type was a contemporary of Mrs. Rowlandson named Benjamin Church, a man whose intimate knowledge of Indians and skill in adapting their tactics enabled him to defeat and kill King Philip. Church is the prototype for a version of the American hero-as-Indian-fighter that reached full historical expression in the career (and public celebrity) of Daniel Boone (1784 and after), and in the literary mythology of the nineteenth century. In the various historical narratives associated with Boone, the narrative formulas and ideological themes of the captivity tale (redemption through suffering) are integrated with the triumphalist scenario of the Indian-war story to make a single unified Myth of the Frontier in which the triumph of civilization over savagery is symbolized by the hunter/warrior's rescue of the White woman held captive by savages.[25]

The frontier romances of James Fenimore Cooper, published between 1823 and 1850, codified and systematized the representations of the Frontier that had developed haphazardly since 1700 in such diverse genres as the personal narrative, the history, the sermon, the newspaper item, the street ballad, and the "penny-dreadful." Cooper's palpable intention is to create a genetic myth that "accounts for" the fundamental ideological and social oppositions dividing the society of Jacksonian America by projecting them backward into a fictionalized past.[26]

Cooper recognizes that the racial opposition of Whites and Indians is (for an American) the most basic and definitive of historical tropes, that the ideological justification of American history hinges somehow on the Indian question. His Leatherstocking novels amplify this basic imagery systematically, using White/Indian opposition as the key to interpreting other fundamental oppositions: the opposition between "hard" and "soft" understandings of social and class questions embodied in the gendered contrast of Masculine and Feminine ways of thinking about Indian wars, and the class opposition between landed gentry and social-climbing yeomen, masters and slaves, or commanders and subordinates.

In each novel Cooper creates a spectrum of possible racial/cultural compromises, ranging from embodiments of racial purity at both the White and the Indian extremes, and gender purity at the Masculine and Feminine extremes, through characters who mix various elements of gender and race—Indians who acquire White sensibilities, White men raised as Indians, and one woman (Cora Munro in *Last of the Mohicans*) who is both a racial hybrid (Negro and White) and a gender hybrid (female sex, "masculine" courage and rationality). Cooper's characters provided generations of imitators and dime-novelists with a lexicon of social and racial stereotypes which they adapted to changing fashions and audiences.

The hero of the Cooper novel is Hawkeye, a White man who knows Indians so well that he can almost pass for one. Based on the historical Daniel Boone, Hawkeye became the model for future versions of the frontier hero in the writings of antebellum historians, journalists, and politicians interested in the important questions of Indian policy, emigration, and westward expansion. As the "man who knows Indians," the frontier hero stands between the opposed worlds of savagery and civilization, acting sometimes as mediator or interpreter between races and cultures but more often as civilization's most effective instrument against savagery—a man who knows how to think and fight like an Indian, to turn their own methods against them. In its most extreme development, the frontier hero takes the form of the "Indian-hater," whose suffering at savage hands has made him correspondingly savage, an avenger determined at all costs to "exterminate the brutes."[27]

The Frontier Myth as a Theory of Development

Between 1815 and 1870 the United States experienced a period of relatively steady and rapid economic expansion. During that period the country grew from an agrarian adjunct of the European economic system to a leading industrial and financial world power, leading the industrial nations in railroad mileage and approaching leadership in key areas of heavy industrial production. The underlying strength of the economy was such that even the massive destruction of the Civil War did not alter the economic growth curve of the nation as a whole (although it ruined the South for several generations). This cycle of economic expansion coincided with a period of dramatic geographic expansion. The American government acquired land (by conquest and purchase) sufficient to double the size of the nation; and successive waves of settlers, drawn from the burgeoning populations of the States as well as from Europe, colonized the undeveloped land. It was perhaps inevitable that these two dramatic expansions be linked in American historical mythology and that the westward movement of population be read as a cause—even as *the* cause—of American economic development.[28]

In the period of agrarian expansion, the Christian-eschatological substructure of the original Frontier Myth was overlaid with a more secular ideology, whose terms were formulated most powerfully by Jefferson (and the republican ideologists who followed him). They saw the achievement and safety of republican institutions as dependent on the availability of vast reserves of land capable of sustaining many future generations of self-supporting freeholders. The settlement of the Old Northwest and the Old Southwest between 1795 and 1830 for the most part fulfilled the agrarian program, since the character of soil and climate and the state of technology made feasible the exploitation of western resources by individuals (or small families) of settlers, artisans, and entrepreneurs.

But in fact the growth of the American economy owed at least as much to developments occurring within the "metropolis" itself—entrepreneurial and technological innovation, industrialization, changes in public education and growth of the work force, high rates of productivity—as to the acquisition of new resources beyond the borders. The acquisition of the Far West from Mexico, the bringing of new lands into cultivation, and the search for new mineral and natural resources were given a new kind of economic importance after 1820, because they were integrated with a developing industrial economy driven on an expansive course by the reciprocal influences of increasing productivity and expanded trade.[29]

These developments accelerated between 1855 and 1873. The development of the Great Plains and the Far Western frontiers was increasingly dominated by large capital concerns (particularly railroads) rather than by the individualistic settlement patterns of the agrarian frontier. The change was partly a function of the distance of these new frontiers from the centers of population; but more significant was the changing character of the American economy, particularly the increased levels and importance of trade and capital accumulation.[30]

Beginning with the California Gold Rush of 1849, the "bonanza" became the characteristic theme of each new frontier enthusiasm. The bonanza frontier offers the prospect of immediate and impressive economic benefit for a relatively low capital outlay; in effect, such a frontier condenses into a brief term the expectation of profit that the agrarian frontiers of 1795–1830 would require a generation or more to achieve. Where agrarian profit depends on the steady rise of population and land values, bonanza profits derive from the opportunity to acquire or produce at low cost some commodity that has a high commercial value. Gold and other precious metals are the most obviously valuable of such commodities, and the discovery of new lodes of gold and silver produced a succession of bonanza frontiers throughout the Mountain West from 1849 to the 1880s. There were also highly touted bonanzas in agricultural commodities like cotton (1830s and 1850s), cattle (1870–85), wheat (1880s), and dry-land products (1900–20), and in energy resources, like the southwestern oil boom of the early twentieth century.[31]

But despite the social and economic differences that distinguished new frontiers from old, throughout the nineteenth century the essential structures of the Frontier Myth remained apt as a way of symbolizing current history and linking it to the traditions of a sanctified past. The Iron Horse could be seen as merely the latest form of the settlers' technological superiority—the scion of the axe, long-rifle, and mold-board plow. Although the new bonanza frontiers were profitable only because of their integration into an industrial economy, the bonanzas themselves still occurred in those regions originally identified as the frontier of the farmer-pioneer and the Indian savage.

In 1873 the long cycle of American economic expansion ended in a catastrophic bank panic followed by the worst depression in American history and twenty years of chronic economic difficulty.[32] Moreover, the vast landed reserve, twice as large as that which Jefferson thought sufficient for a thousand generations, was seemingly approaching exhaustion after only three or four.

The economic crisis of the 1870s produced a major transformation in American mythology, which I have described in some detail in *The Fatal Environment*.[33] The most important agents of that transformation were the proprietors, editors, and journalists of the great urban newspapers and journals, which had developed (since 1850) into a medium for the nationwide circulation of information and opinion. They addressed themselves to three simultaneous crises, which they saw as organically related, the urban "class warfare" that began with the Tompkins Square "riot" of 1874; the breakdown of Reconstruction in the South and the threat of a "race war" in that region; and the failure of federal policy in regard to the development of western lands—specifically, the failure to police the opening of the territory to exploitation by the railroads and the failure to solve the "Indian question." All three crises would reach a violent climax in 1876–77. Reconstruction would collapse in a last wave of race riots and Ku Klux Klan outbreaks; labor unrest would culminate in the Great Strike of 1877, which seemed a foretaste of proletarian revolution; and the failure of western development would culminate in the outbreak of the Sioux War of 1876 and the catastrophe of Custer's Last Stand.

In addition to their temporal coincidence, these three crises were seen to have a structural kinship. In each, a conflict had arisen between the will and desires of a "lower" human order or class (Indians, Black and immigrant laborers, urban wage-workers) and the imperative requirements of the new industrial system as defined by its owners and managers. Workers, Indians, and freed slaves had asserted in their different ways their desire to control the conditions and terms of their labor and/or the land from which they gained subsistence. The Republican administration was identified with a "philanthropic" (in our terms, "liberal") ideology, which followed the prewar doctrines of "free labor": political authority was to be vested in "the people" rather than in an elite, and the acquisition of both economic competence and political self-control was to be made universally available. But such a wide diffusion of political and economic power seemed incompatible with the requirements of a modern industrial order whose prosperity depended on the expert management of large and complexly interlocking systems of capitalization, production, and distribution. The health of the new corporate order required the willing subordination of worker to manager, and of private ambition to corporate necessity. But this was an ideology logically at odds with the traditional values of self-government and freedom of opportunity and with the political ideology of "free labor" for whose vindication the Civil War had been fought and which the newspapermen shared (or were afraid to openly contradict).[34]

The contradiction was evaded by an act of ideological sleight of hand: the use of race-war symbolism, drawn from the Myth of the Frontier, to interpret the class warfare of workers and managers. The Indian war was at once a current event and a symbol of the primal and genetic strife from which the nation was born. The events of the Sioux War of 1876, culminating in Custer's Last Stand, were treated as a paradigm of the disaster that might overtake "civilization as we know it" if moral authority and political power were conceded to a class of people whose natural gifts were like those of "redskin savages." The basic link between White workers, Blacks, and Indians was their common resistance to the managerial disciplines of industrial labor and to the Malthusian discipline of the labor marketplace, which required men to "work or starve" and to accept starvation wages when the market decreed them. But equally significant was the determination of these groups to use the political power of the national government to defeat the managers and the marketplace. According to the newspapers, Indians "used" the Indian Bureau and powerful lobbies of "philanthropists" to "monopolize" and keep out of development lands that could better be used by White farmers or railroads. Blacks used the Freedmen's Bureau and the same "philanthropic" or "radical" lobbyists to obtain federal funds and troops to sustain their political "monopoly" of Reconstruction legislatures. Workers demanded government support for strikes, subsidized rents, and soup kitchens to feed the unemployed during the depression. Finally, each of these groups appeared to threaten society with violence "from below": the Indians were already on the warpath, southern elections and labor disputes were already marked by racial violence, and labor demonstrations in the cities raised for the newspapermen "The Red Spectre of the Commune."

The newspapers' account of the politics of Indian affairs and Reconstruction policy was distorted, and to some extent fabricated, to suit the polemical needs of the managerial ideology which the editors supported. Their primary objective was to weaken the capacity of organized workers and farmers (and their allies among the "philanthropic" elite) to use the instruments of democratic politics for advantage in their struggle with landlords, employers, and managers. By framing the class conflict as a choice of "racial" identification between "savageism" and civilization, these editorialists hoped to deprive the embattled workers/freedmen/Indians of the sympathy they had hitherto received from the "middle class"—that putative majority of farmers and city-dwellers who had not yet become either proletarians or members of a corporate hierarchy.[35]

The representation of the working classes as "white savages" was facilitated by the large and growing presence of immigrants in American society. As early as 1869, Charles Francis Adams had predicted that the American laboring classes would soon be reduced to three racially defined "proletariats"—Celtic in the North, African in the South, and Oriental in the Far West. Since (in Adams' view) these races were incapable of properly exercising the responsibilities of self-governing citizens, Americans would have to consider restricting their access to voting and other political rights. In the wake of the Great Strike of 1877—four years before the great wave of immigration actually began—the *Nation* would describe the working classes as *predominantly* composed of aliens, "to whom American political and social ideals appeal but faintly, if at all, and who carry in their very blood traditions which give universal suffrage an air of menace to many of the things which civilized men hold most dear."[36]

The substitution of the symbolism of "savage war" for that of "class war" shifts the ground of controversy from the ideological frame of democratic tradition to that of race war, from a frame in which progress and right order are presumed to emerge from the widest imaginable diffusion of property and political power to one in which progress depends on the exclusion/extermination of a congenitally regressive type of humanity and on the aggrandizement of a privileged race or people.[37]

The racialization of class lines became more marked after 1880 as the urban working classes grew in number. As the ethnic composition of the working classes became more clearly marked as "alien" (Italian, Slavic, Jewish), many writers (conservative and progressive) began to fear that the country was sliding toward a second Civil War, which would combine the features of a class war and a race or "savage" war, a Jacobin or Communard "Terror," and an Indian massacre or Last Stand. The possibility of a class/race apocalypse became a staple of political polemics, as in moral reformer Josiah Strong's vision of a racial "Battle of Gettysburg" that might determine the future of America and humanity. A variety of possible scenarios were projected in the newly popular genre of utopian/dystopian fiction, which included such works as Bellamy's *Looking Backward* (1887), Twain's *A Connecticut Yankee in King Arthur's Court* (1889), Ignatius Donnelly's *Caesar's Column* (1890), and Jack London's *The Iron Heel* (1908).[38]

"Progressives" and "Populists"

Within the purlieus of a commercial and increasingly industrialized popular culture, the genres that carried the Myth of the Frontier became the site of a cultural contest between two different schools of American ideology, which I will call the "progressive" and the "populist."[39]

The "progressive" style uses the Frontier Myth in ways that buttress the ideological assumptions and political aims of a corporate economy and a managerial politics. It reads the history of savage warfare and westward expansion as a Social Darwinian parable, explaining the emergence of a new managerial ruling class and justifying its right to subordinate lesser classes to its purposes. The basic elements of this style were developed in the newspaper polemics of the 1870s and were formulated as a systematic doctrine in the frontier histories and political speeches of Theodore Roosevelt (and other political Progressives) between 1883 and 1893. The progressives acknowledged that the decade had produced a crisis in the history of American development in the form of a political struggle between an aggressively monopolistic "big business" and an increasingly radical and potentially violent labor movement. But they also believed that the conflict could be resolved by identifying and following a clear and continuous line which ran through American history: the steady transformation of small individual concerns into large economic and political institutions—small farms into industrial farms, shops into factories and factories into corporate complexes, colonies into provinces, provinces into confederacies, confederacies into nation, republic into empire.

The "populist" style developed in reaction to the emergence of the corporate/industrial economy and the political claims of its proprietors and managers. Its ideological premises combined the agrarian imagery of Jeffersonianism with the belief in economic individualism and mobility characteristic of pre-Civil War "free labor" ideology. Progress in the populist style is measured by the degree to which the present state of society facilitates a broad diffusion of property, of the opportunity to "rise in the world," and of political power. Where the progressive idealizes greater centralization and efficiency and sees these as the basis for America's assumption of a Great Power role in world affairs, the populist values decentralization, idealizes the small farmer-artisan-financier, and either devalues (or opposes) the assumption of a Great Power role or asserts that the nation derives both moral and political power from its populist character.[40]

The unifying element in these variants of the populist style is the conception of "the closing of the Frontier" as a historical crisis or disjunction that breaks the hitherto straight line of American development and imperils America's democratic values and social peace. The classic populist vision defines the crisis of modernization as a loss of the democratic social organization, the equitable distribution of wealth and political power of the agrarian past.[41] Where the progressive sees the transformation of the American economy as gain, the populist emphasizes loss; and in the contrast between past and present—America before and after the "break"—the populist finds grounds for a critique of the American present and prospective future.[42]

The progressive style is the more politically coherent of the two. Its spokesmen in the 1890s tended to come from a well-defined segment of the Republican party, and its language has acquired greater authority in the twentieth century as the political economy itself has become more centralized and managerial. The basic ideological premises of the populist style were shared by a variety of thinkers, writers, spokesmen, and partisans who differed substantially (and fatally) in their attempts to apply their critiques of "big business" to specific political cases. Yet the tropes of populist rhetoric have been basic to many if not most of the radical movements and social/political critiques of our post-Civil War history, including the Grangers and Greenbackers of the 1870s, Henry George and the Single Tax movement of the 1880s, the Farmers' Alliance of the 1890s, the Popular Front of the 1930s, and the counterculture of the 1960s. In each case populist style and imagery lent myth/historical resonance to radical polemics while imposing certain limitations on the analytical power of their social and political critiques.

However, it is important not to schematize the ideological map by seeing "populism" and "progressivism" as irreconcilable polar opposites, on the order of Marxist concepts like "capitalism" and "feudalism," or as ideological positions so disparate that any given writer or spokesman must make an exclusive choice between them. Rather, they represent two distinctive styles of usage which draw on a common myth/ideological language in which there is substantial agreement on such central concerns as the exceptional character of American life and history, the necessity and desirability of economic development, the vitality of "democratic" politics, and the relevance of something called "the Frontier" as a way of explaining and rationalizing what is most distinctive and valuable in "the American way." It is the existence of this common mythic language, to which all sides can appeal, that makes the conflict of progressive and populist interests a coherent political discourse—a political culture—rather than a clash of mutually uncomprehending and irreconcilable tribes.

As the political struggles of the twentieth century intensified, the genres of mass culture became crucial as a common site in which Americans could imagine (or observe others imagining) the basis for a new (or renewed) cultural consensus on the meaning and direction of American society. In the fictive or mythic "space" defined by the genres of mass culture, the primary contradictions of value and belief embodied in the ideological styles of progressives and populists were continuously "entertained"—imaginatively played out in story-forms that either tested ideological propositions against the traditional values embodied in myth or invited the projection of utopian visions of a "possible" or "alternative" outcome to the nation's historical travail.

This ideological struggle on the grounds of mass culture is the main subject of *Gunfighter Nation.* The discussions that follow will focus on the ways in which ideological controversy affected the language of American myth as reflected in the forms and practices of commercial culture-producers: writers of literary fiction and popular history, producers of dime and pulp novels, mass-circulation editors and journalists, movie-makers, and so on. Those discussions will require a reciprocal movement between analyses of developments internal to the mass media and of crises arising in the larger social realm of which the media industries are a part. By this method I hope to show that reciprocity characterizes the functional relation between cultural constructions and "material" experience, that our myth/ideological systems shape our apprehension and provide the terms for our response to reality and in the event—in the process of actual use—are themselves revised and transformed.[43]

It is impossible in a study of this kind to treat every important aspect of American history in the period covered or to do full justice to complex movements like the Populist "crusade" of the 1890s or policies like the New Deal or Cold War "containment." I have necessarily limited myself to those aspects of twentiety-century history and politics which have had a demonstrable effect on either the content or the form of our mass-culture mythology. Studies of this kind also have to strike a balance between textual and contextual (or intertextual) concerns if they are to show how myth and ideology appear in and work through the various forms of cultural production.[44] Textual study is also vital as a way of demonstrating that myth and ideology are created and recreated in the midst of historical contingency, through deliberate acts of human memory, intention, and labor—that myth has a human/historical rather than a natural or transcendent source and is continually modified by human experience and agency.

By definition, the structures of myth and ideology pervade the life of a culture and all its varied forms of expression. The Myth of the Frontier has found expression through media as varied as the pamphlet, the dime novel, the nineteenth-century historical romance, the stage melodrama, the Wild West show, the movie, the modern paperback, and the TV miniseries. Moreover, the influence of the Myth is such that its characteristic conventions have strongly influenced nearly every genre of adventure story in the lexicon of mass-culture production, particularly science fiction and detective stories. It would be physically impossible for a single study to trace the Myth through all these various forms of expression. I have chosen, therefore, to limit this study to genres that may be described as "Westerns": story-forms whose connection to the characteristic images, characters, and references of frontier mythology is observably direct. The influence of frontier conventions on other genres will be suggested through a look at some early twentieth-century detective stories and science fiction, in which the influence of Western scenes, heroes, and themes is explicitly acknowledged; but I will not attempt to provide a full account of the differentiation, development, or significance of these genres. I have also chosen to limit my discussion of twentieth-century Westerns to the movies and to omit all but passing reference to the literary Western. The emphasis is justified by the centrality of moving pictures in modern culture and by the pervasive influence of moving-picture images on the language of both literature and politics.[45]

The central (though not the exclusive) concern of this study is the *political* significance of myth and the way in which mythic formulations affect and reflect political beliefs and practices. This emphasis reflects my belief in the central importance of power-relations in determining the course of public events and the reshaping of the cultural landscape.

The book begins with an examination of Theodore Roosevelt's development of a "progressive" version of the Frontier Myth between

1883 and 1900 and compares Roosevelt's version to Turner's Frontier Thesis. Both of these texts are treated as attempts to systematically apply the "lessons" of our frontier past to the task of interpreting and developing a response to the cultural and political crisis of industrial development, which came to a head in the panic and depression of 1893–94. Although Turner's work has had the greater influence on academic historiography and has received the greater acknowledgment from historically minded policy-makers, Roosevelt's version of the Myth is closer in style, emphasis, and content to the productions of industrial popular culture and (as the body of the study will show) has had a greater (though unacknowledged) impact on the ideological underpinnings and policy-practice of twentieth-century administrations.

We will then turn to developments in turn-of-the-century mass culture to examine the populist mythologies that were developed in dime novels at the same time that Roosevelt was developing his progressive myth-history and then turn to the emergence (in Buffalo Bill's Wild West) of a commercial cultural form in which both populist and progressive myth/ideologies could find expression. Thereafter, we will trace the developing forms of modern popular culture, first in the "formula fiction" of 1900–1940 and finally in the genres of Hollywood cinema, and will show how these forms reflected the crises of national ideology provoked by the initial phase of American imperialism (1898–1904), the Boom and Depression of 1920–40, the Second World War, the Cold War, and the Vietnam War.

PART I

The Mythology of Progressivism, 1880–1902

1 The Winning of the West

Theodore Roosevelt's Frontier Thesis, 1880–1900

On July 12, 1893, in an event that has come to symbolize a turning point in American history and historiography, Frederick Jackson Turner delivered his address on "The Significance of the Frontier in American History" to a meeting of American historians at the World's Columbian Exposition in Chicago. Turner himself asserted that he and his audience stood at the end of the first and formative epoch of American history: an epoch whose triumphs of democracy and economic power he associated with the development of the agrarian frontier, an epoch that had ended in 1890 with the disappearance of the vast reserve of undeveloped land that had constituted that frontier.[1]

The address marked the beginning of Turner's own rise to the top of the historical profession. His methods of analysis, which emphasized the study of material forces (especially economics) in the shaping of society and culture, became the basis of the academic discipline; and his general thesis, which asserted the exceptional character of American history and politics, became the central premise (or problematic) of American historiography.[2]

Turner's immediate contemporaries, however, did not perceive the "Frontier Thesis" as revolutionary in either method or content. Theodore Roosevelt defined the situation precisely when he praised Turner for having "put into shape a good deal of thought that has been floating around rather loosely."[3] Indeed, Roosevelt himself had promulgated a frontier Thesis of his own—one that was far better known than Turner's. Turner was pleased to be recognized by the author of the multivolume *The Winning of the West* (1885–94), a man who (though not yet a major figure in national politics) was his senior as a historian.

Roosevelt's praise seemed all the more generous since Turner had criticized Roosevelt's historiography in a review of his first two volumes. However, Roosevelt considered that Turner's work supplemented and corrected, but did not contradict, his own, and Turner did not dissent. Indeed, they saw themselves as sharing basic assumptions, a belief that the Frontier was a vital element in shaping American institutions and national character, and a concern that the passing of the agrarian frontier marked the beginning of crisis in American history. Both understood the historian's mission as that of public teacher, applying knowledge of the past to the analysis and resolution of present difficulties. Their agreement extended to the political application of ideas: Turner supported most of Roosevelt's political initiatives from the mid-nineties until 1912, when he rejected Roosevelt's "New Nationalism" for the "New Democracy" of Woodrow Wilson.[4]

Many of the elements of the "Frontier Thesis" put forward by Turner and Roosevelt already belonged to the complex of traditional ideas that had accumulated around the idea of the "Frontier" since colonial times, including the concept of pioneering as a defining national mission, a "Manifest Destiny," and the vision of the westward settlements as a refuge from tyranny and corruption, a safety valve for metropolitan discontents, a land of golden opportunity for enterprising individualists, and an inexhaustible reservoir of natural wealth on which a future of limitless prosperity could be based.

Turner's and Roosevelt's Frontier Theses differ from earlier versions in their theoretical self-consciousness: the deliberation with which they attempt to systematize earlier traditions and to create a historical account with the explanatory authority of scientific demonstration. And their impulse for this undertaking arose from their sense of crisis, that the closure of the Frontier, and the bonanza economy its existence had fostered, was no longer a prospect but an accomplished fact.

That conclusion was premature, however. As a purely material entity, the Frontier was far from closed. More public land would be taken up and brought into production between 1890 and 1920 than during the supposed heyday of the western frontier in the decades that followed passage of the Homestead Act (1862). Superior techniques of irrigation produced a bonanza in dry-land farming in the early twentieth century. During the Great War, favorable markets and improved technology led to the cultivation of acreage previously considered inarable or unprofitable. There were also bonanzas on various "resource frontiers," in the timber ranges, the new oil fields of Texas and Oklahoma, and the Alaskan gold rush. But the political, economic, and social conditions under which these new "frontiers" would develop differed radically from those that pertained on the agrarian and mineral frontiers of 1800–70. Individual entrepreneurs and settlers on the new frontiers of the industrial and railroad eras had to contend (on increasingly disadvantageous terms) with large capitalist enterprises for control of the new resources.[5]

The apparent closure of the old agrarian/artisanal/entrepreneurial frontier coincided with a crisis in American social and political history, and Roosevelt and Turner were not alone in seeing the two phenomena as significantly, perhaps causally, linked. The social order envisioned in republican ideology and the Frontier Myth was one in which class tensions were disarmed by the broad diffusion of wealth and power, by the relatively slight differentials between wealthy and working classes, and by the promise of upward mobility. By 1890 it was clear that the industrialization of the economy had produced a social order in which wealth and power would increasingly be concentrated in the hands of a relatively few men, and a few powerful (and even monopolistic) industrial and financial "trusts."

Interpreters of the political economy disagreed on the meaning and desirability of this tendency toward concentration, but they recognized its centrality to the epoch and its potential for producing social and political crisis. By 1895 the concentration of wealth in the agrarian sector had undone the achievements of the "pioneers" of the Homestead era. Independent farmers on the Plains lost their land to debt and became tenants or sharecroppers on industrial farms or plantations, and their resentment had taken a radical and political form in the "populist" movements of the previous decades.

The concentration of industrial wealth and power produced similar resistance among small businessmen and workers in the cities, milltowns, and mining towns of every region. The labor movement was increasingly radicalized by its experience of "degradation" in the workplace and victimization in the marketplace, and management defended its interests with escalating levels of force and violence. Resentments that had festered during the twenty-year cycle of relatively depressed economic activity reached a crisis in the wake of the Panic of 1893 and in the wave of factory closings, lay-offs, and wage rollbacks it provoked.[6]

For Turner and Roosevelt the crisis posed a profound question about the meaning of the American past. How had the history of the

American republic produced this squalid new "metropolis" of the 1890s, in which greedy monopolists and sullen, degraded proletarians wrestled for advantage in an environment of chronic economic stagnation? And was it possible for the nation to maintain the republican forms and democratic values of its traditional political culture under the new conditions? Both men believed that their role as historians was not merely to establish the facts of the historical case but to apply historical knowledge to the ideological task of defining and projecting resolutions of contemporary crises.[7]

Their historiographical projects conform precisely to the function we have ascribed to mythic narrative in modern culture: they deploy a language of traditional ideological symbols and narrative structures as a means to understanding a social/political crisis. The histories they produced portrayed the Frontier as the source of exemplary tales that provided a model of the workings of natural, social, and moral law in history. From these tales they derived a paradigm of interpretation and a model of social behavior which, if understood and followed, would keep Americans true to the values and practices of republican democracy despite the transformation of the economy.

But despite their common sources and concerns, the historical mythologies and the Frontier Theses formulated by Turner and Roosevelt were actually antitheses. If we look closely at their myth/historical practice, we see that they offer very different visions of the shape and meaning of the frontier past.

Sources and Premises

Turner and Roosevelt were drawn to the history of the Frontier by an "intuitive" sense of its importance. The literature of the Frontier had played a significant part in their respective childhoods. But there were important differences in the kind of frontier stories each received and in the form of historical storytelling each preferred.[8]

Turner grew up in Wisconsin, a well-established agricultural region only two generations past its own frontier phase and separated by the width of Minnesota from the "cutting edge" of the Great Plains frontier in the Dakotas. The folklore of his region's frontier past was communicated to him directly, and it explained the meaning of that past by seeing it as foreground to the prosperous agrarian present. As a reader, he was less interested in literary fiction than in the writing of the philosophers, historians, and panegyrists of agrarianism and the "yeoman farmer." His academic career in the East distanced him from the agrarian landscape and enabled him to analyze his home region with a degree of theoretical rigor. The goal of his historiographic method was to achieve a fully materialist understanding of the Frontier in which abstractions like "American values" and "national character" would be related to the concrete matters of land acquisition and agricultural production.[9]

Roosevelt was imaginatively engaged by the literary mythology of the Frontier, especially Cooper's *Leatherstocking Tales,* and he favored historians like Francis Parkman, who portrayed history in Cooperian terms as a real-life "romance" in which heroes representing national virtues test and vindicate the "character" of their people in "savage war." While Turner went east to think about frontier economics, Roosevelt went west to his Dakota cattle ranch to escape personal grief and disappointment by living out his Hawkeye fantasies as a frontier hunter. (The ranch itself was more of an agribusiness, complete with absentee owner, than a yeoman's freehold such as Turner knew and praised.)[10]

Turner assigned to farmers the leading role in the historical legend of American development. But the literary mythology preferred by Roosevelt offered a different historical protagonist and a different historical scenario. The primary agent of American expansion in this literature is "the man who knows Indians." Consequently, Roosevelt's pantheon of heroes included both the fictional Hawkeye and historical figures like Daniel Boone and Davy Crockett, Robert Rogers of the Rangers, Kit Carson, Sam Houston, and even Andrew Jackson. In this his preferences were shared by the readers of American nineteenth-century popular fiction, for in romances and dime novels the farmer was a secondary figure while the hunter/Indian-fighter was at the center of action.[11]

The significance of this difference in literary taste becomes clear when we look at "hunter" and "farmer" as figures in a myth/ideological scenario. In its traditional form, the Myth of the Frontier emphasizes the necessary linkage between two themes as the basis for spiritual and secular regeneration, taking up the "free" or "virgin land" of the wilderness, and defeating the savage natives in a war of races. The "virgin land" theme symbolically addresses the economic aspects of ideological concern, while the "race war" or "savage war" theme addresses political concerns (the use of force, the right of conquest). When a novelist or historian privileges one theme (or figure) at the expense of the other, the harmony of the original formula is broken, and two alternative versions of the myth—two different readings of historical dynamics—appear.

The yeoman farmer described by Turner and the earlier agrarians is not an individual hero but a Whitmanian hero *en-masse*. "His" ambition belongs to no particular person but is an abstraction of the motives that drive any modern economy: the desire for a better living standard to be achieved through labor and the accumulation of wealth. "His" great achievement—the establishment of the agrarian republic, the regeneration of society—is the outcome of a large collective process in which nearly everyone participates. Though some political leaders are accorded prominence for their fostering of agrarian development, their achievements (as Turner envisions them) do not take the form of heroic adventure. Not only is the result of this process democratic, the process itself is democratic in form. The agents of historical achievement in Turner's world are not the great captains and men of daring exploit but the small entrepreneurs, artisans, and farmers, the little men in their average and aggregate.

To the husbandman's life of laborious cultivation, the hunter-hero opposes the ideal of a life lived by and for individual exploit. And the history that proceeds from the activity of such heroes is one in which certain actors are accorded a moral privilege: to act on their own initiative, perhaps for the sake of the democratic *en masse* but without being bound by the constraints of moral or civic order which the social collective must observe. In the literary mythology of the nineteenth century, the function of such a hero is to make the wilderness safe for a civilization in which he is unsuited (and disinclined) to participate. He lives outside the cash nexus of commercial society, in a pre-capitalist Eden; yet he gives his life, or destroys his own "natural" mode of living, for the sake of bourgeois society whose rewards he does not value and whose manner of earning bread he despises. He is American ideological ambivalence personified: he reproaches commercial values by his purifying regression to the primitive, but that regression itself is accorded moral privilege only because it initiates the regime of democratic progress, that culminates in turn to the commercial "metropolis" of modernity.

Roosevelt and Turner resolve this paradox in different ways. Turner's approach is essentially "nostalgic." By dwelling on the naive perfection of the pre-modern frontier past, Turner implies a critique of the corruptions of the present. The Frontier of the past appears as the place in which, once upon a time, the political and social life of a European people was transformed, morally regenerated, and given a distinctively democratic direction. Roosevelt's historiography has a different premise and structure. The present social order, despite its evident dangers and corruptions, represents the culmination of civilized progress. To ground that belief required a historiography that would allow him to see the industrial/urban order of the present as the direct, logical, and hence desirable outcome of a frontier past. The choice of a man of violence and conquest as the representative frontiersman was appropriate to the kind of history he wished to write and the kind of ideology he wished to justify. For him significant action occurred at the cutting edge of expansion, where representatives of different races contend for mastery, and not in the peaceful regions where the husbandman tills his fields. While Turner locates the crucial dynamism in a democratic collectivity, Roosevelt locates it in successive classes of heroes emerging from the strife of races to earn a neo-aristocratic right to rule.

It was this suggestion of a potentially aristocratic character lurking under the hunter's buckskins that attracted Roosevelt to the figure. In the works of Cooper and his imitators this association had a schematic form, in the repeated plot-formula of an alliance between an "old hunter" of plebian origins and a well-born natural aristocrat—the son of a British nobleman (*The Pioneers*), a Virginia planter and soldier (*Last of the Mohicans*), or a professional military man (*The Prairie*). The dime novelists who developed the Cooper formula after 1860 followed this pattern, but they also gave greater prominence to a hybrid form of frontier hero in which the characteristics of hunter and soldier-aristocrat were combined. After the Civil War this combined figure became more prominent in the mythologization of figures from the contemporary frontier scene by journalists and dime novelists. (The celebrity of General Custer from 1865 to 1876 took this form.)[12]

A similar mythology informs Francis Parkman's monumental history of the colonial Indian wars, published between 1859 and 1892. Parkman was one of young Roosevelt's favorite authors, his model as a historian.[13] Like Cooper, Parkman represents history as a contest between "nations" or "races," each with its distinctive and inherent set of "gifts" and propensities. His accounts of intertribal rivalries established as historical orthodoxy and the idea that Indian warfare was characteristically exterminationist and genocidal in its objectives and tactics. He insists that historical struggles test character as well as might, and that the victory of the Anglo-Americans over the French and Indians is a vindication of the "character" that has produced their institutions. Like Cooper, Parkman offers two types of heroes, exemplifying the virtues of different classes of men. His Hawkeye-like "rangers" (of whom Robert Rogers is the prime example) are useful but problematic figures. His clearest embodiments of Anglo-American (and even of French) virtue are always aristocrats and military professionals—Washington, Wolfe, perhaps Frontenac—who are capable of ruling and managing their lower classes as well as mastering the enemy. Such men are needed to

> resist the mob and the demagogue, . . . the race for gold and the delirium of prosperity . . . to prove . . . that the rule of the masses is consistent with the highest growth of the individual; that democracy can give the world a civilization mature and pregnant, ideas as energetic and vitalizing, and types of manhood as lofty and strong, as any of the systems which it boasts to supplant.[14]

Roosevelt's interpretation of frontier heroism built upon these developments in literary mythology and extended their implications.

The Historian as Hunter

Roosevelt's inchoate enthusiasm for and intuitive identification with the Frontier became central to his self-image during his immersion in the "real West." Then, in the period of intensive literary labor that followed his return to the East, he developed his ideas into a systematic historical theory and a personal mythology. His motives for going west in 1882 reflect his internalization of the myth of regeneration through wilderness-going; he fled to his cattle ranch to escape the grief and despair that followed the sudden deaths of his wife and his mother. After two years of ranching, big-game hunting, and service as a deputy sheriff, he was sufficiently restored in spirit to return to the East and to re-enter politics with an abortive (but instructive) run for mayor of New York.[15] While his political prospects were germinating, he set out to earn his living and a share of public attention as a writer, with the West as his chief subject. Between 1885 and 1895 he published numerous articles on the West, three books recounting his adventures as a hunter and a rancher, a biography of expansionist Senator Thomas Hart Benton, and the seven volumes of *The Winning of the West*. He also collaborated with Henry Cabot Lodge on a collection of *Hero Tales from American History*, to which he contributed sketches of the heroes of westward expansion and Indian warfare.

As Roosevelt reflected on his western experiences in these books and connected them with historical antecedents, he began to see a sanctifying relation between his own adventures and the larger patterns of history. His Dakota experience suggested that he possessed latent qualities not unlike those of pioneers like Boone and Crockett, figures that became feasible role models as well as heroic ideals. He felt he had acquired, through immersion in the wilderness, a capacity for "strenuous" life and achievement that set him above the selfishness and sloth of the leisured and moneyed classes whose political impotence he accused. He began to see himself as the representative man of his class, embodying its essential energies and latent virtues. Roosevelt characteristically projected his personal psychology into public affairs, equating his own early struggle with physical debility with his country's rise to power. But his new identification with the Myth of the Frontier gave a larger shape to this tendency. He began to see his own ranching and hunting experience as a model for regenerating the lost manliness and vigor of his class.

His most palpable gesture in this direction was his co-founding (with Lodge) of the Boone and Crockett Club in 1887. It was to be an organization for gentleman hunters like himself, a social club and an agency for fostering conservation policies. The members included many of the most prominent and influential men of the time: political leaders like Lodge, Roosevelt, and Redfield Proctor; industrial magnates like John Rogers, Jr.; professionals and amateurs of history and social science like Francis Parkman, Madison Grant, and Henry Fairfield Osborn; Clarence King, a leading figure in western exploration; the anthropologist George Bird Grinnell; painters of western scenery (Albert Bierstadt and Frederic Remington); the novelist Owen Wister; and the conservationist Gifford Pinchot. In addition to sponsoring hunting expeditions and a system for establishing records in trophy-taking, club members lobbied for conservation measures and national parks, helped establish the American Museum of Natural History, and undertook programs of education to foster public appreciation of hunting as an exercise that produces "vigorous and masterful people" who possess "energy, resolution, manliness, self-reliance, and a capacity for self-help"—qualities "without which no race can do its life work well."[16]

For Roosevelt and his fellow clubmen, the ritual veneration of archetypal frontiersmen like Boone and Crockett was an American equivalent of the Victorian gentleman's playing at medieval chivalry.

But their choice of ancestors, and the rituals through which they affirmed their connection, reflected the ideological needs of a distinctly American gentry. For by identifying with these ancestors, who were plebeian in their origins, these new aristocrats sought to affirm an organic and legitimating connection between their own privileged state of wealth, power, and knowledge and an original "democracy" in which such privilege was unknown.[17]

Roosevelt was not only the founder of the Boone and Crockett Club; in the autobiographical hunting tales and histories he published between 1885 and 1895, he was the author of its myths of origin. His first two books—*Hunting Trips of a Ranchman* (1885) and *Ranch Life and the Hunting Trail* (1888)—were similar in structure and subject matter. They reflect his initial responses to his rediscovery of the Frontier and his rapid assimilation of his experience to a systematic historiographical scenario. His opening chapters identify the grand theme of frontier history as an American recapitulation of the "stages of civilization."[18] He uses the history of the West to illustrate first the succession of savages by civilized races and then the succession of different classes or subdivisions of the White or Anglo-Saxon race that represent progressively higher stages of development. He presents his personal development as typical of the experience of the latest, most civilized, and most self-conscious of these successor-classes. Thus he makes his own history the fulfillment of the larger historical processes he has invoked.

The mythic subtext of Roosevelt's account is a version of the theme of regeneration-through-regression—here, the passage of a highly civilized man through a revivifying return to the life of an earlier historical "stage." After Roosevelt's emergence as a popular politician, this experience was usually presented as an immersion in the democratic life of the cowboy—a version Roosevelt himself espoused in his *Autobiography* of 1913.[19] But in his earlier works Roosevelt insists on the importance of class differences and characterizes them in almost racial terms. He identifies the competition of race-like classes as the force that drives civilization upward through its several stages. At each stage, the demands of the historical moment foster the emergence and triumph of a distinctive biosocial "character" or "type." The type is identified by its distinctive social attributes, which suggest that it is effectively a *class* or cultural entity, but Roosevelt assumes that its differences must be rooted in "blood" or heredity and that it is genetically transmissible to future generations.

As civilization develops and becomes more complex, primitive race/classes give way to superior forms. Thus the tribal Indian hunter gives way to "The old race of Rocky Mountain hunters and trappers, of reckless, dauntless Indian fighters . . . archetypes of freedom"—a race that is "now fast dying out," to be replaced by more advanced types like the cowboy, the rancher, and the farmer. The cowboys are the nearest in spirit to the hunter-race and are therefore "much better fellows and pleasanter companions than small farmers or agricultural laborers; nor are the mechanics and workmen of the great city to be mentioned in the same breath." Roosevelt ignores the racial and ethnic diversity that actually characterized cowboys during this era and represents the whole class as essentially Anglo-Saxon. Unlike the workmen of the cities, Roosevelt's cowhands are uncontaminated by alien influences, immune to the poison of labor unionism, and (as Roosevelt tells it) eager for a vigilante neck-tie party to lynch the Haymarket anarchists. But they cannot be pure archetypes of freedom, because they are hired hands, "hard-working, faithful fellows."[20]

The best of the cowboys form the nucleus of the successor-class of ranchers. However, as the ranching business becomes engaged with the larger economy, leadership of the ranchers passes to a new class of proprietors, ranchers borrow eastern management skills and sophistication, and the emigrants discover in themselves "ruder, coarser virtues and physical qualities" appropriate to the conquest of a new territory.[21]

As stage succeeds stage and class succeeds class, those who do not form part of the newly empowered elite are either destroyed or subordinated. Roosevelt's West is a Darwinian arena in which "races" representing different phases or principles of social organization contend for *mastery*. Mexicans and White hunters displace Indians; Texan cowboys displace hunters and Mexicans and are subordinated by the most efficient Texans—who in turn bow to the superior managerial skill of eastern capitalists. But even these new classes will go the way of Boone and Crockett when different conditions and superior forms of organization appear. The lesson Roosevelt draws from his historical fable is that no class or race can stay the march of history, and that those who seek to do so are the foes of progress. Thus he links his own class of gentleman-ranchers to the vanished Indians of Cooper's romances and pronounces a stern epitaph prophetic of his later trust-busting:

> In its present form stock-raising on the plains is doomed. . . . The great free ranches, with their barbarous, picturesque, and curiously fascinating surroundings, mark a primitive stage of existence as surely as do the great tracts of primeval forests and, like the latter, must pass away before the onward march of our people. . . . The doctrine seems merciless, and so it is; but it is just and rational for all that. It does not do to be merciful to the few at the cost of justice to the many.[22]

The Indians are the primary representatives of the anti-progressive principle in Roosevelt's West. He is merciless in his ridicule of the "foolish sentimentalists" who seek to protect and preserve the land titles and cultures of reservation Indians and even argues against shielding Indians who took up homesteads under the provisions of the Dawes Act from the chicaneries by which Whites defrauded them of their freeholds on the grounds that their inability to help themselves proves their inaptitude for even the agrarian stage of civilization. At times the Indian appears as a primitive anticipation of the worst of the robber barons, a would-be monopolist of the free land. More typically, the Indian is associated with lower-class Whites who are unable to survive in a society which demands that they "work or starve":

> Give each Indian his little claim; if, as would generally happen, he declined this, why, let him share the fate of the thousands of white hunters and trappers who have lived on the game that the settlement of the country has exterminated, and let him, like these whites, who will not work, perish from the face of the earth which he cumbers.[23]

By associating "savages" with the class of White "failures" under the rubric "cumberers of the earth," Roosevelt was working within a tradition of public discourse that dated to the newspaper editorials of the mid-1870s, when labor disorders attending the depression of 1873 coincided with a period of Indian hostilities over the Black Hills of Dakota (not far from Roosevelt's ranch). For example, the New York *World* of January 18, 1874, offered a "solution" to the Indian problem in much the same terms:

> The Indians have their choice of incorporation with the general mass of the population and a life of civilized industry, which in the great majority of instances they decline to lead[;] or else of betaking themselves to such regions as are not needed for the maintenance of civilized men, there to remain unmolested until either the land they live on is needed, in which case they must be removed, or else they issue from it to molest civilized settlers, in which case they must be punished with death if no

> less penalty will avail. The country is not yet so crowded that the Indian must be told to work or die; but it is so crowded that he must be told to behave himself or die.

Ten days later, in response to the labor demonstration in Tompkins Square, the paper used the same terms to deride the demands of the workingmen: "Every man is capable to do something which the world wants enough to keep him alive while he is doing it. If he will not do that something, he ought to starve."[24]

The difference between Roosevelt's formulations and the *World*'s is his belief that America has at last become so crowded that both Indians and workmen must be compelled to accept the disciplines of "work or starve, behave or die." But the mechanism that will enforce this discipline is not the crude application of military force envisioned by the exterminationist editorials of the 1870s. Roosevelt expects genocidal effects to be achieved "naturally," without any deliberate human agency, through the operation of Social Darwinian natural selection.

Roosevelt "naturalizes" force and violence by representing it chiefly through stories of his big-game hunts. By helping to exterminate the buffalo, Roosevelt indirectly plays a role in the warfare that would subjugate the Indians.[25] The hunting chapters also follow a program of hierarchical and historical stages as Roosevelt stalks and kills ever more dangerous quarry, from deer at the bottom, through grizzly bear and panther near the top. The "most dangerous game" is man himself; Roosevelt figures as a man-hunter in the episodes dealing with his term as deputy sheriff. This pattern follows the pattern laid down by Cooper in *Deerslayer*, one of Roosevelt's favorite books; as in *Deerslayer*, the stages of hunting function as preparation for the higher function of the warrior. But Roosevelt would not complete his quest until the Cuban war gave him the chance to "get his Spaniard."[26]

Roosevelt's hunting also has a "class" character. He insists that he is not a "game butcher" who hunts animals for profit or subsistence. Like the fictional Hawkeye, he sees himself as a man at odds with the sordidness of trade, who kills only for simple need or to complete a ritual test of manhood. This is clearly an aristocrat's and a sportsman's approach to hunting. Roosevelt's plebeian hunter-heroes, Boone and especially Crockett, were certainly game-butchers by Roosevelt's definition. But Roosevelt is only interested in Boone and Crockett as putative ancestors for his own developing hero-persona and for the new aristocracy he sought to represent. In his last hunting book, *The Wilderness Hunter* (1893), Roosevelt symbolizes history itself as a series of great "hunts" in which a succession of representative hunter-heroes and political leaders carry the nation from colony to world power. The sequence begins with Daniel Boone, the "archetype" of the hunter, and continues on through Crockett and Houston to Buffalo Bill and the officer-gentlemen of the Plains cavalry (Custer, Sheridan). The stages of our political development are marked by the careers of three hunter-presidents, Washington, Jackson, and Lincoln. And from the prominence given to Roosevelt's own exploits, it is clear that he himself is eligible to cap both the game-killing and the political sequences.[27]

The Winning of the West: *A Progressive Myth of Origins*

In the hunting books Roosevelt develops a personal mythology, linking his own role and character to the historical and natural forces he saw at work in frontier history. In *The Winning of the West* he attempts a more systematic study of his "myth of origins," designed to provide an authoritative rationale for the hegemony of the new elites. Like Parkman's histories, *The Winning of the West* treats the Indian wars as the central matter of American history. His account begins where Parkman's ends, with the Anglo-American settlement of the trans-Allegheny region after the last of the French and Indian Wars. As originally designed, Roosevelt's history would have dealt with the Indian wars of the revolutionary and early national periods and would have ended with the opening of the trans-Mississippi frontier.

The success of American arms is the means by which progress and nationality will be achieved, and that success (as in Parkman) depends on the heroism of men whose virtues represent and impose on the course of events the latent virtues of their "race." But Roosevelt adopts a theoretical apparatus, drawn from the diverse fields of biology, social science, and linguistics, that is far more systematic than anything invoked by Parkman. He tries to give a quasi-scientific authority to his historical account of the development of an American "racial" character. Social Darwinism is perhaps the most important element in his system, the ideological extrapolation from Darwin's theory of evolution by natural selection which held that the "struggle for existence" tended to pass power on to "higher" biological forms, races, and social classes. But Roosevelt's theory of heredity is Lamarckian; he believes that human races acquire new traits through historical experience which are incorporated in their "blood" and passed on to succeeding generations. His typology of human races is derived from the linguistically based theories of Aryanism and Teutonism, which held that one common racial ancestor or master-race is the root of all those peoples whose languages belong to the Indo-European family and that in some races (that is, the Teutons) the line of inheritance runs truer.[28]

But the personal motives and the ideological dilemmas that gave rise to this ambitious theorizing are also important to understand. Roosevelt's desire for "system" and "rigor" arises from his sense that to define a truly racial or *volkisch* basis for an American nationality is an extraordinarily difficult task. Parkman assumed that the preponderant majority of "Americans" were essentially English or British and that the Anglo-American culture and political society of the colonies was the appropriate expression of their racial or national character. Roosevelt cannot take that much for granted, because he lives at a moment when the traditional definition of American nationality is being tested by demographic change. He had at least to acknowledge the element of heterogeneity that he himself represented as an "intensely American" scion of Dutch-American rather than Anglo-American ancestry.

According to Roosevelt, the strife of races on the frontier produces first of all a generalized "type" or "race" of "fighters and breeders." Within this frontier folk heroic virtues are broadly diffused, as are political power and wealth. The racial endowment, under these social circumstances, fosters a government that can only operate through a broadly based mutual consent, a society in which class divisions are miniscule and fluid, and a political culture that invites individuals pre-eminent among their fellows for particular merits (tactical skill, sagacity, virtue) to step forward and take the lead. Such leaders serve only for the duration of the crisis or occasion that has called them forth; they do not at first form a permanent leadership class. Having served the community, they return to it. But as the frontier community grows and as the pressure of Indian hostilities becomes greater and more enduring, the "best men" of the frontier are called to lead more often, and for longer periods of time. And as the community itself becomes more complex, higher leadership skills are required. In the end, a new leadership class emerges from the race, the double-distilled product of the hero-making environment of the wilderness, and this new class *replaces* the original democratic mass as the chief agent of historical progress.

The Winning of the West begins with the Teutonic barbarians emerging from their northern forests to invade the Roman Empire. It culminates in the latter-day expansion of the English-speaking peoples "over the world's waste spaces." The Teutons triumph because of their martial virtues, their love of independence, and their tribal patriotism (the germ of nationalism). But their conquest of Rome is followed by a racial and cultural interbreeding that corrupts or "Latinizes" their blood and culture. Only in the British Isles (says Roosevelt) is "a lasting addition to the Germanic soil" achieved; for only in the isolation of the European periphery can their racial germs develop without alien admixture.

In the wilderness of Britain, the Germanic settlers are exposed to invasion by warlike barbarians of the same racial stock but of more primitive social development. Thus the blood of the original settlers is continually refreshed and regenerated by infusions from peoples whose military vigor has not been vitiated by civilization. The resulting British race is not unmixed or pure, but all of its elements (aside from a small Celtic input) are in some sense "Germanic": Saxon, Anglian, Friesian, Norse, Danish, and Norman-French. Under the special conditions of isolation and underdevelopment that pertained in Britain, a hybrid super-race emerges from the interbreeding of these Germanic constituents in which the specialized qualities, attainments, and historical memories of the tribal variants are harmonized and blended while their common "Germanic" root-qualities are reinforced and made into the basis of political unity. Thus Roosevelt reads into the primitive history of the American "race" the essential structures of the Frontier Myth—regeneration through regression, isolation, and savage war—and the contemporary notion of America as "melting pot."[29]

In the settling of America this paradigm of ethnogenesis is reenacted. The most vigorous offspring of that British "race of races" return to an environment very like the one that produced their original ancestors: a wilderness, isolated from civilization, in which the forces of nature and the hostility of native barbarians compel them to renew their latent capacity for self-government and military conquest. Since the conditions of the Frontier are so difficult, only the most hardy and adventurous folk will venture there; and as in ancient Britain, they will tend to be of "Germanic" stock. The largest element are the Protestant Scots-Irish, joined by Dutch and German settlers, and by French Huguenots (whose Protestantism allows Roosevelt to suggest that their racial gifts differ from those of the "Latin" and Catholic French). From the blending of these select and kindred "bloods" the uniquely American racial "stock" is composed. The American character that emerges in the wilderness is a recrudescence of German racial traits, as in his comparison of Daniel Boone to Siegfried.[30]

Roosevelt's special brand of Teutonism was derived from an eclectic mixture of sources. The theory as such was derived from the work of European historians and social scientists, including the French philosopher Gobineau and the English historians Freeman and Stubbs, who developed an implicitly racialist interpretation of the "Whig" historiography of Macaulay. In both instances a racialist historiography emerged from the attempt to respond to an ideological problem: In an age of rapid and violent social and political change, what basis exists for belief in the continuity of "the nation," in the particular distribution of wealth and power that characterized that nation's life? Freeman and Stubbs suggested that the parliamentary/bourgeois regime of Victorian England was indeed the culmination of a progressive history; they showed that its organization conformed to the predilections of an innate Anglo-Saxon racial character whose rudiments could be discerned in the earliest stages of English history. English history then becomes the fable in which that race—like the individual hero in a tale—realizes its latent true identity through action. Although individuals die, racial character persists through time and its consciousness of identity is ratified and continuously preserved by a racial memory that somehow passes on knowledge of past experience.[31]

A popularized form of Whig Anglo-Saxonism had entered American political discourse before the Civil War. And, despite the deep ideological divisions of American society in the middle of the nineteenth century, there was broad agreement on its usefulness in explaining the course of history. Figures as diverse as the expansionist promoter and politician William Gilpin, the abolitionist and anti-Mexican War activist Theodore Parker, the pro-slavery expansionists George Fitzhugh and William Walker used Anglo-Saxonist concepts to describe and justify American expansion into Mexican and Latin American territory. Gilpin represented the vast untapped reserves of western land as a field on which would be worked out "the untransacted destiny of the American people," and he found the shape of that destiny in the correspondence between the special resources of the West and the racial gifts of the American people, expressed in their Anglo-Saxon love of democracy and their industrious energies. Parker also declared that expansion was inevitable as a consequence of racial gifts and that it would bring with it a regime of Anglo-Saxon dominance.

> Of all races, the Caucasian has hitherto shown the most of this instinct of progress, and though perhaps the youngest of all, has advanced the farthest. . . . [They are] the most aggressive, invasive, and exclusive people on the earth. . . . The history of the Anglo-Saxon, for the last hundred years, has been one of continual aggression, invasion, and extermination.

Fitzhugh—Parker's ideological opposite in most respects—characterized American expansion in nearly identical terms.

> [For] what people can stand free competition with that race? . . . The Indian is exterminated . . . the Spaniard is hardly heard of in Florida, and Peonage alone can save the Mexican from extermination. From the days of Hengist and Horsa to those of Houston the same adventurous, rapacious, exterminating spirit has characterized the race.

To which William Walker, the filibuster-conqueror of Nicaragua added:

> Whenever barbarian and civilization . . . meet face to face, the result must be war. . . . That which you ignorantly call "Filibusterism" is not the offspring of hasty passion . . .; it is the fruit of the sure, unerring instincts . . . in accordance with laws as old as creation.[32]

The use of "Anglo-Saxon" rather than "White" signaled the emergence of a crucial distinction in the language of American racialism, a need to differentiate not only Whites from Blacks and Indians but to distinguish between different classes of Whites—for example, to mark a difference between Anglo-Americans and the Irish or German immigrants or the Mexicans in Texas and the Far West that would entitle Anglo-Americans to subordinate or subjugate them.[33]

Roosevelt's version of Teutonism developed the logic of these distinctions into a more systematic theory of the origin and meaning of social differences, and he provided a more sophisticated account of the putative historical origins of a specifically *American* type of Anglo-Saxon. Here he was influenced by Social Darwinism, which transformed "cultural" Teutonism into a biological/hereditarian explanation of the "Germanic roots" of Anglo-Saxon liberty.[34] Instead of simply accepting the inevitability of racial conflict (and White victory) as a practical justification of recent events, he constructs an imaginative model of the process of race-formation in which the Indian—the uniquely American race-enemy—plays a crucial and creative role.

For the purposes of "ethnogenesis," the crucial difference between the American Frontier and that of ancient Britain lies in the character of their respective savages. In both cases, battle with invading savages evokes the latent valor and race-consciousness of the Germano-British settlers. But the racial difference that separates Indians and Whites is insuperably great, different in kind even from the distinction between invading Saxons and native Celts. Where the ancient British settlers could renew their racial vigor by interbreeding with Germanic barbarians, American settlers must regain that vigor by repelling and exterminating their barbarians. Instead of biological exchange with savages of another race or folk, the Americans participate in a *spiritual* exchange, taking from the enemy certain abstract ideas or principles but accepting no admixture of blood. But since the Americans already possess a powerful racial endowment, passed down from the British/German/Viking crossings of the past, this spiritual exchange is able to reinvigorate the American race by arousing forces latent in its "blood."

The initial exchange involves purely tactical knowledge. The frontiersmen become "men who know Indians" and learn to fight savages according to "savage" rules that echo those of the Norman knight and Viking Berserker.[35] But the Indians teach more than tactics. Their fanatical determination to maintain their lands and tribal integrity provides a model of nationalist patriotism that the Whites will have to relearn: White patriotism has been undermined by the spirit of self-interestedness and materialism that is endemic to the commercial civilization of Britain.[36]

The root of that "patriotic" teaching is the principle of race-loyalty, and the Indian war is the necessary means by which it is learned. While the Whites are divided against each other by the pursuit of individual and class interests, for the Indians race and nation are synonymous. They therefore make war on *all* Whites, acting on the principle that "Each race [must stand] by its own members, and . . . [hold] all the other race responsible for the misdeeds of a few," without distinction of age or sex let alone of class or wealth.[37] Although this violates even Roosevelt's notion of justice and produces a war marked by atrocities on both sides, this kind of "savage war" is inevitable given the conditions of the Frontier and the confrontation between two races of such dissimilar "gifts." Since mutual assimilation is impossible, the war can only end with the extermination or removal of one race or the other. Hence the centrality of attacks on the women and children of both sides: the object of the war is to destroy the enemy root and branch (through the murder of mothers and children) or to corrupt and alter his seed (through captivity and rape).

The character of Roosevelt's frontiersmen is less like the mild, nature-loving model of Daniel Boone or Cooper's Hawkeye and more like the type of the "Indian-hater."[38] But what was dangerous and reprehensible in literary characters like Jibbenainosay or John Moredock becomes a necessary and justifiable basis for historical agency when it is enlarged into a racial trait. Roosevelt explicitly urges his reader to ignore the pleas of "sentimentalists" whose consciences are made uneasy by the dispossession of the Indians:

> [T]he struggle could not possibly have been avoided . . . [U]nless we were willing that the whole continent west of the Alleghanies should remain an unpeopled waste, *war was inevitable*. . . . It is wholly impossible to avoid conflicts with the weaker race.[39]

The law of nature and of progress requires that those unsuited for civilization either give way to those who bear the germs of progress or be destroyed. The same principle applies in contemporary America to the struggle between those classes of Whites who are capable of advancing the race and those who are unable to succeed in a modern society or who espouse antiprogressive values. As Frontier becomes civilization, the frontiersmen's understanding of race as "color" must be elaborated into an understanding of race as class.[40] Roosevelt suggests this application of the frontier precedent by describing the Indians in terms that link them to modern "antiprogressives." The "cumberers of the earth" formula is one such device, but in *The Winning of the West* Roosevelt develops a more complex set of analogies.

The key passages occur in a section of the first volume devoted to an ethnographic overview of the Indian tribes, modeled on a similar section of Parkman's *Conspiracy of Pontiac*. Roosevelt tells us that the Creek Indians possessed a federal system of government somewhat like our own before the Civil War; and like the antebellum United States, they encouraged slaveholding. However, "the tillage of the land was by communal labor; and, indeed, the government, as well as the system of life, was in many respects a singular compound of communism and extreme individualism." The analogy with American federalism suggests that the reader see the Creeks as a metaphoric representation of the United States (or certain aspects of it). The evils of the Creek systems are likewise analogous to tendencies that Roosevelt condemned in American culture. In fact, the Creeks are a perfect scapegoat for those evils, since their culture comprehends both political/economic extremes: the "communist" collectivism of the socialists and the "extreme individualism" of the Robber Barons.[41]

On the White side of the racial divide, Roosevelt finds the germs of modern class divisions. The early warfare with the western Indians fused the varied White stocks into "the kernel of the distinctive and intensely American stock who were the pioneers . . . the vanguard of the army of fighting settlers." They are the pick of the most vigorous elements of a British race that was itself the pick of the German racial stocks: the cream of the cream of the conquering race. Their characteristics anticipate the virtues of the "strenuous life," which Roosevelt would later preach to his own class. They were "fighters and breeders," with a simple and ideal family government. "The man was the armed protector and provider, the bread-winner; the woman was the housewife and child-bearer. They married young and their families were large, for they were strong and healthy, and their success in life depended on their own stout and willing hearts." There was little inherited wealth but there was enough land for every virile man to maintain his family, so "courage, thrift, and industry were sure of their reward." Although they were farmers, and hence figurative precursors of the Jeffersonian yeoman, they were also hunters, and hence exemplars of those virtues which the Boone and Crockett Club promoted for the new aristocracy.

Their hunting was not ritual or sport; it was a form of productive labor and a preparation for their historical role. "No form of labor is harder than the chase, nor none so excellent as a training school for war." It is their character as hunters, not their role as farmers, that gives the frontiersmen the power to make history. The virtues of the farmer are not those of the shaper of history: "A race of peaceful, unwarlike farmers would have been helpless before such foes as the red Indians. . . . Colonists fresh from the old world, no matter how thrifty, steady-going, and industrious, could not hold their own on the frontier; they had to settle where they were protected from the Indians by a living barrier of bold and self-reliant American borderers."[42]

This relationship between active agents of progress (hunters) and passive developers of progressive gains (farmers) is an embryonic form of the distinction between those modern classes gifted for direction, management, and enterprise and those gifted only for subordination and drudgery. A further symptom of class differentiation appears among the hunters themselves. "All qualities, good and bad, are intensified and accentuated in the life of the wilderness," and the freedom and violence of frontier life proves congenial to the expression of criminal propensities among the Whites. The prototypes of the modern "dangerous classes" and "cumberers of the earth," like the "southern crackers and poor whites," had their origin among the borderers.[43]

But for most frontiersmen, the experience of savage war becomes the basis of a renewal and strengthening of the social compact. "The first lesson the backwoodsman learnt was self-help; the next, that such a community would thrive only if all joined in helping one another." The first generation of political leadership produced by this experience is typified by Daniel Boone—a figure whose virtues are greater in degree, but not different in kind, from those of the general public. His notion of government is theirs, and it envisions nothing more than an *ad hoc* agency for mutual assistance, operating only when self-help has manifestly failed. But by 1774 "the pioneer work of the hunter was over, and that of the axe-bearing settler was about to begin." In this more complex social setting, a different and more managerial model of political leadership was required. The heroes and representative men of this second stage are a succession of military-aristocratic leaders, most notably George Rogers Clark and Anthony Wayne. These men are distinguished from the public they serve by superior birth, education, and technical training, and (as Roosevelt tells it) they insist quite openly on the reality and significance of their class difference. Clark handpicks the men he will enroll in his army, ignoring the democratic customs of militia companies. (Roosevelt would do the same in recruiting his Rough Riders for the Spanish–American War.) The victory of Clark's army is therefore not attributable to the democratic mass; rather, it "belongs" personally to Clark as "their leader." In 1794 Wayne was to achieve a similarly personal triumph by overcoming the weakness of the democratically elected national government and the indiscipline of his troops to defeat the Indians at Fallen Timbers and to bring "peace by the sword."[44]

Thus the end product of the Frontier is the production of a new kind of ruling class whose skills and values reflect the lessons of both Indian warfare and frontier government, and whose authority is ratified by both natural law (their success in the Darwinian strife with the Indians) and the consent of those they govern. That consent is gained from a people with a gift for self-government and self-reliance whose subordination is willing and informed because it is based on the experience of savage warfare and the recognition that racial solidarity and social discipline are necessary to victory.

If Roosevelt had been able to carry his history as far as originally projected, he would have taken this process of political succession one crucial step further, to the opening of the trans-Mississippi frontier and the Texas Revolution. Crockett's death at the Alamo would have symbolized the transfer of all those qualities that the hunter personified to a new field of struggle in which the primary enemy is not a "savage" race but a civilized (or "semicivilized") nation formed by an inferior race in which Indian and Latin stocks are mixed. The shift from one form of Frontier expansion to another would also have provided a metaphoric anticipation of Roosevelt's polemic on behalf of overseas imperialism, which he saw as the necessary continuation of the "Winning of the West."[45]

Recovering the Frontier: Regeneration Through Imperialism

The logic behind this extension of the Frontier Myth to foreign affairs can most clearly be seen in Roosevelt's speeches and writings about the Spanish–American War. The most famous of these, "The Strenuous Life," is addressed not to the public at large but to the wealthy conservatives of Chicago's Hamilton Club—"Men who pre-eminently and distinctly embody all that is most American in the American character." Their role is analogous to that of the earlier frontiersmen, who had "formed the kernel of that distinctive and intensely American stock who were . . . the vanguard of the army of fighting settlers." It is to these men that Roosevelt "wish[es] to preach, not the doctrine of ignoble ease, but the doctrine of the strenuous life, the life of toil and effort, labor and strife." For them, the problem of a closed Frontier is not the lack of economic opportunity but the loss of those conditions that allowed their class to acquire the virile character that entitles and enables them to rule giant corporations or a modern nation-state. To renew their virility and to save their class from leisured inanition, they must take up the challenge of empire.

The stakes in this challenge are not merely economic and political but racial. The virility of a race, its "fighting spirit," is its sole safe reliance in the Darwinian competition that has been and is to be our history. One of Roosevelt's chief anxieties during this period was the decline in the birthrates of the White, Protestant middle and upper classes relative to those of immigrants and the underclass. He characterized this tendency as "race suicide," because it promised the ultimate extinction of his class/race in the Darwinian struggle, and he once likened women who refused to bear children to soldiers who dropped their weapons and fled the field of battle. By recovering the martial discipline and mission of the frontiersmen, the upper classes will also regain their model of family government, their energy as "fighters and breeders," and the productive advantages that go with these qualities:

> The man must be glad to do a man's work, to dare and to endure and to labor; to keep himself, and to keep those dependent upon him. The woman must be the housewife, the helpmate of the homemaker, the wise and the fearless mother of many children. . . . When men fear work or fear righteous war, when women fear motherhood, they tremble on the brink of doom; and well it is that they should vanish from the earth. . . .[46]

The test of true virility is willingness to engage in "righteous war," the archetype of which is the Indian war or "savage war" of *The Winning of the West.* In a companion piece to "The Strenuous Life" titled "Expansion and Peace," Roosevelt argues that a war against savages is inherently the most righteous of wars, because it brings "peace by the sword." The necessity for such wars arises from the racial character of the contending parties, and the triumph of civilization is always to be seen as both a moral and a secular bettering of the world.

> On the border between civilization and barbarism war is generally normal, because it must be under the conditions of barbarism. Whether the barbarian be the Red Indian on the frontier of the United States, the Afghan on the border of British India, or the Turkoman who confronts the Siberian Cossack, the result is the same . . . without force, fair dealing usually amounts to nothing.

Peace is possible only between nations that "feel the same spirit." But so long as we had an Indian frontier, "the chief feature of frontier life was the endless warfare between the settlers and the red men." In the larger, worldwide perspective, the growth of peace and progress has been "due solely to the power of the mighty civilized races which have not lost the fighting instinct, and which by their expansion are gradually bringing peace to the red wastes where the barbarian peoples of the world hold sway."[47]

Those who question or seek to oppose the imperial mission are therefore agents of potential "race suicide" who would doom their folk to political and biological impotence. Roosevelt clinches this point by linking the anti-imperialists with those "foolish sentimentalists," philanthropists, and Indian-lovers whose policies once enraged and encouraged the American Indians to slaughter settlers and resist the advance of civilization:

> I have scant patience with those who fear to undertake the task of governing the Philippines, . . . [or] shrink from it because of the expense and trouble; but I have even scanter patience with those who make a pretense of humanitarianism to hide and cover their timidity, and who cant about "liberty" and "the consent of the governed" in order to excuse themselves from their unwillingness to play the part of men. Their doctrine, if carried out, would make it incumbent upon us to leave the Apaches of Arizona to work out their own salvation, and to decline to interfere on a single Indian reservation. Their doctrines condemn your forefathers and mine for ever having settled in these United States.[48]

Applying the Frontier Myth to the imperial project begins with a metaphoric extension of Frontier categories to a new situation in which Asians become figurative Apaches and the Philippines become a symbolic equivalent of Boone's Kentucky or Houston's Texas. But it also requires the final abandonment of the democratic political principles that had been so prominent a feature of the original frontier. That abandonment appears most strikingly in Roosevelt's sarcastic dismissal of "liberty" and "consent of the governed" as concepts applicable in the contemporary situation. The immediate distinction is of course racially based: these democratic concepts are irrelevant to the Filipinos because their racial gifts and state of development preclude their making civilized use of them. But an equally undemocratic assertion of class privilege is implicit in Roosevelt's polemic and in the policies he supported. For the new imperial frontier could not, by definition, be a recreation of the old egalitarian frontier of Boone and Crockett. The opportunities for advancement it offered could only be seized by those with capital to invest, or with the skills and training to act as proconsuls managing the affairs and ruling the destinies of an alien population. These elites act as surrogates for the mass of the American public, who can only participate vicariously in the new frontier.

But this undemocratic development is consistent with the course of frontier history Roosevelt traced in his progressive myth of origins. Although the initial phase of frontier life fostered an egalitarian democracy, the course of savage war and social development progressively winnowed and narrowed the class of those invested with heroic, history-making capacities—the "race of heroes" that produced Boone, with Boone deferring to Generals Clark and Wayne, and so on to Jackson, Lincoln . . . and Roosevelt. What was once the common heritage and power of a race of heroes became, because of progress itself, the property of a class within that race. Roosevelt would dramatize this new phase of republican heroism in *The Rough Riders* (1900), the account of his recruitment and command of a highly select volunteer cavalry regiment composed of aristocrats and cowboys with whom he charged to glory and the presidency in the Spanish–American War battle of San Juan Hill.

Roosevelt's interpretation of history reifies his class bias: he can think of nothing better to say of the frontier past than that it has produced and entitled a new ruling class, of which Theodore Roosevelt may well be the representative man. The virtues of the frontier hero are not (as Cooper implied) a rebuke to the values of a commercial society but are in fact an embryonic form of those values. The point of studying frontier history is not to develop a critique of progress by glorifying the past but rather to learn from the past the necessity of acquiescing in the forward movement of history, which once required greedy men to seek monopoly but which now requires (as Roosevelt sees it) the subordination of private profit to public interests and projects of national aggrandizement. The son of the banker or industrialist who reads Roosevelt's lesson aright will exchange mere coupon-clipping for membership in a new class of vigorous and virile rulers bent on the consolidation of class rule at home and the extension of empire abroad. Through this teaching, it will become possible for Americans to *reconstitute* a "Frontier" in terms appropriate to the modern era.

It is at this turn—the moment when historical fact is transformed into precedent for future action—that Roosevelt's history begins to function as myth. And it is at this juncture that his differences with Turner become more significant than their initial agreements.[49]

Their most fundamental disagreement concerns the role of race as a determinant of history. Like Roosevelt, Turner was influenced by Teutonism but preferred to emphasize the importance of environment and to assert that "Too exclusive attention has been paid . . . [to] Germanic origins."[50] Racial and Social Darwinian ideas continued to influence Turner's work, and in his private writing Turner expressed doubts about the capacity of Negroes and certain of the European "races" (Jews, "Mediterraneans," Slavs) to properly adapt to American life. He believed that the alien ethnic character of the urban working classes exacerbated the estrangement between labor and capital. Nonetheless, as he developed as a historian, he became a more consistent and thoroughgoing "environmentalist." At a time when progressives tended to favor the exclusion of immigrants (particularly those from non-Anglo-Saxon or non-Teutonic "racial stocks"), Turner publicly insisted that immigrants had always produced more of economic and even moral value for the nation than the costs their presence imposed.[51] The older immigrants had brought to the country as a whole, and to the West in particular, a moral and political idealism that had reinforced and enriched native democratic tendencies, and Turner insisted that the "new immigrants" who were the objects of racial scorn—even "the hordes of recent immigrants from southern Italy"—were just as idealistic. "He who would take stock of American democracy must not forget the accumulation of human purposes and ideals which immigration has added to the American populace."[52]

Turner's rejection of racialism also entails a rejection of the mystique of privileged violence that informs Roosevelt's historiography and the political ideas he derives from it. For Roosevelt the history of the Indian wars *is* the history of the West; Turner's work is remarkable for the degree to which it marginalizes the role of violence in the development of the Frontier. Most of Turner's references to Indians are concerned with economic matters, and he pays far more attention to the legal, legislative, and commercial struggles of the settlements than to events on the "cutting edge" of expansion. One can legitimately argue that Turner actually obscures the historical role of violence and thereby weakens his analysis. But his antipathy to a war-oriented historiography is more significant as the mark of his disagreement with the ideology of power implicit in Roosevelt's *The Winning of the West*. By rejecting the idea that racial violence is the principle around which both individual character and social organization develop, Turner devalues violence as a political symbol. Turner's and Roosevelt's different appreciation of the significance of violence is directly reflected in the proposals they made for developing civic rituals and institutions through which the "spiritual" or ideological essentials of the lost frontier could be recovered.

From the perspective established by Roosevelt's myth-history, the closing of the Frontier does not signify the loss of an economic resource or "safety valve" but the loss of those elements in national life that made Americans virile and vigorous, stimulated their taste and aptitude for competition, and gave them a strong and unifying sense of racial solidarity. The problem for a post-frontier America is how to preserve and develop those leadership virtues that were fostered by hunting and Indian-fighting in a world without wilderness or savages.

In *The Wilderness Hunter* (1893) Roosevelt describes a public policy that would provide the moral equivalent of Daniel Boone's Indian war or Bill Cody's buffalo slaughter. He proposes the creation of national hunting parks, financed by taxes and open to the public, in which wilderness could be preserved and in which new generations could live "the free, self-reliant adventurous life" of the hunter, "with its rugged and stalwart democracy, [and] wild surroundings, . . . [which] cultivates that vigorous manliness for the lack of which in a nation, as in an individual, the possession of no other qualities can possibly atone." These enclaves of preserved wilderness might be the site (for qualified individuals) of a ritual re-enactment of the frontier experience in which the appropriation of the frontier's ideological essence would substitute for the loss of its material reserves of unappropriated wealth. Instead of bagging dinner for the family, hunters in the parks would bring down and carry home an ideological lesson.[53]

Roosevelt was democrat enough to envision public parks that would include a much larger spectrum of social classes than the game preserves owned by the Boone and Crockett and other hunting clubs. But even so, the benefits of the hunting ritual would hardly be available to all classes of Americans. Nor does he believe that the experience itself would produce what Turner would recognize as a "democratic" ideology. Rather, the hunting parks would teach that life and politics are a Darwinian struggle in which superior types not only triumph but are justified in their hegemony. Roosevelt's first concern was not with the loss of hunter-virtues in the general public—such virtues had never been universal, and even on the Frontier there were "farmers"—but with the loss of those virtues among his own class. For this cultural and social elite, the ritualized violence of the hunting park was merely a preparation for the higher enterprise of imperial war: the extension of the frontier dynamic beyond the American continent.

Turner also understood that the passing of the Frontier had destroyed the "material forces that gave vitality to Western democracy," and that to prevent the "concentration of economic and social power" from rendering "political democracy an appearance rather than a reality" Americans would have to look to "the realm of the spirit, to the domain of ideals and legislation." But he did not regard hunting or warfare as an especially valued part of those exercises; and though he accepted imperialism as a commercial necessity, he did not see imperial warfare in Roosevelt's terms, as a spiritual exercise valuable in itself as a builder of racial character.

Turner located the "domain of ideals" and spirituality in the institutions of public and higher education, whose task it would be to promote the conscious recognition of the value and historical provenance of democratic ideology.[54] He put particular emphasis on the role of the great midwestern land-grant universities, the most "democratic" of the nation's institutions of higher learning, because of their historical origins (as stepchildren of the Homestead Act), their institutional structure, and the demographic range of their faculties and student bodies. Although the scions of industrial managers and laborers could no longer learn democratic values by farming an actual freehold, such an education would give them a conceptual or symbolic knowledge of the nature and importance of agrarian values.[55]

Turner also asserted that this intellectual project was useless unless it eventuated in action in the material world of politics and economics. The "spiritual" exercises of education were to be augmented and enacted through deliberate programs of "legislation"—the articulation and enactment of an informed popular will through the forms of democratic politics.[56] Turner's choice of Wilson over Roosevelt in 1912 turned on his belief that the "New Democracy" would assert the power of a democratic collective to regulate an economically concentrated economy, while the "New Nationalism" promised an inconsistent mixture of heroic "trust-busting" with the chronic Republican bias in favor of big business.[57]

Roosevelt saw the preservation of American "democratic" values as paradoxically dependent on the power and virtue of a heroic elite class. Turner rejected that paradox as contradiction and asserted that the preservation of democratic values would depend (as it had in the past) on the existence of material and political conditions conducive to democratic political practice. Even in the face of a closed frontier, American society retained two elements capable of sustaining that practice, both of which derived directly or indirectly from the experience of frontiering. The first of these was a general ideological consensus, which Turner saw as pervading all classes of society, in favor of the *idea* of democracy as a moral and political value.[58] The second element had a more material character: in his "Sectional Hypothesis" Turner asserted that the political culture of the West and the Midwest was directly derived from the values of the old frontier. Hence, through the West's pursuit of its sectional interests, the traditional values of the Frontier might be ensured potent and enduring representation in American politics.[59]

As a description of American politics Turner's vision of a democratic consensus is deeply flawed. By attending only to the widespread use of the term "democracy," he underestimates the critical differences dividing the contending parties, interest groups, and classes—conflating the "democracy" envisioned by elite figures like Harvard's President C. N. Eliot and Andrew Carnegie on the one hand, and Debsian socialists (or the Populist Party) on the other.[60] Likewise, western sectionalism was a weak reed on which to rest the responsibility for sustaining democratic values attributed to the agrarian era. The same forces that had brought about the closing of the Frontier would also dissolve the cultural autonomy of the sections in which the spirit of the Frontier still ruled. The political economy of the different regions or sections was already fully integrated into a national and international market system. The farmers of the Midwest were directly concerned with developments in New York, London, the Ukraine, and India, and their political behavior reflected this engagement. In such an economy, localities could not preserve either the cultural integrity or the political authority needed to maintain their ideological traditions uncompromised, even if they were so inclined.[61]

The analytical "softness" of these ideas is, in large part, the consequence of the contradiction between knowledge and desire in Turner's thinking. If the historian was correct in identifying the frontier phase as a distinctive epoch responsive to particular historical and material contingencies, then the ideologist's wistful attempt to create a new frontier by merely invoking "spirit" must be logically doomed to frustration.[62]

But the weakness of Turner's program for recovering the last frontier should not obscure the important value differences that distinguish his recuperative projects from Roosevelt's visions of managerial hegemony. Turner's rejection of racialism and the mystique of violence thus points to a more fundamental difference with Roosevelt in the ideological value each assigns to *democracy* and *power*. While conceding the necessity of greater centralization and the direction of commerce by an elite of experts, Turner still defines the objective of politics as the preservation and extension of "democracy" as traditionally conceived: a social order in which all classes have equal access to wealth and power, and to the education that will (in the new order) be the basis of personal independence and social mobility; a politics not merely paternal in its care of the people, but open and responsive to initiatives arising from the "grass roots." Turner's way of reconciling the competing imperatives of democracy and power is "populistic" in its style and symbolism. Its key terms of value refer to the agrarian past, and it assigns a significant share of power to structures closer to the community level than to the grand structures of the state and the corporation. But it differs from true populism in substituting a geographical entity—the former frontier region—for the social class or economic interest group as the basis of significant political action. Where Roosevelt wishes to preserve as much of traditional democracy as is compatible with the interests of a new kind of American nation-state, Turner treats democratic ideas and practices as good in themselves and looks to republican politics (with a populist flavor) as a means to preserving or creating a set of conditions under which democracy in something like the traditional sense can continue to thrive.

Roosevelt's concern as both ideologist and historian was to explain and rationalize the development of American economic and political power. By his account, the replacement of frontier democracy by a corporate order headed by a managerial elite is not to be regretted so long as it fosters the continued growth of national wealth and power. The culmination of American development would be reached with the emergence and empowerment of a new, progressive managerial class which was not the product of frontier "democracy," nor even the representative of popular will, but rather a "third force" standing apart from and sometimes against the contending parties of capital and labor or banker and farmer, asserting against their class interests the interest of "the nation." Democracy remains one of the important elements of American society, and it is in the "national interest" to preserve it; but the imperatives of political democracy are no longer accepted as self-evident moral absolutes but as an important interest that must be balanced against the managerial necessities essential to the maintenance and growth of national power. In the name of that "national" interest, Roosevelt progressives sought to limit the economic power of the Robber Barons in the marketplace, and the ballot-box power of democratic movements—Populists, Socialists, labor unionists, African-American resistance to Jim Crow, and immigrant-based political associations—that threatened the nation's corporate solidarity.[63]

The power and influence of Roosevelt's Frontier Thesis has been obscured by Turner's pre-eminence among the founders of modern American historiography. Roosevelt's career as a historian and man of letters was substantially complete by 1899, while Turner was just then emerging as a leading figure among academic historians. Between 1893 and 1903 Turner developed and systematized his Frontier Thesis with a major book and a series of influential essays. By 1902 his assertion that the Census of 1890 had marked an epoch in American history had been widely recognized as valid, not only by historians but in the mass media as well. Frank Norris's "The Frontier Gone at Last," published in *The World's Work* in 1902, declared that the end of the Frontier marked an epoch in American letters as well. *The World's Work*—one of the leading progressive journals—hailed Turner as one of the nation's "most important living historians," and Woodrow Wilson (an academic historian turned politician) named him "the coming man in American history."

Turner continued to develop and extend the Frontier Thesis (and the related "Sectional Hypothesis") over the next quarter-century. His work became the basis of the "progressive" school of historiography, which shaped academic research at least until 1945. And a Turnerian theory of economic development, linking economic growth to the discovery of various kinds of "bonanza," has been (as we shall see) a major strain in American economic policy-making for most of the century.[64]

But Turner's eclipsing of Roosevelt's reputation only obscures their original (and persistent) intellectual affinities. Although Turner moved away from his earlier Teutonism, many of his disciples retained key elements of a racialist historiography that allowed them to combine elements of Roosevelt's war-centered and racialist historiography with Turner's socioeconomic analysis. However, they did so (for the most part) without crediting Roosevelt, whose work no longer met the canons of professional historiography.[65]

Although Turner exercised far more overt authority as a political ideologist, in this realm there is a degree of parity between the two. Turner's ideas, for all their confusion, were important influences in the development of a liberal critique of both big-business conservatism and Roosevelt's brand of corporate progressivism. Their effect is apparent in the writings of Woodrow Wilson and in the cultural critiques of American political culture developed in the 1920s, 30s, and 40s by scholars and critics like V. L. Parrington, Charles and Mary Beard, and Van Wyck Brooks.

But Roosevelt's influence is paramount in the cultural realm that we are concerned with here: the realm of mass-culture mythology. For dime novelists, Wild West show impresarios, the writers of Western fiction, and the makers of Western movies Roosevelt's hero-centered narratives and his affirmative use of the figures and symbols of the traditional literary mythology had far more appeal than the complexities, criticisms, and depersonalized sociology of Turner's histories. The influence of Turnerian ideas in shaping American academic historiography after 1900 has an exact parallel in the influence of Roosevelt's progressive ideology on American mythology; and that mythology, in turn, became one of the major constituents of cultural and political discourse in the new century.

In 1893 the Frontier was no longer (as Turner saw it) a geographical place and a set of facts requiring a historical explanation. Through the agency of writers like Turner and Roosevelt, it was becoming a set of symbols that *constituted* an explanation of history. Its significance as a *mythic space* began to outweigh its importance as a real place, with its own peculiar geography, politics, and cultures.

The Frontier had always been seen through a distorting-lens of mythic illusion; but until 1893 it had also been identified with particular geographical regions, actual places capable of generating new and surprising information as a corrective to mythic presupposition. As a region with a distinct geography, ecology, and social landscape, "the West" has continued to exist. But after 1893 regional realities no longer affected the development of the mythology identified with "the West." For most Americans—to the perpetual dismay of westerners—the West became a landscape known through, and completely identified with, the fictions created about it. Indeed, once that mythic space was well established in the various genres of mass culture, the fictive or mythic West became the scene in which new acts of mythogenesis would occur—in effect displacing both the real contemporary region and the historical Frontier as factors in shaping the on-going discourse of cultural history.

It was in that mythic space, defined by the genres of commercial popular culture, that the rival ideological claims of the "school of Turner" and the "school of Roosevelt"—of the populist and the progressive versions of liberal ideology—would be played out.

2 The White City and the Wild West

Buffalo Bill and the Mythic Space of American History, 1880–1917

A map of that "mythic space" was already available in the composed landscape of the World's Columbian Exposition of 1893, where Turner delivered his famous address. Visitors to the fair entered an elaborately structured space. Those who followed the paths prefigured in the Exposition's map and program were engaged by symbols, displays, and rituals that visualized the rapid course of American progress. The centerpiece of the Exposition, and the culmination of the typical itinerary, was the "White City," an architectural extravaganza in ersatz marble representing the pinnacle of Euro-American civilization, the original "alabaster city . . . undimmed by human tears," "a little ideal world" prophetic of "some far away time when the earth should be as pure, as beautiful, and as joyous as the White City itself." The main road from the railroad station to this New Jerusalem lay through the "Midway Plaisance," a street lined with restaurants and souvenir shops, "kootch-dance" palaces side by side with exhibition pavilions and "villages" displaying the wares and folkways of other nations, ethnological displays superintended by Franz Boas of the Smithsonian Institution cheek by jowl with sideshows of the "Wild Man from Borneo" variety.[1]

The antipode of the White City was Buffalo Bill's Wild West. Officially it was not a part of the Exposition, but its advertising did its best to obscure that fact. Moving up the Midway to the White City, the visitor passed from the Wild West to the metropolis of the future, and from the low culture to the high; from *caveat emptor* commercialism at its most blatant to a place of classical order; from displays of primitive savagery and exotic squalor to a utopia of dynamos and pillared façades. It was easy to construe the lesson implicit in the tour. More than one journalist observed that the exhibits featuring more "advanced" races (Celts and Teutons) tended to appear closer to the White City end of the Midway while the non-White Dahomeans and American Indians appeared at the farthest remove from utopia. "You have before you the civilized, the half-civilized, and the savage worlds to choose from—or rather, to take one after the other." The stroller "up" the Midway traces "the sliding scale of humanity" according to a Social-Darwinist program. Reporter Denton Snider advised his readers that "undoubtedly the best way of looking at these races is to behold them in ascending scale, in the progressive movement. . . . In that way we move in harmony with the thought of evolution."[2]

There actually were two ways of walking the grounds and reading the parable. The novelist and social critic William Dean Howells took the tour-program as a prophecy of the nation's eventual transcendence of the present crisis of social and industrial relations. The association of African and Indian "savages" with the rampant vulgarity of American commercialism suggested an analogy between primitive savagery and "primitive" capitalism. The "pitiless economic struggle" characteristic of the regime of *laissez-faire* was (for Howells) a commercial variant of "savage war," in which the objective is to either exterminate or utterly subjugate one's business rivals and compel the proletariat to "work or starve." In Howells' view, the aims of revolutionary socialism were no true alternative to but a vengeful mirror-image of the extermination/subjugation scenarios of monopoly capitalism. But the White City suggested a third alternative: that at the end of this course of savage war lay the potential for a utopia in which the relations of labor and capital (and of rival capitalists) would be cooperative rather than competitive.[3]

Most interpreters of the Midway/White City map did not share Howells' genteel socialism. Henry Adams saw the White City as symbolic of the ultimate and necessary triumph of capital over labor, of managerial intelligence over the licensed anarchy of democracy. The esthetic and moral "harmony" of the White City expressed the victory of capitalists as a class. In the struggles of the previous two years, "All one's friends, all one's best citizens had joined the banks to force submission to capitalism" and in the process had carried the country from a "simply industrial" condition to a fully "capitalistic, centralizing [and] mechanical" order, where democratic practices and moral imperatives were out of place. The achievement of the White City was proof that if a modern society is "to be run at all, it must be run by capital and capitalistic methods." Adams' particular targets are the constituents of the Populist and labor movements ("Southern and Western farmers in grotesque aliance with city day-laborers"); but his more general point is to discredit "democracy" and advance the claims of managerial ideology.[4]

To Frederick Douglass, the aging "Black Lion of Abolition," the White City was a "whited sepulchre," concealing the reality of the nation's abandonment of Negroes to impoverishment, social segregation, and political degradation, maintained and enforced by a recrudescence of Reconstruction's "White terror"—the lynch mob, the Klan raid. Black labor had been excluded from the work gangs that raised the White City, and the historical presence and labor of non-Whites was represented only in the "repulsive" and degrading displays of savagery in the Midway. The American Indians in the Midway were the objects of overt hostility from the White crowds; the Dahomeans were greeted with more derision than hostility, but mass-circulation journals like *Harper's Weekly* used them to reinforce White contempt for Negroes. A series of caricatures titled "Coons at the Exposition" offered grotesque stereotypes of American Blacks in ecstasy over the antics of their "cannibal" brethren.[5]

The relation of White workingmen to the White City was little better. Although organized labor had cooperated with the Exposition's planners, its contribution was presented as an entirely dependent and morally insignificant one as measured against the contributions of capital and management. Labor leader Eugene Debs complained that while labor was "quite willing to admit the alliance between money and labor in the accomplishment of great undertakings," it was unwilling to accept the premise that the rights and deserts of capital were prior to those of labor. Debs (quoting Lincoln) asserted that labor is "prior to capital" and gives it its value, and that therefore "greater credit is due to labor, because it is the creator of capital."[6] But Debs found employers impervious to the moral claims of "free labor" republicanism and unwilling to treat labor as a negotiating partner, let alone as an "ally." The building of the White City followed two decades of slack employment, the increasing oppressiveness of workplace conditions, declining standards of living, and intensified union-busting. It coincided with the Panic of 1893 and a national business contraction, with "labor wars" in Colorado and in the Coeur d'Alenes and the Homestead steel mills, and with the Johnson County War of small ranchers against a private army hired by the big cattleman of the Wyoming Stock Growers' Association. In the year following the Exposition, Debs himself would lead the railroad workers in the greatest "labor war" of the century, the "Pullman Strike"—which would be broken by federal troops (including regiments drawn away from Indian country) sent by President Cleveland over the objections of Illinois' pro-labor governor Altgeld. During that strike the White City itself would mysteriously burn to the ground.

While it was certainly possible to imagine the White City as a utopia of civility and shared progress, it was easier, in that depression year, to dismiss its "whiteness" as a utopian illusion and to imagine the inescapable city of the future as a grim and squalid Chicago divided between its few rich and its many poor, the prospective site of an apocalyptic confrontation between "civilization" and the forces of savagery and regression—between the social imperatives that Mark Twain had called "the spirit of progress" and "the spirit of massacre."[7]

Turner and Roosevelt saw "history" as the ineluctable flow of persons and events in a single, determinate direction toward the White City. But in fact, traffic on that symbolic road flowed both ways. Frederick Remington, the painter of western scenes and journalist, was in principle as committed as his friend Theodore Roosevelt to progressive politics. But he was more like Turner in the emphasis he placed on what was lost in the passing of the Frontier. On his visit to the Exposition (which he wrote up for *Harper's Weekly*) he turned away from the modernity symbolized by the White City to walk the Midway in the direction of the "Wild West," which for him fulfilled "its mission as a great educator." What it teaches "the universal Yankee nation" is the value of "that part of the world which does not wear Derby hats and spend its life in a top-and-bottom tussel with a mortgage bearing eight per cent." Despite his contempt for non-Whites, on the Midway Remington found glimpses of a real and somehow regenerative "savagery" beneath the fakery of costumes and carnival hype. The sight of an armed Turk awakens "the sense of admiration . . . that if you were not an American you would be a savage of that type." It is contact with savagery, the White City's opposite, that Remington craves as an antidote to civilized discontents, and thus his itinerary is to do "all the savages in turn, as every one else must do who goes there, and Buffalo Bill's besides, where I renewed my first love."[8]

"Buffalo Bill's Wild West" was for more than thirty years (1883–1916) one of the largest, most popular, and most successful businesses in the field of commercial entertainment. The Wild West was not only a major influence on American ideas about the frontier past at the turn of the century; it was a highly influential overseas advertisement for the United States during the period of massive European emigration. It toured North America and Europe, and its creator William F. Cody became an international celebrity on terms of friendship with European royalty and heads of state as well as with the leaders of the American military establishment. With its hundreds of animals, human performers, musicians, and workmen, its boxcars filled with equipment and supplies, it was nearly as large and difficult to deploy as a brigade of cavalry; and since it went everywhere by railroad (or steamship) it was far more mobile. The staff of the Imperial German army was said to have studied Buffalo Bill's methods for loading and unloading trains in planning their own railroad operations.[9]

William F. Cody, "Buffalo Bill," was the creator, leading manager, and until the turn of the century the chief attraction of the Wild West. Over the years he worked with a series of partners whose ideas and decisions influenced the development of the enterprise and who often assumed a greater share of control over the design of the production. But it was Cody and his ideas that provided the most coherent and continuous line of development. Certainly Cody himself was primarily responsible for establishing the Wild West's commitment to historical authenticity and to its mission of historical education.[10]

The management of Cody's enterprise declared it improper to speak of it as a "Wild West show." From its inception in 1882 it was called "The Wild West" (or "Buffalo Bill's Wild West"), a name that identified it as a "place" rather than a mere display or entertainment. A "Salutatory" notice that was added to the Program of the 1886 Wild West and that appeared in every Program thereafter, declared:

> It is the aim of the management of Buffalo Bill's Wild West to do more than present an exacting and realistic entertainment for public amusement. Their object is to PICTURE TO THE EYE, by the aid of historical characters and living animals, a series of animated scenes and episodes, which had their existence in fact, of the wonderful pioneer and frontier life of the Wild West of America.[11]

The Wild West was organized around a series of spectacles which purported to re-enact scenes exemplifying different "Epochs" of American history: "Beginning with the Primeval Forest, peopled by the Indian and Wild Beasts only, the story of the gradual civilization of a vast continent is depicted." The first "Epoch" displayed Plains Indian dancers but represented them as typical of the woodland

Indians who greeted the colonists on the Atlantic shore (a tableau depicting either the Pilgrims at Plymouth Rock or John Smith and Pocahontas). The historical program then cut abruptly to the settlement of the Great Plains, displaying life on a Cattle Ranch, a grand "Buffalo Hunt," and Indian attacks on a settler's cabin and the "Deadwood Stage." Between these episodes were displays of "Cowboy Fun," of trick riding and roping, and spectacular feats of marksmanship by featured performers like Annie Oakley ("Little Sure Shot") and Buffalo Bill himself.

The historical rationale of the Wild West was carefully described in the elaborate Program; but all visitors, whether or not they purchased the Program, were admonished that "Attention to the Orator [announcer] will materially assist the spectator in his grasp of the leading episodes." The authenticity of the historical program was vouched for by letters of recommendation from leading military officers published in the Program and by the use of figures publicly recognized as actual participants in the making of history: "The hardships, daring, and frontier skill of the participants" was "a guarantee of the faithful reproduction of scenes in which they had actual experience." Over the years Buffalo Bill managed to engage such figures as Sitting Bull and Geronimo as performers, and a great number of Indians who had fought against the cavalry less than a year before, as well as the services of regular units of the U.S. Cavalry to perform opposite them. But the center of the Wild West, as both premier performer and veteran of historical reality, was Buffalo Bill himself:

> The central figure in these pictures is that of THE HON. W. F. CODY (Buffalo Bill), to whose sagacity, skill, energy, and courage . . . the settlers of the West owe so much for the reclamation of the prairie from the savage Indian and wild animals, who so long opposed the march of civilization.[12]

It is the most extraordinary tribute to the skill of the Wild West's management that its performances were not only accepted as entertainment but were received with some seriousness as exercises in public education. The leading figures of American military history, from the Civil War through the Plains Indian wars, testified in print to the Wild West's accuracy and to its value as an inculcator of patriotism. Brick Pomeroy, a journalist quoted in the 1893 Program, used the newly minted jargon of the educational profession to praise Buffalo Bill with the wish that "there were more progressive educators like William Cody in this world." He thought the show ought to be called "Wild West Reality," because it had "more of real life, of genuine interest, of positive education . . . [than] all of this imaginary Romeo and Juliet business."[13]

But despite its battery of authentications, the Wild West wrote "history" by conflating it with mythology. The re-enactments were not re-creations but reductions of complex events into "typical scenes" based on the formulas of popular literary mythology: the "Forest Primeval" Epoch reads colonial history in Fenimore Cooper's terms, the Plains episodes in terms drawn from the dime novel. If the Wild West was a "place" rather than a "show," then its landscape was a mythic space in which past and present, fiction and reality, could coexist; a space in which history, translated into myth, was re-enacted as ritual. Moreover, these rituals did more than manipulate historical materials and illustrate an interpretation of American history; in several rather complex ways, the Wild West and its principals managed not only to comment on historical events but to become actors themselves.

Staging Reality: The Creation of Buffalo Bill, 1869–1883

Until 1869 William F. Cody had been a minor actor on the stage of western history, a frontier jack of all trades who had been a farmer, teamster, drover, trapper, Civil War soldier in a Jayhawk regiment, Pony Express rider, stagecoach driver, posse-man, meat hunter for the Kansas Pacific Railroad, and army scout. The upsurge of interest in the Plains that accompanied construction of the transcontinental railroads brought numerous tourists to the region, along with journalists, gentlemen-hunters in search of big game, and dime novelists looking for material. There was money to be made guiding such folk on hunting trips, and fame (and more hunting clients) to be garnered when the trips were written up back east. Wild Bill Hikock and Cody both achieved early fame in this way—Hikock as the subject of an article written for *Harper's Weekly* by G. W. Nichols, Cody in a Ned Buntline dime novel published in 1869 and a stage melodrama that premiered in 1871. Cody had already acquired a word-of-mouth reputation as an excellent scout and hunting guide, but after 1869 his newly acquired dime-novel celebrity made his name familiar to a national audience while linking it with spectacular and utterly fictitious adventures.[14]

In 1871 James Gordon Bennett, Jr., editor and publisher of the

New York *Herald*, hired Cody as a guide on one of the more elaborate celebrity hunting trips of the era (covered of course by a *Herald* reporter). The next year General Philip Sheridan named Cody to guide the hunting party of the Russian Grand Duke Alexis, who was in the country on a state visit. General Custer was among the American notables who accompanied the expedition, and Cody again figured prominently in the elaborate press coverage of the event. When Bennett, hoping to capitalize on this journalistic coup, urged Cody to visit him in New York, Cody, encouraged by his army superiors and friends, seized the opportunity to cash in on his celebrity. The visit was a turning point in Cody's career. In New York he took control of the commodity of his fame by forming a partnership with Ned Buntline for the production of Buffalo Bill dime novels and stage melodramas.[15]

Between 1872 and 1876 Cody alternated between his career as scout for the U.S. Cavalry and his business as star of a series of melodramas in the East. His theatrical enterprises prospered, so that by 1873 he was able to form his own "Buffalo Bill Combination" with Wild Bill Hikock and "Texas Jack" Omohundro. The plays themselves were trivial and the acting amateurish, but the success of the "Combination" was evidence of the public's deep and uncritical enthusiasm for "the West," which could best be addressed through a combination of dime-novel plots and characters with "authentic" costumes and personages identified with "the real thing."[16] A poster for the 1877 edition of the "Combination" advertises the main feature of the entertainment as a performance of *May Cody or, Lost and Won*, a melodramatic variation on the captivity narrative featuring both Indians and Mormons as villains. An actor impersonates Brigham Young, but two genuine Sioux chiefs appear in the play and in the dance performances "incidental" to the drama which "introduc[e] . . . THE RED MEN OF THE FAR WEST." The play featured a series of "THRILLING TABLEAUX" in "Panoramic Order" depicting the famous "Mountain Meadows Massacre" (in which Mormon fanatics abet Indians in wiping out a wagon train) and recreations of "Brigham Young's Temple" and his residence, the "Lion House." In addition, there was a display of marksmanship by the "Austin Brothers."[17] The mixture of elements anticipates the program of the Wild West, although these performances did not approach the scale of ambition of the Wild West.

Combinations of this kind were not unprecedented. In 1766 Major Robert Rogers, the famous commander of "Rogers' Rangers," wrote and staged in London a tragedy titled *Ponteach* based on the recently concluded Indian war and featuring authentic Indian dances, costumes, and performers. In the 1830s and 40s George Catlin's touring "Indian Gallery" combined displays of Indian dances with exhibitions of paintings. Similar authenticating devices were used by the various panoramas and cycloramas—aggregations of painted scenes with a narrative program of one sort or another—which toured the country between 1850 and 1890.[18] Cody's creative achievement was his organization of these various conventions and media around a coherent set of plot formulas drawn from a literary mythology whose structure and language were (by 1870) well developed and widely recognized.

Cody's continuing engagement with the Plains wars strengthened his claims of authenticity and in 1876 provided him with a windfall of public celebrity. The outbreak of war with the Sioux and Northern Cheyenne had been expected since the failure in 1875 of government attempts to compel the sale of the Black Hills, and preparations for three major expeditions into "hostile" territory began in the winter of 1875–76. Cody was then performing in the East, but his services as Chief of Scouts had been solicited for the column led by General Crook out of Fort Fetterman. His theatrical engagements prevented his joining Crook, whose command moved out in May, but General Carr had also been trying to recruit him for the 5th Cavalry. On the 11th of June Cody announced from the stage in Wilmington, Delaware, that he was abandoning "play acting" for "the real thing" and within the week had joined the 5th (now commanded by Merritt) in southern Wyoming. While the three main columns under Terry (with Custer), Gibbon, and Crook attempted to encircle and engage the main body of "hostiles," Merritt's command moved toward the Black Hills to prevent additional warriors from leaving the reservation to join Sitting Bull and Crazy Horse. On July 7 the command learned of Custer's disastrous defeat at the Little Big Horn (June 25). Ten days later a battalion of the 5th under Captain Charles King—a professional soldier with literary ambitions—caught up with a band of off-reservation Cheyenne which it had been tracking. In a rapid sequence of ambush and counter-ambush, Cody and his scouts engaged a small party of Cheyenne outriders. Merritt and his officers, watching from a low hill, saw Cody and one of the Cheyenne meet—seemingly in mutual surprise—and spontaneously fire. They saw Cody's horse stumble and fall (the horse had stepped in a prairie-dog hole). But Cody extricated himself from the saddle, took a kneeling position and deliberate aim, and shot the charging Indian from his horse. Then, as King's advancing troopers swept by him, he walked over to the corpse, scalped it, and waved his trophy in the air.[19]

This scene became the core of the Buffalo Bill legend and the basis of his national celebrity. Before the year was over he would be hailed as the man who took "The First Scalp for Custer." It would be claimed that the Indian he slew was a leading chief, one of the leaders at the Little Big Horn, and even that Cody had announced his intention to avenge Custer from the stage in Wilmington—an absurdity, since the Last Stand did not occur until three weeks later. Although the fight itself had elements of exciting drama, it was in fact a small skirmish in a dusty, empty place. The Signal Corps observer who had the best sight of the action said only that he saw "just a plain Indian riding a calico or a paint pony." But the dusty details were immediately transformed into melodrama by Captain King, whose literary ambitions reveal themselves in the sensational prose with which he described Cody's fight in his official report (and later in a book). King's report was given to a correspondent of Bennett's New York *Herald*, who added his own touches.[20]

But the chief mythologizer of the event was Cody himself. That winter he would star in *The Red Right Hand; or, The First Scalp for Custer*, a melodrama in which the "duel" with Yellow Hand becomes the climax of a captivity-rescue scenario. (The story also appeared as a dime novel.) Moreover, it seems that Cody approached the event itself with just such a performance in mind. On the morning of July 17, knowing that the proximity of the Indians made battle probable, Cody abandoned his usual buckskin clothing for one of his stage costumes, "a brilliant Mexican *vaquero* outfit of black velvet slashed with scarlet and trimmed with silver buttons and lace"—the sort of costume that dime-novel illustrations had led the public to suppose was the proper dress of the wild Westerner. He was preparing for that moment when he would stand before his audience, wearing the figurative laurels of the day's battle and the *vaquero* suit, able to declare with truth that he stood before them in a plainsman's authentic garb, indeed the very clothes he had worn when he took "The First Scalp for Custer." In that one gesture he would make "history" and fictive convention serve as mutually authenticating devices: the truth of his deeds "historicizes" the costume, while the costume's conventionality allows the audience—which knows the West only through such images—to recognize it as genuine.[21]

Cody also displayed the relics of Yellow Hand—a warbonnet,

shield, gun, and scabbard, and the dried human scalp itself—outside theaters in which the "Combination" performed, as indisputable evidence of his claims as a historical actor. Their impact was augmented when the display was condemned as obscene and barbaric by the self-appointed keepers of public morality. Even the anti-Indian and sensation-loving *Herald* criticized Cody; and in Boston, where Friends of the Indian were numerous and influential, the "Combination" was banned. The effect of this action was roughly the same as the banning of *Huckleberry Finn* by the Boston Library Committee—or better, the advertisement in that novel of "The Royal Nonesuch" as a show to which women and children would not be admitted. It brought sensation-seekers to the show in droves.[22]

Here the Buffalo Bill signature appears clearly, in its characteristic confusion of the theatrical and the historical or political. The deed itself is unquestionably real—blood was shed, a battle won—but the event is framed by fiction from start to finish, and its ultimate meaning is determined by its re-enactment in the theater. It soon ceased to matter that the skirmish itself was unimportant, that Yellow Hand was not a war chief, that his was not "the first scalp for Custer," and that the "revenge" symbolized by Cody's deed had no counterpart in reality (since the Indians he fought had not been at the Little Big Horn). Cody and Custer had been associated very briefly (and distantly) in the Southern Plains war of 1867–70 and the Grand Duke's buffalo hunt; but beginning in 1876 Cody (and his associates) exploited his connection with the Last Stand and Custer by every means available. In addition to *The Red Right Hand*, Cody appeared as Custer's trusty scout in a series of dime novels, figuring (in terms of the Cooper formula) as a kind of Hawkeye to Custer's Duncan Heyward, or Kit Carson to Custer's Fremont. The Yellow Hand fight was transformed from a lucky accident to the climax of a program of deliberate revenge.[23] The "duel" itself became even more sensational in Cody's 1879 autobiography, where it culminated in a hand-to-hand knife fight. The image of Cody waving the scalp in the air was reduced to a crude woodcut, which became a permanent feature of Buffalo Bill iconography. It appeared in most of the Wild West Programs, as a dime-novel cover, a poster, and—elaborated in oils—as the centerpiece of several heroic paintings.[24]

After 1876, the Buffalo Bill mythology developed in two forms, the dime novel and (after 1882) the Wild West. Buffalo Bill was the protagonist of more dime novels than any other character, real or fictional, with the possible exception of Jesse James.[25] But after 1883, the Wild West was the basis of his fame and of his increasingly legendary status. The early Buffalo Bill dime novels (written by Cody himself, as well as by Buntline and Prentiss Ingraham) were based (loosely) on his frontier exploits; they placed Buffalo Bill in the traditional pantheon of frontier heroes derived from Boone, Hawkeye, Carson, and Crockett. But the Wild West framed Cody in a mythic spectacle that enlarged and transformed this legend; eventually even his dime novels celebrated him as the proprietor of the Wild West rather than as an old-time plainsman.[26]

The Wild West and the Ritualization of American History

The Wild West itself was Buffalo Bill's most important myth-making enterprise, the basis of his later celebrity and continuing dime-novel fame. It began in 1882 as part of a July 4th celebration in Cody's hometown of North Platte, Nebraska. Its primary features were rodeo-like displays of cowboy skills—feats of marksmanship, riding and roping, horse races—framed by an elaborate parade. To this base were added elements that would appeal to the larger audience that had been drawn to the Buffalo Bill Combination, scenes "typical" of Western life, developed around a standard melodramatic narrative scheme like the captivity/rescue. Many of these scenes were drawn from Buffalo Bill dime novels: the attack on the Deadwood Stage, the Pony Express display, the raid on the settler's cabin, the "Grand Buffalo Hunt on the Plains." As in the Combination, authentic historical celebrities were recruited to lend credibility and to exploit public curiosity: Major North and his Pawnee battalion were early favorites, Sitting Bull appeared in 1884–85, *metis* veterans of the Riel Rebellion in Canada (1886). In later years the Wild West would feature appearances by Rain-in-the-Face ("the Indian who killed Custer"), chief Joseph of the Nez Perce, Jack Red Cloud (son of a famous Sioux chief), and (over the years) assorted sheriffs and outlaws whose exploits had attracted the attention of the newspapers.

In 1886 the Wild West program was reorganized and publicized as "America's National Entertainment," an exemplification of the entire course of American history. The different scenes were now presented as typifications of the stages of frontier history, although their content remained virtually unchanged. Costumes and staging were more elaborate, and spectacular "special effects" were developed, including a prairie fire, a "sunset," and a "cyclone." The historical program, and the patriotic purpose Cody and his associates claimed for it, was intended to distinguish the Wild West from other competing circus-like displays, to give it the gloss of respectability, and thus to increase its appeal. The emphasis on the Wild West as an exemplification of American history may also have been a response to the prospect of the company's first European tour (1887–89). The appeal of the Wild West could only be enhanced by representing it as a kind of cultural embassy from the New World to the Old—an exhibition of all the exotic American types that had piqued European imaginations since Cooper, if not since Columbus.[27]

Cody's stage persona was now given a more elaborate definition designed to present him as the archetype of the American frontier hero. Buffalo Bill is presented in the 1886 program as "the representative man of the frontiersmen of the past." He is "full of self-reliance" and acquires scientific knowledge through the necessary operations of his native curiosity and engagement with nature. The history of the West is, in effect, his "lengthened shadow." "His history, in fact, would be almost a history of the middle West, and, though younger, equalling in term of service and personal adventure Kit Carson, Old Jim Bridger, California Joe, Wild Bill, and the rest of his dead and gone associates." (It is worth noting that with the exception of Bridger, all these figures were as well or better known as dime-novel heroes than as historical personages.) "Young, sturdy, a remarkable specimen of manly beauty, with the brain to conceive and the nerve to execute, Buffalo Bill *par excellence* is the exemplar of the strong and unique traits that characterize a *true American frontiersman*."

Like Hawkeye, Cody is of plebeian and agrarian origins, and therefore knows the value of democracy and hard work. As "a child of the plains" he inevitably becomes acquainted with the wilderness and with the strife endemic to a border region. These "accident[s] of birth and early association" bring him (like Hawkeye) into intimate knowledge of the wilderness and the "implacable Indian foe." But where Hawkeye is disabled by this knowledge from living a civilized life, Cody's experience prepares him "to hold positions of trust, and without his knowing or intending it made him nationally famous." Cody is able to overcome Hawkeye's limitations because he possesses an innately superior moral character whose powers go beyond the primitive virtues of loyalty, truthfulness, and honor. Cody's virtues are those of the manager and commander as well as the soldier. Though "full of self-reliance" he also possesses the moral qualities associated with a good ship's captain. His incipient gentility is attested by the certified "gentlemen" of the officer corps, particularly Generals Carr and Merritt, who praise him as "a natural gentleman in his manners as well as character." Sherman figuratively ennobles Cody as "King of them all [that is, the army's scouts]." As Cody aged and prospered, the Wild West Programs would present him as a patriarchal figure of fully achieved gentility, a natural aristocrat able and worthy to socialize with royalty.[28]

In 1886 a re-enactment of "Custer's Last Fight" was added to the Wild West's repertoire, and it eventually became not only the most spectacular of the "epochs" but the center of a reorganized program. Unlike the "Deadwood Stage" and "Settler's Cabin" scenes, "Custer's Last Fight" referred to a struggle that was not yet concluded. Geronimo was still on the warpath, and most of the Indians who had fought Custer were still alive, living uneasily on the reservation. Sitting Bull, widely regarded as the mastermind who had defeated Custer, was still regarded as a dangerous man.

Cody's presumption in addressing "history" so directly was of course defended by his insistence that the re-creation was authentic. A visitor to his tent noted that he had only three books in his working library, a scrapbook of newspaper clippings, a manual of infantry drill and tactics, and Frederick Whittaker's 1876 illustrated biography of Custer. He dressed his cowboys as cavalrymen and gave them proper drill; the Indians he hired were Sioux and Cheyenne and included veterans of the Custer fight. But the "script" which these "genuine" performers played out ended in fictional melodrama, with Cody's appearance on the stricken field before a transparency bearing the motto, "Too late." The suggestion that Cody might have saved the Boy General had he only arrived in time was pure "dime novel": Cody never approached the battlefield in 1876 and had had no knowledge of (or concern with) Custer's column until July 7.

Cody's role in the "Last Fight" was at once self-abnegating and self-aggrandizing. The suggestion that he might have saved Custer implicitly inflates his heroic stature. But by featuring Custer, the "Last Fight" scenario reduces Buffalo Bill to the role of elegiac commentator—he no longer acts the role of avenger taking the "first scalp for Custer." However, for this new role Cody invested himself with a new imagery and aura which suggested that he was not merely Custer's would-be savior and chief mourner, but in some sense a reincarnation of the heroic general. He had begun to cultivate a resemblance to Custer, doffing his famous *vaquero* suit for fringed buckskins, high boots, and a broad-brimmed hat, like those worn by Custer in popular illustrations of the battle. He trimmed his long hair, beard, and mustache to resemble Custer's. The difference between his dark hair and Custer's famous "Long Yellow Hair" was not at all jarring in an age of black-and-white illustration, and as Cody's hair became gray with age the difference disappeared. The most significant testimony to this resemblance was provided by Mrs. Custer herself, who saw the Wild West in New York (probably in 1886 or 1887). In her book, *Tenting on the Plains* (1887), she endorses the observation of Eliza, the Negro maid who had served the Custers since the Civil War, "Well, if he ain't the 'spress image of Ginnel Custer in battle, I never seed anyone that was."[29]

Cody was of course well aware that his representation of historical events was inaccurate, to say the least. But he seems to have been sincere in his belief that the Wild West offered something like a poetic truth in its representation of the frontier. His "truth" had two aspects, the pictorial and the moral. Within the boundaries of good showmanship he strove for the greatest accuracy of detail, because he wished to memorialize a period of his own life (and a regional life style) which he loved and from which time increasingly estranged him. This concern pervades both his public and private writing and shows as well in the care and consideration with which he treated his Indian performers and the wild animals used in the Wild West.

But the "moral truth" of the frontier experience, which the Wild West emphasized, was its exemplification of the principle that violence and savage war were the necessary instruments of American progress. Even the displays of marksmanship by Buffalo Bill and Annie Oakley are framed by the Program's essay on "The Rifle as an Aid to Civilization":

> [While it is] a trite saying that "the pen is mightier than the sword," it is equally true that the bullet is the pioneer of civilization, for it has gone hand in hand with the axe that cleared the forest, and with the family Bible and school book. Deadly as has been its mission in one sense, it has been merciful in another; for without the rifle ball we of America would not be to-day in the possession of a free and united country, and mighty in our strength.[30]

Cody's sense of the Wild West's educational and ideological mission was sharpened during the European tours he undertook between 1887 and 1892 by the responses of European audiences and reviewers to this "typically American" display.[31] He was therefore well prepared for the opportunity presented by the World's Columbia Exposition to place the Wild West in a strategic and profitable situation. His success is attested by the achievement of over a million dollars in profit from the 1893 season.

The show itself was larger and more spectacular than anything seen in America before, and Cody undertook an elaborate schedule of promotional activities to arouse and maintain public interest in the Wild West. The Program was far more elaborate in its framing of the Wild West's historical significance: the re-enactment of the Last Stand would feature performers on both sides who had been actual participants in the battle; other survivors, even Mrs. Custer, were "consulted" in preparing the performance.[32] Cody himself now appeared as a hero whose authenticity as "representative man" was attested in two different worlds. Wild West posters and publicity blazoned his triumphs before "The Crowned Heads of Europe," his success as an exemplar and promoter of American values and national prestige on the world stage. In addition, his reputation as a genuine Indian-fighter had been recently refreshed by his service during the Ghost Dance troubles of 1890, first as a would-be peacemaker between his friends Sitting Bull and General Miles, then (after the massacre of Ghost Dancers at Wounded Knee) as a member of Miles' staff.[33]

Cody exploited his connection with Wounded Knee in advertising posters which alternately showed him overseeing the making of the Peace Treaty and charging into a village to rescue White captives. He also reconstructed on the Wild West's grounds the cabin in which Sitting Bull lived at the time of his assassination. There Cody staged a ceremony of reconciliation between cavalry and Indian veterans of the two battles of the Little Big Horn and Wounded Knee. The Crow scout "Curly," famed as the last man to see Custer alive, shook hands with Rain-in-the-Face, the Sioux who had been unjustly accused (and immortalized by Longfellow) as the man who killed Custer and then cut out his heart and ate it. These ceremonies of reconciliation transfer to the Indian wars a species of public ritual previously associated with the reunion on Civil War battlefields of veterans of the Blue and the Gray. Of course, the Indian-war ceremony ocurs not on the "real" battleground of the West, but on the fictive "battleground" of Buffalo Bill's Wild West. Nonetheless, the ideological import of the gesture was seriously intended. Cody framed the ceremony with a set of overt appeals for reconciliation between Whites and Indians.

The Program now represented the "savages" as "The Former Foe—Present Friend—the *American*."[34]

This shift in the role assigned to the Indians signaled a change in the historical scenario enacted by the Wild West. In its original appearance, "Custer's Last Fight" had concluded the Wild West's first half and was followed by scenes displaying the peaceful life and labor of the ranch and mining camp.[35] In the new program, the "Last Fight" was the last act in the Wild West and served as an elegy for the *entire* period of American pioneering. What followed it was a vision of America assuming a new role on the world stage as leader of the imperial powers: the parade of the "Congress of the Rough Riders of the World."

The Ritual Frontier and the Sanctification of Imperialism

The term "Rough Riders" had been applied to western horsemen in dime novels before 1880, and Cody had adopted it during the European tours to characterize his White American horsemen. But the appeal of the "Last Fight" sequence had led the partners to increase the representation of military drill in the show. Military drill and trick-riding teams had been a regular feature of American fairs and circuses since the antebellum period; such teams, drawn from regular army units, performed in European nations as well. Cody had obtained the services of such units in the countries visited by the Wild West between 1887 and 1892, and he brought a selection of them back to the States to provide an exotic and appropriately international note for the Columbian Exposition edition of "America's National Entertainment." These units were added to the American cowboys and cavalrymen to form the "Congress of the Rough Riders of the World," whose grand parades opened and closed each performance and whose displays of horsemanship became featured acts between the historical scenes.[36]

But the full "Congress" included other kinds of horsemen as well. Beside each American or European unit rode representative horsemen of the non-White tribesmen recently conquered by the imperial powers. At the head of this "Congress" rode Buffalo Bill, identified in the Program and by his precedence not merely as "Prince of the Border Men" or "King of the Scouts" but as "King" of all the Rough Riders of the World. His pre-eminence was not merely personal but national, signifying the American assumption of a leading role in world affairs.[37]

The display of horseback skill by the Rough Riders was partly a development of the intervals of "Cowboy Fun" that had previously punctuated the staged "epochs." But the intensity with which the Wild West now pursued its historical program soon invested even these performances with ideological symbolism. If the "Custer's Last Fight" re-enactment was the funeral rite of the old frontier, then the Rough Rider contests and pageants were the ritual games that looked to the beginning of a new age. This suggestion was given substance in the greatly expanded text of the 1893 Program. All the standard features of earlier Programs were reprinted, but new essays were added, including one by Colonel T. A. Dodge, which declared that the warfare of the future would primarily engage civilized nations with barbarian races, and that therefore the American Indian-fighting cavalry would become the "pattern of the cavalry of the future." Cody's abortive embassy to Sitting Bull on the eve of Wounded Knee becomes the basis for an assertion that Buffalo Bill's mission offers a model for international diplomacy that might well be applied to the approaching Franco–German crisis over Alsace-Lorraine.[38]

Buffalo Bill's potential as a force for "universal peace" is attested by the ease with which he can move from the "red wastes" to the "great cities of Europe," and from the mixture of military skill and peace-making wisdom he brings to both settings. In moving rapidly between Dakota and Europe in 1890–91, Buffalo Bill had had a unique opportunity to contrast the might of industrial civilization with the lowest ebb of savagery; a similar experience (the Program suggests) is available to the visitor who passes freely between the Wild West and the White City of the Columbian Exposition. But as the essay explores the meaning of this juxtaposition, an ideological embivalence appears in the historical role assigned to violence. On the one hand, the contrast between Wild West and White City teaches us that the war-making spirit is an attribute of man in the "savage" state and that civilization requires the substitution of peace for war. But though war is denigrated as an end of civilization, it is exalted as a means to peace and progress.[39]

The basic thesis of this historical argument is essentially the same as that of Theodore Roosevelt's advocacy of American imperialism in "Expansion and Peace" (1899): that "peace" can be imposed on the "barbarian races" of the world only by the armed force of a superior race. The history of the Frontier has been one of Social-Darwinian racial warfare, "years of savage brutal wars conducted with a ferocious vindictiveness foreign to our methods." It was inevitable that the Red man's "once happy empire (plethoric in all its inhabitants needed)" be "brought thoroughly and efficiently under the control of our civilization, or (possibly more candidly confessed) under the Anglo-Saxon's commercial necessities."

> [T]he practical view of the non-industrious use of nature's cornucopia of world-needed resources and the inevitable law of the *survival of the fittest* must "bring the flattering unction to the soul" of those—to whom the music of light, work, and progress, is the charm, the gauge of existence's worth, and to which the listless must harken, the indolent attend, the weak imbibe strength from—whose ranks the red man must join, and advancing with whose steps march cheerily to the tune of honest toil, industrious peace, and placid fireside prosperity.[40]

But the Wild West's historical ritual has a double effect: it signals the integration of the Indian into "American" life as "Former Foe—Present Friend"; and it re-awakens the "savagery" or warrior spirit that is latent in the civil sons and daughters of the heroes who won the West. A reporter for the Chicago *Inter-Ocean* declared that the 1893 performance of the "Deadwood Stage" and "Last Fight" scenes made him aware of "the aboriginal ancestor" that remains "in us after all the long generations of attempted civilization and education." David A. Curtis, writing in the *Criterion* in 1899, notes that the spectacle of "struggle and slaughter" produces effects like those of Roosevelt's "Strenuous Life": it awakens "the hidden savage," the "ineradicable trace of savage instinct" that lurks in the blood of all the great fighting races; it "stirs the thinnest blood and brightens the dullest eye" in the genteel Anglo-Saxon audience. The only "lack is that this . . . fighting is not real."[41]

As if anticipating Curtis' regret that its bloodshed was not "real," the publicity of the Wild West after 1893 asserted more strenuously than ever its claim to "realism" of detail. And it linked that claim to a more assertive statement of its educational mission. The copy attached to the Wild West's gigantic billboard of 1898–99 offered the clearest and most assertive definition yet of the Wild West's educational purpose. The billboard invited the viewer to "LOOK UPON THIS PICTURE" and behold "the VARIOUS EPOCHS of AMERICAN HISTORY, from the primitive days of savagery up to the memorable charge of San Juan hill," all reproduced with "remarkable fidelity." This epic image and performance is not merely a "show" but:

> AN
> OBJECT
> LESSON
>
> Differing as it does from all other exhibitions, BUFFALO BILL's WILD WEST and CONGRESS OF ROUGH RIDERS OF THE WORLD stands as a living monument of historic and educational magnificence. Its distinctive feature lies in its sense of realism, bold dash and reckless abandon which only arises from brave and noble inspiration. It is not a "show" in any sense of the word, but it is a series of original, genuine and instructive object lessons in which the participants repeat the heroic parts they have played in actual life upon the plains, in the wilderness, mountain fastness and in the dread and dangerous scenes of savage and cruel warfare. It is the only amusement enterprise of any kind recognized, endorsed and contributed to by Governments, Armies and Nations; and it lives longest in the hearts of those who have seen it most often, since it always contains and conveys intensely inspiring ideas and motives, while its programme is a succession of pleasant surprises and thrilling incidents.[42]

The function of realistic presentation is first to memorialize the real past in a "living monument," preserving not only the details of past heroism but also the moral truth that such "bold dash" can only arise "from brave and noble inspiration." Having memorialized true history, the Wild West's next task is to translate history into useful instruction, conveying to the public "intensely inspiring ideas and motives." Whatever these ideas may be, they are of a kind that is "endorsed and contributed to" by the official apparatus of the modern nation-state, for the Wild West's ultimate distinction is that it is the only "amusement enterprise" to be "recognized" by "Governments, Armies and Nations"—as if the fictive "place" that was Wild West had achieved something like diplomatic recognition.

The Wild West's conflation of the Frontier Myth and the new ideology of imperialism was fully achieved in 1899 when "Custer's Last Fight" was replaced by the "Battle of San Juan Hill," celebrating the heroism of Theodore Roosevelt—whose First Volunteer Cavalry regiment was best known by its nickname, "The Rough Riders."

By incorporating Roosevelt into the Wild West, Cody would seem to have conferred the very honor Roosevelt sought through his energetic hunting, soldiering, and writing about the West: a place in the pantheon of frontier heroes whose founder is Daniel Boone and whose latest demigod is Buffalo Bill. But Roosevelt somewhat ungenerously denied his own real indebtedness to the Wild West for the regimental sobriquet of "Rough Riders." The 1899 Wild West Program reprints an exchange of letters between Cody and Roosevelt in which the latter denies having borrowed the name from Cody's Congress, asserts that it was spontaneously bestowed by local citizens, and that Roosevelt himself was unaware of its reference. This (as Cody rather modestly points out) was hardly credible, given the fame of the Wild West (which Roosevelt had certainly attended), and the presence of some of the show's cowboys and Indians among Roosevelt's recruits. Roosevelt offered a mollifying compliment to the effect that, however it had come about, he was proud to share the name with those "free fearless equestrians, now marshalled under the leadership of the greatest horseman of all."[43]

This exchange of names between the agents of real-world imperialism and the myth-makers of the Wild West defines a significant cultural and political relationship. In performances, programs, and posters "San Juan Hill" was substituted for "Custer's Last Fight." It was the climactic act of the Wild West performances in 1899, where it was hailed as a battle equal in significance to Lexington and Concord, opening a new phase of America's history. The colossal 108-sheet billboard poster that advertised the 1899 Wild West restated the point in panoramic iconography. The poster illustrations recapitulated the historical "epochs" from "Attack on the Settler's Cabin" at the extreme left, to "San Juan Hill" at the extreme right; and the whole was flanked with "bookends" of text that proclaimed the Wild West as "An Object Lesson" in American history. This substitution of an imperial triumph carried off in "Wild West" style, for a ritual re-enactment of the catastrophe that symbolized the end of the old frontier, completes the Wild West's evolution from a memorialization of the past to a celebration of the imperial future.

By the terms of this exchange, the categories of myth shape the terms in which the imperial project will be conceived, justified, and executed; and the imperial achievement is then re-absorbed into the mythological system, which is itself modified by the incorporation of the new material. One effect is clearly that of glorifying the "imperialization" of the American republic. But the use of Wild West imagery also has the effect of "democratizing" the imperial project—or rather, of investing it with a style and imagery that powerfully (if spuriously) suggests its "democratic" character. The point is visualized in an 1898 Wild West poster, "Art Perpetuating Fame," which compares Buffalo Bill with Napoleon Bonaparte as "The Man on Horseback of 1796" and "The Man on Horseback of 1898." At the center of the poster is the black-cloaked figure of an old woman sitting before an easel: the French portrait painter Rosa Bonheur, who had painted well-known equestrian portraits of both the Emperor Napoleon and Buffalo Bill. The two men sit on white horses, facing away from the center. Napoleon (on the left) is in uniform, but he appears paunchy and looks sidelong out of the frame; Buffalo Bill is slightly more frontal, appears young and trim, has an erect seat, and wears civilian clothes. The identification of the two as "Men on Horseback" associates them not only as soldiers but as embodiments of the military principle in civil politics. The tag-phrase comes from French politics in the Dreyfus-case era to identify the conservative glorification of the army and hopes for a military assumption of civil power. The American version of this political type is youthful rather than decrepit, and "civilian" rather than military; his triumphs (the caption tells us) are peaceful rather than violent (Wild West show tours vs. military conquests). If Buffalo Bill is America's "Man on Horseback," then the American empire will be a peaceful and republican one, animated by youthful energy rather than depressed by tyrannical conservatism.[44]

Cody's version of the charge of Roosevelt's Rough Riders of course featured "the very heroes and horses who were a part of what they portray" and invited comparison with the Last Stand by describing the attack as a forlorn-hope assault against superior numbers. But those who followed "Roosevelt and the flag" reverse the Custer scenario and triumph over the lurking Spaniards. It is also characteristic of Cody that he emphasizes the ethnic and racial diversity of the soldiers, "white, red, and black," who followed Roosevelt. In this too the showman's generosity exceeds the politician's: Roosevelt does not emphasize the Indian presence in the regiment and denigrates the contributions of the Black regular infantry regiment that charged beside the Rough Riders.[45]

Both the historical program of the Wild West and its intricate play with racial categories were transformed by its identification with imperialism. In subsequent years the military elements of the show—the cavalry drills, the display of new-model artillery and Gatling guns (a feature of the San Juan Hill attack)—began to eclipse traditional western elements like "Cowboy Fun." The racialist ideology implicit in the inter-ethnic horse races is more sharply defined. In the 1893 Program the non-White riders had been identified by nationality; in 1894, as "primitive riders"; and in 1898 their competition (always one of the first five acts) was described in terms suggestive of Social Darwinism as "The Race of Races."[46]

Percival Pollard, writing in the *Criterion,* found that the outbreak of the war with Spain made the familiar scenes of the Wild West seem "freighted with a newer meaning." If the Spaniards doubted we were "a manly race . . . they might do themselves good by viewing Buffalo Bill and his cohorts." Wartime performances of the Wild West were announced in terms that deliberately echoed war news: the headline "City Capitulated" was used for both the surrender of Santiago and the announcement of a Wild West box-office triumph. In an interview given to the New York *World* in April 1898, Cody proposed a "Wild West" approach to the coming war: "Buffalo Bill Writes On 'How I Could Drive the Spaniards from Cuba with 30,000 Indians" assisted by such chieftains of the "noble but dying race" as Geronimo and Jack Red Cloud. Wild West performers were sought out for pro-war quotations, and Buffalo Bill made the show an instrument of propaganda by developing acts featuring Cuban and Filipino insurgents. However, these "savages" of the new frontier presented some of the same ideological difficulties as the old. When the Filipinos rebelled against an American takeover of the islands in 1899, the Filipinos in the Wild West became objects of hostility. Buffalo Bill himself was identified as "an avowed expansionist" and was quoted as declaring that the American Indian "Outranks the Filipino in the Matter of Common Honesty." His assertion that "Their Fighting Tactics Are Almost Identical" affirmed the polemical position taken by Roosevelt and other expansionists, that the Filipinos were "savages" like the "Apache." In a reversion to mythic origins, they were replaced in the San Juan Hill re-enactment by the Wild West's Indians.[47]

In 1901 San Juan Hill was replaced by a more recent imperial adventure, "The Battle of Tien-Tsin," a re-enactment of the capture of that city by the Allied army that suppressed China's "Boxer" Rebellion and rescued the "captives" in the Peking Legation Quarter. In this performance, the Indians assumed the role of the Boxers, and the Wild West's soldiers and cowboys represented all of White civilization storming the citadel, from which flew "the Royal Standard of Paganism . . . proudly defiant of the Christian world," to place there "the Banners of civilization." After running "Tien-Tsin" in 1901–2, Cody reprised "San Juan Hill" in 1903–4, taking advantage of (and perhaps assisting) Roosevelt's run for re-election.[48]

It is appropriate that Cody and Roosevelt should have benefitted materially from each other's activities, because their contributions to American culture were complementary and mutually reinforcing. The Wild West's casting of its cowboys and Indians as Rough Riders and Cubans, Allies and Boxers, makes literal and visible the central tenet of Roosevelt's racialist myth of progress: that the struggle between Red Men and White on the American frontier is the archetype and precedent for the world-wide struggle between "progressive" and "savage" or "regressive" races that shaped the modern world. The Wild West performed as myth and ritual the doctrines of progressive imperialism that Roosevelt promulgated as ideology. By dramatizing the imperial frontier as the logical extension of the continental frontier, Cody lent mythological support to Roosevelt's Frontier Thesis: that the American "savage" and his Anglo-Saxon foe were the archetypes of the universal and world-wide opposition of "progressive" and "regressive" races; and that empire was merely the continuation of Wild West democracy "by other means."[49]

After 1905 the Wild West fell on hard times: managerial errors were made, competition with other shows was keener, rising costs made the business less profitable. Cody believed that the Wild West had erred in allowing its traditional "frontier" elements to fall out of use. He revived "Custer's Last Fight" in 1905, and in 1907 offered a new frontier spectacle, "The Battle of Summit Springs," which featured Cody killing a chief named Tall Bull one year after the Little Big Horn. The plot and materials of this scene were a rehash of elements already present in the "Last Fight" and "Settler's Cabin" scenarios. In 1908 he attempted to appropriate specifically Western current events by staging a version of "The Great Train Hold-Up and Bandit Hunters of the Union Pacific"—a subject which had already been treated with great public fanfare in the new medium of moving pictures, in Edwin Porter's *The Great Train Robbery* (1903). Porter "scooped" Cody on this theme, and the success of movies would prove fatal to the Wild West, because films could provide similar excitements without having to maintain the huge stock of transportation, livestock, performers and technicians, or the geographical mobility that the Wild West required.[50]

From 1908 to its end in 1917 the Wild West suffered a marked decline in profitability and popularity. There was no longer a margin to cushion the effects of bad management. Cody lost control of the enterprise but remained obligated to it, because the failure of his other investments severely reduced his private fortune. Through the years of its commercial decline, the various managements of the Wild West persisted in following the practice established in 1899 of incorporating current events and concerns. For instance, in 1916, on the eve of Cody's death, the entire program was built around the theme of "Preparedness" for entry into the Great War. But its particular way of presenting those concerns had become hackneyed and predictable; other forms, like the movies, now had greater novelty, and the power to shock and surprise.[51]

But the ultimate financial failure of Buffalo Bill's Wild West should not obscure its unparalleled success as a myth-making enterprise. From 1885 and 1905 it was the most important commercial vehicle for the fabrication and transmission of the Myth of the Frontier. It reached large audiences in every major city and innumerable smaller ones throughout the United States. The period of its European triumph coincided with the period of massive immigration to America. As many immigrants testified, the Wild West was the source of some of their most vivid images and expectations of the new land. The Wild West also invented and tested the images, staging, and themes and provided much of the personnel for the motion-picture Western, which succeeded to its cultural mantle.

Nothing reveals Cody's skill and achievement as a myth-maker better than his manner of leaving the stage. His last years were marked by a seemingly endless cycle of "Farewell Performances." His personal motives for undertaking this long good-bye were undoubtedly financial and egotistical. But they also reveal the extent to which the Myth of the Frontier had become independent of the historical reality that produced it. In Cody's farewell tours, that nostalgia for the "Old West" that had been the basis of his first success gave way to a new form of the sentiment: a nostalgia not for the reality, but for the myth—not for the frontier itself, but for the lost glamour of Buffalo Bill's Wild West.[52]

3 Mob, Tribe, and Regiment

Modernization as Militarization, 1883–1902

We resort to our myths not merely to evade the discontents of our historical moment, but to find something—a precedent, a bit of wisdom, a new perspective—that will allow us to imagine a way of coping with and even transforming the present crisis. Mythic space is a metaphor of history, and the heroes in a functioning mythological system represent models of possible historical action. The increasing emphasis on military displays in Wild West scenarios after 1893—and the popularity of the Rough Riders sequences—suggests that the readiest way to modernize the frontier hero was to militarize him. Buffalo Bill the "scout" represented an antique type of heroism. Even within the framework of the Wild West, his Indian-fighting exploits are presented as restored relics of an age that is now gone. But Buffalo Bill as King of the Rough Riders, the commander of an elite regiment of regiments, becomes once again a potential model for modern heroism.

This approach was not peculiar to Buffalo Bill. It was responsive to an important strain in progressive ideology, developed in the aftermath of the Civil War, which saw in military organization a possible model for good management in an age of gigantic enterprises, intense competitive struggles, and massive social unrest. This "military metaphor" of American social organization was linked with the Myth of the Frontier by a group of "progressive" writers and artists who invoked the Indian-fighting regiment as an ideal model of American society and who deployed a new, "militarized" version of the frontier hero as an effective protagonist in the two forms of social conflict that would be characteristic of the new century—the "labor wars" at home, and the wars of imperial conquest abroad.

Origins of the Military Metaphor

The Civil War was the great crisis of American national development, and for many generations after it was an ideological benchmark against which all current crises and large-scale enterprises were to be measured. Nostalgic memories of the Civil War suggested that, at their best, the Civil War armies had modeled a social solidarity capable of transcending personal selfishness and class interest, with all hands working willingly, each according to his abilities and powers, toward a noble common goal. Amid the corruption of the Gilded Age, this aspect of the war was retrospectively idealized, producing such formulations as William James's call for a "Moral Equivalent of War" to mobilize patriotism and Edward Bellamy's utopian vision (in *Looking Backward*) of a society built around the just and efficient workings of an "Army of Industry."[1]

The boom times that gave the Gilded Age its name also were seen as a consequence of wartime achievements. The Civil War had been the means by which a generation of political and business leaders learned the management of large enterprises, mastering and improving on existing methods of capital formation, debt management, logistics, and productivity, and the value of a systematic partnership between business and government. The transcontinental expansion of the American railroad network after 1865 was achieved through the application of all these wartime lessons, so that it might almost be said (with apologies to Clausewitz) that railroad-building was war carried on by other means. Competition between rival railroad corporations and developers during the 1870s and 1880s was described in terms that identified them as the moral (or at least the peaceable) equivalent of combat: there was a "war" between Jay Gould and his rivals for control of the Erie Railroad, the "Short Line War" for control of midwestern railroad business, and so on. Strikes also were described as "railroad wars," as were Indian attacks directed against the transcontinental lines and radical attempts at regulation like those promulgated by the grangers in the Midwest.[2]

In this context, an industrialist's or financier's assumption of the title "Captain of Industry" was a significant conceit. David A. Wells, an economist and Treasury official, wrote in *Recent Economic Changes* (1889):

> When once a great association of capital has been effected, it becomes necessary to have a master-mind to manage it—a man who is competent to use and direct other men. . . . Such a man is a general of industry, and corresponds in position and function to the general of an army.[3]

The consolidation of economic enterprise in the large corporate "trusts" produced a class of men able to carry this role. The same tendencies also caused initiative and craftsmanship to decay as working-class virtues. Laboring men as a whole were "brought into a condition analogous to that of a military organization, in which the individual no longer works independently . . . but as a private in the ranks, obeying orders, keeping step as it were, to the tap of a drum."[4]

It is hard to believe that a generation that had lived through the Civil War could have taken seriously the concept of "military efficiency." Wartime logistics on both sides had been marked by waste and corruption on a colossal scale, and the same might be said of the postwar railroad business. But what attracted businessmen, politicians, and journalists to the "military metaphor" was not its aptness as a model of economic efficiency but its usefulness as a model of an industrial politics governed by the principles of command and subordination. The administrative lesson of the Civil War was taken to be the proof that the accomplishment of great projects, national in their scale of operations, required a more hierarchical organization of power in which those of greater ability and merit were entitled to subordinate and command those who were best suited to serve as instruments for achieving the grand design. John W. Draper, in his *Thoughts on the Future Civil Policy of America* (1865), believed that the war provided a crucial lesson for the modernization of national life: the necessity to "learn subordination [and] be made to appreciate order. It may be true . . . that men secretly love to obey those whom they feel to be their superiors intellectually. In military life they learn to practice that obedience openly."[5] Marshall M. Kirkman's *The Science of Railways* (1896), written in the aftermath of the Pullman Strike, asserts that "The force that operates a railway is like an army. It is methodically organized and drilled. It has its commanders, its rank and file." Strikes are therefore a form of mutiny: "insubordination among railway men is as great an offense as insubordination in an army," and "a country thus cursed is in as great danger as if its soldiers were traitorous." Loyalty to one's employer and his property interests ought to be as absolute as loyalty to the flag and uniform of the regiment. "Equality ends" at the moment of hiring (or enlistment), and therefore obedience should be implicit, disobedience punished by a special "criminal code."[6]

The politics implicit in the "military metaphor" is managerial rather than democratic; the leadership of the society is not unconditionally required to rule by and with the consent of those they govern, but it is licensed to use coercive force in order to maintain order within its ranks. But assertions of managerial authority in both the workplace and the polling booth met with organized resistance from workers, and in the culture as a whole the appeal of more traditional notions of democracy and government by consent remained potent throughout the 1890s.

In the face of such internal division the traditional recourse of American mythology is the invocation of the threat of "savage war." By representing politically active or "radical" representatives of labor as instigators of "savage" and anarchistic social strife, the exponents of managerial ideology vindicated their military metaphor as an essential component of "Americanism."

Writing in 1903, David M. Perry, President of the National Association of Manufacturers, summed up three decades of conservative polemics that equated strikers and savages:

> Organized labor know but one law, and that is the law of physical force—the law of the Huns and Vandals, the law of the savage. . . . It is, in all essential features, a mob power owing no master except its own will. Its history is stained with blood and ruin. . . . It extends its tactics of coercion and intimidation over all classes . . . strangling independence of thought and American manhood.[7]

A series of mass immigrations from Europe that began after 1881 drew on regions and ethnic groups not hitherto represented in the United States, including Italians, Germans, Slavs, and Jews from Eastern Europe. Now the identification of the working class as an alien mob acquired new force.[8] Thus in 1886 the New York *State Sun* responded to the Haymarket "riot" by calling for the exclusion of further immigration from Europe because "Such foreign savages, with their dynamite bombs and anarchic purposes, are as much apart from the rest of the people of this country as the Apaches of the plains are."[9]

These formulations equate the savage "tribe" with the urban "mob" as twin enemies of industrial society, and of the very "manhood" of the race. To defend itself against savage anarchy, society must organize itself as if it were an embattled army or a regiment of Indian-fighting cavalry. This way of symbolizing the social struggles of industrialization was realized in the events of the Pullman Strike of 1894, which saw cavalry regiments—among them Custer's 7th Cavalry, late of the Little Big Horn and Wounded Knee—drawn from the garrisons of Apacheria and the Sioux country to put down the strikers. Their presence led writers like Frederic Remington and the soldier-novelist Charles King to envision a new kind of American hero, a military/managerial version of "The man who knows Indians," who shows that the lessons learned in fighting savage tribes are superb preparation for asserting control of savage mobs.

Cavalry in the Streets, 1890–1896

An early sketch of this heroic scenario is provided by John Hay's anti-strike novel, *The Breadwinners* (1883–84), set during the Great Strike of 1877. Hay had been Lincoln's personal secretary and became a leading figure in Republican politics, serving as Secretary of State under both McKinley and Roosevelt. Hay's hero, Captain Arthur Farnham, is an ex-cavalryman of aristocratic antecedents who has served in the recently concluded Indian war over the Black Hills—Custer's war. When an inheritance makes him rich he returns to the metropolis of "Buffland," to a society whose wealthiest citizens have become effete and politically passive, while the lower orders have become jealous of the wealthy classes and are prepared to use politics to despoil them. Farnham seeks to infuse his own class with "virile" energy, and to re-engage it with party politics. His ideological mission is identified with his assertion of his own "manhood" and the principle of political "virility" against the "effeminate" principles espoused by the corps of powerful females who dominate the culture of the upper classes. His political success is prefigured when the "refinement" in which his beloved has been indoctrinated is overwhelmed by the desire generated by his virile sex appeal. When the Great Strike breaks out, threatening the city and his beloved's family with rape and ruin, Farnham organizes a vigilante company of ex-soldiers and with them manages to defeat the strikers. Hay's hero resolves the labor crisis by applying to the city lessons learned in Indian warfare and military life. His eye, trained in assessing the difference between "hostiles" and "friendlies," is adept at recognizing the distinction between "honest" (that is, compliant) workmen and would-be Communards. His experience as a soldier has taught him that in the presence of such enemies, sudden and direct action is better than temporizing or "moral suasion." And his experience as an officer has taught him that in all endeavors—whether running a corporation or suppressing disorders—subordination and organization are essential to success.[10]

The novels of Captain Charles King make a more literal translation of the Indian-fighter into the managerial hero. King had commanded the battalion Buffalo Bill was serving when he killed Yellow Hand, and his dispatches and reminiscences of the campaign had contributed substantially to Cody's fame. He became a writer of fiction after his retirement. He was also director of the Michigan Military Academy, where one of his pupils was the young Edgar Rice Burroughs.[11] King's plots follow a standard formula: the usual complications of status and jealousy initially divide a young romantic pair—a Farnham-like military aristocrat and a refined young lady—but in the end, after captivities and rescues, love and virtue triumph and the couple is united in love and devotion to performing "the work of the world." The special appeal of the novels is their description of the world of the regular army: a world apart from the metropolis, in which honor and service matter more than wealth, and duty is heroically simple.

In 1893 King published *Foes in Ambush*, the first of three novels that feature Indian fighters drawn from the Apache wars who do battle with strikers.[12] King's officer-hero is embroiled with a series of evil-doers who represent a sampling of every enemy faced by the American government from the Civil War to the Pullman Strike. The list includes Mexican bandits, Apaches, and Socialists; they are all linked by their common "savagery" and are led by the same evil genius, an ex-Confederate renegade named Bland. The regiment ultimately settles with Bland when it is called to Chicago to suppress a mob of strikers—the "lowest of the masses . . . 'toughs'—Chicago's vast accumulation of outlawed, vagabond, or criminal men." Bland is finally shot down by the tough Irish sergeant who has been playing the Cooperian "old scout" to the hero's "young aristocrat" throughout the novel.[13] *An Army Wife* (1896) reprises the theme, as an Indian-fighting regiment suppresses "savage" strikers in a setting reminiscent of the strike-torn Cripple Creek district of Colorado.[14]

A Tame Surrender (1896) is King's most ambitious treatment of the theme, and here the Pullman Strike forms the center of the action. Lieutenant Floyd Forrest is an aristocratic young officer; his beloved is the daughter of the wealthy and refined Allison family, who object to Forrest as a suitor because of his military profession. For Mr.

Allison, the man of arms does not follow the forms of productive labor valued by a commercial society: soldiers are neither merchants nor skilled workmen. Moreover, they represent the power of the government to intervene in civil society, which violates Allison's *laissez-faire* principles. Finally, the family is repelled by the idea of the soldier as a man whose profession is violence. The Allisons' objections thus summarize all those commercial, genteel, "philanthropic," and effeminate values that were condemned by the editorialists of the 1870s, by Hay, and by Roosevelt as inimical to the proper internal ordering of an industrial society and to the necessities of an expanding frontier or a progressive economy. The Allisons' false consciousness makes them vulnerable to the suasions of a German *factotum* named Elmendorf (giving the symbolic enemy of order an ethnic or racial cast).

Forrest answers the Allisons' objections in both theory and action. In a masterful analysis of the issues of the day, he overwhelms Mr. Allison with his knowledge of affairs. He finds Allison too complacent about the state of society and politics. The growing power of the Grangers, Populists, Anarchists, and Socialists presages a systematic attack on Property. Already these forces have used their political power (especially among the foreign-born) to gain control of the statehouse: Governor Altgeld's pardoning of the surviving Haymarket anarchists is cited as proof. When the inevitable crisis comes, only the power of the federal government, represented by the army, will be able to save Allison, his daughter, his class, and the system of private property from the mob.

Looking beyond the crisis, Forrest offers a military man's solution to the conflict between labor and capital. These twin constituents of the industrial and commercial order are both at fault (though labor is the more dangerous party). Though the Pullman Company has acted legally in its treatment of the workers, it has exceeded the limits of what is practically advisable and morally desirable and so has driven its workers into the arms of the agitators. What is needed to resolve the issue and establish social peace is an appeal to an authority that stands outisde the labor/capital dichotomy—an authority identified with the nation as a whole, imbued with the ideal of a disinterested pursuit of the nation's good, devoted to its duty and detached from the world of trade, trained in the expert management of large projects and masses of men—in short, the army.[15]

But this meliorative rhetoric—this appeal for moral equivalents of war—is voiced by a soldier who shows himself willing and able to deploy coercive force. In King's scenarios, this force is applied with restraint and is limited to mutinous troopers, renegades, and savages who live outside the social compact. However, the myth of "savage war" holds that such struggles are inherently limitless. To avoid defeat in such a war, the hero must be licensed to use whatever forms of violence may be necessary. The taboos and moral prohibitions that limit the use of force within civil society do not apply.

The implications are vividly realized in Frederic Remington's account of the intervention by Indian-fighting cavalry regiments in the Pullman Strike of 1894. His articles on the strike are vivid and extremist in their assertion of the likeness between strikers and savages. But Remington's attitudes toward "savages" were complex; they reflected the larger society's ambivalence about reconciling democratic values and practices with the presence of a proletariat marked by ethnic and racial difference.

Remington was one of three prominent easterners whose work shaped national images of the West between 1885 and 1910, including Theodore Roosevelt and the novelist Owen Wister, who created one of its most enduring literary legends. All three came from families of wealth and social standing and were members of the educated elite. They saw their class as the trustee of traditional American values imperiled by the struggle between the proletariat below and the plutocracy above. After meeting Remington, Owen Wister wrote that he was an "excellent American" who shared the belief "that this continent does not hold a nation any longer, but is merely a strip of land on which a crowd is struggling for money." All three had gone west to renew ties with a better, more primitive, and vanishing phase of American history.[16]

Although Remington shared many of Roosevelt's and Wister's biases and commitments, his temperament, artistic style, and financial circumstances were quite different. Roosevelt or Wister could afford to go west as gentleman-ranchers. Remington invested and lost his small patrimony in a sheep ranch and was dependent on his earnings as writer and artist in a way that the other two were not. Journalistic assignments brought out the ideologue in him; but in his fiction, painting, and drawing he expresses himself as an ironist whose moralizing tendencies are continually undermined by contrary inclinations.[17]

Between 1886 and 1891 Remington covered the West for *Century Magazine* and *Harper's Weekly*, providing correspondence and illustrations on the Apache wars, life on the great cattle ranches, and the

Ghost Dance troubles in Dakota. At the same time he began to achieve success as a painter and illustrator of western scenes. It was through this work that he became friends with Roosevelt and Wister.[18]

Remington identifies the vanishing freedom and purity of the Frontier with the "Vanishing American," and in his early treatments of Indians he tries to imagine a way of preserving savage freedom within the new "progressive" order by taking the management of affairs away from philanthropic civilians and politically appointed bureaucrats and assigning it to the men who really "know Indians"—the officers of the Plains cavalry.[19]

This vision is elaborated in an article published in *Harper's Weekly* during the Ghost Dance troubles of 1890–91 but written some time earlier. "Indians as Irregular Cavalry" notes that through incorporation as scouts in the regimental structure of the army some Indians have been made useful members of civilized society; and in the extension of this regimental socialization, in which the Indians are maintained as "children in their relation to us," Remington sees hope of the Indian's final integration into American society. It is worth noting that his thought-process mirrors the proposal for "civilizing" freed slaves put forward by Charles Francis Adams during the Civil War, which envisioned the establishment of military colonies whose firm hierarchical discipline would keep the Blacks under control during the course of their civic education. Remington imagines the new regimental order as a utopia in which the noblest aspects of savagery are preserved to serve as reminders to the White man of the primal virtues of a warrior race.[20]

Remington contrasts the prospects of this soldierly regime for the Indian with those of the misgoverned democracy of the metropolis. Though in racial endowment Indians are not much better than the "lowest type of Italian or Hungarian immigrant" who is unable to "tell the difference between the Constitution and a coal scuttle," they are not swayed by democratic cant or the promises of elected officials ("they know that [the government] never keeps its word"). Rather, they trust the strong managerial hand of professional soldiers, who are warriors like themselves. Thus while Chicago's laborers seethe with disloyalty, those Indians who wear the uniform resist even the appeals of Sitting Bull's "jihad." While the urban workers will never be anything but a dangerous class, the Indians may ultimately become for us "a semi-military industrial force, much after the fashion of the Cossacks," whose colonies would stabilize our border with Mexico. The regimental partnership of the two warrior races might produce a new kind of frontier settlement in which military management replaces Wild West license.[21]

But the new order envisioned in the article has no place for a continuation of the warfare through which both Indians and cavalrymen acquired and expressed their warrior virtues. As metropolis replaces wilderness and as the primal Anglo-Saxon military virtues are adulterated by commercialism, democracy, and immigration, the heroic soldier no less than the wild Indian becomes a Vanishing American. From this perspective, the Indian's fate mirrors that of Remington's chosen people; and when he is using the Indians to symbolize this decline, his diatribes against their brutal savagery give way to a form of romantic primitivism. This ambivalence appears most clearly in his essay on the death of Lieutenant Casey, who was for Remington a paragon of the new-model soldier: an "Indian thinker" as well as fighter, a military manager. Remington's anger at the "nasty" savage who murdered Casey is countered by his paradoxical recognition that, as warriors, some of the Sioux had a better appreciation of Casey's virtues than did his own people: Americans seem to "lack a virtue which the military races of Europe possess," the soldierly virtues that (as Roosevelt would have it) are vitiated by commercialism and excessive gentility.[22]

On the classic ground of savage warfare, Remington's imagination plays freely with the symbols of Indian and cavalryman, sometimes identifying with the savage for the purpose of expressing his admiration of warrior virtues and his sense that heroic values are doomed before the advance of modernity. But when the Last Stand is transferred to an urban setting, Remington's ideological ambivalence disappears. His published work shows contempt for the immigrants, his private correspondence something worse:

> Jews, Injuns, Chinamen, Italians, Huns—the rubbish of the earth I hate—I've got some Winchesters and when the massacring begins, I can get my share of 'em, and what's more, I will. . . . Our race is full of sentiment. We've got the rinsin's, the scourin's, and the Devil's lavings to come to us and be *men*—something they haven't been, most of them, these hundreds of years.[23]

Remington's dispatches for *Harper's Weekly* on Chicago during the Pullman Strike realize the scenario for massacre suggested in the letter. "Chicago Under the Mob" represents him entering the city with Custer's old regiment the 7th Cavalry, "born on the Platte River" and never having come "far enough East . . . to buy a fine-tooth comb or hear a hand-organ." But now they have come to redeem Chicago, the degraded symbol of everything our ancestors strove for, "the middle of civilization," and the site of "the great Fair, the fame of which told even Kalmuck Tartars that of all, Chicago was greatest." Like countrymen at the Exposition, the soldiers are, in a sense, innocents and even "primitives" in this modern city, though Remington's polemic will forbid likening them to Indians. They represent primal Anglo-American virtues—patriotism and the fighting spirit—returning to a metropolis that has alienated itself from such things. The mob is a "malodorous crowd of anarchistic foreign trash," and the soldiers' idea of handling it is "to create about eleven cords of compost out of the material at hand." Like Indians, the strikers are moved by unaccountable impulses, inexplicable to a civilized White American.[24]

The antipathy between strikers and soldiers is racial as much as it is moral:

> The soldier mind doesn't understand this Hungarian or Polack, or whatever the stuff is; he will talk to a real American striker in an undertone, and tell him it is best to go home and not get shot, but he tells me in his simple way, "Say, do you know them things ain't human?—before God I don't think they are men."

Remington attributes to the soldier the sentiments he had voiced in his letter-diatribe against the immigrants, using many of the same phrases:

> Chicago is a social island; there is nothing like it elsewhere; it has the "scourin's, the rinsin's, and the clanin's, . . . and it's had some politics for twenty years that would make a moral idiot suck for breath.

The embodiment of Chicago's political evils is Governor Altgeld, whose sympathy for labor identifies him as one who has taken "the raging, savage, unthinking mob, as it stands in front of the police and the soldiers, into partnership. . . ." The result has been a "rape of government," a figurative captivity to strikers from which the cavalry must rescue the "real Americans" of Chicago as once they rescued White women from Indians. After the mob has been driven off, "a real workman" appears to cheer the soldiers and cry, " 'Kill 'em—kill every one of 'em . . . they ain't got no wives and children, and they do me harm who have . . .' Whereat Uncle Sam's troopers felt refreshed morally."[25]

It was a standard joke of the 1870s that Indians were so dirty as a race that the surest way to either civilize or exterminate them was by giving them soap. Remington echoes this joke in his assertion that "There is a big foreign population here in Chicago that isn't American in any particular. . . . Eventually this unlicked mob will have to be shot up a little, or washed, before it will get into a mental calm."

But the orders to shoot never come, because (as a half-smart, American-born agitator notes) "no-one's got the sand." The soldiers' healthy instincts are restrained by a high command that is too subservient to a corrupted democratic polity. But the "decent people" of Chicago instinctively recognize that the army is more to be trusted than "their" government: there is "always more or less doubt about all the forces of law" because they are controlled by the democracy that elected an Altgeld; but "no one doubts the 'regulars' " because "The regulars hate the scum," and "their presence alone keeps the social scum from rising to the top." If martial law had been immediately declared when the strike broke out, and "a few rioters shot, . . . this would all have been over before now."[26]

The violence that will bring "Chicago Under the Law" is administered first by the army. But the work of the soldiers is supplemented by a vigilante movement among the "decent people." Here Remington invokes another aspect of the Frontier Myth, related to the savage war scenario but not restricted to it: vigilantism or lynch law, which (like Indian-killing) envisions the use of private violence for public ends, especially the elimination of criminal elements from a Frontier society. Remington specifically compares the Chicago movements to the vigilance committee in Hayes City, Kansas, before that cattle town was "tamed"; and to the campaign of the Wyoming Stock Growers Association against the "rustlers" in the Johnson County War (see Chapter 5):

> The ease with which much beer is obtained in America has inflamed the imagination of this Central European peasantry . . . and they imagine they own the town. Even now there will be isolated acts of vandalism . . . in which case the people will hunt them as the stockmen used to hunt horse-thieves out West.[27]

Remington admires the vigilantism of the "decent folks" of Chicago as a sign of their renascent virility. Their visceral outrage and hatred for the "scum" testifies to a recrudescence of an essential virtue, as does Remington's own declaration that he has his own Winchester ready to use. But personal or local vigilantism is insufficient remedy for the ills the strikers represent. In "The Affair of the —th of July," published in *Harper's Weekly* two months after the Pullman Strike dispatches, Remington indulges in a genocidal fantasy in which the *army* acts as the instrument of vigilante justice or lynch law.

The story is framed as a letter written by a staff officer named "Jack," who tells what "might very well have happened if the mob had continued to monkey with the military buzz-saw." The mob in the story is not disorderly, but it has prepared for revolution with dynamite bombs and battle plans. This time someone has the "sand" to order the army to shoot. As the "real workman" of "Chicago Under the Mob" had declared, they have no women or children—and are therefore legitimate targets of army firepower. The artillery fires indiscriminately into clusters of people; it bombards streets and neighborhoods, not just formations of strikers. The captain of the cavalry troop orders a charge, telling his men "No prisoners . . . no prisoners!" Those prisoners who are taken are sent before drumhead court-martial—the situation envisioned in Kirkman's suggestion that railway workers be treated as enlisted soldiers for purposes of discipline.

What happens next is adapted from descriptions of the mass execution of supposed Communards after the suppression of the Paris Commune of 1871:

> I saw some of the executions of those hundreds of prisoners next day, but I didn't care to see it much. They piled them on flat cars as though they had been cordwood, and buried them out in the country somewhere. Most of them were hobos, anarchists, and toughs of the worst type, and I think they "left their country for their country's good." Chicago is thoroughly worked up now, and if they keep with the present attention to detail, they will have a fine population left. The good citizens have a monster vigilance committee, and I am afraid will do many things which are not entirely just, but it is the reaction from lawlessness, and cannot be helped. They have been terribly exasperated by the rioting and license of the past. . . .[28]

Thus to save civilization for "decent folks," it becomes necessary to set aside the forms of law and both the ideological framework and the traditional practices of democratic government. Those who perform the work of rescue are licensed not only to act outside the norms of civil law and the Law of War (which forbids indiscriminate killing of civilians), but to deploy violence on a a scale never hitherto permitted in any other contexts but those of "savage war" and "servile insurrection."[29]

"The Affair of the —th of July" is both a polemic and a projective fantasy. Its nominal aim is to warn the government, the decent citizens, and the strikers of the possible consequences of their social conflict and to help them avoid the cataclysmic violence that the story depicts. But as a work of fiction its function and effect are more ambivalent. The fantasy of a massacre allows Remington to vent in public his private rage against the increased share of American social space, cultural influence, and economic and political power that was being taken up by immigrants and the labor movement. It also allows him to envision a more heroic resolution for the social crisis than the one that actually occurred.

But as a model for modern heroic adventure, the cavalry-in-the-streets scenario has severe limitations. From Remington's perspective, the setting is too squalid and the enemy too base for urban warfare to produce in its heroes the spiritual regeneration that the cavalryman can achieve in combat with his savage opposite in the Homeric country of the West. And even in his ideological rage, Remington (through his narrator) expresses a sense of queasiness at the kind of slaughter that occurs.

But the sympathies of the mass-culture audience were far more divided than Remington's on these issues. Figures like King's Captain Forrest or Remington's narrator in "The Affair of the —th of July" were designed as heroes for a public that no longer existed (if it ever had): a mass audience which homogeneously identified itself as White Anglo-Saxon Protestant and middle class and which was willing to dispense with its traditional notions of democracy, equality, government by consent, and America as the refuge of the oppressed.

But if the regimental hero was problematic when engaged in a domestic social conflict, when projected into an imperial conflict against the non-White peoples of Asia and Latin America he could be credibly represented as the embodiment of American virtues.

Roosevelt's Rough Riders: The Regiment as Social Microcosm

The use of the regiment to symbolize American society gained wider currency with the outbreak of the Spanish–American War. Regular officers and regiments came in for a far greater share of praise and news coverage than they had in the Civil War. The difference is partly a reflection of the different composition of the armies: while the small regular army was lost in the mass mobilizations of the Civil War, it made up a larger and more visible component of the small army that invaded Cuba. War correspondents like Remington, Stephen Crane, and Richard Harding Davis praised the courage, professionalism, and gentlemanly character of the professional officers, and Crane and Remington extended that admiration to the men in the ranks.[30]

Nonetheless, the most celebrated single regiment of the war was not a regular outfit but the First Volunteer Cavalry or "Rough Riders," the "cowboy regiment" recruited and commanded by Theodore Roosevelt. The story of the "Rough Riders" has three phases: the actual process of its formation, training, and service; its treatment in the press while the war was being fought; and its apotheosis in Roosevelt's own book on the subject, *The Rough Riders* (1900). In each of these phases, Roosevelt played the role of "author": he composed his regiment with an eye to its symbolism that is reminiscent of Buffalo Bill's organization of his own "Congress of the Rough Riders"; he used political influence first to get the regiment assigned to Cuba and a combat role and then to get the regiment returned to the States; he shaped press coverage of its battles by assiduous attention to correspondents; and finally he authored its official history.[31]

Roosevelt's book was serialized before publication and was his most successful literary endeavor. Although it effectively exploits current events, *The Rough Riders* is also thematically continuous with Roosevelt's earlier books on the Frontier, and it thus suggests that Roosevelt's adventure represents the culmination of that mythic history. His regiment is offered as a microcosm of the progressive order: a military society inhabited by professional soldiers, genuine frontiersmen, and aristocratic converts to "The Strenuous Life"; governed by and obedient to an officer class whose place and powers are earned by native merit and the proof of action; selflessly devoted to a patriotic objective. Roosevelt himself is both the regiment's representative man and its unquestioned leader.

Enthusiasm for the war created competition for places in many of the volunteer regiments, a phenomenon compounded for the Rough Riders by the publicity the regiment enjoyed from the moment of its conception. In Roosevelt's account (as in practice) the regiment's recruiting therefore becomes a ritual of selection in which Roosevelt deliberately composes the band of heroes he will project against the racial enemy.

Certain symbolic gestures define the process of creating the regiment, and the exercise of authority within it, as "democratic." But these symbols are ultimately co-opted to the service of a managerial model of social relations. As Roosevelt tells the story, the regiment is a utopia of meritocracy in which distinctions of birth and wealth are set aside in favor of military aptitude. The regiment's officers are therefore to be seen as a "natural aristocracy" of merit and virtue whose men follow them unquestioningly because they recognize their worthiness for command. Once it is trained in Roosevelt's system, the regiment realizes the vision of a new order first articulated by Draper in 1865: the *recognition* of the officers' intellectual or professional superiority makes even the rugged individualists of the Rough Riders willing to submit to their authority. The social compact that binds the Rough Riders substantially modifies the notion of consent envisioned in democratic theory; it is not obtained through political negotiation or the clash of asserted wills but through a training process that makes men accept the idea that consent to obey is implicit once superiority is recognized in a commander.

Since consent depends on recognition of superiority, the commander of a democratic regiment must project a distinctive kind of heroic persona to give substance to his merely official powers. Although Roosevelt praises the regular army discipline imposed by the regiment's first commander, Colonel Leonard Wood, when he himself assumes command he deliberately adopts a more democratic *style* of leadership: he tells us he prefers to explain matters to the troops and to lead by example, to be firm but not snobbish or punctilious about his social or military rank.[32]

The rank and file are primarily drawn from those classes that figure as supporting players in Roosevelt's hunting books or *The Winning of the West*: cowboys, hunters, scouts, sheriffs, Texas Rangers. They include some men who have been outlaws, and a larger number who had served as vigilantes acting outside the law in "those bodies of armed men with which the growing civilization of the border finally puts down its savagery."[33] He even accepts Indians from Buffalo Bill's Wild West and the Indian Territory—the latter, he said, wanted to learn through soldiering how to act "civilized." Roosevelt even suspends his usual prejudice against racial intermarriage long enough to praise a "half-breed" as coming "of soldier stock on both sides and through both races." The Rough Riders thus partly fulfill Remington's vision of the regiment as a refuge in which both sides of the primal heroic warfare of the wilderness can coexist and become productive in a modern sense. However, the Indians are segregated in their own company.

Yet Roosevelt accepts in the regiment only those social types who had figured as parts of his mythic "Frontier." No mechanics, no sodbusters or sharecroppers, no clerks or factory operatives, no immigrants, no bankers or merchants—none of the characteristic folk of modern society are included. The only exceptions are four New York policemen who had served Roosevelt during his term as Police Commissioner, whose race is not specified but "in whose veins the blood stirred with the same impulse which sent the Vikings over sea."[34] The new frontier, like the old, will be won by the same racial stock that won the West.

Leadership of this wild assortment of self-reliant fighters is vested in a mixture of professionals with "natural" leaders of plebeian origin, like the Arizona sheriff Bucky O'Neill.[35] Nonetheless, various types of "aristocracy" are over-represented among the regiment's officers and in the pages of Roosevelt's book. Particular emphasis is given to recruiting among each of the aristocracies of birth, education, and military service. In addition to Roosevelt's northeastern neighbors, there were requests from Europeans and from southerners like ex-Confederate Fitzhugh Lee and Thomas Nelson Page, a novelist noted for his nostalgic portrayals of antebellum slavery and later an apologist for southern vigilantism.[36] Roosevelt is proud of his ability to recruit a cadre of regular officers like Leonard Wood and Allyn Capron (who would give the regiment its good discipline), of the large contingent of Ivy League scholar-athletes, and even of the presence of some sons of noted businessmen, who qualified by showing "the traits of hardihood and a thirst for adventure"—signs of their aptitude for the "strenuous life." Capron is Roosevelt's ideal, a West Pointer, "the best soldier in the regiment," the scion of a long and distinguished military line, a superb athlete, horseman, marksman, and scholar, "the archetype of the fighting man," blond and blue-eyed. Yet Capron is also "Hawkeye" enough to be given command of the Indian company, whose "wild spirits" he commands by example. But if Capron is to be praised for taming the Indians, what are we to think of Roosevelt, who proves himself able to command cowboys, Indians, athletes, scholars, vigilantes, outlaws, and West Pointers all together?[37]

The Rough Riders, then, are a matured version of frontier democracy in which the necessities of warfare have produced a natural leadership or aristocracy that directs its course by command. The governed consent to be so ruled because they are spiritually (and for the most part racially) homogeneous: all are drawn from stocks in which the blood and spirit of warrior ancestors are marked. Through the test of battle, this Rough Rider community—initially treated with condescension by the regulars—not only proves its virtue but attains a commanding position among the regiments of the army. At the battles of San Juan and Kettle Hills the wounding or death of senior officers leaves Roosevelt the Volunteer in command of the main assault. His Rough Riders will charge and fight alongside two regular regiments but will (in his account) eclipse both in skill and aggressiveness.

But this comparison between regulars and Rough Riders is actually a proof of the importance of race, for the two regular regiments are composed of Negroes. Their racial inferiority makes them peculiarly dependent on their White officers, many of whom have fallen in the attack:

> Occasionally they produce non-commissioned officers who can take the initiative and accept responsibility precisely like the best class of whites; but this cannot be expected normally, nor is it fair to expect it . . . whereas with the white Regulars, as with my own Rough Riders, experience showed that non-commissioned officers could usually carry on the fight themselves if they were once started, no matter whether their officers were killed or not.[38]

It should be noted that Roosevelt's assessment of the quality of the Black regulars is not supported by other accounts, which emphasize their good performance and the generally high level of competence among Black non-coms. Because they offered relatively better standards of living, dignity, and protection from Jim Crow, these regiments had higher-than-average rates of re-enlistment, with concomitant advantages to their state of training and unit pride.[39]

The racial distinction suggests a contrast between two kinds of regimental society. Where the mass of the population are racially inferior, a more rigid and paternalistic form of governance is necessary, and a less stable and effective form of society is the result. In comparison, the White regiments appear models of democratic self-government, with all ranks capable of exercising some degree of leadership. However, within the White camp there is a further distinction between those who can keep an action going after it has been started and those who are capable of taking the initiative. The Rough Riders are "wholly exceptional" among the regiments, because their subordinate officers, non-coms, and even privates are so versed in self-reliance and self-government that each can take responsibility for maintaining the regiment's forward drive.[40] But Roosevelt's capacity is superior even to theirs: in the midst of battle Roosevelt takes the initiative by assuming command of all the forces and modifying the orders of the high command. Thus the parable of the regiments produces an allegory of Roosevelt's own worthiness for supreme command: to be a leader of leaders, directing officers who are themselves the pick of a rank and file that has been selected out of the American mass on the basis of military virtue.

The Philippine "Insurrection" as Savage War, 1898–1902

This allegory of command has two political references: the first, and most obvious, is to Roosevelt himself and justifies his seeking the highest political office; the second is to policy, Roosevelt's belief that seizure and conquest of an overseas empire beginning with the Philippines was essential to the establishment of a commanding position for America among the "great fighting races." In 1898 he had exerted pressure from within McKinley's administration for the adventure in Cuba; after his return from Cuba he made the Philippine question the centerpiece of his gubernatorial campaign. In addresses like "The Strenuous Life" and "Expansion and Peace" he used the symbolism of the Frontier Myth to argue that imperialism was the logical and necessary extension of the nation's "westering" course of development, the fulfillment of our destiny among the "fighting races" of the world, and the means to personal and racial re-invigoration. By likening the Filipinos to "Apaches" and the anti-imperialists to "Indian-lovers," he suggested that those who resisted imperialism were traitors to their race and recreant to their sex—emasculators of American manhood.[41]

With his nomination as McKinley's running mate in 1900, Roosevelt was able to make the Philippine issue central to the presidential campaign. The strength of the Democratic opposition lay in its critique of big business and in the Republicans' support of the banking interests and the trusts against the demands of Populist farmers and organized labor. But their candidate, William Jennings Bryan, was also a leading anti-imperialist; and through effective and unremitting demagogy Roosevelt and the Republican press were able to defeat Bryan by focusing attention on this unpopular position. In cartoons, editorials, and speeches, Bryan was identified as a supporter of Aguinaldo, the leader of the Filipino "insurrection" against American control. Bryan was given a "shadow cabinet" of "three traitorous A's": Aguinaldo, Atkinson, and Altgeld—the Filipino guerrilla, the Populist "radical," and the pro-labor governor who pardoned the Haymarket anarchists. Roosevelt was particularly effective in dramatizing this connection. His speeches were given added drama by the appearance of "hecklers" who would be identified from the platform by Roosevelt himself as "rowdies and anarchists" and "Bryan's friends" before being ejected by Republican stalwarts who were usually identified as "veterans."[42] These were, in all likelihood, prearranged dramas—the Wild West technique of historical ritual translated to the political arena.[43]

American participation in the suppression of the "Boxer Rebellion" in China provided an additional occasion for this kind of polemic. *Harper's Weekly* equated the Chinese with the Filipinos as excluded from the "peoples of the civilized world," because despite their long cultural history their racial character is still so marked by "tribal" qualities (cruelty, superstition, irrationality, etc.). The cover of the June 23, 1900, issue features a political cartoon in which the anti-imperialist Bryan is identified as "The Vanguard of the Boxers," and an editorial on July 28 terms the Democratic convention the "Boxer Convention." The cover cartoon on July 28 shows McKinley and Uncle Sam wrapped in a torn American flag charging against caricatured Orientals who brandish knives over the bloody corpses of a woman and child—the caption asks, "Is this imperialism?" The iconography is nearly identical to that of an anti-labor cartoon published on June 16th, which shows caricatured Irishmen leering like cartoon savages as they stomp on the bloody female form of "St. Louis"—a comment on the streetcar strike in that city. Another on August 25th shows "What Might Have Happened if the Original Thirteen States Had Never Expanded": Bryan dressed as an Indian chief and supported by a grinning horde of ethnic types (also dressed as savages) menace a tiny Uncle Sam beleaguered in a coastal fortress.[44]

The point of this exercise in symbolism was not simply a general defamation of Bryan as the putative ally of Aguinaldo. By linking Aguinaldo, Atkinson, and Altgeld, Republican propaganda suggested that domestic radicalism was a form of guerrilla warfare conducted by "White savages" and aimed at the destruction of civil order and private property. In this context, anti-imperialism appeared as more than resistance to a dubious overseas adventure: it was a means for "enemies of order" to overthrow the "ordered liberty" of Republican rule, for "Desperate Democrats" to "Sow . . . Seeds of Anarchy, License, Mob Rule."[45] As in the 1870s, a "savage war" on the border provided the symbolism through which one party could discredit the other in the battle for ideological supremacy and political power. And once again, the distinction between savages and civilized Whites provided the symbolic basis for a justification of managerial privilege against the claims of democracy and the rights of labor.

In transferring the reference of the Myth of the Frontier from continental to overseas expansion, imperialist polemics translate the "democratic" features of the original myth into "managerial" terms. Senator Albert Beveridge invokes a Turnerian view of the Frontier when he asserts that seizure of the Philippines "means opportunity for all the glorious young manhood of the republic—the most virile, ambitious, impatient, militant manhood the world has ever seen."[46] According to the Turnerian or democratic understanding, such opportunities had been available to mankind in general on the old Frontier; on the new, they belong only to the most "virile" races of mankind. Racial virility in turn is identified not only with military skill but with managerial ability: our right to rule the Philippines derives from our character as "the most administrative race in history":

> God has not prepared the English-speaking and Teutonic peoples for a thousand years for nothing but vain and idle self-contemplation . . . No! He has made us the master organizers to establish system where chaos reigns. He has given us the spirit of progress to overwhelm the forces of reaction throughout the earth. He has made us adepts in government that we may administer government among the savage and senile peoples of the earth.[47]

Anti-imperialists err when they assert the injustice of governing Filipinos without their consent, because the issue is not one of political philosophy, it "is elemental. It is racial."[48] American nationality is not constituted by adherence to a set of universal principles, like those in the Declaration of Independence, which all rational men can be expected to understand. Rather, to be American is to belong to a particular and exclusive race whose understanding and exercise of democratic liberty are privileged by nature. When races of unequal endowment occupy the same social space, the defense of civilization replaces the development of democracy as the highest social priority.

Within our borders we have recognized this principle in governing without their consent such dependent classes as Indians, children, lunatics, and even the White peoples of unorganized territories. The Indian example is a particularly important one, because the dispossession and subjugation of the Native American was the precondition for establishing an American nation; hence those who argue that savages have a right of self-government reduce "the patriots of 1776" to "a swarm of land pirates." But if we accept the racialist reading of our history as a valid model of progress, then we will see that in seizing the Philippines we do not violate the Declaration of Independence: "We do but what our fathers did—we but pitch the tents of liberty farther westward . . . we only continue the march of the flag," and those who oppose this march are "infidel to American power and practical sense."[49]

Even if one accepted the idea that "savages" were not entitled to the natural rights belonging to a "people" (in the Jeffersonian sense), it ought to have been difficult to prove the Filipinos savages. The islands had been ruled by Spain since the sixteenth century and possessed a substantial urban culture supported by peasant agriculture. James H. Blount, who served as an administrator in the islands, notes that according to the census of 1903, only 7 percent of Filipinos could be classified as wild or savage; he turns Beveridge's argument on its head by asserting that it was as reasonable to withhold independence from the Philippines on account of these "savages" as it would have been to withhold it from the American colonies in 1776 on account of the mere presence on our territory of uncivilized Indians.[50] Some imperialist polemics did distinguish between the better classes of Filipinos and the savage or barbaric masses.[51] But the more extreme expressions of the "savage war" thesis saw the savage element as comprehending all classes of Filipinos, including the educated and propertied elites who supported the nationalist Aguinaldo.[52] Once that principle had been established, American commanders could even concede that Aguinaldo represented a genuine popular resistance to the American takeover without imperiling the rationale of the imperial mission. After all, Crazy Horse and Sitting Bull had been popular leaders.[53] *Harper's Weekly*, which had praised Aguinaldo in January, excoriated him in March as a savage who had ordered his men to "exterminate . . . without compassion" or distinction of age or sex all of "the civilized race" in the Islands.[54]

This demonstration of Filipino savagery licenses the Americans to respond in kind, transforming the struggle from a civilized war for politically defined objectives to a race war, whose objective must be the utter destruction or subjugation of the enemy; a war demanding absolute loyalty from all who would not identify themselves as racial renegades:

> The war has developed into a race war. After this let no one raise his voice in favor of Aguinaldo's government or army. For be it understood that Sandico [the official who wrote the order] is not an ignorant savage, but a native educated in Europe—the type of what we can hope for in educating the native. . . . I had a great deal of sympathy with the native, however mistaken might be his ideas of liberty. To-day I understand that to them liberty means the opportunity to give unbridled license to their mad racial instincts.[55]

Correspondent John Bass goes on to argue for the unrestrained use of force in suppressing the rebellion and governing the Islands in the language hitherto used in debates over Indian policy between hard-liners and "philanthropists":

> Let no mistaken philanthropic movement at home interfere with our government here, or many of our brave men will die in consequence. I have learned to be an ardent anti-annexationist; now, however, that we have undertaken the herculean task of establishing a stable government here, self-preservation requires, for the time being at least, an autocratic government.[56]

In the ensuing months of fighting between American troops and Filipino guerrillas, *Harper's* developed the Indian-war analogy in detail. Frank D. Millet, in an article on "The Filipino Leaders," compares their tactics to those of the Indians and their religious practices to those of the Ghost Dancers. An article on "Philippine Ethnology" by Marrion Wilcox asserts that "our North American Indians so thoroughly interpret to us this type of humanity" that we may find "that some of our present hostiles are blood-relations to the poor foes of the Pilgrims and Puritans."[57] Although there were no serious Indian hostilities at the time, disorders on the reservations were juxtaposed with accounts of Philippine battles.[58]

The journalistic use of Indian-war terminology was reinforced by the commanding generals and field officers who had learned their trade in the Plains and Apache wars, and by officers and bureaucrats whose first experience in managing refugee camps and pacified districts had been on Indian reservations. The high command was rife with ex-Indian fighters, including generals Otis, Merritt, Lawton,

Bell, Jacob Smith and Chaffee; and there were numerous junior officers like Funston and John Pershing, whose techniques for combating Moro tribesman and organizing Filipino scouts had been learned in Apacheria. It was second nature for someone like Otis to speak of Filipino casualties as "400 Indians," and for the press to report the "Success of the Moment Against Filipino Braves."[59] An article in *Harper's Weekly* on "The Regulars" quoted one of "Custer's scouts" to the effect that the best way to suppress the savage Filipinos was to find a Philippine equivalent of the buffalo and destroy it.[60]

To suppress the insurrection these soldiers applied doctrines drawn from the Indian wars and from Civil War anti-guerrilla campaigns along the Missouri-Kansas border—the region in which the James Gang later operated (see Chapter 4). Their model statutes were General Orders No. 11 and No. 100, which declared the guerrillas in violation of the laws of civilized warfare and licensed extraordinary measures against them. Although the targets were White, the orders were justified by a rhetoric which insisted that the guerrillas had inaugurated a "savage war" and had thereby made themselves liable to treatment like that which was already recognized as legitimate when fighting Indians. Acceptable measures included the refusal to grant quarter, the right to summarily try captured guerrillas as murderers, and the right to burn out and dispossess guerrilla families and place them in camps or reservations where they could be controlled—measures that had earlier been employed against the "Civilized Tribes" during the Indian Removals of the Jacksonian period. These methods, systematized in 1863–65, were then re-applied to the Indians during the Plains wars of 1865–90. The adoption of policies that held all off-reservation Indians (including whole villages) as liable to attack, coupled with the extermination of the buffalo, destroyed the resource and population base on which the hostiles depended and compelled the Indians to accept concentration on reservations.[61]

When the Spanish imperial administration in Cuba used similar techniques against the native independence movement, depopulating the countryside and incarcerating civilians in "reconcentration camps," American public opinion had been outraged. Such treatment was only appropriate for savages, like the Plains Indians, not for the civilized Cubans. But once the Filipinos had been identified as "savages," they became eligible targets of campaigns aimed at destroying hostile districts and re-concentrating peasants on reservations where Americans could police them.[62]

"1008 Dead Niggers": The Logic of Massacre

By the terms of the Frontier Myth, once imperial war was conflated with savage war both sides become subject to the logic of massacre. The savage enemy kills and terrorizes without limit or discrimination in order to exterminate or drive out the civilized race. The civilized race learns to respond in kind, partly from outrage at the atrocities it has suffered, partly from a recognition that imitation and mastery of the savages' methods are the best way to defeat them. A cycle of massacre and revenge is thus inaugurated that drives both sides toward a war of extermination. Only an American victory can prevent actual genocide: the savage enemy would indeed exterminate all of the civilized race, but the civilized carry massacre only as far as necessary to subjugate the savage. To achieve victory in such a war, Americans are entitled and indeed required to use any and all means, including massacre, terrorism, and torture. This is the argument implicit in war correspondent Henry Loomis Nelson's account of the soldiers' thinking about the course of the war:

> The soldiers reasoned that, as the United States have imposed upon them the duty of putting down the insurrection, these brown men must be overcome at all hazards; while the war against them must be conducted upon the principles of savage warfare, since most of those who are fighting against us are classed as barbarians. . . . There are but two possible conclusions to the matter. We must conquer the islands or get out. . . . If we decide to stay, we must bury all qualms and scruples about Weilerian cruelty, the consent of the governed, etc., and stay. We exterminated the American Indians, and I guess most of us are proud of it, or, at least, believe the end justified the means; and we must have no scruples about exterminating this other race standing in the way of progress and enlightenment if it is necessary.[63]

The use of exterminationist rhetoric by American commanders and correspondents was not intended as the literal promulgation of a policy of genocide. Rather, it was a polemical device by which American leaders hoped to nerve their troops and the public at home to accept the new political measures and changes in our ideological tradition that imperialism would require.

The commission of atrocities by American troops was admitted by both pro-imperialists and anti-imperialists. Indeed, some of the most effective propaganda of the anti-imperialists consists of quotations from journalists who cite such incidents with approval. The correspondent of the Philadelphia *Ledger* offered graphic descriptions of American atrocities but cited them as the inevitable and appropriate methods for prosecuting a savage war:

> The present war is no bloodless, fake, opera bouffe [*sic*] engagement. Our men have been relentless; have killed to exterminate men, women, children, prisoners and captives, active insurgents and suspected people, from lads of ten and up, an idea prevailing that the Filipino, as such, was little better than a dog, a noisome reptile in some instances, whose best disposition was the rubbish heap. Our soldiers have pumped salt water into men to "make them talk," have taken prisoner people who . . . peacefully surrendered, and an hour later, without an atom of evidence to show that they were even insurrectos, stood them on a bridge and shot them down one by one, to . . . float down as an example to those who found their bullet-riddled corpses. . . . It is not civilized warfare, but we are not dealing with civilized people. The only thing they know and fear is force, violence, and brutality, and we give it to them.[64]

This sort of frank avowal, not only of the fact but of the logical necessity of "atrocious" behavior by American troops, ran the risk of providing ammunition for the anti-imperialists. Advocates of the war ran that risk in order to bring the American public to something like an informed consent to the principle of imperialism: the necessity for a superior people to impose its will on a weaker race or nation.

The psychological basis for public acceptance of the logic of massacre is the expectation, born of continual cultural reinforcement, that a people defined as savage will inevitably commit *atrocities*: acts of violence so extreme that they seem to violate the laws of nature. By defining the extreme limit of permissible uses of human power, a culture's way of defining and responding to atrocity reveals a good deal about the concerns that shape its value system. The recurring themes in accounts of savage war atrocities are those of massacre and torture, particularly by rape and/or sexual mutilation. What rape is in the myth of the "White woman's" captivity, torture and mutilation are to the story of the White male's potential victimization by his "blood enemy." In these acts, the White victim is held powerless, while his/her body is cruelly manipulated, invaded, and destroyed by a race that—according to "natural law"—ought to be subordinate to the White. The White woman's body and blood are "polluted" by the sexual invasion of her genitals and womb; the White man is emasculated, deprived of his manhood through figurative or literal castration. The politics of torture/rape/mutilation are also a parody of revolution in which a natural and legitimate order of subordination is violently and (from the White man's perspective) inappropriately reversed.

To prevent or avenge such an atrocity, to restore the social balance in which the hegemony of Whites could be taken for granted, the White man must respond with a similarly extraordinary level of violence; for only such a reciprocal atrocity can balance the shame of the original "rape." Hence the prevalence of sexual mutilation and rape of Indians when Whites succeeded in surprising a major village, as happened at Sand Creek (1864), the Washita (1869), and White Mountain (1870). But the same rationale, and the same propensity for mirror-image atrocities, characterizes American behavior in those struggles we define as similar to savage warfare, particularly (as we shall see) in southern lynching campaigns since 1865; and in extreme circumstances, in vigilante attacks on labor organizers, like those on IWW agitators in 1917–20.[65]

The parallel between the logic of massacre in the Philippines and the lynching of Blacks in the South and Midwest was a fact of contemporary life and rhetoric. If "Indian" was the racial epithet for Filipinos preferred by the high command, the second most popular—and the one preferred by the rank and file—was "nigger." The former emphasized the danger the Filipino presented as an armed enemy capable of "exterminating" the American army as Sitting Bull had exterminated Custer's men. The latter identified the Filipino as more contemptible than the Red Man, a member of a servile race well suited for subjugation, whose presence is *polluting* as much as menacing.

This dual identification was inherently murderous in its implications. "Extermination" was the traditional revenge visited upon rebellious Indians; and the Philippine war coincided with a period of widespread violence directed against Blacks marked by hundreds of terrorist incidents and lynchings annually increasing in number, territorial range, and sadism. While Black troops were still serving with the army in Cuba and Manila, there were bloody race riots in Illinois, South Carolina, and Wilmington, N.C. These incidents reflected not only the racial prejudice that divided the poor of both races, competing for a limited number of economic opportunities, but a systematic campaign to disenfranchise southern Blacks, stripping them of rights they had clung to since Reconstruction. Joe Wheeler, the ex-Confederate cavalryman, referred to the *insurrectos* as "Aguinaldo's Dusky Demons"; and a hard-line correspondent mocked the

Philippine Commission's attempts to establish the rudiments of a native judicial system by deriding those "who have the 'welfare' of the poor nigger at heart. . . . Fancy a court in the South presided over by a Negro judge and a white man as prisoner!"[66] After an advance against Aguinaldo a newspaper reported a soldier as writing:

> In the path of the Washington Regiment . . . there were 1008 dead niggers, and a great many wounded. We burned all their houses. I don't know how many men, women, and children the Tennessee boys did kill. They would not take any prisoners. . . . At the best, this is a very rich country; and we want it. My way of getting it would be to put a regiment into a skirmish line, and blow every nigger into a nigger heaven.[67]

"Almost without exception, soldiers, and also many officers, refer to the natives in their presence as 'niggers'; and the natives are beginning to understand what the word 'nigger' means."[68] Those meanings were already well understood by the large contingent of Black regulars serving with the army in the Philippines. Their own experience, and news from home, informed them of the violence committed against Black civilians, not only by lynch mobs but by gangs of soldiers from the volunteer regiments with which they served. The turn of the century was the midpoint of a forty-year period of southern terror directed against Blacks, during which lynchings averaged one per week. (See Chapter 6.) Some proponents of segregation suggested that American Blacks be deported en masse to colonize the Philippines. The idea that the two kinds of "nigger" might make common cause occurred to Whites, and the few cases of Black defection to Aguinaldo's forces generated rumors of guerrilla bands led by Black renegades. But Black troops (and community leaders at home) were not notably disaffected from the war on the Filipinos until it began to appear that the task of uplifting "little brown brother" substantively detracted from attempts to reform race relations and "uplift the Negro" at home.[69]

Invocations of savage war may have helped build public support for the Philippine War. But real campaigns based on the logic of massacre had other consequences. Warfare of the kind waged by Bell and Smith may have terrified Filipinos by convincing them of the mercilessness of the Americans; but, like similar actions in the Civil War and Indian wars (and later in Vietnam, they also helped produce an escalating cycle of reciprocal cruelties. American excesses increased the likelihood of countervailing atrocities by the other side by creating motives for revenge, by making the denial of quarter a norm of the struggle, and by making the guerrilla war more desperate by decreasing an *insurrecto*'s interest in giving himself up.

Moreover, the commission (even under official license) of "atrocities"—acts that radically violate the norms by which a soldier (or the member of a lynch mob) has lived—can create a psychology that fosters compulsive repetition. While some soldiers or mob members who participate in an act of collective torture and/or murder may be deterred by feelings of shame or guilt, others feel compelled to affirm the correctness of their original act by repetition. In the cases cited above—massacres of Indians and Filipinos, the lynchings of Blacks—the initial act of violence was often motivated by a projective fantasy in which the "savage" character of the enemy was understood as implying a threat of extreme and atrocious violence. Some of the worst massacres of this kind (Sand Creek, MyLai) were committed by troops whose experience of Indian or enemy atrocities was minimal or largely second-hand. Anticipatory vengeance certainly characterized the initial pre-emptive attack on Aguinaldo, which was justified as an act to forestall the Filipinos' attempt to "exterminate" the American army and every member of the White race in Manila. Our troops' mistreatment of captured *insurrectos* was justified by the assertion (contrary to known fact) that Aguinaldo's "savages" would torture American POWs.[70]

But once such a *threatened* or rumored atrocity has been avenged with an *actual* atrocity, the mechanisms of projection become more (rather than less) powerful. Although we hopefully assert that our vengeance has had a chastening effect on the enemy, our belief that the enemy is "savage" suggests that we may merely have given him an additional motive for vengeance. The torments or indiscriminate slaughter we have inflicted make the image of what the enemy may do to *us* all the more vivid; and to the extent that we feel guilt for the action we may even feel that our action has made us morally liable for similar mistreatment. The mechanisms of projection continue to work, and the perpetrator of an atrocity now attributes to the Filipino, Indian, or "nigger" the desire to do to the White man exactly what has been done to him (or his likenesses) in the way of torment, emasculation, and unjust slaying. And if we deal with this fear by a further act of pre-emptive cruelty, we merely begin the process again, at a higher level of murderousness. Indeed, even General Order 100 warned commanders that "unjust or inconsiderate retaliation" might produce an escalating cycle of atrocity and revenge, causing the entire struggle to degenerate into a "war of savages"—that is, a war in which *both* sides behave like savages.[71] But a proximate if not identical matching of savagery with savagery was precisely what was meant by equating the Philippine campaigns with the Indian wars.

After the "massacre" of an American garrison at the town of Balangiga in September 1901—an event the press likened to Custer's Last Stand—it became official policy to identify the struggle as a form of "savage war," and the ensuing campaign against the guerrillas was marked by the kinds of battlefield atrocities and attacks on native civilians associated with Plains campaigns like those that ended at Sand Creek (1864), the Washita (1868–69), White Mountain (1870), and Wounded Knee (1890).[72] The Balangiga garrison was commanded by a Lieutenant Connell, whose lenient treatment of the natives caused his men to identify him as a "nigger lover." His laxity had allowed guerrillas disguised as women to infiltrate the town, surprise the garrison, and kill or wound all but six of his men. The retaliatory force that recovered the village found that the bodies of the dead had been "mutilated and treated with indescribable indignities," including castration. Although these mutilations were probably committed on the dead, Army propaganda had asserted from the start (despite considerable evidence to the contrary) that Filipino guerrillas tortured and castrated their prisoners.[73]

The circumstances of the massacre were certain to produce a desire for retribution in the troops immediately involved. It is no surprise to learn that the first troops into Balangiga took spontaneous revenge, killing their prisoners and shooting up the town. But the army command used the massacre to obtain material and moral support for a broader and more systematic policy of "retributive" terror, through which they hoped to cow the local population, drive peasants into "reconcentration" areas, and thus deprive the rebels of their base of support. The commander of American forces, General Chaffee, responded to press criticism by blaming the "mollycoddling of treacherous natives" by "false humanitarians," just as Sheridan and the conservative press had blamed the "philanthropists" and President Grant's Peace Policy for Custer's defeat. Some reporters attributed the natives' success to the expert leadership of David Fagen, a black renegade from the Colored 24th Infantry—a figure whose rumored role corresponds to that assigned to White "squaw men" and renegades in Sitting Bull's camp.[74] Sensational journalistic accounts of the massacre (and the subsequent campaign) served the army's purposes, although many of the newspapermen who wrote about Balangiga cited it as proof that the army's earlier claims of success in suppressing the insurrection had been fatuous or exaggerated. Thus even critics of the army concurred in the view that Balangiga showed the need for sterner measures and more systematic use of force.[75]

Just as in the aftermath of the Little Big Horn, the army determined to avenge Balangiga with a systematically merciless campaign. Under Chaffee's direction, General J. Franklin Bell issued a new set of orders and rules of engagement for troops operating on the island of Samar. Formulated in the language of a legal brief rather than a set of military instructions, Bell declared that the Filipinos had departed from the usages of civilized war and cited precedents in military law (including General Orders No. 11 and No. 100 from the anti-guerrilla campaign in Civil War Missouri) which entitled the American army to "severely punish, in the same or lesser degree, the commission of acts denounced in the aforementioned articles." A series of circulars elaborated these orders, authorizing commanders in the field to retaliate in kind against guerrilla actions (for example, responding to the "murder" of an American by shooting a guerrilla P.O.W. chosen by lot), to act without hesitation even where the innocent suffer with the guilty, recognizing that "a short and severe war creates . . . less loss and suffering than a benevolent war indefinitely prolonged," and to act when necessary without waiting for higher authorization.[76]

As Stuart Miller has said, Bell's order "should never have appeared in writing," because its legal rationale was inadequate—Filipinos were being punished for violating an executive order of which they had never heard, an order promulgated by Lincoln in 1863—and because the measures it called for were in violation of the existing laws of war, even as they pertain to "savage war."[77] However, the kind of warfare sanctioned by these orders was permitted and even required by the myth/ideology of savage war as formulated in the hard-line or exterminationist polemics of the 1870s; it was justified too by the belief systems of the Indian-fighting army from whose ranks Chaffee and Bell had come. Moreover, the formal adoption of this line of attack occurred under the aegis of Theodore Roosevelt, a president who identified himself with the Indian-fighting cavalry and against the "foolish sentimentalists."[78]

The Samar campaign that followed Balangiga was characterized by what Secretary of War Elihu Root called "Marked Severities," and it became celebrated (or notorious) for its cruelty when several officers were court-martialed for atrocities committed during its course. The trial of Major Waller (U.S.M.C.) revealed that he had received verbal orders from General Jacob Smith requiring him to wage a war of extermination:

> "I want no prisoners. I wish you to kill and burn: the more you kill and burn the better you will please me." And, further, [Smith said] that he wanted all persons killed who were capable of bearing arms and in actual hostilities against the United States, and did, in reply to a question by Major Waller asking for an age limit, designate the limit as ten years of age. . . . General Smith did give instructions to Major Waller to "kill and burn" and "make Samar a howling wilderness," and he admits that he wanted everybody killed capable of bearings arms . . . over ten years of age, as the Samar boys of that age were equally as dangerous as their elders.

Although Waller was court-martialed for killing some of his prisoners, he seems actually to have resisted carrying out the worst of Smith's orders.[79]

Although the Samar campaign provided the occasion for a public examination of the methods and reasons of "savage war," it was not the first or the most terrible of these campaigns. Smith came to Samar from Batangas, where (serving under General Bell) he had been responsible for a particularly murderous campaign that depopulated large sections of the province and brought most of its population into reconcentration camps.[80] Anti-imperialists cited Bell's own figures in estimating that one-sixth of the population of Luzon had died—616,000 persons—and quoted Bell's officers boasting that their general had found "the secret of pacification of the archipelago. . . . They never rebel in Northern Luzon because there isn't anybody there to rebel."[81]

In fact, Bell overstated the murderousness of his campaign in an attempt to disprove assertions that the army's anti-guerrilla campaign was ineffective and thus inadvertently gave the anti-imperialists good grounds for protest. But the real figures are only comparatively less monstrous. Later estimates based on army records suggest that between 16,000 and 20,000 rebels were killed in action and that an additional 200,000 civilian deaths resulted from the campaigns of 1899 to 1902.[82]

According to James H. Blount, who served as a private under Bell before becoming a colonial official, the inflation of body counts may also have been part of a calculated campaign of terror, which also included forced labor and the destruction of villages, designed to frighten the villagers into abandoning the guerrillas. Bell's orders were taken by the soldiers as license to "devastate" rebel territory, to avenge the deaths of comrades slain in ambush, and to wreak on the natives their resentment of the guerrilla war and the way officials wanted it fought. "The American soldier in officially sanctioned wrath is a thing so ugly and dangerous that it would take a Kipling to describe him." While Bell may have exaggerated his "severities" in Luzon, when coupled with his orders to Smith they had the effect of encouraging an "exterminationist" approach to the pacification of Samar and other embattled districts.[83]

Although tales of American atrocities created a public scandal that led to the court-martials of Waller and Smith, Roosevelt and his allies were able to turn the Samar massacres from a potential embarrassment into a renewal of public support by insisting more vehemently than before on the "savage" character of the *insurrectos*. Once that was established, all but the most extreme actions and words became excusable. The Congressional investigation into the Philippine war sought by the anti-imperialists produced testimony that ought to have been damning, including Governor Taft's admission that the "water cure" torture had been freely used and that "inhuman conduct" was a normal part of warfare between superior and inferior races, and General Hughes' admission that the punitive measures taken by American forces were not within "the ordinary rules of civilized warfare." But only the egregious brutality and rhetorical excesses of General Smith aroused public outrage of a significant kind, and even that did not prove durable.[84] General Bell noted that he had never been rebuked for taking similar measures during his campaigns against the Indians.[85] General MacArthur turned his testimony before the committee into an occasion for detailing his belief that America was fulfilling the destiny of our "Aryan ancestors."[86] Frederick Funston, whose heroic capture of Aguinaldo matched Roosevelt's San Juan Hill exploit, lambasted the anti-imperialists in the same terms that had been used against the pro-Indian "philanthropists" in the 1870s and added the suggestion that those who had petitioned Congress for peace ought be taken out and lynched. Here was the logic of "savage war" and southern "race war" come home with a vengeance.[87]

Although Roosevelt denied that American troops committed atrocities, he privately endorsed the "water cure"; and he supported Secretary of War Root's lenient response to General Smith's conviction, citing the "well-nigh intolerable provocation" of Balangiga and the Filipinos' "cruelty, treachery, and total disregard of the rules of civilized warfare."[88] In the political campaign of 1904, the Samar massacres and Roosevelt's handling of Smith did not produce a widespread revulsion against imperialism, and Roosevelt was able to turn the Philippine issue against Bryan once again.

In these ideological contests, Roosevelt and the imperialists enjoyed an important advantage: they could invoke the Frontier Myth to support their position and do so in the most straightforward and traditional way simply by substituting "Filipinos" for "Apaches." Their opponents had the more complex task of denying the validity of America's most potent national myth and then of explaining why it had been wrong for our ancestors to dispossess the Indians; or why Filipinos, who seemed quite primitive, should not be thought of as Indians; or how it was that forms of oppression perfectly suitable for American "niggers" were unsuited to Filipino "niggers." Their task was further complicated by the fact that many anti-imperialists shared the racialist theories of Anglo-Saxon superiority that the imperialists invoked and opposed acquisition of an empire because colonial intermarriages and immigration would compromise American racial purity.[89]

The myth of the Indian wars was thus used to justify the prosecution of the Philippine war, and the terms of that justification were then translated into a revision of domestic political ideology. The same principles that justified "marked severities" administered by soldiers in the Philippines could be called upon to justify the imposition of regimental discipline at home, through acts of extraordinary violence. The persistent linkage of Bryan, Altgeld, and Aguinaldo—Populism, Anarchism, and Anti-imperialism—collapses the distinction between domestic enemies of order and the savage enemy beyond the borders, as it collapses the distinction between a class-based partisan division and the racial distinction between "Whites" and "savages," "mobs" and "tribes." Whether the battle is fought on the Little Big Horn, in the streets of Chicago, or in the Philippine jungle, the *war* is the same. If Sitting Bull, Bryan/Altgeld, or Aguinaldo triumph, then the scenario resolves itself as a "Last Stand": the cavalry behind their hedge of swords waiting for death on the Plains, the American army "exterminated" in Manila's "Night of Terror," Company C massacred at Balangiga, the scum of the earth ("Jews, Injuns, Chinamen, Huns") ruling the city of Chicago. To avert the Last Stand, society must vest all its hopes and its moral authority in "the regiment": a microcosm of progressive America organized into a military hierarchy, composed only of those who share the same blood or racial spirit, administered by trained professionals and natural aristocrats, and commanded by a hero—who is licensed to shoot first and ask questions later (using the water cure if necessary), and to "exterminate the brutes" if that is what the preservation of civilization requires.

PART II

Populists and Progressives: Literary Myth and Ideological Style, 1872–1940

4 Mythologies of Resistance

Outlaws, Detectives, and Dime-Novel Populism, 1873–1903

To translate the ideology of progressivism into the language of popular myth, writers like Roosevelt, Hay, King, and Remington had to "modernize" both the character of the traditional frontier hero, and the setting of his adventure. They resolved the problem by transforming the "man who knows Indians" into a military aristocrat representative of managerial values and by transferring him direct from the wilderness to an urban or imperial frontier, where immigrants, strikers, and *insurrectos* were merely allegories of the savage Apache. This modernized Frontier Myth licensed the new hero to repress these dissident classes with the mercilessness belonging to "savage war" and to govern the defeated without their consent, as if they were children, criminals, lunatics, or reservation Indians.

They thus made explicit an ideological distinction latent in earlier versions of the Frontier Myth: that the "civilization" defended by the American hero was not necessarily the same thing as a universalized "democracy" of the kind envisioned in the Declaration of Independence and the Gettysburg Address. The ideology of managerial progressivism declared that under modern conditions "civilization" and perfect "democracy" were incompatible, and that the extension of democratic rights to classes and races unfit for self-government might destroy civilization "as we know it."

While the appeal of the progressive myth/ideology was great enough to make imperialism a winning issue for Republican presidential campaigns from 1900 to 1908, its dominance of politics and culture was far from complete. Its values and ideals were offset by the persistent power and appeal of traditional concepts of democracy and equality and by the new schools of democratic socialism and populism, which both appealed to democratic tradition and sought to modernize its application. This countervailing ideology was mythologized in a "populist" revision of the frontier hero developed in the genres of the "cheap literature" or "dime novel" industry. In the "detective story" the "man who knows Indians" is replaced by a "man who knows strikers"; in the "outlaw story" a social bandit uncovers and attacks the dark side of modern capitalism. Both genres register, in different ways, the discontent of lower-class readers with the division of wealth and power in modern society.[1]

Between the Revolution and (roughly) 1850 the story-types we have identified with the Myth of the Frontier were developed in a variety of "cheap" formats ranging from the penny broadside and pamphlet to inexpensive clothbound books and the precursors of the paperbound dime and nickel novels. Improvements in the technologies of printing and distribution and the rapid growth of an urban audience produced a postwar boom in the cheap-literature business and made it a precedent for the emergence of modern "culture industries" after 1890.[2]

The low cost and minimal literary pretension of this type of literature has led some historians to identify it with "popular," specifically "lower-class," tastes and preferences; while others have noted the "elite" status of both writers and publishers and have argued that this literature became an instrument of ideological control during the period of intense labor/capital struggles between 1873 and 1893. However, it is more accurate (as Michael Denning has argued) to see the cheap-literature business as a site of cultural conflict and its product as the result of elaborate compromises between the different interests and concerns of publishers, writers, editors, salesmen, and readers.[3]

The proprietors of the fiction factories sought the broadest possible audience, and the low cost of their wares made them available to the lowest income levels of society. But this did not forbid their enjoyment by the relatively well-to-do; and even if a cultural bias against vulgar literature may have made them unappealing to adults of the educated elite, dime novels appealed to the unsupervised young of all classes. The potential market for cheap fiction was as large as American democracy itself, comprehending all those who belonged to the "producing classes"—excluding only slaves barred from literacy at one end of the spectrum and the snobbish aristocrat at the other. Although sensationalism was the key to their commercial success, the publishers of popular books also continued the tradition which saw popular literature as an occasional instrument of propaganda for moral and patriotic causes.[4]

The "cheap literature" that specialized in tales of the Frontier had a particular place and function. From the 1840s through the Reconstruction period, most cheap frontier stories followed the formula of Cooper's historical romances, using Indian warfare and captivities (actual or threatened) and a colonial or Revolutionary War setting to provide a "historical" context for the action of the plot. The cast nearly always included a Hawkeye-type hunter and his faithful Indian companion; a monstrous savage, aided by a White renegade; and a set of ingenues, male and female, awaiting rescue by the "man who knows Indians." But a large number of these tales were set in the very recent past or in the contemporary West and used frontier settings to address concerns and difficulties arising from life in the metropolis, such as the defrauding of an honest youth by a greedy uncle or a crooked financier. The characters' experience of the Frontier has been both violent and regenerative, and the West has functioned (metaphorically) as a safety valve for metropolitan social conflicts.[5]

After 1875, however, many of the most popular new dime-novel series abandoned Indian-war settings in favor of conflicts between "outlaws" and "detectives," and the struggle between classes.[6] The hero of these postwar dime novels is no longer the protector or vindicator of the "genteel" values of order and respectability, as Hawkeye and his dime-novel successors had been. In fact, some of the most popular of these heroes are criminals drawn to banditry by a mixture of social injustice and an innate propensity or "gift" for antisocial behavior. As Michael Denning notes, "For a short period between 1877 and 1883, outlaws defied the law and got away with it, escaping the moral universe of both genteel and sensational fiction."[7]

The hero of the outlaw/detective dime novel is not just a more sensationally violent version of the traditional western hero. He stands in actual opposition to the moral values embodied in the Cooperian mythology and therefore to the ideological values of the "progressive" mythology that Roosevelt constructed on the Cooperian base. The two most popular dime-novel outlaws of the 1877–83 period—the fictional "Deadwood Dick" and the half-legendary Jesse James—are social bandits whose outlawry was a response to injustices perpetrated by corrupt officials acting at the behest of powerful moneyed interests.

The ideological implications of these tendencies in the dime novel were taken seriously by moralists and educators concerned about the values of American youth. The celebrity accorded crime and violence in cheap fiction, and the supposed tendency of young readers to imitate heroic models, were cited by critics in the 1870s as a factor contributing to the rising rates of juvenile crime in the cities. When the fictional "Deadwood Dick" was joined by Frank Tousey's "The James Boys"—genuine criminals who were still active when the first series began—the attack became more serious and more credible. As a result, the Postmaster General forced the temporary withdrawal of the James Boys series in 1883, just as Frank James was coming to trial in Missouri. (Publication was resumed in 1889 and continued until another, more substantial movement against dime novels destroyed the business in 1903.)[8] Michael Denning attributes this "moral panic" on the part of cultural officialdom to an implied understanding that the dime-novel outlaw of 1877–83 was indeed a distinctly modern form of *social bandit* defending the integrity of an old-style agrarian/artisanal community against the aggressions of advanced capitalism represented by the corporation.[9]

But Jesse James and his dime-novel counterparts differ from traditional social bandits like the Italian *banditti* or Spanish *bandoleros* of the eighteenth and nineteenth centuries because their greatest significance was not developed in the folklore of the provincial community whose resentments and resistance they initially symbolized. After 1873 Jesse James was taken up by national media as the central figure in a mass-cultural myth of social banditry. It was not his true and *local* history that made him a modern and *American* social bandit but the pseudo-history that was fabricated for him in the mythic space of the dime novel. It was not the historical (and now defunct) Jesse James that the Postmaster General banned, but his fictional incarnation. When he became a subject for national media, the form and meaning of his social banditry were transformed and enlarged and at the same time were separated from the specific social and political context that had given his banditry a "social" character. The case of Jesse James suggests that in modernizing or adapting the *ideology* of social banditry to capitalism, mass culture gradually replaces real historical deeds and political struggles with generic mythologies.

Social Banditry in Fact and Fiction: The Reconstruction Outlaws, 1865–1880

The myths of social banditry are symbolic dramatizations of real social conflicts, and their terms and references reflect the experience and idiom of specific localities and/or cultural regions. Between 1865 and 1880, the divisions and upheavals of modernization and resistance were experienced with significant differences in each of hundreds of communities and regions throughout the nation. However, from the national perspective there were two major variations on the theme, one of which can be characterized as "southern," and the other as both "northern" and national. The "northern" type sees society divided by issues arising from the conflict between labor and capital in the industrializing cities and towns and along the nationwide network of railroads. The characterizing events of this conflict were the series of scandals that revealed the power, political corruption, and monopolistic ambitions of the new industrial "robber barons"; and the series of violent strikes that began with the "Long Strike" of 1873–74 in the Pennsylvania coal fields (which gave birth to the "Mollie Maguires") and culminated in the Great Strike of the railroads in 1877. The experience of industrialization in the western states followed a similar pattern after 1877: as western railroad and mining businesses consolidated and incorporated, communities of workers and small businessmen organized in more militant fashion, sometimes in the manner of frontier "regulators" but more frequently as members of radical unions.

In the South, this kind of conflict was overlaid by others arising from the northern-imposed "Reconstruction" of the former Confederacy: a complex of racial, political, and economic conflicts between freed slaves, poor Whites, former masters, and new plantation owners. Here the major characterizing events were the series of race and election riots that arose from the use of Klan terrorism by the South's would-be "Redeemers." Although the most violent of these incidents had a clearly racial character, the South was also riven by conflicts between those classes of Whites who benefited greatly from the processes of "modernization" and those who were damaged by those processes or were politically excluded from enjoying their fair share of the New South. This latter type of conflict produced the James Gang.

In each region there were characteristic forms of resistance to the processes of incorporation and modernization, many of which involved clandestine organizations and/or some form of extralegal violence. The racial cast of the struggle in the South produced the KKK and kindred organizations, whose roots lay in the "slave patrols" of the antebellum period (and perhaps in the tradition of "regulator" movements in the backcountry). The justification and formal organization of the armed resistance mustered by railroad strikers in Pittsburgh and East St. Louis in 1877, and by steel workers at Homestead in 1892, were based on the traditions (and experience) of community self-defense embodied in the militia system and on Civil War volunteer service. In the coal fields of Pennsylvania and similar communities, the ethnic composition of the miners made Irish clubs and fraternities centers of union activity. In western mining communities, like Cripple Creek in the 1890s, union organization was combined with community-based movements that closely resembled the "regulator" and "vigilante" organizations of the antebellum Midwest. Small farmers and ranchers in the Midwest, West, and California drew on similar traditions in forming local "leagues" to resist foreclosures by banks or landholding corporations, the imposition of excessive rents or railroad rates, and the like. Although justification of the right to violent resistance was important to all such organizations, the practice of violence took a variety of forms: from the armed occupation of a struck mine or contested property to acts of sabotage, terrorism, assassination, and lynching.[10]

As local economies became engaged in trade networks national in scale and corporate in organization, these conflicts acquired national significance and were re-interpreted by editorialists in the national-circulation newspapers and magazines. Local understandings of the conflict were often transformed beyond recognition as they were translated to national media and contexts—and so too were the heroes of local folklore. The dime-novel mythology of outlaws and detectives is the culmination of a myth-making process that began with the "local" translation of two historical actors—Jesse James and Allan Pinkerton—into the terms of regional folklore. One of the earliest references to Jesse James in the national press is a story published in the New York *World* in 1874, which described a gunfight between the James Gang and a pair of Pinkerton detectives. The story identifies the Gang as "The Western Lowrys." The Lowrys were a southern gang of mixed-race "swamp outlaws" whose "savage" resistance to the White government of North Carolina had been the subject of a series of sensational articles in the New York *Herald* and of a recently published book.[11]

The Lowry and James stories began to develop in the national-circulation daily newspapers in 1872–74, in the midst of the political crisis of Reconstruction.[12] After 1872 there had been a marked weakening of support for the so-called "Radical" plan of Reconstruction and for the Grant administration that espoused it. Conservative northern newspapers reflected a mood of generalized disgust with southern affairs, especially with the continual violence between "savage" Klansmen and "brutish" Blacks. The Congressional elections of 1874 would mark the Democrats' re-emergence as a party capable of mustering a national majority for the 1876 presidential election. But Democratic and conservative prospects were threatened by the likelihood of further Klan outrages in the few states still struggling for "Redemption." To counter this threat, conservative polemicists took the line that the Grant administration was responsible for the "savagery" of both Negroes and Klansmen: by making Blacks equal or politically superior to Whites, the administration had incited the violent desires of Blacks and had provoked the "savage" resentment of Whites. James Gordon Bennett, editor and publisher of the sensationalist and conservative New York *Herald*, saw in the Lowry case a journalistic opportunity ideally suited to the development of this thesis, and in 1872 he sent a famous reporter, George A. Townsend, to investigate the Lowrys.[13]

The Lowrys were a band of Lumbee Indians from Robeson County led by Henry Berry Lowry. Like the James and the Younger families, the Lowrys belonged to a "middling" sector of their society rather than to the poorest class. However, for the Lowrys racial identification was more significant than social condition. Although identified from the eighteenth century on as "Indians," a specific tribal origin has never been established for the Lumbee. Their society seems to have been formed by refugees from bands fleeing intertribal warfare in the early eighteenth century who intermarried with White traders and settlers. The establishment of slavery in North Carolina added African-Americans to the mix, and some slaves—purchased, or escaped to the forests and swamps of the Lumber River—may have interbred with the Lumbee. However, as soon as state authorities attempted to regularize racial identification (as a means of enforcing slave codes), the Lumbee protested against any act that would identify them as "mulatto." Their immunity from enslavement before 1863, and their civil rights afterward, depended on this distinction.[14]

One of the crucial tests of their status concerned the right to bear arms and to serve in the militia. According to his own account, Henry

Lowry and other Lumbee attempted to enlist in the Confederate army but were instead compelled to work with slaves on the fortifications of Wilmington. In response, Lowry and his followers took to the swamps and skirmished with Confederate troops until 1865. Their proscription ought to have ended with the collapse of the Confederate government. But the Lumbee lands were coveted by both carpetbaggers and "redeemers," so it was never in anyone's interest to amnesty the Lowrys. Their resistance to wartime conscription had earned them a kind of folk-hero status in the region, even among some Whites; but they opposed the Klan's terror campaign on behalf of the state's Redemption (1869–72), which identified them with the cause of the Negroes.[15]

It was during this turn of postwar politics that Townsend (the *Herald*'s reporter) arrived in Robeson County. He interviewed officials and local notables and was able to interview Henry Lowry himself in his swamp hideout. Townsend's articles ran in the *Herald* in February-March 1872 and were later published as "cheap literature" under the title *The Swamp Outlaws* (1872).[16] Townsend's newspaper articles were usually accompanied by items that enlarged the Lowry story into an allegory of the failure of Republican "philanthropy" toward the South, Indians, and Mexicans. Bennett used such stories not only to stir sympathy for southern Whites but to characterize Blacks (and other groups, like Indians and Mexicans) as inherently bestial and to suggest that if they were fully enfranchised the southern "race war" would soon infect the North.[17]

Townsend's articles gave substance to Bennett's vision of Lowry as the embodiment of the evils of Reconstruction. In dime-novel format, the Lowry portrait was given some appealing suggestions of romance, as in Townsend's comparison of the swamp outlaws to Rob Roy's clansmen and Robin Hood's merry men. But Lowry and his men are also made unimaginably "cruel" by a literally monstrous racial heritage: "in their veins the blood of Indian and Negro strangely commingled" with that of White slavemasters, the villains of the Secession War, so that "Indeed, it seems as if the white *Frankenstein* by his crimes has raised a fearful monster that will not down at the bidding of his affrighted master."[18] Lowry himself is a "natural leader," at once "the Nat Turner, the Osceola, and the Rob Roy . . . of the South"; but his savagery shows in "that light, fiendish, enjoying smile, which shows a nature at its depths savage, predatory and fond of blood."[19] He answers the terrorism of unruly White trash with its exact counterpart: "The black Nemesis is up, playing the Ku Klux for himself." Only the assumption of authority by a true Anglo-Saxon aristocrat, like Virginia's Governor Walker—"the handsomest man in the South . . . every inch a lord lieutenant in the oldest of our shires"—can restore class and racial order.[20]

By identifying the James Gang as "The Western Lowrys," the conservative *World* linked these White outlaws to the racial and social disorder of Reconstruction and identified them with the forces of "savagery"—both Black and Ku Klux—that radical "philanthropy" allowed to run wild. But journalists in western Missouri saw the Gang's operations in a different light, as an extreme but morally justifiable form of resistance to the invasion of their region first by Yankees and then by banks and railroads chartered by the Republican government of the state. The legend of Jesse James's social banditry, which they fabricated, uses the same terms of value employed to demonize Lowry: Jesse is presented as an exemplar of the primal values of his "race," a man of the wilderness, a natural leader, a character marked by both "nobility" and a propensity for savage violence and merciless revenge. But the meaning assigned to these qualities is inverted: what was evil in Lowry becomes heroic in James, and a tale of fanatical opposition to progress becomes a myth of justified resistance.[21]

Like the Lowrys, the James Gang was a family or clan operation, and its outlawry was a by-product of the border warfare in "Bleeding Kansas" and the Civil War. The nucleus of the original gang were the James and Younger brothers. Frank James invaded Kansas as a "Border Ruffian" in 1855–56, and this service blended seamlessly into his and Jesse's enlistment with the guerrilla leader William C. Quantrill after the outbreak of war. Jesse was only sixteen when he joined, but he soon became known as one of the deadliest and most skilled of the guerrillas.[22] As northern forces occupied large regions of the South, guerrilla and partisan warfare inevitably became a more prominent aspect of the conflict, bringing with it acts of terrorism and reprisal against public officials, civilians, and prisoners. General Orders No. 11 and No. 100 (1863) defined the activities of Confederate guerillas as violations of the laws and customs of civilized warfare and licensed the treatment of guerrillas and their supporters according to the usages of "savage war." A significant part of the civilian population of the embattled Missouri counties was dispossessed and incarcerated by federal authorities, and captured guerrillas were subject to summary trial and execution.[23] Ex-guerrillas like the Jameses had reason to suppose that the victorious Unionists would continue to attack their enemies under the cover of the Reconstruction government. In any case, by 1869 they had definitely turned to robbery and had been identified as outlaws.

The Missouri outlaws were distinguished from common criminals by the sympathy extended to them by the regional press and political leadership. Their chief supporters, and the class whose resentments and interests they symbolically represented, were not poor Whites but rather the region's antebellum leadership, now displaced by the Reconstruction government—men like newspaper editors J. N. Edwards and A. C. Appler, the ex-planter and Confederate general J. O. Shelby, and the wealthy Hudspeth clan. Such supporters aided the Gang by sponsoring a series of amnesty bills in the state legislature, often in the teeth of new evidence of the Gang's criminality. Moreover, they mythologized the Gang's exploits, affirming Jesse's espousal of conservative values, as a means of enhancing their polemical assault on the state government.[24]

The myth they fabricated for Jesse identified him as a "guerrilla" rather than an outlaw, whose postwar deeds were to be seen as the "Lost Cause" carried on by other means. J. N. Edwards' *Noted Guerrillas* . . . (1877) sees Jesse and his comrades as a southern version of the frontier hero whose "gifts" combine elements of the Noble Savage and the "man who knows Indians," the Jeffersonian yeoman farmer and the "natural aristocrat." These diverse and even contradictory attributes are fused into a single super-heroic character engaged in a fiery struggle, which Edwards represents as both a revolution and a "savage war."

Like the archetypal Indian-hater of Bird's *Nick of the Woods*, Edwards' guerrillas are peaceful yeomen who are maddened by the massacre of their families and the violation of their homes:

> Pastoral in many cases by profession, and reared among the bashful and timid surroundings of agricultural life, he knew nothing of the tiger that was in him until death had been dashed against his eyes in numberless and brutal ways, and until the blood of his own kith and kin had been sprinkled plentifully upon things that his hands had touched. . . .[25]

The Union and Reconstruction governments embody *both* of the negative ideological poles of the Frontier Myth: their civil order takes the excessive form of a tyranny; and the violence through which they impose order is "savage" in its excess, making war without respect to age or sex or to the laws protecting citizens in their private property.

Thus motivated, the guerrillas become "an organization whose history might well have massacre put over against it as an epitome." Like Nick of the Woods, their "mission was not to kill, alone, but to terrify," and their practice extended to the taking of scalps from the slain.[26] Massacre was typical, and the combat was joined by men expecting to "receiv[e] no quarter and giving none." Edwards emphasizes the Indian-like quality of their skills, particularly their extreme skill and patience in ambush, watching a road for weeks "alert as the red deer and crouching as the panther" until the quarry appears. Then "the long ambuscade [is] broken by a holocaust."[27]

In this regression to savagery, a new sort of democracy is forged as the conditions of warfare bring humbly born men of merit to the fore. As in Roosevelt's Myth of the Frontier, the war-born meritocracy produces a new "aristocracy of daring wherein the humblest might win a crown or establish a dynasty." Their superior proficiency as killers, and the cruelty with which they use their powers against lesser men, are linked to a chivalric manner that identifies them as a knightly warrior class. Their courtesy and chivalry toward women are emphasized, as is their exhibition of "refined" and even "female" sensibilities. The aristocratic bias is particularly evident in Edwards' description of Jesse James, who is cited for "a face as smooth and innocent as a school girl" and a form "tall and finely moulded"—conventional hallmarks of an aristocratic nature. But when combined with their "savage" ferocity, these traits create a perverse and striking mixture: "At times he mingled the purr of the tiger with the silkiness of the kitten. . . . The softer the caress the surer the punishment."[28]

The terms in which Edwards mythologizes Jesse James have particular significance in the violent discourse of local politics. But they also draw on elements of the *national* literary mythology, and they anticipate key elements in Roosevelt's adaptation of that tradition to the requirements of a *progressive* ideology. Edwards' account of Jesse's regression to the primitive and consequent rise to personal and racial dominance follows precisely the same scenario as the progressive ruler's myth of origins envisioned in Roosevelt's *The Winning of the West.* Edwards' characterization of Jesse's rise to dominance anticipates the progressive version of the cowboy hero developed by Roosevelt's friend Owen Wister in *The Virginian* (see Chapter 5). Some of the guerrilla-hero's gifts became hallmarks of the movie-cowboy and gunfighter: his superb horsemanship and love for a favored animal, and his almost fetishistic preference for the pistol as a weapon and his "preternatural" skill with it.[29] Although Edwards and Roosevelt differ radically in their ideological *usage* of the language of myth—Edwards uses it to justify resistance to the kind of management Roosevelt glorifies—the language they use draws on a vocabulary of myth and symbol that they hold in common. Their agreement on the mythic terms in which their historical fables are articulated reveals a limited but significant degree of ideological consensus between the southern proto-populist and the northeastern progressive on such matters as the significance of race as a force in human affairs, the necessity of heroic leadership, and the progressive or regenerative role of violence in history.

Frank Triplett's *Life, Times and Treacherous Death of Jesse James*, which appeared just after Jesse's assassination in 1882, was the foundation of the outlaw's literary mythology. Triplett characterizes Jesse as a type of the progressive neo-aristocrat whose purity of race sets him apart from the average *White* as well as from all non-Whites—a prototype of the neo-aristocrat envisioned by Roosevelt. Where Edwards sees Jesse's "aristocratic" refinement as typical of "middling" southern culture, Triplett identifies Jesse as the incarnation of racial virtues. He and his comrades unite "the infinite physical endurance of the Western Indian and the indomitable soul and mental qualities of the Anglo-Norman." (The Norman reference suggests that their origin is more aristocratic than that of mere Anglo-Saxons.) The antislavery forces, whose cruelties drive Jesse to rebellion and outlawry, are described as "white trash," jealous of the Jameses' refinement. Trained in Quantrill's "school of rough riders" and "Anglo-Norman Comanches," Jesse becomes a tigerish avenger of his family's wrongs. When Yankees invade the "soft sylvan idyll" of the prairie, he attacks with a war cry "as much more terrible than the Red man's as the vices and virtues of the Anglo-Norman exceed those of the Indian."[30] His refusal to abandon Clay County after the war is linked to those racial virtues that, in Theodore Parker's formulation, had made the Anglo-Saxon pre-eminent among the human races for extermination and conquest: "It is not in the blood of the Anglo-Norman, the born ruler of the world, to submit to such oppression and become a slave."[31] In his outlawry Jesse remains true to his racial gifts, avenging the rape and murder of a young girl by Indians and treating all women chivalrously. In contrast, the suborning of Jesse's assassination by Governor Crittenden is an unchivalrous act, "recreant to the laws of civilization and the spirit of the Anglo-Norman race."[32]

These echoes of Fenimore Cooper and Theodore Roosevelt indicate the degree to which the mythology of national literary culture shaped discourse in Jesse's locale. They also suggest Jesse's aptness for translation into a hero appropriate to that larger mythological system. The James Gang finally made the leap from local to national myth in 1873–74, when they switched from robbing local banks to holding up trains. As a result, they ceased to figure as "southern" outlaws and became both a national and a western phenomenon: national, because the railroads were an interstate enterprise and the leading sector of the industrial economy; western, because the postwar development of the railroads had been most dramatically identified with the development of the great transcontinental lines.[33]

The first result was to make the Gang targets of an investigation by the Pinkerton World-Wide Detective Agency, an agency noted for both wartime counterespionage and postwar railroad work, and the only police force able to operate on the scale of the nation.[34] Pinkerton's operatives came a cropper when they attempted to enforce national laws in the teeth of local culture: the people of the district protected Jesse even after his men had killed two Pinkertons. It was this incident that brought them to the attention of the New York *World*, which called them Lowrys and saw them as analogous to Sioux Indians and radical "grangers" in their barbarous opposition to progress. When the Agency responded with a bomb attack on the James household, in which Jesse's mother was maimed and a young cousin killed, the James Gang's fame became national, under circumstances not unfavorable to the outlaws.[35]

The celebrity of these robberies was such that Jesse was falsely credited with inventing train robbery. Modern movie treatments of the outlaw have identified the railroads as the chief agents of persecution that drove him to outlawry, and Jesse himself as an antirailroad guerrilla. In effect, his public legend was rewritten after 1880, and his conflict with the railroad was featured at the expense of struggles that were more germane to his career. It was this rewriting that transformed the local hero and Reconstruction outlaw into a figure of western or frontier mythology and the hero of a *national* myth of resistance.

These new themes are prominent in Joseph A. Dacus' *The Life and Adventures of Frank and Jesse James and the Younger Brothers*, one of the most popular book-length treatments of Jesse's career, which first appeared in the wake of the Glendale train robbery (1880) and was periodically updated to include new events (including Jesse's assassination). Dacus was a St. Louis journalist and author of books of spiritual guidance and self-help; his most famous work was a study of the railroad strikes of 1877, which in East St. Louis had actually produced a "commune" government—the nightmare of the New York dailies. Like many commentators on the strikes, Dacus is compelled to acknowledge the justice of the workingmen's grievances while condemning the violence of the strikers and their more radical political assertions. Both books are linked by Dacus' concern with the negative effects of the great railroad corporations on American life. In the end, concern for private property and social order compels Dacus to condemn the strikers; but in his account of Jesse he can express criticisms of the railroad corporations in a form that leaches them of political danger by identifying them with a set of noble, but doomed, outlaws.[36]

A similar spirit pervades the first appearances of the James Gang in dime novels. Between 1881 and 1883, Frank Tousey published two dime-novel series which included stories of the "James Boys." Seventeen titles appeared in *Frank Tousey's Five Cent Wide Awake Library* (1881–83), and four in *Boys of New York Pocket Library* (1882).[37] The *Wide Awake* stories were entirely fictional, though one or two had nominally historical settings (for example, *The James Boys as Guerrillas*, #457). Many of these stories follow the early Deadwood Dick formula, presenting the outlaws as Robin Hoods victimized by the law and awake to chivalrous impulses. Others show them as cruel and violent criminals but mitigate their villainy by showing them as the objects of violence by social organizations more violent than themselves (*The James Boys and the Ku Klux*, #466; *The James Boys and the Vigilantes*, #462). The *Boys of New York* series offers a four-volume "history" of the Gang that emphasizes the "guerrilla" and "social bandit" aspects of their career.[38] The Gang members are glorified as rebels on behalf of a preindustrial America whose peculiar skill and courage enable them to do what the strikers had failed to achieve: to "set steam and telegraphs, improved detectives, and all modern ingenuities at defiance . . . [to] make the iron horse . . . stand and deliver."[39]

As historical social bandits, the James Boys had been a distinctly local and partisan phenomenon whose careers ended in failure. But in the dime novel their historical defeat is transformed into a kind of perpetually embattled success, and their parochial significance is enlarged to the dimensions of a national symbol. Local conditions and parochial values defeated the attempts of Allen Pinkerton's national detective agency to capture the real James Boys. But Pinkerton, no less than Jesse, understood the importance to his cause of having a positive public myth; and like Jesse, he was quite deliberate about fabricating his own legend. In effect, he carried the pursuit of Jesse James into the mythic ground of the dime novel and in the process developed the "detective" as the counterpart and antagonist of the mythic outlaw.

The Pinkerton Detective: Hawkeye Among the Communists

The origins of the "detective story" as a genre of nineteenth-century popular culture are diverse.[40] But the detective story of American cheap literature is primarily a story of practical rather than theoretical detection—a fictional development of figures first met in the pages of daily newspapers as perpetrators of sensational crimes. Some early examples of the type are set on the Frontier—the story of Virgil Stewart's infiltration and exposure of John Murrell's "vast conspiracy" in the 1830s is a prominent case. But after 1840 virtually all stories centering on the social drama of crime and punishment have a metropolitan location, if not in the heart of the city's mean streets then in country districts closely adjacent. These adventures shared important structural features with the frontier romance. But when the corruption of civilization replaces wilderness as the scene of the drama, and the "urban savage" replaces the Noble Red Man, Hawkeye is transformed from a saintly "man who knows Indians" to a figure whose consciousness is "darkened" by knowledge of criminality.[41]

The writings of Allen Pinkerton gave the development of this genre a distinctively American and political twist. Pinkerton's detective agency was not only the largest provider of investigative and protective services in the United States between 1858 and 1898; it was also the only instrument of police power to function throughout the nation. Pinkerton built his agency's reputation by aiding antebellum railroad corporations in their efforts to deal with embezzlement and defalcation by employees and with robbers who preyed on trains or railroad facilities. His work for the Illinois Central and B&O railroads brought Pinkerton to the attention of the Lincoln administration and of Union General G. B. McClellan. Pinkerton organized wartime equivalents of the FBI and CIA, infiltrating "copperhead" organizations in the North and directing espionage and intelligence operations in the South—the former a great success, the latter an utter fiasco. After the War, Pinkerton was again engaged by the railroads in capturing robbers and embezzlers; it was as a consequence of this work that his agency was engaged in the hunt for Jesse James.

Pinkerton's methods of "detection" went beyond the use of "clues" to identify and convict culprits. Pinkerton operatives often acted as *agents provocateurs* or instigated vigilante-style violence against the criminals they hunted and the labor organizations they sought to break. Pinkerton's probably instigated the lynching of the Reno gang of train-robbers, because they feared the robbers would be freed by sympathetic juries in their home district. A similar problem complicated their pursuit of Jesse James: the detectives were identified with outside interests resented by the local community, which therefore protected the outlaws. Pinkerton responded by attempting to suborn Jesse's assassination and by bombing the James household in 1873—an act that brought the Agency public obloquy for blowing up Jesse's mother instead of the outlaw himself.[42]

The bomb fiasco occurred at a low point in the Agency's fortunes. The Panic of 1873 hurt Pinkerton's business, and he himself had suffered losses in the stock market. He therefore approached Pennsylvania coal magnate B. F. Gowen and proposed that he use the Agency to infiltrate and destroy the labor organizations whose "Long Strike" against Gowen had good prospects of success. Pinkerton's program called for operatives to spy out the plans of the strikers and urge them to commit criminal acts that would diminish public sympathy. Operatives would also provide evidence to sustain Gowen's assertion that the union masked a conspiracy by the "Mollie Maguires," a secret terrorist society within the Ancient Order of Hibernians.[43] While terrorist and criminal organizations may have existed within the mining communities, there is little evidence that a long-lived master organization existed, under the "Mollie Maguire" designation or any other. The "conspiracy" that was "unmasked" was in significant part a fabrication of the Pinkerton Agency and of B. F. Gowen to discredit the Irish miners' unions.[44]

The Pinkerton-Gowen campaign in the coal fields had its counterpart in literature, and from the Agency's perspective this was not the less important of the two enterprises. Pinkerton saw "cheap literature" as an ideal medium for promoting his Agency's work to potential clients, and for building public admiration and support for detectives as professionals and for corporate clients as a class. (Jesse James had certainly benefited from that sort of publicity, at Pinkerton's expense.)[45] Pinkerton's first essay in the form, *The Detectives and the Expressmen* (1875), was an inflated account of the Reno case.

But in 1877 he cashed in on public concern about labor violence with two books, *The Mollie Maguires and the Detectives* and *Strikers, Communists, Tramps and Detectives* (the latter an account of the railroad strikes). The former is the pattern-setter for the genre: it follows a clear narrative line and centers on the adventures of a single heroic detective whose persona is carefully built up as a new model of the anti-labor detective as hero.[46] The new elements are given resonance by devices that implicitly link the detective hero to the hero of the frontier romance. The coal fields are first represented as a kind of frontier: an almost foreign world set apart from the normal life of the metropolis among wild mountain scenery "inhabited by a mixture of races" not found elsewhere.[47] The Agency's struggle in this region is both a savage war and a variation on the theme of the Civil War, a defense of freedom against the conspiracy which aims to "rule our people with a rod of iron." That conspiracy is powerful because the people of the state, and their democratic institutions, have been corrupted and infiltrated by a poisonous ideology promulgated by the conspirators:

> Even the political sentiments of the commonwealth are moulded by them, and . . . they elect or defeat whomsoever they please. They control, in a measure, the finances of the State. . . . Wherever in the United States iron is wrought, from Maine to Georgia, from ocean to ocean—wherever hard coal is used for fuel, there the Mollie Maguire leaves his slimy trail and wields with deadly effect his two powerful levers: secrecy—combination. Men having their capital locked up in the coal beds . . . have for some time felt that they were fast losing sway over that which by right should be their own to command.

Thus the Mollies threaten not only the Schuylkill mines but the nation as a whole and the sacred principle of private property. If successful they will make of the state "a very golgotha . . . from which law-abiding men and women might be forced to flee."[48]

Belief in the existence and power of the Mollies owed a good deal to the racialist characterization of the "Celts" as a relatively primitive "race" with "gifts" for superstition, anarchic violence, and tribalism. Pinkerton exploits these sentiments by emphasizing the ethnic or racial basis, the Celtic tribalism, of the organization. To infiltrate, expose, and defeat them Pinkerton requires a detective who is enough of an Irishman to pass as a Mollie and enough of an "American" to keep faith with Pinkerton and civilization. In Detective MacParlan he finds the Irish equivalent of Hawkeye, the White man raised among Indians, partaking of their "gifts" yet true in the end to his own race. He is also a frontiersman of sorts: we are told that he followed Horace Greeley's advice to "go west." MacParlan is an Ulsterman—Irish, but not Catholic-Irish. The religious or ethnic distinction takes the place of the simple racial distinction that finally keeps Natty Bumppo "White." This implies that to be Catholic-Irish, Mollie-Irish, is to be of a lesser race. Pinkerton tells us that MacParlan will have to "consent to . . . degrade [himself] that others might be saved," to separate himself from all his civilized ties, and to be "as one dead and buried in the grave," having merged his "individuality" in the criminal tribe.[49]

MacParlan's experience among the Mollies is treated in the conventional language of the frontier romance and captivity narrative. Like Mrs. Rowlandson's, his adventure is also a spiritual journey which tests his conscience through infernal temptations and a descent into hell, a "darkness" in which the "singing, dancing and fighting" of the Mollies echoes the "roaring, danceing, singing of those Black creatures in the night" that made Rowlandson's captivity "a lively resemblance of Hell." One particularly vicious group of Mollies is known as the "Modocs"—the name of a tribe of Indians noted for their murder of an American general while under a flag of truce.[50]

The "savage" character of the enemy licenses MacParlan to go beyond civilized norms in combating them. He not only adopts Mollie/Modoc disguise, he imitates their treachery, breaking his oath of loyalty and obedience to them, and actually suborning them to acts of violence for which he will later convict them. It is worth noting that in dealing with White "savages," the hero is allowed to violate codes of honor that the heroes of Indian-war romances adhered to. Hawkeye's moral nobility is proved by the scrupulous way in which he keeps promises made to enemy Indians, even those made under duress, and by his refusal to imitate Indian tactics that are contrary to "White gifts."[51]

Detective stories published by Allen Pinkerton and his son continued to appear for the next twenty years. Their influence on the dime novel was profound, and their treatment of the detective's character, mission, and milieu became the basis of the so-called "hard-boiled" detective story—the characteristic form of the genre after 1920. Dashiell Hammett, the most important figure in early hard-boiled fiction, was a former Pinkerton detective, and his first series of stories featured an operative for the "Continental" detective agency—a thin disguise for Pinkerton's. But the detective's rise to heroic stature did not reflect back on the Agency as an institution. Pinkertons' involvement in the labor-spy and union-breaking game was not universally acclaimed by a society whose public opinion and politics continued to insist on the value and democratic rights of labor, to note the growing disparities between rich and poor, and to be outraged by scandalous revelations of the corruption of politics by Big Money.

A crucial turning point in the agency's reputation followed its engagement in the Homestead Strike of 1892. The striking steelworkers in the Pittsburgh area enjoyed strong support from the local community and a relatively favorable national press, which regarded the Steel Trust with suspicion. Pinkerton attempted to break the strike by sending in a private "army" of detectives and strikebreakers. The army first suffered a humiliating defeat by the strikers and was then widely condemned for committing an unnecessary act of aggression—populist journals accused the Agency of hiring "Hessians" and of initiating a "war of extermination" against labor. Even the anti-union editorialists of *Harper's Weekly* criticized the Agency by equating the vigilante-like violence of its operatives with the Indian-like savagery of the strikers.[52]

Harper's discomfort at having to choose between detectives and anarchists—between the excesses of order and the excesses of liberty—is a reflection of a basic ambivalence in American political culture at the turn of the century. The same contradiction is reflected in the world of mass culture by the opposition of the "James Gang" and "The Pinkertons" as models of American heroism. But the function of a mythological system is to reconcile ideological contradictions of this kind; in the dime novels of 1877–1900 this is achieved by the development of a hybrid hero who combines elements of the outlaw and the detective.

The Outlaw/Detective: Heroic Style as Ideology

The logic behind the development of this paradoxical figure can best be seen in the evolution of Edward Wheeler's Deadwood Dick, the original good-badman of the dime-novel world.

In the first novels of the series, Wheeler frames the outlaw as a new variation on the traditional frontier hero. The title *Deadwood*

Dick, the Prince of the Road; or, The Black Rider of the Black Hills (1877) suggests that we are in for a tale with a conventional Indian-war setting. The Black Hills region was inescapably linked with the Indian war of 1876–77 and with the fame and death of General Custer, and Sitting Bull and the Sioux are a menacing presence in the story. The cast of characters is based on Cooperian models. There is a romantic pair (Alice Terry and Fearless Frank) who have the hallmarks of aristocracy. Like the well-born Oliver Edwards of *The Pioneers* Frank has lived with the Indians, and he will rescue Alice from Indian captivity. Deadwood Dick himself is a "Hawkeye" type, a dialect-speaking veteran of the Frontier who knows the wilderness and the Indian and possesses extraordinary skills. Like the Indian-hater, Dick has been driven over the border by the desire to avenge his victimization. However, the agents of victimization are not Indians but rich White men, and Dick's vengeance is not enacted through Indian-killing but through stagecoach robbery. His enemies are not savages but a set of well-dressed eastern dudes who represent the corrupt wealth and effete characteristics of a contemptible aristocracy of pelf.[53]

This pattern of association persists through most of the early volumes in the series. References to the Black Hills, Sitting Bull, and Custer abound and establish the drama as belonging to the Frontier. But Indians are rarely the primary villains, and on occasion they appear as allies of the hero in a struggle against a common enemy. That enemy is usually identified with the wealthy classes in general, and with stockbrokers, industrial capitalists, and managers in particular. In *Deadwood Dick on Deck* (1878) the outlaw helps a community of independent miners evade the machinations of an effete British aristocrat ("Hon. Cecil Grosvenor"), owner of a large corporation that seeks to engulf them.[54] The miners explicitly identify themselves as "enthusiast[s] on the labor question" and draw a defiant parallel between the struggle in the Pennsylvania coal fields—where the owners were able to grind the workers down and concentrate the wealth in their own hands—and the West, where the workers are strong enough to fight for their rights and "this delectable Black Hills kentry."

> No doubt there are capitalists who would like to step down into the little city of Whoop-Up, and grasp the tyrant's reins in their hands; but they'll be mightily disappointed when they find that very few poor men are so poor but what they can stand firm for their rights.[55]

Unlike the "progressive" hero, the "civilization" he defends is still identified with the values of agrarian/artisanal democracy.

The publication in 1879 of three Deadwood Dick tales set in Leadville coincided with the founding of a chapter of the Knights of Labor in that town and the beginning of a bitter strike that was ended in favor of the mine owners when the government sent in the militia.[56] Wheeler's stories incorporate the struggle and use the outlaw to provide a fictive solution. As "Deadwood Dick, Jr.," the outlaw hero first leads the miners' union and then uses his heroic achievements to gain a managerial role (as superintendent) from which vantage he can work to win "fair" wages for the workers. However, he must also defeat the sinister enterprise of a "communistic" labor organization whose programs imply the necessity of a war of extermination between the opposing classes.[57]

By transferring the labor struggle to a western setting, the dime novel is able to imagine a "utopian" resolution for the labor strife of the metropolis. The border between labor and management proves permeable to Deadwood Dick, and his upward mobility restores a just relation between the classes that makes "communistic" solutions unnecessary. The "frontier" setting allows Wheeler to imagine an alternative industrial order in which all the evils of the actual system are avoided. Pastoral values are preserved without sacrificing the advantages of industry: commerce turns "Paradise . . . into a 'gold-mine' . . . of active industry and labor" yet somehow fails to destroy the natural beauty of the scene.[58] The asperities of class division and labor discipline are negated. In *Deadwood Dick, Prince of the Road*, White labor is liberated from onerous toil by the classic racialist device of assigning all mine work to Ute Indians (who nonetheless are well paid); but in *Deadwood Dick on Deck* the miners run their enterprise as a cooperative commonwealth in which the proceeds are equally divided among the workers.[59] Although the West still serves as the site of an imaginary future, what the mythic Frontier of the dime novel actually embodies is a world in which the values and practices of the pre-industrial order are given renewed life: a place in which machines still stand in gardens and in which the only social category of real importance is that of the all-inclusive "producing classes."

It is only within this kind of framework that the outlaw can function unambiguously as a "hero" and an exemplar of the use of justified violence. He has been driven to outlawry by men who represent forces inimical to the values of the pastoral community and the interests of the "producing classes"—men who would divide and degrade those classes into slavish proletarians working for "Chinamen's wages."[60] In this conception, the outlaw is not the savage enemy of order or civilization as such but the defender of a particular kind of civilization: the agrarian democracy of our mythical Jeffersonian past. In identifying with him, the reader can indulge sentiments of resentment and rebellion without having to adopt a radically alienated stance toward his society and its traditional ideology.

As the series progresses, this conservative aspect of the outlaw's character is recognized by the community. In his early adventures, Deadwood Dick is often pursued by vigilantes or "regulators"—armed citizens out to suppress banditry who often enact (wittingly or not) the will of the wealthy villain. Later in the series, Dick himself appears in the role of "regulator," defending community interests against evil outsiders. This tendency reaches its final development when the outlaw himself becomes a detective. In *Deadwood Dick as Detective* the outlaw (his gang are called the "Archangels") disguises himself as a detective in order to infiltrate the conspiracy of "Sal Savage," an evil saloon-keeper who has upper-class cohorts. In the end he destroys the conspiracy, rescues the romantic hero from jail, and is himself reconciled with society, pardoned, and married to a good woman. In *The Frontier Detective* and *The Detective Road Agent* his frontier outlaw persona is simply merged with his new character as detective; and in *Gilt-Edged Dick, The Sport Detective* he defeats a false accusation that he has lapsed into criminals ways.[61]

The evolution of Deadwood Dick from outlaw to detective is the logical development of that side of the dime-novel outlaw that expresses a wistful yearning for a social order that could be happily defended. But what is logical in the formal evolution of the myth is paradoxical in the world of political reference that the myth invokes. By identifying outlaw and detective, Wheeler was suggesting an identity of interest between those who resisted the new industrial order and those who sought to enforce that order by all available means. The power of this mythic resolution is attested by its ability to transform not only the imaginary Deadwood Dick but the "historical" James Gang and the Pinkertons into a new, hybrid hero that combines elements of the detective and the social bandit.

This development occurred in the most important of the Jesse James series, produced between 1889 and 1897. Frank Tousey's *New York Detective Library* featured a revised version of the fictive Jesse James and a set of fictional private detectives headed by an Irishman named "Old King Brady." At the same time a rival dime-novel house, Street & Smith, began publishing James Boys stories as part of their *Log Cabin Library*. These series marked the return of "the Boys" to dime novels after a five-year hiatus following the Postmaster General's informal ban.

The two series have many features in common. Stories featuring the outlaws alternate (in no regular pattern) with stories featuring detectives; and in both series "western" or "Log Cabin" settings alternate with eastern/urban or "New York" settings. Historical and fictional stories are closely linked in both series, and their materials are freely mixed. Historical figures from the outlaw saga (the "boys" themselves or Sheriff Timberlake) appear in purely fictional settings, and Old King Brady turns up in the Ghost Dance War.[62] Both series also used the authenticating device of attributing authorship to detectives who had hunted Jesse James: Street & Smith's "Capt. Jake Shackleford" is identified as "the Western Detective," and "A New York Detective" is listed as the author for many of the volumes in Frank Tousey's series.[63]

Within the frameworks of these series, "New York" and "the Frontier" (or city and country) initially appear as two contrasting types of American mythic landscape, each with its own geography, its own peculiar social forms and ethics, and its own peculiar type of story. But as the series develop, certain common elements in the two settings begin to appear, reflected in the recurrence of situations and narrative patterns; and the relationship between the two scenes—the world of the outlaw and the world of the detective—becomes closer, as figures from one setting begin literally to infiltrate the other.

The world of the outlaw is usually identified with the natural wilderness, in terms reminiscent of Fenimore Cooper; in this environment, the outlaw is a kind of Noble Savage: "Those hunted outlaws had some poetry in their souls. Like the savage of the forest and the plain, they had really become children of Nature, and if ever they had any good impulses it was when they approached nearer to her."[64] American frontiersmen have become outlaws because, like the Noble Red Man, they had been reared in a culture that places personal honor, proud "manhood," and an intuitive code of "justice" above the rationalism and restrictions of civilized law. Frank Tousey's Jesse James is driven into guerrilla warfare and crime by the whipping of his stepfather—a motive similar to that of Cooper's Magua in *Last of the Mohicans*.[65] He is able to operate freely in the West because the ethical codes of the region give singular importance to courage and manhood—an attitude which the eastern detective, "Old King Brady," is unable to understand or accept.[66]

The detectives are unambiguously heroic in these series, whether they appear as protagonists or merely as pursuers of the outlaws, and they consistently assert the primacy of law in any civil society. Only a few were seen as having a "frontier" origin: *New York Detective*'s "Man from Nowhere" is a frontiersman in the Hawkeye tradition, a child of nature, an expert tracker and dialect-speaker; Sheriff Timberlake is a figure from the James Gang's history; and "Sam Sixkiller," the Cherokee detective, is a full-blooded Indian whose racial gifts of skill, courage, and ferocity make him the Jameses' most dangerous foe. But neither of these types appeared more than one or two times. The typical detective hero is a figure from a metropolitan setting, literally or figuratively a Pinkerton operative, who infiltrates the Gang by impersonating a criminal.[67]

The archetype of the "New York Detective" is "Old King Brady," who heads his own Pinkerton-like agency in the metropolis. Like the outlaw, and like Pinkerton's MacParlan, Brady has racial "gifts" that link him with those we have identified as "savage"—he is Irish, and therefore intuitive, mystical, combative, and capable of identifying with the underdog. For the most part, this identification takes the form of aiding worthy workingmen and clerks who are falsely accused of crime by crooked employers; occasionally a major corporate scandal is exposed. On the other hand, the detectives periodically assert their hostility to all forms of radicalism, in adventures that pit them against "Reds" or "Anarchists." However, these actions are always presented as responsive to the real feelings of honest workingmen, whose attitude toward radicals (according to the dime novel) is best expressed in the caption on the cover of John E. Barrett's *A Knight of Labor; or, The Master Workman's Vow*: "The Powerful Young Blacksmith Seized the Communist and Shook Him Vigorously."[68]

The obvious differences between outlaws and detectives conceal a certain latent similarity in their valuation of chivalry and courage, and even their practical objectives. They have certain enemies in common, including villainous foreigners and Jews, and certain "exotic" American types more alien and menacing than the traditional outlaw, like Kentucky moonshiners, vigilantes, or Ku Klux Klansmen.[69] The Street & Smith series set quite a few James Boys adventures in Mexico, where the Jameses appear as agents of American/

Anglo-Saxon virtue against the vices of racially "mongrelized" Mexicans.[70]

These common elements begin to appear more strikingly later in the series, when outlaws and detectives begin to invade each other's terrain and figuratively "exchange pulpits." In these stories Old King Brady goes west to hunt Jesse James, becomes embroiled in the struggle between the powerful and the weak, and begins to understand the social motives that might drive a man to crime. Frank and Jesse go to the city, become embroiled in social struggles against capitalists greater than they have known, and engage with a class of oppressed people utterly unlike the farmers of the West. These stories also emphasize the difficulty each hero has in acting in a world to which he does not belong. Old King Brady stumbles (as Pinkerton had done) when he tries to capture the James Boys in Missouri, because he does not understand the westerners' sympathy for courage, even in an outlaw: for the easterner, criminals are simply criminals. Equally, when the James Boys come to New York, Frank complains to Jesse, "Will ye never understand that New York's a different place from St. Louis or Kansas City? Thar we could rally friends in a minute, but hyar we're nobuddy in the crowd."[71]

These exchanges of place were not necessarily motivated by any conscious ideological purpose. There is an implicit pressure for variation in the marketing of any mass-produced formula, and the easiest kind of variation is the mechanical recombination of elements from existing formulas. The idea of sending Old King Brady west or Jesse James east proceeds from the same kind of imagination that produces *Abbott and Costello Meet the Wolfman*—or, for that matter, *Jesse James Meets Frankenstein's Daughter*.[72] Nonetheless, these variations have an ideological effect.

Their appearances on each other's terrain give outlaw and detective a better appreciation, and even a degree of sympathy, for the other's way of life. Their alienation from familiar settings brings out the common element in their characters, which is that they are members of "marginalized" social groups rather than Americans of the main stream. Detectives can, after all, "pass" as outlaws—and outlaws as detectives, as the James Boys prove in *The James Boys and Pinkerton; or, Frank and Jesse as Detectives*. In the West, Brady finds himself in sympathy with workingmen, Indians, and even outlaws victimized by corrupt officials and businessmen. In *A Bag of Shot; or, Old King Brady Out West*, the New York detective plays a role in a miner's strike similar to the outlaw's in *Deadwood Dick on Deck.* Frank and Jesse, trapped by toughs in a New York tenement and compelled to escape via the sewers, find themselves wishing for the police.[73]

As the *New York Detective* series develops, detectives and outlaws become more alike and begin to act in concert. Although they begin from different premises, they find a common enemy in the villainous banker or railroad executive. At first, the discovery appears fortuitous. The James Boys attempt to victimize all capitalists, so it is perhaps not remarkable that they sometimes pick on one who is being pursued by detectives and inadvertently aid in exposing the villain. But the irony of the situation does not go unremarked, and the contrast between outlaw and crooked financier usually ends by suggesting that the outlaw is somehow morally preferable and less of a danger to social peace. Transferred to the city, the outlaw visits a kind of "populist" justice on wealthy malefactors and even appears as a model of heroism for the urban proletariat.[74] In *Frank James in St. Louis; or, The Mysteries of a Great City,* the outlaw rescues a young girl from a Pinkerton who seeks to return her to her wealthy but tyrannical guardian and himself becomes the "angel of the slums." But his role here is not all that different from that of the detective who comes to the aid of unjustly accused workingmen.[75]

The kinship of outlaw and detective appears more strikingly in those stories that send the urban detective west. In *Old King Brady and the James Boys in Missouri,* the two heroes work from opposite sides of the law to help a worthy mechanic (Tom Power) save himself and the railroad's dependents from the machinations of a crooked financier.[76] In *Old King Brady and the James Boys Among the Choctaws; or, A Raid into the Indian Nation in '81,* the detectives and outlaws inadvertently cooperate in exposing a crooked Indian agent who has defrauded the Cherokee of the "Strip money" paid in compensation for the seizure of their lands. (Brady disguises himself as "a sheeny scoundrel" in order to infiltrate the conspiracy.) Carried to the extreme, this tendency finally sees *The James Boys Working for Old King Brady* or outlaws making a complete change of profession, as in *The Ford Boys' Vengeance; or, From Bandits to Detectives.*[77]

By turning outlaws into functional approximations of detectives, these dime novels augment the moral authority of the outlaw as symbol of a critical stance toward the ideology and practice of industrial and finance capitalism. If not the agent of an identifiable class or coherent political party, the outlaw—when legitimated in this way—at least voices a generalized discontent with the managerial order and its leadership. But the critique is voiced more explicitly in those tales that turn the detective figuratively into an outlaw by allying him with groups like the James Boys or with an excluded race like the Indians. Old King Brady's Irish ancestry and his ability to assume the disguise of such racial aliens as the Jews suggest a capacity for sympathy beyond the limits of "Whiteness." The sympathy for mistreatment of the Indians evinced in *Old King Brady and the James Boys Among the Choctaws* is given more pointed expression in *Old King Brady Among the Indians; or, Sitting Bull and the Ghost Dance.* Appearing one year after Wounded Knee and the assassination of Sitting Bull, this dime novel takes a forthrightly pro-Indian stance. The villain of the piece is a crooked railroad baron who underpays his clerks and foments an Indian war to cover his defalcations. Among his devices is the staging of an "attack of the Reds"—not Communists, though the language deliberately suggests them, but White renegades disguised as redskins. The Indian Ghost Dancers, led by Sitting Bull, play the traditional role of the cavalry, riding to rescue the detective and his young associate. Brady's role in the narrative suggests a comparison between the detective and Buffalo Bill: both are friends of Sitting Bull and have special knowledge that might (with better luck) have averted the Wounded Knee massacre. In the end, Brady represents Sitting Bull's death as "Murder by the United States government" and declares with pride that he is the only man in New York who mourns "Custer's slayer. . . . [He was] a good friend to me, and while I was among the Indians I learned some things to make me ashamed to call myself an American citizen." Though hardly unique, this expression of sympathy is rather strong, measured against the editorial opinion of the day.[78]

The Significances of Dime-Novel Populism

The history of the outlaw-and-detective dime novel indicates that the media of commercial mass culture have purveyed not only the mythologies of the cultural elite but mythologies of lower-class resistance—including a legitimation of the use of force and violence. If Deadwood Dick and the James Gang represent "the adaptation of social banditry to capitalism" (as Hobsbawm and Denning suggest), then part of that adaptation requires the substitution of the fictive framework of a mass-culture medium for the "real world" as the site of that banditry. Of course, all social banditry is in some sense as much an ideological construction as an objectively defined set of practices. But the processes and outcomes of ideological construction in the "dime novel" culture are fundamentally different from those that shaped the construction of the James Gang myth in local lore. In western Missouri, Jesse James was in some sense a symbol created for and by a particular "people" or community. But the dime-novel social bandit is created for the people by "outsiders," in a medium owned and managed by urban capitalists and staffed by professional writers. The culture of this producing community gives a distinctive bias to the construction of a mythology of resistance to modernization. Although these dime-novel outlaws express class resentments against the wealthy and powerful, the genre contains those resentments by distinguishing "outlaws" from "Communists" and by identifying the outlaw's moral perspective with pre-industrial political culture rather than with radical prescriptions for future reform. Moreover, the act of projecting labor and agrarian class conflicts into a western-outlaw setting implicitly discredits the more active forms of class struggle by displacing them to the outer margins of civil society. The substitution of the outlaw for the Mollie Maguire or the communard licenses the expression of class resentment, but at the price of rendering the actual politics of working-class and agrarian resistance invisible.

Despite this limitation, dime-novel outlaws preserved at least the nominal forms of democratic ideology as a part of mass-culture mythology. They asserted a "producing class" vision of social order in which classes enjoy a rough equality of conditions and a genuine equality of political rights, and in which the lower classes are self-governing, hard-working, and virtuous and share essential interests with good, small capitalists. Indeed, it can be argued that the role of the fictional Jesse James was at least as important to the ideology of populism (and to genuinely populist forms of social banditry) as was the real career of the James Gang.

Some surviving members of the Gang understood their status as figures in a national mythology and consciously revised their public personae and their history to make them equal public expectation. James Younger, captured at Northfield in 1876, became a socialist while in prison. And Frank James identified himself with the rising Populist movement after his release from prison. In 1897 he claimed that the Gang's activities had served to keep mortgage-bankers out of Jackson County and so had forestalled the tyranny of the metropolitan financiers. He also declared,

> If there is ever another war in this country, which may happen, it will be between capital and labor, I mean between greed and manhood, and I'm as ready to march now in defense of American manhood as I was when a boy in defense of the South. Unless we can stop this government by injunction, that's what we are coming to.[79]

Statements like this allowed the Jameses to become models for would-be social bandits in the early twentieth century, during the long period of struggle over the transformation of the agrarian economy (1880–1920). Between 1912 and 1915, radical newspapers in Oklahoma like the Socialist *Appeal to Reason* identified professional bank robbers like Henry Starr as guerrillas in the war between labor and capital; and Starr—who was distantly related to members of the James Gang—played up that identification in his public statements.[80] But the legend of Jesse James invoked in these contexts also owed as much or more to the dime-novel hero as to regional folklore. Organized farmers and individuals resisted foreclosure and dispossession by acts of violence ranging from individual acts of sabotage to intimidation, to the formation of armed bands or leagues for collective resistance. But resistance of this kind differs from social banditry, in that those who engaged in it usually did not adopt outlawry as a career; these groups did not appeal to the symbolism of the James Gang but to the traditions of vigilantism or the platforms of their political parties.

Moreover, it is important to note that Frank James' populism and Jim Younger's socialism were not the affirmations of active social bandits but rationalizations long after the fact: it is Populist Era hindsight that allows Frank James to declare that the Gang's raids were a campaign against mortgage-bankers when the original targets of their partisans' polemic were carpetbaggers and scalawags. We may suspect that Henry Starr's use of populist rhetoric was equally opportunistic. Moreover, the terms in which James identifies his politics owe at least as much to his internalization and assertion of dime-novel values as to his understanding of populism. The principle he defends is not that of the farmer or the workingman but that of a generalized "American manhood," an ideal of masculinity so abstract that it makes no distinction between the defense of southern slavery in 1861 and the defense of agrarian freeholds and workingmen's rights in 1897. But "manhood" is not a distinctively "populist" value. Indeed, it is the same principle to which Roosevelt appealed in calling for imperialist expansion in "The Strenuous Life," the same to which the President of the National Association of Manufacturers appealed in 1903 in his condemnation of organized labor as a form of savagery.[81]

As I have already suggested, in the discussion of the Anglo-Saxonist versions of Jesse James' myth, this convergence in the language of values used by populists and progressives indicates the presence of an underlying consensus on a number of important ideological principles. This consensus, which is national in its scope and in its concerns, finds its clearest and most pervasive expression in the mythology developed and purveyed by the media of mass culture. The commercial prosperity of those media depends on their power to incorporate a wide range of social and political referents and to entertain fantasies that express all sides of the public's contradictory desires and beliefs. The outlaw and detective genres of the dime novel began as representations of conflicting social imperatives—the contest between labor and capital, outlaws and detectives—projected into a mythic space disconnected from the political culture of specific, embattled communities, in which the moral and political referents points are always generic and national rather than specific and local. Because it exists only to conceive and purvey public fantasies, the same producing community that indulges the outlaw's dream of resistance entertains the detective's dream of ordered progress. And since this community deals with an entirely fictional world, it is free not only to indulge these fantasies separately but to combine them. Indeed, the logic of formula fiction—the need to continually vary the same story materials—makes such combination inevitable.

Hence, through continual play with the roles and moral categories associated with the figures of outlaw and detective, the dime novelists evolved a composite heroic type in which the two figures, and the political oppositions they represent, are fictively harmonized. The outlaw becomes a hero who resists the forces of order, but in a way that affirms the basic values of American society; the detective defends the progressive social order, but does so *in the style* of an outlaw, always criticizing the costs of progress and often attacking the excesses of the privileged classes. For the facts of social conflict the mass-culture mythology substitutes a persuasive vision of an ultimate reconciliation between irreconcilable opposites: progress is achieved, but traditional values and life-ways are preserved unharmed; farmers and landlords, workers and employers, outlaws and detectives, Jesse James and Allen Pinkerton, all abandon the pursuit of their interests to discover and share their common ground.

That common ground extends not only to the literary figures of outlaw and detective but to the ideologies of "populism" and "progressivism" they represent. Behind their nominal oppositions is a set of common understandings on the basic terms in which the myth and ideology of American nationality would be formulated in the new century: an agreement that the American social struggle be seen, not as a class war of proletarians and capitalists, but as a struggle between the "free labor" values of the old agrarian/artisan/entrepreneurial order and the monopolistic tendencies of the corporation; an acceptance of the language of racial difference as the best way to interpret social and political difference; and an affirmation of the "virile Anglo-Saxon" as hero of the American myth and exemplar of its primal values. These agreements were to constitute the basis of a consensus on the basic structures and vocabulary of the mythologies that were created and purveyed by the mass-culture industries of the twentieth century.

After the turn of the century, this mythological language was given a distinctly anti-democratic interpretation by writers who worked at a "higher" literary level and whose works provided the basic material for the new century's most important mass medium, the motion picture.

5 Aristocracy of Violence

Virility, Vigilante Politics, and Red-blooded Fiction, 1895–1910

In the May 1903 number of *The World's Work*, the critic W. Churchill Williams hailed the emergence of a new generation of writers: "It was only the other day that one of our ablest critics remarked in effect that American fiction is emasculated," but the turn of the century has seen a recrudescence of virility and "Red Blood in Fiction." The "red-blooded" school includes writers now recognized by literary historians as founders of American "realism" and "naturalism" (Frank Norris, Hamlin Garland, and Jack London). It also includes a number of "minor" authors whose works enjoyed a wide popular and "middle-brow" readership, including Owen Wister, the southern novelist (and would-be Rough Rider) Thomas Nelson Page, and Stewart Edward White (an author of western adventure stories and a great favorite of Roosevelt's). James Fenimore Cooper is cited as their ancestor, creator of the archetypal red-blooded hero, and an early critic of literary effeminacy. The "emasculated" include all those writers (male and female) whose works belong to the sentimental and idealistic tradition that had dominated the market for "serious" or "genteel" popular fiction (as distinguished from the dime novel) for much of the nineteenth century.[1]

Williams' gendering of literary categories articulates a basic ideological opposition that informed American literary and political expression in the late nineteenth and early twentieth centuries. For most of that period, women made up the largest and most reliable readership for literary fiction. The developing canons of literature and criticism were therefore influenced by the same social and cultural pressures that shaped the construction of "middle-class womanhood" as a new ideal of gender identity and function—the embodiment and keeper of "genteel" values. In practice, this meant that the values represented in the novel had to fall within the range of conventionally acceptable Victorian notions about what the ideal woman *ought* to think and know and of what matters she should be kept ignorant.[2]

The critical attack on "female sensibilities" as the enemy of "realism" has less to do with the preferences of actual women or even the demographics of the literary marketplace than with ideological animus. The "female" values associated with the sentimental and reformist fiction of writers like Harriet Beecher Stowe, "Fanny Fern," Rebecca Harding Davis, and Lydia Child—broad and emotional sympathy, moral idealism, excessive "refinement" in sexual matters, a distaste for violence and conflict—had become identified with the political idealism of the reformers and radicals of the Gilded Age. The conservative journalists who had denigrated strikers, Indians, and Blacks by defining them as demented "savages" also discredited their friends among the elite by labeling them "philanthropists," unsexed viragos and effeminate "she-males."[3]

The *virilist* realism of the "red-blooded" writers rejects both idealism and sentimentalism for a more "tough-minded" view of the world. They espoused one or another of the varieties of Social Darwinism, which saw life as a struggle between differently "gifted" individuals and groups for social mastery and (limited) control of the amoral force of natural law. Finally, they conceived of this Darwinian struggle as occurring in a "Malthusian" environment, which is to say a "post-Frontier" society in which the supply of land and cheap resources would tend to become more restricted from generation to generation.

This view of reality is no less partial, tendentious, and theoretical than the Christian idealism of reform-minded sentimentalists. Yet "red-blooded realism" was canonized by the critical establishment between 1900 and 1925 as objectively more truthful in its representation of nature and humanity than the critical "reform" novels of a Rebecca Harding Davis, a Harriet Beecher Stowe, or a Helen Hunt Jackson. This acceptance was forthcoming because the world imagined by red-blooded realism embodied the central principles of the dominant progressive ideology. By examining the ideological context and content of red-blooded fiction, we can see how such a literary mythology works: how it entertains and imaginatively enacts an ideological program, and how that literary enactment affects the discourses of real-world politics.[4]

"Men Who Do the Work of the World"

The *World's Work,* whose critic defined these writers as a "school," was itself an important organ of the Progressive movement. Its glossy pages, filled with photographs (reproduced by a new printing process), were devoted to praising and disseminating the ideas of men who "do the work" of our "newly organized world": statesmen, scientists, captains of industry, great soldiers and farsighted colonial bureaucrats.[5] The magazine saw organization and the concentration of wealth and power as necessary and beneficial but recognized the difficulties entailed by "the general tightening of the hoops of the world." "The Doctrine of 'Room at the Top' " would no longer apply as widely as before. "It is misleading to hold up to young men conspicuously great rewards as so many plums hanging high on a tree which the best climbers may pluck," for in an economy controlled by great corporations rewards are carefully dispensed by the wise and powerful to the diligent and well-trained.[6] Yet far from corrupting American character, concentration has revealed a new kind of heroic virtue in the power of captains of industry to manage great affairs greatly. The first number of the magazine published Rev. William Lawrence's famous essay on "The Relation of Wealth to Morals," which argues that "The accumulation of wealth tends not to moral decay but to the development of character." And what is true of the individual is true of the nation: Frederick Emory's article on "The Greater America" argues that though seizure of the Philippines may create a "drift towards imperialistic ideas—the concentration of power in the hands of a privileged few—" it will compensate by arousing the nation to a sense of its responsibility for doing "the work of the world."[7]

But the new order could not be "democratic" in the sense of a broad diffusion of power. *The World's Work* consciously spoke "In Behalf of Those in Authority" in an editorial which portrayed the leaders of the new order in frankly paternalistic terms. Its editorial response to the scandal of massacres in Batangas and Samar was to assert their faith that the gentlemanly character of our soldiers and administrators in the Islands was sufficient guarantee that no atrocious or unnecessary violence had been committed. But the editorial went on to acknowledge that sometimes extraordinary measures had to be taken to keep order; and it offered as examples the defeat of southern secession, the suppression of the Blacks after their brief period of power during Reconstruction, and the repression of violence among the dangerous classes of the modern city.[8] It therefore found Bell's proclamation that more than one-sixth of Luzon's population had perished as a result of his activities merely "a startling measure of the severity" of American policy and reasserted its belief that Bell was doing "a good deed for civilization."[9]

Whether in the Philippines or at home, gentlemen must sometimes use violence because so large an element of "the People" has become morally and racially degenerate. America's earlier success in combining democracy with progress resulted (in Frederick Emory's formulation) from "The Homogeneity of Our People," our derivation from "a single race, with substantially the same political and social instincts, the same standards of conduct and morals, the same industrial capability." The only notable exceptions were "the Negroes and the Jews." But the new immigration threatens both "The Purity of the American Race" and the solidity of our institutions. The magazine therefore favored restriction of further immigration by other than British or Teutonic racial stocks and took a favorable view of attempts to disenfranchise "the ignorant."[10]

In this new order, the role of red-blooded fiction was potentially crucial as a means of public education, offsetting the cheap and potentially corrupting influence of the dime novel among members of the new working classes. Even in the ghettos of the city, says Williams, Yiddish-speaking children are being Americanized by reading the works of Fenimore Cooper, and it could be hoped they would also acquire "the unlimited view" of American life that "readers get from [Owen Wister's] 'The Virginian,' and some of Bret Harte's and Hamlin Garland's Western stories."[11]

But the "Americanism" propounded by most of the red-blooded writers was a racial gift identified with the possession of Anglo-Saxon "blood" rather than a cultural attainment. Most of them regarded the mixture of races and ethnic groups in the modern city as a sign and cause of America's degeneration:

> No rod of modern ground is more debased and mongrel with its hordes of encroaching alien vermin, that turn our cities to Babels and our citizenship to a hybrid farce, who degrade our commonwealth from a nation into something half pawn-shop, half broker's office.[12]

Wister himself believed that projects of cultural "Americanization" could never change the fundamental character of the aliens: Yiddish-speaking Jews might read the novels but were incapable of emulating heroes like Hawkeye and the Virginian:

[To] survive in the clean cattle country requires spirit of adventure, courage, and self-sufficiency; [hence] you will not find many Poles or Huns or Russian Jews in that district; it stands as yet untainted by the benevolence of Baron Hirsch.[13]

The subject matter of red-blooded fiction had the same sort of appeal that the dime novel enjoyed: it was oriented to action and adventure, sensational in its treatment of violence. Yet these works were also seriously didactic and polemic in their style and organization, and they developed at length the central ideas and historiographic scenarios of such ideological systems as Social Darwinism, Positivism, and even Marxism.

What the red-blooded writers proposed to teach the immigrant was acceptance of a particular ideology of political force, in which the use of violence becomes the legitimate monopoly of a privileged class, and the identification of the Anglo-Saxon "natural aristocracy" as the proper vessel of that privilege. They systematically link the myths of regenerative violence to an ideology of class and race privilege—an emphasis different from that in the more "democratic" dime novel, in which the right to behave like a red-handed avenger is accorded to persons of every class, and occasionally to women and people of color.

Indeed, in its own version of the Frontier Thesis *The World's Work* represents the dime-novel worldview as the cultural expression of that democratic frontier epoch which has closed forever. Frank Norris' "The Frontier Gone at Last," published in *The World's Work* in 1902, describes dime novels as the eddas and sagas of a Rooseveltian race-history:

When we—the Anglo-Saxons—busied ourselves for the first stage of the march, we began from that little historic reach of ground in the midst of the Friesland swamps, and we set our faces Westward, feeling no doubt the push of the Slav behind us. Then the frontier was Britain and the sober peacefulness of the land where the ordered, cultivated English farmyards of today was the Wild West for the Frisians of that century; and for the little children of the Frisian peat cottages, Hengist was the Apache Kid and Horsa Deadwood Dick—freebooters, law-defiers, slayers-of-men, epic heroes, blood brothers if you please to Boone and Bowie.[14]

But though American Anglo-Saxons as a nation may conquer or dominate lesser breeds and nations, the new order of industry will also require a division of power and privilege between different classes of Anglo-Saxon in which some of the ruling race will sink to the level of "Poles or Huns or Russian Jews." The critical problem for American ideology in this period of transition is to reconcile the principle of Anglo-Saxon superiority—the ideological basis for imperialism abroad and for the subordination of immigrant and Black labor at home—with the need to justify the subordination of some classes of Anglo-Saxons to others.

This is one of the themes of Norris's great fiction, particularly of *The Octopus* (1901), the epic novel based on the "war" between farmers and railroad interests that ended in the Mussel Slough "massacre" of 1880. The embattled farmers of *The Octopus* are (for the most part) classic embodiments of the Anglo-Saxon drive for progress and domination. Yet they are defeated because under the new regime of commerce the race-gifts of pride, ambition, will, and aptitude for violence are not enough by themselves to ensure dominance. Their expression must be consistent with the requirements of "the market," whose operations Norris represents as a law of nature, as irresistible as the sex drive or the processes of natural fecundity. In a fully incorporated industrial order, where giant monopolies contend for worldwide markets, the future belongs to those (Anglo-Saxons or not) whose racial gifts can be modified to find expression through a powerful corporate entity.[15]

The West of the Progressive Era was recognized by contemporary journalists, sociologists, and red-blooded novelists as a particularly useful setting for the exploration of such matters. As the sociologist Emma Langdon wrote in 1905, "[The] labor war being waged in the west is a fight not to be considered lightly by the progressive man or woman of today—and war it has been and is still—for the end is not yet."[16] What made western class struggles important were their high levels of violence, their combination of agrarian and industrial aspects, and the fact that the opposed classes were led and predominantly constituted by native-born Whites. The conflicts that figured most prominently in red-blooded fiction were the Central Valley "war" in California between farmers and the railroad in 1880, the "Johnson County War" between small and large ranchers in Wyoming (1892), the gold-mining strikes in the Coeur d'Alene (1892) and Cripple Creek (1893–94) districts, and the coalmine "wars" in Colorado (1903–14) between the Western Federation of Miners (and later the IWW) and the corporation owned by J. D. Rockefeller.[17]

Like the *World's Work* editorialists and correspondents, red-blooded writers interpreted these struggles by applying the insights of an eclectic mix of generally "progressive" theories in which a Turnerian understanding of economic change is blended with a Social Darwinist (*cum* Roosevelt) understanding of the connection between racial character and class attainment. Studies of the Colorado labor wars prepared by professional social scientists Emma Langdon (1905) and Benjamin Rastall (1908) described these conflicts as a last recrudescence of Anglo-Saxon violence in its Frontier-democratic form—the final stage described in Roosevelt's Myth of the Frontier, in which the social power and entitlement to force that had once belonged to the White American race as a whole passes to an elite or managerial class within that race. In the West, both capitalists and workers are descendants of the conquering race who "explored the West and reared a golden empire" and who "know not the word compromise." The workmen are

> of the characteristic frontiersman type, come not so much to find work as to seek a fortune. Rough, ready, fearless, used to shifting for themselves; shrewd, full of expedients; reckless, ready to cast everything on a single die. . . .

The capitalists have corresponding virtues; they are more daring entrepreneurs and more stubborn contenders for power than their eastern equivalents. Western labor wars therefore have all the violence to be expected of savage war, in which one side or the other must be destroyed or subjugated.[18]

But despite their conviction that the corporate order is bound to triumph, Langdon and Rastall are strongly sympathetic to labor. Like Norris in "The Frontier Gone at Last," they lament the loss of that promise of personal independence and democratic equality which must follow the closing of the Frontier. And in this ambivalent mixture of democratic nostalgia and progressive conviction they reflect the ideological division of their society.

Recovering the Savage: Remington, London, Garland

That ideological division is addressed by the most popular and influential works of "red-blooded fiction." These novels are not chiefly concerned with the loss of democratic opportunity entailed by the closing of the Frontier, but with the potential loss of opportunities for exercising the peculiar warrior virtues of the Anglo-Saxon race. Some question whether the racial vigor of the

Anglo-Saxon can survive the passage from the age of conquest to the age of trade; others offer imaginative programs for the renewal of that vigor, in which the civilized hero is transformed through an experience of "the strenuous life."[19]

Frederic Remington's is the most dismal version of the Anglo-Saxon hero's historical prospects. He sees the exhaustion of the wilderness and the Indian as a permanent loss of the material conditions that fostered the growth of a vigorous and heroic American race. In his later writings, Remington increasingly identified with the Indian. But his nostalgia for lost red savagery is really a disguised lament for the loss of the primal, and hence "savage," essence of Anglo-Saxon racial virtue.[20]

This theme is most systematically developed in his novel, *John Ermine of Yellowstone* (1902). Ermine is a modern Hawkeye, who, though raised among Indians, is of impeccable Anglo-Saxon lineage. He aids civilization by serving as a scout for the cavalry. Ermine is a Rooseveltian Hawkeye whose gifts make him both a fighter and a would-be breeder; as a scion of the ruling race, he chooses the best available woman for his mate—the Colonel's daughter. But the rank-order of the regiment mirrors the hierarchy of modern society: because of his low birth and Indian upbringing Ermine is considered socially unacceptable despite his Anglo-Saxon blood. Since for Ermine race is the sole valid basis of social distinction, he understands this rejection as a denigration of his blood and character. Forbidden to stand equal with his race-fellows, he chooses to stand *apart* from them and returns to the wilderness.

But the regiment has made such a separation impossible, for it has impressed its values on Ermine's psychology: he can't get it out of his head. To prove himself equal to the officers, he must use the only means he understands—armed violence, which is the Anglo-Saxon's gift and the basis of his power in the historical struggle for hegemony. Ermine does not fight for the *democratic* principle, for he does not believe all men are created equal; rather, he is asserting his entitlement to a racial privilege: the right to marry a woman of the best class and lineage. In the final gunfight the archetype of primitive Saxon virtues is shot down by an officer who represents the new, "regimental" expression of racial character.[21]

The alternative to this tragic view of racial destiny is the "strenuous life" scenario: a man softened by modern civilization is immersed in a wilderness and thus recovers his race's latent capacity for mastery—

or discovers, just before his final ruin and death, that he lacks such gifts.

Jack London's Alaskan stories and novels present this "strenuous life" scenario in its most fundamental terms. In "The White Silence" (*The Son of the Wolf*, 1900) London finds one last frontier of opportunity for the descendants of the pioneering races to get wealthy (on gold) and become heroes through success in savage war—and "savage marriage." In *The Son of the Wolf* the Anglo-Saxon proves his worth as fighter and breeder by defeating Indian rivals for the hand of an Indian bride, thereby establishing spiritual dominance over the savages that he will then enforce and reproduce through the woman he has taken from them. London thus breaks a fundamental taboo of the Fenimore Cooper tradition by apparently endorsing White-Indian marriages. But he does so in the interest of a different kind of racialism, in which *virility* is identified as the most important racial "gift" or virtue. The power and character of the *male* determines biological and social destiny in London's mythology, and from such a red-blooded "virilist" position the distinction of gender works exactly like the distinction of race—all women stand in relation to superior men as Indians stand in relation to Anglo-Saxons.[22] All marriage that dilutes or compromises virility is "miscegenate"; and since Indian women value warrior-manliness, marriage to an Indian may, in some circumstances, be better for "the race" than marriage to an excessively "feminine" White woman.[23]

Most of London's short-story heroes, drawn from a range of social classes, are in some way ennobled by the way in which they meet the challenge of the wilderness. But several stories, and the novels *Call of the Wild* (1903), *The Sea Wolf* (1904), and *The Adventures of Smoke Bellew* (1914), feature men (or dogs) of "gentle" birth who show a special gift for leadership in the wild. Occasionally London reverses the parable and suggests that the virility that is re-energized by the wilderness may return to civilization and place its power at the service of genteel heroines and social values. But (like Remington) he tends to see civilization as the enemy of that savage virility that is born in the wilderness. In *The Iron Heel* (1908) he takes the John Ermine plot and gives it a subversive twist. This dystopian novel imagines a future in which the divisions of class collapse into a genuinely racial division. Society is torn between a wealthy race/class of highly endowed and empowered rulers ("the Oligarchy") and a laboring class whose capacity for self-government and self-defense has degenerated. The Oligarchy lives by the creed of *The World's Work*:

> They, as a class, believed that they alone maintained civilization. It was their belief (inculcated in childhood) that if they ever weakened, the great beast would ingulf them and everything of beauty and wonder and good in its cavernous and slime-dripping maw. Without them, anarchy would reign and humanity would drop backward into the primitive night out of which it had so painfully emerged. . . .[24]

The workers' struggle against the Oligarchy is as foredoomed as the Indians' resistance to the Whites, because they too are racially deficient. London compares them to "the small groups of Indians that survived, . . . dancing ghost dances and waiting the coming of a Messiah of their own," only to be massacred in an industrial version of Wounded Knee.[25]

Such a working class must depend on superior types for leadership. It finds such a leader in Everhard, a truly "red-blooded" hero—virile, attractive, masterful:

> He was in every respect a natural aristocrat—and this in spite of the fact that he was in the camp of the non-aristocrats. He was a superman, a blond beast such as Nietzsche has described, and in addition he was aflame with democracy.[26]

However, Everhard's democracy is not the expression of his nature, merely the result of circumstance: he is a superior man born and raised among the lower classes, like a White man raised by Indians. Like Ermine, he must choose whether to submit to a subordinate place in a regimented society or to make war on society and court his own destruction. The difference between them is that where Ermine stands alone and is fundamentally anarchic, Everhard possesses the Anglo-Saxon gift for "administration," which enables him to become the leader of a revolutionary working class.

But Everhard's leadership ironically discredits the "democracy" he professes, since it is based, not on his equality, but on his superiority to the people he leads. In a sense, his success as a socialist confirms the Oligarchy's progressive belief that ruling classes arise from superior human types. The Oligarchy recognizes danger in Everhard, because he is so clearly one of them.[27] They therefore begin a war of extermination in which (like John Ermine) Everhard perishes along with most of his class.

London's work exaggerates the ideological ambivalence of progressive political culture, pitting extreme expressions of democratic and managerial principles against each other (and Nature) in apocalyptic strife. A more normative resolution of this ambivalence appears in the work of Hamlin Garland, whose development as a writer shows how readily populist sympathies could develop into progressive convictions.

Garland made his reputation as a "realist" with the publication of *Main-Travelled Roads* (1891), which portrayed the hard lives of farmers on the Great Plains frontier of the 1870s. He was deeply interested in a variety of reform movements, and much of the work he produced between 1890 and 1894 was intended as a contribution to the Populist cause. But in response to the events of the 1890s—the labor wars of 1892–94, the absorption of the Populists by the Democratic Party, America's emergence as a world power in 1898—his political and literary concerns took on a more "progressive" cast. This is particularly evident in the series of novels he published between 1900 and 1902, which focus on the Far West and develop a fictional history of the process by which those frontier regions were ultimately civilized.[28]

The passage between "populist" and "progressive" frontiers is the subject of the first novel in the series, *The Eagle's Heart* (1900). This "strenuous life" fable tells the story of Harold Excell, the son of a midwestern minister who abandons the safety and respectability of his home for the risks and dangers of the West. As his name suggests, Excell has an inborn gift for mastery, which the West will call forth. He has the conventional hallmarks of the Anglo-Saxon race hero: he is exceptionally virile and attractive, has more energy than his little community can use, chafes under discipline but possesses self-control, and exhibits (when frustrated) a "Berserker's" temper—which testifies to his descent from Viking and Crusader. That rage makes him an outlaw, but his crime is mitigated by its being committed in defense of a good woman: his instincts are not merely combative but chivalric.

Like Roosevelt, he decides to go west, not to make his fortune but to become something like a hero of "knight-errantry." (Garland, *The Eagle's Heart*, 1900, pp. 12, 14). The news of Custer's Black Hills expedition (1874) is fresh, and Excell's first idea is to scout for Custer in the Sioux war.

> Of the Indians he had mixed opinions. At times he thought of them as a noble race, at others—when he dreamed of fame—he wished to kill a great many of them and be very famous. Most of the books he read were based on the slaughter of the "redskins," yet at heart he wished to be one of them and to taste the joy of their poetic life.

Excell's unconscious aim in seeking to find and join "the Indians" is to acquire, through a regression to "the primitive," a new and more authentic conscience and sense of self. He will become a "man who knows Indians" without being either an Indian-hater or a John Ermine, because his gifts prove to be those of a progressive manager.

Excell's is a *faux naif* version of Garland's own attitude toward the Indians. In the mid–90s he had become interested in the Indian side of the Custer battle, and in 1897–98 he made frequent visits to the Sioux and Cheyenne reservations to interview participants. His sympathy for the Indian was an extension of his populism: he identified them as victims of the same forces of corporate greed that oppressed and impoverished the Plains farmers.[29]

Like all metaphors, this one was reversible. If the likeness of Indians to homesteaders made them eligible for greater sympathy, the likeness of homesteaders to Indians suggests that the decline of the "primitive" small farmer was as inevitable as the disappearance of savagery before the advance of civilization. The imaginative development of his populist metaphor thus pointed Garland toward a Rooseveltian reading of development in which savages, ranchers, and finally farmers progressively give way to higher forms of social organization.

When Excell, like Roosevelt, abandons dreams of Indian-fighting for the ambition of becoming a "Cattle King," Garland's hero finds himself in a crisis. Cattlemen begin contesting homesteaders' rights to the range. The homesteaders' encampments are likened to Indian villages; their anger at the cattlemen's seizure of their water rights is compared to Indian rage at the slaughter of the buffalo; they whoop like Indians when they attack the cowboys; and the farm girl who loves Excell violates his notion of femininity by showing she can "ride like a Sioux."[30]

But when Excell befriends a homesteader and discovers that "These 'red devils' were people," Garland reverses the racial metaphor to identify the cattlemen as the savages: like the Indians in *The Winning of the West* and *Ranch Life and the Hunting Trail*, they are would-be monopolists of government land who "stand to keep out settlement."[31] Because he has now identified the homesteaders as the agents of progress, Excell puts his skill with weapons at their service and becomes a kind of guerrilla or social bandit resisting the vigilantism of the cowboys—the sort of figure the movies would later identify as a "gunfighter." He takes the rather dime-novelish alias of "Black Mose."

The pattern of the narrative requires Excell to undergo periodic regressions to the primitive as preparation for each new advance of his moral consciousness. His fall from minister's son to convict sends him west as a cowboy; his sympathy for the Indian/farmers makes him a populist gunman. Then a gun battle with a cowboy lynch mob (in which another Berserker rage helps Excell triumph) forces him to hide among cowboys on a cattle drive—a regressive identification, according to Garland's symbolism. The cattle drive ultimately takes Excell to Chicago, the center of modern civilization. Here he suffers a further regression, this time to the ranks of the urban savages. He becomes a wage-slave subject to the "tyrant[s] of labor" and then falls "into the ranks of the poor." In his misery Excell reverts to his romantic or populist vision of savagery as an alternative to this sort of progress: " 'My God, if I was only among the Injins,' he said savagely; '*they* wouldn't see a man starve, not while they had a sliver of meat to share with him; but these Easterners don't care."[32]

But what Turner had said of the lost frontier is also true of Excell's solution. It no longer exists as a material option, a way of life that can be successfully followed and perpetuated; but it retains its significance on the spiritual or mental plane as the symbol of certain moral and political ideals which can be perpetuated through education. As soon as Excell has recovered and has married his redemptive woman, he returns to the West to manage an Indian reservation, to educate his savage charges in civilized arts, and to interpret the Indian's natural morality to a capitalist society in need of reform.

The cycles of regression and advance have thus carried Excell from populist outlaw to progressive bureaucrat, peace officer, and husband of a well-born woman. The manner of his rise has been "populist" and "democratic" in its style. Yet in the end, what he achieves is a kind of aristocratic status in which a privileged social position and political power are united.

Garland's *Captain of the Gray Horse Troop* (1902) picks up where *The Eagle's Heart* left off, with the hero in charge of an Indian reservation. However, Garland replaces Excell the redeemed outlaw with Captain George Curtis, a heroic idealization of the progressive bureaucrat: a soldier and a professional, a man with all the skills to be a captain of industry, who for reasons of conscience places himself at the service of the nation, the People, and even of the oppressed. Under the regime of progressivism, Curtis is empowered to function effectively against both "mobs" and "tribes." He succeeds in protecting his wards from lynch mobs and from the attempts of the demagogic Senator Brisbane to drive them into a war of extermination (and captures the heart of Brisbane's daughter).[33]

The novel is polemical, a muckraking attack on corruption in the Indian Bureau which is said to have roused President Theodore Roosevelt to reform that agency. (It was also one of Garland's most popular books, selling over 100,000 copies and earning critical praise as well.)[34] However, there is no suggestion of a populist liberation for the Indians. The Captain's success merely confirms the necessity of vesting authority in a paternal elite whenever an inferior race or class is to be managed.[35] But Garland is unwilling to apply the logic of managerial progressivism to the problem of class warfare in the American metropolis. When he addresses the labor issue in *Hesper* (1902), set during the Cripple Creek strike of 1894, he invents a Turnerian safety valve to evade a seemingly inescapable class war. He maintains a fairly hopeful view of the prospects for traditional democratic values in a post-frontier America by evading or denying the issues of class interest and industrial governance that troubled Remington, Norris, and London.

A third type of red-blooded story offers an alternative to the evasions of Garland and the gloomy prophecies of *The Iron Heel* and *The Octopus*. Owen Wister's *The Virginian* (1902) and Thomas Dixon's *The Clansman* (1904) recreate the frontier hero in terms exactly suited to the role of progressive overlord of a modern nation-state. Wister's novel presents the cowboy as a Rooseveltian hero; Dixon's historical romance shows the Ku Klux Klansman as the hero of a modern form of "savage war." The cultural impact of these novels sets them apart from the work of the other red-blooded writers: not only were they best-selling novels, they were widely imitated, reproduced in versions for the stage, and finally translated into the new medium of motion pictures. Wister's novel became the paradigm text of the Western film genre, and Dixon's provided the script for *Birth of a Nation*, the film that established motion pictures as the century's pre-eminent popular art form.

The Virginian *(1902) and the Myth of the Vigilante*

Like his friends Roosevelt and Remington, Wister was a wealthy, well-born, well-educated easterner who went west (in 1885) to escape a metropolitan career and live the strenuous life. He was also indulging a social grudge, which he shared with Remington, against the debased political culture and racial character of the polyglot metropolis. Like Roosevelt, he was anxious about the ability of his own class to maintain its power and values against the numbers and ambitions of the lesser breeds. He feared that the American elite of the Atlantic coast was doomed to "vanish from the face of the earth" because (unlike the English peerage) "We're no type, no race," merely "a collection of revolutionary scions of English families and immigrants arrived yesterday from Cork and Bremen." Roosevelt had seen the old Frontier as the crucible of race formation, and Wister hoped the nascent aristocracy of the great cattle ranches might provide the "permanent pattern" for a new American racial type.[36]

The ranching business on the northern Plains had experienced a boom in the 1880s: rising urban populations raised the demand for beef, the new railroads made it feasible to ship it in large amounts, and the low fees charged for using public grazing range made costs relatively low. The "beef bonanza" that had been actively promoted by western developers since the 1870s now found ready investors among bankers and industrialists in the eastern states and Europe, who became the absentee owners of vast cattle ranches. In addition to profits, the ranches also provided summer recreation for the owners, their sons, and invited guests, and an opportunity for the dilettante heir (or his chum) to improve himself by acting as manager of the operation. In Wyoming the social life of the big ranchers centered on the Cheyenne Club, which offered civilized amenities fairly close to the range and provided an organizational center for the Wyoming Stock-Growers' Association (WSGA), which had been formed by the big ranchers to protect their interests against the banks and railroads, the demands of labor, and competing small ranchers.[37]

The Cheyenne Club, and not the working ranch, provided the model for Wister's ideas of "frontier democracy." To a scion of Philadelphia's aristocracy, the mingling of the heirs of eastern fortunes on terms of social equality with the rough-hewn founders of the range cattle business seemed a radical type of egalitarianism. To identify himself as part of it, Wister had only to accept (and to whatever degree he would, adopt) the plebeian style of the western ranchers. But this democracy of style encompassed only those who had gained entry to the Cheyenne Club—men who had proved themselves fit in what Wister (like Roosevelt) saw as the Darwinian competition of western life. The majority of the Club's members were aristocrats of Wister's own kind, "clubbable" even in the East. The importance of social position in that milieu is attested by the fact that within a few months of his arrival in Cheyenne Wister was serving as manager of the Teschemacher and de Billier Cattle Company, a large ranch owned by two of his Harvard classmates.[38]

As a result of his ranching experiences, Wister revised his hopes for racial regeneration. The characteristic native type of westerner—the cowboy—lacked the instinct and desire for *social* power which is the essential trait of a would-be ruling race. But the West could contribute to regeneration by awakening the primal racial vigor of metropolitan aristocrats and by arousing a desire for mastery and conquest and achievement that would offset the contemptible and enervating imperatives of a commercial society. In "The Evolution of the Cow-puncher," in *Harper's Monthly* in 1895, Wister shows the regenerative effect on an English aristocrat of the experience of managing a western cattle ranch and working with American cowboys:

> Directly the English nobleman smelt Texas, the slumbering Saxon awoke in him, and mindful of the tournament, mindful of the hunting-field, galloped howling after wild cattle, a born horseman, a perfect athlete, and spite of the peerage and gules and argent, fundamentally kin with the drifting vagabonds who swore and galloped by his side.[39]

But though "the bottom bond of race" unites cowboy and aristocrat, the no less significant qualities of class divide them. The cowboys are fighters but will not be successful "breeders" of a new class: "These wild men sprang from the loins of no similar father, and begot no sons to continue their hardihood." They leave neither estates nor institutions behind them, and their politics are tainted with populism. The line of racial heritage is therefore rooted in the aristocratic ranchers, who are the end product of "The Evolution of the Cow-puncher" from "the tournament at Camelot to the round-up at Abilene."[40]

In their approach to the cattle business the members of the WSGA were more like captains of industry than Texas cowboys. They brought to their operations the skills and biases of big businessmen; and when the cattle business finally dried up, they returned to become managers of corporations like the Morgan Bank, U.S. Steel, the Seligman Bank, the American Surety Company, the First National Bank of New York, and the North American Copper Company.[41] The scale of their operations required the large investments of capital and organizational skill associated with contemporary trends in manufacturing, mining, and railroading. In 1902 *The World's Work* praised a similar group, the Cattle Raiser's Association of Texas, for having created a capital enterprise rivaling "the great Standard Oil Company, and almost as strong in point of money as the world-famous

Steel Trust." The Association members were "an avalanche of men who mean business and who get what they go after, from a band of rustlers to a national act of legislation."[42]

"Rustlers" had been a problem for the WSGA as well, and during Wister's stay its members began a private war to suppress them. However, the real objectives of the anti-rustler campaign went beyond the suppression of cattle-thieving. The campaign arose from a complex set of labor, interest-group, and party conflicts that were in some respects unique to the cattle ranges but that also belonged to the general pattern of conflicts arising from the concentration of economic power.

In Wyoming, the small ranchers dominated the county politics of the hilly north-central part of the state while the WSGA controlled the wealthier and more populous plains of the southern and eastern counties. Their rivalry over grass and water rights was exacerbated after 1884 by hard times in the range cattle industry. Demand for beef softened, rail rates rose, and overgrazing reduced the quality and quantity of the product. The terrible winter of 1886–87 decimated the herds, and bad management made the situation worse: absentee owners did not trim their productivity expectations, and many managers met quotas by shipping cattle that ought to have been saved for breeding. Rather than blame their own faulty operations for the reduction of the herds, managers accused the small ranchers of "rustling." (There was some justice in their complaint, but not as much as they asserted.)[43]

The accusation was one the large ranchers were well prepared to believe. The small ranchers of Johnson County were not only economic competitors. Many of them (and particularly their leaders) were ex-employees of the big ranchers who had managed to save enough of their meager pay to purchase government Homesteads and set up as rivals to their former bosses. The desire to gain land figured prominently, along with "chuck-wagon" issues and wage disputes, in labor-management conflicts on the range and was a major factor in two large strikes by cowboys, in the Texas Panhandle in 1883 and in Wyoming in 1884 and 1886. Jack Flagg, a leader of the 1884 strike, later figured as a leader of the "rustlers" in the Johnson County War—the event that forms the background for *The Virginian.*[44]

The WSGA moved against the "rustlers" by using its control of the legislature to establish regulations nominally intended to prevent "rustled" cattle from being shipped or sold. But the regulations amounted to a policy of deliberate discriminations against the interests of small ranchers as a class. The latter responded by entering the electoral lists as Grangers and Populists, taking control of individual towns and counties and eventually uniting within the Democratic Party to contest control of the legislature with the WSGA-oriented Republicans. Johnson County was dominated by these small ranchers and provided a political base for the Democratic opposition.

The response of the WSGA was to act *outside* the framework of law and electoral politics, through a campaign of private violence. Between 1884 and 1892 WSGA cowboys lynched key figures in the illicit cattle trade as well as leaders of the Johnson County ranchers. The "war" reached a crisis in 1892 when a majority faction of the WSGA hired an army of "Texas gunslingers," augmented them with their own armed cowboys, and invaded Johnson County with the intention of "exterminating" the rustlers and "deporting" their elected officials. The lynchers and invading gunslingers identified themselves as "vigilantes," borrowing their name from earlier organizations of "decent citizens" formed in the frontier towns of California, Montana, Idaho, and Nevada between 1854 and 1870.

Vigilantism has been used to describe a number of local movements occurring at various times that have in common the use of extralegal force by an organization of citizens to suppress "criminal" threats to the civil peace of prosperity of a community. Although some of these movements invoked British, Scottish, or Teutonic precedents, the vigilante phenomenon seems to be peculiar to "settler-states": political communities established on the periphery of a colonizing "metropolis" in which the forms and powers of government are initially tenuous.[45] The simplest and earliest type of frontier vigilantism involved the application of "lynch law" (mainly banishment and corporal punishment) against criminals and "undesirables." More complex (and violent) were the various forms of "regulator" movements, in which vigilante actions against individuals were part of a larger pattern of resistance to government authority—for example, the South Carolina "Regulators" of 1767–69, and the Whiskey Rebellion of 1794. The latter type of vigilantism was, in effect, a rudimentary exercise of the "right of revolution" asserted in the Declaration of Independence.[46] But after 1865 vigilantism acquired broader significance as a means of justifying new forms of social violence directed against the "dangerous classes" of the post-Frontier, urban, and industrial order. As a result, the vigilante ideology itself was transformed from an assertion of a natural and democratic right-to-violence to an assertion of class and racial privilege.[47]

The WSGA's war in Johnson County was a vigilante campaign in a more modern sense. Its "respectable men" were not natives of the community whose "criminal elements" they attacked, but the citizens and elected officials of a different county.[48] The campaign was statewide, aimed at establishing the WSGA's dominance in Wyoming politics, and in that way begs comparison with the activities of the Klan in the Reconstruction South. But the specific tactics used by the WSGA more closely resemble those used to break the Coeur d'Alene and Homestead Steel strikes in that same summer of 1892. At Homestead, Andrew Carnegie's corporation paid the Pinkerton Agency to hire a private "army" of detectives and strike-breakers, which attempted to drive the strikers out of the factories and arrest their leaders. The invasion of Johnson County was characterized by similarly deliberate planning, the use of spies, the recruitment of an "army" of hired guns (cowboys instead of detectives), and the development of a "dead list." The WSGA army was well equipped, and special trains were arranged to transport it. Telegraph companies gave tacit approval for the cutting of their lines to isolate the "rustlers" and to provide cover for sympathetic state officials who did not wish to be summoned for aid by Johnson County officials. The Republican state government provided some arms, a mustering place, and a guarantee that the National Guard would not be used in Johnson County. The WSGA's newspaper urged its army to "WIPE THEM OUT" and invoked the language of the Indian wars to assert that "All honest citizens are in hopes that the cattlemen will Exterminate the rustlers."[49]

As in the Homestead affair, this large-scale use of a private armed force ended in defeat. At Homestead the Pinkerton "army" was outfought and captured by the strikers. The WSGA's invaders surrounded the isolated cabin of a rancher named Nate Champion but were held at bay until county forces could rally; shortly after killing Champion, the "army" was surrounded and forced to surrender. Both defeats were humiliating and scandalous, and in their wake many independent newspapers turned against the Pinkertons and the WSGA. In Wyoming, prominent members of the Association were indicted and the Democrat/Populist alliance took control of the legislature. But as in the Homestead strike, these gains were short-lived, the courts freed all the invaders, and the WSGA and its supporters regained control of the state government and by more indirect means of intimidation were able to drive their severest critics (like journalist Asa Shinn Mercer) out of the state. Publication of Mercer's book on the "war," *The Banditti of the Plains, or The Cattlemen's Invasion of Wyoming in 1892, the Crowning Infamy of the Ages,* was legally suppressed in Wyoming, and copies of it were burned. The WSGA's failure to regain its former economic and political dominance, and the reduced engagement in the business by eastern financiers after 1892, had more to do with the state of the industry than with the political power of its opposition.[50]

Ten years after the "invasion," but during a time when similar struggles were still occurring in the range-cattle regions, the WSGA's side of the affair was written into the canon of American literary mythology by Owen Wister in *The Virginian.* Wister himself had worked on the margins of the struggle during his term as manager for Teschemacher and de Billier and was intellectually a WSGA partisan.[51] But the novel moves beyond a partisan representation of the range war to project a larger vision of the "significance of the Frontier" for a post-Frontier world order.

Like Roosevelt, Wister sees the primary achievement of the Frontier as the production of a new racial type, selected from among the Anglo-Saxon "democracy" and trained by the frontier experience in the skills and psychology of command. But Wister goes further, to show that his hero—who represents a uniquely "American genius"—can succeed by taking a principled stand *against* democracy (in its traditional formulation) and becoming part of a class order whose power is greater in progressive potential than that of popular government.[52]

In *The Virginian* a young man born in poverty rises through the social ranks by the exercise of exceptional skills and the display of a superior moral character. These bring him the favor of wealthy folk who encourage and employ him, offer him access to education (which he has the innate good sense to seek), and eventually promote him to a "partnership in the firm." Wister's hero takes the further step of becoming a captain of industry in his own right by investing his savings in land that would be wanted by developers of coalmines and railroads. Wister seeks to uncover the hidden causes of "success" and to develop the political consequences of an economic order divided between "those who move up" and those who fail.[53]

The cattle range is represented as a Social Darwinian laboratory, perfect for testing hypotheses about human nature. The lawlessness and opportunities for gain offered by the Frontier are invitations to all sorts of ambition, both industrious and criminal. But to succeed at anything in the West you must be extremely good at it, and success is the only measure of personal or moral value. "Now back east yu can be middling and get along. But if you try a thing in this Western country, you've got to do it well. . . . Failure is a sort of treason to the brotherhood, and forfeits pity."[54] The Virginian takes nature's standard as his own when he says that the only equality he recognizes is being "equal to the situation."

In his youth the Virginian had himself been an "outlaw" of sorts. But unlike his contemporaries, Steve and Trampas, he has the "genius" to recognize that the wild West is changing, that civilization and law are arriving in the territory, and that the imperative to be equal to the situation therefore requires him to change his way of acting and thinking.

His "genius" is an attribute of his nature or heredity, although his actual parentage is far from aristocratic. But his identity as a Virginian, even of the poorer classes, suggests his participation in a kind of "natural aristocracy." Virginians had been identified in the historical romances of Cooper and his imitators as the Americans closest in status and breeding to British nobility.[55]

But in Wister's novel the primary sign of social and moral superiority is not nobility but *virility*; and on this score the Virginian is pre-eminent. As readers, we are brought to an understanding of his superiority, and an appreciation of its basis, by observing him through the eyes of three aristocratic easterners: the narrator, a gentleman who comes west for recreation; Judge Henry, the Virginian's employer and owner of a large ranch; and Molly Stark Wood, the daughter of impoverished gentry who comes west to earn her living as a "schoolmarm." The Virginian proves his worth to each of these in turn and finally earns from each an acknowledgment of his *superiority*.

The language of gender and sexual relations signals the Virginian's dominance. In each of these relationships he appears as the virile male engaged in courting or seducing a "female" who must eventually submit to him. The theme of sexual conquest is first sounded comically, in the Virginian's seduction of the hotel-keeper in Medicine Bow; it is triumphantly concluded with his successful courtship of Molly. But the courtship structure also defines the hero's relations with the male narrator and with Judge Henry. Although the narrator will fancy himself (for a brief moment) the Virginian's superior, his first sight of the man (joking with a new bridegroom) indicates their true relation: "Had I been the bride, I should have taken the giant, dust and all." And later, responding to the hero's intense gaze, he says, "Had I been a woman, it would have made me his to do what he pleased with on the spot."[56] Judge Henry is a more masterful person, and the Virginian has to work harder to win his acknowledgment: "[How] cleverly he caused me to learn the value of his services. . . . He is pretty nearly as shrewd as I am." Knowing that such capacity is "rather dangerous in a subordinate," the Judge raises him to foreman and eventually partner in the ranch.[57]

The Virginian's relationship with Molly is a more extended and elaborate courtship or seduction, in which he overcomes her own pretense to mastery and makes her both his lover and his subordinate. Wister uses their relationship to articulate a gendered allegory of politics in which the Virginian's virile "realism" is opposed by Molly's inconsistent mixture of genteel class snobbery and philanthropic-sentimental "egalitarianism"—which Wister takes to be the ideology of an emasculated and intellectually exhausted American upper class. She initially sees herself as superior to the Virginian by birth and culture. Hence, as a would-be lover he is supposed to look but not touch (or hope to marry), and as an intellectual companion to be her pupil rather than her teacher. But her sense of class superiority and sexual reserve are "unmanned" by the cowboy's overwhelming masculine sexual appeal. The demands of Darwinian nature, which urge her to breed with the most virile male of her race, conflict with the values of class. Wister of course values both, and his game is therefore to show that class privilege is as "natural" a phenomenon as sexuality; that the difference in the gifts and powers belonging to the sexes is a paradigm for distinctions between different orders of men; and that biological urge that drives Molly to subject herself to the virile mastery of the Virginian is therefore her best guide to both thought and action.

The Virginian's courtship of Molly is played out as an ideological dialogue in which the Virginian's arguments compel Molly to alter her beliefs and produce a revised version of the ideology of social dominance. The central theme of her argument with the Virginian is the idea that "equality" is and ought to be the basis of American politics and values. "Equality is a great big bluff," he says, "and it's easy called." He reminds her of the different intellectual capacities of the scholars in her class and then extends the analogy:

I know a man that works hard and he's gettin' rich, and I know another that works hard and is gettin' poor. He says it is his luck. All right. Call it his luck. I look around and I see folks movin' up or down, winners and losers everywhere. All luck, of course. But since folks can be that different in their luck, where's your equality? No, seh! Call your failure luck or call it laziness, wander around the words, prospect all yu' mind and yu'll come out the same old trail of inequality. . . . Some hold four aces . . . and some holds nothin'; and some . . . gets the aces and no show to play 'em; but a man has got to prove himself my equal before I'll believe him. . . . I am the kind that moves up. I am goin' to be your best scholar.[58]

Wister elaborates his hero's suggestion into a new political doctrine in the opening paragraph of the crucial set of chapters titled "The Game and the Nation":

There can be no doubt of this:—

All America is divided into two classes,—the quality and the equality. The latter will always recognize the former when mistaken for it. Both will be with us until our women bear nothing but kings.

It was through the Declaration of Independence that we acknowledged the *eternal inequality* of man. For by it we abolished a cut-and-dried aristocracy . . . [and] decreed that every man should hence have liberty to find his own level. By this very decree we acknowledged and gave freedom to true aristocracy, saying "Let the best man win, whoever he is." Let the best man win! That is America's word. That is true democracy. And true democracy and true aristocracy are one and the same thing. If anybody cannot see this, so much the worse for his eyesight.[59]

Democracy is not a value in itself but the means through which a naturally qualified ruling class can make its way to the top. And once in place, the neo-aristocracy is entitled to maintain itself by force. It may be implicit in Wister's argument (as it was in Roosevelt's "Great Rule of Righteousness") that the newly empowered classes would remain open to those energetic members of the lower class who could (in the Virginian's words) prove themselves equal. But it is clear from the rest of the novel that the terms of proof would never be easy, that government had no business correcting the disadvantages (or "bad luck") under which the "equality" labored, and that indeed the ability to overcome actual disadvantage was a valid test of admission to the "quality." Wister's "democracy" thus provides a biosocial rationale for class privilege.

In the narrative sequence that completes "The Game and the Nation," the doctrine is proved by its application to a "western" problem with distinctly metropolitan overtones. As a final test before his promotion to partner by the Judge, the Virginian is called upon to manage the sale of a large consignment of cattle and their delivery in Chicago. To achieve this he must show abilities beyond those of a range foreman, first in his handling of complex business and legal arrangements and then in maintaining control of his workers under novel conditions.

The Virginian's adventure parallels that of Excell in *The Eagle's Heart*, but the ideological intent of the passage is opposite: where Garland uses the city episode to evoke sympathy for the working class by comparing the natural morality of savages with the unnatural injustices of industrial sosciety, Wister uses it to affirm the necessity of strong managerial governance of a degenerate working class. His workers are an irresponsible lot, some merely wild cowboys reflexively defiant of authority, others—like Shorty—men of weak moral and mental endowment, easily misled. The misleader is Trampas, a villainous rustler whose name suggests both "treason" (from the Spanish) and "tramp"—the term that had identified the most rootless and "dangerous" segment of the working class since 1877.[60]

The Virginian's mastery of Trampas and the cowboys proves his "quality," and that proof becomes a metaphoric validation of the larger view of class (and race) relations that Wister has promulgated. Thus the ultimate stakes of the "game" between Trampas and the Virginian have to do with "the nation" itself. If the Virginian and his class triumph, progress and civilization will be achieved; if Trampas and Shorty triumph, the "equality" in power will reverse the course of progress. To make this point, Wister truncates his account of the Johnson County War, omitting the "invasion" and ending with the political triumph of "rustler" democracy rather than extending the story to the return of Republican control; and he attributes the ruin of the Wyoming cattle business to this democratic triumph (which causes wise investors to withdraw) rather than to economic factors.

The "game" with Trampas proves the Virginian's quality as a "fighter." But his quality as a "breeder" is tested by his courtship of Molly. To earn her love and consent to marriage he must revolutionize her effeminate values, her sentimentalized ideas of "equality," and her deference to the codes and persons of a "cut and dried aristocracy." When she finally surrenders to her love for the Virginian, "true aristocracy" and democracy are united. Her acceptance provides a social, class-based ratification of the Virginian's entitlement to the name "aristocrat," while at the same time it "democratizes" Molly, who has married "beneath herself" as the cut-and-dried aristocracy measures such things. The democratizing gesture of her marriage is one of the most appealing features of the story, and in the film versions that popularized it after 1929 it becomes the central theme of the romantic plot. In the novel, however, it is the Virginian's achievement of "true aristocracy" that gives the marriage its real value.

Moreover, the politics of their marriage is not "democratic." The courtship is completed only when, after two episodes of intense struggle, Molly accepts the Virginian as her "master" in crucial matters of moral and social judgment.[61] Both episodes frame moral and political problems as a question about the entitlement of the "quality" to use violence in a privileged manner. The lynching of the rustlers (Wister's representation of the start of the Johnson County War) frames the question in social and political terms: What must a good man do to protect civilization? The final gunfight with Trampas puts the question in more primal terms: What may (and must) a real man do to vindicate the principle of manhood itself? In both instances the Virginian's actions are questioned by Molly, who initially regards them as proof of the Virginian's lack of civilization and moral scruple.

Molly argues with Judge Henry that lynching rustlers is a barbarous and anarchic act, like the lynching of Negroes in the South. Judge Henry distinguishes the Virginian's act from southern lynchings by noting the difference of manner: the southerners torture their victims and make a public display of them, violating the boundaries of gender by inviting women and children; the vigilantes simply hang their rustlers and do it in private, intending to protect the sensibilities of women and children.[62] This proves that the lynchers are men of good character, a fact that is in itself a sufficient guarantee of the rightness of their action. This is the same principle evoked by *The World's Work* in defense of the "marked severities" in Batangas and Samar. Molly responds that although the Virginian may be a good man, she cannot accept his character as sufficient justification for his assumption of the privilege to punish and kill outside the forms of law.

The Judge answers by reverting to first principles. In a further revision of the Declaration of Independence, he develops the consequences of the "quality/equality" distinction. The most fundamental principle of the Declaration is its idea that the law is merely the expression of the will of "the people," and that when government becomes corrupt it is the right of the people to remake the law through revolutionary action. In punishing the rustlers, the Virginian acts in the name of "the people," who (through him) take back the power that once they gave the state.[63]

Judge Henry's argument works only if we accept a radical revision of the Jeffersonian concept of "the people." The government of the state has not been imposed by a foreign power or distant bureaucracy; it is elected. "The people" who are attempting to "take back" the power are not the whole or even a majority of the electorate; they are but a minority of the "quality" acting as if they were "the people"—or the only people that ought to count, politically. This potential flaw in the argument is evaded by a shift of ground in which the Judge asserts that in effect the state is still in a frontier condition in which savage-war conditions pertain:

> We are in a very bad way, and we are trying to make that way a little better until civilization can reach us. At present we lie beyond its pale.[64]

Wister's primary concern (expressed through Judge Henry) is not with the preservation of democratic legislative and judicial forms, but rather with the establishment and protection of "civilizaton"—tasks that can be performed only by the races and classes who possess the proper "gifts." As Judge Henry sees it, the South already enjoys the benefits of a system of government which privileges the "decent" (i.e., White) classes at the expense of the "dangerous classes" (the Blacks). Rustlers sitting on Wyoming juries can turn rustlers free, but Blacks cannot sit on southern juries. Therefore "The South has never claimed that the law would let [a Negro] go." The Judge does not object that all-White juries might (and did) act as judicial lynch mobs, treating accusation as tantamount to guilt. Indeed, that exercise of privilege and discrimination is exactly what is necessary whenever a civilization is threatened by its dangerous classes.

In the traditional terminology of the Frontier Myth, the coming of "civilization" and the establishment of a legally constituted government were regarded as virtually synonomous. Wister distinguishes "civilization" from "government" by arguing that certain forms of democracy produce a degenerate form of politics: one in which mongrels and failures, the "equality," are enabled to assert against the "quality" their claims for power and a redistribution of wealth. The crucial battle of the mythic Frontier is therefore not simply the struggle between White republican and Red savage but the struggle between "true aristocracy" and false democracy. This latter internal struggle is what literally threatens the existence of "civilization" as such; savagery proper was never more than a figurative threat, although savage war has been the school in which the defenders of civilization have acquired their "manhood" and all the attributes of skill and character that define heroic virility.

Wister emphasizes the latter point in an episode in which the Virginian is wounded by Indians and rescued by Molly. This reversal of the usual captivity/rescue pattern has a crucial role in Wister's polemic against Molly's false and "effeminate" values. To save the Virginian's life she must bind his wounds, and to do that she must overcome her female distaste for gore and her sentimental unwillingness to cause pain even in a good cause. The Virginian urges her not to fail "from being still too gentle." "You've got to be the man through all this mess," he tells her; and when she brings him back, the Doctor affirms that she "had not done a woman's part, but a man's part."[65]

In the end, the only sort of "manliness" available to her is that of heeding the call of her nature in accepting the Virginian and accepting as valid the ideology of manliness which he embodies and articulates. Her final acceptance of this principle is not complete until she passes one last test: her acceptance of the code of honor that compels the Virginian to accept Trampas' challenge to a gunfight. Unlike the lynching, higher political and social considerations play no part in this argument. The issue between them is simply one of manly honor—an insult that must be answered simply because (in effect) *a man's gotta do what a man's gotta do.* In accepting the slaying of Trampas as moral and necessary, Molly finally accepts the masculine principle *as such* as a valid guide to moral action; her conversion and subjection are complete. Manliness thus becomes the single symbol in which all the novel's various moral and ideological principles are reconciled.

The political allegory around which Wister builds his narrative thus moves from the proof of his Darwinian thesis, that all men are created unequal, to the demonstration that "the quality" are naturally entitled to rule "the equality." He proves the latter point by showing that "civilization"—a higher value than any particular form of politics—can be defended from the forces that menace it only by an armed and virile elite that is willing and able to take the law into its own hands and substitute itself for the will of the people. But "virility" itself has a value that is nearly equivalent to that of "civilization," as something that must be defended at any and all costs. Thus, to paraphrase Wister, "true civilization" and "true manhood" are one and the same thing: although women retain their value as symbols of the vulnerability of civilization, it is the spirit of virility—the power of the "great fighting races" (as Roosevelt called them)—that is the essence of the civilization our new heroes defend.

Democracy or Civilization: Dixon's The Clansman *(1904)*

The lynchings in Wyoming were part of a relatively short-lived political movement. But in the South, lynchings and the ideological rationale that sustained them were a central feature of political and social life between 1880 and 1920. Although these rationales reflected the peculiar history and culture of the South, they shared important elements of the progressive ideology espoused by writers like Roosevelt and Wister; and they used the vigilante and savage-war themes of the Frontier Myth in similar ways. These cognate features appear most strongly in the work of Thomas Nelson Page and Thomas Dixon, Jr., the leading figures in the southern branch of the "red-blooded" school. Their work is important, not just because it reflects the New South's way of receiving the national Myth of the Frontier, but because the southern variant of that myth would become a major influence on twentieth-century mass culture through D. W. Griffith's adaptation of Dixon's novel, *The Clansman*, for his epic movie *The Birth of a Nation*.

The period that White American historians have dubbed the "Progressive Era" has also been termed the "Nadir" of African-American history. After two decades in which the political achievements of Reconstruction were undermined and undone, southern Blacks faced a powerful social and political movement aimed at their formal exclusion from southern politics and their more systematic segregation from social and economic life. This movement had many sources, including (after 1895) the scapegoating of Blacks by frustrated White populists, but its political and economic particulars, and the speed with which it moved, varied from state to state. In each case, however, it culminated in both a state constitutional convention that legislated Black disenfranchisement and segregation, and in an increase in the frequency, range, and cruelty of White terrorism against Blacks.[66]

A contemporary scholar, James Cutler, noted in *Lynch-Law* (1904) that in the peak years of political struggle over disenfranchisement (1882–1903) there were 3,337 recorded lynchings in the United States, 2,585 of them in the South, of which 1,985 were of Blacks—an average of just under two Blacks lynched in the South each week for 20 years.[67] The trend persisted in later decades: in 1918 the NAACP verified the occurrence of 63 lynchings and cited an additional 12 that had probably occurred but could not be verified. Herbert Shapiro's study, *White Violence and Black Response from Reconstruction to Montgomery* (1989), concludes: "In the United States after 1900, lynchings continued as weekly phenomena, and mob assaults, comparable to European pogroms, against Black communities became commonplace occurrences in both the North and the South." The act of lynching itself became more atrocious toward the turn of the century: victims were not merely shot or hanged but were routinely subjected to torture, including eye-gouging, castration, flaying alive, and burning to death.[68]

It was in this context that Wister offered his distinction between western and southern lynchings. The western lyncher-hero represents a superior class of American Anglo-Saxon who is privileged to use violence with a freedom hitherto granted only to the Indian fighter, because the very existence of civil society is imperiled by the threat of a numerous "dangerous class." Southern lynching fails to meet this test, because government there already privileges the superior race at the expense of the presumed dangerous class, the Blacks, and because the manner of lynching argues that those in charge belong to the worst classes, who are as dangerous as Trampas.

But Wister's southern counterpart among the red-blooded writers, the novelist Thomas Nelson Page, was able to defend southern lynching in terms appropriate to *The Virginian*'s ethical scheme. In *The Negro: The Southerner's Problem* (1904), Page sees contemporary lynching as a consequence of the carpetbaggers' attempt to establish a Negro dictatorship during Reconstruction.[69] Because the Blacks were essentially savages in their moral development, this regime combined features of both "savage war" and political despotism; the White terrorists who "redeemed" their section therefore enjoyed the double sanction of the Indian fighter and the revolutionary patriot. But Redemption could not eliminate the central problem of southern society: the necessity for two races of different and inimical "gifts" to share the same territory—a situation which (by the tenets of the "savage war" myth/ideology) requires the subjugation or extermination of one or the other. The remnants of political liberty retained by Blacks, and the sympathy of northern supporters, have (according to Page) prevented Blacks from accepting subjugation and have led to political radicalism among the better classes and the rape of White women by the lower. Southern Whites possess in abundance the proverbial "exclusiveness" of the Anglo-Saxon and respond to any threat of miscegenation with instinctive violence.[70] Where the poor Whites take the lead, violence takes an extreme and atrocious form, because these classes are themselves "semi-savage" in moral development. What is needed in the New South is a restoration of some modern equivalent of the Old South's aristocratic government, in which the "quality" would take full charge of the apparatus of power, and democratic agitation on behalf of the "equality" (Black *and* poor-White) would cease.

This view of lynching and this recipe for the reform of southern politics appealed to values shared with those northern progressives who favored a managerial regime in government and economics. Page's criticism of the barbarity of poor-White lynch mobs, and the disrespect for law produced by toleration of the practice, parallel the views of Progressives like Roosevelt and Cutler—who (in their different ways) expressed understanding and even sympathy for the motives of the mobs in terms similar to Page's. They too saw lynch law itself as the expression of an important racial trait, the will to self-government, inherent in the Anglo-Saxon/Teuton and given distinctly American attributes by the Frontier. Moreover they believed that (in Roosevelt's words) "the greatest existing cause of lynching is the perpetration, especially by black men, of the hideous crimes of rape—the most abominable in all the category of crimes, even worse than murder." (In fact, *accusation* of rape figured in less than 20 percent of the lynchings during the period covered by Cutler's study.)[71] Cutler, like Page, uses the lynching epidemic as an argument for vesting greater power for social control in the hands of the better classes.[72]

But the appeal of such an obviously self-interested polemic on behalf of "government by the quality" has clear limits in the arena of commercial popular culture, whose primary audience is, after all, the "equality." Successful myth-making in the United States requires bridging or covering-over ideological dichotomies, like that between the democratic and the managerial models of good politics. When Wister's work was imitated by dime-novelists and pulp-novelists and adapted for the movies, the Virginian's lynching of Steve and his killing of Trampas appear as the triumphs not of a racial aristocrat but of an uncommon common man. Southern lynching was "Americanized" by a similarly "populist" revision of Page's apologia for aristocracy in Thomas Dixon's *The Clansman* (1904).

Dixon was not included in the 1903 article on "red-blooded writers" in *The World's Work* because his career had barely begun. But his political and literary concerns and values clearly mark him as a member of the school of Cooper, Wister, and Page. Dixon uses the events of the Reconstruction period as Cooper had used the colonial Indian wars: as a "historical" scene in which we can see the origins of present-day conflicts of power and value. Dixon's myth of Reconstruction specifically addresses the issues of the "disenfranchising" era in the South. The Populists attempted to reform southern politics and agricultural economics by organizing the agrarian poor of both races, but they were defeated by the race-baiting campaigns of their conservative or "Bourbon Democrat" opponents. A political accommodation was finally reached which accorded some Populists a share of power in exchange for moderation of their radical program and which compensated the class resentment of White Populists by the disenfranchisement of Blacks and the imposition of a Jim Crow regime. Dixon's novels provide a historical mythology for this new regime by dramatizing the processes through which Whites of different classes and parties come to understand the primacy of racial distinction.[73]

But although Dixon was a lifelong Democrat, his myth of southern regeneration owes an unacknowledged debt to Rooseveltian progressivism. The debt is most obvious in his first novel, *The Leopard's Spots* (1902), a parody of *Uncle Tom's Cabin* in which poor White southerners (rather than Black slaves) are the saintly victims of cruel oppression. Simon Legree, the Vermont Yankee turned planter who had murdered Uncle Tom, has survived the war, has made a fortune as a "scalawag" helping carpetbaggers oppress and exploit the South, and has used his ill-gotten wealth to become a robber baron. He returns to the South to exploit a division in the ranks of the Whites created by a "demagogic" political faction (read "Populists"). With their help, Legree begins to create a regime of "egalitarianism" whose nominal democracy is merely a mask for the "Africanizing" of the southern working class. Belief in "equality" and "democracy" undermines public understanding of the importance of racial purity and stimulates Blacks to forward Legree's plan by raping and impregnating White women. The most significant victims of this campaign are the daughters of a poor White named Tom Camp, whose Uncle Tom–like adherence to Christianity prevents him from protecting or avenging his raped daughters.[74] Thus Dixon subjects Populists to a double discredit: their doctrine of egalitarianism fosters miscegenation, and the ultimate "purpose" (or paradoxical effect) of their movement is to subjugate the farmer to his arch-enemy, monopoly capitalism.

Legree's regime recreates in the South the same conditions of Black empowerment and race war that had existed under Reconstruction. A second "redemption" of the South is therefore required, and Dixon's hero, Gaston—a southerner of good birth and culture—will have to become both a vigilante/guerrilla (that is, a Klansman) and a revolutionary to achieve it. Although Gaston's cause is originally southern, the novel's development reveals its national significance. Gaston's Anglo-Saxon "racial fury" has been roused by a Negro's rape of Camp's youngest daughter. But Gaston's revenge produces a movement that finally awakens northerners to the Black menace: "You cannot build in a Democracy a nation inside a nation of two antagonistic races. The future American must be an Anglo-Saxon or a Mulatto."[75]

Gaston's second "redemption" is completed through a vindication of the vigilante principle embodied in the Klan: "Nations are made by men, not by paper constitutions and paper ballots."[76] American law is merely the enactment of the will of "the People," but only Anglo-Saxons are comprehended in that category. "This is a White man's government, conceived by White men, and maintained by White men through every year of its history—and by the God of our fathers it shall be ruled by White men until the archangel shall call the end of time." False democracy, which dogmatically asserts "equality," is replaced by true democracy, which is based on *race*. When northerners heed Gaston's message and begin to form their own Klans and to lynch Negroes, "The Anglo-Saxon race is united and has entered upon its world-mission."[77]

The outbreak of the Spanish–American War unites American Whites of North and South behind this new sense of mission:

> America, united at last and invincible, waked to the consciousness of her resistless power.
>
> And, most marvellous of all, this hundred days of war had re-united the Anglo-Saxon race. This sudden union of the English-speaking people in friendly alliance disturbed the equilibrium of the world, and confirmed the Anglo-Saxon in his title to racial sway.

Gaston seems likely to be a leading force in this movement, for his southern experience has enabled him to recognize the struggle as the opening gun of a universal war of color in which the races "like thousand-legged beasts" will meet in final conflict.[78]

The Clansman develops the vigilante myth more systematically and concisely than *The Leopard's Spots*. Dixon constructs *The Clansman* around a simple set of oppositions. As in *The Virginian*, sex and gender key our discrimination between the parties of right and wrong. The southern male hero is more virile and attractive than his northern counterparts, and the northern heroine (Elsie Stoneman) is wooed from her infatuation with the unnatural doctrines of racial equality (espoused by her father) by her desire to love and be loved by the manly southerner. Elsie's father, the leader of the Radicals, is physically deformed, which "explains" his hatred of the healthy southern male and his desire to cripple and deform the southern race through miscegenation. Only when his own daughter is threatened with enforced marriage to a mulatto and his own blood-line is threatened, does Stoneman recover some inkling of "natural" race-consciousness.

Dixon represents Black Reconstruction as both a historical aberration and a model of the fate that might befall civilization should Radical, "philanthropic," or egalitarian principles triumph. Because power has been given to a class that has no genius or capacity for real productivity, the Reconstruction governments become kleptocracies whose sole purpose and means of survival is to impose ruinous taxation on those who are productive: the Whites, and especially the former planters, in whom resides most of the region's managerial genius. Although the specific referent is historical, Dixon suggests that Reconstruction exhibits the defects of agrarian democracy and socialist systems (the kind advocated by turn-of-the-century radicals), and that in order to save themselves Americans must choose between the values of "Democracy" and the safety of "Civilization."[79]

The difference is fully articulated in a conversation between Stoneman and the southern leader, Dr. Cameron. Stoneman asserts the primacy of democratic ideology: "Manhood suffrage is the one eternal thing fixed in the nature of Democracy. . . . The Negro must be protected by the ballot. . . . The humblest man must have the opportunity to rise. The real issue is Democracy." Cameron replies, "The issue, sir, is Civilisation! Not whether the Negro shall be protected, but whether society is worth saving from barbarism." Cameron condemns Blacks as a "leprous" race whose touch is defiling, a "creature . . . half-child, half-animal," a "senile" race, like the Chinese in Roosevelt's "Strenuous Life," whose capacity for natural evolution has been exhausted. On the other hand, the White race is still in mid-career, and its youth suggests the nature of its mission. "There is a moral force at the bottom of every living race of men," and that of the Anglo-Saxon is to rule and command. The proof of this, says Cameron, is to be found in the struggles through which we achieved the winning of the West—his terms echo Roosevelt's:

> This Republic is great, not by reason of the amount of dirt we possess, the size of our census roll, or our voting register—we are great because of the genius of the race of pioneer white freemen who settled this continent, dared the might of kings, and made a wilderness the home of Freedom. Our future depends on the purity of this racial stock. The grant of the ballot to these millions of semi-savages and the riot of debauchery which has followed are crimes against human progress.[80]

To punish that crime and to deter the criminals from attempting to repeat the infamy, the best representatives of Anglo-Saxon virtue are permitted to use whatever instruments of violence they may need. The rise of the Ku Klux Klan is presented as a literal recrudescence of an ancient race-"civilization" from the threat of savagery, whose means of attack range from the jungle ambush to the "abuse" of the ballot box.[81]

The Political Uses of Symbolic Violence

The southern version of progressive myth and ideology differs from the national version in some important respects. The history from which southern ideology draws its signifying symbols is less engaged by the myths of the western Frontier than by the mystique of the Old South and the Lost Cause. The enactment of that ideology in politics produced a modernization process that was in many ways exceptional, particularly in its establishment and long-term maintenance of a Jim Crow racial regime. But these differences should not obscure the similarities with national progressivism. Page and Dixon sought to justify Jim Crow by appealing to a system of ideas developed by northern Progressive Republicans like Roosevelt and Wister, and some northern Progressives combined the southern myth and the Frontier Myth in their ideological program for subjugating their own "dangerous classes." The most significant expression of this tendency was the movement to limit the role of immigrants in politics and to halt, or radically restrict, immigration by peoples of "inferior" racial stock.

During his second term, President Roosevelt formed the U.S. Immigration Commission to consider the social and political problems presented by unrestricted immigration and to propose reforms. Roosevelt's disposition is suggested by his appointment of Jeremiah W. Jenks to head the Commission—a proponent of the "Nordic supremacy" theory and a leader of the Immigration Restriction League. But the Commission also employed John R. Commons, a Turnerian liberal.[82] Commons' report, *Races and Immigrants in America*, published in 1907 as a contribution to the beginning of Congressional debate on restriction, was reissued in 1920 when the last and most restrictive of the Progressive immigration bills was debated and passed.

Commons is "Turnerian" to the extent that he recognizes the potential crisis created by the closing of the Frontier; however, his insistence that the capacity to use resources progressively is an attribute of race rather than a universal gift of nature is pure Roosevelt.[83] His account of the basis of American prosperity is taken whole from *The Winning of the West*: the conquest of the wilderness is merely the most recent phase of the worldwide expansion of the Teutonic peoples.[84] The racial gifts of Americans are those of organization, executive ability, and above all "manliness, which the Romans called virility, and which at bottom is dignified self-respect, self-control, and that self-assertion and jealousy of encroachment which marks those who, knowing their rights, dare maintain them."

> These are the basic qualities which underlie democracy—intelligence, manliness, cooperation. If they are lacking, democracy is futile. Here is the problem of races, the fundamental division of mankind. Race differences are established in the very blood and physical constitution. They are most difficult to eradicate, and they yield only to the slow processes of the centuries. Races may change their religions, their forms of government, their mode of industry, and their languages, but underneath all these changes they may continue their physical, mental, and moral capacities and incapacities. . . .[85]

Commons follows Wister in revising the Declaration of Independence to assert that the prevalence of "true democracy" (equality of rights and opportunities) during the formative years of our history has merely allowed nature to take its course and produce a set of unequal classes whose different levels of achievement reflect different biological capacities. Now the weaker members of the original American stock have been joined by other races even less well endowed, the new immigrants and southern Negroes. These races are so fundamentally different from Anglo-Americans (or Teutonics) that their capacity for "manliness," productivity, and "Americanization" is extremely problematic. As industrial society becomes more complex and demanding, the unfit races/classes fall further behind. Breeding within communities segregated by ethnicity, race, class, and poverty, the incapable are becoming a permanent sub-race or "caste" of inferior genetic endowment.

Given the limitation of their racial gifts, their growing numbers—and the corresponding decline of the Anglo-American middle-class birth rate—constitutes a threat to the very basis of American national character and identity.[86] The problem becomes crucial in the Malthusian economy of a post-Frontier America, where any class's gain is another's loss. To protect *American* civilization, it will be necessary to restrict access to American resources and the levers of political power. Such discrimination and exclusion should not be arbitrary but should be based on a rational or scientific analysis of racial capacity.

Commons echoes *The Iron Heel* (published the following year) in suggesting that the United States may be evolving into "a class oligarchy or a race oligarchy" like that which already exists in the South. As if following the suggestions of Page and Dixon, Commons compares the corruption and political upheavals of urban political machines to the malfeasance and disorder of Black Reconstruction and finds that a common cause underlies both: the attempt to base a democratic government on the racially unfit under the guidance of spoilsmen and impractical idealists. If the southern example holds, we will have no practical choice but to "despotize our institutions in order to control these dissident elements."[87] Commons' southern analogy has particular force and resonance in light of the fact that serious and systematic movements to "despotize" southern politics had been underway for nearly a decade.

But the scenarios of extraordinary violence in the work of Remington, Wister, and Dixon were not taken as literal prescriptions for murder and genocide. Rather, the exaggerations of mythic violence prepared the public mind for the acceptance of a greater license for the use of *force* and *violence* against "dangerous" social elements. The effects of this preparation can be seen in the tendency of politicians and journalists to sympathize with the perpetrators of extraordinary acts of violence (for example, lynchings and massacres) committed against racial or cultural "aliens" during a political or economic crisis. The number and kind of groups regarded as proper targets of such "understandable" (if excessive) violence grew substantially during the "Progressive Era." Although Blacks remained the primary targets of lynching, between 1900 and 1925 other ethnic groups—particularly Jews, Italians, and Asians—were identified as legitimate targets for vigilantism, as were political dissidents and union organizers. In the industrial and commercial cities of the other sections, discriminatory legislation and administrative practices—sometimes buttressed by Klan or vigilante activities—limited the ability of immigrants to obtain naturalization, to organize unions, and to vote. These measures did not ultimately prevent White ethnic minorities from entering and gaining a share of power in the American political economy. Unlike African-Americans, Native Americans, and Hispanics, they were able to make use of the relative openness of the urban political system, to appeal (as fellow Whites) to traditional concepts of democracy and fair play, and finally to compel a revision of that tradition toward a new ideology of the democratic "melting pot." However, the discrimination these communities suffered was real and enduring, and they were unable to prevent invidious legislation against new immigrants from their homelands, or to protect themselves from the deportations and jailings—a form of official vigilantism—that accompanied the Red Scares of 1918–20 and 1948–52.

In part because of its identification with immigrants, unionized labor was subjected (1910–30) to new forms of discrimination and suppression. The use or support of spies, *provocateurs*, and strikebreakers became an important function of federal law enforcement during the Great War when the Wilson administration sought to suppress antiwar agitation and strikes that might affect war production. Judicial means were used to break up most of these movements and jail their leaders, but agents of the Wilson administration were also partly responsible for such illegal acts as the lynching of IWW organizer Frank Little in 1917. Wilson himself was sympathetic to the impulses and fears that produced southern lynching and viewed the Ku Klux Klan in much the same terms as did Thomas Dixon. For his part, Theodore Roosevelt—rejected for membership in the Dakota vigilantes in the 1880s because he was too hot-headed—helped form an organization whose purpose was to drive the corrupting presence of German culture from schools and concert halls and to push for American intervention against the Kaiser. The group was named "The Vigilantes."[88]

It is the nature of mythic symbolism to exaggerate, to read particulars as universals, to treat every conflict as Armageddon in microcosm. The primary social and political function of the *extraordinary* violence of myth is to sanction the *ordinary* violence of oppression and injustice, of brutalities casual or systematic, of the segregation, insult, or humiliation of targeted groups. And, as we shall see, when the nation faces a challenge from a power beyond its borders, the mythology of vigilantism reminds us that extraordinary violence by privileged heroes, often acting in despite of law, has been the means of our national salvation.

6 From the Open Range to the Mean Streets

Myth and Formula Fiction, 1910–1940

The writers of "red-blooded" fiction brought respectability to the materials and themes of the dime-novel adventure story, and their achievement was exploited in its turn by the writers of "pulp fiction"—a form of cheap literature named for the low-quality paper on which it was printed.[1] Like the dime novel, pulp novels and magazines developed series around particular heroes or story-types, but their repertoire was augmented by genres with distinctly twentieth-century subjects, like aviation and science fiction. The tale of frontier adventure retained its popularity, but it was now identified as "the Western," distinguishing it from other types of borderland adventure, such as the "Oriental" or "African" adventure set on the new frontiers of imperialism.[2]

Of the numerous genres of pulp fiction that were popular in the early part of this century, three have remained staples of cheap literature and have been successfully adapted to movies and television: the Western, the science fiction/fantasy, and the hard-boiled detective story. Although each has its own conventions of form and linguistic style, all three have roots in a common literary-mythic tradition; and their differentiation reflects the ramification and spread of that mythic tradition through modern mass culture.

Like the red-blooded novel, pulp fiction addressed the problem of adapting the traditional concept of democratic heroism, based on the Myth of the Frontier, to a post-Frontier America. Many of the most important of the early pulp writers were themselves the children of the middle-to-upper classes—the "quality"—but their audiences were of the "equality" (according to Wister's measure). Pulp heroes have many of the distinctive attributes of red-blooded "neo-aristocrats": they are "dominant" within their fictional worlds and supreme in fighting skills and sexual attractiveness. However, pulp heroes are not consistently assigned the specific attributes and functions of a contemporary ruling class. As often as not, their origins are unspecified, or are vaguely identified with "the People," the plots frequently have a distinctly "populist" bias against malefactors of great wealth. The pulp adaptation of red-blooded myth and ideology appealed to its audience by finding a way to re-confound the distinctions of class and heredity that Wister, Dixon, and the red-blooded social scientists had labored to define. The new mythic space of pulp fiction therefore became an imaginative equivalent to the old mythic space called "the Frontier." Within its boundaries the "equality" readership could imaginatively identify with the "quality" without consenting to class subordination and in the most appealing stories could even identify itself as possessing in the small the same virtues of "manhood" that the pulp hero displayed in the large.

Edgar Rice Burroughs: The Virginian in Outer Space, 1911–1925

Edgar Rice Burroughs is perhaps the most important of the pulp authors. His work has been consistently popular since his first book appeared in 1911, and much of it is still in print. "Tarzan of the Apes" has become a permanent addition to the language of Western culture, and Burroughs must also be credited as a seminal figure in the development of American science fiction. But Burroughs' most extraordinary attribute is his range: he worked in nearly every major pulp genre, including the Western, the spy story, the tropical or Oriental adventure, and science fiction/fantasy.[3] Other famous pulp writers tended to specialize in a particular genre or even a single character: Zane Grey and Max Brand wrote Westerns, Maxwell Grant produced the "Shadow" series, and the contributors to *Black Mask* wrote hard-boiled detective fiction. Burroughs' work is therefore the best place to see how the new pulp genres used the mythic traditions of the dime novel and red-blooded fiction in creating a new kind of mythic space for twentieth-century formula fiction.

Burroughs was born in 1875 in Chicago to an upper-middle-class family. His father, the owner of the American Battery Company (which manufactured automobiles), was a strict disciplinarian who thought his sons should work hard and strive for greater achievement. Burroughs was his youngest son, and the least reconciled to his father's regimen. His rebellion took the form of failure at school and work. He later described himself as an "escapist" who preferred dreams of fantastic adventure to reality. The "strenuous life" on the family's Idaho cattle ranch bored him; he was happier driving tourists around the World's Columbian Exposition (1893) in one of his father's demonstration models, savoring the technological fantasia of the White City and the make-believe Indian wars of Buffalo Bill's Wild West.[4] Custer was one of his boyhood heroes. The big illustrated biography by dime novelist Fred Whittaker represented the Boy General in terms Burroughs could recognize, as a rebellious schoolboy, always in trouble for fighting and practical jokes, who nonetheless lived a life of romantic adventure that culminated in a splendid and heroic act of sacrifice.[5]

In 1892 Burroughs enrolled at Michigan Military Academy, intending to major in "Cavalry." During his first year, the commandant of the school was General Charles King, the soldier-novelist who had captained Buffalo Bill's troop at Warbonnet Creek. While King knew Burroughs for only a year, and that unfavorably—as an unhappy and insubordinate freshman, guilty of "desertion"—Burroughs nonetheless regarded him as a mentor and wrote to him several times for advice and encouragement over the course of a dozen years.[6]

In 1896, after graduating from Michigan Military and failing the entrance exam for West Point, Burroughs enlisted in the 7th Cavalry as a private. His romantic expectations were undone by the squalid life at Fort Grant, Arizona Territory, and by the convict-labor of road-making that occupied most of the regiment's time. After less than a year (and a bout with dysentery), Burroughs wrote home begging his father to use money or influence to get him out of his enlistment, which was done.[7]

But with the demoralizing reality of Fort Grant behind him, his dream of military glory revived; only now he understood it would be best to be an officer. Between 1898 and 1906 he made several attempts to realize this dream. But his application to join Roosevelt's Rough Riders in 1898 was turned down, and he refused the opportunity to enlist in the Idaho regiment then forming for service in the Philippines because he felt himself a "better" man than his company commander. In 1902 he inquired about rejoining the 7th Cavalry in Samar, currently famed as the scene of General Smith's "marked severities," and sought a command in the Chinese army then being reformed under foreign officers in the aftermath of the Boxer Rebellion.[8] But all these attempts to enter the world of Indian-fighting and imperial warfare ended in failure, and Burroughs spent the years between 1898 and 1911 working by turns as a railroad-yard cop, a door-to-door salesman, head of the Sears, Roebuck stenographic department, and a construction supervisor—never prospering or holding any job for very long. At last he decided to make fantasy his life's work. The success of his first fiction—*Under the Moons of Mars* (1911), reissued as *A Princess of Mars* (1912)—proved that he could support his family by writing, and he pursued that career with devotion, energy, and success until his death in 1950.[9]

Although his experiences had acquainted him with the reality of cowboy life and military service, Burroughs' literary fantasies found their primary sources of inspiration, and their world of reference, in other peoples' books. Burroughs' "indebtedness" to other writers sometimes smacked of plagiarism, as in his recasting of Anthony Hope's *The Prisoner of Zenda* (*The Mad King*, 1914).[10] But the most important of his borrowings involved a highly imaginative processing and integration of the themes and styles of a number of romantic and red-blooded writers. Among the influences he later acknowledged were Rudyard Kipling, Charles King, Owen Wister, and Jack London. Burroughs appears to have known Remington's work for *Harper's Weekly* in the 1890s. Jules Verne's influence shows in Burroughs' technological and hollow-earth fantasies, and H. Rider Haggard's tales of lost White races in the African jungle influenced the Tarzan books.[11]

Burroughs once said that he read nothing but fiction as a youth and nothing but works of history and science as a man. Although he became an enthusiast for both serious and popular works in these areas, his approach to nonfiction was shaped by the same concerns and themes that informed his reading of fiction. He moved from novelistic fantasies of racial strife and progressive conquest to the literature of Social Darwinism and the historical and anthropological literature that applied the theory of evolution to human affairs. He was already committed to belief in the social application of the "survival of the fittest" dogma when he read Darwin's *Origins of Species* in 1899. As an avid student of mythology he may have known at first- or second-hand the work of Lewis Henry Morgan and James George Frazer. But his anthropology was primarily based on popularized versions of Aryan or Nordic theories which traced the evolution of the several modern European (or superior) races from a pure and primal master-race. He certainly admired Theodore Roosevelt as a public figure, and it seems likely that he knew *The Winning of the*

West—the imaginary history of Burroughs' "Barsoom" (Mars) parallels Roosevelt's account of the rise, decline, and rebirth of the great "fighting races." His work after 1916 was directly influenced by the work of two racialist historians: Madison Grant, *The Passing of the Great Race* (1916); and Theodore Lothrop Stoddard, *The Rising Tide of Color Against White World Supremacy* (1920) and *The Revolt Against Civilization* (1922).[12]

Burroughs' genius was to find in these various sources the paradigmatic elements that unite them into a coherent world view and, having found the paradigm, to invent new and more attractive ways of framing them for a large popular audience.[13] The thread that links his preferred fiction to his taste in science and pseudoscience is the theme of the White man's adventure in the wilderness and his struggle to master savage nature and savage men—the theme of the Myth of the Frontier.

Burroughs' relationship to the work of Grant and Stoddard is interesting, because it reveals the ways in which ideological polemics are received and used by mass-culture artists. Their common sources are the basic books of the progressive myth/ideology, the "Darwinist" social science of Sumner and Spencer, the historiography of Roosevelt, and red-blooded fiction.[14] Grant and Stoddard merged Roosevelt's historiography with the lingo of Darwinian "science" to project apocalyptic scenarios of worldwide race-war, which were used in their political campaigns for White supremacy, immigration restriction, and eugenics. Burroughs developed similar scenarios from the same material but projected them into a succession of fantasy-worlds and imagined a range of possible resolutions for the apocalyptic course of American and race history.

Grant was a wealthy amateur anthropologist, a friend of Theodore Roosevelt and with him a founding father of the Boone and Crockett Club and the American Museum of Natural History in New York (where some of the big game he killed can be seen, stuffed and mounted in the display cases of the North American Mammals room). A minister's son, Stoddard earned a doctorate in social science. His dissertation on the *The French Revolution in Santo Domingo*, published as a book in 1914, identified the Haitian revolution as the first act in a worldwide "conflict of color" that would be "the fundamental problem of the twentieth century."[15] Grant and Stoddard were active participants in the contemporary academic debate between racists and culturalists in the fields of sociology, anthropology, psychology, and genetics. But the main purpose of their books was to shape public opinion. Their political influence was considerable. They were leaders of the eugenics movement, whose legislative initiatives contributed to the network of laws and attitudes that sustained segregation. They were also leading figures in the Immigration Restriction League during its victorious legislative campaigns (1917–24).[16]

Grant and Stoddard see world history as merely the lengthened shadow of an eternal and unremitting war of "colors." Civilization itself, as the highest expression of man's potential, is the unique product of the White race: "When I say 'Man,' " says Stoddard, "I mean the White Man"—and civilization has developed and expanded through the White conquest of the Colored world: the "Lands" of Africa, Asia, the Near East, and the Americas, which produced the Black, Yellow, Brown, and Red Races. "The white man could think, could create, could fight superlatively well. No wonder the redskins and negroes feared and adored him as a god, while the somnolent races of the Farther East offered no effective opposition." They agreed with Roosevelt in seeing the American conquest of the frontier as part of this "world-wide expansion of the white race during the four centuries between 1500 and 1900 . . . the most prodigious phenomenon in all recorded history."[17]

The White/Colored distinction in the world at large is matched by distinctions within the White race between superior and inferior types. Grant and Stoddard take pains to distinguish "Nordics" from darker Whites ("Alpines" and "Mediterraneans"), adopting a more restrictive definition of the superior race than either Roosevelt's "Teutons" or Wister's "Anglo-Saxons." Nonetheless, the qualities that distinguish their Nordics are the classic "gifts" of the progressive race-hero: "a race of soldiers, sailors, adventurers and explorers, but above all of rulers, organizers and aristocrats."[18] Like Roosevelt, they emphasize the superiority of the White American racial stock, which has been highly "selected" from the best of the Nordic peoples:

> The colonial stock was perhaps the finest that nature had evolved since the classic Greeks. It was the very pick of the Nordics of the British Isles and adjacent regions of the European continent—picked at a time when those countries were more Nordic than now.[19]

The purity of American Nordics had been defended by "outer" and "inner dikes": the outposts of empire, which subdued the Colored Lands; and the legal impediments to immigration and race-mixing, which protected Nordic purity at home. But these "dikes" have been breached by a combination of capitalist greed—which imported slaves and non-Nordic immigrants as cheap labor and exported industrial technology to the Colored World—and democratic ideology, which undermines racial instinct with false doctrines of equality.[20] In addition, the commercial rivalry of the Great Powers fosters "civil wars" among the Whites that will allow the Colored races to escape subjection. Thus (in the words of Stoddard's and Grant's most popular titles) the "Rising Tide of Color Against White World Supremacy," coupled with the dilution of Nordic purity through democracy and immigration ("race suicide"), may end in "the Passing of the Great Race" and the fall of civilization as "we" know it.[21]

Given its gifts for dominance and exclusivity, how could the Great Race have succumbed to the intellectual seductions of democracy and the physical temptation of miscegenation? Grant and Stoddard augment Roosevelt's vague account of past episodes of White degeneration with an elaborate theory of the "psychological" factors that underlie racial conflict and degeneration. This theory codifies and modernizes (and caricatures) a set of beliefs that had been implicit in the racialist mythology of the Frontier Myth almost from the start. Puritan writers had seen the Indian as the incarnation of devilish propensities inherent in sinful human flesh; romantic writers from Cooper to Melville had seen dark-skinned peoples as incarnations of the "dark" side of human character, embodiments of both the poetic creativity and the erotic peril of the libido. Stoddard translates this metaphor of psychic and social dualisms into his own language of race/class difference. He sees our human nature divided into elements corresponding to Nordic qualities (the "Over-Man") and Colored qualities (the "Under-Man"): "The basic attitude of the Under-Man is an instinctive and natural *revolt against civilization*."

> Each of us has within him an "Under Man," that primitive animality which is the heritage of our human, and even our prehuman, past. The Under-Man may be buried deep in the recesses of our being; but he is there, and psychoanalysis informs us of his latent power. This primitive animality potentially present even in the noblest natures, continuously dominates the lower social strata, especially the pauper, criminal, and degenerate elements—civilization's "inner barbarians." Now, when society's dregs boil to the top . . . in virtually every member of the community there is a distinct resurgence of the brute and the savage, and the atavistic trend thus becomes practically universal.[22]

Our susceptibility to democratic dogma is merely the political expression of our susceptibility to "The Lure of the Primitive." The

Bolshevik Revolution is just such a boiling-up of the "inner barbarian." Its leaders are "half-breeds," of mixed European and Jewish bloods, who have fought and won a war of extermination against the Russian aristocracy and now envision a similar war against White world supremacy.[23] The end product of democracy and socialism will be a "cacocracy," in which the "fecal classes," the "ordure of humanity," constitute political society.[24] Grant specifies the political lesson to be drawn from Wister's assertion that "true aristocracy" and "true democracy" are the same thing: "True aristocracy or a true republic is governed by the wisest and best, always a small minority of the population."[25]

In the past, the effects of racial decline were overcome by the existence of "sane [White] barbarians," racially pure and committed to "the basic truth that inequality and not equality is the law of nature."[26] Racial vigor and purity could be regenerated either through a conquest of civilization by these barbarians, or through the regression to barbarism that occurs when a new frontier is opened (as in Roosevelt's *The Winning of the West*). But in a thoroughly metropolitanized world, these possibilities are foreclosed. Hence the Great Race must win the present struggle or vanish from the earth:

> "Finally perish!" That is the exact alternative which confronts the white race. For white civilization is to-day coterminous with the white race. The civilizations of the past were local . . . confined to a particular people or group of peoples. If they failed there were always some unspoiled, well-endowed barbarians to step forward and "carry on." But to-day *there are no more white barbarians*. The earth has grown small, and men are everywhere in close touch. If white civilization goes down, the white race is irretrievably ruined . . . carrying with it to the grave those potencies upon which realization of man's highest hopes depends.[27]

Although their apocalyptic fulminations made Grant and Stoddard influential as advocates in immigration restriction, the regime they envisioned for a frontier-less White America was too radical to attract a wide following. They demanded acceptance of a eugenic regime that put both "true love" and family structure under the governing oversight of genetic science. Their implicitly genocidal approach to birth control required the use of forced sterilization and other measures to achieve "the obliteration of the unfit," for "human life is valuable only when it is of use to the community or race." They equated democracy with "the suicidal ethics which are exterminating [their] own race" and urged (in Commons' phrase) a "despotization" of American institutions to guarantee recognition of "privilege of birth" and "privilege of wealth" as legitimate entitlements to rule.[28]

Burroughs' imagination was powerfully affected by the ideas of Grant and Stoddard. He shared their racial anxieties, used their color symbolism and race-historical scenarios, and even followed their vision of race-heroism to the extreme point of speculating "what a humanitarian Hitler might accomplish for Germany and the world."[29] But he would not be bound by the Malthusian logic that reduced the Great Race's choices to extinction or eugenic repression. If Earth has lost its regenerative barbarian wildernesses, then Burroughs' heroes find new ones in outer space or at the Earth's core or in the latent "savagery" of their own nature. Where Stoddard fears and wishes to repress the "inner barbarian" who succumbs to the "lure of the primitive," Burroughs sees the inner barbarian as the repository of the racial energy that will sustain, and if need be regenerate, the hegemony of the Great Race.[30]

A Princess of Mars shows Burroughs at his imaginative best, beginning his exploration of the themes that most concerned him. The story is told by its hero, "Captain John Carter," whose body is now entombed but whose manuscript has come into the hands of his "uncle," Burroughs. Carter's crypt is designed to open only from the inside, for the hero expects that he will soon be resurrected; from the manuscript we learn that he has indeed risen from the dead once before. Putting this together with his initials (J.C.) and Burroughs' tendency to describe his arrival anywhere as an "advent," we should not be surprised to learn that Carter is also a kind of Messiah—not on Earth, but on Mars, which is known to its people as "Barsoom." Carter's origins are also superhuman: he was apparently born full-grown (like Athena) and thus has never been anything other than a fully developed adult male; nor does he show any signs of aging. If he is a Christ-figure, he brings peace only by the sword. He is not the son of a common carpenter but a scion of the Virginia aristocracy who follows the profession of arms in the spirit of the age of chivalry. As an antebellum planter, he was the perfect patriarch, whose "slaves fairly worshipped the ground he trod." He has also been a professional soldier, serving the Confederacy and the armies of three foreign republics and one empire (probably Maximilian's in Mexico).[31]

Carter, then, is the perfect embodiment of the virtues of the White race as represented in the Myth of the Frontier, "red-blooded" fiction, and the social science of Roosevelt, Grant, and Stoddard. He is an adult among the childish races (who worship him), a knight among hinds. He is not merely a Virginian like Cooper's Duncan Heyward, or "the Virginian" like Wister's hero: he is *The* Virginian, the type abstracted into an allegorical absolute. The virtues that in Stoddard's Nordics are merely god-like become in Carter the attributes of something like a man-god.

But although Carter clearly embodies the "masterful" qualities of the Anglo-Saxon, Burroughs also links his heredity to the American Indians. As a descendant of the First Families of Virginia he is not ashamed to include the blood of Pocahontas in his lineage, and he has lived with the Sioux as a warrior among warriors.[32] Thus Carter is a "man who knows Indians." This will allow him to understand the savage thought processes of Barsoomian cultures and to fall passionately in love with the red-skinned Martian princess, Dejah Thoris. But though his bloodline is mixed in one sense, it is pure in the only sense that matters: both sides of his ancestry derive from races whose love of war and honor is distinctly "archaic."[33] Hence even his "Under-Man" has heroic attributes; and when he reverts to his most primitive instincts, his character as a progressive hero is not degenerated (as Stoddard would have it) but *regenerated.*

Burroughs begins Carter's adventure by deliberately locating it in relation to the Myth of the Frontier. In a world made peaceful by the growth of the great civilized nations, Carter decides to prospect for gold in Arizona, not because he needs money but because Apache country is one of the few places left in which he can exercise his talents—albeit on a meaner scale than he has known. This last and most diminished of frontiers sees Carter's power shrink to the smallest possible compass: his partner is killed and he himself is cornered in a cave. As the Apaches close in, he falls into a death-like trance and his spirit rises out of his body. He sees the planet Mars and prays to it as symbol of the War God he has served all his life.

When Carter awakes he finds himself in a desert of reddish sand, which he mistakes for Arizona until his capture by a gigantic, six-armed Green Martian tells him that he has somehow been transported to the Red Planet. Barsoom itself is an oddly distorted mirror-image of Earth in which the symbolism by which we have interpreted our passage through historical time is reflected back to us in an "alien" disguise. Barsoom is divided into realms ruled by beings of different color and shape, in ways that anticipate Grant and Stoddard's division of the world into "White Man's Land," "Black Man's Land," "Yellow Man's Land," and so on. Each realm is protected by defensive "dikes" and canals which divide the race-realms and nourish a dying planet. However, on Barsoom racial difference is exaggerated into something more like *species* difference.[34]

The first two races Carter meets define the range of difference and the inevitability of "savage war" that results from it. The Green Martians of the Red Planet correspond to the redskinned Apaches of Earth, the Green Planet; the highest Barsoomian race, which corresponds to the white-skins on Earth, are the Red Martians. All Martians are warlike, to such an extent that they almost never die a natural death. But the Red Martians are also civilized: they have a high technology, a literary culture, a code of laws, and an innate sense of fair play. They respect the sanctity of the nuclear family and of private property. And they are capable of romantic love. The Green Martians fit the general stereotype of Indians as elaborated in works like *The Winning of the West* and are described in passages that paraphrase Cremony's *Life Among the Apache* (1868). They are cruel by nature, enjoy inflicting torture, are incapable of feeling love, abhor manual labor, and carry tribalism to the extreme point of communism—they have no private property and no nuclear families.[35] The exception is Tars Tarkas, the only Green Martian who has known a mother's love. Though this compromises the purity of his racial gifts, it allows him to play Chingachgook to Carter's Hawkeye throughout the series.[36]

The primal oppositions of the Frontier Myth, and of the imperial ideology that succeeded it, are thus preserved on Mars. But the usual color-coding is altered. A simple color reversal identifies Red Planet greenskins with Green Planet redskins. The first white-skins Carter meets are the six-armed White Apes, whose color is that of Earth's master-race but whose qualities are those stereotypically identified with earthly Blacks. This pattern of reversal is repeated in *The Gods of Mars* (the second novel in the series), in which a degenerate white-skinned race is harassed and enslaved by black-skinned air-Vikings. The only Barsoomian race whose color and character correspond directly to their earthly equivalent is the Yellow Race in *Warlord of Mars*, whose qualities are consistent with those of Oriental racial stereotypes.[37]

Burroughs also invents a history of Barsoom in which the themes and premises of racialist historiography are allegorized. The present races of Mars are the more-and-less degenerate successors of an original White Race, whose characteristics (like those attributed to Teutons, Anglo-Saxons, and Nordics) were those of a military nobility. This Great Race perished because of an excess of the very virtue that made them masters of their world: an insatiable appetite for combat. Their numbers diminished by incessant warfare, their blood vitiated by intermarriage with lesser racial breeds whom they conquered, the White Barsoomians are eventually overwhelmed by the colored races they themselves begat and empowered. These include the savage Green Martians, the Yellow Race, and a degenerate White Race. The White Race is devoted to religious fanaticism and is subjected to the will of a race of airship-riding Black Vikings—a striking inversion of the qualities attributed to White and Black on Earth.

The Red Race is the closest to the original uncorrupted Whites in gifts and capacities. Like the "American race" in Roosevelt's history, the Red Martians are a mixture of the best and most warlike elements of the White and certain other Martian races. (Burroughs is clear about the fact of mixture, vague on the specifics.) But even the Red Race represents a decline from the power of the original Whites. Racial decline is mirrored in the environment: Mars is a dying planet whose very air must be manufactured in an Atmosphere Factory. Martian life thus exaggerates the Malthusian conditions of a closed or closing frontier dependent on a factory system and cut off from the regenerative power of unspoiled and untapped Nature. Instead of open frontiers, Martians gaze out across irrigation dikes that circumscribe dwindling arable districts and define a world in which one race's gain must be another's loss.

Carter brings with him the promise of both racial and planetary regeneration. His role approximates that of a lone Cortez on an Aztec planet: his white skin and extraordinary powers lead the natives to revere him as the returning form of a god (or superhuman figure) who left them eons ago. The difference is that Carter proves worthy of their trust. He will emerge through his adventures as the Jeddak of Jeddaks, the "Warlord of Warlords"—as one might say, the King of Kings—of Barsoom. Through his victories and his marriage to Dejah Thoris, the best woman of the Red Race, he will ensure the planet's domination by its most progressive race. Since Carter is himself "White" and embodies the best qualities of the original White Race of Mars, the mingling of his bloodline with hers suggests the renewal of the Red Race's tie to its "Aryan" origins. Like the "White barbarians" in Roosevelt's and Grant's race-histories, the Red Race is regenerated by being reconnected to its White Barsoomian origins. And, since the Reds are "savages" from Carter's perspective, his marriage to their Princess restores his attenuated connection to his own primal nature.

Dejah Thoris is Burrough's solution to the classic "miscegenation" problem of American literary mythology. Like Cooper's Cora Munro in *Last of the Mohicans*, she combines the sensuous and erotic appeal of the "dark woman" with the spiritual gifts of the White or "redemptive" woman. Burroughs' first description of her follows so closely the paradigm of the "tragic mulatto" embodied in Cooper's Cora as to argue direct influence. The racial heritage of Cora is half-concealed behind the negative statement that her complexion was "not brown" and did not show any "want of coloring"—that is, the inability to blush, which was taken as the biological sign of shamelessness in non-Whites. Her hair is "shining and black, like the plumage of the raven," and her "dark eye" is captured by the naked body of a savage. Although her costume seeks to conceal and control her sensuous and womanly character, the sexuality of her "finely moulded" figure continually asserts itself and arouses lust in Indian men (though not in White). Though morally innocent, she is betrayed by her racial/sexual nature, the "rich blood" which seems to "burst its bounds."[38]

The "dark" sexuality that is Cora's dirty secret becomes fully explicit in Dejah Thoris. Carter does not have to surmise her shape through her costume: she appears completely naked and is both frankly non-White and frankly sexual:

> Her features were finely chiseled and exquisite, her eyes large and lustrous and her head surmounted by a mane of coal black, waving hair, caught loosely in a strange yet becoming coiffure. Her skin was of a light reddish copper color, against which the crimson glow of her cheeks and the ruby of her beautifully molded lips shone with a strangely enhancing effect.
>
> She was as destitute of clothes as the green Martians who accompanied her; indeed, save for her highly wrought ornaments, she was entirely naked, nor could any apparel have enhanced the beauty of her perfect and symmetrical figure. (pp. 45–6)

Women of this kind are destroyed in novels of the Cooper tradition, because they tempt the White hero to a miscegenate union that would compromise the White and civilized character of the new American nation. In the thinking of Dixon, Grant, and Stoddard they are demonic presences, because their erotic appeal rouses the Under-Man within the Nordic psyche and tempts him into unions that spell racial suicide. But Burroughs has a different scenario of racial regeneration in mind, which requires the White hero to recover his racial potential for "fighting and breeding" through the recognition and realization of his latent potential for "savagery." Such a hero requires a fully sexualized woman as his counterpart and "rescue-object," because she excites the fighter/breeder in him. She is non-White because sexuality (in the language of American myth) has been coded as racially "dark."[39] But having established her as a symbol of regenerative primitivism, Burroughs then proceeds to "Whiten" her by making her the rescue-object in a classic Indian captivity scenario. Carter meets her when both are being held captive by the savage Green Martians, and he will prove his heroism and earn her love by rescuing her from captivity—a plot device that is endlessly repeated throughout the series.

Thus Dejah Thoris is a perfect reconciliation of the contradictory values attached to women in the Frontier Myth. Her Indian qualities make her an appropriate object for the indulgence of erotic fantasies, while her aristocratic lineage and status as both virgin and Indian captive identify her as a "redemptive" White woman and an appropriate mate for the White hero. Burroughs even makes her (and her species) oviparous, so that she does not have to make a choice between Roosevelt's twin imperatives of fighting and breeding.

Burroughs was a prolific and inventive writer, and it is difficult to do justice to the variety of his work in any brief summary. Some of his series played through dozens of books, others through only one or two. Although most are built around distinctive imaginary worlds, Burroughs liked to have characters from one series show up in another—partly for variety, partly for advertisement, and partly to foster the oddly effective illusion that the series were somehow part of a larger system and were mutually authenticating. The recurrent theme in his fantasies is the Darwinian play of racial struggle as the shaping force of history. His most popular series, *Tarzan of the Apes* (1912 *et seq.*), is an extended Darwinian parable, the argument of which is the absolute primacy of heredity over environment in shaping individual and racial development.

Burroughs' treatments of racialist themes became more systematic and polemical between 1915 and 1925. The Great War made Burroughs a rabid anti-Prussian and a foe of immigration—particularly after the Russian Revolution led him to suspect that every immigrant carried the "bacillus" of Bolshevism.[40] Most of his on-going series touch on the Great War, but the racial stakes of the conflict are the central themes in *Beyond Thirty* (1915), *The Land Time Forgot* series (1917–18), and—most significantly—the *Moon Maid* trilogy (1922).[41]

Burroughs saw the Bolshevik revolution as a movement more threatening to the survival of Western civilization than the victory of the hated Huns. His first fictional diatribe against Bolshevism, "Under the Red Flag," (1919) was rejected by several publishers. Under the influence of Stoddard's *Revolt Against Civilization* (1922), he recast the story as a science-fiction trilogy and achieved immediate success.[42] *The Moon Maid* (1922) begins fifty years after the Great War in a world now completely civilized and peaceful under Anglo-Saxon hegemony. But the Great Race, forgetting the inherent wisdom of its warrior instincts, is persuaded by sentimental idealists and egalitarian populists to accept universal disarmament—an implicitly degenerate decision that will expose Earth to conquest by subhuman Kalkars from the Moon.[43] The heroes of the trilogy, which spans nearly a millennium, are all named "Julian": in effect, the Julians are a race of heroes, since each is the virtual reincarnation of the original. In *The Moon Maid* Julian V voyages to the Moon, where his adventures parallel those of John Carter but end in disaster. He must rescue his princess from the destruction of her civilization by an uprising of Lunar Under-Man led by a traitorous Earthman named Orthis. Julian V attempts to warn Earth of an impending Lunar invasion, but is ignored. When Julian IX takes up the story in *The Moon Men* Earth has been ruled by the Kalkars for four generations and the achievements of Anglo-Saxon civilization have been undone.

The Kalkars combine the traits of several different rivals to the Great Race. They are blond and fair, which links them to the hated "Huns" of Burroughs' wartime fiction; but their other traits draw more directly on stereotypes of American Blacks and the "lower sort" of immigrant. Their "calculating" intelligence is a common feature in anti-Semitic stereotypes, particularly those invoked by Grant and Stoddard.[44] Kalkar ideology and government are parodies of communism or socialism and of the program of organized labor in general. The demand for the eight-hour day is met by permission to work only four whenever the worker "felt like it," and the demand for democracy produces a system in which workers spend so much time "making new laws" that production ceases. Resentment of management is pandered to by a campaign that exterminates the engineers and technical experts—"the more intelligent class of earthmen."[45] Even after the passage of generations, the class conflicts that divided and weakened the Great Race persist in the hackneyed recriminations that the descendants of ruined managers and ruined workers hurl at each other—managers blaming workers for succumbing to the "Brotherhood" doctrine, workers echoing Roosevelt's accusation of the wealthy classes as "too rich and lazy and indifferent to vote . . . while they waxed fat off our labor."[46]

However, the primary model for Burroughs' Kalkar/communism is not socialist Russia but the "Black Legend" of Reconstruction as promulgated by Thomas Dixon. Like the "tainted geniuses" of Radical Reconstruction (for example, Stoneman), Orthis has created a society in which an inferior and indeed subhuman race rules over a superior one. Since the inferior is incapable of real productivity, it can maintain its power only by forcibly subjugating the superior race, depriving it of education, and imposing a confiscatory tax on its productivity. As a result, industrial production ceases and technological civilization falls into ruinous decline. The Kalkars preside over the ruins with a carpetbagger-style government complete with shinplaster currency, a corrupt militia, and regular sexual assaults on White women. The Whites have become the "niggers" and even the slaves of these "brutes." White "marriages had long since become illegal" so that Kalkars could have their "pick of our young women and girls."[47]

The primal energies of the Great Race still lurk in the genes of White Americans and display themselves in childhood rebelliousness and play—although "the brotherhood of man had almost . . . kill[ed] the spirit of childhood."[48] That spirit survives in great strength in the children of the Julian line, as does race pride. Despite his training, Julian IX has "manhood" enough to resent Kalkar tyranny and to express himself in terms like those of Dixon's Doctor Cameron:

> My God! I cannot stand it. I shall go mad if I must submit longer to such humiliation. I am no longer a man. There are no men! We are worms that the swine grind into the earth with their polluted hoofs. . . . I stood there while the offspring of generations of menials and servants insulted me and spat upon me and I dared say nothing but meekly to propitiate him. . . . In a few generations they have sapped the manhood from American men. My ancestors fought at Bunker Hill, at Gettysburg, at San Juan, at Chateau Thierry. And I? I bend this knee to every degraded creature that wears the authority of the beasts at Washington—and not one of them is an American—scarce one of them an earth man. To the scum of the moon I bow my head—I who am one of the few survivors of the most powerful people the world ever knew."[49]

Julian IX mounts a revolt whose ideological basis is cultic reverence for the only two symbols that can still unite American Whites: the Flag, and White womanhood. But the power of the Kalkars and their allies (the descendants of Orthis) is too great. Julian IX perishes in yet another "last stand" after vindicating the sacred principle of "manhood" and passing his genes on to another generation.

In the last book of the trilogy, *The Red Hawk* (1925), this genetic heritage finally triumphs. The Kalkars' ineptitude has destroyed civilization, and each race reverts to its barbarous origins. This restores the advantage to the Americans, whose genetic endowment is superior. A war of extermination ends in the slaying of the last of the Kalkars by the last of the Julians, "the Red Hawk." He then marries a daughter of the last Orthis, and their marriage reconciles the divisions that destroyed the Great Race. The precondition for this regenerative violence and the full restoration of American "manhood" is the regression of the Julians and their race to a savage condition, like that of the "sane" and "pure" White barbarians in the histories of Grant and Stoddard. But the form of Julian's regression is not Germanic or Saxon—it is American Indian. In reverting to his "origins," in recovering the energy of his "inner barbarian," the American goes back to the savagery of his own peculiar myth of origins—the Myth of the Frontier.[50]

What is gained by Burroughs' transformation of ideological polemics into the terms and conventional imagery of literary mythology is the power to reconcile the contradiction between a fundamentally undemocratic vision of politics and political reform and the conventional pieties of democratic liberalism. Stoddard and Grant are compelled by the logic of their argument to advocate a series of discomforting positions: the puritanical repression of sexual passion and the desire for sensual gratification (an uncomfortable doctrine in a society based on consumerism); abandonment of the canonical rhetoric of American republicanism in favor of frankly aristocratic doctrines; acceptance of the moral principle that war is a higher good than peace, and intolerance better than tolerance; and the adoption of a eugenic regime repellent to both traditional religion and the mystique of romantic love. Burroughs is able to get his readers to identify with his *übermenschen* because he frames the emergence of his neo-aristocracy as the consummation of an adventurous insurgency, an escape from or rebellion against a metropolis based on Malthusian economics and oligarchic politics. This insurgency is both psychosexual and political: it allows the hero to enjoy the fantasies of erotic love, married love, and mother love across racial (and even species) lines, to indulge liberal sentiments of tolerance, and to overthrow a tyrannous political order. But these insurgent passions and liberal impulses can be enjoyed without suggesting that race-mixing and revolution are a "good thing." The adventures occur in a place outside history, the marriages are always motivated by the need to regenerate the powers of a "high" race (like the marriage of the Virginian and Molly Wood), and the rebellions are always against a tyranny in which "Under-Men" or nonhumans rule their racial betters. Indeed, the Burroughs formula allows the reader the double satisfaction of affiliating with an ethic of tolerance while enjoying the violent expression of racialist antipathies.

Although the worlds of Burroughs' pulp fantasies began as extensions of the mythic space of the Frontier Myth, Burroughs' way of reproducing the Myth transforms its character. Burroughs abstracts the essential structures and symbols of the Myth from their original "historical" context. This allows him to project an almost limitless range of possible resolutions to the historical scenario envisioned by the Myth—to adapt the myth to shifts of political concern and mood—while retaining enough of the ideas and images made familiar in the original to lend credibility and resonance to the most fantastic variations.

Burroughs' procedure is not unique. It is characteristic of the adaptation of nineteenth-century mythic traditions in twentieth-century mass culture. A similar kind of abstraction even characterizes the genre that is most continuous with the traditions of the dime novel and frontier romance: the pulp Western, whose seminal author is Zane Grey. Although Grey's "West" is rich in references to western landscape and to particular periods of regional history, his themes, images, and characterizations have as much or more in common with Burroughs' Barsoom as with the "real West" of Wister's *Virginian*.

Zane Grey: The Formula Western, 1911–1925

Zane Grey is perhaps the most popular Western writer of all time. His most popular novel, *Riders of the Purple Sage* (1912), sold over a million copies in its hardcover edition. Only once between 1915 and 1924 did he fail to place a book among the top ten annual best-sellers, and much of his work is still in print. Generations of successful pulp and paperback Western writers, from Max Brand in the 1930s to Louis Lamour in the postwar period, imitated his style and story-forms.[51]

Grey's knowledge of the Frontier was almost entirely literary. He was born in Ohio in 1872, where his ancestors had come as settlers at the end of the eighteenth century. Stories of his pioneer heritage undoubtedly intrigued him, but they did not influence his choice of career. His adolescence and early manhood were spent in New York City, where he studied and practiced dentistry, played baseball, and dreamed of becoming a writer. He did not go west until he was in his 30s, and then he went as a tourist, hitting scenic high spots like the Grand Canyon and sampling a "dude ranch" version of the strenuous life. His West had few attributes of the Frontier: where Roosevelt had hunted the last of the wild buffalo, Grey labored to preserve the species from extinction by crossing them with domestic cattle.[52]

Grey's knowledge of the Frontier came from an amalgam of family legends, the "forest" romances of Cooper and Bird, dime novels, and the "cowboy" stories of Wister.[53] But unlike Cooper and the red-blooded novelists, Grey is not concerned to develop a historiographical or racial theory. For him, the central symbols of the myth/ideological system are not representations of real-world values and conflicts but literary properties whose meaning is established by well-understood conventions. And since he usually has no stake, either personal or ideological, in the outcome of the struggles he depicts—Indians vs. Whites, rustlers vs. cattlemen, Mormons vs. Gentiles—he is able to play freely with some of the most basic myth/ideological conventions, including politically loaded categories like race and sex.[54]

The Zane Grey Western usually features a "White woman" of wealth and "high" birth; a wealthy and powerful villain, whose conspiracies enmesh her and threaten her inheritance; and a wandering mysterious stranger bent on private vengeance, whose purposes converge with the "White woman's" needs. The problem is usually resolved through the hero's use of some spectacular act of violence, which is morally redemptive because it rescues the "White woman" (who then accepts the hero as lover and husband). The "conspiracy" is often a simple matter of big ranchers cheating small ones, or of malevolent relatives defrauding proper heirs of their inheritance. Yet many of the books have vague but ominous political overtones, as in the combination of corporate greed with religious fanaticism in *Riders of the Purple Sage* (1912), and the alliance of Imperial German espionage with IWW radicalism in *The Desert of Wheat* (1919). This basic plot structure was already a staple of cheap literature when Grey began using it, but his gift for inventing variations on the theme made the formula a literary program through which he could run all sorts of characters, settings, and situations.

His first two novels, *Heritage of the Desert* and *Riders of the Purple Sage*, set the pattern. *Heritage of the Desert* (1911) introduces us to a West that is as strangely formed and peopled as Burroughs' Barsoom. Grey's is a tourist's West; there is no ordinary terrain, only scenic attractions—hidden valleys and secret springs, freakish rock-forms, queer pinnacles of twisted red and yellow rock. Its inhabitants live (Burroughs-fashion) in lost worlds and hidden "empires," beyond metropolitan power and outside history, ruled by weird patriarchs, governed by religious beliefs as strange as the Barsoomian cult of Iss.

The hero of *Heritage* is an easterner who has come west for his health, gets lost in the desert, and is rescued by a Mormon patriarch named Naab who rules an isolated "empire" in the wilderness. Naab is a fantastic variation on Ishmael Bush, the head of the squatter clan in Cooper's *The Prairie*, crossed with elements of Judge Henry from *The Virginian*. He has two sons, one a good Mormon-Christian, the other an evil and greedy man with a "savage" streak of cruelty. His half-Indian daughter Mescal is betrothed to the evil son. Naab's cultish insistence on an incestuous marriage identifies the Mormons as an entirely exotic religion whose central oddities are sexual. It allows Grey to give his tale biblical resonance, specifically with Cain and Abel (and possibly the Rape of Tamar). In the course of the novel Naab's sons destroy each other, the rustlers are "exterminated" like so many Amalekites, and the hero marries Mescal and is adopted as heir to Naab's hidden empire. A marriage of the kind that ends *Heritage* is inconceivable in Cooper's or Wister's fiction, because it would negate the race-historical thesis that underlies their fiction. But Grey's West is no more "historical" than Burroughs' Barsoom, and the eastern gentleman's marriage to Mescal has no more political weight than Carter's marriage to Dejah Thoris.

But Grey was not wedded in principle to such meliorative resolutions of racial and religious difference.[55] The plot of *Riders of the Purple Sage* (1912) features the implacable opposition between the tyrannous patriarchy of the Mormons, the Christian and womanly values of Jane Withersteen, and the code of the justified avenger which motivates the gunfighter hero, Lassiter. Jane is a female Naab who has inherited a vast ranch-empire from her father, a Mormon "proselyter" and polygamist. Her herds cover the valley in which the town of Cottonwoods is located and are divided according to color to facilitate scientific breeding. Her wealth is based on Amber Spring, a great reservoir discovered by her father and dammed by him to irrigate the whole valley and to form three lakes, with oases of trees and waterbirds amid the desert. Her empire is threatened from the side of anarchy and wilderness by rustlers, who conceal themselves in a hidden valley behind "Deception Pass," and from the side of order and civilization by the Mormon Elders—a fanatical oligarchy who exploit her piety and seek to engorge her lands by forcing her to marry the evil Elder Tull. The Elders also use terror to drive all non-Mormons (Gentiles) from the Valley, while Jane (like a good Christian) not only tolerates but employs them.

Grey's description of the political economy of Jane's "Valley" mixes elements from several periods of Western development and different varieties of red-blooded fiction. The "coloring" of the herds and the wonderful irrigation projects refer to the contemporary movement for scientific breeding and dry-land farming, which had produced (between 1900 and 1920) a "bonanza" in arid land development and dam-building. The villainy of the Mormons is also an abstraction and combination of several standard types of literary "evil." Their treatment of women links them to the savage enemy of the Indian war romance: they seduce and/or kidnap and rape Gentile women or coerce them into polygamous marriages. Their monopolistic politics and economics link them to the oligarchs of the "populist" dime novel. Like the railroad in *The Octopus* their power is a "great invisible hand . . . secret, intangible," which enmeshes Jane in "a cold and calculating policy thought out long before she was born, a dark immutable will of whose empire she and all that was hers was but an atom."[56] The Gentiles' quarter in Cottonwoods is an embryonic urban hell of the kind envisioned in Donnelly's *Caesar's Column* and London's *Iron Heel*: like the laborers of *Caesar's Column*, the Gentiles have been impoverished and driven into a "ghetto" by the Mormons, who behave like Donnelly's "Hebraized" race of robber barons. Jane's foreman, Venters, is threatened with lynching and castration for having "looked the wrong way" at a Mormon woman. All these elements suggest a vaguely contemporary political reference for the story. But they are projected into a historical period identified as "1871," which allows these "progressive" and modern developments to be treated in a cowboy-adventure framework.[57]

The hero of the tale is Lassiter—Grey's most famous literary creation, the prototype of generations of black-clad two-gun gunfighters, steely-eyed and lightning-fast on the draw. Like the Virginian he is a master cowboy; but like the Indian-hating Jibbenainosay he is an implacable avenger who hunts down the men who massacred his family and ravished his sister—not Indians, but Mormons, whose foul religion turns White men into savages. The characters and conflicts of the novel are not attempts at representing distinctive frontier types or situations but a distillation and abstraction of literary conventions. Lassiter shows every sign of being a natural aristocrat like the Virginian, but Grey does not bother to give him a real past beyond his motive for revenge and his use of a conventional verbal formula—that where he comes from a woman's word is law.[58] Jane Withersteen's "Christian" qualities are cartoon exaggerations of the standard features of the "redemptive heroine": her hatred of violence and willingness to turn the other cheek are treated as evidence both of her purity and her inability to cope with the demands of a red-blooded world. She must learn to love the "good" violence that is inherent in "true manliness."

Grey exaggerates the terms of Jane's test by sensationalizing and sexualizing Lassiter's violence, particularly in the climactic scene in which bullets from his "big black guns," fired one by one, penetrate and destroy a screaming Bishop Dyer (the man who raped Lassiter's sister). This is a long way from the disciplined and ideologically rationalized killings of Hawkeye and the Virginian. But Grey is able to represent overtly the *pleasure* in violence that belongs to the myth-justified killer, because Lassiter's perhaps excessive enjoyment of the killing does not discredit a social type or ideological thesis. Nor is the reader's identification with Lassiter's revenge a threat to social peace, because it cannot even shake the fictive society of "Utah." Like the robber barons of Norris's novel and Donnelly's and London's dystopian fantasies, the Mormons are too powerful to be overthrown by an individual avenger or band of outlaws. But with Jane's technical assistance, Lassiter inflicts an apocalyptic vengeance by destroying the great irrigation works, leaving the Mormons—like the victors of *Caesar's Column* and *Iron Heel*—to monopolize the scorched earth of a ruinous war of extermination.

But the mythic landscape of Grey's fantasy-West provides an escape from the apocalypse: the discovery of "Surprise Valley," an Edenic haven hidden behind "Deception Pass," with natural gardens of wild flowers and herds of game surrounded by walls lined with veins of gold ore. In the end Jane and Lassiter will flee from the world of "Mormon" monopoly power and seal themselves away in Surprise Valley, where they will presumably be safe. In a sense, Grey's conclusion is an allegorical use of the old Myth of the Frontier to answer the dilemma of a post-Frontier, metropolitan society. His description certainly draws on the language of post-Civil War land promotions used by writers like William Gilpin and General Custer (in his Black Hills dispatches), which proffer the new frontier of the Plains as the antidote to contemporary class strife.[59] But Surprise Valley does not *function* as a safety valve in this version of the West: it is not the site of a general social renewal but a hidden or lost world into which Lassiter and Jane withdraw forever. Thus the best "safety valve" in Grey's fictive West is not a real place of any kind but a never-never land disconnected from history.[60]

Like Lassiter, Grey's heroes are generally "populist" in their ideological style. They are freedom-loving individualists who defend worthy folk who are oppressed or dispossessed by powerful men and combinations bent on monopoly. Sometimes, as in *Vanishing American* (1922, 1925), the populist style is matched by populist content. But in other fictional contexts that same style is called upon to vindicate conservative values and to oppose practical or organized "populism." *The Desert of Wheat* (1919) is a case in point. Published during the "Red Scare" that followed the conclusion of the Great War and loosely based on contemporary incidents, *The Desert of Wheat* applies the standard Grey formula plot to a tale of patriotic farmers fighting against a conspiracy of Teutonic immigrants and the "pro-German" radicals of the IWW.[61] Yet despite its modern referents, the conspiracy that threatens Golden Valley has the same essential character as the Mormon plot against Jane Withersteen: it is a "long hidden . . . nameless force . . . looming dark and sinister," whose motives are monopolistic greed and a desire for dominance energized by fanaticism and perverse sexual lusts.[62] Grey's hero (Kurt Dorn) is a half-German "man who knows Indians" (in this case "Huns"). Before he can rescue his beloved and Golden Valley he must play out a Stoddardean psychodrama, subjugate the Hun/Under-Man in his own character, and (like Burroughs' "Red Hawk") tap the potential for good or chivalric violence latent in the American side of his race character.[63] He can then lead a vigilante war of extermination that leaves the placarded corpses of lynched Wobblies dangling from the cottonwoods.[64]

By translating the West into a purely mythic or fantasy-space, Grey made western settings available for a range of stories unlimited by the constraints of historical or conceptual consistency. In such a mythic space, style is indistinguishable from content. A hero who acts in a "populist" style may be taken as the representative of liberal or democratic values (for example, racial tolerance or anti-monopoly) even though he acts on behalf of a conservative, repressive, or corporatist program. Although the purpose of this combination (as in *The Desert of Wheat*) may be to co-opt the outlaw hero to the side of authority, such a procedure also indicates the persistent power and appeal of genuinely populistic, liberal, or democratic values in the society addressed by mass culture, as well as the necessity felt even by conservative writers to square their views with democratic ideas and myths. Any shift of ideology or perspective, any variation in costume or setting, is permissible so long as the story remains true to the essential structures of the Grey formula: the conspiracy, the revenge-rescue plot, the sanctifying burst of violence that resolves all issues—the Frontier Myth abstracted to the most basic of formula plots.

The Virginian in Nighttown: Origins of the Hard-boiled Detective, 1910–1940

Like the fantasies of Burroughs and the pulp Westerns of Zane Grey, the hard-boiled detective story began as an abstraction of essential elements of the Frontier Myth. The detective's adventure follows a formula of heroic action similar to that of Grey's steely-eyed avengers: he rescues the victims of criminal plots that range in scale from muggings to international conspiracies. But the "mythic space" of the detective story differs in being identified with the "real" scene of urban crime. Like the West of the nineteenth century, the modern city is a living entity capable of generating events (crime waves, scandals, new rackets) that may require incorporation with, and modifications of, the formulas of literary fiction. Thus the detective's mythic space is governed, to a greater extent, by rules consistent with those of realistic red-blooded fiction. And paradoxically—considering both his literary roots and his historical provenance—the hard-boiled detective has become a more consistently "populist" hero than either Burroughs' supermen or Grey's cowboys.[65]

The most eloquent definition of the hard-boiled worldview, and of the type of American hero best suited to it, was offered by Raymond Chandler in his preface to *The Simple Art of Murder*:

> The realist in murder writes of a world in which gangsters can rule nations and almost rule cities, in which hotels and apartment houses and celebrated restaurants are owned by men who made their money out of brothels, and in which . . . the nice man down the hall is boss of the

> numbers racket. A world where a judge with a cellar full of bootleg liquor can send a man to jail for having a pint in his pocket. Where the mayor of your town may have condoned murder as an instrument of money making. Where no man can walk down a dark street in safety. . . . It is not a fragrant world, but it is the world you live in.[66]

The detective hero who fights for whatever good and justice exists in such a world is a figure not unlike the Virginian. He is an uncommon common man, a "man who knows Indians," which in this world means a man who knows the world of crime as if from the inside but who also has a chivalric sense of "honor" or justice, which identifies him with aristocratic values and with the values of an earlier, cleaner America:

> Down these mean streets a man must go who is not himself mean, who is neither tarnished nor afraid. . . . He must be a complete man and a common man, yet an unusual man. He must be, to use a rather weathered phrase, a man of honor. He is neither a eunuch nor a satyr. I think he might seduce a duchess, and I'm quite sure he would not spoil a virgin. If he is a man of honor in one thing, he's that in all things. He is a relatively poor man, or he would not be a detective at all. He is a common man or he could not go among common people. He has a sense of character or he would not know his job. He will take no man's money dishonestly, and no man's insolence without due and dispassionate revenge. He is a lonely man, and his pride is that you will treat him as a proud man or be very sorry you ever saw him.[67]

His character is liminal with respect to *all* class identifications: his lineage and style are "equality," his character and values "quality." But Chandler's suggestion that he would "seduce a duchess" is the sign of a "populist" bias that informs the work and consciousness of this genre hero—a bias echoed in the line from Chandler's *The Long Goodbye* (1953): "There ain't no clean way to make a hundred million bucks."[68] The hard-boiled detective's answer to the constriction and corruption of the post-Frontier landscape is to labor with wit and violence to create a small space or occasion in which something like traditional justice can prevail and in which the "little man" or the "good woman" can be protected against the malignity of the powers that be.

Chandler's description distills the central elements of the "mature" hard-boiled formula, which we can recognize in the series detective fiction of postwar writers like Ross MacDonald (Kenneth Millar), Robert B. Parker, and John D. MacDonald. Their work builds on that of Chandler himself, particularly the novels (and critical essays) he published between 1939 and 1953, in which he codified and elaborated on the achievements of *his* predecessors— particularly Dashiell Hammett—who wrote for the pulp magazine *Black Mask* in the 1920s. Hammett in turn built on the themes and characterizations developed in the dime-novel detective series, in which "outlaws" and "detectives" define alternative ways of imagining American justice.

In the hard-boiled detective, the characters and roles of dime-novel outlaw and detective—Jesse James and Old King Brady—are *fully* combined, and their ideological opposition reconciled. The hard-boiled detective is both an agent of law and an outlaw who acts outside the structures of legal authority for the sake of a personal definition of justice, which often takes the form of a private quest or revenge. In the myth/ideological landscape of the industrial metropolis he thus represents a "third force," identified neither with the propertied and managerial classes nor with the "dangerous classes" and radicalized labor organizations (socialists, anarchists). In Chandler's novels, and in the best work of his successors, the hero maintains this position of precarious and delicate moral/social balance with the grace of a practiced performer. But this balance was not immediately or easily achieved, and it is the difficult evolution of the detective's liminal position that concerns us here.

The career of Charles A. Siringo provides some insight into the dynamics of the transition from the dime-novel outlaw-detective to the urban hard-boiled pulp series, and into the connection between this type of pulp fiction and the politics of industrialization in the Far West.[69] Siringo was an Italian-American, born in Texas in 1855, who began working as a cowboy on his family's small ranch at age eleven. After losing the ranch and enduring a brief experience of urban poverty while looking for work in the East, he returned to Texas and worked fifteen years as a cowboy, saving money to buy himself a store and storing up material for a book he hoped to write. His business failed, but *A Texas Cowboy* (1885) brought him a bit of fame and some money. However, in 1886—motivated (he said) by patriotic disgust with the Haymarket anarchists—he abandoned literature for a job as a Pinkerton detective, which he held until 1910.

As an ex-cowboy who had occasionally "thrown the long rope," Siringo "knew rustlers." So Pinkerton's sent him to the cattle ranges.[70] Although he was not involved in the Johnson County War, as a range detective hired by big ranchers he was inevitably involved in similar anti-rustler campaigns elsewhere in the West. Later in his career he was engaged in the Pinkerton Agency's war against the Western Federation of Miners and the IWW—the "anarchists" he had originally signed on to fight. He worked under an operative known to him as "McCartney" in breaking the Coeur d'Alene miners' strike (1892) and the framing of IWW leaders for the assassination of Idaho's ex-Governor Steunenberg in 1905. He later discovered that "McCartney" was none other than James McParlan, the agent who had infiltrated and destroyed the Mollie Maguires in 1874.

In his first book of reminiscences, *A Cowboy Detective* (1912), published after his retirement, Siringo proudly details the clever ways in which he (and the Agency) overcame all obstacles to achieve their objectives, including instances in which detectives stretched or broke the law to entrap, capture, or kill those they were paid to hunt. But the book revealed more about the Agency's methods than was good for its reputation. Pinkerton's had the first edition suppressed and recalled, and Siringo had to settle for publishing a revised edition in which all names were altered (for example, Pinkerton becomes "Dickerson"). Siringo counterattacked in 1915 with a polemical paperback titled *Two Evil Isms: Pinkertonism and Anarchism* and a second autobiography, *Riata and Spurs*, in 1927. But Pinkerton's intervened once more and forced him to excise the whole middle section of the book.

In *A Cowboy Detective* Siringo dramatizes a distinctly "hard-boiled" approach to the pursuit of rustlers, renegade bank officials, and "anarchists." He is a complete pragmatist who uses whatever means are necessary to get the job done, and he recounts his actions with dry, ironic humor. He is proud of his ability to pass as a bandit among bandits, a rustler among rustlers; he even enjoys his time on the other side of the law, because cowboy outlaws are generally "good fellows."[71] His attitude toward "woman" violates the proprieties of conventional literature and anticipates the hard-boiled approach to sexual relations. He confesses that he seduced the eighteen-year-old daughter of an outlaw while his own wife was recovering from an operation. His justification is that such "tricks" are necessary to his "profession."[72]

He brings the same hard-boiled attitude to the fight against anarchism." He notes with approval the use of bribery and corruption by Chicago businessmen to frame and convict the Haymarket anarchists:

> A million dollars had been subscribed by the Citizens' League to stamp out anarchy in Chicago, and no doubt much of it was used to corrupt justice. Still, the hanging of these anarchists had a good effect and was worth a million dollars to society.[73]

The passage concludes with a warning against unrestricted immigration which attributes the growth of radicalism to the presence of alien elements among the population. In this, and in his animadversions elsewhere against Mexicans, Jews, "mix-bloods," and Irishmen, Siringo reflects the biases of progressive ideology and anticipates the portrayal of the urban underworld as an ethnic stew in the early hard-boiled detective stories.[74]

Siringo represents himself as a "man of the people" whose instinctive "sympathy was with labor organizations as against capital." But he is converted to an implacable foe of "anarchism" by the "savagery" of the strikers in the Coeur d'Alene. In his account they are "Mollie Maguire type[s]" who make war on the wives and children of nonunion miners and murder fourteen men, concealing the corpses by disemboweling them, filling them with rocks, and sinking them in the river.[75]

But when Siringo himself becomes a victim of the Agency's penchant for overriding constitutional rights, his moral perspective is completely inverted. In *Two Evil Isms* his "tough-minded" understanding of the anarchist menace is transformed into a "hard-boiled" understanding that *all* the orders and powers of the metropolis—cops and robbers, capitalists and unionists, bankers and embezzlers, detectives and anarchists—are corrupt.[76] The detective, at his best, offers a disinterested alternative to "the greedy capitalists and bloodthirsty labor union agitators."[77] He is a man of skill and moral independence, with traits of character linking him to traditional frontier heroes, employed by an agency whose resources allow it to apply the most sophisticated of modern methods to the task of facilitating "progress." But at his worst the detective is merely the slave of capital treated as a piece of machinery by his own "money-mad" employers, who sell his services to other greedy and unscrupulous men.

Siringo dramatizes his own condition in terms reminiscent of the populist outlaw: he is a simple cowboy whose good faith is violated by clever city slickers who entrap him in a powerful and widely ramified system that he is helpless to escape. Like the dime-novel outlaw, he wishes to vindicate his "manhood" by some form of protest, but he knows too well the strength of the system that engulfs him:

> The question might be asked why I did not show my manhood by resigning and exposing this crooked agency in the beginning. Exposing it to whom, pray? Not to the officers of the law, I hope. In my cowboy simplicity I might have been persuaded to do so at that time. But I am

glad I did not, for, with my twenty-two years behind the curtains, I can now see the outcome . . . many "sleeps" in the city bull-pen, and a few doses of the "third degree" to try and wring a confession for blackmailing this notorious institution.

Up to the time of the Homestead riot, and since the moral wave has been sweeping over the land, the Pinkerton National Detective Agency was above the law. A word from W. A. Pinkerton or one of his officers would send any "scrub" citizen to the scrap heap, or the penitentiary. This is no joke, for I have heard of many innocent men being "railroaded" to prisons, and my information came from inside the circle.

A man without wealth or influence trying to expose the dastardly work of the Pinkerton National Detective Agency would be like a two-year old boy blowing his breath against a cyclone to stop its force. . . .[78]

This corrupt and all-encompassing system anticipates the terms of Chandler's characterization of the world of the hard-boiled detective: a world of constricted opportunities in which all money is "big" and big money is "dirty," in which the few rich dominate the many poor, and in which the systems of justice and political representation have been systematically suborned by Big Money. Although Siringo does raise his voice in protest against the system, as a writer he has no alternatives or resolution to project. But the hard-boiled detective genre developed by the *Black Mask* writers projected such an alternative in mythic terms, in the figure of the private detective who is free to pursue his animus against both overworld and underworld, unscrupulous banker and immoral criminal, "greedy capitalist" and "bloodthirsty agitator."

The "hook" which drew readers into the seedy world of the detective was its promise to acquaint them with a world that was both exotic and hidden (like one of Burroughs' or Grey's secret empires) and undeniably "real"—a world of lurid evils, realizing one's worst suspicions about city hall and big business, which were nonetheless credible visions of a threat to American civilization.

Like the dime-novel outlaw and detective, the hard-boiled dick exposes defalcating bankers, crooked speculators, the usurpers of inheritances. But the more sensational and appealing exposures are those that come when the detective delves into the urban criminal underworld. This is where the key to our social disorder is found, where the trail of an upper-class malefactor can be picked up, where the detective confronts the gang-bosses who constitute the elite of urban crime.

The concision demanded of the *Black Mask* writer required the use of racial/ethnic stereotyping to provide instant characterization of the villain and his milieu—a practice that emphasizes the "grotesque" qualities of the ethnic "other." This convention and its effects are best displayed in Hammett's "The Big Knockover" (1927), in which the hero meets and sends to the morgue a succession of characters whose racial and class character is completely defined by the mere listing of their names: the "Dis and Dat" Kid, Sheeny Holmes, Spider Girucci, Nigger Vojan, and Paddy the Mex.[79] These are the "Indians" whom our scout-detective "knows," and his understanding teaches him that in the end we will have to use violence against them. *Black Mask* detectives approached this necessity more or less in the spirit of the Indian-hater.

Carroll John Daly, the most popular *Black Mask* writer before Hammett's arrival, wrote a series of stories featuring "Race Williams," a detective whose first name suggests the kind of warfare in which he was engaged. Race Williams speaks of himself as living on the "border" between "outlaws" and the police, and his enemies are almost always the racially or ethnically alien bosses of the underworld. Williams is less the tracer of clues than the executor of a vigilante type of justice who operates in the moral and social isolation of the "Indian-hater" and usually solves his case with gunplay.[80]

Hammett's stories for *Black Mask* feature an operative of the Continental Detective Agency, a fictional Pinkerton known only as "The Continental Op"—as if he has no identity apart from his employment. But this absorption of the man in the company paradoxically empowers the Op, giving him the wherewithal to act as a disinterested professional independent of "labor," "capital" and all local powers and interests. Although his identity is thus bound up with the corporate apparatus of law, he expresses himself and achieves his goals in an "outlaw" style. His profession licenses him to act like the "man who knows Indians," to learn and use the cynical wisdom and violent methods of the underworld so that he can turn them against their makers. But the moral order in which the Op works is far more corrupt than that in the Indian-war romance or Western: greed and the evil it causes are so pervasive and dangerous that none of the conventional symbols of good can be trusted. The Op's cynicism is the mark of his realism as a judge of men and women and of his pragmatic professionalism.[81]

Daly's stories and Hammett's early work stay within the ideological boundaries of the "vigilante" Western and the Pinkerton detective tale. Although they treat the criminality of the rich, the corruption of the poor and the foreign is more spectacularly displayed. Moreover their animadversions on crooked politicians are not inconsistent with the anti-democratic political bias of *The Virginian*. But Hammett's later stories, and the novels he produced after *Red Harvest* in 1929, go beyond the "Pinkerton" ideology to devlop a more complex use of the crime story as an allegory of social and political conflict.

Hammett himself had been a Pinkerton operative around the time of the Great War. By his account, his years with Pinkerton taught him a good deal about the realities of the detective business and the complex underside of human behavior. He also claimed that in 1916 or 1917 an official of Anaconda Copper offered him $5,000 to assassinate IWW organizer Frank Little. Although Hammett refused, Little was later tortured and killed by a lynch mob in Butte, Montana, during a labor battle in which Pinkertons were also employed. The incident is said to have caused Hammett's revulsion against the Agency, and by the late 1920s he had gone over to Little's camp, becoming a Marxist of sorts.[82] But Hammett's account conceals or omits a good deal. Although he left Pinkerton's for army service in 1917, he may have returned to the Agency for a brief time after the war; and his Continental Op stories idealize the detective agency as a disinterested force for justice. But whatever the process of his personal development may have been, *Red Harvest* does turn the agency-detective story inside out.[83]

The Op is called to the western mining town of "Personville" by newspaper editor Donald Wilsson to expose the gangsters who have taken over the city, but his client is murdered before they meet. Donald is the son of old Elihu Wilsson, the robber-baron industrialist whose mining/smelting business is Personville's reason for being, and who has controlled the city's politics for decades—until the gangsters took over. Now the city is known as "Poisonville," a name that symbolizes its decline from a pastoral pioneer mining community to its present condition of moral and environmental pollution. The Op discovers that the gangsters were originally brought in by Elihu Wilsson to break a strike by the IWW. In pursuing the murderer of his client, he uncovers and destroys the network of corrupt bargains that makes the town's economic and social elite, the political leadership, and the rackets bosses partners in rulership and crime.

The "Poisonville" setting returns the Op to the original terrain of the Pinkerton detective story, the strife between unions and employers in mining towns—more specifically, to the mines of Idaho and Montana in which Charlie Siringo had worked against the "anarchists." It also sends the Op to a town very much like Butte, where vigilantes and private detectives performed the assassination Hammett himself refused. In *Red Harvest* the Op solves the crime and restores something like a right order of things by using against the established order the very methods of the labor spy, *agent provocateur*, and vigiliante that a Pinkerton operative like Siringo or MacParland would have used against the Western Federation of Miners or IWW.[84]

The Op gets a line on Poisonville politics from Bill Quint, head of the WFM, whose red tie marks him as a Wobbly. The Op identifies himself by flashing an IWW Seaman's card—one of several false credentials he carries. The use of the card reminds us that the normal role of an Op would be to infiltrate and break the union. Quint actually spots the phony, but the Op is so good at his masquerade that Quint assumes he is dealing with an undercover agent of his own national organization. This suggests a Siringo-esque parallel between the detective agency and the revolutionary union: both are national organizations with a mission they will achieve through conspiracy and "direct action." The parallel is reinforced by personal similarities between the two men: both are professionals with an unromantic understanding of the way the world works and of virtue's prospects for ultimate victory over vice. Quint even shares the Op's belief that the strike was an act of historical grandstanding by the union's national leadership. Further, Quint's way of defining the differences between the union and Wilsson invokes the principle of "manhood," the moral ideal of dime-novel and red-blooded heroes. Wilsson is condemned because he "hired gun-men, strike breakers, national guardsmen and even part of the regular army" to do his bleeding for him; "the wobblies had to do their own bleeding."[85] These affinities suggest the appropriateness of the practical alliance that develops between Quint and the Op, who after all share the same enemies. But helping the union is not the Op's mission, and his ideological stance toward the "red tie" boys is problematic.

Like Personville/Poisonville, "Elilhu Wilson" is a signifying name. The surname recalls the President whose Attorney General conducted a wartime *jihad* against radical labor organizations and did not scruple to incite vigilante violence against antiwar agitators, and who after the war presided over the nation's first major "Red Scare," attended by massive violations of civil rights.[86] "Elihu" suggests a connection to Elihu Root, Roosevelt's Secretary of War, a leading exponent of the seizure of the Philippines and of the "marked severities" by which we enforced our imperial regime in 1900–02. To his idealistic son Donald, Elihu Wilsson appears the embodiment of a traditional order in which political and social leadership was vested in the most respectable citizens. But the "Czar of Poisonville" is a parody of the progressive captain of industry: a man so corrupted by greed that he poisons the air and land of his city, and so determined to control the town that he is willing to hire gangsters to threaten and kill his opponents and to connive in the cover-up of his son's assassination (if not in the murder itself).

The perversion of all "normal" ideological values is the norm in Poisonville and in the world of hard-boiled fiction in general. Conventional expectations imported from more romantic types of popular literature are certain to be violated. The wealth, breeding, and respectability that guarantee worthiness in a Western are usually masks for corruption in the detective story: to paraphrase Chandler, in the hard-boiled world all streets are mean and there is never a clean way to make a hundred million bucks. But perhaps the most significant inversion of convention is the genre's treatment of women.

In the conventional romance, the hero's love for the redemptive woman reveals his aptitude for goodness and signals his instinctive choice of the right side in the racial, political, or social struggle that engages him. By the beginning of the twentieth century it had become possible to see "good women" as sexual creatures, arousing and even experiencing erotic desire, rather than as symbols of an asexual spirituality; at its most extreme (in London, Grey, and Burroughs) this development even permitted the representation of a redemptive woman as racially "dark." But the sexualizing and darkening of these "good" women is still circumscribed by the devices of plot and characterization that identify them with the most essential elements of female respectability. Within their setting and context they are still identified as being of noble blood and character (princess, heiress), and their passion is entirely monogamous and fixed on the hero. The hard-boiled detective story takes the further step of identifying the "fallen" or sexually experienced woman, the woman who has herself had adventures, as the repository of values the detective finds "good"; while the more respectable-seeming women, who appeal to the detective for rescue, often stand for a kind of naivete that amounts to moral cowardice (like Donald Wilsson's wife), or are revealed to be the source of evil itself, like Brigid O'Shaughnessy in *The Maltese Falcon* (1930), Eileen Wade in Chandler's *The Long Goodbye* (1953), or Daisy Buchanan in Fitzgerald's *The Great Gatsby* (1927).[87] (As the last example suggests, in this undoing of a central trope of Victorian literature and ideology, the hard-boiled detective story identifies itself as part of literary modernism.)

The closest thing to a "redemptive woman" in *Red Harvest* is Dinah Brand, a physically imposing "dark" woman who has slept with nearly every powerful man in town, established her independence (and a measure of prosperity) by using her sexuality as tool, and gained a share of power by blackmailing her lovers. The Op admires her and feels for her the same sensed of affinity that connects him to the Wobbly/outlaw, Bill Quint: she too is a professional and a pragmatist who has the courage to risk her life for what she wants or believes in. Of course, the Op is better than she is in all of these areas, as he is better than Quint. But his kinship with the "fallen woman" is important, because when she is killed the detective turns against the party of order and inclines, slightly but significantly, to the party of outlawry.

The Op decides to pursue a private vendetta against the murderers of Donald Wilsson and Dinah Brand, using his skill as a trained *agent provocateur* to foment a civil war between Wilsson, the gangsters, and the corrupt political bosses, hoping that the Governor will then send in the National Guard—as he did during the strike. This is precisely the strategy for strike-breaking followed by Pinkerton's and other organizations since the "Mollie Maguires." The Op uses rumor and deception to provoke a complexly interacting series of assassinations, jail-breaks, and shoot-outs that has crooked Police Chief Noonan muttering, "Everybody's killing everybody. Where's it going to end?" The purification of Poisonville can begin only after its rulers have regressed into the "war of each against all" that is the Hobbesian version of the state of nature.[88]

The Op himself, caught up in the Wild West atmosphere, experiences a regressive urge for violence and revenge and breaks so many rules that even the Agency considers him an outlaw (until he succeeds). Violence and even assassination have been instruments like any other in his work, to be used with the restraint and purposeful rationality of the professional: "I've arranged a killing or two in my time, when they were necessary." But the social warfare of Poisonville engages the Op's passions and makes him hungry for a "red harvest" of revenge and retributive justice: "this is the first time I've ever got the fever. It's this damned burg. You can't go straight here." The Op contemplates vengeance with the same cruel pleasure shown by Lassiter:

> I don't like the way Poisonville has treated me. I've got my chance now, and I'm going to even up. . . . There was a time when I wanted to be let alone . . . But I wasn't. . . . Now it's my turn. . . . Poisonville is ripe for the harvest. It's a job I like and I'm going to do it.[89]

The Op's "red harvest" is a revolution of sorts, but with distinct limitations. Elihu Wilsson's power is broken but not destroyed. The National Guard takes over and cleans up the mess left by the Op; but the Guard has been used to break the strike, so it is doubtful that the new order will be of any use to Bill Quint and his "red tie" men. The justice which the detective achieves affects persons, not classes; it changes situations but does not transform orders.

Red Harvest marks the beginning of the modern hard-boiled detective series: a genre whose basic unit is not the magazine story or short pulp "novel" but the longer novel form, which lends itself to a more detailed and complex development of character, situation, milieu, and theme. Hammett's later novels, and the work of Chandler that built on Hammett's achievements, elaborated on the *Black Mask* formulas and developed the interesting innovations of *Red Harvest* into a new and richer set of conventions. The inversion of conventional female characterizations in these later works has already been noted. Of equal significance is the identification of the detective as a *private* eye, an independent entrepreneur rather than the employee of a Pinkerton-like corporation. The shift realizes the implication of Hammett's vision of the detective as a moral free agent, an outlaw for the sake of a higher law, a man disillusioned enough to survive in a modern world but still capable of believing in and acting on a traditional concept of honor. And it embodies that moral consciousness in a figure whose economic condition harks back to the "populist" economy of small, independent farms and businesses.

Thus the hard-boiled detective, for all his mean-streets manner, is no less a recrudescence of the frontier hero than John Carter and Lassiter: an agent of regenerative violence through whom we imaginatively recover the ideological values, if not the material reality, of the mythic Frontier.

PART III

Colonizing a Mythic Landscape: Movie Westerns, 1903–1948

7 Formulas on Film

Myth and Genre in the Silent Movie, 1903–1926

Edwin S. Porter's *The Great Train Robbery*, produced for the Edison Company in 1903, has long figured in the folklore of American mass culture as the progenitor of narrative cinema: "the first story film," the first to use a close-up, "the first Western."[1] In fact, many of its technical and narrative innovations had been anticipated in earlier productions. The legend is closer to truth in identifying *The Great Train Robbery* as the foundation of the Western as a movie genre. The film was a commercial success on a scale that no single movie had previously achieved. And in an effort to reproduce and extend that success, the Edison Company and its competitors turned out a series of films that imitated Porter's movie: *The Great Bank Robbery, The Bold Bank Robbery, The Little Train Robbery, The Hold-Up of the Rocky Mountain Express.*[2] By 1908 the genre was so well established that distributors' catalogues listed their products under the headings " 'Drama,' 'Comic,' and 'Western.' " By 1914 reviewers were complaining that Westerns were already old hat—"a style of motion picture that we had hoped was a thing of the past"—and went on to identify as tiresome clichés the very devices that W. S. Hart and his successors would profitably exploit for the next dozen years: "sheriffs, outlaws, bad Indians, good Indians, Mexican villains, heroic outlaws, desperate halfbreeds, etc."[3]

The history of the Western as a film genre begins with the decision to imitate Porter's work and repeat its success. In reproducing the successful pattern the production companies reified it *as a formula*; in so doing, they carried over into a new medium the processes of formula and genre formation that had already been systematized in printed forms of mass media. However, while similar processes shaped the development of literary mass media and movies, the differences between print and film as media made a difference in the way stories are told and in the way patterned associations of image and idea are developed. To understand the way in which movie Westerns function as works of cinematic art and as vehicles for mythography, we need to look briefly at the elements that go into the making of movie genres and at the development of the Western during the era of silent films.

Genre as Mythic Space

Despite the appeal of visual presentation, movies (particularly silent movies) have certain liabilities as a narrative medium when compared with novels. Because movies deal primarily in pictures, it is difficult to represent the intricate processes of thought and feeling that literary convention requires for the development of character. Dependence on the visual also creates in both viewer and filmmaker a bias toward literal readings of the observed action—metaphors are harder to make in movies than in novels. Finally, the success of movie narration depends on a set of optical and psychological deceptions through which a discontinuous series of "still" images creates the impression of continuous motion and sustains the illusion of narrative continuity.

The speed with which the film-frames move sustains the illusion of continuous motion, but the illusion of narrative coherence depends on a set of prior understandings. Some of these derive from the basic conventions of the medium. We expect our written language to be printed from left to right, and there are similar conventions in film which teach us how to "read" continuity through the various kinds of transition that link a series of shots or scenes. But more sophisticated understandings depend on the viewer's prior experience with stories in general, and with filmed stories in particular. Experience and custom teach us what kinds of narrative to expect from different kinds of storyteller. Once we learn them, the recognition of a few signs or clues tells us what category the tale belongs to and allows us to anticipate the kind of thing that will happen.[4] Filmmakers, like other artists, manipulate these understandings for various effects. "Normative" usages help in building suspense, creating tension, achieving the suspension of disbelief, bridging discontinuities, establishing plausible motives; while violation of norms can surprise, amuse, or frighten the reader/viewer into heightened attentiveness.[5]

In cinematic storytelling these mnemonic cues are given visually through a set of images that invite the viewer to associate the story with others of a similar kind of "genre" that he or she may know. The most essential cues are established through the development of a powerful association between particular kinds of setting and particular story-forms. This interdependence of setting and story may be unique to cinema, because the power of the visual medium depends on its ability to place the viewer in a visible world and to unify the picture with an idea or feeling with minimal explanation.

The history of a movie genre is the story of the conception, elaboration, and acceptance of a special kind of space: an imaged landscape which evokes authentic places and times, but which becomes, in the end, completely identified with the fictions created about it. The "mean streets" of gangster movies, the horror-movie castle rearing up into a stormy sky, the backstage of a Broadway show or Hollywood sound stage, the white picket fences of Andy Hardy's small-town America, the western town of false-front saloons and board sidewalks are as instantly familiar to us, as recognizable, and as dense with memory and meaning, as the streets we grew up on. We know that they mean, on some level, to be representative of places that historically existed. Yet genre worlds are also never-never lands whose special rules and meanings have more to do with conventions, myths, and ideologies than with historical representation.

The genre setting contains not only a set of objects signifying a certain time, place, and milieu; it invokes a set of fundamental assumptions and expectations about the kinds of event that can occur in the setting, the kinds of motive that will operate, the sort of outcome one can predict. If setting does not absolutely determine story, it at least defines the range of possible plots and treatments. As stories accumulate and are mnemonically linked to a particular visual setting, the imaginative possibilities of the generic terrain are both expanded and mapped for future reference.

Genre effects also allow movies to engage the viewer on levels other than the visual, to overcome the limiting notion that movie-images are merely documents of action, and to provide visual narrative with the metaphoric resonance that is achieved in printed literature. Scenes evocative of past Westerns give depth and resonance to the later movies of John Ford and enrich the ironies of *The Wild Bunch* just as Melville's appropriation of the rhythms of Shakespeare and the King James Bible lend *Moby-Dick* the cultural resonance of epic. When fully developed, the mythic space of a genre invests even the sketchiest characterization or setting with resonance, as if it were part of a larger culture, with its own special architecture, manners, folkways, and politics.

Genre space is also *mythic space*: a pseudo-historical (or pseudo-real) setting that is powerfully associated with stories and concerns rooted in the culture's myth/ideological tradition. It is also a setting in which the concrete work of contemporary myth-making is done.[6] This is particularly true of the Western, whose roots go deeper into the American cultural past then those of any other movie genre.

The Western developed so early in the history of American film-making that its origins have been confounded with those of the medium itself. But in fact the Western may be more dependent on pre-cinematic forms and conventions than any of its rivals. The West was already a mythologized space when the first moviemakers found it, and early Westerns built directly on the formulas, images, and allegorizing traditions of the Wild West show and cheap literature.[7] No other genre has pre-cinematic roots of comparable depth and density. The characteristic iconography, material settings, and historical references of the gangster or detective film, the police procedural, the suburban domestic comedy, the "woman's picture," the musical comedy, and the combat film all belong to the "age of movies." But for American audiences, their traditions do not compare in density, currency, and ideological presence to those associated with the Myth of the Frontier.[8]

Like any pioneer in a new territory, the movies began by adapting to the environment, which in the case of the Western was both a real place and a set of myths associated with that place. In the end they colonized this space and altered it to suit their needs and preferences. For Americans raised in the middle decades of the twentieth century, the most memorable images of the historical frontier are drawn from the mythic landscape of the Western movie rather than from the pages of Francis Parkman, Frederick Jackson Turner, James Fenimore Cooper, Owen Wister, or even the dime novel and its literary successors.[9] But the early development of the genre was shaped by the problems and opportunities arising from the filmmaker's need to adapt existing images and ideas associated with the West to the new medium.

The most characteristic of these problems is the *dilemma of authenticity*. Cultural tradition defined "the West" as both an actual place with a real history and as a mythic space populated by projective fantasies. Expectations about Western stories were therefore contradictory: they had to seem in some way realistic or "authentic" while at the same time conforming to ideas of setting, costume, and heroic behavior derived from literary fantasy. The cultural tradition the movies inherited was based on successful resolutions of this problem, in the forms of the historical romance, the dime novel, and the Wild West. But one of the unique appeals of early cinema was its claim (derived from photography) to be a direct and true representation of "the real thing."[10]

This aspect of the medium was particularly useful to makers of Westerns, because many of the sites and personages celebrated in frontier fiction and the Wild West were still in existence; the dress, weaponry, and life-styles of modern cowboys had not changed much since the 1880s. The crime on which Porter's *Great Train Robbery* was based occurred in 1900, only three years before the film appeared. "The real West" itself became readily accessible after 1909, when—in response to the Patents Company's attempt to monopolize film production and distribution in the East—the center of movie production began to shift to the West.[11] Although production would eventually center in Hollywood, in the 1913–20 period several other western towns and cities were bidding to become centers of film production, including Pawnee and Tulsa, Oklahoma, Chicago, and various towns in Texas and Colorado. Los Angeles itself was a distinctly "western" city, with strong cultural and commercial links (via railroad) to the cattle and mining frontiers of Arizona, New Mexico, and West Texas. Unemployed cowboys and hungry reservation Indians looked to regional and Hollywood movie companies for work, as once they had looked to the Wild West. Before 1903, brave lawmen and famous desperadoes (after release from prison) could cash in on their celebrity by performing in Wild West shows, as Sheriff Con Groner and outlaws Frank James and Cole Younger had done. The movies presented similar opportunities to ex-lawmen like Bill Tilghman and ex-bandits like Emmett Dalton, Henry Starr, and Al Jennings.[12]

But the filmmaker who exploited these advantages found that his license for invention might be circumscribed by the public's well-formed notions of what an "authentic" Western story or setting had to be. The cowboys who signed on as movie extras and technical advisers also constituted an in-house pressure group with a bias toward authenticity.[13] Early filmmakers dealt with the dilemma of authenticity by following the Buffalo Bill recipe. They combined scenes and stories drawn from the traditions of the dime novel and stage melodrama with authentic details of costume and scenery. Thomas

Ince's *Custer's Last Fight* (1912) is little more than a cinematic version of Cody's Wild West re-enactment. Its melodramatic "plot" is more elaborate than Cody's (an advantage of the new medium), and filming on location makes for greater realism of setting than could be achieved in an arena. But Ince uses the Wild West's characteristic methods of "authentication" to enhance his film's appeal: the insistence on screen and in a lengthy, printed program that participants in the original battle (or their children) had served as actors and technical advisers.[14]

The appeal of "original participant" Westerns and the fatal limitations of this approach to moviemaking appear most clearly in the career of Al Jennings, a reformed Oklahoma bankrobber. Jennings found employment in the regional film industry that, between 1907 and 1920, was centered in Tulsa—before Hollywood's dominance was established.[15] He eventually went on to a professional moviemaking career in Hollywood, which lasted from 1908 to 1920 (he died in 1962). The key to his success (according to director Alan Dwan) was his ability (derived from his standing as "the real thing") to play on Holllywood's insecurity about the authenticity of its product. "As soon as they knew he was Al Jennings, they opened the doors. . . . If you wanted something done in a Western the way it ought to be done, you asked him." And his characteristic answer would be: "Not the way you see it done in the movies."

Jennings appears to have been sincere in his desire to achieve realism in the representation of detail. He also had a personal stake in the authenticity of his films: he hoped to rehabilitate his own character and history by representing himself as a genuine populist outlaw. (Jennings actually stood as a Democratic candidate for governor in 1914.) But the closer he got to achieving authenticity, the less successful his movies were. The problem was that Jennings' standard of realism was regional, his outlaws and Indians look as they did in Oklahoma at the turn of the century—the outlaw in a battered fedora and jacket that suggest a city tramp rather than a cowboy badman, the Indians living in small cabins and dressing like dirt farmers rather than feathered warriors on painted horses. Such images might be received as authentic by a regional audience, but in the nation at large the cues signifying "realism" were those that belonged to the iconography of commercial mass media: dime novels, Wild West posters, illustrated magazine articles, and the early Western based on these images.[16]

While a "yearning" for "the real thing" remained an integral part of the Western, its power to both enable and constrain cinematic myth-making was bound to diminish with the passage of time. As the links to the past attenuated, they were replaced by the accumulation of movie images purporting to represent American history and the West—vivid, "authenticated," and above all *memorable*. What became essential to the creation of an illusion of authenticity and historicity was not the presence of a "real old-time outlaw" or "Last Stand Survivor," but the establishment of a set of habitual associations between image and idea that would ultimately constitute a code or language of cinematic symbols, understood by both filmmaker and audience as referring to or symbolizing "the historical West" or "the real thing." In the end, the culture as a whole would remember the West in terms of movie images and would "validate" new representations by measuring them against the "authority" of genre conventions. Codes of this kind were being developed for a wide variety of story-forms throughout the first decades of movie production as a logical and inevitable result of the developing practice of cinematic narration.

Cinematic Form and Mythographic Function: Griffith's Birth of a Nation *(1915)*

The desire for historical authenticity that is so marked among the makers of early Westerns is a sign of their mythographic ambition: a desire that their functions be received as imaginative engagements with the matter and meaning of the nation's history. In 1902 Frank Norris had half-humorously suggested that dime novels might be the American cultural equivalent of the Norse sagas. The red-blooded writers had expanded the sensational adventure-tale into a kind of heroic "lore" through which they hoped to inculcate nationally characteristic notions of high motive and right action. In *The Art of the Motion Picture* (1915) the poet and visionary Vachel Lindsay carries this idea one step further. He sees "The whirlwind of cowboys and Indians with which the photoplay began" as evidence that "this instrument, in asserting its genius, was feeling its way toward the most primitive form of life it could find"; and this suggests that movies might be able to satisfy the modern nation's "hunger for tales of fundamental life" which had once been the province of epic poetry and sacred myth.[17] In fact, a mythographic program of this kind was being consciously realized in D. W. Griffith's *Birth of a Nation*, which appeared in the same year as Lindsay's book.

Critics and scholars have justly and sufficiently described Griffith's contribution to the history and art of cinema. Here our primary concern is with Griffith's response to, and solution of, the problems of cinematic myth-making. Griffith was the most consciously and ambitiously mythographic of artists, and the conception, construction, and marketing of *Birth of a Nation* were informed by his desire to create a completely authentic and convincing historical myth.

Griffith's purpose was to be accepted as a serious "writer" (the term by which he described his role as cinematic author) working in a medium as capable of high artistic creation as literature or painting.[18] In the American tradition, to be a serious writer was also to be a "moral painter," a historical fabulist, and an interpreter of the conundrums of American "national identity," and to work in the largest and most respected forms, like the novel or the large canvas.[19] The scores of one- and two-reel films Griffith produced between 1908 and 1914 (including several Westerns) were technically inventive and increasingly sophisticated in form, but as narratives they were little more than kinetic dime novels.[20]

In 1911–12, movie companies in Europe had begun producing "feature films"—elaborately costumed epics based on historical or literary subjects like *The Fall of Troy*, *The Crusaders*, and *Homer's Odyssey*. On the American side, Thomas Ince entered the field with re-creations of *Custer's Last Fight* and *The Battle of Gettysburg* (1912). The critical and commercial success of *Quo Vadis?* (1913), based on a best-selling historical novel, confirmed Griffith's sense that the "feature" format was the one in which he had to work.[21] As Griffith's biographer Richard Schickel notes, these early feature films were less sophisticated in their cinematic technique than the one- and two-reelers that Griffith's company cranked out in quantity. What gave features their prestige and impact was the combination of greater length and more impressive production values and cinematic effects with large moral themes and historical settings drawn from religious and literary classics, popular history, and historical fiction.[22]

In 1913 and 1914 Griffith searched for a subject or literary property that would serve his purposes and justify the expense of money and time of a feature production. He chose Dixon's novel *The Clansman*, which had been a best-seller and a popular touring melodrama. While it was undoubtedly controversial, the main tenets of its historical thesis had been accepted by the most influential academic historians and by White politicians of both major parties.[23]

Griffith's intention was to re-create a historical episode in terms that would display its moral significance. As the project went forward, this implicitly mythographic intention became more self-consciously ideological and polemical. The title was changed from *The Clansman* to *The Birth of a Nation* to evade the anticipated charge of pro-southern bias, but the effect was to nationalize the racial allegory's frame of reference and thereby heighten its effect. The controversy that followed the film's release heightened Griffith's consciousness of the ideological mission of the project. In response, he added several explanatory and self-justifying title-cards, cut or modified certain scenes (the rape, the castration of Gus) that provoked excessive hostility, and began a polemical offensive on behalf of *Birth of a Nation* and film in general. He defended his work not merely on First Amendment grounds but on the substantive assertion that movies had a unique potential for public education. His argument parallels that of the Wild West's "Salutatory" exhortation, asserting that this new mode of expression can be vital to the development of the public's awareness of the meaning and direction of the nation's history, hence an aid to the achievement of democracy and progress:

> Fortunes are spent every year in our country teaching the truths of history, that we may learn from the mistakes of the past a better way for present and future. . . . The truths of history today are restricted to the limited few attending our colleges and universities; the motion picture can carry these truths to the entire world, without cost, while at the same time bringing diversion to the masses.[24]

Griffith later declared, "The cinema is the agent of Democracy. It levels barriers between races and classes."[25]

Although Griffith's colleagues testify to his sincerity on this score, it is hard to see this film as anything but an assertion that "democracy" depends on the *maintenance* of barriers between the races. That was certainly Dixon's view. He saw the film as a way of enlarging the audience for his ideas and of compelling public acceptance of his political program, and promoted the film assiduously through his excellent connections to the Democratic Party. On the eve of the film's general release, Dixon sought an appointment with President Wilson, who had been his classmate at Johns Hopkins and whose candidacy he had actively supported. He convinced Wilson to view the film by asserting that Griffith's work "made clear for the first time that a new universal language had been invented . . . a new process of reasoning by which will could be overwhelmed with conviction." In a subsequent letter to the presidential secretary Joseph P. Tumulty, Dixon named the conviction he had in mind: the film would "revolutionize Northern sentiments by a presentation of history that would transform every man in the audience into a good Democrat," which for Dixon implied membership in a "White Man's party."[26] Wilson's reaction to the film—as the public heard the tale—endorsed both its political thesis and the idea that movies were a form peculiarly suited to representing (and in our sense of the term, mythologizing) history: "It is like writing history with Lightning. And my only regret is that it is all so terribly true."[27]

Most critics would assert that the movie's power to compel conviction derives primarily from the skill with which Griffith uses elements of cinematic form—the composition of shots, and the skillful editing technique that gives the narrative rhythm and pace and keeps the viewer locked into the flow of images.[28] But Griffith himself did not think these elements sufficient to compel the sort of belief he wanted. He therefore buttressed his visualizations with appeals to the authority of historical writing and iconography. He used the "literary" side of the medium—text laid out on title-cards, and tableaux drawn from traditions of magazine illustration and popular prints—to give the images moral and ideological authority.[29] Turns of the story that are crucial to his thesis are supported by "footnotes" and assurances that a given scene is a precise re-creation of an actual event based on verbal and photographic evidence. Among the works cited is Woodrow Wilson's own *History of the American People* (1902).[30] Griffith buttresses Dixon's assertions of Black inferiority by drawing on the vocabulary of more "scientific" forms of racism, specifically the "Aryan" theories that became current after the publication of Houston Stewart Chamberlain's *The Origins of the Nineteenth Century* (1899).[31]

The film gained a different kind of authority from Griffith's use of images associated with Western movies. Westerns had already developed a characteristic and well-recognized set of narrative and iconographic tropes which were both visually exciting and "coded" as somehow "historical." In thinking about the cinematic form of his myth-in-the-making, Griffith deliberately drew on both the formal conventions of the genre and its mythic content:

> We had had all sorts of runs-to-the-rescue in pictures and horse operas. The old United States Cavalry would gallop to the rescue—East, one week; West, the next. It was always a hit. . . . Now I could see a chance to do this ride-to-the-rescue on a grand scale. Instead of saving one poor little Nell of the Plains this would be a ride to save a nation.[32]

The visualization of that rescue as a struggle between men of White and Dark races for the body of a White woman is of course a fundamental trope of the Frontier Myth. Griffith emphasized the connection by setting the climactic struggle as a Reconstruction version of the "Attack on the Settlers' Cabin" scene that had been a staple of dime-novel illustration, Buffalo Bill's Wild West, and Griffith's own early Westerns.

For movies to succeed as a mythopoetic medium, they had to develop a more comprehensive form of that visual coding of image and meaning that the Western enjoyed by virtue of its extensive pre-cinematic history. *Birth of a Nation* extended the rhetorical reach of existing visual codes (the Western structure is enlarged to contain a larger historical subject), and it invented new codes and ways of investing images with intellectual content. For our purposes, the most significant of these inventions is the discovery that when history is visualized by a camera the audience will receive it as if it were *realized*.[33] The mobs of Blacks rioting in the streets of Piedmont do not just symbolize or refer to the concept of "Negro Rule"—they *are* Negro Rule made visible, just as hooded Klansman massing on horseback to redeem Piedmont from Negro Rule *are* the White race's instinctive response to oppression and racial degradation. The power of historiographic and political hypotheses, which written history represents abstractly as the interaction of large "forces," becomes concrete on the screen in the spectacle of masses of troops in battle and crowds in violent movement. Through repeated usage, "spectacle" itself became a visual sign whose presence the audience would recognize as signifying the presence of "the historical."[34]

As we have seen, the Western had inherited some ready-made icons of historical authenticity—Indians, covered wagons, cowboys—and had augmented the authority of these images by advertising its use of "real" locations and "original participants." As real connections to the Old West became more tenuous, and as moviemakers evolved their own habits and preferences in the matters of landscape, setting, and costuming, they developed their own equivalents of Griffith's spectacles and mob scenes: a set of visual signs signifying the presence of "History" and imparting the suggestion of mythic significance.

But unlike Griffith, the maker of Westerns could not transform "History" into "Lightning" in one grand, unified work of art. In the movie business, even at this early date, habits tended to form quickly and die slowly. The Western movie had developed as the visual equivalent of the series dime novel, and there would be no attempts at epic historical treatment until *The Covered Wagon* in 1923. Rather, the mythic charge of the Western was constituted by the genre as a whole—by the habitual connection of image and idea in a series of closely related productions.

The viewer's perception of an intertextual bond between Westerns depended on the strength of two visual elements, the Western setting and the Western star. Moviemakers modified the received images of western towns and ranches to suit the requirements of filming, explored the visual possibilities of more "authentic" locations, and gradually established their own distinctive "Western" iconography. This development was closely linked to the development of Western "stars"—actors peculiarly identified with Western roles and settings.

Icons of Authenticity: The Movie Star as Progressive Hero

In the most elementary sense of the term, the *star* is the protagonist of the movie. But "stardom" became a peculiar feature of both the corporate structure of the movie business and of the kinds of film Hollywood would produce. The first stars were film actors who acquired celebrity through a succession of appealing roles in which they developed and projected a consistent screen persona by which they could be readily identified. When movie production was incorporated in a studio system, the phenomenon of stardom was recognized and systematically commodified. Screen personae were "typed" and systematically exploited. Some stars were inescapably associated with particular genres; others embodied a type that was both general and highly personal—for example, the "romantic lead" or "Clark Gable" type—which allowed them to appear in a variety of genres. But stardom as a cultural phenomenon is not contained by the films on which it is based. It involves an apparently inescapable confusion between actor and role, between "real life" and the fiction made about it, that mimics the conceptual structure of myth.

This confusion is particularly significant in the case of the Western star, because he is a hero in two different mythic traditions: the celebrity-generating mythology of Hollywood, and the Boone–Crockett–Cody–Virginian tradition of the Frontier Myth. Actors whose stardom derived primarily from Westerns often found themselves "type-cast" into a narrow range of roles. But the repeated association of a performer with a single genre like the Western or (later) the gangster film fostered the illusion that the star continuously "inhabits" that fictive world, and his passage from film to film is mistaken as a kind of biography, the development of "his" character, the figurative history of "his" life.[35] The more significant the star as a figure in national culture, the deeper the confusion. The supreme example of the type is John Wayne, whose role as movie hero became so important to our culture after the Second World War that Congress authorized a medal honoring him as the embodiment of American military heroism—although he had never served a day in uniform. The cultural structures through which Wayne would rise to the stature of myth-hero were established between 1914 and 1920 in the work of the most important silent-Western star, William S. Hart. Although he was born in the East, was a professional stage actor rather than a cowboy, and was even older than Zane Grey when he finally became a "westerner," Hart became so powerfully identified with "the real West" that he was "cast" as the model for the statue of "The Range Rider of the Yellowstone" (Billings, Montana), which memorializes the range cattle frontier.[36]

Hart was both a star actor and a director, and in both capacities he exercised genuinely authorial supervision over most of the productions with which he was associated. He also brought to the movies a clear and well-established vision of the West as region and the Western as a story-form, coupled with a serious, almost preacherly commitment to moralizing through his art.[37] "Authenticity" and "realism" were Hart's trademarks from the first, putting him squarely in the filmmaking tradition of Ince and Jennings. However, except for a brief excursion to the northern Great Plains in the 1870s, Hart did not personally experience the "cowboy-and-Indian" West until he began to make Western movies at the age of forty-nine.

Hart was born in Newburgh, New York, in 1865, and his father—an itinerant miller—moved the family from town to town throughout the northern Midwest. When Hart was fifteen they moved to New York City, where they lived in poverty. After trying a variety of jobs, and after considering an application to West Point, Hart became a professional actor and spent thirty years touring the United States and England playing a variety of roles in classical drama, contemporary plays, and melodramas. His success in the supporting part of the cowboy in *The Squaw Man* led to his most successful role as the lead in the stage version of *The Virginian*. According to his autobiography, these roles gratified his oldest childhood fantasies, and they certainly gave him credibility when he came to Hollywood to act in Westerns.[38]

What Hart brought to the genre was not the experience of a Tilghman or a Jennings, but the theatrical sense of a professional trouper energized by a powerful affection for, and a psychological investment in, the "real Wild West." As his fame grew, and as the authenticity of his screen persona became an important feature of his art, he revised the story of his own early life, exaggerating his connection with the West of cowboys and Indians.[39] He condemned Westerns made by other producers and even asserted (somewhat ungratefully) that Wister's work "is at variance with cowboy life as I knew it," although Wister knew both the relevant period and the range cattle business far better than Hart.[40] In articles and interviews for the trade press he displayed his expertise to justify his way of costuming and dramatizing his stories. He sought technical advice and cultivated friendships with "original participants" like Wyatt Earp, "Bat" Masterson, Charley Siringo, Bill Tilghman, and Al Jennings and seems to have been geninely popular with working cowboys, especially (though not exclusively) those in show business or rodeos.[41]

But Hart's "realism" was a conscious compromise between his sense of "the facts" and his understanding of formal conventions. In an interview given in 1920, Hart said that although the true stories told by these men were better than any of his own scripts, neither the critics nor the public would recognize them as the real thing. The public's canon of "realism," as Hart understood it, was determined by the language of convention, and a filmmaker could push audiences only so far without losing their interest and their belief in the film's reality. Hart's sincere devotion to creating a Western cinema of perceived authenticity and realism paradoxically demanded that he offer only those versions of truth that conformed to the expectations generated by a "false" but culturally prepotent mythology.

The plots of Hart's movies were pure dime novel and nickelodeon, very much in the Deadwood Dick pattern. Hart almost always played a "bad man" of one kind or another—an outlaw, gambler, or just a hard customer—who finds redemption through the love of a good woman (or a pure young girl). The formula was used over and over, with minor variations. Sometimes the hero would be unjustly accused of crime; sometimes he would be a genuine criminal who redeems himself through some charitable act. The settings varied somewhat but were generically Western.

What set Hart's films above the dime novel and other Westerns was their visual style, which critics identified as realistic but which might more accurately be described as consistently austere. His costumes were designed to look more utilitarian and gritty than the stage cowboy's garb; his towns are scruffy and mean-looking; and his landscapes are desert-like—sparse grass and brush, wide blanks of sky. His view of western society is similarly "hard-boiled." His opponents are only rarely Indians, who might have been construed as Noble Savages. More often, his opponents are figures reminiscent of the dangerous classes and human "scum" of the metropolis: cardsharps, brothel-keepers, and racketeers, many of them half-breeds or "Mexicans."[42]

Hart matches his screen persona precisely to the style of this unforgiving landscape. Spareness and austerity are the salient features of his face, which is long and bony and marked with vertical lines, the mouth thin-lipped and grimly set. His clothing is rough and simple. Though sometimes varied with a preacher's or gambler's frock coat, it is usually a cowboy rig—pants stuffed into high boots, checked shirt with leather bracers at the wrists, wide-brimmed hat, and two guns slung low on crossed gunbelts, with something in the line of the belts and the jut of the pistol butts suggesting the size and weight of the revolvers. Man and landscape complete each other, as even the early reviewers of Hart's films observed. The review of *On the Night Stage* (1915) in the *New York Dramatic Mirror* ignores the film's nominal plot to locate its power in the visualizations of landscape and character:

> It is almost useless to dwell on the silvery landscapes that tell the wild story of this rugged period. Long stretches of wandering road for the racing coach are unmarred by any anachronisms such as modern buildings as are usually present. One may truly picture the West of boundless prairies and hill tracts, with here and there a town where . . . things were "wide open." . . . Doubtless the success of William S. Hart in the role of the gruff, almost forbidding looking cowboy in previous pictures has rightfully suggested that he play the lead here. Mr. Hart's is a face that photographs to a nicety. Small wonder, then, that he should be able to monopolize the action, for one follows his movements with the fascination that a snake has upon his feathered prey. . . .[43]

Hart's screen persona became the primary symbol of authenticity in his own films, and this identification of the man with the role defines the character of movie stardom. The figure of Hart and the landscape he inhabits effectively authenticate each other. The face is credible as the "type" of the western man because it so obviously belongs in that landscape where nothing that glitters is gold. Yet this aesthetic consistency has nothing to do with realism as such. The West is not all arid sagebrush; and western men—even outlaws and revengers—sometimes looked more like Friar Tuck or Caspar Milquetoast than Savonarola. Hart's face works because it matches the kind of West he has chosen to envision, and that West is primarily a mythic space in which a special kind of moral drama can be imagined as occurring.

Birth of a Nation influenced Hart's understanding of the medium, particularly in *Hell's Hinges*, produced during the fall of 1915 in the wake of *Birth of a Nation*'s spectacular success, and released in February 1916. At $32,676.43 it cost nearly four times as much as any other film Hart had ever made.[44] The story-line follows what was by then the standard Hart formula, in which Hart plays the badman redeemed by the love of a good woman. But Hart's sophisticated handling of the generic story and pictorial elements gives the work complexity, irony, and resonance with the larger structures of myth and ideology.

The film begins in an eastern city rather than in the West. The Rev. Robert Henley, a young candidate for the ministry, preaches a sermon in the basement chapel of an urban mission. His examining board notes evidence of spiritual weakness and vanity: he plays to the young ladies in the audience with flourishes of hands and eyes, to the dismay of his sister Faith. The board decides that he is not strong enough to cope with the temptations of city life; so they send him to the Far West, where (they suppose) people live pure lives, close to Nature and to Nature's God. Faith accompanies him to help him in his labors and to keep watch over his weakness. The scene then jumps directly to Placer Gulch—a typical western town seen at first from above, with false-front saloons and covered board sidewalks, and a raw-looking clapboard church set in an arid plain. The streets are filled with a violent rout of cowboys, and a title informs us that the town has earned its sobriquet "Hell's Hinges."

The opening sequence invokes, in the most economical manner, the fundamental opposition of civilization and savagery and the fable of redemption through immersion in the wilderness that lies at the heart of the Myth of the Frontier. The examining board invokes the "pastoral" version of the Frontier Myth, which sees the wilderness as more innocent than the city and as a place for spiritual regeneration.

But as soon as the Myth is invoked it is cast in doubt. The denizens of Placer Gulch are not red savages whose brutality might be the result of a kind of innocence, but Whites corrupted by the freedom the West gives to the indulgence of animal nature. This West is not an alternative to the city but the field in which the evils of society have found their freest play.

Two men stand at the head of this evil society, each representing a side of its character. Silk Miller is the owner of the largest saloon, the center of the town's institutionalized evil. He dresses in black frock coat and hat, string tie and vest, and he sports a black mustache. His is a refined corruption, belonging to towns and dependent on the power of money, insidious and indirect in pursuit of its aims. The script gives this image of an urban-western corruption racial overtones by describing Silk as having "the oily craftiness of the Mexican."

The other pillar of evil is "Blaze" Tracey (played by Hart), whose membership in the party of disorder is the by-product of his intense individualism, his Anglo-Saxon self-will and impatience of restraint, his masculine pride, and his disdain for weakness and effeminacy. He wears cowboy clothes and two guns on crossed gunbelts, which mark him as a range rider rather than a townsman like Miller. His name associates him with the noblest kind of "wild Westerner," the scout or blazer of trails (i.e., "traces"), in the tradition of Boone, Leatherstocking, and Buffalo Bill. His "badness" is different from Miller's, because it has to do exclusively with himself, with his way of living his own life, while Miller's evil aims always at the achievement of power and control over others. Tracey may be a kind of Noble Savage—perhaps the only one in this version of the West—who has an intuitive recognition of "the good" and a code of personal honor. However, aside from his propensity to violence, the signs that mark his difference from civilized norms are not "Indian" signs but rather the habits that mark his kinship with the "White savages" of the dangerous classes who inhabit the urban "saloon culture": smoking, drinking whiskey, and gambling.

Tracey initially supports Miller and his rowdies in their attempt to scare off the new minister. But when Faith Henley defies the mob and appeals for help, Blaze is knocked off balance by a vision of goodness beyond his experience—but not beyond his imagination or desire. After an exchange of intense glances (a visual cliché even in 1916) we know Faith and Blaze have fallen in love and that the good woman will redeem the bad man. Hart's narrative is designed to distinguish Tracey's "virilist" or "red-blooded" Christianity from the merely conventional piety of Rev. Henley.

The narrative of Blaze's conversion is paralleled in mirror-image by the tale of Henley's degeneration. Blaze learns to desire faith by experiencing desire for Faith: the virile Anglo-Saxon man's sexual love of the pure White woman is the instinctive basis of his "natural" or innate capacity for civilization and progress. Given his nature, his salvation is not imperiled by his rude training or physical disposition to vice. Although he lubricates his Bible studies with shots of whiskey and puffs of a cigarette, his *motives* are seen to be absolutely sincere, because they are based on "true love" for a "White woman." He reads the Bible simply because it is "Her Book." In contrast, Henley's respectable habits cannot restrain his inherently vicious character when it is tempted by the licentious freedoms of Hell's Hinges. His character weaknesses are visualized in racial terms: Silk Miller (part Mexican, part rattlesnake) seduces Henley into subjection to the demon rum and then turns him over to his half-breed prostitute, who completes the minister's moral ruination. In the end, Henley will be killed at the head of a drunken mob while putting the torch to his own church. The image of its burning cross borrows one of the most dramatic of Griffith's symbols—although here it signifies the ruin of society rather than its coming redemption.

The parallel narratives make it clear that closeness to nature does not determine moral character: West or East, human society is corrupt. But neither does culture determine character and fate: eastern culture and Bible-reading cannot make Henley a good man, nor can saloon culture make Tracey an entirely bad one. What makes Tracey capable of good is that aspect of his nature which determines that his sexual passions will be fully aroused only by a woman like Faith Henley, while the moral weakness of the minister is equated with his racially indiscriminate passions. This racial dimension allows us to see that the idea of "character" with which Hart is working is drawn from the traditions of Cooper's historical romances and the more recent literature of Anglo-Saxonism. In those traditions, sexual passion is seen as the most fundamental expression of racial consciousness or instinct, and the characteristic of the true Anglo-Saxon is represented as an intense exclusivity in preferring women of his own race, the purer the better.

The amalgamation of Christianity and western manhood in Tracey's character makes him an Old Testament type of avenger, ready to answer burning with burning. "Hell needs this town," he says, "and it's goin' back, and goin' damn quick!" All alone, with both guns drawn, Tracey stalks into Miller's saloon, shoots Miller and two of his henchmen, and holds the entire male population of the town at bay with his six-guns. Then, having demonstrated his dominance and their cowardice, he shoots the oil lamps down, sets the place ablaze, and lets them flee. The fire spreads to the whole town, and we see what appear to be hundreds of people fleeing the smoke and flame and their fear of Blaze Tracey out into the desert.

The scene evokes the destruction of Sodom and Gomorrah. But Hart has his character reach this Old Testament conclusion by a non-canonical route: his action arises not from obedience to any external book-learned code but from his Anglo-Saxon nature and his western nurture—from the nature of his race and character as a man. Thus it arises from the same part of his nature that engaged him with Faith Henley in the first place. Love and violence—the passion that draws the Anglo-Saxon man to his woman and that forces him to defend her at all costs—are twins. As the saloon burns, Tracey lingers inside and the camera follows him around. It is a beautiful, striking set of images, the two-gun man walking meditatively through the fire, shadowed in front, lit only from behind by sudden flares of fire as spilled whiskey or a dry board ignites. It is impossible to know what he is thinking, but the beauty of the images suggests that there is a kind of pleasure for him in lingering there, savoring his victory, or perhaps just savoring the power of destruction, the sheer "blaze."[45]

In that image the movie completes its abstraction of the mythic and historical figures and situations with which it has been playing. Every element of the historical mythology, which Griffith and Hart share, is pared down, in the Western, to its most elemental terms. The economy of this symbolic language facilitates the making of allegories, with all the weaknesses and strengths of allegorical forms. But that paring-away is also a form of critique of the more elaborately structured systems of rationalization. There is an ideological stance implicit in this way of telling the story—a stance that vests moral power only in the individual and denies the possibility of larger forms of social redemption. At the end, Blaze and Faith ride away from the ruins of Placer Gulch heading for California. Their gesture is like Huck Finn's "lighting out for the Territory," or Lassiter and Jane Withersteen sealing themselves away from the world in their hidden valley. It invokes the Frontier Myth in the assumption that beyond the border is a better, more redemptive place, but it does so at the end of a story that suggests that there is no way to evade the corruption of the world. The only thing that has been validated by the story is the hero's character itself, now raised nearly to the status of a moral principle: Virtue, goodness, and right are to be found wherever there is a man like Blaze Tracey—intensely "masculine," proud, self-willed, strong, hard-headed, capable of effective violence—and White.

So formulated, Hart's persona is the perfect *visualization* of the progressive hero whose qualities and ideological significations had been established by Roosevelt, Grant and Stoddard, Wister, and the red-blooded school.[46] Indeed, these connections are explicitly developed in Hart's next two films, *The Aryan* and *The Patriot*, both released in 1916.

The Aryan (1916), made right after *Hell's Hinges*, is Hart's most explicitly racialist film.[47] Hart plays a young miner, Steve Denton, who is enticed into a roulette game by a prostitute named Trixie. In the midst of the game a telegram arrives from Denton's mother, who is gravely ill; but Trixie lies about its contents and keeps Denton drinking and playing till his money is gone. He discovers the telegram next day, but before he can respond he is informed of his mother's death. Denton then shoots up the town, repeating the ending of *Hell's Hinges*. But instead of turning his back on violence and riding off to marry the good woman in California, he abducts and enslaves (rapes) the prostitute who betrayed him. Denton becomes an odd variant of the old Indian-hater figure: "He has sworn vengeance on the whole white race, and especially its women." His moral fall is expressed as a loss of racial identity: the woman's crime has "left its black impress on his very soul." He now treats White women as only the bad Indians and renegades of dime novels do and leads a band of Mexican and half-breed renegades in attacks on wagon trains full of White pioneers. Denton is redeemed when a young girl from one of the wagon trains comes to his camp to plead with him. She risks herself among the Mexican renegades, confiding implicitly in the fact that Denton is an "Aryan" and as such instinctively bound to protect all women of his race, especially the pure and innocent: "He is a White man, she can see that, although he lives among half-breeds and Indians, and she knows he will run true to the creed of his race—to protect its women."[48]

In *The Patriot* (1916) Hart treats the same theme in a more overtly political way. Hart plays Bob Wiley, a veteran of the Spanish–American War who is cheated out of his homestead by a pair of crooked politicians. When the authorities in Washington fail to help, he becomes bitter against the nation that has so miserably rewarded his patriotism. He crosses the border and joins the bandit and revolutionary "Pancho Zapilla," who is planning a raid on the border town in which Wiley has lived. The bandit's name is a compound of two peasant leaders of the Mexican Revolution of 1910–20, Pancho Villa and Emiliano Zapata. The plot clearly refers to Pancho Villa's 1915 raid on Columbus, New Mexico. In the end, Wiley is recalled to patriotism by the "racial" appeal of a child who reminds him of his own dead son. Hart thus uses the terms of the Western to address the issues of social justice and abuse of power from which modern revolutions arise; and through those terms he is able to acknowledge the fact of injustice while discrediting revolutionary solutions by linking them with the racially alien and criminal Mexicans.

Hart's career shows how "star-persona," created through performances in individual films, can become a cultural artifact whose signifying power transcends both the single film and the boundaries between fictive screen-worlds and "the real thing." The development of a star-persona of this kind is a mythographic act: the creation of a distinctly modern form of culture hero who appears as the representative man of his people or nation. Through Hart, the Western genre-hero achieved broad acceptance as a historically "authentic" and morally valid representation of a specifically "red-blooded" version of American character. This is the sense of a review of Hart's *Breed of Men* (1919) by Louis Reeves Harrison: "The ruling idea . . . is that the American type is one of strong protective instincts and sympathy for the weak; a fine theme, and admirably exemplified by Hart in his own personality. . . ." The same reviewer praises Hart's portrayal of an outlaw in *The Toll Gate* (1920) for transcending the simplest categories of type to represent "the combined daring and cunning of the American fighting male." And reviews of *The Testing Block* (1920) saw that Hart's theme is really "an evolution of manhood," beginning with a representation of the "tigerish" and "intensely animal" primitivism of the outlaw—his most vivid representation of "the lawless male"—but ending with his redemption through the love of a woman and her child.[49]

Although the critics understood that Hart's films were meant to represent archetypes rather than to reconstruct history, they persisted in praising Hart for being the authentic cowboy that he assuredly was not: "No actor before the screen has been able to give as sincere and true a touch to the Westerner as Hart. He rides in a manner indigenous to the soil, he shoots with the real knack. . . .[50] Critics who disliked his films represent him as the "Blaze Tracey" of Hollywood, a man whose preoccupation with crime and violence has made his "pictures . . . a most dangerous weapon in the hands of our enemies [the censors]."[51] One critic suggests that Hart is a kind of Hollywood Hawkeye, a primitive who has no place in a modern, progressive society:

> A large number of the roles he has assumed in the past have been those of the vagrant outlaw of equally vagrant morals brought to a conversion of character through the [effect] of a woman's influence. While the reformation of wandering outlaws may be occasionally edifying, their lack of importance in any civilization, particularly one so progressive as our own, is apt to rouse but faint interest in the story.[52]

Although the individual Western had less obvious impact on public discourse than a *Birth of a Nation*, in the aggregate the impact of the genre-based mythology was probably greater. Its images were more pervasive and entered public awareness without the troubling aura of political controversy. Moreover it became part of the general idiom and vocabulary of contemporary references—as "Charlie Chaplin," apart from any single performance, came to stand for a particular human type or comic style. To critics and audiences a succession of Westerns, bound to each other by the carry-over of character-types, individual actors, and common settings, taking up in turn a range of possible responses to the given problem, made a kind of aggregate statement whose meanings were taken as broadly applicable to "American society." No critic of the period would have seen the popularity of *Birth of a Nation*, *Ben-Hur*, or *The Ten Commandments* as a measure of public taste and morals, although the production might be read as a sign of seriousness in the company or the industry that produced it. But public response to Westerns as a group was taken as a symptom of the state of American taste, morals, and self-image, and it is this implication of a significant interplay between what occurs on screen and what occurs in "the real world" that signals the presence of an active mythographic enterprise.

The Epic Western, 1923–1931

The popularity of formula Westerns eventually encouraged Hollywood production companies to produce Western "feature films."[53] Although there were some respectable literary works on which a Western could be based—*The Virginian* was one—the obvious way to aggrandize a Western would be to enlarge upon its implicit historical referents. This had been attempted in early films like Ince's *Custer's Last Fight* (1912), but in the post-Griffith era the scale and sophistication of the historical epic were incomparably greater.

James Cruze's *The Covered Wagon* (1923), based on a well-known novel by Emerson Hough, was "the first American epic not directed by David W. Griffith."[54] The film's plot was formulaic melodrama, and some important episodes—the buffalo hunt, the Indian attack—were movie versions of Wild West standards. But Cruze made extraordinarily efective use of location shooting, which established the grand image of western landscape as a strong cinematic sign of the presence of "history"—a Western equivalent of Griffith's mob scenes and architectural spectacles.

Other production companies of course attempted to replicate Cruze's success. Fox urged Hart to revive his waning fame by attempting his first "historical" Westerns, *Wild Bill Hickok* (1923) and *Tumbleweeds* (1925). Cruze followed *Covered Wagon* with the cattle-drive epic *North of 36* (1924) and *The Pony Express* (1925). John Ford's first feature film, *The Iron Horse* (1924, with Thomas Ince), told the story of the building of the transcontinental railroad, and his *Three Bad Men* (1926) used an elaborately staged version of the Oklahoma Land Rush as background for a sentimental "good badman" story (later remade as *Three Godfathers* [1940, 1949]).

These epics expanded the repertoire of the genre beyond the allegorical simplicities of the moral melodrama. It was now possible to set a dignified and "significant" historical fable in Western dress. The "epics" also suggested that there was more to the Western than the character of the hero-star: that some *stories* had "star quality"—enough intrinsic power or symbolic weight to invest relatively unknown actors with Hart-like stature. The epics also promulgated a consistently "progressive" interpretation of frontier history—a reading which ironically makes for characterizations that have fewer moral complexities than the heroes of Hart's potboiler allegories, and portraits of society that lack Hart's grim realism and critical edge.

The Western rose in popularity throughout the boom years of the 1920s and reached its peak in 1926, when the advent of "talking pictures" sent it into a brief decline (1927–29) as the studios scrambled for properties designed to exploit the sensation of the new technology. But silent Westerns retained their popularity during the transition, and between 1929 and 1931 the Western again became a staple of sound-movie production.[55] The series and feature films produced continued to develop along lines laid down in silent Westerns. Fox's *In Old Arizona* (1929) enlarges a character from a silent series (the Cisco Kid); Paramount's *The Virginian* (1929), starring Gary Cooper, was a remake of a silent film. MGM's *Billy the Kid* (1930), directed by King Vidor, achieved what Hart had failed to accomplish: the integration of a tightly focused portrait of a man torn between good and evil within a large, historically defined framework. Despite the beginning of the Great Depression in 1929–30, Hollywood was willing to expand its investment in Westerns to epic scale. Raoul Walsh's covered-wagon epic, *The Big Trail* (1930), was an expensive failure that ruined John Wayne's initial bid for stardom. But Cecil B. deMille's *Cimarron* (1931) successfully continued the epic formula developed by Cruze and Ford. In addition to its box-office success, the film won Oscars for best picture, best adaptation, and best set decoration.

The emergence of the Western as a genre for feature films in 1926–31 marked the culmination of the genre's first cycle of development. In the years following *The Great Train Robbery*, works in the Western form had a significant impact on the development of the new medium and of the industry that produced it. They helped shape producers' understanding of the importance of setting and reference, the possibilities of location and action shooting, and the appeal of the star. At the same time, the new medium and the industry succeeded in appropriating the literary and historical tradition of the Myth of the Frontier and translating its symbols and references and its peculiar way of blending fiction and history into cinematic terms. As a result, Western movies were established as a primary vehicle for the transmission of that myth/ideology, rivaling or exceeding in importance the pulp novel.

But the continuity of genre development was broken in 1931. As the Great Depression deepened, Hollywood virtually abandoned the Western as a subject for feature films.

8 The Studio System, the Depression, and the Eclipse of the Western, 1930–1938

Given the precedent of *The Covered Wagon,* the spectacular success of deMille's *Cimarron* in 1931 ought to have been followed by a wave of big Westerns. Despite the Depression, the newly consolidated studio system now centered in Hollywood was better equipped than it had been in 1923 to exploit such a triumph with a series of follow-up productions. Instead, the Western entered a period of eclipse that lasted for most of the Depression decade.[1] "B" Westerns remained staples of Hollywood production during this period and were part of most afternoons at the movies.[2] But after 1931 the seven major studios became extremely skeptical about the market for feature-length Westerns, and their investment of money and resources went into the development of other genres that seemed more likely to appeal to the "general public."[3]

The drop-off in the production of "A" Western features was sudden and precipitous. In 1930 "A" Westerns made up 2.6 percent of films produced by the seven major studios, and 21.4 percent of all Westerns. In 1931 these figures dropped to 1.6 percent and 16.7 percent, although Westerns (both "A" and "B") continued to comprise 16–17 percent of all Hollywood films (major studios and independents). In 1932 the Western share of all Hollywood films actually rose to 22 percent; but "A" Westerns dropped to 0.6 percent of major studio production and 4.7 percent of all Westerns. The nadir was reached in 1934, when *no* "A" Westerns were produced. Between 1932 and 1934, though Westerns continued to average 17 percent of all Hollywood productions, "A" Westerns averaged only 0.3 percent of all major studio productions and 2.4 percent of all Westerns. In 1935–36 the studios attempted a revival of the genre, but public response did not seem adequate and production dropped sharply again.[4] In absolute numbers, there were fewer "A" Westerns made in 1937 and 1938 (three and four, respectively) than had been made in 1931 (five), the first year of the genre's decline—this in an industry that generally increased the annual number of films produced through the decade.[5]

But in 1939 there was a "renaissance" of the Western. Every studio made a major and nearly simultaneous commitment of resources to the production of "prestige" feature Westerns. From a total of four "A" Westerns in 1938, production by the major studios jumped to nine in 1939 and fourteen in 1940—2.3 percent and 3.5 percent of the majors' total production in those years, a level exceeding that of the previous peak in 1930. The "renaissance" inaugurated a thirty-year period—briefly interrupted during the war years 1942–45—in which the Western was the most consistently popular and most widely produced form of action film and a significant field for the active fabrication and revision of public myth and ideology.[6]

This sequence of events poses some important problems for the study of mythographic processes in mass-culture industries. Why did the Western genre fall from favor when and how it did, and why were attempts to revive it unsuccessful until 1939? What happened to the mythographic charge of the Western during its eclipse? And what kind of history does a form or genre like the Western have when it is not an active, primary field for the projection of major ideological and political concerns?

The crisis of the Depression undoubtedly had something to do with the genre's decline. The formulas of the silent Western (and especially of the epic) had developed during the boom times of the 1920s, and the historical or literary references of these films evoked a mythology ineluctably linked with the heroic age of American expansion and the dream of limitless growth. In 1932–35 it may have seemed that that vision of history was invalid, or no longer useful, that to speak to the needs of the moment projective fantasies had at least to entertain the possiblity of historical catastrophe, the failure of the progressive dream that had been embodied in the Myth of the Fronter.

Indeed, an explicit rejection of the progressive interpretation of Turner's Frontier Thesis was part of the ideology of the New Deal administration. President Franklin D. Roosevelt himself, and other members of his "Brains Trust," used Turner's theory of frontier closure to describe the new condition of the American economy. But they rejected the "progressive" gloss on Turner, which looked to new frontiers of imperial conquest or unlimited industrial growth to replace the lost Frontier. As FDR himself declared in a 1932 address,

> Our last frontier has long since been reached. . . . There is no safety valve in the form of a Western Prairie. . . . Our task is not the discovery or exploitation of natural resources. . . . It is the less dramatic business of administering resources and plants already in hand . . . of distributing wealth and products equitably.[7]

But the "negatives" that attached to the Western may have been less important than the "positives" that the studios found in other kinds of story. The pressure to find (or create) and exploit new types of story, and to systematically assess the degree to which they aroused public interest, was inherent in the new studio system that evolved after 1927—and prospered, despite the Depression.

The Studio as Genre-Machine, 1930–1938

The corporate consolidation of the Hollywood studios, the growth of their market, and the economies of scale that the studio system made possible pointed the industry toward the mass production and marketing of great numbers of films; and this in turn facilitated the proliferation and development of film genres by maximizing the benefits inherent in the systematic repetition of successful productions and formulas. At the least, such repetition enabled the studios to re-use such properties as sets and costumes; more important, it allowed them to fully and efficiently exploit the popular recognition of consistent screen personae (both stars and character actors) and story-types.

But the profitability of the studios' vast investment of capital and labor depended on their ability to read and anticipate fine shifts in the balance of public enthusiasm for given types of story. Although they had incomparable facilities for flooding the market with films of a certain type and for manipulating public preferences, the studios could not control those preferences. Studios prospered by learning to anticipate shifts in the public's interest in particular kinds of story and by their industrial capacity to exploit a discovered preference by reproducing the successful story-type speedily and in quantity. New stories, and innovative treatments of older stories, were continually tested in the marketplace, evaluated for their appeal to the public, and then imitated and reproduced as many times, and for as many years, as their apparent popularity warranted.[8]

Thus one of the important threads in the history of the film industry in the 1930s is the appearance, growth, and decline, the alternate waxing and waning, of movie genres. In fact, the 1930s was the founding decade for many if not most of the specific forms that are now identified as "Hollywood movie genres." The musical comedy, the gangster film, the screwball comedy (with its mix of sound and sight gags), and the hard-boiled detective film had no real equivalents in the silent era. And though the Western, the "swashbuckler," the war film, and the Bible epic existed before 1929, their characteristic story-forms and iconography were radically revised after 1932.

Story-type was not the industry's only operative category for defining the production and marketing of films. The studio star system gave certain actors and actresses a persona that transcended the limits of performance in a single film and gave them a public identity that was both dependent on and larger than their on-screen role-playing. The commercial drawing power of certain stars made them, in effect, the premise of their own genre of star vehicles. However, the achievement of stardom was not, in most cases, independent of the processes that produced story-and-setting-centered genres. Indeed, most stars acquired their screen personae through early success in particular kinds of setting followed by persistent type-casting; their personae remained associated, in greater or lesser degree, with these roles and settings. The star persona of a Clark Gable or a Bette Davis could be successfully used in a variety of stories and settings, but Errol Flynn did not seem usable outside a certain kind of adventure film and James Cagney was so powerfully identified with his gangster roles that his work in musicals is sometimes forgotten.

Some of the genres the studios exploited in the 1930s were already well established. The studios recognized differences in types of comedy and drama according to setting and subject matter: contemporary or historically costumed; domestic, romantic or sentimental; verbal or slapstick. The epic was also understood in its several variants—historical, literary, and biblical. And there were two kinds of Western, the Hart/Mix type of formula Western and the historical epic.

This genre mix was modified by the industry's need to reflect timely concerns and current sensations. In this they followed the precedent of their precursor culture industries, the purveyors of dime-novel and pulp fiction. But under the studio system, the process of connecting formulas to current concerns became far more self-conscious and systematic. Warner Bros.' initial experiments with films that referred directly to the social setting of the Depression may have arisen spontaneously from the traditional mass-media practice of ransacking contemporary journalism for timely stories. But the public response to these movies, registered at the box office, convinced the Warners that what the general public wanted (in 1931–35) were films that spoke more or less directly to the setting, concerns, and dark mood of the Depression. The studio responded by developing the new genres of the "gangster film" and the "social drama." But appeal of timeliness and sensational effects was also available to less political genres. Sound technology made new kinds of comedy possible, combining the verbal with the physical in ways that were innovative and highly appealing. The movie musical and the "swashbuckler" took advantage (in their different ways) of the sensational possibilities inherent in the new technologies of movie production to produce films of "magical" appeal. The new wave of "horror" films offered a fantastic take on the darkness of the time.

The thirties also saw the development of new genres that arose in response to changes in the industry (the shift to sound) as well as to the social crisis of the Depression. The genres that spoke most directly to the crisis of the 1930s were the crime film and the social drama. The latter category included films that dealt explicitly with Depression-era problems of poverty, unemployment, and social displacement (*I am a Fugitive from a Chain Gang* [1932], *Wild Boys of the Road* [1934], *Grapes of Wrath* [1940]) or with more general issues of social justice and political ideology (*Gabriel Over the White House* [1933], *Fury* [1936], *Black Legion* [1936], *Meet John Doe* [1941]). The crime category centered on the most popular new action genre of the early 1930s,the gangster film; but it includes as well urban "police procedurals" and stories of crusading newspapermen who expose civic corruption. These films reflected on the dark side of the American dream, which the Depression had revealed. The gangster film offered a dark parody of the Horatio Alger success story in which the characteristically American dream of success is perverted by the hypocrisy and greed of the Roaring Twenties.

Two of these newly active genres developed on the terrain of the Western and took over some of its mythographic function: the gangster film, and certain related types of crime film, which became suddenly and phenomenally popular in 1931–32; and the "Victorian Empire" adventure film, which became a prominent type of production between 1935 and 1940. These two genres achieved remarkable popularity at different ends of the decade. Their pattern of development reflects a shift in the emphasis of ideological concern through the course of the 1930s. When the Western was revived as a feature genre in 1939 and became once again a major focus of mythographic energies, it built upon the achievements of these two Depression genres.

The Two-Gun Man of the Twenties: Gangster Films, 1931–1939

The gangster film was invented as a distinct category of production in 1931, following the somewhat scandalous box-office successes of Warners' *Public Enemy* and *Little Caesar*. Life and crime on the mean streets had been treated in films before—as early as Griffith's *Musketeers of Pig Alley* (1912). What was new about the gangster film was its insistence that the gangster was a predictable, even a probable, product of modern American life, and its assignment of a quasi-heroic role to a figure who, in the end, remains a criminal. Gangster films also emphasized their timeliness, linking their action directly to the world of current events, to headlines of the day or of the recent past. *Public Enemy*, *Little Caesar*, and *Scarface* (1932) referred to well-known public figures or events. *Scarface* uses episodes from the career of Al Capone, such as the St. Valentine's Day Massacre (1929) and the "Pineapple Primary" (1928)—which would seem to be the source of the gangster-film icon of the hand-grenade hurled from the speeding car to blow up the storefront. *Public Enemy* generally dates its episodes to an earlier epoch but refers to recognizable events from 1924 to 1928. Moreover, these films address an active public issue: the Roosevelt administration's commitment to do away with Prohibition and to confront organized crime. This was hardly the most radical or controversial measure of the New Deal, but for that reason it provided the movies with a relatively safe way for commenting on the historical background of the Depression crisis.

But below these surface innovations of the genre, the narrative and mythic structures of the gangster film were continuous with those of the Western, particularly the good-badman action-formula developed by William S. Hart. Both types of film focus on the career of a social outlaw in a narrative that is generally terse, "gritty" in style, and "realistic" in its pretensions. They take a hard-boiled view of male character and motives in general, and of politicians in particular, and they deploy female figures (mothers, "good women," and "bad girls") as the symbols of moral force that point the hero toward redemption or damnation.

The parallels between the Western and the gangster film are particularly strong in the seminal gangster film *Public Enemy*. The linkage begins in the source material on which the film was based. One of the most memorable episodes in the film is the assassination of a horse by the gangster-hero Tom Powers (James Cagney) and his sidekick Matt, after the animal has thrown and killed their boss "Nails" Nathan, a Jewish gangster modeled on Arnold Rothstein. The incident was based on an incident that actually occurred in Chicago and that involved members of Dion O'Banion's Irish mob. The man who was actually killed by the horse was "Nails" Morton, who was neither Jewish nor the leader of the gang; transforming Morton into Nathan emphasizes the "alien" ethnic element in Prohibition gangsterism. The real-life horse-killer was a man named Louis "Two-Gun" Alterie, whose Italian-sounding alias masked his French origins (his real name was Leland Verain); and he was not raised on the mean streets but on a ranch in Colorado. He gained his nickname from his distinctly Wild West game of shooting out the lights in a saloon with pistols held in both hands. After the Torrio-Capone gang assassinated O'Banion, Alterie became a celebrity of sorts by challenging the killers to a Trampas/Virginian style gunfight, telling the newspapers: "I would die smiling if only I had a chance to meet the guys who did [it], any time, any place they mention and I would get two or three of them at least before they got me. . . . I'd shoot it out with the gang of killers before the sun rose in the morning."[9] Alterie's challenge was never answered, but it is acted out by Cagney's Tom Powers in the climactic shoot-out of *Public Enemy*.

Hell's Hinges and *Public Enemy* begin in the same setting, an urban slum, just before the Great War, and then move to a "wide-open" boom-town setting—Placer Gulch in the Western, Roaring-Twenties Chicago in the gangster film. Both films frame their moral and social problem by contrasting images of Christian morality with the low life of the slum: Faith Henley's image in *Hell's Hinges*, and *Public Enemy*'s opening juxtaposition of the beer-drinking culture of the street and the invasive march-through of the Salvation Army Band. Blaze Tracey and Tom Powers are both identified as "badmen" from the start and are associated with criminal systems headed by racketeering saloon-keepers, Silk Miller and Paddy Ryan. Miller enlists Blaze to prevent the "psalm-singers" from ending his wide-open regime; Paddy enlists Tom and his pal Matt for much the same reasons when Prohibition threatens Ryan's power as a ward heeler and rackets boss. The historical or political stakes of the drama are similar: we stand on the border between two regimes and eras, one bound to a violent past, the other looking to a progressive future. However, the gangster film takes a more ironic view of American pieties: the Christian forces that promise redemption to *Hell's Hinges* are responsible for the moral and legal hypocrisy of Prohibition and the gangster regime that follows.

The good-badman of the Western is also a more abstract image of criminality than the gangster. We know nothing of substance about Blaze Tracey's past; but Tom Powers' childhood is sketched in some detail, because *Public Enemy* needs to explain why and how a potential American hero has gone wrong. Powers' father is an authoritarian policeman-patriarch who disciplines Tom cruelly with the strap. His mother is correspondingly weak and passive, dreamily naive and sentimentally doting. The brutal father makes Tom a rebel against any and all forms of authority; the only things he respects are muscle and money, especially the latter, since his father has none. Overindulgence by his mother spoils Tom and gives him his arrogant style, his sense of being the apple of someone's eye. But the inadequacies of his family shape his fate: Tom seeks and finds surrogate fathers in criminal bosses like Paddy Ryan and "Nails" Nathan. And his affairs with women are complicated by the memory of that ever-gratifying but finally unsatisfying mother.

Tom's romantic problems are significant because the gangster film follows the Western in identifying virtue and redemption with a woman. Three different women offer a kind of salvation to Tom Powers, but the form of each offer reveals that, in the "new" America, even the symbols of redemption have become problematic. Tom's first affair, with a girl he picks up in a speakeasy, opens the possiblity of domestication (though Tom's girlfriend is "no better than she should be"). But Tom rejects domesticity in the famous scene in which he pushes a grapefruit in the woman's face.

Where Blaze covets the moral salvation that Faith represents, Tom desires the secular redemption of "class," equated in this film with the moneyed power, glamour, and self-assurance of "Nails" Nathan and Gwen—a "gent" rather than a gentleman, and a "classy dame" rather than a "lady." Gwen, played by "sex symbol" Jean Harlow, offers Tom more complex and ambiguous gratifications: she seductively admires his violent manliness in one breath and in the next calls him her "little boy"—she is the perfect mate for Tom, an impossible combination of whore and mother. Like Faith Henley, Gwen requires the badman-hero to chose between his love for her and his loyalty to the criminal fraternity of men—but her method is that of sexual seduction, and it does not redeem Tom.

Before the seduction can be consummated, Tom receives word that "Nails" Nathan has been killed and that a war with the rival gang of "Schemer" Burns has begun. Tom immediately abandons Gwen and rejoins "the boys," affirming his loyalty to the criminal fraternity of men. The significance and finality of his choice are registered in the last of his relationships with women, which amounts to a mockery of his "redemptive" romance with Gwen. The "boys" are hidden out in a hotel room, commanded by Paddy Ryan to stay off the streets until he can reorganize things. Frustrated by his separation from Gwen and by the enforced inactivity, Tom gets drunk and is undressed and put to bed by the prostitute whom Ryan has provided for the entertainment of his boys. The prostitute seduces Tom—indeed, he is so helplessly drunk that what happens between them amounts to something like rape. Yet the seduction also involves mothering: the woman speaks about her age and treats Tom like a baby who needs to be tucked in. Tom's revulsion the next morning is so extreme that he disobeys Paddy and returns to the street, where Matt is gunned down by the Burns mob.

Both movies resolve their narratives in a climactic shoot-out, with overtones of the Last Judgment, in which the hero appears as an avenging angel-demon armed with two guns and enters the saloon/speakeasy headquarters of the enemy to confront the whole "mob" alone. Blaze Tracey's confrontation ends in success and in the destruction-purgation of the town by fire. Tom Powers stalks into Schemer Burns's headquarters through a drenching downpour—Noah's flood mirroring apocalyptic fire—but we do not see his vengeance. We see only the flashes of his guns behind blinded windows and hear his lingering cry from off-screen as he comes staggering out into the storm, terribly wounded, and falls into the flooded gutter saying, "I ain't so tough."[10]

Blaze Tracey's fire purges the world of evil and sends Placer Gulch back to the Hell that spawned it. But despite his perverse heroism, Tom Powers' vengeance fails: Burns's men kidnap Tom from the hospital; Paddy Ryan, affirming the code of gang loyalty, agrees to quit the rackets if Tom is released; Tom is returned as a corpse, with a suggestion that he has been tortured to death. The contrast with the ending of *Hell's Hinges* is not simply one between the success of "Western" justice and the failure of "gangster" vengeance. The meanings of success and failure in the worlds envisioned by the two genres are utterly different. The Western hero's redemption and success are linked to the triumph of progress and civilization over a criminality linked to barbarism. In the world of *Public Enemy* the party of order and progress is marginal; the real battle is between a "good" gang that lives by the code of masculine loyalty and brotherhood, and a "bad" gang that "schemes" its way to power and tortures the helpless instead of going at it with straightforward violence. After the apocalypse of *Hell's Hinges*, hero and redemptive woman can ride together down an open road to a new and better territory; for the gangster-hero all women are snares and all streets are dead ends.

The popularity of the early gangster movies produced a spate of imitations at Warners and other major studios. By 1933 the conventions of the genre were well established, and a group of stars and supporting casts became thoroughly identified with gangster roles. The most important were Edward G. Robinson, James Cagney, and (to a lesser extent) Humphrey Bogart, all of whom worked for Warners. Cagney's films in particular set the pattern for the genre and constitute most of its classical canon. In the developed genre, iconography and characterization were highly conventionalized. The opening tracking-shot through the streets of an urban immigrant slum became the visual sign that evoked the historical and social rationale of the genre: gangsterism arises from the gap between urban poverty and the opportunity for wealth offered by the Prohibition era. The glittering world of wealth is visualized in the posh nightclub or speakeasy—a device which associates wealth and class with the entertainment industry itself and with the imagery of "stardom." The hero's childhood is usually represented or referred to as a way of explaining his motives. The hero's choices are symbolized as a choice between masculine friendship (and criminal loyalties) on the one hand, and the love of a redemptive woman on the other. The redemptive women are of two kinds, pure maidens and whores-with-hearts-of-gold. The final resolution, as in the Western, is a shoot-out motivated by a mixture of revenge motives and an urge for redemptive sacrifice. These shoot-outs were particularly important in Cagney's films, where they followed the pattern set in *Public Enemy* of sending the hero up against overwhelming odds, as in *Angels with Dirty Faces* (1938), or all alone into the headquarters of the enemy, as in *Roaring Twenties* (1939). The latter film stands in the same relation to *Public Enemy* as the epic Westerns stand to *Hell's Hinges*: it treats the hero as a historical type who belongs to a wilder epoch that has been tamed and reformed by civilization (the New Deal).

The continuity of theme and structure that links Westerns and gangster films is, I think, primarily the result of their common function as vehicles for a continuously developing mythology. The gangster genre absorbed a central element of the mythic charge of the Western and adapted its mythic material to the concerns and imagery of the Depression and the New Deal. The story of the good-badman had been the conventional device for exploring the meaning of the transition from Frontier to Civilization, from the regime of wild male freedom to that of order and domesticity. In its Indian-fighter variant it had posed the civilization/savagery dichotomy in stark and racial terms; in its outlaw variant, it queried more specifically the difference between "natural" and instinctive codes of honor, justice, fair play, and revenge on the one hand and civilized law and order on the other. But although the gangster film modernized the imagery and historical referents attached to the mythic story, it did not fundamentally transform the underlying structure of the myth itself; nor did it drastically depart from the narrative conventions of the Western genre. As we will see, this continuity of development would carry over and back into the Western when the genre was revived in 1939.

The World-scale Western, "Victorian Empire" Movies, 1935–1940

If the gangster film may be thought of as the heir of the Hart tradition in Western movies, the "Victorian Empire" film may be thought of as the New Deal successor to the epic Western. Where the Hart Western and the gangster film focus intently on a microcosmic conflict within an implied historical frame, the "Empire" film deals explicitly with historical conflicts on the largest scale. The stake of struggle in these films is not merely the possession of the American West or the local rackets but the defense of Western civilization (represented especially by the women and children of the White race) against savagery (represented by non-White natives and European tyrants). Although some of these films had a roughly contemporary setting, they were more typically located in the historical past. Nonetheless, the themes and settings of this kind of film made it an appropriate vehicle for allegorizing public concerns about foreign affairs: specifically, the rise of anticolonial movements in Asia, Africa, and Latin America; the Great Power rivalries that divided Europe and Asia into democratic, Fascist, and Stalinist camps; and the programs of political and military expansion undertaken by the

Fascists in Spain, Japan in China, Italy in Ethiopia, and Germany on the Continent.

The founding works of the Victorian Empire genre were Parmount's *Lives of a Bengal Lancer* (1935) and Warners' *The Charge of the Light Brigade* (1936), directed by Michael Curtiz.[11] The success of these two films was exploited in a series of imitations made between 1936 and 1940, chiefly at Warner Bros. and Paramount. Representative titles include *Wee Willie Winkie* (1937), *Drums* (1938), *Four Feathers, Beau Geste*, and *Gunga Din* (1939). Certain Westerns made during the forties are also modeled on these movies, most notably the Flynn/de Havilland Westerns made by Warners, *Santa Fe Trail* (1940) and *They Died With Their Boots On* (1941). Through periods of popularity and relative obscurity, the genre persisted through the fifties and sixties in movies like *Kim, King of the Kyber Rifles, Guns at Batasi, Zulu, 55 Days at Peking, Khartoum*, and the like.[12]

Thematically, these movies deal with a crisis in which civilization—symbolized by the Victorian Empire or its equivalent—is faced by a threat from an alliance betwen the opposite extremes of savage license and totalitarian authority. The Victorian or civilized order is embodied in a regiment or a military outpost whose values are nominally those of a liberal and progressive imperium but whose heroes are warriors and whose politics are those of a justified and virile patriarchy happily exercised over consenting White women and childlike brown faces. A fanatical and perhaps even pseudo-messianic chieftain (usually a "Khan" of some sort) is uniting the hill tribes against our regimental utopia, and the bloody politicians in Whitehall or Washington are too corrupt, inept, or locked into bureaucratic red tape to do what needs to be done about it. There is often a foreign power, an evil empire (Russia, Germany, Imperial China) working behind the scenes. As a result the British army and civil service (wives and children included) and all the little brown people who depend upon "us" are in peril of massacre by the chieftain and his deluded barbarians. The only one who can save us is the hero, a soldier who knows the natives well enough almost (or actually) to pass for one—a man who straddles the border between savagery and civilization, fanaticism and religion, brown and white, them and us. And we *are* saved—though typically at the cost of the hero's sacrificial death, in company with his picked band of men, in some heroic last stand or suicidal charge.

There is a striking and not fortuitous resemblance between this formula and the classic Indian-war scenarios of the Myth of the Frontier. In a sense, these movies merely flesh out in fiction the ideological implications of the Roosevelt thesis, which envisioned the transformation of the racial energies that won the West into the basis of an Anglo-Saxon alliance for the conquest and control of the undeveloped world. Although the settings and characters are nominally British, these were essentially American productions, conceived, designed, scenarized, and marketed by and for Americans. British actors and actresses played principal and especially character parts, but it is worth noting that the stars of *Lives of a Bengal Lancer* were Americans (Gary Cooper and Franchot Tone), and that Errol Flynn was a colonial (from Australia) rather than "the real thing."

The Charge of the Light Brigade—the lavishly produced epic that transformed a successful film idea into the basis of a genre—was an entirely Americanized version of a British historical subject. The Americanization of this story reveals a good deal about the way in which the language of myth shapes the discourse and productions of artists in mass media. The *Light Brigade* project began with Warners' decision to imitate and exceed the success of Paramount's *Lives of a Bengal Lancer*, a film about the adventures of three young officers defending India against the machinations of the Russians and the rebelliousness of Moslem hill tribesmen.[13] To top *Lancer*, Warners designed a production in which everything would be bigger, more spectacular, more glamorous. It would feature the newly fledged romantic stars Errol Flynn and Olivia de Havilland and would deploy all of Warners' substantial resources for costuming, set design, and spectacular outdoor action. The male rivalry and camaraderie of *Lancer* would be enlarged to a full-blown romantic love triangle setting brother against brother. Where *Lancer* emphasized the obscurity and isolation of modern imperial service, *Light Brigade* would explicitly link events on the border to a grand historical confrontation of the Great Powers culminating in the Crimean War.[14]

The Charge was the film's reason for being, and therefore the sole function of its yet-unwritten script would be to provide a rationale for the ultimate catastrophe. The event itself, as mythologized by Tennyson, offered an opening for creative invention because it contained a mystery: Who was the "someone" who had "blundered"? What *was* the "reason why" for which the soldiers never asked? It was understood that the scenarists would have to invent plausible answers and that the "reason why" (when invented) would have to be a *good* one. With the values of so lavish a production investing him, Flynn could not merely "blunder" into glorious failure. Yet his reason would have to be a "secret," a privileged truth concealed from the general public and unknown to "History"—a reason sufficiently in tune with higher laws to do the hero credit but transgressive enough to warrant a cover-up. And although the historical mystery itself belonged to British culture, the scenarists' solution would have to satisfy an *American* audience.

In searching for a reason of that kind, the scenarists reverted to the basic myths of their own culture. They explain the European catastrophe as the consequence of events that occurred on the Frontier, where civilization confronts a savage non-White enemy whose culture combines ignorance with fanaticism and blood-lust.[15] The movie transfers us to a mythical borderland on the Northwest Frontier of India, where the 27th Lancers confront the Surat Khan, Emir of Suristan (that is, Afghanistan), and his wild Moslem tribesmen. The Emir has the speech and manners of a gentleman; yet as he himself smugly admits, he has the love of cruelty and blood-sport that is innate to his "ancient race." Internal divisions will weaken British efforts to control him. The opening scenes reveal a sharp split between the politicians and diplomats—a set of elderly and effete armchair warriors—and the soldiers, particularly Captain (later Major) Geoffrey Vickers (Flynn), who is not only brave but a realist who knows the enemy well. He and the Khan are old acquaintances, hunters of great skill; during the course of a hunt Vickers earns the Khan's gratitude by saving him from a leopard attack with a superb shot. But the diplomatic mission to Suristan fails.

Surat Khan makes a secret alliance with the Czar, and with the aid of a Russian military adviser (Count Volonoff), who is a Stalin look-alike, leads an uprising of the hill tribes against the Chukoti garrison while most of the regiment is on maneuvers. When the Colonel surrenders on promise of safe conduct, the Khan orders a horrific massacre of the men, women, and little children of the garrison, complete with implications of rape, mutilation, and torture. Vickers rescues Elsa Campbell (Olivia de Havilland)—his Colonel's daughter, who is also his fiancée—from the massacre, but he succeeds only because he is spared by the Khan, who thus repays his debt of honor. Although the British defeat the Suristanis and hound the Khan out of India, the massacre remains unavenged. Vickers is ready to protest the command's transfer to the Crimea until he discovers that Surat Khan is in Sebastopol with his former adviser, Count Volonoff.

And *here* is the reason why: Vickers learns that Surat Khan and Volonoff are actually on Balaklava heights. He forges his commander's signature to change a retreat order into a suicidal attack and then sends a belated warning to the commander so that he can use the attack as a diversion. He leads the Charge in person and kills Surat Khan amid the Russian batteries with a cast of his lance just before he falls mortally wounded by the Khan's pistol shot.

In the final scene, we learn how and why the secret history has been concealed from us. Sir Charles Macefield—the army Chief of Staff and the most "military" of the political officers—decides to burn Vickers' confession because it would taint the public memory of his heroism. Macefield knows that in the absence of the confession the Charge of the Light Brigade will appear to be a blunder, and he himself will be blamed for it; but this noble fib is as close as a political officer can come to partnership in Vickers' heroic transgression.

Thus the Charge turns out not to have been a blunder at all. It is justified by two very good albeit totally imaginary reasons: a tactical one, by which the fatal Charge becomes a successful military diversion; and a mythic or spiritual one, based on the American myth-ideology of Indian warfare, whose values place the imperative of consummating an act of racial revenge or rescue ahead of obedience to military orders or political law.

The "secret history" part of *Light Brigade*—the Indian part—closely resembles the classic Indian-war novel, Fenimore Cooper's *Last of the Mohicans*, the centerpiece of which is the massacre of Fort William Henry led by a vengeful Indian fanatic in alliance with a European general. In both stories, world and class politics are treated through the metaphor of racial conflict beyond the borders and are amplified by a sexual politics that divides civilization into a female "heart" moved by sentiment and naive idealism and a hard masculine "head" moved by soldierly realism.[16] Although he is an aristocrat, Errol Flynn in *Light Brigade* is also the man who knows Indians (Suristanis) so well that he can pass for one; and in the final battle he uses the "primitive" lance against the Khan's modern pistol.

As in the historical romance, historical events are made to function as an allegory of contemporary political and social concerns. The figure of the Russian adviser, and the premise that the frontier massacre is causally related to a war between the Great Powers, bind the frontier romance metaphorically to the politics of Europe in 1935–36. It was by no means clear that the enemy of the West in the next war would be the Fascists: Stalinist Russia, then entering the time of the Great Purge and heavily engaged in Spain, was a likely candidate, and Bolshevism was the preferred enemy for many Western conservatives (and remained so even after the war with Germany was actually engaged). Thus the explanatory fiction offered by the movie can be read not only as a rendering of the historical past but as a use of a mythologized past to interpret a present crisis. At the same time, the displacement of the crisis into "history" clouds the allegory and avoids the danger of offending any of the movie's potential European audience.[17]

Light Brigade unites and reconciles its diverse ideological concerns and its mixture of real and imaginary politics through its narrative rather than through any sort of discursive logic—although argumentative and explanatory discourse occurs frequently enough. The predicted and predictable narrational drive that moves everything toward the mayhem of the final Charge suggests the operation of a force of historical determinism through which White triumphs over non-White, freedom over tyranny, and justice over crime. Those characters who speak for or embody this force, in whatever degree, appear insightful and heroic; and it is interesting that on this score the hero Geoffrey Vickers is closer in thought to the savage Surat Khan than to his military and political superiors—this is very much in the Fenimore Cooper tradition. In contrast, the viewpoints and value-systems that disable the regiment from acting—the calculations of politicians, the hidebound rules of the military hierarchy—are identified with women or with femininity. Diplomats and bureaucrats are played in an effete manner; the ineffectual General Warrington is shown as a henpecked husband; and in an elaborate and brilliantly staged "Grand Ball" scene the treacherous double-dealing of the Oriental Khan is systematically likened to the inconstancy of the romantic heroine—who is betrothed to the soldierly Captain Vickers but has fallen in love with his prissy younger brother, who has been transferred from his regiment to serve as "a diplomat of sorts." Thus the play of gender differences in the "romance" plot supports and enlarges the play of racial difference in the historical/political plot, and both plots together constitute the whole "secret history" that "explains" the Charge of the Light Brigade.

As the comparison with the Cooper formula suggests, this type of movie was well designed to absorb the concerns and symbols traditionally associated with the Myth of the Frontier and the Western and to recast them in a new, more exotic and spectacular and even a more timely disguise. They also enlarged the studios' historical vocabulary and frame of reference. The success of these films, and the perpetual search for new variations on successful formulas, made inevitable the turn toward American subjects that occurred in 1939. However, that turn was also shaped by the changes in American culture arising from the politics of the New Deal, the "rediscovery of America" by the Popular Front, and the crisis of world politics that would lead to American engagement in a second "Great War"—developments that made an intense re-examination of the American past a central item on the national agenda.

In rediscovering American history, Hollywood necessarily returned to its own preferred form of historical myth-making—the Western movie. However, the revived genre did not simply revert to pre-Depression traditions. The new Westerns drew on and modified the mythographic and iconographic achievements of the major genres of the 1930s, particularly the gangster film and the historical romance. And although the Western itself had been in eclipse for most of the decade, the ground for the genre's revival had been prepared by changes in the "B" Western—a steady accumulation of small-scale innovations made between 1931 and 1939 that had the effect of restoring the genre's metaphorical connection to contemporary concerns.

"Meanwhile, Back at the Ranch . . .": "B" Westerns, 1931–1939

Within its medium, the "B" Western had the same product status and role that the dime and pulp novels had in the field of literary production. Since it served an audience that delighted in a particular kind of story, it was designed to be reliable rather than strikingly original. Like dime/pulp novels, "B" Westerns were developed in series based on recurring characters or performers. Plots were developed by making minor variations in a basic formula (for example, giving the hero an odd disguise or a mistaken identity), by adapting some notorious current event to the terms of the series (as dime novels did with Jesse James), or by doing a cheap knockdown of a feature film (as dime novels had often done with the plots of romances by Cooper, Simms, and Bird). Many of the recurrent character types in these films had dime-novel and pulp-novel antecedents. The villains tend to be figures of authority corrupted by greed: crooked bankers or politicians, or wealthy ranchers plotting to do a worthy heir or heiress out of an inheritance or conspiring with outlaw gangs preying on outlying communities or ranches. The heroes are very much in the "young hunter" mode which the dime novel had perfected and which *The Virginian* had developed to apotheosis: good with weapons and wise in Western ways, but with the manners of a gentleman and the disposition of a chivalric knight, even when (like Zane Grey's heroes) they were bent on vengeance.[18] Typically, the hero is paired with a humorous sidekick, often an old cowboy, who speaks in a heavier Western dialect and is distinctly more plebeian than the hero—an echo of the tradition of heroic pairing that dates back to Hawkeye and Oliver Edwards in Cooper's *The Pioneers* (1823).

The key to establishing a viable "B" series was the creation of a series star: an actor with a distinctive style whose real identity is more or less completely merged with his screen persona. Johnny Mack Brown's style suggested the tough guy more than the gentleman; Ken Maynard's films exploited his spectacular trick-riding skills; George O'Brien was noted for the athleticism of his fight scenes. Bill Elliot often adopted a historical guise and setting, and singing cowboys like Tex Ritter, Roy Rogers, and Gene Autry dressed to the show-business standard established by Tom Mix. Many series encouraged a confusion of identities between the actor and his role. Some "B" actors followed Wild West practice and sought to borrow the mystique of the "original participant" by assuming "historical" names like "Buffalo Bill Junior," "Bob Custer," and "Buddy Roosevelt."[19]

But the confusion of the real and the fictive was usually achieved by simpler devices. Bill Boyd played Hopalong Cassidy for so long that the two became virtually indistinguishable; other actors, like Ken and Kermit Maynard, simply used their real names (or names very like them) in their films. This was the method used to establish John Wayne's persona when he began making "B" Westerns for Warners in 1932. The studio's idea was to suggest that what the audience saw on the screen was not just "an actor in a role" but somehow a "real" cowboy-adventurer named John Wayne. In the six Westerns he made for the studio in 1932–33, Wayne's character was always named "John"; and in *Three Musketeers* (1933)—a Yanks-in-the-foreign-legion serial—Wayne's character is "Tom Wayne."[20] In one sense, this attempted confusion of the mythic and the real is only an elaboration of practices developed by Buffalo Bill fifty years before. The difference is that Buffalo Bill's performance authenticated itself by referring to our memory of or belief in his relation to the historical or real "Wild West," whereas John Wayne's "authenticity" is established by confusing an actor with his role and by mistaking references to other movies for references to a world *outside* the movies.

Self-referentiality was built into the product-design of the "B" Western. These films not only repeated plot formulas but continually recycled actual footage from earlier productions, particularly for recurrent scenes like horseback chases or displays of trick riding. Stunt footage from Ken Maynard's silent Westerns was used in John Wayne's early films for Warner Bros., because Wayne was a less accomplished rider. The historical resonance of a "B" film could be (and was) cheaply enlarged by splicing in footage from a silent or early sound epic—often with only the most perfunctory efforts at matching the lighting, costuming, or speed of the original. Thus the visualized landscape of the "B" Western was, to a considerable extent, made out of pieces of other movies rather than out of scenes newly observed or constructed to recreate a particular historical setting.[21]

This confusion of the real and the fictive, the historical and the Hollywood setting, made possible some very interesting interaction between icons symbolic of the past and those referring to the present. Most "B" Westerns used the cattle-ranch and cowtown setting of the late nineteenth century, with plots appropriate to that era, featuring claim-jumping, range wars, homesteaders vs. ranchers, attempted land grabs by would-be "barons," or rivalries between "Old West" enterprises like stagecoach lines, railroads, and the Pony Express. Films of this kind followed the norms of the traditional Western as to costume, setting, and conflict. However, a great number of "B" Westerns were produced in which cowboys vested with the aura of the Old West did battle with problems and villains from the modern world—gangsters, corrupt political bosses, counterfeiters, greedy corporations, enemies of conservation, and (after 1936) Nazi agents. In these films, the Western story is aggrandized by the appropriation of bits of other genres: the gangster film, the social drama, the spy story, science fiction, and (in the case of the singing cowboy) the musical. Some of these films show cowboys indistinguishable from nineteenth-century prototypes fighting crime in a modern setting; others project conflicts or problems typical of the 1930s back into a nineteenth-century setting.[22] The practice created a useful confusion of temporal references that had the effect of expanding the mythic space of the Western, making it a kind of cinematic fourth dimension in which heroes from an earlier epoch battled the evils of the present time.

Perhaps the best illustration of this confusion—and of the creative possibilities inherent in it—is Republic Studio's *Three Mesquiteers*, one of the best-mounted and most successful of the "B" series. The Mesquiteers were an Americanized version of Dumas' heroic team based on characters in a pulp-Western series by William Colt MacDonald, the first of which was published in 1933.[23] The movie series ran from 1935 to 1950 and featured a variety of performers in the three roles. Ray Corrigan, Bob Livingston, and Max Terhune established the original personae of the group, but other actors were later inserted in the roles like interchangeable parts, including (at various times) Raymond Hatton, Bob Steele, Tom Tyler, Duncan Renaldo, and John Wayne. However, the roles themselves were carried over from film to film: an "old hunter" type (called Rusty or Lullaby Joslin) to provide comic relief; "Stony Burke" (originally played by Livingston, later by Wayne), a wild young cowboy, hot-tempered and prone to falling in love; and "Tucson Smith" (originally played by Corrigan), a figure whose age and temperament split the difference between the other two.

The Mesquiteers are joint owners of the 3M Ranch, but their pursuit of business—trail drives, cattle-buying excursions, etc.—leads them into adventures in a variety of settings. Initially presented as chivalric cowboys-errant, their continuous engagement with law enforcement leads to their acquisition of semiofficial status as part-time government agents. The first entries in the series are set on the ranch, costumed as "cowboy pictures," and are indeterminate as to period, though clearly suggestive of the open-range era of the 1880s. But starting with *The Three Mesquiteers* (1936), the time references become mixed: the three are represented as returning veterans of the First World War but find themselves aiding a covered-wagon train—a visual sign that contradicts the nominal periodization of the film. As the series was extended, it developed the elaborate intertextual connections that unite films in any series. These connections did not resolve the problem of just where in time the Mesquiteers operated, however, since later installments were set in periods as various as the generic "Old West" (for example, *Covered Wagon Days* [1940]), the range wars of the late nineteenth century (*Range Defenders* [1937]), the Indian wars of the 1870s (*Saddlemates* [1941]), the Civil War, and the 1940s (*Call the Mesquiteers* [1938]). In this expanded "Western" space, past and present are superimposed on each other—or, more precisely, confront each other—and through their conflict produce a moral drama. The heroes are chivalric cowboys out of the historical hinterland of *The Virginian*, but their enemies are city men, twentieth-century men, whose corruption is linked (via costume) with their modernity.[24]

The political dimension of this confrontation of the Old West and the contemporary was treated most directly in the Mesquiteers movies made after John Wayne entered the series in 1938. Of the eight Mesquiteers films made in 1938 and 1939, only *Santa Fe Stampede* (1938) has a routine Western plot. *Overland Stage Raiders* and *Red River Range* (1938) sound like routine Westerns, but the former concerns air-transport hijackers rather than stagecoach bandits, and the rustlers in the latter use refrigerated trucks. *Pals of the Saddle* (1938) is more pointedly political. It engages the Mesquiteers with a female undercover agent who is working to prevent a foreign spy ring from acquiring a mysterious metal called "monium," from which a new kind of poison gas can be made. The film plays on fears of Fascist subversion on the eve of the Second World War and anticipates the fascination with new superweapons that would be so important to the war effort. But the Mesquiteers are still cowboys on horseback, and when they summon aid it is the U.S. Cavalry they appeal to. *New Frontier* (1939) engages the Mesquiteers in a scenario evocative of contemporary debates over the TVA's dam-building programs.[25] *Wyoming Outlaw* (1939)—based on the case of a young Cody, Wyoming, poacher who was killed resisting arrest—weaves together a number of New Deal themes, including conservation and the abuse of federal work-relief.[26] *The Night Riders* (1939) translates the ideological and political response to the spread of Fascism into Western movie terms: in 1881, the Mesquiteers have to save their valley from a megalomaniacal gambler and his gang of black-shirted gunmen.

As the war came closer to the United States, "B" Westerns incorporated war-related issues more and more explicitly. There was some precedent for this: Hart had made two short films during the First World War, in one of which he arrives in Berlin in full cowboy regalia to confront Kaiser Bill. But Hart's films were tongue-in-cheek; he knew, and as a filmmaker lived by, the difference between "then" and "now." The "B" Westerns of the 1940s persisted in conflating "cowboys and Indians" space with "Yanks and Nazis" space. In *King of the Texas Rangers* (1941), horseback cowboys confront Nazis operating out of a Zeppelin over Texas. In *Riders of the Northland* (1942), the problem is German submarines. The Three Mesquiteers fight

Nazi spies in *Valley of Hunted Men* (1942) and black marketeers in *Black Market Rustlers* (1943). The Range Busters—competitors of the Mesquiteers—expose a Filipino spying for the Japanese on a journey to deliver cavalry horses to the Philippines in *Texas to Bataan* (1942); and in *Cowboy Commandos* (1943) they prevent Nazi subversives from seizing the secret "magnesite" ore from which a new superweapon could be fabricated.[27]

If the "B" films conflated the symbolic "issues" of the past with those of the present, they also necessarily obscured the distinction between contemporary political action and the heroic, Wild West manner of resolving conflicts. One of the premises of the traditional Western had been the distinction between the primitive conditions of the Old West and modern civilization. If the Western represented the act of taking the law into one's own hands (vigilantism) as heroic, it also circumscribed the allegory of vigilantism as belonging to an earlier state of society. Wister's *The Virginian* had gone to great lengths to elaborate this point, and the formula Westerns of Hart implicitly respected it by identifying the Western setting as primitive, socially unformed, and distinctly *past.* By obscuring the distinction between then and now, the "B" Western effectively dissolved the implicit limitations that historical location placed on radical or violent solutions to the problems of social injustice, economic oppression, or political privilege. The "B" Western thus heightened the allegorical qualities of the genre and converted the stock villains of the Frontier Myth into symbols of present-day evils. The continual confusion of past and present in the "B" Western suggests that the heroic ethic of Western vigilantism had a kind of timeless validity as a means of resolving a social or political impasse. Is a film like *King of the Pecos, Lawless Range, Wyoming Outlaw,* or *Night Riders* to be taken as an exercise in populist nostalgia, a kind of Wild West version of old-fashioned trust-busting? Or is the vigilantism of the cowboy the historical model and sanctified symbol of a valid form of present-day revolution?

This is not to say that the "B" Western was a major medium for making moral and ideological statements. Overt social commentary was appropriately (and therefore safely) made within the boundaries of the "social drama," "problem" film, or "prestige" costume drama. The "B" Western picked up political concerns as it picked up the idea of singing cowboys, through the continual efforts of the producers to keep their product as timely and attractive as possible. But the consequences of the appropriation for the Western of the language and concerns of New Deal politics was the creation of some new possibilities for the hackneyed formula. It became possible to see the mythic space of the Western genre as an appropriate field for the projection of real questions about the state of the nation and for the cultivation of fictions embodying possible answers to those questions.

9 The Western Is American History, 1939–1941

In 1938–39 the major studios decided to revive the Western as an important genre of feature film. In 1938 "A" Westerns had constituted 1.1 percent of Hollywood's total production and 6.9 percent of all Westerns. In 1939 that percentage more than doubled to 2.3 percent of all films, and 18.8 percent of all Westerns, and in 1940 to 3.5 percent of all productions and 21.7 percent of all Westerns. During the three-year "renaissance" of the Western (1939–41) "A" Westerns made up an average of 18.6 percent of all Westerns and 2.7 percent of all productions. The new films were also larger in scale and ambition; many were in color, and all were more lavishly produced and promoted than previous Western epics.[1] Although the development of the new Western was interrupted during the Second World War, it was resumed almost immediately after the conclusion of peace and was continuously pursued until 1973. The "renaissance" thus inaugurated a thirty-year period in which the Western movie became pre-eminent among American mass-culture genres as a field for the making of public myths and for the symbolization of public ideology.

The pressure for a revival of the Western was generated from within the industry itself, in anticipation of change in public taste rather than in response to a clear market signal. Historical costume dramas and "prestige" biographies, most with European subjects, had enjoyed great success. Given the studios' normal procedures for exploiting successful genres, it was inevitable that similar treatment be extended to American historical subjects.[2] The industry's sense of the genre's potential was also heightened by the renewed seriousness with which critics, scholars, and fiction writers in the late 1930s began to take up the matter of American history and the Frontier. This larger movement was driven by a widely felt need for a renewal of that sense of progressive and patriotic optimism that had been punctured by the Depression. The New Deal fostered these tendencies through the patriotic propaganda with which it promoted the policies of the National Recovery Administration (NRA), the WPA's support of regionalist painters, and the folklore-studies and state guidebooks programs of the Federal Writers' Project. Although the effects of the Depression lingered, Franklin Roosevelt had largely restored public faith in the viability of the government as the instrument of the popular will and as a vehicle for positive social and economic change. These developments suggested that American history could once again be read as a kind of "success story," rather than (as in the gangster film) a tale of inevitable corruption and decay.

The need for such a positive view of the American past was augmented by the apparent intrusion of "alien" radicalisms (Fascism and Communism) into mainstream electoral politics during the crisis over early New Deal policies in 1934–37, and by the rising threat of a war between the Western powers and the totalitarian and militaristic powers of Japan, Germany, and Soviet Russia.[3] This was the ideological crisis of the late New Deal: How far did Americans want reforms to go? What was our proper role among the world powers? To resolve the crisis, writers, historians, scenarists, and politicians of varying political and social affiliations looked to American history and mythology for precedent and direction.

The Rediscovery of American History

The cultural program implicit in this endeavor was articulated by Howard Mumford Jones in a 1938 *Atlantic Monthly* article titled "Patriotism—But How?"[4] Jones observed that the fascist nations were united and energized by their governments' manipulation of patriotic myths. At the same time, Americans' belief in their own national myths had been undermined in more than a decade of systematic debunking by the intellectual elite. Historians had undone the myths in the name of empiricism; social critics had attacked them as barriers to reform. Jones did not want writers (or the American government) to impose patriotic ideology by deliberately falsifying history or suppressing inconvenient facts. The truths of the historians, the new perspectives developed by the social critics, were now part of cultural memory and could not be simply dispensed with. But these projects had been shaped by an intellectual bias that privileged the most jaundiced views of the past and sought to reduce all historical events and motives to the mean and prosaic. Jones called for the development of a countervailing perspective that would deliberately focus on the positive elements in our history. Writers should actively seek out "thrilling anecdotes" and "glamorous" episodes from the past—episodes in which the audience could see the heroic expression of American and democratic virtues without the "chauvinism, economic self-interest, or racial snobbery of the totalitarian states." Jones recommended the history of the Frontier as one of the obvious places to seek such stories.

This was exactly the recipe for the kind of Western the Hollywood studios began planning and researching in 1938–39. But their efforts were part of a broad spectrum of similar activities in other sectors of cultural production. Writers of literary fiction had in fact anticipated this cultural turn. Beginning in the mid–1930s the "big historical novel" became an increasingly notable presence in both mass-market best-sellers and in serious modernist fiction. Margaret Mitchell's *Gone with the Wind* (1936) is the best remembered of these books. But these years also saw the beginning of two notable series of historical novels dealing with the Frontier—Kenneth Roberts' series on the forest battles of the French and Indian and Revolutionary wars, and Stewart Edward White's four-volume "Saga of Andy Burnett." Howard Fast began his career as a writer of historical fiction with a Marxist perspective, recovering and celebrating lost heroes and episodes of the radical tradition for offering revisionist views of figures from the American pantheon like George Washington.[5]

Among modernist writers, John Dos Passos' trilogy *USA* (1930–37) gave mythic resonance to the story of America's cultural coming of age by constructing a collage of novelistic narrative, fragments of popular song and journalism, and poetic biographies of representative historical and contemporary figures. William Faulkner's *Absalom, Absalom* (1936) inaugurated that writer's "myth of the South" by rooting the fabled plantation culture in a legend of wilderness conquest; and the stories that finally made up *Go Down, Moses*, written between 1940 and 1942, developed a complex, nearly allegorical working-out of the symbolism of the Frontier Myth in southern terms. John Steinbeck's *The Grapes of Wrath* (1939) highlighted the irony of the Dust Bowl migration to California by aligning the wanderings of the Joads with traditional images of covered wagons heading west. Poet and folklorist Carl Sandburg's best-selling biography of Abraham Lincoln represented its subject as the hero of western folklore as well as history and made of Lincoln a current mythic symbol of great power.[6]

The ideology of American exceptionalism, and its Turnerian underpinnings, had traditionally informed the rhetoric of conservatives and isolationists, who had used it to discredit the radical critiques of American society developed by the Left. Now that ideology became the ground of a loose consensus, as leftist artists and intellectuals sought to join the New Dealers in a "Popular Front Against Fascism." In *Mainland* (1936), Gilbert Seldes developed a sort of "left-Turnerism" which emphasized the Frontier and the West as the cultural sources and regional base of an indigenous American radical tradition, characterized by such movements as the Whiskey Rebellion, Jeffersonian agrarianism, Jacksonian leveling, John Brown abolition and Lincoln Republicanism, Populism, and the radical unionism of the IWW.[7]

This intellectual tendency was reflected in the cultural sphere in the work of artists and writers for the WPA's public mural program and the Federal Writer's Project. The FWP's famous series of state guidebooks developed the themes and images of America and "Americanism" and invited the citizenry to connect with its diverse past through informed tourism. The mural program sponsored the work of artists like Thomas Hart Benton and Grant Wood, whose paintings linked regionalist concerns and images with an iconography evocative of populist radicalism. The scholars and writers who canvassed the nation's rural and urban backwaters for government-sponsored oral history and folklore projects discovered the genuinely popular roots of the nation's history and culture. The folk-music projects played directly into the popular culture through radio performance and recording, which gave the music of rural Blacks and Whites the kind of currency hitherto reserved for the products of Broadway and Tin Pan Alley. Singers like Leadbelly and Woody Guthrie made the transition from folk artist to mass-culture performer and then linked their music to political action for radical causes and the Popular Front movement. Their style was imitated, elaborated, and eventually re-commercialized by professional performers within the movement. Oklahoma-born Guthrie made the most extensive use of frontier motifs and cowboy ballads, particularly in the series of songs he wrote about western outlaws, in which Belle Starr, Billy the Kid, and Jesse James figure as social bandits. In "Jesus Christ" he even sets a depiction of Jesus as social revolutionary to the "Ballad of Jesse James."[8]

But most of these radical adaptations of historical mythology give a populist gloss to a structure of ideas whose basic principles remained "progressive," in Teddy Roosevelt's sense of the term. The persistence of this structure is apparent in the FWP state guidebooks, where New Deal perspectives on immigration, industrial regulation, and unionism are framed by histories that conform to the Turner/Roosevelt models of progress. The historical chapters in the guidebooks associate the steady growth and development of the states with the succession of Indians by Whites, and of Hispanics and the French by Anglo-Americans. Almost all of them emphasize the development of "popular" and democratic institutions under the kind of frontier conditions described by Turner. Some praise the "melting-pot" and follow Turner's suggestion that the new immigrants from Asia and from eastern and southern Europe are legitimate successors to the Anglo pioneers.[9] But the racialism implicit in progressive historiography reappears in treatments of Native Americans and Mexicans. The historical sketch of Arizona is more blatant than most in its description of the movement from "hairy aborigines who stoned to death the giant sloth" to cliff dwellers lacking "even the rudiments of agriculture" [*sic*], to "pastoral tribes," "fierce raiders," "swashbuckling *conquistadores* and gentle priests." The sketch culminates in the arrival of "the last of these modern interlopers, the Yankees, who leveled mountains for their copper, laced the face of the land with ribbons of concrete, dammed rivers to make the desert bloom, and in less than a century worked changes vaster than their predecessors had wrought in thousands of years."[10] Angie Debo's chapter on the history of Oklahoma was suppressed by officials in charge of the state project because it took a favorable view of the state's development under Indian home-rule and gave a devastating account of the way in which Indians had been abused by Anglo-American proponents of statehood and economic modernization. A different text was substituted which asserts that the "red thread" of "Indian blood" made the territorial leadership recalcitrant to progress. "Because of this long period of Indian occupation, Oklahoma presented for generations the picture of an area of arrested development," and rapid progress became possible only when Whites took power from the Indians on this "last American frontier."[11]

Though less radical in their use of myth than Popular Front figures like Seldes, Guthrie, and Fast, these New Deal historians still belong to the school of "left-Turnerism." Their political ideology conforms to the "populist" style in its advocacy of democracy, praise of the political wisdom of the common people, and hostility to "Big Business." They conclude that, since the Frontier is indeed "gone at last," democracy can be preserved only through a just redistribution of wealth and power.

There was, however, a more conservative way of reading the myth/history of American development: a "right-Turnerism." Its chief spokesman was Charles A. Beard, the pre-eminent figure in the American historical profession between 1913 and 1940, author of an epoch-making economic interpretation of the Constitution, and (with his wife Mary) of a series of textbooks and historical surveys that shaped historical education for thirty years. In their monumental *The Rise of American Civilization* (1927) and its sequel, *America at Midpassage* (1939), the Beards revised the economic and political assumptions of the Turner Thesis in ways that made it more amenable to the requirements of progressive or managerial ideology.[12]

Charles Beard shared with Seldes and Franklin D. Roosevelt the Turnerian assumption that the existence of the Frontier had given America an exceptional history and a unique political economy. He too saw the Frontier as the historical site of the genetic ideological struggle between "popular" (or "western") and "centralizing" (or "eastern") forces, in which the origins of present-day conflicts could be seen. However, Beard saw industrialization as a more than adequate substitute for the cheap land frontier, because it promised a continuous and inexhaustible increase of resources for each succeeding generation and for every nation irrespective of its size.

Beard develops this thesis through a mixture of discursive argument and poetic use of mythological language. He mixes metphors associated with "Nature" and "Industry" to suggest that industrialization is itself an expression of "natural law," and that the development of industry was implicit even in the characteristic scenes and labors of the agrarian pioneers. And he suggests a rough equation between "invention" and "discovery" which suggests that industrial development follows the paradigm of the Turnerian Frontier. The industrial goods and processes invented by an Edison or a Ford transform society in ways analogous to Boone's discovery of Kentucky or the gold strike at Sutter's Mill: a concentrated lode of potential wealth is discovered/invented by venturesome heroes, and the benefits are suddenly diffused throughout society, revolutionizing expectations and social relations.[13]

Beard uses the language of Fenimore Cooper to celebrate the "marvelous empire of virgin country," the "pathless forests" as "cathedrals" with "Gothic arches" of trees, and "the man with the rifle—grim, silent, and fearless" who stalks in the vanguard. His pioneers are a "rugged" Rooseveltian democracy of fighters and breeders, "hardy men and women, taut of muscle and bronzed by sun." But he describes their lives in terms of labor and productivity rather than hunting and war-exploit. They work "with their hands in abundant materials" and form "a social order without marked class or caste, a society of people subtantially equal in worldly goods, deriving their livelihood from one prime source—labor with their own hands in the soil."[14]

In the twentieth century the democratizing influence of the developing West can no longer offset the monopolistic and centralizing tendencies endemic to "capitalism" in the eastern metropolis. But industrialism has imperatives different from those of capitalism: its primary value is not monetary gain but *productivity*, and bonanzas of productivity are achieved only through technological innovation. The "invention of invention" has allowed the industrial system to, in effect, incorporate the essence of the Frontier by making all monopolies vulnerable to competition and entrepreneurial initiatives and by diminishing the authority of monopolistic owners as enterprises become dependent on technical experts and a better-educated (and therefore more self-willed) work force.[15] Properly understood, the triumph of industrialism could mean the restoration of a modernized version of the Turnerian Frontier in which the opportunity to "rise" would be available to a broadly constituted "producing class." But to achieve this, production would have to be "nationalized"—not through the public ownership of the means of production but through the use of regulatory and advisory agencies managed by disinterested experts to assert national and patriotic purposes against the selfish concerns of particular classes and special interests.[16] With this idea in mind, Beard initially supported the New Deal, but he broke with the Roosevelt administration when its policies took a seemingly "leftward" and internationalist turn after 1934.[17]

Implicit in the Turnerian basis of Beard's ideas was the assumption of American "exceptionalism." Hence his use of "nationalization" implied not only the assertion of national over special interests but an exclusivist and exclusionary approach to industrial reform. The frontier tradition made the achievement of democratic industrialism feasible for Americans. But the prospects were unfavorable for those nations abroad, and for those races living here, who were not direct heirs of that unique American experience, and any attempt to include or accommodate them in our reforms would fatally compromise us.

In *The Idea of National Interest* and *The Open Door at Home* (1934) Beard reverted to a milder version of Stoddard's and Grant's racialist vision of history: the American Frontier Eden had been undone by the importation of alien masses and the annexation of territory inhabited by alien races, which diluted and displaced the native producing classes of farmers and mechanics. Beard describes the "new immigrants" of the late nineteenth century as "less adapted to the national heritage than many races later excluded by law" (that is, Asian); and he asserted that national identity, as embodied in figures like Washington and Jefferson, was racial as well as cultural, requiring homogeneity of "blood and language" and an inborn capacity for self-government. Beard saw the legislation of 1921 and 1924 that restricted immigration as a turning point in the development of American culture, involving a "revulsion" against the "Oriental and European invasion" of American civilization and the beginning of a determination to "build a civilization with characteristics sincerely our own."[18]

Beard's isolationism put him at odds with the internationalist outlook developed by the Roosevelt administration. By 1935 it had become clear that monetary and trade policies could not successfully be pursued in isolation; and with the rise of Hitler and the spread of Japanese imperialism in Asia, it became obvious that America's safety required engagement in a world-power role. By 1934 it was also clear that the New Deal's political elan and base of support came in significant part from its mobilization of ethnic and immigrant minorities, who benefited from its distributive programs and support of the labor movement and supplied the Democratic Party with a new cadre of leaders as well as an augmented rank and file. This shift in political demography was both signal and instrument of the integration of the post–1880 ethnic immigrants into American social and cultural life—an integration that was peculiarly important in the movie business, where first-generation and second-generation immigrants figured so prominently among owners, managers, workers, and creative artists.

Thus despite their agreement on the significance of the Frontier as a formative epoch and an ideological symbol, there was a fundamental opposition between the "progressive" Turnerism of Beard and the left-Turnerism of the Popular Front and the more radical New Dealers. The latter emphasized the post-Frontier aspect of the American present and the need to establish some form of social justice through the redistribution of wealth and power. They looked to the Myth of the Frontier for historical fables that would give weight and resonance to their critique of corporate capitalism and an air of heroic glamour to those who in the past resisted or attempted to overturn it. The Beardian "progressives" followed the tradition articulated by Theodore Roosevelt, in which the past was romanticized as a prelude to an attempt to reproduce, under industrial conditions, the mythical order of an the idealized Frontier.

The Renaissance of the Feature Western

Faced with these alternative visions, Hollywood preferred, as always, to assimilate competing ideologies to a common language of myth and genre. The new wave of Western features drew on both Beardian progressivism and Popular Front populism to produce three different ways of resolving the problem of making movies out of American mythology.

The "historical epic" was the most prestigious of the three and featured the most expensive and spectacular productions. True to the canons of the "historical romance," "costume epic," and "bio-pic," the ideological thrust of these films is relentlessly "progressive" in its reading of history, celebrating all persons, tendencies, and crises that yield higher rates of production, faster transportation, more advanced technology, and more civilized forms of society.

The ideological antithesis of the progressive epic is the group of historical Westerns that centered on the exploits of western outlaws like Jesse James. These films also referred to the canons and icons of progressive history, particularly the railroad, but they adopted the "populist" perspective of those victimized by technological and industrial progress and treated their outlaw-heroes as social bandits. This subgenre of the Western was so immediately popular, and so many versions of the type were produced over the next ten years, that film historians Fenin and Everson properly refer to it as "The Cult of the Outlaw."

The basis of a third type of feature Western was promulgated in John Ford's *Stagecoach* (1939). In a formal sense it is the antithesis of both the progressive epic and the Cult of the Outlaw, since it eschews the insistent historicism of those forms for the formal austerity and poetic allegory of the W. S. Hart tradition. This type of Western might be described as "classical" or perhaps "neo-classical," because of its knowing use and modernistic adaptation of traditional and relatively "archaic" styles and story-structures. Because it has no obligation to historicize, it offered a field in which the ideological oppositions of "progressive" and "outlaw" Western could be simultaneously entertained and played off against each other.

The progressive epic was the most imposing and important of the new forms, because it inherited the market niche previously occupied by the historical romance and the bio-pic. It also inherited the stars, directors, supporting casts, and writers associated with those films. Studio research departments were assigned to develop for the new Westerns the kind of historical authenticity they had lent to productions like *Light Brigade*, and, although they drew on a wide range of primary and secondary sources, the structuring premises of their historiography are Beardian. The dominant themes of the "epic" Westerns associate the Frontier with the heroic phase of America's industrial and democratic progress. They revolve around advances in technology, like the building of transcontinental railroads or stagecoach lines; advances in productivity, including the replacement of hunting economies by ranching (or ranching by farming); and in general the achievement of a better life through mobility (especially westward migration) and the overcoming of natural, savage, and criminal obstacles to progress. Although, like Beard's histories, these films praise the virtue and wisdom of the common people, they represent heroic individuals as the real initiators of historical change. and they prefer villains who are racially or ethnically alien, or snobbish "fat cats" more interested in luxury, leisure, and power than in production.

The railroad is the dominant symbol of progress in "renaissance" Westerns. Cecil B. deMille's *Union Pacific* is the most traditional in its treatment of the theme, following Ford's 1924 silent *The Iron Horse* in its mixture of history and melodrama. Warners' *Santa Fe Trail* (1940) sets the enterprise of railroad-building as a counterpoise to the ideological tensions that would lead the nation into the Civil War. *Dodge City* (1939) links the coming of the railroad to the modernization of pioneer society. Other films celebrate advances in technology like the stagecoach (*Stand Up and Fight* [1939]), the wagon-freight business (*Arizona* and *Twenty Mule Team* [1940]), and the telegraph (*Western Union* [1941]).[19] The entrepreneurial activities of pioneer cattlemen are seen as agents of progress in *The Texans* (1938), *American Empire* (1941), and *The Great Man's Lady* (1941). There was also a series of Western bio-pics that featured the likes of Brigham Young, Kit Carson, and George Armstrong Custer.

The Indian wars figured prominently as subjects for epics. But the political allegory implicit in these films is complex, mingling images of war as historically necessary or heroic with wishful scenarios of war-avoidance that have a contemporary reference. *Drums Along the Mohawk* (1939) and *Northwest Passage* (1940) treat the woodland Indian wars as major tests of America's national integrity and ability to survive. *Geronimo* and *Northwest Mounted Police* (1940), *Badlands of Dakota* (1941), and *They Died with Their Boots On* (1941) all deal with attempts by military officers to *avoid* an Indian war. To do so they have to fend off the Indians' savage propensity for bloodshed on the one hand, while on the other exposing and defeating the machinations of American politicians, land-grabbers, and war profiteers.[20]

How these epics managed their mythographic task can be illustrated by a brief discussion of Warners' *Dodge City*, directed by Michael Curtiz, the film that was to mark the studio's grand re-entrance to the Western field. The production and its promotional campaign were lavishly supported; the studio's leading romantic stars, Flynn and de Havilland, were translated—with some labor and cajoling in Flynn's case—from British aristocracy to pioneer Americans.

The movie's premiere—"one of the biggest things that has ever been put on in the history of show business"—was staged in Dodge City itself and was covered by newsreel and NBC radio. The dignitaries included the Secretary of War and the Secretary of Agriculture (a happy conjunction for a movie about the Frontier). A parade deploying 400 horses and 45 marching bands, "stagecoaches, buckboards, [and] Indians" entered Dodge City with a replica of an original 1860s locomotive chugging alongside and an overflight by 50 "decorated planes." There was a beauty contest, a rodeo, and a mock attack by 50 "masked horsemen . . . sweep[ing] out of the prairie shooting guns and pacing the train." The entire Hollywood delegation were made honorary deputies, and the citizens of Dodge agreed to wear "frontier costumes"—and "all . . . are growing beards." By taking the premiere "on location," the authenticity of the film's portrayal of western progress would be affirmed, and the movie itself would be framed by a patriotic pageant/Wild West show in which present-day citizens assumed the personae of their mythical ancestors—whose "history" it was the movie's business to relate.[21]

The film's historical subject is the modernization of the Frontier after the Civil War. The coming of the railroad means the end of the old buffalo-hunting life of the Indians and the development of the ranching and trail-driving business. The small Indian-fighting outpost of Fort Dodge will become a city where vigorous western productivity meets the eastern capitalist and consumer. This nascent metropolis will also be the site of ideological confrontation: the overt antagonism between northern and southern veterans of the Civil War; the political opposition between the forces of corruption and civic virtues; and the ideological opposition between the frontier principles of rugged individualism and masculine violence, and the refinements of a civilization presided over by women. Through the course of the narrative these oppositions will be resolved and a new and more perfect western society created.

The historical framework is established explicitly through the use of a rolling title that places us in Kansas just after the Civil War and establishes the central premise: that the coming of the railroad marks an epoch in the history of American national development. These words are immediately translated into pictures. A group of dignitaries is riding into Dodge City on the first train to travel along the newly laid tracks. They discuss the railroad's meaning for the West in terms redolent of a history textbook—*America at Midpassage*, let us say. As they talk, a stagecoach appears on a road parallel to the tracks and challenges the train to a race. After a brief scare, the train easily outdistances the coach: new technology must replace the old. The moral is verbalized, again in Beardian terms: "That's the symbol of America's future. Progress! Iron men and iron horses, you can't beat 'em."

The next scene amplifies this theme. We see a prairie dotted with buffalo and are introduced to the hero, Wade Hatton (Errol Flynn) and his sidekicks, Rusty and Tex (Alan Hale and Guinn Williams). The three have been hunting buffalo to feed the railroad workers and are about to trap a group of hide-hunters led by the villain Jeff Surrett (Bruce Cabot) who have been illegally (and wastefully) killing buffalo on Indian land. The arrest of Surrett presents Hatton as the protector of Indian rights; and this, taken with the end of buffalo hunting, tells us we are witnessing the last act of the Indian-fighting phase of frontier history. Indians and buffalo alike are now under the protection of well-disposed White men like Hatton. Surrett's stolen hides will be sold and the money will be given to the Indians.

These two scenes (erroneously) place the drama of Dodge City at the end of the wildest phase of Wild West history—the time of the buffalo, the hunter, the great Indian wars. The new age will demand a hero different from the individualistic old-time plainsman, a conservationist rather than a free hunter, a redistributor of misappropriated wealth rather than an exploitative entrepreneur—a New Dealer on horseback. The script next raises the question of whether Hatton is that sort of man. Colonel Dodge offers him the job of marshal, but Hatton declines. He prefers trail driving, the only work in these times whose freedom compares with that of the old scouting and buffalo-hunting days.

There are actually two problems in the character of Hatton. The scripted problem concerns his unwillingness to put aside his personal freedom in order to serve his society. But there is also a tacitly acknowledged problem about the star persona of Errol Flynn. Both Flynn and his co-star Olivia de Havilland had been thoroughly identified with "Merrie England" and "Victorian Empire" films—*Captain Blood* (1935), *Charge of the Light Brigade* (1936), and *The Adventures of Robin Hood* (1938)—which like *Dodge City* had been made under the direction of Michael Curtiz.[22] *Dodge City* turns difficulty to advantage in a bit of expository dialogue, offered by Hatton's sidekick Rusty, which "explains" Hatton's past: he is an Irish-born gentleman (which accounts for his accent) and has been a soldier of fortune fighting with the British in India and in the Confederate cavalry in the Civil War. In other words, Hatton's "past" consists of Flynn's previous movie roles (especially *Light Brigade*). The script thus borrows the authority and appeal of Flynn's "historical epic" persona to aggrandize the Western.

If Flynn's character connects the film to the romantic heroism of imperial epics like *Light Brigade* and *Captain Blood*, the plot connects it to the disillusioned view of urbanization and "the big money" promulgated in the gangster film. Titles inform us that the new city soon becomes the "wide-open Babylon" of the Frontier, "rolling in wealth from the great Texas trail-herds . . . the town that knew no ethics but cash and killing." This description may remind us of *Hell's Hinges*. But its more immediate reference is to the wide-open cities of gangster films like *The Roaring Twenties* (also made and released in 1939). The criminal boss of Dodge City, Jeff Surrett, is a saloon-keeper like Silk Miller (and Paddy Ryan). But his operation is more like that of the rackets-bosses of *Roaring Twenties* and *Little Caesar*, who have their offices in nightclubs. The dance-hall numbers in Surrett's saloon are simply Western translations of the nightclub numbers that punctuate gangster movies with visions of the glamour to which the criminal aspires.[23]

As in the traditional Western, women incarnate the Christian moral principles essential to a civilized order. Those principles are set off against the "male" propensity for violence—although the safety of female order will depend on the assistance of at least one violent male. *Dodge City* works within this mythic paradigm, but it multiplies and elaborates the oppositions of gendered codes for purposes that are both comic and ideological. The initial opposition between Hatton and the female lead is presented in the most traditional terms, Hatton is the rough trail boss, and Abbie Irving (Olivia de Havilland) is the eastern girl come west (like Molly in *The Virginian*) along with her morally incompetent brother (like the minister's sister in *Hell's Hinges*). Like Molly, she is instantly attracted to the gentlemanly cowboy, but she rejects him when, in an act of rough but necessary justice, he kills her brother. So far the story simply parallels *The Virginian*, suggesting that the woman's code is too rigid to comprehend the real necessities of life in the West.

This easy interpretation is rendered problematic when Hatton refuses to take the job of town marshal. The audience is well aware that, for both ideological reasons and for the fulfillment of plot-generated expectations, putting on the badge is the right thing to do. Now Abbie's rebuke acquires genuine authority. If Hatton's code demands that he execute violent justice in the individual case, how can he ignore a whole community's need for law? Moreover, as the story develops, we see that Abbie is not the passive female icon of *Hell's Hinges*, nor the morally subordinate schoolmarm of *The Virginian*. She is instead a Western movie version of the "new woman," determined on a career in journalism (albeit writing a fashion and gossip column), and more than capable of standing up to Hatton's attempts to "put her in her place."[24] One exchange between them ends with Hatton knocked, literally and figuratively, on his ass. Abbie is not opposed to violence as such; she merely wants Hatton to (in Beard's terms) "nationalize" his use of it.[25]

In the movie's terms, the "progressive" character of Hatton's socialization is conveyed by the metaphor of "growing up." While the marshal's job has been vacant, the little son of a cattleman (murdered earlier by Surrett) has been wearing a paper badge and playing marshal. When the little boy is accidentally killed in a street brawl, the paper badge confronts Hatton with the image of his own childishness, his adherence to a primitive and infantile notion of freedom. His conversion is pictured in the image of the paper badge dissolving into a metal star pinned to his gunbelt.[26]

Dodge City set the pattern for the new "historical epic" Western. The three Westerns made by Flynn and de Havilland after *Dodge*

City—*Virginia City*, *They Died with Their Boots On*, and *Santa Fe Trail*—were all very much in the *Light Brigade* tradition, deploying the standard elements of the historical romance to answer questions about the proper response to the world crisis of the late 1930s. In these films, as in *Light Brigade*, Flynn is the central figure, the effective commander of the regiment in combat, the "man who knows Indians," and whose knowledge allows him to break the rules and win. The movies provide "secret histories" which explain American crises as the product of forces originating on the Frontier and offer historical models for defining and confronting present crises. *Virginia City*, set during the Civil War, sees Unionists and Confederates compelled to unite against the sort of racially alien enemy the Frontier typically produces—a gang of Mexican renegades led by a sadly miscast Humphrey Bogart. *Santa Fe Trail* (1940) pits Flynn as Jeb Stuart and Ronald Reagan as Custer against radical leftists (abolitionists) and a Hitlerian John Brown in Kansas before the Civil War.[27] In *They Died* . . . (1941), a biography of George Custer, the army represents the virtues of American democracy and meritocracy imperiled by the war-mongering and profiteering of bureaucrats and financiers, whose machinations cause the Last Stand.

These films develop and extend the *Light Brigade* formula for describing the political issues of war and peace. The "enemy" is identified by turns as savage and brown-skinned, fanatical and allied with non-Whites, and bureaucratic or corrupt. The narrative proceeds along much the same course, alternating dances with battles, romantic with political conflicts, using gender signals as a key to the interpretation of morality, and engaging the hero in a misunderstanding that threatens both his romance and his political mission. And the movies end with a climactic cavalry charge or a grand battle, with overtones of apocalyptic catastrophe. War-avoidance, however, is the theme and the unspoken wish of the two Western "cavalry epics": progress, usually symbolized by the railroad, can be achieved only if war is avoided. True to the logic of Beardian progressives, the development of the epic during the "renaissance" ends on an isolationist note.

But Hollywood movies—like the community that produced them—entertained more radical sentiments as well.

The Cult of the Outlaw

The new "outlaw Western" addressed the dark side of progressive history which the epic evaded or subsumed, and which had hitherto been the province of the gangster film and the social drama. This large, popular, and thematically coherent group of films celebrated the careers of famous western outlaws, particularly those associated with Jesse James and his gang. They adopted the historicizing narrative, iconographic devices, and historical referents of the "progressive" epic but exposed them to criticism by showing how progress can lead to injustice, oppression, and crime. But there is more to the translation of gangster to outlaw than a simple change of costume and setting. The shift of genres expressed a change in the industry's attitude toward social criticism, from a disposition to indulge the gloomiest of critiques to more positive and patriotic interpretations.

Warners' *The Oklahoma Kid* (1939) best illustrates the formal and ideological dynamics of this shift. The stars are James Cagney and Humphrey Bogart, in a plot which—despite its western setting—clearly invokes their past association with the classic gangster film and their current engagement in *Roaring Twenties*, which was to be released later that same year. In making *The Oklahoma Kid*, the studio was responding to the demand created by the revival of the Western in charactetristic fashion by adapting proven story-formulas and re-costuming established stars.

Clichés of genre iconography are used to bring the different myth/ideological frameworks of the gangster and the Western film into conversation. Among the gangster-film conventions are: the subplot conflict between the outlaw kid (Cagney) and his respectable brother, which echoes the relationship of Tom and Mike Powers in *Public Enemy*; the staging of a Western-style "pineapple primary," with a gangster-like use of thugs to strong-arm opponents and fire-bomb stores and offices; and the use of newsreel-like montage—blending newspaper headlines, violent scenes, and narration—to establish the historical frame in which the plot unfolds. Connection to western history is provided by stock footage of the 1889 Oklahoma land rush, which had been a well-established icon since the silent era.[28]

The opening titles ominously inform us that this "last free frontier" has been acquired through an act of economic and racial injustice—the unfair expropriation of Indian land by a government devoted to the advancement of Whites. A similar abuse of power will set one class of Whites above another. As the pioneers line up for the land rush, we see "the Judge" and his son planning to stake claims to an outsized tract of land where they will build the city of Tulsa. The Judge is a domineering patriarch, like Cooper's Judge Temple or Wister's Judge Henry or *Dodge City*'s Colonel Dodge, a progressive and "nationalist" in the Beardian sense, whose mission is to bring "civilization" in its most advanced form to the West—cities, banks, railroads, industry. But his idea of pioneering is "plowing up new empires" rather than breaking ground for a simple agrarian freehold. He silences his critics by pointedly asking, "What sort of *American* are you?"

But his values and methods are called in question. To get the extra land he needs the Judge must make a deal with the corrupt interests represented by the black-clad McCord (Bogart). By this bargain ("What's a few hundred feet of frontage to an empire-builder like you?") McCord and his associates are given a monopoly of saloons and gambling halls; and with control of the rackets, they drive the farmers into debt and gain control of the land.

The politics of "Tulsa" are clearly derived from the gangster film. But *The Oklahoma Kid* projects the model backward in time and presents it as part of the genetic myth of American progress. A montage then illustrates the development of Tulsa from the Judge's bargain to the roaring-twenties-style prosperity of the oil boom. The montage is accompanied by narration which explains that "land-grabbing" and "empire-building" are what drive the process and that violence and theft are endemic to it. The Whites steal Indian land by the gun; the "immigrants" arrive to "carve a civilization" on the stolen land; then "grafters" arrive, with hired guns to help them, to reap the ultimate benefits—a process illustrating the principle that "the strong take from the weak, and the smart from the strong." McCord and his gang rule the territory as a "closed corporation of closed mouths"—a metaphor that makes the gangster connection explicit.

The Oklahoma Kid (Cagney) responds to this systematic injustice by becoming a "good outlaw," a Robin Hood who robs from the rich and gives generously to the poor. His first robbery makes the political allegory plain. A stagecoach carrying money that corrupt officials have stolen from the Cherokee is held up by McCord, and McCord in turn is held up by the Kid. McCord's theft has in effect "laundered" the gold, diluting the criminality of the Kid's theft and preparing us for the Kid's ultimate redemption. The Kid's generosity guarantees the money's return to "the poor" by one route or another and symbolically corrects the original injustice.

The casting of Cagney and Bogart and the transfer of "gangster" imagery to the West follows the pattern set in *Dodge City* of borrowing appealing elements from an older genre to aggrandize a Western. But the consequences of the mixture are different in the two cases. The ideological premises of a romance like *The Charge of the Light Brigade* harmonized with the progressive premises of an epic like *Dodge City* or *They Died with Their Boots On*; but the basic premise of the gangster film had been to question the easy equation of material and moral progress and to see corruption as the necessary adjunct of America's rise to the economic heights. Shifting the setting of the social critique from the modern city to the Old West "softens" the critique by setting its objectives at a distance. But at the same time it widens the scope of the critique to include mainstream industries and businesses whose "progressive" and respectable character the gangster film never challenged. And it deepens the critique by locating the source of modern problems, not in the aberration of Prohibition, the intrusion of immigrants, or the innovations of the modern city, but in the very scene that Turner and Roosevelt identified as the site of America's exceptional genesis—the nineteenth-century agrarian frontier. By juxtaposing the symbolic referents of the gangster film with those of the Western epic, Warners was effectively questioning the fundamental assumptions of the "renaissance" Western.

The most influential of the outlaw Westerns was Henry King's *Jesse James* (1939). The film was both a critical and a commercial success, and Hollywood registered its value by promoting its principal players (Tyrone Power and Henry Fonda) to major stardom and by turning out numerous imitations in rapid succession.

King's hero, like the Oklahoma Kid, owes something to the gangster film. The intensity of his family bond (especially to his mother) and his rivalry/partnership with a "good" brother echo the key relationships in *Public Enemy* and *Scarface*. As Jesse become a professional outlaw, he acquires more of the gangster style: a mustache, a more elegant and citified wardrobe, and six-guns worn in shoulder holsters rather than hip-slung in cowboy fashion. But *Jesse James* is a more complete departure from the conventions of the gangster film than *The Oklahoma Kid*. The revisionist reading of the West in *The Oklahoma Kid* is achieved through the contrast of anachronistic elements—characters and situations identified with *The Roaring Twenties* invade and corrupt the terrain of the Western. *Jesse James* takes its primary language from the vocabulary of images and historical references established by the "progressive" Westerns of the "renaissance" and makes its critique of the "progressive" reading of the Frontier by offering a new perspective on the emerging conventions of the Western movie.

The project was first proposed to King by the screenwriter Nunnally Johnson, who had been working on a Jesse James screenplay since 1938 and had been researching the story for a good deal longer than that. Following the practice of the WPA folklorists, King and Johnson went to Missouri to visit the original scenes of Jesse's career, to interview people who had known Frank and/or Jesse (including Frank's son), and to gather local color and Jamesian lore. According to King, the final screenplay did not reproduce anecdotes uncovered in his research; rather, it relied on printed sources, which were adapted rather freely. But King's field work gave him a vivid sense of the flavor and tone of Jesse James folklore and shaped his treatment.[29]

King's movie begins with a prefatory title similar to that which introduces *Dodge City*. We are in post-Civil War Missouri, and the nation is turning its energies to the building of transcontinental railroads. But where *Dodge City* sees railroads as progressive and corruption as the work of criminal interlopers, *Jesse James* sees the railroad itself as corrupt and its building as a criminal invasion of an agrarian community.

The film opens with the image of the railroad agent Barshee (Brian Donlevy) riding in a four-wheeled buggy surrounded by henchmen on horseback. As the gangsters in *Public Enemy* bullied Chicago bartenders into buying "Nails" Nathan's beer, Barshee will pressure Missouri farmers into selling their land to the railroad at ruinously low prices. The first farm they visit is a poor log cabin whose illiterate owner is overwhelmed by Barshee's fast talk. The second looks somewhat more prosperous (there is a flower garden in front); Barshee obtains the widow's signature by beating up her son and threatening to do worse.

The third house they visit belongs to the James family, Frank (Henry Fonda), Jesse (Tyrone Power), and Ma (Jane Darwell). Theirs is a two-story frame house with a porch—the Jameses are more prosperous, perhaps more middle-class, than Barshee's earlier victims. Ma James won't be cajoled or bullied into signing: she is intelligent, knows her rights, and is backed by two grown sons who prove more than a match for Barshee and his goons. But the boys recognize the seriousness of the threat and send their Negro servant Pinky to summon the other farmers to a political meeting.

A warning is brought to the farmers' meeting by Major Cobb (Henry Hull), the fiery editor of the local newspaper and the uncle of Jesse's fiancée, Zee (Linda Darnell): the railroad corporation controls the law, and Barshee has obtained a warrant for the arrest of Frank and Jesse. Ma convinces the boys to hide until the Major can get them a lawyer. She is a good Christian woman, a tender mother who fears the consequences of resistance for her sons and who has a weak heart. Barshee and his men arrive and refuse to believe the boys have escaped. When Ma—fainting with a heart attack—knocks over a lamp, Barshee hurls a hand bomb through the window, blowing up the front of the house and killing her. Jesse hears the news from Zee and leaves his hideout in the hills. With a band of armed friends to cover him, he confronts Barshee in the saloon and kills him in a classic Western draw-down.

King thus provides Jesse with a double justification for becoming an outlaw. The initial impulse is given by a confrontation with the railroad and the law it has corrupted. But the crucial shift from legal resistance to rebellion or guerrilla warfare is motivated by the murder of the mother—the central symbol of Christianity and of the values of harmony and decency represented by the family. Thus Jesse's attack on the railroad appears to be a defense (or at least an avenging) of the principles of justice and civility that law was created to protect.

The meaning of this characterization is reinforced by King's combination of elements of the yeoman farmer and the middle class in his representation of the Jameses. Though Jesse is first seen swinging a scythe, their house is clearly that of a more prosperous sort of farmer and they have what appears to be the only Negro servant in town. The narrative movement from the illiterate man's poor cabin, to the widow's slightly better cabin, to the Jameses' frame house suggests that the normal development for farms is that of progressive improvement, upward mobility. Its populism is really a defense of that American dream which culminates in the achievement of the middle-class home—which the railroad will destroy. The railroad thus marks itself as the exponent of a false "progress," inimical to the natural growth figured in the move from cabin to frame house; and its signature is the throwing of the bomb through the window—an icon of the gangster film.

This thematic inversion of the railroad's role in the "progressive"

Western is developed iconographically in the next phase of the narrative, in which Jesse and his gang begin their guerrilla warfare against the railroad. The railroad president himself—a "meeching" little man, played by Donald Meek—boards the Missouri Midland train for its inaugural run from the state capital to Jesse's hometown of Liberty. The train gets a celebratory send-off, reminding us of the festivals of progress that framed the opening of railroad lines in *Dodge City* and *Union Pacific*. Night descends on the train, and in the darkness Jesse's gang strikes.

The robbery sequence is extraordinarily well designed, featuring some dramatic stunt work and one spectacular visualization. Jesse, who has jumped from his horse to board the train, runs crouching along the roofs of the passenger cars towards the locomotive, his hunched form silhouetted against the evening sky as he leaps from car to car, while below him we see through the lighted windows the unsuspecting faces of the passengers and the railroad president. The athletic movement of the figure emphasizes Jesse's energy and power; the silhouette of his ape-like crouch suggests his potential "darkness" and a kind of feral quality (Zee fears he will become a "wolf"); and the contrast between the warm, crowded interior and the shadow on the roof signals his coming isolation from the community.

The robbery sequence establishes Jesse's characteristics as a hero and a counterforce to the railroad. He is first of all the incarnation of the principle of direct and pragmatic action. When he orders the engineer to stop the train, the engineer asks, "What are you planning on doin'?" Jesse replies, "I'm not planning on doing anything; I'm *doing* it." In a sense, he represents a heroic form of pragmatism. He solves problems without resort to litigation or abstract theory, confronting each question on its own terms and resolving it in the handiest, most efficient way. His problem is the excess of this virtue: the most direct way is often a violent way.

The second element of characterization is Jesse's association with folklore and folkloric style. Jesse himself will become a part of folklore and legend while still alive, as the movie itself shows. But that development is prepared by the way in which bits of folklore and folkspeech are associated with Jesse from the start of his outlawry. Two "preacher jokes" made in the film illustrate this point. As the gang walks through the cars relieving the passengers of their money, Bob Ford (John Carradine) greets each "contribution" with an unctuous "*Thank* you, brother"—as if he were taking up a collection in church. The line suggests the peaceful, even church-going origins of these robbers. But King doubles the humor, and the irony, in a later scene, when the outlawed Jesse and Zee interrupt a service and ask the preacher to marry them. The preacher then praises Jesse for his attacks on "that danged railroad," which robbed him of his fine farm and forced him to take up preaching when he could have been doing "honest work." The passage echoes a standard irony of American folklore, which often shows preachers as less than honest men. But it also suggests that in certain circumstances robbing trains may be as natural an expression of Christian virtue as preaching or passing the collection plate. By associating Jesse with folkloric scenes and speech, King emphasizes what we might call his "populist" character—his role as armed representative of "the People."[30]

To achieve this characterization King substantially modifies the history of the James Gang, which he and Nunnally Johnson had been at pains to research. The most crucial alteration is the suppression of the brothers' Civil War service as guerrillas under Quantrill, their postwar proscription, and their early shift to bankrobbing in 1865–66. King emphasizes the purity of their motives by shifting the bomb attack on the James household from 1871 to the very beginning of Jesse's career as an outlaw and by having Jesse's mother killed rather than badly wounded in the incident, when in fact she outlived her son by several years. As far as we can tell, Frank and Jesse are peaceful farmers thrust into outlawry by the violence of the railroad.

King visualizes the *social* character of Jesse's outlawry by testing his use of violence against the moral standards of domesticity and civilization embodied in a set of female figures. Jesse's wife Zee is the most important of these figures, but her espousal of "female" values is supported by the more maternal figure of Ma and by the Uncle Tom–like servant Pinky, whose style is distinctly maternal. Zee accepts Jesse's initial step into outlawry as justified first by his defense and then by his avenging of his mother. But she opposes his war on the railroad, believing that outlawry will get "in his blood" and make him "wild," like an animal—so that he will undergo a kind of racial degeneration toward savagery. With the aid of Will Wright (Randolph Scott)—a federal marshal independent of the railroad, who represents the national government and the possibility for justice within the law—Zee arranges for Jesse to surrender in exchange for a pardon. If he accepts, she will marry him and wait out his prison sentence; if he refuses, she is through with him. His acceptance once again indicates that Jesse's appetite for "wild justice" is subordinate to the principles of the redemptive woman. Thus, when the railroad violates the terms of the surrender and Frank breaks Jesse out of jail, Zee follows Jesse. Her action tells us that Jesse is still to be seen as justified in his outlawry.

But the impossibilty of reconciling outlawry with domesticity is demonstrated almost immediately. Jesse returns at night to the cabin in which he will begin living with Zee and Pinky and finds a scene of suburban domesticity. The returning breadwinner, dressed in suit and tie, embraces his wife while their Negro "maid" (Pinky in an apron) blesses them with an indulgent smile. The husband praises the little woman's nice decorating touches, especially the "Home Sweet Home" sampler above the mantlepiece which she has embroidered herself (Pinky made the frame). Then, suddenly, the narrative takes a drastic turn. Someone calls from the yard—a farmer, wife, and children in a wagon, inquiring the way to "the Wilson place." When they go, Jesse turns grimly to Zee and tells her to pack; when she pleads that they were "only farmers," he answers: "How do you know?" With this economical sequence of images and words a line is drawn that marks the beginning of Jesse's alienation from Zee and from the community of farmers for whose sake he had fought the railroad.

Jesse's development from social bandit to professional outlaw is then sketched in montage. Wanted posters register his "success" by raising the cash value of his death; and as Jesse's star rises, Zee's hope of domesticity sinks. The nadir is quickly reached. Jesse is "away on business" when his son is born, and Zee is now so miserable that she wishes she were dead and her baby as well. Jesse has forced the redemptive woman almost to repudiate motherhood itself—the source of her redemptive power. Zee and the Major return to Liberty, leaving Pinky to tell Jesse that Zee does not wish to see him again.

The degeneration of Jesse as consort of the redemptive woman is echoed in the change in his relations with his brother and his gang. Where before he had led by example in a cause they shared equally, he now rules by the authority of his fame and skill with a gun. He has become an embodiment of the principle of tyranny against which he rebelled. When he tells Frank that he'll ride his horse up the steps of the state capitol if he wants to, the words have overtones of megalomania—they belong to a would-be dictator, not to a populist rebel. When Frank manages to mitigate Jesse's grandiosity and the rage and disappointment that feed it, the male camaraderie of the gang-family is restored. But the result is only to make possible the catastrophic robbery of the Northfield Bank.

Jesse's fall from the standard set by Ma and Zee is mirrored by the partial rehabilitation of the railroad itself. The turn becomes visible in the Major's office: the editor is playing with his young nephew, Jesse James's son, who pulls a little toy railroad train while he and his uncle go tooting around the presses. They are interrupted by the arrival of a pudgy, drummer-looking man, who is really the railroad detective Remington (that is, Pinkerton) in disguise. This conjunction of images signals Jesse's doom. The railroad detective's unctuous manner and city clothes remind us of the railroad president and the evil of which railroads are capable; but if Jesse's son is playing railroad trains, then perhaps the future belongs to the railroads after all.[31]

But the railroad's rehabilitation is incomplete and ambiguous. The railroad's last action is to suborn Jesse's assassination by the "coward and traitor" Robert Ford. Jesse himself achieves a measure of redemption when, after the failure of the Northfield robbery, he returns to Zee, promises to go straight, and makes plans to "start fresh" in California. This plan is the traditional resolution proposed by a "good-badman" after his redemption by the good woman—it is the ending of Hart's *Hell's Hinges*, *The Oklahoma Kid*, and *Stagecoach*. The railroad's assassins prevent his fulfilling the plan, but we are given good reason to think he is sincere about it. He is shot in the back while attempting to take the "Home Sweet Home" sampler down from the wall. Thus the film ends, as it began, with Jesse as the (now martyred) defender of the values of woman, child, and home against the rampant commercialism of the railroad.

King's vision of Jesse James as a historically authentic American social bandit was immediately taken up and imitated by other studios and producers. A sequel—*The Return of Frank James*—was produced the following year, directed by Fritz Lang and starring Fonda and most of the supporting cast from the original. Other studios and producers set their research departments to gathering material for stories on other outlaws of the same era, especially those who had some direct ties to the James Gang. The films they produced either referred to Jesse by name, featured him in a walk-on or supporting role, or employed an actor who had been either a principal or a supporting player in the original film. Among the features of this type produced in the next two years were *When the Daltons Rode* (1940), *Bad Men of Missouri* (1941), *Belle Starr* (1941), and *Billy the Kid* (1941). Over the next twenty years a Jesse James "canon" developed in which themes, figures, scenes, and characters clearly derived from King's original treatment were continually varied, reprised, and reinterpreted. Many of these films borrowed images or cribbed actual footage from King's film, as if his images had become authenticating "historical" references.[32]

The populist outlaw figure became an important symbol in the lexicon of movie mythology. Motifs, figures, and performers identified with the "cult" could be used to give mythic/ideological resonance to other kinds of story. The development of Henry Fonda's casting type and star persona illustrates the ways in which such resonance could be used. King had cast Fonda for the role of Frank James over the strenuous objections of studio head Daryl Zanuck and screenwriter Nunnally Johnson. Fonda had previously been cast as a romantic lead in melodramas like *Wings of the Morning* (1937) and *Jezebel* (1938). The exception to this pattern was his casting in *You Only Live Once* (1938) as a man framed for murder who escapes from prison and flees for the state line (accompanied by his wife) only to be shot down on the brink of safety. The film looks back to *I Am a Fugitive from a Chain Gang* (and anticipates *They Live by Night*), and it evoked comparisons with the contemporary careers of midwestern bank robbers Bonnie Parker and Clyde Barrow. King recognized Fonda's performance as the basis for the characterization of Frank James: an initially or fundamentally decent man driven by injustice to the dark side of American life who becomes increasingly alienated, angry, grim, and capable of violence and crime.[33] Where Tyrone Power's Jesse swung from the romantic heights to the megalomaniacal depths, Fonda projected an alternative vision of a populist outlaw who has achieved emotional and moral stability. His performance in *The Return of Frank James* (1940) established "Frank James" as the basis of his star persona: an uncommon common man, laconic, folksy, commonsensical, basically decent, yet quick, skillful, tough, unsentimental, and capable of effective and violent action. Memories of the role gave resonance, and a potentially violent edge, to subsequent performances, and these in turn enlarged the ideological significations of the original role. The roles for which Fonda was cast immediately after the Frank James films include: another innocent man framed for a crime (*Let Us Live* [1939]); the title role in Ford's *Young Mr. Lincoln* (1939), in which he stops a frontier lynching and defends a poor farmer framed by a rich man; an embattled Revolutionary War farmer fighting Indians and Tories in Ford's *Drums Along the Mohawk* (1939); and finally, and most notably, Tom Joad in Ford's

The Grapes of Wrath (1940). (His co-star from *Jesse James*, Tyrone Power, had been considered for the role.)[34]

In *The Grapes of Wrath*, Fonda's Tom Joad brings these variations on the populist hero together in a single heroic figure—agrarian, Lincolnesque, a fugitive and an outlaw—who is finally able to articulate the social and political meaning for which the outlaw has been a metaphor. The symbolic resonance produced by this intertextual echoing is most palpable in Fonda's last scenes, in which Tom says good-bye to his mother and sets out his vision of what a man has to do to set things right. Ma Joad is played by Jane Darwell, who had played Ma James; and her response, like Zee's and Ma James's, is to worry that Tom's choice of an outlaw life will make him wild or "mean." Tom reassures her by affirming his belief in the words of Preacher Casey, that "a man ain't got a soul of his own, just a little piece of a great big one." The role of Casey is played by John Carradine, another member of the *Jesse James* cast. Tom says that since he is an outlaw anyway, he might as well try to talk to the people as Casey had done—to become, in effect, an organizer and agitator for some unspecified movement of the dispossessed to get decent jobs and (the Western movie's vision of utopia) "a piece of land." We last see him walking along over a hill toward a sunrise—an image that echoes the final shot of *Young Mr. Lincoln* and suggests the essential unity of the populist outlaw and the Great Emancipator.

The Apotheosis of the "B" Western: John Ford's Stagecoach (1939)

John Ford's *Stagecoach (1939)* represents an alternative approach to the feature Western. Ford understood the epic Western quite well: the basic elements of the progressive epic *Union Pacific* were already present in his silent epic, *The Iron Horse*. But he chose instead to work with the elements of the "B" formula, taking advantage of genre-based understandings—clichés of plot, setting, characterization, and motivation—to compose an *exceptional* work marked by moral complexity, formal elegance, narrative and verbal economy, and evocative imagery.[35]

Though identified with Westerns during his early career, Ford had not made a Western since the advent of sound. He had made his reputation in the 1930s as a director of prestige productions and social dramas for major studios.[36] His return to the Western genre was undertaken with revisionist intentions: he wanted to develop and expand the latent capacities of the old form as a vehicle for cinematic expression. Moreover his reputation ensured a more serious sort of critical attention for his film than would be accorded a routine Western. In the event, *Stagecoach* was both a critical and a commercial success.[37]

The basic ingredients of the film are recognizable variations on standard "B" Western formulas. The most patent of these is the spectacular stagecoast-and-Indian chase scene with cavalry riding to the rescue. The iconography and riding stunts of this scene hark back to Buffalo Bill's "Attack on the Deadwood Stage" (1883). The main plot is a variation of the classic "good-badman" formula. The hero (Ringo Kid), who has been framed for a killing, escapes from prison to seek revenge and on the way meets "the girl" who will redeem him through love. John Wayne, who stars as Ringo, was an actor thoroughly identified with "B" movie roles. The supporting characters likewise represent common "B" Western types—the apparently respectable banker who turns out to be a crook, an eastern lady out west who needs the aid of a gallant stranger, the comic drunk, the rough-mannered frontier doctor, the effete eastern drummer, the southern gentleman too much on his dignity, the murderous gambler, the sheriff who sympathizes with his prisoner, the "rube," the whore with the heart of gold.

Ford invokes our knowledge of these stereotypes quite deliberately, presenting them concisely and with an apparently naive forthrightness that invites viewers to accept the film as a folk tale or fable rather than as a serious attempt at historical realism. But Ford's deliberate play with type-casting categories is a way of invoking the memories that such movie-stereotypes contain, the framework of associations with earlier stories that defines each character's meaning and mode of action. The effect is mythographic: "each character . . . represents a culture or a class in microcosm."[38]

Ford builds a feature movie, and a more complex work of art, by the elaborate way in which he extends, combines, and juxtaposes these elements of formula. "Doc" Boone is both the frontier sawbones and the resident drunkard, but the generally comic rendition of his type is punctuated by brief glimpses of alcoholic abjection. The figures of the gentlemanly Virginian and the murderous gambler are joined in Hatfield, a combination that realizes the implicit cruelty in the aristocrat's assumption of superiority. The redemptive woman is a prostitute, not a minister's sister or a schoolmarm. The plot is composed by the weaving together of three or four story lines, each of which might have made a "B" movie. But Ford's point is not merely to enlarge his script by multiplying plot devices. The stagecoach journey will be a temporary meeting-ground where the different characters and their movie-stories interact in ways that alter and enrich the meaning of each. This narrative device supports the central theme of the script, which concerns the passengers' forging of a temporary community to defend themselves against the Indians and the desert.[39]

The movie's landscape likewise mixes elements of formula with innovations aimed at using the tale to open a fresh perception on "reality." The narrative begins and ends in the frontier towns of Tonto and Lordsburg. These terminal points are representations of the "civilization" that has come to the West. They resemble familiar studio or backlot spaces whose like we have seen in a hundred "B" movies. But on the journey from Tonto to Lordsburg, as the characters pass into the desert wilderness and leave civilization behind, the audience passes from "backlot" space to a "real" location—the sort of setting that would be chosen to lend authenticity to a historical epic.

Ford emphasizes this shift by his choice of Monument Valley as the movie's location. Monument Valley has become so well established as a "typical" landscape, emblematic of "the West," that it is difficult for modern audiences to recognize that in this film (and in his subsequent Westerns) Ford is *inventing* the Valley as a cinematic (and American) icon. The Valley is in fact as unique a landscape as can be imagined. The "monuments" are huge red monoliths of volcanic stone shooting up out of rubble-piles, shaped like open hands or towered skylines or phallic spires, surrounded by the flat plane of a barren rocky desert. In *Stagecoach* it is the landscape's visual oddity that gives it authenticity—this is not a landscape anyone could invent or build in the San Fernando Valley. Its peculiarity effectively represents the alien quality of the Frontier—which had been in its time as uncanny a place for pioneers as a moonscape might be.

The main plot concerns Ringo Kid (John Wayne) who has broken out of prison to seek revenge on Luke Plummer and his Lordsburg gang—who had murdered the Kid's father and brother and had framed the Kid himself. We learn of the Kid's escape at the outset of the film, just after an interrupted telegraph message announces that Geronimo is on the warpath between Tonto and Lordsburg. The marshal (Curly) decides to ride shotgun on the stage because he knows the Kid will head for Lordsburg to shoot it out with the Plummers. Ringo—whose horse dies on the trail—will be picked up en route and carried to Lordsburg as a prisoner.

We are next introduced to the secondary plots. "Doc" Boone (Thomas Mitchell) and Dallas (Claire Trevor) are being expelled by the respectable ladies of Tonto—the former for alcoholism, the latter (implicitly) for being a prostitute.[40] To this group is added Mrs. Lucy Mallory, an army wife journeying to join her husband at his outpost in Indian country; she is pregnant, though this is not visually apparent. The southern ex-gentleman/gambler Hatfield (John Carradine) decides to take the coach to offer his protection to "the lady"—a chivalrous gesture with which he evades the necessity of confronting the sheriff of Tonto, who wants him out of town. Also on the coach is an eastern whiskey-drummer named "Peacock," a fussy effeminate little man to whom Doc Boone attaches himself and whom he calls "Reverend."[41]

Dallas and Doc have been expelled by a set of female vigilantes, the "Law and Order League," led by Banker Gatewood's wife. Like the "Petticoat Brigade" of *Dodge City*, they represent the values of respectable society in a way that discredits those values as stuffy and "schoolmarm-ish." But where the Dodge City matrons are treated comically and see their values ultimately triumph through the hero's actions, these women are represented as a lynch mob. Their pretension to true decency is undermined by Doc Boone's remark that they are driven by social prejudice. But their moral authority is utterly undone when we see Banker Gatewood emptying his own vault and absconding on the Lordsburg stage to escape an audit.

If the movie has a villain, it is Gatewood. The Indians are a menacing abstraction for most of the film, and their final eruption into the frame is so predictable, so conventionally treated, and so visually stimulating that it seems as much a release of tension as the arrival of a crisis. Luke Plummer and his gang are even more distant from the visualized action that engages us. But Gatewood is with us from the beginning, a constant source of irritation, disunity, and weakness in the coach—the passenger from Tonto who clearly represents its "civilization" and who is not at all improved by the journey. Ford and Nichols enlarge the usual "B" stereotype of the crooked banker by making him the conscious incarnation and ideological spokesman for everything that is oppressive, self-righteous, hypocritical, and corrupt in "civilization." His dialogue is marked by standard chamber-of-commerce slogans: "What's good for the banks is good for the country." He tries to bully a young cavalry officer into disobeying orders by asserting that the army's main purpose is to protect people like himself.

The narrative of the journey—the passage of the characters from point to point—is stylized in ways that emphasize its allegorical, archetypal, and legendary quality. Scenes of the coach in movement alternate with scenes at the various way stations.[42] At the first stop (Dry Fork) the basic structures of politics and social hierarchy that initially govern the journey are developed. Curly informs the passengers that although he, Buck, and Ringo are obliged by law to continue the journey, the others are not; but whatever they do, the passengers must act as a unit, since none can survive alone. Curly therefore holds a vote, from which only his prisoner Ringo and his deputy Buck are excluded. Curly invites "the lady" (Mrs. Mallory) to vote first—in this frontier democracy suffrage is not restricted to men. But he ignores Dallas and starts to ask the men for their votes. Ringo interrupts, "What about the other lady?" The question points up Dallas' anomalous status. Curly's omission suggests that she is not "a lady" and relegates her to the class of criminals and servants to which Ringo and Buck belong. Ringo's question tells us that he is an "innocent" in matters of social distinction and sex. He has no idea what Dallas' profession is, as Doc Boone brings out when (in another scene) he pointedly asks the Kid how old he was when he went to prison. But the Kid's innocent question has a healthy political result: it pushes Curly to follow through on the principle, implicit in his plebiscite, that when all are equally endangered each must have an equal say and take an equal share of responsibility for the group's actions.

With the vote taken, the passengers arrange themselves at the dinner table, and a carefully choreographed passage defines the state of the social microcosm. Lucy Mallory is obviously repelled by the idea of sitting next to the tainted Dallas; Hatfield reads her expression and rescues his "lady" by suggesting they eat apart—a gesture whose implicit insult is not lost on Dallas. Hatfield and Lucy Mallory are joined by Gatewood, whose spurning of Dallas and Ringo is motivated by snobbish self-importance rather than "gentility." By associating Gatewood with this aristocratic pair, Ford implicitly questions the social code on which their sense of honor and position is based.

Of all the people in the room, only Ringo does not understand and tacitly accept the propriety of the triad's judgment. Like Huck Finn, Ringo is an innocent when it comes to civilized niceties and thinks of himself as a bad boy. He therefore assumes that the aristocrats are snubbing him because he is a criminal; and since he sees Dallas as "the other lady," he assumes that his proximity must also be offensive to her and rises to go. Dallas checks him, although she is visibly embarrassed because his misunderstanding simply underlines the social whipping Hatfield has so quietly administered. Ringo mistakes her complexly motivated action for a simple act of lady-like courtesy, which exactly matches his own innate sense of manners. The brief exchange displays Ringo's innocence and Dallas' dark knowledge, but it also marks her as Ringo's match in true courtesy or "natural gentility" and underlines those standards as something by which we can judge the different class values represented in the coach. To Ringo *all* women are ladies to be treated with deference and courtesy and offered protection; to Dallas, the basis of courtesy is kindness. Ringo is thus characterized as a "natural gentleman" whose instincts are in tune with the spirit of chivalry that underlies the mannered codes of honor, and Dallas is characterized as a "true woman" whose nurturing instincts are not checked by social convention.

The next way station, appropriately named Apache Wells, is deeper into Indian country and is ruled and inhabited by non-Whites. Here Nature itself sets the terms of testing: Lucy Mallory goes into labor, and the group learns that the raiding Apaches are now quite close. The ordeal of Lucy's delivery brings to the fore the virtues and capacities of hitherto weak or despised characters. Doc sobers up and delivers the baby, with the strong advice of Peacock. But it is Dallas whose response is the most virtuous and even heroic as she assists Doc, cares for the baby, and lends Lucy some of her courage when the "lady" nearly gives way to despair. At the same time, the romance between Dallas and Ringo ripens, and Dallas cleverly gets Ringo the rifle and horse he needs to make his getaway. Thus the second way station adds to the basic principle of democracy (shared responsibility and one–person–one–vote) the ideal of meritocracy: that any distinctions within the community must be based on demonstrated skill and virtue rather than on wealth or social position. Three characters in some sense fail these tests and remain a source of weakness and division in the community. Hatfield is not a harmful presence, but he is useless at such moments. Gatewood remains obstreperous, outraged that the course of nature has the temerity to impede his schedule. The outer boundaries of the community are defined by the wall-eyed Mexican station-keeper and his treacherous Apache wife. Here, at the nadir of the journey, Ford uses the imagery of racial difference and physiognomical deformity to define the boundaries of his community of concern.

It is the growing threat of the Apache that pushes the community to an ultimate test of its various principles of solidarity. At the river crossing (Lee's Ferry) Ringo has to choose between his chance for escape and the completion of his vengeance, and his responsibility to his fellow stagecoach-citizens. Although they need Ringo's gun, Curly will not unshackle him or let him play a man's and a citizen's part in the struggle unless he gives his word not to escape. When the Kid agrees, he becomes both an adult and a citizen, and his skilled violence can be exercised for the benefit of all.

In *Stagecoach* Ford uses the language of the Western as a tool of inquiry and analysis, exploring and questioning the fundamental assumptions about American communities that underlie self-congratulatory formulas of the epic Western and the history textbook. The little society of the stagecoach is both a microcosm of American society and the model of an ideal alternative to that society's normal patterns of human relations. The stagecoach community is democratic without being indecisive; familial without the dangerous passions and tribalism that attend the ties of blood; purposeful and coherent without being authoritarian. It is neither mob, nor tribe, nor regiment, though it borrows virtues from each of these orders.

But the historical status of the stagecoach utopia is problematic, because it does not describe any specifiable "stage" on the continuum of the progressive historical scenario. In the historical epic, the achievement of the heroic quest would have been presented as a metaphor for the triumph of modern America over its youthful poverty, wildness, or moral disarray; and while the journey goes forward, the possibility exists that the stagecoach might constitute a model of some future America at which we will "arrive." But this possibility is utterly undone when we get to Lordsburg.

If this were a progressive historical epic like *Dodge City*, we might expect to find in Lordsburg an improvement on the social order of Tonto: a town in which better laws forestall bank embezzlers, a town in which respectability is based on a more just standard than "social prejudice," the sort of town in which our heroes would have earned a place through their testing on the trail. Instead, Lordsburg is merely the perfection of Tonto's hypocrisies and incipient corruption. As Lucy Mallory says good-bye to Dallas, her voice fills with emotion when she says, "If there is ever anything I can do for . . ." But the sentence breaks off: there is of course nothing she can do for Dallas now that "civilization" surrounds them again. The Petticoat Brigade is already impatient for the strumpet to move along. Dallas's reply to Lucy—"Sure!"—simultaneously accepts the kind thought and dismisses it with bitter irony.

In the wake of this disillusioning scene the picture of Lordsburg as "Night-town" begins to unfold, filmed in an expressionistic style that suggests an urban-Western nightmare. Though the architecture is recognizably "Western," we move through a gas-lit darkness; Ford fills the streets with such crowds of people that even the open spaces have a claustrophobic quality. As Ringo walks Dallas "home" through these mean streets, the bars and whorehouses they pass—brief bursts of garish light and harsh sound, hysterical laughter, cries—suggest a journey into hell. Each new street is darker and more threatening than the last. Each brings closer to the surface the truth that Dallas cannot voice to the innocent Ringo: that she is a whore, that she is returning to a whore's life, and that from here on things will only become more vile for her. Tonto was one wide street in harsh daylight, the darkness was in the minds of its Petticoat Brigade; in Lordsburg the darkness is more complex, layered and ramified in street after street winding back out of sight.

Lordsburg justice is just good enough to punish Banker Gatewood, but it cannot provide the more positive sort of justice required by Ringo and Dallas. The law still holds Ringo guilty of the crime for which the Plummers framed him, as well as for his jailbreak; and social prejudice will continue to treat Dallas as a whore no matter how her actions transcend that name. The only justice they get is what they make for themselves, with the aid of a few friends: Ringo "rescues" Dallas by declaring his love for her in the midst of the red-light district, and kills the Plummers (with a little help from Doc Boone). Curly and Doc then render justice to Ringo and Dallas by allowing them to escape to Ringo's little ranch across the border in Mexico.[43]

Ringo's description of his Mexican ranch as a place to raise both cattle and kids suggests that they may be going to a new and better frontier, a recovered Garden of Eden for an Adam and Eve soiled by history—he by murder, she by sexual exploitation. We first learn of the ranch at Dry Fork, and from that moment we are aware of the presence of the "Mexican border" as a region that runs the length of the road to Lordsburg—a refuge that is just over the horizon no matter where we are on the journey. But the suggestion is briefly made, and "Mexico" is disembodied, known by words alone. "Mexico" is mythic space par excellence: outside the frame of "history," which is visibly constituted by the "progressive" drive that carries us from Tonto to Lordsburg, from frontier settlement to metropolitan modernity. When Dallas and Ringo ride out of the movie frame they are riding out of American history, as the Western understands it. Like Twain at the end of *The Adventures of Huckleberry Finn*, Ford in *Stagecoach* sees no hope within American "sivilization" and sees beyond it only the dream-shape of freedom in "the Territory"—a dream that may dissolve as soon as we attempt to realize it.

Thus *Stagecoach* completes its ironic commentary on the "progressive" Myth of the Frontier. The "progress" achieved through the journey-ordeal belongs only to the isolated individual—it has no social realization, finds no historical home. Democracy, equality, responsibility, and solidarity are achieved—are *visible*—only in transit, only in pursuit of the goal. When the goal is reached they dissolve, and society lapses into habitual injustice, inequality, alienation, and hierarchy. Our only hope is to project a further frontier, a mythic space outside American space and American history, for the original possibilities of our Frontier have used up.

Thus the concentrated outpouring of Western productions in 1939–41 effectively restored the Western as a viable genre for feature productions and as a significant site for the fabrication of myth and ideology. It established as a basic given of the form that the Western is "about" American history, and it developed a range of approaches that facilitated both celebrations and critiques of that history. Although the real-world referents of these films were nominally of the past, the new historical Western presented them as part of "genetic myth" that could clarify present-day ideology dilemmas by explaining their origins. *Stagecoach* adds another possibility to the repertoire of those who would work in the genre: that one can look through cinematic formula and stereotype to discover archetype: the fundamental or root structures of thought and imagination that shape American cultural mythology in all its forms, from the products of the commercial mass media to the literature and historiography of the cultural elite.[44]

But before these possibilities could be pursued very far, the normal course of American life—and of Hollywood production—was altered by our entry into the Second World War. Wartime rationing of resources limited the kind and number of productions Hollywood could mount. At the same time, the government's need for films to popularize the war effort and the audience's desire to learn about the war through the mass media reshaped the genre map of Hollywood production, creating new genres like the combat film and redirecting older genres like the women's picture, the musical, the gangster film, and the Western to war-related themes and symbols.

10 Last Stands and Lost Patrols

The Western and the War Film, 1940–1948

The Second World War plunged American culture into a crisis of unprecedented scope and intensity. The resources of society were comprehensively mobilized and directed against an enemy whose success seemed to threaten "civilization as we know it." Mobilization affected every aspect of American life, accelerating and transforming the processes of modernization and reform whose interaction had shaped political life and economic development since 1890. The war economy ended the Depression and boosted American productivity to levels beyond the benchmark GNP of the boom years of the 1920s. The United States emerged from the war as the richest and most powerful nation on earth with a rapidly expanding economy driven by the consumer demands of an increasingly prosperous public.[1]

During the war the movie industry, like the larger culture of which it was a part, looked to its heritage of myth for moral and historical precedents that would give it a "handle" on the crisis and indicate the best course of action. The society as a whole had to learn how to make war; the movie industry had to learn how to make war movies. Moviemakers initially addressed the developing crisis by trying to reduce its issues to the kind of symbols that could be projected into the mythic spaces of existing genres. Within these frames a variety of possible interpretations and resolutions could be imaginatively entertained through the systematic matching (in Geertz's formulation) of "the states and processes of the world."[2] The production of culturally useful representations of war required the continual comparison and adjustment of inherited or traditional symbols (genre formulas) to the "information" provided by the events of a developing crisis—for which (by definition) no *existing* symbol could be entirely adequate. This cultural processing of events produced a double result: the "real war" was partly assimilated to the categories of myth, which necessarily distorted public understanding (and memory) of the experience; but at the same time the application of myth to the task of representing a real war "stretched" and partly transformed the existing structures of genre and myth.[3]

None of the genres developed in Hollywood since 1927 presented war in a manner that seemed appropriate to the present conflict. Historical epics like *The Charge of the Light Brigade* and *Gone with the Wind* treated war as romance. There was a tradition of realism embodied in a small genre of films depicting the Great War; but from *The Big Parade* (1925) and *What Price Glory*? (1927) to *All Quiet on the Western Front* (1931) and *Dawn Patrol* (1938), "realism" meant the representation of war as cruel, dirty, and ultimately futile. Archibald MacLeish, the first director of the Office of War Information (OWI), was so dubious about the industry's ability to aid the war effort that he discouraged the studios from making war pictures and suggested that they lift public morale by continuing to produce escapist entertainments (with some acknowledgment of wartime concerns).[4]

But even if the OWI had kept to those restrictive guidelines, Hollywood would have insisted on treating the war as a subject for fictional moviemaking. It was the subject above all others that engaged most Americans and could not be escaped even in the cloistered space of the movie theater. This was a war covered by newsreel for an audience raised on movies—an audience which believed that film could let it "see for itself" the reality of war without the polemical distortions of the written word. That the filmed image had its own distortion and polemics was less important than the fact that its images represented something actually seen: the exploding ship, the dead body, the soldier's face, the Zero dissolving in the frame of the gunsight cameras. But it also mean that movie versions of the war would have to be able to stand comparison with the images of reality represented in newsreel and photojournalism and with the firsthand written narratives sent from the battlefronts by war correspondents and by friends and relatives in the service.[5]

Fiction films about the war would have to address the large questions of ideology and strategy: Why are we at war? How shall we fight it? Moreover, they would have to engage these issues not only on the level of abstract statement but on the personal level: Why should this character—representing myself, or my son, husband, or father—risk death in this war? What will happen to him? What will he have to do to win the war? Newsreels could represent part of that reality. But fiction films could imagine those crucial events that the newsreel photographer could not record: the actual moment of combat when soldier kills soldier or is killed himself. By anticipating and fulfilling the audience's need to "know" the real war, fiction films worked as rituals of vicarious initiation into war. Hollywood satisfied this public demand and made the war into movies by abandoning the grand historical scale of the "epic," focusing instead on the intimate scene of small-unit combat, and by making initiation a central theme of the narrative.

The development of the combat film was responsive to the unfolding *cultural* crisis of the war years: the war's problematization of the values, beliefs, and symbols of the nation's mythic/ideological system, especially that part of it which we have called the "Myth of the Frontier." We can see how this process worked by looking at movie treatments of the cultural problems associated with four basic stages of the war crisis: the pre-Pearl Harbor problem of engagement (whether and why we should join the struggle against Germany and Japan); the problem of morale arising from early defeats; the problem of defining the form and meaning of our imminent victory; and the problem of war-memory and postwar adjustment.

The Problem of Engagement: For Whom the Bell Tolls *(1939)*

Between the outbreak of war in Europe in 1939 and the attack on Pearl Harbor at the end of 1941, the United States avoided direct engagement in the European war between Hitler and the democracies of France and England and in the Asian war between Japan and China. Although the Roosevelt administration believed that vital American interests were at stake in both struggles, the public was too deeply divided to make an overt campaign for intervention supportable.

Of all the Hollywood genres, the Western, whose story-lines had been coded as fables of American history, registered most clearly the public's reluctance to go to war. The historical Western drew its mythology from the exceptionalist reading of American history developed by Turner and modernized by Beard; and the genre's concerns looked inward, away from the international arena. Only in the prewar "B" Western, where historicity could be blithely disregarded, did cowboy heroes confront a foreign enemy; but until 1942 their task was to protect America from infiltration, not to confront the enemy overseas. The historically oriented feature Western was actually the genre in which Hollywood entertained the most appealing fantasies of war-*avoidance*. The Westerns most notable for their attempt to address the international crisis were Warners' cavalry epics, *Sante Fe Trail* and *They Died with Their Boots On* (1941), both of which represent war as something that fanatics and profiteers provoke but that principled and civilized soldiers seek to prevent.[6]

The culture's passage from war-avoidance to mobilization is registered in the change in Hollywood's usage of Western symbols: in 1940–1 they express the wish that war will pass us by; by 1943, many of the Western's distinctive stars, settings, plots, and characterizations had been drafted for service in the combat film. From 1942 to 1947 the combat film effectively replaced the "renaissance" Western as the most popular, prevalent, and mythologically significant movie genre, but it did so by incorporating the Western's mythic charge.[7] As the two genres developed after 1945 their kinship became more marked. Finally the mythic landscapes of "War" and "The West" became metaphorical twins in the language of American mythology, and the cowboy/gunfighter became the alter ego of the top-sergeant/Green Beret.

But in 1939–41, the most systematic use of frontier symbolism to support an interventionist polemic is found not in movies but in literary fiction. Ernest Hemingway's *For Whom the Bell Tolls* (1939) uses the Frontier Myth as a way of redefining America's relation to the struggle against Fascism. His hero, Robert Jordan, is from the ranch country of Montana—a cowboy who has become an intellectual, a writer, and a dynamiter for the Loyalists in the Spanish Civil War. The action is set in the hills behind Fascist lines, among guerrilla bands who (like Geronimo and the James Gang) operate on horseback against enemy trains and roads. Jordan's comrades-in-arms are also "primitives," by and large, from the earth-mother Pilar, to the feral Pablo, the "Indian princess" Maria, and the noble-savage-like Anselmo, who plays Chingachgook to Jordan's Hawkeye.

Jordan is a lone American in a war his countrymen would find inconceivably alien. But Hemingway makes his war resonate with American history by continually discovering and comparing cognate features in Loyalist Spain and the idealized America of the Frontier Myth. Listening to the Fascist planes destroying El Sordo's band, Jordan is reminded of Custer's Last Stand. Spanish peasant guerrilla and American cavalier are equals in courage and sacrifice; but Sordo is a superior version of the American type, since his defeat results from bad luck and devotion to his mission rather than from glory-hunting folly.[8] Jordan's account of the American Homestead Act strikes his Spanish comrades as the perfect model of democratic land reform. But as he pursues the analogy, he is forced to recognize that the ideals and principles for which his American ancestors contended are more readily to be found in Spain than in an America grown morally and politically flaccid. His grandfather had fought in the Civil War as a guerrilla and thus was a counterpart of Quantrill and the James Boys and the *gente* of Pablo; he had been a Republican, a supporter of Lincoln and the Union, and hence a liberator of the slaves. But America has degenerated since his grandfather's time. Jordan's father was a weakling who killed himself "to escape torture" of a lesser kind than that endured by the Spanish Loyalists; and "Republican" no longer means what it did, in a nation that now lynches Negroes. Only in Spain is the old meaning of "Republican" still valid; the true "Party of Lincoln" is the Lincoln Battalion.

Hemingway invokes the Myth of the Frontier primarily for purposes of irony and therefore inverts the self-congratulatory "progressive" historiography implicit in the epic Westerns of 1939–41. But his novel also offers a recipe for adapting the Myth as a rationale for intervention. For Jordan, the Spanish war is a new "frontier" on which he can achieve a spiritual regeneration that is no longer possible in a metropolitan and morally compromised America. His journey requires an exile from home and an initial regression to more primitive and "natural" terms of life. Paradoxically, the journey puts him in touch with the forces that must shape a progressive future. Although he is fighting for the Spanish people, the war also enables him to perfect himself as both an American (or democrat) and a hero. Finally, although he is aggressively projecting his (American) power into a foreign scene, the narrative absolves him of any imperialist taint by placing him in a "last stand" scenario. He does not die conquering. Rather, he dies defending his woman and her family/tribe from an enemy whose character combines the worst aspects of barbarism, aristocracy, and corporate tyranny.

In fabricating the combat film Hollywood would use Western-movie myth and the Myth of the Frontier as Hemingway uses it in his novel: drawing implicit comparisons between the present war and the wars of our heroic past, especially the Indian wars; centering the action in a small, isolated, ethnically diverse band, which often contains "natives" and which fights in guerrilla or commando style; building the story around a "last stand" scenario in which heroic representatives of American civilization sacrifice themselves to delay the advance of a savage enemy; and, above all, representing the war scene as one in which American cultural values are tested and *systematically perfected* through a regression to the primitive.

The Problem of Defeat: Bataan *(1943) as Last Stand*

The themes and structures of the combat film developed in response to the series of military disasters with which the war began. The destruction of the American fleet at Pearl Harbor was followed by months of humiliating defeat at the hands of the Japanese, who seized American-held islands in the Western Pacific and conquered the Philippines. It was six months and more before Japanese advances were checked at Midway and Guadalcanal, and a year before the first successful American counteroffensives in the South Pacific were completed.

The shock of these defeats was augmented by the fact that it was the Japanese who had inflicted them. Before Pearl Harbor, most of the public concern and debate over intervention centered on the European war, which the administration also considered the more crucial. (Even after Pearl Harbor, the European Theater had priority over the Pacific Theater.) But in Hollywood that priority was reversed. The industry would approach the war by telling stories of combat, and from 1941 to early 1943 the most important engagements of American ground troops occurred in the Pacific. Moreover, by concentrating on those battles, the movies could also address the problems of morale arising from our initial defeats. The Pacific war also provided settings and enemies that were uniquely appealing to the visual imagination of moviemakers, since the heroes of American action movies had often had to fight non-White enemies in wilderness and jungle.

Since Japanese faces figured more prominently than Germans in the first wave of visualizations of the enemy, an element of racial symbolism became an essential part of the combat film's symbolic code. These images drew their initial force from the racist ideology that still informed the language of American political culture. The Japanese advance graphically confirmed the direst fantasies of a "Rising Tide of Color." That a non-White people who had been stereotyped as racial and technological inferiors should be capable of inflicting such defeats went against the expectations ingrained in Americans by the racist imagery of our preferred mythology.

No comparable reversal of mythic expectations had occurred since Custer's Last Stand in 1876, and it was to that myth that the media reverted in their search for an explanatory model. By an extraordinary coincidence, *Life* magazine's issue for December 8, 1941, featured both a cover photo of General MacArthur ("If war should come he leads the army that would fight Japan") and a photo-spread on Warners' Custer biography, *They Died with Their Boots On.* (The next issue, December 15, covered the attack on Pearl Harbor.) The April 13, 1942, issue of *Life* explicitly uses the "Last Stand" metaphor to rationalize the defeat of MacArthur's army on the Bataan peninsula as a heroic sacrifice intended to buy time. The battle is described as a form of "savage war": the tactics resemble "old-time Indian fighting," with cavalry patrols, ambushes by Filipino "scouts," and Japanese torture of prisoners.[9] But these tactics are merely a microcosm of the war's more profoundly "savage" aspect: for a triumph by the Axis would mean a "rever[sion] to barbarism and brute savagery."[10]

Though defeated in battle, MacArthur's last stand makes him the heroic symbol of the Great Race's willingness and ability to stand against the rising tide of color and the totalitarian ideologies (Fascism and/or Communism) that lie behind it:

> [MacArthur] stopped the Japs. "By God, it was destiny that brought me here," he had said. . . . It was more than destiny that in the whole sad panorama of white men's bitter failure in the Far East, the only men who did not fail were Americans. . . . In holding Bataan . . . MacArthur wrote as clearly as if he had dictated it, the history of America's future relations with Asia. War is the pay-off, and MacArthur, of all the white men in the Far East, paid off."[11]

The imputation of savagery linked the Japanese to the oldest of our mythic race-enemies, the Indian. This may explain the War Department's decision in the spring of 1942 to print 2,000 copies of the famous "Budweiser lithograph" of the Last Stand and distribute them to army posts around the country.[12] But the imagery and rhetoric of wartime propaganda also invoked the analogous myths of Negro "savagery" and "Black Reconstruction." Poster images of Japanese as ape-like monsters raping and murdering White women draw more heavily on the iconography of Black stereotypes (from films like *Birth of a Nation*) than from the images of Western-movie Indians.[13] Nor was the parallel unrelated to domestic social and political tensions. The beginning of the war coincided with emergence of a new African–American political movement that took a more militant stand on civil rights and pressed the administration for action against "Jim Crow" legislation, economic discrimination, and lynching. In response, southern Democrats like John Rankin and Theodore Bilbo of Mississippi identified civil rights with Bolshevism and asserted that Blacks might be as inclined to subversion against "the White man" as the Japanese-Americans then segregated in internment camps.[14] Although the demagogy of Bilbo and Rankin was addressed to concerns that were peculiarly regional, the fear of "race-mixing" which they voiced was not restricted to the South. Nor was racial violence. There were major race riots in Detroit and Harlem in 1943, followed in 1944 by the "Zoot Suit" riots directed against Hispanics in Los Angeles.[15]

But the war also brought into sharp focus the fundamental contradiction between racialism and the values of democracy. The traditional values of democracy and equality had been re-energized in the 1930 by the New Dealers, the labor movement, and the left; but in the context of the war, they constituted the ideological rationale for our armed opposition to the totalitarian and racist systems of Nazi Germany and Imperial Japan. The perception of the likeness between Hitler's racial laws and the segregation codes which sustained Jim Crow in the South began the process of breaking down the consensus that had sustained segregation. Ideological change was reinforced by the ethnic and racial mixing that mobilization fostered and by the mobility (geographic and social) that the expansion of war industries promoted.

America's war-fighting ideology thus contained a potent racist element and at the same time required an explicit disavowal of racism. One of the great achievements of the Hollywood war film was its successful integration of these contradictory pressures. It profoundly altered the ideological content of national ideology by substituting the multi-ethnic platoon for the representatives of White supremacy in the classic "Last Stand" myth-scenario.

The mixture of ideological and technical concerns that shaped this achievement can be seen in the archetype of the combat film, *Bataan*, released by MGM in 1943. The movie was widely praised for its "gritty realism," which gave credibility to its inspirational message; it became the pattern for virtually all of the infantry combat films that followed.[16] It is hard to recover the impression of "gritty realism" when viewing the film today. The movie was shot on a sound-stage, and its potted-plant jungle suffers by comparison with the location shooting in later films like *Objective Burma*—or, for that matter, the "forest Western" *Northwest Passage* (1940). The movie's real claim to "grit" is the skill and consistency with which its script introduces us to the moral "dirtiness" of this new kind of war: its insistence on showing us the harsh and "dirty" fact of defeat; the enemy's "dirty" savagery; and the necessity of our learning to *match* savagery with savagery to achieve victory.

The prevalence of "savage war" structures in characterizations of the Pacific war owes something to firsthand accounts of fighting against the Japanese, whose adherence to the code of *bushido* often made their troops unwilling to give or take quarter and led them to mistreat or kill their prisoners.[17] But in conceiving a narrative and imagistic framework in which to tell the story, the filmmakers were also guided by precedents drawn from the film genres of the 1930s, particularly those of the Western and the "Victorian Empire" film. The most important source of *Bataan* was *The Lost Patrol* (1934), directed by John Ford. Far from concealing its debt to Ford's movie, the studio specifically identified the earlier film as a source in the trade papers. Even reviewers who praised the realism of *Bataan* informed their readers that it was "Just like *The Lost Patrol*."[18]

The Lost Patrol is nominally a movie about the First World War. But it involves a lost patrol of British cavalry in the Mesopotamian desert, with costume and setting like those in a Victorian Empire film. The patrol consists of a variety of British social types, including a fanatic Dissenter, a "fallen" gentleman, a Scotsman, an Irishman, and a Cockney. The patrol is lost in the desert when its officer is killed by a sniper, leaving the soldiers under the command of their hard-boiled professional sergeant (Victor McLaglen). The desert space is utterly blank and barren. They are without orders or knowledge of their mission or means of contact with the army and the civilized world it represents. The only proof of that world's existence is the black-comic visit of a British airplane, which flies over the oasis and then incredibly sets down. A foppish pilot with a swagger stick steps out, begins to speak ("I *say* . . ."), and is immediately killed by an Arab sniper. It is altogether a nicely visualized existentialist dilemma: the external desert encroaches and makes itself a metaphor for the emptiness and absurdity which overcomes each of the men in turn. It is a theme for which the Great War setting is certainly not inappropriate; yet it is clearly outside the historical frame of Great War movies, which is conventionally identified with the familiar horrors of the Western Front.

In *Bataan*, the absurdist landscape of military blunder and defeat in alien and unknown settings is systematically transformed into a comprehensible landscape of defensible spaces. The opening scenes establish clear moral and spatial boundaries. The savage character of the enemy is immediately revealed when we see Japanese planes bombing a column of Filipino refugees protected by Americans. The platoon forms immediately after this attack; its mission will be to destroy a bridge and delay the enemy as long as possible. Although the officer in charge is killed early on by a sniper, the sergeant who takes over (unlike his counterpart in *Lost Patrol*) knows what the orders are and why they must be carried out.

Having established the ideological frame, the movie defines its symbolic landscape. A jungle clearing/oasis becomes a surrogate for "home." It contains a hut and pool of water, and the platoon sets up housekeeping there. Corporal Ramirez (Desi Arnaz) has a portable radio, and they can even hear jazz broadcasts from Hollywood. The rituals of roll calls, guard duty, and other assignments define this as an orderly place, but when Japanese snipers violate it we learn that this is a war in which no place, however homelike, is safe. As the battle proceeds and the platoon loses man after man, a series of burials fills out a line of graves and the platoon is united by the recurrent ceremony of burial.

The movie carefully defines the social microcosm of the platoon which defends the home-space. The social divisions of America in the 1930s must be acknowledged through representation, but the ideological point of the film is that the test of war will produce unity out of division. Here for the first time we see that detailed representation of ethnic types that became the hallmark of the combat film. The platoon includes a Jew, an Irishman, a Pole, a Hispanic, and two Asians—the Filipinos Salazar (the Moro) and Katigbak. Although the army was racially segregated, there is even a Black (Epps), whose presence is plausible because this is a pick-up platoon. Epps is brave and dignified, though comfortably within the range of accepted racial stereotypes. A would-be preacher, he does most of the grave-digging and hymn-singing. His death is uniquely gruesome, and he is the only member of the platoon who screams as he dies.

Others in the platoon represent combinations of ethnicity and class. The commander, Captain Lassiter, is a WASP and a West Pointer, and so is the pilot, Lieutenant Bentley (George Murphy). The tough top-sergeant's name, Bill Dane (Robert Taylor), suggests Viking or Nordic derivation, though like the Virginian he is a man of "the ranks." But the other WASPs in the platoon represent a range of social types and, in some case, the imaginary worlds of pre-war movie genres. Corporal Todd (Lloyd Nolan) is a kind of gangster figure; Purckett (Robert Walker) is the small-town, "Andy Hardy" kid, naive, eager, versatile; Ramirez is a Hispanic and also a link to the fictive "culture" of the pop-music scene. Each of the men also represents a different branch of the service. Bentley is Army Air Force; Purckett is Navy; Lassiter, cavalry; Dane, infantry. The medic Hardy is a conscientious objector. Others represent the signal corps, tank corps, chemical engineers, army engineers, motor transport, Philippine Scouts, and Air Corps—only the artillery and the Marines are left out.[19]

Later films, drawing on the achievement of *Bataan*, could be more economical in their symbolization of American diversities. But the overdetermination of types in *Bataan* is worth attention because it reveals the conscious strain behind the composition of the mythical platoon. It is also worth noting, as a reflection of the cultural power of movies, that real-world and movie-world referents are accorded equal authority as sources of American social types.

The story line of *Bataan* provides two structuring fables that give larger meaning to the tale of the lost patrol's last stand. The first is the overt ideological premise that the war is just and that the platoon's mission is both a necessary sacrifice and a real contribution to eventual victory. But the more powerful subtext is the story of the platoon's—and by analogy America's, initiation into war. Only Sergeant Dane and Corporals Feingold (Thomas Mitchell) and Todd are veterans of active service. Captain Lassiter is only four months out of West Point, and the rest of the platoon are (in Dane's words) a bunch of kids and raw recruits. As the combat develops they will prove their worth to the veteran sergeant and the audience.

The central lesson that they have to learn is that war is "dirty."[20] The word is used in a number of different ways in the film, and it becomes one of the genre's most resonant terms. The dirtiness of war begins with its physical squalor and hardship, but it is moral dirtiness that is really meant: the war is dirty in its unfairness and cruelty and in its remorselessness—one can never relax, never call time or plead unreadiness. Good men and bad are killed alike; sometimes the deaths seem useless or absurd. Good men have to kill and have to suppress their natural impulses to kindness or fair play. The dirtiness of war is personified by the enemy, called "monkeys," who sneak up to kill from behind; who torture and mutilate captives. In the enemy's case, this moral dirtiness—this willingness to do anything to win—is also the sign of an incredible energy and commitment. The Japanese never get tired, never stop coming at you, never ask for a respite let alone for quarter. Like the Apache in *Stagecoach*, they compel the diverse types that make up the platoon to unite; and the monstrous proportions of their savagery are indicated by the fact that they compel Americans to unite across lines of race as well as across lines of class. Yet these monsters teach the Americans the war-fighting techniques they need to win.

The Americans have to get dirty too if they are to win. The key character here is the kid, Purckett, the most naive and childlike member of the platoon, straight from a high-school movie full of sock hops and malt shops. Purckett's initiation represents the audience's own loss of innocence, and it is important that he is as much (or more) a movie type as a social species.[21] On sentry duty, unnerved by a shape in the mist, Purckett fires his machine gun only to discover he has shot at the tortured corpse of the platoon's own "savage," Salazar.[22] "Dirty dirty *dirty*!" he mutters, hunching over his gun. Purckett is also the figure through whom *Bataan* reconciles the implicit racialism of its characterization of the Japanese with the ideology of multi-ethnic tolerance around which the platoon's democracy is built. Earlier in a famous two-shot, Purckett glares over his machine gun and snarls about his desire to kill lots of these "monkeys"; but just next to him is the "oriental" face of Corporal Salazar, whose rage against the "monkeys" is every bit as great. The expression of racial hatred is thus framed in a way that allows us to disclaim racism.[23]

The racial limits of tolerance are defined by the conditions of savage war. In hand-to-hand combat, Purckett learns where and how to draw the line of humanity: a Japanese soldier offers to surrender and then tries to kill him. Purckett strangles the Japanese, lifting and shaking the body in rage—the Japanese have fully taught Andy Hardy how to fight dirty. He returns to the home-clearing besmirched with blood, both his own and the enemy's, bewildered and distraught by what he has done. He then reverts one last time to kid-like innocence and writes a letter to his "Mum." In that mood he becomes vulnerable and is killed by a sniper.

At the end of the film, only Sergeant Dane is left. He has buried the last of the platoon, has dug his own grave at the end of the row, and has made it into a machine-gun nest. The last stage of our initiation into the "dirtiness" of war engages what is best described as "the horror"—figured in the horror-movie fog that pervades the set and through which the Japanese swarm toward the weary, depressed Dane. He now knows (as the audience does) all the terrible things the enemy is capable of; he knows, too, that for this platoon there is no hope of victory, rescue, mercy, or escape. As the enemy creep closer, Dane rouses himself to a fury, that mounts to eye-rolling madness. He yells and curses at the charging Japanese while firing his tripod-mounted machine gun at them. At last he fires it directly into the camera's eye as the final title declares our intention to return to Bataan.

Thus the enemy's last lesson is about the power of madness, the willingness to kill promiscuously in an overpowering rage. Like Kurtz in Conrad's *Heart of Darkness*, Dane's knowledge of the enemy makes him wish for the magic power to "exterminate the brutes." Conrad unmasks Kurtz's genocidal rage as a magical device for evading his sense of subjection—of *likeness*—to an enemy whose racial character he despises. But the propaganda purposes of *Bataan* require us to see Dane's berserker rage as a potentially successful model for fighting and winning the jungle war. Rage makes the doomed sergeant seem invulnerable—for though we know he is about to die, we never see him fall.[24]

Although Dane is fiction, the kind of rage he visualizes was an inescapable part of both motivational propaganda and of the experience of war-fighting itself. Samuel Eliot Morison's official history of naval operations around Guadalcanal in 1942–43 describes a sign at fleet headquarters in the South Pacific that urged "KILL JAPS, KILL JAPS, KILL MORE JAPS!"

> This may shock you, reader: but it is exactly how we felt. We were fighting no civilized, knightly war. . . . We were back in the primitive days of fighting Indians on the American frontier; no holds barred and no quarter. The Japs wanted it that way, thought they could thus terrify an "effete democracy"; and that is what they got, with the additional horrors of war that modern science can produce.[25]

But despite the racist "savaging" of the Japanese, the "war-world" imagined by Hollywood is markedly more liberal, tolerant, and integrated than the one in which most of the movie audience lived. Henry Luce's *Life* editorialists claimed Bataan as a moral victory for the "White race": *Bataan* claims it a moral victory for a melting-pot

America. The Hollywood platoon was more than a representation of an idealized America; it was a utopian projection or reification of the kind of nation that Hollywood—acting as keeper of the symbols of public ideology—thought we should and could become through the testing and transformation of war. This exercise in reification had a significant impact on the national culture that emerged from the war: it made the realization of "melting pot" values *at home* the symbolic equivalent of a war aim—a domestic analogue of FDR's "Four Freedoms." After 1943, whatever the divisions of local politics, when one looked to those media that mirror the life and ideal values of "America at war," what one saw was not *Birth of a Nation* but the multiethnic platoon of *Bataan, Sahara, Gung Ho, Objective Burma, A Walk in the Sun.*[26]

But the ferocity of the last images of *Bataan* also poses a moral and ideological problem. To match the ruthless violence of the enemy may be proof that democracy is virile, not effete. But how far can such imitation be pushed without fatally compromising the values of civilization and melting-pot democracy?[27] All wars, however "just" and popular they may be, inevitably raise certain questions of belief and value, certain doubts about the balance between means and ends. War requires people to endure and inflict terrible suffering; and once the pressures of crisis have passed, individuals and societies alike experience a reaction against the war, against the things war has compelled them to do and endure. Even in the victorious nation, such a reaction may take the form of a rejection of wartime political leadership, as it did in the United States after the Great War and in Great Britain in 1945. At the very least, the reaction calls into question ideas and practices that the wartime society had been willing to take on faith.

The Problem of Victory: Objective Burma *(1945)*

The film that poses (and answers) the problem of victory in the most appealing terms is Warners' *Objective Burma* (1945), directed by Raoul Walsh. The film deploys the by now familiar iconography of the combat film interestingly and economically. We are presented with a range of ethnic types played by a mixture of familiar character actors and authentic-looking "unknown" faces. Walsh mixes references to newsreel-reality with allusions to movie conventions and icons. An old newspaperman, played by Henry Hull (the editor in *Jesse James*), acts a *rapporteur*, interpreting the "big picture" for the soldiers and asking the men in combat the questions those at home might want answered. The film's "realist" intentions are underscored by casting Errol Flynn as the commander, Captain Nelson, and then costuming him *against* his romantic type.

Unlike the platoon in *Bataan*, Nelson and his paratroopers are on an offensive mission. The first part of the film traces their swift and efficient execution of their orders. With grace and skill they assassinate the sentries, massacre the surprised and unarmed Japanese as they pour out of their mess hall, and destroy the radar station that threatens the allied offensive. Thus far the narrative shows the Americans as having effortlessly incorporated the "fight dirty" lesson and having converted it into a "clean" and efficient set of moves. But our platoon pays for its easy victory by being abruptly returned to the moral terrain of *The Lost Patrol*. The Japanese disrupt the attempt to lift the raiders out, and the mission degenerates into an increasingly desperate flight through the jungle with the Japanese in pursuit.

Once again we regress to a wilderness condition at increasing removes from "home." Mission and objectives become obscure, the high command's purposes undecipherable, and the map references increasingly abstract, lacking all meaningful relation to the one point all strive to reach—not even home, merely "the base."

The platoon is split, and half of it is massacred. When Nelson's troops discover their bodies at a temple-village in the jungle, a nadir of "the horror" imposed by the enemy is reached. The Japanese have mutilated the men beyond recognition and have (presumably) castrated and tortured to death Lt. Jacobs, Nelson's best friend. The old reporter is suddenly infected with "the madness" that "the horror" imposes on those who learn it. Kurtz wanted to "exterminate the brutes"; the reporter cries, "They're moral idiots! . . . Wipe 'em out, I say, wipe 'em off the face of the earth!"[28] Bill Dane's fury is thus fully verbalized, only seven months before Hiroshima and Nagasaki. But *Nelson*'s response reflects both an awareness of the horror and an ability to preserve the core of humane feeling from the contamination of racist rage. His words are solely of grief for his friend, and when he turns to action he is not thinking about an apocalyptic last stand but about getting his men out of the jungle.

The film gets *us* out of the jungle and away from "the horror" by getting us to "follow Nelson." Though the troops have lost faith in the army, the high command, perhaps the nation, and certainly "the mission," they believe in Nelson's virtue and power. He cares about them and takes care of them; he doesn't just give orders, he leads.

Walsh's combination of Flynn's aristocratic/swashbuckler persona with plebeian dress and democratic style makes Nelson a modern version of the Virginian: the natural leader who rules others because of the innate qualities of his character. "I'd follow that guy down the barrel of a cannon," says one of the men, in a sly allusion to *The Charge of the Light Brigade*.[29] The traditional hero (in "realist" mufti) saves the platoon by leading them back to the primary ground, the original mythic space of the combat film: a clearing on a hilltop, a place they can defend—perhaps a place for a last stand, but still, a place to *defend*. We have, in a moral sense, indeed come "back to Bataan." The crucial difference is that now the gesture of digging in, of *willingness* to fight to the last man, leads to redemption, rescue, and even transcendence: the platoon is saved by the massive paratroop drop that precedes the "liberation" of Burma and then is literally snatched into a shining heaven as a plane picks up their glider and soars them homeward.

But though *Objective Burma* thus affirms both the essential structures of our traditional heroic myths and the ideological premises of the *Bataan*/Last Stand platoon movie, its last scene poses a question about the cost and meaning of the war that is left unanswered. When his commander congratulates him on a job well done, Nelson drops into his hands the dog tags of all the men he has lost and says, "Here's what it cost." In the context of the film's careful delineation of the platoon's personnel, this image—fifty men reduced to a stack of tin tags—is devastating. If the war has been worth *this* cost (Nelson's gesture says), the margin of profit is damned thin.

The Problem of Memory: Fort Apache *(1948)*

The climax of the "victory"-oriented combat film is an image that promises completion of the mythic ordeal through escape from battle and a return "home." But "home" itself is almost never seen in the combat film. It exists abstractly, at a terrible distance from the action, and is invoked in words rather than pictures. But though unseen, it remains the supreme symbol of value, the sacred thing for whose safety the platoon undergoes its ordeal. It is usually identified with women—Mom, Sis, the girlfriend whose name always seems to be some variant of "MaryLou." Nor is the utopian dream of that return compromised by any suggestion that "home" may be less than perfect; that the world of *Dead End* and *Grapes of Wrath* still exists; that while the platoon has been dirtying itself with blood, civilians have been living clean and comfortably and politicians and profiteers have been making "The Good War" into "a good thing." The sharpest criticism of the home front is occasional sarcasm about the "hardships" of rationing or the rhetoric of war-bond drives. Though some war films suggest that after the war we will have to work even harder to realize our ideals, they hardly imply the need for profound social or political transformation.

The achievement of victory in 1945 brought both euphoria and a rush to fulfill the promise of the myth of return. The armed forces were demobilized with astonishing and perhaps excessive speed. But the war produced radical changes in American social conditions, in the structure of economic and political institutions, and in the orientation of domestic and international politics. The nation that emerged from the war, and to which the veterans returned, was not the place they had left. It was certainly not the "home" that lay just beyond the last frame of the combat film. Nor did the peace for which they had fought take the form that had been popularly imagined for it.

The reformist agenda of the New Deal was not merely postponed by the war; it was fundamentally transformed. The original principle of New Deal ideology was the belief that the Depression had permanently discredited the regime of "big business" capitalism. Government regulation, based on scientific planning, was seen as necessary not only to relieve the immediate distress caused by the contraction of business but to effect a redistribution of power and wealth. The goal of these policies was to restore the productive power and expansiveness of the economy. As Franklin Roosevelt's invocation of Turner's Frontier Thesis suggests, however, there was also a tacit assumption that a certain limit of growth had perhaps been reached, and that the just redistribution of limited resources was now a more realistic goal than the opening of some new economic bonanza. After eight years of the New Deal, the GNP had still not quite returned to its pre-Crash levels.

It was the war that ended the Depression and inaugurated a colossal economic expansion underwritten at first by government spending but sustained by dramatic increases in domestic consumption. Between 1941 and 1945 American income, aggregate wealth, and production more than doubled over pre-war levels; at the same time, the wealth and productivity of the European and Asian industrial powers was substantially reduced or obliterated by war damage. Memories of the postwar recessions of 1919–20 caused some apprehension that the war boom might be followed by another bust, but the anticipated contraction did not materialize. Instead, the most "utopian" predictions of postwar prosperity seemed to be near realization. The marvels of wartime productivity suggested that a new frontier of potentially limitless wealth had been discovered in a Keynsian partnership between government, consumers, and big business. Government support for public and higher education, low-interest financing for housing, and the underwriting of basic security would be supported by progressive taxation. This would make possible higher levels of consumption, which would drive demand upward and support increasing industrial productivity and higher employment and (therefore) still higher levels of consumption.[30]

The phrase that best describes the vision was, perhaps fittingly, coined by Eric Johnson, president of the Motion Picture Association, in a 1946 address titled "Utopia as Production," delivered to a union of movie technicians and later distributed in pamphlet form.[31] Johnson began by addressing the public fear that wartime prosperity would be succeeded by a return to the conditions of the 1930s, with "rough and rugged" industrial strife and with contending classes "fighting over the dry bones of famine." The struggles of the thirties had brought us "dangerously close to the cliff of collectivism," and government control of economic activity during the war economy had eliminated that strife at the cost of economic freedom. Now, said Johnson, "People are tired of death, trouble, and all the sundry woes of war. . . . We want bacon and butter and beefsteaks. We're in a hurry to decontrol." But the public is also weary of class warfare, "fed up to the eyebrows with some of labor's indefensible practices" and demands, and as ready to turn against labor now as it had been ready to turn against capital in 1930.

For Johnson, "the public" is seen almost exclusively as a body of consumers driven by its desire for "more" of everything and willing to exert political power against any group or class that impedes the fulfillment of its desire. "What threatens production threatens our whole economy. It threatens our futures. It threatens our hopes of an ever-rising living standard." On the other hand, "Having the things we want spells Utopia." But higher consumption is possible only with ever-increasing productivity: "We've got to make what we want before we can have it. . . . [Therefore] Utopia now and always is production." And the only way to achieve such production is through the substitution of union/corporation cooperation for the adversarial relationship of the thirties.[32]

The wealth of this new frontier was to be enjoyed by all. But it was not to be achieved by "populist" (or in Johnson's term "collectivist") means, which would require government regulation of big business to support the claims of small entrepreneurs, farmers, and organized labor. The wartime expansion that opened this new frontier was the work of big business—one-third of all war orders had gone to ten large corporations—and its success had given corporate capitalism a higher ideological standing than it had enjoyed since the days of Calvin Coolidge.[33]

Johnson's vision was consistent with the ideological direction taken by the most influential American intellectuals and policy-makers in 1945–47, and it anticipates the "consensus" ideology that dominated public discourse in the 1950s.[34] However, its immediate context was not one of harmony and consensus but of dissonance and conflict. The malaise Johnson refers to, the anticipation of future class conflict, reflects an emerging conflict between those individuals and groups who were committed to completing the New Deal's social and political agenda and those who believed the New Deal reforms had gone far enough and that further "leftward" movement had to be stopped.

The rightward shift was reflected in the growth of public hostility toward union militancy. The Republican majority in the Congressional elections of 1946 was built, to a considerable degree, on successful union-bashing. The passage of the Taft-Hartley Bill in 1947 by a conservative majority that included Democrats and Republicans was a major blow to the power of unions. President Truman became embroiled with labor when strikes by coalminers, railroad and steel workers challenged his authority and threatened his programs for economic adjustment and European recovery. But the labor movement itself was taking a rightward turn. The CIO abandoned its radical critique of American capitalism and craft unionism and moved closer to the AF of L. Organized labor purged its "leftists," neglected the organization of unorganized workers to pursue a "partnership" with business, and finally joined the anti-Communist "crusade."[35]

Nonetheless, the labor movement was still capable of militancy (as Truman's union troubles showed), and there was a growing constituency for civil rights. The "populist" slogans, symbols, and critiques of fat-cat capitalism that characterized the spirit of the later New Deal were still as current in the public's ideological lexicon as the vision of a corporate utopia.

There were other dissonances as well. The nation had nominally fought in the name of democracy and equality against dictatorships founded on racist premises, yet racial inequality was still a marked feature of American life. The former slave states, and parts of the West and the Southwest, lived under regimes of segregation that legally deprived Blacks (and in some cases Indians and Hispanics) of the most basic political rights and subjected them to vigilante terrorism. The war inaugurated major demographic shifts that brought racial inequities into more prominent focus. Blacks improved their economic position and achieved geographic and economic mobility by working in war plants. Black soldiers from the South learned that alternative ways of living existed elsewhere in the United States and in Europe; as soldiers of democracy they not only learned how to organize and fight but became convinced that they had earned the right to enjoy the liberties they fought for. Changes in Black consciousness were matched by corresponding shifts in the political ideology and priorities of White liberals. The war against Hitler had changed their awareness of the significance of racial injustice in ways that the labor battles of the thirties never had. The civil-rights movement and the restructuring of race relations would become the dominant theme of domestic politics in the decades ahead.

But the most profound gap between the expectation and the reality of victory was opened by the breakdown of the wartime alliance between the United States and the soviet Union. Whatever else victory was supposed to mean, the establishment of permanent peace and a rational world order was the irreducible minimum. Although the war had made the United States the pre-eminent military power in the world, it had also revealed the nation's essential vulnerability. Until 1941–45 it had seemed feasible for the country to choose between isolation from world politics and active but limited engagement. Hitler's conquest of the European continent and Japan's strike at Pearl Harbor proved that in the modern world isolation was no longer feasible, even if it were desirable. Russia's acquisiton of atomic weapons in 1947 merely confirmed a condition that was already acknowledged even by the remnant of the isolationist bloc in Congress. Peace could not be achieved by American withdrawal behind the shield of the oceans, but only through the active maintenance of the wartime unity of the Western Powers.

But these countries were themselves caught up in costly attempts to recover their pre-war colonies in Asia and Africa. Although the United States was committed in principle to decolonization, in practice we supported the efforts of the British and French to suppress nationalist uprisings, particularly those that appeared to be influenced by Communism. Nelson and his men help liberate *Objective Burma* and then fly home, obviously wanting no part of any colonial reconquest—but that was one of the things their sacrifice bought. At least one combat movie, made late in the war, entertains this ideological question more or less explicitly. *A Walk in the Sun* (1946) is a highly stylized version of the platoon movie in which pairs of characters serve as a kind of Greek chorus commenting on the action through the reiteration of formulaic phrases. The best remembered of these is the wishful/ironic "Nobody dies"; but a close second is the repeated declaration of one soldier-cynic that the war will never end, that after Italy they will fight in France, in Germany, and ten years from now in "the battle of Tibet."

By 1948 a battle of Tibet was more than just a rifleman's nightmare. The establishment of Communist regimes in European countries occupied by the Red Army, the apparent intransigence of Stalin, and the advances made by Communist parties in war-ravaged western Europe aroused American fears of Soviet domination of the Continent. The success of the Communist revolution in China and the outbreak of rebellions in the Asian and African colonies of France, England, and the Netherlands suggested that the Communist threat might in fact be worldwide. In the spring of 1947 the Truman administration responded with the articulation of the "Truman Doctrine" and the establishment of the Marshall Plan. The conservative drift of economic policy was now linked with a policy of containing Communism in Europe, and perhaps in the whole world.[36]

The movies responded to the crisis of victory as they had to the crisis of defeat. They reverted to their generic maps in search of ideological reference points, which meant, for the most part, a return to the home terrain of the Western. Only eight Westerns with running times of 80 minutes or more had been produced in 1945. However, in 1946 there were 12; in 1947, 14; in 1948, 31; and after a drop to 25, 80+ Westerns in 1949, production increased every year until 1955 and remained high until the end of the 1960s.[37]

At first, the new Westerns attempted simply to recover the mood of the *ante-bellum* genre. Feature films were produced in all the categories developed during the "renaissance" of 1939–41: good old "cowboy pictures," progressive epics celebrating technological advances, town-taming lawmen bringing law and order to wild cattle towns, good-outlaw tales and reprises of *Jesse James*.[38] But as the shape of postwar concerns became clearer, there were more substantive changes in Western styles and content.

Beginning in 1947—Year One of the Cold War—a new and darker style of the Western appeared, anticipating the style known as *film noir*. This style centered on themes of revenge and featured psychologically damaged and alienated heroes, often played by either Robert Mitchum or Randolph Scott.[39] Others offered an ironic or inverted version of standard "progressive" themes. *Red River* (1948) starred John Wayne as a classic progressive empire-builder who metamorphoses into a megalomaniacal tyrant in the course of masterminding the first great cattle drive from Texas to Kansas. *Silver River* (1948) starred Errol Flynn as a corrupt politician in a perverse revision of *Dodge City*. *The Furies* (1950) treated cattle-ranching in *film noir* style, and Samuel Fuller's *The Baron of Arizona* (1950) framed the "epic of statehood" as the tale of a confidence man. Both *The Fabulous Texan* (1947) and *The Man from Colorado* (1948) deal with the imposition of tyrannies by Reconstruction carpetbaggers in the post-Civil War West. On one level, these films reprise the anti-Fascist conventions of prewar films like *Night Riders*; they may be read either as reflections on the war just ended or as extensions of wartime formulas to the new totalitarian threat from abroad. Yet the settings of these films are domestic, and they are as easily read as critiques of postwar militarism and the advantages gained by corporate war profiteers.[40]

What these films have in common is the use of mythical tropes drawn from movie genres to pose questions about the meaning of our victory. In a variety of settings, these films played variations on the same basic concern: How had America's achievement and exercise of pre-eminent power affected our commitment to the democratic ideology for which we had nominally fought the war?

In 1948 John Ford added a major variation to the Western genre by uniting the conventions and concerns of the combat film and the Western in a single coherent fable. In his cavalry trilogy—*Fort Apache* (1948), *She Wore a Yellow Ribbon* (1950), and *Rio Grande* (1950)—Ford used the time and resources of three productions to create and intensively develop a single set of themes, characters, and images. His success was such that he and his many imitators were able to draw on the formulas developed in the sequence to make numerous cavalry Westerns over the next two decades. By transferring the ideological concerns of the World War and its aftermath from the terrain of the combat film to the mythic landscape of the Western, Ford proposed a mythic response to the crisis of postwar ideology that is at once a moral critique of our "victory" and an affirmation of the importance of the patriotic solidarity that made victory possible.

Ford's experience of the "real war," as a filmmaker for the navy and Naval Intelligence, was more extensive than that of most of his Hollywood contemporaries. Yet of all the major directors, he was the most reluctant to make fiction films about combat. His only generic "combat film," *They Were Expendable* (1945), was made under some official duress.

Ford later explained his unwillingness to fictionalize the war as a reaction against wartime censorship, which forbade his telling the truth about combat or his criticizing American tactics and policies. He may also have needed to distance himself from painful memories of war experiences before he could treat those memories in the terms of his art.[41] On the other hand, the Indian-fighting cavalry offered a setting that naturally lent itself to the consideration of military issues in Western guise. But that setting was a novel one in 1948. It had been sixty years since Remington's illustrations had given the cavalryman as prominent a place as the cowboy in Western iconography; and thirty-five since the Wild West's last re-enactment of Custer's Last Stand and Ince's *Custer's Last Fight* (1912).[42] Though the cavalry often rode to the rescue in formula Westerns, few films made the cavalry itself the central subject. Of more immediate relevance to his project were the Victorian Empire movies of 1935–40, like *The Charge of the Light Brigade*, and their American equivalents, *Santa Fe Trail* and *They Died with Their Boots On*. In these films the order of the regiment symbolizes the values of civilization (and in the American case, of democracy) imperiled by the assaults from without of a fanatical race-enemy and from within by the weakness (or corruption) of a political order ruled by "female" sentiment.[43]

But *Fort Apache* develops into an ironic undoing of the naive racial-imperial ideology of these films. Most of the thematic and formal elements typical of the Victorian Empire formula are present: the regiment, the savage foe, the fanatic villain, the tyrant representing antidemocratic values, the border outpost, the dance scene, the massacre, the fatal cavalry charge. But in *Fort Apache* the meaning of the symbols is inverted: the colonel of the regiment is the fanatic and tyrant who breaks the code of warrior honor, women's values stand equal to men's, the Indians are victims and honorable fighters rather than savage rebels or aggressors, and the film's last stand is less a glorification of Western civilization than the culmination of a subtle critique of American democratic pretenses.[44] The undoing of this particular genre-ideology is achieved by applying to the romantic formula the "gritty realism" of the combat film. But Ford's critique in *Fort Apache* undoes more than the conventions of an outdated genre. By building his story around a "Last Stand"—the sanctifying trope of the combat film and the Western alike—he extends his critique to contemporary American ideology and to the mythological roots of that ideology in the Myth of the Frontier.[45]

The primal division of space in the Western and the war film is usually the border between the defended "home" of the clearing (or settlement) and the savage wilderness; and that division is usually complemented by the distinction between the civilized men (and women) who inhabit (or depend on the defense of) the clearing and the dark-skinned savages who lurk without. In *Fort Apache* it appears in the spatial division betwen the emptiness of the desert and the replete social life of the Fort. The setting recalls the "classic" West of *Stagecoach*; but in the wake of *Bataan*, *Sahara*, and *Objective Burma*, the monolith-desert also evokes the jungles and deserts of the combat film; a vision of Nature as intractable and inhuman, the home of a terrible and implacable enemy, impossible to imagine as the site of a future agrarian paradise, a place we fight in but not necessarily a place we fight for.[46] However, in *Fort Apache* the threat of wilderness and savage is not sufficient to overcome the differences of class, race, and gender that divide the Fort community.[47]

The world of *Fort Apache* is recognizably related to that of the platoon movie. The first section of the film deals with the initiations of several characters (the new Colonel and his daughter, young Lieutenant O'Rourke, a group of recruits) to the army and its war. Likewise, the men in the ranks are all "ethnics" who represent a range of social and political divisions in American society. But instead of the obligatory representation of almost every contemporary ethnic group by at least one soldier, the historical setting permits a simplification: all the ethnics are Irish. The Western setting allows Ford plausibly to abstract from the practice of ethnic representation the *principle* that the army, as a metaphor of American society, is an institution in which the melting-pot ideology works. It also allows him to poke fun at the convention by having Sergeant Mulcahy (Victor McLaglen) favor anyone from County Cork; ethnic chauvinism is as much a feature of the melting pot as intergroup cooperation.

The second most identifiable class among the soldiers consists of ex-Confederates, whose leader is the only non-Irish sergeant, Beaufort (Pedro Armendariz), a Mexican–American despite his French name. Here the shift from combat to Western adds a new element of potential division to the platoon mix: political differences serious enough to have caused a Civil War.[48] Ex-rebels may find a home and honor and comradeship in serving the regiment against the Indians, but they still retain a separate and suppressed political identity.

The abstraction and simplification of ethnic and ideological difference leave Ford room to explore an aspect of American society that the platoon movie typically evades: the structure of class and hierarchy. In *Fort Apache*, ethnics and southerners are—with two exceptions—relegated to ranks of sergeant and below. The officer corps are almost exclusively WASP; their style, their households, their speech, and their code of honor mark them as *gentlemen*. Captain Kirby York (John Wayne) may be an exception: he has the Virginian's sense of courtesy and protocol and gamecock sense of honor, and he will fight duels if insulted. But he is *not* a Confederate. His most distinctive traits are those that make him the Fort's "man who knows Indians." He is a professional soldier who despises mere parade-ground smartness, a "scout" type rather than a "Lancer." He is, in fact, the culmination of a number of traditional themes in American heroism—a "natural aristocrat" who is also well born and well educated, a frontier Indian fighter who is capable of presiding over a civilized world.[49]

The more important exception is Lieutenant Michael O'Rourke, Jr. (John Agar), who is not only Irish but the son of the Sergeant Major at Fort Apache (Ward Bond). He has been raised in the Fort and so "knows Indians." But his father, with the other sergeants helping, have worked to put the boy through West Point. Young O'Rourke embodies the central trope of the melting-pot ideology: that the children of immigrants may rise as high in American society as their merit will take them, even into the ranks of officers and gentlemen—where they will nominally command the fathers who paved their way to power.

However, the political culture of Fort Apache enables its citizens to evade the consequences of such unequal and unnatural divisions of authority. Although young O'Rourke is an officer, the sergeants still treat him as a child, giving him a mock-spanking when they first meet and helping him out when his technique with recruits shows him to be "too much the gentleman." In the symbolic speech of politics, the contradiction between liberty and power is conventionally concealed under the metaphor of family relations. But in Ford's fort that metaphor is literalized, with the result that genuine familial elements rise to counteract official power. The relation of the sergeants to the young officer illustrates this, but a stronger case is that of the women of Fort Apache.

The two dominant architectural frames of Fort Apache are the Colonel's office and the row houses of the married officers and sergeants. These represent two worlds, the army and the home, a patriarchy (whose authority will fall into the hands of tyrant) and a matriarchy. At the head of the patriarchal order stands Colonel Owen Thursday (Henry Fonda), an aristocratic and intellectual officer, bitter over his lack of promotion and his posting to "this godforsaken desert," a martinet, a glory-hunter, and a caste-snob.[50] Thursday is the representative of power and authority in general and (as he tells the crooked Indian Agent Meachum) of the United States government and, therefore, of the law. At the head of the matriarchy stands the wife of Sergeant Major O'Rourke (Irene Rich), mother of the young lieutenant—a powerfully maternal figure, evocative of Ma Joad, to whom even the officers' wives defer in matters concerning the women's world in Fort Apache.

The presence of the women, and of their powerful emotional and ideological counterweight to patriarchal authority, is another creative possibility made plausible by the transfer of the war story to the landscape of the Western. Ford's women play a far subtler, more complex, and more significant role in the cavalry-world than do the women in the three prewar Flynn/de Havilland cavalry epics produced by Warners. In *Fort Apache* the female or matriarchal side is assigned a moral weight equal to the authority vested in Thursday. The women are entrusted with the preservation of the fundamental rituals that bind Fort society together; they are identified with the principles of democratic egalitarianism, which they pose as a countervailing principle against the claims of Thursday's power.[51]

Until the arrival of Thursday, the different orders of Fort Apache live in harmony and mutual support despite their differences. Their symbolic meeting ground is the post recreation hall, where they enact an annual series of dances—rituals that symbolize and recreate their communal bond. That Thursday will disrupt the tribal utopia that is Fort Apache becomes clear when his arrival breaks up the Washington's Birthday dance. That he is a danger to the community is confirmed when he violates the democratic spirit of the Noncommissioned Officers' Dance, which is the climax of the year's ceremonial cycle. Here the Irish sergeants preside as hosts and are permitted to dance with the officer's wives and daughters—a reversal of role and rank that makes this the ceremony above all others which validates the ideology of democratic meritocracy and the familial values vested in Mrs. O'Rourke.

Thursday's caste-snobbery is identified by Ford as a species of racism. He despises the Apaches as a race, which makes him less able to combat them effectively; and he despises the Irish. Although Thursday is professional enough to recognize O'Rourke's skill as a soldier, he continually "forgets" his name, calling him Murphy, O'Brien . . . as if to him all Irishmen (like Indians, Asians, and Blacks) look alike. Racism and caste-snobbery put Thursday at odds with the ideology of true meritocracy by which Fort Apache's citizens live. The value of meritocracy is attested, not by a mere legal formula, but by the experience of a just-completed war—in the movie the Civil War, although the allusion to the Second World War is clear. How did young O'Rourke ever get into West Point? an incredulous Thursday asks the Sergeant-Major, who does a slow burn at the implied insult. The answer is, "By Presidential appointment." But, Thursday says, he thought such appointments were open only to the sons of winners of the Congressional Medal of Honor. The Sergeant-Major answers, "I had myself fancied that was the case, sir." The exchange establishes the fact that Thursday has not learned to recognize the war's great lesson: that race and class are irrelevant in the face of merit, and that national success depends on the recognition and promotion of merit from all ranks.[52]

When the young man and the Colonel's daughter Philadelphia (Shirley Temple) fall in love, Thursday bursts uninvited into the O'Rourke quarters and rudely forbids them to see each other, on the grounds that young O'Rourke is her social inferior. Mrs. O'Rourke answers that her son is an officer, a West Pointer in fact (like the Colonel). Thursday replies that in the army it would not be forgotten that his father was *not* an officer; that this makes a marriage socially impossible and by implication renders O'Rourke unlikely to be promoted to high command. The O'Rourkes resist this assertion and rebuke Thursday for entering their house uninvited. They invoke the protocols of military law and of courtesy, both of which recognize the household as a privileged space within whose bounds the sergeant's authority is equal or superior to the Colonel's. Their assertion affirms the basic rule of democratic and constitutional government, which guarantees a substantial degree of autonomy to the domestic and social spheres against the power of the state and its officials. Mrs. O'Rourke clinches the point by quietly reminding Thursday to remove his hat. Home space enjoys the moral privilege that myth accords to the White woman and implicitly commands the respect of all good men.[53]

But despite this invocation of rules and customs, and despite our knowledge that the romance will be consummated, it is important to note that no one contradicts Thursday's declaration of army prejudice. Outside the utopia of Fort Apache, the world may well be as Thursday represents it, divided by unbreachable lines of race and class, neither a democracy nor a meritocracy. Here again, the projection of the war story into the Western frame serves an important purpose. *Fort Apache* uses the language of the Frontier Myth to play an ironic variation on the relationship of Home Front to War Front. What lies outside Fort Apache is not the Home Front of the war film—the unseen utopia in which everything is or will be perfected—but rather that Old World of class oppression from which the frontiersmen fled. The civilian America of *Fort Apache* is that civilization which (in the elegiac mode of the Frontier Myth) fatally overtakes and destroys the liberating play of freedom in the Wild West; yet it is *also* that Home Front for whose sake the soldiers of the war and the combat film make their sacrifice.

Fort Apache is less an America-in-microcosm than a utopian idealization of America as it *ought* to have been. In its original eighteenth- and nineteenth-century context, the Frontier Myth suggested that whatever America's corruptions or limitations, our potential for self-perfection was as unlimited as the open spaces waiting for us over the border. But in *Fort Apache* that sort of suggestion is limited. There are, for example, no settlers to be seen in or near Fort Apache, no families making a new life except those like young O'Rourke and Miss Thursday, who will make it inside the Fort. Fort Apache stands at the outer edge of society and overlooks a permanent desert.

By bringing (corrupt) "home" values to Fort Apache, Thursday has divided the society of the Fort, eventually weakening its power to deal with the external enemy. At first the Indian war appears to bring out the best in Thursday and to create the basis of mutual understanding between the Fort and its commander. Thursday earns York's respect by ambushing a war party and exposing Meachum's criminal abuse of his charges. York—who knows the Apache well—therefore approaches Thursday with an offer to undertake a lone mission to Mexico to bring the Apaches in for negotiation. Thursday jumps at the offer but spoils the effect of professionalism by musing about the fame and promotion that would come to "the man who brought in Cochise" (obviously thinking of himself rather than York).

York's mission marks his character as the White man who does indeed know and sympathize with the Indians and is not afraid to go among them disarmed. His ceremonious entry into the Indian stronghold contrasts strongly with Thursday's disruption of the Non-commissioned Officer's Dance at the Fort. But Thursday—true to his role as breaker of ceremonies—refuses to abide by York's treaty. Instead of meeting Cochise man to man, as York has done, he rides out with the whole regiment to provoke a battle. He rejects York's assertion that as a man and a soldier he is bound to keep honor with Cochise. Thursday's honor is a thing of rank and caste, not shared with lesser classes or races. He also rejects York's military advice against attacking Cochise, accuses him of cowardice, and sends him back to defend the wagon train.

Thursday then leads the regiment on a spectacular cavalry charge which carries them into a box-canyon ambush and ends in a "last stand." York attempts to rescue Thursday, who has fallen just outside the canyon. But the Colonel proves his courage as a soldier by riding in to die with his men after telling York, "When you command this regiment . . . be sure you *command* it." In the box canyon, surrounded by the sergeants and officers he has despised, Thursday is reconciled with the regiment in a final democracy of death—although the expression on his face when Sergeant-Major O'Rourke prophesies that they will share a set of grandchildren suggests that he is still galled by the idea.

In a last ceremony of mutual recognition, Cochise rides up to York's laager of wagons, stabs the guidon of York's own B Company in the ground at York's feet, warrier to honorable warrior, and then disappears with all his men in a forward-sweeping cloud of dust. This exchange suggests the completion of a tragic ritual, and the mutual recognition of warrior-honor between races suggests that Thursday's "last stand" has been after all a potentially redemptive or regenerative act of violence. It purges the worst elements from the army by killing Thursday (while bringing out the best element in his character) and by leaving York in command, it promotes the best qualities in the regiment.

The movie does not end with this tragic reconcilation, however. It moves on to an epilogue in which we see York, now a Colonel, about to lead the regiment out against the Apache once again. The guidon-ceremony notwithstanding, an eternal round of wars has followed Thursday's last stand. A group of eastern reporters ask York about the legendary charge, which is the subject of a heroic painting in Washington. Though York knows the picture to be false, he tells the reporter it is "true in every detail." He defends Thursday as legend, because the myth has been good for the regiment. For York (and for this movie) the regiment is the center of the world of values—more important even than the Home Front which it nominally serves. Only those in the regiment—and in the privileged audience of the movie—can share the knowledge that to an outsider might discredit the regiment. The last image is of York leading his men out, wearing a distinctive uniform hat earlier worn by Thursday. He thus affirms Thursday's dictum that right or wrong the commander is the final and supreme embodiment of authority to whom obedience is as central to the health of the Fort as any of its other sacred signs and democratic ceremonies.

Ford thus visualizes and verbalizes the process by which truth becomes myth and by which myth provides the essential and socially necessary meaning in our images of our history. This he would later translate into an ideological imperative—the famous epigram that commands a writer faced with a choice between truth and legend to "print the legend" (*The Man Who Shot Liberty Valance* [1962]). But the irony in this epilogue does not entirely discredit its polemic intent and effect. Through York, Ford makes a plea for the willed retention of patriotic belief in the teeth of our knowledge that such belief has been the refuge of scoundrels and the mask of terrible death-dealing follies. It is our ability to continue to believe in what "the regiment" and "the flags" stand for—and to hold that belief in the face of what we know of Thursday's abuse of authority and to repress our knowledge of the truth behind the legend—that converts an unnecessary and even criminal massacre into an act of redemptive sacrifice.[54]

Ford thus reconstitutes mythological thinking, but on a novel basis. We are to continue to believe in our myths despite our knowledge that they are untrue. For the sake of our political and social health we will behave as if we did not know the history whose truth would demystify our beliefs. Ford makes us willing to accept this principle by using the terms of the Frontier Myth and the Western movie to show how necessary are the rituals and symbols that bind a society together in the face of the desert and the Indian. In the framework of art, this way of thinking matches the proverbial dictum that true intelligence and creativity depend upon one's ability to entertain two different and opposed ideas at the same time. In political terms. York's plea comes perilously close to the advocacy of doublethink:

though we recognize the gap between idealistic war aims and the disappointments (or betrayals) that followed from the victory, we agree to think and act as if no such gap existed.

Fort Apache is a seminal work of mythography. It signals the completion of one cultural transformation and the beginning of another. In Ford's film the problematic world of the combat film—the new ideas about American identity gained from our experience of defeat, our mastery of war's "dirtiness," and our dependence on hitherto oppressed classes—is reconciled with the traditions of our national myth. But this return to the mythic ground of the Frontier is not only a way of coming to terms with memory; it also provides us with the mythic basis for a new ideology, designed to build national solidarity in the face of the threatening advance of Soviet Communism—an ideology which (if Ford is a true prophet) would ultimately rest on a deliberate and consensual falsification of history.

PART IV

Democracy and Force: The Western and the Cold War, 1946–1960

11 Studies in Red and White

Cavalry, Indians, and Cold War Ideology, 1946–1954

The beginning of the Cold War in 1948 inaugurated the Golden Age of the Western: a 25-year period, regularly punctuated by the appearance of remarkable films, that saw the genre achieve its greatest popularity and that ended with its virtual disappearance from the genre map. The rise and fall of the Western mirrors the development of the Cold War and its sustaining ideological consensus from its seedtime in 1948–54 to its fulfillment in the years of the liberal counteroffensive under Kennedy and Johnson, to its disruption by the failure of the war in Vietnam. During this period there was a more or less continual exchange of symbols, themes, and concerns between the discourses of politics and movie production. The genre provided a frame in which alternative approaches to the political and ideological problems of the Cold War era could be imaginatively entertained.

The Western's exceptional position in the post-war genre map is attested by the remarkable level, continuity, and duration of its popularity. From 1947 to 1955 the number of feature productions (running time of 80-plus minutes) increased markedly, from 14 in 1947 to 31 in 1948; after a decline to 25 in 1949, the number rose to 38 in 1950, 40 in 1952, 36 in 1954, and 46 in 1956.[1] Years of high production usually alternated with years of adjustment to the market. But even bad years saw many more feature Westerns than had been produced in 1947, and the overall trend was upward. There was a sharp decline between 1955 and 1962, but the drop reflects an industry-wide contraction in response to competition from television and the collapse of the legal and economic structures that had sustained the studio system, rather than a negative response to Westerns.[2]

The drop-off in Western movies was more than compensated by increases in prime-time television productions. In 1955, the peak year in the decade for Western movies, Western TV series constituted 4.7 percent of the prime-time hours programed by the three national networks. From 1955 to 1957 that share rose to nearly 15 percent, and in 1959 to slightly more than 24 percent. Over the next decade the level fluctuated between highs of 18 to 20 percent (1962, 1966–67) and a low of 9.5 percent (1964), with an average of 15.6 percent. Westerns were consistently among the top-rated TV shows for most of the 1955–70 period. The average audience share for Western series from 1957–58 to 1960–61 varied between 32.5 percent and 36 percent, reflecting a phenomenal level of audience interest. Although the genre did not sustain these levels through the sixties, it maintained a substantial presence—typically with four shows among the top 25, with Neilsen shares of about 24 percent. No other type of action/adventure show in this period (detective/police, combat, and the like) commanded so consistently high a share of prime time over so many years.[3]

These figures do not take into account the great number of Western productions that were shown outside regular series. Many anthology shows, including those that specialized in live theatrical performance, included Western episodes. Westerns (especially "B" and series films) also figured prominently in children's programing, and feature Westerns were regularly broadcast by networks and local stations both in and out of prime time.

After the period of adjustment (1955–62), the genre's popularity in one medium reinforced its appeal in the other. After 1962 big-screen productions revived to levels comparable with those of 1950–55, and this rise was matched by a second surge of Western productions on TV in the mid–sixties. The boom lasted until 1971–72, when both movies and television abandoned the genre. But despite television's importance as a medium for disseminating mass-culture mythology, for most of the 1950–70 period movies remained the most important source of myth-making. Television profited by reproducing and adapting concepts or figures developed by the movies to series format, with production values scaled down to the requirements of the small screen. In a sense, television is to the movie Western what the dime novel was to the historical romance or the red-blooded novel.[4]

One of the factors that made the Western movies of this period so appealing was the remarkably high quality of the product. The postwar Western attracted some of the best new writers and directors in the industry (like Mann and Boetticher). It retained or renewed the interest of old hands like Henry King and awakened the interest of veterans like Howard Hawks, who had never made a Western until he directed the classic *Red River* in 1948. John Ford now gave the greater part of his time to directing Westerns, in part because they were so lucrative, but also because the genre's highly formalized terms, "fraught with myth, irony, and double-leveled narratives," suited the highly personal, poetic, increasingly "acerbic" statements he now wished to make.[5] The 1948–56 period—beginning with *Fort Apache* and ending with *The Searchers*—is extraordinarily rich in Westerns that are formally sophisticated, intellectually interesting—and *seminal*, in that some of them inaugurated major revisions of or additions to the genre's vocabulary.

The long and relatively continuous development of the Western—especially during 1939–41—had provided the genre with a visual language of great force, variety, resonance, economy, and thematic reach that invited both cinematic virtuosity and critical intelligence. As a result, the genre was now developed intensively and with a high degree of consciousness by filmmakers who sought to use its vocabulary to allegorize a wide range of difficult or taboo subjects like race relations, sexuality, psychoanalysis, and Cold War politics.[6]

Real-World Problems in Mythic Spaces: Dramatizing the Problem of Force

The period between the end of the Second World War and the Korean War was one of ideological crisis in which the political assumptions that had shaped American policy from 1937 through 1945 were radically revised. The Truman administration worked to maintain an alliance with Western Europe and to "contain" Communism, but it did so without the assurance of public understanding or Congressional support for sustained engagement in foreign affairs. At the same time the recently "liberated" colonial empires of our allies began to break up in response to indigenous nationalist movements with revolutionary agendas. It was not clear whether these movements should be encouraged as the fulfillment of American hopes for a world of self-governing nations or opposed as threats to Western economic interests or as cases of Communist aggression.

Nor was there a domestic consensus on the New Deal's legacy of reform.[7] Although Truman favored the continued development of social programs, the rejection of his Fair Deal by conservative Congresses (1946–50) put him on notice that the public mood and the political balance had shifted. Truman himself came into conflict with labor over strikes in the steel, coal, and railroad industries; and in response to the Cold War he began a hunt for "subversives" in government and the unions. After 1950 that hunt would lead to a full-blown "Red Scare" under Republican auspices and the leadership of Senator Joseph McCarthy.[8]

But even as politics tilted to the right, there was a renewed demand for completion of the New Deal's most significant piece of unfinished business—the reform of race relations, especially in the South, to restore civil and political rights to Blacks and guarantee them a share of the economic pie. The battles fought over the complex of issues and movements associated with the term "civil rights" would emerge over the course of the next two decades as the most crucial and divisive concern of domestic politics.

In the midst of this ideological turmoil, the Western and its informing mythology offered a language and a set of conceptual structure rich in devices for defining the differences between competing races, classes, cultures, social orders, and moral codes. It incorporated these definitions in pseudo-historical narratives which suggested that human heroism could shape the course of future events. Moreover, the preoccupation with violence that characterizes the Western and the Myth of the Frontier made its formulations particularly useful during a period of continual conflict between the claims of democratic procedure and Cold War policies that required the use of armed force.

This is not to say that Western movies provided American leaders with their marching orders, nor even that Western movies became mere allegories of contemporary politics. Even in films shaped by explicitly allegorical intentions, political ideas do not monopolize or exhaust the range of possible references and concerns. Rather, there is a pattern of reciprocal influence in which the preoccupations of politics shape the concerns and imagery of movies, and in which movies in turn transmit their shapely formulations of those concerns back to political discourse, where they function as devices for clarifying values and imagining policy scenarios.

When an ideological issue or problem is projected into a Western-movie setting, the range of possible and plausible resolutions is shaped by the rules and expectations that inform the mythic landscape of the genre. These are neither arbitrary nor inflexibly prescriptive. Rather, they are the practical result of a continuous process of revision, and they permit a range of interpretation broad enough to give moral license to heroes as politically opposite as Jesse James and George Armstrong Custer. The mythic space of the genre should be thought of as a field for ideological play which is attractive precisely because a wide range of beliefs and agendas can be entertained there. However, the peculiar conformation of the mythic landscape shapes and limits the ways in which issues can be conceived and pressures the flow of action toward particular kinds of resolution.

The geography of the Frontier represented in Western movies is that of a world divided by significant and signifying borders, usually marked by some strong visual sign: the palisade of the desert fort; a mountain pass or a river, especially one whose name is recognized as a boundary marker, like the Rio Grande; the white empty street of the town. Finally the hero must leave a good woman and a place of safety, enter that street, and confront the enemy who advances from the opposite end. Through persistent association, these border signs have come to symbolize a range of fundamental ideological differences. The most basic of these is that between the natural and the human or social realms, "wilderness vs. civilization." This opposition is given depth and complexity by metaphors that liken it to social and ideological divisions: between White civilization and Redskin savagery; between a corrupt metropolitan "east" and a rough but virtuous "west"; between tyrannical old proprietors (big ranchers) and new, progressive entrepreneurs (small ranchers, homesteaders); between the engorged wealth of industrial monopolies (railroads) and the hard-earned property of the citizen (farmers); between old technologies (stagecoaches) and new (railroads); between the undisciplined rapacity of frontier criminals and the lawman's determination to establish order. The borderline may also be construed as the moral opposition between the violent culture of men and the Christian culture associated with women. It is nearly always understood as a border between an "old world" which is seen as known, oppressive, and limiting, and a "new world" which is rich in potential or mystery, liberating and full of opporunity.

The action of the narrative requires that these borders be crossed by a hero (or group) whose character is so mixed that he (or they) can operate effectively on both sides of the line.[9] Through this transgression of the borders, through combat with the dark elements on the other side, the heroes reveal the meaning of the frontier line (that is, the distinctions of value it symbolizes) even as they break it down. In the process they evoke the elements in themselves (or in their society) that correspond to the "dark"; and by destroying the dark elements and colonizing the border, they purge darkness from themselves and from the world. Thus the core of the mythic narrative that traverses the mythic landscape is a tale of personal and social "regeneration through violence."

Finally, the mythic space of the Western is identified with the American past and with a traditional, progressive narrative of national history. In watching a Western, we are asked to think of ourselves as looking across the border that divides past and present in order to recover a "genetic" myth which displays the (putative) origins of our present condition and by so doing suggests ways of understanding and responding to that condition.[10]

By the time of the Korean War the mythic geography of the Western had been differentiated into distinct sub-regions, each with a characteristic setting and scenario of heroic action, organized around different themes and aspects of Western history. The town-tamer Western provided a field onto which metropolitan issues (crime and punishment, division and solidarity, conformity and individualism) could be heroically projected; films about epic cattle drives, or the building of great ranches or railroads, explored the economic rationales for corporate gigantism and entrepreneurial freedoms; "cult of the outlaw" films offered a critique of corporate society; the cavalry Western provided a way to merge the language and concerns of the war film and the Western.[11]

But the organizing principle at the heart of each subdivision of Western genre-space is the myth of regeneration through violence; the cavalry Western has its Indian massacre or charge into battle, the gunfighter or town-tamer movie its climactic shoot-out in the street, the outlaw movie its disastrous last robbery or assassination, the romantic Western its bullet-riddled rescue scene. Each has its own special ways of explaining or rationalizing the culminating shoot-out. But in general, when we are told that a certain film is a Western, we confidently expect that it will find its moral and emotional resolution in a singular act of violence. Moreover, since the Western offers itself as a myth of American origins, it implies that its violence is an essential and necessary part of the process through which American society was established and through which its democratic values are defended and enforced.

The Western's handling of violence represents the culmination of the mythic ideological project begun by turn-of-the-century progressives like Roosevelt and Wister—the development of a revised version of the Frontier Myth as a way of justifying a "modern" distribution of social power between the managerial and laboring classes and a new balance between *force* and *consent* in the ideology and structure of republican government. More Westerns adapted the traditional mythology of "savage war" to interpret modern forms of industrial and ethnic strife and to rationalize the development of the republican nation-state into an imperial Great Power. In both the domestic and the imperial spheres, Westerns asserted the entitlement of representatives of the "better" or "decent" classes to a privileged form of violence. The perceived imperatives of the Cold War would lead a series of American governments to assert a similar privilege for the use of armed force and to justify, in the name of national security, the evasion, abuse, or overriding of the official procedures and social institutions through which the American public registers its consent.

The problem of reconciling democratic values and practices with the imperatives of power is both the central contradiction of American Cold War ideology and the classic problem of democratic politics. And it was precisely this issue that the "Cold War Western" addressed.[12]

Cult of the Cavalry: Rio Grande *(1950) and the Korean War*

In the development and articulation of Cold War policy, the Truman administration had to fight a two-front war. Beyond the borders it had to apply persuasion and threat in varying proportions to cope with the recalcitrance of the enemy and with the weaknesses of various allies. But its ability to project both the image and the reality of American power depended on the creation of a public consensus capable of sustaining that policy over the long term. That consensus did not exist in 1950. Although Republicans hurt the administration by attacking it as "soft on Communism" and riddled with "subversives," anti-Communist enthusiasms did not automatically translate into support for increased military expenditures or overseas interventions.[13]

Truman and Secretary of State Dean Acheson believed that the American public was ignorant of world politics, war-weary, and reluctant to sacrifice for the sake of foreign-policy objectives. They also believed that the nature and immediacy of the Communist threat made it impossible to wait for public opinion to come around. They therefore employed on the home front tactics similar to those used against the foreign enemy: they used the power of the executive branch to manipulate information and to create "facts" that would compel recognition and acceptance of their policies. The political initiatives of the Marshall Plan and the Truman Doctrine were taken without extended public debate. Opposition was disarmed by high-level talks with leaders of the isolationist and conservative blocs in Congress, particularly the legendary conversation between Acheson and arch-isolationist Senator Vandenberg. Public acceptance of the new direction followed the *faits accomplis*, just as it had after Pearl Harbor. The administration believed that while Americans might be inconclusive and divided when debating theory and principle, their response to events would be immediate and strong.[14]

Therefore when a North Korean Communist army attacked across the 38th Parallel armistice line in June 1950, Acheson and Truman responded with an immediate exercise of presidential authority. Within twenty-four hours the administration had decided to use military force to halt the invasion—preferably with United Nations support, unilaterally if necessary. Acheson believed that the United States faced a situation comparable to that in Central Europe on the eve of Munich: a dictator bent on world conquest (Stalin) was testing the will of the democracies, and failure to "call his bluff" would be taken as a license for further aggression and would lead inevitably to a third world war. The UN Security Council, dominated by European countries who shared Acheson's understanding of the folly of appeasement (and with Russia boycotting the session), passed a resolution condemning North Korean aggression and calling on member states to respond. The administration chose to construe the UN's vague resolution as a mandate for military action, and the next day Truman ordered the Air Force and Navy into action in Korea.[15]

News of these orders was withheld from the public for twelve hours. When Congressional leaders were summoned to a meeting on June 27 (the third morning of the war) they raised no procedural objections. They had feared Truman would fail to act and were pleased he had done "much more than he was expected to do, and almost exactly what most individuals seemed to wish he would do." Opposition leaders voiced second thoughts on succeeding days, blaming Truman's "vacillating" policies for inviting attack and complaining that he had confronted them with a *fait accompli*. But even the

Republicans did not think Truman's high-handedness sufficient reason to question what he had done. Whatever the procedure, they applauded its result.[16]

Congress maintained this stance in the ensuing weeks, even though the terms of the original commitment grew to include ground troops from the garrison in Japan. Still mistrustful of public and Congress, Truman minimized the significance of this escalation, tacking its announcement to a press release read at the end of a meeting with Congressional leaders: "General MacArthur has been authorized to use certain supporting ground units." The Congressmen mildly suggested that perhaps Truman might wish to obtain formal approval of his action. But after some discussion, Truman and Acheson rejected a proffered Congressional resolution as both unnecessary and dangerous: The administration already had "complete acceptance of the President's policy by everybody on both sides of both houses of Congress—we were going ahead with it; everything was in good shape." To submit the matter to further questioning might muddy the waters, weaken support, and perhaps even force reversal of the policy.[17]

The collapse of South Korean and UN forces when struck by the initial Communist advance brought heavy criticism of the administration for underestimating enemy strength and for overestimating the quantity and quality of the force the country could bring to bear on such short notice. But despite these errors and the unanticipated and undesired results of the intervention—a major ground war, mobilization of the Reserves and National Guard, the expansion of the draft—the policy aims and the decision to use force were still regarded as correct. Nor was there a serious challenge to the principle that war could legitimately be made by presidential fiat without obtaining the formal consent of the people or their elected representatives.[18] The ideological imperatives of maintaining American world power outweighed the principles and practices of democratic and republican ideology. The government's performance in the new role of world power was to be judged by its objectives rather than by its methods, by the results it achieved rather than by its adherence to democratic forms and values in the process. And the measure of "good results" would be primarily a military one: how had a given policy affected the world balance of force between the United States and the Soviet Union?

While Truman and his policy-makers were fashioning their response to the crisis of the Cold War, John Ford was completing the last of the group of Monument Valley Westerns that occupied him from 1946 to 1950—*Wagonmaster*, and two more cavalry movies, *She Wore a Yellow Ribbon* (1949) and *Rio Grande* (1950). It was especially in the last of these that Ford entertained the question of war and peace in the aftermath of the "Great Crusade."

In *Rio Grande* Ford takes up and pushes to a conclusion the unresolved questions of the cavalry pictures: Which is more to be valued—war or peace? Authority or principled rebellion? Military necessity or the rituals?[19] He initially saw the film as a "potboiler" demanded by his studio (Republic) as a precondition for funding his production of *The Quiet Man*. He therefore built the film's concept around ideas and images that were ready at hand. The plot of embattled lovers was suggested by his prospectus for *The Quiet Man* (in which *Rio Grande* principals John Wayne and Maureen O'Hara were also slated to star). To give the story variety and timeliness, he invoked current concerns about war-preparedness. He also borrowed themes, characters, and images from the earlier cavalry pictures—which made *Rio Grande* begin to seem interesting as a further commentary on the cavalry world. Once engaged in the work Ford became "enchanted" by its thematic and visual possibilities.[20]

Rio Grande distills the themes and images of the cavalry film to their formal and ideological essentials. The powerful opening sequence, in which the cavalry returns to the fort after a long patrol, establishes with the utmost formal economy the entire structure of the social microcosm. The battalion, led by Colonel Kirby Yorke[21] (John Wayne), rides in through the gate of the fort slowly and wearily, their worn and dusty appearance cast in a heroic light by the way they are framed in low-angle shots. A bell rings and schoolchildren come pouring out to meet them; women gather in statuesque groupings to watch anxiously for their men. The wounded are brought in on litters; a woman runs beside one of them holding her husband's hand. We see bound Indian prisoners and Indian scouts in uniform. Despite the urgency of personal and domestic feeling, Yorke halts the troop in formation, offers a laconic word of praise, and orders the men to walk their horses before they retire. We understand that these are men who do a dirty job with discipline and skill; that they are implicitly heroic but make no parade of the fact; that they defend the fort, which is a world of women and children, care and vulnerability and affection; that the Apache are their enemies, but that they do not hate Indians (the scouts belong to the fort).

The enlisted men's quarters in *Rio Grande* are divided from officers' country by a deep streambed crossed by a bridge. The class division which this arrangement suggests is borne out in the movie's theme: Yorke's son Jeff has flunked out of West Point and has enlisted in the cavalry (lying about his age), and the film makes an issue of his apparent loss of class. Class division is paralleled and contrasted with racial distinction: the Indian prisoners are confined, as if in a pit, below the bridge that spans the social "Rio Grande." These are not the Indians of *Fort Apache*. No Cochise speaks for them to rationalize (however poorly) their cause. Indeed, these Indians speak no intelligible words in English or Spanish. They utter only war cries when they attack, and wild falsetto chants in ceremonies that Ford invests with a horror-movie quality. Once again Indians have become identified with "the horror," to which Ford will give a more explicit expression than in any of his earlier Westerns.

As in *Fort Apache*, gender difference signals a difference in ideology. The central figure in *Rio Grande* is Colonel Kirby Yorke, which suggests that this is a sequel to *Fort Apache*, the further adventures of the rebellious subaltern and "man who knows Indians" who had been promoted to command of the regiment after Thursday's Last Charge.[22] Yorke's estranged wife Kathleen (Maureen O'Hara) comes to the fort to buy her son's way out of the ranks. Like Mrs. O'Rourke, she speaks for family solidarity and love against the authority of the army, and she is a strong Irish woman. However, Kathleen is a plantation owner, more Scarlett O'Hara than Mrs. O'Rourke. "Bridesdale" is her "Tara," burned during the Civil War by her own husband under orders from General Sheridan. She has singlehandedly rebuilt the plantation, and she has remained proudly separated from her husband for fifteen years, the whole of young Jeff's childhood. Her pride, competence, and independence make her a match (in every sense) for her husband. Moreover, her indictment of Kirby has principle as well as personal outrage behind it. She puts it best when she tells her son that his father is a great soldier but adds, "What makes a soldier great is hateful to me." It is not simply the soldier's tasks of death and destruction but his devotion to duty itself that makes him repress and even destroy every human feeling, even love, if it impedes the achievement of his mission. Some of Kathleen's critique is granted validity: Kirby *has* steeled his heart against the claims of love and must be softened by the recovery of his wife and son. Nonetheless, we also understand the implicit nobility of Yorke's action: he was not only obeying orders but demonstrating his willingness to put duty ahead of personal interests. If he erred then in withholding the sympathy Kathleen deserved, she has matched his steeliness by perpetuating their estrangement.

As the narrative proceeds, it appears that Ford may have stacked the deck against Kathleen. Unlike Mrs. O'Rourke, she is unsupported by any other female character. The other women in the film are not persons but icons whose identification with the fort and their husbands is complete. Against her are ranged a set of strong male characters, including Kirby, Jeff, and Jeff's comrades—particularly the two strong supporting roles of Tyree (Ben Johnson) and Daniel "Sandy" Boone (Harry Carey, Jr.). All the males speak eloquently of the army and what it means, and they attain heroism by living up to the spirit as well as the letter of their oaths of duty.

Ford also devalues the woman's ideological stance by changing its political identification. In *Fort Apache* Mrs. O'Rourke had stood for democracy and meritocracy against the aristocratic pretensions of Colonel Thursday. Here it is the Colonel who speaks for democracy and merit. Although he is sorry his son failed at West Point, he respects his decision to serve in the ranks: the soldier's calling is honorable in itself and offers a chance to rise by the exhibition of real merit. Kathleen, on the other hand, feels the sting of her son's loss of the status of "gentleman." Kirby's critique of her position is harshly put but accurate: "special privilege for special born." That was Colonel Thursday's ideology.

The narrative provides a series of shocks that convert Kathleen from an anti-militarist to a good soldier's wife. As her appreciation of military virtue and necessity grows, she becomes more "O'Hara" and less "Scarlett." The change is particularly marked in the scene in which she washes clothes for her son and his friends to the accompaniment of "The Irish Washerwoman." Thus as she becomes more "military," she also becomes more "ethnic," which in Ford's language means more "democratic."

The identification of military values with democracy is further developed in the movie's "outlaw" subplot.[23] The other southerner in the troop is Tyree, who has attributes of both the outlaw hero and the "man who knows Indians." He is arrested for killing "a Yankee" who had seduced his sister, and Kathleen shares his fears that he will not get a fair trial by the standards of "Yankee justice." But the army responds more effectively, although it must break civilian rules to do so: Tyree's sergeant connives at his escape from arrest (which Kirby tolerates), and even though he is outlawed Tyree responds in kind by continuing to serve his comrades against the Indians. Thus the ideological oppositions of law and justice, progressive and populist, Colonel Thursday and Tom Joad, are dissolved in the idealized army.

Rio Grande develops to an extreme the logic inherent in the combat film's representation of the platoon as a metaphorical "America." Here metaphor becomes metonymy. The cavalry is not merely the "representative" of American democracy—the agent of its policy, the metaphoric expression of its values. Democracy and nation are now entirely identified with the military. Cavalry ideology incorporates and assigns a proper place to all the significant characters of the western landscape, Indian and White, man and woman, outlaw and law-bringer. Cavalry codes and practices provide sure guides to the resolution of every ideological opposition: democracy vs. authority; civilian vs. soldier; egalitarianism vs. hierarchy; justice vs. law; civilization vs. savagery; masculine vs. feminine. *Rio Grande* also develops the political implications of this identification. If the cavalry subsumes "democracy," then the rules that govern the cavalry are indistinguishable from the ideological imperatives of democracy. Therefore we must consent to the replacement of traditional or "civilian" codes and practices by the military principle of doing whatever is necessary to complete our mission—even when that mission is so questionable has to be a "Mission with No Record."[24]

These ideas, initially developed in the gender-opposition of Kirby and Kathleen, are enlarged to the dimensions of political allegory in the promulgation of a final solution to the Apache problem by General Sheridan (J. Carroll Naish). Force is the only language the Apache understand. The army cannot subdue them because civilian bureaucrats and diplomats will not allow troops to cross the Rio Grande in pursuit of raiders. Sheridan and Yorke have wondered whether Washington's spinelessness signals a larger degeneration in American society, a general unwillingness among the American people to join or even to support the military.[25] The action they contemplate will test the nation's will by confronting the people and their leaders with a choice like that envisioned in Theodore Roosevelt's "Strenuous Life"—a choice between willingness to engage in the toil and strife of "the world's work" and the loss of membership among "the great fighting races." Roosevelt had used Imperial China to illustrate the emasculate impotence of a degenerated nation; Ford uses Mexico, the sister republic on the other side of the movie's clearest borderline, the Rio Grande. Yorke and his command, in pursuit of the Apache, are halted at the river by the apperaance of three Mexican soldiers, one of them wounded. The Mexicans are unable to stop the Indians—there are only seven men to police the whole region—but the courtly Mexican lieutenant is unwilling to let the American cross to help him. Yorke even offers to put himself under the lieutenant's command, forgoing the privilege of rank (and the weight of numbers) to defeat the common race-enemy. But the Mexican refuses to break his government's rules, and obedience to Washington reduces Yorke to comparable impotence.

The doubts expressed by Yorke and Sheridan about the reluctance of Congress and the people in general to support a military buildup are the same as those voiced by Acheson and Truman in1949–50 and echo the Republican critique of the administration's supposed "softness on Communism," which was said to have encouraged the Communist attack. In the fictional frame of *Rio Grande*, Sheridan proposes to resolve the problem by taking pre-emptive action on his own authority, without consulting the civilian government. He orders Yorke to cross the Rio Grande and strike the Apache in their sanctuary, in direct and conscious defiance of the national government's policy and of American and international law. Since the orders are manifestly illegal, says Sheridan, they cannot be written; if Yorke fails in his mission, Sheridan will deny having issued them. If he fails, Sheridan promises to subvert the judicial system on his behalf by packing his court-martial with men who "rode with us down the Shenandoah"—comrades in arms who understand the necessities of war and the impotence of legalisms and mere diplomacy. However, if Yorke succeeds in his mission, then (Sheridan implies) no questions will be asked. Success will retroactively justify their transgresssion of the boundary and the law.

In the real world, the Truman administration dealt with the Korean crisis of June–July 1950 by methods similar to Sheridan's. The intervention was begun on the President's initiative, which preempted the mechanisms of popular debate and Congressional consent. In the fall, after the Inchon campaign had routed the North Koreans, Truman and General MacArthur (commanding UN forces in Korea) similarly stretched or exceeded the terms of the UN mandate by attacking north of the 38th Parallel in an attempt to unite Korea by force. MacArthur would carry the "Sheridan" principle to the point of deliberately exceeding Truman's instructions as well.

The conception and presentation of Sheridan's solution probably owes very little to the actions taken and the rationales put forth during the Korean crisis. The story on which the film was based had been published in 1949, and the film itself was completed during the summer of 1950 while the crisis was in progress. It was released on November 15, when the issue before the public was no longer whether or not to fight in Korea but how far north MacArthur should be allowed to go. Which parallel of latitude or river barrier would MacArthur's government decree as the limit of his advance: the 38th Parallel? the Chongjon? the Yalu? Or would MacArthur be allowed to cross the Yalu as well and attempt the reconquest of China? Newsreels shown in theaters along with *Rio Grande* would have presented MacArthur staring through binoculars across one or another of those barriers, in fortuitous parallel with Kirby Yorke's angry glare at the redskin sanctuaries across the Rio Grande which a week-kneed administration prevents him from attacking.[26]

But in the fictional scenario, the rationales for action are not subject to the corrective of events. Yorke and Sheridan are spared the necessity of acting on their transgressive plan when the enemy provides them with an unanswerable argument for crossing the river. In preparation for Yorke's campaign, the women and children are sent by wagon train to Fort Grant. But the Apache attack the train, capture the wagon containing the children and the wife of Corporal Bell, and carry them across the border into Mexico. Rescuing the captives is the strongest of mythical imperatives, a self-evident "higher law" that supersedes government regulations and is far more appealing as a basis of action than Sheridan's military *realpolitik.* Even Kathleen is converted. She tells Kirby he must get those children back, no matter what. Thus Yorke's is a double victory: he gets license to attack across the Rio Grande, and he converts the most recalcitrant element of "public opinion" to the acceptance of his views.

That conversion is made more emphatic by the revelation of the enemy's "horror." On the first night out, the troops discover Corporal Bells' wife raped and mutilated. Yorke restrains Bell from seeing the corpse, and it is hidden from us as well. All we see is the reaction on the face of the officer who finds her, the wagon-wheel to which she was perhaps tied for torture, which sits in a steaming pool of water. The darkness, the hidden body, the viscid setting all invoke responses that belong to the horror movie. But the scene also works exactly like the discovery of Lieutenant Jacobs in *Objective Burma,* and such precedents make it unnecessary for Ford to articulate our response ("Wipe 'em out! wipe 'em off the face of the earth!"). We already know what "a man's gotta do" about something like this.

The Indians occupy what appears to a Mexican village—a street lined with adobe houses and ending at a steepled church. It is early morning. The children are in the church, the Indians have been drinking and dancing all night, and we know that when they are done they will come up the street in a body and commit the most unimaginable atrocities on the children. The Indians are all men, without a single woman or child in sight. And the men are all monsters, toothless, dressed in scraps of women's and soldier's clothes, uttering unintelligible menaces in oddly pitched voices, numbed and staggering with drink or madness. Troopers Tyree and Boone, with Jeff Yorke, infiltrate the church and will defend the children until the regiment can charge to their rescue. Ford loads the defense of the church with symbolism: both the Alamo and the Last Stand are referred to (two of the little boys wear 7th Cavalry numbers on their caps); it is a Catholic edifice still, with an intact altar (before which Sergeant Quincannon will genuflect later in the battle); and a cross cut into the front door serves as both religious symbol and rifleman's firing-slit.

Thus when Yorke and the regiment come charging into the village, shooting "everything that moves," their aggression is construed as both rescue and as defense of a sacred place against an utterly monstrous enemy. The transgresssion of civilian orders and of the Rio Grande boundary is thus fully, even apocalyptically, justified. Not only does Yorke wipe out the Indians (we see no prisoners when he returns); his victory and its form resolve every theme or conflict in the story. Kathleen ceases her resistance and critique and becomes a soldier's wife, walking beside the wounded Kirby's litter when they return. Yorke admits to some human vulnerability and need and becomes a less lonely and therefore a more perfect man and hero. Jeff becomes a man. Corporal Bell avenges his wife. Tyree gets a medal and his commander's cooperation in his continued avoidance of "Yankee law."

But although Indians are the objective of Yorke's attack, the visualized setting suggests that he is also in some sense attacking "Mexico." This imagery is consistent with the logic of Ford's narrative premises: Yorke has implicitly attacked Mexico's status as a sovereign nation by crossing the Rio Grande. But the moral onus of that violation is visually negated by the fact that there are no longer any Mexicans to be seen; the Apaches have completely replaced them, even to the extent of taking over this entire village with its church. What has become of the Mexicans? We can invent a variety of plausible scenarios in which the original inhabitants are killed or driven away. But Ford gives us no way of knowing whether this happened recently—in which case Indian occupation may be thought of as temporary—or long ago, in which case it may reflect a permanent change in the character of the village. The film's ambiguity on this score reinforces the suggestion that in a war of this kind, between two races (savage and civilized), the very existence of one society or the other is at stake, and one or the other will be exterminated. The fate of the Mexican village suggests that a nation that is weak, lacking the political will to take up arms on its own behalf, will be extinguished as a nation, its land occupied by aliens, its posterity defiled by the rape or terminated by the slaughter of its women and children.

The imagery here is clearly genre-specific and draws on the traditional language of the Frontier Myth. Its use of sexual imagery to dramatize the character of racial warfare follows the tradition of ideological argument laid down in "The Strenuous Life." But language of this kind had already been absorbed into the ideological conception of the Cold War. As a slogan, "Better dead than red" takes off from the same premises as the nineteenth-century cavalryman's "Save the last bullet for yourself." At a less public, more personal level of discourse, Marine Colonel Lewis "Chesty" Puller voiced similar ideas and similarly invoked the precedents of savage war in a speech he made to his troops in Korea:

> I want to tell you something straight. Just do one thing for me—write your people back home and tell 'em there's one hell of a damned war on out here, and that the raggedy-tailed North Koreans have been shipping a lot of so-called good American troops, and may do it again. Tell 'em there's no secret weapon for our country but to get hard, to get in there and fight.
>
> I want you to make 'em understand. Our country won't go on forever, if we stay as soft as we are now. There won't be an America—because some foreign soldiers will invade us and take our women and breed a hardier race.[27]

Puller and Ford were friends—Ford would later make a filmed biography of Puller, which was never released for public showing. But there is once again no possibility of direct influence between the film and the speech. (Puller spoke on November 10, 1950, five days before the premier of *Rio Grande*.) As with the parallels between Truman's Korea decision and Ford's version of Sheridan's orders, each man was responding to the same crisis in the terms provided by his culture's mythology.

Yorke's character incarnates the ideological problem of "American power" in both a personal and a social sense. He has the knowledge and the skill necessary to "solve the Indian problem" for good and all, and he commands an instrument which (despite his doubts) is equal to the task. His problem is not lack of power, but lack of the authority to use it. His government's refusal adds a burden to his conscience, because those who have the power to avert evil also have the responsibility to do it. By crossing the Rio Grande Yorke not only executes a necessary policy, he fulfills a moral imperative that is built into his character as hero. His heroic character, and the stern necessities of the situation, entitle him—and the institution he represents—to the moral and ideological privilege of the vigilante.

The ideology that informs Yorke's mission and Sheridan's orders is the same as that which would govern the rationales and procedures of "covert action" and "secret war," which would be typical features of American Cold War tactics in the ensuing forty years.[28] In operations of this kind, officials of the government—in the executive branch, the military, or the CIA—undertake a mission deemed vital to national security that cannot be successfully initiated or completed without violating the letter or spirit of the Constitution and/or Congressional statutes, formal treaty obligations, or international law. The covert operations of the CIA in Guatemala and in Iran in 1953–54, the Bay of Pigs (1961) and the secret war against Castro (1962–65), the formation of secret armies and the concealment of bombing campaigns in Laos and Cambodia during the Vietnam War, and certain of the *Contra* operations in Nicaragua (1981–87) are cases in point.[29] The parallels with *Rio Grande* are particularly striking in the Iran-*Contra* affair of 1985–87. The words and deeds of key NSC officials echo Sheridan's rationale for illegal action, his demand for "plausible deniability," his promise of official influence to prevent a full judicial inquiry and/or penalty, and his belief that success would make their methods invulnerable to question. Yorke clearly lives by Oliver North's dictum that the essence of a lieutenant colonel's function is to charge when his commander tells him to charge—whether the order is legal or not. Though both are soldiers, they also play the role of the vigilante who breaks rules for the sake of a higher law identified with the interests of the state.[30]

Rio Grande thus appears to be in some sort of dialogue with history.

Film and event "speak" to each other—event lending political resonance to the fiction, the fiction providing mythological justification for particular scenarios of real-world action. They did so in the first instance (summer–fall, 1950), not because one necessarily caused or influenced the other, but because the conceptual categories which shaped the scenarios developed by both movie-makers and policy-makers were drawn from the same cultural lexicon, the same set of mythological models. But once the "cult of the cavalry" was established as a major division of American mythic space and was seen to be responsive to the course of political events, its fictive rationales and heroic styles of action (especially as embodied in the symbolic persona of John Wayne) became functional terms in public discourse and symbols of the correct or heroic response to the challenges of the Cold War.

Over the next decade the themes and images developed in Ford's "cavalry trilogy" were reproduced, varied, and extended by other studios and producers. These films retained the essential elements of Ford's original myth: the use of the cavalry as a microcosm of embattled American values, the representation of the Indian as the supreme enemy of those values, and the resolution of all the personal and ideological divisions of the microcosm in the process of defeating that enemy. The lost patrol/last stand motif was a structural element in most of these films, and many of them dealt directly with Custer and the battle of the Little Big Horn, proffering rescue fantasies and historical might-have-beens filled with suggestion for avoiding such defeats.[31]

Cavalry Westerns established the Indian war/Cold War metaphor as a convention of the genre. However, the "cult of the cavalry" did not exhaust the possibilities of the genre or the myth, nor was the militaristic and "exterminationist" solution the only alternative imagined by Hollywood filmmakers. Beginning in 1950 a second "cult" developed, centered on a sympathetic portrayal of the Indian side of the cavalry/Indian wars. The iconography and ideological stance of this "cult of the Indian" was the mirror image of the "cult of the cavalry." Its terms offered a safe and effective vehicle for a liberal critique of the Cold War and the unfulfilled promises of the New Deal.

Cult of the Indian: Devil's Doorway *and* Broken Arrow *(1950)*

The decision to produce a new, "pro-Indian" type of Western was shaped by the convergence of a number of tendencies in the movie industry and in the political culture. The pressure for variation which is native to the mass-culture form perhaps made it inevitable that at some point the industry would experiment with an inversion of the standard formula. But the studios were also registering the aftereffects of wartime propaganda, which emphasized the difference between the racism of the Nazis and the Japanese and the supposed tolerance of the democracies. It was clear that some permanent revision of standard racist stereotypes and social practices was required to redeem the promise implied in both the New Deal and the "Four Freedoms." Anti-Semitism was the first target of postwar "problem films" dealing with racism (*Gentlemen's Agreement*, 1947). In the wake of the fight over a civil-rights plank at the 1948 Democratic Convention, two successful films were produced that dealt with anti-Black racism: *Pinky*, the story of a Black woman passing as White; and *Home of the Brave*, a combat film based on an adaptation of a Broadway play (which had originally dealt with anti-Semitism).[32] It was standard procedure to attempt to borrow the cachet of the "race problem" film by adapting it to a Western setting.

An additional impetus was provided by the "Red Scare," which became a national preoccupation after February 1950, when Senator Joseph McCarthy launched his campaign against "twenty years of treason" and creeping socialism.[33] Hollywood experienced the effects of this ideological *jihad* directly, and at an early stage. Leftist tendencies in the studios had been the subject of a blundering inquiry by the Dies Committee in 1940. Abandoned in 1941–43, when the Soviet alliance was most crucial to the war effort, the search for "subversives" in Hollywood began to revive in 1944. The Motion Picture Alliance for the Preservation of American Ideals was one of a number of similar organizations formed for this purpose, and its officers included such Western and war-movie stalwarts as John Wayne and Ward Bond. Anti-Communism and red-baiting became more overt in a series of postwar union battles which involved technical unions as well as the Screen Actors Guild—whose president, Ronald Reagan, led a purge of supposed leftists.[34] In the midst of these internecine battles (1947), the House Un-American Activities Committee conducted a "show trial" hearing in Los Angeles, with the intention of creating a public impression of massive Communist subversion of the media. Its activities had the effect of scaring industry management into conducting its own purge of "pinkos" and establishing the notorious blacklist. The expression of suspect political sentiments in private conversation or in one's work as scenarist, screenwriter, dialogue specialist, story developer, or director became grounds for expulsion from the industry. Thus the anti-Communist crusade directly affected the language of cinema by imposing limits on the expression of liberal ideas.

The Western was a safe haven for liberals, because its identification with the heroic fable of American progress covered its practitioners with a presumption of patriotism that was essential in Hollywood during the years of the "Red Scare."[35] Because it was safely "in the past," the tale of White-Indian conflict and peace-making allowed filmmakers to raise questions of war and peace and to entertain the possibility of coexistence without the kind of scrutiny to which a film set in or near the present would have drawn. Moreover, the same setting would allow them to address the race question without offending southern sensibilities.[36]

Like the cavalry Western, the Cult of the Indian was an elaboration of one of the constituent elements in the complex mixture of *Fort Apache*. Ford's sympathetic treatment of Cochise in that film anticipated both the general phenomenon of the pro-Indian film and the specific figure who would be its primary symbol. Both Fox and MGM planned movies for 1949–50 that would represent the Indian side of the conflict sympathetically, emphasizing the culpability of Whites in starting and perpetuating hostilities. MGM's *Devil's Doorway*, directed by Anthony Mann, was completed first; but its story was so uncompromising in its presentation of White greed and bigotry that the studio delayed its release until the success of Fox's *Broken Arrow* indicated that the public was ready to accept it.[37] The success of these films (and especially of *Broken Arrow*) inaugurated a new and permanent addition to the Western genre-scape comparable in its appeal (and its ideology) to the "Cult of the Outlaw."

Sympathetic depictions of Indians and polemics for Indian rights were not without precedent in Western literature and earlier movie traditions. The "Indian romance" had been a staple of nineteenth-century fiction. In 1911–14 Thomas Ince had made a number of Westerns that treated Indians sympathetically, and successful feature movies had been made of *The Squaw Man*, Helen Hunt Jackson's *Ramona*, Oliver LaFarge's *Laughing Boy*, and Zane Grey's *Vanishing*

American. Warner Brothers' *Massacre* (1934) presented contemporary Indian problems in the muckraking terms of the social drama.[38] But the new Indian Westerns had a larger cinematic vocabulary to work with. Both *Devil's Doorway* and *Broken Arrow* gave the theme ideological point and symbolic resonance by their integration of more traditional "good Indian" conventions with the terms of the populist outlaw Western and the combat film.

Devil's Doorway is the more radical of the two in its depiction of racial politics, and the more innovative in its manipulation of genre formulas. Director Anthony Mann and his screenwriter, Guy Trosper, tell the story of Indian dispossession primarily from the Indian perspective. The hero is Lance Poole (Robert Taylor), a Shoshone Indian who returns home from service in the Union Army to find that a White land-grabber named Coolan (Louis Calhern) is trying to dispossess his family. The Pooles are not reservation Indians but independent ranchers, like heroes of the standard populist-outlaw Western. Coolan is identified with the forces of "progress" (the railroad, statehood) that are "civilizing" Wyoming Territory. These forces envision the complete subjugation and expulsion of the Indians from their lands, and Coolan seems to want nothing less than extermination.

Our identification with Poole is facilitated by the mixture of signals with which his racial identity is first presented. Though his skin is dark, he is not immediately identifiable as non-White; he wears his hair cut short, and he is greeted warmly by the old marshal (who was his father's hunting companion). His status as a returning veteran automatically ennobles him and may remind us of Taylor's role in *Bataan.* When Coolan abruptly and gratuitously insults Poole and his uniform, he seems to be insulting a returning vet, a "regular Joe." Even when Poole's Indian identity is acknowledged, we understand that he is "just like ourselves"—that is, just like the movie heroes with whom we are accustomed to identify. We recognize Coolan as violating the "melting pot" ethic and the expectation of a "happy return" that belong to the combat film.

But after Poole leaves, there is a chilling note: Poole's White friends, the sheriff and the bartender, seem afraid to rebuke Coolan when he sneers: "Did you notice how sour the air got? You can always smell 'em." Coolan's line invokes a stereotypically racist insult, most commonly associated with prejudice against Blacks and Jews. The Anti-Semitic connection may be particularly important here, as another device for easing the audience into sympathies across the color line. Its use suggests a parallel between Coolan's color prejudice and a type of bigotry associated with standard movie-villains, primarily Nazis and upper-class American snobs.[39]

But Coolan's influence increases in step with the town's material progress. When Poole returns to the saloon five years later, the bar is crowded with Whites who (we are told) are offended by his success. A sign over the bar proclaims that by act of the legislature, whiskey can no longer be sold to Indians. The loss of this right signals a more fundamental dispossession: the legislature has also declared that Indians may not own land, take up homesteads, or live off the reservation.[40] This time Coolan's insults provoke an attempt to throw Poole out of the bar. When Poole fights back, Mann's camera shows the White crowd watching the desperate battle with a cruel coldness. A gap appears, a cognitive dissonance between the expectations born of progressive myth and the evidence of our (fictive) experience. Instead of producing a more perfect moral order, victory and progress have brought evil into the valley.

The scenario of Indian dispossession in literary and cinematic tradition usually involves a conflict between the tribal organization and hunting economy of the Vanishing American (or savage) and the progressive culture (perhaps marred by greed) of the Whites. But *Devil's Doorway* uses instead the conventions of the populist outlaw film to frame the conflict. The Poole family is more like the Jameses than like the Indians of *They Died with Their Boots On* or *Fort Apache*. They have adapted to and are living the American/agrarian dream. They own a ranch, and they are continually improving their condition and the productivity of their land.[41] Their success also disproves the racialist premise that Indians are capable of civilization.

The structural principle of *Devil's Doorways* is its development of the dialectic between the sad and well-known historical facts of Indian dispossession and the dream-desire for a utopian resolution that is embodied in myth-archetypes and the conventions of the genre. The power of archetypal fantasy appears most clearly in the depiction of the Poole ranch. The little ranch over the border in *Stagecoach* and the little piece of land in *Grapes of Wrath* were standard symbols for an agrarian utopia, a perfect refuge where the hero dreams of building a new and better life—although we rarely see him actually achieve it. The Poole ranch is the achievement of just such a utopia. It is described as "paradise," which literalizes the Edenic implications of the original agrarian vision. That it is also a too-perfect dreamland is emphasized by its physical setting, which deliberately incarnates elements of archetype and convention: it is a refuge from bigotry and want, a hidden valley, an "enclosed garden" surrounded by mountains, reachable only by a narrow pass called "the Devil's Doorway."[42]

The juxtaposition of "historical" with "archetypal" elements is the basis of a fundamental tension in the narrative. The historical referents remind us of the hard facts of our case—that we have despoiled paradise wherever we found it, and that the mistreatment of the Indian went on to the point of their destruction despite all efforts at reform and accommodation. But the image of the archetypal paradise invokes a world of possibilities limited only by our capacity to imagine alternatives to our history and its politics, and it reminds us that our democratic and ethical ideals (the code by which these *Indians* live) provide a clear language in which these possibilities can be expressed. Thus the formal tension between archetype and history defines the ideological gap between American ideals and our political practice.

However, the film's opposition of the ideal and the actual does not translate simplistically into a struggle of good vs. evil. Although the Pooles are clearly the party more sinned against than sinning, the film insists on humanizing both sides of the conflict. For Poole the valley is a refuge from bigotry and a place from which Indians can rise to a position of equality with the advancing Whites. This vision is initially private, but it acquires social force when a group of Indian refugees arrives, fleeing starvation and oppression on their reservation. The Poole ranch becomes a microcosm in red-face of the United States itself, welcoming "huddled masses yearning to breathe free."

But a similar vision drives the White sheepherders whom Coolan entices to settle in the valley.[43] They are farmers like the Pooles, and like them victims of Coolan's manipulation. Although they recognize the unfairness of dispossessing the Pooles, they have no choice but to go forward—if they stop, their sheep will starve. Their hope lies in some sort of compromise that will allow them to share the valley. Poole refuses, at first insisting on the capitalist's right to exclusive use of his property. But after the arrival of the Indian refugees, this legalistic and self-interested motive is replaced by a more generous one—the valley cannot sustain all of the refugee Indians who are fleeing there and the sheepherders as well.

Thus both sheepmen and Indians are caught in a trap, in which the determination to defend legitimate ideals, principles, and interests combines with economic conditions to make conflict inevitable.

This is not the limitless West of the progressive Western, but an enclosed valley, a West of limited resources for which hungry masses must contend. The Indians cannot compromise with the Whites, because to do so would make it impossible for them to give refuge to their oppressed brothers. The Whites cannot back off, because if they do they will starve. Thus each side must seek to exterminate the other, because neither can abandon the struggle.

Mann's film thus depicts the sort of social catastrophe that populists like Donnelly and racialist progressives like Grant and Stoddard, writing at the turn of the century, had seen as inevitable once the closing of the Frontier had cut off the promise of a continual expansion of productive resources. This is precisely the kind of social cataclysm that New Deal liberalism was designed to avert, and that ideology is specifically invoked when Lance Poole goes to law to seek validation of his claim and the overturning of the discriminatory statute. The liberal lawyer to whom he takes the case turns out to be a woman, Ory (Paula Raymond)—a fact that shocks Poole into expressing a classic set of gender prejudices. But unlike Coolan, the Indian sees the parallel between his case and hers and modifies his views. Ory will fight his case through the federal courts: she is the voice of the New Deal, believing in the essential justice of the American system and in the government's willingness and power to provide a remedy.

Romance will bloom between Poole and Ory, which invokes another archetype and constructs another vision of possible utopia. In envisioning this interracial romance Mann and Trosper draw on literary traditions at least as old as *Last of the Mohicans* and *Hobomok*—and they draw on the most radical strain in this tradition, in which the non-White partner is male. Romances involving White men and Indian "princesses" have the saving grace of preserving the political and moral hierarchy of a male-dominant ideology. In the reverse case, the non-White male assumes a tutelary and commanding role over the White woman and is implicitly permitted to penetrate her body and to mingle his sperm (figuratively his blood) with her "blood." This is a situation that reproduces the central "horrors"—figuratively political, literally sexual—of the captivity myth, or, more proximately, of Chesty Puller's fantasy of tough Oriental Communists breeding a hardier race out of "our" women. In *Devil's Doorway* the racial taboo inherent in that tradition is partially offset by the power of one of the most fundamental conventions of Hollywood cinema: the resolution of the story-problem in the marriage of the romantic stars. In this sense the film once again invokes archetype and fictive convention as a way of inviting us to imagine an alternative history more closely matched to our professed ideals.

This "invitation" is not merely offered as a seductive suggestion; it is made a central problem of the action and dialogue. Ory is seen to be caught between ambivalent impulses: she is attracted to Poole, she may love him, but she is held in check by her awareness of their difference. Her uneasiness prevents us from simply indulging a liberal sympathy on behalf of the Vanishing American. Why does she hesitate to live out the romantic scenario? Are we to understand that there is something unassimilable about the Indian? Or should we question the values the White woman represents?

The problem is complicated by the close connection between romantic and political issues. Faced with an intractable legal situation, Ory must continually return to Poole to beg him to compromise, to stop insisting on his rights. Here too her role is consistent with the politics of the New Deal: she tries to use government authority to effect distributive compromises that will avert social cataclysm. When Poole becomes more adamant, we are at first invited to see him as a capitalist who will not admit the moral bankruptcy of *laissez-faire*, or (in genre-specific terms) as a classic cattle baron who will not let the sheepmen share his land. But the authority of Ory's liberal criticism of Poole is offset by mounting evidence that White society offers nothing to the Indian but the choice between the degradation of the reservation and a doomed "last stand" in which he can at least die with dignity.

The film's presentation of the problem is all the more powerful for its refusal to offer a simple resolution of the difficulty. Ory comes to the besieged ranch under a flag of truce to tell Poole that the government has refused her plea for justice and has affirmed the Pooles' dispossession. When she pleads again for him to surrender, he asks her whether, to save his life, she would love him, kiss him. A close-up catches their faces barely apart, and although she is passive it is not clear that she is unwilling to *be* kissed. It is Poole who now recognizes the hopelessness of the situation and turns away. By suspending and refusing to resolve the moment of maximum ideological and erotic tension, the film invites the audience to finish the tale and the thought, to answer the question for itself. Do we wish the White/Indian marriage to take place? Do we want Poole to surrender to injustice and accept degradation as the price of survival? Poole's last words to Ory suggest that the time for a different answer (or a better set of choices) ought to have arrived by now: "A hundred years from now it might have worked."

Although the script denies us easy (romantic) answers, the narrative creates an implicit pressure for identification with Poole as against Coolan's bigotry and Ory's ineffectual faith in liberal government and compromise. At the same time, it moves from finding likenesses between Poole and "ourselves" to images that emphasize Poole's otherness, his Indian difference. At the beginning of the film Poole indicates his willingness to play by White men's rules: he has fought in their army for their flag, dresses like a White man, insists that his people speak English, and is a successful businessman. It is White bigotry, not racial atavism, that drives him to define himself more and more as *Indian* rather than American. Nonetheless, the change in his ideological stance is signaled by racial imagery. As he refuses Ory's penultimate plea for compromise, he moves out of the shadows that have hidden him and we see that he now wears his hair long, with a band across the forehead, Indian-style. If we began identifying with Poole as a White/Indian, by the end we are clearly asked to accept him as a distinctly Indian hero.

Poole's emergence as fully "Indian" is followed immediately by the return of combat-film references, all of which identify Poole and the Indians with the archetypal American platoon. When the settlers invade the valley, Poole arms everyone, including the women and children, and the ranch becomes a surrogate for the defended clearing in *Bataan*, with Robert Taylor starring once again as the veteran sergeant who must organize and lead a battalion of rookies against overwhelming odds. But if the physical situation mirrors the setting of the combat film (as well as the traditional pioneers-vs.-Indians Western), the moral situation inverts the standard references: this time it is the non-Whites who form the platoon (or the defenders of the ranch) and the Whites who lurk in the bushes threatening massacre. This inversion of the racial metaphors that establish the normal moral or ideological reference points of the action film is the single most original and important contribution of the "Indian Western" to the mythological vocabulary.

After an extended fire-fight, in which most of the Indians and many of the settlers fall (Coolan is killed), the cavalry arrives and interposes itself between the two forces. Poole puts up flag of truce and allows the women and children to surrender. Finally Poole himself appears, walking steadily toward a "firing squad" line of soldiers, wearing his old blue cavalry jacket and his Medal of Honor with his long hair and Indian headband. The camera views him from a low angle, making him seem monumental as he salutes the cavalry officer, who asks him where the rest of his men are. "We're all gone," he says, and still at attention pitches forward and out of the frame. If the ending echoes that of Bill Dane in *Bataan*, it also suggests a contrast: for the Indians there will be no "return to Bataan"—their last stand is a final one.

Devil's Doorway is the most complex and also the most radical of the Indian Westerns. A more meliorative vision was developed in *Broken Arrow*, directed by Delmer Daves and written by Michael Blankfort, whose treatment established the basic conventions followed in most subsequent cult of the Indian films.[44]

As in *Devil's Doorway*, the Indians in *Broken Arrow* are presented as victims of aggression and double-dealing by the Whites, whose motives are a mix of rational greed and irrational racism. Once begun, the war becomes a reciprocal exchange of atrocities; and since the Whites have never acknowledged their culpability in starting the exchange, the war has only confirmed their original prejudices. Daves' way of conceiving the issues is simpler and more readily accessible than the tragic mix of competing moralities that shape the Mann film. Since the conflict's origins can be understood in legalistic terms (Whites started it and have matched atrocity with atrocity), it becomes possible to imagine that a legal formula (the treaty) can resolve the conflict. The rationalistic permises of this analysis are borne out in the narrative form of the film, which depends on frequent face-to-face exchanges of argument between the various principals. Talk means as much or more than action for most of this film, but ultimately action will have to prove the validity of the spoken arguments.

The Indian arguments are authenticated and made accessible to us by the hero of the film, Tom Jeffords (James Stewart). Virtually the whole of the film is seen from his perspective; even when he is absent, his voice-over assumes responsibility for the narrative. He first appears as a lone prospector in Apache country and tells us he is a veteran weary after years of fighting. An encounter with a wounded Apache boy evokes a surprising sympathy with the enemy: he had not thought that Apaches could cry like White men. He heals the boy, who saves him in turn from a band of warriors led by a young war chief who, we later learn, is Geronimo.

Jeffords can conceive the possibility of peace with the Apaches because he can overcome race prejudice and recognize the humanity of his enemy. This recognition begins (for Jeffords and the audience) with the characterization of the enemy as child and mother, symbols that conventionally speak of weakness and dependency. This sentimental motive is augmented by a rational calculation of economic interest. If he can negotiate an agreement with Cochise to spare from attack the non-military mail service Jeffords runs, he will profit; at the same time he will be conducting a public test of Cochise's good faith and of the feasibility of a treaty with him. Jeffords rides alone (like John Wayne in *Fort Apache*) into the Apache's "Stronghold" to settle the treaty terms with Cochise. That Jeffords profits from his personal deal with Cochise at first arouses the prejudices of the townsfolk, who nearly lynch him. But gradually all but the most incorrigibly bigoted and irrational are converted to recognition of Cochise's trustworthiness as a "partner."

In *Devil's Doorway* the *failure* of a liberal peace is attributed to a combination of race prejudice with intractable underlying economic pressures. *Broken Arrow* shows us a successful peace being achieved through the combination of liberal principles and economic interest in an expanding or "open frontier" economy.[45] Moral appeals undermine racist emotion, but the mutual recognition (by White and Indian) of a common set of economic understandings is potentially a basis for coexistence and peace. Once Jeffords' experiment works, those who oppose his efforts for peace are identified as *irrational* and fanatic in their bigotry. They cease to function as representatives of a racist society and are seen as a marginal group excluded from the rational and (now) tolerant majority.

We in the audience are convinced much sooner than the citizens because we get to meet Cochise along with Jeffords. He acts as Jeffords' (and our) interpreter of Apache life, conducting a little "National Geographic" tour of folkways—dances, rituals, customs, taboos. As played by Jeff Chandler, Cochise is a classic modern instance of the Noble Savage. "Cochise" was already identified (in *Fort Apache*) as an Indian with whom peace was possible. Chandler's portrayal fixed that image and established it as an icon—he would portray Cochise (and other similar figures) in "Indian Westerns" for the rest of the decade.[46] His Cochise is immensely dignified, stern, laconic, and philosophically "eloquent" by turn. He is treated by his people as a king; he looks and acts the natural aristocrat. He is an Indian we can trust, because he is literally and figuratively "White"—that is, he acts up to "White" standard of nobility and honor, and he is played by a White actor whose pale eyes are not concealed and whose color and physiognomy are distinctly different from the Indians in his encampment. When the final confrontation comes between the peace and the war factions of his people, Cochise's opponents are all played by Indian actors—most notably Jay Silverheels as Geronimo, better known for his portrayal of Tonto on the *Lone Ranger* TV series (1949–57).

Thus the racism that the film banishes on one level returns on another. We can trust the Indians and make peace with them because they are "just like us"; but to demonstrate that "truth" we have to transform them into Whites and expel or suppress the ethnic Indian from the picture.

This theme is carried through in the interracial romance between Jeffords and Sonseeahray (Debra Paget), the Indian maiden whom he loves and marries. Their marriage is a symbolic proof of the possibility of integrating the two cultures and races. She represents the transfer of the role of the "redemptive woman" from the White to the Indian side of the racisl spectrum, a gesture meant to convey the movie's determination to change our conventional ideas about Indians. As Cochise reincarnates the classic Noble Savage, Sonseeahray is the traditional "Indian princess" out of nineteenth-century literary romance.[47] She is virginal and innocent of civilization. The use of a mirror and the concept of kissing have to be explained to her. To make her moral status even clearer, she is also a returned captive who had been taken prisoner by other Indians.[48] At first the movie uses makeup and lighting to emphasize her "Indian" appearance; but as the romance progresses, her skin and eyes appear lighter. This progression subtly visualizes the premises of "tolerance," which ask acceptance of the Other by (in effect) denying difference.

Sonseeahray is taken with Jefford's white ways and tools and keeps asking him to teach her about them. Her response conforms to the racialist belief that "inferiors" instinctively love and seek to emulate "superiors," and thus seems to assure Jeffords' dominance—especially since he is male, and hence (by the normal standards of gendered politics) the dominant partner in the marriage. Nonetheless, there is a threat of Jeffords' "Whiteness": the bigotry and selfishness of White society so disgust him that he declares his intention to live as an Apache and must be recalled to a rational sense of his difference by the noble Cochise.

In *Rio Grande* a similar gender-dilemma was resolved by the woman's conversion and subordination to the values of the male cavalry-culture. In *Broken Arrow* it is resolved by the murder of Sonseeahray by White bigots, which occurs in the middle of her Edenic honeymoon with Jeffords. But her death proves "redemptive" in a way her life might not have been: the handling of the murderers by Cochise, Jeffords, and the White authorities proves that the treaty is workable. The bigots are defeated and expelled, and peaceful coexistence is established.

This ending allows the viewer to entertain two contradictory understandings of the fate of the "good" Indians and the meaning of their tale. On the literal level, the film tells us that the treaty has succeeded, and we are to presume that its aims of providing a good future for the Apache will be achieved. But at the same time, the possibility that "peace" might lead to full integration ("marriage") has been eliminated. Jeffords tells us that he will return to his former life as a lone wanderer, and that Sonseeahray "survives" as an idea in his mind, recalled by the beauties of Nature.[49] At the same time his counterpart, Cochise, has had to exchange his masculine freedom for the "broken arrow" of peace.

But the inconsistencies that make *Broken Arrow* inadequate as an imaginative antidote to the mythology of racism also gave it broad appeal. Its formulas permitted the audience to indulge, and congratulate itself on, a "liberal" attitude toward non-Whites without having to abandon the fundamental assurance of their own superiority.[50]

Like the "Cult of the Cavalry," the "Cult of the Indian" continued to develop after 1950. Between 1950 and 1965 usage of the two forms diverged: the cavalry film tended to remain responsive primarily to Cold War issues, while the Indian film provided a setting for stories related to the domestic struggle over civil rights. The Cult of the Indian was particularly active during periods of intensified civil-rights activism, in 1950–55 and 1960–64. After 1965, the two genres would show a tendency to "merge," in response to the simultaneous and interrelated crises over "Black Power" and the Vietnam War.

But the capacity of cavalry Westerns and Indian Westerns to represent ideology is constrained by their military subject matter. They represent conflicts of power and value as social or collective in character, and the heroic resolutions they propose feature the kinds of operation that are characteristic of nation-states: diplomatic negotiation, treaty-making, and the mustering of tribes and regiments for war. The combat-film ideology that informs these Westerns also gives them a bias toward socially meliorative resolutions and the subordination of individual rights, beliefs, needs, and desires to some greater good. In the classic cavalry film Whites merge their differences to present a solid front to the enemy, and in later "civil rights" variations (like Ford's *Sergeant Rutledge* [1960] Blacks are integrated into the regimental society that opposes the demonized Apache.[51] In the Indian film opposing races are asked to abandon their special beliefs and interest for the sake of peace. A different kind of Western was required to entertain more critical questions about the character of the American social compact under conditions of Cold War and to raise issues of social justice and individual conscience for which meliorative or common-front solutions could not readily be found. These were the issues formerly addressed by the New Deal outlaw Western; they would become the concern of a Cold War variation on the outlaw theme, the Cult of the Gunfighter.

12 Killer Elite

The Cult of the Gunfighter, 1950–1953

The "renaissance" Westerns provided two story-forms which addressed the complex of ideological problems that we may call "social justice": What is the proper balance between the rights of the individual citizen and the interests or opinions of the majority? Between the ideal of justice and the practical operation of the laws? Between the property rights of the haves and the legitimate needs of the have-nots? The "town-tamer" Western, of which *Dodge City* and *My Darling Clementine* are classic examples, offered a "progressive" answer: social injustice is imposed by powerful criminals; the hero must defeat them and thus empower the "decent folks" who bring progress to the Frontier. The "outlaw" Western proposes a critique of this model by locating the source of injustice in the powerful institutions (railroads) that are also the agents of "progress."

In the postwar decade two variations on the "town-tamer" and "outlaw" Western emerged: the "psychological" or *film noir* Western, in which pathological elements in the hero's character are emphasized at the expense of his character as lawman or social rebel; and the "gunfighter" Western, in which professionalism in the arts of violence is the hero's defining characteristic. These new takes on the Western were shaped by the internal logic of genre development, which fostered a certain kind of *stylization* of the Western and its hero, and by the pressures and anxieties of the postwar/Cold War transition, which gave that stylization a particular kind of ideological significance. The consonance between the formal character of the gunfighter Western and its ideological content is a genuinely poetic achievement. It gave the gunfighter films ideological and cinematic resonance and made the heroic style of the gunfighter an important symbol of right and heroic action for filmmakers, the public, and the nation's political leadership. For that reason we need to review the pressures and trends that shaped the gunfighter Western and look closely at the three films that created the gunfighter as a character: *The Gunfighter* (1950), *High Noon* (1952), and *Shane* (1953).

Postwar filmmakers who returned to the Western had a more highly developed sense of the genre *as genre* than their predecessors during the "renaissance." This awareness of the conventionality of their working language liberated them from the obligation to treat the Western as a historical script and encouraged them to take odd or innovative slants on the old stories. A late-genre film might be built around events marginal to more celebrated episodes—for example, the various films dealing with army units trying to warn Custer or dealing with the aftermath of his defeat.[1] A familiar tale might be re-told from an unfamiliar or reverse angle, as in *I Shot Jesse James* (1949), where the outlaw's story is seen from his assassin's point of view.

Or one might take a "deeper" look into a mythic figure, emphasizing psychological analysis over "action." The "psychological Western" was particularly appealing to filmmakers and critics who sought to make the mature genre a vehicle for works of a "literary" seriousness. If much of the "psychology" in these Westerns could be dismissed as the substitution of canned Freudianism for canned history, the same could be said of a good deal of the popular and even "serious" fiction during this period. For the general public, and even for some important critics, the use of recognizable psychological concepts and complexes had the desired effect of altering audience expectations and making the genre seem more "serious" and worthy of "adult" attention.

The common denominator in all these approaches is a particular kind of abstraction and stylization. A single element of the Western is isolated from its original context and made the subject of exaggerated attention and concern, even to the point of fetishization. The tendency is most obvious in a group of Westerns that fetishized particular kinds of weapon: *Colt .45* (1950), *Springfield Rifle* (1952), *Winchester '73* (1953), and *The Gun That Won the West* (1955). The new figure of the "gunfighter" similarly exaggerates a skill that had been merely one of the standard attributes of all cowboy heroes. Jesse James used his quickness with a gun to avenge his mother and to rob trains; Ford's Wyatt Earp shot it out with the Clantons in *My Darling Clementine*. But if we focus on the two figures *purely* as gunfighters, the ideological clichés of the historical Western give way to a new view of the Western myth in which the difference between lawman and outlaw is obscured by their kindred gift for violence and is rendered problematic by their characterological difference or alienation from their communities.

The Revised Outlaw: From Rebel to Psychopath

In an esthetic view, the shift to a psychodynamic perspective was both necessary and productive, since it opened the genre to a more searching and complex engagement with characterization. But it was accompanied by the de-emphasis (and for a while the virtual abandonment) of those social/historical formulas of motivation that had previously shaped Western scenarios. Characterizations of Jesse James are an index to this change in the myth of the populist outlaw. *Kansas Raiders* (1950) treated Jesse as a troubled young man warped by his oedipal engagement with the charismatic father-figure of Quantrill; in *The Great Missouri Raid* (1951) and Nicholas Ray's *The True Story of Jesse James* (1957), Jesse is played as the historical ancestor of the 1950s juvenile delinquent—a "rebel without a cause" other than his emotional response to the twisted values of his mother.[2]

By rooting their explanation of the hero's actions in his own psychology or in the dynamics of his family during his childhood, these films lifted the burden of responsibility for outlawry from the shoulders of an unjust society. The emphasis on psychology is achieved by the dismissal of politics, social criticism, and the idea of revolution from the field of mythological play. This shift of emphasis was perhaps a self-protective gesture at a time when the postwar "Red Scare" in Hollywood made political statements of any kind potentially dangerous. But it is worth noting that this way of constructing myth-historical narratives gained favor at the same time that American intellectuals and historians were turning away from radical forms of social analysis and heralding the "end of ideology."[3]

The substitution of psychology for theories of social causation is more marked in a newly refurbished Western formula that might be called the "revenger" plot. The new revenger Westerns differ from the Zane Grey and W. S. Hart models in their emphasis on the neurotic element in the hero's makeup and in the highly stylized *film noir* atmosphere with which the action is invested—deep shadows, claustrophobic settings, and grim and hostile landscapes embodying a dim view of human nature and human possibilities. "Historical" characters and settings are rarely important. This West is abstracted even further from the historical frame than was the west in the psychologized outlaw film.[4]

The psychology of the revenger has its roots in the outlaw Western. Passionate anger and desire to avenge a murdered parent had also been part of the complex of motives that drove the hero of *Jesse James* into outlawry. Indulgence of that passion and satisfaction of that desire finally obsessed Jesse and turned him into a "wolf." But the turns of Jesse's psychology are always given value by the way in which they affect his society. Avenging his mother is inseparable from his determination to fight the railroad on behalf of the farmers; his moral decline is linked with the separation from society that the outlaw's life requires; his death is seen as a sacrifice which teaches the virtues of skill, courage, and resistance to oppression. The revenger Western isolates this passion and privatizes it. Mann's *Winchester '73* is the tale of a "good" brother's obsessive search for revenge against his evil sibling, who shot their father in the back and stole the perfect rifle that the hero had won in a shooting match. But the film's central questions concern the psychology of the avenger, not the parricide (whose badness is a given). His obsession with revenge and the fetishization of the rifle that is its symbol suggest that he may be driven by a madness akin to his brother's malice and that only by slaying his dark brother can he be free of it.[5]

In such a tale, the redemption of the hero from the darker side of his own nature has little or no meaning for a larger society. Where the outlaw Western sets the adventure amid strong and persistent visualizations of social life, the revenger Western gives us a landscape that mirrors the hero's introvert psychology. Often it is a desert landscape through which the hero, the enemy, and a small group of supporting players must journey, driven by some pressure of time, pursuit, or desire. The revenger always faces a world in which social authority and community support are lacking; he must rely on himself, and perhaps one other person, for the fulfillment of his obsessional quest and/or redemption. Thus the revenger Western also fetishizes "psychology," isolating the private dimension of the original story and replacing social with exclusively personal motives, insisting (in effect) that the private dimension determines the whole significance of the story.

The Invention of the Gunfighter

The gunfighter Western adopts the *noir*-ist sensibility of the revenger and its concern with character; but it also addresses the outlaw film's task of providing social commentary. It therefore offers an opening for assertive ideological statements. Like the revenger, the gunfighter is psychically troubled and isolated from normal society by something "dark" in his nature and/or his past. But that "darkness" is bound up with and expressed by his highly specialized social function: he is a killer by profession, usually for pay. The existence of his profession is in itself an implicitly hard-boiled commentary on the nature of American society; and the psychic isolation his profession begets gives the gunfighter the alienated perspective he needs to articulate such a critique: What sort of society is it in which those who have money can hire a killer? And what kind of people are we, that our strong men find such work to their liking? But more important than his critical function is the gunfighter's embodiment of the central paradox of America's self-image in an era of Cold War, "subversion," and the thermonuclear balance of terror: our sense of being at once supremely powerful and utterly vulnerable, politically dominant and yet helpless to shape the course of crucial events.

Fittingly, the seminal film in the development of this new subgenre was *The Gunfighter,* written and directed by the same team that had produced *Jesse James*—Nunnally Johnson and Henry King. The project was shaped from the first by a deliberate intention to make a film that would impress and surprise critics and audiences with innovations in style and subject matter. Daryl F. Zanuck, the head of 20th Century Fox, was looking for a "prestige" Western with the same claims to "seriousness" as the studio's critically acclaimed *Ox-Bow Incident* (1943) or Ford's *My Darling Clementine* (1946), but with broader popular appeal.[6] He assigned the project to Andre De Toth, noted for his work in the *noir* style. De Toth went to history for his story, but to a source and subject that were distinctly marginal. Eugene Cunningham's *Triggernometry: A Gallery of Gunfighters* (1934) was a collection of brief biographies of Westerners noted for their skill with weapons. These same figures—Wild Bill Hickok, Calamity Jane, Jesse James, Wyatt Earp, and the like—had been treated in similar compilations in the past, under the rubric of "plainsmen," "border outlaws," "noted guerrillas," "frontier scouts," "heroes of the Plains," and so on.[7] Rather than repeat those formulas, Cunningham focused on the single attribute of their skill with a pistol. He added his own "technical notes on leather slapping as a fine art, gathered from many a loose-holstered expert over the years"—a device that emphasized and exaggerated this aspect of their lives, suggesting that "gunfighting" was a kind of art or profession. In fact, the "classic" model of the gunfighter portrayed by De Toth was an artifact of Cunningham's intense and specialized focus on the technique of the fast-draw. Cunningham's subjects were not (for the most part) professional killers. But they pursued a variety of trades—peace officer, gambler, robber, saloon-keeper—that often engaged them in violence.[8] Some of the men who served as "hired guns" in Western range wars, like Frank Canton and Tom Horn, were professional assassins who killed from ambush or under cover of a vigilante expedition. But most—like the "army" that invaded Johnson County—were working cowboys, no more than usually proficient with weapons, or outlaws like the Evans gang in the Lincoln County War, whose willingness to kill was at the service of merchants and ranchers who fenced their stolen goods or otherwise profited from their criminal labors. Such men were not called "gunfighters." They were variously (and properly) described as "mercenaries" and "banditti" or as "regulators" and "vigilantes," depending on the politics of the writer. The image of the gunfighter as a professional of violence, for whom formalized killing was a calling and even an art, is the invention of movies like *The Gunfighter*, the reflection of Cold War-era ideas about professionalism and violence and not of the mores of the Old West.[9]

De Toth chose for his subject "Johnny Ringo," one of the most obscure figures in Cunningham's book, a member of the Clanton gang which opposed Wyatt Earp and his brothers in the "Gunfight at the O.K. Corral" in 1881. The national fame of that incident was itself an artifact of Hollywood culture. Neither Earp nor the gunfight had enjoyed any great notoriety outside Arizona until 1920, when the aged Wyatt appeared on a movie lot in Pasadena hoping to cash in on the enthusiasm for "authentic" Western figures. The belated spotlight cast on this event found little record of Ringo beyond the name, accounts of a few vicious murders, a reputation for heavy drinking, and a couple of intriguing mysteries. He was said to have had a cultured manner (evidenced by an ability to quote Shakespeare) and to have been the scion of an aristocratic southern family ruined in the Civil War. He also died mysteriously, murdered by someone who gave him no chance to draw, and his reputation was such that the chief suspect bragged that he had done it.[10]

De Toth was intrigued by the idea that Ringo's killer could gain stature by claiming to be "the man who killed Johnny Ringo." Celebrity of that kind had been part of frontier culture and its fictional representation from a very early date. Mark Twain, in *Roughing It* (1872), says that to become a notable personage in frontier Nevada it was good to have it known that you had "killed your man." But De Toth—following Cunningham's suggestion—imagines a different and more stringent system for according reputation, drawn from the contemporary worlds of sports and movie celebrity. Cunningham's book suggested that gunfighting was a profession like modern prizefighting, a highly technical game or "gentle art" with distinct rules; it followed that one could gain a reputation by defeating a higher-ranked opponent. To be a champion was therefore to become the mark of perpetual challenges, not only from fellow professionals but from the random and spiteful aggression of ambitious amateurs. De Toth counted heavyweight champion Joe Louis and the actors Humphrey Bogart and Errol Flynn among his friends; and he noticed that whenever these men appeared in public, they were likely to be challenged by a drunken citizen who needed to show how much tougher he was. In this regard champions and movie stars were alike: centers of a public fantasy-life so powerful that those in its spell had to seek somehow to become—and failing that, to destroy—the idealized figure. De Toth's gunfighter was therefore not only a formal abstraction from the conventions of the outlaw hero, but a self-conscious reflection on the nature and meaning of "the star" as an element in both cinematic form and public life. De Toth envisions the gunfighter as a killer-celebrity who finds himself trapped in the role and reputation he has spent his life seeking. That mood of entrapment was to shape the narrative and the landscape through which the gunfighter would move, seeking refuge or escape from his special history and failing to find it.

Although Zanuck appreciated the originality of De Toth's idea, he disagreed with his innovative design for the production, which called for the use of the expensive technicolor process but aimed at a somber, almost colorless look. He gave the project to King and Johnson, who reworked De Toth's script, preserving most of its essential features.[11]

The movie opens with a title that echoes the conventions of the historical Western. But the historical allusions here are deliberately vague and devoid of "progressive" associations. The place is no more specific than "the Southwest," the time is "the 1880s," and there is no issue of national progress at stake. We are simply told that "the difference between death and glory was often but the fraction of a second," and that familiar figures like Wyatt Earp, Wild Bill Hickok, and Billy the Kid were "champions" in that line. We are told that "the fastest man with a gun who ever lived, by many contemporary accounts, was a long, lean Texan named Ringo" (renamed "Jimmy" Ringo for the film). Though we are not expected to recognize him as a historical personage, we may remember the fictional "Ringo Kid" of *Stagecoach*.

Before we learn anything about Ringo we are presented with the essentials of his identity as a "gunfighter": his loneliness, his skill, his fatal celebrity. He enters a town, alone and at night, to get a drink at a saloon. The bartender immediately hails him as "Jimmy" and begs recognition, which Ringo grants with a quick, false grin and an expression of terrible weariness—he is the "star," sick of recognition but wise enough to know that it is useless to resist. The reason for his distaste is immediately revealed. No sooner is his name uttered than a smart-aleck kid has to challenge him to draw, playing to the audience in the bar and rejecting every attempt by Ringo to evade the inevitable killing.

Ringo is pursued by the kid's three brothers, and the film will cut back and forth between the oncoming avengers and the town of Cayenne, where Ringo goes in quest of his lost wife and son and a new beginning. The pursuit runs on a timetable, which is laid out in a conversation between the brothers; their progress marks the steady encroachment of Ringo's past on his future prospects.

Ringo arrives in Cayenne and once again goes straight to the saloon, where there is a repetition of the recognition scene with the bartender. Ringo establishes himself at a corner table, and this single interior becomes the center of the movie. The enclosed, finally claustrophobic space of the saloon takes the place of the normally open space of the Western. Like the jungle clearing in the war film, the saloon is a space we leave only when danger threatens, or to accomplish some brief mission. And like the jungle clearing, the saloon's enclosure is threatened by powerful forces. Though these are most obviously indicated by the brothers' progress across the desert, they are embodied as well in the passage of time and Ringo's continual references to the clock. Time and space are thus equated, and both are closing in on the gunfighter. Ringo's seat in the corner of the saloon is beneath the Budweiser lithograph of Custer's Last Stand.

Ringo is passive for much of the narrative, sitting or pacing the saloon like a caged tiger, waiting for something to happen. The sense of suppressed violent energy is the essence of Gregory Peck's characterization of Ringo, and King emphasizes it by continually prolonging that suppression, promising release and frustrating that promise. As the narrative proceeds, we see that this mood is more than just a symptom of the occasion. Ringo lives in an atmosphere in which the expectation of violence is never absent; his character has been deformed by his response to the demands of his violent world. His movements are slow but efficient. He is always watchful, eyes always moving—even when he seems to be staring fixedly at his hands we see that his peripheral vision misses nothing. He always sits in the corner, never with his back exposed. He lives according to a discipline of watchfulness, preparedness, and restraint—the marks of his professionalism and signs of his isolation.

The saloon enclosure is also a theater. Its open board floor suggests a stage, and the action that occurs there could easily be transferred to a proscenium setting. Thus even when Ringo is just sitting at his table waiting for something to happen, he is still a celebrity, still "on stage." The townspeople, especially the children, press their faces hungrily to the windows for a look at him, hoping "something will happen," that they'll get to see a killing. Their attitude mirrors our own conventional expectations about what will occur on screen, and through this device the film construes our expectation as desire: the wish to see Ringo kill and/or be killed. Although there will be talk of motives and reasons here, we know that in some sense motives are rationalizations. There is a necessity or fatality at work that cannot be controlled by the conventional and historistic rationales of the "renaissance" Western, and it has something to do with an almost abstract will to violence.

The most perverse representative of that will is the local "fast kid," Hunt Bromley: a brilliantly visualized version of the type, whose arrogant sneer is carried on a most unappealing late-adolescent face, with the barest smear of mustache dirtying the upper lip. Though he is quite particularly nasty, he is also a social symptom: a vile boy given license to bully by the admiration that any capacity for or disposition to violence evokes in the town's menfolk. He is the dazzled spectator who can't see the difference between the play and the real world, who persistently invades the stage to threaten, insult, and finally assault the actors in an attempt to become a star in his own right.

Ringo's character and history are revealed slowly, through a series of encounters with people from his past. These include the town's old marshal, Mark Strett; the widow of Ringo's best friend Bucky Harris, now reduced to working as a saloon singer; a local version of the generic Petticoat Brigade, led by Mrs. Pennyfeather; a crazed avenger of a father, who believes (erroneously) that Ringo killed his son; and his estranged wife and son. Each of these encounters is based on some more or less traditional element of the genre, some of them as old as *The Virginian.* But King emphasizes the conventionality deliberately, and sometimes comically. The stylization of these encounters suggests the artificiality of the hope of redemption that they seem to promise Ringo.

The marshal is the first and most important of these stock characters. Mark Strett had ridden with Ringo years before, apparently in an outlaw gang that robbed banks, but he abandoned that life after a raid (which sounds like the James Gang's Northfield fiasco) in which a little girl was killed. This classic image of evil—the assault on innocent children—fills Mark with self-disgust (it wasn't his bullet, but it could have been), and compels him to go straight. That same disgust and weariness now fill Ringo: he is sick of his life and wants to change it; he has come to Cayenne to reconcile with his wife and start over. But he doesn't know what name she is using, and Mark refuses to tell him. Like Will Wright in *Jesse James*, this sympathetic lawman is in love with the outlaw's woman. But his motive is not jealousy. Rather, he has promised to keep the woman's secret, especially from Ringo; and in any case he does not believe Ringo can start over—Mark Strett could disappear only because he was never famous.

That Ringo is famous is clear enough, but just what kind of work he did to achieve fame is not at all clear. Although he robbed banks, he was not a Jesse James. He seems also to have worked as a "big, tough gunny," but we are never told exactly what that work entails. At some point his skill with a gun became more important than the tasks for which he nominally used it. The tool and its use became ends in themselves, and he has spent most of his time defending (and so extending) his reputation in a series of unremunerative encounters like the one we witnessed earlier. As he tells Bucky's widow, they may have gotten into the gunfighting trade for fame and money, but the fame is a burden and "the truth is it don't pay very well . . . I ain't even got a decent watch."

Ringo's wife is a highly conventional take on the "redemptive woman." Like Molly Wood in *The Virginian*, she is a "schoolmarm." Like Zee in *Jesse James*, she leaves her husband after the birth of their son when he refuses to change his way of life. Of course (like Zee) she still loves her outlaw, but she is more skeptical than Zee of his ability to change, even though she is moved by the sincerity of Ringo's self-disgust and desire for a new start. In the outlaw Western, such a change of heart would have earned Ringo at least a figurative redemption, though it might not save him from Jesse's tragic fate. But the gunfighter's sincerity is beside the point. His desire to change is rendered meaningless by the completeness with which his identity and his imagination have become merged in his role and profession.

While Ringo waits for his wife to arrive, a young rancher enters the saloon, orders a drink, and buys one for Ringo. The rancher's innocence is marked by his hayseed dress, but more importantly by the fact that he alone does not recognize Ringo. We learn that he was formerly a wild cowboy, but a good woman has domesticated him, and now (like the lovers at the end of *Stagecoach*) they've got a little ranch with a few head of cattle and some horses. Until this moment, Ringo has not said what he plans to do to "start over"; but in the next scene he will tell his wife that he has an idea about a little ranch somewhere, he doesn't know where he got the idea, it just "come over" him. His wife believes that this is a sign of his change of heart, and in a way it is. But we know that the idea is not really his own; and we recognize the dream itself as a movie-formula, not a solution suited to the harsh "reality" of Ringo's world.

In the end, space and time close down and run out. Hunt Bromley shoots Ringo in the back, as Robert Ford shot Jesse James. But instead of a eulogy and a monument that would translate tragedy into a legend of heroism, *Gunfighter* ends with a curse. The dying Ringo declares that Hunt outdrew him, thus insuring that Hunt will live the kind of life Ringo himself has led—a life he now sees as a terrible doom. At Ringo's funeral—a celebrity's send-off in a packed church—his wife takes her place as chief mourner, acknowledging her relation to Ringo and offering a kind of posthumous reconciliation. But its meaning is personal rather than social; it is not clear how the town will respond. The final image, of a lone rider disappearing into the sunset, suggests a passage into immortality, perhaps that of legend. But this is not as ideologically specific as the final passage of *Jesse James*, which shows the hero's reconciliation with the myth of progressive history.

Ringo's relation to that myth is fundamentally ironic. His career, like that of the gangster-hero in the 1930s, is a darkened mirror-image of progressivism, but now with a distinct postwar emphasis.

His fate is not primarily a critique of capitalist excess, but of power and world preeminence. Ringo has striven to rise in the world by the development of his skill; he has become a leader in his profession, the best at what he does and renowned for doing it. Having achieved the pinnacle of success and power, he discovers that the achievement is meaningless, even poisonous. The disciplined self-restraint that is the essence of his professionalism has become an imprisoning shell that cuts him off from human connections. Despite his discipline and skill he is still vulnerable, the target of every man and boy with a gun. His fame and power are profitless, unless he is willing to accept them as values in themselves. In the past he has done so, but the cost has been a steady dehumanization of his own life, which has finally become unbearable. He would like to transform his role and values, but he can't see how to do that. He is trapped by his history and his identity.[12]

This sense of entrapment makes the gunfighter a resonant figure on several levels. One should not underestimate the appeal of the homely analogy between Ringo's situation and that of the 1950s archetypal "Man in the Gray Flannel Suit." Ringo renders as heroic tragedy the malaise of the middle-class man grown weary of the "rat race" through which he has prospered. But Ringo's situation is also a parody of Cold War, nuclear garrison-state psychology; he is at once the most powerful and the most vulnerable man in the world. He realizes the disillusionment of the transition from postwar to Cold War—the sense that all our accumulation of power and great wartime victories had somehow failed to produce the world we expected, or even to give us the assurance that we, as a political society, could control our own destiny.

In a larger ideological view, the gunfighter Western entertains the idea that the "progressive" rationale for both political action and violence may in fact be a chimera. The gunfighter enters the narrative already knowing that the Wild West's promise of fame and power (or of redemption) is an illusion; that the vision of the Frontier as limitless in its possibilities for personal and social perfection is a mirage; and that he himself has been rendered isolated and vulnerable by the very things that have made him victorious in the past.

High Noon (1952): *The Hero in Spite of Democracy*

The ideological implications of this approach to the Western were developed with striking clarity in Stanley Kramer's production of *High Noon,* directed by Fred Zinneman and written by the blacklisted screenwriter Carl Foreman. The film was both a critical and a commercial success. Academy Award nominations went to the film (as Best Picture) and to both Zinneman and Foreman; Gary Cooper won an Oscar as Best Actor. The film editors and Dmitri Tiomkin's score received Oscars as well. It was also an extremely influential film, spawning many imitations (including the TV series *Gunsmoke*) and one major "rebuttal": Howard Hawks' *Rio Bravo* (1959). Although nominally a "town-tamer" Western, its hero is envisioned in ways that link him to King's Jimmy Ringo, and the formal structure of the film mirrors and exaggerates *The Gunfighter's* clock-driven narrative.

The hero of *High Noon* is Will Kane (Cooper), who is about to marry and then retire as Marshal of Hadleyville. Kane is a lean, dour, iron-gray man who wears the lawman's costume of white shirt and gray vest like a set of vestments. His wife (Grace Kelly) is a good deal younger and is a Quaker; it is because of her religion that he is giving up his gun and his badge. As the two are about to leave, they learn that Frank Miller is out of prison and will return on the noon train. Miller had ruled Hadleyville from his saloon and had terrorized the town with his penchant for insane cruelty until Kane decided to put on the badge and clean up. Now Miller is returning to kill Kane and the others who had a hand in his overthrow. The townspeople insist that Kane not change his plans, assuring him that they can take care of themselves and that Kane's callow deputy Harvey (Lloyd Bridges) can protect them till the new marshal arrives. But after starting off on his journey, Kane turns back, despite his wife's passionate objections and her insistence that she will leave him if he decides to fight.

From this moment the film begins a dramatic countdown in pace with the real passage of time—one minute on screen equals one minute closer to "high noon." As Kane tries to rally his old deputies to oppose Miller's return and to talk his wife out of leaving on the train that will bring Miller back, the camera continually refers us to the clock, to the narrowing time/space within which Kane's heroism (like Ringo's fame) has entrapped him.

Like Ringo, Kane is isolated from society by the very qualities that have given him honor. The difference is that Ringo is alone from the moment we meet him; Kane does not discover his alienation until, through the action of the narrative, he tries to engage his community's sense of solidarity and decency in defeating Miller. One by one, everyone he approaches refuses to take up arms against Miller's return. (The series of encounters parallels the narrative plan of *Gunfighter* and even engages the hero with some of the same conventional types.) Kane's mentor and predecessor is too old and arthritic; most people (like the judge who sentenced Miller) are simply too frightened. Some cover their fear by professing to believe that Miller may have grown soft in prison. The young deputy is jealous of Kane. The minister is in a snit because Kane was not married in his church.

The crisis arrives when Kane addresses the townspeople in the church and reminds them of what life was like under Miller's rule—asking, in effect, if they have learned the lesson of their history. What follows is a parody of democracy. At first the townspeople are all for helping Kane; then "cooler heads" prevail, particularly the mayor (Thomas Mitchell). The defeat of Miller (he says) meant progress for the town, and that progress is about to culminate in a wave of new investment—important people in the state capital have heard about Hadleyville! But if a gunfight takes place in the streets, Hadleyville will seem like "just another wide open town." Thus the traditional sanctions of "progress" become motives for cowardice rather than incitements to heroism. The community, in a virtual town meeting, declares that it does not want Will Kane to fight its battles a second time.

But just as he rejects the moral authority of his wife's religion, Kane rejects the "will of the people" and prepares to face Miller and his henchmen alone. At this moment, he has been deprived of the classic sanctions that authorized the town-tamer's use of violence. He has no official entitlement to the badge he has re-assumed after retiring that morning; the Mayor has defined his action as anti-progressive; and the town meeting has made it clear that it no longer wants him to act as its agent.[13] He is, in effect, a vigilante: a private man assuming the power of the law without submitting himself to the democratic process. In these circumstances, what principles can justify his decision to face Miller?

There is a personal element in his decision, which at first predominates. Kane knows that Miller will pursue him wherever he goes and prefers to face him now rather than spend a lifetime looking over his shoulder. But other feelings and ideas move him as well. He is a professional: his badge was his calling, the expression of his pride and honor, and Miller's expulsion was his most meaningful victory. He can't leave the job unfinished, and Miller's return will undo the work of his life. There is also a social component among Kane's motives. His work was meaningful because it transformed Hadleyville into a "progressive" little town where it is safe for women and children to walk the streets. He cannot permit society to revert to the savage regime of Miller, even if the people who constitute that society are willing to permit it. In effect, the principle on which he acts is the same as that to which Wister's and Dixon's vigilante heroes and Ford's cavalrymen appealed: that the defense of "civilization" is more important than the procedures of "democracy."

But Kane's ultimate appeal is to the authority of his "character" and his "manhood"—the same "red-blooded" principles to which Judge Henry and the Virginian appealed in justifying the lynching of rustlers. Kane is the only man with knowledge, skill, and power enough to defeat Miller; and his conscience, like that of Sheridan and Yorke, holds that (in cases like this) possession of the power to act entails an absolute responsibility to act, whether or not the action is legal or acceptable to the public. But Foreman and Zinneman do not provide an excuse like the capture of the children to cover his action. Kane forthrightly asserts the need for pre-emptive violence to prevent atrocities which he (apparently alone) believes are certain to follow Miller's return.

Kane understands Miller's savage character, because, like "the man who knows Indians," there is a side of Kane's nature that is akin to Miller's. The hint is there in the name "Will Kane," which combines the suggestion of "will" as the drive to power with a homonym of the Bible's first murderer. When Kane talks to the old marshal who first persuaded him to put on the badge, their conversation confirms that Kane might have gone "bad" if the marshal hadn't turned him around. But the dark potential in Kane is most vividly defined by Helen Ramirez (Katy Jurado), who owns the town's saloon (and presumably its attendant gambling and prostitution). Helen was originally Frank Miller's moll and is presently the mistress of Kane's deputy Harvey. But she was once the lover of Will Kane, who freed her from Miller's sadistic control and may have enabled her to replace Miller as owner of the saloon, become a wealthy woman, and repay the town's scorn of her for being a "Mexican woman." Helen is therefore to be believed when she tells Harvey that the difference between him and Kane is that Kane "is a *man*." The emphasis and context of the remark identify Kane's manliness as a lover with his power to confront and overcome Miller.

There are precedents in earlier Westerns for the sharing of a woman between hero and villain, and if we are aware of these (as an audience) Helen's suggestions will carry a bit more resonance. A similar quartet of figures—gunfighter, gambler, Mexican woman, Christian woman from the East—set the terms of the moral drama in Hart's *Hell's Hinges* (1915); but Hart's turn-of-the-century morality insists on the (racial) purity of Blaze Tracey's sexual inclinations. The foursome of marshal, gambler, Mexican woman, and virginal Anglo maiden also forms the central group of the Wyatt Earp/O.K. Corral story, most recently remade by John Ford in *My Darling Clementine* (1946).[14] In that film Wyatt (Henry Fonda) becomes marshal of Tombstone in order to avenge the killing of his brother and the rustling of his cattle. Far from "cleaning up" Tombstone, Wyatt forms a close friendship with the murderous gambler Doc Holliday (Victor Mature), who owns a saloon and keeps as mistress the Mexican singer Chihuahua. Although Ford's movie ultimately reaffirms an essentially "progressive" view of the town-tamer, the Earp/Holliday relationship suggests an element of darkness and violence in Earp that belongs to an earlier stage of civilization. Earp, however, is moving toward a more civilized way of life, a direction indicated by his falling in love with Clementine, an aristocratic easterner who is virtually the reincarnation of the Virginian's Molly Stark. But Clementine was once Doc Holliday's fiancée, and his abandonment of her indicates that his path will be the reverse of Wyatt's, toward atavism and death.

Foreman and Zinneman use the same group of characters but alters their relationships to emphasize the "dark" and "Miller-like" aspects of Kane's past. The sympathetic Holliday becomes the vicious Miller (whose name is the same as that of the villain in *Hell's Hinges*), and the woman they share is not the pure Anglo maiden but the "dark" Mexican woman. The capacity for "dark" sex and "dark" violence is the key to Kane's power, the definition of the virility Helen praises. Kane can defeat Miller because he could have been Miller. He too is willing to impose his will on the citizens. The difference between them is Kane's latent instinct for goodness, which shows in his jilting of Helen and his love for a Quaker woman. Like the Virginian, the "essential" goodness and manliness of his character provide the only "authority" to which he can appeal in justification of his actions. And the movie says it is enough.

The gunfight is the center of the film's formal structure, the iconic moment toward which the clock-driven narrative inexorably drives and its moral resolution as well. Only the gunfight can prove that Kane really does "know Indians" and is therefore morally entitled to set his will against that of the townspeople. The gunfight itself has a ritual quality. Kane's preparations and his solitary walk up the empty street tell us not only that he *must* fight Miller but that he has to do it in a certain way, playing by certain rules. Even Miller and his henchmen move in formal order and make symbolic gestures, the most significant of which is a gunman's shattering a shop window to steal a woman's bonnet—an act that validates Kane's prediction that if Miller wins neither women nor property will be safe, and that coincidentally warns Kane of the gang's presence. The ritual proceeds through passages of quick-draw confrontation, chases, and ambushes (which visually echo similar passages in earlier Westerns).[15] At the end, Kane's moral vindication is perfected, first by the "conversion" of his Quaker wife—who grabs a gun and shoots one of Miller's men in the back—then by a "captivity/rescue" in which Kane kills Miller while Miller is holding Mrs. Kane as a shield.

In the classic town-tamer Western, Kane's personal redemption would have been mirrored in the triumph of the community. But the social implications of Kane's victory are anti-canonical. Instead of vindicating Kane discredits the community, which proves itself unworthy of the sacrifices he has made for it. At the end, Kane contemptuously drops his badge in the dust at the mayor's feet and rides out of town. The people have been saved, but they have less value than the man who saved them.

High Noon is usually interpreted as an allegory, from a leftist perspective, of Hollywood's surrender to McCarthyism. From this perspective Miller's return is a metaphorical way of identifying McCarthyism with Fascism: the same people who in an earlier and less prosperous time had risen up to defeat the enemy have now grown too comfortable or complacent to risk their lives and fortunes for the public good. This reading is true to Foreman's intentions, and it makes sense; but it does not exhaust the film's ideological utility. The same reading works equally well from a rightist or Cold War perspective: the new aggressions of totalitarian Communism represent a "return" of totalitarian Fascism, and the fatuous self-interestedness of Hadleyville's citizens makes concrete those fears about the American public's will to fight that darkened the thoughts of Truman/Acheson and Sheridan/Yorke.

The popular impact of *High Noon* was undoubtedly helped by the fact that its political suggestions incorporated both ends of the ideological spectrum. But it is important to note that the film does not resort to ambiguity to resolve its ideological dilemma. It forthrightly adopts a solution that emphasizes the moral privilege and entitlement to power of the man of superior knowledge, courage, and capability, and it denigrates the moral and historical claims of popular democracy. Beneath the "left" perspective of the gunfighter film and the "right" perspective of the cavalry film is a common ideological structure that devalues "democracy" as an instrument of progress and declares that the only effective instrument for constructive historical action is a gun in the hands of the right man.

A Good Man with a Gun: Shane *(1953)*

This principle is rendered as an aphorism or slogan in one of the most successful Westerns of the 1950s, George Stevens' *Shane*. In response to the "redemptive woman's" wish that all guns and violence be banished from the valley, Shane replies: "A gun is just a tool, Marian. It's as good or as bad as the man that uses it." The underlying message of the narrative is even stronger: a "good man with a gun" is in every sense the best of men—an armed redeemer who is the sole vindicator of the "liberties of the people," the "indispensable man" in the quest for progress.

The narrative of *Shane* takes off from what appears at first to be a conventionally "progressive" premise. The homesteaders in "the valley" are fighting for their land against Ryker, an old-fashioned cattle baron. Ryker's wealth depends on the "wasteful" system of open-range grazing, and all the law he has ever needed was made with his guns. The homesteaders represent both economic advancement and political democracy. Their farms prosper through the intensive use of irrigation and scientific cattle-breeding, and their society is based on cooperation and is directed by democratic community meetings. The farmers are led by Joe Starrett (Van Heflin), father of little Joey (Brandon DeWilde) and husband of Marian (Jean Arthur). Starrett is headstrong and willful, a natural leader who through most of the narrative leads by persuasion and consent. Ryker, on the other hand, rules by pure intimidation. He is so used to living by the gun that he congratulates himself that up till now he has never had anyone murdered; but the pressure to fill a big government beef contract has him over a barrel, and he must win at all costs.

This is the situation into which the lonely figure of Shane (Alan Ladd) comes riding. Seen from the first through the worshiping eyes of the boy Joey, he is instantly recognizable as a special man, a hero. He wears neat buckskins and a gunbelt that is quietly (but noticeably) elegant. The impression of latent gentility is confirmed by the quiet courtesy of his speech, the smoothness of his manners. The Starretts treat him with a deference that is as much due to his air of refinement as to his generosity and steely courage in aiding them against Ryker.

Shane incarnates the suggestion of "nobility" that invests all such characters, beginning with the Virginian. Suggestions of his aristocratic nature were part of the characterization in the Jack Schaefer novel on which the film was based. But Schaefer's Shane wears the fine clothes associated with high-toned gamblers like Doc Holliday in *My Darling Clementine*. Stevens preserves the distinction of class but gives it a different inflection by dressing Shane in buckskins, which make him seem a figure from America's buffalo-hunting frontier past, rather than a refugee from the urban future. Nor is there any clear indication (as with Ringo) that he has ever been an outlaw. Ryker calls him "gunfighter," and the abstract purity of that identification is not compromised by association with any specific kind of work.[16]

Thus quite early in the narrative, the historistic and naturalistic references are offset by a perspective (identified with Joey's point of view) that insists on abstracting and stylizing every person and action and looking through history to find a mythic archetype. This tendency is given force by Stevens' alternation of naturalistic and folkloristic scenes (the July 4th dance, the funeral of Stonewall) with scenes whose elements are exaggerated and distorted to achieve an "epic" effect. When the principal males in the story are in troubled throught, the skies darken; when they fight, the animals in the corral go crazy, leaping over the fences as lightning flashes in the sky—as if they were Homeric demigods and Nature itself were responsive to their power. So too with Wilson (Jack Palance)—the huge, cold-eyed, evil gunfighter whom Ryker has hired. As he enters Grafton's saloon, a dog gets up and slinks away. Wilson's slow passage into the room is viewed from a low angle that makes him look gigantic. His movement is broken by a "wipe," a formal device that usually suggests an extended passage of time, as if time itself were deformed by Wilson's weight and menace.

In *Shane*, stylization of dress, movement, and behavior is the visual sign that identifies both the powerful and the professional. And the value that is vested in the men who have these attributes is apart from and perhaps higher than the "progressive" and "democratic" values the film nominally espouses. This principle is visualized in the first meeting between Shane and Wilson. Ryker has come to give Starrett one last chance to "be reasonable"—that is, to sell his land on extremely favorable terms and to become an employee of Ryker. All Starrett will have to sacrifice is his personal independence and his democratic principles—none of the other farmers will get the same deal. Ryker's paternalist intentions are revealed by his addressing his speech to little Joey. Starrett replies that he is a grown man, proud enough to work for himself, and too honorable to betray his community. Their argument degenerates into polemics about "rights" and "progress." Ryker reminds Starrett it was men like him who cleared the Indians off the land; Starrett answers that Ryker is a primitive himself, that farmers use the land more efficiently. . . .

And while this palaver is going on—raising matters that would be at the heart of any "progressive epic"—the camera is watching Shane and Wilson size each other up. They say nothing; they merely look and smile a little smile. They know that the talk of rights and wrongs has become meaningless. Pride and economics make it certain that neither Ryker nor Starrett can back down. Violent force alone will settle the issue, and the gunfighters are the ones who best understand that truth. Ryker and Starrett and their original objectives are reduced to the mere premises from which the action will arise, but the action itself will be entrusted to professionals.

The connection between stylization, professionalism, and power is emphasized in the gunfight between Wilson and Stonewall (Elisha Cook, Jr.). Stonewall is a gamecock ex-Confederate who believes that words matter and is therefore vulnerable to Wilson's provocation. The exchanged insults ("Southern trash," "Low-down Yankee liar") mean nothing to Wilson: words (like guns) are merely tools for accomplishing his task. As they move toward the moment of drawing pistols, Stonewall picks his way through the slop but Wilson moves gracefully across an elevated "stage" (the sidewalk). His stylishness is the sign of his power. The evil inherent in his beautiful display is not fully manifest till the end. Wilson is so much faster that he can hold the gun on Stonewall for a long second, savoring the little man's horrible amazement before he blows him into the muck with one shot. Shane has the same elegance, but he lacks Wilson's self-indulgent sadism.

The politics of "saving the valley" now become "stylized" as well—reduced to the formally necessary confrontation of two professionals who belong to neither of the contending classes. Wilson has now taken Ryker's place as the farmers' most significant enemy. Although he is nominally Ryker's "tool," he is in fact the objectification of Ryker's power, which has always been based on force. But only Shane is "equal" to Wilson in professionalism. It follows that Starrett too must abdicate his role as leader and potential hero in favor of his "hired man," Shane. Those who have the power to act have the responsibility to act, perhaps in the name of the community but if need be against the will of the community. Starrett himself acts on that principle when he puts himself ahead of the community and insists on going alone to confront Wilson. But Shane, knowing that Starrett cannot hope to beat Wilson, substitutes his own will for Starrett's and takes the burden of Starrett's fight on himself. When Starrett tries to stop him, Shane defeats him by unfairly drawing his gun and knocking him out. Once again the hero breaks the law (the code of fair play) and risks his standing with the community or family (Joey) in order to meet the responsibilities of the pre-eminently powerful man.

Shane's confrontation with Wilson confirms the validity of his knowledge and his principles. He and Wilson face each other in the bar. Though there is talk with Ryker, the camera tells us that the sole point of the talk is to create the proper occasion for the final shootout. The exchange between Shane and Wilson is formal and stylized, and both men appear conscious that they are going through a familiar, predictable, and even trite, but nonetheless essential, ritual. Shane says he's heard of Wilson; Wilson asks what he's heard. Shane smiles and deliberately repeats Stonewall's phrase: "I heard that you're a low-down Yankee liar." Wilson smiles back: "Prove it." The exchange of smiles establishes their equality as professionals, and that equation remains valid despite the moral difference between them. All that will count now is action, and action follows in a rapid series of cuts as Wilson draws and Shane kills him. Shane then spins and cuts down Ryker and his foreman.

These killings are sanctioned as acts of sacrifice, because Shane does not stay to enjoy the fruits of triumph. He rides off alone, with Joey crying after him, begging him to "Come back!" Shane's words to Joey declare that the value of his action lies in its saving Joey's parents, their farm, and (implicitly) the progressive and domestic order they represent. But Joey doesn't seem to accept the sacrifice as given, because Shane means something to him that weighs equal with his love of his parents. And Joey's feeling is echoed by Marian's. We understand from the beginning that though she is committed to husband and child, she has fallen in love with Shane, and he with her. Joey's naive final cry, "Mother wants you!" reminds us of this and emphasizes this aspect of Shane's sacrifice. Their sublimated romance reproduces the exact Western equivalent of chivalric love, with Shane as a stainless Lancelot and Marian a chaste Guinevere—a suggestion that reinforces the impression of Shane's nobility. Even Joe Starrett understands this, in his paternal fashion. Contemplating the likelihood of his own death in the gunfight with Ryker and Wilson, he tells Marian that he understands her feelings for Shane and that if he dies Shane will take better care of her than he ever could. Indeed, Shane's nobility, his perfection of style and manner and *virtu*, are so much beyond the human scale of Starrett that we (like Joey) tend to value him equal to (if not above) the nominal objectives for whose sake he makes his murderous sacrifice.[17]

Like the populist outlaw, Shane acts as the farm community's surrogate in its confrontation with propertied evil. But the pseudo-history and politics of heroic surrogacy in the gunfighter movie are very different from those in the outlaw Western. *Jesse James* spends most of its narrative describing and analyzing the outlaw's response to oppression and injustice and relates those concerns to the life of the outlaw's community, showing how Jesse emerges from the heart of that community, serves it, then goes too far and is cast out of it. The hero of *Shane* is also a skilled fighter who assists small farmers against a tyrannical proprietor. But Shane arrives from outside, and his past is concealed. His motives for helping the farmers are chivalric and romantic. He is the only character in the movie who never acts (or hesitates to act) from self-interested motives. But because Shane's motives for helping the farmers are unique and arise from no visible history or social background, they appear to be expressions of his nature, signs of a nobility which is independent of history, like the attributes of a "higher race."[18] Shane is never part of the community, and his superior values are not seen as belonging to the community. He is an aristocrat of violence, an alien from a more glamorous world, who is better than those he helps and is finally not accountable to those for whom he sacrifices himself.

The Gunfighter Mystique

The success of *Shane* ratified the prominent position of the gunfighter in the Western movie pantheon, and Westerns featuring figures modeled on Ringo, Will Kane, and Shane proliferated over the next decade. As a heroic type, the gunfighter was both apt as a representation of contemporary moods and conflicts and adaptable enough to serve a wide range of plot-types, situations, historical periods, and geographical settings. Unlike a Wyatt Earp or a Jesse James, the gunfighter was not identified with or restricted to a particular historical period or social function. King was vague about what Ringo actually did for a living; King's imitators found it possible and credible to imagine many different kinds of working life for men of Ringo's style, temperament, and professional skill. The list includes such occupations as bounty-hunter, hired assassin, mercenary, and even certain kinds of lawman.

What establishes their kinship to Ringo is first of all their speed with a gun and the professionalism they bring to the use of weapons. Next is the fact that we see them operating in a "terminal" environment, standing on a historical border between the world in which things were still "possible" for them and a world in which they and their profession are becoming outdated. Their story will have to reach its climax in a fast-draw shoot-out, in which their calling will reach its pinnacle of achievement—followed by its exhaustion. And they will become critically conscious, before the end, of just what has gone wrong with them and their world. Irony is as essential to the gunfighter's heroic style as his skill with weapons. It tells us that, like the "man who knows Indians," he has "seen through" the mystifications of society. But the object of his irony is American society itself—the sacred "people" of the democracy for whose sake the hero of the "progressive" Western idealistically risked his own life and took the lives of enemies.

It may be more useful to think of the term "gunfighter" as describing a style of action appropriate to a certain kind of world-view rather than a specific social role in a particular historical frame. The "cults" of the outlaw, the Indian, and the cavalry are constituted by the repetition of a particular kind of story, setting, historical reference, and ideological problem. The "cult of the gunfighter" is constituted by the use of a particular character and style of action to resolve a wide range of conflicts in a nearly limitless variety of settings. The outward form of the gunfighter style emphasizes artistic professionalism in the use of weapons, but what justifies and directs that professionalism is a particular state of mind, a "gunfighter" understanding of "how the world works." That understanding is essentially "hard-boiled": the world is a hostile place, human motives are rarely good, and outcomes depend not on right but on the proper deployment of might.

The fictive politics of gunfighter Westerns is worth attending to, because its symbols contribute to a public discourse on the role of power and force in American political and social life. The substitution of a glamorous and/or hard-bitten professional—at once a knight-errant and a mercenary—for a populist rebel as the model of an American hero is consistent with the rightward ideological shift we have already noted in the war-mythology of the cavalry film. To the extent that the movie-making community may be taken as a representative cultural elite, it suggests a drift of the ideological imagination away from the populist values and symbols of the late New Deal toward a politics based on hierarchy and the empowerment of expertise. In the traditional Western, the imperative for violence was usually balanced by countervailing values, often identified with women: the moral superiority of peace to war, cooperation and free consent to compulsion. Although female symbols retain their nominal sanctity, in Cold War Westerns—particularly the cavalry and gunfighter Westerns—the moral balance shifts decisively in favor of male violence and force. In the world of the gunfighter and the "man who knows Indians," moral suasion without violent force to back it is incompetent to achieve its civilizing ends; it is foolish at best, at worst a species of complicity with evil.

Over the next decade the gunfighter figure recurred in a wide variety of films. The *Shane* plot-formula of a gunfighter from outside aiding a helpless community was perhaps the most frequently used. Representative titles include *Man Without a Star* (1955); *Tall T* (1957); *Proud Rebel* (1958); *At Gunpoint* (1955); *Johnny Concho* (1956); *Man from Del Rio* (1956); *Fury at Showdown, Gun for a Coward, Gun Glory* (1957); and *Last of the Fast Guns* (1958). There were also numerous films that showed ex-gunfighters who had retired into sheriff-ing or even civilian pursuits (doctor, lawyer, editor, storekeeper) but had taken up the gun again when their town (or a good woman) is threatened: *Fort Worth* (1951); *Fastest Gun Alive* (1956); *Hanging Tree* (1959). Imitations of *High Noon*, and recastings of the OK Corral story which emphasized the quick-draw side of Earp and Holliday, were also popular; *Law and Order* (1953), *A Man Alone* (1955), *Top Gun* (1955), *Wichita* (1955), *Gunfight at the OK Corral* (1957), *The Tin Star* (1958), *Rio Bravo* (1959), and *Warlock* (1959). There were also new versions of classic outlaw stories which emphasize gunfighter style, as in *Cole Younger, Gunfighter* (1958) and the growing list of Bill the Kid films, including *Parson and the Outlaw* (1957) and *Left Handed Gun* (1958). The professional bounty-hunter figured in a number of films—a type that combined aspects of the "revenger" and the mercenary-killer, whose problems and worldview are essentially those of the gunfighter: *Naked Spur* (1953), *The Bounty Hunter* (1954), and *The Tin Star* (1958). In addition to law-and-order themes, these films took up psychological concerns like father/son and sibling rivalry, the relationship of an old gunfighter to a young one, or the paranoia born of a life of violence: *Saddle the Wind* (1958), *Gunman's Walk* (1958), *No Name on the Bullet* (1959).

As the civil-rights movement began to have an impact on American politics and culture in the late 1950s, racial issues were addressed in "gunfighter" terms. The subplot of Anthony Mann's *The Tin Star* involves the bounty-hunter/gunfighter (Henry Fonda) in a romance with a White woman ostracized by the townsfolk because she has been married to (and borne a child by) an American Indian. An equally interesting case is Paramount's *Walk Like a Dragon* (1960), which deals with an interracial love-triangle involving a rancher, the Chinese woman he saves from sale as a prostitute, and the Chinese man who loves her. Much energy is devoted to exploring the town's bigoted response to the girl and the prospect of her marriage to the rancher. Before he can claim the woman, the Chinese must become able to confront the rancher as man to man; and he must also become an American, since the woman refuses to return to China. He accomplishes both by studying to become a gunfighter. He apprentices himself to a black-clad fast-draw artist who instructs him so well that he is able to kill his teacher. Then, dressed in the all-black "uniform" of the gunfighter, he confronts the rancher, who (it turns out) was the teacher's teacher in the fast-draw arts. Tragedy (and interracial marriage) is averted when the woman declares her love for the Chinese man. But the role of gunfighting is crucial to the outcome. It is the means by which the oppressed victim gains equality and the immigrant is Americanized. The terms of American equality and identity are defined by the arts of the gunfighter.

But from an ideological perspective, the most significant expression of gunfighter style was the new subgenre of the "Mexico Western," which sets the gunfighter in a story-frame redolent of foreign-policy issues, blends his traits with those of the cavalry commander, and envisions him as an American "freedom-fighter" battling the forces of oppression and "alien ideologies" in the Third World.

13 Imagining Third World Revolutions

The "Zapata Problem" and the Counterinsurgency Scenario, 1952–1954

In 1953 Cold War politics took a decisive turn. The successes of the Marshall Plan and NATO effectively limited Communist expansion in Europe, and the West's refusal to intervene in the Eastern Bloc uprisings of 1953–56 made it clear there would be no attempt to "roll back the Iron Curtain." The nuclear balance of terror and the Korean War stalemate suggested that military confrontation between the major powers was unlikely to yield advantage to either side. The death of Stalin and his successors' preoccupation with internal difficulties disposed the Soviet leadership to a "thaw" in political relations with Europe. But the stakes of superpower rivalry remained potentially unlimited, and it was logical for each side to perceive any conflict, in any region of the globe, as directly affecting the bipolar balance of power.

It was also apparent that Cold War competition would be transferred to the "Third World," where underdevelopment and the disorders of decolonization provided a favorable environment for anti-Western and Communist political movements. The postwar wave of anticolonial and nationalist revolutions began in China and Southeast Asia in 1945–50 and then spread to Africa and Latin America. In particular, the successes of anti-American and leftist parties in Iran and Guatemala threatened Western access to Persian Gulf oil and American economic and strategic interests in Latin America.[1]

The Communist victory in China in 1949 was an ominous precedent for the kind of struggle that might emerge in the Third World. Under the leadership of Mao Tse Tung, the Chinese Communists had vindicated a major revision of Marxist/Leninist doctrine. The orthodox or Soviet theory held that revolutionary change must be based on an urban proletariat, with the peasantry playing a passive or regressive role. Mao turned this orthodoxy on its head by basing his successful revolution on the peasantry and using control of the countryside to isolate and overwhelm the urban power centers held by the Kuomintang.

Although American policy-makers perceived Maoism as the addition of a new technique to the Soviet Union's offensive assets, events would show that this interpretation was simplistic. Maoist China would emerge in the next decade as the Soviet Union's rival, with its own agenda for political revolution and economic development.[2] But although American planners may have overestimated the unity of the Communist powers and their ability to direct and subordinate revolutions in the emerging nations, they were correct in perceiving that revolutionary movements based on the peasantry were bound to develop and that their colonial histories would probably give them an anti-Western bias.[3]

Like the Truman administration, Eisenhower and his advisers believed that the United States would have to develop a strategic response to this threat, since the nation's European allies lacked the resources and the political will to do so. But the attempts of the Eisenhower administration to reorient policy were complicated by a lack of clear precedents and the contradictory character of its political mandate. Although the 1952 Republican campaign had scored the Democrats' supposed "softness" on Communism, the Republicans owed their electoral victory in part to public reaction against the war in Korea. Traditional isolationism was discredited, but the leadership of both parties believed that the American public was still profoundly reluctant to support the higher taxation and expenditure, and the risk of war, entailed by our Great Power role. It had taken the USSR's development of atomic weaponry, Stalin's aggressive moves in the Berlin crisis of 1948, and Communist political successes in Western Europe to create the sense of peril that won public support for the Marshall Plan and NATO. It had taken the invasion of Korea and Truman's pre-emptive use of presidential power to gain public support for the re-mobilization of military strength. But it was by no means clear that the public would support with equal consistency and understanding a broad-ranging and expensive competition with Communism in a swarm of new nations across three continents.[4]

Nor was it clear what the specific terms and procedures of that competition would be. Unlike the protection of Europe, this problem could not be handled by maintaining an overall balance of military forces. The Korean experience was taken as a warning that the use of American arms in such regions produced ambiguous results at nearly intolerable costs. What the American government needed to discover or create in the decolonizing world was a "third force," neither "Communist" nor colonialist, that would function as a native "counterpart" to American leadership and that would embody the historic compromise between capitalism and socialism which the United States had achieved in the New Deal.

However, it was not yet clear whether "discovery" or "creation" was the appropriate metaphor for the American task. Had the indigenous cultures of the emerging nations already produced counterparts in business and government who would be naturally drawn to American values and methods and who would be ready and able to work with us? Or would it be necessary to create counterparts where none existed? If the former, then it might be possible to achieve the Americanization of the Third World relatively cheaply, by supporting those counterparts with financial aid, or even (in extreme cases) by engineering a *coup* on their behalf, as the CIA would do in Iran and Guatemala. But such surgical operations would succeed in the long term only if the "American" element represented a substantial and genuinely native tendency. In the absence of such a counterpart class, it would be necessary to engage in what would later be called "nation-building"—a task difficult to conceive, let alone budget, which the Eisenhower administration was therefore reluctant to undertake.

At this relatively early stage in the development of postcolonial political conflict, extrapolation necessarily ran ahead of the available data. Before the American government could formulate a policy toward revolution in the emerging nations, it would be necessary to *imagine* a scenario of the normal causes, composition, and course of such a revolution and the kinds of party and leader it might produce, and to project a role for the United States to play in determining the course of the developmental scenario.

The policy-makers faced an imaginative task analogous to that of a screenwriting team which has been given a setting and a situation and is asked to turn them into a narrative that can be acted out. For the movie scenarists, the problem could be resolved by canvassing the conventions of genre, in which mythic narratives are encoded as a set of standard models for heroic action. Imaginative work of this kind involves both the interpretation of "hard data" according to "objective standards" and the speculative canvassing and deployment of the full range of available interpretive procedures, including those that we have identified with the processes of myth-making. Mythic symbols encode paradigms or programs of real-world action, drawn from past experience or historical memory, which are projected as hypotheses about the outcomes of prospective action.

Historical precedents are also encoded and recalled in the form of myths, and policy-makers canvass them for the same reasons that scenarists review the generic repertoire: to sample a range of interpretive models and alternative resolutions.[5]

A case in point is the discussion at an inauguration-eve meeting of President-elect Eisenhower and his top advisers. The immediate question was whether Eisenhower should name Moscow as the directing intelligence behind all modern revolutions. But the discussion soon moved to address the ideological and political impasse that hindered the development of a coherent policy toward the Third World. On the one hand (as Eisenhower at first suggested), the revolutions then in progress seemed clearly inimical to American interests. Most were directed or strongly influenced by Communists; and whatever their nominal leadership, they tended to polarize the political alternatives into a choice between a Red terror and a colonial or military despotism—neither of which produced regimes that were both stable and friendly to the United States. On the other hand, to simply oppose all such revolutions would be to deny the genuine grievances and irrepressible political aspirations they expressed, and to confirm the Communists' claim that socialism and anticolonial nationalism were one. Though they disliked the revolutions they knew, Eisenhower's advisers were unwilling to concede that the word "revolution," with its connotations of rapid, liberating, and progressive change, could no longer be used by an American President with safety and authenticity.

To resolve the paradox, they canvassed their repertoire of historical cases in search of a usable paradigm of decolonization. The Philippines might have occurred to someone as a model, but it did not—perhaps because the active Communist insurgency there made the Philippines an instance of the problem rather than a model of the solution.[6] It was Eisenhower himself who invoked the Mexican Revolution of 1910–34 and found in it a metaphor of the present situation. A peasant revolution had developed there in response to the Diaz dictatorship's abuses of power and the immiserated condition of the countryside. Although that revolution had experienced Red and White Terrors and phases of socialist radicalism, in the end a regime had emerged that was both responsive to popular needs and compatible with American interests: "In Mexico today they still talk about the revolution like the second coming of the Lord. While it hasn't worked out too well, nevertheless it is better than they had."

The Secretary of Defense-designate, industrialist Charles Wilson, amplified the suggestion that revolution might be productive of necessary change and suggested that there was a counterpart in our own traditions: "We had a little revolution in our own country. . . ." Wilson thus raised the possibility that the proper role for the United States was to counter Communist revolutions by fostering American-style revolutions. But this provoked rejoinders from Eisenhower and Secretary of State-designate John Foster Dulles that our revolution had hardly been "little" and had certainly been violent. The discussion thus came back to the initial premise: that the tendency of modern revolutions was toward Communism and the imposition of a "Red Terror" rather than an American-style compromise of class differences.[7]

The discussion ended with a decision to evade the issue by excising the word "revolution" from the text of Eisenhower's inaugural address. But the invocation of revolutionary Mexico as a metaphoric representation of the problem opens a view of the underlying ideological ambivalences that influenced the imagination of policy alternatives.

The appropriateness of the metaphor derives from the appearance of important cognate features linking Mexico to both the Third World and the United States. The metaphor of kinship in the epithet "sister republic" works in two directions. It allows Charles Wilson to read the relative success of the Mexican Revolution as a validation of the positive worth of the American revolutionary tradition. But when Eisenhower and Dulles focus on the negative elements of revolution (radicalism and "violence"), the metaphor suggests that the critique of Mexican revolutionary practice applies as well to our own *American* revolutionary tradition. As an ideological symbol, "Mexico" is a *double-acting* metaphor. In speculating on and developing the ideological and political implications of the metaphoric representation of Mexico as a "model" of revolution, Eisenhower and his advisers were not only imagining a scenario of Third World revolution; they were also forwarding the process of criticizing and transforming our own domestic ideology to make it more compatible with the demands of playing our world-power role.[8]

At the same time that Eisenhower's administration was developing a policy scenario for American engagement in the Third World,

Hollywood was inventing the scenario for a new kind of Western whose plot and setting would address the same ideological concerns. Hollywood also remembered the Mexican Revolution and found it especially apt as a setting in which timely questions could be addressed through the traditional symbolism of the Western. The result was the creation of a subtype of the Western in which a group of American gunfighters crosses the border into Mexico during a time of social disruption or revolutionary crisis to help the peasants defeat an oppressive ruler, warlord, or bandit.[9] In the process they transform "Mexican" society, and the American values they bring with them across the border are subjected to a searching test and a critical revision. The plot-premise of the "Mexico Western" mirrors the concrete themes and problematics of American engagement in the Third World, and its reflexivity mirrors the transformation of our domestic ideology and institutions in response to the exigencies of Cold War power politics.

This "Mexico" scenario differs radically from the border-war scenarios of Ford's cavalry trilogy. Those films treat the Rio Grande as a fixed and perilous border, the home or refuge of red savages whose raids threaten the safety, even the existence, of American society. In *Fort Apache* the river is a figurative Elbe, across which enemies can still negotiate (as Soviets and Americans could before 1948). In *Rio Grande* the river is a Yalu or an Iron Curtain, which can only be crossed in arms for battles of rescue and/or annihilation. The "Mexico" of counterinsurgency films is a potentially "Americanizable" land.

The elements that would constitute the "Mexico Western" formula began to appear in the late 40s and early 50s and were brought together in the production of *Vera Cruz* (1954)—the same year in which the Eisenhower administration formulated the doctrine of counterinsurgency and covert operations that would define future policy toward revolution in the Third World. The evolution of the "Mexico Western" proceeded in step with the development of American policy in the struggle for hearts and minds in the Third World and reached its height of popularity during the Vietnam War.

The Mexico Western may be likened to a "thought-experiment," similar in kind to the hypothetical scenario-projection that characterizes the conceptual phase of policy-making. Although it was at best a proximate representation of the empirical reality of counterinsurgency warfare, as a thought-experiment it nonetheless highlighted contradictory elements in that policy and anticipated their destructive effect on its practice.

This is not to say that changes in the Western genre were determined by the political agenda of the Eisenhower and later the Kennedy/Johnson administrations; nor that the transformations of public mythology effected in the movies determined the Eisenhower administration's choice of priorities and its operational style. Imaginative processes in the policy-making and genre-making communities differ in the way they define their initiating problems and in the outcomes they envision. Policy scenarios are dominated, first and last, by real-world referents which may be interpreted by the use of metaphors drawn from the fictive structures of myth and ideology but which begin and end with action in the material and political world. Movie scenarios arise from attempts to resolve problems native to the world of fictive referents that constitute the genre-map of the industry at a given moment; they issue in works of fiction, whose projections and revisions *primarily* refer to the fictive world. If in the conceptual stage both policy scenarios and movie scenarios may be likened to thought-experiments, they are nonetheless subject to radically different kinds of proof. While the movie scenario is played out in the controlled environment of a purely hypothetical or fictional world, the policy scenario is played out and tested in the unforgiving and finally uncontrollable medium of material reality and human action.

What we see during this 1950–57 period is the parallel response of two different ideology-producing communities to the dilemmas and contradictions of the new Cold War. The policy scenarios of counterinsurgency and the generic scenarios of the Mexico Western developed in parallel, deriving their cognate features from the fact that, as citizens of the republic in the 1950s, their manufacturers shared a common knowledge of recent history and a common set of social and political concerns and as participants in American culture shared a common language of myth and ideology.

Coloring the Looking-Glass: Mexico as Mythic Space, 1912–1952

Like Eisenhower, Hollywood was reminded of Mexico when it thought about the problem of Third World revolutions. Mexico was the Third World country Hollywood knew best, both as a place in which to make movies and as a subject.[10] The earliest images of Mexico in American fiction films (1910–16) were based on dime/pulp-novel stereotypes and the regional prejudices of California and the Southwest. Mexicans are seen as a mixed or "mongrel" race, combining Indian and Latin elements, by turns comic and cruel, sensual and indolent.[11] Mexicans and half-Mexicans were favorite villains in the formula Westerns of William S. Hart, and the Rio Grande was seen as a moral as well as a physical border. The land across the line was primarily a refuge for renegades.[12]

This racial symbolism was given a specifically political charge by the outbreak of the Mexican Revolution in 1910. As a revolution nextdoor it became a favored subject for both documentary and fiction filmmakers. The presence of newsreel cameras was tolerated by federal generals and was actively courted by the rebel Pancho Villa, who recognized the propaganda value of the new medium. At first, Hollywood expressed its friendly response to the Revolution by assimilating its heroes to the formulas of pulp-novel and nickelodeon melodrama.[13] Its attitude changed, however, after 1913, when the murder of President Madero and the dictatorship of General Huerta destroyed the hope for reform under a moderate or liberal regime. Huerta's coup provoked an increasingly radical revolutionary movement with numerous factions, several of which had social and economic agendas that directly threatened American interests. With the outbreak of the Great War in 1914, German agents became active in Mexico, hoping to create border problems that would keep the United States out of the European struggle. When Villa's forces raided Columbus, New Mexico, in 1915, American hostility to the Revolution became overt. In 1916 President Wilson dispatched the Punitive Expedition against Villa under cavalryman John J. Pershing, who had distinguished himself in the Apache country and as a counterguerrilla fighter against the Moros in the Philippines.[14]

Fiction films made during this period reflect the political shift but suggest that it was motivated as much by fear of domestic radicalism as by concern with Mexico. In W. S. Hart's *The Patriot* (1916) an American veteran, dispossessed by an unscrupulous capitalist and an unjust government, joins the revolutionists under "Pancho Zapilla" (a conflation of Villa and Zapata). He redeems himself by resisting Zapilla's attack on an American border town (a reference to the Columbus raid).[15] Antipathy for the Revolution was also expressed in a reversion to earlier stereotypes of *Barbarous Mexico* (the title of a 1913 documentary).[16] The Hearst newspapers described, and the Hearst Motion Picture Company depicted, Pancho Villa and Emiliano Zapata as respectively a "barbarian" and "The Attila of the South," implying that the struggle in Mexico mirrored the savage war of Huns and Romans, with civilization itself at stake.[17] The 1916–17 serial *Patria* sees Mexico as a key battle in what Stoddard later called the "rising tide of color"; it represents Mexican revolutionaries as agents of a Japanese plot to make Mexico a base for the "mongolization" of the United States.[18] A similar interpretation of the Revolution was developed by Blair Coan, a salesman in Mexico for Bronco Billy Anderson's Essanay Film Company. Coan "uncovered" a plot to use revolutionary Mexico (and "certain of [our] big labor organizations") as a base for the Bolshevization of America: "Mexico is today, was yesterday, and will be tomorrow the most fertile incubator of Bolshevik revolution on the American continent."[19] This would be a recurrent theme in antirevolutionary polemics throughout the 20s and 30s, as Mexican governments nationalized American-owned oil companies and sheltered exiled revolutionaries like Leon Trotsky.[20]

Hollywood lost interest in Mexican politics after 1920, and until 1934 its treatments of Mexico were shaped by the requirements of genre. In the Western, Mexico remained the ultimate "border," a refuge for outlaws and renegade Indians.[21] But the revival of radical politics during the Depression also revived interest in our sister republic's experience of revolution.

In 1933 MGM purchased the rights to *Viva Villa! A Recovery of the Real Pancho Villa, Peon . . . Bandit . . . Soldier . . . Patriot*, written by Edgcumb Pinchon, an English leftist and sympathizer with the movements of Villa and Zapata.[22] MGM's film of *Viva Villa*! (1934), directed by Jack Conway and written by Ben Hecht, follows Pinchon's interpretation of Villa but transforms the historical figures into allegorical types. Madero is both the liberal reformer and "the Christ-fool," a sacred martyr for "democracy" who prefers to let himself be killed rather than seek protection in an immoral or unconstitutional use of power. The military men who kill Madero are jack-booted incarnations of the principle of might and of the bigotry and caste-pride of "bad" aristocrats. Although Villa is presented as the archetype of the modern peasant revolutionary, Hecht's script and Wallace Beery's performance interpret the revolutionary through the standard comic devices of ethnic stereotype: he is a slob, a womanizer, a buffoon, alternating between indolence and violent action, emotionally erratic and subject to fits of unthinking cruelty. Nonetheless, this "primitive" exterior masks the serious and consistent vision of a genuine class warrior.

But though the Mexican inflection makes Villa's ideas seem alien and radical, we sympathize with them because they are in fact "primitive" expressions of ideas that are recognizably (North) American.

Villa becomes a bandit and a rebel after his sister is raped and his father whipped to death by the *hacendado* who has stolen his people's land. His revolutionary agrarianism is not very different from the "movie-populism" of *Jesse James, Stagecoach*, and *Grapes of Wrath*. Its goal is still "a little piece of land," a "place of my own" on which to raise corn and cattle and children. Villa's politics of direct action merely anticipates Jesse James's "I'm not *thinking* about doing anything. I'm *doing* it!"[23] His strategic and moral doctrine are eminently "pragmatic." If the end is good, one must use any means that will work in order to achieve it, even if this requires violating the rules of conventional warfare and the Geneva Convention.[24] In all this Villa is the opposite of the idealistic "Christ-fool" Madero. But his amoral pragmatism is justified, first because he literally worships the "Christ-fool" and makes himself the instrument of Madero's purposes, but finally because history proves him right.

The most significant difference between the Mexican and the American versions of the social bandit is expressed through the metaphor of sexuality, which functions in both *Viva Villa*! and *Jesse James* as a way of characterizing the hero's relation to the conventional values of his society. Jesse's monogamous love for Zee is a potentially redemptive link to middle-class and domestic values. Villa's sexuality is rampantly *macho*, the erotic expression of the willful violence that makes him an effective revolutionary fighter. The script acclimates us to this unfamiliar heroic attribute by treating Villa's lust comically. But after Madero's assassination, Villa marks his commitment to a more uncompromising class warfare by sexually assaulting the aristocratic sister (Fay Wray) of a liberal landowner (Donald Woods)—former supporters of Madero who had reluctantly acquiesced in Huerta's *coup*. The sanctity of the "White woman" is partly reaffirmed by the conclusion of the film, which attributes Villa's assassination to the landowner's need to avenge his sister. But in the assault scene itself, Villa's hatred of the landowners is presented sympathetically, and the assault is seen as a tragic necessity of revolution rather than a savage or gratuitous act of cruelty.[25]

Viva Villa! was an extremely successful film whose images and narrative formula shaped all future treatments of Mexico and the Revolution.[26] The combination of *bandido* style and populist politics in Beery's Villa became the standard Hollywood interpretation not only of Villa but of Mexican revolutionaries in general. In a "Villa" figure, American producers and audiences could identify as "revolutionary" ideas that were not really very far left of the tenets of movie-populism and New Deal reform. And they could excuse, even enjoy, the radical violence of "Villa's" methods, because they were identified with the alien mythic space called "Mexico."

The political utility of the Mexican setting was elaborately developed and extended in *Juarez* (1939), a Warner Bros. production whose genesis shows how close relations between the policy-making elite and the Hollywood elite could become. In 1938 Jack Warner (with other members of the Producers' Association) accompanied the U.S. delegation to an inter-American conference in Lima, called to further Roosevelt's "Good Neighbor" policy. Discussions at this conference led to the development of *Juarez* and several other projects designed to persuade Americans of the importance and appropriateness of our Latin ties and (through international distribution) to "take Latin America for the U.S.A."[27]

Juarez approaches the task by making a contemporary political allegory of the Mexican struggle against the French occupation (1863–68), with Emperor Napoleon III as a Gallic Hitler, alternately comic and sinister. The two poles of Mexican politics are represented by Juarez (Paul Muni) and Maximilian (Brian Ahern), the Austrian archduke who becomes Napoleon's puppet-emperor in Mexico. Maximilian and his empress Carlotta (Bette Davis) are represented as sincere and well-meaning representatives of the principle of aristocratic government who become in the end a pair of "Christ-fools." Like Madero, Maximilian promulgates policies of land reform and racial tolerance and pursues them even against the Mexican conservatives who support him.[28] But the fundamentally undemocratic nature of his government and its identification with foreign rule finally compel him to abandon reform and rule by force and cruelty.

Muni's Juarez combines elements of the "Madero" and "Villa" characters, with the latter predominating. He dresses and speaks the enlightened language of a Madero, and his amenability to American liberal values is signified by his veneration of President Lincoln. But he is identified as an Indian, exhibits Villa's iron determination to win his revolution at all costs, and is implacable in his destruction of the "Christ-fool" Maximilian. Thus *Juarez* ratifies the myth of Mexican revolutionary politics promulgated in *Viva Villa!*, which sees the revolutionary as having to choose between ineffectual idealism and the violent pragmatism of the guerrilla chieftain.[29]

Juarez and *Viva Villa!* established "Mexico" as a mythic space in which certain kinds of political themes could be credibly projected, heightened by the association with a historical revolutionary movement, and played out as a thought-experiment in the problems of modern revolution. The typology of Mexican political leadership developed in these films established the imaginative categories with which most future movie versions of the Revolution would operate. It also anticipates the categorization of political leaders and options developed during the 1950s by policy-makers concerned with the problem of Third World Revolution. This typology sees "Mexico" as a nation (and race) whose innate character and economic condition inevitably generate a radical division of society between the wealthy and cultured and the immiserated, primitive peasants. The party of wealth, order, and (corrupt) civilization is represented by a dictator whose style and costume are explicitly military and implicitly fascist. When he is called "Santa Anna" or "Diaz" or "Huerta," he represents either the pure authoritarianism and militarism of the army or the rapacity of the native commercial and landed classes—progressivism gone awry, perhaps because Mexican *bourgeoises* lack the rationality and moderation of our own "middle class." When he is called "Maximilian," he represents the combination of an aristocratic class-tyranny with the alien or "un-American" ideologies of Europe. The peasant revolutionary or "Villa" type represents a polar alternative to the dictator. He expresses both the legitimate aspirations of the peasantry and their terrible rage—the passion that drives them to uncompromising extremes and in the end perverts their own revolution through terror and excess.

Between these two extremes stands the liberal or moderate reformer who offers the hope of a compromise between the excesses of dictatorship and those of a "red terror." When he is called "Madero," this figure links liberal ideology with the mystique of Christian sacrifice; but since "Madero" always fails to achieve his goals, he may also represent the inherent weaknesses of "Mexican" political culture. When he is described in terms suggestive of "Juarez," he links the struggle for democratic procedures with the ideals of racial toleration. *In both versions, this figure incarnates a "double-acting" metaphor: he validates the ideals and practical methods of United States politics by applying them to the Mexican case and thus offers a model of heroic leadership that can work on both sides of the border.*

Although the categories of this political typology can be isolated and defined, they do not always appear in a simple allegorical relation to each other. In creating specific characterizations for new versions of the Mexican story, filmmakers mixed and matched aspects of these different types to give a particular political inflection to their treatment of the theme. As we have seen, the characterization of Juarez as both an American-style liberal and a successful revolutionary was in part achieved by mingling in his character elements of "Madero" and "Villa."

When Hollywood returned to the "Mexico" theme after 1945, these conventional figures were adapted to suit current concerns. Two notable films, John Ford's *The Fugitive* (1947), based on Graham Greene's best-selling novel, *The Power and the Glory*, and John Huston's *Treasure of the Sierra Madre* (1948) indicate the central ideas that informed Mexico as "mythic space." *The Fugitive* is an anti-Communist allegory, set in an unnamed, presumably archetypal Latin American nation (Mexico in the novel), in which a revolutionary regime has asserted totalitarian power. The chief spokesman for the revolution is a soldier/policeman (Pedro Armendariz) who blends elements of the "Villa" figure with attributes of a "Huerta." His opponent is a "Christ-fool," the failed priest played by Henry Fonda, who was still strongly identified with the populist roles he had played since *Jesse James*.

The delineation of "Mexico" as mythic space in *Treasure of the Sierra Madre* has had the strongest influence on subsequent treatments, because of the consistency with which Huston conflates Mexico and the archetypal landscape and images of *gringo* mythology. Behind a screen of "gritty realism," Huston schematizes Mexico so that its landscape will answer the requirements of an American moral and/or political allegory. Mexican society is abstracted to four social settings, in which the classic oppositions of movie-Mexico appear: the city of Tampico, divided between unscrupulous wealthy capitalists (many of them American) and the utterly immiserated poor; the primitive pueblo, where a rough but simple justice rules under the eye of a patriarchal mayor; the wilderness mining camp, where no law exists but self-interest and the gun; and the Indian village, which offers a vision of pastoral paradise. In the end, the two surviving prospectors are able to laugh at the absurdity of their quest for gold and return to their different versions of the populist utopia. The older prospector returns to the pastoral utopia of the Indian village, where he will be treated like a White god; the younger prospector returns to the States to realize the same sort of ambition that motivates Tom Joad and the Ringo Kid—a small ranch, a peach orchard, a good woman, and some kids.

Huston's romantic view of Mexico as the scene of Americans' moral regeneration formulates what would become an important theme in postwar Westerns. Theme and imagery link *Treasure* closely to the "Cult of the Indian," which also sees engagement with the world of the racial/ethnic Other as a utopian alternative to the corruption of American "civilization" as well as the site of a potentially redemptive spiritual/sexual experience.

The "Zapata Problem": The Strong Man Makes a Weak People

Since Hollywood's "Mexico" was merely a screen for the mirroring of certain kinds of American political concerns, interest in the Mexico setting and this lexicon of political "types" waxed and waned with the right/left shifts of American politics. America's entrance into the Second World War gave a new cast to Mexican-American relations and lent a new intensity to American concern with the problem of Mexico's revolutionary political tradition. This concern was characteristically expressed in Anita Brenner's illustrated history of the Revolution, *The Wind That Swept Mexico* (1943). The mixture of text and photographs recalls the Margaret Bourke-White/Erskine Caldwell collaboration, *You Have Seen Their Faces*, and the book was received in a similar spirit—as a work at once accessible to a mass audience and serious in its critical understanding of a major problem. The opening sentence declares, "We are not safe in the United States, now and henceforth, without taking Mexico into account."[30] Beyond the need for Mexican support in the war against Fascism, Brenner envisions a postwar order in which the United States and Latin America will become more interdependent and in which all the Americas will be menaced by new enemies, to whose power our oceans will be no barrier. But Latin America suffers from poverty, social injustice, and the prevalence of dictatorship. "Before this war is over . . . and certainly when it is ended, there will be uprisings and upheavals in many American countries."[31] For all these nations, the Mexican Revolution will serve as the chief example, and Americans must study it, because:

> It puts questions to us our government will have to meet, and is already in the midst of; questions which the American people cannot safely leave to deals and power-barters and accident and intrigue. Policies shaped for export have their internal consequences. For we are not safe, either, from the inner struggle tearing other peoples.[32]

Brenner reads the Mexican Revolution in ways that emphasize its resemblance to the political battles of the New Deal. Mexico acts out in violence a script that the more prosperous and fortunate North can play through the electoral process.[33] This struggle seemingly confronts Mexico with a choice between radical socialists or Communists on the one hand and crypto-Fascists on the other. Brenner's solution to this revolutionary impasse is the development of a liberal center, modeled on the New Deal, in which pragmatic and moderate leaders temper the extremism of left and right, adopting some socialistic objectives and measures to achieve social justice, but avoiding terrorism, expropriation, and social violence, and opening the country to investment without delivering it into the hands of foreigners.[34]

Brenner's telling of the story of the Revolution traces the emergence of a "third force" out of the primal rivalry between the principles of the "Strong Man" and "democracy." Reliance on the Strong Man is the besetting weakness of Latin politics, a desperate response to poverty and injustice that in the end merely reproduces the conditions it was invoked to solve. The idealistic Madero overthrows the weakened Strong Man Diaz but cannot resist the Strong Man Huerta. Against Huerta four revolutionary chieftains arise, each of whom represents a different resolution to the revolutionary impasse. Carranza is a classic Strong Man of the Diaz type. Villa is a sincere revolutionary whose penchant for personal rule makes him an incipient Strong Man. Zapata is the most doctrinaire revolutionary, master of guerrilla warfare and exponent of the radical "Plan of Ayala." Although Zapata too is a potential Strong Man, his is the strength of a revolutionary party on the Bolshevik model. The destructive potential of this approach is suggested by Brenner's use of the epithet "Attila of the South" for Zapata.

Against these three representatives of "strength" stands Obregon, who is described by Brenner in terms that link him with FDR, although their actual policies were often at odds. He is "his own brain trust," but he makes no political or military move without elaborate consultations with his "boys"—a council that includes Yaqui Indians (the core of his forces), labor leaders, and "socialist" intellectuals. Where Carranza and Villa try to maximize their personal power, and Zapata follows the ideological dictates of his revolutionary program, the Plan of Ayala, Obregon is pragmatist rather than ideologue, dealmaker rather than Strong Man. "What Obregon decided to do was always a combination of desirables and practicables . . . that is, a shrewd, immediate political adaptation of the boys' radical demands." In the end, this approach produces results analogous to those in the United States: the rejection of both "bolshevism" and Fascism.[35]

Brenner's praise of Obregon had no effect on Hollywood's "Mexican" vocabulary, which continued to feature Villa (or Zapata), Madero, and Huerta (or their cognates) as political symbols. But the political values that Brenner identifies with Obregon were absorbed into postwar readings of the Mexican Revolution and were eventually embodied in the hero of *Viva Zapata!* (1952).

Viva Zapata! was the culminating film of the small genre that dealt with the Mexican Revolution as a historical phenomenon in its own right. (Later films treat Mexican matters as adjuncts of the Western.) Political concerns figured importantly and explicitly in the shaping of the production. At about the same time that Warners was planning *Juarez*, Edgcumb Pinchon and Gildardo Magana approached MGM with a proposal for a film biography of Zapata, who was to Morelos and south-central Mexico what Villa was to the north. Pinchon pitched the film as one that would "revivify the waning flame of Democracy in the English speaking world" and alter the balance of

> [a] World . . . teetering between the enticements of dictatorship and democracy. . . . It could light, like a torch, the almost unkindled fires of democracy in Latin America. It could be the answer—beautiful, sweeping, unanswerable to Mr. Hitler and Mr. Mussolini. . . . It could take Latin America for the U.S.A.!

The film's politics were potentially more radical than those of *Viva Villa!* Magana was a senior leader and polemicist of Mexican socialism and one of the architects of Zapata's radical land-reform program. Nonetheless, MGM bought the property in 1940 and planned a production to be called *Zapata, the Unconquerable*. In the interim, the Roosevelt administration had established the Office for Co-ordination of Commercial and Cultural Relations between the American Republics, headed by Nelson Rockefeller, to guide Hollywood (and other export businesses) in dealings with Latin America. The studio submitted the project to the head of the agency's motion-picture division (John Hay "Jock" Whitney), whose researcher found Zapata to be a radical and controversial figure, the particular enemy of the Catholic Church and American interests. MGM dropped the project.[36]

But the Zapata scenario was revived at MGM in 1946, and the outline of a screenplay with a "rather radical and decidedly altruistic bent" was developed by Lester Cole. Management remembered the unfavorable report of Rockefeller's agency, however, and saw Zapata as "a goddamn commie revolutionary." When Cole was subpoenaed by HUAC, the studio sold the property to 20th Century Fox, whose own Zapata prospectus had languished for years.[37] Although the film was produced during the height of the Red Scare in Hollywood (1950–52), *Viva Zapata!* was given generous support—a prestigious director (Elia Kazan), the commissioning of John Steinbeck to write the screenplay, and the newly famous Marlon Brando to play Zapata.

It has been said that *Viva Zapata!* evaded the accusation of radicalism by representing the hero as a "land reformer" rather than a revolutionary. Though it is true that the movie soft-pedals Zapata's quasi-socialist program, it is well to remember that while the film was in production the State Department's China specialists were being decimated for having identified Mao Tse Tung as an "agrarian reformer." The film would not have been undertaken if its makers wished simply to evade political controversy. It is more accurate to see *Viva Zapata!* as an attempt to make a positive political statement that would distinguish the essential values of American liberalism from both Stalinist Marxism and right-wing conservatism and that would claim for those values a "revolutionary" or liberating world mission. Both Kazan and Steinbeck had been associated with left and liberal groups and causes in the 30s and 40s (though neither was a Communist). By 1950 both had come to regard their earlier political enthusiasms as mistaken. Yet it was important to both Kazan and Steinbeck to separate their rejection of Communism from repudiation of the commitment to social justice which they had once associated with the left.[38]

Theirs was hardly a unique ideological position. Rather, both participated in a broad and general "turn" against Marxism (and socialism), which shaped the thinking of intellectuals, historians, and policy-makers in the postwar years. This turn was responsive to the "negative" stimulus of Soviet behavior, beginning with the Hitler–Stalin pact of 1939 and culminating in the outbreak of the Cold War and revelations about the Stalinist terror of the late 1930s. But it was also affected by the revelation of American moral and economic strength in the victory of 1945 and our emergence as the dominant political and economic power in the world. This produced a new and highly sophisticated form of "American exceptionalism," which—when fully developed in the 1960s—would constitute an "Americanist" ideological program that Godfrey Hodgson has termed the "Liberal Consensus." Such a consensus hardly existed in 1950, but its terms had already been formulated by some of the leading younger theorists of post-New Deal liberalism. In 1949 Daniel Bell had written of "America's Un-Marxist Revolution," and Arthur M. Schlesinger, Jr., had asserted that "Keynes, not Marx is the prophet of the new radicalism." The "progressive" or "consensus" historians of the post-war period extended the Turner/Beard tradition of exceptionalist historiography. The special conditions of American life (of which the old Frontier and the new productivity are the most prominent) were seen to have produced a history remarkably devoid of class consciousness or class politics of any kind.[39]

In *Viva Zapata!* Kazan and Steinbeck formulate this incipient "Americanist" ideology as a heroic myth which they project as a thought-experiment in the fictive space of "Mexico." Their Zapata offers an "exception" to the rule of revolutions—Mexican and otherwise—which sees as inescapable the pendulum swing between upheaval and dictatorship. Although he is identified as "Mexican," many of the values that make Zapata exceptional are drawn from the conventional vocabulary of the American Western (and allied genres). These similarities determine the degree to which Zapata succeeds in breaking the cycle, or symbolically demonstrate how such a break could be achieved.

Western movie images pervade the film, linking the drama of revolution to the iconography of the genre. Steinbeck and Kazan transform the radical "Plan of Ayala" into the familiar "little-piece-of-land" dream of the populist Western. One Mexican peasant virtually quotes the passage from *Grapes of Wrath* in which a farmer's hunger for land is likened to his love for a woman, and delivers another passage in which dispossessed farmers sneak out to plant corn in fields they cannot own.[40]

The use of horses and horseback action sequences is particularly effective, and Kazan integrates this Western-movie imagery with the themes of his narrative in subtle and complex ways. For example, the recurrent imagery of horses and eggs becomes, through continual repetition and variation, a poetic metaphor for the crucial oppositions that shape the revolution. Horses are identified with male sexuality, eggs with women in their role as feeders and nurturers. The injustice of the Diaz regime is represented in a scene in which a rich *hacendado* washes his horses in a bath of egg whites while starving peon children are whipped for stealing grain from the horses' stalls. Later, the revolutionaries turn the tables when peasant women (at the sacrifice of their lives) plant dynamite concealed in baskets of eggs at the door of a federal fort. Zapata's desire for Josefa (his middle-class beloved, played by Jean Peters) and his almost erotic passion for the revolution are both voiced by the white horse with which he is identified. When the horse keeps interrupting his enforcedly decorous courtship of Josefa, we know that Zapata's tension comes from both unfulfilled sexual desire and the unfinished revolution. At the end, the white horse, which has escaped to the mountains, becomes the symbol of Zapata's spirit—a symbol which Steinbeck and Kazan intended seriously but which is strongly reminiscent of the "B"-Western hero's preference for his horse over "the girl." The final image of the white horse in the mountains might have been clipped from a "B" Western of the *King of the Wild Horses* variety.

The script also insists on Zapata's Indian identity. Makeup gives his eyes an oriental look and a darker skin tone, especially early in the film, and Zapata's Indian identity arouses the bigoted scorn of the middle-class father of Josefa. The Indian/peasant linkage of course recalls *Juarez*, but the Josefa/Zapata romance is more strongly evocative of the White/Indian romances of *Broken Arrow* and *Devil's Doorway*.[41]

As the "redemptive woman," whose role parallels those of Zee James and Sonseeahray, Josefa validates the hero's use of violence through most of the film. She never condemns the principle for which Zapata is fighting, so that she never has to repudiate him as Zee repudiates Jesse. Still, Zapata's death occurs immediately after he rejects her tearful plea that he not leave their refuge. The moral standard represented by the redemptive woman is given a different emphasis in each film: in *Jesse James* she stands for civilized law and morality and for the sanctity of the family; in *Broken Arrow* she stands for a kind of natural Christianity. In *Viva Zapata!* the "womanly" principle is identified with the bourgeois culture: the second thing they do on their wedding night is that Josefa teaches Zapata how to read. Their romance suggests a reconciliation not only between Spaniard and Indian but between the peasant revolutionary and an enlightened middle class.

Steinbeck and Kazan thus draw a distinct line between Zapata and Villa as revolutionary types. Villa's rampant male sexuality and Strong Man tendencies are assigned to Zapata's brother Eufemio (Anthony Quinn), who eventually becomes a local Strong Man, robbing the peasants of both their land and their women. Zapata's "freakish" (according to Eufemio) fidelity to one woman thus gives this revolutionary the most important caste-mark of the middle-class American and of the Hollywood romantic hero and explains his ultimate rejection of the Strong Man role.

The Steinbeck/Kazan interpretation of the Strong Man/"Christ-fool" contradiction is made plain in three parallel scenes in the Presidential Palace. In the opening scene of the movie a delegation of farmers from Morelos comes to petition President Diaz for protection from the *hacendados* who have taken their land. Although he is costumed as the incarnation of tyrannical authority, in a military coat slathered with braid and decorations, Diaz is also a former revolutionary who had fought under Juarez against Maximilian. Moreover, Diaz is made up to look like Joseph Stalin, with close-cropped iron-gray hair and large mustache, a chestful of medals, and a colossal portrait of himself on the wall. Diaz puts the farmers off with a pretense of fatherly benevolence, calling them "my children"; he is defied by Zapata, who asserts the authority of nature and of justice—the planting season won't wait while the courts decide the case, and neither will hungry families. Diaz responds by drawing a circle around Zapata's name, marking him as an enemy of the regime. The former revolutionary has become the tyrant.[42]

In the second scene, Zapata meets Madero in the Presidential Palace. The exchange between them reveals Madero to be less the "Christ-fool" than an ineffectual Caspar Milquetoast who is too caught up by the sound of his own idealistic pieties to heed the advice of the practical bandit-revolutionary. He is, as his enemies say, a "mouse," and unlike the Madero of *Viva Villa!* he dies without dignity.

The third scene replicates the first, with Zapata in the President's chair after Villa and Zapata have captured Mexico City and won temporary control of the revolution. This time the delegation from Morelos comes to complain that Zapata's brother has seized their lands and their women and won't let them plant. Zapata puts them off just as Diaz had, although he calls them *compadres* rather than "children." When a man named Hernandez throws in his face the same words he had used to Diaz, Zapata circles his name . . . and then tears up the paper, grabs his rifle and sombrero, abandons the presidency, and returns to Morelos. With this gesture he rejects politics as such, declaring (in effect) that the achievement of power through revolution inevitably makes tyrants. He returns to the role of permanent revolutionary, operating in an "outlaw" framework where politics is "replaced" by direct action and simple justice.

Zapata's transcendence of the role of Strong Man carries him into the condition of the "Christ-fool." However, the emphasis given Brando's virility, the number of guns and bandoliers he carries, and the extraordinary violence that is needed to martyr him make him a *muscular* "Christ-fool."[43] When Zapata is enticed into the courtyard of a fortress, the battlements are suddenly filled with armed riflemen who shoot him down and pour volley after volley into his dead body—a spectacular and memorable scene whose visual arrangement would become an icon of Mexico Westerns. His body is then dropped in the town square, where it lies in a composition suggestive of a deposition of the body of Christ, with a stream of water gushing from a pipe just below its right side. The people refuse to believe Zapata is dead. They say he is "in the mountains" and will return when they need him.

The movie thus provides a mystical solution to its political dilemma and consciously opposes its Christological mystique to alternative solutions, which it identifies as "ideological." The voice of ideology in the film is provided by Fernando Aguirre (Joseph Wiseman), a revolutionary organizer and polemicist whose weapon is the typewriter, "the sword of the mind." As Zapata's aide and adviser he continually reminds Zapata of the "logic" of revolution, which requires first of all the systematic use of force and violence to win and hold power. Through most of the film Aguirre's cold ruthlessness is balanced by the passion of Zapata's brother, suggesting that Zapata himself represents an ideal mean between the two extremes. However, the movie's positive values are always identified with symbols expressive of Steinbeck's characteristic primitivism and nature-mysticism, suggesting that the excesses of natural (revolutionary) passion are less dangerous than the intellectual perversions of an ideologue. Eufemio's betrayal of the revolution is merely venal, and Zapata easily undoes it. Aguirre ends by serving a new military regime, which considers the extermination of the Morelos peasantry a permissible (if impractical) tactic in suppressing Zapata's insurgency, and he invents the plot that betrays Zapata to his death. Through Aguirre, the film discredits not ony a specific revolutionary ideology but the systematic style of thought that generates ideology.

It is important to note that this characterization of the intellectual as ideologue is not idiosyncratic. Rather, it represents a major tendency in American political thought during the decade of the 1950s, which accompanied the development of the "Americanist" or "Liberal Consensus." The characterization of Aguirre prefigures the school of political analysis that would later be associated with Daniel Bell's *The End of Ideology* (1960), in which the specific failure of Marxism justifies a broad denigration of systematic theorization about politics and society in favor of a "pragmatic," problem-solving approach derived from and suited to "the special American conditions."[44]

But in *Viva Zapata!* the practical effect of this rejection of "ideology" is to rule out all rational and secular approaches to the dichotomy of killer and "Christ-fool." We are left with a mythic and religious vision of a resolution beyond the power of people to articulate. If the ending works at all, it is because Zapata is a *Mexican* hero whose world is visually coded as "Catholic"—a religious framework that (in Hollywood's interpretation) is not governed by the hard-boiled rationalism of the Protestant/Anglo North.[45] But as a version of politics, the Christological resolution merely affirms the inescapability for "Mexico" of the Hobson's choice between "Christ-fool"/failure and the poisonous triumphs of the Strong Man.

The one bit of practical doctrine that Zapata offers us is his aphorism, "The strong man makes a weak people." To be finally free, the people must somehow learn to "lead themselves." The movie does not define what a society or a government ordered in this way would be like—a universalized town meeting? an anarchist utopia? But the idea is clearly a restatement of the very traditional American ideological principles of self-reliance and self-government. If we take the film seriously as political allegory, then what makes Zapata viable as the symbol of a "third force" alternative to dictatorships of the right (Diaz) and dictatorships of the Communist left (Aguirre) is his "exceptional" and essentially "American" character.

Moviemakers addressing problems similar to those that engaged policy-makers thus produced a thought-experiment that parallels the course of thinking about American policy in the emerging nations during the decade of the 1950s. Indeed, there is evidence that at least some in the policy-making establishment were directly influenced by the "Zapata" myth. Peculiarly valuable testimony on this score comes from an article written by Arthur M. Schlesinger, Jr., the historian and adviser to John F. Kennedy.[46] In an essay published in the British journal *Encounter* just after Kennedy's election, Schlesinger addressed the question of Third World revolutions in terms drawn directly (though without attribution) from *Viva Zapata!* The essay was titled "On Heroic Leadership and the Dilemma of Strong Men and Weak Peoples." Although it specifically addresses the need to blend strong leadership with democracy in the emerging nations, it makes the more general assertion that even American democracy occasionally requires the heroic guidance of the Strong Man.[47] If such a Strong Man were a true "Zapata"—able to use force ruthlessly and effectively to win his war but willing to return power to democracy in the end—he might (with American aid) be able to provide an effective third choice between the ruthless efficiency that ends in revolutionary terror and the idealistic "Christ-fool" policies that end in failure and a resumption of dictatorship by the right.

Schlesinger's argument is important as an indication of the direction of liberal thinking on policy toward the Third World. But it is also important to note that the article reproduces in political discourse the same "double-acting metaphor" that informs the "Mexico" movie. Schlesinger not only reads the politics of those he terms "weak peoples" in American terms; he uses that reading to articulate a set of political ideas whose primary application is to the United States. Sometimes *Americans* behave like, or find themselves in the condition of, "weak peoples"; and when that occurs, they too have need of a Strong Man or Heroic Leader who will save for them the "democracy" they might lose if left unled. The argument about the "Other" is in fact an argument about ourselves; "Mexico" is the mirror in which we appear to ourselves in a glass, darkly.

The Man Who Knows Communists: The Heroic Style of Covert Operations (1953–54)

Hollywood's answer to the question posed by the Zapata thought-experiment was to "propose" the sending of American specialists to aid the "Zapatas" in overcoming both their enemies and their own self-destructive tendencies. The heroic type best suited for such a project was the gunfighter: the quintessential American pragmatist, a specialist in the arts of violence, who could relieve the Third World leader of the necessity of being his own "Villa"; a man whose character as a foreigner, a "loner," and a man who has outlived his time is a guarantee that he will not himself remain in "Mexico" to become a "Maximilian" or a "Huerta."

Hollywood evolved this answer by following its usual methods for making timely new stories out of tried and true properties. Given the successes of the gunfighter Westerns and *Viva Zapata!*, the obvious compatibility of their settings, and the timeliness of "revolution" as a subject, it was perhaps inevitable that someone would bring all these elements into the frame of a single film.[48] The Hecht-Lancaster production of *Vera Cruz* (1954), directed by Robert Aldrich, doubles its myth-historical framework by bringing the gunfighter movie to Zapata's territory; and it doubles its box-office appeal by bringing together Gary Cooper and Burt Lancaster, two major stars whose screen personae represented distinctly different versions of the Western hero.

There were some recent precedents for the story-premise, such as *The Eagle and the Hawk* (1950) and *Wings of the Hawk* (1953).[49] What makes *Vera Cruz* different from those earlier films is its innovative, and controversial, treatment of the Americans' motives and methods. Instead of being obvious White Knights in killer's clothing, the heroes of *Vera Cruz* seem to incarnate the most hard-boiled aspects of "gunfighter style." They are hard-bitten mercenaries, amoral pragmatists who will break any rule—no matter how sacred—to achieve their sordid goals. Their adventure in Mexico poses the question of how far the gunfighter or the "man who knows Indians" can go in imitation of the enemy without becoming morally indistinguishable from the enemy.

At about the same time, the same sort of question was being asked—and similar answers arrived at—by policy-makers in secret discussions concerned with defining and rationalizing a new strategy for prosecuting the Cold War. At this anticipatory stage of policy-making, government officials dealt with abstractions and collectivities rather than specific personages. But they too had to imagine the scenario of the coming struggle, conceive a response that would be both effective and acceptable to the public, and develop a model of effective or heroic action. They too drew on both myth/ideological tradition and analysis of current events in imagining a new stance or style for the exercise of American power under the conditions of the Cold War. The parallel between the processes and results of these different and independent projects are worth noting, first because it is a sign of the pervasive influence of the symbols and ideas carried by our culture's myth/ideological system, but also because those parallel features prepared the public to accept the results of the secret discussions when the policies they envisioned became manifest. It is therefore useful to look briefly at this covert policy debate before analyzing the public "counterinsurgency" scenario developed in *Vera Cruz*.

In 1953–54 a series of secret studies, discussions, and reports was undertaken which reconceived the mission of the Central Intelligence Agency (CIA) and made it the President's chosen instrument for the active prosecution of the Cold War. There were several motives for this change: the need to use indirect and subversive means of competition against a rival superpower armed with nuclear weapons; economic and political constraints that militated against high military budgets; and President Eisenhower's leadership style, which "valued the facts of power over the appearance of power" and aimed at avoiding open conflict and public controversy as much as possible.[50] The CIA was manned by professionals, many with military experience, who specialized in the secret accumulation of information and the clandestine exercise of power. Its capacity for covert action allowed it to apply force at strategic points, on a cost-effective scale, in a way that avoided large-scale military intervention; and it did so without the necessity of provoking controversy in Congress or aggravating the public's proverbial resistance to policies that risked war or required increased taxation. The Agency was therefore the "natural vehicle" for America's counterthrust against advancing Communism.[51]

During the first year of Eisenhower's tenure, covert intelligence operations scored major successes in the Philippines (1953), Iran (1953), and Guatemala (1954). In the latter two cases, the CIA overthrew unfriendly governments by the adroit use of "smoke and mirrors" and the subornation of a small number of local military leaders with minimal expenditure and with relatively little (immediate) bloodshed. The use of clandestine measures meant that accusations of imperialist aggression could be plausibly denied.

To make it a more effective instrument, the CIA was given a bigger budget and a new charter, which added covert operations to the task of intelligence-gathering as the Agency's primary mission.[52] The Doolittle Report of 1954, which revised the CIA's charter, began by re-defining the setting and scenario of intelligence work. The Report asserted that this new stage of the Cold War was a conflict different in kind from any the public had supported in the past. It was a struggle against the threat of annihilation, as the World War had been; yet it would not be fought in the open, against the primary enemy. Rather, it would be waged indirectly and secretively, through espionage and subversion and a kind of clandestine warfare that was at odds with American moral and martial traditions. To win that war, the nation would have to choose between fighting in an American way that is presumed to be fair, decent, and innocent, but ineffective, and fighting in an enemy way that is brutal, deceitful, and repugnant, but highly efficient:

> It is now clear that we are facing an implacable enemy whose avowed objective is world domination. There are no rules in such a game. Hitherto acceptable norms of human conduct do not apply. If the United States is to survive, longstanding American concepts of fair play must be reconsidered. We must learn to subvert, sabotage, and destroy our enemies by more clever, more sophisticated, and more effective methods than those used against us. It may become necessary that the American people be made acquainted with, understand and support this fundamentally repugnant philosophy.[53]

The terms in which the Report conceives and presents the Cold War are the same as those which shaped the political typology of "movie Mexico": the traditional American concepts of fair play correspond to the methods of the "Madero" or "Christ-fool"; those of the enemy correspond to the ruthless pragmatism of a "Villa" or "Huerta." Beneath these oppositions are more primal categories of the Frontier Myth's scenario of "savage war." The Doolittle Report's language echoes the eighteenth-century description of the American Indian war as

> a rigid contest where all is at stake, and mutual destruction the object. . . . [Where] everything is terrible: the face of the country, the climate, the enemy. . . . [Where] victories are not decisive but defeats are ruinous; and simple death is the least misfortune which can happen."[54]

It adds to this base the idea (most eloquently stated by Theodore Roosevelt) that the nation's ability to continue on a "progressive" course is at risk in this kind of struggle, since the enemy is identified as inherently incapable of and opposed to progress; and that a war of this kind is therefore not only ju t but even "righteous." The ultimate character of the stakes in such a struggle permit—or rather require—that the side of progress and civilization meet the enemy on his own ground and fight on the enemy's terms without quarter and even without scruple. The normal restraints of civilized custom and morality cannot be allowed to impede a defense of this kind. As Thomas Dixon says in his fable of racial warfare, the defense of "civilization" must take precedence over adherence to the forms of democracy. Although originally invoked against the Soviet threat in Europe, this doctrine would be immediately applied to the more primitive environments of the Third World, where the circumstantial parallels to the wars of the American wilderness gave the association with the Frontier Myth force and emphasis.[55]

The "savage war" scenario traditionally carries with it a particular vision of heroic style. To defeat a savage enemy who will not fight by civilized rules or limit his ferocity to "legitimate" objectives, civilization must discover and empower "the man who knows Indians"—an agent of "White" civilization who is so intimate with the enemy's way of thinking that he can destroy that enemy with his own weapons.[56] In the clandestine struggle against the Soviet Union itself, this scenario required American secret agents who mirror their Communist counterparts in professional skill, ruthlessness, and willingness to engage in espionage, subversion, sabotage, subornation, and betrayal. In the counterinsurgency warfare that would characterize operations in the Third World, the scenario required the development of an American counterguerrilla capable of matching the enemy in jungle warfare and in the use of force, terror, and civic action to transform Asian peasants into partisans. It was implicit in this scenario that a necessary part of the "mirroring" process might be the (presumably temporary) abandonment of such traditional American notions as "fair play," "democracy," or "government by consent of the governed." Theodore Roosevelt had invoked much the same metaphor in appealing for an American takeover of the Philippines in 1899, when he contrasted sentimental "cant" about government-by-consent with the frontier hero's toughmindedness about taking the shortest way with "savages." This doctrine would in fact be applied, first in American support of "friendly" dictatorial regimes in Iran, Guatemala, and South Vietnam, and finally in the government's efforts to circumvent the consensual procedures of the American constitutional system itself.

Although the Doolittle Report uses the kind of language that we would expect in propaganda intended to persuade the public, it was in fact intended only to persuade an intra-governmental audience. It assumes that members of the public are not prepared to understand the nature of the struggle they are inescapably engaged in. The Report therefore recommends that the scenario of Cold War as "savage war," and the scenarios of heroic response that might be developed to win such a war, be explored in secrecy. Implicit in the aversion to public debate was the by now traditional belief that under normal circumstances the American public would not consent to the costly measures necessary to carry out the role of a world power. But a more fundamental motive for concealment was the administration's belief that (as the language of the Doolittle Report suggests) the public was likely to find the "philosophy" of the new CIA mission "fundamentally repugnant" because the recommended techniques of espionage and subversion violated American canons of "fair play" and "honor." Moreover those techniques, and in many cases the ends at which they aimed (for example, the support of "friendly" dictatorships) violated fundamental principles of democratic ideology and the often muted but still persistent tradition of anticolonialism, which since 1910 had paradoxically managed to coexist with the imperialist methods of "Dollar Diplomacy."[57] For all these reasons, the Eisenhower administration sought to evade Congressional investigation, debate, and consent in pursuing its necessarily dirty war.

Two of its evasions proved crucial to the pattern of political and military conflict that would emerge in Vietnam. The administration decided to block full implementation of the Geneva accords that had ended the French war in Indochina by using the interim regime established in South Vietnam to prevent the nationwide elections which the accords required—and which the Communists, led by Ho Chi Minh, were sure to win. Having thwarted the "consent of the governed" in Vietnam, Secretary of State Dulles then evaded it at home by giving vague and misleading answers to Congressional demands for assurances that the new SEATO treaty (which constituted a regional alliance) would not legally bind America to intervene against an indigenous revolution in South Vietnam.[58] With the SEATO treaty ratified, and with a moral obligation to the region established, the administration expected that, if and when regional affairs reached a crisis, it would confront Congress and the public with a choice between "standing firm" and "backing down" in the face of a Communist challenge.[59] That both would choose to "stand firm" was predictable, given the convergence of so many ideological strains: the myth of "appeasement and its evil consequences" derived from the Munich agreements of 1938; the experience of the recent war and the public's militant response to Pearl Harbor; and not least, the images of virtue and manliness purveyed in the mass media, particularly in Western movies—images that incarnated the ideological imperative that "a man's gotta do what a man's gotta do," that it's wrong to leave town when Frank Miller is coming back, and that you are the only one who can stop him.

In effect, the administration applied "Doolittle" ethics to the United States as well as to Vietnam. In both countries, the pursuit of a tough-minded Cold War policy was achieved by setting aside or evading the legal forms and the ideological values of democracy. Here the political consequences of the double-action metaphor ("Mexico" = U.S.) become apparent. The political rationale that justifies anti-democratic policies among the "weak peoples" is the reflection of our (or our leaders') loss of faith in *our* entitlement to the full exercise of self-government. That being so, when we project "Strong Man" ideology onto the "Other," we also prepare to enact it upon ourselves.

Nonetheless, the administration's need for evasion still bespeaks the importance of democratic ideology as a constraint on policy: Could the United States use the techniques of a totalitarian enemy without itself ceasing to be a democracy? Put the question in Western-movie terms and you have the premise of *Vera Cruz*: How far beyond the boundaries of traditional idealism can a hero or a policy go without forfeiting public sympathy? And how far could Will Kane go in answering evil with evil without becoming Frank Miller?

Fast Guns for "Zapata": The Counterinsurgency Scenario and Vera Cruz (1954)

V*era Cruz* (1954) is the story of a team of American gunfighters, ex-solders, and outlaws who go to Mexico to advise and assist the Mexican government in suppressing a radical revolution—a fictional adventure that mirrors the administration's contemporaneous decision to launch a counterinsurgency mission in Southeast Asia. *Vera Cruz* transfers the problem of the "revolutionary impasse" or the "Zapata problem" to the familiar terrain of the Western and translates the problem of defining an American role in Third World revolutions into a question about the nature of Western movie-heroism.

The question is embodied in the casting of its two stars. Gary Cooper brought to the film the look of an older generation of Western heroes *(The Virginian, The Westerner)* whose essential idealism was taken for granted and whose world offered stark contrasts between right and wrong. His performance in *High Noon* had made a powerful impact, because it represented the confrontation of the older Western hero with the ambiguity and cynicism of postwar America and dramatized the process of his disillusionment. His role in *Vera Cruz* in effect takes up the story of this transformation where *High Noon* leaves off: Cooper's Ben Trane has been a traditional Western idealist, but defeat in the Civil War and the loss of his plantation have made him disillusioned and cynical. Nonetheless, his experiences in Mexico will plumb the depths of his cynicism and will restore his idealism on a new and more realistic basis.

Burt Lancaster, on the other hand, was both a younger star and a performer whose screen persona linked romantic glamour, erotic appeal, and an enthusiasm for violent action. In *Vera Cruz* this side of Lancaster's persona is given full expression: his Joe Erin has completely eroticized his propensities for violence and takes sensual pleasure in the exercise of his skill and of the power over men and women that his speed with a gun gives him. But what gives Erin his power to intimidate is his absolute amorality. It is clear that he values nothing but his own power and pleasure, that he respects nothing and no one outside himself (with the possible exception of Ben Trane), and that he is capable of any degree of violence against any and every kind of person—helpless or strong, man, woman, or child—in his quest for satisfaction.[60]

These heroic styles also play-act the alternative rationales for action promulgated in the Doolittle Report. Erin represents the side of clandestine warfare that Doolittle represented as "repugnant" and contradictory to "longstanding American concepts of fair play." He incarnates the proposition (which we may also identify with "Villa" and "Aguirre") that in a revolutionary struggle the ends justify any means that will be effective. The limits of that proposition are tested by Ben Trane, whose moral intelligence justaposes traditional ideas of chivalry and fair play with the stern necessities of war, tests the limits of pure instrumentalism, and finds a new balance between moral restraint and the exigencies of revolution.

The film opens with titles that place us in a political and historical context: it is after the American Civil War, and the Mexicans under Juarez are fighting for freedom from the imperial regime of Maximilian. The struggle attracts Americans who enlist as mercenaries on both sides—men who have been either psychologically or socially displaced by the Civil War and who come to Mexico in search of adventure and/or fortune. The post-Civil War setting is a convention which signals a parallel between the theme of the movie and the concerns of post-World War America: the nation has completed a great political and ideological struggle that threatened its vital center; Americans now turn to the Third World periphery and through the course of their adventure discover that a struggle of equal significance is being waged there.

The Americans go to Mexico in search of private gain. They care nothing about Mexico or about the freedom for which the Juaristas are fighting. The chivalric idealism associated with the cowboy heroes of the 30s and 40s, or with gunfighters modeled on Shane, is dismissed as soft-headedness. This treatment of motive is deliberately anti-conventional, designed to surprise and even to shock. The contrast between traditional cowboy chivalry and the actual motives of our heroes is continually reiterated in scenes that are alternately humorous and serious. Although this approach makes for an exceptionally varied and entertaining film, it drew criticism from reviewers for its blithe cynicism.[61]

The two protagonists represent distinct variations on this hard-boiled motivation. Burt Lancaster's Joe Erin is a "pure" mercenary who prides himself on his cynicism. His aim is to make money, and he is willing to do anything necessary to do so. His technique is to take the nearest way, which usually involves force and fraud in some combination. Human relations are simply a contest for advantage in the quest for money, and the possession of superior force is the ultimate advantage. Erin's approach is to get the drop on his rival whenever possible, by fair means or foul. Not only does he act on these beliefs; he is a kind of folk-philosopher of cynicism who turns humorous anecdotes from his past into parables of his version of the Golden Rule, which is to do unto others before they do unto you. So devoted is he to the principle of playing dirty that he is in fact a perversely idealistic figure whose one weakness is to be taken by surprise when anyone acts out of moral principle. Erin is also brave, and supremely skilled with weapons. He wears all-black clothes and an elegant gunbelt, and he holsters his pistol with a twirl: signs that identify him as a professional gunfighter, a younger, coarser Jimmy Ringo.[62]

Gary Cooper's Ben Trane is Erin's colleague and rival, an older man in distinctly plainer clothes, whose solemnity is more like that of the disillusioned gunmen of *Gunfighter* and *High Noon*. Unlike Erin, he has the good, quiet manners we identify with characters like the Virginian, natural aristocrats in cowboy garb. But he too appears at first to be a man in search of the main chance. When he and Erin meet on the way into Mexico, a series of exchanges establishes that neither can get the drop on the other and that both will benefit by teaming up. Their equality as gunfighters and men of skill seems to suggest a kinship beneath their differences of manner and breeding. Whatever else they are, they are the best of their kind.

Like Erin, Trane has come to Mexico to sign up with whichever side will pay him better for his services. But his motives, we learn, are not purely mercenary. Trane needs money to rebuild his plantation, which is more to him than a mere asset: a plantation, he says, is "people who depend on you," by which he must mean his ex-slaves (since he is unmarried and never refers to a family). Thus Trane's mercenary pragmatism is not a true reflection of his moral nature but the expedient means to an end we recognize as moral, according to movie canons.

But *Vera Cruz* proposes to see just how dirty, how like the enemy, an American hero can become and still remain an American hero. The first real test comes when Trane, Erin, and their little "platoon" of mercenaries arrive in the pueblo where the two sides will bid for their services. The forces of Maximilian, represented by the aristocratic Marquis (Cesar Romero), can pay well and in gold; the Juaristas led by General Ramirez can offer little pay and appeal to the love of freedom and independence which Americans are supposed to share. Erin refers Ramirez to Trane, "our expert in Lost Causes"—a gesture that identifies the ex-slaveholder with the cause of freedom, because he has fought for the independence of the South. Ramirez accepts Erin's equation of the Confederate cause with that of Mexico, praises Trane for the South's gallant fight, and asks him for aid. This perverse use of the Civil War referent is consistent with the downgrading of populist versions of democracy implicit in the Doolittle Report.

When Trane too refuses Ramirez, the Juarista signals to his hidden troops, who suddenly line the high walls surrounding the plaza. Ramirez fights by Doolittle-like principles, taking "unfair" advantage when he can—although like Trane he does so only out of necessity. But Erin's treachery tops that of Ramirez: two of his men seize some children and hold them hostage in a church. The scene puts us into the moral framework of the climax of *Rio Grande*, only now it is "our" men who hold the hostages and the non-Whites who are the would-be rescuers. When Ramirez retreats, we learn that the Mexicans are not utterly amoral, that there are limits they will not transgress even to win their war. But we are not at all sure how far Erin will go. Trane answers the question empirically: the children are still alive—perhaps the hostage-taking was merely a bluff. But not only has Erin violated a "longstanding American concept of fair play"; he has nearly transgressed the supreme taboo of the Western movie—the "Apache" deed of deliberately killing children and/or women. In this light Trane's response appears to be a rationalization, and we are prepared to find it increasingly untenable.

Trane's moral development is aided by a "redemptive woman," a Juarista pickpocket and spy named Nina with whom he falls in love. Joe Erin forms a corresponding liaison with a French countess and courtesan (Denise Darcel), who is his female counterpart and goads him to new heights of cynical treachery. The female pair is an inversion of conventional light-woman/dark-woman pairings like the one in *High Noon.* Nina's character signals the presence in this Cold War Western of the liberal values identified with the "Cult of the Indian" and the "civil rights Western." Her role unites the associations of the Mexican saloon girl with those of the Indian princess in the *Broken Arrow* tradition. She introduces the hero both to the life of passionate love and sexuality and to the life and moral perspective of another race and culture.

This "liberal" approach to racial imagery is also reflected in the composition and development of the group of mercenaries led by Erin and Trane. Like the "platoon" of the combat movie, the group is a mixture of social, ethnic, and racial types—a gambler, an Irishman, a working-class thug named Pittsburgh (Charles Bronson), and a Black ex-slave and Union veteran named Ballard. But the members of this new, postwar platoon are too mercenary and self-interested to be credible as "liberators." Their spirit is typified by Bronson's Pittsburgh. This representative of the working-class American is an unthinking brute who is interested only in loot. He is playful one moment with a Mexican fiesta band and in the next he is leading the attempted gang-rape of Nina.[63]

Ballard's presence in the "platoon" is significant as a gesture toward integration at a critical moment in the renewal of the struggle for civil rights. The liberal intentions behind his role are also reflected in Ballard's rescue of Nina from the rape—a scene whose clear intention is to invoke and then rebuke the normative rape-scenario of racial bigotry in which the Black male is always the aggressor. Since it would damage this "liberal" gesture to present Ballard as a Black "Pittsburgh," Ballard becomes the one man in the platoon who identifies more closely with Trane than with Erin.

The movie's ideological self-contradictions are reflected in the conflicting elements of Trane's character—aristocratic and democratic, paternalistic and mercenary. Trane's relationship with Ballard is proof of a "democratic" spirit of racial tolerance. But what kind of value can "democracy" have if its representatives (Erin and Pittsburgh) are utterly mercenary, unprincipled, and uncivil?

The reconciliation of these ideological oppositions is achieved through violent action. The Americans finally shift to the revolutionary side, but their reasons are still mercenary: they want the gold that has eluded them. The rebels accept them despite their service with Maximilian and their lack of principle, because the Americans are masters of a vital military technology. The rebels lack artillery, and the Americans can use their brand-new Winchester repeating rifles as a substitute. Trane is the only American who has begun to soften toward the revolution as such. The process begun by his love for Nina is completed by what he sees of the rebels in the assault on Vera Cruz. The courage of the rebels, their willingness to fight and die for their cause, awakens his respect for them and their beliefs as no other kind of appeal had done.

This change of heart makes explicit the standard of ideological value that has been implicit throughout the movie but has been masked under the contrasting claims of "democracy," "self-interest," "honor," and the like. What makes men admirable and equal in each other's eyes, what makes them willing to recognize and respect each other's dignity and need, is their capacity as warriors. Trane the paternalist is not moved to moral action by the helplessness of the Mexican children whom Erin takes hostage, or by the sight of peons abused by the French. He enlists in their cause only after they prove themselves according to the standards by which he and Erin measure and respect each other. That standard is the one articulated by the Virginian in 1902—the only equality is that of being equal to the occasion. In 1954, that standard is identified with the specific characteristics of the gunfighter: the professional man of arms, cool, isolated, self-sufficient, capable of self-defense under any circumstances, who measures all things and all men by the canons of his calling.

But according to that standard, there is no real equality between Anglos and Mexicans. The Americans are so superior that the Mexicans cannot win without them. Mere will and courage are not enough without fast guns and sharpshooters to fire them. In *Vera Cruz* as in *The Virginian*, the triumph of "true democracy" is equated with the empowerment of a "true artistocracy" founded on superior skill and developed and revealed through the test of battle. By this measure, the final confrontation of Erin and Trane is a more significant conflict than the struggle of the revolutionaries against the French. This is a battle between giants, supermen capable of reversing any historical verdict. But when Trane finally proves he is "the better man" by outdrawing and killing Erin, none of the moral differences between them are resolved, nor is their mutual admiration and friendship entirely undone—Trane clearly regrets Erin's death. Trane does not win because he is a *morally* better man, but because he is a faster man with a gun. The world of the traditional Western, and the myth of American history which it embodied, appeared to be one in which right and might were necessarily linked. That was why the opponents of "progress" inevitably failed in the end. But in *Vera Cruz* no such historical providence is at work; progress, like politics, comes out of the barrel of the fastest gun.

The triumph of Ben Trane enlarges the significance of the gunfighter. Instead of being a remnant of the Old West whose skill and bravery have outlived their usefulness, the gunfighter is now the expression or personification of a valid heroic style that provides the key to success in a "modern" revolution. Although the cause for which he fights is still identified as an idealistic one, gunfighter style emphasizes the inadequacy of right to conquer in a contest with might. It insists on the necessity of bringing to an idealistic cause an absolutely hard-boiled and even cynical appreciation of the division of political and military power and a willingness to measure means by their effectiveness rather than by their conformity to "longstanding concepts of fair play." Moreover, the adoption of gunfighter style implies the assumption of a kind of aristocratic privilege. The style assumes a broad gulf of difference between those who can "do what a man's gotta do" and those who are either too cowardly or simply too inexpert to do it effectively. In the Mexican or Third World setting, this difference between gunfighter expertise and civilian incompetence becomes a metonymy of the different racial endowments of White Americans and brown-skinned "natives."

As a "thought-experiment" in the development of a response to the problem of Third World revolutions, *Vera Cruz* is suggestive but incomplete. The film takes the moral and ideological stance implicit in policy projections like the Doolittle Report, gives it flesh and form, and connects it to the traditions and current practices of our mythology. It resolves the Hobson's choice of "Mexican" revolutionary politics—Villa or Huerta or Madero, the killer or the tyrant or the "Christ-fool"—by substituting a team of American killers for a Villa or a Zapata. But it does not attempt to envision the consequences of this substitution. We are not told what happens to Trane after the battle. Does he stay in Mexico because the Mexicans will still be dependent on his help? If he returns to his plantation, how will the Mexicans do without him?

Critics have differed in their evaluation of the effect this ambiguous ending has on the film's formal structure. It can be seen as a failure (or a refusal) to carry the script's revisionist view of heroism through to its logical conclusion. Or it can be seen as the perfect reflection of that revisionist view, whose essential point is the ambiguous and contingent character of heroism and virtue. But from the perspective of genre movie-making, the ambiguity of the film's conclusion is the sign that the film has not exhausted its theme—that interesting possibilities for characterization and alternative scenarios remained to be explored.

The irresolution of the ending of *Vera Cruz* also mirrors the unresolved character of counterinsurgency policy in 1954, which would be pushed forward in the intra-governmental policy debates of 1954–61 on counterinsurgency strategies. Likewise, Westerns made over the next six years canvassed the range of possible solutions to the interesting myth/ideological problem inherent in the gunfighter-in-Mexico scenario. The range of character types developed in *Vera Cruz* would become standard for the subgenre—the chivalric mercenary (the Han Solo type), the true mercenary, the mixed "platoon" of Americans, the revolutionary *Mexicana* of dubious virtue, the German officer who assists the tyrant, the Zapata-like Indian revolutionary bandit. The scenario of the gunfighter and/or mercenary in Mexico was imitated and extended over the next six years in a series of films, including *Treasure of Pancho Villa* (1955), *Bandido!* and *Santiago* (1956), *Last of the Fast Guns* and *Villa!* (1958), and *The Wonderful Country* (1959).[64] The series culminated in 1960 in the epic production of *The Magnificent Seven*, a film that set the pattern for future Mexico Westerns and linked the subgenre even more closely to the concerns of counterinsurgency.[65]

14 Gunfighters and Green Berets

Imagining the Counterinsurgency Warrior, 1956–1960

At the same time Hollywood was imagining an errant American gunfighter as the solution to the "Zapata problem," the Eisenhower administration was developing a scenario for an American response to anti-colonial revolutions. The immediate task was to assist the new anti-Communist government of South Vietnam (GVN), headed by Ngo Dinh Diem. The 1954 Geneva accords that ended France's colonial war in Indochina had divided Vietnam into two armistice zones, with the GVN controlling the South and the Vietminh the North; unification of the country under a single government was to be the subject of an election scheduled for 1956. There was little doubt that Ho Chi Minh, leader of the Vietminh, would win that election. To prevent the Communists from gaining control of the South, the administration advised and aided Diem's efforts to abort the election and establish South Vietnam as an independent nation. Before its legitimacy or administrative structure was well established, however, Diem's regime faced a renewed Vietminh insurgency. That development provided the first test of America's counterinsurgency policy.

American Guerrilla in the Philippines: The Lansdale Scenario

The recently concluded campaign against the Communist *Hukbalahap* or "Huk" guerrillas in the Philippines (1949–53) offered an appealing model of successful counterinsurgency. The campaign had been led by Ramon Magsaysay, a strong, liberal Philippine nationalist who perfectly fulfilled the vision of a native "counterpart" to American leadership. But behind the scenes,

Magsaysay had been secretly assisted by a former OSS officer, Colonel Edward Lansdale. The administration appointed Lansdale to head the CIA's operations in Indochina and to apply his methods to Diem's counterinsurgency problem.[1]

It was perhaps inevitable that the administration should see the Huk campaign as *Lansdale's* victory. Since 1898, American policymakers and colonial administrators had assumed that the Filipinos were culturally, and perhaps racially, unready for self-government; that American tutelage was needed to transform the feudal, tribal, and family-centered polity of the natives into the political culture of a modern democratic nation-state. This attitude persisted, even though the Philippines had been declared ready for independence in 1942 and were actually freed in 1946.[2] The original colonialist concept of Philippine political culture was never subjected to systematic and sustained critique in American cultural or political discourses. After the wave of imperialist enthusiasm that had enabled Theodore Roosevelt's administration to subjugate the islands, the "White Man's Burden" ceased to be a major subject for either political agitation or popular fiction. Colonial administrators pursued their tasks without public attention, and indeed without the assurance of public interest and support. There was no Philippine equivalent of the Western dime or pulp novel, and (with the exception of *The Real Glory* [1939]) no feature films dealing with imperial adventures in the Philippines, our largest and richest colonial possession. (Compare this with the dozen or so major features devoted to the British imperial administration of India.) Only in the combat films of 1943–50, where the Filipinos appear as subjects of American stewardship and liberation, do the Philippines figure as an important subject for mass-culture mythography.[3]

But it was a serious mistake to see the Lansdale/Magsaysay partnership as a tutelary one. In fact, Lansdale and Magsaysay worked effectively because the relationship was balanced; and Magsaysay, as both a native leader and an expert on his own political culture, shaped the objectives and overall course of policy. Magsaysay was a genuine reformer who was as much the opponent of the corrupt post-colonial government of Elpidio Quirino as he was the enemy of the Huks. The Quirino government, which had received independence as an American gift, was a confederacy of political cliques built around wealthy families and their clients. Its members used political office to enrich themselves and maintain control over their tenants and workers; dissent was stifled by stuffing ballot boxes and by making extensive use of political violence. It did little to help the islands' economy recover from the ruinous effects of invasion and Japanese occupation. Many of the older generation of non-Communist native nationalists, who had opposed U.S. colonialism, had been compromised by collaboration with the Japanese. In this setting the Huks were able to co-opt a wide range of social and economic discontents and make a credible bid to become the heirs of the anti-colonial nationalism of Aguinaldo.[4]

When Magsaysay began his work as Quirino's Defense Minister, he already represented a substantial native constituency for reform. He used his office to revamp the Philippine military and to undertake programs of "civic action" aimed at improving the living conditions of peasants in the threatened provinces. He emerged from this counterguerrilla operation as a national hero and the leader of a movement for national reform. The real secret of "Lansdale's success" was his early discovery and cultivation of Magsaysay and his self-discipline in keeping within the boundaries of his role as adviser and sometime provider of material support. His advice was perhaps less crucial in the struggle against the Huk than in the organizational work through which Magsaysay built his political movement; he helped Magsaysay win the Presidency by using the influence of the American government to guarantee two relatively honest elections (in 1951 and 1953).

By interpreting the victory over the Huks as the product of Lansdale's professionalism and genius, American policy-makers blinded themselves to the real dynamics of that counterinsurgency operation. When they transferred Lansdale to Vietnam in 1956 to apply the lessons of "his" victory, the error was compounded. In the Philippines Lansdale had had advantages that would not be found in Vietnam: a longstanding historical and linguistic tie between the imperiled country and the United States, a relatively stable native government, a popular native leader to head that government, and a reliable native military force whose institutional structure and traditions were compatible with American methods.[5]

The situation was very different in South Vietnam, whose people and leaders had no ties to the United States, whose government lacked popular legitimacy and administrative experience, and whose sense of nationality was either problematic or identified with the Communist-led Vietminh. The political problems of the South Vietnamese regime might have proved intractable even to advisers knowledgeable about Vietnamese history, culture, politics, and military doctrine. Lansdale and his colleagues had no such knowledge. Moreover, their mission was not to analyze Vietnamese society but to ensure the survival of the Diem regime by every technique at their disposal, since it was the only visible alternative to a Communist takeover.[6]

In practice, this required the Americans to support the anti-democratic actions through which Diem established his power. American policy-makers expected that such measures would become unnecessary once the regime had dealt with the immediate threat of Communist takeover and that under American tutelage Diem would begin a transition to genuine democracy. But these expectations were based on a misunderstanding of Vietnamese political culture and Diem's place in it. Because of the circumstances of its birth, the regime faced almost insuperable difficulties in establishing its legitimacy among its own people. Those difficulties were compounded by Diem's weaknesses as a leader.[7]

In 1956–57 Diem instituted the Denunciation of Communists Campaign. Although the name disarmingly suggested a parallel with Congressional hearings on "Un-American Activities," the operation in fact involved the widespread use of imprisonment, torture, and execution against all those constituencies which either opposed Diem or favored national elections.[8] The result was a narrowing of Diem's popular political base and a renewal of guerrilla activity by remnants of the Vietminh and new cadres sent from the North. This in turn induced the regime to rely still more heavily on armed force to maintain itself and required the American administration to increase the military side of its operations.[9]

Instead of reinforcing a genuine native "third force," an alternative to both Communism and to the dictatorship of an imperial "puppet," the Americans found themselves committed to support a regime that could maintain itself only by forcibly suppressing all political opposition. This was a position at odds, not only with the democratic pretensions of American political ideology, but with the real goals of counterinsurgency policy, which envisioned the development of a South Vietnamese nationality as democratic and pro-American as the Magsaysay government in the Philippines.[10]

Because Diem's regime was unable to muster an authentically "national" resistance to the Vietminh, the American administration was confronted with four choices: to allow the GVN to continue on a ruinous course; to abandon the GVN to its fate; to take power from the GVN and impose an American regime; or to bring in more American troops to stave off military disaster and buy more time for the GVN to reform itself. The first two alternatives would (it was thought) do irreparable harm to the American policy of containment and deterrence by proving the United States a "paper tiger." Most policy-makers believed that an outright American takeover was unlikely to succeed and was in any case precluded by the prevalence of a national and international consensus against colonialism. The logic inherent in this way of conceiving the alternatives pointed to the steady increase of military activity and the transformation of the struggle from a Vietnamese counterguerrilla war with American advisers to a thoroughly Americanized war. This was precisely the result that the Eisenhower administration had hoped to avoid when it began systematic development of a counterinsurgency policy in 1957.

But the tendency toward militarization was not simply a response to circumstances in Vietnam; it was driven by the institutional biases of the agencies that formulated American counterinsurgency doctrine. The most pervasive of these biases was the tendency to interpret all problems as arising from the Cold War confrontation between a Free World led by the United States and a Communist World led by the Soviets and to calculate the success or failure of any operation by quantifying the amount of military strength added to or subtracted from the enemy camp by "winning" or "losing" this or that country. This conception of the Cold War reduced analysis of indigenous social and political cultures to the barely instrumental and rejected nationalist movements with a "neutralist" bent.

The military bias in counterinsurgency policy was initially reinforced by the absence of any systematic theory of "development" or "modernization" around which a more flexible and comprehensive policy could be based. But between 1956 and 1962, theories of "nation-building" were being developed. And as evidence of Diem's failures accumulated, these theories became the basis of a transformation in the conception of the American mission. Instead of seeing ourselves as "advisers" to a viable nation-state, our task now was to *create* the kind of nation whose independence we could legitimately be asked to protect—a paradoxical sort of mission, to say the least.[11]

Although administration policy required the establishment of a legitimate and (more or less) democratic national government in the South, its strategy for achieving that goal was a complete inversion of American democratic theory. From the time of the Revolution that theory had insisted that the only valid (or permanently viable) government is one generated by and/or expressive of the will of the nation's people. The South Vietnamese "nation," however, was to be created from the top down. First the government was to be established and empowered, then it was to attempt to win the full consent of its subjects, and only when it had created (with our help) "a people in which it could have confidence" would fully free elections be held.[12]

From its inception under Eisenhower to its full development under Kennedy, American counterinsurgency doctrine held that "the organic and unsponsored insurgency was [not] a viable possibility." It was "the American political shibboleth that insurgency could not be organic" but must depend absolutely on an "external sponsor," not only for the material of war but for the political will and motivation to initiate and sustain a durable revolutionary movement. It was this belief that blinded policy-makers to the political character of the North Vietnamese regime and to the nature (even the existence) of an indigenous political culture in the South. If there was no native political culture, it followed that the American task would be to supply something in the place of nothing: to inscribe the forms of national organization on the "blank slate" of a pre-nationalist culture.[13] Thus the various programs of "reform" and "nation-building" tended to become programs of Americanization. But since there was in fact a strong and intractable political culture in Vietnam, Americanization of the war served only to alienate the people it was intended to protect and to allow the Communists to identify themselves with the defense of the indigenous culture and Vietnamese nationality.[14]

The language and conceptual categories of the Frontier Myth were particularly important during the formative period of counterinsurgency doctrine. That myth taught us that historical progress is achieved only by the advance of White European races/cultures into and against the terrain of "primitive," non-White "natives." The native races are inherently lacking in the capacity to generate "progress." The best of them are seen as passively willing to subordinate themselves to the progressive Whites. The worst are seen as savagely opposed to progress, preferring extermination to either civilization or subjugation.

The myth of savage warfare also provided an imaginative model of the kind of historical actor who is needed in a struggle of this kind. Since the new enemy does not fight by civilized rules, he can only be defeated by someone who combines the amoral pragmatism and technical expertise of the gunfighter with the skill in handling natives that belongs to the "man who knows Indians." To answer the challenge of the Marxist "war of national liberation" required the creation of American guerrilla specialists whose skills as tacticians and as organizers of peasant militias mirrored those of the enemy. Such men, backed by the greater resources of the United States, could presumably beat the Communists at their own game.[15]

To develop a scenario of military and civic action, American planners had to predict the kinds of problem that were likely to occur and the sorts of measures that would be needed to resolve them. Since there was so little knowledge of Vietnam, these predictions (and the war-games in which they were tested) had to be based on generic concepts derived from our past experience in similar situations. But that historical past was itself encoded in the terms of myth. Hence, despite their official auspices, the scenarios and game-models developed by the policy-makers were not very different from the imaginative projections that were developed by fiction writers and filmmakers interested in counterinsurgency during the same period. We have seen this parallel in the broad definitions of operational doctrine and "heroic style" formulated in the Doolittle Report and *Vera Cruz*. Other works of fiction and film from this period also offered thought-experiments that tested certain possible interpretations of the counterinsurgency problem by imaginative projection. Some of these thought-experiments were in several respects more accurate than the policy papers and counterinsurgency manuals in their understanding of the logic and anticipation of the future course of counterinsurgency.

Imagining a Counterpart: The Ugly American *(1958)*

One of the most influential critiques of the Eisenhower administration's lack of counterinsurgency policies was developed in a novel called *The Ugly American* (1958), written by two journalists, William Lederer and Eugene Burdick. In some ways this book was the *Uncle Tom's Cabin* of counterinsurgency: it put into vivid novelistic prose a convincing interpretation of the crisis of Communist expansion in Asia and offered an appealing scenario of how we might master the situation. As late as 1963 the novel was still regarded as a counterinsurgency primer, even by knowledgeable men like John Paul Vann, who were attempting with little success to apply counterinsurgency doctrine in Vietnam.[16]

But the novel's wide appeal owes more to its conformity to literary and mythic conventions—the standard by which we are used to determining the plausibility of a given story—than to its analysis of Asian society. Lederer and Burdick treat "Asians" as Hollywood (for the most part) treated "Indians"—as if they had a unitary racial character transcending differences of culture and nationality. The hero of the novel is a "man who knows Indians," Colonel Hillandale, based closely on Lansdale. Hillandale (like the real Lansdale) is summoned to organize counterinsurgency in "Sarkhan" (that is, South Vietnam) because he understands "the Asian personality and the way it play[s] politics" and has demonstrated this by defeating the Huk uprising in the Philippines. Given the ethnic and historical differences between the two countries, it is difficult to imagine two situations more unlike; but for Lederer and Burdick, and indeed for Eisenhower, Dulles, Lansdale, Taylor, and Kennedy, those differences weighed less than the essentially literary conception of an "Asian character."[17]

"Character" is also the determinant of victory in the novel's scenario of counterinsurgency. According to Lederer and Burdick, America is failing in Asia because our agents there do not represent our best national characteristics. Though we can, and do, provide more material aid to the Third World than do the Communists, we lose to them in the area of "symbolism," which is of paramount importance to "the Asian mind." The problem is stated in the first chapter of *The Ugly American* in an argument between an American who has set up a dairy for the benefit of a peasant village and a Communist guerrilla named Deong who sabotages the operation. The American and Deong were originally comrades in the war against Japan—an OSS Hawkeye and his Asian Chingachgook. But Deong has turned against the American who "took [him] off the back of a water buffalo" and taught him how to fight for freedom, because (he says) "the side with the most brains and power wins . . . that's not your side any more. . . . You haven't got the power or the will." Deong is conceived as a nationalist, but as one who has no specific political beliefs or ideological commitments. His politics are reactive or passive. He is a Communist only because the Communists have displayed brains, power, and a will to fight. To win (or win back) the hearts and minds of people who think this way, it is only necessary to demonstrate a different character, more insistent on exerting its will and able to display more brains and power.[18]

This new display of American character is effected through the rest of the novel in the stories of a series of other counterpart pairs which suggest ways of repairing the breach symbolized by Deong's rejection of his American mentor. The Americans include engineers, soldiers, agronomists, and diplomats, all of whom have in common a "first rate" character, a plebeian style, an ability to relate "unaffectedly" and sympathetically to the natives, a belief in "can-do" pragmatism, and a professional approach to their duties. Each finds his native counterpart in an Asian who is representative of racial character but who is exceptional in his possession of a latent gift for American-style progress. His "Asiatic" suspicion of the foreigner is overcome because he recognizes in the American the fully realized expression of his own inarticulate yearning for self-improvement. He has an *instinctive* affinity for capitalism and an appreciation of technology. Above all, he has transcended the tribal and "selfish" views characteristic of "the Asian peasant" to identify with the (potential) "nation." Left without an alternative, he would undoubtedly have followed Deong into the Communist camp. It is vital to the dramatic point of the story, and appropriate to the polemics of counterinsurgency, that the counterpart be seen as a "hostile" who is converted into a "friendly" by the White American's display of honor and competence.

This kind of relationship conforms to the pairings of frontier heroes and Indian companions in the mythic tradition. From the earliest Indian-war narratives down through Fenimore Cooper to the dime novel and the Western movie, the best allies of American myth-heroes have always been wild Indians rather than tame or reservation Indians. Admiration is reserved for those Indians whose thoughts mirror the Whites' understanding of the terms of conflict—either civilization or savagery must be wiped out—and whose actions are consistent with that belief. This was what General Custer had in mind when he made his famous declaration that if he were an Indian, he would prefer dying with the hostiles to living on a reservation. It underlay Remington's vision of militarized Indian colonies serving as a buffer between the United States and Mexico.[19]

The immediate appeal of the counterpart pair is novelistic and mythic. It makes for an effective drama, and it domesticates an exotic adventure by aligning the adventure with familiar story-devices. But the reality of counterpart relationships in Vietnam was radically different—as (for example) John Paul Vann discovered in the Delta in 1962, when he attempted to make a Lederer/Burdick-type counterpart out of Colonel Cao. Instead of accepting the tutelage of the American adviser and adapting to his concept of military and political priorities, the Colonel persisted in acting in accordance with values and priorities indigenous to the South Vietnamese political culture—just as the insurgents were doing.[20]

The Ugly American also anticipates the drift or bias toward militarization that we have noted in the development of counterinsurgency policy as a whole. Lederer and Burdick clearly intended to emphasize the importance of "civic action" as a way of forestalling or limiting an insurgency. But war stories form the spine of the narrative. The novel's thesis is that in the Cold War, and especially in counterinsurgency, the Clausewitzian maxim is inverted and politics is merely war carried on by other means. Many of the civic-action scenarios in *The Ugly American* are seen to depend on or to result in the establishment of a counterguerrilla military force, usually led by a Westerner or a Westernized native. Particular emphasis is laid on the military successes gained by a native counterguerrilla militia led by a French priest who forms his unit by working on the peculiar religious temperament and susceptibility of "Asians."

The most extended of these episodes concerns the activities of a group of American observers and counterguerrilla advisers with the French Foreign Legion during the last stages of the French Indochina War. But the key terms in the account are drawn from the Frontier Myth, the Western, and the combat film. The hero of the episode is the American military observer, Major Tex Wolchek, whose characterization draws on the conventions of both the Western and the combat film. His family "had always dreamed of the American frontier; they had found the American magic in Texas," where his immigrant father became a self-made millionaire. Tex himself is the incarnation of a stereotype, the model "of what Texans thought Texans looked like," and he has risen through the ranks during combat in Normandy and on Pork Chop Hill in Korea. (These references invoke battles that were particularly celebrated in commercial popular culture and film.)[21] In his time with the French, Tex works with two Foreign Legionnaires, an aristocratic French officer named Monet, and an African-American named Jim Davis—a college athlete who had dropped out of UCLA to look for adventure in the Legion. The Foreign Legion was indeed prominent among the French forces in Vietnam, but frequent and favorable cinematic treatment also made it the only French unit with which an American audience could be expected to readily identify. Combat-film conventions also are important here: the trio of heroes is an alliance across lines of nationality (French/American), class (aristocratic/self-made bourgeois), and race (White/Black). Davis' college background and his service in a unit consisting mostly of Whites (including former Nazis) link him suggestively with Jackie Robinson, the star UCLA athlete who served as an officer in the Second World War before integrating major-league baseball in 1947.

Although Monet and Davis have been fighting in Vietnam for months, Tex turns out to be the only one of the three who truly "knows Indians." He tries unsuccessfully to get Monet to study the Communists' battle doctrine, as laid out in the works of Mao Tse-tung, and to learn to fight the enemy in his own style. Tex's knowledge is not the product of experience but of an instinctive recognition of the correct way to fight such a war. Although his American identity and background have not taught him anything about this particular war, they have taught him everything he needs to know about this *kind* of war.

Monet is converted to Tex's wisdom by the same kind of incident that converts Kathleen to Kirby Yorke's militarism in *Rio Grande*. Davis and another soldier are sent out on a scouting mission and are captured and tortured by the Vietminh; Davis has an eye gouged out, and his companion has his voice box cut out. The companion is a Vietnamese native whose nickname is "Apache." Like Kirby Yorke, Monet responds with an instant decision to punish the enemy and to break the regular army rules that have constrained him. He and Tex re-read their copy of Mao, which contains the recommendation that a guerrilla headquarters be a certain distance from the field of action. By process of elimination they are able to deduce which village, and even which building, the headquarters "must" be in. They then improvise a mobile rocket-launcher and race through enemy lines to hit the target with surgical precision and maximum firepower. Although their victory comes too late to save the French colonial regime, Lederer and Burdick clearly intend it as a model of how to fight guerrillas.

Lederer and Burdick's thesis is that we must "read Mao's book" to understand the nature of the enemy. But their own reading completely (and, for an American, characteristically) misconstrues the principles and tactics of the so-called wars of national liberation. The first of these principles is the primacy of politics in determining the character and objectives of military action: guerrilla war makes sense only when it represents a powerful indigenous political tendency. At the level of tactics, the primary principle of guerrilla warfare since the seventeenth century has been mobility, improvisation, dispersion of forces, and evasion of open battle. Tex and Monet succeed in their raid because Lederer and Burdick have imagined for them a guerrilla army that rigidly follows a military doctrine laid down in a manual—

in fact, a guerrilla army that fights like a regular army. Tex's assault on the Vietminh town anticipates the wishful dream of American commanders who tried to transform the guerrilla war into a conventional battlefield, with an enemy army found and fixed in place and vulnerable to the application of a maximum dose of firepower.[22]

Lederer and Burdick intended *The Ugly American* as a critique of the presumed lethargy and passivity of the Eisenhower administration, which had allowed the Russians and the Chinese to win a series of cheap victories among the emerging nations of the Third World. But the approach to counterinsurgency which they imagined so vividly in this novel was already being formulated as a tactical doctrine and put into practice by army counterinsurgency specialists. Unfortunately, these specialists also anticipated the novelists' misinterpretation of Mao's so-called handbook of revolution.

In his post-revolutionary writings, Mao described a three-phase strategy by which (he said) his movement had triumphed, and he asserted that peasant revolutions could triumph anywhere by following the Chinese model. In Phase I the insurgency secures political and military bases among a discontented peasantry. In Phase II units begin protracted guerrilla warfare in many localties, gradually forcing the government out of the countryside and establishing themselves as protectors of the villages. Finally, with the countryside effectively governed by the insurgents, an offensive can be opened against the government in the cities (Phase III). In every phase, terror tactics are employed to destroy the institutional infrastructure of the regime, to evoke repressive measures by the regime (against which the revolution can offer a defense), and to repress dissident or counterrevolutionary movements within areas controlled by the revolutionaries. After the revolution, terror is used to destroy "class enemies" and to complete the process of economic transformation.[23]

In fact, Mao's three-phase "model" was as much a literary artifact as an account of "Maoist strategy." The apparent theoretical rigor of his strategic doctrine was possible because it was not a historical description but a rationalization, after the fact, of the revolutionary tactics Mao and his followers had evolved through trial and error. The theoretical model ignored or discounted the historical contingencies (most notably and exceptionally the eruption of a world war) that had contributed to Mao's victory. Moreover, the pretense of theoretical or strategic omniscience in these writings was exaggerated beyond the usual self-congratulation of a triumphant party, because Mao's purposes were polemical rather than historical or technical.

His statements were weapons in the ideological battles he waged against competing factions in his own party and in the emerging competition between China and the Soviet Union for leadership of the "socialist camp" (a rivalry American planners also failed to appreciate). Nor was Mao taken as a master of revolution by either Ho Chi Minh or Fidel Castro, who led the two most successful peasant revolutions of the Cold War era.[24]

Americans misread a literary-polemical performance for a description of practice, because—following the institutional customs of the military planning agencies—they themselves were looking for a strategic doctrine that could be abstracted as a set of techniques and maneuvers, taught to an elite corps of counterguerrilla specialists, and applied by them to any insurgency that might occur in any post-colonial or peasant society. In "Mao's book" they found the perfect *counterpart* of their own project, and, following the doctrine of Indian fighting—you need "White savages" to combat "Red"—they promulgated a theory of counterguerrilla warfare and "nation-building."

By reading Mao as an authority on *tactics*, American planners made a fundamental error that proved fatal to the counterinsurgency mission. They presumed that it was possible to separate the tactics of a revolutionary movement from the politics that such a movement necessarily entails and to entrust the development of tactics to specially trained soldiers.

The Ranger Mystique and the Origin of Special Forces

During Eisenhower's second term the Army Special Forces or "Green Berets" were created to answer this particular need. These units were originally conceived as auxiliaries to regular NATO forces whose mission would be to organize and direct partisan and resistance movements behind enemy lines in case of a Soviet attack on Western Europe. But the increasing American involvement in Vietnam and the need for military specialists to direct the fighting against Communist guerrillas transformed the Special Forces mission from partisan to counterinsurgency warfare.[25]

In this formative period of counterinsurgency doctrine (1956–60), military planners did not possess any systematic theory of guerrilla warfare in post-colonial settings. In the absence of specific knowledge, they had to teach prospective counterguerrillas a generalized technique of operations, an overall attitude or style of approach that would meet the necessities of "unconventional warfare." Like their civilian counterparts, they scanned their institutional history in a search for useful precedents on which to base a program for training the kind of officers and enlisted men who could be victorious in a counterguerrilla battle.

As an institution with its own historians and system of historical education, the army had its own special myths: traditional concepts of war-fighting and leadership embodied in exemplary tales of military success and failure. But these were only specialized versions of the same myths that shaped the culture of civilian society, and they featured many of the same legends of heroism and disaster—Washington at Braddock's Defeat, Custer at the Little Big Horn—that were celebrated in popular and mass culture.[26] But where fiction-writers and journalists drew general moral and ideological lessons from these legends, the army's interpretations naturally emphasized lessons about strategy and tactics, the character and role of military leaders, and the ideal forms of command and control on the battlefield.[27]

In some respects the army's experience in "unconventional" wars was both practical and extensive. During the wars of the colonial period, the primary and perennial enemy faced by American soldiers were the Native Americans; and throughout the nineteenth century, service on the Indian frontier was the school in which combat officers learned their craft. Thus the kind of warfare that modern military theorists identified as "unconventional" was in fact the most typical form of military operation during most of the army's history.

During the colonial period American militia and (later) ranger units had served as auxiliaries of professional or regular army units organized by the British. In conventional campaigns rangers provided scouts and harassed the flanks and rear echelons of the enemy; in Indian campaigns (like the attack of Rogers' Rangers on St. Francis in 1758), ranger-type units sometimes constituted the main striking force. Units of this kind had acquired a special mystique in the United States, because they were distinctly *American*, distinguished from the British by both nationality and style of warfare. This distinction became particularly important during the last French and Indian War and the Revolution, as Americans sought to differentiate themselves from the British. American accounts of these wars increasingly emphasized the difference between the stand-up tactics of the British and the "ranger" style in which even uniformed American units fought (for example, at Braddock's Defeat, Concord, Bunker Hill, and New Orleans) and noted that the ranger's was truly a "native" style, adapted to the peculiar conditions of warfare in the American wilderness.[28] The ranger mystique thus involved a complex identification with the Indians, whose character as natives marked them as the original and quintessential "Americans" but whose character as "savages" marked them as the ultimate enemy. By dressing and fighting as Indians, the ranger appropriated the savage's power and American nativity for himself and turned it against both savage and redcoat.[29]

The ranger mystique was elaborated and developed in both popular/commercial culture and military culture during the nineteenth century. The spectacular successes of Confederate cavalry raiders and guerrillas during the Civil War added luster to this image, although the atrocities committed by guerrilla bands in Missouri also added to the aura of "darkness" and savagery attached to this kind of warfare. The persistence of Indian wars throughout the nineteenth century made Indian fighting and policing the army's constant task, the practical training ground in which many if not most of each new generation of combat officers—and commanding generals from Winfield Scott to John J. Pershing—learned the essentials of combat command. The combat style of the Indian-fighter and the Civil War partisan guerrilla emphasized pragmatic improvisation, borrowing tactics from the enemy, and disdain of parade-ground regularity; and this style became an important strain in the complex of institutional traditions that shaped the American officer's concept of his own character and role.

The ranger mystique defined an alternative leadership style, different from but no less conventional and traditional than regular-army spit-and-polish. Differences between these styles could produce serious internal disagreement over tactics, training, and entitlement to promotion—real-world versions of the conflict between Thursday (the regular) and York (the ranger) in *Fort Apache*. But as the characterization of Yorke in *Rio Grande* suggests, the two styles were not necessarily incompatible. Like real-life Generals Custer, Pershing, and Patton, Yorke exemplifies a command style that we may think of as "profesionally irregular": rigorous in establishing the chain of command and maintaining troop discipline, but willing to get dirty, to learn from the enemy, to adapt to the irregularity of war.[30]

But the differences between "regular" and "ranger" styles were also the cause of conflict within the army over the development and use of Special Forces (1957–61), and, during the Vietnam War itself, over the methods of counterinsurgency and those of a "big unit" war.[31] York's disagreement with Thursday hinges on the *distinction* he draws between the Civil War and the Apache wars and on the assertion that tactics applicable in a conflict between civilized peoples will not work in a savage war. (It is worth noting that he advocates negotiation and a type of "pacification" that includes political reform as substitutes for a big-unit attack.) Thursday's denial of the importance of the distinction reflects more accurately the viewpoint of the army's institutional culture, which saw the two kinds of war as different phases in a single spectrum. "Regular" wars can be won by the use of "irregular" tactics and Indian wars can be won by applying lessons learned in regular warfare. Grant and Lincoln had defeated the Confederacy by treating civil war as savage war. Compromise on vital questions was ruled out, making negotiated peace impossible and "unconditional surrender" the definition of victory. The war was "totalized" through systematic attacks on civilian economic tragets. After Appomattox, Sherman and Sheridan systematically applied these same methods to the subjugation of the Plains Indians.[32]

After 1865, the army's strategic doctrine was essentially an extrapolation from the Grant/Lincoln strategy. The doctrine assumed that war was a necessary and logical extension of politics whose object was the imposition of one's political will upon the enemy. However, the American army's adherence to the principle of civilian control, coupled with an industrial society's drive for specialization, fostered conditions in which army planners were unable to consider anything but the "purely military" elements in a war situation. Since "politics" was "not their business," it followed that for military planners "victory" could only be understood as the destruction of the enemy's capacity to make war through the attrition of continuous battle coupled with destruction of the civilian economy—the method by which "unconditional surrender" had been won by Grant and Sherman in 1865 and by Eisenhower, Nimitz, and MacArthur in 1945. This was a strategy based on the lavish use of firepower, the maximization of destruction, and the seeking of large "set-piece" battles in which the enemy could be fixed, fired upon, and destroyed—even at the cost of heavy casualties to our own forces.[33]

This orientation made it difficult for army planners to fully understand and utilize the principles of combined civic and military action that lay behind the recent successes of Magsaysay and Lansdale in the Philippines and the British in Malaya. Interservice rivalry and bureaucratic divisions insulated army planners from the highly relevant experience of the Marine Corps during the "Banana Wars" of 1915–34, which de-emphasized the idea of achieving victory through persistent combat, minimized the use of heavy firepower that might cause civilian casualties, and insisted on the centrality of what would later be called "civic action" or "pacification" to any counterinsurgency operation.[34] Army training inevitably centered on the purely military aspects of these successes, leaving the political dimension to civilian officials whose knowledge of Vietnam was limited and who were themselves reluctant to challenge their host regime.[35] Not until 1962, when the counterinsurgency campaign in Vietnam was well launched, would army training manuals acknowledge the central importance of civic action in a counterinsurgency campaign; and even then it was asserted that "civic action must not be looked upon as a substitute for military power and combat capable forces."[36]

Two different approaches to irregular or unconventional warfare were developed during the Second World War: the partisan warfare of resistance movements behind the battle lines in occupied countries; and the operations of elite commando (that is, "ranger") units trained and equipped to perform extraordinarily difficult missions on a conventional battlefield. Partisan operations were based on political resistance movements of varying strengths and allegiances. They ranged in size and scale from the efforts of individual saboteurs and spies, to small-unit warfare in the rural regions of France and Poland, to large-scale uprisings (the Polish Home Army in Warsaw) and campaigns conducted by irregular armies (Yugoslavia). Once the Allies began to advance, the partisans became valuable as military auxiliaries, harassing German lines of communication and supply. But the distinctive feature of partisan warfare is its basis in a popular movement of resistance to an occupying power, and this political dimension was acknowledged in the bureaucratic arrangements that had originally assigned supervision of partisan warfare to the intelligence services.

Ranger or commando units were designed for a different type of unconventional warfare.[37] They were not partisans, but regular troops trained for special tasks. Their missions, which were usually coordinated with conventional operations, involved the infiltration of enemy positions prior to an assault, the seizure (by speed and stealth) of objectives too strong to be taken by conventional assault, and various types of raids designed to divert enemy forces or damage vital facilities. Their training and morale also made them useful as shock troops in an infantry assault and as last-ditch defenders of vital positions.

Implicit in these partisan and ranger/commando types of unconventional warfare are two different models of the relation between politics and force. The partisan movement may be aided by an external power, but its primary source of strength is a popular and indigenous resistance movement, and its military activities are an extension of its civic role and political character. The ranger/commando is trained to operate as an interloper with an external armed force as his base of support; his character and objectives are specifically military and bear no necessary relation to the customs and purposes of the civilian politics of the territory in which he operates.

The designers of American counterinsurgency forces began with a vision of the unconventional warrior derived from ranger/commando tradition: he was to be a professional soldier, trained in techniques of raiding, scouting, and harassment. The American practice of designating these forces as "ranger" and "raider" battalions reflects the association of this kind of unit with the military tradition of the Indian wars and with the partisan cavalry and guerrillas of the Civil War. That association carried over into the new counterinsurgency units that were formed in 1954. The designation of these troops as "Special Forces" made specific reference to the Canadian/American 1st Special Service Force (also called "the Devil's Brigade"), which had fought in North Africa and Italy. That unit had been assigned as its combat badge the crossed-arrows insignia of the now-defunct regiment of Indian Scouts (celebrated by Remington), which had been formed to assist the cavalry during the Plains wars.[38] The Indian symbolism was intended to mark the "otherness" of these units: their kinship with the traditional enemies of their own society and civilization; the distinction between their rule-breaking practice as warriors and the conventional, rule-bound fighting habits of regular troops; and their willingness to fight the enemy in the enemy's style.

This mystique carried over to the Special Forces, and its Indian-war elements became more marked when "New Frontier" became the identifying symbol of the American government. The Green Berets were seen as combining the character of an elite military force, able to make sophisticated use of modern technology and "nation-building" techniques, with the fighting style of frontier rangers "from the French and Indian wars through Marion in the Revolution, Mosby's Rangers in the Civil War and Merrill's Marauders in World War II."[39] But the Indian and ranger mystique confuses guerrilla style with guerrilla substance. These were not truly "savage," irregular, or partisan organizations but elite units of a professional regular army; and despite the peculiarities of their style of operations, their tactical doctrine followed regular army ideas about reliance on a chain of command, firepower, technology, and fixed systems of communications and support.[40]

The partisan *tactics* that most interested and concerned American planners were those designed to disrupt, discredit, and overthrow a regular army or a standing regime. These were the guerrilla tactics in which American Special Forces became expert, on the theory that it takes a thief to catch a thief, a poacher to catch a poacher, and a "White Indian" to catch a "Red" one. The problem was that while counterinsurgency units were designed and trained to think and fight *in the style* of a revolutionary army, their mission was not to make a revolution but to suppress one. Thus soldiers trained to act as thieves, poachers, and Indians had to play the role of policemen, gamekeepers, and garrison troops.[41] But in a war like that in Vietnam, with elements of both a social revolution and a war of national independence, the key to victory is the ability of one side or the other to achieve a successful integration of politics and war. The test of that integration is the ability to maintain a *partisan* army—a military force that can continue to exist only if the population (or its most active element) identifies its own interests with it and proves that willingness by feeding and manning and suffering losses for the partisans' sake. If they were to succeed, the Americans would have to create an army of genuine Vietnamese "partisans"—a task made insuperably difficult by the character of the Diem regime. Failing that, they would have to transform *themselves* into partisan fighters—partisans "on behalf of the Vietnamese," since they could not be partisans "of the Vietnamese." But that would put American troops in the absurd position of substituting themselves for the political entity they were supposed to be protecting.

The advantages and limitations of their approach can be illustrated by a brief jump forward in time to look at a relatively successful counterinsurgency operation: the Special Forces' organization of several Montagnard tribes as Civilian Irregular Defense Groups (CIDG) in 1961–65. Here the mystique of the Indian fighter as a revolutionary partisan provided an appropriate orientation toward the problem. The Montagnards were the closest Vietnamese equivalent to the American Indians of the Frontier Myth. They were semi-nomadic tribesmen, without a written language, technologically primitive, with a shamanistic religion and a political structure based on family clans. As a racial and ethnic minority, they had been persecuted by Vietnamese governments for centuries and felt threatened by the power of any Vietnamese government, Communist or otherwise. They were in rebellion against Diem when the Americans first arrived, but it was not too difficult to redirect their hostility: the Communists were advancing, Saigon was the weaker force, and as patrons of the Montagnards the Americans could be expected to avert Saigonese persecution. By learning the basics of their language and culture, and by giving evidence of power and willingness to aid them in maintaining themselves against Vietnamese encroachment, the Americans were able to bring many of them into the CIDG program. With the Montagnard CIDGs the Americans could function as both revolutionary partisans and as supporters of the Diemist political order. They could utilize their tactical skills as disrupters of communications by raiding out of Montagnard villages against the Ho Chi Minh Trail while employing their civic-action techniques to turn those villages into economically viable and defensible outposts.[42]

But as soon as the CIDG mission was completed, the paradoxes at the heart of counterinsurgency policy reasserted themselves. The whole point of the exercise was to develop the Saigon regime into a genuine national government, on the American model, with authority over the whole of South Vietnam. The final stage of CIDG therefore required the Americans to turn over their role as "Indian agents" for the Montagnards to their Vietnamese counterparts. But as soon as they did so the original political conflicts reappeared with all their original force: the Saigon troops abused or neglected the Montagnards, and the Montagnards rose in rebellion.[43]

The counterinsurgency soldier thus found himself trapped in an insoluble contradiction, a microcosm of the larger dilemma of American policy. The successful application of his tactical doctrine did not provide a way of resolving the endemic problems of South Vietnamese political culture. The only way the Americans could save the fruits of their tactical victory among the Montagnards was to substitute their own regime for that of the Vietnamese. But to do so would have been to admit the impossibility of realizing the larger and more essential goal of American policy, which was to establish a South Vietnamese nation. Moveover, such substitution could only work in a peripheral area among a marginal section of South Vietnam's population. To attempt it on a country-wide scale would be, in effect, to take on the role of a traditional imperial power—a role the American people and government were unwilling and unable to sustain, and against which the Vietnamese (given their history) would probably have rebelled. Yet this was the direction in which the logic of counterinsurgency seemed to drive the course of policy.[44]

The American government went from advising Diem in 1955 to providing the sinews of his power by 1959. Disillusioned with Diem in 1961–62, it would overthrow and replace him with a military regime in 1963. Dissatisfied with that regime's failures, in 1964–65, it would Americanize the conflict through the wholesale substitution of American for Vietnamese forces on the battlefield. Each step in the process of escalation and substitution appeared to be a logical and practical response to well-defined tactical problems. But the basic contradiction at the heart of the counterinsurgency policy was never resolved; and in pursuing its logic, the American mission in Vietnam found itself compelled to continually escalate both the level of American involvement and the scale of violence.

The sources and consequences of this "logic of massacre" were explored in the two most powerful and influential Westerns of the 1956–60 period. John Ford's *The Searchers* (1956) explores the myth of "savage war," and the racism that informs and energizes that myth, at a level of sophistication no previous fiction film had achieved. And John Sturges' *The Magnificent Seven* (1960) applies the race-war symbolism of the Western to a "Mexico" story that is an allegory and a prophecy of the course of counterinsurgency in Vietnam.

Search and Rescue/ Search and Destroy: The Indian-Hater as Counterguerrilla

The Searchers returns us to the primary ground and the original generic form of the Frontier Myth: the Indian wars, the tale of the White woman captured by Indians, and her rescue by the quintessential American hero, "the man who knows Indians." But Ford does not simply reproduce this myth. He explores and exposes its informing structures, especially the complex of thought and feeling that constitutes racialist hatreds; shows how these develop and operate at the level of individual psychology and in the behavior of communities; and shows above all how racialist structures of thought produce a "logic" which, if we accept and pursue it, traps us in cycles of violence and retribution without limit and beyond all reason. Although the concern with racism suggests that we see the film as addressing the domestic or "civil rights" side of contemporary ideological concern, *The Searchers* is also a "Cold War" Western which addresses issues of war and peace from the perspective of a microcosmic community forced literally to choose between being "Red" and being dead. *The Searchers* brings these two concerns into the framework of a single, coherent, highly compressed fable and thus makes a crucial connection between the ideological basis of domestic racism and the ideological premises of the new, "counterinsurgency" phase of the Cold War.

The racialist charge that underlies the original myths of "savage war" and "Indian captivity" is incarnated in the character and consciousness of the film's hero, Ethan Edwards (John Wayne)—a recrudescence of the classic "Indian-hater" first depicted in popular literature in James Hall's historical sketch of the life of Colonel John Moredock (1835) and portrayed most notably in Robert M. Bird's *Nick of the Woods* (1837) and Melville's *The Confidence-Man* (1857). The "Indian-hater" is the evil twin of Cooper's Hawkeye whose knowledge of Indians engenders profound and undying hatred rather than sympathetic understanding. He is the most primitive type of Anglo-Saxon pioneer, whose love of war and hunting and appetite for conquest correspond to the "savage" propensities of the Native Indians. He is also "Indian" in his tribalism, which is a primitive form of racialism: he is "exclusivist" in his claim to the land, which makes conflict with the natives inevitable; and he holds all members of an enemy tribe accountable for the deeds of any individual, which transforms every individual dispute into the grounds of race war. The Indian-hater is set apart by his suffering an atrocious loss at Indian hands—for example, the loss of wife and child in a massacre. This experience of "the horror" converts him into a demon of revenge who "never in his life fail[s] to embrace an opportunity to kill a savage" and who desires to inflict on the Indians a "horror" exactly equivalent to what he himself has suffered—to answer mutilation with mutilation, rape with rape, massacre with massacre.[45] There are two possible outcomes for this type of hero. Some Indian-haters exterminate the savages and then return to become useful parts of the "pioneer stock." Others (like Bird's Jibbenainosay) are carried so far into the "dark" side of the wilderness by the indulgence of a "savage" passion that their identities become dependent on perpetual engagement with the objects of their hatred, and they can never return.

Ethan Edwards is an Indian-hater, and his hatred takes an unambiguously racialist form; yet he is also clearly the "hero" of the film. Ford's casting of John Wayne as Ethan deliberately invokes the star's heroic screen persona, borrowing elements from many of his Western and combat-film performances. Ethan's point of view also determines the way in which much of the action is seen, and it is rendered "sympathetically," in the literal sense of that word. It has therefore been easy to mistake Ethan's racism for John Ford's.[46] Ford could have avoided this sort of misunderstanding by scripting a polemical rebuke of Ethan's bigotry. But to do so would have falsified the characters and the "heroic" pseudo-culture whose style and values he means to represent: a culture in which heroism is identified with a laconic nobility of gesture and action and with the deliberate refusal of elaborate polemics. Moreover, by postponing the unmasking of Ethan's hatefulness and by refusing to entirely dispel the suggestion that his hatred of Indians is legitimate grounds for sympathy, Ford prevents the audience from adopting a position of comfortable disdain toward Ethan. As the terrible logic of Ethan's vision unfolds and begins to be questioned by other characters, we may distance ourselves from him; but because we have begun in sympathy, we retain a sense of kinship with him and may discover that we share (in some degree) Ethan's obsessions.

The film begins with the return of Ethan Edwards to his brother's ranch after years of wandering. Although he is secretive about what he has been doing, we learn that he is an unreconstructed ex-Confederate who never surrendered or took the oath of loyalty to the Union. He may have recently robbed a "Yankee" stagecoach—as if he were still fighting the Civil War, a one-man Confederacy. He has certainly been in Mexico, because he gives his little niece Debbie a medal he won there. Its colors and design suggest he fought for Maximilian against Juarez, a cause perfectly consistent with his racism. (He is in fact a more credible and historically accurate representation of the role of ex-Confederates in Mexico than is *Vera Cruz*'s Ben Trane.)

Although Ethan's "history" is a plausible one for his place and time, its chapters also correspond to different kinds of Western movie. The "Union stagecoach" reference invokes a frequently used plot formula for Civil War Westerns. Ethan's Confederate past and postwar criminal record link him to Jesse James and the cult of the populist outlaw. He comes from the Juarez/Maximilian war (*Vera Cruz*), where he has been a mercenary/gunfighter. We will learn that he has been a cavalryman (for the South), a Texas Ranger, and an Indian-fighter. Ethan thus combines attributes of nearly all of the heroic types developed in the Western since 1939, and particularly of the prior movie roles of the star who plays him: the hard-bitten, unforgiving rancher of *Red River* (1948), the hard-boiled Sergeant Stryker of *Sands of Iwo Jima* (1949), the cavalryman/Indian-fighter of *Rio Grande* (1950), the knowing Indian scout of *Hondo* (1953), the good outlaw of *Stagecoach* (1939) and *Three Godfathers* (1948). Ford has deliberately cast his actor and structured his character to make Ethan Edwards a "hero of heroes" whose character and fate are therefore commentaries on American heroism in its historical and its cinematic forms. And although Ethan's mission does not require that he be a fast draw, there is a suggestion of the gunfighter in the way he draws and twirls his pistol when the Ranger Captain arrests him during the wedding scene.[47]

Setting, theme, and characterization are presented in ways that advertise and make us conscious of their mythic, archetypal, and generic sources. The effect is to enlarge our sense of the action's significance by giving it an "epic" resonance; but the effect is also to bring the "sacred" and "eternal" values of myth and archetype into play in a setting that will test their validity and find them wanting. *The Searchers* is nominally set in Texas just after the Civil War, but Ford shot most of the exteriors in Monument Valley—the terrain he had made into an iconic archetype of the West. On the Western's map of mythic space, Ethan comes not from Mexico but from Jesse James by way of Vera Cruz. Behind him lie the unresolved conflicts of those two scenarios: How far beyond the legal and the customary can a hero go and still be a hero? How far can "longstanding American concepts of fair play" be stretched without changing their nature? *The Searchers* shifts the terms of these questions back to the old, classic ground of progressive pioneers vs. savage Indians; but its answer goes beyond the limitations of the classical myth by developing a psychological critique of its hero.

The opening scenes seem to be preparing us for a domestic tragedy. Through a wordless language of gesture and glance, Ford tells us that Ethan is in love with his brother Aaron's wife Martha, that she is aware of his love and returns it, but that neither will ever speak or act upon these powerful feelings because to do so would violate the most fundamental obligations of kinship and conscience. The tension generated by repressing this tacit passion is implicitly identified as the primary cause of Ethan's grim, angry, solitary character.

At this moment in the narrative, Ethan's return figures as the first step toward resolution of the romantic tension so vividly established. But the possibility of such a resolution is almost immediately aborted by a Comanche raid, led by a chief named Scar, in which Aaron Edwards and his family are massacred. Aaron and his son are killed, Martha is raped and horribly mutilated, daughter Lucy is carried off (to be tortured, raped, and killed on the trail), and little Debbie is preserved to be raised as an Indian. Ethan embarks on a search that will last seven years. He is accompanied only by Martin Pawley, Martha's adopted son, who is the survivor of an earlier massacre and partly of Indian blood ("one quarter Cherokee").

The partnership of Ethan and Martin Pawley (Jeffrey Hunter) echoes a heroic convention older than those of the outlaw and the gunfighter—the classic pairing of White man and Indian companion, in Fenimore Cooper's Leatherstocking Tales and its numerous imitators. However, in *The Searchers* the conventional roles are reversed. Ethan's knowledge of the ways of the wilderness and "the savages" far exceeds Martin's, and Martin is a far more civilized and Christian character than the race-proud Ethan.

At first we view Ethan through Martin's eyes, as a hero whose cruelty and harshness may be necessary attributes of his strength and power. Ethan is clearly "the man who knows Indians," the best of the Rangers at trailing, the most proficient fighter, the best at "thinking like an Indian," and (therefore) the best tactician. But his knowledge also includes an intimate acquaintance, even an identification, with stereotypically "savage" qualities. Ethan's desire for revenge is limitless, permitting and even requiring him to kill his enemies any way he can, by fair means or foul; to kill without regard for age or sex; to exterminate the living; and, through mutilation of the dead, to humiliate and degrade even the ghosts of the enemy. We are invited to suppose that Ethan's is a kind of sacred madness, the kind that is actually "Heaven's sense," giving access to deeper insights and higher wisdom than rational logic can attain.[48] Ethan's most profound source of power is his mastery of the most terrible and magical of the Comanche's powers—their capacity to imagine and create "the horror," which enables them to destroy the souls of White men and women by driving them mad.

Ford's narrative strategy requires that we see the world first through Ethan's eyes; nonetheless, the images are so unforgettable that it is easy to see why the film has been charged with propagating the racialism it sets out to demystify. The Comanches' stealthy approach to the Edwards ranch evokes the atmosphere of the horror film. It culminates in the sudden zoom-closeup of Lucy Edwards' face as she realizes what is about to happen and shrieks. As in *Rio Grande*, Ford conceals the bodies of the Comanches' mutilated victims in ways that invite us to imagine the worst things possible. Lucy's fate is so terrible that we are not even allowed to see Ethan discover her body. "The horror" is registered in the look on Ethan's face when he returns, in his harsh command that his companions never ask him what he has seen, and above all in the suicidal madness that overtakes Lucy's fiancé, Brad, when he finally imagines what has happened to her.

Ethan's determined hatred of the Comanche, his fierce and limitless rage, is a psychic shield that allows him to look on Lucy's naked body without losing his self-control. Ethan's "look" is a highly charged image. Its hatefulness signals a total repudiation of "the horror" and its perpetrators. Yet it also reproduces "the horror": since the bodies are hidden, Ethan's expression is our only way of knowing (or guessing) what is there. Moreover, as the narrative develops, it becomes plain that the hatred in his face is the visible sign that he is himself a "horror" and that his apparent immunity to "the horror" is merely another form of the disease. From the start of the search, love and hate are confounded with each other in Ethan's mind. He loves Debbie not only as his niece but as the only surviving daughter of his beloved Martha. But his feeling for Martha has also been twisted by guilt into the rage that keeps him solitary and at odds with his society. Now all that rage can be focused on Scar, whose rape of Martha and destruction of Aaron's family is a horrific, nightmare enactment of Ethan's repressed desire. By rescuing a pure and unsullied Debbie from Scar, Ethan can symbolically expiate his own guilt toward Aaron and in a sense redeem Martha's sin as well, since her living avatar will be a virgin daughter.

Thus far Ford's rendering of the basic structure of Ethan's psychology follows the classic paradigm of racial scapegoating. But Ford takes the logic of that psychology a step further by showing that Debbie herself inevitably becomes an object of his murderous rage. Ethan's dream of absolution is viable only so long as Debbie remains a little girl, untainted by the sexuality that "darkened" Ethan's relationship to his brother. Once she becomes a woman, Scar will take her as his wife, and she will then be doubly polluted or darkened. In Ethan's eyes she will be racially "Indianized" by the sexual incorporation of Scar's "blood" (semen). Instead of being an alternative or antidote to the dark dreams of which Scar is the symbol, as a "woman" she will become, like the dead Martha, their vessel. The same motives that drive Ethan's obsession with killing Scar will then drive him to kill Debbie. He will have to destroy the captive in order to save the idealized "virgin" symbol he has made of her. He will have to destroy her in order to save her.[49] Thus for Ethan the objective of the quest or mission gradually changes from "search and rescue" to "search and destroy."

Ford's interpretation of the captivity myth brings to articulation an aspect of the myth that for the most part is repressed in the canonical versions of the story. On the surface, these versions idealize the captive woman as an embodiment of White and Christian values, and they envision her rescue *intact* as the vindicating climax of the hero's mythic endeavor. But this ideal of "rescue intact" is the expression of a wish rather than the representation of belief in a real possibility. From the time of Mrs. Rowlandson's captivity in King Philip's War to the captivities of the nineteenth-century Plains Indian wars, most returning captives were treated as pariahs, on the assumption that they had been sexually and spiritually "polluted" or racially transformed by their intimate contact with Indians.[50] They thus became objects of the very same racial antipathies that had been invoked to motivate their rescue.

Through Ethan, Ford unmasks the true relation of the female "rescue object" and the male rescuer. The woman is only his nominal objective or excuse. His true and only objective is to kill the Indian. As in *Rio Grande* the rescue of captives is merely the cover story which justifies an attack that Sheridan and Yorke had intended to execute in any case. Ford's fictional account accurately represents the processes of moral judgment and tactical planning that went into such military operations as Custer's attack on the Cheyenne at the Washita River in 1869, ordered by General Sheridan. Although the rescue of captives was nominally an aim of the campaign, Sheridan's orders to Custer declared that since the women had already suffered a fate worse than death (having certainly been raped by the Indians) no special pains need be taken to prevent their being accidentally killed during an assault on the Indian village—as indeed happened to the captive Mrs. Blynn during Custer's assault.[51]

The Washita example is directly alluded to in *The Searchers* and marks a turning point in Martin's understanding of Ethan.[52] The Washita passage culminates in a vivid scene in which the searchers confront the most horrible image they have yet seen of Debbie's possible fate. This is the group of White women and girls who have been rescued from the Comanche by the cavalry. Their contact with Indians has infected them with horrible and degrading forms of madness or idiocy. Ethan equates their madness with Indianization by declaring that "they were White—*once*." The images we see appear to validate the specifically *racialist* element in Ethan's obsession and to confirm his worst suspicions about what captivity will do to Debbie.

But although the horror Ethan and Martin feel in the scene temporarily overwhelms other feelings, the sequence that leads up to this passage plants a number of ideas that begin the process of subverting the authority of Ethan's vision. The sequence begins when Martin inadvertently acquires an Indian wife named Look. The passage at first seems a vulgar parody of the "Indian marriage" theme that *Broken Arrow* invests with so much liberal sentiment: the two men treat Look in a comically abusive fasion. But the comedy ends abruptly when they question her about Scar and Debbie. When she flees in the night, the searchers discover that they may have misunderstood the seriousness with which she takes her role as "Mrs. Pawley." They cannot be sure if she has fled from Martin or has gone to find Debbie for him. The two White men never find out, because Look herself is massacred, along with other Indian men, women, and children, by the same 7th Cavalry that brings the White captives home. Martin is appalled by the mentality the massacre reveals in his own people—they are no better than Comanches. This perception chimes with his growing realization (in the buffalo-killing passage) that Ethan is motivated by the same "spirit of massacre" that drives both Scar and the cavalrymen. Martin's Look opens a perspective on the "Other" that is closed to Ethan. The hatred that "immunizes" him and allows him to "look" the horror in the eye forbids him from seeing anything *but* "the horror."

Other visual and thematic parallels between Scar and Ethan, and between Comanches and Texans, have been accumulating steadily from the beginning of the narrative. Their function is usually to suggest a kinship or likeness behind a façade of opposition, like the parallel lines in which Rangers and Comanches ride before their first melee. The most important of these parallels link Ethan to Scar—because they allow us to escape from Ethan's identification of Scar as the demonic "Other." We learn that Scar is as much an obsessive revenger as Ethan: the original raid was mounted to avenge the death of his two sons. This alters our perception of Scar as demon by providing him with a "human motive"—that is, with a motive just like that of our White Indian-hater hero. On the other hand, it alters our respect for Ethan's moral authority by establishing his likeness to a figure we have identified as evil. The logic here is perfectly circular: to humanize Scar we compare him to a White man, who is dehumanized by his likeness to Scar. But the circularity has a point: it highlights the absurd illogic of the categories by which we define "us" and "them," and it suggests that the hidden logic of these categories is to tempt us into a cycle of victimization and revenge from which it is possible that no one will escape alive and untainted.

The nadir of the cycle of revenge is reached in a moment of ironic mirror-inversion when Ethan and Martin finally catch up with Scar and Debbie (Natalie Wood) and attempt to ransom her. Their negotiations are broken off when Ethan sees that Debbie has become a grown woman and is the wife of Scar. When she appears at their camp to warn them of Scar's ambush, Ethan tries to kill her—"She ain't Debbie, she's Comanch'!" Martin tries to stop him, but Debbie's life is in fact saved by Scar, the Indian rapist who (in effect) saves her from her White "rescuer."

This meeting with Debbie also retrospectively revalues the scene with the White captives rescued at the Washita. Whatever else may have changed in her, Debbie has not been driven to madness by her captivity. For Martin, this resolves the most terrible implication of the earlier scene: Debbie is still Debbie and therefore still worthy of love and rescue. Her acceptance of an Indian identification and her resentment of Martin's failure to rescue her are understandable and adaptive responses to her situation and are more than offset by the fact that she leaves Scar's camp to warn them of an impending attack. But for Ethan, the fact that Debbie does *not* go mad like the other White captives is the most terrible revelation of all. It suggests that Debbie's nature was somehow insufficiently "White" to begin with, because in Ethan's scenario the Comanche are so alien and horrible that intimacy with them *must* make genuinely "White" people mad. Moreover, Debbie's organic susceptibility to the "pollution" of her racial consciousness is mirrored by her development of a woman's sexuality—the propensity for racial pollution is synonymous with her femininity. Ethan therefore sees her as welcoming Scar's sexual penetration, as a willing convert to the Comanche identity, and thus a traitor in the most fundamental war of all, the Darwinian race-war which is fought in the womb and the blood—a traitor whose criminal transformation can only be redeemed through her destruction.

Ford thus reveals the dream of "intact rescue" as a myth which conceals the true motive and character of the White male hero's quest. The captive woman is significant only as a "rescue object," a totem whose seizure sanctifies as "Christian" and "peace-making" a project that is inherently un-Christian and aggressive. Moreover, the realization of the White man's quest for power and justification can *only* be achieved through her victimization. The engendering condition of the captivity myth is the abduction or "rape" of the White woman. Without the violence done to her, there is no motive or justification for the hero to vindicate his manhood by attacking and destroying the Indians.

The revelation of Ethan's "madness" (and consequent kinship to Scar) frees Martin to assert his different evaluation of Debbie's captivity and their responsibility to her. For Martin she is still "Debbie," still the person they all loved, and still worthy of that love. Being Indian or being with Indians makes no difference. But it is important to note that Ford voices this view through a character who is himself part-Indian. Most of the other Whites agree with Ethan that she is "better off dead" now that she is "red." That the men should feel this way is perhaps predictable, but even Laurie (Martin's love, and a classic "redemptive woman") thinks Martin is crazy to want to bring her back. This harsh perspective on Laurie reveals Ford as merciless in his willingness to show how the dehumanizing cruelty that racism breeds can poison everything in the culture that espouses it.

Ford's own views are suggested by the fact that from the moment Martin stops Ethan from killing Debbie Ethan becomes less of a hero, physically weaker, more fallible in his tactical judgments. Martin's power as both strategist and warrior grows to equal or exceed Ethan's. The test of their differences comes when Scar and his people return to Texas on another vengeance raid and Ethan and the Rangers determine to attack him. Martin argues that if the Rangers simply assault the village as they intend, Debbie could easily be killed by Scar or shot by accident. He clearly has in mind a repetition of the 7th Cavalry assault in which Look was killed. Ethan and the others are willing for Martin to infiltrate the village and rescue her before the battle. But the rescue simply does not mean as much to them as it does to Martin. They still believe that the destruction of Scar is more important than the rescue of the captive.

In the event, it is Martin who kills Scar and Ethan who rescues Debbie. Martin's victory completes the demystification of Ethan's heroism by showing that hate-madness is not the only possible basis of heroism. Ethan cannot entirely abandon that hatred—he must take

Scar's scalp after Martin has killed him. Therefore when Ethan pursues Debbie as she flees from the attacking Rangers, neither Martin nor we are entirely sure that he does not mean to kill her. But the moment in which Ethan seizes Debbie, holds her aloft, and then embraces her marks his acceptance of a limit to his hitherto boundless rage. It is worth noting that this is Ford's ending, substantially different from the ending of the novel by Alan LeMay that was his source. In LeMay's book the "Ethan" character (whose name is Amos Edwards) is killed by a squaw whom he fails to shoot because he thinks it may be Debbie—which suggests that Ethan's merciless racialism may have been correct. Ford's film works toward the opposite meaning: it is the substitution of hatred for love, the contempt for differences of blood, the repression of "softness," that destroys both Whites and Indians.

However, Ford backs away from fully visualizing the implied parallel between the Ranger attack and the cavalry's massacre of the Indians at the Washita. We enjoy instead a tactical fantasy in which violence is used both massively and with miraculous selectivity. The Rangers charge at top speed through the village, firing left and right as the 7th Cavalry did at the Washita—the composition of individual shots in fact mirrors the image of Custer's battle in popular prints and posters.[53] Nor do we see any Indian prisoners—not even women and children—in the comic after-battle scene. Yet in the battle itself we see only Indian men falling from the shots, as if the Rangers had special powers to kill both comprehensively and selectively. This tactical fantasy, coupled with Debbie's rescue, indicates the limits of Ford's demystification of the savage war and rescue myth. Though rejecting race-hatred and the spirit of extermination it begets, Ford accepts as valid and even sanctifying a more "meliorative" kind of violence which he confounds with a certain kind of love: the gently paternal love which condescendingly recognizes Look's humanity, wishfully spares Comanche women and children while slaughtering the men, and (through Ethan's rescuing embrace) forgives Debbie the "transgression" of her Indian captivity. But once the captive is rescued, it appears that we no longer need to worry about the morality of attacking villages and are licensed to treat this one as a free-fire zone. The consequence is that Ford's own narrative reproduces the deadly shift of Ethan's mission from "search and rescue" to "search and destroy"—though the destruction Ford envisions is conceivably limited, even "surgical," rather than total.

The moral confusion of the ending is responsible for two recurrent misreadings of the film. A "left" misreading sees it as an exemplar of the very racism it decries. A "right" misreading sees Ethan Edwards as an entirely heroic figure whose harsh manner and personal isolation are the consequences of his devotion to his mission and his unique understanding of the red menace. Both misreadings were and are responsive to the ideological crisis over civil rights and foreign policy that began in the mid-fifties and culminated in the era of the Vietnam War. Through Ethan Edwards, Ford metaphorically explores the logic of the "savage war"/Cold War analogy, which he himself had so eloquently stated in *Rio Grande*, and finds that it produces an overwhelming, and finally malign, pressure to choose "destruction" over "rescue." American policy-makers would explore that same logic in articulating and putting into practice a new doctrine for counterinsurgency in the Third World. They too would have to decide whether American counterinsurgency operations would be designed as "search and rescue" or "search and destroy" missions. And having determined on the equivalent of "rescue," they would have to develop ways of preventing the inescapable violence of the "search" from creating an irresistible pressure for tactics that would "destroy the captive in order to save her."

In the end, as we know, the response to Vietnamese events by soldiers on the ground and policy-makers in Washington eventually took an "Ethan Edwards" direction. That their response was not merely personal but reflected tendencies of American culture as a whole is suggested by the strength which the "pro-Ethan" misreading acquired in the immediate aftermath of *The Searchers*. Between 1956 and 1964 the "Cult of the Indian" lost ground to a recrudescence of more traditional "savage war" renditions of White/Indian conflicts. Although sympathetic portrayals of the Indian continued to appear, they were outweighed in number, popularity, and scale by movies that emphasized Indian savagery and the inevitability of wars of extermination.[54] Among the most vivid of these films were two senstaional versions of the "captivity myth": Huston's *The Unforgiven* (1960) and Ford's *Two Rode Together* (1961). *A Thunder of Drums* (1961) and *A Distant Trumpet* (1964) offered more or less "orthodox" cavalry/Indian conflicts; Budd Boetticher's *Comanche Station* (1960) and Sam Peckinpah's *Deadly Companions* (1961) use Indian savagery as the background of a formulaic journey or revenge plot. John Wayne's "Mexico Western," *The Comancheros* (1961; a virtual remake, *Rio Conchos*, appeared in 1964), brings the Cold War subtext of these films to full articulation. Even the "civil rights" Westerns produced in the 1960s address the problem of anti-Black racism by contrasting good and heroic African-Americans with a "genuinely" *savage* race-enemy, the Apache.[55]

The role of Ethan powerfully enhanced John Wayne's movie stardom and marked his emergence as a major symbol in the language of public discourse. Ford's handling of Wayne in *The Searchers* developed levels of complexity and intensity hitherto missing from Wayne's screen persona. But perhaps more persuasive with the general public was the film's treatment of Wayne as virtually a one-man pantheon of heroic types—gunfighter, outlaw, cavalryman, sergeant, rebel, Indian-fighter, rancher. Though Ford means to demystify the pantheon through Ethan, the appeal of the originals remains potent. It is extremely easy for viewers to take away from this film an admiration for Ethan's skill and power, and even for his merciless rage and ruthless "realism," akin to that which Martin feels during the first half of their quest. The heroic associations of Wayne's screen persona reinforce our tendency to give Ethan's actions the best possible interpretation. Moreover, Wayne's "Ethan" does not die or dissolve with the final fade-to-black: he is re-absorbed into the on-going life of John Wayne-as-movie-star and becomes part of an ever-growing heroic persona that would finally make Wayne a "living legend," a cultural symbol whose role in public mythology is akin to that of figures like Daniel Boone, Davy Crockett, and Buffalo Bill. Ethan is also the incarnation of the counterinsurgency fighter envisioned by the Doolittle Report: a man who intimately knows the ways of an enemy whom he identifies as the supreme embodiment of evil and with whom he fights a battle to the death, but who nonetheless is willing to imitate that enemy in order to defeat him.

No wonder, then, that in the decade that followed the production of the film, what proved most memorable about Ethan Edwards was not Ford's critique of savage war but Wayne's powerful incarnation of "the man who knows Indians"—a role that became an essential element in the heroic style and public image of America's counterinsurgency warriors.[56]

The Magnificent Seven (1960) and the Counterinsurgency Paradox

The Searchers explores, in a highly formalized generic setting, the nature of the hatred, fear, and rage that inform and energize the myth of savage war. John Sturges' *The Magnificent Seven* (1960) rejects "hate" as a proper motive for heroes and develops the possibilities of "love," combined with toughmindedness and gunfighter expertise, as a basis for heroism. This is a "liberal" Western whose heroes will rescue a hapless Mexican village from bandits and who will themselves be redeemed by the experience, drawn out of the psychic alienation of a society based on self-interest, greed, and power. The scenario of their adventure mimics rather precisely the theoretically ideal form of a counterinsurgency mission. As a thought-experiment or "war-game," it is surprisingly prophetic in anticipating the kinds of problem the actual practice of counterinsurgency would develop. But with all these differences, *The Magnificent Seven* follows a logic of escalating violence that is nearly as remorseless as that in *The Searchers*, and its final "rescue"-gunfight bears an unintentional and disturbing resemblance to the Rangers' attack at the end of Ford's movie.

Sturges' film was officially an American remake of Akira Kurosawa's *Seven Samurai*—a film that itself owed a great deal to American Westerns and had enjoyed critical and commercial success during its run in the States. *The Magnificent Seven* was successful in ways that go beyond its considerable box office: it became the basis of imitation and a rich source of commercial iconography. The main theme of Elmer Bernstein's score became the theme of the Marlboro cigarette commercials, one of the major advertising triumphs of the era, which ended by identifying the whole West as "Marlboro country." Yul Brynner and Eli Wallach saw flagging careers revived, and Steve McQueen emerged immediately as a major star, to be followed by Horst Buchholz, James Coburn, Robert Vaughn, and Charles Bronson. Several sequels and numerous imitations of the film were made in Europe and the United States over the next twenty-five years in the combat and science-fiction genres as well as in the Western genre, and many of them starred one or more of the original players.[57]

The narrative of *Seven Samurai* counterpointed two kinds of conflict: the tactical struggle of the samurai to save the peasants from the bandits, and the class conflict between the fading military aristocracy and the peasantry. The premise for *The Magnificient Seven* begins with the classic trope of American myth/ideology: the translation of class difference into racial difference, and the projection of an internal social conflict into a war beyond the borders.[58]

A poor Mexican village is being raided and tyrannized by Calvera (Wallach), a brutal but complex villain who acts like a bandit but speaks the language of paternal authority—"I am a father to these men; they depend on me"—to justify his rape of the village. Driven at last to resist, the villagers send a delegation to the United States to buy guns. But they discover that in the States men are cheap and guns are dear; the taming of the frontier has thrown a lot of gunfighters out of work. The peasants show their aptitude for American-style capitalism by their (well-advised) decision to hire an American mercenary.

Their decision is aided by a drama to which they are audience. The town drunk, an Indian named Old Sam, has died, and the town's bigots will not let him be buried in Boot Hill. The situation invokes the conventionally ironic connection of "civilization" with bigotry that Ford had used in *Stagecoach* and that had figured so prominently in the Cult of the Indian. But in 1960, this scene also reminds us of the civil-rights battles of the previous five years, some of which concerned the integration of Southern military graveyards.

At this point two gunfighters step forward, drive the hearse to the cemetery, stand off the bullies, and bury the Indian. The gunfighters are Chris and Vin (Brynner and McQueen). Chris is a solemn, ironic, black-clad figure; Vin is a laid-back, easy man, with a Mark Twain style, full of folk-sayings and tall tales. It is not clear why they do what they do. Nothing is said about racism, and they accept no money, though both are out of funds. It appears that the sight of injustice, and of an important job undone, is more than they can resist. In this they resemble Shane and the cowboys-errant of the traditional Western, and they anticipate the New Frontier's call for citizens to "ask not what their country can do for them, but what they can do for their country." However, the script emphatically disparages all romantic and sentimental suppositions about their character and motives. These are men "without illusions" who nonetheless fulfill the most idealistic expectations. When the peasants come to hire Chris, the paradox is invoked and resolved with the suggestive brevity of a ritual gesture. The gunfighter at first dismisses their few coins and gold watch. Mercenary values function in this film as one of the signs of "realism." But Chris's sentiments are obviously chivalric, and he squares them with the mercenary code by declaring, "I have been offered a lot for my services before, but never everything."[59]

Chris then recruits six other gunfighters through an elaborate series of tests and rituals which recall the recruitment and training rituals of the combat film—particularly those dealing with commando or ranger units, like *Gung Ho*. The narrative thus makes clear that the force that must aid the Mexicans is a killer elite, carefully chosen by means that are technically and morally sophisticated. The common denominators are tough-mindedness and professionalism, which are expressed by the gunfighters' adherence to the formulas of self-interest. The good work of saving "Mexico" is not to be undertaken in the sentimental or idealistic spirit of romantic missionaries; it is to be firmly based in "realism," the implication being that pure idealism is too rare and perishable a quality to sustain a long, dirty, "twilight" struggle.

The contrasting motives that impel gunfighters and peasants are presented as the signs of both class and racial difference. Although the peasants believe they have bought the Americans for a few dollars and all the tortillas and beans they can eat, there is actually only one pure mercenary in the crowd—Chris's oldest friend, Harry, who refuses to believe that there is not some hidden treasure Chris is angling for. For the rest, professionalism (as an ideal and as social status) weighs equally with cash values. Vin joins because he is out of money and must choose between killing for low wages or clerking in a store—"good, steady work," one of the Mexicans tells him. But Vin despises that kind of work and the loss of status and dignity it suggests. He paradoxically demonstrates his *contempt* for the Mexican's values by immediately enlisting in the villagers' cause. The maintenance of professional status outweighs the "farmer" considerations of cash value and security. Thus right from the first we see that the differences between Mexicans and Americans have both a racial and a class aspect: the Americans are a White aristocracy or elite whose caste-mark is their capacity for effective violence; the Mexicans are non-White peasants, technologically and militarily incompetent. Gunfighter professionalism is thus a metonymy of the class and ethnic superiority of Americans to Mexicans.

As the recruiting of the gunfighters proceeds, this definition is developed and extended. The most professional of the crew (James Coburn) is like a Zen master gunfighter; he joins solely to test himself and perfect his skills. For him, professionalism is a religious discipline or calling. Lee (Robert Vaughan) is a neurotic gunfighter who joins to escape his past and the vengeful Johnson brothers. For him, professionalism is the last virtue of failure, the last strength of the psychically damaged. The youngest and least competent of the gunfighters, Chico, or the Kid (Horst Buchholz), is a child of Mexican peons who wants desperately to be one of the elite; for him, professionalism is the means to Americanization and higher status. This theme is emphasized by the role of Bernardo Riley (Bronson), the child of a Mexican mother and an Irish father, whose identity is split between pride in his status as American killer-professional and nostalgia for the maternal and familial values represented by Mexico.

In these seven, Sturges gives us a sampling of the major types of gunfighter developed by the movies in the preceding decade—the wild "Kid," the crazed neurotic, the aristocratic loner, the folksy populist, the ethnic outsider seeking acceptance. By multiplying the heroes in this way, he enlarges a form that had canonically focused on the single gunfighter. He gives us a platoon of isolatoes whose psyches map the range of heroic motives and even take in a range of ethnic possibilities. In effect, he has merged the conventions of the Western and the combat movie—the adventure of the lonely man and the adventure of the representative platoon.

Once in the village, the gunfighters begin to train the Mexicans in self-defense. As in the combat film, comic scenes contrast the imcompetence and innocence of the recruits (peons) with the expertise of the sergeants (the gunfighters). But here the contrast has a racial/ethnic dimension that also produces mutual suspicion. The farmers hide their wives and daughters and otherwise show their distrust until action proves the worth of the gunfighters. Likewise, the gunfighters maintain a professional reserve; they keep reminding themselves that it is a canon of their code not to get emotionally involved with their work. But each party modifies the other. Association with the tribal life of the village softens the gunfighters, specifically by evoking paternal feelings.

The key figure here is Riley, who becomes a father-figure to a group of children and who will be killed at the end because of them. For Riley, acceptance of the children means accepting the part of himself that is Mexican; but he does this in a style that affirms his own higher paternalism—the paternalism of violence—even while he denies it. When the children ask to go away with him because they despise the cowardice of their peasant fathers, Riley spanks them and orders them to believe that their fathers are not cowards because they cannot fight, that it takes more courage to be a good father and breadwinner than to be a gunfighter.

But this nominal ideology is undercut by the whole structure of the film, which shows frame by frame that the gunfighter like the hunter-hero of Roosevelt's myth is both technically and morally superior to the farmer. This clash of nominal and actual ideology is brought to full articulation in a scene late in the film in which the gunfighters—questioned by Chico—voice their code in a formal chorus. The gunfighters begin to get sentimental about the village and its families—lonely technocrats dreaming of a lost pastoral. But Chico breaks into the mood and reminds them that "you owe everything to the gun"—no false pastoral for Chico, he knows the dark side of peon life all too well. Chico's question provokes the gunfighters to think things over, and each answers him in turn, at first emphasizing the emptiness of their life—"Home? None. Wife? None. Kids? None." But then Chris and the others chime in, and the balance shifts toward the pride and power of their calling: "Places tied down to? None. Men you step aside for? None." Although the litany is meant to underline the ideological premise that the solid family life and working-class virtues of the Mexicans are morally superior to gunfighting, it becomes a paean to rugged individualism. The audience's emotional response is voiced by Chico, the peon who would be a gunfighter: "This is the kind of arithmetic I like!"

Thus the film's visual and stylistic apparatus valorize the hunter/gunfighter ethic of violence, mobility, and individualism at the expense of the farmer-values, the peon-values. The gunfighters are "good paternalists." Their order conforms to the *Camelot* slogan, which describes the ideal world order as one in which "the strong are just, and the weak are protected." But the movie is consciously ironic in its deployment of this chivalric/paternalistic structure. The most eloquent spokesman in the movie for paternalistic ideology, the most eloquent sloganeer for the party of order, is none other than Calvera the bandit.

The characterization of Calvera is very different from Kurosawa's bandit chief, who is virtually an abstraction of evil ferocity. Calvera has complexity and irony, and sardonic humor of a kind that has great appeal on the screen. He has a mouthful of cynical proverbs: "If God did not mean them to be sheared, he would not have made them sheep." There is even a kind of perverse innocence in his belief that all men—and especially all thieves and mercenaries—can be trusted to act on a rational calculation of self-interest. He is more than a simple bandit. The movie's imagery links him to figures like Villa and Zapata, who (in their movie biographies) are transformed from horseback bandits to social revolutionaries.[60] But if Calvera looks like Villa or Zapata, he talks like Porfirio Diaz or General Huerta, cynically mouthing paternalistic slogans and religious pieties while he "taxes" the village. Clearly he is more accurately described as a "warlord" than as a bandit. But since we cannot limit Calvera's type specifically to either the revolutionary left or the patriarchal right, he becomes an abstraction of the tyrannical potential inherent in the "extremes." This paradoxical combination makes Calvera the perfect enemy, the enemy counterinsurgency always sought and never found. He is the enemy who is native but is more hated by the people than the alien Americans are, who represents simultaneously the principle of excessive order (tyranny) and excessive disorder (banditry, revolution), and who embodies two "extremes," leaving the center to the Americans.

Calvera is a savage parody of paternalism; but as such he also offers a critique—implied and stated—of the character and motives of the Americans. Like them, he is a professional, which is to say a man whose actions are motivated by pure pragmatism, self-interest, and an advanced understanding of weapons and tactics. This parallel is perceived by every Mexican, from Calvera to Chico to the villagers themselves. And when Calvera appeals to the understanding of self-interest and pragmatism common to all professionals, he expects the seven gunfighters to understand; he is mystified when they persist in acting "unprofessionally." "We are in the same business," Calvera says plaintively. They are thieves—why do they pretend to be policemen?

The gunfighters cannot vindicate their own moral character unless they establish clearly the difference between Calvera and themselves, and the only way to do that is by negating Calvera's assumption of their fundamental likeness and confronting the bandit as if they represented diametrically opposed principles of good and evil. This is, in effect, the resolution adopted in *Vera Cruz* when Ben Trane redeems himself from kinship with the ruthless Joe Erin by a full conversion to the Mexican cause. *The Magnificent Seven* suggests that a tendency toward a transformation of this kind exists within the gunfighters. It is particularly marked in Chris, who is seen passing through several stages of conversion, each of which takes him further from the ruthless instrumentalism of the mercenary and brings him closer to the familial warmth and self-sacrificial nurturance of the

Mexican villagers. His name suggests his Christ-likeness, a suggestion that is given particular emphasis in the final battle scene when he grants an ironic absolution to the dying Harry. The point is worth insisting on, because of the specifically political implications such Christ-likeness has in a movie about Mexico. To the extent that Chris is converted to "Mexican" values, he also becomes an American version of the "Christ-fool"—the incarnation of the ideal of a liberal, Christian, nonviolent government, promising a utopian escape from the Hobson's choice of Red Terror and White Dictatorship. (Calvera certainly thinks, and says, that Chris's return to the village is the act of a fool rather than of "men like us.") The movie thus raises the possibility that perhaps the problem with Madero was not his "Christ-foolishness" but his "Mexican" weakness and incompetence. Perhaps if we could substitute an American "Christ-fool" for a Mexican one, the American's superiority in the martial arts would allow him to contend successfully against the violence of both left and right.

This is an appealing suggestion, and one with which (in the end) counterinsurgency policy could not dispense. But in the film, the idea of a killer-Christ is treated ironically and problematically through the parallel handling of Chris and Calvera, which becomes more strongly marked as the film approaches its climax.[61] After Calvera's first attack is repulsed, the villagers realize that they will have to fight to the death against the outraged bandit. A party of appeasement arises, and Chris suppresses it by demanding that the peasants choose now between fighting and surrender. He holds a pseudo-plebiscite right there in Sotero's bar. When those present (some of whom are intimidated by his glare) choose to fight, he tells them that they are now committed and that if anyone tries to back out he will shoot him. Chris deals with Sotero and the Mexican fathers as Riley deals with the children: he "spanks" or disciplines them coercively, replacing their authority with his own in everything but name. Yet he asserts that this paternalistic coercion will make them free and independent adult men. He has, in effect, substituted his own authority for that of the villagers and has become a "White Calvera."

The paradox in Chris's response to Sotero reproduces the contradiction on which the "nation-building" project in Vietnam would founder. That project was based on the assumption that Americans had to provide Vietnam not only with technical assistance and advice but with the most basic constituents of nationality, including an entirely new type of political culture—one capable of sustaining the regime the Americans had chosen to recognize. When the Vietnamese displayed an unwillingness or inability to act up to American standards, the Americans felt they had to "step in and take over," substituting their own power and authority for the incompetent native polity.

This is effectively what happens just after the "plebiscite" in Sotero's bar. At the moment when Chris asserts his dominance, the narrative of *The Magnificent Seven* departs radically from the plot of Kurosawa's *Seven Samurai.* The samurai and the villagers achieve a kind of comradeship, and their solidarity is never broken. But after the "plebiscite," the gunfighters dictate to the villagers, and the weakest peasants betray the Seven to Calvera, who captures and disarms them. For at least some of the villagers, Chris and Calvera are now morally equivalent, and Calvera is in some ways preferable—or at least, he seems the more powerful and inescapable of the two. Though some of the Seven's allies remain loyal (and have become Calvera's prisoners), at this moment it appears that the village, as a society, has repudiated and betrayed them.

Calvera now offers the Seven a sort of "Geneva settlement." He allows them to live and regain their guns in return for their promise to leave Mexico. His reasons are thoroughly rational, according to the movie's version of the code of mercenary "professionalism." He recognizes that the Seven probably have friends in the States who would avenge them, and he doesn't need gringo trouble. He's won his point, proved the mission futile; he expects men of similar professionalism to recognize and bow to the facts in a rational and disinterested spirit. All they must sacrifice is pride and honor.

From this point, Calvera and the Seven play out a set of motives which arise from the conventions of the genre but which also anticipates several aspects of the American approach to the Vietnam War. The logic of Calvera's "settlement" is a version of the "deterrence" theory that governed American atomic warfare policy (and "containment" in general): if the nation demonstrates its capacity and willingness to impose "excessively high" costs on the enemy, then a rational enemy will think twice about attacking. Further, Calvera's treaty follows the logic of the "End of Ideology" value system: if the gunfighters give up the abstractions called pride and honor, they will receive the real benefit of survival. This was just the sort of pragmatic stick-and-carrot deal that President Johnson would offer the North Vietnamese in his speech at Johns Hopkins in April 1965. He promised substantial economic aid, including a TVA-style development of the Mekong River valley, if the North would abandon the nationalist (and Communist) goals for which they had fought for thirty years; but if they refused, he threatened to respond with extraordinary violence.[62]

But the Seven are "magnificent" because they follow the imperatives of pride and "honor" rather than the ethic of rational self-interest. At work here is an ideological double-standard which sees Americans and their (non-White) enemies as governed by fundamentally different motives and standards. What is sanity and reason for the enemy is "madness" and dishonor for Americans; what is "selfless idealism" in the Seven would appear as irrational fanaticism in an enemy. Thus for the United States to persist in fighting an excessively costly war without (after 1970) expectation or realistic hope of victory is "rational *realpolitik*" and an act of unselfish nobility; while a similar persistence on the part of North Vietnam is mere "fanaticism." Moreover, it is clear that the American/chivalric standard is the higher of the two: carrots and sticks appeal only to a lower order of moral intelligence, the kind that puts family and material interests before those of the larger polity—the kind that has not learned to ask first what they can do for their country.

The decision of the Seven to return to the village heightens the distinction between hapless Mexicans and powerful Americans. The gunfighters will go back and redeem the village *in spite of* the villagers' betrayal, in the teeth of evidence that the village polity does not fully sustain them and that its culture is alien to them. We know from an earlier scene that some of the gunfighters have developed a real affection for the villagers. But in this moment of decision the only reasons they voice are those that belong to their pride as professionals and as Americans: "Nobody takes my guns away and then hands them back to me. . . . Nobody!" By avenging their loss of face they will also rescue the villagers. But that rescue is not their stated objective, nor does it provide the ideological justification of their mission. They will return because their feelings of affection for the village and their desire for symbolic vindication now coincide precisely. They do not have to choose between making love and making war—these have become the same thing.

In this accounting of motives, the movie anticipates the rhetoric of Kennedy's New Frontier, with its insistence that idealistic projects be rooted in a ruthlessly hard-headed analysis. But the transformation of "self-interest" into a rationale of chivalric rescue is achieved (in both film and presidential rhetoric) by identifying the American "self" with the aristocratic pride of a self-consciously professional elite for whom devotion to abstract symbols of achievement has replaced desire for the material attributes of wealth. But the film also explores the consequences of applying this "gunfighter style" of action to a counterinsurgency struggle. In the process, it predicts the direction in which rationalizations of American policy would move: from an assertion that Vietnam must be defended for material reasons of national interest to the assertion that the war is necessary as a "symbol" of American determination, down to the strident and pathetic demands of Nixon and Kissinger that the war must be continued and extended—through bloody infantry assaults on symbolic targets, through "signals" in the form of massive bombing campaigns—to prevent our being *perceived* as "a pitiful helpless giant."[63]

The climactic shoot-out requires critical examination, because of the importance such scenes have in the paradigmatic structure of the Western movie. The narrative plan of the Western always works toward the resolution of plot tensions in a final gunfight, and it rationalizes the conclusion by investing it with powerful and appealing ideological and mythological overtones. This structural principle, inherent in both the genre and its substructure of myth, establishes a framework of expectation which we bring to the narrative. As the plot unfolds, our expectation that it *must* end in violence becomes by implication a *requirement* or a demand that it do so. If it does not, we are disappointed. Moreover, this violence will be "total." Chris has told us from the start that a struggle of this kind is a form of savage war; once begun, the killing must continue till one side or the other has been exterminated.

The Seven stage a commando-style attack on the village in which bandits and townsfolk are completely intermingled. Yet so expert is their technique that they never kill any townspeople; they only and precisely kill bandits. The narrative situation and the visual representation of the attack link it to the climactic battles of John Ford's cavalry foray into Mexico in *Rio Grande*, and the rescue-raid that ends *The Searchers*. In both films a rescue is effected through an assault *en masse* on the village in which the "rescue-objects" are held captive, with a liberal use of firepower that puts the "rescue-objects" in distinct jeopardy. But both films evade the troubling suggestion of a cavalry massacre by elaborate plot devices which isolate the rescue-objects before the battle begins. In *The Magnificent Seven* the situation is still more problematic. The villagers are not only physically intermingled with the bandits; they are morally complicit with Calvera through their betrayal of the heroes to a humiliating "captivity." They are in the condition that Ethan imagines for Debbie: someone once worthy of protection who has "allowed" herself to be penetrated and possessed by the enemy.

The literal representation of the attack as an extermination of the bandits is offset by the visual impression that this is indeed an attack on the village that has betrayed the Americans. The gunfighters charge in at top speed, kick in doors, and blaze away into darkened interiors. Until the sequence is well advanced, we receive no *visual* confirmation that (incredibly) they are killing *only* bandits. The ambiguity of the initial visualization of the attack suggests a potential within the gunfighter/Green Beret scenario for interpreting our *difference* from the people we have come to aid as proof of their identity with the enemy. That suggestion was already present in the scene in Sotero's bar in which Chris threatens to shoot anyone who even speaks a word against the completion of their mission. In the final assault the threat is very nearly carried out.

The "tactical fantasy" with which the movie climaxes represents the final development of a generic convention. But it is also a fictional representation of the tactical doctrine for the use of firepower which American commanders hoped to apply on the ground in Vietnam. The mythical "surgical strike," so central to the fantasies of military scenario-makers, and the counterinsurgency fantasy of blasting the guerrillas with bomb and shell without harming the peasants, are here visualized. The selective identification, isolation, and elimination of guerrillas from among the civilian population by American-advised native troops was an extraordinarily difficult procedure, even when the tactics used involved small-scale, intelligence-centered operations. As American operations in Vietnam became more military in character, the "surgical strike" and various methods of selective targeting became the besetting fantasy of combat operations. But neither smart bombs nor radar sites nor electronic fire control were capable of producing results as perfect as those obtained by the Magnificent Seven, and (for reasons discussed in the following chapters) only results of comparable quality would have justified the use of massive firepower to fight a counterguerrilla war. The last assault in *The Magnificent Seven* is one step away from the terrible rationale associated with the nadir of the Vietnam War: "We had to destroy the city in order to save it." If such a scene had been filmed a few years later, it would have raised echoes of Mylai.

In the end, it is clear that Chris's superiority to the Mexicans makes it impossible for him to play the role of "Madero." He is so much more powerful than the villagers that if he were to stay he would inevitably produce the political tragedy envisioned by Zapata, in which "the strong leader makes a weak people." The dilemma is resolved by having the surviving American gunfighters (Chris and Vin) return to the States. The Americans can help this world but they literally have no interest in it. They are not hewers of wood and drawers of water. They are professionals. Their retention of this difference signals not only their continuing loneliness but their maintenance of the power and superiority of the killer elite. In contrast, the gunfighters who identify most intimately with the Mexicans are marked as weaker than Chris and Vin (though not as weak as the villagers). Riley's love for and identification with the Mexican children gets him killed; and when Chico chooses to stay with his love and the village, he has to hang up his guns and abandon the freedom and individuality of the gunfighters.

This ending resolves the problem of the movie's plot. It also fulfills in fantasy the scenario of counterinsurgency, which envisioned the victorious Green Berets—like Washington after the Revolution—declining the mantle of imperial rule. With the old colonial power gone and the new Communist takeover defeated, the Green Berets could safely turn power back to the natives, or rather to a new counterpart class of Americanized leaders. The war done, the Americans leave the scene—either to go back home, or, like the Lone Ranger, to ride on to similar adventures in yet another imperiled town.

By restoring the gunfighters to America and leaving Mexico to the Mexicans, the movie evades the question that is most dramatically posed in the Seven's final attack on the village: What is the real relation of American power to peasant society in that moment of the conflict when the Americans *cannot* simply leave Mexico but must choose between the acceptance of defeat and the renewed exercise of power? Sturges goes out of his way to show that, in the crisis, the peasants are helpless, dependent on the violent incursion of the Americans outside—dependent on the chivalric *caritas* of men who owe them nothing, except perhaps contempt.

The Magnificent Seven is, as I've presented it, nearly an allegory of American policy in Vietnam.[64] Like the traditional Westerns that preceded it, it appears to offer a "genetic myth" or fictive history in which a crisis in the fictive "Old West" appears as a primitive anticipation of some contemporary crisis—as if "gunfighters" historically "grew up" to be Green Berets. But it is vital to recall that the film was made before the Kennedy administration took office and made

Vietnam a test case of counterinsurgency warfare. There is no prophetic gift involved in the process. Movie and policy address similar ideological concerns and use the same mythological language, the same ideologically loaded images of heroism and savagery, the same narrow and essentially racist views of non-White peoples and cultures, the same hope that all problems can be solved by a burst of action and a spectacular display of massive yet miraculously selective firepower.

The Western "thought-experiment" thus brings to the surface the imperatives for violence that were implicit in the program of "nation-building" in Vietnam and anticipates the actual transformation of our objectives there from a campaign to win Vietnamese "hearts and minds" into a military assault on the countryside. Calvera's savagery and the villagers' moral and political weakness are both symptoms of the "primitive" development and practical inferiority of their "race." And their identification as "Mexican" masks the fact that these are the characteristics attributed to the two non-White races that are the chief antagonists of the Anglo-Saxon in American myth: Indians and Blacks. These stereotypes are not only conventional expressions of a casual bigotry; they are symbols in which important ideological dilemmas about social, racial, and political relations are condensed—symbols impacted in a mythic narrative whose structure insistently drives toward resolution in an all-encompassing, satisfying, purifying, spiritually regenerative act of violence.

PART V

Gunfighter Nation: Myth, Ideology, and Violence on the New Frontier, 1960–1970

15 Conquering New Frontiers

John Kennedy, John Wayne, and the Myth of Heroic Leadership, 1960–1968

John F. Kennedy's 1960 Presidential campaign slogan expressed in symbolic shorthand a new approach to the use of American power.[1] The "New Frontier" administration (and its successor, Lyndon Johnson's "Great Society") rejected Eisenhower's conservative assessment of American economic resources and political strength. Kennedy and Johnson intended to make full use of the tremendous aggregation of political and economic power that had been centered in the federal government since 1932. Three aspects of the new Democratic agenda were of particular importance:

> to "get America moving again" in an economic sense, by dealing with the emerging problems of the balance of payments and international economic competition and with the recessive tendencies of the domestic economy;
>
> to complete the unfinished agenda of the New Deal, by filling the gaps in the social welfare safety net, dealing with "pockets" of persistent poverty, and addressing at last the long-postponed question of civil rights for southern Negroes;
>
> to improve our military ability to "contain" the Soviets in Europe and to turn back the advance of Communism in the Third World.

The last of these was Kennedy's deepest concern and the one he regarded as the ultimate test of his capacity as a leader. Economic policy came second, for one of the central tenets of Kennedy's New Frontier was the belief that the best guarantor of social peace and prosperity was a continually growing economy. The liberal wing of his party expected a good deal more from Kennedy's social and civil-rights agenda than the President was able or inclined to deliver.[2]

Kennedy's invocation of the Myth of the Frontier was more than an advertising ploy. It was designed to suggest the kind of "heroic" action that was to be expected of the new President and to establish the terms in which the historical and moral significance of those actions might be appreciated. In several important respects, the administration's approach to policy was based on premises adapted from Turner and Theodore Roosevelt. Like Roosevelt, Kennedy projected a vision of the President as a heroic figure tested and qualified for power by deeds in battle and prepared to take a militant stance toward the nation's concerns. Like Roosevelt, he saw the United States as standing on the edge of a "frontier," facing a new world of vast potential for either unlimited progress or ultimate disaster—"the frontier of the 1960s, a frontier of unknown opportunities and paths, a frontier of unfulfilled hopes and threats."[3] But unlike Roosevelt, who summoned the wealthy members of the Hamilton Club to engage in political life, Kennedy's inaugural called on a whole "new generation of Americans" to face up to its "destiny," to "ask not what your country can do for you, but what you can do for your country," and to commit its energies to serve the Republic in its "long twilight struggle" against the worldwide forces of oppression and poverty. Kennedy's foreign policy called for a counter-offensive against Communism on the "frontiers" of the Third World: the New Frontier's frontier; the stage for the expansion of American influence and power; the site in which the ideology of the "liberal consensus" would be proved; the scene in which an American model of development would be tested.[4]

The new administration also shared Roosevelt's disposition to formulate all issues (foreign and domestic) as warlike conflicts, tests of character requiring some sort of heroic resolution through vigorous executive action. But the substance of the New Frontier economic policy was rooted in a revised version of the "progressivism" and "exceptionalism" of Turner and Beard. Before we examine the structure and meaning of Kennedy's heroic myth, we must describe the myth/ideological "landscape" in which that heroism would be enacted.

Modernizing Turner: The Ideology of the New Frontier

The Kennedy administration brought to power a group of "New Economists" whose approach combined Keynesian theory with ideas drawn from the American experience of recovery and postwar prosperity.[5] They believed that with a proper mixture of government regulation and private enterprise, it was possible to produce a capitalist economy that would enjoy more or less continuous expansion and growth, and that the productive capacity of such a system would in the end abolish poverty and render class antagonisms trivial. This way of construing the social task of an economic system is fundamentally Turnerian. The difference is that the "safety valve" is no longer provided by "free land," nor even by the raw productivity increases that Beard had seen as an alternative, but by a new and almost magical quality, a capacity for unrestricted exponential growth ("take-off") inherent in the fully modernized economy. The powers of the New Economic Frontier were to be tapped by grand-scale manipulation of fiscal policy and taxes—government-directed operations based on scientific abstraction, masterminded by experts, occurring at a remove from the arenas of production and distribution. The New Economists had, in effect, worked out the macroeconomic techniques through which Turner's and Beard's vision of "progressive history" could be realized.

This view of American prospects was not merely a mathematical model. The nation's emergence from both Depression and World War with an intact democracy and an economy many times stronger than it had been in 1929 suggested that something in our politics, culture, and circumstances was indeed historically exceptional. The "consensus" historians, who succeeded Beard's "progressives" as the dominant school of American historiography after 1945, refurbished and updated the Roosevelt/Turner/Beard myth-historical script to provide the New Economists and the "modernization" theorists with an explanation for America's exceptional success.[6] David Potter's *People of Abundance* (1954), one of the most sophisticated and thoroughgoing of these revisions, finds that the characteristic forms of American culture and politics—democracy, individualism, constitutionalism, immunity from social radicalism—derive from our more or less continual experience of actual or prospective "abundance" in land, food, manufactured goods, and (finally) finance capital.[7]

In the new ideology of the postwar "liberal consensus" America's "exceptional" status is interpreted as proof of our vanguard or pioneer status among modern nations, and the history of American progress (based on a revised Turnerian script) is seen as a normative model for "modernization" that must be followed by any other emerging (or rebuilding) nation that seeks a similar prosperity.[8] Walt Whitman Rostow's *The Stages of Economic Growth: A Non-Communist Manifesto* (1960) was the most influential formulation of this theory. Rostow became a key adviser on national security policy in both the Kennedy and Johnson administrations, and his theory of the relation between economic stages and nation-building shaped the development of policy toward the Third World.[9]

"Americanist" models of modernization also followed Turner in their concentration on economic matters and in their neglect or evasion of the dark side of the Frontier Myth: the close connection between the development of American resources and the violent destruction of those who opposed the dominant forms of economic and national organization—the southern Confederacy, the alliance of Radicals and Freedman during Reconstruction, the populist and labor movements of 1875–1915, the"Wobblies" and "Reds" of 1917–20 and 1948–53. The Indian wars provided the only historical case in which the connection between progress and violence could be acknowledged; and the Indian-war metaphor acquired new significance after 1960, when American engagement in the "underdeveloped world" seemed to reproduce the basic elements of frontier conflict.

The consensus historians' view of Indian wars reinforced the ideological dispositions of the administration's modernization and nation-building theorists. Their interpretation of the confrontation between "progressive" White civilization and the barbarism of non-White "primitives" followed the paradigm formulated by Theodore Roosevelt in "Expansion and Peace" (1899). Wherever races representing these principles come in contact, war is the inevitable result and the primitives are inevitably either wiped out or subjugated. The American experience of Indian wars is not taken as a special historical case but as representative of a general and universal principle. Native resistance to the imposition of a "progressive" regime is presumed to be irrational and hence not subject to negotiation. For example, Alden Vaughan, in his critically acclaimed *New England Frontier* (1965), asserts that the New England Indians rejected the Puritans' proffer of civilization because they were the dupes of superstitious and self-interested "shamans":

> No society of any appreciable magnitude has ever chosen to reject westernization. . . . There is no reason why the Indians should not have shared in this almost universal trend if they so chose. There is some evidence that the far greater number of them would have thrown off the shackles of the Stone Age if their sachems had not been so reluctant to jeopardize their own power and wealth.[10]

Faced with native resistance, the progressive colonists have no choice but to apply force to keep the natives in subjugation: "In a frontier society, someone has to impose a semblance of justice and order."[11] If the colonists fail to maintain themselves, the consequence is a historically significant setback to the growth of civilization. Thus Samuel Eliot Morison, in his *Oxford History of the American People* (1965), suggests the significance of the French withdrawal from Algeria in 1958 by likening it to a hypothetical case of American refusal to contest an Indian war: "It was as if the Tecumseh Confederacy of 1811 had succeeded in forcing all white Americans to return to Britain."[12] The Indian-war model insists that when faced with such a reversal of historical destiny compromise is unthinkable; "progress" can and must be defended by "savage war," prosecuted till one side or the other is annihilated or subjugated.

If modernization on the Americanist plan represents the only valid path to historical progress, resistance to that model is equivalent to an attempt to reverse the course of history. Thus the State Department's 1965 "White Paper" could only construe the widespread destruction and political deformation of South Vietnam by American power as "nation-building"; and the indigenous Communist-led movement for independence and national unification as motivated merely by jealousy or fanatical opposition to the progress of the South.[13]

The Indian-war metaphor became increasingly prominent in the rhetoric of counterinsurgency after 1961, in part because of the parallels between these two kinds of fighting—both of which took place in a "wilderness" setting against a racially and culturally alien enemy. But the real power and relevance of the Indian-war metaphor are rooted in its appropriateness as an expression of the New Frontier's basic assumptions about the relation between "primitive" and "advanced" peoples: that the natives ("savages") of "fledgling" or "less developed" nations lacked anything like the equivalent of the political culture of a Western nation-state.[14] This bias, reinforced by a systematic study of the counterinsurgency policy that was undertaken in 1961–62, became the official doctrine of the New Frontier. Its effect was to distort American responses to both political events and to tactical developments on the battlefield.

One of the most important aspects of the counterinsurgency study was the study of "Training under the Mutual Security Program," by General Richard Stilwell, which recommended the development of tactical and strategic doctrine for the Special Forces' war. The review began with a vivid restatement of the Doolittle Report's vision of a war to the death between "East" and "West" being fought out in the shadows and jungles of the world. It asserted that the vulnerability of "fledgling" nations to Communism derived from their lack of political culture; modernization had "uprooted most of the symbols, beliefs and concepts" on which such societies had been based—beliefs that were themselves little more than "superstitions."[15] It followed that the Vietnamese peasants were inherently "passive," incapable of either generating a political movement of their own or of giving an informed consent to a movement on their behalf. To win them over one had to overawe them by the display of superior force and become the masters of their "superstitious" view of the world.[16] But in practice, their political passivity required the representative of progress and civilization to impose an order where none existed by using American power to check Communist insurgency nd by building up an American-style national leadership—one that would likely be based (at least initially) on an American-trained officer corps.[17]

This kind of underestimate of native politics was a logical consequence of the settlers-vs.-Indians myth that informed the administration's concept of "modernization," and it affected the understanding of both military tactics and the political tasks of counterinsurgency. In 1962, counterinsurgency specialist Roger Hilsman gleefully reported that helicopters were such a "terrifying sight to the superstitious Viet Cong peasants" that they would flush from cover and be shot down as they fled.[18] In fact, their panic was simply that of raw troops faced with a weapon for which they were unprepared. Within months of the beginning of the helicopter war the Viet Cong had developed a new set of tactics for dealing with helicopters, which they successfully applied in defeating a major South Vietnamese drive in the battle of Ap Bac (January 1963).[19] The same misreading of the actual level of Vietnamese cultural and political development made American advisers impatient with the apparent illogic of local politics and created a pressure, which finally proved irresistible, for an American takeover of the war.[20] American planners understood the war in terms similar to those Vaughan had applied to the study of war on the Indian frontier: "In a frontier society, someone has to impose a semblance of justice and order."[21] The necessity of forcible *imposition* thus suggested itself quite early. But when Vietnamese society (North and South) proved resistant to that imposition, the same logic created a pressure for the acceptance of a "*semblance* of justice and order" [emphasis added] in place of the real thing.[22] The coup of November 1963, in which Diem was overthrown and killed, marked a definitive step in this direction. The logic of that decision was realized slightly more than a year later, with the arrival of massive American reinforcements to take control of the fighting.[23]

The metaphoric association of counterinsurgency with the mythic "Indian wars" became more explicit as the level of violence and American involvement in Vietnam increased.[24] One of the most prevalent images was that of the pioneer "stockade" or cavalry fortress, which provided shelter for the "civilized" from the "savagery" outside. Harold H. Martin, writing in the *Saturday Evening Post* (November 24, 1962), applied the metaphor to the "strategic hamlets" in which South Vietnamese peasants were being concentrated to protect them from Viet Cong influence (and to bring them under government control). This was the same "stockade idea our ancestors used against the Indians," and "The 'Old Stockade' Idea Works." Maxwell Taylor (Ambassador to South Vietnam under Kennedy and Johnson) used the same figure in testifying before Congress four years later, but in a somewhat more defensive manner (since Congressional criticism of the failures of such programs had grown). Said Taylor: "It is very hard to plant corn outside the stockade when the Indians are still around. We have to get the Indians farther away. . . ."[25]

The adjective "savage" and the "captivity" symbolism were used freely throughout this period to characterize the Communists' use of terror against South Vietnamese civilians (and later against American POWs). For example, in December 1961 Kennedy wrote to Diem to tell him that Americans had become increasingly angered by "the deliberate savagery of the Communist program of assassination, kidnapping, and wanton violence."[26] In 1965 Lyndon Johnson repeatedly essentially the same figure, in more graphic language, to justify his escalation of the war:

> It is a war of unparalleled brutality. Simple farmers are the targets of assassination and kidnapping. Women and children are strangled in the night. . . . And helpless villages are ravaged by sneak attacks. Large-

scale raids are conducted on towns, and terror strikes in the heart of the cities.[27]

The heading of a notice posted in the "war room" of Admiral Felt's headquarters in Hawaii put it most succinctly: "Injun Fightin' 1759. Counter-Insurgency 1962." The text of the notice was a reproduction of the standing orders of Rogers' Rangers, including the warning that "Dawn's when the French and Indians attack."[28] Early journalistic treatments of the New Frontier's plans for the Special Forces emphasized their status as the shock troops of Kennedy's New Frontier and compared their fighting style with that of frontier rangers "from the French and Indian wars through Marion in the Revolution, Mosby's Rangers in the Civil War and Merrill's Marauders in World War II."[29] Similarly, the agents employed by the CIA for its clandestine war against Castro's Cuba (after the Bay of Pigs) were known as "cowboys."[30] This language acquired a potent new spokesman when Kennedy was succeeded by Lyndon Johnson, whose rhetoric—authenticated by his Texas background—was thick with allusions to a frontier past. He urged American troops to "bring the coonskin home" from Vietnam and "nail it to the barn"; and he told Hugh Sidey that "he had gone into Vietnam because, as at the Alamo, somebody had to get behind the log with those threatened people."[31]

To the extent that the myth/ideology of "modernization" invokes the Frontier as a historical precedent, it denigrates as "primitive" the cultural character of the emerging nations with (in some expressions) an implication of racial deficiency. But the overt and systematic racialism of Theodore Roosevelt's original plea for imperialist engagement was (by 1960) no longer an acceptable part of public ideology. Whatever the social or cultural prejudices or implicitly racialist assumptions they may have had as individuals, Kennedy and his advisers were committed to a liberal reform of race relations in the United States. Thus the administration's Third World projects, including its counterinsurgency war, were seen as perfectly consistent and continuous with programs aimed at "modernizing" the remaining pockets of poverty and racist superstition in the United States.[32] Indeed, under Johnson those programs would be reorganized as a "War on Poverty"—the domestic counterpart of the War in Vietnam.

Thus both the domestic and the foreign policies of the New Frontiersmen (and the "liberal consensus") contained a fundamental contradiction or ambivalence. The "liberal" strain in their thinking made them genuinely desirous of improving the living conditions of "the poor" by engaging them in the dynamics of "progress" and by extending the benefits of political democracy to those who had been prevented from enjoying them by tyranny, discrimination, and their own ignorance. But their way of defining progress incorporated the very structure of thought which justified the subjection of "nonprogressive" races and peoples "for their own good." This contradiction was played out most dramatically in policy toward Asia and Latin America, where, despite the original emphasis on political and economic reforms, there was a steady drift toward militarization through support of native military elites, covert operations, or overt intervention.[33] But there was a parallel in domestic politics: the tendency to treat American citizens according to the "subjugation" paradigm through the transformation of the "War on Poverty" to a "war on the poor"; the increasing reliance on secrecy and falsification to preserve public and Congressional support for administration policy (especially the war in Vietnam); and the use of armed force, police powers, and covert operations against domestic dissidents.[34]

This contradiction was inherent in the concept of the "heroic presidency" that informed the politics of the New Frontier and its successors and that became central to our politics again under Reagan and Bush after a hiatus (1974–80) caused by reaction to the defeat in Vietnam, "Watergate," and a prolonged economic crisis. To understand the meaning and power of this political myth, we need to look more closely at Kennedy's heroic style; for it shows how such a myth can appeal to us by appearing to resolve the cultural and political ambivalences that it merely expresses.

Heroic Leadership and the Cult of Toughness

Kennedy's projection of himself as "hero-president" was built on two basic structures. His heroic style was that of the warrior. He gave this character historical resonance by drawing on three specific forms of warrior-myth, each of which had both a *historical* reference and a reference to contemporary movie genres. His campaign identified him with the heroes of the combat film through invocations of his wartime heroism ("P.T. 109") and with the heroes of the Frontier Myth. The "regal" style of his White House led to his identificaton with the myths of chivalric knighthood (*Camelot*), a venerable historical structure.

But the form of his heroism is as significant as its content. Like his folkloric ancestor, the hero of a modern mass-culture myth is offered as the embodiment of certain natural and historical principles or forces, as an idealized representation of his people's characteristic traits, and as a model for emulation. When the heroic character is assumed by a modern political leader, its representational function becomes political as well as symbolic. To the extent that the hero-leader "represents us," we license him to act *on our behalf*, to achieve things that are beyond us. If we can also believe that he represents our own best selves—if we actively identify with him, as we identify with the protagonist of a movie—then his unilateral decisions will seem to be enactments of our will (or at least of our wishes). From the perspective of a President who conceives himself as a hero, the actions he wishes to take will seem to be "representative" of things the people wish for—or would wish for if they shared the superior knowledge and courage that make him a hero. He therefore feels empowered to act beyond the expressed or legislated will of the people and sees in such action nothing inconsistent with his function as the agent or representative of the people. During his brief administration, Kennedy had considerable success in achieving public credibility as a *hero*. The power of Kennedy as symbol was augmented by his tragic assassination in 1963, and in subsequent years he has become the center of a public "cult": a heroic symbol to be invoked by politicians from both ends of the political spectrum.[35] That heroic "cult" has been for most of his successors a problematic legacy: a vision of the power they might exercise if only they could capture for themselves the heroic afflatus that (in hindsight) seemed Kennedy's natural gift.

But Kennedy's heroic myth owed as much to careful construction as to his unquestionable gifts as a performer. His campaign staff was marked by its sophisticated understanding of the power and function of "political imagery." One of the first advisory papers Kennedy read as President was the Rand Corporation's "Political Implications of Posture Choices," which emphasized the importance of projecting the *appearance* of power when dealing with the Soviets on the one hand and with the American public on the other.[36] A "heroic" style enhances the appearance of power by indicating that the President is confident that he possesses strength and is willing to use it to further national and personal objectives, even at great risk.

Although Kennedy was elected by the narrowest of margins, once in the White House he became the dominant figure on the political scene, and his growing popularity produced a midterm Congressional election extraordinarily favorable to the administration. The key to his persuasive power was his ability to engage a significant percentage of the American public (particularly among the college-educated) in personal identification with him, to see him as a genuine representative of the ideals and aspirations of the younger political generations, and to accept, either personally or vicariously, his invitation to participate in the "long twilight struggle."

Kennedy was not less committed than Eisenhower to the secret use of presidential instruments like the CIA and to the evasion of the mechanisms of Congressional consent. But he differed from Eisenhower in his belief that it was necessary to establish a climate of public opinion that was openly supportive of "dirty war" operations and the "stretching" of constitutionally limited powers that such operations entailed. To a remarkable degree he sought (and obtained) *consent* for the use of "Doolittle" methods—and thereby won the complicity of a broad spectrum of the intellectual and political elite, and of the general public, in such projects as the "Secret War" against Castro and counterinsurgency in Vietnam.[37]

His inaugural address, and the policy formulations that followed it, framed the New Frontier's project as one of personal moral regeneration achieved through action in a particular heroic style. The goal was not merely to survive or maintain our national and personal standing but to achieve "greatness" as both individuals and as a nation. Kennedy's rhetoric is filled with recurrent assertions of his belief that the American nation, and himself as the nation's leader, have a "high destiny," that this is "a time for greatness," and that his ambition as President is not merely to do a decent job but to achieve and promote that "greatness."[38] Under modern conditions, greatness was to be achieved, not by a single romantic Errol Flynn-like cavalry charge, but by close engagement in a "long twilight struggle" against tyranny and poverty. But though the means and styles of action might be those of the "gritty" combat film or the cynical gunfighter Western, the idealism of the ends was evoked by the language of chivalry: the vision of a world polity "in which the strong are just, and the weak are protected." The line was paraphrased from Teddy Roosevelt, but it owed something to the Arthurian slogan "might in the cause of right" from the script of the contemporary Broadway musical, *Camelot.*[39]

War was a primary symbol of political value on the New Frontier. Its symbolic importance was first registered in Kennedy's request that Robert Frost read "The Gift Outright" during the inaugural ceremonies—a poem in which Frost describes the emergent nationality of Americans as the people's "gift outright" of themselves to "the land vaguely realizing westward" and ties that process to necessary violence: "The deed of gift was many deeds of war."[40] The senior personnel of the Kennedy and Johnson administrations shared a common mystique of "war," similar in both its sources and its content to that which had informed the intellectual life of the post-Civil War generation. War was identified as the supreme expression of American values, in which the society "as one man" assumes the moral burden of a struggle (on the grandest scale) for justice and against a great evil, submerges petty and individual concerns in a collective and patriotic effort, and in pursuit of victory develops, organizes, and directs the full potential of the American political and economic system. When so construed, war comes to seem an appropriate metaphor even for programs as pacific as the "War on Poverty."

But the mythology of war prevalent in American culture also sanctifies a hierarchical and highly "command-centered" version of democratic or republican ideology. When the war metaphor is invoked for a national project (containment of Communism, the war on poverty), the people as a whole become the platoon and the President becomes the commander in whom (at least for the duration of the crisis) we must repose *implicit* confidence. The paradox of the New Frontier was that it aimed at achieving democratic goals through structures and methods that were elite-dominated and command-oriented.

The Kennedy administration cultivated an image of "tough-mindedness" and scorn for the "sentimentality" and hide-bound routine of the Eisenhower regime.[41] Its style was "to advocate restraint, and yet to despise softness and to admire a willingness to use military power; to feel conscience, but by no means allow it to paralyze one into inaction; to walk softly with one's big stick, in fact, but to be ready to crack heads with it."[42] Like the "gunfighter style" of the Magnificent Seven, the Kennedy style was a mixture of "idealism and cynicism"—idealism as to ends, and cynicism as to means.[43] Thus the definition and resolution of most important international issues tended to emphasize the element of the "force" involved: What sort of military threat did a given political development pose? What sort of force could be deployed to meet it? Kennedy's administration had "a conviction of the efficacy of force amounting almost to romanticism [and] a strategic doctrine that, while nominally designed to make nuclear war less likely, had the practical effect of making every other kind of war less unattractive."[44] Problems were perceived as "challenges," and it was important that the administration be perceived as being "disposed to act forcefully."[45]

The projection of a President as "heroic" is not merely a play of images but a way of construing presidential power. Father John B. Sheerin, writing in *Catholic World*, voiced what had become conventional wisdom in regard to the President's license to respond to threatening situations abroad: "The fact is that he does have a mandate to solve our international problems by means of any device that will work."[46] But the assertion of such a "mandate" ran the clear risk of undoing both the consensual mechanisms on which the Constitution insists and the ideology of democratic consent that is one of the fundamental bases of American national cohesion.

This was the ideological problem Arthur M. Schlesinger, Jr., addressed in his 1960 article "On Heroic Leadership and the Dilemma of Strong Men and Weak Peoples." Though nominally addressed to the "Zapata problem" of Third World societies, the article offers a general theory of democratic leadership which asserts the necessity of Strong Men even in a fully matured constitutional democracy. Schlesinger's conception of the heroic president had real authority: he was a leading member of Kennedy's intellectual cadre, and he was (and is) a distinguished historian whose prize-winning biographies of Andrew Jackson and FDR used the lives of two notably "strong" Democratic presidents as occasions for exploring both the theory and the practice of democratic leadership.[47] The article deplores the neglect of "leadership" in democractic theory. Schlesinger asserts that the experience of the Western democracies has shown that in times of severe crisis democracy itself has been saved by strong leaders who stretch or exceed the norms or bounds of executive power for the public good. In the emerging nations, where political culture is primitive and unformed, such Strong Men deform the political order and weaken the emergent "people" by encouraging their dependence. But the Western democracies, and some of the more "mature" Third World states (he cites Mexico in particular), "can risk an interlude of crisis because the great preponderance of national values and institutions can be relied on to require reversion once the crisis is over."[48]

Schlesinger defines the license a "hard" leader may exercise very broadly: "While the executive should wield all his powers under the constitution with energy, he should not be able to abrogate the constitution *except* [emphasis added] in face of war, revolution, or economic chaos."[49] Although Schlesinger meant this formulation as a definition of the *limits* to which an executive can go, these "limits" (as

Dwight MacDonald pointed out) go far beyond anything that even the strongest presidents had attempted, even during the dire crises of the Civil War and the Great Depression.[50] In effect, Schlesinger finds that when a mature democracy is in crisis, "the people" are likely to become (for the moment at least) "weak," in ways that are analogous to the weakness of Third World peoples; and for their good, and the good of the nation, the heroic President must control public action with something like the willful rigor and extralegal authority of a Strong Man. It is not necessarily the peoples' will or intelligence, but the "strength" and "maturity" of the institutions that govern developed democracy that assure us that the authority of such a Strong Man will be temporary and will pass with the crisis.

But Schlesinger weakens the force of this limitation on heroism by suggesting that even under normal circumstances a democratic nation is dependent on the hero for those rule-breaking innovations that are the basis of "progress." He is drawn to this notion by his adoption of the Emersonian concept of the hero as "representative man," who incarnates the genius of his people and expresses it in ways that the mass of men cannot: "From the start, democracies have been able to concert their energies and focus their aspirations only as strong individuals embodied and clarified the tendencies of their people."[51] Modern leaders play the same creative role, even though they are not (as Emerson would have had it) the spontaneous expressions of native genius but the crafted and largely falsified products of a manipulative manufacturing process. Indeed, such falsification is, in Schlesinger's view, a necessary precondition for the effective functioning of heroic leadership in a modern society; and the necessity of such falsification should be recognized in principle. (This is the same ideological position that is promulgated at the end of *Fort Apache*.)[52]

The heroic President is not merely the instrument of popular or majority will. Rather, acting out of a higher and more perfect sense of the nation's mission and necessity than any popular majority could possess, he helps his race or nation to realize its latent destiny by leading it forward in directions it might not have chosen by or for itself. What Schlesinger says of Third World leadership therefore applies with equal force to American leadership:

> The real division in these countries is not between left and right; it is between hard and soft—between leadership which has the will to do what must be done to lay the foundations for economic growth, and leadership

which falters before the vested interests of traditional society or the peremptory challenges of rising social groups.[53]

This model of leadership dovetailed with the tradition of "closed politics" in which most of Kennedy's advisers had been reared.[54] It also conformed to the Cold War doctrine embodied in the Doolittle Report, which held that it was incumbent on the government to act in advance of or even in opposition to an expression of popular will in order to respond effectively to the "dirty war" tactics of the enemy.

As the administration's chief spokesman and representative man, Kennedy's role was to "alert" the public to its danger and to summon it to join him in an act of heroic self-sacrifice.[55] By heeding his call, one could identify with the hero-President and imitate his action on one's own level. Such identification worked in two directions: it validated Kennedy's belief in his own representative character, and it taught the most politically engaged elements in American society to identify Kennedy's "chivalric" style with "American democracy." The most demanding form of identification was to accept (in one way or another) Kennedy's summons to public and political service. But even where the public's identification with Kennedy-as-hero was no more profound than that which bonds the audience to the characters in a movie, it gave force and validity to his belief that by acting on his own inclinations he was representing the will of the nation.[56]

By identifying with the complex of chivalric and gunfighter/Indian-fighter imagery that invested the New Frontier Americans as a people gave their consent to the project of "caring for" the poor of the Third World. But with their consent given, the deeds of charity would be vicarious. The actual work would be entrusted to small, elite cadres of volunteers who would live among the natives and learn their ways but who would resist the temptation to "go native." Instead, they would begin the process of modernizing—which is to say, Americanizing—the indigenous cultures. The Peace Corps and the Green Berets were the political instruments most closely identified with Kennedy-style heroism. Both would pride themselves on their volunteer spirit and their radical pragmatism—their ability to improvise techniques on the ground and to overcome hidebound regimes of red tape and bureaucratic restraint. Both would begin by achieving mastery of the local rules, mirroring the wiles of the native enemy to defeat that enemy on his own ground. The Peace Corps, like the heroes of *The Ugly American*, would work directly with village counterparts on local projects, using "small" technology and "getting their hands dirty." In the case of the Green Berets,"fighting dirty"—fighting "like the Indians"— was part of the original charter, and in Vietnam this style of warfare was expected to prove itself in the field.[57] These two organizations put in practice the "neo-Turnerian" and the "Rooseveltian" aspects of the administration's myth of choice. The Peace Corps and the *Alianza para el Progreso* in Latin America aimed at achieving economic abundance and political reform through the peaceful infusion of American capital, energy, and expertise; while the Special Forces made a Rooseveltian connection between counterinsurgency warfare and the processes of nation-building.[58]

Kennedy's public persona thus represents a political realization of the myth/ideology of "progressivism," and particularly of its literary mythology, which Owen Wister formulated in *The Virginian* in the paradoxical assertion that "true aristocracy and true democracy" are "the same thing" and that success is the only just measure of a man's or a nation's value. ("The only equality I recognize is being equal to the situation.") Just as Wister's appealing fable of the "progressive cowboy" obscures the essentially anti-democratic implications of the novel's ideology, so the powerful appeal of the "New Frontier" and the Kennedy style obscures the elitist and anti-democratic implications of "Camelot," with respect to both the treatment of "weaker" peoples and nations abroad and to the management and control of public opinion and Congressional consent at home.

Defending the West: Epic Cinema and the New Frontier, 1960–1965

Kennedy's heroic myth derived much of its force and resonance from the symbolism of the combat film and the Western. But the evolution of that myth from 1960 to 1965 developed in dialogue with a new and more spectacular form of movie myth-making: the so-called "blockbusters," whose scale and ideological ambition mirrored the sense of world-mission that informed the New Frontier. Blockbuster productions emerged in the mid–1950s as the movie industry's answer to competition from TV. They tried to offset the appeal of the small screen by exaggerating the differences of scale through the (highly publicized) use of new widescreen technologies, incredibly lavish production values, epic subject matters and lengths, and huge costs of production. After 1959, the breakdown of the domestic studio system and the development of advanced filmmaking facilities in other countries made it feasible to cut the cost of large productions by filming abroad, particularly in the disadvantaged economies of Mexico, Spain, Italy, and Yugoslavia.[59] But while the technology of the blockbusters was new, their stories represented a reversion to the traditional "epic" and "big picture" formulas of the 1920s and 30s: epic treatments of "western" history, recreations of best-selling historical novels, lavish musicals, "Bible" and "Roman" epics, and grandiose treatments of the Victorian Empire after the manner of *The Charge of the Light Brigade*.[60]

Blockbuster epics made the movie-house the scene of a series of vivid engagements with "history" in terms well suited to the themes of the New Frontier. The grandiose scale of these epics and the worldwide scope of their production techniques and historical references corresponded to the administration's vision of an incomparably wealthy and powerful America confronting global issues in "a time of greatness." Moreover, the recurrent themes of the epics promulgated the worldview that closely corresponded to Kennedy's sense of America's place in the world as a nation noble and strong but sorely beleaguered in a "darkened" and hostile political environment. The typical epic of this period centers on a "hard" and self-willed White male hero—often played by Charlton Heston—who stands for the highest values of civilization and progress but who is typically besieged from without by enemies (often non-Whites and/or savages) who greatly outnumber him and beset from within by the decadence, corruption, and "softness" of his own society.[61] The story often ends with the hero's martyrdom (*Spartacus*, *The Alamo*, *Khartoum*), and even when he gains a victory (*Exodus*, *Fifty-five Days at Peking*, *Zulu*) his battle is seen as a "Last Stand." The epics with non-American settings add to the traditional "savage" stereotypes the element of "fanaticism"—an irrational devotion to a cruel religion or ideology which impels them to a frenzy of devotion and battle-madness.

El Cid (1961), the first of the Kennedy-era epics, draws on the *Camelot* imagery that came to invest the New Frontier. It casts the "long twilight struggle" backward in time to the age of chivalry and the wars of the nascent Spanish Christian kingdom against the Moors. Heston's Ed Cid is a larger-than-life abstraction of chivalric honor whose early speeches and battles are highly stylized to suggest his embodiment of an archaic nobility. Like the gunfighter, whose legendary reputation becomes a code he must live by—and like Zapata, whose moral triumph is achieved when the man and the revolution he symbolizes become one—El Cid has power because he becomes the mythic embodiment of his people's aspirations. His chivalry is demonstrated by his sacrifice of love for the sake of honor. This medieval code is given a modern and liberal inflection, however, by El Cid's insistence that his personal honor requires him to act as the "champion" of national values—the defense of the Spanish state—against the private and selfish considerations of rival contenders for the throne. He acts the role of a Lansdale, asserting an American's larger view of nationhood ("Ask not what your country can do for you, but what you can do for your country") against the "feudal" clannishness of "Spanish" (that is, Vietnamese or Philippine) ruling elites.

The safety and honor of the nation also require a compromise of racial and religious differences between the Moslems and Christians who share the soil of Spain. El Cid makes himself the instrument of this primal "integration,"[62] because he recognizes the threat of an alien power, inimical to Spanish Moslems and Christians alike: a fanatical Islamic movement, originating in Africa, whose dark-skinned, black-robed hordes have been commanded by their megalomaniacal prophet and leader to exterminate or forcibly convert the Christians and subject the (light-skinned) Spanish Moslems to a rigorous fundamentalist regime. The distinction between African Moslems and Spanish Moslems represents as racial difference the distinction between Communist and non-Communist Asians or Latin Americans: the latter are well disposed, but weaker than the White Christians; the former are crazed devotees of a cruel ideology.

El Cid attempts to halt the Africans' advance by turning the city of Valencia into a medieval Alamo. When he receives a mortal wound, it appears that the city and the nation are doomed. But the death of the man merely gives power to the symbol. The dead hero is mounted on a white horse to lead a final charge from the city gates, and the *superstitious* Africans flee in panic (as Hilsman's superstitious peasant-guerrillas flee from American helicopters). At the end, El Cid and his white horse are seen riding down the beach into a distance that suggests eternity—and that echoes the use of the white horse to symbolize the legendary status and redemptive capability of Zapata.

An epic with a similar theme and structure, but with more obvious relevance to contemporary politics, is Samuel Bronson's *Fifty-five Days at Peking* (1962), directed by Nicholas Ray, which deals with the siege of the "Legation Quarter" of Peking during the Boxer Rebellion of 1900–01. The film begins (and ends) with an image of international discord and rivalry, as the legation bands simultaneously play their national anthems. However, during the crisis all the European powers and Japan are forced to unite to save themselves from the savagery and fanaticism of the Boxer-led Chinese hordes. That moment of cooperation is offered as a wishful prophecy of a future international order in which civilized nations will forget trivial rivalries to confront the profound danger which the Boxers symbolize. One of the most notable features of the story is the role of the Russians, who figure as allies of the Americans, West Europeans, and Japanese. The political scenario of *Fifty-five Days* thus mirrors the new vision of the Communist threat which had begun to emerge in the aftermath of Stalin's death. In that vision the possibilities of co-existence with the Soviets appeared more plausible, while the onus of ideological fanaticism and aggressive support for the "wars of national liberation" was identified with Mao and "Red China." This tendency would reach a climax of sorts during the following year (1963), with the resolution of the Cuban missile crisis and the taking of important initiatives for detente, including the Nuclear Test Ban Treaty.[63]

Like the African-Moslems of *El Cid*, the Boxers combine elements of primitivism or "savagery" (which symbolizes the *racial* difference of our enemy) with an ideological fanaticism that is a metaphor for Communism. The Boxers also have a more distinctive identity as a "class" movement (representing or seeking to represent the peasantry), and as a nationalist movement that seeks to free China from foreign domination. The difference between "our" nationalism and "theirs" is that ours is based on "reason" while theirs is based on superstitious fanaticism and racial resentment. The script answers a well-stated Chinese critique of imperialism through the British ambassador (David Niven), who counters that under Western control China has made more economic progress in fifty years than it had in fifty centuries; and while national independence is a worthy goal, it would be more rational and realistic for China to allow the West to complete its tutelage before attempting an independent course. Moreover, if China throws off the foreign yoke before it is prepared to sustain independence, it will touch off a new round of international rivalry that will end only in worldwide conflagration. Thus the ideal of national self-rule for a Third World or a non-White nation takes second place to a calculation of economic and political interest whose "rationality" is measured by its conformity to Western principles: the value-systems of capitalism and the European balance of power.

As in *El Cid*, the primary signifier of moral and political difference is race, and the hero is recognized by his ability to master the terrain in which contending races meet. Major Lewis, the hero of *Fifty-five*

Days (Charlton Heston), deals with the problem in the style of Cooper's Hawkeye. Although Lewis is a Marine, we first see him riding into Peking on a horse, wearing a white slouch hat and a blue tunic—the garb of the Western cavalryman. As a disciplinarian he follows the pattern set by John Wayne in *Sands of Iwo Jima* and *Rio Grande*; as a fighter he is a pure pragmatist who prefers direct action to diplomatic temporization (*Rio Grande*) and is willing to fight dirty, like the enemy. He is represented as a "man who knows Indians," but it is emphasized that his knowledge does not derive from intimate acquaintance with the Chinese. Rather, like Tex Wolchek in *The Ugly American*, he masters the Chinese by applying the general principles of direct action and tactical surprise derived from the pragmatic lore of American military professionalism, and more specifically from the mystique of the "ranger."

His ability to think and fight like an Indian is forcibly illustrated in an early scene in which the fanatical Chinese Prince Tuan turns a display of Boxer acrobatics and martial arts into an occasion for humiliating the American. Tuan challenges the Major to strike the unarmed Boxer with a sword, an exercise that will certainly end with the Major disarmed and tossed on his rear in front of the entire diplomatic community. The Major escapes the trap by suddenly shifting his attack from the Boxer acrobat to a muscle-bound Boxer guard (who has been complacently watching the scene with arms akimbo), humiliating him (and the Prince) by forcing him to fall backward onto a table of refreshments. Although the British diplomats are dismayed by this provocation of Tuan, the American believes he has given a convincing demonstration of Western strength and cleverness that will deter aggression—an idea perfectly consonant with the Rand Corporation's 1960 recommendation of symbolic "Posture Choices" in the foreign-policy strategy.[64]

But, although the Major is a past master in the lore of force, he is at first too cold and distant to be a perfect counterinsurgency warrior. Like *The Magnificent Seven*, *Fifty-five Days* asserts that the capacity to love is as important as the warrior's knowledge and skill, for it is love that converts the Western project in China from an exercise in pure exploitation to a true "civilizing mission." The Major's capacity for love is tested by two females: the little half-Chinese girl who is the daughter of a captain in his command, and the Russian countess (Ava Gardner) who becomes his lover.

The Major's relationship to the little girl is a paradigm of the paternal relation that the West bears to China. Her mother is dead, and her father is so often away on duty that she has been living in an orphanage run by a Catholic priest. But her father has promised that when he retires he will take her home with him to America. The Major regards this promise as sheer sentimentality. As a "realist" he knows that she would be regarded as a racial alien in the States, and her father as a miscegenate renegade. Yet after her father is killed, the Major inherits the father's promise and the emotional appeal of the little girl's plight forces the Major to question the premises of his "realism." Perhaps his hard-headedness is merely a mask to conceal his fear of emotional involvement and intimacy, and his expectation of racism a projection of his own bigotry. In overcoming these inhibitions, he will become a better and more loving man and a better exemplar of American values. Having repudiated his own biases, he will take a more hopeful view of his countrymen's capacity for tolerance and become willing to do something toward reforming American society along "liberal" lines.[65] The Major's acceptance of his paternal obligation to the child becomes the symbol of the larger obligation articulated by the British Ambassador for the United States to meet its responsibilities to the wider world by helping to westernize China and maintain the balance of power.

But there are limits to the degree of intimacy and love which this ethic requires. Those limits are explored through the character of the Countess (Ava Gardner). If the Major is a New Frontier version of Hawkeye, then the Countess is a modern recrudescence of Cooper's Cora Munro: an aristocratic, sensuous, sexually mature White woman who—because of the power of her sexuality— is associated with a racial "taint." Cora is part Black, and the taint registers in her rampant femaleness and its erotic hold on the non-White males who surround her. The Countess is White, but she has acquired a racial taint by becoming the lover of a Chinese, General Yung Lo—the most rational and "British" of the Empress's ministers.[66] The Countess is first presented as a woman whose cynical realism matches the Major's; their affair begins as a hard-headed liaison of convenience between a sophisticated woman and a soldier looking for a temporary mistress. But the Countess moves beyond the cynical mode in which they began to "true love" for the Major; he, however, is unwilling to move beyond the instrumental into genuine intimacy. His love affair thus mirrors his problem with the little girl.

But the Countess represents a level of intimacy with the Chinese "Other" that is no more acceptable in *Fifty-five Days* than Cora's marriage to Uncas would have been in *Last of the Mohicans*, or Debbie's marriage to Scar in *The Searchers*. According to the racialist imagery in which blood and semen have the same value, the Countess has been racially polluted or transformed by her intimacy with Yung Lo. Her death is caused, not by the bullet, but by a mysterious "germ" that neither medicine nor cruelly repeated surgery can remove from her system. The Countess' tormented death permits a resolution in which the American Major can express his paternal "love" for China by lifting the little girl onto his horse as he rides out of Peking and taking her back to America. He thus expresses love, but (like the gunfighters at the end of *The Magnificent Seven*) preserves both his paternal authority and his distance from the nation he has rescued instead of accepting "marriage," with its implicit "bondage" to a life of intimate absorption in the life of the racial and the female "Other."

In *Khartoum* (1964), the last of Heston's "last stand" epics, the racial implications of his heroic persona are presented in their starkest form. Heston plays "Chinese" Gordon, the defender of Khartoum against the fanatic Afro-Moslem horde of the Mahdi (Laurence Olivier). The movie is heavily indebted to the 1936 *Charge of the Light Brigade*.[67] Khartoum exaggerates the earlier film's distinction between political soft-headedness and military "realism." The British government that sends Gordon to Khartoum is utterly cynical about exercising its imperial responsibilities. Unwilling to risk its tenure of office by seeking taxes to support a real intervention against the Mahdi, it sends Gordon as a sop to public sentiment. This ploy backfires when Gordon's inspired defense of Khartoum arouses a demand for genuine action. But relief comes too late, and Gordon's death completes the process of arousing the public and transforming the policies of the corrupt home government.

As in the earlier film, the White hero is in some ways a mirror-image of his opposite number. But the kinship here is based on biosocial superiority rather than on similar codes of honor. Gordon and the Mahdi are both heroic visionaries who see themselves as representatives of their respective gods and of their race's destiny. They are superior men, "aristocrats" of a kind—perhaps even "supermen"—and their mutual recognition confirms this status in each of them. Of the two, Gordon is the greater: his spiritual ascendancy over the Mahdi is indicated by the horror with which the Mahdi greets the sight of Gordon's head impaled on a pike and by his superstitious belief that if Gordon is killed his own destiny will be altered for the worse.

This exaggerated conception of the hero as an innately superior human type is consistent with the conventions of the "epic." However, the heroic imagery of *Khartoum* has a more immediate source in the theories of a new and revised form of Social Darwinism (a precursor of the theories of sociobiology that emerged in the late 1970s), which sought a biological explanation for the stages and differences of social and cultural development observable among human beings. During the 1960s the most prominent spokesmen for this approach were not academics but popularizers like Konrad Lorenz (*On Aggression*), Desmond Morris (*The Naked Ape*), and Robert Ardrey—author of *African Genesis* (1961), *The Territorial Imperative* (1966), and *The Social Contract* (1970)—and author of the screenplay of *Khartoum*.[68] Ardrey begins by assuming that control of territory is the necessary precondition of social organization and that control rests on the demonstration of a relatively superior endowment in the motives of aggression. Since aggressive capacity is inherited, societies will tend to divide into classes based on biological types, which Ardrey calls "alpha" (dominant) and "omega" (subordinate).[69] Beneath their pseudoscientific neologisms, Ardrey's theories are structurally identical with the Social Darwinism of Roosevelt and Wister. The significant factors in human behavior are identified as racial "gifts," and a superior endowment of aggression and territoriality—the qualities most celebrated in both Anglo-Saxonist theory and the Myth of the Frontier—are seen as the basis of society and a rational division of power and privilege. In Heston's Gordon of Khartoum the "alpha" type is allegorized, and we see his superiority to both the "alpha" competitors of a lesser race and the "omegas" of his own society—that is, the politicians empowered by a decadent electorate.

The range of heroic styles portrayed by Heston in these three films is an index of sorts to the leadership style affected by Kennedy, which combined elements of the chivalric hero, the charismatic visionary, and the counterinsurgency warrior—part frontier cavalryman, part Marine, and always the "man who knows Indians." It is also a recurrent theme of this heroic style that the hero achieves his final victory only by suffering a Last Stand and risking or actually undergoing a personal martyrdom. In a sense, these films also established (or at least reinforced) the mythic paradigm through which commercial, popular, and political culture would interpret the historical accident of Kennedy's own "martyrdom" at the hands of an assassin. The numerous claimants to Kennedy's political authority represented him as a hero in terms similar to those that invest El Cid or Gordon: he is a visionary particularly gifted in discerning foreign threats, a charismatic leader who summons his people to moral regeneration through dedication to public service, and a warrior who thrives on conflict. The best-selling account of the assassination, *The Death of a President*, by William Manchester, made the mythic connection overtly in its discussion of parallels with figures from Arthurian and archetypal mythology.[70]

Allegories that were more narrowly partisan were framed by Lyndon Johnson, who represented Kennedy's murder as a sacrifice to the irrationalism of racist bigotry and used it to build the bipartisan coalition that finally passed the civil-rights bills of 1964 and 1965. In subsequent years Kennedy's death would serve as a myth for opponents of the war in Vietnam who asserted that Kennedy would never have let things get out of hand as Johnson did; and by proponents of the war who claimed that Kennedy would have spoken more effectively than Johnson against the implicit "isolationism" and "sentimentality" of the antiwar movement. In the long run, this usage made Kennedy a hero of the culture in terms that were broadly inclusive rather than partisan. A 1988 *Times-Mirror* survey of the American electorate found that Kennedy was recognized and accepted as a symbol of American heroic style by a range of citizens constituting roughly three-quarters of the electorate.[71] Divorced in this way from the specifics of his political goals and achievements, the hero-president has become a symbol no different in kind from a Charlton Heston—or, perhaps more to the point, John Wayne.

John Wayne Syndrome: The Cult of "The Duke"

The period of Kennedy's campaign for the presidency coincided with the transformation of John Wayne from a major Hollywood star to a powerful cultural icon. Since 1949, Wayne had been perhaps the most widely and consistently popular Hollywood actor. But the most striking peculiarity of his stardom was its generic limitation. His screen persona was identified with his roles in combat films and Westerns, and even when he was cast in other kinds of film his role was usually designed to refer more or less explicitly to his soldier/cowboy persona. This concentration of screen activity created a particularly strong link between Wayne's screen persona and his off-screen role as celebrity and public figure.[72] Such linkages are (as we have seen) a normal feature of movie-stardom. But Wayne's identification with war and the West linked him with a highly specific set of myth-historical referents. And over time he came to be identified with those referents—came to be seen, not as a player in cowboy and combat pictures, but as an authentic representative of "the Old West" or of "the American soldier."

By the end of the 1960s, Wayne would be so identified with the West that his presence in a Western was taken as a guarantee of authenticity, similar to that which "original participants" had provided for Wild West shows and early movies—even though his "participation" was as a movie actor, not as a working cowboy or actor in frontier history. The ultimate development of this paradox is nicely represented by P. F. Kluge's laudatory 1972 article in *Life*: "First and Last, a Cowboy / Half myth and half movie star, John Wayne rides a lost frontier." Kluge wants us to see Wayne as an "authentic" representative of the Old West, and of "19th Century values," although Wayne's knowledge of both derives entirely from roles played in fiction films. So Kluge describes the filming of Westerns on location as a form of pioneering (a "community of men . . . [doing] rough work in remote awesome locations, [living in] tent cities . . . ") and has Wayne complaining, like a crusty old cowpoke or mountain man, how "everything has gotten built up so, it's hard to find distant locations for roughing it, like we did before."

Kluge identifies Wayne's movie roles as historical performances in order to lend authority to Wayne's angry polemic against contemporary American values and politics: "He has been a leatherneck and he has been a Green Beret, but he has gone on being a cowboy. But now he sees his kind of cowboy, his kind of western as part of a legacy which is increasingly threatened."[73] When Kluge asks, "What frontiers will replace the West, which is all won and closed and settled and where locations for a western film are getting scarce?" Wayne replies with a diatribe that is both a reprise of the classic Teddy Roosevelt version of the Myth of the Frontier (from an essay like "Expansion and Peace") and a direct response to the contemporary politics of decolonization:

> "Your generation's frontier should have been Tanganyika . . . It's a land with eight million blacks and it could hold 60 million people. We could feed India with the food we produced in Tanganyika! It could have been a new frontier for any American or English or French kid with a little gumption! Another Israel! But the do-gooders had to give it back to the Indians!
>
> "Meanwhile, your son and my son are given numbers back here and live in apartment buildings on top of each other."[74]

Wayne's version of the "New Frontier" differs from the Kennedy version in being an excessively explicit and credulous reproduction of the mythic tradition. But the two have important cognate features of style and content. Wayne's Third World Frontier is literally and naively Turnerian, with its scenario of individual "kids" establishing the farms whose wheat will feed starving India. But Kennedy also saw the Third World as a frontier in which the kids of "this generation"—acting as agents of the nation rather than as individual settlers—could justify their moral character and bring waste spaces into productivity. Wayne's distinction between "blacks" and "people" openly applies to contemporary Africans the original colonists' characterization of land occupied by American Indians as an "unpeopled waste." The administration's belief in the "primitivism" of Third World cultures was a more sophisticated application of this classic analogy between American Indians and non-White natives elsewhere—although it would never express these ideas in language so frankly racist. Wayne's formulation differs only in its explicit anger from Samuel Eliot Morison's likening the French surrender of Algeria to a putative American surrender of Ohio to Tecumseh. His use of the standard of productivity to define the qualitative difference between Euro-Americans and natives is both a traditional aspect of the Frontier Myth and an essential premise of the New Frontier's "modernization" and "nation-building" strategy, and "do-gooders" was nearly as much a term of contempt among the President and his men as it is for Wayne.[75]

Wayne's connections to the figures of "leatherneck" and "Green Beret" were every bit as fictive as those that identified him as a nineteenth-century cowboy. Wayne never served a day in the military, although he contributed to the war effort as a civilian entertainer of troops overseas and as an actor in films designed to spur the war effort.[76] But the movie-myth that developed around Wayne became a more than adequate substitute for his lack of real military experience. In a speech before the American Legion Convention, General Douglas MacArthur praised Wayne's performance as the hard-boiled Marine sergeant in *Sands of Iwo Jima* (1949) by declaring, "You represent the American serviceman better than the American serviceman himself"—a statement which suggests that Wayne's mythic figure is not merely a representation but a valid substitute for and even an improvement on the real thing. This confounding of myth and reality would reach its culmination in Congress's authorization of a John

Wayne medal, identifying the lifelong civilian as the embodiment of American military virtue.[77]

The essential elements of Wayne's cowboy/soldier persona are visible in his earliest "B"-Western roles and in the spate of wartime action films he made between 1942 and 1945. But Wayne achieved the most complete and powerful development of that persona in the postwar films he did for John Ford and Howard Hawks. Ford and Hawks constructed the powerful screen persona Wayne came to inhabit and taught him how to use that persona effectively. As his career prospered, Wayne sought to apply what he had learned by taking greater control of that image. He used his leverage as a star to negotiate with producers for particular roles and for the choice of scriptwriter and director. He produced two of his own pictures in the late 1940s, and in 1952 he formed a production company of his own, Wayne-Fellows. That company produced three films, including two trademark Wayne performances in *Hondo* (1953) and *The High and the Mighty* (1954).[78]

In 1955 Wayne formed his own production company (Batjac) and began serious work on a project that had interested him since 1946—an epic treatment of the defense of the Alamo.[79] The picture was to be a "blockbuster," but Wayne also intended it as both a personal and a political statement. He risked his own and his company's fortunes on the production and pushed it to completion despite mounting financial difficulties. When he insisted on independent production, his former studio (Republic) vindictively attempted to pre-empt the subject by rushing *The Last Command* (1955) into production.[80]

Wayne wanted *The Alamo* to be received as a serious historical epic that gave an authentic picture of the historical event and linked it to an impeccable and uplifting moral and political message. He wrote much of the publicity for the film, defining his purposes in terms that echo Buffalo Bill's "Salutatory" assertion of historical authority and educational purpose:

> We want to recreate a moment in history which will show to this living generation of Americans what their country really stands for, and to put in front of their eyes the bloody truth of what some of their forebears went through to win what they had to have or die—liberty and freedom.

He hoped that the film would play a role in the struggle against Communism in the emerging nations, that through it he could "sell

America to countries threatened with Communist domination . . . [and] put new heart and faith into all the world's free people. . . ." But his more immediate purpose was to "sell America" to the American people, whose patriotism had gone flabby: "I think we've all been going soft, taking freedom for granted."[81]

As the reviewer for the *Los Angeles Times* noted, this rhetorical line—which might have seemed a cliché a year or two before—seemed very timely. Wayne released the film on the eve of the 1960 presidential election, in which Kennedy and Nixon vied with each other in asserting their commitment to a more vigorous opposition to Communist advances. Although Wayne was a Republican, his "going soft" remark, and the heroic persona that lies behind it, corresponds more closely to the rhetorical style and ideological stance of Kennedy. The difference between them was that while Kennedy identified "softness" with the regime of an aged Republican general, Wayne blamed intellectuals: "those pseudo-sophisticates, the people who belittle honor, courage, cleanliness." But that sort of intellectual—by implication leftist and critical of American policy in the Cold War—was just as antipathetic to Kennedy and the "tough-minded" academics who advised him."[82]

Wayne's choice of the Davy Crockett role for himself was a way of buttressing his moral authority in the narrative.[83] *The Alamo* was developed in the midst of the "Crockett Craze" spawned by Disney Studios' three-part TV serial, *Davy Crockett, King of the Wild Frontier* (1954, released as a movie in 1955, and followed by sequels in TV and theatrical release).[84]

Wayne's Davy Crockett borrows the "populist style" of the Disney version—folksy humor, frankness, preference for substance over formality—but uses it to sanctify an essentially undemocratic set of political manipulations. Wayne's Crockett has brought his volunteers to Texas under the pretense that they are merely hunting, but he plans to inveigle them into enlisting in the Texan cause by means of an elaborate psychological ruse. He tells us that his Tennesseans are too independent and hard-headed to simply enlist in someone else's fight or to succumb to highfalutin' patriotic rhetoric. To persuade them, he will first have to show them that the Texans are their kind of people: brave, Anglo-American (for the most part), and opposed to the kind of government oppression any Tennessean would naturally resent. He then supplements fact with deceit, producing a forged letter supposedly from Santa Anna, which implicitly insults the Tennesseans' manhood. Having aroused their ire, he then unmasks his deceit and restores his standing as a truthful man. But his falsification has been persuasive in opening the men's eyes, and they agree to stay and fight. (Crockett's procedure here mirrors John Ford's play on truth, falsification, and belief at the end of *Fort Apache*.)

Wayne's relation to his men is a good metaphoric rendering of the public relations problem faced by American policy-makers and their methods for dealing with it. The Tennesseans are as isolationist and self-interested as the public imagined by the policy-makers. Their leaders must define a mission that they would not choose for themselves and trick them into accepting it as if it were their own. The trick is not unmasked until they have emotionally committed themselves, and its exposure merely adds a corollary to the ideological imperatives of their leaders—namely, that they give their free consent to be ruled by a set of procedures which require that crucial information be concealed from them "for their own good."

This message is amplified in the relationship between Colonel Travis (Laurence Harvey) and the soldiers in the Alamo, particularly the Hispanic Texans who are serving with him. Travis believes that if his troops learn that they have been ordered to fight to the last man and are certain to be overwhelmed by Santa Anna's army, they will simply bolt. He therefore conceals the true situation, even though this requires him to contemptuously dismiss intelligence brought to him by Hispanic Texans. At this point in the narrative, Travis appears to be a "martinet" figure: he relies too much on formal authority and lacks Crockett's warmth and plebeian touch. However, although his manner is repellent, his method of command is vindicated by its similarity to Crockett's own deceptive procedures. Even his insulting manner toward the Hispanics is accounted for as an expression of paternal concern. He knows that when the Alamo falls, Santa Anna will be merciless to any Mexicans who have fought against him, and he wishes to spare them by driving them away.[85]

The politics of *The Alamo* thus mirror the emerging politics of counterinsurgency in their insistence on the legitimacy of falsification and manipulation to evade (until commitment is an established fact) a skeptical public scrutiny, and in the tendency to substitute American for non-American forces in an approaching crisis. The movie also addresses the question of military "style," in the conflict between the "regular" command principles of Travis and the "irregular" methods of Bowie and Crockett. Although the movie gives Travis and command authority their due, it clearly regards the "irregular" style as the most effective as well as the most "American," and it signals that emphasis by making Wayne's Crockett the figure who effects the compromise between Travis and the *excessively* "irregular" Bowie.

Wayne equated dislike of the film with the eastern "pseudo-sophisticates'" distaste for his message.[86] But the film's formal defects contributed to a critical reception that was at best lukewarm and at its harshest contemptuous of both Wayne's polemics and his film-making. For the most part, the film's jingoism was less problematic even to liberals of that era than was the fatuous, self-important, and doctrinaire tone in which Wayne delivers his opinions on patriotism, courage, religious faith, "Woman," race relations, the marriage bond, the balance of military and civilian authority, and so on. Wayne's handling of the theme of slavery drew on a recognizably denigrating stereotype of the faithful black servant and reiterated one of the oldest of pro-slavery myths by having Bowie's servant resist his own manumission and elect to die with his master. His treatment of gender follows the model of patriarchal dominance (modified by chivalry): at one point the script declares that "a man without a woman is half a man, but a woman without a man is nothing." His religious enthusiasm reaches a point of absurdity when one of the soldiers declares that he is unwilling to die with anyone who doesn't believe in God. It is not enough that, as the proverb says, there are no atheists in foxholes—Wayne wants it understood that if an atheist appears he will be asked to leave.

But despite the weaknesses of *The Alamo*, Wayne's performances during the 50s and 60s, and the linkage of his screen persona and his role as a public figure, made him a public icon whose ideological resonance nearly matched the ambitions of his Crockett portrayal. As the public perceived him, he was not only the actor who had played all those Western and Marine Corps heroes; he was somehow, in his own person, a breathing incarnation of the personalities and consciousness of Ringo, Kirby York, Colonel Jim Madden, Tom Dunson, Sergeant Stryker, and Ethan Edwards.[87] His roles in *The Longest Day* (1962), *How the West Was Won* (1962), and *The Greatest Story Ever Told* (1965) are almost purely iconic in their use of Wayne to invoke military and Western associations.[88]

These iconic cameos were merely one aspect of a public persona that had transcended the movie roles from which it had derived its identity and force. By 1960 "John Wayne" had become a kind of folk-hero, his name an idiomatic expression, a metaphoric formula or cliché that instantly invoked a well-recognized set of American heroic virtues—or, from a different perspective, inflated American pretensions. His triumph over cancer and his return to the screen were hailed in cover stories in both *Life* and *Newsweek*; *Time* compared him favorably with the Hemingway ideal of heroism in "John Wayne Rides Again." Reviewing two Wayne vehicles in 1967, Richard Schickel treats Wayne as a mythic figure, "a kind of natural phenomenon, rather like a spectacular geological remnant of a vanished age," representing a heroic past which is at once that of the Old West and of an older Hollywood:

> For some of us who have grown up in his shadow, measuring our changing personalities against his towering constancy, Wayne has become one of life's bedrock necessities. He reminds us of a time when right was right, wrong was wrong, and the differences between them could be set right by the simplest means.
>
> There used to be many like him, but death and age . . . have robbed him of most of his competition—and robbed us of the opportunity to regress . . . to the mythic days of yesteryear. . . . If anything, he has improved with age. . . . Most men of his paunch have given up righteous violence in favor of guileful acquiescence in the world's wickedness; the Duke is still banging away at it . . . an unconscious existential hero. . . . [89]

(Two years later, Schickel would write a scathing and contemptuous review of *The Green Berets*, scoring both its politics and its incompetence as an action film.)[90]

Within the special subdivision of the culture that belongs to the military, the John Wayne image also had important meanings. Its most obvious role was its "recruiting poster" idealization of military heroism, which attracted many young recruits (like Ron Kovic) to the Marine Corps.[91] But it also had meaning for the professional officer corps, as a way of expressing the intangible qualities that give a commander authority: "[Colonel] Porter, who was somewhat in awe of Harkins, thought that he resembled John Wayne."[92] The necessary concomitant of this role was the use of Wayne as symbolic scapegoat when patriotic heroism led to personal or collective catastrophe, as in the crippled veteran Ron Kovic's bitter cry, "Nobody ever told me I was going to come back from the war without a penis. . . . Oh God, Oh God, I want it back! I gave it for the whole country. . . . I gave [it] for John Wayne."[93]

The double-edged quality of the Wayne icon appears in the complex of war-related stress disorders identified by Vietnam veterans and their doctors as "John Wayne Syndrome." The common feature of the syndrome was the soldier's internalization of an ideal of superhuman military bravery, skill, and invulnerability to guilt and grief, which is identified at some point with "John Wayne." The identification is not necessarily with a specific Wayne film or group of films, but with Wayne as a figure of speech, signifying the suppposed perfection of soldierly masculinity. Since that ideal is, in fact, impossible to live up to, "John Wayne Syndrome" often took the form of excessive guilt or shame for feelings of guilt or grief, or for responding to battlefield stress with a normal human mix of fear and bravery. Disillusion with the Wayne ideal, or recognition of its inapplicability in the real world of combat, could transform the heroic symbol into its opposite, a metaphor of false consciousness, pretension, and military excess, as in the statement attributed to a Marine in I Corps, "There are always two ways to do something—the right way and the John Wayne way. We might as well do it the right way." The phrase is actually a variation on the army folk-saying that distinguishes "the right way, the wrong way, and the army way," in which a symbolic "John Wayne" takes the place of the military institution itself. It is also worth noting that the I Corps Marine identified the "John Wayne" approach with the abandonment of successful Marine pacification campaigns ("the right way") in favor of the more destructive big-unit operations.[94]

While this weight of public symbolism is indeed "a heavy weight to lay on a movie star," Wayne invited such readings of his performances by his deliberate efforts to use his screen image as an instrument of political persuasion. The tendency to increasingly explicit political polemics is marked in the movement from *The Alamo* to *The Comancheros* (a 1961 "Mexico Western") and *McLintock!* (1963).[95] The culmination of his efforts in this line was reached in 1966 when, after returning from a trip to Vietnam, he decided to make *The Green Berets*.

Blockbuster Tactics: The Green Berets *(1968) and the Big-Unit War*

The Green Berets was conceived from the start as a work of propaganda to convince the American people that "it was necessary for us to be [in Vietnam]." Despite his antipathy for the liberalism of the Democratic administration, Wayne sought the President's support for the project. Jack Valenti (Johnson's press aide) pleaded Wayne's cause, telling Johnson that although Wayne's political views were otherwise antipathetic, "so far as Vietnam is concerned his views are right . . . he would be saying the things we want said."[96]

Such a propaganda project was particularly appealing in view of Johnson's own reluctance to engage in a full-bore campaign for public support of the war. This reluctance sorts oddly with the fact that as early as the summer of 1964 Johnson and his advisers had decided to escalate (rather than terminate) the war and after the election had authorized aerial bombing of the North and a steady augmentation of the numbers and combat roles of American ground forces in the South. But it was important to Johnson's larger policy concerns that the war be rhetorically minimized (or at least limited) even as it was being materially augmented. One of the reasons he gave for this procedure was fear that dramatic mobilization measures would make intervention by the Chinese or Soviets more likely, while a slower and more surreptitious sort of escalation might somehow arouse less anxiety. But his primary reason was concern that excessive emphasis on the war might distract attention from and reduce support for the Great Society social measures, which reflected Johnson's real priorities and embodied his hopes for "a place in history." Moreover, like his predecessors, Johnson mistrusted the American public's willingness to accept the social and financial burden of the long struggle the Vietnam War was clearly becoming. To maintain support for the war and the Great Society it was necessary to minimize the likely costs of both by resisting the temptation to make war propaganda the central theme of administration rhetoric.[97]

Thus the task of making propaganda for the liberal President's war devolved on the arch-conservative John Wayne. This was the first of a series of "displacements" which the film embodies, the most important of which is the displacement of the real war into the fictive space of the "John Wayne movie." Wayne interprets the war in terms provided by the movie-mythologies in whose creation he had played a major part. The fictive counterinsurgency struggle is organized on the "star" principle. Although teamwork is much talked about and elaborately displayed, the plot, the dialogue, and the framing of sequences and even of individual shots all emphasize the absolute centrality of Wayne's character, Colonel Mike Kirby, to the successful prosecution of the war. This is also a fundamental weakness in the film, for despite the John Wayne "aura" his casting is utterly implausible: he (and several of his colleagues) are simply too old for the parts. Wayne himself was 60 when the film was made, had recently lost a lung to cancer, and *looks* it.

The film's narrative is divided into two major sequences, each of which is built around a standard combat-movie plot. In the first, Kirby's A-team defends a beleaguered Montagnard outpost against the assault of an overwhelming number of VC and Northern regulars. The second part centers on a paratroop drop and commando raid "behind enemy lines," drawing on elements of *Objective Burma* and *The Dirty Dozen*. These combat-film conventions are augmented by Western-movie references, most obviously the identification of the Montagnard outpost as "Dodge City." Less obvious, but equally important, are the references to Wayne's cavalry Westerns, carried by the name "Kirby" (reminiscent of Kirby York) and by the central role of the ethnic sergeants—here including a Black man (Raymond St. Jacques) as well as the obligatory Irishman, Muldoon (Aldo Ray).

Finally, Wayne tries to arouse sympathy for the Vietnamese and a willingness to "rescue" them by using a wounded Montagnard girl and an orphaned Vietnamese boy as his primary symbols for the Vietnamese people. Through the children, the Viet Cong are identified with "the horror" by standard Indian-war movie means: they massacre the Montagnard village and rape to death the little girl who had been saved by the Black Green Beret medic. The child's death converts the liberal antiwar reporter (David Janssen) to immediate and full identification with "the mission." The orphan boy Hamchunk brings off a similar conversion when he engages the symphathy of the most cynical of the Green Berets (Peterson, played by Jim Hutton). The killing of the child's little dog by the VC during their assault on "Dodge City" converts Peterson's sympathy into a fatherly adoption. When Peterson is killed in a particularly horrible VC boobytrap, Hamchunk is adopted by Kirby himself in a scene whose dialogue makes literal the ideological implication of the child symbolism—the Vietnamese are orphaned children who have luckily fallen to the paternal care of the paragon of strong American men.

Critics scored *The Green Berets* for its "dishonesty," its simpleminded preachiness, and its propagandistic use of imagery.[98] Wayne's Western and combat-movie references were seen as blatant attempts to invest the Vietnam War with the sanctity of movie-myths and as misrepresentations of the purpose and character of American operations. There is a good deal of validity to the latter criticism, but the dishonesty of *The Green Berets* is not wholly Wayne's fault. In a number of crucial areas, Wayne's film errs in good faith by its too-credulous acceptance of statements from official sources about what our tactics were and how they actually worked. What is interesting about the film is not its misrepresentation of the war-as-fought but the accuracy with which it reproduces and compounds the official misunderstanding and falsification of the conflict.[99]

Wayne's good faith in relying on delusory or deceptive government information is attested in the opening scene of the movie, as the Green Berets conduct a briefing for a group of civilian tourists and hostile journalists from the "liberal media." At one point a display of captured weapons (supplied by Czechoslovakia and "the Chicoms") is used to prove that the Viet Cong are not indigenous insurgents but invading agents of a worldwide Communist conspiracy. The briefing may be taken as a generic phenomenon, providing exposition of the historical background; but it corresponds rather closely to an actual briefing given to the President and his advisers in February 1965 by the CIA, in which evidence (including Czech and Chinese weapons) was produced in support of the assertion that the insurgency was inspired and supplied from outside Vietnam. It was later acknowledged that the evidence had been falsified to buttress the case for "drawing the line" in Vietnam.[100]

Both Wayne's briefing and the CIA's misrepresent the manner in which the Southern insurgents had actually been arming and supplying themselves during the period leading up to the action of the film (1964). Between 1961 and 1963 the VC were able to expand and maintain their supply of modern weapons from *American* arsenals via the capture or abandonment of arms supplied to the ARVN and the infiltration of American-equipped hamlet militias. As Neil Sheehan has written, "By January 1963, the United States had potentially furnished the Vietnamese Communists with enough weapons to create an army in the South capable of challenging and defeating the ARVN."[101] American planners failed to register this information, because belief in an externally maintained insurgency was both a shibboleth of counterinsurgency doctrine and the foundation of the political rationale through which support of South Vietnam was justified to the Congress. But their failure or refusal to acknowledge this intelligence had ensured our persistence in policies whose results were the opposite of those we intended.

Wayne's "adoption" of Hamchunk is the film's most notorious "dishonesty," a predictable and shameless exercise in sentimentality and blatant propaganda. It was exposed to ridicule when critics pointed out that it occurs as the sun sets over the South China Sea, which lies due east of Vietnam—proof that Wayne knew a good deal less about "Indian country" than he pretended, and that his war was pure Hollywood. The gesture itself, and the implicitly racialist paternalism that underlies it, is a conventional icon of the "epic" movie, from *Charge of the Light Brigade* and *Gunga Din* to *El Cid* and *Fifty-five Days.* It is also (as I have noted) a perfect allegory of the ideological rationale for American engagement in Vietnam. But its key iconic elements had been part of the mythology of counterinsurgency since *The Ugly American*, and by 1962 its symbolism was already a well-understood and widely accepted element of public discourse. An early story on the growing American engagement in Vietnam by reporter Scott Leavitt, published by *Life* in March 1962, describes the nature and purpose of our role in three concise images: "The American colonel on the remote Vietnamese ridge top . . . , the dead child in the burned village and the snarling guerrilla in the upland jungle." For Leavitt, there is only one possible narrative that can relate these images: the guerrilla has killed the child and the American colonel on his commanding ridge is determined to avenge that killing and prevent its repetition."[102] So basic is this structure that it would be used in *precisely* the same way in antiwar movies like *Soldier Blue* and *Little Big Man*—which few criticized for false sentiment.

Wayne used Western and war-movie imagery because they were (so to speak) his native tongue. But that same imagery, drawn from the same sources, was also current "in the field," as Wayne observed it in 1966–67. As we have seen, by 1966 the use of Western-movie and frontier references had become typical of official discourse. [103] Of particular relevance to Wayne's project is the report made by the retiring commander of 5th Special Forces in June 1966 (the period of Wayne's visit to Vietnam), in which he praises his NCOs by comparing them to "the tough, self-reliant, combat-tested soldier who fought on the Indian frontier of our country during the 1870s."[104] When the counterinsurgency phase of the war gave way to the "Big-Unit" war in 1965 such terms became even more prevalent, in part because of the prominent role played by the elite 1st Air Cavalry Division, whose operations came to typify the "Big-Unit" war as the Special Forces' CIDGs had typified the counterinsurgency phase. The regiments of the Air Cavalry traced their lineage directly to the cavalry of the Plains Indian wars and included such famous outfits as Custer's 7th, Buffalo Bill's and Wesley Merritt's 5th, and the "Buffalo Soldiers" of the (formerly "Colored") 9th and 10th Cavalry. When one company of the 7th was particularly hard hit in the Ia Drang valley in 1965, the connection to Custer's Last Stand was inevitably made both by journalists and by survivors of the fight. These units still affected cavalry regalia and insignia when not in combat, and their operations often had code names like "Crazy Horse," "Davy Crockett," and "Sam Houston."[105] In this context, Wayne's "Dodge City" seems a tame and entirely appropriate invention.

Likewise, Wayne's concept of the Green Beret as a "character type," though based on such movie models as his own Kirby York(e) and Ethan Edwards, was very much in the spirit of the counterinsurgency warrior envisioned in the Doolittle Report and the early Special Forces formations. The phrase "self-reliant" occurs in practically every summary of Special Forces characteristics. Shelby Stanton, in his history of the Green Berets, describes them as "rugged individualists," thoroughly professional yet capable of going beyond standard operating doctrine and of staring down bureaucratic sneers at "crackpot non-Army" methods, ready for "insertion" anywhere in the world, "able to survive the most hostile environment, and to take care of themselves and others . . . to be independent thinkers, able to grasp opportunities and innovate with the materials at hand," to fight the enemy with his own weapons, in his own style, on his own terrain.[106] Thus Wayne can be excused for thinking that in casting himself as a Green Beret he was not violating the Special Forces' own sense of their character and role.

Wayne's film adds a new and disturbing element of racialist iconography to the war/Western mixture by initially giving the Green Berets a distinctly "Germanic" style. We first see these elite soldiers standing at rigid attention under a banner that identifies the place as the John F. Kennedy Special Warfare Center. But when the soldiers introduce themselves they speak in German and in a mechanical monotone which, when combined with their mask-like WASP-standard faces, suggests an association between the young President's elite corps and the classic Nazi stormtroopers of Hollywood iconography. Why are these soldiers, who are presumably to fight a jungle war against Asians, speaking German? Is there a suggestion that the proverbial toughness and fanatic anti-Communism of the Nazis is a positive model for American emulation? Is there even a suggestion that the war in Vietnam is as much about race as it is about ideology?[107]

Whether or not Wayne intended to give his Green Berets a bit of the stormtrooper-elite aura, his "German" reference is actually an allusion to the historical antecedents of Special Forces. These units were originally planned to operate in Germany and Eastern Europe behind the lines of a possible Soviet invasion. For this reason, many of the early Special Forces recruits were refugees from Iron Curtain countries; some had fought as soldiers or partisans against the Germans, and others had fought *with* the Germans against the Soviets.[108] Robin Moore's novel *The Green Berets* (1965), on which the film was based, describes the role played by these "Foreign Legion" types, emphasizing their Nordic racial character and even their Nazi associations. His language and the paradigm of racial qualities he uses are strongly reminiscent of Theodore Roosevelt's Teutonism, with its contrasts between German soldierliness, Latin decadence, and the barbarism of non-Whites. Moore's first chapter celebrates the exploits of a Special Forces officer named Kornie (based on a real-life SF major named Thorne), a "Nordic giant" who leads an "all-Viking A Team" against the VC and who was also a decorated veteran of the Finnish army which fought the Soviets in alliance with Hitler in 1941–45. Another of Moore's heroes is described as a former Hitler Youth whose family had emigrated to the United States before the war. One of the hardest and most battle-loving of Moore's characters, he takes particular delight in physically destroying a Frenchman who has betrayed his fellow "Whites" by collaborating with the VC. The scenario allegorizes, and projects into Vietnam, the Nazi conquest of a "decadent" France and appropriates the Nazis' military virtues for our side.[109]

Nonetheless, Wayne's handling of this material is more "liberal" than his source's. With the exception of the opening sequence, Wayne's handling of racial imagery eschews Teutonist exclusivism and follows the assimilationist model of the Hollywood combat film. He offsets the implication that this is a war of Whites against non-Whites by emphasizing the roles of the Vietnamese counterparts and by integrating his A-Team through the addition of a Black medic—a procedure that parallels the composition of the platoon in *Bataan*, which includes two Filipinos and a Black engineer.

Wayne was opposed to affirmative action in principle, and his responses to accusations of racial prejudice often betrayed the very White-supremacist biases he was attempting to deny.[110] However, tokenism was important to the patriotic message of both *The Alamo* and *The Green Berets*, and Wayne provided Blacks with what he described as the "correct" number of places in the cast: that is, a number supposedly proportional to their percentage of the population. In fact, neither he nor any other filmmaker has represented Blacks in anything like their actual proportion of the working cowboys in 1880–1900 (perhaps 25 percent), of the Indian-fighting army of the 1870s, or of the combat troops in Vietnam (where they served and took casualties in numbers greater than their proportion of the population). Nor does the number of Blacks in either film equal their share of either the historical or the present population. But in the case of *The Green Berets* Wayne may actually err on the "liberal" side. For Blacks were notably underrepresented in elite units and especially in Special Forces before 1966. Special Forces verteran David D. Duncan has testified that during the early years of Special Forces, Blacks were the objects of deliberate discrimination in the selection and assignment process.[111]

Wayne's contribution to the racialization of the struggle is to give it a distincitve "Hollywood" inflection. His Vietnamese are seen in terms of a set of stereotypes which are explicitly "Oriental" but also generically related to earlier stereotypes of American Indians. Three types of women appear: the Oriental seductress Li and the little Montagnard girl define two ends of the spectrum, and the ubiquitous mama-sans define the peasant average. Among the men, Colonel Kai (Jack Soo) is a slightly comic figure who does not quite meet the Green Beret standard he emulates, while General Ti is a classic Hollywood version of the Oriental warlord. The VC are "savages," and Captain Nim (George Takei) is a "savage for our side," like Chingachgook. It is their native savagery that defines the terms of battle.

But Wayne's racialism merely dramatizes a set of racialist concerns that the government itself took quite seriously. Throughout the series of meetings in 1964–65 during which Johnson and his advisers debated the question of terminating or escalating the war, the racial aspect of the struggle was a continual preoccupation. Part of their concern was over appearances and public impressions—the kind of consideration that led Wayne to integrate his A-Team and emphasize the roles of Asian counterparts in the film. George Ball, who opposed escalation, worried that by increasing our troop levels we would "give the appearance of a White man's war." McGeorge Bundy, who favored escalation, stated the problem as one of substance rather than appearance when he expressed concern about the consequences of "our getting into a white man's war with all the brown men against us or apathetic." But Ball also wondered whether "an army of Westerners can successfully fight Orientals in an Asian jungle," which restates the problem as a comparison of the relative prowess of two racial or ethnic stocks. This way of defining the problem was echoed by Lyndon Johnson: "Can Westerners, in the absence of accurate intelligence, successfully fight Asians in jungle rice paddies?"[112]

The answer to a question put in these terms is provided by the experience of jungle combat in the Second World War, in which American soldiers proved themselves capable of fighting Asians in "jungles and rice paddies." But the success of Americans in that trial by combat was the basis of the combat-film mythology on which Wayne's scenario was based. Wayne's fictive projection of the combat-film resolution onto the Vietnam conflict was thus no more (and no less) egregious or inappropriate than the administration's way of defining and handling the problem. The administration's error was not its miscalculation of the capacity of "American boys" to defeat Asians on a jungle battlefield but its mistaking the infantry battlefield as the crucial arena of struggle. In the event, American troops proved capable of winning most of the tactical engagements, but the war was lost because those engagements were subsumed by a misconceived strategy.[113]

The torture and mutilation of the helpless and innocent are the symbols by which the film identifies the VC as evil, and the same symbols figure prominently in the characterization of VC "savagery" by both Kennedy and Johnson.[114] But in one of the film's most controversial scenes, Colonel Kirby permits and justifies the torture of a captured VC infiltrator by his counterpart Captain Nim. Four kinds of justification are asserted or suggested: a "Western-movie" rationale, which asserts that in Vietnam as on the frontier "due process" comes from the barrel of a gun; a "savage war" rationale, which recognizes that in a war whose objectives do not balk at extermination, the worst of means will inevitably be used; a racialist rationale, in the Fenimore Cooper manner, which suggests that torture is customary with Vietnamese, a kind of "racial gift" like the Indian propensity to scalping, which Hawkeye accepts as appropriate to "red skins"; and a revenge justification, invoked when Kirby discovers that the captive is carrying a Zippo lighter taken from the body of a Green Beret who had been mutilated and tortured to death by the VC. Wayne's response is therefore framed by several different streams of mythology, in each of which his action would be read as both justified and exemplary of tough-minded "realism" about the way such wars must be fought. Moreover, Wayne's rationalization reflects an attitude that was influential among American officers from the earliest period of American involvement, an attitude which, as the war was prolonged and frustration with the South Vietnamese grew, produced a steady increase in the use of torture and (more generally) in the indiscriminate use of violence.[115]

Far from being evidence of "tough-mindedness," American acceptance of our ally's use of torture was regarded by counterinsurgency experts like John Paul Vann as both repugnant and counterproductive to the efforts being made to gain popular acceptance for the regime. American mythology, and the heroic style based on that mythology, thus provided American officers with the wrong set of symbols for measuring "tough-mindedness."[116] A similar attitude underlay the pressure for a wider and more merciless use of force and firepower—tactics that were incompatible with the goals and methods of counterinsurgency.

Wayne's plot develops a "tactical fantasy" that is absurdly inappropriate: a parachute drop "behind enemy lines" to capture General Ti in his palatial plantation headquarters.[117] By 1968 it was quite obvious that there were no "lines" in Vietnam, that Viet Cong generals did not locate themselves in plantation mansions where they could be easily fixed and attacked, and that if such a mission were mounted helicopters would be used, not parachutes. But though Wayne gets the details wrong, his film actually reflects the drift of tactical doctrine in Vietnam away from the small civic/military missions of Special Forces and CIDG and toward the massive operations of a "Big-Unit War," designed to reduce enemy military strength through battlefield attrition. Wayne's scenario enacts the wishful thinking of the army's high command, which built its strategy on the premise that it was possible to turn the insurgency into a Second World War movie by forcing the VC and the NVA to fight a conventional military campaign that could be defeated by the same tactics that had beaten Japan and Germany.[118]

The strategy of the Big-Unit "war of attrition" was designed by General William Westmoreland, commander of the Military Assistance Command in Vietnam (MACV), and his staff. It envisioned the assumption of the burden of ground combat by the large and growing American expeditionary force that had begun arriving in 1965. The mission of American forces would shift away from the task of "pacifying" peasant villages and gaining their allegiance for the Saigon regime to that of seeking combat with "main force" VC and NVA units along the borders and in those regions of the country whose isolation and difficult terrain had made them ideal guerrilla base areas. Like Grant in his campaign against Lee, Westmoreland hoped to engage the enemy in more-or-less continual combat, draining the enemy's resources of men and equipment until a "cross-over point" was reached beyond which those losses could no longer be replaced. American troops would also have to suffer significant losses in men and materiel. But since the United States was incomparably richer than Vietnam and had more than fourteen times the population, it was obvious that the enemy would run out of men and money long before we did.[119]

MACV pursued attrition by the offensive tactic of continuous small "search and destroy" missions around American-held areas and by larger missions into guerrilla base areas (like the Air Cavalry's incursion in the Ia Drang Valley in 1965). These missions were costly and not as productive of large body counts as the strategy of attrition required. However, MACV believed that its tactics had succeeded in damaging the indigenous guerrilla movement, and that this success, coupled with the Vietnamese Communists' supposedly rigid adherence to Mao's "three phase" program for a war of national liberation, would dictate a massive conventional military assault in 1968. American planners also assumed that the Vietnamese would adhere rigidly to the paradigm of victory provided in their own revolutionary mythology and would attempt to repeat their victory of Dien Bien Phu by isolating and destroying the Marine combat base at Khe Sanh, which "threatened" the invasion and supply routes entering South Vietnam from the northwest. American firepower guaranteed that such an assault could be defeated with ruinous losses as soon as the Vietnamese came out of the jungle, producing a Dien Bien Phu in reverse.[120]

Wayne's treatment of the "Dodge City" battle is clearly determined by movie conventions, particularly those of *The Alamo* and its kindred "last stand" epics. Like the Alamo, or the Peking Legations, or El Cid's Valencia, "Dodge City" is both a home (to women and children) and a fortress; its defenders represent an alliance that transcends racial, religious, or national lines to combat a massive assault by an inhuman enemy. But the defense of Khe Sanh was being planned at the same time that Wayne was scenarizing the defense of "Dodge City," and the movie scenario mirrors MACV's expectations of why and how such a battle would develop. Because of "Dodge City's" strategic location, Wayne's VC are compelled to attack it with both VC and NVA regular troops. So desperate are those troops that they assault in a "human wave," taking massive casualties from the guns and pre-planted "infernal machines" of the defenders. Even when the camp is reinforced by a "Mike" force, the enemy keeps coming and finally forces evacuation of the camp. Green Berets and Vietnamese counterparts form the rear guard and blow up their own buildings (destroying the village to save it), while women and children escape to the choppers. Finally, with "those people" in control of the camp, Wayne summons "Puff the Magic Dragon"—a C-47 with a modern Gatling gun—which shoots the enemy to pieces. The decimated VC/NVA abandon the ruined camp, and the Green Berets and their counterparts return and—like the pioneers in *Drums Along the Mohawk*—"start all over again."

In the event, MACV's Khe Sanh scenario never materialized. The North Vietnamese were not compelled to attack the combat base by logistical necessity; instead, they bypassed it to deliver the Tet Offensive to the population centers. Nor were they inclined to attack it out of some "superstitious" reverence for and ritual compulsion to repeat the Battle of Dien Bien Phu. A mythological understanding of the coming campaign was more characteristic of MACV, which had become wedded to a scenario derived in part from the French defeat and in part from fantasies of The Alamo.[121] But in one respect, Wayne's movie was predictive of the event: in order to defeat the VC/NVA and rescue "Dodge City," its defenders have to destroy it. In *The Green Berets* this outcome is presented as proof of the strength and commitment of the Americans and their counterparts and deliberately evokes the pioneer spirit evinced in films like *Drums Along the Mohawk* and *The Searchers*, in which settlers whose farms have been destroyed by Indians vindicate their moral character by their determination to rebuild. However, in Vietnam itself, in the aftermath of Tet 1968, the idea that "We had to destroy the city in order to save it" came to symbolize the war's absurd futility and even "madness."[122]

The public response to Wayne's film was an odd mixture of acceptance and rejection. Despite a generally unfavorable critical reception, the film did well at the box office in 1968 and continued to do steady and profitable business in subsequent years. But some of its success was due to the fact that it was for nearly a decade the only combat film to treat the Vietnam War directly. This testifies to the limits of Wayne's success, for unlike *Bataan* this war film was not followed by a wave of imitations. On the contrary, it made barely a ripple in the veil of Hollywood's avoidance of Vietnam as a subject. Nor did the film succeed in its propaganda aims. Public support for the war continued to diminish at the same steady rate it had followed since the end of 1965.[123]

The film's limited acceptance is not attributable to its falsification of events, nor to its use of conventional symbols, themes, and story formulas. Defects of a similar kind had not limited the appeal of films like *Bataan* or *Retreat, Hell!* If there is a problem with the film's credibility, it is not so much Wayne's failure to represent the war's reality as it is the fidelity with which he represents the officially authorized version of events. The film's credibility gap is identical with the gap that had opened between the administration and the public, which was becoming increasingly skeptical of the accuracy and even the honesty of the administration's account of how the war was going. Despite assertions of continuous progress in counterinsurgency and pacification, despite the massive infusion of men and money and equipment, despite the statistics of crippling losses suffered by the enemy, Americans perceived a steadily mounting rate of American casualties, a South Vietnamese government riven by corruption and bedeviled by repeated *coups*, and above all the persistence of guerrilla attacks and control of the countryside.

By the time the film appeared we were in the third year of the "Big-Unit" war, apparently no nearer to victory, and beginning to feel the negative effects of the "war of attrition." American casualties increased drastically, a steady drain of casualties from search-and-destroy, punctuated by major assaults with large "butcher's bills," and very little of a concrete nature to show for the cost, except the increasingly suspect statistic of the "body count"—a measurement of success that many Americans found morally repugnant. Moreover, the new tactics in the South and the massive bombing in the North produced heavy civilian casualties and floods of refugees whose immiseration argued against administration claims of "progress." There was a growing sense of the disproportion between the limited objectives of the war and the ever-increasing levels of violence its prosecution seemed to demand.[124]

A series of newsfilm images—beginning with Morley Safer's 1965 report on the Marines' firing on Cam Ne with their "Zippo" lighters and culminating in *Life* magazine's 1969 publication of the pictures of the Mylai massacre—provided the symbolic iconography of a growing uneasiness about the ways in which the American military effort was affecting the "little people" it was our "mission" to rescue.[125] Although the media have been criticized (from 1965 to the present) for emphasizing such scenes, for most of the war ample screen-time was also allotted to the representation of pacification and civic-action projects. The Cam Ne images were striking and memorable because they were *exceptions* to the normal way of telling an American war story. They identified an abnormal extreme to which this war might occasionally drive American soldiers, as the experience of Indian warfare turns some Americans into Ethan Edwards. But between

1965 and 1969 the public's understanding of the "Vietnam war story" underwent a transformation, which became visible in the shock of recognition (as well as horror) that greeted the revelation of the Mylai massacre. The public had accepted "Doolittle rules" to the extent that they saw the killing of civilians by American troops as a regrettable necessity of a dirty war. But such killing was acceptable only so long as it appeared to be necessarily and rationally related to the use of effective tactics in pursuit of worthy goals. But in the "war of attrition," the level of killing continued to rise without evidence of tactical success, to levels that began to appear excessive and unrelated to our war aims.

In 1962 Scott Leavitt had been able to provide *Life*'s readers with three photographic images which instantly and with minimal interpretation conveyed a comprehensible and thoroughly credible answer to the question, "Why are we in Vietnam?" The pictures showed "The American colonel on the remote Vietnamese ridge top . . . , the dead child in the burned village and the snarling guerrilla in the upland jungle," and in 1962 it would have been clear that the guerrilla had killed the child and that the American had come to save other children by killing the guerrilla. But in 1968 the same three pictures were as likely to generate a story in which the child is killed by American bombs or has been shot in the cross fire between the colonel and the guerrilla, or, more demoralizing still in its irrationality, that the colonel has "killed the child in order to save it."[126]

That was precisely the point the war had reached when *The Green Berets* was released in June 1968.

The juxtaposition of the film's heroic fantasies with the televised realities of the war of attrition spoiled Wayne's mythographic project. But it is vital that we see *The Green Berets*, not as a misconceived failure, but as the logical fulfillment of the myth of charismatic leadership and counterinsurgency—of the weak people needing to be rescued by the Strong Man—that was so appealingly voiced in John F. Kennedy's inaugural and so vividly portrayed in the epic cinema of *El Cid*, *Fifty-five Days*, and *The Alamo*.

16 Attrition

The Big Unit War, the Riots, and the Counterinsurgency Western, 1965–1968

In 1965 the counterinsurgency phase of the Vietnam War ended, and the big-unit war began. Instead of countering Communist guerrillas with an American-led partisan movement, the Johnson administration decided to use conventional forces to gain control of crucial regions, decimate enemy combat troops, and force the NVA to abandon the war or "come out and fight in the open." On paper, the war of attrition must have seemed like a winning strategy. Given the disparity of wealth, force, and population between the United States and North Vietnam, it appeared that so long as the American government was tough-minded enough to apply force unstintingly over a period of years, it could hardly fail to bring the war to a "cross-over point."

Similar considerations suggested that the War on Poverty, which President Johnson had declared in 1964, was destined for success. The pockets of poverty and inequality would certainly yield once the full battery of public resources was brought to bear on them. By the spring of 1967 a series of new agencies and programs had been created, funded, staffed, and sent into the field to fill gaps in the social welfare system; to upgrade pre-school, public, and vocational education; to create a domestic Peace Corps; and to reorganize poor neighborhoods for self-improvement.

Less than a year later—in March of 1968—public and official confidence in the logic that governed strategy in these two presidential wars had begun to break up in response to a series of violent shocks. In Vietnam, the countrywide Tet Offensive mounted by the VC and NVA in January/February 1968 gave the lie to a year's worth of statistics ostensibly showing the enemy growing weaker and South Vietnam more secure and to official predictions that a successful end to the war was in sight. Indeed, the numbers, equipment, and morale of the enemy appeared (if anything) greater, and his presence in every region of the country more ubiquitous than before the war of attrition began.

In the United States, the summer of 1967 saw the climax of a series of riots that had been occurring since 1965 in urban ghettoes *outside* the South. These "uprisings" were more extensive and violent than any other American civil disorders in this century, and they seemed to belie the administration's assumption that legislative guarantees of civil rights coupled with an expansion of the welfare state would guarantee the nation's social peace. Though their causes were the subject of elaborate sociological studies and intense partisan debate, the net effect of the riots was to suggest that—in the War on Poverty as in the war in Vietnam—American political leaders had misunderstood the nature of the forces with which they were dealing and/or had deceived the public about their ability to direct the course of events.[1]

Two sets of images, conveyed in print and television photography, symbolized the undoing of these paired strategies. The first showed armored vehicles and paratroopers drawn from divisions fighting in Vietnam battling with Black rioters in the burning streets of Detroit in July 1967. The second showed American and ARVN soldiers fighting desperately to defend the core installations of regions that were supposedly secure, including the American embassy in Saigon, and then turning their artillery and bombs against the very cities they had been defending in order to recapture them (at heavy cost) from the enemy. The absurd inversion to which the logic of our policies had brought us was inadvertently rendered as a slogan by the American officer who explained the army's evacuation and destruction of the town of Ben Tre by saying, "We had to destroy Ben Tre in order to save it."[2]

The seven-month period that began with the Newark and Detroit riots in the summer of 1967 and ended with the Tet Offensive signaled the eruption of a major crisis of politics and ideology which ultimately fragmented the conceptual and political consensus that had shaped our history since 1945. A political and ideological crisis of this magnitude naturally affected nearly every aspect of our cultural life and expression by calling into question some of the most basic elements of our belief structures, most particularly the belief that our political leadership and institutions of government are generally reliable, rational, and trustworthy, and that our political discourse provides both a reasonably truthful accounting of events and useful mechanisms for articulating and giving effect to the wisdom and will of the public.

This broad cultural impact was of course registered in the mythographic media of the commercial culture, including movie and television Westerns. Given its importance in the lexicon of American mythology, a study of the impact of these events on the Western movie provides a useful indicator of the cultural effects of the crisis. But there are also reasons for thinking that the genre played an exceptional role in the cultural production of the period. Through most of the New Frontier/Great Society era, and most markedly between 1965 and 1972, the Western—and particularly the "Mexico Western"—was the only one of the standard Hollywood genres whose practitioners *regularly* used genre symbolism to address the problems of Vietnam and to make the connection between domestic social/racial disorder and the counterinsurgency mission.[3] Many of the films produced in this period used the symbolic codes of myth and genre in highly complex and sophisticated ways to articulate a sense of crisis, define its elements, critique existing patterns of response, and develop a moral stance or style of action that would promise some kind of resolution.

To appreciate the ambition and mythographic accomplishment of these films, we need to look first at the nature of the crisis they addressed and the symbols, slogans, and icons through which the journalistic media represented and interpreted that crisis.

The Road to Ben Tre: The (Il)logic of Attrition

Beginning in 1966, journalists remarked a steadily growing cognitive dissonance (or "credibility gap") between two incompatible visions of reality: that promulgated by the rhetoric of the administration and enforced by the higher levels of the Military Assistance Command, Vietnam (MACV), and that perceived by the soldiers and journalists at ground level (and by the public, who received mail from the soldiers and read or watched the journalists' stories). American planes regularly staged heavy bombing raids in both North and South Vietnam, and American soldiers for the most part took over the task of ground combat from the South Vietnamese army (ARVN). But despite the skill and determination with which American forces were used and the mounting toll of American casualties, and despite the optimistic statistics that flowed out of MACV, the enemy's capacity to make war did not appear to be substantially weakened. And instead of recruiting its strength behind the shield of American forces, the South Vietnamese government appeared to become weaker, less popular in the countryside and even in the cities.

Yet the administration persisted, not only in the policy direction it had taken, but in the assertion that its understanding of the war was now, and always had been, correct. In fact, however, public uneasiness with the level of violence corresponded to the most informed and hard-headed analysis available to MACV and Washington in 1965–67. This analysis revealed that instead of the "cross-over" Westmoreland envisioned, American tactics had produced a "looking-glass" effect, yielding results almost diametrically opposite from those they were designed to achieve. A study by the State Department's intelligence office (June 29, 1965) of the effect of the bombing of North Vietnam found that there were "no significantly harmful effects on popular morale. *In fact*, the regime has apparently been able to increase its control . . . perhaps even to break through the political apathy and indifference . . . of the average North Vietnamese." Far from deterring and demoralizing the Hanoi regime, American bombing had aided its efforts to arouse the Northern population to a greater sense of outrage at American intervention and had increased its identification with and engagement in the struggle to the South.[4]

A more painful paradox was apparent in the South. Here the combination of "search and destroy" tactics with the establishment of "Free-Fire Zones" was supposed to allow the Americans to attack Communist strength directly, to break the bonds between guerrillas and peasants, and to genuinely "pacify" crucial regions. Free-Fire Zones were defined in regions where support for the VC was so ingrained that the only way to "pacify" it was to "remove the people and destroy the village." Once such a removal had occurred, anyone remaining in the village became, by definition and without regard to age or sex, an enemy combatant and therefore a legitimate target of American firepower. As the war was prolonged, and as the depth of VC support in the countryside revealed itself, these zones were extended, creating more refugees to fill the government compounds or crowd the alleys of the major cities.[5]

The refugee crisis produced a public-relations backlash which MACV addressed in December 1965 by changing the designation to "Specified Strike Zone," which suggested a more "surgical" use of firepower. This ploy merely helped to discredit MACV with both the press and with soldiers in the field, who felt that the spirit of the policy was better expressed by the original name. But the concern with public relations masked a more dangerous contradiction.

Although Westmoreland had not intended so large a displacement of the rural population, he was not displeased with the result, which he saw as "depriv[ing] the enemy of population." He deemed the refugees to be "under government control," because they were now well within the zones covered by the major military bases of the ARVN and the American army. From the administration's perspective, the uprooting of the peasantry was a sign of progress, even a symptom of "nation-building" and "modernization." The political scientist Samuel P. Huntington, a civilian analyst who studied the refugee problem for the administration, described the process in quasi-Turnerian terms, with the urban slums, "which seem so horrible to middle-class Americans," becoming "a gateway to a new and better way of life" as part of the modern sector of the country's economy, devoted to services, retailing, and industrial labor.[6] The refugee experience is thus assimilated to the model of immigrant acculturation and success idealized in the myth of the "melting pot." In fact, the refugees were under no one's control. Their presence strained the GVN's resources and contributed to the corruption and demoralization of the cities; yet the refugees remained available for recruitment as active or passive agents of either South Vietnamese gangsters or of the VC.[7] The merciless absurdity of this misreading of Vietnamese society and history is ironically highlighted by its juxtaposition with the urban riots of the late 1960s, which suggested that the administration's understanding of its own society was not much better than its understanding of Vietnam.

From the perspective of counterinsurgency experts like the army's John Paul Vann and the Marine Corps' Victor Krulak, the more massive the firepower, the *less* likely it became that we would achieve the sort of "victory" the counterinsurgency policy had envisioned: the establishment of an independent South Vietnam with a viable economy and a government legitimated by broad acceptance among the peasantry and urban managerial and working classes. The logic of MACV's war of attrition was the uprooting of the peasantry, the defoliation and abandonment of the countryside, and the absurdity of a government "based" on a population of refugees.[8] As Krulak argued, "The real war is among the people and not among these mountains," and "Every man we put into hunting the NVA was wasted."[9]

Westmoreland's concept of attrition was flawed in both theory and practice. The ability of a society or an army to sustain battlefield losses is not solely dependent on the numbers and materiel available. Cultural and political factors may determine an army's motivation and make it willing to fight despite hardship and losses. Westmoreland's strategic models were the Civil War and the Second World War, in which the side with the bigger battalions and the deeper resources had finally worn down and overwhelmed the weaker enemy. However, experience in both wars had also demonstrated the capacity of high-morale units and armies to sustain extremely heavy losses without breaking while numerically stronger units lost combat effectiveness after suffering much lighter casualties. And both wars gave evidence that the morale and willingness to resist of both armies and civilian populations substantially increased when combat was seen as defense of the homeland. Indeed, the Union and Allied armies were able to survive early and disastrous defeats and persist until victory was achieved because they were sustained by the public's belief that they were fighting to defend society from destruction.

In Vietnam the relationship between numbers and motivation was inverse. The United States had incomparably greater numbers, but its stake was defined as "limited" even by the war's strongest advocates. To the public, from whose ranks the soldiers were drawn, neither victory nor defeat in Vietnam promised any very direct benefit or severe threat to the integrity of their communities, their standard of living, the sanctity of their values, or the safety of their institutions. The North Vietnamese were outnumbered, but their leaders regarded success as absolutely vital to their own survival, to the vindication of their political culture, and to the completion of the nationalist project they had begun in 1940. This project, and the Viet Minh leadership identified with it, enjoyed substantial support in both the North and the South before the American intervention on behalf of Diem in 1955–56, and as the war became more Americanized the hard core of that support became more intense (at least in the North).[10]

The failure of policy-makers to understand the relationship between political motivation and the ability to sustain attrition was the logical consequence of their original failure to recognize the existence and strength of the indigenous political culture. Such misunderstandings led even the most rational of strategists into confusion and mystification when they tried to account for (and develop a tactical response to) the persistence of the VC and the NVA. Thus in the discussions that preceded the troop escalations of the summer of 1965, Maxwell Taylor declared, "The ability of the Viet-Cong continuously to rebuild their units and to make good their losses is one of the mysteries of this guerrilla war. . . . Not only do the Viet-Cong units have the recuperative power of the phoenix, but they have an amazing ability to maintain morale."[11]

Taylor's resort to "mystery" signals the failure of counterinsurgency theory to account for the reality of Vietnam; or rather, its failure to provide an account that was both rational and politically acceptable. For if the "phoenix-like" regenerative capacity of the VC was in any significant measure due to indigenous political strength, then it would have to be accepted and admitted that the political premises on which the counterinsurgency and nation-building projects in Vietnam were based were intrinsically flawed. In the absence of such a critical analysis the military/political strength of the opponent could not be accurately assessed, and the measures taken to defeat him could not be effectively designed. Three years after Taylor noted the "mystery," the Marines in I Corps were still noting with dismay that, despite the fact that enemy thrusts into the region were always repulsed with heavy losses, the Communists would always return after a brief respite with more men and equipment than before.[12]

This failure to recognize and address the political contradictions inherent in the "mission" limited the usefulness of even the best internal policy critiques and made the intelligent revision or adjustment of strategy and tactics more difficult. On the eve of the Tet Offensive in 1968, even the statistical measures preferred by MACV and the administration were indicating (to disinterested analysts) the failure of the war of attrition. Studies done for the Defense Department by its Office of Systems Analysis (OSA) showed that, even if the highest current rate of attrition could be maintained, it would require *ten years* to reach the cross-over point beyond which enemy losses would be mathematically unsustainable.[13] But the most damaging statistics were those derived from studies of the types of engagements fought by American troops. The OSA study of combats in 1966 showed that in 85 percent of all engagements the enemy determined the time and place of battle either by initiating an attack or by standing to fight in a fortified position. In nearly 80 percent of the engagements the enemy had an initial advantage of surprise, while American officers had enjoyed adequate intelligence of enemy positions and strength in only 5 percent. This proportion remained roughly the same through the period of the Tet Offensive and its aftermath.[14]

These statistics had devastating implications for the strategy of attrition, because they revealed that the North Vietnamese were able to *limit* their rate of losses by *controlling* the number and type of engagements to which they would expose themselves. If the North Vietnamese could not be fooled into abandoning this strategy for more conventional combat *in the South,* then no conceivable increase in either the numbers of American ground troops or of sorties flown against the North could impose on the North Vietnamese a rate of attrition they would be unwilling or unable to sustain.[15] But information of this kind was too much at odds with the logic of the military commitment we had already made. Good statistics were misinterpreted (or not interpreted at all), displaced or offset by corrupt or incorrect figures which had become embedded in the bureaucratic record, or simply suppressed in favor of figures that would justify the course of action on which we were already determined.[16] Over the years a steady accumulation of misconceptions, self-delusions, and deliberate falsifications had combined and compounded themselves into a system of maddening paradoxes, contradictions, and double-binds. On the eve of the Tet Offensive of January–February 1968, "war-managers lived [in a world defined by] multiple systematic falsifications, some created by subordinates at ground level . . . [and] still more systematic falsifications imposed by senior officials at MACV, the Pentagon, and the White House."[17]

Falsification and mystification were the responses of men committed to achieving the mission in the face of mounting evidence that the premises of our engagement in Vietnam had been flawed from the start, founded on a misconstruction of indigenous Vietnamese politics. South Vietnam did not lack a political culture and sense of nationality; the problem was that the form its political culture took would have produced a result contrary to American security interests (as these were defined under Eisenhower and Kennedy). The implicit, unacknowledged premise of American policy was our intention to negate the extant political culture of Vietnamese nationalism and to substitute a more-or-less Americanized model in its place.[18]

The gap between what could be privately acknowledged and what could be publicly stated became wider the longer the war persisted and the more closely the prestige of the nation (and of the individual policy-makers) became identified with the war. To salvage that prestige, the administration committed itself more fully and frankly to the manipulation of appearances, hoping thereby to maintain public belief in the project and to erect a screen behind which they might yet be able to create the sort of GVN they needed. While Ambassador Taylor knew that "there is no George Washington in sight" among the leaders of the GVN, "nothing is more important than to exert every effort to make the present leadership *appear* to be inspired leadership."[19] The problem with such deceptions was that the reality they sought to conceal was incorrigible: a series of junta heads would emerge and be hailed as the answer to American prayers only to be displaced (with American aid or acquiescence) in a hail of unsavory revelations of personal corruption, failure, or surreptitious "neutralism."

But if the GVN could (or would) not transform itself into a genuinely popular government, and if American attempts at indirect management were always foiled by the recalcitrance of the GVN's leaders, what alternative remained? In a paper written in the summer of 1965, John Paul Vann argued that it was still possible to capture the social revolution from the Communists by making the GVN "responsive to the dynamics of social revolution." But Vann's experience in Vietnam since 1962 had taught him that no such changes would be forthcoming from the Saigon regime. It followed that to win the hearts and minds of the South Vietnamese peasantry for the GVN, it was necessary for Americans to take the conduct of the war, politically as well as militarily, directly into their own hands. He added, in suitably tough-minded terms, that it was only our sentimental "fear of tarnishing our own image" by appearing to act as a colonial power that kept us from adopting this necessary measure. Although his immediate proposals envisioned the countryside as the locus of American control, Vann was clear that if the Saigon regime did not accept the new policies willingly "then GVN must be forced to accept U.S. judgment and direction."[20]

Although Vann's rhetoric was uniquely forthright, his line of thought was not inconsistent with the direction of government policy since 1963, and even earlier. From the inception of American involvement under Eisenhower, policy-makers had insisted in public that the South Vietnamese government was a genuinely national regime while recognizing privately that its legitimacy was only *potential.* The strategy of "nation-building" was implicitly an acknowledgment that a South Vietnamese nationality was something that had to be constructed. The American-engineered coup against Diem in November 1963 was an acknowledgment (as the administration saw it) that that potential would never be fulfilled under Diem.[21] But the military juntas that succeeded Diem proved just as intractable in resisting the Americans' demands for political and military reform and more active prosecution of the war by the ARVN. In August 1964 Ambassador Taylor informed the President that the GVN would not be able to transcend certain "definite limits of performance" and would have to depend on the United States to "take the major responsibility" for fighting the VC; in March 1965 he acknowledged that South Vietnam lacked a "truly national spirit" and recommended that the United States take action to "establish an adequate government in SVN."[22] Taylor's analysis describes the regime as a political nullity, unrepresentative of a national political culture. In fact, the Minh and Khanh juntas did represent the political mood prevalent in the regions and the military cadres they controlled. But once again the problem was that a government expressive of the will of those they represented would have produced a political outcome unacceptable to the Americans. At this moment, since the public mood was one of "war weariness and hopelessness," that result would have been a triumph of "neutralist" politics, which would have sought a negotiated accommodation with the North—an arrangement that would inevitably end in the unification of the country under Communist leadership. To forestall this, the United States engineered a coup against Diem's original successor (Minh) and a few months later found it necessary to repeat the operation with Minh's replacement, General Khanh.[23]

The most maddening paradox in the situation was that the weaker the Saigon regime became, the less power Americans had to insist on fundamental political reforms. The coup against Diem, Minh, and Khanh revealed that the American government's commitment to the war was perhaps greater than that of the GVN itself. This circumstance was confirmed after the "Tonkin Gulf Incident" of October 1964, in which the Johnson administration presented Congress with a deliberately distorted version of a supposed attack on American naval forces in order to obtain Congressional authorization for the bombing of the North. The purpose of the deception was to win from a reluctant Congress "an act of irreversible commitment by the United States" that would bolster the flagging morale of the GVN with "a confident sense of victory."[24] The GVN's morale could not be permanently raised by one such gesture, because its decline was a rational response to its inability to defend itself against the VC on the one side and the Americans on the other. Therefore, each escalation undertaken to bolster the regime had the real-world effect of making the GVN more dependent and the war more of an *American* commitment, an *American* liability.

The "cross-over point" in this paradoxical relationship was reached after the Tet Offensive with the GVN's recognition of the way in which those acts of "irreversible commitment" had made the administration vulnerable to blackmail.[25] If America needed to win the war that much, then the GVN and its leaders could limit American control of the affairs that most concerned them by threatening (openly or implicitly) to sabotage the *American* war effort through private negotiations, public revelation of their disagreements with Washington, or the like. By 1970 it was clear that the American administration had, in effect, to submit to its ally's blackmail so that it could continue to fight that ally's war.

The impasse to which affairs in Vietnam had come on the eve of Tet was described in a long essay by Theodore H. White on the Vietnamese elections, published in *Life* in August 1967. White was a veteran Far East correspondent and political reporter, a journalistic elder statesman whose prestige and popular reputation had been established by his "inside" account of Kennedy's electoral victory, *The Making of the President, 1960*—a success he repeated in 1964 and would attempt again in 1968. White shared the American government's hope that the Vietnamese elections would provide some genuine legitimacy for the regime, and he believed that a successful election there would affect the American election in 1968, which might well be a referendum on the war. White saw the GVN's lack of legitimacy as the sign of a troubling and perhaps fatal limitation of American policy and power: "Progress, in American [that is, military] terms, has been spectacular. . . . We can do almost anything we want in this country—except govern." Despite our destruction of enemy forces, the political power and popular appeal of the VC (the "romance-terror web of the Vietcong") remains unbroken, for "The Vietcong, in ultimate analysis, is the first native institution created and shaped by the Vietnamese themselves in this century."

As White's description of the Vietnamese political crisis develops, he finds himself framing American alternatives in terms of the "savage war" or "race war" scenario, which he initially rejects as morally and politically repugnant:

> American policy thus faces two choices: either to adopt a policy of extermination, the classic way of ending guerrilla wars; or to invite into being a native counterforce. . . . And, since extermination has been decisively rejected, the American effort today is pinned to the great adventure of fostering a political alternative to the Vietcong . . . an alternative between slavery to white men and Communism.[26]

Our ability to reject the logic of a "war of extermination" depends on our success in tactically isolating the enemy's forces. But as White recognizes, that tactical goal may well be unattainable, because the VC are indeed an indigenous political movement supported by the peasants in the countryside. They are therefore able to evade attempts to isolate and destroy them by disappearing, not merely into the landscape of jungle and paddy, but into what White calls the "web" of Vietnamese culture—that culture which had invented them as its first native political institution. Thus "It is an environment we fight—not an army." To imagine the defeat of such an enemy in such a place, White is forced to revert to the "savage war" or exterminationist model and to imagine violence on the scale of eco-cide: "It is this environment we must liquidate before we will be able to silence the guns."

Clearly, the idea of a "war of extermination" or a "liquidation of the environment" is something White finds horrifying and unacceptable. Yet it is also clear that what he has seen in Vietnam has convinced him that a struggle of this kind is a real possibility, and he underscores the feasibility of "extermination" by suggesting that this is the "classic" solution to a guerrilla war. In fact, "extermination" and "attrition" were "classic" strategies only in the Plains Indian wars; neither the British victory in Malaya nor the American/Filipino victory over the Huk was achieved that way. The drift of White's discussion thus follows the drift of American policy: from the limited combat of counterinsurgency, with its balance of military and civic action, to the war of attrition, whose logic points to what we may think of as a war of "limited extermination" in which most or all of the enemy's military-age males are killed or wounded. But against this logic, and in sharp dissonance with it, is the obvious moral repugnance White feels for such a war. This sentiment was no less potent than the pressure for perpetual escalation, and no less apt or consistent as a response to both the "facts" of Vietnam and the myth of "savage war."

The moral/tactical dilemma defined by White also had consequences among soldiers in the field. Here the cognitive dissonance between the pretensions of command rhetoric and the practical application of attrition tactics had a "crazy-making" effect on combat officers and soldiers. The high command spoke in two voices: in one it promulgated a model "Rules of Engagement" designed to minimize civilian casualties; on the other, the use of terms like "Free-Fire Zones" and the fetishization of "body counts" inherent in the war-of-attrition strategy suggested that what the army actually *wanted* was for the soldiers to kill as many Vietnamese as quickly as possible. The result was a continual expansion of the levels of violence and the range of permissible targets and the loss of any real sense of the logical (or even the practical) relation between the violence and its nominal objectives. Something of the range of responses is suggested in Michael Herr's *Dispatches*:

> . . . A lot of men found their compassion in the war, some found it and couldn't live with it, war-washed shutdown of feeling. . . . People retreated into positions of hard irony, cynicism, despair, some saw the action and declared for it, only heavy killing could make them feel so alive. . . . Some people just wanted to blow it all to hell, animal vegetable and mineral. . . . A lot of people knew that the country could never be won, only destroyed, and they locked into that with breathtaking concentration, no quarter, laying down the seeds of the disease, roundeye fever, . . . until a million had died from it and millions more were left uncentered and lost in their flight from it.[27]

Tropes and symbols derived from Western movies had become one of the more important interpretive grids through which Americans tried to understand and control their unprecedented and dismaying experiences in Vietnam. The infusion of large numbers of American ground troops between 1965 and 1968 brought to the scene a generation for whom the imagery of Western movies and television programs (no less than rock 'n' roll) provided a ready-made set of metaphors that seemed quite appropriate to the war in which they found themselves. The original "stockade" metaphor was modified to suite the new situation. However, instead of referring to protected villages of Vietnamese farmers, as if the peasants were "settlers" in a film like *Drums Along the Mohawk*, it now invoked structures like those in *Fort Apache*, in which White soldiers and their dependents "fort up" for protection in a place they explicitly identify as "Indian country."

But under the stress of application to Vietnam, the saving simplicities of Western-movie symbolism broke down, revealing internal contradictions and ambivalences that made them problematic as guides to "what a man's gotta do." The initial terms of the mission defined the American role as that of the heroic rescuer, saving "settlers" from "Indians." But in Vietnam, "settlers" and "Indians" were often indistinguishable, and more than half the "settlers" were justly suspected of sympathizing with (and sometimes working for) the "Indians."[28] But beneath that ambiguity the structural principle of both the mythic and the historical versions of the Indian-war scenario is the primary distinction between "Red" and "White"—a distinction that overrides the fine discrimination between "hostiles" and "friendlies." When in doubt, it is safer to assume that all Indians are actually or incipiently hostile. This dictum was particularly apt in Vietnam, where the population of the countryside was in fact deeply enmeshed in the Viet Minh/Vietcong network, and where hostility to and suspicion of the Americans were rife. When this attitude was coupled with the body-count imperatives of the war of attrition, it became easy for soldiers in the field to drop the pretense that they were on a search-and-rescue mission and to become "Indian-haters," with a mission to search and destroy. In movie terms, they abandoned the John Wayne role in *Fort Apache* for the John Wayne role in *Rio Grande* or even *The Searchers*, becoming savage in order to defeat savages, committing massacre in order to avenge or deter massacre: "Some people were on an Indian trip over there." Here was a different and larger form of the "John Wayne Syndrome." It was traumatic to discover that one could not live up to the John Wayne model of on-screen military heroism. And it was maddening to realize that the moral categories by which we had identified the hero's role were slippery and unstable to such a degree that the roles and values of Indian-fighter and savage, hero and enemy, could be exchanged at any moment.[29]

The loss of relation between the normal objectives and rationales of "the mission" and its actual practices and achievements became manifest in the wake of the Tet Offensive. Tet has been variously interpreted as a brilliant use of force to expose the fallacies of American policy and cripple public support for the war, as a cynical effort by the Northern government to expose and decimate its non-Communist allies in the South while simultaneously ravaging the GVN, as a failed attempt to realize Mao's Phase III, and as a military blunder caused either by overconfidence or the triumph of American tactics in which the Communists suffered ruinous battlefield losses—only to be saved by the American press's overreaction to the enemy's temporary success.[30] By striking in such strength against the cities that were supposed to be the inner core of the GVN's support, the offensive discredited MACV's assertion that the combats undergone by American troops since 1965 had brought more of the country under GVN control and had pushed the arena of enemy operations out into the hinterlands and border regions. The numbers, equipment, and morale of the enemy appeared higher than ever; units long since counted as "destroyed" reappeared at full strength, attacking outposts and towns hundreds of miles from the base camps in which they were supposed to be hiding. VC and NVA units from the countryside, supported by local guerrillas, seized provin cial capitals and the Citadel of the old imperial capital of Hue. Attacks were pressed against the big American bases in and near Saigon, and insurgents seized substantial sections of the city itself and even assaulted the American embassy, the mission's command central.

Public uneasiness over the increase in civilian casualties, which had been troublesome to American consciences from the start of the war of attrition, now reached a crisis as American and ARVN forces were compelled to bombard and assault the cities and citizens they were supposed to protect in order to liberate them from the VC and NVA: to "destroy the city in order to save it." Colonel William R. Corson, a Marine counterinsurgency specialist who saw the war of attrition in the same terms as Vann and Krulak, interpreted this statement as evidence of a descent into "the language of madness, a madness which if allowed to continue will destroy not only the people of Vietnam, but also the moral fabric and strength of America."[31] Yet this madness was inherent in the original logic of the war of attrition, which had abandoned the effort to create a viable popular government in Vietnam in favor of a "limited war of extermination" against the North Vietnamese. Now that logic seemed also to encompass the destruction of the South as well—the defoliation of the countryside, the removal of the peasantry to economically unproductive refugee reservations, and the leveling of the cities to root out the hidden enemy.

The Race War Comes Home: Watts, Newark, Detroit (1965–1967)

The crisis of disillusionment produced by Tet came on the heels of a similarly violent crisis in domestic affairs. The Johnson administration had followed through on the agenda suggested by Kennedy's inaugural by linking the militant pursuit of counterinsurgency abroad with an equally systematic assault on the problems of social welfare and justice at home. Indeed, Johnson's commitment to the social agenda was stronger than Kennedy's. He had soft-pedaled discussion of the military crisis in Vietnam in 1964–65 to protect that agenda, and he persisted in hoping that the Vietnam war could be prevented from interfering with the War on Poverty. But the summer of 1965 that saw a major escalation of the Vietnam fighting also saw the first of a series of urban riots that would be repeated every year between 1965 and 1969, in Watts, Detroit, Newark, and even Washington, D.C. As the scale of violence escalated in Vietnam, so too did the levels of urban violence. National Guardsmen and regular army paratroopers, in tanks and APCs, were called on to suppress the Detroit riots in 1967; and the following year, in the wake of Martin Luther King's assassination, the violence would spread to the nation's capital. The title of one popular study of the phenomenon brought back into currency a term first used for domestic violence during Reconstruction: *The Race War.*[32]

The ghetto riots began in the North and in California just as the civil-rights movement was achieving its greatest legislative victories at the national level with the Civil Rights Act of 1964 and the Voting Rights Act of 1965. Most White journalists and politicians responded to the riots with surprise and/or aggrieved outrage similar to the shock reaction that followed Tet. The makers of the counterinsurgency and "nation-building" policy had underestimated the strength and endurance of the Viet Minh/Viet Cong because they were ignorant of the particularities of Vietnamese political history; because the general theories of development on which they based their policies were artifacts of American ideology, neo-Turnerian theories of modernization projected onto the Third World; and because these theories, coupled with the implicitly racialist belief in something called "the Asian character," induced them to discount historical and cultural particularities in favor of a unitary model of development.

The War on Poverty was similarly based on general theories of development and assimilation that were themselves merely reifications of the experience of those immigrant groups which had, in earlier times, succeeded in entering the American middle class. It was based as well on the traditional assumptions of American ideology, which see the possession of civil rights as the key to "equality" and the guarantor of economic opportunity. These theories (and the policies based on them) did not sufficiently take into acount the peculiar character of African-American historical experience as a whole—the long and complex history, not only of slavery but of "Jim Crow," which differs from the immigrant experience in both the severity and the duration of social exclusion. The theories also erred in assuming that something like a single "Negro community" existed and that it had more or less the same character in North and South, rural and urban areas. So they failed to anticipate or understand the hostility that arose in northern and western ghettoes after the "victory" of the civil-rights movement. Civil-rights bills did not address the economic distress and social exclusion of northern Blacks; and whatever their intentions, Great Society programs did not make an immediate or widespread impact on the poverty and joblessness that afflicted the ghettoes. But this situation was invisible to a public and to mass media for whom "Negroes" were a single category, undifferentiated by class, culture, or region.[33]

In the summer of 1967 riots occurred on an unprecedented scale in a score of major cities. In Newark and Detroit they reached a level of violence which begged comparison with Vietnam and produced a public revulsion against the administration's domestic policies comparable to the disillusionment with the war that would be produced by the Tet Offensive less than six months later. These two "war" stories developed simultaneously and were reported in parallel on nightly television news programs. But a more explicit working out of the parallel can be seen in *Life* magazine's photojournalistic coverage of the stories.

Life's cover on July 28, 1967, shows a twelve-year-old Negro boy lying on the street bleeding from an invisible wound, his glazed eyes suggesting death, though (the story inside would reveal) in fact registering shock (he would survive his wounds). The title above him proclaims "Shooting War in the Streets / Newark: The Predictable Insurrection." The group of stories on the riot ("Negro Revolt Echoes to the Ugly Crack of Sniper Fire") suggests that what is occurring is not merely a riot but something akin to insurrection. The narrative emphasizes the theme of insurrection and implicit parallels with Vietnam (snipers, "civilians" killed in the crossfire) and follows the Vietnam prescription by asserting, "Only force—sometimes brute force—could end the insurrection." National Guardsmen are summoned because they can deploy greater force than city police.[34] *Life* interviews the snipers, whom it identifies as would-be revolutionaries, some of whom have crossed the border (from New York) to get there. The story shows them as clever guerrillas who shoot not to kill but to provoke a violent response from "trigger-happy" and bigoted policemen—a response that will radicalize the ghetto. And it suggests that the snipers have the tacit support of the community, which conceals them from the police. The parallels with VC techniques and their protection by the peasantry are obvious.[35] Moreover, the police are *shown* as trigger-happy in the story of their shotgun killing of an unarmed Black man who had looted a six-pack from a liquor store. The same shot that kills the looter wounds the boy whose picture we have seen on the cover, which suggests an *indiscriminate* use of firepower by the police.[36]

Taken together, pictures and story give us a divided perspective on the event. The talk of "insurrection" suggests that the riots present a danger of American society, and that "brute force" is needed to suppress them. Yet "brute force" turns out to be morally dubious when its use endangers the innocent (civilians), and politically counterproductive to the degree that it fulfills the aim of the revolutionary snipers. An editorial by Shana Alexander, "A Message from Watts to Newark," amplifies the revolutionary implications of Newark by describing Watts as:

> the turning point, a moment as significant in the long agony of American Negro history as John Brown's raid. . . . In a flash of flame, . . . the forces of violence and non-violence were polarized. And traditional Negro passivity in the Northern ghettoes came to an end.

But Alexander identifies as objects of revolutionary rage not only the predictable conservative and racist targets but the liberal programs of the Great Society: "The ghetto has become a gigantic pork barrel, a place where anti-poverty opportunists can get rich quick and split." She quotes one antipoverty worker as agreeing with a radicalized client who "claims that what we're really doing is fooling our own people, betraying them. He says the next time they burn anybody down here, what they ought to do is burn us."[37]

The Detroit riot was the worst of the series of uprisings that followed Newark, and the next week's issue (August 4) devotes an even more luridly colored picture-story to "Detroit / City at the blazing heart of a nation in disorder." The "Detroit insurrection" is part of a nationwide "Negro revolt." Its proportions are such that Governor and Mayor request federal troops. "Paratroopers from the 82nd and

101st Airborne Divisions—many of them veterans of Vietnam—rolled into the continuing fray" and suppressed the riot with the same weapons used against the VC. The destruction committed by looters is paralleled by the destruction inflicted by those suppressing them—a foretaste of the fate of Ben Tre, the city that had to be destroyed "in order to save it." As in the Pullman Strike of 1894, the "regiments" had been recalled from fighting "Indians" to put down an "insurrectionary mob." This time, however, the putative "racial" difference between soldiers and strikers was literally realized, and the race war of the border was reproduced in a "revolutionary" race war at home.[38]

Life's editorial explains the spread of rioting by invoking the same political myths (for example, "Munich") that Johnson's advisers had used to rationalize continued escalation in Vietnam. Things are out of hand because federal and local authorities have adopted a policy of "appeasement" toward radicals and rioters. Encouragement of nonviolent civil disobedience and a generally soft attitude toward rioters, first displayed in the refusal of Philadelphia's mayor to allow the police to shoot looters during a riot in 1964 have deprived the laws of moral authority. *Life*'s logic thus exactly mirrors the logic by which the Johnson administration had decided to abandon counter-insurgency, with its emphasis on civic action and minimal firepower, in favor of the big-unit war.[39]

Letters to the editor in subsequent issues showed that at least some readers had picked up the implication of likeness between the two wars. A letter to the editor in the August 25th issue, responding to coverage of the Detroit riot, laments:

> It is like a nightmare from which one will not awaken. . . . Isn't this a civilized country . . . ? Must innocent citizens—and firemen and policemen who are doing their duty—be murdered before there are "peace talks"? It is overwhelming to know that Vietnam veterans are needed to help the police fight the people of their own country.[40]

And the editorial page of the September 16th issue paired advocacy of peace talks following the Vietnamese election ("A Vietnamese Mandate to Talk") with a call for programs to meet the implicit demands of the Negro "insurrection" ("Jobs Are a Must for Negroes").[41]

In the issue of August 25th, the two crises are explicitly linked as cases of counterinsurgency. Three stories are of particular importance: Theodore H. White's essay on the Vietnamese election (cited earlier); the cover story on Marine pacification teams in I Corps,

"The 'Other War' in Vietnam / To Keep a Village Free"; and a trailer to that story, "The 'Other' Pacification—To Cool U.S. Cities." We have already seen the way White's piece uses the language of "savage war" to define the issues in Vietnam. But when we set his article in the context of this issue of *Life* (and of the riot stories that had dominated the magazine for a month), his implicit paralleling of the crisis of legitimacy in the Vietnamese and American elections becomes more striking. The public mandate for Johnson's administration was more immediately imperiled by the war in the streets than by the one in the jungle. In this context, White's description of the impasse in Vietnam acquires an ironic relevance to the American scene: "Progress, in American terms, has been spectacular. . . . We can do almost anything we want in this country—except govern." The riots had revealed that what was true of Saigon was also true of cities like Newark and Detroit; and just as the alternative to government success in Vietnam was seen to hold the potential for a war of unlimited destructiveness, so the failure of the Great Society in the cities might mean (in Robert Conot's phrase) "rivers of blood, years of darkness."[42]

The story on pacification in I Corps ("Their Mission: Defend, Befriend") offers a detailed study of the work of a Marine CAP unit, whose work comes across as an ideal balancing of aid and enforcement.[43] The Vietnam story then feeds its central metaphor of "pacification" to the story on post-riot urban reforms, "The 'Other' Pacification—To Cool U.S. Cities." Thus policies designed to win the war abroad and end the strife at home are linked by the common name of "pacification." But both of these pacifications/wars are identified as "other"—that is, as exceptional, problematic, out of the mainstream of military and civil events. And both are presented in an "ironic" tone or frame, which undermines each story's nominal message: that our government is taking these parallel problems in hand. The "other war" in Vietnam (pacification) can be seen as the "other" or flipside of the military struggle, supplementing and supporting the main project. The identification of urban reform as "the other pacification" is overtly ironic in its suggestion that the main or central action of urban life in America is analogous to the guerrilla war in Vietnam. The hidden irony in the story is that MACV regarded the CAP operations as "other" in the negative sense, a distraction from the "real war," and was about to pull the Marines away from CAP for the war of attrition in the "boondocks."[44]

As the American administrations had misjudged the character of Vietnamese society and the depth of popular hostility to the government and the policies they had sponsored in Vietnam, so they had misjudged the nature of the problems of race and poverty and the deep social divisions these engendered. These two perceptions come together in *Life*'s issue of March 8, 1968, in which a "Special Section" on "The Cycle of Despair: The Negro and the City" is paralleled by an account of city fighting during the Tet Offensive. The Vietnam story offers an opportunity for a concise and vivid statement of the ironic impasse of government policy: "The Battle That Ruined Hue" exemplifies "The sickening irony into which the war has fallen—the destruction of the very things that the U.S. is there to save." Although the urban story (based on the Kerner Commission Report, released in March 1968) deals with the domestic situation, its theme develops the same irony: policies designed to make American cities like Newark and Detroit into sites of democracy, racial tolerance, and economic improvement have instead produced a situation in which the citizens burn down their own neighborhoods while the army shoots the city to pieces in order to "protect" it.[45]

Thus the metaphor of "madness" invoked by Corson (and others) signifies more than an observation of the disjunction between means and ends in Vietnam. It testifies to a sense that in all our national affairs rational control of both concept and event has somehow suddenly been "lost."[46] The Democratic administrations had begun the public discourse about counterinsurgency with a rhetoric whose metaphor of "surgical strike," "gradual escalation," and "specified strike zones" implied that violence could be used as an effective instrument of policy, subject at all times to rational control, and always proportional to the values to be defended and the goal to be achieved. But by the summer of 1968 there was no evading the perception of disproportion between policy ends and violent means. For the bloodletting of Tet and riots in the mean streets had been followed by the assassinations, in the midst of the presidential campaign, of Martin Luther King and Robert Kennedy—the most prominent political leaders identified with the movements for civil rights, social justice, and an end to the war. In this context, the idea that events were driven by some form of collective insanity, a congenital flaw in the American "national character" that produced an irrational "propensity to violence," gained currency and credence.

Exceptional Violence: Official Revisions of the Frontier Myth, 1967–69

The growing sense of a disproportion between the levels of violence and the ends for which it was being deployed made "violence" itself—as an abstraction larger than the particular violence of the war and the riots—an object of intense public concern. In the wake of the 1967 riots, President Johnson had convened a National Advisory Commission on Civil Disorders to investigate the causes of that particular form of social violence. But before the Commission's final report was presented in June 1968, the assassinations of Martin Luther King and Robert Kennedy (and a further series of urban disorders) compelled the administration to extend the level of inquiry and generalize its concern by forming a National Commission on the Causes and Prevention of Violence. The "Violence Commission" made its final report in June 1969, but its taking of testimony was covered by the press throughout most of 1968.[47]

The preface to the Report's historical volumes defines the character and tone of the ideological dilemma which the Report addressed:

> [S]o disturbing is today's civil commotion and its attendant widespread disillusionment that it invites a reaction against the comfortable old certitudes. Contemporary Americans, confronted as they are with overseas war and domestic turmoil, may be tempted to overcompensate for past patriotic excesses by equating the American experience instead with slavery and imperialism, Indian genocide, and Judge Lynch. Similarly, some contemporary European intellectuals, such as Jean-Paul Sartre, have come to regard "that super-European monstrosity, North America" as a bastard child or satanic mutation of degraded Europe.[48]

The Report had the paradoxical tasks of criticizing those aspects of American life and history that have produced such frightening levels of social violence while defending American society from its demonization by leftist and European critics. It had to awaken Americans to a realization of what was wrong in their history and culture without intensifying their mood of angry despair—a mood that would make constructive reform impossible.

Most of the scholars who reported to the commissions attempted to demystify the historical and political mythology that sustained the "liberal consensus." They used statistical and historical evidence to show that the liberal vision of America as a prosperous, essentially classless, and basically tolerant society was an illusion; that the society had been, and remained, chronically divided between increasingly inimical classes (or "cultures") of have and have not, and also of White and Black. The Violence Commission specifically criticized the exceptionalist myths by which Americans had rationalized their social violence. Its studies used both American and European data to show that civic violence is the product of specific historical contingencies that arise in a variety of cultures and societies in times of rapid political and social transformation.

But the form of the study, and the public concerns that provoked the establishment of the Commission, distorted the way in which its findings would be formulated and understood. Despite the explicit rejection of an exceptionalist or "national character" approach, the Violence Commission's almost exclusive preoccupation with American matters inevitably appeared to document the existence of "characteristically American" forms of violence. Most of the Commission scholars were concerned to refute the notion that modern social violence represented a survival of the violence of the nineteenth-century Frontier. They showed that characteristic forms of violence had been prominent in "metropolitan" culture in every phase of our history, and they related the provenance of social violence to the persistence and spread of social, economic, and racial injustices and inequities—aspects of American life which textbook historiography in the exceptionalist tradition had treated as transient phenomena or had relegated to the margins. Nonetheless, these critical elements in the Violence Commission's historical report are undercut by the persistence of a new sort of exceptionalism—an inverted Turnerism in which *negative* aspects of American national life and character (especially racial violence) are attributed to "our frontier heritage."[49]

Richard M. Brown's study of vigilantism is particularly important, because it emphasizes the primacy of political and social factors in shaping the social violence of particular epochs in national history and the primacy of the violence-prone cultures of particular regions. Brown shows that vigilantism was not an exclusively western or "frontier" phenomenon. Further, he clarifies the class basis of the most important vigilante movements, which were usually based in a propertied or well-established class and directed against various classes of "have–nots." In a section on "Indian Wars," Brown asserts, "It is possible that no other factor has exercised a more brutalizing effect on the American character than the Indian wars. . . . It has done much to shape our proclivity to violence."[50] But Brown treats this idea as a historical commonplace and does not attempt to integrate data on Indian wars with his carefully researched studies of vigilante movements and the history of "violence-prone" communities.

Indian wars are more central to the explanatory model developed by the political scientist Louis Hartz in his study of the United States as a colonial "fragment culture." Hartz sees American society as a collection of (mostly) European emigrant "fragments" united by the "exceptional" elements of their New World history. The most important of these (for the student of violence) is the experience of Indian warfare, which Hartz (like Brown) describes as a form of social struggle more basic and violent than the class struggles of Europe, from which the emigrants escaped:

> One thing, in any case, is clear. Whether the European fragment destroys, isolates, or incorporates the aborigine, the record is vivid with bloodshed. Here is the ironic compensation [the fragment culture] experiences for leaving its enemies in Europe behind, that it encounters even stranger antagonists abroad. This encounter brings out all of the . . . hidden Europeanism, and in doing so, unleashes a violent energy that transcends even that which produced the guillotines of the Old World.[51]

Hartz's description of the peculiar social, psychological, and cultural stresses to which a colonial and emigrant society is subject is an astute and useful one; he is accurate in his assertion that the encounter of colonists or emigrant settlers with the Indians ("strange antagonists") produced expectations of extraordinary violence. But even if one takes into account all the Anglo-American Indian wars since the attack on Jamestown in 1622, it is simply not true that they were as violent and destructive of human life as the French Revolutionary Terror or the wars that followed it; nor were they (after 1780) a common experience for most (or indeed very many) citizens of the Republic. The most costly and violent American conflicts have been those arising in the "metropolis," beginning with the political disorder of the pre-Revolutionary period and the Tory/Patriot conflict during the War of Independence. The events that were most important in shaping American understandings of the nature and meaning of social violence, and of the levels of destruction it could attain, were those associated with Bleeding Kansas, the Civil War, and Reconstruction.

This is not to say that the Indian wars were trivial in their costs, their cruelty, or their influence on American history and culture. But the ritual invocation of Indian wars as an explanation of contemporary metropolitan violence obscures the complex etiology of that violence. The crucial sources of modern American social violence are found, not in the "exceptional" environment of the Frontier, but in "the peculiar conditions" of life in the American "metropolis"—the settled core of American society in which most Americans, then and now, have lived.[52] Although the "frontier experience" is not a *cause* of American metropolitan violence, the elaboration and use of a Myth of the Frontier is one *effect* of the culture's attempts to explain and control the various forms of violence which originate in the social conditions of the metropolis. For the vast majority of Americans and American communities, the expectation that extraordinary violence will arise from encounters with "savages" has been primarily an artifact of cultural representation rather than a remembered experience or even an episode of family lore. For the most part, the "heroes of the Frontier" are not "our" ancestors; we know them as figures in books and movies, and we are their readers rather than their lineal descendants—or even their cultural heirs, since what we have of them are not stories passed down within the family or tribe, but commercial fictions. The invocation of Indian wars as a primary cause of metropolitan (and post-colonial) violence serves to diminish, obscure, or excuse the operation of more proximate social, economic, and political causes by "scapegoating" the supposed ancestors of "American national character."

The emotional ambivalence and ideological contradiction of "inverted Turnerism" is most apparent in Joe B. Frantz's "The Frontier Tradition: An Invitation to Violence," which alternately condemns western violence as the root of our present troubles and apologizes for that violence as a necessary instrument of American progress and democracy. The patterns of vigilantism learned on the Frontier "continue . . . right into these days of the 1960s." Frantz condemns such aspects of the "frontier tradition" as the "heedless" exploitation of resources, the lynch mob, the KKK, and lawmen of the "shoot first" variety as "misuses" of an essentially good and characteristically American system of values and practices. He assumes the primacy of the self-reliant, self-made man as the classic frontier "type" and asserts that this fictive man is "our" ancestor:

> . . . [men of] independent action and individual reliance . . . taking what

> was there to be taken. The timid never gathered the riches, the polite nearly never. . . . It was a period peopled by giants, towers of audacity with insatiable appetites. The heroes are not the men of moderate attitudes, not the town planners and commercial builders, not the farmers nor the ministers nor the teachers. The heroes of the period, handed along to us with all the luster of a golden baton, are the mighty runners from Mt. Olympus. . . . We revere these heroes because they were men of vast imagination and daring. We have inherited their blindness and their excesses.[53]

Frantz places Indian wars among the worst examples of frontier violence and sees them as the origins of present-day racial antipathies. To characterize the racialism of frontiersmen, he poses the problem of Indian wars as if in their voice: "How do you handle an element for which there is no positive use? You exterminate it, especially if in your eyes it has murderous propensities." But he cannot himself dispense with the notion that this doctrine, while morally repugnant and productive of atrocities, was nonetheless a realistic and historically necessary way of responding to life on the Frontier. Unlike the excesses of the Klan, violence against Indians was (in his view) "reasonably straightforward, and could perhaps be condoned as inevitable conflicts. But individual atrocities have no justification. . . . This latter statement holds true for both sides." He thus adopts the self-contradictory position of justifying savage war in principle while condemning the individual atrocities that such war entailed.

Although Frantz's paper is the least rigorous in this section of the Commission's report, its author's concern to vindicate (even as he critiques) the myth/ideology of the Frontier responds most directly to the concerns of the political leaders who appointed the Commission and of the wider public whose fears the politicians had to address. Some aspects of contemporary violence seem to him disproportionate, to such a degree that questions must be raised about the way our culture works and the things it stands for. But he is unwilling to simply abandon or discredit the myth of American history that has defined our national political culture; he wants to analyze it, so as to preserve what is good and makes sense and to rebuke what is bad and irrational. Since violence plays a central role in that myth, he must distinguish between rational and irrational forms of violence. He does so by insisting that despite their cruelty and tendency toward "extermination," the primal or paradigm American wars were "inescapable." But while slaughter in the largest or strategic scale may be excused and even justified by "historical inevitability," Frantz declares that massacres and "atrocities" at the particular or tactical level are inexcusable. Frantz's moral argument is both torturous and illogical, but its inconsistencies reflect the ambivalence of the American public toward the violence being done in its name and anticipate the terms in which that public would respond to news of the Mylai massacre.[54]

Recovering the Mission: Mexico Westerns, 1965–1968

The Westerns of the 1965–68 period incorporate the sense of *trouble* that informs the editorial and scholarly response to the crisis. They attempt to develop a revised version of the myth of regeneration through violence that will acknowledge the force of the questions that have arisen against the tradition but that will still permit effective and admirable heroic action. Moreover, the Western was nearly alone among genres in providing such a field for mythic play with the themes and categories of the historical moment. A number of revisionist combat films were made, set during the Second World War but reflecting a Vietnam-era sensibility. Aldrich's *Dirty Dozen* (1968) is the most notable of these. But these films did not match in number or ambition the "Vietnam Westerns," and Aldrich's film no less than Wayne's derives some of its perspective and thematics from contemporary Westerns.[55]

The violence in these films is "extraordinary" in several respects. First, their heroes tended to be utterly cynical and cold-bloodedly instrumentalist about their reasons and methods for shedding blood. Second, the representation of violence became increasingly realistic, elaborate, and sensational—the result of a combination of technical innovation by special-effects artists, the wider license for all sorts of sensationalism characteristic of the arts in the 1960s, and the evident success of spectacularly violent scenes in particular films (for example, *Bonnie and Clyde* [1967]). Taken together, these developments constituted an important change in the formal representation of violence. Mayhem could now be abstracted from its normal narrative and explanatory contexts and presented as something "beautiful" or worthy of attention in and for itself. But the "abstraction" of violence was not merely an artifact of changes in cinematic form. It corresponded to, and was reinforced by, the "abstraction" of social violence in "Vietnam" and "Detroit" from the normative logic of American ideology that had previously explained and justified it.

Two variants of the Western were prominent during this period:

a group of cavalry/Indian films, which linked the "domestic" theme of racial dissension with the "foreign" theme of savage war, and a series of "Mexico Westerns" that critically explored the counterinsurgency script. The cavalry/Indian films are interesting as a group, because the changing distribution of pro-Indian and pro-White treatments during this period seems responsive to the twin crises provoked by the escalation of the war and racial violence at home. Between 1965 and 1970, pro-Indian films gave way to conventional "savage war" versions of the cavalry/Indian struggle. Of eleven cavalry/Indian films produced during this period, only three represent Indians as heroic or sympathetic, or present Whites as aggressors. *Duel at Diablo* (1966) takes the rebuke of racial prejudice as its theme but nonetheless demonizes the Indians as "savages" and as race-bigots whose intolerance matches that of the worst Whites. *The Stalking Moon* (1968) pits a scout-hero and a redeemed captive woman against a truly demonic savage who manages to track his enemies back to their home country—a device which realizes the nightmare of the guerrilla war migrating to America's home streets.[56]

No such simple correlations can be made with the Mexico Westerns of this period. Where the cavalry/Indian theme lent itself to relatively singleminded responses (pro-cavalry or anti-cavalry), the Mexico Westerns deal in ambiguity and contradiction as they attempt to reconcile the contradictions of value and practice that were tearing the "liberal consensus" apart. Two remarkable films began this new cycle: Sam Peckinpah's *Major Dundee* (1965), a combination of the cavalry/Indian and Mexico Westerns; and Richard Brooks' *The Professionals* (1966), which tranlates the Western gunfighter into a prototype of the Green Beret. Both films pose searching questions about the motives and character of the American heroes' mission in "Mexico"/Vietnam, and both move through these questions to a disillusioned reaffirmation of a (modified) version of that mission. This same period also saw the first of the official sequels to *The Magnificent Seven*: in *Return of the Seven* (1966) Yul Brynner's Chris once again rescues a village of peasants.[57] At the same time, European-made Westerns began to make a significant impact on the American market; after 1964, the dominant theme of these "spaghetti Westerns" was a highly stylized version of the gunfighter-in-Mexico.[58]

Major Dundee translates the political and ideological paradoxes of the Vietnam War into mythic terms. In Vietnam the transition from counterinsurgency to the war of attrition was making apparent the disparity between the means and the ends of the American mission.

In Peckinpah's film, the "mission" is the classic imperative of the cavalry film, drawn directly from *Rio Grande*, to avenge the massacre, rescue the captive, destroy the savage, and in the process vindicate the values of the cavalry as family and the regiment as democratic utopia. But by his way of accomplishing this mission, Major Dundee (Heston) calls in question the heroic and Amercian values he embodies.

The film is set on the Mexican border during the Civil War. A troop of Union cavalry has been wiped out at the Rostes Ranch by Sierra Charriba's band of Apache. The wounded soldiers and male civilians have been tortured to death and the women have been raped, mutilated, and murdered. The two Rostes boys are carried captive into Mexico by Charriba, who challenges Major Dundee to pursue him. Dundee has been sent to his post as punishment for some unspecified act of glory-hunting insubordination at Gettysburg; his inadequate garrison is charged with protecting the territory from Rebels as well as from Indians and with maintaining a prison for Rebel POWs. Dundee decides to violate his orders by pursuing Charriba. Since he cannot take many men from the garrison, he recruits a mixed company that includes civilian horse-thieves and jailbirds, Black ex-slaves tired of playing jailer to their former masters, and a squad of Rebel POWs under sentence of death for murder led by their own Captain Tyreen (Richard Harris), who has a personal grudge against Dundee that is older than their Blue/Gray enmity. Once in Mexico, the pursuit of Charriba will be complicated by involvement in the revolutionary struggle between the Juaristas and the occupying French army that supports Maximilian.

The narrative of *Major Dundee* is overlaid by a collage of references to classic war films and Westerns which are designed to give the film mythic and ironic resonances and to create expectations of heightened symbolic significance. The initial impulse of the mission takes off from a situation which invokes the heroic motives of both *The Searchers* and *Rio Grande* (revenge/rescue). The combination of Union and Confederate soldiers against Indians is a standard Western plot formula.[59] Many of the men come from the mythic terrain of the movies rather than from the categories of contemporary sociology: the fighting preacher is a Ford standard; the tough ethnic sergeant, the rigid West Point shavetail, and the innocent kid-trumpeter are recognizable Fordian and platoon-movie types. Once in Mexico, references to the Villa and Zapata biographies and to earlier Mexico Westerns multiply. "Viva Dundee!" appears painted on the wall of a liberated village; fiesta scenes and the relationships of Dundee and his men with Mexican women mimic relationships in *Vera Cruz* and *The Magnificent Seven.*[60]

At first Dundee's mission appears to have the same character and justification as Yorke's in *Rio Grande.* Although he is breaking the rules by crossing the border in pursuit of Charriba, his transgression is justified by the higher law which demands the rescue of captives (and the avenging of rape, castration, and massacre). But Dundee's character, and the myth/ideological imperatives that drive him, are called into question as soon as he crosses into Mexico. Almost immediately, Charriba turns loose the two Rostes boys, thereby depriving Dundee of the captivity/rescue rationale for his mission. (Not only are the boys unhurt; they seem to have enjoyed "playing Indian.") When Dundee continues the pursuit, it is clear that the "mission" is a personal obsession driven by a mixture of hatred, desire for revenge, a thirst for glory, a careerist calculation that success will restore his standing with the army—and perhaps a more obscure desire for vindication of his character as man and as fighter. This transformation of the "mission" suggests that the "captivity" scenario was never anything more than a cover story justifying an act of violence on which we (or our "commanders" and "heroes") had already determined.[61]

In Mexico, Dundee finds another kind of civil war and a more vivid presentation of the moral and political dilemma inherent in his quest for power and revenge. In need of supplies after his defeat, Dundee attacks and captures a French outpost. As a necessary but unintended consequence, he becomes the liberator of the Mexican village, whose people the French have been abusing, starving, and murdering. The Mexicans make a complex set of claims on the Americans. As an oppressed people covered by the imperatives of the Monroe Doctrine, they present an implicit claim for liberation from a European tyranny. As a village of women, children, and aged or helpless men, they qualify for paternal protection from the French by the same moral standard already invoked against the Apache on behalf of the women and children of New Mexico. These appeals are personalized in the characters of two women: a widow who acts as assistant to an Austrian doctor (Senta Berger) and who falls in love with Dundee; and a girl of the village who falls in love with Trumpeter Ryan (the troop's "kid" and voice-over narrator) and "makes a man of him" via sexual initiation.

But Dundee is incapable of love. The sexual act, which is for the "doctor-lady" and the village girl an act affirming life and giving effect to human kindness, is for Dundee merely an instrument whose sole utility (as he understands it) is the contribution it makes to the operational effectiveness of the commander and the fulfillment of his desire for triumph over the Apache. Although it takes some time for the narrative to reach this conclusion, the outcome (and its political significance) is anticipated by the sardonic Captain Tyreen in a conversation that follows the liberation of the village. Tyreen observes the beginnings of Dundee's romance and sees how his temperament thwarts the need to give and take affection. But Tyreen couches his reading of Dundee in political terms: as Dundee lounges on the ruined wall inscribed with "Viva Dundee!," Tyreen sardonically informs him that he hasn't "the temperament of a liberator." His self-centered and obsessive sense of mission make him fit (as Tyreen has earlier said) only to be a "jailer" or a tyrant. If Dundee has chosen to "liberate" (or make love to) the Mexicans, it is only because doing so is necessary to the completion of his obsessive quest for personal vindication and the destruction of the Apache. Even when he makes love, Dundee is only making war. The consequence is that, as his lover finally tells him, he will never achieve the peace that is the ostensible aim of his warfare: "For you the war will never end." The disproportion or disjunction between means and ends in Dundee's pursuit of Charriba suggests his likeness to Melville's Captain Ahab, whose tactics (like Dundee's) are sane but whose objectives are "mad." Destroying the Apache cannot satisfy the moral principles Dundee and his society nominally espouse (democracy, love, rescue of the helpless) nor bring Dundee the kind of personal redemption he seeks.

Like Ahab, Dundee would be a "democrat" to all above him, a "despot" to all below. He asserts for himself alone the "right of revolution" (or of civil disobedience) which is the root of democratic theory. Like Ahab, his moral sense combines a Puritanical sense of the absolute distinction between good and evil with an egotism that transforms morality into self-righteousness and the identification of personal desire with divine will.

Dundee's heroic egocentricity, his desire for both glory and moral vindication, and his rigid insistence on the authority of command make him incapable of love. That incapacity in turn limits his power to realize the mythic imperative of the combat film and cavalry Western, which is to provide platoon/society with a firm basis of communal solidarity. His problem (as Peckinpah presents it) is probably more difficult than that faced by mythic ancestors like Kirby Yorke and *Objective Burma*'s Captain Nelson. The constituents of his society are not merely ethnically different, they are sworn blood-enemies ("white trash" Confederates and ex-slaves in Yankee blue); their divisions are those of the era of Selma and Watts, not the era of the Popular Front and the Fair Deal. But Dundee can give his troopers no basis of unity beyond hatred of the common race-enemy and the legalistic code that requires them to keep the oaths of obedience they have given him. This is "his" mission: he will define its terms and its limits, and its victory will be his. Whatever unit solidarity the command attains is developed in spite of, or in actual opposition to, the will of its commander.

The limitations of Dundee's imagination mirror those that shaped the decisive turn in Vietnam from counterinsurgency to the war of attrition. Though buttressed by the most "rational" calculations, our tactics in the end produced the "mad" paradox of "destroying the city in order to save it." In the light of this outcome, the original motives of our mission become questionable: Were we in Vietnam to rescue or liberate the peasants and enable them to choose their own political destiny? Or were we there to confront and destroy the Apache/Communists and vindicate our national character as a "heroic" actor on the world stage? In Peckinpah's film, such an approach to the American "mission" has disastrous consequences, first of all for Dundee as a man, in the revelation of his incapacity for love, but ultimately in the fate of the mission itself.

Dundee regards the actual politics of the Mexican revolution/civil war as irrelevant to his mission and tries to limit his engagement with the French and the Mexicans to tactical exercises. He seeks to follow his own script of rescue, revenge, and personal redemption; his actions inscribe the personal myth on the terrain of Mexico, which he prefers to conceive as a blank slate—useful only as a setting or instrument for his purposes, without significant purposes or powers of its own. But his actions engage him willy-nilly in the revolution, first as liberator of the village, then as a Juarista legend (*el Tigre*) whose exploits boost morale for the struggle against the French. Like the American mission in Vietnam, Dundee finds that he cannot impose his script on the "native" world; rather, he himself becomes a figure whose value and function may be equally determined (or at least affected) by the native script of revolution. But because Dundee does not understand the native script, he can make no use of it. He does not join the Mexicans but continues his obsessively focused pursuit of the Apache—now with French cavalry in hot pursuit.

Dundee's situation is ironic and even absurd. But it is also a situation that mirrors the classical position of the American hero in the cinematic and literary mythology whose formulas can be traced back to Fenimore Cooper. He stands between, and at deadly odds with, the symbolic extremes of European civilization (imagined as corrupt and oppressive) and primitive savagery (imagined as bloody and anarchic). As the pursued pursuer, his situation also replicates that of Ahab in *Moby-Dick*, who passes Sunda Strait closely pursued by Malay pirates as he enters the last stage of his obsessive hunt for the white whale. And as in *Moby-Dick*, the climax arrives when the roles of pursuer and pursued are exchanged.[62]

The only way Dundee can see to escape the Mexican script is to return to the obsessive chase of Charriba and reverse its course so that it will carry us back to the States rather than deeper into Mexico. Dundee is no more able to catch the elusive Apache than American forces were able to find and fix the guerrillas in Vietnam. However, through the long engagement Dundee has come to "know his Indians" and therefore to recognize that Charriba's prestige—no less than his own—is at risk. Thus if Dundee runs for the Rio Grande, Charriba will be forced to follow and attack him and Dundee will be able to fix him in position and defeat him with superior firepower.

His tactical thinking thus mirrors the hopes MACV entertained for the big unit war and anticipates the plan to trap the enemy into attacking the "pseudo-Dien Bien Phu" at Khe Sanh. It is worth noting that Peckinpah is able to imagine an American victory only by "crossing over," or "passing through the looking-glass," and reversing the roles and positions of the Big Unit and the guerrilla. The guerrilla is induced to think like an American planner and thus can be tricked into abandoning guerrilla fight/flight tactics for frontal assault in which Charriba and all his men will be killed. The American becomes the guerrilla, abandoning search-and-destroy for retreat-and-ambush. Dundee's obsessive and single-minded pursuit of Charriba has already discredited or destroyed every "decent" or rational motive for action, including those of rescue, liberation, and the reconciliation of American divisions. Now he paradoxically achieves victory by abandoning the tactics for which he sacrificed everything.

But no sooner are Charriba and his men buried than the value of the victory and the tactical genius that produced it are immediately called into question by the appearance of the French, whom Dundee has forgotten. A strong force now holds the *American* side of the Rio Grande, blocking his return, while an even stronger force closes in from the Mexican side. Another reversal has occurred, mirroring the reversal of pursuer/pursued, Americans/Apaches. The French defend "America" from her returning renegades, who can get home again only by hacking their way across the border. In the end, Tyreen will receive his death wound rescuing the American flag (which he despises) from the French and will die in a single-handed charge against the pursuing Lancers, saving the man he hates and the mission he was blackmailed into undertaking. His ironic and absurd fate is a realization of the consequences of the moral imperative laid down by Kirby York at the end of *Fort Apache*: that for the sake of a higher principle (patriotism, personal honor) we must act as if our myths were true and valid, even when we know and believe them to be false or mistaken.

The relationship between the three contending societies—European, American, Indian—is thus resolved in a series of increasingly bloody and arguably meaningless battles. In Fenimore Cooper and the mythological tradition he engendered, this kind of battle is usually read as a tragic but necessary means to historical progress: the surviving Americans may emerge chastened but also purified by their ordeal and justified as agents to future progress. Peckinpah's reading is very different. The Indians are annihilated, as are at least half of the French; the Americans emerge with a Pyrrhic victory in which many of the characters we have come to value are destroyed. Dundee signals his satisfaction by lighting a cigar and asking the trumpeter to "whistle up a tune." But we have learned to suspect Dundee's character, particularly his willingness to take things of human value for tactical advantage. The ending deliberately leaves us with the central questions about the character and value of the mission in doubt. It is nonetheless clear that the American capacity for regular/irregular violence is matchless and is capable of gaining victory even in such dubious battle.

Peckinpah's film is a sprawling, episodic narrative filled with powerfully stated ambivalences, rich in metaphors that suggest connections between American sexual psychology and violence—tremendously rich in implication but confused in achievement. A more orderly and disciplined treatment of the theme is Richard Brooks' *The Professionals* (1966). The film imagines the problem of the gunfighter/counterguerrilla in Mexico in terms that look back to the origin of the American mission in Vietnam, when the Special Forces were conceived as potential organizers of an authentic but American-style democratic revolution in the Third World. Like *Major Dundee*, *The Professionals* begins as a standard captivity/rescue tale, but the standard moral reference points are inverted at the very moment of rescue. The Professionals pass "through the looking-glass" and discover that the premises behind their mission are false. From that point on their task is to re-imagine and revise their mission, and this time to get it right.

The period of the film is roughly 1915–16, when the Mexican Revolution (as the film has it) has begun to degenerate into a seemingly meaningless cycle of political fragmentation and violence.[63] The young Mexican wife of Mr. J. W. Grant (Ralph Bellamy), a railroad and mining baron with holdings in Texas and Mexico, has apparently been kidnaped and held for ransom by a revolutionary with the resounding name of Jesus Raza (Jack Palance). "Jesus," says Grant, "what a name for the bloodiest killer in Northern Mexico." The woman's name is, inevitably, Maria. To rescue her, Grant hires three "professionals," each specializing in a skill essential to the success of the mission. The formation of this team follows the pattern set in *The Magnificent Seven* and *Major Dundee*. But the simplicities of the original model have been elaborated. Instead of a set of minor variations on the quick-draw, we have a systematic and detailed account of different specializations and how they will work together. The balance between "combat film" and "Western" elements in the formation of the heroic group is thus shifted toward the military, and in particular toward a Special Forces or "commando raid" concept.

The commander is Rico (Lee Marvin), a professional soldier and weapons specialist turned mercenary. He is very military in dress and style and gives orders like a platoon commander. He is also the "man who knows Indians," in this case, Mexicans. He was married to a Mexican woman and had been Raza's comrade-in-arms under Pancho Villa. Jake (Woody Strode) is a Black bounty-hunter whose specializations mark him as the team's Indian scout: he is the best tracker in the West, and his preferred weapon is the bow. Jake's presence, and the dialogue that introduces him, also connect the film with the "civil-rights Western." The weakest of the team is the finest horse-wrangler in the country (Robert Ryan), a man whose professionalism is tempered by the tenderness that makes him so good with animals. He becomes the team's "house liberal," a spokesman for softer values that prove dangerous as guides to action.

To provide an "equalizer" against Raza's advantages in men and weapons, Rico recruits a dynamite expert named Dahlberg (Burt Lancaster), who served the Revolution with Rico and Raza. Dahlberg is a variation on the hero of Hemingway's *For Whom the Bell Tolls,* a Robert Jordan who has survived "the bridge," his improbable romance, and even the minimalist idealism of the Hemingway hero. Dahlberg is the platoon's libido. He is (in Jake's words) "a lovin' man" for whom sex and violence are different aspects of the same action. Both involve "explosions," and both (he says) create life. His language establishes a metaphoric equation between sexuality and "good action," which becomes (as the story develops) the key term through which Rico and Dahlberg interpret the meaning of the Revolution and of their relation to it.[64]

To reach Raza's base they have to cross a bleak, sterile desert, an environment whose cruelty can be borne only by "men of steel," men like Raza, Rico, Dahlberg, and Jake. The desert is a metaphor for a Darwinian view of life and struggle in which the worldview of the Doolittle Report is fully realized: whether the enemy is nature or Mexican guerrillas, the only way to survive is to be ruthlessly pragmatic. Living by "traditional American concepts of fair play"—kindness to dumb animals, giving quarter to enemies—will get you killed.

We also learn that Rico and Dahlberg were once committed soldiers of the Revolution, realist-idealists in the Kennedy mold who used their gift for ruthless pragmatism in the cause of liberation. But both have left the Revolution, disillusioned with its "degeneration." The revolutionary army had been reduced to a collection of bandit-like guerrilla outfits whose violence seemed to have lost its original connection to meaningful political struggle.

Rico's despair with the Revolution is clarified when the team observes Raza's men ambushing a train—an inescapable scene in nearly every film set during the Mexican Revolution. The train is filled with *Colorados,* sadistic stormtroopers of the conservative regime. Raza kills them all, hanging the officers and shooting the men after they surrender, an action Rico approves. When the "liberal" raises predictable objections, Dahlberg answers with the story of how the *Colorados* tortured Rico's wife (also named Maria) to death while her *compadres* did nothing. Dahlberg then offers the first formulation of the ideological problem that he and Rico are grappling with. In all times and countries, says Dahlberg, there has been only one revolution, "the good guys against the bad guys. . . . The problem is, how do you know which is which?"

Dahlberg's parable raises a question about the meaning of the mythological fable of captivity/rescue that informed the ideology of the American mission in Vietnam (and had most recently been restated by President Johnson in his Johns Hopkins address).[65] Its function here is to remind us of the fundamental difference between the revolutionaries and the government. The scene establishes the moral authority of the "tough-minded" standard of judgment used by Rico and Dahlberg against the sentimentality of the be-kind-to-animals "liberal." It thus places us firmly within the frame of values and references that justified the original program of counterinsurgency and the use of ruthless and "immoral" means to achieve its ends.

The identification of the enemy as *Colorados*—as "reds"—aligns the scene politically with the American enterprise in Vietnam and allows us to read it as an apology for atrocities committed by our side. To anyone familiar with the iconography of the war, the image of Raza shooting his prisoners now recalls the TV footage of the Saigon police chief summarily executing a bound prisoner during the Tet Offensive. However, that event occurred two years later; in 1966 the burden of official rhetoric was that our side did not commit such atrocities. If the scene is an apology of our atrocities, it can only be an apology made as if in anticipation of the fact, an assertion that in order to win "the good guys" may have to commit "atrocities" just like the enemy.

But another aspect of the scene complicates this reading: the *Colorados* represent the government forces, while Raza's men are the guerrillas. If we translate this situation as an allegory of Vietnam, then Rico/Dahlberg are justifying atrocities committed by the equivalent of the VC. The reflection of Vietnam in *The Professionals* is thus literally a mirror-image in which the real-world alliances are reversed. This device opens the story to imagine possible resolutions that are not limited by the "facts" of Vietnam: specifically, to the possibility that we can somehow "go back" and reverse the errors that compromised the originally "liberating" and even "revolutionary" purposes of counterinsurgency; that instead of becoming enforcers for a corrupt government, we can become partisans of a genuine revolution by and for the "good guys."

The team reaches its moral "cross-over" point, and passes through the looking-glass, at the moment it completes its mission. The professionals stage a well-timed commando attack on Raza's base, with Rico and Dahlberg penetrating Raza's headquarters to effect the rescue. Until the last moment, everything they see reinforces the premise that this is a classic save-the-woman scenario. Maria (Claudia Cardinale) appears to be a sad captive, deprived of all clothing but a robe, staring moodily out the window. When the gigantic Raza enters the room, orders the female attendant to leave, strips to his waist, and advances on the bed, we see Maria as an Indian captive about to suffer yet another brutal rape . . . when suddenly she throws off her robe, embraces Raza passionately, and angrily asks him why he took so long getting there. "Brother, we've been *had*," says Dahlberg—they, and not the woman, have been "screwed." But before this suggestion of sexual rôle-reversal can be explored, the commando attack begins. It is too late to retreat. And Rico in any case is determined to fulfill his contract with Grant. He may be a mercenary, but he insists on retaining a mercenary's honor. They grab the girl, and, though Rico spares Raza, more than a dozen of his men are killed as they shoot their way out of the camp.

As they head for the border the Professionals learn just how badly they have been "screwed" and begin to see the narrative of their expedition from the other side of the mirror. The moral poles represented by Grant-as-victim and revolution-as-rapist are reversed by two traumatic shocks. The scene in Raza's bedroom suggests that Maria is not a captive "virgin" but a "whore," Raza's accomplice in an attempt to fleece Grant. Yet the "whore" shows herself worthy according to the values of "professionalism": she loves and will do anything to aid Raza and the Revolution and is willing to play the whore if that will help them.[66]

Having challenged their ideas about the potential heroism and professionalism of women, Maria then unmasks the lie that has shaped their mission. It was not Raza but J. W. Grant who "kidnaped" and "raped" her, by using his wealth and power to frame Raza for outlawry and to compel Maria to marry him. This revelation forces Rico and Dahlberg—and the audience—to revalue the scenes through which they have passed, looking for signs they ought to have spotted before. Grant's appealing invocation of the conventions of the captivity myth has masked other signs which Rico and Dahlberg, as men of the world—and the audience, as people familiar with Western-movie conventions—ought to have recognized. In outlaw/gunfighter movies, and in Mexican Revolution movies, it is almost always the case that "good guys" ride horses and "bad guys" ride trains; this convention is reinforced by Raza's ambush of the *Colorados*, who are riding on a J. W. Grant train. Moreover, ever since *Jesse James* it has been a given of such films that railroad barons are by nature and inclination tyrants who prosper by stealing land from small farmers or peasants.

From this new perspective, Grant's sarcastic dismissal of Raza's name is discredited. "Jesus Raza" can be seen as a name combining a symbol of self-sacrifice and willing martyrdom with a word identifying the whole of the Mexican people as his family. La Raza—literally "the race"—was and is the term used to identify the Chicanos of southern California, and especially the farmworkers organized during the 1960s by Cesar Chavez in the movement called La Causa. Our heroes' hearts have been telling them from the start that they were on the wrong side; we now recognize that part of their misgiving has a basis in politics and class—as American heroes, they ought to have known that their "side" was that of "the people," not the side of the corporation. By enlisting in Grant's cause, they have themselves become the thing they most despise: kidnapers of a woman.

The consequences of this discovery are worked out through the integration of the discourse of "love" and "women" with the discourse of "violence" and male "professionalism." Dahlberg is the vehicle for this integration. He begins by reformulating the original problem of ideological and political allegiance ("good guys/bad guys") in sexual terms. Instead of querying the political relations of Grant and Raza, he says he wants to find out "what makes a woman worth a hundred thousand dollars" (the ransom Grant would have paid for Maria). He gets his answer through an exchange of bullets and kisses with Lieutenant C. C. Chiquita, a buxom *soldadera* with bandoliers crossed between her breasts. Like Raza, she is a former battle-comrade, of whom Dahlberg admiringly says "she never says no." She is Dahlberg's female twin, someone for whom sexuality and violence are equal as sources of pleasure and creative energy, who indulges both passions with delighted promiscuity and is very good, very "professional," in both love and war. She is, for Dahlberg, a more valued woman than Maria, because she uses the instruments of her professionalism as a man would—as he himself does.

The consummation of their relationship comes when Dahlberg stays behind to hold off Raza and the seven remaining pursuers in a single-handed rear-guard action. With fearsome competence Dahlberg wipes out all of Raza's group except for Chiquita and the wounded Raza himself. As the two Mexicans plan their final attempt to kill Dahlberg, there is a three-way conversation between these former comrades about love, sex, and revolution. Raza asks Dahlberg why he and Rico, who fought so well and were so committed to the cause, deserted the Revolution; when Dahlberg speaks of his disillusionment, Raza answers by comparing the Revolution to "a great love affair" with a beautiful woman. At first, you worship the beloved as a goddess; then, when she proves a sinful mortal, you dismiss her as a whore. But she is really neither: it is your own illusions that make you demand she be one thing or the other. Having associated "revolution" with a symbol of mythic "Woman," at once "whore" and "virgin," Raza then offers a catechism that covers the problems of both love and revolution and asserts that a truly tough-minded man will commit himself to love/the cause with an open-eyed awareness of "her" imperfections:

> We fight because we believe. We leave because we are disillusioned. We return because we are lost. We die because we are committed.

As Raza finishes, Chiquita launches an attack on Dahlberg, exposing herself because she believes "he won't shoot a woman." She underestimates Dahlberg's professionalism. He breaks the taboo and shoots her off her horse. But when Dahlberg shows a soft side by bringing water to the dying Chiquita, she turns the tables again. First, she greets him affectionately, showing no malice toward her killer. She understands that "a man's gotta do what a man's gotta do," and that he must do it well no matter what cause it serves. Her warmth even suggests that between professionals the give and take of death is of a piece with the exchange of pleasure in sex. But in a last gesture Chiquita proves her mastery of Dahlberg's discipline. When Dahlberg lifts the canteen to her mouth, she raises her pistol and points it at his head—only to have the hammer click on an empty chamber. "I have no luck," she says with a smile, and dies with Dahlberg's kiss on her lips.

Dahlberg (it will turn out) has been converted to the possibility of reaffiliating with the Revolution by this sexual encounter. In his words, he has discovered "what makes a woman worth a hundred thousand dollars." A similar process of conversion has been at work on Rico, but its terms are more abstract, even ideological. He must square his new understanding of the real political relations of Grant and Raza (America and Mexico) with both his personal disillusion and the formal terms of his contract with Grant. He does this by delivering Maria to Grant, but when Grant abuses her and admits the truth of her accusations, he seizes her, gives her back to the wounded Raza, and returns with them to Mexico. This inversion of his original mission is justified, because he had contracted his honor "to save a woman from a dirty kidnaper"—only he has discovered that Grant ("us") rather than Raza ("them") is the kidnaper.

The last image suggests that the four Professionals return to Mexico to rejoin Raza and make a disillusioned, tough-minded act of reaffiliation with the Revolution. Given the skill of the Americans—Jake and Dahlberg can turn a bow and arrow and a few sticks of TNT into a battery of howitzers—we can guess that their aid will help the right side to win. The Americans' exceptional capacity for extraordinary violence has made the process of their revolutionary education extremely costly for the Mexicans. They have killed both Chiquita and Raza's right-hand man, and an estimate of the total "body count" racked up by the Professionals in the course of their mission is in excess of thirty. But the movie suggests that this cost has been worth it, for both Americans and Mexicans: the former because it has reawakened their commitment to heroic action on behalf of a moral order, the latter because now those American guns will be drawn on their side.

The movie thus recuperates the original project of counterinsurgency after taking account of the grounds for disillusion with its failure. The Green Beret mission is not demystified and rejected but reformed and reoriented: this time, the Americans will pick the "right" side. The movie also suggests that we can use traditional myth-sanctioned signs to recognize which side is right: the good guys will be "populists," not corporate fat cats or government officials; they will use primitive technology (horses), not modern (trains); they will show extraordinary loyalty, and exceptional skill (professionalism) in combat; and in their company there will be no dichotomy between "making love" and "making war"—they will feel like the same thing.

Both *Major Dundee* and *The Professionals* raise questions about the war and the counterinsurgency project, and both identify American heroism with a propensity for violence that is presented as extraordinary in its methods and scope—a shocking willingness and ability to give and take death without stint or limit. But in both films the suggestion of a disproportion between violent means and moral ends is first voiced and then abandoned for endings that suggest that an American victory justifies the methods used to achieve it. The films that took up this theme over the next three years developed and elaborated these recuperative strategies.[67]

Mexico Westerns made in this 1966–68 period for the most part develop the "recuperative" side of the *Dundee/Professionals* reading of the "mission"; but at the same time they give increased prominence to the presence of cynicism and corruption on "our" side, and to spectacular and literal displays of *excessive* violence by both sides. In 1968 five major American films—*Villa Rides*, *Guns of the Magnificent Seven*, *Bandolero!*, *Blue*, and *100 Rifles*—dealt with the matter of Mexico, for the most part with a growing self-consciousness about the political implications of the story.[68]

The most elaborate and interesting attempt at recuperating the "mission" of the counterinsurgency Western was *100 Rifles* (1968). Like *Major Dundee*, the film crosses the Mexico Western with the "Cult of the Indian" and attempts to merge the "civil-rights" theme with that of counterinsurgency. The American gunfighter is a Black man (Jim Brown); the "peasants" are identified as Yaqui Indians; the enemy is a fascistic military dictator aided by a railroad corporation; and in addition to helping the Indians save themselves from genocide, the American breaks the most important of cinematic racial taboos in a much ballyhooed "soft-core" sex scene with Raquel Welch.[69] But its recuperative version of the Amercan mission is undercut by humorous exaggeration and by the suggestion that, in the end, cynical motives and "special interests" will deprive the mission's victory of meaning.

Although the American is reluctant to get involved with the Yaqui, like the heroes of *The Magnificent Seven* and *Green Berets* he is won over by an appeal to his paternalism by the peasant children. Like the "typical" hero he is, Brown cannot refuse the appeal of the captivity/rescue scenario; and when he rescues hostage children from the dictator's fortified ranch (the *Rio Grande* scenario), the Yaquis themselves recognize their need for his expertise and make him their General. The movie thus plays out a fantasy of counterinsurgency in which the paradox of American power and peasant democracy is overcome: the peasants freely choose the American to lead them.

Although Brown's "blackness" is emphasized in the characterization and the love scene, for the most part his relationship with Welch follows the conventions for White/Indian love affairs laid down in *Broken Arrow*. Her passion for him threatens to turn a fighting rebel woman into a domestic angel; his love for her threatens to bind him to Mexico and deflect him from his ambition to succeed as a Black man in White America. The death of Welch's Sarita repeats the traditional pattern, which we have remarked in both Fenimore Cooper's work and in *Broken Arrow*, in which the non-White woman plays her "redemptive" role by vanishing from the scene, leaving the hero free to fulfill his destiny among his own people. Nonetheless, there are differences in the use of this convention: Sonseeahray dies as a victim, and her death enables peace between Reds and Whites by eliminating the possibility of sexual intimacy and equality between them. Sarita dies as a warrior who leads men in battle for the revolutionary salvation of her race—an implicitly feminist gesture in the scenario, although Sarita is still very much the objectified "sex goodess." It is worth noting that when, as in *Little Big Man*, the Western becomes a vehicle for overtly antiwar polemics, the role of the woman is once again that of the victim—as if sympathy for figures identified by the racial stigmata of the enemy can be fully and unambivalently evoked only when they are transformed into pure victims incapable of aggression or even of self-defense.

The death of Sarita at the moment of victory deprives Brown's character of his emotional stake in the Yaquis. Like Jeffords at the end of *Broken Arrow* (and Chris at the end of *The Magnificent Seven*) he returns to the States, leaving a reconstructed native order behind. However, at this juncture the movie's wish-fulfillment scenario is deflated by an ironic denouement. Brown is succeeded as leader of the revolution by Yaqui Joe (Burt Reynolds), a half-American Yaqui who seems a slightly roguish version of Chico or Bernardo Riley from *The Magnificent Seven*: an Americanized native who remains to solidify the achievements of the counterinsurgency professionals. But as Yaqui Joe turns to his task, he is approached by the corrupt railroad agent, who has been aiding the military dictator. The railroad operates in the spirit of capitalist pragmatism: if the Revolution is in power, it will make a deal with the Revolution. But the making of the deal requires that Yaqui Joe arrogate to himself the power of the Revolution, imposing an "order" which his people would not be able to achieve by themselves and using his authority to make a deal with the railroad—from which he will, of course, benefit personally. The movie ends with the implication that the Revolution will not be succeeded by Indian/peasant democracy but by another form of dictatorship, in which rational corruption and simple greed replace the excessive and self-indulgent sadism of the old regime.

Thus the drift of these Westerns paralleled that of ideological polemics in responding to the twin crises of counterinsurgency and the War on Poverty. Like the scholars and policy-makers who contributed to the work of the presidential commissions and to the more routine labors of the various federal agencies and private "think tanks," moviemakers used the languages of their profession to represent the concerns of the moment and to reconsider the basic assumptions of value and historical fact on which our culture's sense of its "mission" had been based. Like the Violence Commission, the movies even entertain the possibility that that "mission" (or important aspects of it) may in fact be corrupt or in some way "mad"—rooted in delusion and/or expressed in a pathologically violent manner. Like the makers of policy and ideology, the movie myth-makers tried to contain these darker suggestions within frameworks that would recuperate the essential purposes (while critiquing the methods) of the "mission" and preserve some model of "heroism" —of an American style of effective and principled action on the stage of history. In both the ideological and the mythological discourse of 1965–68 there was a rough balance between the desire for recuperation and the sense that the "mission" was both wrong-headed and doomed to failure. That balance was disrupted, first by the Tet Offensive in early 1968; then by the violence-marred presidential campaign that followed; and finally by the revelation of the massacre at Mylai.

17 Cross-over Point

The Mylai Massacre, The Wild Bunch, *and the Demoralization of America, 1969–1972*

The Mission joined hands and stepped through the looking glass.

MICHAEL HERR, *Dispatches*

In April 1967 General William Westmoreland had announced, "It appears that last month we reached the cross-over point" in all but two provinces, and that from now on enemy "attrition will be greater than additions to [his] force."[1] But the shock of Tet in January 1968 brought the war to a very different kind of "cross-over point" from the one envisioned by Westmoreland. The "hard figures" of the attrition strategists were revealed as illusions or outright fabrications, and the victory that was about to complete the official narrative suddenly vanished into an indefinite future. It became impossible to say with any authority whether we stood near the end of the Vietnam scenario, in the middle, or had been pushed back to "square one."[2]

Disorientation within the frame of history (as we understood it) was matched by a spatial disorientation, lived out by the troops and experienced vicariously by the television audience, in which American troops had to attack and recapture at heavy cost some of the very cities they had so recently (and "successfully") been defending. "We had to destroy the city in order to save it" was not a rallying cry like "Remember the Alamo"; it was an absurdly self-negating rationalization, speaking of the loss of any logical relation between aims and methods, deeds and reasons. If that was what our mission had come to, then we had indeed "crossed over"—into a "looking-glass" world where everything was inverted, where rational analysis and planning were merely exercises in delusion, where salvation was destruction, where those whose mission it was to subdue and expel "the horror" became its agents. As Marine Corps counterinsurgency specialist William Corson said, this was "the language of madness . . . which if allowed to continue will destroy not only the people of Vietnam, but also the moral fabric and strength of America."[3]

The antiwar movement gained in numbers, militancy, and respectability. Polls taken during the presidential campaign consistently showed strong public preference for candidates who promised the withdrawal of American troops from combat. Within a month of Nixon's inauguration, polls were indicating that a majority of Americans had come to see the entire enterprise as a "mistake."[4]

A similar skepticism and growing antipathy greeted administration explanations of what had gone wrong with the "other war" . . . the War on Poverty. It was hardly surprising that the ambitious program of social reform had not abolished poverty and injustice overnight. But it was shocking to find that civil-rights acts and Great Society programs had not even managed to buy good will and greater hope in the urban ghettoes but had, on the contrary, provoked the most widespread and violent civil disorders since the Great Strike of 1877.

American ideology envisions electoral politics as the system through which crises of this kind are resolved. But in 1968 the American electoral process itself was irrationalized by surprising insurgencies and eruptions of violence. President Johnson's re-election campaign was upset by the "peace" candidacy of Eugene McCarthy. The assassinations of Martin Luther King and Robert Kennedy eliminated the leading spokesman for nonviolent Black protest and decapitated the liberal/antiwar wing of the Democratic Party. A right-wing insurgency led by Alabama's segregationist Governor George Wallace, which appealed to the "White backlash" vote, would produce the most successful third-party candidacy since the Depression. Finally—with "the whole world watching" on television—the Democratic convention degenerated into a circus of denunciation, demonstration, police repression, and street violence. The hope of counterinsurgency had always been that some day Vietnamese politics would begin to mirror this American political model. Instead, our engagement in Vietnam had carried us to the other side of the looking-glass and had made our politics seem a mirror-image of Saigon's *coups*, conspiracies, riots, and assassinations.

The election of Nixon briefly revived belief in the government's capacity to control events. Nixon had promised to substitute conservative "control" for liberal "anarchy" at home and abroad by getting tough with "crime in the streets" (that is, urban uprisings) and by enacting a "secret plan" for ending the war on favorable terms. Polls suggested that, despite persistent skepticism, the public was willing to give the "secret plan" the benefit of the doubt; it approved the drawing down of American forces and the shifting of the combat role to the ARVN. But these developments were offset by evidence that this administration too did not know how to regain control of events and restore the proportionality between violence inflicted, losses suffered, and results achieved.

The enemy began 1969 with a second "Tet Offensive," which ignored South Vietnamese targets and inflicted heavy losses on American troops and installations. Nixon responded with a "signal" of American resolve—the beginning of a secret bombing campaign in Cambodia. Despite the administration's declared intention to disengage American forces, heavy fighting persisted through the spring and summer. By year's end, American forces had suffered 10,000 casualties, the heaviest annual toll thus far. In May the 101st Airborne suffered heavy casualties in the controversial battle of Hamburger Hill, which seemed to symbolize all the bloody absurdities of the war of attrition. The impression of irrational waste and futility was compounded by the fact that the attrition strategy was even then being officially abandoned by MACV and the administration.[5] A massive "sapper" attack on the Cam Ranh Bay naval base in August reminded the public that despite years of "progress" the Communists were still able to strike in force anywhere in the country. Nor had Vietnamese politics improved: the Thieu regime still resisted reform and since April had been at odds with the administration over "Vietnamization."[6]

A series of large antiwar demonstrations were organized during the summer of 1969 (along with the counterculture festival at Woodstock), and in November there was a massive antiwar demonstration in Washington supported by similar demonstrations across the country. Coverage of these events in "mainstream" and even conservative media (*Life*, the *New York Times*, the networks) was generally favorable to both the style of the demonstrators and their cause—although the administration viewed them with alarm as evidence of a dangerous (for some, a "revolutionary") dissidence. With the rise of more militant and violence-oriented organizations in the African-American community and the antiwar movement, and the corresponding increase in repressive government measures, it began to seem credible that America itself might fall into that cycle of revolution and repression which the New Frontiersman had seen as the besetting evil of Third World societies and from which the American model was supposed to deliver them.[7]

At this moment the public learned of the Mylai massacre. More than any other single event, the revelation transformed the terms of ideological and political debate on the war, lending authority to the idea that American society was in the grip of a "madness" whose sources might be endemic to our "national character." The massacre itself happened during the aftermath of Tet. It might well have had a different significance had it been made public during the period of bloody fighting, sudden imminent peril to our troops, and discovery of the Communist massacre of civilians in Hue.

But the events that had occurred in the eighteen months between the Tet Offensive and the Mylai revelations—the assassinations of King and Kennedy and the violence at the Chicago convention, the Sisyphean assaults on Hamburger Hill, the casualty lists that grew longer under a strategy of "disengagement" than they had been during the war of attrition—augmented the public's sense of being trapped in an irrationally rising tide of violence which signaled "an appalling, indeed frightening deterioration in our national standards of morality and law."[8]

"Indian Trip": The Mylai Massacre

The Mylai massacre was committed on March 16, 1968, by an infantry company of the Americal Division, which deliberately wiped out nearly an entire village, including old men, women, children, and infants.[9] After-action reports suggested that something "out of line" had occurred, but officers of the Americal and MACV discouraged or suppressed attempts at investigation for more than a year. Thus the public did not learn of the massacre until the fall of 1969, when the *New York Times* and *Life* magazine broke the story of the army's internal investigation.[10] The *Life* coverage is worth a closer look, because the shocking color photographs of the massacre by Ronald Haeberle had a powerful impact on public opinion and prepared the ground for acceptance of the story of massacre and cover-up which Seymour Hersh and the *Times* would begin to develop in January 1970; and because *Life*'s "cinematic" way of telling the story translates the massacre into the language of movie-genre, transforming a disruptive military/political event into a crisis of American mythography.

The Mylai material is presented in the format typical of the "big story" in a given issue of *Life*. A central narrative, running over several pages, is framed and supplemented by boxes and add-ons which provide "close-up" treatment of particular individuals or aspects of the story. The major stages of the narrative are given by headings at the top of each page.[11] A "stream" of photographic images runs through the story and provides a rudimentary pictorial narrative, which here begins with the image of a "normal" helicopter landing and ends with an image of huddled refugees. The horrific images of slaughtered civilians that fill the middle pages document a massacre but do not show which side committed it, and the terse captions do not explain how it happened. This information is provided in the verbal narrative that is braided through the image-stream, but the narrative itself is organized in a "cinematic" way as a series of selected "cuts" that jump from one participant-observer to another. There is no omniscient narrator to construe the action for us. As in a movie, the viewer/reader must fill in the blanks between the cuts, and connect prose narrative with photographic image, by making his/her own interpretive construction guided by the suggestive patterning of the scenario and by the writers' use of "genre effects" . . . characterizations, motivations, and plot-lines drawn from movie formulas. This formal organization has the effect of engaging readers/viewers deeply in the task of construing the story for themselves. And since the story is one of atrocity, the effect of this engagement is to make the reader feel responsible for and implicated in the outcome.

The story begins with two color photos on facing pages: helicopters disgorging troops, and a group of civilians—an old woman grimacing while frightened children huddle behind her and a young woman calmly buttons her black "pajamas." These images invoke a stereotypical "norm" of the fighting: troopers hitting an LZ, frightened civilians. The turning of the page makes a "jump cut" to atrocity: a heap of dead women, children, and infants tossed obscenely onto a road. The captions tell us that photographer Ronald Haeberle found the bodies; they do not say that American troops did the killing. The next pair of pages make the attribution of atrocity clearer. The caption below Haeberle's picture of a man and a little boy tells us that they were wounded when they started up from a field and were then finished off at close range after Haeberle left. The picture of troops burning the village is a "normal" image of this war, but it now acquires implications of atrocity. Those implications are realized on the next page in the black-and-white photo of a dead infant shot in the mouth at close range, its mother dead beside it with her head covered in burning straw.

The narrative that explains the meaning of these images is provided by a series of participant/observers. The most important of them is Charles West, a familiar and appealing type of American GI, a civilian in uniform who is nonetheless professional in his approach to combat, careful of the lives of his men, and sympathetic to the Vietnamese (especially children).[12] Like the photo sequence, West's story begins as a "normal" war movie. He recounts the briefing by Captain Medina, who describes the village as heavily fortified and inhabited only by VC, and concludes: "the order was to destroy Mylai and everything in it." West then characterizes Medina in terms that remind us of Kirby Yorke or Sergeant Stryker: his nickname of "Mad Dog" is a mark of respect, and he has made of his men

> the best company to ever serve in Vietnam . . . not just a hundred and some men they call a company. . . . We cared about each and every individual's problems. This is the way we were taught by Captain Medina to feel towards each other. We were like brothers.

Despite his toughness, Medina grieves for the loss of his men; but as with Ethan Edwards and Mike Kirby, his mourning turns to rage: "Captain Medina told us we might get a chance to revenge the deaths of our fellow GIs."[13] A plausible motive for what follows is thus suggested; but as the story develops, the "revenge" motive comes to seem inadequate as an explanation of the massacre.

The opening sequences of the narrative give us a series of "shots" suggesting a gradual buildup to slaughter. The troops enter the village, shooting at figures that appear suddenly, figures that run. But gradually, what could be a series of mistakes by trigger-happy green troops becomes a pattern of deliberate killing.[14] Our two most sympathetic observers, West and the photographer Haeberle, at first just shake their heads over events that seem to them awful but still not too different from things they have seen before.[15]

Through Haeberle's camera/eye we witness a scene that marks the crossing of the line between the "normal" excesses of the war and full-blown atrocity. As Haeberle crouches to shoot a picture of the wounded child, a GI kneels behind him. Then:

> The GI fired three shots into the child. The first shot knocked him back, the second shot lifted him into the air. The third shot put him down and the body fluids came out. The GI just simply got up and walked away. It was a stroboscopic effect. We were so close to him it was blurred."[16]

The scene begins with a striking juxtaposition of the two crouching "shooters": a terribly ironic visual metaphor which aligns observer with killer. This tableau, and the photographic metaphors through which Haeberle describes the killing, remind us that the photographer is our representative in this scene: through him we vicariously enter the event and become witnesses to a crime; and to the extent that we see ourselves crouching and witnessing with Haeberle, we too are implicated in the massacre.[17] The massacre teaches Haeberle, and his photos teach us, that (as Michael Herr said) in Vietnam "you were as responsible for everything you saw as you were for everything you did."[18]

The cognitive play which this quasi-cinematic narrative invites seems designed to make us *feel* that complicity. A series of "reaction-shots" describing the responses of various other participants reflects the range of likely reader/viewer responses (horror, denial) and incorporates (implicates) our reactions in the story. Reactions range from Sergeant Bernhardt's refusal to participate because "I didn't think this was a lawful order," to SP4 Varnado Simpson's defensive assertions: "To us they were no civilians . . . they were VC. They showed no ways or means that they wasn't. You don't have any alternatives . . . they could turn around and kill you."[19] Both types of reaction are presented without editorial comment, and the reader is therefore free to identify with Simpson's apology. But readers who do so will be jolted by the box on the following page in which Simpson's excuses are rejected by his own grandmother. (The box also frames the photo of the murdered infant and mother, described earlier.)

Within the narrative itself, the atrocious character of the event is finally acknowledged in a climactic scene at the center of the village. Private Meadlo describes the gathering of forty to forty-five civilian prisoners—"Men, women, children. Babies"—and Lieutenant Calley's orders to kill them all. Calley then "stepped back about 10, 15 feet, and he started shooting them. . . ." Meadlo's account breaks off and jumps to a ditch on the edge of the village, where another mass killing takes place. The description here is extremely effective, its authenticity emphasized by the imitation of Meadlo's impoverished language, the abrupt transitions as he tries to reconstruct events that deeply traumatized him. But although we are to assume the accuracy of the direct quotations, careful editing heightens their effectiveness. The affecting phrase—"Men, women, children. Babies"—is repeated (as if it were a refrain), and the editor gives the second repetition of "babies" special emphasis by inserting a paragraph break:

"And so we walked over to the people, and he started pushing them off [into the ditch] and started shooting . . . we started shooting them, so altogether we just pushed them all off, and just started using automatics on them. Men, women, and children.

"And babies. And so we started shooting them, and somebody told us to switch off to single shot so that we could save ammo. . . ."[20]

At this moment it can no longer be denied that the troops have "crossed over." Instead of protecting women and children from "the horror," they have themselves *become* "the horror." The story cuts back and forth between images of GIs massacring the helpless with cold faces or expressions of "savage" glee and reminiscences by West (and others) that remind us of the "normal" behavior we have learned to expect of American troops:

"On other missions . . . the GIs would take their fruit and maybe a can of pork and beans and give the rest to the Vietnamese people. I always thought it would be a treat. . . . The people seemed like they appreciated it. . . . Just about anywhere we went on an operation we always had kids following us, and most of the kids we would know by name. . . ."

West then veers to an opposite view, which implicitly rationalizes massacre: "There was a saying that every time we ran into a booby trap, it turned out to be made by a can that we had given the kids." But the apology is immediately undercut by a vivid word-picture in which a toddler sits by a pile of corpses holding the hand of one (perhaps its mother); a GI drops into "kneeling position, 30 meters from this kid, and killed him with a single shot."[21]

The culminating atrocity is a rape scene in which we finally learn how to interpret the image we saw back on the first pair of pages, of the grimacing old woman and the girl in black pajamas. Haeberle comes upon a pair of GIs attempting to rape the girl, who is identified by Haeberle as thirteen years old. "As they were stripping her, with bodies, and burning huts all around, the girls' mother tried to help her, scratching and clawing at the soldiers." When Haeberle appears with his camera the men stop, allowing him to take his picture, which we now understand is of an enraged and terrified old woman who has just defended her daughter from rape. But once the image is frozen on film and Haeberle turns away, shots are heard; when Haeberle returns he sees that everyone in the group, including the children, has been shot.[22] The hopeful expectation of rescue that is raised in the tale of the old woman's courage, and above all by the appearance of Haeberle (and ourselves, as vicarious public witnesses) is horribly negated. Once again, the passivity of the "witness" has permitted an atrocity; indeed, his presence may even have provided a motive for the GIs to eliminate evidence of the attempted rape.

The inversion of the normal war-movie/Western scenario is now complete. Instead of rescuing the woman/child from rape and slaughter, the Americans commit rape—in fact, child-rape—and murder amid the burning buildings of the "settlement." We are back in the symbolic terrain of the captivity myth—the terrain of Mary Rowlandson and Ethan Edwards—only now *we* are the "savages." Jay Roberts' description of the wild cries and increasingly indiscriminate slaughter suggests a descent into madness and unconsciously echoes Mary Rowlandson's description of the Indian massacre of Lancaster in King Philip's War:

> "One soldier was stabbing a calf over and over again. Blood was coming from the calf's nose. The calf tried to move toward the mother cow. The GI was enjoying it and stabbed again. . . . Soldiers stood around and watched. Others were killing the baby pigs. . . . A GI was running down a trail, chasing a duck with a knife."[23]

How can this "madness" be explained? The most rational and authoritative of the combatants, Charles West, is himself confused: "They might have been wild for a while," he says, "but I don't think they were crazy." He tells us that soldiers have to be quick on the trigger when they enter a hostile village but admits "I can't rightly say that I got fired upon." He blames those he calls "yanigans" for getting out of hand, "running around like rookies." But West's ideal of veteran professionalism is Medina, who does not stop the yanigans and murders an old man while West looks on.[24] Since the "madness" has no rational or limiting cause, the reader/viewer is invited (as in a horror movie, or the "concealed rape/torture" images in *The Searchers*) to imagine "the worst": that Mylai represents the upsurge of an evil so "mysterious" that it may well be limitlessly pervasive and may represent (as the Violence Commission debates suggested) a demonic potential inherent in our civilization, a "madness" to which the home front is not immune.

The narrative concludes with the departure of most of the company, leaving West and his platoon to guard the ruins of the village. A quiet dénouement reminds us again of the moral norms that defined the Americans' original "protective" mission: "Children and old papa-sans were hovering nearby. When the GIs opened their

C-rations, they shared their supper with these Vietnamese who had survived the massacre." The cinematic narrative thus ends in a tableau filled with complex ironies and unresolved questions: Do the Vietnamese still see the Americans as benefactors? Or have they been so degraded that they must beg food from their murderers? And how do these Americans deal with and think about the Vietnamese when they recall what they have just finished doing?[25]

We are left to imagine most of the answers for ourselves. However, an add-on story indicates the implicit meaning of the event. An old woman who survived the massacre and is now "in a government corral" says, "Before, Americans always brought us medicine and candy for the children"; now she knows she cannot trust them.[26] Apparently the massacre has ruined our efforts to "win the hearts and minds" of these people; and to the extent that it appears to be a symptomatic rather than an eccentric act, it discredits the whole counterinsurgency mission.

The coverage of *Life* and other journalistic media has been criticized for representing an aberrant episode as typical of American action in Vietnam. Clearly, *Life*'s coverage was only partly "objective." Its organizing principle was the desire to represent the "truth" by deploying all the resources of "art," especially those that allow a reader to experience a subjective illusion of vicarious participation in the emotions of the event. But the validity of the story's artistic "truth" was attested (and delimited) by counterinsurgency experts like Vann and Corson, who recognized that the Mylai massacre was *both* aberrant and typical: aberrant, in that it was rare for that many American troops to massacre so many civilians "point blank," in one time and place; but typical, in that "the normal pattern" of the war of attrition simply spread the same kind of violence "over a larger area [and] a longer period of time."[27] The power of Mylai as symbol derived not only from the cleverness with which the media framed and the antiwar movement exploited the tale but from its appropriateness as a metaphor for what had gone wrong with the war. It resonated not only with the sympathies and sentiments of civilians but with the feelings of normally compassionate officers and soldiers, who were haunted by the killing of civilians and especially children that was a consequence of the big unit war—no matter how unintended or inescapable such killings might have been.[28]

Mylai turned on its head one of the primary symbolic rationales by which the administration had justified the war and its manner of prosecuting it. In his April 1965 address at Johns Hopkins, President

Johnson had justified escalation by identifying the enemy as perpetrators of a savage war "of unparalleled brutality" in which

> simple farmers are the targets of assassination and kidnapping. Women and children are strangled in the night. . . . And helpless villages are ravaged by sneak attacks.[29]

After Mylai, the logic of the captivity/rescue myth required us to identify *ourselves* as the Indians, and by that logic our mission now became one of rescuing Vietnam from "us," or (better) of rescuing us from ourselves, by finding a "cure" for the "American madness" or by withdrawing from the war, and so putting temptation away. In the light of Mylai, this mission of self-rescue began to seem more vital than the original mission of saving the South Vietnamese from a VC/NVA bloodbath.[30]

The same symbolism that had been invoked to engage our protective sympathies on behalf of helpless Vietnamese "women, children, babies" was now transformed into an antiwar iconography. The shift of perspective was described by Hugh Sidey, in a column titled "In the Shadow of Mylai," published in *Life* on December 12, 1969. Sidey describes his changing reactions to a poster that had been carried for months by a Quaker protester named Champney:

> [The poster showed a] tiny child . . . with huge, soulful eyes, scared but trusting. It is an appealing picture. It always brought an inner tug but it also raised a mild resentment against Champney for "using" the kids. . . . All that changed last week when the full weight of the Mylai massacre settled on the city. There were not so many who denounced him. More people took his leaflets. Others looked at the child's picture . . . and then hurriedly glanced away. In microcosm, here on a Washington sidewalk, one could see played out America's shocked reaction to Mylai . . . [a search for the] common things in American life which are hopeful and durable and have not been tainted by the Vietnam war.[31]

But the next issue of *Life* reminded readers that—as the Violence Commission had been telling them for a year now—such actions were not at all outside "the national experience." The cover showed the face of Charles Manson, the cult leader whose followers had just been arrested for the ritual butchery of Sharon Tate and her house guests. The story of "The Monstrous Manson 'Family' " testified to the reality of American monsters whose individual pathology had been given a peculiar shape and direction and empowered by the peculiar conditions of American life. Elsewhere in the same issue, *Life* reprinted forty-eight letters from readers responding to the Mylai massacre.

Although there was some division of opinion among the writers, two-thirds of them cite Mylai as proof that the war is "wrong" and is either cause or symptom of a potential for madness, moral corruption, and cruelty in American life.[32] Most blame the government, public "apathy," and the officers in command; only one blames the soldiers themselves ("God damn them!"). Five of the letters make explicit comparisons between Mylai and Nazi atrocities. Another group invokes some of the critiques of American culture and politics that had been voiced for years by the New Left and critics of the war and had been given systematic expression in the presidential commissions on civil disorder and violence. One blames the massacre on "militaristic" tendencies in American culture; another links it with urban violence; and three blame it on "racism." A Chicago businessman writes:

> We have a thousand Mylais every day right here in America. I am talking about the brutalization of individuals in the everyday life of urban communities. . . . We accept killing, the killing of civilians in Vietnam and the killing here in Chicago of the head of the Black Panthers, as . . . a way of life.

A Native American connects the massacre to the primal race-war of American history: "history repeats itself and this is not the first time that American soldiers have murdered women and children . . . how about Wounded Knee[?]"[33]

Many of the letter-writers emphasize the sense of horror they feel at the inversion of their normative expectations about the behavior of American troops: Americans are supposed to protect women and children, not murder them. An Illinois woman says:

> Several years ago I sent a letter to you . . . in which I stated, "thank God for American soldiers that are fighting to end such agony." I had reference to a picture of a Vietnamese woman and her dying baby. Oh, dear God, how things change.

An ex-Marine uses the same symbolism to describe the effect of the massacre on his pride in military service: "I took the massacre as one would the death of his child." In this context, the letter, which flatly says, "My child . . . is much more precious to me (and should be to *every* fellow American) than the life of any enemy, no matter what the age or condition," appears statistically aberrant and sounds morally insensitive.

The letters reprinted in *Life* were not necessarily an accurate reflection of the range and character of public opinion. They should be seen as a collage selected and composed by the editors to reflect their reading of public opinion and (consciously or unconsciously) their sense of what it ought to be. Although the letters disagree on the specific charges they levy, they represent a consensus view that the war has now become a source of insoluble, deeply troubling, perhaps "maddening" moral and emotional dilemmas, that it produces a sense of moral taint or disease, makes patriotism seem morally obtuse, and vindicates the heaviest accusations levied by the left against our national culture.

Mylai thus became the central trope of the "counter-myth" through which Americans expressed their growing disillusionment and disgust with the myth/ideology of counterinsurgency. But it is vital to note that this counter-myth merely reproduced, in inverted form, the moral/political symbolism of the original myth. The appeal of the counter-myth hinges on a misrepresentation of Mylai's politics that exactly reproduces—albeit with an *opposite* political intention—the original fallacy of counterinsurgency in Vietnam, which was to treat indigenous political culture as a nullity. The villagers are represented as innocent victims who naively trusted Americans and have now been thoroughly disillusioned and alienated by a gratuitous atrocity. Mylai was in fact a Vietminh/Vietcong village, in a region that had neither been friendly to the Saigon regime nor had looked to Americans as liberators. From a moral or legal perspective, the politics of the village did not justify or extenuate the massacre; but from the standpoint of movie-based public myth, the effective representation of an American atrocity required that the victims by *entirely* innocent—void of evil intent as well as guiltless of hostile action.

In effect, the Mylai counter-myth follows the scenario of the old "Cult of the Indian": the standard Western mythology of captivities, rescues, and regenerative violence is reproduced, with the "normal" racial referents reversed, so that the Whites are savages and the Indians are pure and hapless victims. In 1970–71 the logic of this counter-myth would lead to the re-emergence of a new "Cult of the Indian," represented in movie-mythology by films like *Little Big Man* and *Soldier Blue* (1970), which invoke parallels between Mylai and the Washita and Sand Creek massacres of Indians by Whites. However, this "cult" reflected a more profound revulsion against the normative ideology than its predecessor. At least since 1966, Native Americans and their culture had become important symbols of rebellion in the so-called "counter-culture" of college-age White Americans. The connection had been recognized (and propagated) by the mass media since the Woodstock festival in the summer of 1969, and cultural critics like Leslie Fiedler had noted the phenomenon as early as 1967–68. This counter-myth has its own internal contradictions and destructive fallacies. Carried to its logical extreme, it erases not only the real politics of the Mylai peasant but the politics of the North as well, suggesting that to recover one's proper role in the myth of regenerative violence we must actually or implicitly identify with the enemy and see him as an embodiment of those virtues we once claimed as our own. As an imaginative response to a Western movie, this sort of reaction can open up new perspectives on cultural values and past events. But in the real world of American politics, it produced aberrant and extreme forms of protest—uncritical acceptance of Hanoi's politics and its version of the war; and identification with, or participation in, "guerrilla warfare" or terrorism within the United States—which ultimately discredited the counter-myth and its proponents.

However, the brief flowering and sudden collapse of the Cult of the Indian counter-myth developed in response to the crisis of cognitive dissonance that characterized our culture's response to the Mylai massacre. The public's sense of that crisis was mythographically expressed in a group of Mexico Westerns which had been developed in the wake of the Tet Offensive. Since they were released *before* the Mylai revelations, they were current in American movie-houses while the news of Mylai was being assimilated.[34]

The Demoralization of the Western: Peckinpah's The Wild Bunch *(1969)*

The three big Mexico Westerns released in 1969 express (in their different ways) the cognitive dissonance that afflicted contemporary ideology and develop responses (of a kind) to the attendant demoralization of American politics. Two of them—George Roy Hill's *Butch Cassidy and the Sundance Kid* and Peckinpah's *The Wild Bunch*—are among the most successful movies ever made. Even the least successful of the three, Fox's *The Undefeated*, was a major Hollywood event—an epic Western featuring a cast headed by John Wayne and Rock Hudson and including sports celebrities (L.A. Rams quarterback Roman Gabriel and defensive end Merlin Olsen). Each film builds directly on the themes, characters, and conventions developed in earlier Mexico Westerns: Mexican bandit/revolutionaries and military tyrants, gringo gunfighters and hard-bitten soldiers, German aristocrat-advisers and American railroad barons. Like such predecessors as *Major Dundee* and *The Professionals*, these films represent the adventure of "American gunfighters in Mexico" as a mixture of the heroic and the morally dubious. But the negative aspects of the adventure are no longer merely suggested as one perspective on the action. They now form the center of the narrative and suggest an implicit rejection of the ideological projects that motivated counterinsurgency.

The gentlest of critiques is offered in *Butch Cassidy and the Sundance Kid* (released in October 1969), a comic take on the "last of the outlaws" theme. The action playfully recapitulates and subverts the conventions of the *Jesse James* movie—the train-robbing and escape-by-water, the good woman who sets limits to outlawry—until the moment when the outlaws discover that their frontier has closed, and the imaginative Cassidy (Paul Newman) decides to start over again on a new frontier in Latin America. Though the locale is Bolivia, the situation of the *bandidos yanquis* is the same as that of the gunfighters in Mexico: they can triumph at their trade because as Americans they are far more ruthless and expert with weapons than the *peons* and *rurales* who are their prey and pursuers. But Butch and Sundance never consider playing the "counterinsurgency" role. They are professional robbers, in the game for fun and profit. But their success as despoilers of the natives isolates them among a frightened but hostile population. In the end they will be destroyed by a whole regiment of regular Bolivian cavalry—shot down, like Zapata, by riflemen firing into the plaza. The number of *latinos* required to kill them testifies to their superiority as Anglo warriors; yet in the end it is the numbers and solidarity of the natives that destroy them.[35]

Butch Cassidy begins as comedy and ends as comic tragedy. *The Undefeated* reverses the process, through a narrative whose complications reflect the difficulty of imagining a solution (symbolic or practical) to the problem of Vietnam. In the aftermath of the Civil War a war-weary Union colonel (John Wayne) and a dispossessed Southern planter (Rock Hudson) cross the border into Mexico at the invitation of Maximilian and in despite of the Juaristas. The colonel is tired of "causes" and just wants to sell horses to the highest bidder; the Southerner is seeking to revive the paternal order of his plantation in Mexico and has brought his family, the survivors of his regiment, and all of his *White* retainers to establish a colony. With *Vera Cruz* and *The Magnificent Seven* as precedent, we expect a story in which both of our heroes will be converted to the Juarista cause, the colonel abandoning mercenary values for the sake of principle and the Confederate perhaps recognizing the similarity between the Juarista cause and that of the South. Both expectations are disappointed. In the end, Yankee and Confederate discover that both sides of the Mexican Revolution are "un-American" and are willing to use terrorism against women and children to further their ends. The only rational response is for our heroes to abandon foreign adventures and return to the States, where they can get involved in politics and work effectively for reform. Thus, despite Wayne's presence, the film has a distinctly antiwar inflection.[36]

Sam Peckinpah's *The Wild Bunch* is the most complex, controversial, and arguably the most popular of these films. Its critical reception was remarkable for the intense partisanship it aroused. Some saw it as a masterpiece of one kind or another, serious in its ambitions and innovative in its form, a critical allegorization of American political culture; others saw it as a symptom of the American "madness," an exploitative exercise in excessive, inadequately motivated, technologically augmented and estheticized violence.[37]

Peckinpah did make deliberate and sensational use of new special-effects technology to render as literally as possible the effects of bullets on human bodies; and in editing he mixed slow and normal motion, giving the most violent scenes a balletic quality. But these techniques serve a representative as well as a sensational or esthetic function. The "exaggerated" display of bloodshed is in fact a truer representation of the real effects of violence than the conventional and sanitized "clutch your chest and fall" of the Hollywood western and combat film. The mix of slow and regular motion allows the audience to experience the subjective distortion of time experienced by those engaged in violent action—for example, the "stroboscopic" or stop-time images in which Haeberle perceived the killing of the wounded child at Mylai.

Peckinpah's representation of violence owes a good deal to the stylized formal technique of the "spaghetti Western," but his borrowings are never simple imitations. His awareness of generic form, and his self-consciousness in using it, had been displayed in all his previous productions. From the beginning of his career as a director, Peckinpah was disposed to develop new movies as implicit commentaries on the canonical films of the genre tradition. *Deadly Companions* was a dark and ironic reworking of Ford's *Stagecoach*; *Ride the High Country* was as much a homage to old Westerns as to the Old West; *Major Dundee* is in continual dialogue with Ford's cavalry films. Peckinpah had also made the Mexico Western his own field of specialization. *The Wild Bunch* was his third film in this subgenre, following *Major Dundee* and his screenplay for *Villa Rides*, and he had a highly sophisticated understanding of the implicit connection between Mexico Westerns and the war in Vietnam.[38] As a result, *The Wild Bunch* is the *Moby-Dick* of Westerns: a sprawling epic whose powerful poetic and ideological resonance derives from its deliberate combination of strong adventure-narrative with compendious reference to history and the traditions of American mythology—particularly those of the Western. Peckinpah's critique of American myth-ideology takes the form of a counter-myth whose structures mirror and expose the structure of the original. *The Wild Bunch* unites the themes and conventions of the Mexico Western and the Cult of the Outlaw in a single story, thus bringing together the populist mythology of the outlaw story, its concern with the problem of domestic justice, and the counterinsurgency mystique of the gunfighters-in-Mexico, which reflects on America's role in world affairs.[39]

Peckinpah's approach to narrative is essentially poetic, working through implication, allusion, suggestion, and metaphor. We can see how his method works by looking closely at the opening sequences of the film, beginning with the credits. Here Peckinpah establishes his main themes and defines the verbal and pictorial icons that constitute the "language" of his film.

The action begins with the titles, which are displayed over the Bunch's ride through the railroad yards into the town of Starbuck, where they intend to rob the railroad office. An ominous bass drone, punctuated by the *frisson* of a military snare drum, creates a mood of tension. Although the titles identify the Wild Bunch, the riders are not dressed as outlaws but in the khaki uniforms and campaign hats of the U.S. Cavalry, ca. 1914–15. As each credit appears, the image freezes and abstracts to black-and-white. The music emphasizes the break with the "normal" world of color by shifting abruptly to a "chilly," suspended phrase played by strings. Faces in these freeze-frames appear more skull-like and sinister than the colored originals, suggesting a view into some deathly substructure of the normal world.[40]

As the Bunch ride in they pass a circle of children, smiling and giggling, playing with something next to the tracks—an image of innocence, until the freeze-frame abstracts them. The group includes boys and girls, Mexicans and Anglos, an albino whose whiteness emphasizes the importance of skin color as a metaphor of difference;

their expressions are a mixture of slyness, glee, excitement, watchfulness, dreamy indifference. As the Bunch approach, they see the game that is concealed by the circle of "innocents:" a pen of sticks in which the children have set two large white scorpions to battle with a colony of red ants. This image anticipates the violence that is about to occur and prophesies the Wild Bunch's last stand. It is also a visualization of the theory of history and human action on which both standard myth and counter-myth are based. The children serve as an image of ourselves, an audience of "innocent spectators" whose expectation of violence can be construed as consent in or even desire for murderous entertainment.[41]

Following this disconcerting vision of an amoral and disordered universe, we are introduced to three versions of social order: a "normal" civilian or Christian order; the order of law represented by the posse that waits in ambush; and the order of the Bunch, which represents a wild alternative to the two civilized options. The initial images suggest that the two civilized orders are flawed and that the Bunch may offer a better model of human solidarity.

The Bunch enter Starbuck's main street, passing a meeting of the Temperance Union. We hear the preacher (Dub Taylor) ranting against the evils of strong drink and recognize him as a pious flannelmouth who knows nothing of real evil. The Bunch dismount and walk toward the railroad office, in good "platoon" formation, recognizing, as they pass, other members of the gang wearing long linen dusters, like the James Gang in the Northfield sequence of *Jesse James*. One of the Bunch jostles an old lady, who drops her package: Pike Bishop (William Holden), the "officer" commanding this squad, courteously picks it up and offers an arm to help the lady cross the street. This is a visual joke: in their khakis and campaign hats, helping an old woman across the street, the Bunch look like Boy Scouts. But the joke also invokes a traditional expectation about heroic outlaws: that they are actually Robin Hoods who live by a Boy Scout code of chivalry that is nobler than mere obedience to civil codes of law. The suggestion that the Bunch are "the good guys" is emphasized in the next shot: a cut to a rooftop overlooking the scene where the posse has gathered to ambush the Bunch. A few images identify the posse as an undisciplined rabble of murderous rednecks, whose costumes combine elements associated with mountain men, tramps, and "hippies."

As we enter the station with the Bunch we hear the stationmaster bawling out a clerk: "I don't care what you meant to do, it's what you *did* do that I don't like." The Bunch enters in a series of shots that suggests the forward roll of waves, culminating in Pike's slamming the stationmaster against the wall and a close-up of his face saying "If they move—*kill 'em*!"—followed by a final freeze-frame behind Peckinpah's own directorial credit, which identifies him with Pike.

To this point Peckinpah has suggested that we see the Bunch as the embodiment of all the heroic alternatives to a fallen civilization that the Western has celebrated: the cavalry troop, the social bandit gang, the chivalric rescuer of women. Even Pike's mistreatment of the stationmaster can be taken as the rebuke of a petty tyrant. But the stationmaster's words suggest that a gap may exist between what you mean to do and the consequences your actions entail; and Pike's command, if taken literally, must include the helpless women and boyish clerks who are also in the room, an act that would violate the most fundamental taboo of the Western.

The action that follows shows that such a massacre is logically entailed by the kind of heroism (soldierly, outlaw/gunfighterly) that Pike embodies. As the three orders converge in front of the bank, one of the Bunch observes the posse on the roof just as the Temperance Union begins its parade down Main Street. A series of shots in the bank and on the roof informs us that the organizer of the posse—a railroad official named Harrington, whose business suit and watch chain mark him as a fat cat—has not warned the townspeople of the ambush for fear they would spoil the plot by blabbing. Harrington has a Nixonian obsession with "internal security," and Peckinpah is about to reveal the cost of that obsession. Harrington's mercilessness is within the predictable range of behavior for Western-movie railroad barons—Barshee and J. W. Grant are salient examples. But in past outlaw Westerns, the unprincipled ruthlessness of the railroad man was usually offset by the populist chivalry of the outlaws. Here the dialogue in the bank immediately undoes this expectation: Pike makes plain his intention to use the Temperance parade to cover his retreat.

It is still possible to imagine that the escape will pass off bloodlessly, that the posse will refrain from shooting at the Bunch while there are civilians in the way, and that the Bunch will simply back out of town behind that cover. But Peckinpah uses sight and sound to prepare us for an outbreak of violent madness that will overwhelm the taboos and rationales on which the expectation or hope of bloodless escape is based. The parade approaches, the band playing "Shall We Gather at the River." This hymn has long been identified with Ford's

Westerns, where it always serves as the leitmotif of the sanctified community. The music is overlaid by a gradually rising bass hum, a mindless drone overwhelming the ordered sound, and then by a sound like an accelerating heartbeat. The screen gives us a closeup of one of the bounty-hunters whose lunatic excitement is evidently mounting toward an eruption in which the normal restraints of Western shoot-outs will not hold. But his excitement is also a sardonically distorted mirroring of the excitement the audience itself is supposed to be experiencing at this point.

What ensues is a massacre in which the Bunch and the posse blaze away at each other, heedless at first of the citizens through whose bodies they shoot. Then some of the Bunch grab women to use as shields, and the posse shoots down women, bandits, and all. The violence done to bodies by the bullets is treated explicitly. Coupled with the breaking of the taboo against the killing of women, the images take on a character that some critics have found "pornographic." Part of our excitement and terror comes from realizing that what is normally and traditionally concealed will at last be explicitly displayed. This outburst of total mayhem relieves the tension of anticipation that Peckinpah has so carefully created, but our experience of that "relief" creates another kind of tension that will persist throughout the film: the tension that arises from our realization that the normal rules of genre and myth will not necessarily apply. Since Peckinpah does not offer, within the film, an explicit denunciation of this kind of violence, the possibility is left open that the makers of this film will not scruple to show us forbidden actions and ideas, and that the heroes we will be asked to identify with may actually be monsters. The audience is thus engaged with an esthetic equivalent of the ethical problem of violence: How much of this sort of thing are we willing to look at? Is looking somehow a form of "consent"? And if we are willing to let "events" proceed under these conditions (that is, if we stay for the rest of the film), do we have a "good" motive for doing so? To paraphrase Michael Herr: Are we willing to take responsibility for "what we see" and for the curiosity—a form of wish or desire to see the unspeakable—that has brought us to this scene?[42]

Peckinpah concludes the sequence with a reprise of the "child's play" image from the opening credits. We see that the children in the railroad yard have piled burning grass over the slaughter of ants and scorpions; and through the ashes left by the burning, and the suggestion of an amoral apocalypse, the aftermath of the street battle comes back into view. In this street scene Peckinpah extends his violation of conventional limits by flashing images of the ugliness, horror, loss, and misery that "heroism" leaves in its wake. But even as he invokes the conventional symbolism of victimization, he undercuts it. While some children are traumatized, others are playing at bandits-and-bounty-hunters, going *bang!* with finger-pistols at bloody corpses. Their action is mirrored in the action of the posse, men with the mental development of feral children, who descend like vultures to crow and pick over the dead (civilian and bandit), stealing rings, boots, and gold teeth, and squabbling and defaming each other in schoolyard language. Child and killer mirror each other. The possibility arises that the horror of violence is latent in our character (as the report of the Violence Commission seemed to suggest). This bloody souvenir-hunting by the posse might also have reminded a contemporary audience of the recent uproar over the taking of ears from dead Vietnamese by soldiers verifying their body counts or acquiring souvenirs of victory. The street battle is set up in ways that suggest a similarity to the urban battles of Tet, and of Detroit and Newark, in which the forces who (in Harrington's words) "represent the law" destroy an entire community to kill the outlaws/snipers/guerrillas who hide among the citizens.

The narrative that develops out of this vision of amoral apocalpyse explores the possibility of finding or creating a humane and moral answer to the problem of a world governed by unrestrained greed and force. The citizens and the posse embody the failure of traditional American ideology. The citizens are pathetic, but their utter haplessness suggests that theirs is not a moral order that can thrive in a ruthless world. The posse "represent[s] the law" but consists of mercenaries hired by a railroad man who obviously values his company's assets more than human life. The posse is led by Deke Thornton, a former member of the Wild Bunch and Pike's oldest friend, who is blackmailed by Harrington into becoming a "Judas goat." The "gutter trash" who follow him are compelled by their own debts to the railroad, and Harrington insures their "loyalty" to the mission by offering a bounty for Thornton himself if he should show signs of softness. Thus the society that represents the law is one in which greed, force, and mutual suspicion are the only binding ties.

As the Bunch flee across the border into Mexico, we are introduced to its members and its special form of organization. In some respects the Bunch is a business enterprise, like the railroad, whose members cooperate to further their self-interest. But other values weigh heavily (if not always equally) with money in their society. The Bunch is like an all-male family, with Pike as patriarch and Dutch Engstrom (Ernest Borgnine) as his "wife." Dutch is Pike's primary helpmeet who continually reminds headstrong father and rebellious "sons" of their common values and mutual obligations. But "family" is only a metaphor for the special and (implicitly) superior order of the Bunch. "Family feeling" as such is devalued by its embodiment in the Gorch brothers (Ben Johnson and Warren Oates), who are the greediest and most selfish members of the Bunch. Like the "citizens" of Ford's stagecoach community, the Bunch is composed of radically different character-types whose solidarity is based on functional necessity: the need to survive the rigors of a journey, a quest, and/or the hardships of their particular line of work. They are also bound by their mutual enjoyment of the work they do and by professional pride in how expertly they do it. Following the suggestion implicit in their military costumes, we can see that they are held together by "unit pride."

A different kind of social alternative is represented by Angel (Jaime Sanchez), a Mexican youth newly recruited to the Bunch. Angel's loyalties are "tribal" or ethnic, a somewhat larger form of the familial bond that unites the Gorches. In the immediate aftermath of the robbery, Angel and the Gorches nearly kill each other, the Gorches driven by selfishness, Angel by the wounded pride of a Mexican too often bullied by *gringos*. They are prevented from doing so by Pike, who reminds them that if they divide against each other then everything will fall apart and they will become mere "animals." But once they cross into Mexico, the "tribal" alternative (which Angel abandons to remain in the Bunch) emerges more clearly as a standard against which the Bunch's form of solidarity can be measured.

The tribal order is embodied in Angel's village, a place of green trees and pools of water in the midst of a desert, a tribal utopia of innocent and kindly natives ruled by a wise and dignified elder. Peckinpah uses imagery that is as old as the writings of the Elizabethan colonizers, who discovered the natives to be ". . . voyd of guile . . . such as live after the maner of the Golden Age." But it also invokes the iconography of the Western (particularly the "Cult of the Indian"), and of Huston's *Treasure of the Sierra Madre*.[43] This idyllic spot and these innocent people have been ravaged and raped by the forces of General Mapache, a despot who controls the province for Huerta. The conventions of the Mexico Western suggest that our heroes must, sooner or later, aid people like these against the tyrant. But the Bunch at first acts pragmatically and sets out for Mapache's capital of Agua Verde to see if they can sell him their extra horses.

Mapache's city fully realizes the system of order that Harrington's posse represents in potential: a society ruled by force and money in which the strong lord it over the weak, taking the best of food, drink, and women. Mapache (Emilio Fernandez) is a dictator whose brutality is visualized in terms of both bad-Indian and fascist stereotypes. His name suggests "Apache," and Fernandez's appearance is distinctly "Indian" (his nickname is "Indio"), with suggestions of the Oriental despot as well. His uniform is "fascist," and his adviser is a uniformed Prussian aristocrat (and his snobbish adjutant). The Prussian's presence is nominally "historical": German agents and military men assisted various parties in the Mexican Revolution with a view to provoking border troubles that might distract the Americans from intervening in Europe. The Teutonic adviser has a Western-movie source in the Austrian officer who serves Maximilian in *Vera Cruz*; but his presence inevitably suggests a connection with the more recent form of German enmity. Thus Mapache's regime combines in a single structure evil elements drawn from the canons of the Indian-war movie, the combat film, and the Juarez-Maximilian and Villa/Zapata Mexico film.

Peckinpah complicates our response to Mapache by showing him as a brave man admired by the women and young men of his city in a way that mirrors the relationship of the children and the old man of Angel's village, and of Pike and the younger outlaws. Although we understand that Villa/the village are morally preferable to Mapache/Agua Verde, Peckinpah insists that we appreciate the human lives and affiliations on both sides. He represents the Revolution as a genuine "civil war" in which a common thread of cultural and human identity links the *people* on both sides. Although no excuse is offered for Mapache, his inhumanity is presented as a twisted (but predictable) development of a human conflict prosecuted without mercy. Mapache's evil consists in the cruelty with which he (and his people) treat all those who are *not* members of his "tribe"; but if we imagine the "redemption" of Mexico as requiring the wiping-out of Mapache's "village," then we are simply adopting Mapache's "evil" as our own. The logical solution for the problem is for the Bunch to somehow "decapitate" Agua Verde by a "surgical strike" that eliminates Mapache himself. This kind of solution was an essential element of the traditional Western (*Dodge City*, *Shane*), in which the hero triumphs over an evil order by selectively out-shooting its leader (and his immediate cohorts).

The idea of establishing a just society by the isolation and careful removal of a relatively small class of evil men is also deeply rooted in the ideological traditions of American liberalism. We see versions of the scenario in the anti-Tory propaganda of the Revolution, the Free Soil/Republican attack on the "Slave Power," the Populist diatribes against "Jewish" bankers. Twain captures the pattern of thought in *Connecticut Yankee* when his hero attempts to revolutionize feudal England by the use of a technological weapon that will selectively exterminate the aristocracy. But, as Twain suggests, this scenario of revolution fails to achieve the fundamental change it aims at, because it derives from an inadequate understanding of the systematic character of social organization, the complexity of class relations, and the ways in which "irrational" factors of culture obscure the supposedly clear lines of economic and political difference. Because the stakes in such social conflicts are so high, the initial intention to use "surgically" focused or limited violence gives way to a pattern of escalations whose logic points toward general slaughter or the "war of extermination." This is the logic we have seen at work in the Vietnam War, in the movement from the selective and limited violence of counterinsurgency to the comprehensive mayhem of the war of attrition.[44] In conceiving the conclusion of *The Wild Bunch*, Peckinpah would bring together the emotional appeal of the wishful "decapitation" scenario and the war-born expectation of general slaughter.

Given the conventions of the genre, we can guess that the Wild Bunch will eventually turn against Mapache, and that when they do the carnage will be considerable (since the climax will probably have to outdo the opening). What is in doubt is how their conversion will come about, and what motives and meanings will determine it. The script invokes a series of conventional myth/ideological formulas, which at first seem to offer a way for the Bunch to resolve the conflicts of value and allegiance that disturb them. But each formula is ultimately discredited as a way out of the impasse.

At first it seems that their conversion will parallel Ben Trane's in *Vera Cruz*, moving from cynical self-interest to revolutionary commitment through the achievement of sympathy with the people's cause. Like Trane and Erin, the Bunch first sign on with the dictator, who hires them to raid an American arms train and steal the equipment that will allow him to resist Villa's hitherto successful campaign. As in *The Magnificent Seven* and *Vera Cruz*, the Third World regime cannot achieve any complex or difficult goal without the aid of American mercenaries and professionals. But the situation of the Wild Bunch makes a problem of the usual counterinsurgency scenario. First, their mission is directed against the railroad (capitalism) and the army of the United States—a government with which they "share very few sympathies." This suggests that the Bunch be identified with movie-populism, or perhaps with some violent element of the antiwar "left." But from the Mexico Western perspective the Americans are aiding the wrong side. Like the Special Forces in 1960–65, the Bunch are outlaws or revolutionaries in style and perhaps sentiment, but in function they are agents of despotism.

The inadequacy of mercenary values—and by analogy, of American capitalism—as a solution to the problem of the Revolution is articulated in the sweat-bath scene when Pike tells Angel that he can solve his village's problem by using his share of Mapache's gold to move the villagers a thousand miles away and buy them a ranch. The values the village revolution defends are to be translated into cash values, which purchase safety by providing economic and physical mobility. Pike's is a classically liberal solution, akin to the peace program offered by President Johnson in his Johns Hopkins address of April 1965, in which the North Vietnamese and VC were to give over their revolution in exchange for a massive program of American economic aid.[45] Pike's solution is impractical, capable of purchasing only a temporary safety for a few villagers but incapable of resolving the nationwide problems that have produced Villa and Mapache. But Angel rejects Pike's idea even as a solution to the problem of one village: "this is *their* land," their bond to it is not translatable into a cash equivalent, and the only solution that can satisfy them is one that gives them their rights on the land they call theirs. To the alienated *gringos*, the village seems a pastoral utopia to which they can escape from the world of mercenary violence; but the villagers have outgrown whatever pastoral innocence they may have had, and their "primitive" mystique of the soil has now merged with their understanding of and affiliation with the ideology of the Revolution. Their love of the land is a primitive form of the nationalist sentiment that insists on independence when colonial subjection might be more profitable, and their tribal/familial politics is now seen as a form of that just order which must be defended from Mapache and extended to the nation as a whole.

So the Wild Bunch cannot happily resolve the problem of the village, or of their own relation to despotic power, by staying in character as mercenaries. The gunfighter Western offers two conventional bases for the transformation of mercenaries into chivalric heroes: the reawakening of populist ideals beneath the mercenary surface through the establishment of a bond of sympathy with the oppressed farmers (*Jesse James, Vera Cruz, The Magnificent Seven*), and the love of a woman whose values and ties to the oppressed awaken the gunfighter's desire for moral redemption (*Shane, The Professionals*).

Although the Wild Bunch are professional outlaws, and in that sense are more like *The Gunfighter* than like *Jesse James*, the ideology of the populist outlaw is an important constituent of the code that holds them together. The most articulate spokesman for populist values is Dutch, who is also Pike's closest friend and the only member of the Bunch whose code of group loyalty matches Pike's own. Dutch asserts the populist creed at two key moments in the narrative, each time with a memorable slogan. One of them is delivered at the Bunch's first view of Mapache enthroned in the plaza of Agua Verde, when Dutch asserts his sympathy with the cause of the villagers against Mapache, whom he condemns as a murderer and a thief. When Pike jokingly suggests that they are thieves too, Dutch angrily replies, "We don't *hang* nobody!" He then identifies with the Revolution by expressing the hope that one day these people will send Mapache and his kind packing, to which Angel fervently responds, "We will."

The distinction between killing done in the name and style of official power and the "wild" killing done by the Bunch is a crucial one in the myth/ideology of the Western. It echoes the traditional populist distinction between the corrupt legalism of railroads/corporations and the just violence of the outlaw—a theme represented here by an exchange between Harrington and Thornton in which the ex-outlaw scorns the railroad man for hiring his killings with the law's license while keeping his own hands clean. Violence that can be purchased by the wealthy is oppressive; violence that proceeds freely (and in a sense disinterestedly) as a response to injustice is redemptive.

In an outlaw/gunfighter Western the romantic symbolism vested in the redemptive woman reinforces (and sometimes substitutes for) the love of justice and democracy as a guide to the *redemptive* use of violence. The "evil" order is identified by its corporate character, its deliberate assault on the family, and/or its victimization of the redemptive woman. And once the evil order is so identified, the conventional genre-values of "populism" and "true love" authorize the hero to use whatever degree of violence might be necessary to punish and destroy the evil. But in *The Wild Bunch* the linked motives of populist sympathy and redemptive love are first disconnected, then discredited; as a result, the heroes' license to kill is called into question.

The vision of woman as redemptive "Virgin" is first identified with Angel, whose beloved Teresa has left the village to become the whore of Mapache. The village patriarch mocks Angel's romanticism and the view of women it embodies. Women are not angels, he says, but human beings no less susceptible to desire and its corruptions than men. Although Pike joins the Old Man in laughing at Angel's "innocence," Pike himself lives by an equally romantic set of illusions. A flashback tells us of Pike's passionate affair with a Mexican woman who is murdered by her vengeful husband in an attack that leaves Pike's leg scarred and half-crippled. Pike's nostalgia and grief for this loss suggest a latent capacity for redemption through romantic love for a Mexican woman, real or (as with Rico in *The Professionals*) remembered. Yet the redemptive potential of romance is undermined almost as soon as it is articulated. When Angel sees Teresa sitting on Mapache's lap, he screams "*Puta!*," pulls his gun, and shoots her through the heart, spattering Mapache and his officers with her blood. Peckinpah thus visualizes the insane "logic" of the Western's code of romantic love that licenses Angel's instantaneous movement from worship to murder: if women are not virgins, objects worthy of blind worship and rescue, then they must be whores, legitimate objects of violence. The mythic idealization of woman is thus shown to imply a double rationale for murder: murder of the evil man who assaults the "virgin," and murder of the woman herself if she is revealed to be a "whore." Both positions deny that human reality articulated by the village elder, whose negative judgment of Teresa still recognizes her humanity and scoffs at romantic revenge as an appropriate response. But like the opening massacre, this revelation of the potential for evil inherent in the values of the Western hero is followed by scenes that partially restore our belief in the Bunch's capacity for goodness and suggest that they may yet find in one or another of their codes—self-interest, comradeship, populism, or romanticism—a basis for heroic action.

Individual members of the Bunch differ in their adherence to the ideologies of self-interest, populist sympathy, family values, or romantic love. But below these is another ideology that is in effect their "true" ideology, since it is the one they will finally die to vindicate: the inarticulable code of honor, loyalty, and group identification that allows men of such different qualities to maintain their solidarity.

But this ideology can barely be abstracted from the cinematic flow of images and genre reminiscences that express it. The primary signs or symbols of that ideology are the gestures of "male bonding" through which the members of the Bunch resolve the tensions that divide them: sharing whiskey from the same bottle; and sharing laughter, with which they mock the forces against them and dismiss (without addressing) the hostilities and contradictions that divide them. Their laughter is identified as the laughter of men and of victors. Women and children are excluded, and the laughter is enjoyed at the expense of "civilians" in general and the opponents they best in particular. Hence it is a sign not only of the Bunch's solidarity but of its superiority.

But though we recognize the gestures that define and give value to their solidarity, it is not clear just what the actual content of their ideology is, or ought to be. They are defined primarily by what they are not: soldiers, bounty-hunters, or revolutionaries. Neither are they simply thieves. We know what they stand against, but what do they stand for? The question is posed just before the climax by Dutch, the Bunch's "chief ideologist," who condemns Thornton's betrayal of the Bunch. Pike apologizes for his oldest friend by invoking one of the Bunch's (and the Western movie's) standard shibboleths: "He gave his word." Dutch responds furiously: How can you give your word "to a *railroad*!" The railroad, genre convention tells us, is the antithesis of both family and Bunch values, a faceless corporation, the mercenary spirit incarnate, the symbol of all that is wrong with modern civilization, the genre's traditional symbol of the oppressor. "It ain't giving your word" that matters, says Dutch, "it's who you give it *to*!"

To this Pike has no answer. It has now become clear that the members of the Bunch can no longer find any open space—any "frontier"—in which to maneuver and escape the contradictions (ideological and tactical) in which they have become enmeshed. History (in the form of politics) has closed in around them. Nor does their code offer guidelines to "heroic" (that is, effective and morally sound) action. The gestural formulas by which they have lived—"giving your word," making a gesture of sympathy to the revolution by allowing Angel to give his people a box of the stolen rifles—no longer make sense. The world now consists almost entirely of contested ground divided unequally between Harrington, Mapache, and the Revolution. In such circumstances to give your word to the wrong party may destroy you, or make you complicit in an evil you have resisted all your life ("We don't *hang* nobody!"). And this is precisely what Pike has done in giving his word to both Mapache and Angel. Angel's gift of rifles to the rebels is betrayed to Mapache by Teresa's mother, and when Angel comes to collect his share of Mapache's gold he is seized and subjected to torture.

As the film approaches the final crisis, the contradictions inherent in the Bunch's ideology become manifest and all the codes and conventional distinctions that have given the Western its ideological force are undone. Although the conventions of the form demand that we identify the betrayal of someone like Angel as evil, we cannot accept the Bunch's characterization of Teresa's mother as a "Judas," because by killing her daughter Angel himself has violated the taboo against killing women and children. But then again, the sacred status of children is also rendered questionable by the children of Agua Verde, who assist in the torture of Angel, turning it into a game like the ant/scorpion massacre with which the film began. Although the Bunch's code of loyalty would seem to require them to attempt a rescue, their code of pragmatic self-interest—which forced them to seek protection from the posse in Agua Verde—results in their becoming passive witnesses, even accomplices, to the torture of Angel.

But such passivity is not acceptable in a hero, whose status is defined by his power to find the path to "good action" no matter how complex the circumstances. Pike's passivity is the sign of his demoralization, his loss of the ability to connect means and ends, beliefs or values and actions. Despairing of direct, effective action, he accepts Mapache's suggestion that they work off their bad feelings on the bodies of Agua Verde's whores.

But women have a special place in Pike's personal mythology, and his choice of whore reveals that he has not yet abandoned the romantic ideal that informs his sense of the Bunch. We see her after the act is done, framed by iconography which suggests that this "whore" is also the "Virgin." She is extremely young, shy, and innocent-looking; we see her sponging her breasts to cleanse herself; a crucifix is illuminated on the wall behind her; and an invisible infant utters a single cry. This image of every illusion sacred to Pike produces first a sense of self-revulsion (registered in a pained blink of the eyes) and a gesture that expresses his yearning to reconnect with the sacred image—he throws two coins on the table, twice the stated price. But the gesture is too filled with contradiction to be fully redemptive. He has sacrificed to the "Virgin" by paying her as a whore. She casts her eyes down, and he turns away.

The implicitly sordid quality of the transaction is augmented by sounds from the adjacent room, where the Gorches are trying to bilk their whore of her payment and are playfully torturing her pet sparrow as well. Pike ends their whining and bickering by stepping into the room and saying, "Let's go." The Gorches immediately understand that he means to rescue Angel from Mapache.

These actions frame the decision to rescue Angel as a complex attempt at redemption on Pike's part; and if we take the image of the whore-as-Madonna literally, we may regard the massacre that follows as an unambiguously heroic and redemptive act. But given what we have seen of the Bunch's treatment of women in Starbuck and of Angel's murder of Teresa, we ought to suspect that Pike's reverence for the female symbol is a self-delusion masking values and impulses that can (and will) transform reverence to rape/murder by a simple shift of perspective.[46]

The Bunch now resolve their dilemma by following the classic "gunfighter" scenario. They seek a direct and personal combat with the chief of the evildoers. Peckinpah organizes his narrative structure and imagery so that we understand this moment as the final knotting-together of the film's several strands of thematic and characterological development. In his account of Pike's decision and the "long walk" down the street, he invokes the conventions of the gunfighter Western, in effect promising that his resolution will conform to the classic model.[47]

As they enter the plaza and confront Mapache, the Bunch are apparently ready to do the right thing for the wrong reasons, or for reasons of personal honor and loyalty that are at best irrelevant to the politics of Mexico. In these circumstances, it is not enough to know to whom your word should be given—that is, to discriminate between Angel and Mapache, comrade and enemy. In Mapache they confront not a singular enemy of the "Frank Miller" or "Ryker" type, but the leader of a community. Nor is that community simply a collection of marauding "savages" worthy of extermination like the Japanese in *Objective Burma* or the Indians in *Rio Grande*. Rather, it is the other half of a Mexican society divided by civil war and therefore, despite its evident corruption, still a counterpart to the sacred "village." But because their reasons and objectives are so limited, the Wild Bunch have no way of estimating the possible consequences of their action for Angel and themselves; nor do they imagine that the act may have consequences beyond the personal, affecting Agua Verde and the revolution beyond its walls. The myths by which they live have imposed a fatal limitation on their powers of imagination. The only consequences that the myths allow them to imagine are those entailed by their defeat: if they lose, they will die. But what will happen if they "win"? What might "victory" mean in such a context?

The Bunch enter the plaza and find Mapache and his officers feasting and drinking in a loggia set at the top of a broad flight of stairs. The tortured Angel lies near Mapache's table; the plaza below the stairs is filled with soldiers, women, and children. Mapache rises to face Pike, a move in accordance with "gunfight" formalities. But the action that follows is a series of increasingly shocking violations of expectation and convention, and the surprise of the Bunch (and of the audience) is Peckinpah's most effective demonstration of their (and our) myth-determined failure of imagination. The sequence itself moves swiftly forward, the images edited into a rhythmic flow of vivid and violent movements and frozen tableaux—one of the richest and most effective action sequences ever filmed. But below the swift and violent surface Peckinpah is also resolving the thematic concerns of his narrative. To see how he does this we have to "stop" the action at critical points:

1. Mapache seems to agree to give Angel back to the Bunch. He raises him, embraces him from behind, and walks him forward. As Angel's arms extend in a cruciform gesture, Mapache reaches a knife around and cuts his throat. A flash to Pike's face shows his shock and surprise, and in the next instant the Bunch open fire and shoot Mapache down. The representation of Angel as sacrificial lamb recalls the "Madonna" that determined Pike on his mission of rescue. But like the Madonna-icon, the image of Angel as Christ is subverted by our knowledge that he is also a merciless killer of women, the man who has said of the killing of civilians in Starbuck, "They were not my people. I care only for *my* people." Pike's shock and horror bespeak the naivete of his belief in mythic images and his tendency to take certain appealing metaphors (the whore looks like a Madonna) for realities. But if his imagination is excessively strong on some subjects, it is blind to others: his surprise at Mapache's action reflects his failure to understand who Mapache is, and that while surrendering Angel may seem to an American a rational move, it is (in Mexican terms) politically impossible.

2. As Mapache falls (in slow motion), a series of jump-cuts shows that everyone in the plaza has frozen, and there is complete silence.

The image cuts from the officers immobile in the loggia to the soldiers immobilized in the plaza below; then it cuts from face to face, as each member of the Bunch recognizes the stunning fact that in the blink of an eye, with the simplest and most natural of gestures, they have "won the war." As the face-to-face movement continues, we see shock turn to relief, then to glee—and then to a kind of doubtfulness. It is clear that the Bunch have not "thought beyond their guns" to what might follow the moment of victory. They have at least made a kind of *coup d'état* and now "have the drop" on the whole of Agua Verde. If we think in conventional terms, we may even imagine that in "decapitating" the counterrevolution they have thereby achieved the Revolution. But what use will they make of their victory?

3. Pike smiles at the others, and they answer—a gesture which recalls the laughter that bonds the Bunch on other occasions. Then he immediately turns, points his pistol, and shoots the German colonel through the head. The gesture is represented as a spontaneous action, flowing naturally from the smile of bonding and mutual recognition, as if the killing of the German is a necessary consequence of the Bunch's solidarity. The shot breaks the silence, and in a flurry of gunshots the Bunch gun down the rest of Mapache's officers, storm the loggia, and seize its elevated position and the machine gun mounted there.

The shooting of the German is a simple action, but its motives and consequences reflect the complexity of the entire film. Pike's gesture is of a piece with his response to the myth-impacted images of Madonna and Christ. "The German" is the archetype of alien ideology, aristocratic privilege, racism, class snobbery, and militaristic authoritarianism. After Mapache, he is the kind of man Pike would hate most; and since he also represents a movie stereotype which the audience would automatically dislike, the killing also has our "consent" and satisfies our wishes and the expectations native to our understanding of genre convention. This killing, and the consequent wiping-out of Mapache's leadership cadre, is also a logical extension of the program of "decapitation" already begun by Pike.

4. But the killing of the German and the disruption of the "freeze" transforms victory into catastrophe. The soldiers in the plaza, and civilians from the surrounding buildings, now open fire on the Bunch; as more and more of them press into the plaza they storm the loggia from the front, while soldiers and civilians in the building behind the loggia snipe at the Bunch from flanks and rear. The

inadequacy of Pike's imagination is now clear: in seeing Mapache as a "personal" enemy he has misunderstood the man's motives and his importance for the people of Agua Verde.

It is Peckinpah's emphasis on this particular failure of imaginative understanding that makes *The Wild Bunch* exceptional as a commentary on the counterinsurgency project in Vietnam. The Bunch's failures are the fictional counterparts of the failures that crippled the "mission" from its inception, particularly the failure to understand the power and complexity of the extant political culture in Vietnam in the South no less than the North. The decision to settle matters by a personal confrontation with Mapache is an adequate metaphor for the "mission's" response to both Ho Chi Minh and Ngo Dinh Diem. Without understanding the role of Ho (and the Communist-led Vietminh) in the nationalist politics of both North and South, the Americans could not appreciate the civil character of the conflict; they attacked "Communists" in North and South as if they were tyrannical interlopers rather than natives.

But there is a closer analogy between Mapache and Diem, who despite his unquestionably corrupt and dictatorial methods was a figure deeply enmeshed in the political culture of the South, the head of a significant native party, and a "nationalist"—at least to the extent of seeking to limit American control of his country's internal affairs. The Americans could "decapitate" his regime by overthrowing him, but they could not discover or provide a replacement. The succession of generals whose regimes were either overthrown or sponsored by the Americans were chosen for reasons that were (like the Bunch's motives) American reasons. Those generals whose programs were not consonant with the prosecution of an American counterinsurgency war—those like General Minh, who wanted to negotiate a "neutralist" solution to the conflict—were overthrown, although their politics was unquestionably representative of a large and growing tendency in the South.[48]

As with the American "mission" in Vietnam, Pike's "failure of intelligence" leads to a surprising catastrophe. Instead of greeting the *gringos* as liberators, Mapache's people assault them as the enemy. Had the Americans understood the "revolutionary" implications of their role—had they understood the nature of the conflict in which, for their own private reasons, they had enmeshed themselves—they might have predicted the Agua Verdean revulsion against them, and they would certainly have understood that a conflict with Mapache could not be settled by personal duel or even *coup d'état*, that only the power of a social order equivalent to that of Agua Verde—the power of the village/revolution—would be sufficient to the task of undoing Mapache.

5. As the Wild Bunch storm the loggia and seize the machine gun—symbol of technological and military superiority—a complex "cross-over" occurs. What began as a "limited war" has developed into something like unlimited and undifferentiated slaughter. By repeating and enlarging the act that brought victory, the Bunch have ensured their final defeat. What began as an attempted rescue of one man becomes a general massacre in which the original image of the mutual slaughter of powerful white scorpions and swarming brown ants is re-created and augmented. The Wild Bunch use their expertise and technological advantages to "waste" hundreds of attackers, butchering in the process the whores in the loggia. The Mexicans keep firing and attacking until the Wild Bunch are literally shot to pieces.

Within the large structure of this colossal inversion of the gunfight/rescue scenario Peckinpah sets other exchanges and images which enlarge and extend the catastrophe's field of reference. Among the most important is the image of a maddened Pike firing his machine gun into the charging Mexicans: an image which thematically recalls the classic "last stand" motif, particularly that of the Alamo, but which links that Western theme to the specific iconography of the combat film—particularly the ending of *Bataan*, in which a maddened Sergeant Dane fires a nearly identical type of machine gun into the charging Japanese. But Sergeant Dane of *Bataan*, like Crockett of *The Alamo*, were identified as both protectors and as liberators. Good men use guns (and women) to effect a rescue of women and children. But Pike's affiliation with in the "Madonna-icon" is demolished in a swift series of shots which ends with his cursing and shooting a "Madonna-whore." The purely symbolic and instrumental function of women in Wild Bunch mythology is unmasked when Dutch uses a woman as a shield—the gesture is a parodic inversion of Shane's defense of guns, which says in effect that a *woman* is just a tool, as good or as bad as the man who uses her, whether for pleasure, spiritual comfort, or something to stop a bullet.

As Pike fires his machine gun into the plaza, exploding boxes of grenades among the tables, we have no reason to think that he is not killing the women and children whom we have seen take cover there. Instead of the rescuer of children Pike becomes their destroyer; and in a final irony he receives his death wound from the rifle of a little child—the same one Mapache had earlier rescued from Villa's forces.[49]

The completion of the Wild Bunch's last stand does not end Peckinpah's demystification of Western mythic structures. The supreme value which the myth assigns to the climactic battle of gunfight is not simply a function of the ideological rationale that frames the fight. It derives its emotional force and irrational appeal from its role in the narrative structure of the myth. Specific versions of the myth may vary in their ideological rationale, hero type, and choice of happy or fatal ending; but they do not vary in their representation of a consummatory act of violence—*whatever* its motivation—as the *necessary* and *sufficient* resolution of all the issues the tale has raised. If Peckinpah had ended his movie with a doomed Pike firing his machine gun (as in the ending of *Bataan*) or even with a fading image of a dead Bunch (as in the ending of *Butch Cassidy*), it would still be possible to see the Bunch's attack as an act of heroic sacrifice and/or vindication. But Peckinpah extends his narrative to display the consequences of this heroic consummation in a seemingly endless series of images which manifest the ruin the Bunch have inflicted—vultures drifting down into the streets to strut and peck and sit among the dead, a column of refugees and wounded limping out of the ruins into an empty desert, the bounty-hunters descending like human buzzards to strip the dead of boots and gold teeth and to take the heads of the Wild Bunch. If the Americans have rescued Agua Verde from Mapache, they have done so by the "Ben Tre" method, destroying the city in order to save it.

The bleakness of these images is partially repaired by the film's ending, in which old Sykes returns at the head of his revolutionary Indians and villagers to find Deke Thornton at the gate of Agua Verde. They make their peace in a reprise of the Bunch's sacrament of laughter and then ride off (like the Professionals) to join the Revolution. This ending mitigates the extremity of Peckinpah's critique of the myths of regenerative violence by renewing the suggestion that if Americans could only know which side "to give their word to," then with their power and expertise they could make a real and worthwhile revolution. However, the ending also preserves, in terms appropriate to the story, a way of imagining the possibility of effective human action—the merest suggestion that some possibility for viable moral (and political) action remains after all the traditional motives and missions have been discredited.

Peckinpah's way of addressing the ideological problem of social violence is similar to Ford's way of addressing racism in *The Searchers*. His task is not merely to condemn a universally recognized evil but to unmask an evil element that has become part and parcel of the received mythology of our otherwise admirable culture—an evil lurking within our own "innocence." He does not attack this evil polemically but through the construction of a counter-mythology in which all the standard devices of our received mythology are used to gain our identification with the story. Then—by making manifest and graphic the hidden evil—he makes us aware of the errors into which our myths have led us. And finally he makes us aware of the operation of *myth* as such, and of our own susceptibility to its appeals. The advantage of the counter-mythic method (when it works) is that it dissolves the moral distance between public and perpetrator that is inherent in a polemical critique and pushes us toward an emotional as well as intellectual recognition of our complicity in the enactment of our myths. The disadvantage is that the ambiguity with which ideology is represented makes possible a misreading that is opposite to the author's intent. Although many critics recognized the critical character of *The Searcher* and *The Wild Bunch*, others have suggested that they are symptoms of the conditions they affect to critique: that *The Searchers* is a case rather than an exemplum of racism; and that *The Wild Bunch* is simply a cinematic equivalent to Newark/Detroit and Ben Tre, testifying to the failure of American values and beliefs and the rising tide of "insane" violence here and abroad—the most graphic exposition yet of the "American madness" it pretended to critique.[50]

Lunatic Semiology: The Demoralization of American Culture, 1969–1973

A similar irony undermined the Nixon administration's attempts to regain control of the "story" of the Vietnam War: to revise the war-myth in such a way that the public would be able to put down the specter of Mylai and once again see a meaningful connection between means and ends. "Victory," or the fulfillment of our mission, was redefined as the achievement of "peace with honor": a set of negotiated arrangements that would permit the withdrawal of American troops but leave in place a South Vietnamese state able to sustain itself against Communist subversion or assault—for the near term, at least. The terms of peace would be negotiated directly with the North Vietnamese in Paris; while in the field, tactics would be altered to make possible a phased transfer of the burden of combat from American to Vietnamese forces—the so-called "Vietnamization" of the Vietnam War.

Nixon's plan involved a significant amount of mystification. Its vision of "victory" fell far short of the original goal of the mission, since it did not require a Communist admission of defeat and could not guarantee South Vietnam's future freedom from subversion or guerrilla assault. The concept of "Vietnamization" was in itself an admission that we had erred in making the war our own. It offered the GVN a good deal less than the original open-ended commitment to "nation-building," since it required the ARVN to replace American combat forces by a determinate date, whether or not the "building" of the South Vietnamese nation was complete. So long as the Paris negotiations and field operations went according to plan, these mystifications could salve the wounded self-esteem of a public that had had to abandon, under fire, the high hopes and ambitions of the New Frontier. But the recalcitrance of both North and South Vietnamese, and the intractable problems of the battlefield, revealed the mismatch between administration scenarios and rationales and the facts of the case. The dissonance of expectation and image, nominal and real values, can be controlled and esthetically resolved in a film like *The Wild Bunch*; politicians have no comparable power to determine the historical script and control audience response. Within a year of his electoral victory, Nixon was experiencing a "credibility gap" at least as profound as that into which Johnson and the Great Society had disappeared.

Nixon's attempts to negotiate favorable terms of withdrawal with the North Vietnamese were continually undermined by the persistence of three political facts: the original and still unbroken commitment of the North Vietnamese and their southern allies to the goal of unifying Vietnam under "socialist" auspices; the GVN's systemic weaknesses and incapacity for self-reform that had from the first undermined its legitimacy and its power to wage effective war; and the new element, an American consensus for de-escalation and a negotiated settlement.[51] The North Vietnamese soon recognized that the American policy of de-escalation and shifting the burden of combat to the ARVN ("Vietnamization") was driven by the internal dynamics of American politics; and that if they were ruthless and persistent, they could not fail to outlast the Americans. Moreover, they did not have to trim their tactics to appease domestic dissent.

They could therefore afford to be less concessive than the Americans on almost any issue of symbol or substance; and when they conceded a symbolic issue, they could demand in exchange concessions that would materially improve their position.[52]

Deprived of its license to use ever larger increments of force, the administration had to maintain its authority and forward its policies by inflating small successes into great "symbolic victories." But its revision of counterinsurgency mythology was hampered by the necessity of playing the same script for three different audiences: the North Vietnamese negotiators, the South Vietnamese government (which feared an American betrayal), and the increasingly war-weary American public. To offset the disadvantages for negotiation that were inherent in the commitment to "Vietnamization," the administration periodically attempted to bluff the North Vietnamese into concessions by taking (or threatening to take) actions (for example, the resumption or expansion of the bombing regime) that "signaled" the administration's "resolve." But the North Vietnamese were aware that American public opinion was not at all resolved on the indefinite continuance, let alone the re-escalation, of the conflict. To offset this calculation, the administration designed some of its war-symbolism to "signal" that Nixon might be a "madman" capable in his rage of resisting public opinion, ignoring the logic of his electoral mandate, and traducing the canons of "limited war." Such actions typically involved dramatic re-escalations of the level of combat, most often through the renewal or extension of the air war, but also through the expansion of ground combat into Cambodia (1970) and Laos (1971). The administration used similar devices to manage its fearful ally, threatening faster withdrawals or less aerial bombardment than the logic of the original policy seemed to require.[53]

But Nixon's use of bombing campaigns (or their cancellation) to send "signals" of resolve to the enemy were failures of signification, because the Vietnamese used a different political language and calculus of value. So long as American actions did not materially destroy their moral or material capacity to continue the struggle, there was no reason for the North to call off the war. Likewise, these gestures did not convince the South Vietnamese government of American resolve, because the leadership was privy to American demands for "Vietnamization" and was periodically subjected to threats of an early American withdrawal. The American public *was* significantly impressed by the "madman" signals, but this was the audience whose greatest need was to be convinced that the administration was rational and capable of controlling a war in which the cost in blood was no longer commensurate with the kind of victory that seemed possible.[54]

Under Nixon the prosecution of the war degenerated into a "lunatic semiology:" *semiology*, in that military actions were conceived as having a primarily symbolic meaning, as "signals of resolve" to the other side; *lunatic*, in that those symbols referred to a nominal "world" that was increasingly disconnected from the realities of the battlefield and the real state of opinion among its three audiences. However, it would be a mistake to see lunatic semiology as an aberration or the consequence of Nixon's personality defects. The logic of lunatic semiology had been inherent in the original concept of the counterinsurgency mission. Though calculations of national and strategic interest had influenced Eisenhower and Kennedy, they saw the value of South Vietnam as symbolic rather than material: it offered an opportunity to demonstrate our will and ability to contain Communism and repel Maoist insurgencies. By the time of the decision to escalate in 1964–65, the balance of administration opinion held that the American stake in a victory in Vietnam was more than 70 percent "symbolic" and that salvaging American prestige was far more important than helping the GVN to survive.[55] Nixon's exercise in political signification through violence was not in itself more "immoral" or absurd than that of his predecessors. What was different in 1970 was the cultural context in which this symbolism was being received: a context informed and demoralized by nine years of futile bloodshed and unrealized prophecies and by the spreading awareness of the gap between official perceptions and pronouncements and conditions in the field, and informed as well by nine years in which the symbolism that justified the war had first been glorified and then sensationally de-mythologized in the mass media.[56]

With the invasion of Cambodia (April 1970), the "credibility gap" became a full-blown, nationwide case of cognitive dissonance. Since early in the war, Communist forces had used bases in the Cambodian border region for attacks on the Saigon and Mekong Delta regions, and in early 1970 it appeared they would also capture the capital of Cambodia and transform that country from acquiescent "neutral" to active ally. The Nixon administration was pledged to substantial troop withdrawals and feared that stronger Communist forces along the border would be able to take the offensive against the reduced American forces. But the political considerations that made withdrawal necessary made risky any strike against these bases. Given the state of American politics, the invasion would inevitably (and credibly) be perceived as a widening of the war, a reversal of the pledges that had earned Nixon his electoral mandate. Several of Nixon's top advisers therefore urged that the operation be modest in scale, that it be justified as a merely tactical enterprise, and that Nixon be wary of raising the symbolic stakes.

However, Nixon (and members of his advisory staff) believed that under present conditions the symbolic and the tactical battlegrounds were the same, that the primary value of an invasion of Cambodia was not its tactical utility but its symbolic value in negotiations with the enemy. Nixon insisted on the necessity of doing "something symbolic," making a "big play," to signify "we were still serious about our commitment in Vietnam." He invited the new commander of MACV, General Abrams, to expand the role intended for American troops and to broaden the mission to include the destruction of "COSVN"—which Stanley Karnow justly describes as "the legendary Communist headquarters" from which the war in the South was supposedly directed. By making capture of the chimerical COSVN symbolic of the invasion's "mission," Nixon and Abrams aroused unrealistic and excessive expectations, in light of which the actual tactical achievement appeared meaningless. Nixon compounded the problem by responding to the first wave of criticism with an "escalation" of symbolic firepower. Instead of minimizing the significance of the "invasion," he rhetorically transformed it into a symbolic Armageddon in which America's credibility as a world power was at stake: "If, when the chips are down, the world's most powerful nation . . . acts like a pitiful helpless giant, the forces of totalitarianism and anarchy will threaten free nations . . . throughout the world." Such speeches confirmed Nixon's core of supporters in their faith, but they further alienated those who were either committed to opposition or simply repelled by what seemed the administration's continual falsification of the course of events—and the constantly lengthening casualty lists.[57] Any possibility that this "big play" would impress the North Vietnamese as a sign of American resolve was dissipated by the strong negative element in the domestic reaction to the invasion. As some of Nixon's advisers had anticipated, the action was criticized as either a deliberate violation of the pledge to reduce the war or as proof of the government's chronic irrationality.

The invasion also "maddened" the domestic political debate. The antiwar "Moratorium" demonstrations in the summer of 1970 were the biggest and best-attended peace demonstrations so far and received favorable coverage even in relatively conservative mass media like *Time* and *Life*. But behind the peaceful façade of the Moratorium there was evidence of a radical polarization in American politics. Frustrated by failure in Vietnam and stung by the antiwar critique, conservative politicians (and their public) demanded and undertook repressive measures against "leftist" dissent. Within the administration, officials on the President's staff joined with Attorney General Mitchell (and his staff) to develop extensive programs of surveillance and disruption aimed at repressing movements that seemed to them potentially "revolutionary." Conservative governors like Rhodes of Ohio and Reagan of California ordered National Guards and/or state police to use violent means (if necessary) to repress student demonstrations. These measures culminated in the shooting of students by Guardsmen at Kent State University and by state patrolmen at Jackson (Mississippi) and Orange State (South Carolina) and in a series of violent clashes between police and students in Berkeley.

The Cambodian invasion also embittered a significant element of the peace movement and the "New Left" by demonstrating the apparent helplessness of the public to prevent Nixon (in his "madman" guise) from re-escalating the war at will. Some elements of the "New Left," most famously the "Weathermen," turned to terrorism. A mystique of regenerative revolutionary violence, the counterpart of the mythology that informed the "mission" in Vietnam, irrationalized the New Left critique of the war and the liberal ideology that had made it.[58]

A culture or community in a state of high morale exhibits confidence in the power of its symbols to accurately describe the world and in the validity of its myths as explanations and justifications of the course of events. In a demoralized community the effective connection between perception, belief, and action is broken or confounded. No single course of action recommends itself as a way out of the impasse, although inaction also seems intolerable. Language and imagination seem unequal to the tasks of defining the problem, expressing the causes of disaffection, or conceiving a desirable resolution of the crisis.[59] Although the growing gap between Nixonian symbolism and the real conditions of the war did not deter the administration from pursuing its course, it intensified the processes of cultural demoralization that had first become evident in the twin crises of escalation and urban rioting in 1967–68.

Nowhere was demoralization more painful and damaging than in the army itself. It is difficult enough to motivate troops for combat in a war whose overall purposes and justification are widely understood and accepted. That task becomes almost insuperable when the reasons behind the war (and the symbols that embody those reasons) are perceived as inadequate, foolish, or morally questionable. A "limited war" like Korea presents special morale problems because of the inherent disproportion between the war's limited (and perhaps intangible) objectives and the unlimited sacrifice it demands of the individual soldiers. This problem was compounded in Vietnam by the complex character of the "mission" and its peculiar and stringent limitations.

There was from the first a striking disproportion between the limitations accepted by the American army and the latitude permitted the enemy. For example, for most of the war American assaults against certain "civilian" targets in the North and against VC and NVA "sanctuaries" in Laos/Cambodia were forbidden, while the enemy was able to strike any target anywhere in the South and use Laos and Cambodia for staging and re-supply.[60] The Vietcong and the North Vietnamese were quite ruthless in the use of terror and assassination to intimidate neutral and pro-government peasants and to eliminate Saigonese officials. Terror was nominally forbidden by American Rules of Engagement, though some violation or "stretching" of those rules was tolerated in practice and some clandestine programs (for example, the Phoenix Program) deliberately imitated the terror tactics of the enemy. But American terror tactics did not have the same consequences as the enemy's. Such tactics were likely to be condemned by the people at home; and even in country, they failed to frighten the population into accepting the Saigon government. When perpetrated by Americans they reinforced the peasants' sense of being persecuted by foreigners; when perpetrated by the ARVN they merely identified the regime as brutal without altering its reputation for corruption, incompetence, and weakness. The massacre of civilians by the North Vietnamese in Hue during the Tet offensive did not discredit their movement in the South, but "three or four minutes" of abusive treatment by young GIs could "destroy in a few minutes time" all that a counterinsurgency specialist had achieved with months of "civic action programs."[61]

Success in counterinsurgency demanded a high degree of specialized training in which mastery of the techniques of combat was less important than the development of a sophisticated understanding of the political nature of the conflict and of the careful balance between initiative and restraint that made for an effective advisory role. It was a mission that proved difficult enough even for a highly motivated and carefully prepared cadre of professionals like the Special Forces. The sacrifices demanded of the combat soldier in such a struggle are different from those demanded by ordinary combat. The military experience in Vietnam confirmed that even where willingness to die for a cause or the country are weakened, unit pride and loyalty to friends can motivate extraordinary acts of courage and self-sacrifice. But what counterinsurgency warfare demanded was not merely the willingness to "throw yourself on a grenade" to save your buddies but to make a similar sacrifice for the sake of those hostile, alien, bad-smelling peasants in the *ville*. It was utterly unreasonable to expect that a conscript army, whose soldiers were trained for conventional combat, would be able to comprehend and accept such a mission. But in the absence of such comprehension it became impossible for the troops to respond appropriately, and usefully, to hostile villagers like those in Mylai.[62]

Morale problems were compounded once it was widely understood that the entire mission was in process of termination. Within six months of Nixon's inauguration, the Defense Department perceived a morale "emergency" in Vietnam, whose most dramatic expression was the refusal of a company of the Americal Division to obey an attack order (August 1969). By the end of 1970 behavior of this kind had spread and ramified. Search-and-destroy operations often degenerated into "search-and-evade," and there was an alarming and unprecedented increase in "fragging"—assassination attempts against officers who demanded aggressive action from their men. Withdrawal cast doubt on the value of what the troops had done in the past, as well as on their immediate sufferings, and caused professional officers to question the competence of their leadership (civil and military) and even the worth of their service. The increased militancy of the antiwar movement, the growing disaffection with the war in the mass media, and the emphasis given to atrocities all suggested that the war was not merely a thankless task for the soldiers but one for which they would actually be held culpable. The Mylai revelations at the end of 1969 intensified the rhetorical assault on the character of the soldiers. Even prowar Senator Thomas Dodd felt compelled to rationalize the atrocity by characterizing the troops as drug addicts. The revelations also weakened the soldiers' (and their officers') psychological defenses against such accusations.[63]

The army in Vietnam was the expression and instrument of our culture's belief in the efficacy and worthiness of violence as a means to power, progress, and moral regeneration. Its effectiveness as an instrument was vitiated when the men who constituted it (or a preponderance of them) could no longer see a clear and valid connection between the "reasons" and symbols of the "mission" and what was demanded of them as soldiers. The administration attempted to deal with military and civilian demoralization by revising the symbolism and objectives of the "mission." The most significant of the new objectives was the return of American POWs held in the North. The belief that Asians had (like the "Apaches") a racial propensity for torture had been given force and credibility by the Japanese mistreatment of Allied prisoners and by the mistreatment and "brainwashing" of American POWs during the Korean War. The expectation of (at best) severe mistreatment in North Vietnamese prisons was not unjustified by the facts, even those that emerged from inspections stage-managed by the North Vietnamese, and the North Vietnamese statement that American pilots should be treated as "war criminals" was cause for real alarm. However, negotiation on such matters is a normal part of belligerent diplomacy, and in the initial negotiating position defined by the administration in the fall and winter of 1969 concern about the POWs was an appropriately subordinate issue.[64]

But by the end of 1970, the return of the POWs had been elevated to the status of a central war aim. Its symbolic significance was highlighted in November 1970, when a team of airborne commandos attempted to rescue the inmates of Son Tay prison, less than 25 miles from Hanoi. Like other symbolic battles designed by the Nixon administration, this one was a failure in material terms—the camp had been vacated. But the attempted rescue and the new emphasis on POWs at the peace negotiations offered an angry and disillusioned public a new and acceptable way to re-mythologize the Vietnam War, and to do so in terms of the most sacred of the Frontier myths—the tale of captivity and rescue.[65] It was a version of the myth that had helped the New Frontiersmen to engage American sympathies with the project of counterinsurgency. It was the myth to which Johnson had appealed to justify his escalation of the conflict as a rescuing of kidnaped and tortured farmers. Now that that larger project of rescue had failed, politicians and journalists began to see in smaller, more manageable scenarios of captivity and rescue a symbolic redemption of our material failures. Moreover, it was a "rescue" that we could hardly fail to achieve, since a prisoner exchange was inevitable under *any* form of negotiated settlement.

In the short run, this substitution of a symbolic rescue for the original "mission" was extremely effective. The ceremonies of greeting which attended the return of the POWs in 1973 constituted the *only* large-scale public celebration for troops returning from the war, the closest thing to a postwar victory parade that Vietnam veterans would enjoy—an irony that other veterans noted with some bitterness. Two years later, faced with the humiliation of South Vietnam's rapid dissolution following Communist attacks in the Central Highlands, the same kind of "rescue" symbolism was revived and was proffered as the metaphorical redemption of a material disaster. American journalists gave particular emphasis to "Operation Babylift," which became the model for a wave of "orphan-lifts" by which many South Vietnamese children were to be rescued from the fate overwhelming their country. Such actions provided "a welcome outlet for humanitarian action" at a time when America's helplessness to save South Vietnam was completely manifest—although the symbolism of such rescues masked operations that were often hastily conceived and were sometimes corrupted by Vietnamese politics.[66]

The *reductio ad absurdum* of these symbolic "rescues" was reached in the "*Mayaguez* incident" which followed the fall of Saigon. The Ford administration mounted a rescue operation in which 41 Marines died to save 39 sailors aboard a ship seized by Cambodian or Vietnamese troops—a trivial and perhaps unnecessary skirmish which the administration described as a "symbolic victory" demonstrating that the United States was not a "paper tiger." The recapture of a single ship was thus said to outweigh and offset the consequences and significance of the defeat of a national government whose independence we had helped to establish and whose integrity we had supported through nearly twenty years of diplomatic, economic, and military aid and for whose sake we had fought a long and costly war. This may have been the nadir of "lunatic semiology," in which sign and referent have scarcely any proportionate relation at all.[67]

But it is important to note that despite the intensive "de-mystification" of this sort of symbolism by various cultural media, ranging from journalistic exposés and the Congressional investigations of the "Secret War" in Laos/Cambodia to the "counter-myths" of *The Wild Bunch* and *Little Big Man*, the administration retained enough political power to persist in its chosen policy direction. Thus it was able to answer each "de-mystification" of the past by creating new "facts," new event-centered crises around which the damaged belief-structures of its supporters could be temporarily reconstructed. Some of these "facts" were created within the framework of the war itself—

the invasions of Cambodia and Laos, the "Christmas bombing," the Son Tay "rescue," the "babylift," the *Mayaguez.* These event-crises had the effect of rallying support in the face of a traditionally conceived outside enemy. Other artificially created or exaggerated crises had the effect of scapegoating domestic "radicals." A public campaign was mounted that emphasized the "alien" qualities and "revolutionary" ambitions of war-protestors, systematically identifying peace activists as domestic sympathizers with the enemy, and "radicals" (especially those active in the "Black Power" movement) as equivalents of the Vietcong. This campaign enabled the administration to shift some of the blame for American defeat onto those who criticized its policies. It also created a set of circumstances in which various levels and agencies of government assumed a wider license in using power, both covert and openly violent, to suppress dissident organizations—measures which, when extended to "covert action" against the Democratic Party, finally produced a reaction which discredited Nixon and drove him from office.[68]

In the end, none of these symbolic devices could entirely redeem the belief-structures they invoked. The heavy losses and final defeat in Vietnam were material and palpable, and far too substantial to be offset by a babylift and a *Mayaguez* rescue. The scapegoating of domestic dissidents may have helped Nixon win re-election in 1972, but it had the long-term effect of amplifying the experience of defeat. Not only had we "lost Vietnam." Our own society had been successfully invaded, divided, and deformed by "alien" influences which had caused us to "lose" the "youth of the ghetto" and a substantial portion of the "sixties generation."

"De-mystifying" manipulations of the myth within the frameworks of cultural activity could not prevent the administration from "successfully" covering its final operations with the sanctions of myth. But the ultimate consequence of that "success" was the discrediting of the myth itself—a trauma not immediately reflected in the realm of electoral politics but registered over the next decade and a half in the underlying structures of value and belief, the "morale" of Americans as expressed in the forms of their national culture.

Conclusion: The Crisis of Public Myth

Flags are blossoming now where little else is blossoming
and I am bent on fathoming what it means to love my country.
The history of this earth and the bones within it?
Soils and cities, promises made and mocked, plowed contours
of shame and hope?
Loyalties, symbols, murmurs extinguished and echoing?
Grids of states stretching . . . westward, underground waters?
Where are we moored?
What are the bindings?
What behooves us?

Adrienne Rich, "An Atlas of the Difficult World"

The Paris accords signed by the United States, the North Vietnamese, and the GVN in January 1973 were the last of Nixon's "symbolic victories." The brief period of public rejoicing over our escape from the Vietnamese quagmire was followed by a growing recognition of how much the achievement of "peace with honor" had cost the nation in blood, treasure, international standing, and public morale—and how little peace and honor had been won. The war between the Vietnamese continued, and two years later a Communist victory in the Central Highlands tipped South Vietnam, Cambodia, and Laos into collapse like the proverbial row of dominoes. At the same time, the American economy—weakened by the deficit financing through which Johnson and Nixon had funded the war—entered a prolonged period of crisis marked by growing balance-of-payments deficits and an unprecedented combination of double-digit inflation and relative stagnation in productivity and economic growth.

Against this background, defeat in Vietnam, coupled with the Arab oil boycott of 1973–74, symbolized a growing concern that the United States was no longer exceptional among the nations, that it was in danger of becoming a "second-rate" power. A writer in the *New York Times* financial pages described the foreclosure of American prospects in the period following the oil embargo as "The End of the Cowboy Economy," a phrase that aptly characterized the disappointing outcome of the high hopes embodied in the New Frontier. Instead of contemplating a future of limitless economic and political improvement, Americans in the 1970s were asked to accommodate themselves to the limitations of "spaceship earth," a world of exhausted frontiers whose rising and hungry population must draw on limited natural resources—a planetary ecology reduced to a "zero sum game" in which every gain entails a concomitant loss.[1]

The nation's ability to respond to its problems was hampered by a crisis of leadership, reflected in the public's rejection of three successive presidencies. After winning a landslide re-election in 1972, President Nixon was discredited and forced to resign by the "Watergate" scandal. Gerald Ford undermined his own moral authority by pardoning Nixon and failed to respond effectively to the Arab oil boycott, inflation, and the fall of South Vietnam. Democrat Jimmy Carter gained the presidency in 1976 with a promise to restore strong leadership and "decency" in government, but his administration (1976–80) was undone by continuing "stagflation" and by the Iran hostage crisis (1979–80). The hostage crisis was particularly damaging, because it so forcibly reminded us of our defeat by another Third World revolution in Vietnam and the anxiety about the fate of our POWs that had marked the last stages of that conflict.[2] Carter responded to rising public concern with a speech that lamented the nation's succumbing to a mood of "malaise." But his response only served to convince the public that he did not understand the real bases of its discontent—or worse, that he found the causes of that discontent inexplicable and was therefore unable to formulate a cure.

But Carter was astute in identifying the *cultural* character of the crisis. Neither "stagflation" nor the defeat in Vietnam posed as severe a threat to the safety, prosperity, and national interest of the United States as the economic crisis of 1929–33 or the international crises of 1939–41 and 1948–50 had done. Yet in those earlier cases, our myth/ideological system had proved entirely adequate to its task of defining the crisis and providing scenarios of resolution. But along with a weakened economy, Carter had inherited the ruined ideology of liberal progressivism.

A more systematic diagnosis of the ideological disarray of the post-Vietnam decade was made by the distinguished intellectual historian William H. MacNeill in a lead article published in *Foreign Affairs* in the Fall of 1982, "The Care and Repair of Public Myth." McNeill's "public myth" is roughly equivalent to "ideology" as I have been using the term. It refers to a core of common beliefs, maintained by a broad social consensus, embodied in "general statements [based more on faith than on fact] about the world and its parts, and in particular about nations and other human in-groups, that are believed to be true and then acted on whenever circumstances suggest or require a common response."[3] Without the common frame of discourse a public myth (ideology) provides, a society can neither generate authoritative analyses of a crisis nor muster a consensus on behalf of future policy. Political culture then degenerates into a conflict among interest groups, each playing by its own rules for its own advantage. When that happens, the common understandings that sustain both public policy and civil life itself are undone:

> Discrediting old myths without finding new ones to replace them erodes the basis for common action that once bound those who believed into a public body, capable of acting together. . . . [W]hen assent becomes halfhearted or is actively withheld from such myths, obedience becomes irregular, the predictability of human action diminishes, and the effectiveness of public response to changing conditions begins to erode.[4]

Historical events (like the defeat in Vietnam) always call into question the validity of "the guiding myth." In a healthy society the political and cultural leaders are able to repair and renew that myth by articulating new ideas, initiating strong action in response to crisis, or merely projecting an image of heroic leadership.[5] But leaders are recognized and empowered only in an ideological system whose public myth imagines a place and a role for heroic action. According to McNeill, American cultural elites (academics, policy intellectuals, journalists) have made the emergence of such leaders difficult by devoting their energies almost exclusively to criticizing, exposing, scandalizing, debunking, and demystifying the symbols, canons, and understandings that inform public belief—seeing in every foreign-policy initiative the seeds of "another Vietnam," and in every social policy or governmental reform the recrudescence of Great Society bloat and mismanagement. In the process they have created a public anti-myth which substitutes for the progressive myth the demoralizing vision of America as a chronically dysfunctional society incapable of self-government.[6]

McNeill's analysis assigns too great a share of responsibility for the crisis to the perversity of cultural elites and gives insufficient consideration to the possibility that the ideological disarray of the 1970s may have been a necessary and even "healthy" response to a traumatic historical experience—the painful assimilation of a difficult lesson.[7] Moreover, McNeill's prescription for resolving the cultural crisis neglects the genuinely *mythological* component of national discourse that is the product of our mass-culture industries. The power and effectiveness of the liberal consensus had been sustained from 1939 to 1973 by a remarkable consonance in the two primary realms of national ideological discourse: the "political culture" of partisan polemics and policy-making, in which ideology is formulated as concept and doctrine; and the mass culture, in which ideology is projected as generic narrative. The crisis of political culture had its counterpart in the genres of mass culture.

The return of the last American combat forces from Vietnam in 1973 marked the sudden end of the pre-eminence of the Western among the genres of mythic discourse. For most of the century the genre had been a sensitive indicator of the state of public myth. It had reached the peak of its popularity and cultural pre-eminence from 1969 to 1972, with an average release by American producers of 24 feature Westerns per year, with a high of 29 in 1971. But in 1973 only 13 Western features were released, and in 1974 only 7. After a brief resurgence in 1975 and 1976 (13 releases in each year), the number dropped to an average of 4 per year from 1977 to 1982. Western series also disappeared from television screens between 1972 and 1975.[8] While the Western has not entirely disappeared from the "genre map," its share of the terrain has been radically reduced and the terms of its cultural presence drastically altered.

A century ago, Frederick Jackson Turner saw in the closing of the agrarian frontier the end of an epoch in American history, and he addressed himself to defining the significance for modern America of the age that had passed. Now, looking back on the end of the "age of the Western" in commercial popular culture, and on the failure of the ideological consensus that reached its fullest expression in the New Frontier, it may be time for a post-mortem assessment of the significance of the Frontier *Myth* in American history.

But we must ask first whether or not the Myth of the Frontier and the ideology of liberal progressivism have indeed been damaged beyond repair by the traumatic events and social transformations of the last quarter-century (1965–90). Hollywood filmmakers were the cultural producers most directly engaged with the myth as such, and the history of their failed attempts to revive the Western after Vietnam indicate the character and strength of the social and cultural forces that fractured the myth/ideology of the liberal consensus.

Indian Tripping: The Alternative Western, 1970–1976

The revision, repair, and/or revival of the Western has been attempted four times since 1970. In the wake of Mylai and *The Wild Bunch*, Hollywood attempted the revision of a genre what had become too predictable and that predictably was identified with the symbolism of a "bad war." The Westerns produced in 1970–72 are marked by ambitious attempts at formal, thematic, and ideological innovation; but despite some critical and commercial successes, the "alternative" Western did not survive the end of the war. The second (1975–76) and third (1980–81) waves of revision were deliberate and systematic attempts by the studios to revive the Western as a genre.[9] But although each wave produced some critically acclaimed and moderately successful films, neither revival generated the sustained investment or the continuous production in the form that constitutes an active movie genre. Though a fourth revival began in the late 1980s, it is too soon to tell whether the successes of the two *Young Guns* (1988, 1990), *Lonesome Dove* (1990), and *Dances with Wolves* (1991) will restore the genre to anything like its former eminence.

The failed attempt to develop an alternative Western in 1970–72 and the aborted revival of 1975–76 are worth a closer look, because they are symptomatic of the cultural crisis of the post-Vietnam decade. Their failures indicate that what might loosely be called a "New Left" revision of the myth was incapable (under existing circumstances) of replacing the traditional "progressive" Western as the basis of an enduring popular genre.

Three types of alternative Western were produced during the 1969–72 period, which might be called the formalist, the neorealist, and the counterculture (or "New Cult of the Indian") Western. The formalist type has roots in the "spaghetti Western" of Sergio Leone. Clint Eastwood's *High Plains Drifter* and *Joe Kidd* are representative of the type, which features abstract, fairy-tale-like plots, gunfighter protagonists who ignore the normative motives of Western heroes, and landscapes devoid of historical association. The neorealist Western, though it is seriously "historical," looks behind the façade of Western mythology to portray some of the grittier, darker, even meaner sides of cowboy life.[10]

From a political view, the most important of the alternative types were the "counterculture Westerns" that comprised the new Cult of the Indian. But where earlier films of this type had been content to demonstrate the ethical culpability of Whites and appeal for peaceful co-existence until the Native Americans could learn civilized ways, the new films suggested that Native American culture might be a morally superior alternative to "civilization." The renewal of the cult began as early as 1964–65 with John Ford's *Cheyenne Autumn* and Sidney Salkow's *Great Sioux Massacre*. These films appeared just as American critics and scholars were undertaking a broad and thoroughgoing re-evaluation of Native American history and ethnography. Leslie Fiedler's *Return of the Vanishing American* (1966) forcibly reminded academic and public intellectuals of the Indians' significance as both fact and symbol in American history and culture and identified them as embodiments of a set of *alternative* values in sexuality, culture, and politics. Popularizations of the new ethnography suggested that by studying native societies we might discover alternative models of development. This renewed interest coincided with (and was energized by) the revival of Native American political movements, whose emergence on the national scene was signaled by the organization of the American Indian Movement (AIM), formed in 1968, and by the publication of Vine Deloria's *Custer Died for Your Sins* (1969).[11]

But Native Americans were also pressed into service as symbols in political and cultural controversies that chiefly concerned non-Indian groups. For the civil-rights and anti-war constituencies, Indians figured as the archetypal victims of White America's bigotry and imperialism. Proponents of the so-called "counterculture" paid homage to the values they found in various Native American societies. For the new environmentalist movement, the Native Americans' religious bond to nature symbolized an ecological critique of the exploitation and pollution of the natural world that accompanied industrial progress.[12] Some New Left ideologies idealized tribal society as a distinctly "American" and "exceptional" alternative to both the self-congratulatory rationalizations of American capitalism and the totalitarian doctrines of Leninism. Critics of American social and personal psychology, of the deflection or repression of sexual and imaginative energy by the "Protestant" or "work ethic," celebrated Indians as symbols of liberated libido. The drug-culture variant of this symbolism looked to peyote cults (as well as orientalism) for models of a lifestyle based on chemical mysticism. Beads, fringes, and painted faces symbolized the rebellion of Woodstock Nation by signaling the affiliation of the "youth culture" with the long-despised "Other." The ultimate absorption of this revalued "Indian" into the mainstream of American culture was registered by *Life*'s devoting a special section (in 1971) to "Our Indian Heritage," complete with a revisionist account of the Indian wars which emphasized White responsibility and celebrated Indian leaders like Crazy Horse as "great men" not "savages."[13]

Though these usages were well-meaning, most of them subordinated the particularity of Native American values and practices to a (mainly) White agenda of cultural revision which once again construed Native Americans as "the Other," the opposite or negation of Anglo-American culture—only now that difference was seen as healthy opposition to a sick society. There was also a downside to this mystique of "the Other," in which a naive identification with Indians, Blacks, and Third World "natives" became a mythic rationale for the uncritical acceptance of "revolutionary" and even terrorist programs.[14]

The impact of counterculture ethnography was first reflected on screen in *A Man Called Horse* (1969). But the most successful and memorable of the new Cult of the Indian films took their inspiration from public reaction against the Mylai massacre. The scandalously successful *Soldier Blue* (1970) borrowed images from the verbal and photographic record of Mylai to stage its version of the massacre of Indians by Whites at Sand Creek (1864). Arthur Penn's *Little Big Man* (1970), a more ambitious film, attempted to symbolize in a single coherent narrative the political concerns of the anti-war movement and the counterculture's "ethnographic" critique of White American character and values. By casting Dustin Hoffman as the hero, Jack Crabbe, Penn was criticizing not only the ideology of race war but the conventions of the Western genre. Hoffman was widely identified as a personification of the youth culture of the 60s after his performance in *The Graduate* (1966) and he had been featured in a 1967 *Life* article ("Dusty and the Duke") as an alternative to the John Wayne model of American heroism. Hoffman's Crabbe is the complete Western anti-hero: in the course of the film he assumes and satirically deflates the standard Western roles of rescued captive, White Indian, scout, gunfighter, and gambler.

The Indian world of *Little Big Man* is visualized as the fulfillment of the counterculture's vision of a sexually, spiritually, and (consequently) politically liberated society. But this utopia of the liberated libido is bloodily repressed in the re-created Battle of the Washita, when Custer and his men ride in over the white snowfields to massacre the village, mercilessly shooting Crabbe's wife and the infant on the cradle-board as she flees. As in *Soldier Blue*, the visual allusions to Mylai are clear, and the connection is emphasized by the casting of an Asian actress to play Crabbe's wife.[15]

A similar set of liberal and counterculture values informs some of the "Black" Westerns of this period, of which the most important is *Buck and the Preacher* (1971). Native Americans and Blacks are closely linked as exemplars of an essentially communal, ecological, and "populist" democratic form of society, which is radically different from a "White" society governed by mindless bigotry, the spirit of exploitation, and the logic of massacre. This vision distinguishes *Buck and the Preacher* from earlier "Black" Westerns like *Sergeant Rutledge, Duel at Diablo*, and *Red, White and Black* in which anti-Black racism can be undone only by scapegoating the Indians.[16] Instead of ending with the triumph of an all-encompassing, White-dominated "progressive" order, the film imagines its "wretched of the earth" establishing a refuge in the Rocky Mountains—an alternative to and replica of the original "City on a Hill" that exemplifies the values of racial and religious liberalism rather than the austere racial dualism of colonial Puritanism and imperial Anglo-Saxonism.

The rehabilitation of the Native American and the recognition of African-Americans as pioneers were appropriate and long-overdue acts of historical revision.[17] Symbolic exercises of this kind can serve the culture well by providing a language in which to imagine alternatives to the constraints of existing ideologies and social organization. But these exercises in mythological revisionism were weakened by their continuing indebtedness to the version of history inherent in the structures of the traditional Western. In *Little Big Man* no less than in *Broken Arrow*, the death of the Indian woman aborts the possibility of the hero's permanently "going native." Indians are still cast as the cultural/racial "Other," the antithesis of modern civilization; and their cultures are still represented as doomed to destruction by the inexorable advance of a modernity which Indians could never have achieved by their own efforts and to which they were incapable of adjusting. The "Black" Western had to straddle the contradiction between identification with the Indians as another oppressed people of color and the assertion of an African-American role in the "heroic" actions that won the West—and dispossessed the Indians.[18]

But contradictions of this kind had not proved insuperable obstacles to the success of the Western in the past. In 1939 and 1950 the ambivalent ideological premises that informed *Jesse James* and *Broken Arrow* had been taken as an invitation to further exploration and development of the theme. The lack of a follow-on to films like *Little Big Man* and *Buck and the Preacher* can be partly attributed to the public's (or Hollywood's) rejection of the symbols, myths, and values of "sixties liberalism." But assertively traditional or reactionary Westerns like *Two Mules for Sister Sara* and *Ulzana's Raid* were also without imitators after 1972. Their failure suggests that the rejection of the Western had gone beyond antipathy for a particular ideology to a rejection of the very idea that the Frontier could provide the basis of a national public myth.

The failure of Hollywood's attempt to revive the Western in 1975–76 proved—or at least confirmed the moviemakers in their belief—that the public had not only rejected a particular kind of Western but had no more interest in Westerns as such.

The Westerns of the 1975–76 revival built upon the alternative genre forms that were prominent in 1969–72 but abandoned the overtly political concerns of *Little Big Man* and *Buck and the Preacher*. The big Westerns of this period included exercises in formalist innovation (*The Missouri Breaks*), neorealist cynicism (*The Posse*, *The Shootist*), and counterculture sensibility (*Buffalo Bill and the Indians*, *The Return of a Man Called Horse*). The most interesting film of this period is Clint Eastwood's *The Outlaw Josie Wales* (1976). The film's design reflects Eastwood's mythographic ambitions and his considerable skill as a filmmaker. He knowingly integrates the sensational stylistics of the "spaghetti Western" with the historical/ideological concerns of the big Western historical epic. Though it begins as a classic cult-of-the-outlaw/revenge tale, the movie becomes an allegory of post-Vietnam reconciliation. To protect the multicultural commune that has gathered around him, Josie negotiates a truce with a Comanche chief in terms that echo the concepts of mutual deterrence and détente that were so prominent in the diplomacy of 1973–77. Although ex-Confederate Josie is a type of the embittered Vietnam veteran, he figuratively makes his peace with the peace movement by marrying a Yankee "flower-child."[19] And his last words to his forgiven enemy—"All of us died a little in that damn war"—seem intended as an epitaph for the divisive rage of that era in terms appropriate to the genre.

Outlaw Josie Wales is a well-conceived and well-made film and was not an unprofitable venture. It did not, however, fulfill the mission of genre-revival that both Eastwood and the Hollywood establishment had imagined for it. Despite the film's many virtues and the reflected glory of Eastwood's star persona, it was not the kind of film Eastwood or anyone else wanted to repeat very soon, unlike *Dirty Harry* and the other big action pictures of the same period.[20] Its fate is therefore indicative of the declining power and appeal of the genre.

The "alternative Westerns" of this period were not simply a cultural dead end, however. Their innovations substantially altered the visual style and ideological burden of the genre. Westerns made after 1976 are far more likely to follow an "alternative" scenario in respect to race or class relations than to revert to the "progressive" model of *Dodge City* or *Rio Grande*. But the effect of those innovations has been to make the Western a rather special form of expression, suitable for formalist exercises (*Pale Rider*, *Silverado*, *Rustler's Rhapsody*) and studied critiques of mainstream ideology (*Heaven's Gate*, *Electric Horseman*, *Young Guns II*, *Dances with Wolves*) rather than a routine resort for tellers of popular tales. The Western has therefore been relegated to the margins of the "genre map," and a succession of new and revamped genres have replaced it as the focus of mythographic enterprise.

Murderous Nostalgia: Myth and Genre After the Western

The displacement of the Western from its place on the genre map did not entail the disappearance of those underlying structures of myth and ideology that had given the genre its cultural force. Rather, those structures were abstracted from the elaborately historicized context of the Western and parceled out among genres that used their relationship to the Western to define both the disillusioning losses and the extravagant potential of the new era. Violence remained as central to these new genre-scenarios as it had been to the Western, but the necessity for violence was no longer rationalized by an appeal to the progressive historical myth of westward expansion.[21]

The fate of the Western in the 1970s is reminiscent of its eclipse during the 1930s, a period similarly marked by economic contraction and social disruption, though on an incomparably larger scale. There are particularly close affinities between the genre maps of the 1930s and the 1970s. In both, the matter of the Frontier was displaced into genres dealing with metropolitan crime, high-seas swashbuckling, and imperial or "oriental" adventure, supplemented by a new wave of "horror films." Between 1971 and 1977 urban crime dramas, featuring as heroes detectives, policemen, and "urban vigilantes," were the predominant type of American-location action film. The success of *Star Wars* in 1977 led to a boom in fantasy and science-fiction epics that were closely related in theme and visual style to the imperial epics of the 1930s. Toward the end of the decade the combat film reappeared, as Hollywood belatedly addressed Vietnam. And throughout the decade, horror and "slasher" films enjoyed consistent box-office success.

The French Connection and Clint Eastwood's *Dirty Harry* series typify the police-centered crime dramas of the period; Charles Bronson's *Death Wish* series inaugurated the "urban vigilante" genre. The heroes in these films are clearly the heirs of the hard-boiled detective, the gunfighter, and the Indian-hater.[22] Eastwood and Bronson made their reputations in Westerns, and their urban gunslingers are steely-eyed, cynical, fast on the draw, and likely to resolve the plot with a climactic gunfight. *Taxi Driver* (1976)—the most artful version of this story-type—uses the captivity/rescue narrative plan of *The Searchers* to give a perversely mythic resonance to its portrait of the violent urban loner, suggesting that he may be as distinctly American a "type" in our day as Ethan Edwards was in his. The police film *Fort Apache, The Bronx* (1981) treats the violence of contemporary racial ghettos in terms of the standard cavalry/Indian paradigm.[23]

What makes the urban vigilante genre different from the Westerns is its "post-Frontier" setting. Its world is urbanized, and its possibilities for progress and redemption are constricted by vastly ramified corporate conspiracies and by monstrous accumulations of wealth, power, and corruption. Its heroes draw energy from the same rage that drives the paranoids, psychopaths, mass murderers, and terrorists of the mean streets, and their victories are almost never socially redemptive in the Western mode. In these respects, the world of the urban gunslinger film is cognate to that of the horror and "slasher" film, typified by *The Omen* and *Texas Chainsaw Massacre*. These films carry to an extreme the premise of *Dirty Harry* and *Death Wish*, that our world is out of control, pervaded by an evil against which we feel helpless, an evil that affronts us from without in the form of disfigured, bloodthirsty strangers and from within in the form of perverse dreams and desires or nightmare versions of the generation gap—our own children suddenly revealed as alien monstrosities, Rosemary's babies. Although horror/slasher movies have their own generic history, they are very much in the captivity-rescue tradition. Many of them invoke bogeys whose ancestors appear in the literature of the Puritan witch trials, like the Indian or voodoo spirits (*Manitou, Cujo*) or murderous backwoodsmen (*Texas Chainsaw Massacre, Friday the Thirteenth*) whose literary ancestors are the Harpes and Simon Girtys of early frontier romances.[24]

However, both the urban vigilante and the horror/slasher genres *invert* the Myth of the Frontier that had informed the Western. The borders their heroes confront are impermeable to the forces of progress and civilized enlightenment; if anything, the flow of aggressive power runs in the opposite direction, with the civilized world threatened with subjugation to or colonization by the forces of darkness.

Although nominally offering an escape from real-world history, the science-fiction and fantasy films of the 1970s and 1980s owe a great and (in the case of the Lucas/Spielberg *Star Wars* trilogy) acknowledged debt to the Western. TV's *Star Trek* was always introduced with the incantation, "Space—the Final Frontier" (which became the subtitle of *Star Trek V*). *Outland* (1981) and *Battle Beyond the Stars* (1982) were science-fiction remakes of classic Westerns (*High Noon* and *The Magnificent Seven*). Beyond such literal imitations, and the *hommages* to John Ford's *The Searchers* in *Star Wars*, both the *Star Wars* trilogy and the *Star Trek* series project a myth of historical progress similar to that in the progressive Westerns and "empire" movies of the 30s and 40s. The tale of individual action (typically a captivity/rescue) is presented as the key to a world-historical (or cosmic-historical) struggle between darkness and light, with perpetual happiness and limitless power for the heroes and all humankind (or "sentient-kind") as the prize of victory. Despite its futuristic setting, *Star Trek II: The Wrath of Khan* (1982) uses a vocabulary that seems drawn from films like *The Charge of the Light Brigade*, *Gunga Din*, and *Santa Fe Trail*: as villain, a despotic chieftain who is half-savage and half-aristocrat; as setting, a desert frontier world, which can also become a colonial paradise through the technical power of the soldier-colonists of the *Enterprise* and the Genesis project; as motive for violence, a massacre with tortures and murder that must be avenged; and as resolution, a suicidal "charge" by the *Enterprise* on Khan's ship.[25]

The worlds of *Star Wars*, and of films similarly set either in fantasy-worlds or galaxies "far far away," are presented to us as alternatives to the historicized spaces of the Western and the pseudo-documentary or "journalistic" space of the crime film. Like fairy tales, they allegorize the condition and etiology of the present world, but they purchase imaginative freedom—the power to imagine the most magical or utopian possibilities—by keeping real historical referents at a distance. It would be inaccurate to describe the genre as entirely anti-historical, however. The *Star Trek* series continually undertakes explanations of how human society developed from its past of war, racism, and ecological crisis to its future of peace, tolerance, and balance under the Federation. In both the TV and the movie series, the crew of the *Enterprise* often go back in time to correct some historical flaw that might abort the utopian future. In the TV series, these excursions are frequently framed as expeditions into the movie-genre space of Westerns, gangster films, or the social dramas of the 1930s. This identification of history with the mythic spaces of film genres has been an important characteristic of both filmmaking and political campaigning since the late 1970s, as I will show in my discussion of public myth in the "Reagan Revolution."

Since 1976 Vietnam has also become a major subject for movie mythography. Cultural crisis is the mother of myth/ideological invention, and the Vietnam War is a particularly appropriate symbol of the catastrophe that overtook the liberal consensus and the New Frontier. It marked the moment when the failure of our latest "Indian war" coincided with the collapse of our expectation of perpetual and universal affluence, as the disappearance of hostile Indians and wilderness or virgin land had marked the end of the agrarian frontier for Turner and Roosevelt. Michael Herr expresses the idea eloquently and concisely: "[M]ight as well say that Vietnam was where the Trail of Tears was headed all along, the turnaround point where it would touch and come back to form a containing perimeter.[26]

The period of suppression and denial, during which the war was treated only indirectly, ended in 1977–78, with the first major Vietnam combat films, and in the 1980s Vietnam war stories became a significant element in commercial popular culture. Print media have produced a steadily increasing number of novels, memoirs, unit histories, even a multivolume Time/Life Books series titled *The Vietnam*

Experience. The number, scale, and prominence of film treatments have grown from the modest success of *The Boys in Company C* (1977), through the epics *The Deerhunter* (1977) and *Apocalypse Now* (1979), to the more recent celebrity of *Rumor of War* (made for TV), *Platoon, Hamburger Hill*, and *Casualties of War*. Major documentaries have been produced for television and for distribution as videocassettes, and two television series have been set in the war (*Tour of Duty* and *China Beach*).

Fictional treatments of Vietnam have developed their own distinctive narrative conventions, centering on a characteristic set of ideological contradictions and concerns. Among the important recurring motifs are: the reality gap between "grunts" and rear-echelon commanders (or soldiers and politicians); racial conflict within the American forces; the power of the domestic anti-war movement to affect combat morale; the alienation of troops from people "back in the World"; the breakdown of normal language in a war where words are deliberately used to obscure reality rather than to define it. Nearly every fictional treatment uses a Mylai-like incident to symbolize the central moral/ideological problem of the war story. Those that do not, usually build narrative crises around some other symptom of "cross-over": the murder of a suspected VC agent, the depredations of rogue counterguerrillas, or the betrayal of troops in the field by their officers, by the home front, or even by each other.[27]

The cultural authority of the Myth of Vietnam is augmented by its continuity with the myth/ideology it seems to have displaced. Allusions to the Frontier and to the Western continually recur in recent treatments, both documentary and fictional. Such references are appropriate to the historical subject, since, as we have seen, the Myth of the Frontier provided so much of the war's original symbolism. *The Deerhunter* (1977) interprets the Vietnam War as an enactment of fundamental American values by drawing on motifs from *The Searchers* and Cooper's Leatherstocking Tales.[28] *Apocalypse Now* (1979) is filled with allusions to cavalry/Indian Westerns, and in the paired characters of Kurtz and Willard it offers a complex interpretation of the darkest side of the "man who knows Indians." Vietnam films usually treat Western elements ironically, simultaneously questioning the war itself, the myths that justified and informed it, and the mass-culture genres that taught us our mythic language. In Stanley Kubrick's *Full Metal Jacket* (1987) several members of "the platoon" respond to the presence of a TV camera with joking invocations of movie myths ("Is that you, John Wayne? Is this me?") and historical mythology ("I'll be General Custer. But who'll be the Indians?"). By making no distinction between the "real" historical figure and the make-believe heroism of movies, the dialogue suggests that there is no "reality" to which one can appeal for an antidote to the poisonous illusion of "John Wayne."

The strong and in some cases deliberate animus with which these newly prominent genres use Western themes and materials is an indication that the rejection of the Western was in significant part a consequence of the reaction against the myth/ideology of liberal progressivism in the backwash of 1960s. But other factors, operating more subtly and over the longer term, seem likely to prolong the eclipse of the Western and promote other historically oriented genres in its place.

The primary function of any mythological system is to provide a people with meaningful emotional and intellectual links to its own past. Although western pioneering was always (after1800) a minority experience, the Frontier was able to symbolize a national past because its major themes—emigration in the quest for new and better things—had close cognates in the experiences of mobility and displacement that belonged both to foreign immigrants and to internal migrants in an industrializing and urbanizing nation. But as I pointed out in my discussion of Roosevelt, Wister, and the "progressive" Western, the twentieth century Frontier Myth was developed in reaction *against* racial and cultural heterogeneity to sanction an exclusive, *völkisch* definition of American nationality. Although immigrants and their immediate descendants shaped developments in the new culture industry of Hollywood, the Western films they made were informed by a desire (and a commercial need) to imitate, and so to acquire for themselves, "real Americanism." They accepted without question the idea that the Old West was an Anglo-Saxon preserve, just as they generally accepted WASP good looks as the standard for casting screen heroes. The WASP monopoly of movie heroism was compromised, to a degree, in the combat films of the Second World War—although through the 1940s and early 1950s the leading player in the ethnic platoon was most often a WASP icon like Robert Taylor, Errol Flynn, or Van Johnson. The bi-polar division of Western demography into cowboys and Indians (and occasional Mexicans) was not seriously enlarged until the emergence of the (shortlived) "civil rights" Western after 1960. Even then Black cowboys, soldiers, and homesteaders were never represented on a scale commensurate with their actual numbers in the West. Other groups have almost never been represented in Westerns, although they made up a significant part of the population of western states and territories from 1848 onward: Germans, Jews, Italians, Chinese, Japanese, Cornishmen, East and Central Europeans, South Americans, and Pacific Islanders. Their exclusion from Westerns is crippling to the genre's project of mythologizing our actual history and to its ability to address the polyglot, multicultural, multiracial folk of the modern United States.[29]

Cultural entities locate themselves in time by recovering and mythologizing their own histories; and if such a recovery is to have meaning in the culture of the nation-state, it must at some point find expression in the commercial media that dominate national culture. Given the increase in the number, population share, political power, and economic resources of peoples of color and the descendants of immigrants, it is not surprising that new non-Western subjects for historical movies have become prominent since 1970 and have begun to develop the kind of recurrent story patterns and stock figures that characterize a mass-culture mythology. These groups must look for their "American" roots in settings other than the Frontier, and (especially for the immigrant-derived groups) in epochs more recent than the 1890s.[30]

The new versions of *immigrant* history are, however, for the most part refracted through a single genre: the traditional "gangster film" and its post-*Godfather* variants. Coppola's epic treatment of the Corleone family saga in the first two *Godfather* films inaugurated what has become a Cult of the Mafia, which serves cultural purposes similar to those of the Cult of the Indian and the Cult of the Outlaw. These films invest the gangster heritage of Italian, Jewish, and Irish immigrants with nostalgia for a lost world of close and extended family ties and with immigrant-group solidarity in the face of poverty, displacement, and discrimination. The lament for the loss or corruption of the immigrant patriarchy in these films parallels, in both mood and ideological function, the idealization of lost pastoral matriarchy in *Jesse James* and the evanescent tribal patriarchy of Cochise in *Broken Arrow* or Lodge Skins in *Little Big Man*. Each of these cults proposes nostalgia for an idealized pre-capitalist past as the basis of a critique of modern American society and culture. Yet each, in the end, sees the power of the modern capitalist state as historically irresistible, doomed to success. To the extent that Hollywood's reading of the immigrant past is determined by the conventions of the gangster film, immigrant history is still conceived of as either marginal to

American life or as a major cause of the nation's fall from grace.

What is new about the Cult of the Mafia is not its myth of American history but its mood of nostalgia, which is both a substantial part of the films' emotional payoff and Hollywood's motivation for returning to old generic themes. Indeed, nostalgia for old styles and forms of expression became, in the late 1970s and early 1980s, one of the most important motives for mass-culture creativity, in movies and elsewhere. The yearning for the old assurances of American progressivism was reflected in the proliferation of theme parks and historical preservation projects, "period" TV series (*Happy Days*), the multiplication of TV reruns on cable, Hollywood's penchant for remaking movies from the 1940s and 1950s—and the election of an old movie star as President. One of the most successful of the new forms is what might be called the "genre genre": artful replicas of 1930s genres like the "B" Western (*Silverado*), the singing-cowboy musical (*Rustler's Rhapsody*), and the cliff-hanger serial (the *Indiana Jones* series). Although these productions invoke images of the American past, their primary appeal is not to the memory of historical experience but to the remembrance of old movies, and above all to the mood of naive acceptance with which these fictions were once (presumably) received. The nostalgia in these films is not only a fondness for the simplicity of old images but a yearning for a lost innocence, regret for the condition or sentiment of belief that (we like to imagine) existed in simpler and "better" times.

Genre-nostalgia disarms audience skepticism by its overt and playful appeal to the conventionality of movie genres. Nonetheless, the underlying structures of these films represent a powerful recrudescence of the old myths of regeneration through violence. This is most obvious in films like *Indiana Jones and the Temple of Doom*, where a 1930s–style "man who knows Indians" contends with a world of savages, both noble and demonic.[31] But the film that is most expressive of the style and content of movie mythography in the Reagan era is the crime drama *The Untouchables* (1987), written by David Mamet and directed by Brian DePalma.

The carefully constructed "period" setting is presented in a way that invites a nostalgic reading of the past. Instead of the Depression's mean streets, it shows us an almost pastoral Chicago of clean streets, its colors brightened by a clear "Morning-in-America" kind of light. This visual presentation augments our natural tendency to see "the past" as a simpler time, when issues could be resolved through the unmediated opposition of heroic virtue and cruel, corrupt villainy.

But despite the obsessive care taken with costume and set design, the 1930s are not the real historical frame to which *The Untouchables* refers. It is first of all a movie remake of a "period" TV series that ran from 1959 to 1963. The version of the 1930s it gives us is not a new attempt at historical representation but a restoration of the historical myth of an earlier generation. In this respect the film mirrors the approach to history taken by commercial theme parks (most notably Disneyworld), which proliferated in the 1970s and 80s: "history" is visualized and physically restored according to the sanitized models provided by contemporary mass-culture genres. The *overt* evocation of nostalgia, which is achieved through *The Untouchables'* elaborate "restoration" of the historical setting, serves the *covert* project of evoking nostalgia for the heroic simplicities of the heyday of the Cold War and the New Frontier.[32]

The film's true ideology is voiced subliminally through the artful use of generic references. The most significant of these link *The Untouchables* to the town-tamer and counterinsurgency Westerns of the 1960s. Eliot Ness (Kevin Costner) is the stranger in town, a Puritan with a hidden gift for violence who has to clean up a city ruled by criminals who have corrupted the authorities. Although he has an official position, like Wade Hatton in *Dodge City* and Earp in *My Darling Clementine* he is really energized for direct action by the killing of a child. Like Chris in *The Magnificent Seven* (a similarly sober Christian hero), Ness assembles a small elite squad of deputies for a classic counterinsurgency scenario, with Italians as the Indians or Mexicans. (Capone is the equivalent of Mapache or Calvera, both of whom employ cutthhroats like Frank Nitti.) Ness's team includes: a WASP "nerd" who shows a native aptitude for gun play and berserker rage; a wise old Irish cop who "knows Indians" and teaches Ness the necessity of "fighting dirty" like the enemy; and a "friendly Indian" (that is, Italian) whose role corresponds to that of Chico in *The Magnificent Seven* and Angel in *The Wild Bunch* and who is also the fastest of Ness's gunslingers. The film shows Ness beating Capone through a series of gunfights, including one on horseback. The image of the four Untouchables walking up a Chicago street carrying pistols, sawed-off shotguns, and pump guns mimics the famous walk of the Wild Bunch to their lat fight with Mapache.

By conflating the "historical" space of the Depression with the "mythic" space of Westerns, Mamet and DePalma gain poetic license for a radical departure from the nominal historical source and the ideological limitations of the TV series—a departure that allows them to make a powerful case for the political necessity of "extraordinary violence." The real Eliot Ness had used careful accounting procedures, rather than axes and tommy-guns, to defeat Capone. The original TV series, by exaggerating the level of police violence, had drawn criticism from public-interest groups for exceeding the norms of contemporary television, but the Eliot Ness of that series was absolutely rigid in his adherence to the letter of the law. By reconceiving their Ness as a counterinsurgency cowboy, Mamet and DePalma are able to assign him the moral and political privilege of the vigilante to take the law into his own hands. To defeat Capone, Ness must learn to play by "Chicago rules," as his Irish mentor tells him: to fight dirty, matching evil with greater evil, "if he pulls a knife, you pull a gun." Ness can win only by breaking the law he would honorably serve—murdering a prisoner and blackmailing a judge. But, though he confesses, "I became what I beheld," Ness (and the script) ultimately affirm the righteousness of what he has done.[33]

The elaboration of nostalgia in *The Untouchables* serves to rationalize and justify an updating of the counterinsurgency-Western scenario of regeneration through violence. In this adaptation, the symbolic conflicts of the "Mexico Western," redolent of an imperial form of savage war, are translated into contemporary domestic equivalents. The evil empire or barbarous bandit-tribe is replaced by a set of "new immigrants," "Latins" (to use Stoddard's term) differentiated by their swarthy skin, tribal code, and conscienceless cruelty from both the native WASPs and the older, "Whiter" Irish immigrants who constitute the civic pastoral of pre-Prohibition "Chicago."

The "post-Western" genre map suggests that, while the Western may no longer provide the most important of our ideologically symbolic languages, the underlying mythic structures it expressed remain more or less intact. Action in the imagined world of myth-symbolic play still takes the form of captivities and rescues, still invokes the three-part opposition in which the American hero stands between the extremes of bureaucratic order and savage license, and still requires a racial symbolism to express the most significant ideological differences. What has been lost is not the underlying myth but a particular set of historical references that tied a scenario of heroic action to a particular version of American national history. The passing of the Western may mark a significant revision of the surface signs and referents of our mythology, but it does not necessarily mark a change in the underlying system of ideology, which is still structured by its twin mythologies of bonanza economics and regeneration through savage war. Indeed, those mythologies provided the structuring principles of the so-called "Reagan Revolution" of the 1980s, which began as a systematic and initially successful attempt to regenerate American "public myth" and ended in a return to something very like the "malaise" of 1978–80.

Back in the Saddle Again?: The Reagan Presidency and the Recrudescence of the Myth

If Ronald Reagan or any of his handlers had read McNeill's diagnosis of the disease of "public myth," they would have wondered why McNeill failed to recognize their administration as the prescribed cure. The mythographers of the Reagan Revolution sought to overcome the "malaise" of the 1970s—the breakdown of public myth that prevented consensus on purposeful action in both domestic and foreign affairs—by substituting for the distressing memory of "the Sixties" a fictive replica of a simpler time: the "Happy Days" when the Cold War was young and the world was divided between an "evil empire" and a TV-pastoral, "Leave It to Beaver" America that a few good men could save by fighting dirty wars. The central theme of Reagan's two presidential campaigns, and of his conduct of office, was the systematic resanctification of the symbols and rituals of "public myth"—a task for which Reagan's experience as an actor was ideal preparation. His 1980 and 1984 campaigns associated him with iconic and idealized American settings drawn from the mythic landscapes of cinema: "Morning in America" (1980) depicted an America of farms, country churches, suburban lawns, the "decent" streets of cities, all seen in a soft early-day light; and many of his most characteristic anecdotes, phrases, and slogans ("Make my day!") were borrowed from movie dialogue. But these patently celluloid backgrounds and gestures seemed both appropriate and authentic as settings for candidate and President Reagan, because they were icons of movie-America, and that imagined space was indeed the historical setting in which Reagan matured and acquired his public identity.

From the beginning of his campaign for the presidency, Reagan was widely (and inaccurately) identified as a "B" Western cowboy actor, particularly (at first) by his detractors. The famous campaign poster, "Bedtime for Brezhnev," which shows a cowboy-clad Reagan holding a six-gun on the Russian leader, illustrates the achievement of the Reagan campaign: it transformed the most ridiculous of pop-culture formulas ("B" Westerns and comedies like *Bedtime for Bonzo*) into recipes for a renewal of the American myth. Reagan acquired a more "serious" heroic aura through images that linked him closely to the two most prominent Western movie stars, John Wayne and Clint Eastwood. The most impressive of these images came at the 1984 convention, when clips of John Wayne introduced a film celebrating Reagan's life and the achievements of his first term.

Reagan had a legitimate claim on this kind of heroic aura. Neither Wayne nor Eastwood had actually been a cowboy or a leatherneck—like Reagan, they had merely played those roles on the screen. The use of mythic allusion to lend a politician the afflatus of a hero was hardly unique to Reagan. William Henry Harrison traded on his Indian-fighting laurels to gain the presidency in 1840, and in 1900 Theodore Roosevelt rode into national office as "The Rough Rider" and "The Cowboy President." But Roosevelt's claim to those titles was proved by reference to his actual deeds as a stockman, sheriff, and Rough Rider, while Reagan's claim to heroic character was based entirely on references to imaginary deeds performed in a purely mythic space. The difference between them indicates the change that has occurred in our political culture over this century: the myths produced by mass culture have become credible substitutes for actual historical or political action in authenticating the character and ideological claims of political leaders. Moreover, the substitution of myth for history serves not only as an advertising ploy for electing the candidate but as an organizing principle for making policy. The obsession of the Johnson and Nixon administrations with symbolic victories was an early exercise in mythopolitics, but Ronald Reagan was the virtuoso of the form. At the height of his powers he was able to cover his actions with the gloss of patriotic symbolism and to convince his audience that—in life as in movies—merely symbolic action is a legitimate equivalent of the "real thing."[34]

The public's favorable response to Reagan's conflation of "cowboy," "star," and "president" suggests that (on some level of awareness) it shared McNeill's belief that a refurbishing of public myth was the proper antidote to the demoralization of American culture. That response also suggests that the key terms of the myth will be drawn from the language of mass media and not from the language of the intelligentsia. However one evaluates the substance of Reagan's policies and achievements, during his term of office he enjoyed perhaps the greatest personal popularity of any president in our history—a popularity that was not affected by the public's disapproval of many of the specific measures and policies of his administration. By the conviction with which he performed his public role, enacted the rituals of his office, and voiced the requisite religious and patriotic pieties, and by his convincing display of innocence of and disdain for the criticisms that were leveled against the traditions he espoused, Reagan *dramatized* or *impersonated* the condition of mythic belief whose loss McNeill laments. Thus by identifying with the President as *dramatis persona*, one could vicariously enjoy the comforts of credulity.[35]

There was more to the myth/ideology of the Reagan Revolution than mere manipulation of surface imagery. The structuring principles of that revolution represented an authentic recrudescence and revision of the Frontier Myth. According to that myth, a magical growth of American wealth, power, and virtue, will derive from the close linkage of "bonanza economics"—the acquisition of abundant resources without commensurate inputs of labor and investment—with political expansion and moral "regeneration" through the prosecution of "savage war." In the "post-industrial" 1980s a similar economic bonanza was to be achieved through the magic of supply-side economics coupled with a regeneration of the nation's spirit through more vigorous prosecution of Cold War (against Russia as "evil empire") and savage war (against enemies like Ghadafy of Libya, Maurice Bishop of Grenada, and the Sandinista regime in Nicaragua).[36]

"Reaganomics" developed in reaction to the failure of the Carter administration to deal with the economic crisis of "stagflation." The Reagan campaign faulted Carter's policy for its vacillation between conservative pro-business policies and conciliation of those labor and minority groups that formed the Democrats' liberal constituency. But the Republicans were equally effective in challenging the intellectual basis of Carter's conservatism: his acceptance of the idea that we had indeed reached "The End of the Cowboy Economy," and that on "spaceship earth" Americans could no longer look forward to high and ever-increasing rates of growth. The Reagan campaign's praise of the bonanza economies of previous "boom" eras was more than just an exercise in nostalgia: it was the prelude to an attempt to revive the "cowboy economy" under "post-industrial" conditions.

The Reagan version of "supply-side economics" represents a recrudescence (with modifications) of the Turnerian approach to economic development. In its original or primary formulation, Turner's Frontier Hypothesis held that the prosperity and high growth rates of the American economy had been made possible by the continual expansion of the Frontier into regions richly endowed with natural resources. As industrial production replaced agricultural and mineral commodities as the primary source of wealth, a revised or secondary version of Turnerism saw rapid increases in industrial productivity as a viable substitute for the land and resource bonanzas of the past—an idea suggested by Turner himself but codified as historical theory by Beard in the 1930s. The theoreticians of the liberal consensus saw the "affluent society" of postwar American as the vindication of this secondary Turnerism and extrapolated from the American model a universal theory of modernization.

"Reaganomics" in effect proposed a *tertiary* Turnerism, in which the multiplication and manipulation of financial capital replaces both agrarian commodities and industrial production as the engine of economic expansion. A "bonanza" of new capital, released through measures favoring business and the wealthy (tax cuts and deregulation), was to act as the magical guarantor of perpetual and painless economic growth, in just the way that the opening of "vast untapped reserves" of free land or gold or cheap oil on the Frontier had energized the economy in the past. At the ceremonies attending his signature of the St. Germain/Garn bill, which deregulated the savings and loan industry, Reagan hailed the measure as one that would cost the taxpayers nothing but would produce limitless benefits for the whole economy by energizing the banking industry and the crucial investment sectors of housing and real estate: "All in all, I think we've hit the jackpot." Although the poor and the middle classes would not benefit directly, some of the newly generated wealth would "trickle down" through the economy. (Even here the parallel with the Frontier held: the opening of new lands had not only benefited the minority who pioneered them, it had contributed indirectly to the prosperity of others by raising the value of land and labor and lowering the cost of food.)[37]

The enactment of tertiary Turnerism was accompanied by the recrudescence of ideas and behaviors associated with the bonanza economics of the old Frontier. The term "frontier" enjoyed its widest currency since 1960–63. Writers on economic subjects and promoters of particular businesses publicized a range of new "frontiers" in marketing and development, while on the left Robert Reich suggested that The New American Frontier lay in the development of human resources neglected by the "politics of greed" that shaped the Reagan program. Proposals for extraterrestrial colonization (on space stations or in lunar or planetary settlements) transformed "outer space" into The High Frontier; and since every American frontier presupposes the threat of Indians, the same term was used in polemics on behalf of a space-based nuclear warfare system, the Strategic Defense Initiative, or "Star Wars." Closer to home, the unexploited realm of the oceans was dubbed our "Last Earthly Frontier," a potentially inexhaustible source of nutriment, mineral wealth, and energy—and of course, an embattled wilderness whose more intelligent natives (the dolphins) might be enlisted as our allies in warfare.[38]

But perhaps the most characteristic use of "frontier" as a term of cultural significance in the Reagan era occurred in the voice-over by Robin Leach that introduced one of the most popular television programs of the decade, *Lifestyles of the Rich and Famous.* Leach invites his viewers to share with him the privilege of a voyeur's peep into the lives of "super" celebrities and the "super" rich, who inhabit "Fame and Fortune—the Final Frontier!" As on other frontiers, minimal investments of labor yield fabulous returns: the most trivial actions are seen to yield the extravagant perquisites of celebrity, especially a license for excessive consumption and conspicuous waste.

In its celebration of wealth and fame as things supremely valuable in themselves, *Lifestyles* seems a self-parody. But the show's abstraction of "wealth" from concrete scenarios of labor, savings, and investment highlights the distinctive character of this most recent recrudescence of Turnerian economics, in which vast speculations in the paper values of real-estate developments, Third World debt, junk bonds, and debt-leveraged corporate takeovers replaced productivity and investment as the calculus of economic value. The economic style of the 1980s has been likened to that of the Roaring 20s. But there is an equally good precedent in Mark Twain's description of bonanza economics during the Nevada silver boom of the 1860s:

> It was the strangest phase of life one can imagine. It was a beggar's revel. There was nothing doing in the district—no mining—no milling—no productive effort—no income— . . . and yet a stranger would have supposed he was walking among bloated millionaires. . . . Few people took *work* into their calculations—or outlay of money either; except the work and expenditures of other people. . . . You could . . . get your stock printed, and with nothing whatever to prove that your mine was worth a straw, you could put your stock on the market and sell out for hundreds and even thousands of dollars. To make money, and make it fast, was as easy as it was to eat your dinner. They burrowed away, bought and sold, and were happy.[39]

Conceiving of our landed, wooded, animal and mineral wealth as inexhaustible, the frontiersmen of the past felt licensed to exploit that wealth without restraint.[40] That same ethic had been applied in the metropolis to the human resource of labor, first in the exploitation of slaves and later in the somewhat more limited exploitation of immigrant and industrial laborers. Under Reaganomics, a marvelous new mother lode of wealth was discovered in the heritage of our society's accumulted savings and in the capital produced by past labor and investment, and a generation of junk-bond financiers and corporate raiders became rich and famous by strip-mining it. As Garry Wills has said,

> Wealth . . . became staggeringly *non*-productive in the Reagan era. It was diverted into shelters. It was shuffled through paper deals; it financed its own disappearance; it erased others' holdings, along with the banks that contained them. It depleted rather than replenished. It shriveled where it was supposed to irrigate. Huge sums were bandied about at art auctions while bridges were disintegrating. Money flew in all directions at home, while seeping almost invisibly abroad.[41]

Although the economy expanded under Reagan, the benefits of expansion were distributed so unequally that, while the richest Americans were acquiring a larger share of the national wealth, the number of persons living in poverty increased and the real income and assets of most of the population declined. The savings and loan deregulation, which Reagan had hailed as a "jackpot" in 1982, proved to be the worst financial disaster since the Great Depression. The government's colossal indebtedness—the result of Reagan's insistence on cutting taxes while accelerating defense spending—seems certain to limit for years to come the government's fiscal resources and its ability to pursue needed policies of social and economic reconstruction at home and to take a leading role in the investments that will shape the post-Cold War political and economic order.[42]

Like the "beggar's revel" of Reaganomics, the "savage war" side of Reagan's revived Frontier Myth shows a disparity between nominal values and real values. The center of Reagan's foreign-policy agenda was the more energetic prosecution of the Cold War against the Soviet Bloc, primarily through a massive buildup of military forces and the acquisition of the most advanced military technology. The renewed Cold War also envisioned the nation's resumption of an active counterinsurgency role in the Third World, both as a means of resisting the advance of Communism and as a way of asserting American interests against those of local opponents. Both policies required the discovery of a cure for "Vietnam syndrome": the public's unwillingness to support military engagement in the Third World for fear of becoming trapped in another "quagmire."

To build public support for defense expenditures, government spokesmen and policy-makers pointed with alarm to the continuing growth of the "Soviet menace." They abandoned the rhetoric of détente for an apocalyptic symbolism which labeled the Soviet Bloc an "evil empire" and "the foundation of evil in the modern world." "Vietnam syndrome" presented a more difficult problem, because engagement in Third World conflicts threatened immediate costs in blood instead of the deferred costs of the anti-Soviet buildup. The administration solved the problem by recognizing that "Vietnam syndrome" could be treated as merely a defective symbolism—a tendency to interpret every Third World contest as a metaphor of the Vietnam War and to conceive of that war as a "mistake" and inherently unwinnable. Reagan himself became the chief spokesman for a revisionist history of the Vietnam War. He represented that war as a noble, unselfish struggle that could have ended in victory if only the liberal politicians in Washington had not tied the hands of the military.

This version of the war was supported (and by Reagan explicitly linked) to a contemporary genre-myth of great currency and power which might be called "The Cult of the POWs/MIAs." *The Deerhunter* incorporated this theme in its epic treatment of the war. But the theme reached its widest audience through the films of the *Rambo* and *Missing in Action* series. The concentration of these films on the captivity formula links them to the most basic story-form of the Frontier Myth, and their obsessive repetition of the rescue fantasy makes them seem like rituals for transforming the trauma of defeat into a symbolic victory. The heroes of these films are military vigilantes, ex-Green Berets who cannot fully return to America until they have completed their failed "mission" and canceled the debt of honor owed to comrades they survived or left behind. The American who, as representative of the world's mightiest army, had been defeated by ragtag, Vietnamese guerillas now gets to play the war movie in reverse: this time he is the guerilla, and he defeats a rigid, regularized, totalitarian enemy who has him outnumbered and outgunned. But the redemption of national honor in these films also requires the defeat of a domestic, American opponent: the most insidious enemies of these rescuer-heroes are officials of their own government who represent those politicians and "big shots" who (as the Nazis said of the Weimar liberals) "stabbed the army in the back" and prevented it from winning the war.[43]

In these Vietnam-rescue films, mass-culture myth plays its classic role, which is not (as critics of media violence fear) to act as a stimulus to individual violence but to justify social violence through the symbolic enhancement of a tale of personal violence. The belief that numbers of POWs/MIAs are still held by the Vietnamese had been a recurrent preoccupation in every administration since 1975 and remains an important factor in our Southeast Asia diplomacy.

But the most significant political referent of these films was not the Vietnam War but the new crisis in America's relations with the Third World symbolized by the series of hostage crises that began with the *Mayaguez* incident and became a major factor in our politics after Iranian Revolutionary Guards seized our Tehran embassy in 1979. The mythic imperative implicit in any hostage "crisis"—that we must rescue or avenge the captive at all costs—has given such events a fatal attraction for public concern, media attention, and political opportunism. Carter's failure to rescue the Tehran hostages helped bring down his administration, and Reagan's obsession with the Beirut hostages distorted our policy in the Levant and encouraged the CIA and the NSC to undertake a series of scandalously illegal covert actions that tainted the last years of Reagan's presidency.[44]

"Standing tall" in places like Central America required the explicit repair of those counterinsurgency myths that had been discredited by Vietnam. The Reagan administration invested a good deal of time, effort, money, and moral capital in justifying its support of the "*contra*" war against the Marxist regime in Nicaragua: a war fought by "Chicago rules" which breached American moral codes and ultimately (in the Iran-*Contra* affair) federal law as well. More recently, the Bush administration's "War on Drugs" has invoked the traditional myths of savage war to rationalize a policy in which various applications of force and violence have a central role. Here the Myth of the Frontier plays its classic role: we define and confront this crisis, and the profound questions it raises about our society and about the international order, by deploying the metaphor of "war" and locating the root of our problem in the power of a "savage," captive-taking enemy.[45]

Once invoked, the war-metaphor governs the terms in which we respond to changing circumstances. It spreads to new objects; it creates a narrative tension for which the only emotionally or esthetically satisfying resolution is literal rather than merely figurative warfare. What begins as a demand for symbolic violence ends in actual bloodshed and in the doctrine of "extraordinary violence": the sanctioning of "cowboy" or (more properly) vigilante-style actions by public officials and covert operatives who defy public law and constitutional principles in order to "do what a man's gotta do."[46]

The mythic scenarios that rationalize and perhaps govern policy no longer take their language primarily from Western movies. They draw as well on the vocabularies of the vigilante-cop film and the Vietnam War rescue-revenge fable. Terms and images derived from Vietnam are used to interpret the "drug crisis" and to project a scenario of response. Advisers are sent to Colombia and Peru, and naval and air power is deployed to interdict supply routes and help the native troops conduct search-and-destroy operations. There are projects for defoliation or coca-crop destruction and efforts to win the hearts and minds of the people (both American drug users and Colombian peasants). The invasion of Panama in January 1990, which literalized the metaphor of the "War on Drugs," was framed by the classic rationales of the Frontier Myth: the tyrannical Manuel Noriega (formerly a paid agent of our own CIA) was characterized not only as a dictator but as a physically repellent man (with pocked face and "Indian" blood), a sexual deviant and a drug addict; and the immediate pretext for the invasion itself ("Operation Just Cause") was the need to rescue American civilians from abuse by Noriega's forces and to avenge the assault on an American officer and his wife.[47]

The most triumphant, and the most disturbing, of these exercises in mythography is the Gulf War of 1991. In justifying the largest deployment of American military force since the Vietnam War, President Bush invoked the classic elements of "captivity" and "savage war" mythology. Saddam Hussein's potential dominance of the Gulf oil fields was seen as a danger to the future of "bonanza economics"; defeating Saddam would facilitate long-term development and save American jobs in the present. Hussein himself was the perfect enemy for a modern Frontier-Myth scenario, combining the barbaric cruelty of a "Geronimo" with the political power and ambition of a Hitler. This characterization was made credible by the oppressive character of the Ba'ath regime, the murderous occupation of Kuwait, and Saddam's ill-managed attempts at hostage-holding. The vivid symbolism and the passions it aroused effectively masked the questionable aspects of American policy in the region, including our earlier complicity with Saddam in his war against Iran.[48]

More disturbing still is Bush's assertion that the violence of the Gulf War has regenerated the national spirit and moral character by expiating the defeat in Vietnam. Mythopolitical exercises of this kind are of course inimical to the successful conduct of affairs, to the extent that they palliate or even justify badly conceived policies. But their most harmful effect may be their distortion of the language and logic that inform the discourses of our political culture. By treating the Gulf War as a ritual of regeneration through violence, and asking us to receive it as redemption for our failure in Vietnam, Bush asks us to conceive our political and moral priorities in *exclusively* mythic terms—with primary reference to the conflicts, needs, desires, and role-playing imperatives that are exhibited in mass-culture mythology, and with secondary or negligible reference to the realities of public and political life. By assuring us that the sentiments we feel when watching a movie-captivity like *Rambo II* or *Missing in Action* are a sufficient basis for engaging in war, the President authorizes the shedding of blood, not as a cruel means to a necessary end, nor as a defense of vital interests or principles, but as a cure for the illness of our imagination—to erase the discomforting memory of our historical experience of error and defeat, and to substitute in its place the lie of "symbolic victory."[49]

The destructive effects of this kind of mythological thinking are not restricted to foreign affairs, but (like counterinsurgency) have their domestic counterpart. The "savage war" paradigm has also been invoked to conceptualize and formulate policy for the social disruption and urban violence that have attended the "drug war" and the "Reagan Revolution" in American cities. The title of a popular novel and film of the early 1980s—*Fort Apache, the Bronx*—vividly captures the public's sense of cities "reverting to savagery" and ruled by semi-tribal youth gangs representing African-American and other Third World "races" or ethnicities.[50] The policy scenarios implicit in this paradigm emphasize "military" over social solutions: the use of police repression and imprisonment—a variation on free-fire zones and "reconcentration camps" or "reservations"—as policies of first resort preferable to more laborious and taxing projects of civic action or social reform.

The political successes of the Reagan and Bush administrations suggest that in the 1980s there was indeed a renewal of public myth: a general disposition to think mythologically about policy questions, substituting symbol and anecdote for analysis and argument; and a specific revival of the ideological structures of the Frontier Myth (savage war and bonanza economics) abstracted from its traditional association with Western movies and the historical Wild West. However, it would be a mistake to see this recrudescence as proof of the restoration of a true public myth capable of organizing the thought and feeling of a genuine and usable national consensus. The iconography, symbolism, and public ritual associated with American patriotism were indeed given new currency and credibility by Reagan's performance of his role. But his repair of public myth was partial and incomplete. He did not (could not) wholly succeed in effacing either the material consequences of our historical experience or its registration in memory.

The magical effects of Reagan's performance began to dissipate with the departure of the performer and with the discovery that some rather costly "due bills" were left behind.[51] Although the economy had revived between 1982 and 1990, the Reagan "boom" was followed by a prolonged recession, by some measures the longest since 1945. Nor has the refurbished myth/ideology of the Reagan Revolution functioned as a unifying or consensus-making tool. On the contrary, as the 1988 presidential campaign made clear, it has helped to polarize political discourse by reviving (in more polite form) the old symbols and codes of racial prejudice, anti-intellectualism, and red-baiting. Reagan sailed into the presidency by smiling and waving Old Glory; his successor won by brandishing the flag, playing "the race card," and deriding his opponent's Americanism.[52]

Despite such triumphs as the collapse of Communism and victory in the Gulf War, polls taken in 1990–91 indicate that most Americans have not recovered their faith in the most fundamental principles of national ideology: the belief that American democracy offers effective means for expressing the will of the people through political action, and the belief in national and personal progress—the idea that each generation will do better and produce more than the one before. There is widespread public skepticism about the ability of the political leadership, Republican or Democrat, to provide an accurate assessment of our problems, a useful set of predictions and policies, or even an honest set of account books. There is a growing awareness that the real bases of American political and industrial strength have been weakened and our culture undermined by the waste and abuse of our human resources in the last fifteen years, in particular our failure to invest in public health and education, in the restructuring of our displaced industrial workforce, in the improvement of our cities, and in measures for reducing the size and permanency of the "underclass." These failures have undermined our capacity to compete with other industrialized nations and have prolonged the crisis of demoralization that has affected our political culture since the end of the 1960s.

Imagining America

Nations, as Benedict Anderson says, are "imagined communities." With all their flaws, the liberal consensus and the Frontier Myth did attempt to imagine—and so to constitute—the nation as a cultural community. Although initially defined in racially and sexually exclusive terms, the mythic "American nation" was always the broadest and most inclusive of our imagined communities; and the most successful movements for democratic reform—abolition, labor and welfare legislation, civil rights—have usually acted in the name of a national community and have achieved their ends through national legislation. The historical experiences of 1965–75 broke up the consensus and discredited the "public myth" of liberal progressivism, and it seems unlikely that a new national consensus can be built on the ambivalent mix of nostalgia, bellicosity, and resentment that characterize the ideology of the Reagan and Bush administrations. But so long as the nation-state remains the prevalent form of social organization, something like a national myth/ideology will be essential to its operations.

We are in a "liminal" moment of our cultural history. We are in the process of giving up a myth/ideology that no longer helps us see our way through the modern world, but lack a comparably authoritative system of beliefs to replace what we have lost. As McNeill notes, a good deal of the creative energy of the intellectual establishment goes into the criticism and demystification of old myths. This critical mood both reflects and adds to a public skepticism that is the product of hard experience. But the history of humanity gives us no reason to suppose that we will ever cease to mythologize and mystify the origin and history of our societies. Critical projects of demystification are, in the long run, merely part of the process through which existing myths are creatively revised and adjusted to changing circumstances.

In that long run, our choice is not between myth and a world without myth, but between productive revisions of myth—which open the system and permit it to adjust its beliefs (and the fictions that carry them) to changing realities—and the rigid defense of existing systems, the refusal of change, which binds us to dead or destructive patterns of action and belief that are out of phase with social and environmental reality. We require a myth that can help us make sense of the history we have lived and the place we are living in. Although myth is a fictive form of expression, its social function is to imagine effective ways of apprehending and controlling the material world. Mythic formulations are therefore, at every moment, implicitly subject to tests of validity or truth. A viable, functioning mythology is one whose truth seems validated by the apparent accuracy with which it accounts for experience and facilitates the design of successful actions. When the language of myth is seen to provide only meaningless, false, or useless representations of the reality to which it refers, myth itself will be discredited.

Myth is the language in which a society remembers its history, and the reification of nostalgia in the mass culture and politics of the 1980s is a falsification of memory. If a new mythology is to fulfill its cultural function, it will have to recognize and incorporate a new set of memories that more accurately reflect the material changes that have transformed American society, culture, and politics in the last forty years. The historical adventure of our national development will have to be reconceived to incorporate our experience of defeat and disappointment, our acquired sense of limitation, as well as the fabulous hopefulness that has perennially informed and energized our culture. Even in its liberal form, the traditional Myth of the Frontier was exclusionist in its premises, idealizing the White male adventurer as the hero of national history. A new myth will have to respond to the demographic transformation of the United States and speak to and for a polyglot nationality. Historical memory will have to be revised, not to invent an imaginary role for supposedly marginal minorities, but to register the fact that our history in the West and in the East, was shaped from the beginning by the meeting, conversation, and mutual adaptation of different cultures.

Our given mythology tends to reduce the parties to the American cultural conversation to simple sets of paired antagonists, and a powerful current of opinion in the academy holds that any attempt to transform our cultural discourse is impossible so long as we continue to work within the grammar and lexicon of that myth. The demand for radical and revolutionary transformation implicit in this approach may be questioned on theoretical and political grounds. As I have been at pains to show, the beliefs and practices that hold societies together are the product of a long historical interaction between ideas, experience, and remembering. To propose significant social change without reference to that language renders the proposal unintelligible; to impose change as if from outside the culture, appealing for authority to values that the culture has not generated and accepted for itself, is to assert dictatorship.[53]

The history we have been tracing suggests that the discourses of myth are not fixed and programmatic—not a "prisonhouse of language" from which conceptual and political escape is impossible. The mythic codes to which we subscribe derive their authority not only (or even primarily) from their linguistic form, but from their historicity—which also renders them vulnerable to modification when they are tested against current experience. The poetics of myth entice the naive audience into false or dangerous identifications, as when the captain in Vietnam invited Michael Herr to play "cowboys and Indians." But the rules of mythic expression are not fixed constraints, like those that govern games. They are more like the structures that define the forms of expressive art: the study and practice of such rules ultimately give the artist the freedom of the form, the power to transgress and transform its regulations. When we understand the history and structure of our mythic language, we acquire the power to innovate and invent in that language—to alter the *practice* of the myth and thereby (potentially) to initiate an adaptation of its basic *structure*. The language of myth allows us to speak in terms that are fully intelligible and rich in historical resonances for the people to whom we speak. Through the discourses of myth we can recover a true (or truer) understanding of our history.[54]

In 1960 Robert Frost helped inaugurate Kennedy's New Frontier with his signifying "gift" of the poem "The Gift Outright," in which he invoked the mythology of savage war to symbolize the processes that had created our nationality. Nothing in the poem would have seemed alien to Theodore Roosevelt. We became Americans, Frost said, by giving ourselves to "the land vaguely realizing westward"—land we claimed in possession but which was not fully ours until we had *given* ourselves to it. And "The deed of gift was many deeds of war." The "we" of the poem is ambiguous, but since the westward movement is the only historical event referred to in the poem, we may guess that it refers primarily to the European settlers who regenerated their identities and generated their nation by violently dispossessing the Native Americans—who are never mentioned in the poem.

But in his last published volume Frost took a different view of our national myth. In "America Is Hard to See" (1962) he recalls the original promise of the Frontier Myth and of American history—that it was to provide the basis for an exceptional future, a new departure from the fatal limitations of human nature and European society:

> Had but Columbus known enough
> He might have boldly made the bluff
> That better than Da Gama's gold
> He had been given to behold
> The race's future trial place
> A fresh start for the human race.
>
> He might have fooled Valladolid
> I was deceived by what he did.
> If I had had my chance when young
> I should have had Columbus sung
> As a God who had given us
> A more than Moses' exodus.

The light of American historical experience has exposed a fatal flaw in the original myth: in its intent focus on the "high purpose" of a single type of hero, an exclusive system of value and belief, the visions of Columbus (and his metaphorical successors) have made the reality of America and American history "hard to see." Against the delusory vision of America as an escape from history and from the limitations of our human and social condition, the poet sets a capsule version of our experience of history:

> But all he did was spread the room
> Of our enacting out the doom
> Of being in each other's way,
> And so put off the weary day
> When we would have to put our mind
> On how to crowd but still be kind.[55]

"The Gift Outright" declares rightly that "we" gained title to "our" nationality through "many deeds of war." But the poem, like the ideological regime Frost helped inaugurate, was too narrow in its understanding of how "we" were actually constituted. From today's perspective, we can see "our" history as including those who once were considered beyond the pale of American citizenship: even the "Indian wars" have proved to be civil wars. Before we can "put our mind/ On how to crowd but still be kind" we must learn to consider *kindness*, not as the charity of the privileged to the disadvantaged, but as an enlarged sense of mortal kinship—the kindness invoked by Melville in *Moby-Dick* when Ishmael, weary of Ahab's apocalyptic quest, imagines the fatal divisions amont people dissolved "into the very milk and sperm of kindness." If our culture is to be responsive to the conditions in which we live, we will need a myth that allows us to see our history as an ecological system: not a false pastoral of pure harmony, but a system bound together by patterns of struggle and accommodation within and among its constituent populations, in which every American victory is also necessarily an American defeat. We need a myth that will help us acknowledge that our history is not simply a fable of sanctified and sanctifying progress, but that our national experience, and the space we inhabit, has been constructed out of what "we" have won and of what "we" have lost by our manner of "winning the West." Adrienne Rich poses the problem for the artist or scholar who wishes to tell critical truths, and still serve as makers of a public myth:

> What if I told you your home
> is this continent of the homeless
> of children sold taken by force
> driven from their mothers' land
> killed by their mothers to save from capture
> —this continent of changed names and mixed-up blood
> of languages tabooed
> disaporas unrecorded
> undocumented refugees
> underground railroads trails of tears
> What if I tell you, you are not different
> it's the family albums that lie
> —will any of this comfort you
> and how should this comfort you?[56]

There is no reason why a myth of national solidarity and progress should not be claimed and used by Americans who envision the nation as polyglot, multicultural, and egalitarian and whose concept of "progress" is not defined by the imperatives of the commercial corporation or the preferences of a managerial or proprietary elite. The history of the Frontier did not "give" Roosevelt or Kennedy or Reagan the political scripts they followed. What they did—what any user of cultural mythology does—was to selectively read and rewrite the myth according to their own needs, desires, and political projects. It follows that our mythology has been and is available, at every moment of our history, to the claims of other constituencies. Indeed, such claims have historically been made both in the folklores of resistant communities and movements and (as the case of the dime novel illustrates) in the specialized sectors of the mass-culture industries as well. The traditions we inherit, for all their seeming coherence, are a registry of old conflicts, rich in internal contradictions and alternative political visions, to which we ourselves continually make additions.

The myth/ideology of a living culture is not a determinate program that endlessly and helplessly reproduces itself but a volatile and ongoing conversation in which the basic value-conflicts, ambivalent desires, and contradictory intentions of the culture's constituents are continuously entertained. It is true that in a modern society, where powerful corporate and political institutions make it their business to "imagine the nation" *for* us, mass-culture myths can be effective instruments for manipulating and directing public opinion. But the demise of Communist regimes in Eastern Europe suggests that no system of cultural hegemony, no matter how perfect its monopoly of the instruments of cultural production, is impervious to the effects of cultural or social change. Hollywood's inability to revive the Western in 1975–76 and 1980–81 is a smaller but no less significant reminder that capitalist culture industries are also unable to monopolize or control the production of myth and ideology, and that no mythic system can be perfectly invulnerable to the rebuke of events. A moment always comes when conditions force us to choose between adherence to a comfortable old formula and successful adjustment to new conditions.

If we wish to contest or alter the myth/ideology produced for us by mass-culture industries and exploited by corporate and political leadership, the full repertoire of cultural and political responses is still available to us. The cultures of media-company board rooms and political bureaucracies are dependent on, and blunderingly responsive to, the shifting moods and preferences of the populations they both exploit and serve. We ourselves can agitate and organize, enlist or resign, and speak, write, or criticize old stories and tell new ones. If the corporate structure of mass culture excludes us, other bases and sites of action remain—the classroom, the congregation, the caucus, the movement, the street corner, the factory gate.

Myth is not only something *given* but something *made*, a product of human labor, one of the tools with which human beings do the work of making culture and society. The discourses of myth are, and have been, medium as well as message: instruments of linguistic and ideological creativity as well as a constraining grammar of codified memories and beliefs. We can use that instrument to reify our nostalgia for a falsely idealized past—to imagine the nation as a monstrously overgrown Disneyworld or Sturbridge Village—or we can make mythic discourse one of the many ways we have of imagining and speaking truth. By our way of remembering, retelling, and reimagining "America," we too engage myths with history and thus initiate the processes by which our culture is steadily revised and transformed.

List of Abbreviations

AQ American Quarterly
AHR American Historical Review
ALH American Literary History
BBWW Buffalo Bill's Wild West
HW Harper's Weekly, a Journal of Civilization
JAC Journal of American Culture
JAH Journal of American History
JAS Journal of American Studies
JPC Journal of Popular Culture
MP Marxist Perspectives
NYDL New York Detective Library
NYH New York Herald
NYRB New York Review of Books
NYT New York Times
NYTBR New York Times Book Review
NYW New York World
RHR Radical History Review
S&S Street & Smith
WHQ Western Historical Quarterly
WW World's Work

Notes

Notes to Introduction

1. Herbert S. Parmet, *JFK: The Presidency of John F. Kennedy*, pp. 8–31, 33, 72–3; and Godfrey Hodgson, *America in Our Time: From World War II to Nixon, What Happened and Why*, pp. 118, 132–3, 463*ff*.

2. *New York Times*, July 17, 1960; Richard M. Drinnon, *Facing West: The Metaphysics of Indian-Hating and Empire Building*, p. 429.

3. Richard Slotkin, *The Fatal Environment: The Myth of the Frontier in the Age of Industrialization, 1800–1890*, pp. 16–18; Drinnon, *Facing West*, p. 369.

4. Slotkin, *Fatal Environment*, p. 18; Michael P. Rogin, *Ronald Reagan, the Movie and Other Episodes of Political Demonology*, pp. 38, 43; Gary Wills, *Reagan's America*, pp. 103–4, 173–4, 205–10, 217, 313, 336.

5. For the theory of myth and ideology used here, see Slotkin, *Fatal Environment*, chs. 2–3; ———, *Regeneration Through Violence: The Mythology of the American Frontier, 1600–1860*, ch. 1.

6. On definitions of terms, see Slotkin, *Fatal Environment*, ch. 2, esp. pp. 30–2; Clifford Geertz, *The Interpretation of Cultures: Selected Essays*, "Ideology as a Cultural System"; Raymond Williams, *Keywords: A Vocabulary of Culture and Society*, pp. 87–93, 153–8, 210–2; Marshall Sahlins, *Historical Metaphors and Mythical Realities: Structure in the Early History of the Sandwich Islands Kingdom*, pp. 7–8, 64–6, 68, 72; ———, "*La Pensee Bourgeoise*: Western Society as Culture," in Chandra Mukerji and Michael Schudson, eds., *Rethinking Popular Culture: Contemporary Perspectives in Cultural Studies*, ch. 8; Morris Freilich, ed. *The Relevance of Culture*. On genre, see Slotkin, "Prologue to a Study of Myth and Genre in American Movies," *Prospects* 9 (1984), pp. 411–3, and ch. 7, below. The concept of a myth/ideological system, and the account of its transformation by historical processes, also draws on the theory of "paradigm" and "paradigm revolution" in intellectual or scientific thought developed in Thomas Kuhn, *The Structure of Scientific Revolutions*, and Peter L. Berger and Thomas and Luckmann, *The Social Construction of Reality: A Treatise in the Sociology of Knowledge*.

7. Slotkin, *Fatal Environment*, p. 23; Northrop Frye, *The Critical Path: An Essay on the Social Context of Literary Criticism*, pp. 35–6, 107.

8. Slotkin, *Fatal Environment*, pp. 23–5; Geertz, *Interpretation of Cultures*, p.

231; Sahlins, *Historical Metaphors*, pp. 68, 72; Frye, *Critical Path*, pp. 38–43; Victor L. Turner, "Process, System, and Symbol: A New Anthropological Synthesis," *Daedalus* 1977, 1:61–80; Roland Barthes, *Mythologies*, p. 110, 129, 142; Claude Levi-Strauss, *Structural Anthropology* 2: 256, 268; on the "logic" of narrative, its fictive character and ideological role, and its problematic status in historiography, see esp. Hayden White, *Metahistory: The Historical Imagination in Nineteenth Century Europe*, pp. 1–42; ———, *Tropics of Discourse: Essays in Cultural Criticism*, "Introduction" and chs. 1–5; Frederic Jameson, *The Political Unconscious: Narrative as a Socially Symbolic Act*, chs. 1, 2, 6; Hazard Adams, "Introduction," in ——— and Leroy Searle, eds., *Critical Theory Since 1965*, pp. 5–11, 15; Louis Althusser, "Ideology and Ideological State Apparatuses," in *ibid.*, pp. 238–50; James A. Henretta, "Social History as Lived and Written," *AHR* 84:5 (1979), pp. 1293–1322; Peter Novick, *That Noble Dream: The "Objectivity Question" and the American Historical Profession*; Arthur C. Danto, *Narration and Knowledge* . . . , chs. 3, 7–9, 11, 15; Robert Scholes, "Narration and Narrativity in Film," in Gerald Mast and Marshall Cohen, eds., *Film Theory and Criticism: Introductory Readings*, pp. 390–403.

9. Sahlins, *Historical Metaphors*, pp. 8, 64–6, 72, ch. 4; Geertz, *Interpretation of Cultures*, pp. 218, 220; David E. Apter, ed., *Ideology and Discontent*. On the renewal of myth following periods of disruption, see Frye, *The Secular Scripture: A Study of the Structure of Romance*, ch. 6; Slotkin, *Regeneration Through Violence: The Mythology of the American Frontier, 1600–1860*, pp. 15–6, 363–4, 370–1; Philip Wheelwright, "The Semantic Approach to Myth," in Thomas Sebeok, ed., *Myth: A Symposium*, pp. 154–68.

10. Geertz, *Interpretation of Cultures*, pp. 211, 214, 231. I have also drawn on some recent developments in cognitive theory which give an account of the operations of individual human memory-systems (and the role of metaphorical thinking) that closely parallels the cultural processes suggested by Geertz and described in detail by Sahlins in *Historical Metaphors*. See the discussion of "script theory" in Sylvan S. Tomkins, "Script Theory: Differential Magnification of Affects," in H. E. Howe and R. A. Dienstbier, eds., *Nebraska Symposium on Motivation* 26 (1979); Dan P. McAdams, *Power, Intimacy and the Life Story: Personological Inquiries into Identity*, chs. 5 and 7. On mnemonic processes and the role of metaphor in cognition, see Roger Schank, *Dynamic Memory: A Theory of Reminding and Learning in Computers and People*, esp. pp. 19, 37–41, and 48ff.; and Earl R. MacCormac, *A Cognitive Theory of Metaphor*, pp. 1–8, chs. 5, 8; Paul De Man, "The Rhetoric of Temporality," in Adams and Searle, *Critical Theory*, pp. 198–222; Paul Ricoeur, "The Metaphorical Process as Cognition, Imagination, and Feeling," in *ibid.*, pp. 423–34. See also Slotkin, *Fatal Environment*, p. 75.

11. Geertz, *Interpretation of Cultures*, pp. 211, 214, 231; Sahlins, pp. 67, 72. Compare H. White, *Tropics of Discourse*, p. 4: "A discourse moves to and fro between received encodations of experience and the clutter of phenomena."

12. On archetype and the collective unconscious, see Slotkin, *Fatal Environment*, pp. 26–8 and fn. 24, p. 539; and ———, *Regeneration*, pp. 9–14. On "grammar of tropes," Martin Green, *Dreams of Adventure and Deeds of Empire*, p. 53. In "From Mythical Possibility to Social Existence," Claude Levi-Strauss sug-

gests that myths propagate themselves in an automatic, almost mathematical fashion within a given cultural system:

> Stimulated by a conceptual relationship, mythic thinking engenders other relationships which are parallel or antagonistic to the first one . . . as though the permutation of multiple axes of terms belonging to the same network were an autonomous activity of the mind, so that any state of a combination would suffice to get the mind moving and . . . produce a cascade of all the other states. . . . The same concepts, rearranged, exchange, contradict, or invert their values and their functions, until the resources of this new combinatorics are dissipated or simply exhausted.

Claude Levi-Strauss, "From Mythical Possibility to Social Existence," ch. 11, *The View from Afar*, trans. by Joachim Neugroschel and Phoebe Hoss, pp. 157–74, 172, 173.

In treating myth/ideological systems as linguistic formulations, one has to take into account the theories of linguistic autonomy in "post-modern" or "post-structuralist" critical theories. At their best, these approaches serve to expose the rhetorical conventions and mythic structures that inform the ideologies of humanism, scientism, capitalist democracy, and Marxian socialism. They also highlight the crucial role of the reader in determining the actual or effective meaning of texts in any given social or historical setting, by asserting that textual meaning can never be determinate but is always "in play." This is an understanding central to any theory that attempts to show ideas as cultural productions engaged in the flux and alteration of history; and the idea that texts have more than one "author"—that successive generations possess both the power and the legitimate authority to rewrite, revise, or re-author their culture—is crucial to the depiction of human "agency" in history. However, the ideology implicit in the more extreme forms of post-structuralism/post-modernism is one that substitutes for the materialist or idealist determinisms it deconstructs a form of "linguistic determinism," in which "Language had come to speak man," and histories "write us." I find the notion of self-generating texts implausible, and the concomitant idea of a linguistic "prisonhouse" both excessively deterministic and inaccurate as a description of the historical activities of cultural production with which I am concerned.

In general, I agree with Sahlins' response to the problem of semiological reference, *Historical Metaphors*, p. 6:

> *In the event* [emphasis added], speech brings signs into "new" contexts of use, entailing contradictions which must be in turn encompassed by the system. Value is truly constituted in a system of signs, but people use and experience signs as the names of things, hence they condition and potentially revise the general conceptual values of linguistic terms and relations by reference to a world. The encounter with the word is itself a valuation, and a potential revaluation, of signs.

See the discussion of post-structuralism and post-modernism in Adams, "Introduction," *Critical Theory Since 1965*, pp. 1–24, esp. pp. 5–7, 9–12, 15, and the essays by Jacques Derrida, Michel Foucault, Paul De Man, Jonathan Culler, Geoffrey Hartman, and Paul Ricoeur; Hayden White, *Tropics of Discourse*, ch.

12; Leon Fink, *et al.*, "A Round Table: Labor, Historical Pessimism, and Hegemony," *JAH* 75: 1 (1988), pp. 115–61; T. J. Jackson Lears, "The Concept of Cultural Hegemony: Problems and Possibilities," *AHR* 90:3 (1985), pp. 567–93; Jean-Philippe Mathy, "Out of History: French Readings of Postmodern America," *ALH* 2:2 (1990), pp. 267–98; Giles Gunn, *The Culture of Criticism and the Criticism of Culture, passim,* and "Beyond Transcendence or Beyond Ideology: The New Problematics of Cultural Criticism in America," *ALH* 2:1 (1990), pp. 1–18; and Scholes, "Narration and Narrativity." I am grateful to Christina L. Zwarg for her advice on applying these theories to my project.

13. On the tendency of commercial mass media to organize stories into genres or formulas, see John G. Cawelti, *Adventure, Mystery and Romance: Formula Stories as Art and Popular Culture*, ch. 1; Michael Denning, *Mechanic Accents: Dime Novels and Working-Class Culture in America*, esp. Part I; Martin Green, *Dreams of Adventure*, ch. 1. On the subculture of popular-culture producers and their relation to audiences, see Herbert J. Gans, *Popular Culture and High Culture: An Analysis and Evaluation of Taste*, and *Deciding What's News: A Study of* CBS Evening News, NBC Nightly News, Newsweek *and* Time; Todd Gitlin, *Inside Prime Time*, esp. ch. 1; Nick Roddick, *A New Deal in Entertainment: Warner Brothers in the 1930s*, esp. chs. 1–2, 4, 9; and Thomas Schatz, *The Genius of the System: Hollywood Filmmaking in the Studio Era*. On the development of culture industries, see Daniel Boorstin, *The Americans: The Democratic Experience*, Book 3, and *The Americans: The National Experience*, pp. 325–90; Albert Johannsen, *The House of Beadle and Adams, and Its Dime and Nickel Novels: The Study of a Vanished Literature* 1: chs. 1–2, 4–6, 11; James D. Hart, *The Popular Book: A History of America's Literary Taste*; Garth Jowett, *Film, the Democratic Art: A Social History of American Film*, and "The Emergence of the Mass Society: The Standardization of American Culture, 1830–1920," Prospects 7 (1983), pp. 207–28; Frank Luther Mott, *American Journalism: A History of Newspapers in the United States Through 250 Years, 1690–1940*, and *A History of American Magazines* (5 vols.); Bernard Rosenberg and David Manning White, *Mass Culture: The Popular Arts in America*; Warren I. Susman, *Culture as History: The Transformation of Society in the Twentieth Century*; Stuart M. Blumin, "The Hypothesis of Middle-Class Formation in Nineteenth-Century America: A Critique and Some Proposals," *AHR* 90:2 (1985), pp. 299–338; ———, *The Emergence of the Middle Class: Social Experience in the American City, 1760–1800*, chs. 1, 8, and Epilogue; John P. Diggins, "Barbarism and Capitalism: The Strange Perspectives of Thorstein Veblen," *MP* 1:2 (1978), pp. 147–8; David Paul Nord, "An Economic Perspective on Formula in Popular Culture," *JPC* 3:1 (1980), pp. 17–32; Richard A. Peterson, "Five Constraints on the Production of Culture: Law, Technology, Market, Organizational Structure and Occupational Careers," *JPC* 16:2 (1982), pp. 143–53; Harold L. Wilensky, "Mass Society and Mass Culture: Interdependence or Dependence?" *American Sociological Review* 19:2 (1964), pp. 173–97; Rosalind Williams, "The Dream World of Mass Consumption," in Mukerji and Schudson, eds., *Rethinking Popular Culture*, ch. 6; Robert Atway, ed., *American Mass Media*.

14. Slotkin, *Fatal Environment*, pp. 28–32; William Bascom, "The Forms of Folklore: Prose Narratives," *Journal of American Folklore* 78:1 (1965), pp. 3–20; Richard M. Dorson, ed., *Handbook of American Folklore*, pp. 1–17, 32–8, 60–85,

326–58; ———, *American Folklore and the Historian*, chs. 1–2, 8–11; ———, *America in Legend: Folklore from the Colonial Period to the Present*, pp. xiii–xv, 1–9; Joseph J. Arpad, "Between Folklore and Literature: Popular Culture as Anomaly," *JPC* 9:2 (1975), pp. 403–23; Alan Dundes, "Folk Ideas as Units of World View," *American Folklore* 84:1 (1971), pp. 93–103; ———, *Interpreting Folklore*, chs. 1–2; ——— and Carl R. Pagter, *Urban Folklore from the Paperwork Empire*, "Introduction." On the conflict between mass and folk culture, see Lawrence W. Levine, *Black Culture and Black Consciousness: Afro-American Folk Thought from Slavery to Freedom*, pp. ix–xiv, 367–445; Lawrence Goodwyn, *Democratic Promise: The Populist Moment in America*, "Introduction," and chs. 1, 5; John Bodnar, *Workers' World: Kinship, Community, and Protest in an Industrial Society, 1900–1940*; Rodger Cunningham, *Apples on the Flood: The Southern Mountain Experience*; Mary V. Dearborn, *Pocahontas' Daughters: Gender and Ethnicity in American Culture*; Stephen William Foster, *The Past Is Another Country: Representation, Historical Consciousness and Resistance in the Blue Ridge*; Gerd Korman, *Industrialization, Immigrants and Americanizers: The View from Milwaukee, 1866–1921*; Werner Sollors, *Beyond Ethnicity: Consent and Descent in American Culture*. A succinct statement of the perspective that shapes this discussion is in Eric Foner, "Why Is There No Socialism in the United States?" *History Workshop: A Journal of Socialist and Feminist Historians*, No. 17 (Spring, 1984), pp. 57–80. On folk/mass culture exchanges in music, see for example Robert Palmer, *Deep Blues*, esp. Prologue and ch. 2.

15. Benedict Anderson, *Imagined Communities: Reflections on the Origin and Spread of Nationalism*, esp. chs. 2–4; Leonard W. Doob, *Patriotism and Nationalism: Their Psychological Foundations*; Anthony Giddins, *The Nation-State and Violence: Volume Two of a Contemporary Critique of Historical Materialism*; Boyd C. Shafer, *Nationalism: Myth and Reality*; Wilbur Zelinsky, *Nation Into State: The Shifting Symbolic Foundations of American Nationalism*.

16. Alan Trachtenberg, *The Incorporation of America: Culture and Society in the Gilded Age*, esp. Preface and chs. 5–6; James Livingston, "The Social Analysis of Economic History and Theory: Conjectures on Late Nineteenth-Century American Development," *AHR*, 92:1 (1987) pp. 69–95; Susman, *Culture as History*, pp. xix–xxx, 1–38; Sollors, *Beyond Ethnicity*, ch. 7; Richard Wightman Fox and T. J. Jackson Lears, eds., *The Culture of Consumption: Critical Essays in American History 1880–1890*, chs. 1–2; Jennifer A. Wicke, *Advertising Fictions: Literature, Advertisement and Social Reading*, pp. 1–18, ch. 2.

17. A more detailed version of this interpretation of the mythology of development, and a more extensive citation of sources, is in Slotkin, *Fatal Environment*, ch. 3. Additional sources and citations specific to this book are indicated below. For discussions of the "Frontier Hypothesis," and the analysis and comparison of frontiers, see Ray Allen Billington, *America's Frontier Heritage*; ———, *Frederick Jackson Turner: Historian, Scholar, Teacher*, ch. 18; David Miller and Jerome O. Steffen, eds., *The Frontier: Comparative Studies*; Roger L. Nichols, ed., *American Frontier and Western Issues: A Historiographical Review*; David W. Noble, *Historians Against History: The Frontier Thesis and the National Covenant in American Historical Writing Since 1830*; William Cronon, "Revisiting the Vanishing Frontier: The Legacy of Frederick Jackson Turner," *WHQ* 18:2 (1987), pp. 157–76; Michael P. Malone, "Beyond the Last Frontier: Toward a New Approach

to Western American History," *WHQ* 20:4 (1989), 409–28; Walter Nugent, "Frontiers and Empires in the Late Nineteenth Century," *WHQ* 20:4 (1989), pp. 393–408; Donald K. Pickens, "Westward Expansion and the End of American Exceptionalism: Sumner, Turner, and Webb," *WHQ* 12:4 (1981), pp. 409–18; Jackson K. Putnam, "The Turner Thesis and the Westward Movement: A Reappraisal," *WHQ* 7:4 (1976), pp. 377–404; Henry Nash Smith, *Virgin Land: The American West as Symbol and Myth*; Martin Ridge, "Frederick Jackson Turner, Ray Allen Billington, and American Frontier History," *WHQ* 19:1 (1988), pp. 5–20; Margaret Walsh, *The American Frontier Revisited*; Donald Worster, "New West, True West: Interpreting the Region's History," *WHQ* 18–2 (1987), 141–56; Walder D. Wyman and Clifton B. Kroeber, eds., *The Frontier in Perspective*. A useful essay on patterns of settlement and population distribution is Wilbur Zelinsky, *The Cultural Geography of the United States*, esp. pp. 41–4.

18. Louis Hartz, "A Comparative Study of Fragment Cultures," in Leon Friedman, ed., *Violence in America: Volume Two, Historical and Comparative Perspectives*, pp. 87–100; Michael Denning, " 'The Special American Conditions': Marxism and American Studies," *AQ* 38–3 (1986), pp. 356–380; Slotkin, *Regeneration*, pp. 40–1, 102–10, 117–8, 557, 563.

19. Slotkin, *Regeneration*, chs. 3, 10, 12; ———, *Fatal Environment*, chs. 3–5.

20. Slotkin, *Fatal Environment*, pp. 53–63; ———, "Massacre," *Berkshire Review* 14 (1979), pp. 112–33.

21. Slotkin, *Regeneration*, pp. 333–7, 344–8; *Fatal Environment*, pp. 74–5, 303–5, 320–1, 496–7, 338–45, chs. 4, 12, 19–20.

22. Slotkin, *Fatal Environment*, chs. 6, 15.

23. Isidor Wallimann and Michael N., Dobkowski, *Genocide and the Modern Age: Etiology and Case Studies of Mass Death, passim*. Rhodri Jeffrey-Jones, *Violence and Reform in American History*, esp. chs. 2, 5, 11, gives a good account of the origins of the myth of the "excessively violent" course of American labor history, attributing its prevalence to the triumph of anti-union propaganda campaigns sponsored by various employers and the National Association of Manufacturers during the Progressive period. Recent studies indicate that American rates of violent crime are much higher than those of other developed nations: the U.S. rape rate is thirteen times greater than that of Great Britain, and the U.S. murder rate is seven times greater than that of Great Britain or Japan. (See for example *Newsweek*, 7/16/90, pp. 23–4.) But this is for the most part private and individual violence, fundamentally different in its scale and political character from the episodes of enormous social violence that have punctuated Europe's (arguably) less violent civil scene in this century.

24. Slotkin, *Regeneration*, chs. 4–5; ———, *Fatal Environment*, pp. 63–4, 86–7.

25. Slotkin, *Regeneration*, chs. 6, 9, 10; ———, *Fatal Environment*, pp. 77–80, ch. 5, pp. 162–73, ch. 12, pp. 290–300, chs. 16–18, 20.

26. Slotkin, *Fatal Environment*, ch. 5; ———, "Introduction," in James Fenimore Cooper, *The Last of the Mohicans: A Tale of 1757*, pp. ix–xviii.

27. See Drinnon, *Facing West*, chs. 13, 15; Slotkin, *Fatal Environment*, pp. 81–2, 100–6. Victor L. Turner, *The Ritual Process: Structure and Anti-Structure*, chs. 1, 3.

28. On the succession of frontiers, see Billington, *America's Frontier Heritage*, esp. pp. 1–22; Slotkin, *Fatal Environment*, chs. 3 and 10, esp. pp. 36–47, 216–9. On the expectation of upward mobility as an element of ideology, and its linkage with the Frontier, see Eric Foner, *Free Soil, Free Labor, Free Men: The Ideology of the Republican Party Before the Civil War*, esp. ch. 1.

29. Slotkin, *Fatal Environment*, chs. 3, 8, 10, 13; Robert P. Swierenga, "Land Speculation and Its Impact on American Economic Growth and Welfare: A Historiographical Review," *WHQ* 8:3 (1977), pp. 283–301; Kermit L. Hall, *The Magic Mirror: Law in American History*.

30. Margo A. Conk, "Social Mobility in Historical Perspective," *MP* 1:3 (1978), pp. 52–69; William F. Deverell, "To Loosen the Safety Valve: Eastern Workers and Western Lands," *WHQ* 19:3 (1988), pp. 269–86; Everett K. Dick, *The Lure of the Land: A Social History of the Public Lands from the Articles of Confederation to the New Deal*; Don Harrison Doyle, "Social Theory and New Communities in Nineteenth-Century America," *WHQ* 8:2 (1977), pp. 167–88; David M. Emmons, "Social Myth and Social Reality," *Montana: The Magazine of Western History* 39:4 (1989), pp. 2–9; Lawrence Goodwyn, "The Cooperative Commonwealth and Other Abstractions: In Search of a Democratic Promise," *Marxist Perspectives* 3:2 (1980), pp. 8–43; Robert V. Hine, *Community on the American Frontier: Separate But Not Alone*; Carlos A. Schwantes, "The Concept of the Wageworkers' Frontier: A Framework for Future Research," *WHQ* 18:1 (1987), pp. 39–56; Robert L. Tyler, "The I.W.W. and the West," in Hennig Cohen, ed., *The American Culture: Approaches to the Study of the United States*, pp. 30–42; Melvyn Dubofsky, *We Shall Be All: A History of the IWW*, chs. 1–3; James R. Green, *Grass-Roots Socialism: Radical Movements in the Southwest, 1895–1943*.

31. Slotkin, *Fatal Environment*, chs. 13–15, 18–20; Dick, *Lure of the Land*, chs. 10, 11, 13, 18, 19; Gilbert Fite, *The Farmer's Frontier, 1865–1900*, chs. 2–6, 11.

32. Slotkin, *Fatal Environment*, ch. 15; Denning, *Mechanic Accents*, pp. 55–7; David Gordon, Richard Edwards, and Michael Reich, *Segmented Work, Divided Workers: The Historical Transformation of Labor in the United States*, pp. 50, 52.

33. Slotkin, *Fatal Environment*, chs. 15, 18, 19.

34. Slotkin, *Fatal Environment*, ch. 13; Reinhard Bendix, *Work and Authority in Industry*, pp. 1–20, 99–116, 198–274; James F. Becker, "The Rise of Managerial Economics," *MP* 2:2 (1979), pp. 34–55; Alfred D. Chandler, *The Visible Hand: The Managerial Revolution in American Business*; Morton Keller, *Affairs of State: Public Life in Late Nineteenth Century America*; Jeffrey G. Williamson and Peter Lindert, *American Inequality: A Macroeconomic History*; Livingston, "The Social Analysis of Economic History and Theory," pp. 69–95; Thomas C. Cochran, *Business in American Life: A History*, chs. 14–16; Robert H. Wiebe, *The Search for Order, 1877–1920*, chs. 1–5; Richard Adelstein, "The Nation as an Economic Unit: Keynes, Roosevelt and the Managerial Ideal," *JAH* 78:1 (1991), pp. 160–87. On the response of workers to the new industrial order, see E. P. Thompson, *The Making of the English Working Class*; Melvyn Dubofsky, *Industrialism and the American Worker, 1865–1920*; Herbert G. Gutman, *Work, Culture, and Society in Industrializing America: Essays in American Working Class and Social History*; David Montgomery, *Beyond Equality: Labor and the Radical Republicans, 1862–1872*; ———, *The Fall of the House of Labor: The Workplace, the State, and American Labor*

Activism, 1865–1925; and Daniel T. Rodgers, *The Work Ethic in Industrial America, 1850–1920.*

35. Slotkin, *Fatal Environment*, chs. 15, 18, 19; M. Blumin, "The Hypothesis of Middle-Class Formation in Nineteenth-Century America: A Critique and Some Proposals," pp. 299–338; Denning, *Mechanic Accents*, ch. 4.

36. Charles F. Adams, Jr., "The Protection of the Ballot in National Elections," *Journal of Social Science* 1:1 (June 1869), 91–111; "The Late Riots," *The Nation* (August 2, 1877), 631:68–70; also "Our Indian Wards," *The Nation* (July 13, 1876), 576: 21–2. And see Slotkin, *Fatal Environment*, ch. 19; Richard L. McCormick, *The Party Period and Public Policy*, Part III.

37. Proposals for the subjugation of Indians, Blacks, women and immigrant workers drew on psychological and biological theories which likened these groups to congenital criminals and insane persons. On this complex matter, see Rogin, "Liberal Society and the Indian Question," in *Ronald Reagan the Movie*, pp. 144–52; Slotkin, *Fatal Environment*, chs. 13–14, esp. pp. 236, 342–3, 358–64.

38. Alexander Saxton, "*Caesar's Column*: The Dialogue of Utopia and Catastrophe," *AQ* 19:2, Part 1 (1967), pp. 224–38.

39. The use of lower case is intended to distinguish these ideological styles from particular parties and movements, such as the People's Party/Farmers' Alliance (the so-called "Populists") or the Republican "Progressives" led by Theodore Roosevelt.

40. Denning, *Mechanic Accents*, 60; David Montgomery, "Labor in the Industrial Era," in *The American Worker*, ed. by Richard B. Morris, pp. 115–6.

41. Goodwyn, *Democratic Promise*; Fred Matthews, " 'Hobbesian Populism': Interpretive Paradigms and Moral Vision in American Historiography," *JAH* 72:1 (1985), pp. 92–115; Bruce Palmer, "American History's Hardy Perennial: Populism from the 1970s," *AQ* 30:4 (1978), pp. 557–66; Glenn Alan Phelps, "The Populist Films of Frank Capra," *JAS* 13:3 (1979), pp. 377–92; Norman Pollack, ed., *The Populist Mind*, "Introduction," and Part 2; ———, *The Humane Economy: Populism, Capitalism and Democracy, passim.*

42. Although Populism was primarily an agrarian movement, there are close connections and analogies between it and parts of the labor movement, especially in the West. See Dubofsky, *We Shall Be All*, ch. 2; Chester MacArthur Destler, *American Radicalism, 1865–1901.* Henry George's analysis of the relationship between the modernization of the economy and the increasing disparity between rich and poor is based on a "populist" (and proto-Turnerian) reading of the Frontier Myth: "land" is the basis of wealth or capital, and the increased value of land is a by-product of frontier expansion and the growth of population; and poverty results when the supply of new land is exhausted and the "rent" from existing lands is concentrated in a single class. Henry George, *Progress and Poverty: An Inquiry into the Cause of Industrial Depressions and of the Increase of Want with Increase of Wealth* (1880), esp. pp. 3–18 and Book VII.

43. Sahlins, *Historical Metaphors*, pp. 6, 67–8, 72.

44. Robert F. Berkhofer, Jr., "A New Context for American Studies?" *AQ* 41:4 (1989), pp. 588–613.

45. Schank, *Dynamic Memory*, pp. 2–3, 26, 40–1; and see Chapter 8, below.

Notes to Chapter 1

1. Frederick Jackson Turner, *The Frontier in American History*, ch. 1.

2. On Turner's life and reputation, see Ray Allen Billington, *Frederick Jackson Turner: Historian, Scholar, Teacher*, esp. chs. 5, 6, 18, 19.

3. Billington, *Frederick Jackson Turner*, p. 130; Edmund Morris, *The Rise of Theodore Roosevelt*, pp. 27, 410, 465–7. Francis A. Walker, a noted economist and former head of the Bureaus of Indian Affairs and Labor Statistics, declared that "the mere title is a success in itself," but apparently felt no need to read the essay.

4. Billington, *Turner*, pp. 27, 130, 438–41; Edmund Morris, *Roosevelt*, pp. 410, 465–7, 459–71; Smith, *Virgin Land*, ch. 22. George W. Ruiz, "The Ideological Convergence of Theodore Roosevelt and Woodrow Wilson," *Presidential Studies Quarterly* 19:1 (1989), pp. 159–78.

5. Everett Dick, *The Lure of the Land: A Social History of the Public Lands from the Articles of Confederation to the New Deal*, p. 303; Paul Wallace Gates, "The Homestead Law in an Incongruous Land System," *AHR* 41:3 (1936), pp. 652–81.

6. *Ibid.*, p. 672; James R. Green, *Grass-Roots Socialism: Radical Movements in the Southwest, 1895–1943*, pp. 1–11, 68–73; Fite, *The Farmer's Frontier*, pp. 193–214.

7. Turner, "Social Forces in American History," in *Frontier*, esp. pp. 322–3, 332–3.

8. Billington, *Turner*, pp. 108–10. Ruth M. Elson's study of American history textbooks (*The Guardians of Tradition*) suggests that between 1820 and the Civil War, the development of the Frontier was presented as a consequence rather than a cause (or even a stimulus) of material and social progress in the metropolis (p. 184). American character, not the material opportunities of the West, determines the development of republican and national virtues. The farmer is accorded pre-eminence as the embodiment of these virtues, and the corruption of urban life is contrasted with rural felicity—a contrast that grows increasingly sentimental, and void of real interest in agriculture itself after 1860 (pp. 25, 27, 30). The texts approve of Manifest Destiny and displacement of the Indians (pp. 37–9, 180–3). References to the Frontier as safety valve begin to appear in the 1880s (pp. 180–1, 280). Social Darwinist ideas became prominent at about the same time (pp. 67–70, 80–1). See also Laurence M. Hauptmann, "Mythologizing Westward Expansion: Schoolbooks and the Image of the American Frontier Before Turner," *WHQ* 8:3 (1977), pp. 269–82.

9. Billington, *Turner*, pp. 9–11, 15–29, and ch. 5.

10. Morris, *Roosevelt*, pp. 386–8; 43–5, 131–3, 300, chs. 8 and 11; Theodore Roosevelt, *An Autobiography*, pp. 15, 19–22.

11. On the myths of hunter and farmer, see Slotkin, *Regeneration*, ch. 10; ———, *Fatal Environment*, pp. 68–76, 103–4, 211–9; and H. N. Smith, *Virgin Land*. On popular literary heroes, see Daryl Jones, *The Dime Novel Western*; and Louise K. Barnett, *The Ignoble Savage*.

12. Slotkin, *Fatal Environment*, pp. 100–6.

13. Theodore Roosevelt, "Francis Parkman's Histories," Literary Essays, *The*

Works of Theodore Roosevelt (1926), vol. 12, p. 247; ———, *Autobiography*, pp. 15, 19–22; Morris, *Roosevelt*, pp. 43–5, 131–3, 300, and chs. 8, 11.

14. Francis Parkman, *Count Frontenac and New France*; ———, *The Jesuits in North America in the Seventeenth Century*, vol. 2:527–49; ———, *Montcalm and Wolfe*, "Preface." See also David Levin, *History as Romantic Art: Bancroft, Prescott, Motley and Parkman*, chs. 6, 9; and Kim Townsend, "Francis Parkman and the Male Tradition," *AQ* 38:1 (1986), pp. 97–113. The aristocratic and chivalrous Montcalm falls short of the ideal because he fails to control his Indian auxiliaries.

15. Morris, *Roosevelt*, 384–7; G. Edward White, *The Eastern Establishment and the Western Experience: The West of Frederic Remington, Theodore Roosevelt, and Owen Wister*, pp. 31–51, 60–7, 79–93.

16. Morris, *Roosevelt*, 285–8, 299, 384–7; G. E. White, 31–51, 60–7, 79–93; George B. Ward, "Bloodbrothers in the Wilderness," Diss. Univ. of Texas, Austin (1981), contains much useful information on the Boone and Crockett Club and other similar organizations.

17. J. A. Mangan and James Walvin. *Manliness and Morality: Middle-Class Masculinity in Britain and America, 1800–1940*, ch. 11, and also 1, 2, 4, 6, 7, 9; John Fraser, *America and the Patterns of Chivalry*, chs. 1, 2, 5–7, 10; compare T. J. Jackson Lears, *No Place of Grace: Antimodernism and the Transformation of American Culture, 1880–1920*, esp. chs. 1, 3.

18. On traditional American versions of the "stages" theory, see Thomas C. Dyer, *Theodore Roosevelt and the Idea of Race*, esp. chs. 1, 2; Rogin, "Liberal Society"; Horsman, *Race and Manifest Destiny*, esp. chs. 4, 6, 7, 10.

19. Roosevelt, *Autobiography*, "In Cowboy Land."

20. Roosevelt, *Ranch Life and the Hunting Trail, Works*, I, pp. 349, 351, 356, 278, 378; ———, *Hunting Trips of a Ranchman, Works*, I, pp. 25–6.

21. Roosevelt, *Ranch Life*, pp. 276, 279, 292–3; ———, *Hunting Trips*, pp. 4–5, 23–5. The new hybrid class reminds Roosevelt of the antebellum southern aristocracy, because of their passion for manly sports and their contempt of mere money-grubbing.

22. Roosevelt, *Ranch Life*, p. 292; ———, *Hunting Trips*, pp. 16–7.

23. *Ibid.*

24. *New York World*, January 18, 1874, p. 4; January 28, p. 4.

25. Roosevelt, *Hunting Trips*, p. 191.

26. Morris, *Roosevelt*, pp. 655–6, 661.

27. Roosevelt, *Ranch Life*, p. 269; ———, *The Wilderness Hunter, Works*, II, 11–3, 16–27, 21–2, 278, 287–8; Morris, *Roosevelt*, pp. 285–7, 299.

28. Dyer, *Roosevelt/Race*, esp. chs. 2, 3; Roosevelt, *The Winning of the West* (1907), I, 20–1, 24.

29. *Ibid.*

30. *Ibid.*, I, 186–7.

31. On the sources of these racial ideas, see Reginald Horsman, *Race and Manifest Destiny: The Origins of American Racial Anglo-Saxonism*; Hugh A. MacDougall, *Racial Myth in English History: Trojans, Teutons, and Anglo-Saxons*; Michael Banton, *The Idea of Race*, pp. 3–7, 13–18, 20–5, 34–5, 48*ff.*; George Sinkler, *The Racial Attitudes of American Presidents from Abraham Lincoln to Theodore Roosevelt.* pp. 386 *ff.*; Dyer, *Roosevelt/Race*, chs. 1, 3.

32. Theodore Parker, *The Rights of Man in America* (1854), pp. 100–1, 434; George Fitzhugh, *What Shall Be Done with the Free Negroes?* (1851), pp. 1–6; William Walker, *The War in Nicaragua* (1860), pp. 259–61, 270, 429–30. Slotkin, *Fatal Environment*, chs. 11, 12. In the North/South controversy, further distinctions were made. Abolitionists asserted that southern Anglo-Saxons had had their racial gifts diluted or corrupted by slavery—had become literally and/or figuratively "Africanized" or "Latinized" (like the Spanish Americans, whose states had been founded on slavery). Southern nationalists asserted that the planter aristocracy had a more aristocratic Anglo-Saxon derivation, from the "Cavaliers" of the seventeenth century; some distinguished those origins as "Anglo-Norman."

33. Roosevelt, *Winning*, I, pp. 231–2.

34. Billington, *Turner*, pp. 64–6.

35. Roosevelt, *Winning*, I, p. 143.

36. Roosevelt's belief that mercantile culture caused the degeneration of martial virtues in a race is based on Brooks Adams, *Law of Civilization and Decay: An Essay on History*, Charles A. Beard, ed., ch. 12; Lears, *No Place*, pp. 107–17, 125–39.

37. Roosevelt, *Winning*, I, pp. 122–6.

38. On Indian-hating as an ideology, see Drinnon, *Facing West*, esp. p. 299.

39. Roosevelt, *Winning*, I, pp. 116–7, 273–4.

40. *Ibid.*, V, pp. 229–30.

41. *Ibid.*, I, pp. 83–4, 119, 274.

42. *Ibid.*, pp. 147–8, 150, 158–9.

43. *Ibid.*, pp. 42–3, 134–7, 166–7.

44. *Ibid.*, pp. 141, 143, 151, 160–3, 170, 176–7, 180–1, 186–7, 237, 239; II, pp. 191, 209; V, p. 226.

45. Morris, *Roosevelt*, p. 387. The place of the Texan Revolution in Roosevelt's overall design is indicated by his essays on Houston and Crockett in Henry Cabot Lodge and Theodore Roosevelt, *Hero Tales from American History, Works*, X, pp. 12–23, 35–9, 83–7.

46. Roosevelt, "The Strenuous Life," *Works*, XII, pp. 3–6, 11; Dyer, *Roosevelt/Race*, ch. 7; Sinkler, *Racial Attitudes*, pp. 406–9.

47. Roosevelt, *Works*, "Expansion and Peace," *Works*, XII, pp. 28–9, 35–6; Lears, *No Place*, pp. 107–17.

48. Roosevelt, "The Strenuous Life," pp. 7–8, 19; ———, *Winning*, III, p. 145.

49. See Chapter 3, below.

50. Turner, *Frontier*, pp. 2–3.

51. Billington, *Turner*, pp. 108–9, 171–3, 436; Turner, "Social Forces in American History" (1910), in *Frontier*, p. 316.

52. Turner, "Contributions of the West to American Democracy" (1903), *Ibid.*, pp. 263–4.

53. Roosevelt, *Wilderness Hunter*, pp. 7–8, 270.

54. Turner, "Contributions of the West," pp. 261, 266–7; "Pioneer Ideals and the State University" (1910); "Social Forces" pp. 322–3, 332–3, in *Frontier*.

55. Smith, *Virgin Land*, p. 302.

56. Turner, "Significance of the Frontier," pp. 24, 27; "Contributions of the West," p. 261; "Pioneer Ideals," in *Frontier*, pp. 276–7.

57. Billington, *Turner*, pp. 438–41.

58. Turner, "Contributions," in *Frontier*, pp. 244–6, 267.

59. See esp. "The Problem of the West," p. 221; "The West and American Ideals"; and "Middle Western Pioneer Democracy," pp. 357–8, in *Frontier*.

60. *Ibid.*, pp. 238–9, 264–7.

61. William Appleman Williams, *Roots of the Modern American Empire: A Study of the Growth and Shaping of Social Consciousness in a Marketplace Society*, chs. 2, 5, 6, 8, 9.

62. Webb, *Great Frontier*, esp. ch. 9.

63. The most stringent and inclusive proposals for the restriction of political rights were not put forward by practical politicians like Roosevelt, who had to be heedful of strong non-Anglo-Saxon constituencies as well as the traditional shibboleths of democracy. An early "progressive" proposal for restriction of the franchise was put forward by Charles Francis Adams, Jr., "The Protection of the Ballot in National Elections," *Journal of Social Science* 1:1 (1869), pp. 91–111, who envisioned the degeneration of the "American people" into "three proletariats": African in the South, Celtic in the North, and Oriental in the West. The most overt form of political exclusion with which Roosevelt had to deal was the disenfranchisement of southern Blacks, a policy that damaged a traditional Republican constituency and therefore drew Roosevelt's criticism. However, Roosevelt was convinced that Negroes, as a group, were racially unfit for full citizenship (though individual Negroes were worthy even of office-holding), and he abandoned even rhetorical resistance to disenfranchisement in his second term. Although he regarded a denial of voting rights based purely on "color" as absurd, he believed that tests (for example, literacy tests) that excluded *all* classes of the "unfit" (including Whites) were permissible. He proposed to "defend the ballot" from ignorant and unfit Whites by the use of literacy tests and quotas to restrict access to citizenship via immigration. See Dyer, *Roosevelt/Race*, esp. pp. 98, 106–10, 121–2; Sinkler, *Racial Attitudes*, pp. 386–8, 378–9; Robert L. Allen, *Reluctant Reformers: Racism and Social Reform Movements in the United States*, pp. 100–2.

64. Billington, *Turner*, ch. 8, pp. 286–7; Frank Norris, "The Frontier Gone at Last," in *Responsibilities of the Novelist*; Richard Hofstader, *The Progressive Historians: Turner, Beard, Parrington*, chs. 4, 12; Noble, *Historians Against History*; Webb, *Great Frontier*; Potter, *People of Abundance*; Billington, *America's Frontier Heritage*.

65. For Roosevelt's influence on professional historians, see below, Ch. 5, fn. 83. For the application of Rooseveltian mythology to popular histories of American participation in the Great War, see for example Tom Skeyhill, *Sergeant York: Last of the Long Hunters*, chs. 1–9, and Theodore Roosevelt, Jr., "The Sword of the Lord and of Gideon," in Ernest Hemingway, ed., *Men at War*, pp. 276–87.

Notes to Chapter 2

1. Trachtenberg, *Incorporation*, ch. 7; R. Reid Badger, *The Great American Fair: The World's Columbian Exposition and American Culture*, pp. 105–7.

2. Robert W. Rydell, "The World's Columbian Exposition of 1893: Racist Underpinnings of a Utopian Artifact," *JAC* (1978), pp. 253–75.

3. William Dean Howells, "Letters of an Altrurian Traveller," in Neil Harris, ed., *The Land of Contrasts, 1880–1901*, pp. 345–62.

4. Trachtenberg, *Incorporation*, pp. 219–20.

5. *Ibid.*, pp. 266–7; see any issue of *Harper's Weekly*, July–August, 1893.

6. Trachtenberg, *Incorporation*, p. 222.

7. Slotkin, *Fatal Environment*, pp. 523–30.

8. Frederic Remington, "A Gallop Through the Midway," *The Complete Writings of Frederic Remington*, pp. 111–3; Ben Merchant Vorpahl, *With the Eye of the Mind: Frederic Remington and the West*, p. 109. "Strange fierce-looking negroes who have evidently not felt the elevating influence of South Carolina pass you. . . . One of Diamond Dick's Indians shuffles along . . . [his] weak-kneed, in-toed plod . . . speaks of the thorough horseman when he 'hits the flat.' "

9. Don Russell, *The Wild West: A History of Wild West Shows*, chs. 1–2, esp. p. 40.

10. On Cody's "authorship," see Don Russell, *The Lives and Legends of Buffalo Bill*, ch. 20, and pp. 300–2, 370.

11. "An Object Lesson" appeared at the right margin of a 108-sheet billboard poster advertising the "Wild West" of 1898. It was, at the time, the largest poster ever displayed. See Jack Rennert, *100 Posters of Buffalo Bill's Wild West*, rear endpaper and p. 16.

12. John M. Burke, "Salutatory," *Buffalo Bill's Wild West*, 1886 and 1887 (hereafter *BBWW*, [date]). All citations from Wild West programs are from copies in the Western History Department, Denver Public Library. I am grateful to Eleanor M. Gehres and the library staff for their assistance.

13. Pomeroy quoted in "Hon. W. F. Cody—'Buffalo Bill,' " a biographical sketch which included sections on Cody as "A Legislator" and "As an Educator." The sketch and its appendices appear virtually unchanged in most Wild West Programs to 1900. See *BBWW*, 1886 for the first version; also 1887 and 1893. The encomia from Cody's former military commanders appeared in different forms over the years, although the same letters of commendation were always cited, and General Carr's praise of Cody as "the King of them all" was given special emphasis. See "Letters of Commendation from Prominent Military Men," *BBWW*, 1886; and *BBWW*, 1887, which adds letters from European royalty and American notables.

14. Russell, *Lives and Legends*, pp. 149–55, 181–4.

15. *Ibid.*, pp. 181–4 and chs. 11–13. On the Grand Duke's hunting party, see Slotkin, *Fatal Environment*, pp. 407–9.

16. Russell, *Lives and Legends*, ch. 15.

17. In Richard Slotkin, "The Wild West," in Leslie Fiedler, *et al.*, *Buffalo Bill and the Wild West*, p. 30.

18. Slotkin, *Regeneration*, pp. 235–40; Robert Rogers, *Ponteach; or, The Savages*

of America (1766); William H. Truettner, *The Natural Man Observed: A Study of Catlin's Indian Gallery*; George Catlin, *Catalogue of Catlin's Indian Gallery of Portraits, Landscapes, Manners and Customs, Costumes, etc.* (1837); Peter H. Hassrick, "The Artists," in Fiedler, *Buffalo Bill and the Wild West*, pp. 16–26; John Mix Stanley, *Scenes and Incidents of Stanley's Western Wilds* (1854); A. J. Donnelle, ed., *Cyclorama of Custer's Last Battle* (1889).

19. Russell, *Lives and Legends*, ch. 17.

20. *Ibid.; New York Herald*, July 23, 1876, p. 1; Charles King, *Campaigning with Crook, and Stories of Army Life*, esp. pp. 36–43.

21. Russell, *Lives and Legends*, pp. 230–2.

22. *Ibid.*, p. 254; *New York Herald*, August 11, 1876, p. 3.

23. Russell, *Lives and Legends*, pp. 407–8; William F. Cody, *The Crimson Trail; or, Custer's Last Warpath, A Romance Founded Upon the Present Border Warfare as Witnessed by Hon. W. F. Cody*, New York Weekly (1876); ———, *Kansas King; or, The Red Right Hand*, Saturday Journal (1876), Beadle's Half-Dime Library, 1877; Prentiss Ingraham, *Buffalo Bill's Grip; or, Oath-Bound to Custer*, Beadle's Weekly, 1883; ———, *Buffalo Bill's Big Four; or, Custer's Shadow*, Beadle's Weekly, 1887; ———, *Buffalo Bill with General Custer*[?]; Grace Miller White, *Custer's Last Fight: A Thrilling Story Founded Upon the Play of the Same Name* (1905).

24. "Death of Yellow Hand . . . ," *BBWW*, 1886; Cody, *The Crimson Trail*; illustrations in Fiedler et al., *Buffalo Bill and the Wild West*, pp. 12, 31; John Rennert, *100 Posters of Buffalo Bill's Wild West*, "A Close Call," p. 56. William F. Cody, *The Life of Hon. William F. Cody, Known as Buffalo Bill, the Famous Hunter, Scout and Guide: An Autobiography* (1879), esp. pp. 343–4. Another example of the "First Scalp" woodcut is the frontispiece to [George A. Custer], *Wild Life on the Plains and Horrors of Indian Warfare* . . . (1891).

25. Russell, *Lives and Legends*, p. 413; Prentiss Ingraham, *Adventures of Buffalo Bill from Boyhood to Manhood: Deeds of Daring and Romantic Incidents in the Life of Wm. F. Cody, the Monarch of the Bordermen*, Beadle's Boys' Library No. 1; reprinted in E. F. Bleiler, ed., *Eight Dime Novels*, pp. 91–105, esp. chs. 1, 29. Ingraham sketches the whole of this development in a single volume, moving through a standard set of dime-novel adventures (loosely based on fact) to Cody's achievement of business success with his Combination—which Ingraham treats as evidence of Cody's ability to surpass that fatal limitation of the Hawkeye-model hero. Cody prided himself on his transformation from frontiersman to modern businessman. In his introduction to Helen Cody Wetmore, *Last of the Great Scouts*, Zane Grey asserts that Cody later characterized his work for the Kansas Pacific as that of a "railroad builder" rather than a buffalo-hunter.

26. Russell, *Lives and Legends*, chs. 20, 27, pp. 494–503; and see for example Prentiss Ingraham, *Buffalo Bill and the Nihilists* (1910), in Western Americana Collection, Beinecke Library, Yale University.

27. Russell, *Lives and Legends*, chs. 21–22; ———, *Wild West Shows*, pp. 1–42; Sarah J. Blackstone, *Buckskins, Bullets, and Business*, chs. 2, 3, 5.

28. "Hon. W. F. Cody—'Buffalo Bill,' " *BBWW*, 1886; and see the succeeding sections on his careers as 5th Cavalry scout, legislator, educator, etc.

29. Russell, *Wild West Shows*, p. 25; Elizabeth B. Custer, *Tenting on the Plains* (1887), pp. 46–7. Compare also the poster "Buffalo Bill to the Rescue" (Rennert,

100 Posters, p. 68) with the illustrations of "The Battle of the Washita" in Custer, *My Life on the Plains*, and Richard Irving Dodge, *Our Wild Indians: Thirty-Three Years Experience Among the Red Men of the Great West*. . . . Cody's "Last Fight" was much imitated by competing shows: see Russell, *Wild West Shows*, pp. 31–2, 45.

30. "The Rifle . . . ," *BBWW*, 1886, 1893.

31. Russell, *Lives and Legends*, ch. 23; Billington, *Land of Savagery*, pp. 48–56, 328–9. Although he returned for a brief American tour in 1888, his main purpose was to recruit more Indian performers and replenish his livestock; the Program for this tour omitted the more spectacular "epochs" he had mounted in Europe. *BBWW*, 1888. A British cartoon shows Buffalo Bill as a conqueror of the Old World, leading a Roman triumph, "The Triumph of the West," *Life*, 12/15/87, in Fiedler, *Buffalo Bill and the Wild West*, p. 44.

32. Russell, *Lives and Legends*, ch. 26. Cody published a newspaper to report on his activities and publicize his promotional schemes. See *Cody Scrapbooks*, Vol. 2, esp. pp. 3, 8, 12, 21, 35, 37, 97–100, 102–7, in Denver Public Library.

33. Russell, *Lives and Legends*, ch. 25; Stanley Vestal, *Sitting Bull, Champion of the Sioux*, ch. 26.

34. *BBWW*, 1893, pp. 10, 31–4, 49–50; *Cody Scrapbooks*, Denver Public Library, Vol. 2, pp. 3, 8, 12, 21, 35, 37, 97–100, 102, 107.

35. *BBWW*, 1887.

36. Russell, *Lives and Legends*, p. 370, identifies John M. Burke as the originator of the idea.

37. *BBWW*, 1887 refers to "American Rough Riders." *BBWW*, 1893, "Programme" and "Salutatory," pp. 2, 4. See also Russell, *Lives and Legends*, 370–85; and ———, *Wild West Shows*, 61–72. See also posters of the parade, Rennert, *100 Posters*, "A Perfect Illustration . . . ," and "The Maze," pp. 101, 104.

38. *BBWW*, 1893, Dodge on p. 36; Cody and Wounded Knee, pp. 32–6, 38–45, 49–53; Alsace on 60–1.

39. "A Factor of International Amity—Carnot," poster of 1893, in Rennert, *100 Posters*, p. 106.

40. *BBWW*, 1893, pp. 60–2. It is worth noting that the Wild West's is a "kinder, gentler" version of the Roosevelt thesis, in that it envisions the integration of Native Americans into American life. This relatively liberal position on racial politics is a consistent one for Cody, who incorporated both Native Americans and African Americans as "American soldiers" in his imperial pageants.

41. "At the Fair," *Chicago Inter-Ocean*, Sept. 12, 1893, p. 3; David A. Curtis, "The Wild West and What It Lacks," *Criterion*, in *Cody Scrapbook*, vol. 7, p. 183.

42. Rennert, *100 Posters*, rear endpaper.

43. *BBWW*, 1899, pp. 32–6.

44. Rennert, *100 Posters*, p. 64. The image of Cody in this poster is far more youthful than that in the Bonheur portrait, p. 63.

45. Cody and Saulsbury attempted to mount a "Black" Wild West in 1895, which toured the South as "Black America," but the experiment was a failure. Russell, *Wild West Shows*, p. 60. Cody also included African-American troopers of the 9th and 10th Cavalry in his San Juan Hill re-enactment (*BBWW*, 1899, p. vi), and treated their exploits as comparable to those of the White Rough

Riders. Cody's relatively liberal treatment of this aspect of the race question contrasts with Roosevelt's account of the battle, which denigrates the achievements and character of the Negro regiments. Compare Roosevelt's attitudes toward the African-American troops who fought with his Rough Riders, below, Ch. 4, and in Dyer, *Theodore Roosevelt and the Idea of Race*, pp. 100–1. On Cody's treatment of Indians, see Vine Deloria, Jr., "The Indians," in Fiedler, *Buffalo Bill and the Wild West*, pp. 45–56; John G. Neihardt, *Black Elk Speaks*; Blackstone, *Buckskins*, pp. 85–8.

46. Rennert, *100 Posters*, "The Race of Races [1895]," p. 65; "Wild Rivalries of Savage, Barbarous and Civilized Races [1898]." It has been argued that the "Race of Races" and the imperialist theme was not Cody's idea; and certainly his control of the Wild West program was weakened after 1895. However, he remained the Wild West's featured performer, and his public statements affiliated him with the imperialist cause—though according to Russell, "his heart was not really in it," *Lives and Legends*, p. 417.

47. *Cody Scrapbooks*, Vol. 7, pp. iii, vii, xx, xxiv–v, 54–5, 65, 69, 73, 95, 97, 104, 107.

48. *Ibid.*, *BBWW*, 1901, "Programme." See also the parallel depictions of frontier and imperial heroes in magazines published by Cody's associates, esp. *The Rough Rider* 1:1 (1900), p. 6; 3:4 (1901), cover and p. 2; *Frontier Guide* 2:3 (1901).

49. *BBWW*, 1901, "Programme." The Wild West rationalized imperialism as an extension of the old "westering" frontier by the simple method of substituting new "imperial" figures in places traditionally recognized as belonging to frontier heroes. The simplest form of this substitution appears in the covers of *The Rough Rider* magazine, published from 1899 to 1907 by Cody's associates. The first issue's cover showed "The Historic Rough Riders of the Sixties"—Sheridan, Cody, Custer and Sitting Bull—but much of the sixteen pages of text was devoted to San Juan Hill. A 1901 issue with a similar cover design replaced Sheridan, Cody and Custer with Cody, Roosevelt, and heroes representing both sides of the Boer War—Petrus Joubert, a Boer guerrilla, and Baden-Powell, the British war-hero and founder of the Boy Scouts. These were "Men Who Have Led the Rough Riders of the World in Civic and Military Conquests." Another, similar publication paired Pawnee Bill (another Wild West impresario) with figures from the Filipino insurrection—the rebel leader Aguinaldo, the American General Lawton, and Frederick Funston, the commando leader who captured Aguinaldo. *The Rough Rider* 1:1 (1900), p. 6; 3:4 (1901), cover and p. 2; *Frontier Guide* 2:3 (1901).

50. "Programme" sections in *BBWW* 1899–1902, 1904–5, 1907–8. Russell, *Wild West Shows*, pp. 62, 72; Blackstone, *Buckskins*, ch. 2, details the logistics of the Wild West. In 1909 the Wild West merged with Pawnee Bill's Far East, an "oriental" spectacle. Despite the Wild West's decline, its literature was updated and expanded. One of the most interesting of the Programs is that for 1909, which follows the suggestion in Roosevelt's *Wilderness Hunter* and *Winning of the West*, that we see our greatest leaders as scions of the Frontier, "scouts" who "wore the buckskin" one way or another. Cody's pantheon includes not only the predictable hunter-heroes like Boone, Crockett and Carson, but also Christopher

Columbus and George Washington, and even Benjamin Church—the usually unrecognized Puritan progenitor of the type.

51. *BBWW*, 1909, 1916; Rennert, *100 Posters*, p. 93.

52. Russell, *Lives and Legends*, pp. 439–72; Rennert, *100 Posters*, pp. 63, 108–9.

Notes to Chapter 3

1. George Frederickson, *The Inner Civil War: Northern Intellectuals and the Crisis of the Union*, ch. 14; Edward Bellamy, *Looking Backward, 2000–1887*; William James, "The Moral Equivalent of War," in B. W. Wilshire, ed., *William James, the Essential Writings*, ch. 15.

2. Slotkin, *Fatal Environment*, pp. 331–8.

3. David A. Wells, *Recent Economic Changes and Their Effect on The Production and Distribution of Wealth and the Well-Being of Society*, p. 93.

4. *Ibid.*, pp. 92–4.

5. Slotkin, *Fatal Environment*, ch. 13; Frederickson, *Inner Civil War*, ch. 14; John W. Draper, *Thoughts on the Future Civil Policy of America . . .* (1865), pp. 200–1; Morton Keller, *Affairs of State: Public Life in Late Nineteenth Century America*, Pt. 1.

6. Marshall M. Kirkman, *The Science of Railways* (1896), pp. 63–7.

7. David M. Perry, *Proceedings of the N.A.M.* (1903), quoted in Reinhard Bendix, *Work and Authority in Industry: Ideologies of Management in the Course of Industrialization*, p. 266.

8. Allen Chase, *The Legacy of Malthus: The Social Costs of the New Scientific Racism*, chs. 6, 11, 12.

9. Quoted in Stanley Feldstein, ed., *The Poisoned Tongue: A Documentary History of American Racism and Prejudice*, p. 258); and compare quote on 1877 strikes from *The Nation*, pp. 20–21, above. Jeffrey-Jones, *Violence and Reform*, pp. 16–19. On immigration statistics and patterns, see Philip Taylor, *The Distant Magnet*, chs. 3, 9, p. 103.

10. Slotkin, *Fatal Environment*, pp. 512–6.

11. Capt. Charles King, *Campaigning with Crook* is his autobiography.

12. The influence of King's novels, coupled with the historical coincidence that saw troops from Apacheria engaged in the Pullman Strike, may have contributed significantly to the permanent aggrandizement of the Apache as symbols of savagery. In 1886, the *Sun's* choice of "Apaches" to symbolize the savagery of the Haymarket "mob" was fortuitous: Geronimo's band were merely the Indians most recently at war with the United States. But after 1894 Geronimo displaced Sitting Bull as "The Worst Indian Who Ever Lived," and his tiny band of Apache replaced the Sioux and Cheyenne as the "savages of first resort" in the new medium of the movies. Rennert, *100 Posters*, p. 99. And see Roosevelt's reference to Apaches in "Strenuous Life," above p. 53.

13. King, *Foes in Ambush*, pp. 250, 252. The novel was published a year before the Pullman Strike, and the disorders it describes do not resemble those that occurred in Chicago at the time of the Haymarket affair. The 1877 strikes are a better historical referent, particularly since King's use of the term "tramps" is

consistent with editorial descriptions of those strikers. However, there were no mass transfers from Apache country to Chicago like those King describes. The novel may be better understood as a projective fantasy, based on the post-1877 agitation for the use of federal troops in strikes, which anticipates the events of the Pullman Strike.

14. King, *An Army Wife*, pp. 146–7.

15. Allison enthusiastically proposes a regime like that suggested in that same year by Kirkman in *The Science of Railways*. But King's hero thinks it ill advised to give such power to private corporations—only the army itself can be trusted with such power. King, *A Tame Surrender*, pp. 151–8. On "welfare capitalism," see James Weinstein, *The Corporate Ideal in the Liberal State, 1900–1918*, esp. chs. 1, 5.

16. Ben Merchant Vorpahl, *My Dear Wister: The Frederick Remington–Owen Wister Letters*, p. 30.

17. G. White, *Eastern Establishment*, chs. 2, 3 and 5; Vorpahl, *My Dear Wister*, pp. 20, 328–9; ———, *Frederic Remington and the West: With the Eye of the Mind*, pp. 3–33; Harold and Peggy Samuels, *Frederic Remington: A Biography*.

18. Vorpahl, *Frederic Remington*, ch. 2; engagement with Custer material, Edward S. Godfrey, *Century* (January, 1892), pp. 358–87.

19. Reprinted in Remington, *Collected Writings*, p. 43.

20. Remington, "Indians as Irregular Cavalry," *Collected Writings*, p. 59. Compare C. F. Adams' proposal to civilize the Black Freedmen by placing them in military colonies, Charles Francis Adams, Jr., in *A Cycle of Adams Letters, 1861–1865*, ed. by W. C. Ford, 1:124–33, 2:194–5, 213–9; Slotkin, *Fatal Environment*, pp. 297–8.

21. Remington, "Indians as Irregular Cavalry," *Collected Writings*, pp. 59–66, esp. pp. 59, 62. See also the interesting juxtaposition (*Harper's Weekly*, April 16, 1892) of Remington's illustration, "An Appeal for Justice," with the article, "The Washington Negro" by Henry Loomis Nelson: the Indian is "dignified" in subjection, the Negro abject. On Lieutenant Casey and the writing of "Lieutenant Casey's Last Scout," see Vorpahl, *Frederic Remington*, pp. 108–112.

22. Remington, "Lieutenant Casey's Last Scout," *Collected Writings*, pp. 70–7; Vorpahl, *Frederic Remington*, pp. 108–12. See also Remington, "On the Indian Reservations," p. 32; "Two Gallant Young Cavalrymen," pp. 47–9; and "Chasing a Major General," pp. 50–6 in *Collected Writings*. Remington's feeling that the old soldierly virtues were doomed is registered in one of his largest works of the 1885–90 period, the oil painting "The Last Stand," exhibited in Paris in 1889, which depicts a group of doomed cavalrymen in a monumental grouping. Though the title alludes to Custer, details of costume and weather suggest a more general or archetypal reference. See *ibid.*, pp. 112–3, 116–7. "The Last Stand" appeared as an illustration in the January 10, 1891, issue of *Harper's Weekly*, centerfold pp. The elegiac suggestions of the picture are reinforced by its appearance in the same issue with an account of the Ghost Dance war by Owen Wister and dispatches from Wounded Knee.

23. Vorpahl, *My Dear Wister*, p. 30; G. White, *Eastern Establishment*, p. 109. The Irish dialect quote is from Kipling's Sergeant Mulvaney, of *Three Soldiers*.

24. And compare Remington, "On the Indian Reservations," *Collected Writ-*

ings, p. 35: "I often think he has no mental process, but is the creature of impulse."

25. Remington, "Chicago Under the Mob," *Collected Writings*, pp. 152–4; reprinted from *Harper's Weekly*, July 21, 1894, pp. 680–1.

26. Remington, "Chicago Under the Law," *Collected Writings*, pp. 156, 155–9.

27. *Ibid.*, p. 155; reprinted from *Harper's Weekly*, July 28, 1894, pp. 703–4.

28. Remington, "The Affair of the ———th of July," *Collected Writings*, pp. 176–83; also in *Pony Tracks* (1896), published the same year as King's *A Tame Surrender* and Kirkman's *Science of Railways*. Compare Twain's critical treatment of this kind of massacre in "The French and the Comanches," *Letters from the Earth*, pp. 146–9.

29. Remington repeats the characterization of strikes as "savage war" in "The Colonel of the First Cycle Infantry" (*Harper's Weekly*, May 18, 1895), a fictional sketch whose nominal aim was to illustrate the potential usefulness of the army's new technology. The occasion for display of the bicycle's effectiveness is an incident set (probably) during the labor troubles in the Coeur d'Alene district of Idaho. The troops attack a strikers' "base" behind "enemy lines." The form of the expedition resembles Custer's Washita campaign: a swift night march; a dawn attack in which the troops fire freely, unable to distinguish "hostiles" from "friendlies"; after which they burn the village and retire. Remington, "The Colonel of the First Cycle Infantry," *Collected Writings*, pp. 190–6.

30. Gerald F. Linderman, *The Mirror of War: American Society and the Spanish American War*, chs. 3, 6; and see Stephen Crane's treatment of the stoic heroism of regulars vs. volunteers in *Wounds in the Rain*, esp. "The Price of the Harness" and "Virtue in War."

31. Morris, *Roosevelt*, chs. 23–6; Roosevelt, *The Rough Riders*, p. 7. Roosevelt had proposed forming such a "cowboy" regiment as early as 1880–81, when war with Mexico seemed possible; but the name and "style" of the regiment—particularly its combination of "cowboys" with representatives of the social and military elite—owe an obvious debt to Buffalo Bill's 1893 Congress of Rough Riders. On the cultivation of correspondents, see Morris, *Roosevelt*, pp. 645–6.

32. Finley Peter Dunne's "Mr. Dooley" punctures Roosevelt's democratic pretenses quite nicely in his review of *Rough Riders*: " 'I wud stand beside wan iv these r-rough men threatin' him as a akel, which he was in ivrything but birth, education, rank and courage . . . Honest, loyal, thrue-hearted la-ads, how kind I was to thim.' " [F. P. Dunne,] "A Book Review," *Mr. Dooley on Peace and War*, p. 15.

33. Roosevelt, *Rough Riders*, p. 20.

34. *Ibid.*, pp. 9–10, 19.

35. *Ibid.*, pp. 16, 17.

36. *Ibid.*, p. 10.

37. *Ibid.*, pp. 3–6. Roosevelt's self-praise is offered in a modest style. The accounts of his adventures in both *Rough Riders* and his 1913 *Autobiography* have a quality that can only be described as self-aggrandizing modesty. Although, as Edmund Morris notes, Roosevelt occasionally gives a humorous view of his action, this too is a standard attribute of the persona of the frontier hero, for

example in Davy Crockett or Cooper's Hawkeye. See Morris, *Roosevelt*, p. 646; Roosevelt, *Autobiography*, pp. 245 *ff*.; and, on the role of humor in constructing a heroic persona, Slotkin, *Regeneration*, p. 166.

38. Roosevelt, *Rough Riders*, pp. 143–4.

39. Dyer, *Theodore Roosevelt and the Idea of Race*, pp. 100–1; Willard B. Gatewood, *Black Americans and the White Man's Burden, 1898–1902*, p. 59.

40. Roosevelt, *Rough Riders*, p. 229.

41. Morris, *Roosevelt*, chs. 26–7; Stuart Creighton Miller, *"Benevolent Assimilation": The American Conquest of the Philippines, 1899–1903*, pp. 22–3.

42. *Ibid.*, p. 144, 149.

43. *Ibid.*, p. 141–2.

44. *HW*, June 23, 1900, cover and p. 596; July 21, 1900, p. 666; July 28, 1900, cover; June 16, 1900, cover; August 25th, 1900, cover.

45. Quoted in Miller, *"Benevolent Assimilation,"* p. 144.

46. Quoted in Amy Kaplan, "Romancing the Empire: The Embodiment of American Masculinity in the Popular Historical Novel of the 1890s," *ALH* 2:4 (1990), pp. 659–90.

47. Albert J. Beveridge, *The Meaning of the Times . . .*, pp. 84–5.

48. *Ibid.*, p. 84.

49. *Ibid.*, pp. 49, 50, 69, 113, 119. The weakness of Beveridge's argument is attested by his use of an absurd debating-point, asking "How do [the Filipinos] know that our government [of them] would be without their consent" until they have given it a fair trial?

50. James H. Blount, *The American Occupation of the Philippines, 1898–1912*, p. 567. Edwin Wildman, an American diplomat, had publically praised Aguinaldo as a Malay of "pure" race who had risen from the common people to become the benefactor of his nation ("General Emilio Aguinaldo—A Character Sketch," *HW*, January 25, 1899, p. 197). Within a month of the outbreak of hostilities, the press was defaming Aguinaldo as a "half-Chinese" barbarian and would-be despot. See Miller, *"Benevolent Assimilation,"* p. 65; Henry B. Russell, *Our War with Spain . . .*, pp. 553–60; and [Moorfield Storey, et al.], *Secretary Root's Record: Marked Severities in Philippine Warfare . . .*, pp. 6–9.

51. "Our Duty," *HW*, February 18, 1899, p. 158. Compare General George Forsyth, "An Apache Raid," *HW*, January 14, 1899, pp. 43–6, in which an American violation of the Mexican border in hot pursuit of Apaches is seen as transgression for which the Mexican "victims" are grateful.

52. Miller, *"Benevolent Assimilation,"* pp. 54–5, chs. 3–4.

53. *Ibid.*, p. 94.

54. John F. Bass, "The Philippine Revolt, Manila's Night of Terror," *HW*, April 22, 1899, pp. 401–4. "Only Filipino families are to be spared. All other individuals, of whatsoever race, are to be killed without mercy, after the extermination of the American army. . . . It will be seen that this historic document orders the murder of all the foreign population of Manila. Neither women nor children were to be spared. First the United States army was to be exterminated, and then all the white non-combatants—men, women, and children—were to be put to the sword." See also Miller, *"Benevolent Assimilation,"* pp. 64, 93; and "Diary of the Revolt," *HW*, March 4, 1899, p. 224. The "extermination" order

was written by an aide to Aguinaldo *after* American troops attacked the Filipinos. Although certainly ill advised and excessive, it was not an actual plan of operations but a piece of propaganda intended to stir Filipino defiance and perhaps create disorder behind American lines.

55. Bass, "The Philippine Revolt," p. 401.

56. *Ibid.*

57. Frank D. Millet, "The Filipino Leaders," *HW*, March 11, 1899, p. 232; "Aguinaldo's Indians," p. 248; Marrion Wilcox, "Philippine Ethnology," May 13, pp. 485, 487; see also Oct. 28, p. 1099.

58. *HW*, May 20, 1901, 496–8. See also pairing of "The Half-Caste in the Philippines" and "Revolt of the Yaqui Indians," January 6, 1900, pp. 14–6. An account of Frederick Funston's daring commando raid which captured Aguinaldo is paired with "The Ute Lands" opened to settlement by farmers—a juxtaposition that suggests what may follow the conclusion of this latest Indian war. A third story ("The Wardner Riot") notes that no troops have been available to send against striking "foreign" miners in Idaho because so many units are in the Philippines. See also "Brigadier-General Funston," *WW* 2:696–98 (1901).

59. Miller, "*Benevolent Assimilation*", pp. 71, 196.

60. James Wallace Broatch, "The Regulars," *HW*, July 1, 1902, p. 653.

61. Miller, "*Benevolent Assimilation*," p. 207; Michael Fellman, *Inside War: The Guerrilla Conflict in Missouri During the American Civil War*, ch. 3, esp. pp. 81–97.

62. Brian McA. Linn, *The U.S. Army and Counterinsurgency in the Philippine War*, 1899–1902, pp. 23–4, 49–52; Drinnon, *Facing West*, ch. 21; Miller, "*Benevolent Assimilation*," p. 209. On Weyler, and the use of captivity mythology to justify the war, see Joseph E. Wisan, *The Cuban Crisis as Reflected in the New York Press (1895–1898)*, esp. pp. 64–6; chs. 5, 9; pp. 220–36; Russell, *Our War*, ch. 17.

63. Quoted in [Storey], *Marked Severities*, pp. 98–9; see also Miller, "*Benevolent Assimilation*," p. 238.

64. Correspondent of the *Philadelphia Ledger*, quoted in Miller, "*Benevolent Assimilation*," p. 211.

65. Herbert Shapiro, *White Violence and Black Response from Reconstruction to Montgomery*, chs. 3–4.

66. *Ibid.*, pp. 93–5.

67. Quoted in [Storey], *Marked Severities*, pp. 10, 67.

68. Quoted in *Ibid.*, p. 67.

69. *Ibid.*, pp. 67, 205; Gatewood, *Black Americans*, pp. 114–5, 280–91, 319, 324; Shapiro, *White Violence*, ch. 3.

70. Slotkin, "Massacre," *Berkshire Review: Special Issue on Culture and Violence* (1979), pp. 112–32; Linn, *U.S. Army and Counterinsurgency*, pp. 143–5; Fellman, *Inside War*, chs. 2, 4 on cycles of atrocity.

71. Miller, "*Benevolent Assimilation*," p. 236.

72. *Ibid.*, p. 204.

73. *Ibid.*, pp. 92–5.

74. *Ibid.*, pp. 204–5.

75. *Ibid.*, pp. 93–4; 203–4. [Storey,] *Marked Severities*, pp. 21–3, 37, 53–4.

76. Miller, "*Benevolent Assimilation*," pp. 207–8.

77. *Ibid.*, pp. 207, 230.

78. *Ibid.*, pp. 206, 236–8.

79. Quoted in [Storey,] *Marked Severities*, p. 33; Miller, *Benevolent Assimilation*, ch. 12, esp. pp. 220, 222, 226–7, 228–32.

80. *Ibid.*, pp. 208–9, 220.

81. [Storey,] *Marked Severities*, pp. 26–7.

82. Glenn Anthony May, *Battle for Batangas: A Philippine Province at War*, esp. chs. 5, 8, 9; Wolff, . . .

83. Blount, *American Occupation*, pp. 378–97. And see Miller, "*Benevolent Assimilation*," p. 206, for the action of a Lt. Rowan, who punished the rape of a Filipina by burning the villages of both the perpetrator and the victim.

84. *Ibid.*, pp. 213–6, 238–52.

85. *Ibid.*, pp. 212–8, 230–8.

86. *Ibid.*, pp. 240, 234.

87. *Ibid.*, pp. 236–8. Though Roosevelt made public statements disapproving the use of torture and excessive force, his private communications to General Chaffee endorsed the use of the "water cure"; he congratulated Bell on his report of 616,000 deaths in Batangas, and (with Secretary of War Root) worked to mitigate Smith's sentence after the court-martial.

88. *Ibid.*, pp. 254–5, 262–3.

89. Miller, "*Benevolent Assimilation*," pp. 15, 121; E. Berkeley Tompkins, *Anti-Imperialism in the United States: The Great Debate, 1890–1920*, chs. 9–10, 15.

Notes to Chapter 4

1. Denning, *Mechanic Accents*, chs. 3–5.

2. Slotkin, *Fatal Environment*, pp. 192–8, 203–7, 307; Denning, *Mechanic Accents*, ch. 1; Christine Bold, "The Voice of the Fiction Factory in Dime and Pulp Westerns," *JAS* 17:1 (1983), pp. 29–46; Albert Johannsen, *The House of Beadle and Adams, and Its Dime and Nickel Novels: The Study of a Vanished Literature*.

3. Denning, *Mechanic Accents*, pp. 57–9; Slotkin, *Fatal Environment*, pp. 28–9; Cawelti, *Adventure, Mystery*, ch. 1.

4. Sensational narratives had served the moral programs of the Puritans and the propaganda needs of the Revolution; and were used in the 1840s and 1850s, by writers like George Lippard, to forward the causes of abolition, labor reform, and temperance. The mix of heroic history-tales and exposes of the "mysteries and miseries" of the metropolis that characterizes Lippard's *oeuvre* has its counterpart in the work of post-Civil War writers like James W. Buel, *The Border Outlaws* . . . (1881, featuring the James Gang), *Heroes of the Plains* . . . (1883), and *The Mysteries and Miseries of America's Great Cities* (1883). After 1860, fiction factories like Beadle & Adams and Street & Smith supplemented their sensational serials with popular histories and biographies of noted Americans. Compare Slotkin, *Fatal Environment*, pp. 151–8, 194–8; Denning, *Mechanic Accents*, pp. 91–100.

5. Slotkin, *Fatal Environment*, pp. 200–7.

6. This is true even of Buffalo Bill dime novels, despite the fact that Cody owed his early fame to the Indian wars.

7. Denning, *Mechanic Accents*, chs. 7–8, pp. 157, 160; H. N. Smith, *Virgin*

Land, pp. 111, 134: "Cut loose first from the code of gentility that had commanded Cooper's unswerving loyalty, and then from the communion with God through nature that had made Leatherstocking a saint of the forest, the Western hero [became] a self-reliant two-gun man who behaved in almost exactly the same fashion whether he were outlaw or peace officer." Daryl Jones, *The Dime Novel Western*, p. 81, asserts that Deadwood Dick was the first practicing criminal to be treated unambiguously in a dime novel. See also Slotkin, *Fatal Environment*, pp. 133–5; William W. Stowe, "Hard-Boiled Virgil: Early Nineteenth Century Beginnings of a Popular Literary Formula," in Barbara A. Rader and Howard G. Zettler, eds., *The Sleuth and the Scholar: Origins, Evolution, and Current Trends in Detective Fiction*, pp. 79–90.

8. Denning, *Mechanic Accents*, chs. 2–4, pp. 159–60.

9. Eric Hobsbawm, *Bandits*, p. 153, questions the identification of the James Gang as true social bandits who classically represent communities of peasants resisting the power of landlords. Hobsbawm sees the James Gang as "an adaptation of social banditry to capitalism," because they were small entrepreneurs of crime, as enmeshed in the capitalist system as their enemies. Denning, *Mechanic Accents*, pp. 159–63, sees the "adaptation" as producing a genuine modern counterpart to Hobsbawm's "primitive" social banditry; and compare Louis Hartz, "A Comparative Study of Fragment Culture," in Leon Friedman, ed., *Violence in America: Historical and Comparative Perspectives*, pp. 91–2.

10. Brown, "American Vigilante Tradition," in Friedman, *Violence in America*, Vol. 2: 51–3; ———, *No Duty to Retreat: An American Theme*, chs. 2–3; Dubofsky, *We Shall Be All*, chs. 1–3, esp. pp. 36–7, 58–60, 146–8, 158–65; John Thompson, *Closing the Frontier: Radical Response in Oklahoma, 1889–1923*, pp. 182–3; Green, *Grass-Roots Socialism*, pp. 360–6 and ch. 8; John Bodnar, *Workers' World: Kinship, Community, and Protest in an Industrial Society, 1900–1940*; Broehl, *The Mollie Maguires*, chs. 1–4. Bruce, *1877: The Year of Violence*.

11. "The Western Lowrys," *NYW* of March 28, 1874, pp. 1–2.

12. Slotkin, *Fatal Environment*, chs. 13–4; Foner, *Reconstruction*, esp. chs. 8–12.

13. Slotkin, *Fatal Environment*, pp. 438–40, 458–9, 464–70.

14. Karen I. Blu, *The Lumbee Problem: The Making of an American Indian People*, esp. p. 135. The speculative suggestion of a late-nineteenth-century White historian that the Lumbee were descended from Ralegh's "Lost Colony" was adopted by the tribe after 1890.

15. *Ibid.*, pp. 49–65.

16. Townsend's story is primarily significant for its thematic content, but it also has interest as an early instance of the emerging form of the dime novel or cheap fiction "detective story." George Alfred Townsend, *The Swamp Outlaws: or, The North Carolina Bandits, Being a Complete History of the Modern Rob Roys and Robin Hoods* (1874), is cheaply printed, and dime-novel series (Sea Romances, the Red Wolf series, and "Black Jokes") are advertised on the endpapers. Townsend himself is the central figure in the narrative, which shows him beginning his investigation, then being kidnaped and carried to Lowrys' camp.

17. *NYH*, January 6, 1872, pp. 4, 6. An article on "The Scuffletown Settle-

ment," *NYH*, January 29, p. 6, which appeared during the Congressional hearings on KKK outrages, distorts context to suggest that testimony had implicated the Lowrys in Klan atrocities, when in fact testimony represents the Lowrys as resisting the Klan. Emphasis is placed on southern disruptions, especially a spectacular account of the "Rochester Riot," precipitated when police attempted to protect an accused rapist from a northern lynch mob:

> [The] atrocious criminal had around him the curse of race. He is a negro. To say that this should have no weight in the case is futile; we are speaking of facts. With all our levelling and pulling down of legal inequalities to place the colored man on a level with white men, the fact remains . . . the idea that he belongs to an inferior race. . . . A crime in one of such a scorned race appears more criminal and revolting than in one of any other, and it would be hard for even the most rational white man to deny . . . that such is the case.

See *NYH*, January 6, p. 6, and joking reference to KKK violence, "Captain Scott Brings Down Two Coons" (January 12, p. 6); "The Ku Klux Klan," January 28, p. 4; "The Ku Klux Investigation," February 19, p. 6. Another group of stories and editorials suggests parallels between the Reconstructed South and Mexico, where racial mongrelization and the breakdown of law and order seem to require rule by the strong hand. See "Manifest Destiny in Mexico," January 11, p. 9; January 6, p. 7. See also Slotkin, *Fatal Environment*, chs. 14–5.

18. Townsend, *Swamp Outlaws*, pp. viii, ix, 9–11.

19. *Ibid.*, pp. viii, ix, 9–11, 14–18.

20. *Ibid.*, pp. 9–11, 24–5, 33–8, 27. Compare Melville's description of the "Indian-hater" Moredock as a "Leatherstocking Nemesis," *The Confidence-Man, His Masquerade*, p. 130.

21. Rollin G. Osterweis, *The Myth of the Lost Cause, 1865–1900*; Gaines M. Foster, *Ghosts of the Confederacy: Defeat, the Lost Cause, and the Emergence of the New South, 1865–1913*.

22. William A. Settle, Jr., *Jesse James Was His Name: or, Fact and Fiction Concerning the Careers of the Notorious James Brothers of Missouri*, chs. 1–3; Michael Fellman, *Inside War*, esp. ch. 6.

23. *Ibid.*, ch. 3, esp. pp. 81–97, 166–91; Slotkin, *Fatal Environment*, pp. 303–7, 384. These measures were invoked even against the regularly enlisted troops of John S. Mosby.

24. Settle, *Jesse James*, ch. 6, pp. 77–84, chs. 12–3; Edwards, *Noted Guerrillas . . .*, pp. 448, 450–1, 456. Like many of Quantrill's men, the Jameses and the Youngers were "middling" rather than poor White: the Jameses' stepfather was a minister, and both families owned large farms and a few slaves and supported slavery because they expected to benefit from it. Fellman, *Inside War*, ch. 1.

25. J. N. Edwards' *Noted Guerrillas . . .*, p. 19.

26. *Ibid.*, pp. 14, 20, 205, 206–7.

27. *Ibid.*, pp. 13, 15, 18.

28. *Ibid.*, pp. 17, 21. Although guerrilla command structures are meritocratic, Edwards asserts that many of the guerrillas were already aristocrats by nature and nurture: Quantrill "attracted a number of young men . . . gently nurtured,

born to higher destinies . . . and fit for callings high up in the scale of science or philosophy."

29. *Ibid.*, p. 15.

30. Frank Triplett, *Life, Times and Treacherous Death of Jesse James*, pp. xxxv, xxxvi, 3–4, 6, 17.

31. *Ibid.*, p. 58, and compare Theodore Parker on "Anglo-Saxons," pp. 45–6, above.

32. Triplett, *Jesse James*, pp. 111–3, 212.

33. Edwards, *Noted Guerrillas*, p. 316; Settle, *Jesse James*, p. 3.

34. *Ibid.*, p. 68.

35. Edwards, *Noted Guerrillas* . . . , pp. 456*ff.*; Settle, *Jesse James*, chs. 8–9, pp. 184–5.

36. *Ibid.*, pp. 184–5; James A. Dacus, *The Life and Adventures of Frank and Jesse James and the Younger Brothers*; ———, *Annals of the Great Strikes in the United States*, esp. chs. 1, 5, 10–12. See also Buel, *The Border Outlaws* . . . (1881) and *The Mysteries and Miseries of America's Great Cities* (1883).

37. Settle, *Jesse James*, pp. 187–9, 229. This series is no longer extant, but most of the titles were reprinted in Frank Tousey's *New York Detective Library* series (1889–97), "The Only Library Containing True Stories of the James Boys," available on microfilm in the Library of Congress; hereafter referred to as "NYDL, No. xx." Street & Smith's series of James Boys adventures is also on microfilm; issues are hereafter identified as "*S&S*, No. xx."

38. *The Life and Death of Jesse James* (No. 76) covers the Gang's career from the Civil War through Jesse's assassination; *Frank James, The Avenger* (No. 81) and *Frank James' Surrender (No.* 105) deal with Jesse's surviving brother, who is ultimately reconciled with the law; and *The Lives of the Ford Boys* (No. 87) deals with Jesse's assassins. These titles reappeared in NYDL as Nos. 466, 467.

39. NYDL No. 466, p. 3.

40. Precedents include the pamphlet and ballad literature of the sixteenth and seventeenth centuries, the "Newgate Calendar" of the eighteenth, Puritan execution sermons, and pamphlet and newspaper tales concerning such American frontier criminals as the Harpes and John Murrell. Frontier romances featured pursuit and rescue plots suggestive of detective-story patterns; crime and detection played a central role in the fiction of urban corruption by Dickens in England, Eugene Sue in France, and George Lippard in America. The tradition of the detective as master of ratiocination has been traced to Poe (if not to Cyrano). William Ruehlmann, *Saint With a Gun: The Unlawful American Private Eye*, pp. 21–31.

41. Slotkin, *Fatal Environment*, pp. 146–57; compare Denning, *Mechanic Accents*, pp. 91–100.

42. Broehl, *Mollie Maguires*, pp. 243–50.

43. *Ibid.*, ch. 6, esp. pp. 144–5.

44. Denning, *Mechanic Accents*, pp. 119–21. The best study of Pinkerton's operations against, and public representation of, the Mollie Maguires is Wayne G. Broehl, Jr., *The Mollie Maguires*, esp. chs. 5–6, 8, and 10 (which treats Pinkerton's operations as a form of vigilantism). See also James D. Horan, *The Pinkertons*, chs. 20, 22–4.

45. Slotkin, *Fatal Environment*, chs. 14–5.

46. Denning, *Mechanic Accents*, ch. 7. Dime novels picked up the Mollies as a subject after the indictments handed down as a result of the Pinkerton investigation; and even where they show sympathy for the union miners, these stories may be considered as exploitations of the Pinkerton scenario rather than accounts originating from the miners' perspective.

47. Allan Pinkerton, *The Mollie Maguires and the Detectives* (1877), pp. ix–xi.

48. *Ibid.*, pp. 15, 16.

49. *Ibid.*, pp. 19–24.

50. *Ibid.*, pp. 73, 181, ch. 10; and compare Mary Rowlandson's famous characterization of her captors.

51. Pinkerton, *Strikers, Communists, Tramps and Detectives* (1877), offers a more apocalyptic vision of labor unions as a national threat and provides Pinkerton with the basis for a more systematic attack on the evils of "communism," the prevalence of anarchic criminality among the lower classes, and the need for a regime of force in which the detective will play a vital role. "Rights are obtained by rates of behavior. They are not inherent in man . . . ," and it is the employer who must judge the proper rate of both rights and wages which his workmen had "earned" (pp. x–xi, 15). "Communistic law boldly assumes that the vagabond is as good as the honest laborer, and that the laziest loafer of the slums has the same claim upon the more fortunate of mankind for bread . . . that the industrious economical citizen has. There cannot exist a more cowardly doctrine than that all men have equal rights in property." (p. 86). Tramps and communists are of course linked with Indian "savages": they are "the scum of creation . . . so devoid of all conscience, pity, or consideration that it is hard to look upon them as possessing the least of human attributes." But they are also likened to the outlaws of the West, to "veritable guerrillas bushwhacking on the outskirts of civilization"—in short, to Jesse James (pp. 67, 85, 88, 90, 229–30, 248–51).

52. James E. Wright, *The Politics of Populism: Dissent in Colorado*, pp. 446–51; *HW*, 1892: July 16, pp. 674–5, 678; July 23, pp. 698, 713–4, 725, 734; August 27, pp. 823, 833.

53. Edward Wheeler, *Deadwood Dick, the Prince of the Road; or, The Black Rider of the Black Hills* (1877), pp. 5, 15.

54. Wheeler, *Deadwood Dick on Deck; or, Calamity Jane, the Heroine of Whoop-Up. A Story of Dakota* (1878), pp. xii, 109, 171.

55. *Ibid.*, p. 4, and Denning, *Mechanic Accents*, p. 164.

56. *Ibid.*, pp. 163–4. "[D]ime novel outlaws . . . are perhaps less sons of Leatherstocking than sons of Mollie Maguire."

57. Smith, *Virgin Land*, p. 112.

58. Wheeler, *Deadwood Dick on Deck*, p. 2; Denning, *Mechanic Accents*, p. 164.

59. Wheeler, *Deadwood Dick, The Prince of the Road*, p. 2; Denning, *Mechanic Accents*, pp. 164–5.

60. *Ibid.*, p. 164.

61. Source is "Deadwood Dick Library," reprinting 1877–84 stories in new format, 1899–1908. Similar shift of concern in Buffalo Bill, *The Columbian Detective* and *Buffalo Bill and the Nihilists* (1910).

62. All *NYDL* "Jesse James" titles are by "D. W. Stevens." *NYDL* Nos. 441,

446, 450, 466, 467, 470, 484.; see esp. *The Last of the Band; or, the Surrender of Frank James* (No. 676, 1895); ———, *The James Boys at Bay; or, Sheriff Timberlake's Triumph* (No. 677, 1895); *The James Boys and the Red-Legs; or, The Great Kansas Raid* (No. 683, 1895); *Old King Brady and the Ford Boys* (No. 420, 1890). *S&S*: No. 175, *Bob Ford, the Slayer of Jesse James; or, The Dramatic Life and Death of a Noted Desperado* (1889); W. B. Lawson, *Jesse James's Successor; or, the Raid on the South Chicago Bank: A Story of the Recent Daring Robbery* (No. 101, 1891); *NYDL: Old King Brady Among the Indians; or, Sitting Bull and the Ghost Dance* (No. 441, 1891).

63. *S&S*: Capt. Jake Shackleford, *Jesse, the Outlaw; A Narrative of the James Boys* (No. 4, 1889); *NYDL, The James Boys and the Detectives* (No. 348), esp. p. 3.

64. *NYDL: The Man from Nowhere and His Adventures with the James Boys; A Story of a Detective's Shrewdest Work* (No. 364, 1889), p. 24.

65. *NYDL: Life and Death of Jesse James and Lives of the Ford Boys* (No. 466, 1891), p. 3–4.

66. *NYDL: Old King Brady and the James Boys in Missouri* (No. 359, 1889), pp. 7, 41–2.

67. "Carl Greene" was the most important recurring figure of this type. *NYDL: Pinkerton's Boy Detective; or, Trying to Capture the James Boys* (No. 491, 1892); *Young Sleuth and the James Boys; or, the Keen Detective* (No. 492, 1892); *The Man from Nowhere and His Adventures with the James Boys; A Story of a Detective's Shrewdest Work* (No. 364, 1889); *Sam Sixkiller, the Cherokee Detective; or, The James Boys' Most Dangerous Foe* (No. 358, 1889), esp. p. 5. *S&S*: Jack Sharp, *The Younger Brothers' Vow; or, Hunted Down in Arkansas* (No. 49, 1890).

68. *S&S*: John E. Barrett, *A Knight of Labor, or The Master Workman's Vow* (No. 85, 1890). "The Powerful Young Blacksmith Seized the Communist and Shook Him Vigorously." Becomes Partner in Steel co. (31); *The Rising Tide; a Story of Nihilism* (No. 108, 1890). *NYDL: Mr. Lazarus of Ludlow Street; or, Old King Brady Among the Anarchists of New York*, (No. 447, 1891); ———, *The Terrible Mystery of Car No. 206; or, Old King Brady and the Man of Gold* (No. 460, 1891), p. 4.

69. *S&S*: Shackleford, *Jesse the Outlaw; a Narrative of the James Boys* (No. 4, 1889); ———, *Jesse James Among the Moonshiners; or, the Train Robber's Trail in Kentucky* (No. 104, 1891); ———, *Jesse James in New Orleans* (No. 110, 1891); ———, *Jesse James in Disguise; or, the Missouri Outlaw as a Showman* (No. 113, 1891); ———, *Jesse James's Hunt to the Death; or, The Terror of Grizzly Hollow* (No. 165, 1889). *NYDL: The James Boys Among the Boomers; or, Old King Brady and Carl Greene Fighting the Outlaws in Oklahoma; The James Boys and the Ku Klux; or, Chased Through Kentucky by Old King Brady and Carl Greene* (No. 771, 1897). Some detective stories make extensive use of frontier romance conventions, like the classic "old hunter/young hunter" pair of heroes; stories set in ex-urban districts are "Westernized" by metaphor. For example, Harlan Hansely's *Flyaway Ned* (1895) pairs "Old Sleuth" with a young sleuth whose motives are those of an Indian-hater, against a gang described as "savage," in a district of Long Island said to be as wild as "Navajoe country," in a style strongly reminiscent of "Southwestern humor" (pp. 11; 17–8, 50–1).

70. *S&S*: W. B. Lawson, *Frank & Jesse James in Mexico; or, Raiders of the Rio Grande* (No. 50, 1890), p. 2; ———, *Jesse James's Oath; or, Tracked to Death* (No.

54, 1890), pp. 2–4, 30; see also Nos. 54, 61, 71, 74, 90, 94. *NYDL: The James Boys in Mexico and the James Boys in California* (No. 419); *The James Boys' Trip Around the World; or, Carl Green the Detective's Longest Chase* (No. 461, 1891), esp. pp. 10–11, 30. The latter is an interesting combination of outlaw/detective tale, utopian fantasy, and plagiarism of Verne's *Around the World in Eighty Days*.

71. *NYDL: Old King Brady and the James Boys in Missouri* (No. 359, 1889), p. 7; *The James Boys in New York; or, Fighting Old King Brady* (No. 673, 1895), p. 10.

72. *Abbott and Costello Meet the Mummy* (1955)—or, for that matter, *Jesse James Meets Frankenstein's Daughter* (1966).

73. *NYDL: The James Boys and Pinkerton; or, Frank and Jesse as Detectives* (No. 396), pp. 7–8; *A Bag of Shot; or, Old King Brady Out West* (No. 332). In the latter, the plot and theme of class warfare in the mines are parallel to Wheeler's *Deadwood Dick on Deck*.

74. *NYDL: James Boys in Boston* (No. 387); *The James Boys and Pinkerton; or, Frank and Jesse as Detectives* (No. 396), p. 10; *The James Boys Afloat; or, the Wild Adventures of a Detective on the MS* (No. 678); *The James Boys and the Bank Wrecker; or, the Mystery of the Missing Bride* (No. 707); *The James Boys and the President's Special; or, Lost in the Benton Forest* (No. 934), esp. p. 30.

75. The Street & Smith series stops just short of a libelous equation between Jesse and the archetypal Wall Street speculator in Jack Shackleford, *Jesse James in New York; or, a Plot to Capture Jay Gould* (No. 74, 1890), esp. pp. 8, 10; while Jesse appears to advantage measured against the vices of wealthy gamblers (*Jesse James at Long Branch; or, Playing for a Million*) (No. 61, 1890), crooked bankers (*Jesse James at Coney Island; or, the Wall Street Banker's Secret*) (No. 71, 1890), and even unprincipled Pinkertons (*Frank James in St. Louis; or, The Mysteries of a Great City* (No. 57, 1890).

76. *Frank James in St. Louis*, pp. 3, 29; ———, *Jesse James in Tennessee*; . . . (631, 1889), p. 23.

77. *NYDL: Old King Brady and the James Boys in Missouri* (No. 359, 1889), pp. 7, 41–2; *The Ford Boys' Vengeance; or, From Bandits to Detectives* (No. 441); *The James Boys Working for Old King Brady; or, Carl Green and the Road Agents* (No. 630, 1894); *Old King Brady and the James Boys Among the Choctaws; or, A Raid into the Indian Nation in '81* (No. 557, 1892); *The James Boys and the Vigilantes and The James Boys and the Ku Klux* (No. 393), p. 28. It makes a difference that the James Boys are the outlaws in question: compare *The Stolen Pay Train* (1895), in which the series detective Nick Carter captures a gang of western train robbers who have many allies among the law officers of their community. After their capture, the gang is lynched by vigilantes, the Carter's evident satisfaction. The story is probably based on Pinkerton's "Reno" case, *The Expressman and the Detectives* (1875); see Broehl, *Mollie Maguires*, pp. 239–42.

78. *NYDL, Old King Brady Among the Indians; or, Sitting Bull and the Ghost Dance* (No. 441, 1891), pp. 3, 4, 23, 27, 30; *Old King Brady and the James Boys Among the Choctaws; or, A Raid into the Indian Nation in '81* (No. 557, 1892).

79. Richard White, "Outlaw Gangs of the Middle Border: American Social Bandits," *WHQ* 12:4, p. 396; Fraser, *America and the Patterns of Chivalry*, chs. 8–9.

80. James R. Green, *Grass-Roots Socialism: Radical Movements in the Southwest, 1895–1943*, pp. 2, 333–44.

81. See ch. 3, fn. 6.

Notes to Chapter 5

1. W. Churchill Williams, "Red Blood in Fiction," *World's Work* 6:1 (May, 1903), pp. 3694–700. Ann Douglas, *The Feminization of American Culture*, esp. chs. 1–3, 5, 7; Jane Tompkins, *Sensational Fictions*.

2. One of the best contemporary descriptions of the kinds of limitations imposed by this genteel tradition is William Dean Howells, *Criticism and Fiction and The Responsibilities of the Novelist*, pp. 148–9. See also Barbara Rush Welter, "The Cult of True Womanhood, 1820–1860," *AQ* 18:2, Pt. 1 (1966), pp. 151–74; Douglas, *Feminization*, pp. 1–16. I do not mean to suggest that women were merely passive in the creation of this model of womanhood; rather, I mean to make it clear that while literature in this tradition was addressed to women, it was not the expression of "women" as a self-conscious class or cultural movement.

3. Williams, "Red Blood in Fiction," pp. 3694–700.

4. Amy Kaplan, *The Social Construction of American Realism*, pp. 1–14; Harold Kaplan, *Power and Order: Henry Adams and the Naturalist Tradition in American Fiction*, chs. 1–2.

5. "The Most Striking Figure in Public Life," *WW* 1 (1900), pp. 21–3. And see for example the portraits of Carnegie and General A. R. Chaffee in *WW* 2: 108, 360.

6. "The Doctrine of Room at the Top," *WW* 3: 1473. See also "Are Young Men's Chances Less?" 1: 170–3; 4: 2359–60; "Froth and Truth About Trusts," 1:1, 18–9. On expansion through applying technology to agriculture and industry, and/or imperial expansion see J. P. Mowbray, "Going Back to the Soil," 1:267–77, 2:690–1 and "Expansion by Irrigation," 1:475–6; 4:2365; 6:3694–700, 3716–7.

7. William Lawrence, "The Relation of Wealth to Morals," *WW* 1:286–92; Frederick Emory, "The Greater America," 2:1321–5; see also 2:502–3; 1:47–54, 65–72; 4:2451; 1:4; 3:1806.

8. *WW* 3:1806–7. Even when proof of General Smith's crimes was made, the magazine warned against extending the condemnation of Smith to a critique of the political authorities or their policies. See "The Lesson of the Philippine Military Scandal," *WW* 4:2135, 2138; "New Force for Peace," 4:2141, 2138. Roosevelt was hailed as "The Most Striking Figure in Public Life," *WW*, 1: pp. 21–3; and an editorial urged that before criticizing Roosevelt's policies, "it is proper for every respectable citizen, whether editor or reader, to remember that President Roosevelt is a frank and approachable man. Any responsible person can see him face to face," 2:1243–4.

9. *WW* 2:141, 230, 802. However, its treatment of the Boxer Rebellion avoided the extremes of racist characterization and demands for revenge. While noting that "Boxer outrages on women of our own blood have indeed been avenged," it condemned allied troops for avenging the outrage "in kind," and

praised General Chaffee for risking a fight with German troops to limit their looting and massacre.

10. Progressives like Roosevelt accepted literacy tests as reasonable barriers to the franchise so long as the barriers were not arbitrarily restricted to Negroes but included unfit Whites as well. On labor issues see for example, *WW* 1:19; 2:1133, 1245–6, 1323; 3:1569; 4:2477–8. Frederick Emory, "The Homogeneity of Our People," 6:3598–3603, 3611–2; 3716–7. On race, see "Changed Opinions on the Race Question," 5:3156–7; also 1:361–2 and 4:2591; and the favorable notice of Booker T. Washington for his advocacy of political and work-place docility for Negro workers, "Rest Cure for the Race Problem," 4:3942.

11. *WW* 6:3476–7; 6:3697; the review of Wister's novel is in 4:5, 2574.

12. Owen Wister, "The Evolution of the Cow-puncher," in Ben Merchant Vorpahl, *My Dear Wister: The Frederick Remington–Owen Wister Letters*, pp. 57–64, 77–96, esp. p. 80.

13. *Ibid.*

14. Frank Norris, "The Frontier Gone at Last," *The Responsibilities of the Novelist. Works*, Vol. 7: pp. 71–2, 74–5.

15. Norris, *The Octopus*, pp. 5, 42, 122, 212–3; Brown, *No Duty to Retreat*, ch. 3. On Gilpin, see Slotkin, *Fatal Environment*, pp. 219–24.

16. Langdon, *Industrial Wars*, p. 467.

17. Representative fictional treatments are (respectively), Norris, *The Octopus* (1901); Owen Wister, *The Virginian* (1902); Hamlin Garland, *Hesper* (1902) and Mary Hallock Foote, *Coeur d'Alene* (1892); Upton Sinclair, *The Coal War* (1915).

18. Emma F. Langdon, *A History of the Industrial Wars in Colorado, 1903–4–5* (1905), p. 467: "Such a struggle between two such contending forces can only be settled one way and that is the complete overthrow of one or the other. . . . [It] has been a struggle between organized labor and organized capital—between the working class and the monied power—right and might—for the complete control of the industrial and political mastery of the situation in the Rocky Mountains." See also Rastall, *Labor History*, pp. 23, 162; Dubofsky, *We Shall Be All*, chs. 1–2; and Winthrop Lane, *Civil War in West Virginia: A Story of the Industrial Conflict in the Coal Mines* (1921), an account of the background to the Matewan "massacre," which treats the hill country as a "frontier."

19. Kaplan, *Power and Order*, ch. 6; Mangan and Walvin, *Manliness and Morality*, chs. 1–2, 6–7, 8, 10. The themes of regeneration through immersion in wilderness violence, which they worked out in more or less elaborate fictions, were echoed in the simpler forms of popular history and biographical writing, in dime and pulp fiction, and in the literature of newly incorporated organizations for boys, like the Boy Scouts, Indian Scouts, etc. Hermann Hagedorn's *The Boy's Life of Theodore Roosevelt* (1918) presents TR himself as a hero in the mold of the protagonist of London's *Sea Wolf*: a sickly eastern tenderfoot who transforms himself into a hero by his deliberate pursuit of the strenuous life. Two town-boys are similarly "regenerated" by their study of Indian lore in Ernest Thompson Seton's *Two Little Savages* (1903)—Seton founded a scouting organization which later merged with the Boy Scouts. The "Lone Scout" organization was entirely based on a pulp series: see LeRoy Ashby, " '*Straight from Youthful*

Hearts': Lone Scout and the Discovery of the Child, *1915–1924*," *JPC* 9:4, pp. 775–93.

20. See for example Remington, "A Sergeant of the Orphan Troop," *Collected Writings*, pp. 256–62. The hero, Carter Johnson, anticipates many features of Wister's Virginian; but Remington's epitaph for the Cheyenne in "A Sergeant of the Orphan Troop" (1896)—"This was the last stand, nature was exhausted"—is the White hero's epitaph as well. In stories like "The Essentials at Fort Adobe," pp. 286–91, and "Massai's Crooked Trail," pp. 277–82, he identifies with hostile Indians for their systematic and uncompromising resistance to civilization. He adopts an Indian persona in the series of stories told by the half-breed Sundown LeFlare (1898), pp. 295–300, 310–9, 322–6, 332–7; and in *The Way of an Indian* (1905), pp. 554–96. This from the man who once lumped "Injuns" together with "Huns" and "Jews" as "the rubbish of the earth I hate."

21. He intended it as a critical response to the more "progressive" myth offered in Wister's *The Virginian*. See Vorpahl, *My Dear Wister*, pp. 306–30.

22. See Jack London, "The White Silence" and "The Son of the Wolf," "An Odyssey of the North," in *The Son of the Wolf* (1900); "An Odyssey of the North" shows the Teutonic or Saxon victor ultimately destroyed. See the critical discussion by James L. McLintock, *White Logic: Jack London's Short Stories*.

23. See for example London, "The Wife of a King," in *Son of the Wolf. Son of the Wolf* was followed by *God of His Fathers* (1901) and *Children of the Frost* (1902), in which the theme of race-struggle is given greater prominence and more orthodox treatment. See especially the title story of *God of His Fathers*, pp. 96–7. In *Children of the Frost*, the Indians' "League of Old Men" teaches Whites the same lesson of racial solidarity that Roosevelt's Indians teach in *Winning*.

24. Jack London, *The Iron Heel*, pp. 256–7. Compare quote from *The Nation* on p. xxx above, and in Slotkin, *Fatal Environment*, p. 496.

25. London, *Iron Heel*, pp. 176, 200–1, 209.

26. *Ibid.*, p. 7.

27. *Ibid.*, pp. 113–5.

28. Parrington, *Main Currents*, Vol. 3: 290; Jean Holloway, *Hamlin Garland: A Biography*; Joseph B. McCullough, *Hamlin Garland*.

29. See Lonnie E. Underhill and Daniel F. Littlefield, Jr., eds., *Hamlin Garland's Observations on the American Indian*. Garland's version of "General Custer's Last Fight as Seen by Two Moon" (1898) has become a standard reference.

30. Hamlin Garland, *The Eagle's Heart*, pp. 71, 107–8, 99, 101.

31. *Ibid.*, pp. 105–8.

32. *Ibid.*, pp. 344, 347.

33. Garland, *Captain of the Gray Horse Troop*, p. 377.

34. McCullough, *Hamlin Garland*, p. 97.

35. *Ibid.*, p. 414. Similar themes and plots are used in S. E. White, *The Blazed Trail* (1902); Mary Hallock Foote, *The Chosen Valley*, about the irrigation frontier; and ———, *Coeur d'Alene* (1892), set during the strike.

36. Vorpahl, *My Dear Wister*, pp. 19–20; White, *Eastern Establishment*, chs. 3, 6, esp. p. 132.

37. *Ibid.*, pp. 123–7; and Gene M. Gressley, *Bankers and Cattlemen*.

38. White, *Eastern Establishment*, pp. 126–8.

39. Owen Wister, "Horses of the Plains," and "The Evolution of the Cow-puncher," in Vorpahl, *My Dear Wister*, pp. 57–64, 77–96, esp. pp. 77–8, 80.

40. *Ibid.*, pp. 81, 93–4, 96.

41. Gressley, *Bankers and Cattlemen*, pp. 278–81.

42. *WW* 4:6, 2685–7.

43. For a full history of the event, see Helena Huntington Smith, *The War on Powder River: The History of an Insurrection*; T. A. Larson, *History of Wyoming*, 272–3; Asa Shinn Mercer, *The Banditti of the Plains, or The Cattlemen's Invasion of Wyoming in 1892, the Crowning Infamy of the Ages*, pp. xxiii, 1–2, 29.

44. Jack L. Weston, *The Real American Cowboy*, chs. 2–4; Gressley, *Bankers and Cattlemen*, pp. 123–4, notes that Flagg's leadership of the strike was marked by an intelligent understanding of the cattle business—he timed it to coincide with what was to be the biggest annual roundup in Wyoming history. For the IWW's attempt to organize cowhands, see William D. Haywood, *The Autobiography . . .*, p. 190.

45. Rosenbaum and Sederberg, *Vigilante Politics*; Brown, *Strain of Violence*, ch. 4.

46. *Ibid.*, pp. 105–9, 111–2, 117, 126–8.

47. *Ibid.*, pp. 103, 205. The model for this new type of vigilantism was the San Francisco Vigilance Committee of 1856, which—despite its western location—was a distinctly urban phenomenon. The San Francisco movement was given a distinctly contemporary gloss by H. H. Bancroft, in his monumental study *Popular Tribunals* (1887), which became a standard reference. Bancroft argues that the use of vigilantism by the "respectable classes" is justified under *modern* and *urban* conditions, when social division approximates the character of "savage war" and "the question [is] no longer whether it [is] right for the people to take law into their own hands . . . but whether the virtuous and orderly element in the community should have any existence at all." See also Thomas Dimmesdale's widely read account of *The Vigilantes of Montana* (1866), which gave the term a new currency after the Civil War.

48. Compare Robert H. Utley, *High Noon in Lincoln: Violence on the Western Frontier*, chs. 2, 3, 5, 15; Brown, *Strain of Violence*, chs. 1, 4, 6.

49. Larson, *Wyoming*, pp. 271, 276; Mercer, *Banditti*, pp. xvii, xxviii–xxxii, 33, 35–6, 47–8; White, *Eastern Establishment*, pp. 128–31. Wister's friend Major Wolcott used the same expression when offering his "nominations" for the "dead list." On Homestead, see Leon Wolff, *Lockout: The Story of the Homestead Strike of 1892*.

50. Mercer, *Banditti*, pp. xvi–xvii, 120–1.

51. In July 1892 he made a somewhat mysterious trip to Cinnibar, Montana. It has been suggested that the trip may have had something to do with plans to free his imprisoned friends, or that his sudden return from Cinnibar was a panic response to the anger in that region against Wister's friends. Whatever the truth of the matter, the trip is the probable model for a key episode in *The Virginian*. (White, *Eastern Establishment*, pp. 128–30, 139.)

52. *Ibid.*, 139–40, 143–4; Philip Durham, "Introduction," in Wister, *The Virginian: A Horseman of the Plains*, pp. viii–x.

53. Slotkin, *Fatal Environment*, pp. 306–8.

54. Wister, *The Virginian* (1902), pp. 243, 240, 256.

55. The best discussion of the literary tradition of "aristocracy" on which Wister drew is still William R. Taylor, *Cavalier and Yankee: The Old South and American National Character*, esp. chs. 4–5; and see Slotkin, *Fatal Environment*, pp. 77–8, 103–4, 118–22, 144–5.

56. Wister, *Virginian*, pp. 8–9, 155.

57. *Ibid.*, pp. 56–7.

58. *Ibid.*, p. 90.

59. *Ibid.*, p. 93.

60. Trampas may also be a fictionalization of Jack Flagg, the leader of the Wyoming cowboys' strike before the big roundup in 1884 who later became a leader of the Johnson County ranchers.

61. Wister, *Virginian*, p. 272.

62. *Ibid.*, pp. 261–2.

63. *Ibid.*, p. 265.

64. *Ibid.*

65. *Ibid.*, pp. 200–7. Note also Molly's remark early in the novel, p. 85, "I've always wanted to be a man."

66. Rayford W. Logan, *The Betrayal of the Negro: From Rutherford B. Hayes to Woodrow Wilson*, chs. 5, 14; C. Vann Woodward, *The Strange Career of Jim Crow*, chs. 1, 2.

67. James E. Cutler, *Lynch-Law: An Investigation into the History of Lynching in the United States* (1904), pp. 171, 181, asserts that the number of lynchings increased steadily between 1882 and 1892, when the violence peaked, and then declined somewhat between 1893 and 1903. Nonetheless, the number of lynchings in 1903 was still double that for 1882.

68. *Ibid.*, pp. 1–2, 152–3, 160–5; Shapiro, *White Violence and Black Response from Reconstruction to Montgomery*, pp. 93, 145, ch. 4. In the period spanned by Dixon's major novels, race riots occurred in Wilmington (1898), New York (1900), Atlanta (1906), and Springfield, Illinois (1908).

69. Lawrence Friedman, *The White Savage: Racial Fantasies in the Postbellum South*, pp. 66–76.

70. Thomas Nelson Page, *The Negro: The Southerner's Problem*, esp. pp. 92–119, and ch. 5 on disfranchisement.

71. Cutler, *Lynch-Law*, pp. 1–2, 6–9, 11, 91, 152–3, 160–5, 268–70. Though he opposed mob lynching, Roosevelt urged that punishment "follow immediately upon the heels of the offense," which—in the context of southern juridical practice—amounted to an apology for summary justice or "legal lynching." See Cutler, *Lynch-Law*, pp. 138, 145–6, 153; Shapiro, *White Violence*, pp. 105–7; I. A. Newby, *Jim Crow's Defense: Anti-Negro Thought in America, 1900–1930*, ch. 5; Theodore Dyer, *Theodore Roosevelt and the Idea of Race*, pp. 110–7. The emotions that underlay this response were more openly articulated by a columnist for *Harper's Weekly* in an editorial on the lynching of Sam Hose in 1899: though horrified at the Black man's public torture and death, E. S. Martin found that the account of the man's alleged rape of a White child "fills the mind with horror, and makes one feel that any means that is effectual to

prevent such crimes is justified." E. S. Martin, "This Busy World," *HW*, May 13, 1899, p. 469.

72. Cutler, *Lynch Law*, pp. v, 153, 191–2, 200–6, 224–6, 264–5.

73. C. Vann Woodward, *Tom Watson: Agrarian Rebel*, chs. 13, 18, 20; ———, *The Strange Career of Jim Crow*, chs. 1–2; Newby, *Jim Crow's Defense*, chs. 4–6. Dixon's conflation of an "old" and a "new" South has a historiographical counterpart in the work of Ulrich Bonnell Phillips; see Daniel Joseph Singal, "Ulrich B. Phillips: The Old South as the New," *JAH* 43:4 (1977), pp. 871–91.

74. Thomas Dixon, Jr., *The Leopard's Spots* (1901), p. 384.

75. *Ibid.*, pp. 386–7.

76. *Ibid.*, p. 442.

77. *Ibid.*, pp. 444–6.

78. *Ibid.*, p. 412.

79. Dixon's portrayal of the "democratic revolution" made by a degraded lower class draws on the literature of Reconstruction and on *Caesar's Column* (1892), the popular dystopian fantasy by the populist writer and politician, Ignatius Donnelly. In Donnelly's novel the degradation of the working classes by the tyranny of capital transforms the People into a race of brutes; and when democratic revulsion comes, it takes the form of a war of extermination that destroys civilization. "Caesar's Column" is the pile of corpses produced by the war of extermination launched by the racially brutalized proletarian leader, Cesare Lombro, in Donnelly's novel. Dixon gives the name "August Caesar" to the Black leader whose rape of a White woman will precipitate the Klan's race war.

80. Dixon, *The Clansmen*, pp. 290–2.

81. *Ibid.*, p. 326. Dixon's later novels extend the lynching scenario to other kinds of conflict. In *The Fall of a Nation* (1916), Dixon plays on the title of the movie version of *The Clansman* to frame a dystopian fantasy in which German immigrants succeed in subverting and destroying the American republic—the New York police are the "boys in blue" who fight a Custer-like "Last Stand" against these savage "Huns." *The Black Hood* condemns "populist" versions of the Klan who pollute the membership with half-breeds: their leader is named "Berry Lowery," after the famous mixed-race Swamp Outlaw of Reconstruction. In *The Flaming Sword* the Klan becomes a weapon against post-Great War socialism.

82. John R. Commons, *Races and Immigrants in America* (1907, revised and reissued 1920), p. 182. Commons was Turner's successor at the University of Wisconsin, founder of the new field of American labor history and a leading figure in the development of academic social science. See also Selig Perlman, *A Theory of the Labor Movement*, and Billington, *Turner*, pp. 445–9.

83. Commons, *Races and Immigrants*, pp. xvii, vii–xiv. Roosevelt and Commons have a common influence in Edward A. Ross, the University of Wisconsin sociologist who coined the term "race suicide." Dyer, *Theodore Roosevelt and the Idea of Race*, pp. 14–5. But the combination of Turnerian economics with a Rooseveltian treatment of race is echoed by other contemporary scholars. See for example the popular treatment of the Frontier by Frederic L. Paxson, *The Last American Frontier* (1910), esp. pp. 14–5; and Archer Butler Hurlbert, *Frontiers*

(1929), pp. 69–73, 225, 228. The editors of Yale University's popular textbook series, "Chronicles of America," assigned the writing of the volume on *The Passing of the Frontier* (1921) to Emerson Hough, a popular writer (*The Covered Wagon*) and an unregenerate Rooseveltian. Hough's frontier is a lost utopia of Anglo-Saxonism, disappearing before the "odious" advance of the immigrants: "There, for a time at least, we were Americans," untainted by "less worthy strains." (pp. 2–3, 172–3).

Woodrow Wilson is another nominal Turnerian whose historiography owes as much to Roosevelt as to Turner, and whose political responses to the racially coded issues of lynching/disenfranchisement in the South, labor "wars," immigration, and imperialism have an ideological basis identical with that of Rooseveltian Progressivism and differ (at least in emphasis) from Turner's theories. For Turner's influence on Wilson, see Billington, *Turner*, ch. 18. But compare Sidney Bell, *Righteous Conquest*, pp. 6–7, 14, 17–25, 191, on Wilson's revision of Turner's economic theory and his adherence to Teutonism, pp. 15–17, 22. See also Woodrow Wilson, "The Course of American History," *Mere Literature*, pp. 230–1. On Wilson's imperialism, see Bell, p. 191, ch. 2; and Wilson, "Ideals of America, *Atlantic Monthly* (1902) 90:721–34. On his Rooseveltian or "heroic" concept of the presidency, see Bell, *Righteous Conquest*, pp. 12–3, 191. On his support of southern movements for segregation and disenfranchisement and his response to lynching, see Bell, *Righteous Conquest*, p. 12, ch. 3; Woodrow Wilson, *History of the American People*, Vol. 5: pp. 58–9; Sinkler, *Racial Attitudes*, p. 186; Logan, *Betrayal of the Negro*, pp. 359–63; Dubofsky, *We Shall Be All*, pp. 385–96.

84. John R. Commons, *Races and Immigrants* (1907), p. xv.

85. *Ibid.*, pp. 6–7.

86. This echoes Roosevelt's fear of "race suicide."

87. Commons, *Races and Immigrants*, pp. 1–5, 8–13.

88. On Wilson's suppression of domestic radicalism and toleration of vigilantism/lynching, see Bell, *Righteous Conquest*, ch. 3; Dubofsky, *We Shall Be All*, pp. 385–96; Brown, *Strain of Violence*, pp. 126–8. Although Roosevelt and his school of progressives would have repudiated the connection, one historian has concluded that, after 1920, "The Klan became the ideal of progressivism for hundreds of thousands of middle class Protestant Southwesterners," because it targeted the new "immoral" and "criminal" classes of the cities and the ethnic groups which either constituted those classes or serviced their vices. Quoted in Green, *Grass-Roots Socialism*, p. 402.

Notes to Chapter 6

1. Richard M. Ohmann, *Politics of Letters*, chs. 9–10; Lizabeth Cohen, "Encountering Mass Culture at the Grassroots: The Experience of Chicago Workers in the 1920s," *AQ* 41:1 (1989), pp. 6–33; David G. Pugh, *Sons of Liberty: The Masculine Mind in Nineteenth Century America*, ch. 4; Blumin, *Emergence of the Middle Class*, chs. 1, 8.

2. Equivalents for most of these genres can be found in the nineteenth century. Technological fantasy was a prominent feature in several types of dime

novel: the "Steam Man" brings robotics to the terrain of the Western, and the detective Nick Carter finds smugglers operating on a submarine. See E. F. Bleiler, *Eight Dime Novels*. Science fiction has a venerable literary pedigree. It enjoyed remarkable popularity in the last quarter of the nineteenth century in the work of writers like Mark Twain, Jules Verne, Jack London, and H. G. Wells. Nonetheless, the development of cheap-literature series devoted primarily to this type of story belongs to the pulp era.

3. See for example Erling B. Holtsmark, *Tarzan and Tradition: Classical Literature in Popular Myth*. Only Robert Howard, creator of "Conan the Barbarian," has a comparable range, and his career was far briefer. See Glenn Lord, *The Last Celt: Robert E. Howard, The Creator of Conan*.

4. Irwin Porges, *Edgar Rice Burroughs: The Man Who Created Tarzan*, Vol. 1: pp. 53–5, 76.

5. *Ibid.*, Vol. 2: p. 124; Slotkin, *Fatal Environment*, pp. 502–10. "Barney Custer" is the hero of Burroughs' *The Mad King* (1914), a two-novel series; and Barney's sister is a Molly Stark Wood-like heroine who, in *The Eternal Savage*, can find an appropriately virile mate only by going back to the caveman origins of the Great Race.

6. Porges, *Burroughs*, Vol. 1: pp. 62, 162–3, 232; and see ch. 3, above.

7. Porges, *Burroughs*, Vol. 1: pp. 103–15.

8. *Ibid.*, pp. 126–7, 135, 164–6. He also applied for a position as cavalry instructor under General King at St. John's Military Academy.

9. *Ibid.*, p. 27.

10. Burroughs and his publishers were following the practice, common in both dime novels and pulps, of "adapting" popular works of "serious" fiction to cheap-fiction format and style. *Ibid.*, pp. 210–9.

11. *Ibid.*, pp. 213, 316, 567. Drawings of cavalry exercises he did at MMA resemble Remington's, and the background of Remington's "Carter Johnson" in "A Sergeant of the Orphan Troop" resembles that of Burroughs' "John Carter." Porges lists Zane Grey as an "early" influence, but since they published their first novels almost simultaneously any such influence must have come later. On "lost races," see Thomas D. Clareson, "Lost Lands, Lost Races: A Pagan Princess of Their Very Own," *JPC* 8:4 (1975), pp. 714–23.

12. *Ibid.*, pp. 126–7, 226, 358, 372. Burroughs had once peddled the bound lectures of Stoddard's father door-to-door.

13. Burroughs' eclectic reading in heroic mythology, and his grasp of the narrative paradigms underlying those myths, produced a "formula" that hews quite closely to the heroic archetype delineated by the myth-critic Joseph Campbell, *Hero with a Thousand Faces*, esp. Pt. I, ch. 4, and Pt. II, ch. 3.

14. Allen Chase, *The Legacy of Malthus: The Social Costs of the New Scientific Racism*, pp. 163–75, chs. 7, 8, 11, 12. Grant and Stoddard were sufficiently well known for Fitzgerald to humorously conflate their names and book titles in *The Great Gatsby*, in which Tom Buchanan cites a book called *The Rise of the Coloured Empires* by someone named "Goddard." The reference is to T. L. Stoddard's *The Rising Tide of Color Against White World Supremacy*, which had an introduction by Madison Grant.

15. Stoddard, *The French Revolution in Santo Domingo* (1914), p. vii.

16. Stoddard was called to testify as an "expert witness" by the Congressional committee which met in 1924 to consider new legislative restrictions on immigration; his testimony was endorsed by political leaders (a letter from President Harding) and by scientists—most notably Havelock Ellis, whose work on eugenics influenced Margaret Sanger. Grant was privately consulted by committee members. (Chase, *Legacy*, pp. 173, 292–5; Morris, *Roosevelt*, pp. 384–7.) Grant dismissed the work of Franz Boas, the leading figure on the culturalist side of the academic debate, as the desperate attempts of a Jew to pass himself off as "White"; and in the 1920s he tried to convince the editors of a leading Protestant journal that "*the Catholic Church under Jewish leadership*, the Jews and the Communist Labor Party" had formed a joint international conspiracy to undermine White supremacy, the principle "*upon which modern Christianity is founded.*" Chase, *Legacy*, pp. 163, 183–90; E. Digby Baltzell, *The Protestant Establishment: Aristocracy and Caste in America*, pp. 96–7.

17. "Where two distinct species are located side by side history and biology teach that but one of two things can happen; either one race drives the other out, as the Americans exterminated the Indians and as the Negroes are now replacing the whites in various parts of the South; or else they amalgamate and form a population of race bastards in which the lower type ultimately preponderates. This is a disagreeable alternative with which to confront sentimentalists, but nature is only concerned with results. . . . " Madison Grant, *The Passing of the Great Race* (1918), p. 77; and Stoddard, *Rising Tide*, pp. 145, 148, 157.

18. Grant, *Passing*, p. 228. Although Grant sees some hybridization between Nordic groups as having occurred during the Middle Ages, Grant disagrees with Roosevelt's emphasis on the tendency of Nordic stocks to mix after their arrival in the New World. See pp. 83, 88.

19. Stoddard, *Rising Tide*, p. 261.

20. *Ibid.*, pp. 149, 165, 226, 231, 236.

21. Roosevelt, "Biological Analogies in History," *Literary Essays. Works* 12: 25–60. Written in 1912, this essay suggests the need for the kind of history Grant was to produce four years later.

22. Stoddard, *The Revolt Against Civilization: The Menace of the Under-Man*, pp. 11, 21–3, 27. The idea that criminality was a symptom of "primitive" racial or genetic endowment had been widely accepted since the 1870s. The leading theorist was the Italian criminologist Cesare Lombroso. See Stephen Jay Gould, *The Mismeasure of Man*, pp. 122–45.

23. *Ibid.*, pp. 1, 2, 11, 21–3, 126, 218–9. On their anti-Semitism, see Chase, *Legacy*, p. 164.

24. Grant, *Passing*, pp. 18, 79. But compare Roosevelt, *Literary Essays*, pp. 35–6, for a more liberal view of up-breeding.

25. See Grant, *Passing*, pp. 5–7, 228, on the evolution of classes from differences in racial endowment. Compare F. W. Heidner, *The Laborer's Friend and Employer's Counselor: A Popular Treatise on the Labor Question* (1895), to see the difference in tone between earlier theories associating race and class and the more strident militancy of Grant and Stoddard. See also Charles E. Woodruff, "Some Laws of Racial and Intellectual Development," *Journal of Race Development* 3:2 (1912), pp. 156–75. Compare also the similar, but more "moderate" argu-

ments on race and nationality in Seth K. Humphrey, *The Racial Prospect...* (1920) and Charles Conant Josey, *Race and National Solidarity* (1923). Racialist theories of class retain their power: Chase, *Legacy*, Parts 3 and 4; R. C. Lewontin, *et al., Not in Our Genes: Biology, Ideology, and Human Nature*, chs. 1–2, 9–10; and see Richard Herrnstein's defense of hereditary IQ in *NYRB*, 28:16, October 22, 1981, p. 16: "The privileged classes of the past were probably not much superior biologically to the downtrodden, which is why revolution had a fair chance of success. By removing artificial barriers between classes, society has encouraged the creation of biological barriers. When people can take their natural level in society, the upper classes will, by definition, have greater capacity than the lower."

26. Grant, *Passing*, p. 79.

27. Stoddard, *Revolt Against Civilization*, pp. 303–4.

28. *Ibid.*, p. 172; Grant, *Passing*, pp. 6, 12, 49.

29. Stoddard, *Rising Tide*, p. 148; ———, *Revolt*, p. 11; Porges, *Burroughs*, p. 917.

30. Stoddard, *Rising Tide*, pp. 303–4; ———, *Revolt*, p. 27. Burroughs' scenarios of recovered White savagery run counter to Stoddard's specific condemnation of the idea: " 'Go back to the woods and become men!' . . . may be excellent advice if interpreted as a temporary measure. [But] 'Go back into the woods and remain there' is a counsel for anthropoid apes." (Stoddard, *Rising Tide*, p. 130). Yet this is precisely the counsel by which Tarzan comes into being. Works by Burroughs in which this sort of primitivism appears include: *Princess of Mars, The Gods of Mars, Warlord of Mars; Tarzan of the Apes, The Return of Tarzan; Carson of Venus, Pirates of Venus, Lost on Venus; Pellucidar, At the Earth's Core, Land of Terror; The Eternal Savage.*

31. Edgar Rice Burroughs, *A Princess of Mars*, pp. 5, 9.

32. *Ibid.*, pp. 9–11.

33. Compare Roosevelt's handling of Indians and half-breeds in *Rough Riders*, pp. 103–5, above.

34. *Princess* also combines features drawn from Bellamy's *Looking Backward* and Twain's *Connecticut Yankee*. His movement through interplanetary space is achieved by means like those used by Julian West and Hank Morgan to travel through time (chemistry and/or metempsychosis) and unlike the technological methods of Jules Verne and later science-fiction writers. Barsoom combines elements of Twain's Arthurian England (a feudal, chivalric, and superstitious culture) and Bellamy's imagined "future" (superior technology and arcane learning).

35. John C. Cremony, *Life Among the Apaches*, pp. 192–3, 195. "Their enmity toward mankind, and distrust of every word or act are ineradicable. As their whole system of life and training is to plunder, murder and deceive, they cannot comprehend opposite attributes in others. He whom we would denounce as the greatest scoundrel they regard with special esteem and honor. With no people are they on amicable terms, and never hesitate to rob from each other when it can be done with impunity. There is no sympathy among them; the quality is unknown. . . . For ninety consecutive years [their] ruthless warfare has been carried on. . . . Thousands of lives have been destroyed, and thousands of women

and children carried into a captivity worse than death. . . . It is both sickening and maddening to ride through that country and witness that far-reaching ruin, to listen to dreadful tales of unequalled atrocities, and note the despairing terror which the bare mention of the Apaches conjures up. . . ."

36. Burroughs, *A Princess of Mars*, pp. 11, 14, 19, 21, 27, 31, 39, 167.

37. See William F. Wu, *The Yellow Pearl: Chinese Americans in American Fiction, 1850–1940*; and Cheng-Tsu Wu, ed., *Chink! A Documentary History of Anti-Chinese Prejudice in America*, esp. ch. 2.

38. Cooper, *Last of the Mohicans*, p. 19. Compare the similar descriptions of Monahsetah in Custer, *My Life on the Plains*, pp. 251–4, and Eliza, the "tragic mulatto" in Harriet Beecher Stowe, *Uncle Tom's Cabin; or, Life Among the Lowly*, ch. 1. See Clareson, "Lost Lands, Lost Races," pp. 714–23.

39. Her non-Whiteness has an "Indian" rather than African quality, which makes it more acceptable. "Indians" for Burroughs are no longer active contenders in the strife of races; they are "Vanishing Americans" who belong to the romantic past. While Burroughs could also use Indians as villains, and could use standard images of Indian savagery to characterize evil races, he often treats Indians as Noble Savages and identifies with them. See for example the fascinating exchange between Burroughs and his publisher over plans for a series featuring a White man raised as an Indian who becomes "War Chief of the Apaches," Porges, *Burroughs*, 1:644. Although most of his heroes are of pure-White ancestry, it is worth noting (as evidence of his belief in the principle of racial tolerance) Burroughs' imaginative inclination to identify with and portray as heroes figures from the other side of a racial and even (as Jane Tompkins has pointed out) in the case of Tarzan, a species barrier.

40. Porges, *Burroughs*, Vol. 1, pp. 452–3, 603–4.

41. *Beyond Thirty* (1915, republished as *The Lost Continent*) envisions a future in which a hero from the isolationist United States rescues a Europe that has descended into barbarism because of the Great War. The story, which is essentially the same as that of *Princess*, ends with Europe and America united against a "rising tide of color." *The Land That Time Forgot* tells of the struggle between the survivors of a German U-boat and a British ship for control of the island of Caspak, a "Lost World" in whose peculiar ecology the processes of evolution are compressed and dramatically displayed. German and Anglo-Saxon are thus figuratively struggling for mastery of evolution itself.

42. Porges, *Burroughs*, p. 461.

43. Burroughs, *Moon Maid*, pp. 5, 12, 18.

44. *Ibid.*, pp. 126–7, 179*ff*. The distinction between merely "imitative" and "creative" racial genius is crucial to Stoddard's system for distinguishing between the races (and classes within a race) and is particularly important in the distinction he makes between the intelligence of "Jews" and true "genius." Chase, *Legacy*, pp. 140–4, 164, 233, 266, 268, 287–95, 359.

45. Burroughs, *Moon Men*, pp. 18, 22.

46. *Ibid.*, p. 30.

47. *Ibid.*, pp. 19, 20, 23.

48. *Ibid.*, p. 55.

49. *Ibid.*, pp. 26–7. Compare Dixon, *Clansman*, cited above p. 189 And com-

pare Stoddard's way of describing the degeneration of America's original "pure" racial stock by the importation of Africans and immigrants. Stoddard blames the selfishness of capitalists for betraying racial purity for the sake of cheap labor (*Rising Tide*, pp. 145, 281).

50. A similar structure informs another extremely popular science-fiction/fantasy series of this period, the comic-strip and pulp-fiction adventures of "Buck Rogers." Rogers is an ex-military aviator who falls asleep in a cave (like John Carter) and wakes up in another time (like the heroes of *Looking Backward* and *Connecticut Yankee*). He finds America has been overrun by "Red Mongols," whose traits combine the worst features of Bolshevism and the "Yellow Peril." White Americans have preserved their racial vigor by reverting to the wilderness; when Buck arrives, they are preparing a rebellion. The novel version follows the *Princess of Mars* scenario, ending with White victory in a war of extermination against the Mongols. However, it is suggested that the Red Mongols are not Orientals but aliens from another planet. Philip Francis Nowlan, *Armageddon 2419 A.D.*, esp. pp. 20–2, 140, 190–2, which shows influence of *Moon Men*. This novel was the basis of the famous "Buck Rogers" comic strip. Compare the dystopian fantasy *Red Napoleon* (1929) by war correspondent Floyd Gibbons.

51. Frank Gruber, *Zane Grey*, ch. 1, pp. 108–9.

52. *Ibid.*, pp. 67, 75.

53. *Ibid.*, p. 13. The historicity of these "forest" adventures is atypical of Grey's work and may reflect a desire to do justice to family history. They also show a greater tolerance than Cooper's for the idea of "Indian marriage," which may have had roots in that history: Grey's ancestors, Isaac and Betty Zane, had been captured by Indians during the Revolution, and (according to family legend) Isaac was saved from death by an "Indian princess" whom he later married.

54. The impulse behind his famously pro-Indian novel, *The Vanishing American* (1922, 1925), was as much that of literary emulation as moral commitment. He had been moved by the portrayal of Navaho culture (and its corruption by Whites) in Oliver LaFarge's *Laughing Boy* and responded characteristically by appropriating LaFarge's subject (and his Navaho lore) and grafting it onto a conventional tale of the Noble Savage's inevitable doom. On the other hand, he was perfectly capable of representing Indians as monsters of cruelty and barbarism, and of condemning the mixture of the races as productive of profound violence and psychic disorder, when to do so served the interests of a particular story-situation.

55. Grey's portrayal of Mormon fanaticism in *Riders* was so grim that he was accused of making anti-Mormon propaganda. Gruber cites the "good" Mormons of *Heritage* against the accusation and asserts that the story is not anti-Mormon but anti-polygamy. But Gruber's defense takes the novel's "polemic" too seriously: the issue of polygamy had been legally resolved more than a decade before. Literary "Mormons" rather than real ones are Grey's subject: he uses them in his writing because they are standard symbols of religious fanaticism, tyranny, and sexual oddity.

56. Zane Grey, *Riders of the Purple Sage*, p. 159.

57. *Ibid.*, p. 33 and ch. 7. For a sample of the enthusiasm for dry-land farming see William E. Smythe, *The Conquest of Arid America* (1899, 1905), esp. pts. 1, 3;

J. P. Mowbray, "Going Back to the Soil," *WW* 1: 267–77, 2: 690–1, and "Expansion by Irrigation" 1: 475–6; see also 4: 2365; 6: 3694–700, 3716–7. A critical history of the movement is Donald Worster, *Rivers of Empire: Water, Aridity, and the Growth of the American West*, pp. 111–25, 191–227.

58. Grey, *Riders*, p. 10.

59. Slotkin, *Fatal Environment*, pp. 219–24, 355–8.

60. Surprise Valley also contains Anasazi ruins, whose presence illustrates Grey's characteristic blending of touristic scenery and literary fantasy in creating his "West." Grey, *Riders*, ch. 8 and p. 127. The ruins were a recently discovered tourist attraction in the Southwest; and like the Mound Builder discoveries of the nineteenth Century (Slotkin, *Regeneration*, pp. 55–6, 455–6), they provoked speculation on Indian origins, and the larger theme of racial rise and decline. These speculations harmonized with the "lost race" fantasies produced in the same period by Burroughs, and earlier by writers like H. Rider Haggard, for ex. *Allan Quatermain* (1887) and *The People of the Mist* (1894). Seen in this context, the ruins in Surprise Valley suggest that the withdrawal of Jane and Lassiter is permanent; but that, in the end, the Valley may be the Eden of a new (and better?) "lost race." See Clareson, "Lost Lands, Lost Races," pp. 714–23.

61. *I.e.*, the vigilante assault on striking miners in Bisbee, Arizona, in 1916, the lynching of IWW organizer Frank Little in Butte, Montana, in 1917, and perhaps the lynching of Wesley Everest in Centralia, Washington, in 1919. See Dubofsky, *We Shall*, pp. 296, 383–92, 455–6. Grey also alludes to the "Preparedness" and "Americanism" campaigns. The latter was directed against immigrants and German–Americans and engaged a number of organizations, including TR's "Vigilantes."

62. Grey, *Desert of Wheat*, pp. 7–8, 69–70, 303. Note parallels between Jane Withersteen and the heroine of *Desert*, pp. 47, 233; and between the good rancher Anderson and Judge Henry, pp. 42–6, 143, 233. Norris's *Octopus* is a source for both books—here, for lyric descriptions of wheat fields, and mystical appreciations of the workings of nature and commerce. See *Desert*, pp. 2, 38, 248–9, 251.

63. *Ibid.*, pp. 13, 35–7, 39, 107, 154–5.

64. *Ibid.*, pp. 90–101.

65. On the genre, see William Ruehlmann, *Saint With a Gun: The Unlawful American Private Eye*; Cawelti, chs. 5–6.

66. Chandler, *The Simple Art of Murder*, pp. 19–20.

67. *Ibid.*, pp. 20–1.

68. ———, *The Long Goodbye*, p. 227.

69. I want to thank Howard Lamar for bringing Siringo to my attention. For an earlier example of the cowboy detective see D. J. Cook, *Hands Up; or Twenty Years of Detective Life* . . . (1882).

70. Charles A. Siringo, *Riata and Spurs*, pp. 15, 55–6.

71. Siringo, *Cowboy Detective* (1912), pp. 57, 65.

72. *Ibid.*, p. 101; Slotkin, *Fatal Environment*, pp. 131–2.

73. *Ibid.*, pp. 22–3.

74. *Ibid.*, pp. 23, 35, 133–4, 161, 187, 497–8.

75. *Ibid.*, pp. 4, 139–40, 161, 181, 187. The "disemboweling" atrocity is a

device identified with John Murrell, an outlaw who figures prominently in southwestern fiction in the 1830s and 1850s. See Slotkin, *Fatal Environment*, pp. 133–7. More objective accounts of the strike, like R. W. Smith's *The Coeur d'Alene Mining War of 1892*, ch. 18, indicate that some of the atrocities cited by Siringo never occurred and that others were committed by ordinary criminals not associated with the union. Siringo's account of these events, and of the union's responsibility for them, repeats the unproven or demonstrably false accusations leveled by the mine owners against the strikers. R. E. Lingenfelter, *The Hardrock Miners*, pp. 197–203. The only criticism of Pinkerton's in *A Cowboy Detective* (p. 46) involves the Agency's work against Ute Indians. The Vanishing Americans are now far less threatening than the anarchists of the city, and Siringo (like Grey) can safely sympathize with their victimization.

76. Siringo, *Two Evil Isms: Pinkertonism and Anarchism*, pp. ix, 2, 3–4, 9, 15, 19, 21, 24, 36–7, 44–8, 94–5, 109. He had expressed similar ideas earlier in *Cowboy Detective*, p. 518, "Every greedy 'Money-bag' in the land should be sat down on hard. I would be in favor of screwing his hands to a long-handled shovel . . . to let him know how it feels to work ten hours a day to keep body and soul together, while such as he do nothing but gloat over gold, and wring the life-blood from humanity." However, this is not a major theme of that book. The "White Caps" case is a litmus test of his changing attitudes toward the detective's role. The White Caps were a Mexican-American vigilante or regulator organization, with a complex. They were dominated by the religious sect of the *Penitentes*, but they also held a charter from the Knights of Labor and were politically oriented toward the Populist Party. Pinkertons were called in by Republican cattlemen, who were embroiled in a range war with sheepmen and farmers as well as in on-going political struggles against Populism and organized labor. They hoped to win the fight by blaming the White Caps for the troubles, and the organization seemed perfectly cast for that role: an armed organization of racial/ethnic "aliens," with ties to the unions, the Populists, and a mysterious and fanatical Roman Catholic sect. Siringo did an honest job of detective work and discovered that the most guilty parties were not White Caps but members of a dissident Republican faction. In *A Cowboy Detective* Siringo cited this case as evidence of the detective's professionalism and sound ethics and suggested that he had achieved a kind of justice. In *Two Evil Isms* the political background of the case is exposed, and the detective appears as the unwilling accomplice of wealthy Republicans who subvert justice and negate Siringo's investigation. Compare *ibid.*, pp. 21, 24, 33; ———, *Cowboy Detective*, pp. 118, 121–2, 133.

77. Siringo, *Cowboy Detective*, p. 518.

78. Siringo, *Two Evil Isms*, pp. 4–5.

79. Ruehlmann, *Saint*, p. 65; Hammett, *The Big Knockover*, p. 372.

80. Ruehlmann, *Saint*, pp. 57–65; Carroll John Daly, "The False Burton Combs," in Herbert Ruhm, ed., *The Hard-Boiled Detective: Stories from* Black Mask *Magazine, 1920–1951*, pp. 3–30. On pulp heroes as vigilantes, see Gary Hoppenstand, "Pulp Vigilante Heroes, the Moral Majority and the Apocalypse," in Ray Browne and Marshall Fishwick, eds., *The Hero in Transition*, pp. 141–4. Thanks to Eric Greene for this reference.

81. Ruehlmann, *Saint*, p. 62. See also Hammett, *The Maltese Falcon*, in *The Novels of Dashiell Hammett*, pp. 437–9.

82. Richard Layman, *Shadow Man: The Life of Dashiell Hammett*, pp. 10–3, 89; Diane Johnson, *Dashiell Hammett, A Life*, pp. 17–21; Dubofsky, *We Shall*, pp. 391–2.

83. Ruehlmann, *Saint*, pp. 65–73; Cawelti, *Adventure*, pp. 168–77.

84. Ruehlmann, *Saint*, p. 9.

85. Hammett, *Red Harvest*, p. 7.

86. An armistice is called "The Peace Conference," sets up a new round of war—poss reference to Versailles.

87. A few examples must serve to indicate Fitzgerald's detailed, complex, and ironic use of mythic formulas in *The Great Gatsby*. Young Gatsby's consciousness is transformed by his sojourn with millionaire "Dan Cody" on a yacht that sails the Great Lakes, a setting reminiscent of the "Ark" and island "Castle" of Lake Glimmerglass in Cooper's *The Deerslayer*. Cody made his fortune as a Western prospector; his names link him to both Daniel Boone and Buffalo Bill. Gatsby himself is a "Virginian" type, who does indeed "hold four aces" but no honest way to play them. Even "good" violence (in the Great War) can't win him a place among the quality; and his Molly Wood is the corrupt and corrupting Daisy Buchanan. The racialism of "progressives" like Grant and Stoddard is explicitly evoked in the reference made by the degenerate Anglo-Saxon aristocrat, Tom Buchanan, *The Rise of the Coloured Empires* by "Goddard"—a play on the title of Stoddard's book, and a conflation of his name with Grant's. The names and descriptions of the "riff-raff" who attend Gatsby's party echo Hammett's grotesque catalogue of ethnic gangster-types in *Black Mask* and the famous "eye" of Doctor Eckleberg that watches the tragedy unfold echoes the logo of the Pinkerton Agency ("The Eye that Never Sleeps"). Finally, the vanished possibilities of a "lost" Frontier are invoked in the narrator's recall of the discoverers contemplating the "green breast of the New World." M. Gidley, "Notes on F. Scott Fitzgerald and the Passing of the Great Race," *JAS* 7:2, pp. 171–82.

88. Ruehlmann, *Saint*, p. 95.

89. Hammett, *Red Harvest*, p. 45.

Notes to Chapter 7

1. George N. Fenin and William K. Everson, *The Western: From the Silents to the Seventies*, p. 47; Lewis Jacobs, *The Rise of the American Films: A Critical History . . . ,1921–1947*, p. 35; David A. Cook, *A History of Narrative Film*, pp. 18–20.

2. Fenin and Everson, *Western*, p. 50; Jacobs, *Rise*, ch. 1, pp. 37, 46; Cook, *Narrative Film*, p. 27; Kevin Brownlow, *The War, the West and the Wilderness*, p. 224.

3. Diane K. Koszarski, *The Complete Films of William S. Hart: A Pictorial Record*, p. 3.

4. Green, *Dreams of Adventure*, p. 53. My understanding of the processes of experience, cognition, and recall in the discussion that follows draws on the work

of Roger Schank, *Dynamic Memory: A Theory of Reminding and Learning in Computers and People*, esp. pp. 19, 37–41, and 48ff.

5. David Bordwell, *Narration in the Fiction Film*, pp. 57–73.

6. This approach to genre follows the theory set forth in the "Introduction," which sees myth, ideology, and genre as *primarily* the results of active, historically contingent construction, and not as the products of a pre-existing set of forms or "grammar of tropes" inherent in either language or psychology. My understanding of film genre has been informed by the work of my colleagues, Jeanine Basinger and Joseph Reed. On genre theory, and its relation to myth, see Slotkin, *Fatal Environment*, ch. 2, and "Prologue to a Study of Myth and Genre in American Movies," *Prospects* 9, pp, 419–23; Jeanine Basinger, *The World War II Combat Film: Anatomy of a Genre*, "Introduction" and chs. 3, 4, 5; Thomas Schatz, *Hollywood Genres, passim*; David Bordwell, *Narration in the Fiction Film*, chs. 5, 8; Cawelti, *Adventure*, pp. 6, 29–30, and ch. 8; Gerald Mast and Marshall Cohen, eds., *Film Theory and Criticism: Introductory Readings*, 3rd ed., Part V; Bill Nichols, ed., *Movies and Methods*, Vol. 1: 111–25, 150–75, and Vol. 2: 165–232; Philip French, *Westerns: Aspects of a Movie Genre*, pp. 17–8; Stuart M. Kaminsky, *American Film Genres: An Approach to a Critical Theory of Popular Film*, p. 11; Carlos Clarens, *Crime Movies: From Griffith to the Godfather and Beyond*, pp. 10–31; I. C. Jarvie, *Movies and Society*, chs. 10–13; R. Williams, "The Dream World of Mass Consumption," in Mukerji and Schudson, eds., *Rethinking Popular Culture*, ch. 6.

7. "The cinema was born, its visual apparatus at the ready, the heir to a venerable tradition of reworking history (the immediate past) in tune with ancient classical rhythms . . ." and (more pertinently) with the symbolic language and formulaic structures of popular literature, drama, and Wild West pageantry. Jim Kitses, *Horizons West: Anthony Mann, Budd Boetticher, Sam Peckinpah, Studies of Authorship in the Western*, p. 15.

8. The horror film and the genre that is sometimes called "the swashbuckler"—the filmic equivalent of the historical romance—draw on literary models that predate films. However, exploitation of the unique powers of the visual medium has radically transformed the conventions of the Gothic novel, and the modern "swashbucklers" are not as indebted to the themes and ideologies of nineteenth-century historical romances as the Western is to its myth-ideological tradtion.

9. Kitses, *Horizons West*, pp. 8–27.

10. Bits of western scenery and action, and scenes from Buffalo Bill's Wild West, were displayed as novelties in vaudeville exhibitions and nickelodeons in the 1890s.

11. Kitses, *Horizons West*, p. ix; Brownlow, *The War, the West*, pp. 237, 253, 257.

12. *Ibid.*, 234–62; Russell, *Wild West*, pp. 67, 127. Dalton stayed in Hollywood as a technical adviser and in 1941 aided in the production of *When the Daltons Rode*—a film that restored the gang's place in movie folklore. Tilghman had been a federal marshal serving Isaac Parker's court in the 1880s; he became interested in film during Tulsa's heyday as a regional filmmaking center and produced *The Passing of the Oklahoma Outlaws* in 1915, starring himself and ex-

bandit Al Jennings. Henry Starr, nephew of the famous Belle Starr who had been Cole Younger's mistress, was also involved in the Tulsa filmmaking scene. On his last parole from prison (1919), he joined a moving-picture company in Tulsa, first as technical adviser, then as actor, and finally as director of his own production—an autobiographical film titled *A Debtor to the Law* (1919). When (as he believed) the company bilked him of his royalties, Starr returned to bank-robbing and was killed in 1924. See Glenn Shirley, *The Last of the Real Bad Men, Henry Starr*, ch. 11; and Green, *Grass-Roots Socialism*, pp. 339–40 for treatment of Starr's reputation as "social bandit."

13. Fenin and Everson, *Western*, chs. 3–5, 7–8; Brownlow, *The War, the West*, pp. 257–69, 275–89, 300–12. The same reviewer who complained about the triteness of Westerns in 1914 praised earlier films as "splendid pictures" because they protrayed "most accurately the life of the early West." Koszarski, *Hart*, p. 3.

14. A copy of the Ince *Custer's Last Fight* pamphlet is in the collections of Little Big Horn National Monument; Everson, *A Pictorial History of the Western Film*, pp. 31–3. Ince made extensive use of Indian properties and actors in both cowboy/Indian and Indian/cavalry stories. In this too his practice follows Buffalo Bill's. His plots drew on the attitudes and symbolism of Fenimore Cooper and the sentimental treatments of the Indian problem developed in novels like *Ramona*. Cody's filmed version of his own re-enactments, *The Indian Wars Refought* (1913), featured a script by another "participant," Charles King, and invoked ethnographic authorities for its sympathetic portrayal of Indians. See Brownlow, *The War, the West*, pp. 234–5.

15. On Tulsa in films, see fn. 12, above. Edward M. Miller, "From Flickers to Todd-AO," is a memoir by a Tulsa projectionist who knew Starr, Tilghman, and others from this era. His manuscript is in the Tulsa County Historical Society; I am grateful to Robert N. Powers, Curator, for bringing it to my attention.

16. Brownlow, *The War, the West*, pp. 287–8. Nonetheless, the desire for "authenticity" was so integral to the Western that even Tom Mix, whose films are considered exercises in "pure showmanship," felt the need to fabricate an "original participant identity for himself." Mix was a Pennsylvania farm boy, army deserter, and rodeo performer who claimed to be "the only honest-to-goodness cowboy in the movies" and invented a biography which included a claim that he was part-Cherokee by ancestry and nurture, that his father was a Captain in Custer's 7th Cavalry, and that he himself was a graduate of VMI and had been a Rough Rider, a veteran of the Filipino Insurrection and the Boxer Rebellion, a marshal, a Texas Ranger, and a volunteer under Pancho Villa. Mix's debt to Buffalo Bill's Wild West is obvious. See *ibid.*, pp. 307–8.

17. Vachel Lindsay, *The Art of the Moving Picture*, pp. 261–63; Koszarski, *Hart*, p. 3.

18. Richard Schickel, *Griffith: An American Life*, esp. pp. 108–9.

19. Slotkin, *Fatal Environment*, ch 5. "Moral painter" is Charles Brockden Brown's prescription for the serious novelist in the preface to *Edgar Huntly* (1794).

20. *Musketeers of Pig Alley* (1912) deals with the life of the slums but finds the same moral genius in twentieth-century street urchins that Alger attributed to Ragged Dick in 1867. Schickel, *Griffith*, p. 33.

21. *Ibid.*, p. 207.

22. Merely extending the length of narrative and spending more on sets and costumes were not enough to distinguish the feature film as a serious artistic enterprise. A review of *The Bargain* (1914), a five-reel Western by Ince and William S. Hart, deprecated their ambition as "a typical Western on an extraordinary large scale. It is as if they took the photoplay recipe that has been found adequate for shorter films and doubled or tripled all the ingredients to make the biggest picture of its kind of record." Koszarski, *Hart*, p. 3.

23. Schickel, *Griffith*, pp. 30–3, 207, 213–4.

24. Quoted in Harry M. Geduld, ed., *Focus on D. W. Griffith*, p. 43.

25. *Ibid.*, p. 56.

26. Schickel, *Griffith*, pp. 268–9; Friedman, *White Savage*, ch. 8.

27. Schickel, *Griffith*, pp. 270.

28. *Ibid.*, p. 247; Michael Paul Rogin, " 'The Sword Became a Flashing Vision,': D. W. Griffith's *The Birth of a Nation*," in Ronald Reagan, *the Movie and Other Episodes of Political Demonology*, pp. 190–235.

29. The image of Christ as "Prince of Peace," which appears near the end of the film, is an example of this use of iconography.

30. Woodrow Wilson, *History of the American People* (1902), 5: 58–62; Friedman, *White Savage*, ch. 8.

31. Chase, *Legacy*, p. 91.

32. Schickel, *Griffith*, p. 213.

33. Like Burroughs and other pulp writers, he had taken up the subject of human prehistory and offered his own myth of man's Darwinian origins in two "cave man" films, *Genesis of Man* and *Brute Force* (1913).

34. The relationship between spectacle and melodrama in Griffith's work has a consistent ideological meaning. The "melodrama" makes the individual (and his or her most intimate circle of relations) the moral center of the world; which is assaulted by "history," editorially associated "with the huge, spectacular environment and with the masses whose mob mind [is] dramatized upon the screen." In Griffith's cinematic universe (*Birth of a Nation*, *Intolerance*, *Orphans of the Storm*), the history made by mass movements is inherently regressive. In Griffith's later films, "spectacle . . . assumed the salient position, and melodrama existed only as a means of exploiting the spectacle." See Geduld, *Focus*, pp. 77, 84, 86.

35. A similar confusion attended the celebrity of the hero of Cooper's five Leatherstocking Tales: after the cycle was completed, the novels were read (and often reprinted) as if they constituted the "biography" of Hawkeye/Natty Bumppo—a man who never existed. See Slotkin, *Regeneration*, pp. 484–508.

36. Brownlow, *The War, the West*, pp. 263–8; William S. Hart, *My Life East and West*, p. 37.

37. Koszarski, *Complete Films of William S. Hart*, p. ix.

38. Hart, *My Life*, pp. 110, 134–5, ch. 12.

39. *Ibid.*, pp. 16, 33–7; 51, 64–5; Indian references on pp. 20, 25, 28, 42–3, 50.

40. Brownlow, *The War, The West*, p. 270.

41. *Ibid.*, pp. 263–8; Hart, *My Life*, p. 37.

42. This vision of the West became a Hart trademark: one early reviewer, in praising *On the Night Stage* (1915), noted that "It is of this combination saloon and dance hall atmosphere that this company has proven itself the masters." Koszarski, *Hart*, p. 7.

43. *Ibid.*, pp. 7, 11, 12, 15, 17.

44. He also borrows two powerful images from Griffith's film: the use of tableaux modeled on iconography from popular and classic religious painting/illustration to visualize the hero's redemption, and the image of the burning cross, discussed below.

45. The "pleasure" here is akin to that which Lassiter displays in consummating his revenge in *Riders of the Purple Sage*, above pp. 214–15.

46. In 1916, in addition to *The Aryan* (discussed below), Hart starred in *The Captive God* and *The Dawn Maker*. In the former he plays a White child adopted by the Aztecs who becomes a god to his tribe by virtue of his Whiteness; in the latter Joe Elk (Hart), a half-breed torn between the religious gifts belonging to his two "bloods," sacrifices himself so that his people will accept the White man's god and ways.

47. His use of the term "Aryan" could have been drawn from either literary sources or the pseudoscience of Chamberlain, Grant, and Stoddard; but a more likely source is *Birth of a Nation*, which also uses the term to identify the White race.

48. Koszarski, *Hart*, pp. 42–3; Fenin and Everson, *Western*, p. 92.

49. *Ibid.*, pp. 103, 121, 126. "Hart in the stellar role is himself at all times, blending action with genuine character work and excellent in the closeups when his facial expressions carry the story unaided. . . ."

50. Koszarski, *Hart*, pp. 7, 10, 81, 39.

51. *Ibid.*, p. 3.

52. *Ibid.*, p. 60. Critics who praised Hart understood and valued his films as exercises in symbolic typology rather than as representations of American life. See the reviews of *Passing of Two-Gun Hicks* (1914), *On the Night Stage* (1915), and *Wolves of the Trail* (1918) cited in Koszarski, *Hart*.

53. Cawelti, *Adventure*, pp. 230–1.

54. Fenin and Everson, *Western*, p. 131.

55. *Ibid.*, ch. 8, pp. 171–2, 174–6.

Notes to Chapter 8

1. Fenin and Everson, *Western*. pp. 178, 203. There were signs that the Western market was "soft" even in 1930–31. *Cimarron*'s success owed something to its having been a best-selling novel. *Big Trail* (1930) and *Fighting Caravans* (1931) were clearly generic Westerns, and both were commercial failures.

2. Western consituted an average of 21 percent of all films produced by

major studios and independents between 1930 and 1938, down from 28 percent in the peak year of silent films (1926), but roughly the same as in the transitional years 1926–30 (20.6 percent). The average for 1926–55 inclusive is 24.7 percent. The three major independent companies (Republic, Monogram, PRC) specialized in "B" pictures and particularly in Westerns. Independents produced 58 percent of the Westerns made in the 1930–38 period, close to the average of 55.8 percent for the 26-year period 1930–55. But there are significant "spikes" in their share of Western production: in 1934–35, at the nadir of the major studios' interest in the genre, they produced 75 percent of all Westerns. There was a comparable shift in 1943–45, when the majors dropped Westerns for war films. Edward Buscombe, ed., *The B F I Companion to the Western*, Tables 2, 4, 5, pp. 426–8.

3. Cawelti, *Adventure*, p. 231.

4. Buscombe, *B F I*, Tables 2, 4, 5, pp. 426–8. The Western share of Hollywood production rose to 27 percent, and "A" Westerns to nearly 2 percent of all major studio productions in 1936; but "A" Westerns fell to 0.7 percent of major studio productions in 1937 and 1.1 percent in 1938.

5. *Ibid.*, Table 5, p. 428; Phil Hardy, *The Western: The Film Encyclopedia*, pp. 18–89. The seven major studios produced 350 films in 1930 and 411 in 1937 (the peak year of the decade); they averaged 351 films a year between 1930 and 1938. The BFI tables distinguish "A" productions from "B" productions; Hardy's listing defines the "Western" somewhat more liberally, which adds a few titles each year but does not alter the general pattern derived from BFI's tables. In the post-studio era (after 1955) the "A"/"B" distinction is less useful, and I have used running time as an alternative way of suggesting relative differences from year to year in the scale and ambition of Westerns. The use of running time as a criterion in comparisons for the 1930–42 period increases slightly the number of productions that might be rated as "larger than 'B' " but does not affect the pattern indicated by the BFI's tables.

6. Buscombe, *BFI*, Tables 2, 4, 5; Hardy, *Western*, pp. 150–245. From 1946 to 1955, 28.5 percent of all Hollywood films were Westerns. The collapse of the studio system after 1955 makes other methods of evaluation preferable to the "A"/"B" and studio production-share comparisons.

7. Billington, *Turner*, pp. 440–3, 446–51, 462–3.

8. The account of the studio system which follows is based on Nick Roddick, *A New Deal in Entertainment: Warner Brothers in the 1930s*, and Thomas Schatz, *The Genius of the System: Hollywood Filmmaking in the Studio Era*.

9. Carl Sifakis, *The Encyclopedia of American Crime: Abbandando to Zwillman*, p. 17.

10. There is a formal likeness between the isolation of pure sound (without a corresponding image) in this scene, and Hart's esthetic abstraction of the fire as a purely visual element—that is, an image whose sensuous effect is not expressible by any verbalizable meaning.

11. Slotkin, "The Continuity of Forms: Warner Brothers' *Charge of the Light Brigade*," *Representations* 29: 1–23.

12. *Ibid.*

13. Rudy Behlmer, ed., *Inside Warner Bros. (1935–1951)*, pp. 28–39; Clive

Hirschhorn, *The Warner Bros. Story*, pp. 82–171, and esp. 82–3, 171; Ted Sennett, *Warner Brothers Presents: The Most Exciting Years—From the Jazz Singer to White Heat*, ch. 6; Dooley, *Scarface to Scarlett*, ch. 17; Hirschhorn, *Warner Bros. Story*, pp. 82–3. Francis C. P. Yeats-Brown, *The Lives of a Bengal Lancer* (1930), refers to events in India, 1907–13.

14. Roddick, *New Deal*, chs. 1–3, 12; Behlmer, *Inside Warner Bros.*, p. 29; Hirschhorn, *Warner Bros. Story*, p. 171. The producers even used replicas of authentic period postage stamps, though these would not be visible on film, in order to foster a feeling for the project's authenticity among the cast and crew.

15. This is in striking contrast to standard British treatments of the battle, from 1854 down to Tony Richardson's film of 1966, in which the primary stakes are those of Great Power rivalry and the ideological problems arise from British class distinction and military incompetence. Cecil Woodham-Smith, *The Reason Why*, pp. 258–71. From the American perspective, there was also some historical and mythological warrant for interpreting the Charge as an Indian war story. The battle was already strongly associated with Custer's Last Stand in popular history and literature, as it has been since the first journalistic accounts of the Battle of the Little Big Horn in 1876; the appeal or logic of that connection is attested by Warners' further development of the association, culminating in the Custer biography, *They Died with Their Boots On* (1941). Slotkin, *Fatal Environment*, p. 455.

16. *Ibid.*, ch. 5; ———, "Introduction," in Cooper, *The Last of the Mohicans*, pp. ix–xviii.

17. Roddick, *New Deal*, chs. 2, 5, 8, 12, and pp. 249–54. Among the more explicit allusions to contemporary politics are the Stalin-like appearance of Volonoff, and the use of the rhetoric of appeasement by Macefield, who tells his commanders "We must have peace [in India] at any price"—so that England can prepare for war against Russia. See also Sinclair Lewis and Dore Schary, *Storm in the West*, which gives the writers' account of a 1943 project for a Western allegorizing the events leading up to the Second World War.

18. The Old West settings often involve revenge plots and cases of mistaken identity, in the dime-novel and W. S. Hart tradition: *Sagebrush Trail* (1933), *West of the Divide* (1933), *Randy Rides Alone* (1934), *The Star Packer* (1934), *The Trail Beyond* (1934), *Blue Steel* (1934), *Lawless Frontier* (1935), *Texas Terror*, (1935), *The Dawn Rider* (1935), and *Westward Ho* (1935). See entries for these films in Hardy, *Western*.

19. *Ibid.*, pp. 88–9.

20. Allen Eyles, *John Wayne and the Movies*, pp. 31–2.

21. *Ibid.*

22. Some exemplary titles in the "gangster" category are *Broadway to Cheyenne*, *Texas Tornado* (1932); *Crossfire* (1933); *Racketeer Roundup* (1934); *Western Racketeers*, *Sunset Range* (1935); *The Last Outlaw* (1936); *Gambling Terror*, *Headin' East*, *Secret Valley*, *Sing Cowboy Sing* (1937); *Racketeers of the Range* (1939). Exemplary FBI/Border Patrol/Secret Service stories are *Blazing Sixes*, *Border Phantom*, *Public Cowboy No. One* (1937); and *Phantom Ranger* (1938). In *The Lucky Texan* (1934) John Wayne rides both a horse and a Model T, and in other films he is an undercover agent working against crooks at a rodeo (*The Man from Utah* [1934]

and *Desert Trail* [1935]). *Riders of Destiny* (1933) and *Paradise Canyon* (1935) are both set as nineteenth-century Westerns, but the Wayne character is an undercover agent operating out of Washington on cases evocative of "Secret Service" or "G-Man" movies in particular. "B" Westerns also poached on the territory of the social drama: both Roy Rogers and Gene Autry made Westerns that adapted the plot of Frank Capra's *Mister Smith Goes to Washington* for a singing cowboy: *Under Western Stars* (1938) and *Rovin' Tumbleweeds* (1939). *'Neath Arizona Skies* (with John Wayne [1934]) exploited the success of Warner Bros.' *Massacre* (1934), a "social drama" about racism and Indian rights. *Phantom Empire* (1935) and *Ghost Patrol* (1936) presented Western heroes in science-fiction settings. See entries for these films in Hardy, *Western*.

23. Bernard A. Drew, Martin H. Greenberg, and Charles G. Waugh, *Western Series and Sequels: A Reference Guide*, pp. 126–7.

24. Everson, *Pictorial*, pp. 141, 6; Fenin and Everson, *Western*, pp. 222–3.

25. Eyles, *Wayne*, pp. 52, 55; Hardy, *Western*, pp. 53, 94; TVA-related scenarios were used in other films of the same period, including Gene Autry's *Red River Valley* (1936) and *Gunsmoke Ranch* (1938). *Heroes of the Hills* (1938) varies the pattern by focusing on an attempt to profit illegally from the projective building of a prison. See entries for these films in Hardy, *Western*.

26. Thanks to my students and the staff at the Buffalo Bill Historical Center, Cody, WY, for bringing the poaching incident, and local articles on it, to my attention.

27. Fenin and Everson, *Western*, p. 261, and see entries for these films in Hardy, *Western*.

Notes to Chapter 9

1. Figures compiled from Hardy, *Western*, pp. 89–125 and Appendix 8; and Buscombe, *BFI Companion*, Tables 2, 4, 5. During the Depression years 1930–38, "A" Westerns averaged 9 percent of all Westerns and 0.7 percent of all productions. Westerns constituted more than 27 percent of all films in 1939–41, compared with 21 percent for 1930–38. Scale of production: in 1939, 11 feature-length Westerns were released with running times of 80 minutes or more, of which 5 had running times of 100+ and 4 had running times of 90+. In 1940 there were 20 films running 80+, including 8 at 100+ and 3 at 90+. The roster of features includes some oddities: 4 were comedies, starring the likes of Jack Benny and the Marx Brothers—unorthodox as genre pieces, but a sign of Hollywood's belief in the appeal of Western settings. Hart's silent classic *Tumbleweeds* was also re-released, with a spoken introduction by Hart that emphasized the historical significance of the film and its subject. New "B" series were also developed, including a new group of "historical" Westerns, some of which display unusually generous production values.

Note on statistics: Hardy, *Western*, defines the genre in a more liberal way than Les Adams and Buck Rainey, *Shoot-em-Ups: The Complete Reference Guide to Westerns of the Sound Era*, or Buscombe, *BFI Companion*. In my view, Hardy errs by including films like *Shepherd of the Hills* but is correct in including certain "forest" Westerns set in Revolutionary or Colonial days, like *Drums Along the*

Mohawk. Buscombe and Adams and Rainey use a different standard of classification—for example, excluding *Drums/Mohawk* but including *Allegheny Uprising*, which has a similar setting. Hardy's system (in my view) offers a more sensible and consistent reading of the public understanding of Westerns during the period: genre boundaries were not so fixed in 1939 that an Indian war film set on the forest frontier would have appeared to belong to an utterly different category from a film with a similar theme set on the Plains.

2. Returns from the attempted revival of "big" Westerns in 1936 and 1938 were extremely modest. The spate of successful feature Westerns early in 1939 had an immediate impact on production; but major commitments obviously had to be made to these first productions in advance of a clear set of box-office returns. Planning for *Dodge City* began in August 1938. Behlmer, *Inside Warner Bros.*, p. 80; Roddick, *New Deal*, chs. 1–2, 9–10, pp. 249–54; Fenin and Everson, *Western*, ch. 13; Dooley, *From Scarface to Scarlett*, chs. 14–17. On "costume" as a genre, see Reed, *American Scenarios*, chs. 1, 12.

3. Richard H. Pells, *Radical Visions and American Dreams: Culture and Social Thought in the Depression Years*, pp. 310–1. On the New Deal in general I have used William E. Leuchtenberg, *Franklin Delano Roosevelt and the New Deal*; and Arthur M. Schlesinger, Jr., *The Age of Roosevelt, III: The Politics of Upheaval*.

4. Howard Mumford Jones, "Patriotism—But How?" *Atlantic Monthly* 162 (November 1938), pp. 585–92; cited by Cecilia Whiting, "American Heroes and Invading Barbarians: The Regionalist Response to Fascism," *Prospects 13*, pp. 295–324.

5. See for example Kenneth Roberts' series on the forest battles of the French and Indian and Revolutionary wars; Margaret Mitchell's *Gone with the Wind* (1936); Howard Fast's *Citizen Tom Paine* (1943); and Stewart Edward White's four-volume "Saga of Andy Burnett," which began with *The Long Rifle* (1932). See Lee Coyle, "Kenneth Roberts and the American Historical Novel," in S. C. Austin and Donald A. Koch, eds., *Popular Literature in America*.

6. Pells, *Radical Visions*, p. 315.

7. *Ibid.*, pp. 316–7; Gilbert V. Seldes, *Mainland*, ch. 1, pp. 138–46, 172–6.

8. *Ibid.*, ch 8, esp. pp. 314–5; Joe Klein, *Woody Guthrie: A Life*, ch. 5; Jerre Mangione, *The Dream and the Deal: The Federal Writers' Project 1935–43*, chs. 2–3, 7; Ronald Brownstein, *The Power and the Glitter: The Hollywood–Washington Connection*, chs. 2–3; Leonard Quart, "Frank Capra and the Popular Front," in Lazere, Donald, ed. *American Media and Mass Culture: Left Perspectives*, pp. 178–83.

9. Christine Bold, "The View from the Road: Katharine Kellock's New Deal Guidebooks," *American Studies* 29:2 (1988), pp. 5–30. Federal Writers' Program, Colorado, *Colorado: A Guide to the Highest State* (1941), pp. 25, 42, 44, uses such standard elements of the myth as the association of historical progress with the succession of peoples or races, esp. the elimination of the Indians; but it extends these themes to the era of immigration and accepts the "melting pot" as a continuition of the ethnic progression. See Richard Weiss, "Ethnicity and Reform: Minorities and the Ambience of the Depression Years," *JAH* 66:3 (1979), pp. 566–85. Similar themes appear in the historical chapters of Federal Writers' Program, *Arizona: A State Guide* (1940); ———, *California, A Guide to the Golden*

State (1939); ———, *Texas, A Guide to the Lone Star State* (1940). The guides acknowledge social and labor problems in the history of several states. The Colorado and Texas guidebooks, for example, deal with ethnic and labor troubles, and detail the struggles of Grangers and Populists against the "money trust" and the railroads. But such accounts usually end with the adoption of "reforms" that anticipate or belong to the New Deal. Thus the tale of industrial poverty and strife becomes a genetic myth of the New Deal. Federal Writers' Program, *Colorado*, pp. 50–1; ———, *Texas*, pp. 50–1; ———, *California*, p. 59.

10. ———, *Arizona*, p. 3.

11. Edward Everett Dale, "The Spirit of Oklahoma," in Federal Writers' Program, Oklahoma, *Oklahoma: A Guide to the Sooner State*. (1941), p. 3; compare [Angie Debo], "History," in *ibid.*, second edition (1981), pp. 20–36.

12. On Turnerism in the 1930s see Stephen Kesselman, "The Frontier Thesis and the Great Depression," *Journal of the History of Ideas* 29:2, pp. 253–68. On the relation between Beard's progressivism and the ideological constituents of FDR's administration see Otis Graham, *Encore for Reform: The Old Progressives and the New Deal*; Richard Hofstader, *The Progressive Historians: Turner, Beard, Parrington*, Part 3; John P. Diggins, "Power and Authority in American History: The Case of Charles A. Beard," *AHR* 86:4 (1981), pp. 701–30; Nancy F. Cott, "Two Beards: Coauthorship and the Concept of Civilization," *American Quarterly* 42:2, pp. 274–300; David W. Noble, *Historians Against History: The Frontier Thesis and the National Covenant in American Historical Writing Since 1830*, chs. 4, 7; and ———, *The End of American History: Democracy, Capitalism and the Metaphor of Two Worlds in Anglo-American Historical Writing, 1880–1980*, chs. 2–3. On managerial economics in the New Deal see Adelstein, " 'The Nation as an Economic Unit,' " pp. 160–87.

13. *Ibid.*, pp. 56–7.

14. *Ibid.*, pp. 48–9; Charles A. and Mary Beard, *The Rise of American Civilization* 1: 514–7, 534–5.

15. Noble, *End*, pp. 57, 59.

16. *Ibid.* pp. 48–50, 56–9.

17. Noble, *Historians*, p. 127.

18. *Ibid.*, pp. 129–30, 137.

19. Progress of this kind is often related to the development of political and/or urban corruption, for example in *Destry Rides Again*, *Dodge City*, *Frontier Marshal*, *Let Freedom Ring*, and *Oklahoma Kid* (all 1939), and *Honky Tonk* and *Lady from Cheyenne* (1941).

20. The Civil War is treated in Western fashion in *Dark Command*, *Virginia City*, and *Santa Fe Trail* (1940). Several epics were set in the eastern woodlands during the colonial and Revolutionary Indian wars—for example, *Allegheny Uprising* and *Drums Along the Mohawk* (1939), and *Northwest Passage* (1940). These are usually listed as Westerns in critical histories; the studios promoted them as Westerns and used their Western actors and directors to make them. John Wayne starred in both *Allegheny Uprising* and John Ford's *Stagecoach* in 1939. Ford directed Henry Fonda and John Carradine in *Drums Along the Mohawk* (1939); Carradine had had supporting roles in both *Stagecoach* and *Jesse James* (1939), in which Fonda had starred. However, the imagery of these "eastern" Westerns

has never been as important to the genre as the images that belong to the Far West, especially the "cowboy" era.

21. Behlmer, *Inside Warner Bros.*, pp. 80–1.

22. The choice of Curtiz (who had never directed a Western) suggests that the studio saw the film as a historical costume-drama akin to those earlier projects.

23. There is also a montage of Dodge City's growth/corruption that is similar to the montages in *Roaring Twenties* and other gangster films, which represent the Prohibition era in alternating images of speakeasy/nightclubs and gunplay in the gutters.

24. Compare *Lady from Cheyenne* (1941).

25. There is a suggestion here that these two have the potential to make a sexually mixed pair of adventurer-comrades, rather than a simple domestic pair, when the adventure is done—a suggestion made explicit in the final scene, which sends the newly married pair off together to tame yet another town. The conclusion was a set-up for *Virginia City*, Flynn/de Havilland's next Western; but in the event, *Virginia City* starts a new story, which requires the Flynn and de Havilland characters to go through the "boy meets girl" scenes again.

26. Gender imagery is used in complex and interesting ways to characterize the moral universe in which Hatton must make his choice. See the discussion of the "Pure Prairie League" sequence in Slotkin, "Violence," in Buscombe, ed., *BFI Companion*, pp. 233.

27. The opening scenes link the politics of the 1850s to those of the 1930s through an abolitionist ideologue named Rader (Van Heflin), who uses the language of the contemporary left (his preferred epithet for southerners is "plutocrats"). Raymond Massey, who played Brown, had played a fanatical Moslem Khan in *Drums* (1939).

28. See Hart's *Tumbleweeds* (1925) and deMille's *Cimarron* (1931), for example. The scene in which the Kid hides out with a Mexican family is similar to one in King Vidor's classic *Billy the Kid* (1931).

29. Walter Coppedge, *Henry King's America*, pp. 93–4; author's interview with Henry King, July 2, 1976, Symposium on Western Movies: Myths and Images, Sun Valley, Idaho.

30. Other folkloric/mythic touches include the phrase-repetitions in the jailer's dialogue in the rescue sequence, and Frank's use of money to distract pursuers, which invokes the myth of Atalanta and the Golden Apples.

31. The editor is an important secondary character who serves (like Rusty and Tex in *Dodge City*) as a comic mirror of the heroic action. He is first seen as a comically apoplectic but principled "populist" whose standard diatribe against various malefactors of wealth and power (railroad presidents, sheriffs, lawyers, etc.) begins, "If we are ever to have law and order in the West, the first thing we must do, is take out all the [fill in blank] and shoot 'em down like *dawgs*!" As Jesse's social banditry is discredited, the rantings of his chief apologist also become more ridiculous; in this scene his target has been dentists. Young Jesse's play in the last scenes of the movie is also inadvertently "prophetic" of his father's death.

32. Coppedge, *Henry King's America*, pp. 110–1. The social bandit theme is also treated without explicit reference to Jesse James. See, for example, *Let*

Freedom Ring (1939); the Wallace Beery vehicles, *Wyoming* (1940) and *The Bad Man* (1941); and *The Westerner* (1940), which starred Gary Cooper. In addition to features, Jesse James and other historical outlaws figured prominently in "B" Westerns after 1939, the most notable of which were the series starring Roy Rogers as Jesse and as Billy the Kid.

A partial list of movies more or less specifically referring to the James Gang or their allies (Youngers, Daltons, Quantrill) includes *Badman's Territory* (1946); *Belle Starr's Daughter* and *The Fabulous Texan* (1947); *Four Faces West* and *Return of the Badmen* (1948); *Calamity Jane and Sam Bass, The Doolins of Oklahoma, Fighting Man of the Plains, I Shot Jesse James*, and *The Younger Brothers* (1949); *Kansas Raiders, The Return of Jesse James* (1950); *Al Jennings of Oklahoma, The Best of the Badmen*, and *The Great Missouri Raid* (1951); *Montana Belle, The Lawless Breed* (1952); *The Woman They Almost Lynched, Vanquished*, and *The Stranger Wore a Gun* (1953); *Jesse James vs. the Daltons* and *Jesse James' Women* (1954); *The Dalton Girls* and *The True Story of Jesse James* (1957); *Cole Younger, Gunfighter* and *Quantrill's Raiders* (1958); *Young Jesse James* (1960); *Jesse James Meets Frankenstein's Daughter* (1966); *The Great Northfield Minnesota Raid* (1971); *The Outlaw Josey Wales* (1976); and *The Long Riders* (1981). Closely related to the James films are the numerous "Billy the Kid" films, which include Roy Rogers' series, *Billy the Kid* (1941), *The Outlaw* (1943), *Texas Kid, Outlaw* (1950), *Parson and the Outlaw* (1957), *Left-Handed Gun* (1958), *Chisum* (1971), and *Pat Garrett and Billy the Kid* (1973).

Among the most important image-icons taken from King's film are Jesse's nighttime run across the railroad cars, used or imitated in numerous films; and various images and episodes from the Northfield sequence, particularly the long linen dusters worn by the outlaws when they ride in; the gun battle between posse and citizens ambushed in buildings, and the robbers on their milling horses caught in the middle of the street; Frank and Jesse crashing their horses through a store window and riding through the store to break out of encirclement; and the final escape by water as they jump their horses off a cliff into a river. Among the feature films that use these elements are *The True Story of Jesse James, Butch Cassidy and the Sundance Kid, The Wild Bunch, The Great Northfield Minnesota Raid*, and *Long Riders*.

33. Coppedge, *Henry King*, pp. 96–7; John Springer, *The Fondas*, pp. 68–9. Fonda had also appeared in the Spanish Civil War drama *Blockade* (1938), whose political references are unintelligible but vaguely populist; but this performance seems not to have influenced King's casting of Fonda. *Jesse James* also impacted the screen persona of Brian Donlevy, who also appeared in the 1941 remake of *Billy the Kid* and as Quantrill in *Kansas Raiders*; Randolph Scott reprised his role (or a close analogue) in both *Belle Starr* and *When the Daltons Rode* (1941).

34. Gallagher, *Ford*, p. 180. Other forms of movie populism espoused values similar to the outlaw Western—opposition to "bigness" and corporate greed, admiration for "the little man," and uncommon-common man heroes—but dispelled the populist hero's potential for violence. See especially Frank Capra's *Mr. Deeds Goes to Town* (1936), *Mr. Smith Goes to Washington* (1939), and *Meet John Doe* (1941); and Pells, *Radical Visions*, pp. 277–84.

35. But its success was not a "cause" of the renaissance of the genre; many of the major productions released in 1939 were developed during 1938, while

Ford was planning *Stagecoach* (released in March, 2, 1939). Tag Gallagher, *John Ford: The Man and His Film*, p. 143; Behlmer, *Inside Warner Bros.*, pp. 80–1. As I suggested earlier, it is probably more accurate to describe the film as a "neo-classical" work, in the sense that the work of Stravinsky and Balanchine is neo-classical: a deliberate attempt to translate an archaic form into the idiom of modernism. The film was a critical and commercial success. It was also a major contributor to the renewed enthusiasm for Westerns and to the emergence of John Wayne as a major Hollywood star and a public icon of some weight.

36. His work had included film versions of important literary and theatrical works, including Sinclair Lewis's *Arrowsmith* (1931), Sean O'Casey's *The Plough and the Stars*, and Maxwell Anderson's *Mary of Scotland* (1936), and Sean O'Faolain's *The Informer* (1935). See Gallagher, *Ford*, ch. 3.

37. The project was controlled by Ford from conception through execution, and is even more of an *auteur*'s piece than the average of his work (see *ibid.*, pp. 120–1, 145–6). The pregnancy and birth scenes stretch the Code a bit, as do the characters of Dallas and Ringo (pp. 145, 150–1). Ford's sophistication in the use of the genre language owes something to genius and something to practice: he had been making Westerns longer than any other major director in Hollywood, with the possible exception of Raoul Walsh.

38. *Ibid.*, p. 149.

39. *Ibid.*, p. 148.

40. This scene borrows the same premise as the Bret Harte short story (and 1937 "B" film), "Outcasts of Poker Flat."

41. The comic exchanges between Doc and the Reverend turn on Ford's and Nichols' consciously ironic play with their chosen stereotypes: the man who looks like a minister is a whiskey-drummer; the doctor is killing himself with the reverend's medicine; but the effeminate little drummer—along with the equally effeminate and oafish stage-driver Buck (Andy Devine)—turn out to have fathered over a dozen children between them.

42. As Tag Gallagher has noted, in the coach scenes Ford cycles through the same sequence of long and close-up, interior and exterior shots nearly a dozen times. In the way stations, he stages set-pieces which dramatize and develop the relationships between the passengers. The structure is reminiscent of the alternation of town and raft-passages in the river-journey section of *Huckleberry Finn*.

43. The ending recalls that of the original "outlaw kid" movie, King Vidor's classic *Billy the Kid* (1930).

44. Gallagher, *Ford*, pp. 149–52.

Notes to Chapter 10

1. Hodgson, *America*, pp. 18–20.

2. Geertz, *Interpretation*, pp. 211, 214.

3. Sahlins, *Historical Metaphors*, pp. 6, 67, 72. "In the event, speech brings signs into 'new' contexts of use. . . . At the extreme, what began as reproduction ends as tranformation."

4. John Morton Blum, *V Was for Victory*, pp. 21, 29, 37; Basinger, *World War II Combat Film*, pp. 83–107. The antiwar conventions of Great War films were

reversed to serve a "preparedness" and perhaps an interventionist message in *The Fighting 69th* (1940) and *Sergeant York* (1941); the former combines the war theme with "good gangster" conventions; the latter has elements of the Western.

5. Famous newsphotos were sometimes duplicated or "quoted" in films as authenticating devices, and these were not necessarily the grand iconic images of battle (like the sunken Arizona or the flag-raising on Iwo Jima): a *Life* portrait of army nurses was "duplicated exactly" for *So Proudly We Hail*. (David E. Scherman, ed., *Life Goes to War: A Picture History of World War II*, p. 116.) Griffith recreated famous photographs and engraved illustrations for similar purposes in *Birth of a Nation*.

6. *Juarez* (1939), which is often listed as a Western, uses the Mexican struggle against the puppet regime established by Napoleon III to represent the threat to democracy posed by European Fascist dictators and elitist ideologies. However, the film is more a "bio-pic" than a Western, and it evades the issue of intervention. Hollywood also made films that articulated American sympathy for the Allies and suggested the desirability of intervention, ranging from the contemporary *Yank in the RAF* (1941) to *Sea Hawk* (1940) from Warners' "Merrie England" genre—but there are no obviously interventionist Western features.

7. Although the Western percentage of total Hollywood production in wartime remained near its thirty-year average of 25 percent, when compared with 1939–41 a disproportionate share were "B" films produced by independents rather than by major studios. Between 1936 and 1940 the independents' share of Western production averaged about 53 percent; their share was 55 percent in 1941, 57 percent in 1942, 67 percent in 1943, 64 percent in 1944, and 67 percent in 1945. This situation persisted through 1946–47 (64 percent), after which the majors returned to the genre and the independents' share dropped to 54 percent. See Buscombe, *BFI Companion*, Tables 3, 2, and 4. The independents' devotion to the genre had an economic basis: Westerns made up more than half of their production, and unlike the majors they could not afford to "mothball" Western stars and sets or convert all resources to "war" production.

8. Hemingway's interest in Custer is attested by the frequency with which he uses him as a symbol. See for example the selections in his anthology of war stories, *Men at War*, pp. 461–82, 221–2, 238–75, 288–301; *To Have and Have Not*, p. 123; *Across the River and Into the Trees*, pp. 16, 169, 265; and *Islands in the Stream*, p. 459.

9. *Life*, December 8, 1941, pp. 75–8, 122–139; April 13, 1942, "Philippine Epic: General MacArthur and His Men Make a Thermopylae of Bataan," pp. 25–37, esp. pp. 32–3. Other "cavalry" and Last Stand references are in Capt. John Wheeler, "Rear Guard in Luzon," March 2, 1942, pp. 51–2, 55.

10. Francis B. Sayre, "War Days on Corregidor," *Life*, April 20, 1942, pp. 94–105; quote from p. 105.

11. *Life*, April 13, 1942, "Philippine Epic: General MacArthur and His Men Make a Thermopylae of Bataan," pp. 25–26, 36.

12. *Life*, December 8, 1941, pp. 75–8, 122–139; Slotkin, *Fatal Environment*, p. 14, and fn. 2.

13. Dower, *War Without Mercy*, chs. 4, 6, pp. 181–90; Scherman, *Life Goes to War*, pp. 125–7.

14. Dower, *War Without Mercy*, ch. 7; Hon. John A. Rankin, "Speech of . . . , February 23 and March 10, 1942," *Congressional Record 1942*, Appendix A: 768–9, 931; Shapiro, *White Violence*, ch. 12.

15. *Ibid.*; Howard Odum, *Race and Rumors of Race: Challenge to American Crisis, passim*; Blum, *V Was for Victory*, check riots, esp Zoot.

16. Basinger, *World War II Combat Film*, pp. 50–1, 73–6.

17. Dower, *War Without Mercy*, chs. 8–10; *Bushido* is explicitly referred to in *Bataan*.

18. Basinger, *World War II Combat Film*, p. 46. The original title was to have been *Bataan Patrol*.

19. *Ibid.*, pp. 107–19. The references are both to the immediate need for teamwork and to the conventions of pre-war "service" comedies, which emphasize inter-service rivalry.

20. "Recreation Officers at Fort Meade Learn 'Dirty Fighting,'" *Life*, June 15, 1942, p. 73.

21. See Blum, *V Was for Victory*, p. 59.

22. In the original script, the "scout" role was assigned to a Native American private named Evening Star, whose "grand-dad always claimed he was with *Sitting Bull* at *Custer's Last Stand*. I always doubted it. But he talked a swell Wild West." Salazar is a Moro, proud that he comes from "one *morderin'* race," who strips to breechclouts and blackens his face before leaving on a mission. Such "friendly savage" characters act, in effect, as tutors who inform the innocent Whites of the "dirtiness" of the racial "Other" and teach the arts of "savage war." Basinger, *World War II Combat Film*, p. 45.

23. *Guadalcanal Diary* (1943) resolves the problem by having its "least White" ethnic—the Hispanic 'Soos (Anthony Quinn)—become the prize student at learning to fight dirty. After playing the same trick on a Japanese that had been played on him, 'Soos charges off giggling insanely and is shot down. As with Bill Dane, those who come to "know the Indians" too well risk their sanity, become potentially threatening, and are eliminated through death. But this use of a non-WASP as a "scapegoat" for exorcising the moral pollution of war was not a "typical" solution of the problem in 1943–46.

24. On the importance of this kind of fantasy for troops in combat, see Glenn Gray, *The Warriors*, pp. 125–6.

25. Samuel Eliot Morison, *et al.*, *The Struggle for Guadalcanal, August 1942–February 1943: History of United States Naval Operations in World War II*, 5: 187. John Dower's recent study of wartime propaganda, *War Without Mercy*, suggests that the prevalence of racial animosity—more than reciprocated by the Japanese—made the actual practice of warfare against the Japanese more indiscriminate in its violence than that deployed against Germany. Certainly Japanese–Americans as a group were subjected to greater discrimination than naturalized German– or Italian–Americans. Critics of Dower's work have pointed out that vicious anti-Japanese racism gave way rather quickly to more positive stereotypes after the war; and the bombing of German civilian targets by the Allies was on a scale comparable to that directed against Japan. Japanese refusal to surrender turned many engagements into battles of annihilation; and their abuse of American POWs was in many ways comparable to German treatment of Russian POWs,

another case in which the enemy was perceived as racially alien and inferior. But the choice of Japan, rather than Germany, as the target for the atomic bomb was dictated by events. See John Dower, *War Without Mercy: Race and Power in the Pacific War*, esp. Parts 1 and 2. Although Nazis were described as "savages," the absence of infantry combat with American forces led to an emphasis on tales of espionage and Gestapo/resistance struggles for films set in the European Theater. The German enemy was therefore characterized by its "aristocratic" tyrants, agents of an excessively order-conscious idea of civilization (Blum, *V Was for Victory*, pp. 46–7)—a stereotype that linked them to domestic class snobs like the villains of *Keeper of the Flame* and *Meet John Doe*, or certain types of mad scientist or obsessed policemen from horror films like *Frankenstein*. There are fewer negative images of ordinary German footsoldiers than of Japanese troopers.

26. *Sahara* (1943) and *Gung Ho* (1944) reflect the range of possible political allegories the platoon structure made possible. *Sahara* internationalizes the theme, with a pick-up platoon drawn from most of the Allied nationalities, led by an American sergeant. *Gung Ho* offers a distinctly leftist take on the theme: the Marine raider platoon is headed by a man who learned guerrilla tactics with Mao Tse Tung in China and is composed of a range of "outlaw" types, including one veteran of the Spanish Civil War. The implicit radicalism of *Gung Ho* was not developed, although an overtly political message is the center of the "problem"/combat film hybrid, *Home of the Brave* (1949).

27. Blum, *V Was for Victory*, p. 13

28. In *Jesse James*, Hull's character is also known for his murderous rants, which finally become absurd.

29. Earlier, Walsh has Flynn synchronize watches for an attack at "Eighteen-fifty-four," the year of Balaklava.

30. Hodgson, *America*, ch. 2; Blum, *V Was for Victory*, pp. 249, 325–7.

31. The address was drawn from arguments Johnson had made in a 1944 book titled *America Unlimited*. My thanks to Lary May for bringing the speech to my attention. See also Dana Polan, *Power and Paranoia: History, Narrative and the American Cinema, 1940–1950*, "Introduction," chs. 2, 3. 6.

32. Eric Johnson, "Utopia Is Production," *The Screen Actor* (August, 1946), pp. 14–5.

33. Blum, *V Was for Victory*, ch. 4; Hodgson, *America*, p. 50.

34. *Ibid.*, p. 77.

35. *Ibid.*, pp. 90–2.

36. *Ibid.*, pp. 17–8, 95; Noble, *End*, chs. 5–6.

37. Hardy, *Western*, pp. 146–85 and Appendix 8. From a wartime low of 23 percent of all productions, Westerns rose to 30 percent in 1948, and until 1956 their share of all productions varied between 27 percent and 33 percent. The majors' share of production increased vis-à-vis the independents, reflecting industry trends and signaling the decline of the "B" Western (hurt by TV) and the increasing emphasis on bigger productions. Buscombe, *BFI*, Table 4. At the same time, there was a three-year hiatus in the production of combat films. See Basinger, *World War II Combat Film*, pp. 153–4.

38. Films representative of these categories include: *Along Came Jones* (1945), an old-fashioned "cowboy picture"; historical epics of pioneering, *Unconquered* (1947), *California* (1946), *Northwest Outpost*, *Wyoming*, and *Cheyenne* (1947), and *Fighting Kentuckian* (1949); railroad/transportation epics, *Dakota* and *Saratoga Trunk* (1945), *The Plainsman and the Lady* and the musical *The Harvey Girls* (1946), and *Canadian Pacific* (1949); town-tamer stories, *San Antonio* (1945), *Abilene Town* and *My Darling Clementine* (1946); good-badmen formulas, *Bad Bascomb* (1946) and *Angel and the Badman* (1947); the Jesse James canon, *The Daltons Ride Again* (1945), *Badman's Territory* (1946), *Belle Starr's Daughter* (1947), *Return of the Badmen* (1948), *Calamity Jane and Sam Bass* (1949), *Doolins of Oklahoma* (1949), *Fighting Man of the Plains* (1949), and *The Younger Brothers* (1949); cattle empires, *Duel in the Sun* and *The Virginian* (1946), and *Sea of Grass* (1947).

39. *The Gunfighters*, *Pursued*, and *Ramrod* (1947); *Blood on the Moon* and *Coroner Creek* (1948).

40. A similar revision also began to occur in the combat film. Although celebratory versions continued to appear, the new wave in combat films took a critical look at the more romantic conventions of the genre. 1949 was a notable year in this respect. See Basinger, *World War II Combat Film*, pp. 154–72.

41. Gallagher, *Ford*, pp. 221–4; Peter Bogdanovitch, *John Ford*, pp. 86–7; Gallagher, *Ford*, pp. 244–5. It is also worth noting that *They Were Expendable* goes farther than any other combat film in attempting to domesticate and Americanize the alien space of jungle warfare. See especially the scene in which an American shipowner (Russell Simpson) prepares to defend his Philippine freehold in the same mood and manner, and to the same musical accompaniment, as the populist farmers in *Grapes of Wrath*.

42. Remington images appear again and again in the trilogy. Slotkin, "Buffalo Bill's Wild West," pp. 34–44; Brownlow, *The War, the West*, pp. 253–63; Fenin and Everson, *Western*, pp. 67–72.

43. Gallagher, *Ford*, pp. 139–41. Ford himself had contributed to the genre, but *Wee Willie Winkie* (1937) is exceptional in showing an innocent American girl (Shirley Temple) as the means to avoiding an exchange of massacres between the regiment and the disaffected Khan. Temple returns as an older ingenue in *Fort Apache*.

44. Gallagher, *Ford*, pp. 246–54; J. A. Place, *The Western Films of John Ford*, ch. 6.

45. The cavalry trilogy scripts were based on a series of stories published in *The Saturday Evening Post* by James Warner Bellah. The title of "Thursday's Last Charge" obviously invokes Custer, but the original painting by Von Schmidt which illustrates Bellah's story is titled "Fetterman Massacre," and the painting seems to have influenced the composition of the last stand in *Fort Apache*. Both Custer and Fetterman died fighting the Lakota and Cheyenne; but Apaches are the savages of choice by Western movie convention, and Ford follows Bellah in transferring the battle to the Southwest. Ford "justifies" the transfer in a bit of dialogue which asserts that the Apache were better fighters than the northern Indians: when they invaded Apache country "you could follow their trail by the bodies they left behind."

46. On Ford and Monument Valley, see Sinclair, *John Ford*, pp. 81–3, 146, 149; Reed, *Three American Originals: John Ford, William Faulkner and Charles Ives*, pp. 84–5, 111–3, 176–9, 181–2.

47. In addition to these generic references, *Fort Apache* also refers specifically to Ford's own essay in the combat-film form, *They Were Expendable*. PT boats and cavalry regiments operate in "squadrons," and there is a strong iconographic parallel between Ford's shots of PTs parading across a flat sea with flying pennants and a rooster-tail of water, and cavalry regiments galloping behind their guidons with the dust boiling up beneath the hooves. John Wayne—who plays the combative but difficult subordinate in *Expendable*—was cast in a similar role in *Fort Apache*, as was Ward Bond, who plays Chief Petty Officer Mulcahy in *Expendable* and a top-sergeant in *Fort Apache*—where the name "Mulcahy" is assigned to Victor McLaglen's character. See discussions of these films in Place, *Western Films of John Ford*, ch. 6; Reed, *Three American Originals*; Andrew Sarris, *The John Ford Movie Mystery*; and Andrew Sinclair, *John Ford: A Biography*, esp. chs. 9–13.

48. A similar ideological distinction is suggested by the presence of veterans of the Spanish Civil War in *Gung Ho* and *Sahara*. However, these films minimize the political differences between such "premature anti-Fascists" and the platoon's consensus.

49. This type of hero is discussed in Slotkin, *Fatal Environment*, chs. 5–6, pp. 290–300, ch. 20, and above, pp. 35–6, 54, 103–6.

50. His military background and abuse of power link him to similar figures in contemporary films, like the tyrannical Reconstruction officers in *The Fabulous Texan* (1947) and *The Man from Colorado* (1948), or the overbearingly patriarchal Tom Dunson (John Wayne) in Howard Hawks' *Red River* (1948).

51. The aristocratic/romantic pair, whose story is the moral center of the Hollywood epic, are relegated to the subplot here.

52. Ford also uses humor as a democratizing device, sometimes (as here) to deflate Thursday's pretensions; while between the Sergeants, the soldiers, and the "good" officers like York there is a give-and-take of mockery, practical joking, and slapstick that takes the sting out of disciplinary actions and permits a degree of symbolic role-reversal between the ranks.

53. The point becomes stronger when we recognize that this scene is both visually and thematically parallel to a similar moment in Ford's *How Green Was My Valley* (1941), in which the owner of the coal mine comes to a miner's house to propose on his son's behalf marriage to the miner's daughter. The father's deference to the owner leads to a bad marriage: unlike O'Rourke, the miner does not use the respect accorded a father in his own home to strike a balance with authority.

54. I suspect, but cannot confirm, that the character of Thursday is Ford's comment on Douglas MacArthur, and that among the criticisms which Ford felt debarred from voicing were errors of judgment and faults of character that would affect the reputation of a Theater Commander and public hero who was also the postwar darling of the anti-Communist right. Ford had served under MacArthur and was well aware of his failings and of the efforts of his public relations staff to protect and enhance his reputation. Thursday shares with

MacArthur aristocratic pretensions verging on snobbery, an inordinate vanity, and pride of rank, offset by a deserved reputation as a student of war and a man courageous under fire. Like Thursday, MacArthur committed his men to a "last stand" (on Bataan); and although he did not have Thursday's degree of culpability for their entrapment, his tactical decisions during the crucial first phase of the Japanese invasion were questionable. But where Thursday redeems military error by the courageous decision to return and die with his men, MacArthur (under FDR's orders) was required to abandon his "last stand" to lead a counteroffensive from Australia. MacArthur's reputation suffered (unjustly) from his departure, and his publicity men worked hard to correct the flaw. Perhaps more damaging, to a knowledgeable insider like Ford, were instances in which MacArthur's troops fought and died unnecessarily to make good erroneous press releases. See Sinclair, *John Ford*, ch. 11, esp. pp. 118–22; William Manchester, *American Caesar: Douglas MacArthur 1880–1964*, pp. 89, 202–5, 368–78, 416–7, 489–89, 499–502, 710–1, 729–30, 756; and Joseph C. Goulden, *Korea: The Untold Story of the War*, chs. 7, 10, pp. 385–95, ch. 18.

Notes to Chapter 11

1. Hardy, *Western*, pp. 188–202, 211–21, 230–6, 245–52 and Appendix 8.
2. Schatz, *Genius*, Part 5.
3. In the three Nielsen years 1957–60 there were 9 to 12 Westerns among the top 25 shows (36–44 percent), and in 1958–9 seven of the top 10 were Westerns. From 1957 to 1961 the top-ranked show was always a Western; in 1958–9 the top 4 shows, and from 1959–60 to 1961–2 the top 3, were Westerns. Figures compiled from information in Tim Brooks and Earle Marsh, *The Complete Directory of Prime Time Network TV Shows, 1946–Present*, esp. Appendix 1.
4. Many series were based directly (*Laramie*, *Broken Arrow*, *Shenandoah*, *Shane*) or indirectly on movies (as *Gunsmoke* and *Wyatt Earp* are based on *High Noon*); others adapted themes made popular by movies to series format, as *Have Gun Will Travel* does with the "gunfighter" figure. And of course television depended on Hollywood for the Western features it broadcast on the various "Early," "Late," and "Late Late Shows" and for prime-time ventures like "Million Dollar Movie." As TV genres developed their own styles and vocabularies, TV Westerns developed innovative approaches to characterization that took advantage of the series format. The success of *Maverick* is a case in point: the comic gambler (anti) hero has no real equivalent among standard Western-movie hero-types. James Garner's performance became the basis of successful movie characterizations in *Support Your Local Sheriff* and *Support Your Local Gunfighter*.
5. Gallagher, *Ford*, p. 244.
6. Basinger, *World War II Combat Film*, pp. 154–219. The increased sophistication and complexity in the handling of generic vocabulary was not restricted to the Western. The last decade of the old studio system (1946–55) saw the maturation of a number of genres whose main lines had been laid down in the 1930s and early 40s. As moviemakers gained practice in the repeatable formulas of genres, and as their audiences became in effect "visually literate" and sophisticated in their understanding of those formulas, filmmakers developed

virtuosic and ironic ways of working with the materials, combining generic properties to achieve different effects, producing more highly style-conscious and stylized works (e.g., *film noir*, the idiosyncratic genre pieces of Samuel Fuller, etc.).

7. Hodgson, *America*, pp. 77–8, 95. A Roper poll in 1942 had shown that 55 percent of the American people either favored socialism or had an open mind about it, while only 40 were percent opposed to it in principle; a Gallup poll taken seven years later showed only 15 percent favoring movement "in the direction of socialism," while 61 percent wanted to move in the opposite direction.

8. *Ibid.*, pp. 90–1.

9. I use the masculine pronoun, because the figures and roles described are—with few and problematic exceptions—represented as male.

10. Frye, *Critical Path*, p. 115.

11. Fenin and Everson, *Western*, ch. 13, pp. 240–3.

12. On the constitutional problems of Cold War foreign policy, esp. covert operations, see Michael J. Glennon, *Constitutional Diplomacy*; Louis Henkin, *Constitutionalism, Democracy, and Foreign Affairs*; Thedore Draper, "Presidential Wars," *NYRB* (Sept. 26, 1991), pp. 64–74; ———, *A Very Thin Line: The Iran-Contra Affairs*, ch. 26.

13. Hodgson, *America*, pp. 34–44.

14. Joseph C. Goulden, *Korea: The Untold Story of the War*, pp. 29–32.

15. *Ibid.*, pp. 62–74, 108.

16. *Ibid.*, pp. 73–4, 84–6.

17. *Ibid.*, pp. 106–7.

18. *Ibid.*

19. On "Cold War Westerns" see John H. Lenihan, *Showdown: Confronting Modern America in the Western Film*, esp. chs. 1, 3; Thomas H. Pauly, "Film: The Cold War Western," *Western Humanities Review* 33:3 (1979), pp. 257–73; and see also ch. 4 on racial issues. Issues similar to those raised in *Rio Grande* also appear in *She Wore a Yellow Ribbon*: the government is guilty of encouraging the enemy through appeasement, the younger generation's aptitude for war and patriotic service is questioned, and the hero must technically violate orders to fulfill a higher mission. However, *She Wore a Yellow Ribbon* is like *Fort Apache* in its suggestion that peace with the Indians may be possible and is certainly desirable, while *Rio Grande* takes a distinctly harder line. I think the movement of Ford's ideas from film to film of the trilogy indicates a clear drift toward the *Rio Grande* model and have therefore centered my discussion on that film.

20. A number of technical flaws in the final print suggest relatively hasty work at various stages of the production. Gallagher, *Ford*, pp. 257–8; Place, *Western Films*, ch. 10.

21. See note 22, below.

22. Some critics find "sequel" too strong a term for describing the continuity between these two films and cite the different spelling of York (a terminal "e" is added in *Rio Grande*) as evidence of Ford's intention to distinguish the two characters and their films. If that is so, the difference between them is no more significant than that between "York" and "Yorke": if Ford had meant to differ-

entiate the characters more strongly, he could have changed the name, as he did in casting Wayne as "Nathan Brittles" in *She Wore a Yellow Ribbon*, the second film of the trilogy in order of composition.

23. The theme is comically reinforced by the role of Tyree's sidekick, Daniel "Sandy" Boone: the joke is that no one in the film recognizes the legendary pioneer hero's name; the more serious point is that on the "modern" frontier, "Daniel Boone" can play his proper role only by shedding his buckskins and individualism for a uniform and a place in the ranks.

24. The title of the Bellah story on which the movie is based.

25. These doubts are expressed metaphorically, in the complaint that government-issue coffee has been getting weaker.

26. Goulden, *Korea*, chs. 8–11; and Bernard Brodie, *War and Politics*, ch. 3.

27. Quoted in Goulden, *Korea*, p. 336.

28. See Prados, *Presidents' Secret Wars*, esp. chs. 1, 5.

29. Analogous missions include pre-emptive sabotage and coup attempts, as in Iran (1953) and Guatemala (1954); the "Secret War" vs. Castro (1962–64); the "Secret Wars" and bombing campaigns in Laos and Cambodia (1967–72); the sabotage and "Contra" campaign in Nicaragua (1981–3). "Surgical strike" operations were proposed vs. Cuban airfields in 1962, executed vs. Libya in 1987. See Prados, *Presidents' Secret Wars*, esp. chs. 11, 12, 16–9.

30. See fn. 12, above; and Harry G. Summers, *On Strategy: The Vietnam War in Context*, ch. 1.

31. The combat-film connection was reinforced by the revival of that genre during the Korean War, many of which used last stand/ lost patrol scenarios. A group of 1951–53 Westerns dealing with the defense of distant outposts or the holding of a vital hill are simply Indian-war versions of Korean combat films of the same period. Representative last stand titles include *Little Big Horn, Warpath* (1951); *Bugles in the Afternoon* (1952). Raoul Walsh's *Distant Drums* (1951) is a Western remake of his own *Objective Burma*; and *Rocky Mountain* (1950), which starred Errol Flynn, is also a variation on the combat film. Compare the combat films *Fixed Bayonets* and *The Steel Helmet* (1951), *One Minute to Zero* and *Retreat, Hell!* (1952), *The Glory Brigade* (1953), *Men in War* (1957), and *Pork Chop Hill* (1959) with Westerns like *Only the Valiant* (1951); *Last of the Comanches* (1953); *Stand at Apache River* and *Charge at Feather River* (1953); *Arrow in the Dust* and *The Command* (1954); *Smoke Signal* (1955); *Dakota Incident* (1956); and *Dragoon Wells Massacre* (1957). Other Westerns use similar themes, although without the combat-film motifs that strongly link certain Westerns to Korea: *Iroquois Trail* (1950); *Fort Ti* (1953); *The Last Frontier* (1955); *Guns of Fort Petticoat* and *Fort Dobbs* (1957). For the "civil rights" period, compare the Korean War film *All the Young Men* (1960) with *Sergeant Rutledge* (1960) and *Sergeants Three* (1962).

32. Basinger, *World War II Combat Film*, p. 296.

33. Hodgson, *America*, pp. 89–94.

34. Gallagher, *Ford*, p. 339; Sklar, *Movie-Made America*, pp. 245, 257–8, 260–7; Garry Wills, *Reagan's America*, Part 5. Lary May.

35. John Ford made effective (and deeply ironic) use of this presumption in a famous confrontation with Cecil B. deMille in 1951; rising to speak against

deMille's efforts to proscribe a number of foreign-born directors for supposed leftist leanings, Ford introduced himself with the words "I make Westerns." Gallagher, *Ford*, pp. 340–1.

36. Interview with Delmer Daves, director of *Broken Arrow* (1950), July 2, 1976, Symposium on Western Movies: Myths and Images, Sun Valley, Idaho. Daves said that his pro-Indian Western, and others like it, offered a safe vehicle for unacceptably liberal ideas on racial and political coexistence. See also Fenin and Everson, *Western*, pp. 281–6. A similar reasoning shaped the more positive views of Indians and Indian-like "princesses" in the work of Grey and Burroughs; see above.

37. Hardy, *Westerns*, p. 192.

38. Slotkin, *Regeneration*, pp. 354–68; Barnett, *Ignoble Savage*; Everson, *Pictorial History*, pp. 31–3.

39. The resentment later expressed against the Pooles' economic success underlines the anti-Semitic theme. But the treatment of prejudice draws on themes and ideas from both *Gentleman's Agreement* and *Home of the Brave*.

40. There is no obvious historical referent for this particular act, although it is conceivable that some actual state or territorial statute is referred to. But the historical specifics are less important here than the reminder that such laws have historically legitimized and enforced regimes of racial exclusion and oppression. Jews had recently been the victims of such an exclusion in Europe. In America, Blacks had been the primary objects of explicit legislation forbidding settlement or landholding in the territories (mainly before the Civil War), and after the war other legal devices were used to obtain the same effect. Some states also attempted to restrict the right of Asian immigrants to own land. A more immediate reference, and one particularly poignant in Hollywood, was the dispossession of Japanese–Americans from their farms and businesses in California, and their internment 1942–45.

41. Thus they have already realized, in this fictional "1865," the program for dividing Indian reservations into individual family allotments that was not in fact developed until the 1880s. Dippie, *Vanishing American*, ch. 11.

42. Slotkin, *Regeneration*, pp. 30–3, 280–1, 522–3, 533–7; and compare "Surprise Valley" in Grey's *Riders of the Purple Sage*, pp. 215–6, above.

43. Coolan himself is presented as sincere (if also fanatical and cruel) in his love for the valley (he is dying of tuberculosis and thinks he can restore his health there), and his belief that the Indians must be pushed aside for the sake of progress—a cause for which he is willing to die.

44. The movie ias based on Eliot Arnold's *Blood Brother*, a historical novel which tells the story of Tom Jeffords, the Indian scout and entrepreneur who negotiated a peace treaty with Cochise's Apaches and became their first Indian agent. Although Arnold's story emphasizes the friendship between the two men and celebrates the peace they made, at the end he implies that Cochise has lost far more by the exchange than he gained. The movie takes a more positive view.

45. *Broken Arrow*'s greater success may have been due not only to its greater optimism, but to a more accurate prophecy of the character of the postwar economy.

46. The "Cochise canon" includes *Battle at Apache Pass* (1951); *Conquest of*

Cochise (1953); *Taza Son of Cochise* (1954); and the TV series *Broken Arrow* (1956–60. *Walk the Proud Land* (1956) rehabilitates Geronimo by treating him according to the "Cochise" formula. Interestingly, Jay Silverheels plays Geronimo, as he did in *Broken Arrow*; but here it is his performance as Tonto that is directly invoked. *Geronimo* (1962), which stars Chuck Connors as the chief, is thematically similar.

47. And would reprise the role in *The Last Hunt* (1956).

48. Mexicans in the novel.

49. Natty Bumppo characterizes his "marriage" to Nature in similar terms near the end of *Deerslayer*, when questioned as to why he will not marry.

50. Elements of interracial romance are most prominent in *Across the Wide Missouri* (1951); *The Indian Fighter* and *White Feather* (1955); *The Last Hunt* (1956); *The Last Wagon* (1956); and *Run of the Arrow* (1957). Indian victimization and/or the desire of "good" White soldiers to make peace is the theme in *Tomahawk* (1951); *The Savage* (1952); *Arrowhead* (1953); *Drum Beat* and *Sitting Bull* (1954); *Chief Crazy Horse* and *Vanishing American* (1955). The "Cochise" and "Geronimo" films listed in fn. 45 belong with this group. *Seminole* (1953) is somewhat exceptional in its characterization of Osceola (Anthony Quinn) as an effective guerrilla fighter, suggesting a kinship with the sympathetic view of revolution in *Viva Zapata* (1952), in which Quinn also plays a guerrilla—see below, ch. 13. Samuel Fuller's *Run of the Arrow* (1957) deliberately inverts the convention requiring the death of the hero's Indian wife; and Aldrich's *Apache* (1954) is closer in spirit to *Devil's Doorway*—only here the Indian warrior makes a successful transition to peaceful farmer, with the aid of a good woman. Almost all of these films follow *Broken Arrow* by implicitly subordinating Indian values, interests, and racial traits to those of the best Whites. A film that captures the essentials of this approach is Walt Disney's *Tonka* (1958), which parallels the tale of an Indian boy and his wild horse: both are treated abusively by the boy's Indian stepfather, but after many vicissitudes, including Custer's Last Stand, they become permanent mascots of the 7th Cavalry. A similar mixture of "sympathy" for Indians and effective preference for Whites marks those films that deal with Whites raised as Indians (for example, *The Savage* [1952] and *Last Frontier* [1955]). This type of story usually ends up insisting that blood will tell, and the hero's choice of woman (as in Cooper) reconnects him to his race. Also compare the treatment of "half-breed" heroes, torn between loyalty to victimized Indians and "civilization"—for example Elvis Presley in *Flaming Star* (1960).

51. Other such films include *Duel at Diablo* (1966), *Sergeants Three* (1962) and *Red, White and Black* [*Soul Soldier*] (1970).

Notes to Chapter 12

1. For example, *Little Big Horn* and *Warpath* (1951).

2. The oedipal theme is also strong in Billy the Kid movies, especially *Parson and the Outlaw* (1957); *Left-Handed Gun* (1958); *One-Eyed Jacks* (1961); and *Pat Garrett and Billy the Kid* (1973). The first two *Billy the Kids* (1931 and 1941) show him as a noble innocent rather than a crazed juvenile.

3. *Rebel Without a Cause* (1955), a story of alienated teenagers which starred

James Dean, was Ray's most famous film, and the basis of both a new genre and a major star-cult. The postwar "James canon" includes: *The Outriders* (1950); *The Return of Jesse James* (1950); *Kansas Raiders* (1950); *Red Mountain* (1951); *Best of the Badmen* and *Great Missouri Raid* (1951); *Montana Belle* (1952); *San Antone* (1953); *The Stranger Wore a Gun* (1953); *The Woman They Almost Lynched* (1953); *Jesse James vs. the Daltons* (1954); *Jesse James' Women* (1953); *Dalton Girls* (1957); *The Lonely Man* (1957); *True Story of Jesse James* (1957); *Cole Younger, Gunfighter* (1958); *Quantrill's Raiders* (1958); *Young Jesse James* (1960); *Arizona Raiders* (1965); *Jesse James Meet Frankenstein's Daughter* (1966); *Great Northfield, Minnesota Raid* (1975); and *Long Riders* (1981). The last two portray Jesse as a psychopath. To this group might be added those that draw on Jesse James motifs to characterize the outlaw as social bandit: *Al Jennings of Oklahoma* (1951); *The Lawless Breed* (1952); *Way of a Gaucho* (1952); *Cimarron Kid* (1952); *Vanquished* (1953); *The Outcast* (1954); and *Seven Angry Men* (1955).

4. *The Pursued* and *Track of the Cat* were early essays in this form, but the possibilities of this approach were most strikingly developed during the 1950s in the Western (mainly "small" productions) of Budd Boetticher and Anthony Mann. See Jim Kitses, *Horizons West*, chs. 2, 3; Basinger, *Anthony Mann*, ch. 4.

5. The self-conscious sense of genre convention shows in Mann's organizing each episode of the quest around the theme or setting of a different subtype of Western, including the "town-tamer," the stagecoach journey, the outlaw Western, and the Cavalry/Indian Western.

6. Coppedge, *Henry King's America*, p. 117.

7. Eugene Cunningham, *Triggernometry: A Gallery of Gunfighters*, esp. pp. 1–11, ch. 18. Compare earlier thematic compilations, for ex. Appler, *Lives of the Guerrillas . . .* ; Buel, *Border Outlaws* and *Heroes of the Plains*. When Siringo was forced to suppress half of his memoirs in *Riata and Spurs*, he was able to replace it with biographies of famous outlaws.

8. Coppedge, *King*, pp. 115–7; Ramon F. Adams, *Six-Guns and Saddle Leather: A Bibliography of Books and Pamphlets on Western Outlaws and Gunmen*, pp. 66–7, 111, 317.

9. Brown, *No Duty to Retreat*, ch. 2, distinguishes "incorporation" gunfighters, hired by landowners and employers to kill or intimidate tenants and employees, and "grassroots" or "resister" gunfighters, who took up arms to defend themselves, their land, or their communities. However, neither type was identified in contemporary accounts as a "gunfighter," in the movies' sense of that term. See also Joseph G. Rosa, *The Gunfighter: Man or Myth?*, pp. v–vii, 5, 11, chs. 3–5, 13; Utley, *High Noon*, ch. 5; Mercer, *Banditti*; Peter Watts, *A Dictionary of the Old West*, p. 153.

10. C. L. Sonnichsen, *From Hopalong to Hud: Thoughts on Western Fiction*, pp. 41, 44, 54–5.

11. Coppedge, *King*, pp. 117–20.

12. The association of Ringo with the icon of the "Custer's Last Stand" lithograph extends the irony by suggesting a parallel between the gunfighter and the hero of the cavalry Western as symbols of American virtue and power.

13. Note the parallel with Brittles in *Yellow Ribbon*, who stretches the terms of his retirement and violates his orders when he assumes his last command.

14. Earlier versions of the Earp story include *Law and Order* (1931), and *Frontier Marshal* and *Dodge City* (1939). Ford's film was officially a remake of *Law and Order*; another remake with the same title appeared in 1953. See also *Gunfight at the OK Corral* (1957), *Warlock* (1959), and *Hour of the Gun* (1967). On *High Noon*, see Lenihan, *Showdown*, pp. 22–4, 117–22.

15. The barn scenes and the escape using stampeding horses are similar to scenes in *Gunfighter, My Darling Clementine*, and *Law and Order* (1931).

16. Shane can also be seen as an enlarged version of the conventional "lone cowboy" of the "B" Western who wanders from film to film like a chivalric knight-errant.

17. It is possible to see Shane as a Christ-figure who miraculously appears to save the farmers, sacrifices for them, is wounded in the side, and disappears—while his truest believer calls for him to make a second coming ("Come back!"). Whether or not this suggestion was intended, Clint Eastwood gives the story a distinctly Christological cast in *Pale Rider*, his own interpretation of the *Shane* story.

18. This was consistent with the novel on which the film was based: "He was the man who rode into our valley out of the heart of the great glowing West and when his work was done rode back whence he had come and he was Shane." Jack Schaefer, *Shane: The Critical Edition*, p. 274.

Notes to Chapter 13

1. Hodgson, *America*, Part I, and esp. chs. 4–5, 8; John Ranelagh, *The Agency: The Rise and Decline of the CIA*, pp. 227–38.

2. Douglas S. Blaufarb, *The Counterinsurgency Era: U.S. Doctrine and Performance*, pp. 15–16.

3. Blaufarb, *Counterinsurgency Era*, pp. 5, 11–5; Walter Laqueur, *Guerrilla: A Historical and Critical Study*, ch. 6; Sam C. Sarkesian, ed., *Revolutionary Guerrilla Warfare*, esp. Nathan Leites and Charles Wolf, Jr., "Selections from *Rebellion and Authority: An Analytic Essay on Insurgent Conflicts*," pp. 537*ff*.; V[ictor] H. Krulak, ed., *Studies in Guerrilla Warfare: Fighting Communist Guerrilla Movements, 1941–1961*, esp. chs. 22, 33, 36.

4. Weigley, *American Way of War*, ch. 15; George McT. Kahin, *Intervention: How America Became Involved in Vietnam*, p. 27; Hodgson, *America*, pp. 115–23.

5. Compare the cognitive theory of political decision-making developed in Yaacov Y. I. Vertzberger, *The World in Their Minds: Information Processing, Cognition, and Perception in Foreign Policy Decisionmaking*, chs. 1, 3, esp. pp. 111–27, 144–60.

6. The absence of the Philippines from both political and myth/ideological discourse is worth noticing. The Philippines never became a popular venue for either pulp or for movie heroism, despite the fact that the Islands were the site of recent (and recurrent) antiguerrilla campaigns. With the exception of *The Real Glory* (1939), I find no pre-war feature films dealing with Americans in the Philippines. Thereafter, the Philippines became a province of the mythic space of the combat film and in this form provided some preliminary versions of a counterinsurgency "genre"—*Back to Bataan* (1945), *An American Guerrilla in the*

Philippines (1950). *Huk* (1956) deals with the Philippine counterinsurgency operations of 1950–53. This neglect of the subject speaks of the weakness of imperialist ideology *per se* in American culture and politics: only when the imperialist project can be completely confounded with a "savage war" is it "popular." See also Theodore Roosevelt II, *Colonial Policies of the United States* (1938), pp. 195–8, which complains of the American public's lack of enthusiasm for colonial administration. It is also worth noting, as a symptom of popular dislike of blatant imperialism, that depcitions of American interventions in Latin America often took quite a cynical view of the role of Big Business in forcing these operations on the military. See for example, *The Cock Eyed World* (1929).

7. Ranelagh, *The Agency*, pp. 274–5.

8. On Mexico in nineteenth-century myth-ideology, see Slotkin, *Fatal Environment*, ch. 9, and pp. 228–36.

9. Representative titles include: *Eagle and the Hawk* (1950); *Wings of the Hawk* (1953); *Border River* and *Vera Cruz* (1954); *The Naked Dawn* and *The Treasure of Pancho Villa* (1955); *Bandido!* and *Santiago* (1956); *The Last of the Fast Guns* and *Villa!* (1958); *The Wonderful Country* and *They Came to Cordura* (1959); *The Magnificent Seven* (1960); *The Comancheros* (1961); *The Savage Guns* (1962); *Gringo* (1963); *A Fistful of Dollars* and *The Outrage* (1964); *Major Dundee* and *Murietta* (1965); *The Appaloosa, A Bullet for the General, Django, The Professionals*, and *Return of the Seven* (1966); *Bandolero!, Blue, Guns of the Magnificent Seven, 100 Rifles*, and *Villa Rides* (1968); *Butch Cassidy and the Sundance Kid, The Undefeated*, and *The Wild Bunch* (1969); *The Bounty Hunters, Cannon for Cordoba, Joaquin Murietta*, and *Two Mules for Sister Sara* (1970). The subject of American heroes in Mexico is also treated in cavalry Westerns (especially John Ford's *Fort Apache* [1948] and *Rio Grande* [1950] and *They Came to Cordura* [1959]), and in films dealing with the battle of the Alamo (*Davy Crockett, King of the Wild Frontier*, and *The Last Command* [1955], and *The Alamo* [1960]). Figures and images from these parallel subgenres were borrowed to enlarge "gunfighter" Mexico Westerns, particularly in post-escalation films like *The Professionals, Major Dundee*, and *The Wild Bunch*. The mixture of Quixotic heroism and racism in the character played by John Wayne in John Ford's *The Searchers* is suggested by his having been not only a veteran of the South's Lost Cause but of Maximilian's fight against Juarez.

10. Brownlow, *The War, The West*, pp. 87–105.

11. Allen L. Woll, *The Latin Image in American Film*, p. 8.

12. See above, pp. 247, 252–4.

13. Raoul Walsh's *Life of Villa* (1915) intercuts actual footage of Villa with scenes of a standard romantic melodrama shot in the studio. Brownlow, *The War, The West*, pp. 101–2.

14. Donald Smythe, *Guerrilla Warrior: The Early Life of John J. Pershing*, chs. 1, 4, 6, 10–11, 15–16.

15. Koszarski, *Hart*, p. 56; Woll, *Latin Image*, pp. 26–7. In *The Americano* (1916) an American mining engineer aids the ineffectual Mexican government by preventing revolutionaries from fomenting a miners' strike.

16. Woll, *Latin Image*, p. 13; Brownlow, *The War, The West*, pp. 87–105.

17. John E. O'Connor and Martin A. Jackson, eds., *American History/American*

Film: Interpreting the Hollywood Image, p. 186; John Steinbeck, *Viva Zapata!: The Original Screenplay*, Introduction by R. E. Morsberger; Ilene V. O'Malley, *The Myth of the Revolution: Hero Cults and the Institutionalization of the Mexican State, 1920–1940*, esp. chs. 1, 3, 5. On Zapata see James A. Womack, *Zapata and the Mexican Revolution*; for general history, William Weber Johnson, *Heroic Mexico: The Narrative History of a Twentieth Century Revolution.*

18. Brownlow, *The War, The West*, pp. 90–1.

19. *Ibid.*, p. 250; Blair Coan, *The Red Web*, pp. 1–2.

20. See also J. R. Mock and C. Larsen, *Words That Won the War: The Story of the Committee on Public Information, 1917–1919*, ch. 15. The use of Mexico or Latin America as the base for a race-based, Bolsehvik-led "revolt of the Under-Man" was also an important theme in pulp fiction. See for example Floyd Gibbons, *Red Napoleon* and compare it to the scenarios of revolution in Stoddard, *Revolt Against Civilization* and *Rising Tide*; Burroughs, *Moon Men*; and Nolan, *Armageddon, 2419 A.D.*

21. Woll, *Latin Image*, pp. 29–41. Outside the Western, "Mexico" appeared as a generic "Latin" country in musical comedies, and "Mexicans" occasionally figured in border-town crime dramas as either pathetic "wetbacks" or evil smugglers and racketeers.

22. Edgcumb Pinchon, *Viva Villa! A Recovery of the Real Pancho Villa, Peon . . . Bandit . . . Soldier . . . Patriot*; Woll, *Latin Image*, pp. 45–9; O'Connor, *American History/American Film*, pp. 164–5.

23. The kinship and compatibility of the two types of movie are suggested by *The Bad Man* (1941), in which Beery (in his "Villa" persona) makes a foray into the terrain of Jesse James, coming to the aid of an American rancher (Ronald Reagan) whose land is being stolen by land-grabbers. Another Villa film of the period is *Under Strange Flags* (1937).

24. Weigley, *American Way of War*, chs. 7, 14.

25. Despite its toughmindedness about class warfare, the movie's ending abandons both history and its own analysis of the logic of social revolution.

26. It was nominated for two Oscars, for its screenplay and as Best Picture. The title of 20th Century Fox studio's planned film on Zapata, *The Beloved Rogue*, suggests that they intended to treat Zapata in terms of the Beery/Villa stereotype. O'Connor, *American History/American Film*, pp. 184–8, 195–8.

27. O'Connor, *American History/American Film*, p. 184.

28. Juarez's own racial (Indian) character and his association with the Great Emancipator are the primary means through which *Juarez* links resistance to imperialism/fascism with a liberal or egalitarian approach to racial questions. However, it is worth noting that Hollywood uses this anti-racialist rhetoric only in the Mexican setting, where "radicalism" in general is permissible. In contemporary films set north of the border, Mexicans were still treated either as buffoons or as a racial enemy half-way between the outlaw and the Indian. For example, Warners' *Virginia City* (1940) shows Union and Confederate Anglos uniting to save a wagon train from Mexican raiders.

29. This idea was literalized in *Kansas Terrors* (1939), a "B" Western in which the Three Mesquiteers aid oppressed peasants and liberals in a generic Latin American country.

30. Anita Brenner, *The Wind That Swept Mexico*, "Publisher's Forward" and p. 3.

31. *Ibid., p.* 5.

32. *Ibid., pp.* 5–6.

33. *Ibid., p.* 9.

34. *Ibid., pp.* 73, 76, 101.

35. *Ibid., pp.* 41–44, 73, 101. Brenner puts "socialist" in quotation marks to indicate that Obregon's advisers were not excessively serious about their socialism.

36. O'Connor, *American History/American Film*, pp. 186–7. See Gallagher, *Ford*, pp. 220–1, for Merrian C. Cooper's affiliation.

37. O'Connor, *American History/American Film*, pp. 187–8.

38. *Ibid., pp.* 187–9, 197–8; Steinbeck, *Viva Zapata!*, pp. 140–2. Kazan had also been a friendly witness before HUAC, an event that required some intellecutal rationalization. Although Kazan and Steinbeck were systematic in their attempt to represent Zapata as a non-Communist rebel, the very idea of rebellion was still so closely identified with the left that it drew strong criticism from conservatives. The film's producer, Daryl Zanuck, was sufficiently queasy about Zapata's radical reputation to hedge the studio's bets by shortening the film's initial run. Nonetheless, *Viva Zapata!* was a commercial and critical success, garnering nominations for Best Picture, Best Actor, and Best Screenplay, and an Oscar for Quinn's supporting performance.

39. Hodgson, *America*, p. 95.

40. Steinbeck, *Viva Zapata!*, pp. xxv–xxx.

41. *Seminole* (1953) is somewhat exceptional in its characterization of Osceola (Anthony Quinn) as an effective guerrilla fighter, suggesting a kinship with the sympathetic view of revolution in *Viva Zapata!*, in which Quinn also played a guerrilla.

42. O'Connor, *American History/American Film*, pp. 197–8. Diaz had been portrayed in the 1939 production of *Juarez* by John Garfield, an actor identified with working-class roles and left-wing causes.

43. His Christ-likeness is presented ironically: the "Judas" who kisses Zapata before betraying him to his death identifies himself as "Jesus Guajarda."

44. Daniel Bell, *The End of Ideology*; Hodgson, *America*, ch. 4.

45. The mysterious and supernatural suggestions of a "Catholic" frame are particularly strong in the assassination and "deposition" scenes, in which stylized, hieratic groups of black-mantled praying women seem somehow to have foreseen the tragic events and begin a sacramental ritual of mourning almost before Zapata's death is enacted. This "Catholic" stylization cues our acceptance of mysteries, transformations, and miracles that we might otherwise see as superstitions or mystifications. Movies about Anglo outlaws and gunfighters often represent their heroes as enacting a sacrifice, which always suggests comparisons to Christ. But rarely is the imagery so explicit. Exceptions are the overt Christography in two Billy the Kid movies, *The Parson and the Outlaw* and *Left-Handed Gun* (1958). But in the latter film the identification is achieved by giving Billy roots in a Mexican community, marked like the Mexico of *Viva Zapata!* by stylized ritual and mystery.

46. Hodgson, *America*, esp. pp. 73, 77, 87, 94, 101, 115, 171; and Dwight MacDonald, "To the Whitehouse" (*NYRB*, 1963), reprinted in Robert B. Silvers and Barbara Epstein, eds., *Selections: From the First Two Issues of the* New York Review of Books, pp. 7–12.

47. Arthur M. Schlesinger, Jr., "On Heroic Leadership and the Dilemma of Strong Men and Weak Peoples," *Encounter* 15: 3–11, esp. 3–4, 7–8.

48. Lancaster and Aldrich took a deliberately revisionist approach to the genre in their first Western, *Apache*, and wanted to push their ideas further in *Vera Cruz*. Edwin T. Arnold and Eugene L. Miller, Jr., *The Films and Career of Robert Aldrich*, pp. 24–5.

49. *Eagle and the Hawk* has an interesting Cold War "secret agent" plot and features a set of character-types that became staples of the Mexico Western.

50. Blum, *V Was for Victory*, esp. chs. 1, 9; Ranelagh, *The Agency*, pp. 237–8; Kahin, *Intervention*, pp. 27–30; Weigley, *American Way of War*, ch. 15; Kahin, *Intervention*, p. 27. He was committed in principle to balanced budgets, and his inclination to thrift was reinforced by two significant economic recessions that punctuated Eisenhower's two terms (1953–4 and 1957–8).

51. Ranelagh, *The Agency*, pp. 237–8, 274.

52. *Ibid.*, pp. 193–4, 202–3, 224–7. On the CIA as an instrument of liberal ideology, see Ranelagh's portrayal of Cord Meyer, who saw CIA operations as the New Deal carried on by other means "a struggle for American liberalism in a world up for grabs."

53. William M. Leary, ed., *The Central Intelligence Agency: History and Documents*, pp. 143–5; Ranelagh, *The Agency*, chs. 3–4, 8–12.

54. Slotkin, *Fatal Environment*, p. 60.

55. On savage war, see Weigley, *American Way of War*, chs. 7–8; and compare Larry E. Cable, *Conflict of Myths: The Development of American Counterinsurgency Doctrine and the Vietnam War*, chs. 6, 9.

56. Slotkin, *Fatal Environment*, pp. 53–4, 59–61.

57. That tradition had been refurbished in the relatively recent past by wartime propaganda against Axis imperialism, and FDR made decolonization a war aim over the objections of Britain and France. On the other hand, Roosevelt's repudiation of American imperialism in Latin America under the Good Neighbor Policy had not precluded support of the 1934 Somoza *coup* in Nicaragua. Nonetheless, America's identification with anti-colonialism was strong enough in 1945 to make plausible Ho Chi Minh's appeal for American suport of Vietnamese independence from the French.

58. Kahin, *Intervention*, pp. 66–70, 73–4, 103. Dulles concealed the administration's intention to interpret the armistice line (the 17th Parallel) as a national boundary rather than as the temporary division of "regroupment zones" which the Geneva accords envisioned.

59. Ranelagh, *The Agency*, p. 238.

60. Edwin T. Arnold and Eugene L. Miller, Jr., *The Films and Career of Robert Aldrich*, pp. 31–6.

61. Hardy, *Western*, p. 236.

62. This film makes the use of black clothing to identify the gunfighter-as-

hero a standard icon, though the usage is not unprecedented, as for example in *Billy the Kid* (1941).

63. This is the original of a role he was to repeat and develop in another Mexico Western, *The Magnificent Seven* (1960), and in the "fifth wave" combat film, *The Dirty Dozen* (1967). The Polish soldier in *Bataan*'s platoon is also identified with Pittsburgh.

64. The latter film sees the American as having to choose between his allegiance to a tyrannical Mexican *patron* and the freedom of American citizenship. However, he does pass through an episode in which he acts as the protector of Mexican villagers from an Indian raid. Other films that use the Mexican setting in related ways are: *Border River* (1954), which plays a variation on the Civil War plot of *Eagle and the Hawk*; *The Naked Dawn* (1955) reduces the scale of the drama to a romance; and *They Came to Cordura* (1959), which uses the American Punitive Expedition against Villa in 1916 as backdrop for a drama of psychological and interpersonal conflict within an American platoon.

65. During the same period Mexican/American history was treated in a set of movies about the Alamo and the Texan War of Independence; but their handling of the material is sufficiently different to warrant separate discussion below.

Notes to Chapter 14

1. A good overall treatment of the development, theory, and practice of "nation-building" (and of its military counterpart, "counterinsurgency") as a model for American policy is D. Michael Shafer, *Deadly Paradigms: The Failure of U.S. Counterinsurgency Policy*; see also Blaufarb, *Counterinsurgency Era*, and Larry E. Cable, *Conflict of Myths*. Vertzberger, *World in Their Minds*, ch. 3 and pp. 265–6, 273–4, offers a useful theory of the role of myth/ideological presumptions in the decision-making process, and on the ways in which our understanding of and response to Vietnam decisions was shaped by a mythologized understanding of American history and the traditions of our "strategic culture" (i.e., the subculture of military planners and historians). On the economic side, see Robert Pakenham, *Liberal America and the Third World: Political Development Ideas in Foreign Aid and Social Science*; Hodgson, *America*, chs. 4, 6, 11. The classic statement of the theory is Walt Whitman Rostow, *The Stages of Economic Growth: A Non-Communist Manifesto* (1960).

2. Michael H. Hunt, *Ideology and U.S. Foreign Policy*, chs. 3, 5; Dean Rusk, *As I Saw It*, p. 423; Hodgson, *The Colonel: The Life and Wars of Henry Stimson, 1867–1950*, pp. 130–1, 171–2, 249–50, 260, 373.

3. The islanders figure as the subjects of liberating Americans, not as autonomous nationalists. See especially *The Bugle Sounds* (1942); *Bataan* (1943), esp. the relationship between the American and Filipino air force men; and the "shipyard" episodes in *They Were Expendable* (1945). Even in *Back to Bataan* (1945) and *American Guerrilla in the Philippines* (1950), it is the American who must convince the Filipino that his nation's cause requires a sacrifice of the selfish pride and interests of the clan or family.

4. Shafer, *Deadly Paradigms*, ch. 8; Blaufarb, *Counterinsurgency Era*, pp. 37,

39. "The major initiatives and strategies [in the campaign] were Magsaysay's."

5. *Ibid.*, pp. 23–4, 27–40.

6. Sheehan, *Bright and Shining Lie*, pp. 142–4; Shafer, *Deadly Paradigms*, chs. 8–9.

7. Not all of those associated with Lansdale and Magsaysay in the Philippines drew the wrong lessons from that experience. See Napoleon D. Valeriano and Charles T. R. Bohannan, *Counterguerrilla Operations: The Philippine Experience*, esp. pp. 89, 95, and chs. 6–7. This account by a Filipino civil-action soldier and an American anthropologist (and member of the advisory mission) insists that, in effective counterinsurgency, military measures are less important than the establishment of responsive and democratic local (and national) government, and that the exigencies of the "dirty war" to suppress the guerrillas are secondary to the political mission. Their account supports the critique developed by Blaufarb, Shafer, and Kahin.

8. Neil Sheehan, *A Bright and Shining Lie: John Paul Vann and America in Vietnam*, pp. 187–90; Kahin, *Intervention*, ch. 4.

9. Kahin, *Intervention*, esp. chs. 3–6, 9–10.

10. *Ibid.*, pp. 78–9.

11. *Ibid.*, p. 121; and see fn. 1, above.

12. The allusion is to Bertolt Brecht's characterization of the East German government's suppression of a revolt in 1953. See Summers, *On Strategy*, chs. 1, 3.

13. Cable, *Conflict of Myths*, pp. 133–4, 142–6.

14. *Ibid.*, pp. 147–8; and on political culture in Vietnam, Frances Fitzgerald, *Fire in the Lake: The Vietnamese and the Americans in Vietnam*, esp. chs. 1–4, 8–10, 14–5.

15. Cable, *Conflict of Myths*, pp. 145–8.

16. Sheehan, *Bright and Shining Lie*, p. 75; Drinnon, *Facing West*, ch. 24.

17. William J. Lederer and Eugene Burdick, *The Ugly American*, pp. 90–1; Rupert Wilkinson, "Connections with Toughness: The Novels of Eugene Burdick," *JAS* 11:2 (1977), pp. 223–40.

18. *Ibid.*, pp. 21–3.

19. George Armstrong Custer, *My Life on the Plains; or, Personal Experiences with Indians*, ed. by Edgar I. Stewart, pp. 19–22; Slotkin, *Fatal Environment*, pp. 409–12.

20. Lederer and Burdick, *Ugly American*, pp. 90–1; Sheehan, *Bright and Shining Lie*, pp. 75–6 and *ff*.

21. Lederer and Burdick, *Ugly American*, pp. 96–8. Second-generation immigrants (usually Italians or Jews, often from Brooklyn) and Texans are standard "types" in postwar platoon movies—for example, *Objective Burma*, which features a "Tex" as well as an Irishman and a Jew from Brooklyn; and *Walk in the Sun*, in which the same range of ethnic types all become "Texans" by serving in the "Texas Division." S.L.A. Marshall's *Pork Chop Hill* was published in 1953, movie version 1959.

22. Weigley, *American Way of War*, chs. 1–2, 18. To be fair, Lederer and Burdick emphasize the importance of using low-level technologies adapted to local conditions and to the peasants' state of education.

23. Walter Laqueur, *Guerrilla: A Historical and Critical Study*; Victor H. Krulak, *Studies in Guerrilla Warfare.*

24. Harry G. Summers, Jr., *On Strategy: The Vietnam War in Context*, pp. 94–5; Larry Berman, *Planning a Tragedy: The Americanization of the War in Vietnam*, pp. 135–8.

25. Shelby L. Stanton, *Green Berets at War*, pp. 11–22; Cable, *Conflict of Myths*, chs. 1, 6; Drinnon, *Facing West*, chs. 21–30.

26. Weigley, *American Way of War*, chs. 5, 6, 9, 13–4; Cable, *Conflict of Myths*, p. 113, "In many essential respects the creation of military doctrine is an exercise in highly selective historical interpretation."

27. See for example R. Ernest Dupuy and Trevor N. Dupuy, *The Military Heritage of America.*

28. Weigley, *American Way of War*, chs. 1–3, 8; Utley, *The Contribution of the Frontier to the American Military Tradition*; John William Ward, *Andrew Jackson: Symbol for an Age*; Slotkin, *Regeneration*, pp. 228–9; ———, *Fatal Environment*, pp. 77–8.

29. John Hellman, *American Myth and the Legacy of Vietnam*, ch. 2.

30. C. Robert Kemble, *The Image of the Army Officer in America: Background for Current Views*, ch. 6; Thomas C. Leonard, *Above the Battle: War-Making in America from Appomattox to Versailles*; and see for ex. Samuel Eliot Morison, *et al.*, *The Struggle for Guadalcanal, August 1942–February, 1943: History of United States Naval Operations in World War II*, p. 200, fn.

31. Marine counterinsurgency specialist General Victor Krulak asserted that the shift of forces from pacification to offensive operations in the hinterlands was a fatal error: "Every man we put into hunting the NVA was wasted." Quoted in Edward Doyle, *et al.*, *The Vietnam Experience: America Takes Over, 1965–67*, pp. 61–5. See also Hellman, *American Myth*, p. 45; Charles M. Simpson, *Inside the Green Berets, The First Thirty Years: A History of the U.S.*, pp. 22–3; Weigley, *American Way of War*, pp. 457–67.

32. Weigley, *American Way of War*, ch. 7; Slotkin, *Fatal Environment*, pp. 301–6, 316–24.

33. Cable, *Conflict of Myths*, p. 113; Weigley, *American Way of War*, pp. 466–7.

34. On savage war, see Weigley, *American Way of War*, chs. 7–8; Slotkin, *Fatal Environment*, pp. 53–4, 59–61. Compare Cable, *Conflict of Myths*, chs. 6, 9.

35. *Ibid.*, ch. 8, esp. 148–52.

36. *Ibid.*, pp. 114–5, 146–7, 151.

37. Like "ranger," "commando" originates in a savage and/or guerrilla war: the Boers of South Africa used *kommando* to describe the irregular companies of varying size and organization organized to fight the Zulu (and other indigenous nations) and to describe the similar guerrilla formations used against the British in the Boer War (1899–1902).

38. Francis J. Kelly, *Vietnam Studies: U.S. Army Special Forces, 1961–1971*, pp. 3–4.

39. Quoted in Hellmann, *American Myth*, pp. 46–8; Simpson, *Green Berets at War*, pp. 69–72; Miroff, *Pragmatic Illusions*, pp. 18–9; Tulis, *Rhetorical Presidency*, pp. 190–1.

40. Cable, *Conflict of Myths*, pp. 144, 147–8, 131–3. The commando skills that were the basis of Green Beret training were designed for the task of harassing the communications of an invading army with the aid of a friendly indigenous population. But the true guerrillas in the South did not have the kind of supply lines that could be disrupted by tactics like these, and the indigenous population was often neutral or hostile to the Americans and the Saigon troops.

41. *Ibid.*, p. 146.

42. Shelby L. Stanton, *Green Berets at War*, pp. 19, 21.

43. Kelly, *Vietnam Studies*, chs. 2–3, esp. pp. 19–28, 32–44.

44. The logic that drove the steady Americanization of the war was most eloquently stated by counterinsurgency specialist John Paul Vann—for example, in Sheehan, *Bright and Shining Lie*, pp. 540–2, 780.

45. Slotkin, *Fatal Environment*, pp. 130–1; and above.

46. Gallagher, *Ford*, pp. 244–5, 324–38, 340.

47. Compare similar spins when guns are re-holstered in *Gunfighter*, *Shane*, and *Vera Cruz* (especially by Erin).

48. The reference is to Pip's madness in *Moby-Dick*.

49. Gallagher, *Ford*, pp. 326–9, 335.

50. Susan Brownmiller, *Against Our Will: Men, Women and Rape*, pp. 140–53; Slotkin, *Regeneration*, ch. 5.

51. Slotkin, *Fatal Environment*, pp. 401–4. Also spelled "Blinn." A similar attitude toward the nominal "rescue object" appears in two notorious domestic rescue operations of the Vietnam period: the suppression of the Attica prison riot (1971), and the attack on the "Symbionese Liberation Army" terrorists who had kidnaped Patricia Hearst (1974). In both cases the use of police force was criticized as either premature or excessive, and as likely to kill as to rescue the captives. The value of the captives' lives was diminished by the suggestion that they had been "polluted" during their captivity: that Hearst had been transformed by sexual congress (coërced at first, later perhaps consensual) into a member of the gang that raped her; and that the Attica hostages had suffered a "fate worse than death" (homosexual rape by prisoners) and were—like Mrs. Blynn—better off dead. I have referred to contemporary accounts of these incidents in *Newsweek* and *Time*. On Attica, see Tom Wicker, *A Time to Die*; on Hearst, Shana Alexander, *Anyone's Daughter*, and coverage in *Time* and *Newsweek*, 1974.

52. The Indians at the Washita were Cheyenne, not Comanche. However, several features link Ford's battle to the Washita: it occurs in Indian Territory, in the wintertime; it involves the massacre of Indians, including women and children, and the slaughter of the Indian pony-herd; and the theme-music for the cavalry passage is "Garry Owen," theme song of Custer's 7th Cavalry, which the bandsmen played during the Washita attack. Although no captives were rescued at the Washita, there was a general return of captives after Custer's follow-up campaign in the spring and summer of 1870.

53. See above, ch. 2, fn. 29.

54. Sympathetic portrayals were: *Tonka* (1958), discussed above; *Oklahoma Territory* (a "B" film) and *Geronimo* (1962). Elvis Presley's portrayal of a half-

breed in *Flaming Star* (1960) is more of a "civil rights" Western in the vein of *Walk Like a Dragon* than a cavalry/Indian Western.

55. See especially Ford's *Sergeant Rutledge* (1960); *Sergeants Three* (1962); and *Duel at Diablo* (1966).

56. The blurb for *Phu Nham*, a novel by Barry Sadler (who wrote the hit "Ballad of the Green Beret"), describes the hero as follows: "An American sniper with the highest record of confirmed hits, as deadly and effective as an M–16, he roams the Vietnam jungle with hate in his heart and blood on his hands. His mission is to strike at the Vietcong—one by one, caravan by caravan—with such skillful precision that the enemy would come to fear him as death itself." And see pp. 24, 228–9.

57. The sequels and imitations are listed with the "Mexico Westerns" in fn. 8, above. *The Dirty Dozen* and its several imitators owe something to both the concept and the style of *The Magnificent Seven*; the made-for-TV *Battle Beyond the Stars* (1982) is a science-fiction version.

58. See Noble, *Historians Against History*, esp. chs. 3–5, 7–8. The populist outlaw films are a partial exception, but outlaws treated as a disadvantaged interest group (farmers) rather than a social class in the Marxist sense.

59. This is also an instance of his "*Christ*-likeness": he will save those who give "everything"—all earthly wealth as well as faith.

60. For example, *Viva Villa!* (1935); *Eagle and the Hawk* (1950); *Viva Zapata!* (1952). *Vera Cruz* (1954) costumes its revolutionary general as a bandit, and the leading spokesman for the cause is a female pickpocket.

61. If Chris = Christ, then Calvera = Calvary; but the allegory (if it is one) is inverted here: Calvera is martyred by Chris, who suffers but survives.

62. Lyndon Baines Johnson, "American Policy in Vietnam," quoted in Marcus Raskin and Bernard B. Fall, eds., *The Viet-Nam Reader*, pp. 343–50.

63. Stanley Karnow, *Vietnam: A History*, pp. 582–3, 588–9, 591–7, 600–2, 652–6.

64. It is probably fortuitous that the "A-Teams," which were the operational units of Green Beret missions, consisted of an officer and six sergeants. Stanton, *Green Berets at War*, pp. 19, 21.

Notes to Chapter 15

1. On the intellectual origins and policies of the New Frontier, see Hodgson, *America*, chs. 4–6, 24; Drinnon, *Facing West*, pp. 429*ff*.; Bruce Miroff, *Pragmatic Illusions: The Presidential Politics of John F. Kennedy*, *passim*, but esp. pp. 35–6 and ch. 1. On the issue of "style," Hodgson, *America*, ch. 6, esp. p. 117; Parmet, *JFK*, pp. 33, 72–3; Halford Ross Ryan, *American Rhetoric from Roosevelt to Reagan: A Collection of Speeches and Critical Essays*, pp. 155–168; and Jeffrey K. Tulis, *The Rhetorical Presidency*, esp. chs. 1, pp. 190–1. On Kennedy's characteristic approaches to decision-making, Vertzberger, *World in Their Minds*, pp. 154, 300–3.

2. Parmet, *JFK*, pp. 50, 53, 96–7, 354 and ch. 11.

3. See "Introduction," above.

4. Quoted in Drinnon, *Facing West*, p. 429; and see Miroff, *Pragmatic Illusions*, p. 35: "Our frontiers today are on every continent. . . ."

5. Parmet, *JFK*, pp. 241, 245; Hodgson, *America*, pp. 78–9, 466–80.

6. *Ibid.*, ch. 4.

7. In 1951 Walter Prescott Webb, Turner's most eminent disciple, had argued that the age of frontier-style development (through the discovery and exploitation of vast untapped resources) was past, and that visions of a "new frontier" were likely to be chimerical and likely to take policy in unproductive directions. (Webb, *Divided We Stand: The Crisis of a Frontierless Democracy*; and Walter J. Rundell, Jr., "W. P. Webb's *Divided We Stand*: A Publishing Crisis," *WHQ* 13:4 (1982), pp. 391–408. By the mid–1960s Turnerian development theory had been revised in ways that made a renewal of the kind of explosive growth and individual upward mobility associated with frontiers seem feasible. For the revision of Turner's theory, see Billington, *America's Frontier Heritage*, ch. 1; and on industrial "abundance" as a substitute frontier, David M. Potter, *People of Plenty: Economic Abundance and the American Character*. For a critique of Potter's thesis, see Hodgson, *America*, pp. 74–5, 86–90, 478–90, 486–7. On the rejection of Marxist approaches and the emergence of the "consensus" school of American historians, see Hodgson, *America*, p. 95; Noble, *End of American History*, ch. 5; William Appleman Williams, *The Great Evasion: An Essay on the Contemporary Relevance of Karl Marx* . . .

8. The most elaborate working-out of this metaphor is Seymour Martin Lipset, *The First New Nation* (1963); Hodgson, *America*, pp. 80–1.

9. Thomas G. Paterson, *Kennedy's Quest for Victory: American Foreign Policy, 1961–1963*, pp. 12–14, 233–8; Hodgson, *America*, pp. 469–71. Walt Whitman Rostow, *The Stages of Economic Growth: A Non-Communist Manifesto* (1960), lays out the theoretical grounding of the approach to Third World development.

10. Drinnon, *Facing West*, pp. 360–4; Alden T. Vaughan, *New England Frontier: Puritans and Indians 1620–1675*, pp. 322–8. And compare Samuel Eliot Morison, in his introduction to a study of King Philip's War published in 1958, in Douglas Edward Leach, *Flintlock and Tomahawk: New England in King Philip's War*, pp. ix–x: "Behind King Philip's War was the clash of a relatively advanced race with savages, an occurrence not uncommon in history. The conquering race (and this is as true of the Moslems and Hindus as of Christians) always feels duty-bound to impose its culture upon the native . . . [who] in the end is either absorbed or annihilated, the only compromise being a miserable existence on a 'reservation.' "

11. Drinnon, *Facing West*, p. 355.

12. Samuel Eliot Morison, *Oxford History of the American People*, p. 1090.

13. Raskin and Fall, *Vietnam Reader*, pp. 152–3, 343–50, esp. 347–50. This is not to say that the Communist movement was a "good thing" in itself, or that its victory was desired by all Vietnamese; only that the Vietminh represented a powerful and authentically indigenous political tendency whose appeal was indeed "rational"—if only in Vietnamese terms.

14. Drinnon, *Facing West*, p. 371. This bias is most vividly expressed in an exchange between SAC commander Curtis LeMay and National Security Adviser

McGeorge Bundy: to LeMay's demand that "We should bomb them into the Stone Age" Bundy replied, "But they're already there."

15. *Ibid.*, pp. 366–7.

16. Scott Leavitt, "The Far-Off War in Vietnam We Have Decided to Win," *Life*, March 16, 1962, pp. 36–45.

17. Drinnon, *Facing West*, pp. 366–7.

18. Kahin, *Intervention*, p. 140.

19. *Ibid.*, p. 142; Sheehan, *Bright and Shining Lie*, pp. 206–8, 262–5.

20. Sheehan, *Bright and Shining Lie*, pp. 67–8.

21. Drinnan, *Facing West*, p. 355.

22. *Ibid.*, pp. 366–7; Paterson, *Kennedy's Quest*, pp. 13–4, 107–8, 110–3, 118–9; Sheehan, *Bright and Shining Lie*, p. 340.

23. Kahin, *Intervention*, pp. 143–4, 188–9, 190–3, 201.

24. Drinnon, *Facing West*, chs. 23–9, gives a compendious account of the use of frontier imagery.

25. Drinnon, *Facing West*, pp. 368–9; Kahin, *Intervention*, pp. 140–1.

26. *Ibid.*, p. 368.

27. Raskin and Fall, *Vietnam Reader*, p. 344.

28. Drinnon, *Facing West*, p. 369.

29. Quoted in Hellman, *American Myth*, pp. 46–8; Simpson, *Green Berets at War*, pp. 69–72; Miroff, *Pragmatic Illusions*, pp. 18–9; Tulis, *Rhetorical Presidency*, pp. 190–1.

30. Drinnon, *Facing West*, p. 435, quoting 1975 testimony. According to Ray Cline, a CIA official involved in the assassination program, "The Russians had cowboys around everywhere, and that meant we had to get ourselves a lot of cowboys if we wanted to play the game." Cline was to become a fixture in covert operations under both official and private cover down to and including the Iran/Contra affair, whose leadership cadre were also called "cowboys." See Russell Watson, *et. al.*, " 'Project Recovery': A handful of 'cowboys' leads Reagan into the biggest blunder of his presidency," *Newsweek* (Dec. 1, 1986), pp. 26–37.

31. Hugh Sidey, "The Presidency," *Life*, Oct. 10, 1969, p. 4.

32. Hodgson, *America*, chs. 8, 11; Drinnon, *Facing West*, p. 372; Lyndon Baines Johnson, "American Policy in Vietnam," in Raskin and Fall, *Vietnam Reader*, pp. 343–50.

33. *Ibid.*, pp. 13–4, 107–8, 110–3, 118–9; Kahin, *Intervention*, pp. 121, 126, 129–32, 135–6; Parmet, *JFK*, pp. 137–8, 213–5, 222, 219, 223–4. The ambiguous mixture of benevolent intent and implicit preference for military solutions is inadvertently suggested by the misquotation of Shakespeare, *King Lear*, "I shall do such things—What they are I know not,—but they shall be / The wonders [*sic* terror] of the earth." (Parmet, *JFK*, p. 8).

34. See below.

35. See for example the 1988 *Times Mirror* survey of the American electorate, which found that Kennedy was considered a "hero" by eight of eleven significant voting groups, representing 71 percent of the adult population. The only groups that did not name Kennedy were the two most right-wing categories (21 percent of the adult population) and a group called "Disaffecteds" who had "no heroes." Norman Ornstein, Andrew Kohut, and Larry McCarthy, *The People, the Press,*

and Politics: The Times Mirror Study of the American Electorate, pp. 13–17. On Kennedy's style and its lingering presence in mass-media symbolism, see for example John Wayne's iconic invocation of Kennedy's name at the beginning of *The Green Berets*; and Tom Mathews, "The Sixties Complex," *Newsweek* (September 5, 1988), pp. 17–21, esp. "Toughness vs. Goodness," p. 18.

36. *Ibid.*, pp. 72–3; Hodgson, *America*, p. 121; Miroff, *Pragmatic Illusions*, pp. 35–6, ch. 4.

37. *Ibid.*, pp. 35–6.

38. Schlesinger, "On Heroic Leadership," p. 10. See also Parmet, *JFK*, pp. 3–4, 33; Miroff, *Pragmatic Illusions*, chs. 1–3; and Tulis, *Rhetorical Presidency*, pp. 190–1.

39. Godfrey Hodgson, *America in Our Time*, chs. 4, 5, 8, and see for example Sheehan, *Bright and Shining Lie*, p. 107. Philip French, *Westerns: Aspects of a Genre*, pp. 28–31, develops a typology of postwar Westerns based on different presidential styles; Lenihan, *Showdown*, ties innovations in Western form and style to specific Cold War issues.

40. Robert Frost, "For *John F. Kennedy, His Inauguration* . . . Gift Outright of 'The Gift Outright,' " *In the Clearing*, pp. 28–31.

41. Parmet, *JFK*, pp. 8, 10.

42. Hodgson, *America*, pp. 118, 132–3.

43. Parmet, *JFK*, p. 88.

44. Hodgson, *America*, pp. 132–3.

45. Kahin, *Intervention*, pp. 126–9, 132. A 1978 study of the use of force as a political instrument found that Kennedy's administration averaged 13 such uses per year; this contrasts with an average of 4 per year for Truman, 7 per year for Eisenhower, and 5 per year for Johnson, Nixon, and Ford. However, absolute levels of military violence (as opposed to number and variety of uses) were greatest under LBJ and Nixon, who presided over the heaviest combat in Vietnam. Barry Blechman and Stephen S. Kaplan cited in Paterson, *Kennedy's Quest*, pp. 5, 10, 14–5; Miroff, *Pragmatic Illusions*, pp. 14–21; Stanton, *Green Berets at War*, pp. 18–9.

46. Parmet, *JFK*, p. 4.

47. Schlesinger's major historical works on the presidency are *The Age of Jackson* and the three volumes of *The Age of Roosevelt* (*Crisis of the Old Order*, *The Coming of the New Deal*, and *The Politics of Upheaval*). His essays on presidential power written in preparation for and during the 1960 presidential campaign are collected in *The Politics of Hope*; his history of the Kennedy administration is *A Thousand Days*. On Schlesinger's intellectual role in the New Frontier, see Hodgson, *America*, pp. 73, 77, 94, 101–1, 115, 124–5; and Dwight MacDonald, "To the Whitehouse," in Robert B. Silvers and Barbara Epstein, eds., *Selections: from the First Two Issues of the New York Review of Books*, pp. 7–11.

48. Schlesinger, "On Heroic Leadership," esp. pp. 3–4, 9–11.

49. *Ibid.*, p. 9.

50. MacDonald, "To the Whitehouse," pp. 10–11.

51. Schlesinger, "On Heroic Leadership," p. 4.

52. Schlesinger acknowledges (*ibid.*, p. 10) that the making of the leadership myth involves a falsification of the man and the role and a degree of cynical

manipulation. But these are to be accepted on pragmatic grounds, as necessary to the effective functioning of the leader. Indeed, cynicism in respect to his own "public myth" is the democratic leader's saving grace: "The first rule of democracy is to distrust all leaders who begin to believe their own publicity." Compare William H. McNeill, "The Care and Repair of Public Myth," *Foreign Affairs* (Fall, 1982), pp. 1–13, and see below.

53. *Ibid.*, p. 8.

54. Hodgson, *America*, p. 121. It was arguably the model of leadership praised by Kennedy in *Profiles in Courage*, a series of sketches in which Senators prove their moral heroism by acting against the will of the majority of their constituents or colleagues.

55. Parmet, *JFK*, p. 8.

56. Hodgson, *America*, p. 153, ch. 5.

57. Hellmann, *American Myth*, p. 44; Terrence Maitland, *et al.*, *The Vietnam Experience: Raising the Stakes*, p. 12.

58. Parmet, *JFK*, pp. 221–4; Paterson, *Kennedy's Quest*, "Introduction," pp. 107–8, 110–3, 118–9, and ch. 5 on Cuba.

59. Cook, *History of Narrative Film*, pp. 422–6.

60. A representative list includes: musicals—*Oklahoma* (1955), *Porgy and Bess* (1959), *West Side Story* (1961); Bible and "Roman"—*The Ten Commandments* (1956), *Ben Hur* (1960), *Spartacus* (1960), *Cleopatra* (1963), and *Fall of the Roman Empire* (1964); Westerns—*The Alamo* (1960) and *How the West Was Won* (1963); Victorian empire—*Lawrence of Arabia* (1962), *Fifty-five Days at Peking* (1962), *Khartoum* (1964), and *Zulu* (1965); best-seller—*Exodus* (1960). A new genre was the "documentary" epic, inaugurated in 1960–2 by the production of *The Longest Day*, an elaborate recreation of the Normandy invasion—a "blockbusterization" of the combat film based on a best-selling work of nonfiction.

61. Heston's "epic" credits include: *Ten Commandments* (1956); *Ben-Hur* (1959); *El Cid* (1961); *55 Days at Peking* (1962); *Khartoum* (1964); *The Agony and the Ecstasy* (1965); and *Planet of the Apes* (1968). The irony of the hero's situation in *El Cid* and *Khartoum* is exactly that alluded to by Kennedy in his first address to Congress, in which he quoted Winston Churchill's lament "that the techniques of a harsh and repressive system should be able to instill discipline and ardor in its servants—while the blessings of liberty have too often stood for privilege, materialism and a life of ease." Parmet, *JFK*, p. 87. Compare T. Roosevelt's animadversions on the "slothful ease" of the American middle classes in "Strenuous Life," above, pp. 37, 51–3.

62. Compare the conversion of "hostiles" to "Friendlies" by a "man who knows Indians," Slotkin, *Regeneration*, 157–9; ——— and Folsom, *So Dreadfull*, 370–90.

63. Parmet, *JFK*, pp. 308–16; Kahin, *Intervention*, p. 287; Raskin and Fall, *Vietnam Reader*, pp. 22–30, 39–46, 180–1. In this same year (1962) the year "Man from Uncle" premiered on TV, pairing a Russian and an American spy against a fanatical war-mongering organization called "THRUSH." In 1965 a Louis Harris poll revealed that 53 percent of the American public considered China to be the driving force behind North Vietnamese attacks, and that on the whole "The American people feel that China is testing our will" in Vietnam.

64. Since the Boxers attack soon after, it might be argued that the Englishman is correct in his criticism of Lewis's methods. The script is certainly sympathetic to this character. But on balance, I think it means to suggest that a little more direct and forceful action earlier on might have prevented the Boxers' gaining such wide influence.

65. The paternal ideology is articulated in the most appealing terms by the priest, who softly rebukes the Major's attempt to wash his hands of the child by saying: "Every man is the father of every child." The priest's character has great authority, because he combines features of the "man who knows Indians" (i.e., Chinese), the soldier, and the man of "love." The "fighting priest" was already an important figure in the literature and journalism of counterinsurgency: the Rev. Thomas Dooley enjoyed some celebrity in the late 1950s for his books on his missionary and anti-Communist work in Southeast Asia; *The Ugly American* included a "fighting priest" among its pantheon of heroes, and in March 1962 the original of this figure was featured in a picture-spread in *Life*. See Leavitt, "The Far-Off War in Vietnam," pp. 36–45, esp. p. 43; and on Dooley's *Deliver Us from Evil* (1956), see Hellmann, *American Myth*, pp. 13–5.

66. Casting choices are interesting. Yung-lo is played by a well-known British character in "yellow-face"; among Gardner's most celebrated roles was her performance as a "tragic mulatto" in the musical *Showboat*.

67. See, for example, the scense dealing with the failed attempt of the hero's friend to summon aid, and the revelation of his death during a conference in the Khan's/Mahdi's tent.

68. On Lorenz and Ardrey, see Chase, *Legacy*, pp. 349, 394–5, 463.

69. Robert Ardrey, *The Social Contract: A Personal Enquiry into the Evolutionary Sources of Order and Disorder*, pp. 63–5, 56–61; ———, *The Territorial Imperative: A Personal Inquiry into the Animal Origins of Property and Nations*, pp. 31, 34–6. However, it is equally important to note Ardrey's assignment of a *comparable* (though not equal) power to the Mahdi. The racialism of American myth and ideology in the 1960s reflects both the persistence of traditional racialist myths and a new and highly self-conscious commitment to the principle of racial tolerance. Thus Ardrey engages in some rather torturous argument to absolve his theories of bigotry—arguing (for example) that the low condition of African-Americans is not the sign of an innate inferiority but the consequence of their unwilling transfer from a "jungle" environment to which their gifts were well adapted, to an urban setting where those "jungle" gifts are useful only in athletics and crime. The argument itself clearly does not escape the onus of racialism, but the expressed desire to evade the taint of racism testifies to a new consciousness of and critical response to racism as an aspect of American society and culture.

70. William Manchester, *The Death of a President, November 20–November 25, 1963*, pp. 1–52, 621–47.

71. See for example, Roger Hilsman, *To Move a Nation: The Politics of Foreign Policy in the Administration of John F. Kennedy*, esp. pp. 577–82; and fn. 35, above.

72. Emanuel Levy, *John Wayne: Prophet of the American Way of Life*, pp. xvi, xvii, 17.

73. P. F. Kluge, "First and Last, a Cowboy/Half myth and half movie star, John Wayne rides a lost frontier," *Life* (January 28, 1972), pp. 42, 44, 45.

74. *Ibid.*, p. 46.

75. See fns. 10, 13, and 23, above.

76. The explanations of Wayne's civilian status offered by his admiring biographers are contradictory. Levy and others agree that enlistment was impossible for Wayne because of an old football injury, but few consider that explanation sufficient in itself. Levy asserts that as a father of four, Wayne was "Beyond the reach of the armed forces"; another declares that he was (at 34) too old for the draft, which was not the case. In any case, age and parenthood were no barriers to enlistment: Ronald Reagan, two years older than Wayne, enlisted and served stateside. Tomkies asserts that Wayne was "rejected," which implies an attempt at enlistment; and Levy confuses the issue by asserting that "Even the connections of John Ford . . . did not help to get him drafted." Levy does not actually say that Ford made such an attempt; and in any case, one did not need connections to get drafted, although they might be useful in getting around medical rejection of an attempted enlistment. The attempts at apology are more remarkable than the facts of the case: without the identification of myth and man, there would be nothing extraordinary in the refusal to enlist of a man in his mid-thirties with a bad knee and a large family to support, whose government has formally recognized his problems by assigning him a low draft priority. Levy, *John Wayne*, pp. 23–4; George Carpozi, *The John Wayne Story*, p. 75; Mike Tomkies, *Duke: The Story of John Wayne*, p. 60.

77. Levy, *John Wayne*, pp. 39–40; Gallagher, *Ford*, p. 256.

78. Jeanine Basinger, "John Wayne, An Appreciation," *American Film* (1976), pp. 50–3.

79. Levy, *John Wayne*, pp. 112, 115, 313.

80. *Last Command* is not an epic like *The Alamo*. Its story-line centers on Jim Bowie rather than Crockett, and its plot hinges on the supposed friendship of Bowie and Santa Anna. But there are strong echoes in characterization and even dialogue, especially in the romantic exchanges between Bowie (*Last Command*) and Crockett (*Alamo*) and the female lead on the subject of love and marriage.

81. Levy, *John Wayne*, pp. 313–4.

82. *Ibid.*, pp. 314–6. Compare the hostility evinced by "hawks" like Rostow and Bundy toward "intellectuals," Miroff, *Pragmatic*, 5–6, 15–9.

83. Wayne had originally intended to stay behind the cameras and was pressured into starring by the film's backers; but once in, he gave himself the best role, the best lines, and the best camera angles.

84. Disney's treatment of Crockett also informed the handling of the character in Republic's *Last Command*. Between the TV series, the Disney movie, and Republic's film there were three "Crockett at the Alamo" treatments in less than two years. Margaret J. King, "The Recycled Hero: Walt Disney's Davy Crockett," in Michael J. Lofaro, ed., *Davy Crockett: The Man, the Legend, the Legacy, 1786–1986*.

85. In fact, Houston begged Travis to abandon the Alamo and join his command, and Travis refused for reasons that were in part political.

86. Levy, *John Wayne*, pp. 316–7.

87. Kluge, "First and Last, a Cowboy," p. 43: ". . . every John Wayne picture

is a new chapter . . . in a book that is already a classic. . . . His career . . . has made him, in fact, into something considerably larger than it, or him: an authentic American legend, a man who ties together strands of dreams and nostalgia for us simply by existing." Roles referred to are those in *Stagecoach, Fort Apache/Rio Grande, Back to Bataan, Red River, Sands of Iwo Jima.*

88. Levy, *John Wayne*, chs. 9–10, pp. 19, 208; Basinger, *World War II Combat Film*, pp. 192–3.

89. Richard Schickel, "Duke Packs a Mean Punch," *Life* (August 4, 1967). p. 8. Compare Miroff, *Pragmatic Illusions*, ch. 1, on JFK as "An Existential Hero?"

90. A 1969 issue of *Life* set Wayne off against Dustin Hoffman as stars offering of "A Choice of Heroes" to the American public (right/tough-minded vs. left-liberal). *Newsweek*, March 1, 1965; "John Wayne Rides Again," *Life* (May 7, 1965), pp. 69–70; John Dominis, "Dusty and the Duke," *Life* (July 11, 1969), pp. 36–45; Hemingway, "John Wayne at 60," *Time* (June 9, 1967), p. 67. J. Barthel, "John Wayne, Superhawk," *NYT Magazine* (February 24, 1967), pp. 4–5; and reply, in *ibid.* (January 14, 1968). A *Time* story published on the eve of his Academy Award nomination in 1969 hailed "John Wayne as the Last Hero" and offered admiring quotations from political conservatives and spokesmen of the New Left. *Time*, July 8, 1969, pp. 53–6.

91. Levy, *John Wayne*, p. 226.

92. Sheehan, *Bright and Shining Lie*, p. 117.

93. Quoted in Levy, *John Wayne*, p. 226.

94. Robert Jay Lifton, *Home From the War: Vietnam Veterans, Neither Victims Nor Executioners*, pp. 219–20, 231–6, 249–57; Edward Doyle, *et al.*, *The Vietnam Experience: American Takes Over, 1965–67*, pp. 19–20.

95. Levy, *John Wayne*, pp. 326–7.

96. *Ibid.*, p. 319.

97. Berman, *Planning a Tragedy*, pp. 125–6, 146–7. But Johnson's approach did more than falsify the language of politics: it also entailed a refusal to take the kinds of political action that would have given his pretenses away, such as calling up the Reserves or proposing a wartime tax increase. These refusals would ultimately distort the military effort and damage the nation's fiscal structure.

98. Levy, *John Wayne*, pp. 319–26; Eyles, *John Wayne and the Movies*, pp. 217–21.

99. Simpson, *Green Berets at War*, p. 124; Robin Moore, *The Green Berets*, p. 30; Hellmann, *American Myth*, ch. 2. Wayne and his writers based their scenario on information gathered from military advisers, government officials and publications, and journalistic accounts. Their fictional source for characters and incidents used in the film was Robin Moore's best-selling novel, *The Green Berets* (1965); but Moore's book was also based on interviews with Special Forces veterans. It referred to real individuals by fictional names and contained fictionalized episodes reported to Moore or his assistants as having actually occurred.

100. Kahin, *Intervention*, p. 290.

101. Sheehan, *Bright and Shining Lie*, pp. 101, 105, 308; Guenter Lewy, *America in Vietnam*, pp. 29–30.

102. Levitt, "Far-Off War," pp. 36–45, esp. p. 36; and see Table of Contents note, p. 5.

103. See above.

104. Kelly, *Vietnam Studies*, p. 86. Compare "self-reliance" theme in Stanton, *Green Berets at War*, pp. 19, 21.

105. Sheehan, *Bright and Shining Lie*, p. 579; Michael Casey, *et al.*, *The Vietnam Experience: Flags into Battle*, pp. 102, 122, 124, 131; S. L. A. Marshall, *Battles in the Monsoon: Campaigning in the Central Highlands, South Vietnam, Summer 1966*, pp. 25, 82; Richard K. Betts, *Soldiers, Statesmen, and Cold War Crises*, pp. 136–7; "Cavalry Charge to Khe Sanh by Road and Chopper," *Life* (April 19, 1968), pp. 82–3. A covert operation in Cambodia (1967) involving an American team with native auxiliaries was code-named "Daniel Boone." John Prados, *Presidents' Secret Wars: CIA and Pentagon Covert Operations from World War II Through Iranscam*, p. 300.

106. Stanton, *Green Berets at War*, pp. 19, 21.

107. Compare the ironic suggestion that, as we learn to fight a "dirty enemy" like the Nazis, we become Nazi-like ourselves, in films like *Dirty Dozen* and *Play Dirty* (1968).

108. Simpson, *Inside the Green Berets*, pp. 25–7, 124.

109. *Ibid.*, p. 124; Hellmann, *American Myth*, pp. 57–63; Moore, *Green Berets*, pp. 30–2, ch. 5.

110. Levy, *John Wayne*, pp. 292–4; Kluge, "First and Last, A Cowboy," p. 46.

111. Simpson, *Inside the Green Berets*, pp. 27–9; Donald Duncan, *The New Legions*, pp. 152–5, 166–9. Neither Moore nor Wayne acknowledges the other ethnic group which, with the "Foreign Legion" types, gave the early Special Forces their unique character: the relatively large number of Asians, Asian-Americans, and Hawaiians. It is interesting that in this war against Asians, Asian-Americans are excluded from the all-American platoon. The platoon also omits Jews and Italians, two standard constituents of the combat-film cast of types.

112. Berman, *Planning a Tragedy*, pp. 94, 109; Kahin, *Intervention*, pp. 351, 375, 376, 378, 395. Compare with *Life*'s handling of the race-war theme in its treatment of MacArthur in the Philippines, pp. 320 above.

113. Summers, *On Strategy*, esp. 21–9.

114. Johnson, "American Policy in Vietnam," in Raskin and Fall, *Vietnam Reader*, pp. 344–6.

115. James William Gibson, *The Perfect War: Technowar in Vietnam*, pp. 179–86.

116. Sheehan, *Bright and Shining Lie*, pp. 101–2, 107, 115–6.

117. The fantasy also owes something to Tex Wolchek's raid in *The Ugly American*.

118. Wayne's tactical fantasies combine elements that belonged to distinctly different phases of the war: the formative 1962–63 period, covered in Moore's novel, during which the insurgency received minimal support from the North; the 1964–5 period, during which the North increased its levels of support, and the "Mike" forces referred to in the film were first formed; and the 1965–7 period, during which American escalation was matched by the increased en-

gagement of North Vietnamese regulars (the "NVA"). Eyles, *Wayne*, p. 221, gives 1963 as the setting, but the "Mike" forces described in the film were not formed until 1964 (Simpson, *Inside the Green Berets*, pp. 127–30, 141). Moreover, the heavy involvement by NVA regulars described in the film did not become common until after 1965. The conflation of different epochs serves the propaganda purposes of the film by visualizing the administration's thesis that the insurgency was from the start an act of aggression by the North, analogous to the Axis aggressions of the late 1930s and the invasion of South Korea in 1950.

119. Sheehan, *Bright and Shining Lie*, pp. 617, 620–1, 544; 683–4; 635–8; Stanley Karnow, *Vietnam: A History*, chs. 12–3; William R. Corson, *The Betrayal*, is a personal account and critique of big-unit warfare and attrition strategy by a counterinsurgency specialist.

120. Karnow, *Vietnam*, pp. 539–42; Berman, *Planning a Tragedy*, pp. 135–8.

121. Sheehan, *Bright and Shining Lie*, pp. 701, 704–5, 710.

122. There are several variants of this quotation in the literature, reflecting the folkloric status of the saying. Clark Dougan, *et al.*, *The Vietnam Experience: Nineteen Sixty-Eight*, p. 21, quotes the original source, Peter Arnett: "It was necessary to destroy the town in order to save it." See also Michael Herr, *Dispatches*, p. 71, and Corson, *Betrayal*, p. 289.

123. Dougan, *et al.*, *Nineteen Sixty-Eight*, p. 69.

124. Kahin, *Intervention*, pp. 403, 406, 409–10; Blaufarb, *Counterinsurgency Era*, chs. 7–8, esp. pp. 205–6, 242; Betts, *Soldiers, Statesmen*, pp. 131–2, 138.

125. Doyle, *et al.*, *The Vietnam Experience: America Takes Over, 1965–67*, pp. 16–9.

126. Leavitt, "The Far-Off War," p. 36.

Notes to Chapter 16

1. Allen J. Matusow, *The Unraveling of America: A History of Liberalism in the 1960s*, chs. 8–9; Hodgson, *America*, Pt. III. On LBJ's decision-making, guiding assumptions, etc., see Vertzberger, *World in Their Minds*, 78, 114–7, 132, 145, 170–8, 214, 226–7, 243–5.

2. See Chapter 15, fn. 122.

3. This is not to say that the crises of 1965–70 did not register in film and TV production outside the bounds of the Western. Green Beret–like operations and war-related issues were also treated in combat films set during the Second World War (e.g., *Dirty Dozen*). Vietnam-related issues registered indirectly, especially after 1969, in the use of "deranged Vietnam vets" as stock characters in TV crime series. *The Lost Man* (1969) is one of the few films to deal directly with the politics of urban disorder and Black Power; however, it is not a new work but a remake of *Odd Man Out* (1947), a British film on the Irish Rebellion. *The Planet of the Apes* series (1968 *ff.*) translates the symbolism of the racial issue into science fiction/fantasy terms; and in *Conquest of the Planet of the Apes* (1972) it uses an ape/human conflict in a future Los Angeles to allegorize (after a fashion) the Black urban "uprisings" of Watts, Newark, and Detroit. (See remarks by Chief of Police Parker, quoted in Robert Fogelson, *The Los Angeles Riots*, p. 320.

But these treatments do not have the chronological range, continuity, or generic coherence of the 1965–70 Westerns. My thanks to Eric Greene for researching the background of the *Apes* series.

4. Berman, *Planning a Tragedy*, p. 51.

5. Guenter Lewy, *America in Vietnam*, pp. 105–6.

6. Quoted in Drinnon, *Facing West*, p. 372.

7. Gibson, *Perfect War*, pp. 227–8, 236–7; Sheehan, *Bright and Shining Lie*, pp. 617, 620–1, 712.

8. Sheehan, *Bright and Shining Lie*, pp. 539–40, 712.

9. Quoted in Doyle, *et al.*, *America Takes Over*, p. 65.

10. On civilian morale and the morale of the defending troops, see results of the *Strategic Bombing Survey*, conducted in the aftermath of the Second World War, which analyzed the effect of bombing on morale and productivity in Germany: Weigley, *American Way of War*, pp. 336–43, 463–70; Bernard Brodie, *Strategy in the Missile Age*, ch. 4. On the morale of highly motivated units, see for example Gen. William E. DePuy, quoted in Jonathan Mirsky, "Reconsidering Vietnam," *NYRB* (October 10, 1991), p. 46: "[T]he North Vietnamese main forces lost up to 40 percent of their troops every year. . . . I should have known better. In World War II I fought in a unit with casualties like that. The 90th Division had 25,000 casualties in a month, so I should have known." As William Bergerud notes, the key question for American planners should not have been which government did the South Vietnamese prefer, but which were they willing to die for: "Had they asked the second question, they would not have liked the answer."

11. Kahin, *Intervention*, p. 249.

12. Michael Casey, *et al.*, *The Vietnam Experience: Flags into Battle*, pp. 91–2: "Each enemy thrust into the region was repulsed with heavy Communist losses in men and materiel, but each time they kept coming back for more."

13. Other studies suggested that even this prediction was too optimistic, because of flaws in the methods used to calculate enemy losses. Not only did the army accept "body counts" that were (for a variety of reasons) typically inflated, but it routinely *increased* the counts by 50 percent, on the presumption that *half* of the dead were uncounted because they were unfound or concealed, or had been carried off by the enemy. Gibson, *Perfect War*, pp. 157–8, 110–17, 126–8.

14. *Ibid.*, pp. 109, 157–8; Sheehan, *Bright and Shining Lie*, p. 683.

15. Gibson, *Perfect War*, pp. 158–9. Only the use of nuclear weapons or an outright invasion of the North could overcome this tactical advantage, and these options were ruled out by domestic politics and the threat of inaugurating a conflict with China or the USSR.

16. *Ibid.*, ch. 6, esp. pp. 159–62, 166, 169–70.

17. Kahin, *Intervention*, pp. 286–7, 290, 361; and for the acceptance of "semblance" for reality in assessing the status of the GVN, pp. 207, 193, 218–26, 311–3. See also Gibson, *Perfect War*, pp. 162, 166. On the falsification of experience in or from the field, see for example Sheehan, *Bright and Shining Lie*, pp. 76, 92; Taylor quoted, p. 99: "My overall impression is of a great national movement, assisted to some extent, of course, by Americans, but essentially a

movement by Vietnamese to defend Vietnam against a dangerous and cruel enemy."

18. Kahin, *Intervention*, esp. pp. 121, 412–3, 432.

19. *Ibid.*, pp. 207, 237.

20. Sheehan, *Bright and Shining Lie*, pp. 537–40, 542.

21. *Ibid.*, ch. 6; Lewy, *America in Vietnam*, pp. 28–30.

22. Kahin, *Intervention*, pp. 237, 249.

23. *Ibid.*, 188–94, ch. 8.

24. *Ibid.*, pp. 218–9.

25. *Ibid.*, pp. 357, 374–5.

26. Theodore H. White, "The Bell of Decision Rings Out in Vietnam," *Life* (September 1, 1967), pp. 54–8.

27. Herr, *Dispatches*, pp. 58–9; Gibson, *Perfect War*, pp. 179–86, 196–201; Lifton, *Home from the War*, pp. 37–8, 42–4, 167–88; Sheehan, *Bright and Shining Lie*, pp. 94–5, 287–8.

28. Slotkin, *Fatal Environment*, pp. 409–11.

29. *Ibid.*, pp. 16–8, and fn. 7; Herr, *Dispatches*, p. 61; Loren Baritz, *Backfire: A History of How American Culture Led Us into Vietnam and Made Us Fight the Way We Did*; Hellmann, *American Myth*, chs. 2–3; Lifton, *Home from the War*, pp. 42–3, 48–51, 52–55, and ch. 8; Raskin and Fall, eds., *Viet-Nam Reader*, p. 386; Drinnon, *Facing West*, p. 368.

30. For full-length studies, see Don Oberdorfer, *Tet!* and Peter Braestrup and Burns Roper, *Big Story: How the American Press and Television Reported and Interpreted the Crisis of Tet 1968 in Vietnam and Washington*, 2 vols. See also Gibson, *Perfect War*, ch. 16; Karnow, *Vietnam*, ch. 14; Summers, *On Strategy*.

31. Corson, *Betrayal*, p. 289, and ch. 16, fn. 129.

32. Ronald Segal, *The Race War*.

33. Matusow, *Unraveling*, ch. 12, pp. 361–2; Hodgson, *America*, chs. 9–10, 20, esp. pp. 203–4, 211, 361–2, 431–5.

34. "Negro Revolt Echoes to the Ugly Crack of Sniper Fire," *Life* (July 28, 1967), pp. 16–28A. esp. p. 18.

35. Russell Sackett, "In a grim city, a secret meeting with the snipers," *ibid.*, pp. 27–8.

36. Dale Wittner, "The killing of Billy Furr, caught in the act of looting beer," *ibid.*, pp. 21–2.

37. Shana Alexander, "A Message from Watts to Newark," *ibid.*, p. 14B.

38. "Detroit/ City at the blazing heart of a nation in disorder," *Life* (August 4, 1967), pp. 16–29, esp. p. 19: "With exploding heat and violence, the flames of Negro revolt crackled across the nation, bringing federal troops into riot duty for the first time in a quarter of a century . . . the gravest domestic crisis since the war between the States." The parallels between the two non-White revolts are emphasized in a follow-up story on the Black Power "summit" in Newark (pp. 26–9), which takes on an explicitly revolutionary and violent tone. And see Matusow, *Unraveling*, pp. 363–7.

39. "Quench Riots—and Look Beyond," *Life* (August 4, 1967), p. 14; and note in same issue the review of a John Wayne movie which laments the loss of a world of simple choices. See also Hodgson, *America*, pp. 265–7.

40. *Life* (August 25, 1967), p. 3.

41. *Ibid.* (September 16, 1967), p. 4.

42. Robert Conot, *Rivers of Blood, Years of Darkness*; "Measuring Vietnam's Elections," *Life* (September 1, 1967), p. 4; and White, "The Bell of Decision," *ibid.*, pp. 54–8.

43. CAP doctrine rejected the devotion of resources to search-and-destroy missions, air strikes, defoliations, and artillery bombardments; it emphasized village defense integrated with programs of civic action (medical care, help with building projects, the development of personal ties with individual villagers).

44. *Life* (August 25, 1967), Cover: The 'Other' War in Vietnam/ To Keep a Village Free; Don Moser, "Their Mission: Defend, Befriend," pp. 24–28, 58A–62; "The 'Other' Pacification—To Cool U.S. Cities," pp. 30–4. Note that "other" is used to identify the pacification program in Vietnam on the cover, but that, inside, domestic pacification is identified as our "other war."

45. "The Battle That Ruined Hue," *Life* (March 8, 1968), p. 26; "A Special Section," "The Cycle of Despair: The Negro and the City."

46. Albert Rosenfeld, "The Psychology of Violence," *Life* (June 21, 1968), pp. 67–71.

47. Brown, *Strain of Violence*, p. 232.

48. Graham and Gurr, "Introduction," in National Commission on the Causes and Prevention of Violence, *Violence in America*, 8 vols., esp. Hugh Davis Graham and Ted Robert Gurr, eds., *Historical and Comparative Perspectives*, vol. 2, Part I, p. xiii.

49. R. M. Brown "Historical Patterns of Violence in America," pp. 35–64 (revised in *Strain of Violence*, ch. 1); and Charles Tilly, "Collective Violence in European Perspective," esp. pp. 10, 21 in *ibid.* See also James B. Rule, *Theories of Civil Violence*, chs. 6–9.

50. Brown, "Historical Patterns," *Violence in America*, p. 49.

51. Louis Hartz, "A Comparative Study of Fragment Cultures," *ibid.*, pp. 87, 91, 97.

52. This point is acknowledged in yet another contemporary study of *American Violence*, by Michael Wallace and Richard Hofstader. Hofstader, "Reflections on Violence in the United States," p. 12, notes that Indian wars were an experience for a small minority, but he too cites experience of such wars as a primary cause of violence in the American metropolis.

53. Joe B. Frantz, "The Frontier Tradition: An Invitation to Violence," in Graham and Gurr, eds., *Violence in America* 2: 101–2.

54. *Ibid.*, pp. 109, 113–4.

55. Basinger, *World War II Combat Film*, pp. 201–14.

56. When I first saw *Great Sioux Massacre* in 1968, the visual treatment of Indians reminded me of images of Vietnamese refugees from contemporary newsfilm. The screenplay may have been the work of a blacklisted leftist: it is credited to "Fred C. Dobbs," the name of Humphrey Bogart's role in *Treasure of the Sierra Madre* and an obvious pseudonym. For similar treatment of Indians as victims, see *Apache Rifles*, *Cheyenne Autumn* and *A Distant Trumpet* (1964); and *Arizona Raiders* (1965).

57. Hardy, *Westerns*, pp. 364, 365; 298. Marlon Brando's *The Appaloosa* (1966)

deals with similar themes but inverts the class standing and power roles usually associated with Mexicans and Americans.

58. *Ibid.*, p. 283; Hardy's list includes *Savage Guns* (1962); *Gringo* (1963); *Fistful of Dollars* (1964); *A Pistol for Ringo* (1965); *7 Guns for the MacGregors* (1965); *The Big Gundown* (1966); *A Bullet for the General* (1966); *Django* (1966); *Five Giants from Texas* (1966); *For a Dollar in the Teeth* (1966); *A Professional* (1968); *Five Man Army* (1969); *Magnificent Bandits* (1969); *No Room to Die* (1969); *Bounty Hunters* (1970); *Cannon for Cordoba, Companeros,* and *Machismo—40 Graves for 40 Guns* (1970); *A Fistful of Dynamite* (1971); and *Pancho Villa* (1971).

59. See for example *Two Flags West, Rocky Mountain,* and (in a slightly different way) *She Wore a Yellow Ribbon.*

60. The scene in which Dundee finally defeats Charriba is staged like the night battle on the hilltop at the end of *Objective Burma,* while the culminating cavalry battle recalls *Charge of the Light Brigade.* The name of the Rebel Captain "Tyreen" is an echo of the ex-Rebel Captain (now sergeant) Tyree of *Rio Grande* and *Yellow Ribbon*; and the sketch we are given of Tyreen's career links him to Maureen O'Hara's Kathleen in *Rio Grande,* and to Scarlett O'Hara in *Gone with the Wind.*

61. The plot takes some complicated twists here: Dundee sees the return of the boys as a set-up for an ambush and counters by attacking Charriba's camp. But Charriba expected this response and defeats Dundee. Meanwhile, the boys are returned safely to the States. The net result is as I describe it: the original objective of the mission (rescuing the captives) is achieved, but Dundee continues the mission, with the desire to avenge his recent defeat as an additional motive.

62. Melville, *Moby-Dick*, pp. 321, 461.

63. The actual date is not specified, but newspaper references suggest it is after Villa's expulsion from Mexico City (1914). Rico is training troops in the use of machine guns, perhaps for the Great War, which sets the date no later than 1917; but no reference is made to Pershing'a 1916 expedition.

64. Dahlberg's sexualized language also identifies him with certain themes of the so-called "counterculture." His apparently amoral hedonism, his happy anarchism and political frivolity, link him with the "Yippies"; his delight in eroticized violence, and his ironic invocation of the antiwar slogan, "Peace, brother," connects him to the mystique of violence that was emerging in radicalized parts of the counterculture, the Black Power movement and the New Left. Matusow, *Unraveling*, pp. 277–80 and 302–3 on N. O. Brown, and pp. 356–9 and 363–73 on Fanon and H. Rap Brown; Judith Clavir Albert and Stewart Edward Albert, *The Sixties Papers: Documents of a Rebellious Decade*, pp. 38–46, 145–71, 247–70; Gitlin, *The Sixties: Years of Hope, Days of Rage*, esp. ch. 17.

65. It is essentially the same story that John Wayne's Mike Kirby would tell the liberal reporter in *Green Berets*, two years later. See above, p. 522.

66. This suggests a rough equivalency between the vagina and the gun as "tools" which a "professional" will use skillfully and ruthlessly. But the superiority of the gun is attested in an exchange between Maria and Dahlberg, in which she offers to sleep with him if he will let her go, then tries to steal his gun as he kisses her, only to find that he has anticipated her move and has "cocked"

the gun under her chin. Chiquita (see below) is a more potent embodiment of female heroism, because she gives the gun priority.

67. The influence of these films was felt outside the Western genre, most notably in the two combat films most closely connected with Vietnam, Aldrich's *Dirty Dozen* and *Green Berets* (1968). Among other likenesses, the idea of a commando mission manned by criminals and renegades is the plot-premise of both *Major Dundee* and *Dirty Dozen*. In both *Major Dundee* and *Green Berets* the character played by Jim Hutton has to go outside regulations to steal equipment needed for the mission.

68. *Villa Rides* and *Guns of the Magnificent Seven* are of particular interest. The first is a classic "Mexico Western," directed by Buzz Kulik from a script by Robert Towne and Sam Peckinpah, featuring an American gunrunner/airplane pilot in the gunfighter role. *Guns* is the second *Magnificent Seven* sequel, in which the gunfighters are summoned to overthrow a military dictator by a little boy whose name is Emiliano Zapata—the suggestion being that the future hero of the revolution learned his skills from the American gunfighters.

69. The sex scene plays with the idea of Brown's "blackness" in ways that seem intended to titillate: at one moment implicitly reminding the audience of the stereotype of aggressive Black male sexuality, and of the taboo nature of Black/White sex; and in the next, denying or evading the implications of this suggestions. Their verbal exchanges first suggest that she is rejecting him because he is Black, then that she merely wishes to proceed more carefully because she loves him. Their physical exchanges first suggest Brown's use of force, then show Welch's consent; suggest that Brown is hurting her, then show that apparent pain is really ecstasy.

Notes to Chapter 17

1. Quoted in Gibson, *Perfect War*, pp. 157, 162.

2. A June 1968 poll showed that only 18 percent of Americans thought the "mission" was making progress; 25 percent thought that things were getting worse; and just under 50 percent thought that the situation was unchanged despite our efforts and losses. Another poll estimated that only 10 percent of the public still believed victory was possible, while more than two-thirds believed we would have to accept a compromise settlement—something the Johnson administration had hitherto rejected. Hodgson, *America*, chs. 20, 22; Samuel Lipsman, *et al.*, *The Vietnam Experience: Fighting for Time*, p. 23; Karnow, *Vietnam*, pp. 581–2, 594.

3. Corson, *Betrayal*, p. 289.

4. Hodgson, *America*, chs. 20, 22; Samuel Lipsman, *et al.*, *The Vietnam Experience: Fighting for Time*, p. 23; Karnow, *Vietnam*, pp. 581–2, 594.

5. *Ibid.*, p. 601; Lipsman, *et al.*, *Fighting for Time.*, pp. 17–23.

6. Karnow, *Vietnam*, ch. 15; Lewy, *America in Vietnam*, chs. 5–6.

7. Gitlin, *The Sixties*, pp. 413–6; Frank J. Donner, *The Age of Surveillance*, pp. 232*ff*.; Karnow, *Vietnam*, pp. 611–2. The prospect of domestic revolution was the subject of a much-ballyhooed series of articles published in *Life* in the fall of 1969. The centerpiece of this "Revolution" series was a summary and analysis

of Mao's strategy of peasant revolution. Although the series concludes that such a revolution is not likely here, it sees the development of domestic radicalism leading to "savage confrontations" with racial minorities and a disaffected counterculture. "Revolution: What are the causes? How does it start? Can it happen here?" *Life* (October 10, 1969) Part I, pp. 100–12, surveys all revolutions before Mao, cites the prediction of "Trotsky, the great Bolshevik revolutionary," that "the final revolution . . . would consist of a series of small and violent upheavals going on everywhere, lasting perhaps for generations." Part 2, "Out of the East, the People's War" (October 17, 1969, pp. 59–78), treats Mao as the ultimate "professional revolutionary," pp. 59–66B. "Can It Happen Here?," pp. 67–78, suggests that Black nationalist "insurrections . . . would be just super-riots" (p. 74), that countercultural movements undermine moral authority, and that the real danger to democratic institutions would come from a right-wing repression. On this last, see also Hofstader and Wallace, *American Violence*, p. 42; and Hugh Sidey, "The Presidency: Behind Nixon's Vietnam Stand," *Life* (November 21, 1969), p. 4: "An alarming number of people in this (pro-war) counterprotest looked and talked like the sort who would go all the way in any military confrontation, who would sweep all the dissenters from the streets, shave the beards and lock up any kid who wants to have a say in his future."

8. Corson, *Betrayal*, p. 289. Arthur G. Goldberg, "Acts of savagery," *Life* (November 14, 1969), p. 30D, is an editorial on the case of Green Beret Colonel Robert Rheault, dismissed from the service after being accused of having murdered a Vietnamese double agent. See also the story in the same issue, Frank McCulloch, "Colonel Robert Rheault, Ex-Green Beret," pp. 34–9. Rheault's defenders appealed to the ideological rationales of the Doolittle Report: in a dirty war, our side has to fight dirty or suffer defeat. Critics of Rheault, and of the army that had so leniently punished murder, fulfilled the Doolittle Report's prophecy that public reaction to the discovery of actions violating longstanding "American concepts of fair play" might be severe. The irony of Rheault's situation is that he is "A believer in self-reliance and elitism" (p. 36) who understood his mission as being to "kill Vietcong" by any and all means and is then punished for it.

9. The village is sometimes identified as Mylai, sometimes as Son My 4, and the Vietnamese names are spelled in various ways: My Lai, My-Lai, Mylai, Mylai 4, etc. I have used "Mylai" because it is the spelling in the *Life* article I cite at length.

10. Seymour M. Hersh, *My Lai 4: A Report on the Massacre and Its Aftermath*; Joseph Goldstein, *et al., The My-Lai Massacre and Its Cover-Up: Beyond the Reach of Law?*; Lewy, *America in Vietnam*, pp. 325–7, 356–64; Gibson, *Perfect War*, pp. 314–5, 437–41; Lifton, *Home from the War*, ch. 2.

11. Hal Wingo. *et al.*, "The Massacre at Mylai," *Life* (December 5, 1969), pp. 36–45.

12. *Ibid.*, p. 39.

13. *Ibid.*

14. *Ibid.*, "This was going to be our first real live battle, and we had made up our minds we were going to go in and with whatever means possible wipe them out."

15. *Ibid.*, pp. 40–1.

16. *Ibid.*, p. 41.

17. See Lifton, *Home from the War*, pp. 35–71, for a discussion of the guilt feelings among participants in the massacre.

18. Herr, *Dispatches*, pp. 18–20. See fn. 42, below.

19. Wingo, *et al.*, "The Massacre at Mylai," p. 41.

20. *Ibid.*, p. 42.

21. *Ibid.*, p. 43.

22. *Ibid.*, p. 43, photo 37.

23. *Ibid.*, p. 43. Compare Mary Rowlandson's narrative, "It is a solemn sight to see so many Christians lying in their blood, some here, and some there, like a company of sheep torn by wolves. . . . Oh the roaring, and singing and dancing, and yelling of those black creatures in the night, which made the place a lively resemblance of hell. And as miserable was the waste that was there made, of horses, cattle, sheep, swine, calves, lambs, roasting pigs and fowls . . . some roasting, some lying and burning, and some boiling to feed our merciless enemies." In Slotkin and Folsom, *So Dreadfull*, pp. 325–6.

24. Wingo, *et al.*, "The Massacre at Mylai," pp. 43–4. Medina implicitly condones the killing by reporting the dead civilians as VC KIA.

25. *Ibid.*, p. 44.

26. *Ibid.*, p. 45.

27. Sheehan, *Bright and Shining Lie*, pp. 689–90. Lewy, *America in Vietnam*, pp. 326–7, cites good evidence that Mylai was atypical in its scale and systematic quality; but he also cites MACV for "criminal negligence" in not recognizing that their tactics—given the conditions and state of training—were conducive to "atrocities" in the sense of excessive civilian casualties and to systematic neglect of the Rules of Engagement (ROE) by troops in the field (p. 241). See Gibson, *Perfect War*, p. 179, on scapegoating junior officers.

28. Sheehan, *Bright and Shining Lie*, p. 533; Gibson, *Perfect War*, pp. 196–211; Ward Just, *Military Men*, p. 13; Corson, *Betrayal*, p. 289. *Time/Life* editorialists continued to distinguish the deliberate terrorism of the enemy from our inadvertent terrorism but nonetheless concluded that Mylai signified the war's power to produce a national descent into "evil." See "On Evil: The Inescapable Fact," *Time* (December 5, 1969), pp. 26–7; "On the Other Side: Terror as Policy," p. 29.

29. Raskin and Fall, *Vietnam Reader*, p. 344.

30. Karnow, *Vietnam*, p. 530.

31. Hugh Sidey, "In the Shadow of Mylai," *Life* (December 12, 1969), p. 4. Henry Kissinger (who would later describe himself as the "Lone Ranger of American foreign policy") used Western-movie terms to account for his own reaction: he could accept the idea of Green Beret Colonel Rheault murdering a Vietnamese double agent because that was "man-to-man violence. . . . But Mylai was not within the national experience."

32. Paul O'Neil, "The Monstrous Manson 'Family,' " *Life* (December 19, 1969), pp. 20–31. The Mylai letters are on pp. 46–7. About a third of the letters offer exculpatory rationalizations (atrocity is normal in war), denials, and accusations that *Life* has given aid and comfort to the enemy ("Whose side are you

on?"). These letters, strident in tone, reinforce the idea that prejudice against the Vietnamese caused the massacre. A veteran writes, "The responsibility is on the Vietnamese people. They are alike, they dress alike and look alike . . . they are trying to kill you."

33. *Ibid.*, p. 46.

34. Hodgson, *America*, pp. 391–4.

35. That Butch and Sundance are (or have been) out of touch with reality is suggested by their last words, to the effect that if the Anglo lawmen they have been trying to evade for the entire film are not out there, they are not really in trouble. They have lived their lives in terms of expectations derived from a standard outlaw-vs.-posse Western; but they have stumbled into a different sort of movie, in which the expertise that was so useful in the older script is now useless and irrelevant.

36. To which the subplot adds a counterculture/civil rights theme: the romance between the Wayne character's adopted Indian son (Gabriel) and the southern-belle daughter of Hudson's planter-colonel. Aside from the interracial romance, Gabriel's character is continually enjoined to cut his long hair—a standard "hippie" joke of the period.

37. Similar objections were raised to the "eroticization" of violence in Arthur Penn's *Bonnie and Clyde* (1967). Concern about graphic movie violence was part of the cultural background that shaped the work of the "Violence Commission.

38. William H. Galperin, "History Into Allegory: *The Wild Bunch* as Vietnam Movie," *Western Humanities Review* 35:2 (1981), pp. 165–72; Doug McKinney, *Sam Peckinpah*, chs. 1, 4, 5; Garner Simmons, *Peckinpah: A Portrait in Montage*, chs. 6, 7, 8, esp. pp. 105–7; Paul Seydor, *Peckinpah: The Western Films*, chs. 2, 3, 6, 7.

39. Kitses, *Horizons West*, pp. 160–70; Seydor, *Peckinpah*, chs. 2, 7. The *Moby-Dick* connection is figurative, but "Amos Dundee" has a good deal in common with Ahab, and his mixed platoon with the polyglot crew of the Pequod; and the first town hit by the Wild Bunch is named "Starbuck."

40. Paul Coates, *The Story of the Lost Reflection: The Alienation of the Image in Western and Polish Cinema*, pp. 10–13.

41. "As flies to wanton boys are we to the gods:/ They kill us for their sport." Compare the children of Peckinpah's "Starbuck" to the "heartless" and "juvenile" deity Melville's Pip discovers at the bottom of the sea in *Moby-Dick*, p. 347.

42. My interpretation of the "pornography of violence" in *Wild Bunch* was suggested by Michael Herr's account of the process through which he came to realize his "responsibility" for what he merely observed as a reporter in Vietnam. The visual clichés through which death is represented in movies/TV form a kind of veil that impedes full understanding of the "real thing" and of the feelings of attraction, repulsion, guilt, and satisfaction that belong to such experiences. That veil is first torn by a "pornographic" vision of actual death in which the shameful pleasure of finally seeing the real, forbidden, unsanitized thing; but this "pornographic" sense of relation to observed death makes possible a more authentic relation which goes beyond shame or guilt to an informed sense of connection with and responsibility for what has been seen: "I went there behind the crude but serious belief that you had to be able to look at anything, serious

because I acted on it and went, crude because I didn't know, it took the war to teach it, that you were as responsible for everything you saw as you were for everything you did." Herr, *Dispatches*, pp. 18–20.

43. Kitses, *Horizons West*, p. 162. The shot of the old man and Pike lounging against a tree mirrors the composition of a scene in *Treasure*, which has the old prospector as its subject. Peckinpah draws on the old prospector in Huston's film for the character and fate of Freddy Sykes (Edmond O'Brien); and the ending of *Wild Bunch* pays homage to the famous scene of the gold-seekers laughing over the failure of all their striving.

44. John Prados, *Presidents' Secret Wars*, esp. chs. 11, 13, 16.

45. See above.

46. Peckinpah further undermines a "redemptive" reading by limiting the Madonna symbolism to Pike's subjective point of view. The Gorches have no such chivalric ideas about women, and if they choose to join Pike it cannot be for such noble reasons. Seydor, *Peckinpah*, chs. 3, 6, 7.

47. The "classic" and "mythic" quality of the moment is heightened by a number of formal devices, especially the use of a long lens which flattens perspective and so distorts our sense of the time it takes them to walk through the town—though they are walking, they appear to make little spatial progress through the frame until they suddenly *arrive*.

48. Kahin, *Intervention*, ch. 7.

49. This scene appears only in the longer versions of the film; it can be seen in the videotape produced by Warner Bros.

50. See for example Gitlin, *Sixties*, p. 360.

51. Hodgson, *America*, chs. 20, 22; Karnow, *Vietnam*, pp. 582–3, 588–97; Lewy, *America in Vietnam*, chs. 4–5.

52. Karnow, *Vietnam*, p. 593.

53. *Ibid.*, pp. 582–3.

54. Hodgson, *America*, chs. 20, 22; Karnow, *Vietnam*, pp. 582–3, 588–97; Lewy, *America in Vietnam*, chs. 4–5.

55. Kahin, *Intervention*, p. 357, 374–5. Military defense of Vietnam was never considered a "vital" national interest, seriously affecting American security or the world balance of military power, like defense of Europe, Korea, or (after 1979) the Persian Gulf.

56. *I.e.*, in the shift from *Magnficent Seven/Comancheros* (1960–1) to *Wild Bunch/Little Big Man* (1969–70).

57. *Ibid.*, pp. 607–12.

58. The War Powers Act of 1973 and the abolition of the draft were intended to limit the President's capacity to initiate military engagement without Congressional approval.

59. See for example Tamotsu Shibutani, *The Derelicts of Company K: A Sociological Study of Demoralization*, ch. 9.

60. The American government got around these limitations by conducting a covert guerrilla war, using various mountain tribes against the enemy in Laos and Cambodia, and by a "secret" bombing campaign directed against Communist bases in those countries. But the clandestine character of these efforts limited

their scope, and the enemy's effective use of jungle terrain limited their effectiveness. Karnow, *Vietnam*, pp. 589–93.

61. Quoted in Jonathan Mirsky, "Reconsidering Vietnam," *NYRB* (October 10, 1991), p. 48; Eric Beregerud, *The Dynamics of Defeat: The Vietnam War in Hau Nhgia Province*.

62. Gibson, *Perfect War*, ch. 6; Lipsman, *et al.*, *Fighting for Time*, pp. 95–6; Just, *Military Men*, is an extended discussion of the demoralizing effects of the war on the professional officer cadres.

63. Karnow, *Vietnam*, pp. 631–2; Lipsman, *et al.*, *Fighting for Time*, pp. 96–112.

64. Karnow, *Vietnam*, p. 593.

65. Schemmer, *The Raid*; Karnow, *Vietnam*, p. 655; Lewy, *America in Vietnam*, pp. 332–9, Lipsman, *et al.*, *The Vietnam Experience: The False Peace, 1972–74*, pp. 72–81.

66. Dougan, *et al.*, *The Vietnam Experience: The Fall of the South*, p. 106; Frank Snepp, *Decent Interval: An Insider's Account of Saigon's Indecent End . . .*, pp. 298–305; 347–55, 365, 373–6, 402–3.

67. See H. Bruce Franklin, *MIA: Or, Mythmaking in America*, pp. 3–10, 37–75, 127–165. On the *Mayaguez*, see P. Goldman, *et al.*, "Ford's Rescue Operation," *Newsweek* (May 26, 1975), pp. 16–8; "Strong But Risky Show of Force," *Time* (May 26, 1975), pp. 9–14; "Machismo Diplomacy," *The Nation* (May 31, 1975), pp. 642–3.

68. Gitlin, *Sixties*, chs. 13, 17.

Notes to Conclusion

1. Titles representative of this attitude include R. Buckminster Fuller, *Operating Manual for Spaceship Earth* (1969), and Barbara Ward, *Spaceship Earth* (1966); Lester C. Thurow, *The Zero-Sum Society: Distribution and the Possibilities for Economic Change* (1983); Richard Rosencrance, *America as an Ordinary Country: Foreign Policy and the Future* (1976).

2. Arnold Martin and Edward Klein, eds., "America in Captivity: Points of Decision in the Hostage Crisis/An Inquiry by the *New York Times*," *New York Times Magazine* Special Issue (1981).

3. William H. McNeill, "The Care and Repair of Public Myth," *Foreign Affairs* (Fall, 1982), pp. 1–13. *Foreign Affairs* is one of the most prestigious of the major policy-study journals, the vehicle for such seminal works of ideological creation as George Kennan's famous paper on the necessity of "containment," which became the key formulation of Cold War ideology. See also Zelinsky, *Nation into State*, esp. pp. 1–19, 48–68.

4. McNeill, "Public Myth," pp. 1–5, esp. pp. 1, 2, 4.

5. *Ibid.*, pp. 5–6.

6. *Ibid.*, pp. 3–6, 13.

7. Compare McNeill's essay with two similar calls for the systematic revision and renewal of national myth and ideology in a time of crisis: Howard Mumford Jones's "Patriotism—But How?" in 1938, and Frederick Jackson Turner's "Sig-

nificance of the Frontier" in 1893. Turner's essay summoned historians and political leaders to anticipate the ideological consequences of a major transformation in material conditions. Jones, like McNeill, treats the crisis as an artifact of ideological discourse: the supposed negativism of the cultural elite.

8. Hardy, *Western*, pp. 322–63 and Appendix 8, which lists all other Westerns and gives times. The two longest-running TV Westerns, *Bonanza* and *Gunsmoke*, left the air in 1972 and 1975. The only successful Western developed during this period was the hybrid *Kung Fu*, which also ceased production in 1975. *Little House on the Prairie* had a western setting, but its stories belong to the genre of family melodrama. Brooks and Marsh, *Complete Directory*, pp. 756–65.

9. I base this interpretation on my experience at a conference on "The Western" at Sun Valley, Idaho, in 1976, to which I refer later in this chapter. The conference was attended by people from the industry who had been associated with Western productions, members of the critical establishment, and academics. I had extended conversations with David Dortort (producer of *Bonanza*); directors Henry King, King Vidor, Monte Hellman, and Delmer Daves; actors Frederick Forrest, Warren Oates, and Iron Eyes Cody; critics and film historians Arthur Knight and Richard Schickel. And I heard presentations by Clint Eastwood, Peter Fonda, and Colonel Tim McCoy (among others). At a similar conference the following year, I interviewed Arthur Penn and Chief Dan George. All these discussions and presentations made reference to the state of opinion in the industry, which held that the Western had "died"; they differed only on the question of the possibilities for revival. Those with current projects (like Eastwood) cited the genre's perennial appeal and the "normal" cycles of genre popularity; those without such projects asserted that the current decline was qualitatively different and likely to endure. In retrospect, what is remarkable about this general belief in a disastrous decline of the Western is its prematurity: in 1976 the "decline" had lasted only three years, production was on the increase, and a spate of innovative new productions by first-rank directors and featuring major stars was slated for release that same year. So I believe that the intensity of the reaction against the Western was at least as much an artifact of cultural processes within the producing community as of market research. The mythmakers had lost faith and interest in their own project, and the "decline" was a case of self-fulfilling prophecy.

10. For example, see: cowboy as workingman (*Monte Walsh, Wild Rovers, Culpeper Cattle Company*); outlaw as juvenile delinquent (*Bad Company, The Spikes Gang*) or as psychopath (*Great Northfield, Minnesota Raid*); town-tamer as psychopath (*Life and Times of Judge Roy Bean*) or as corrupt weakling (*McCabe and Mrs. Miller*); Indian as ethnic outsider rather than noble savage (*Tell Them Willie Boy Is Here*).

11. See, for example, Peter Farb, *Man's Rise to Civilization as Shown by the Indians of North America from Primeval Times to the Coming of the Industrial State* (1968); Stan Steiner, *The New Indians* (1967); Robert Brunette, *The Tortured Americans* (1971); Carlos Castaneda, *The Teachings of Don Juan: A Yaqui Way of Knowledge* (1968); John G. Neihardt, *Black Elk Speaks* (1961, reprint).

12. Roderick Nash, *Wilderness and the American Mind*, ch. 10; Samuel Haber, *Efficiency and Uplift: Scientific Management in the Progressive Era, 1890–1920.*

13. "Wounded Knee and Mylai," *Christian Century* 88:59 (January 20, 1971); "Our Indian Heritage," *Life* (July 2, 1971), pp. 10–11, 38–67. Dee Brown, *Bury My Heart at Wounded Knee*, a study of the Plains wars with marked sympathy for the Indian, was a best-seller in 1973. My own work in this period (especially *Regeneration*) was strongly influenced by the idea that the Native American perspective held the key to a critique of American ideology. The polemical tendencies in this school of historiography are well indicated in Leslie Fiedler, *Return of the Vanishing American*, and such anthologies as David R. Wrone and Russell S. Nelson, Jr., *Who's the Savage? A Documentary History of the Mistreatment of the American Indian* (1973). The first rock-musical, *Hair* (1969), subsumed the mystiques of consciousness-enhancing drugs, anti-war politics, and the "generation gap" in its subtitle, "A Tribal Love-Rock Musical." Among the "Indian" films are *Smith!* (1969); *Tell Them Willie Boy Is Here* (1969); *Flap!* (1970); and *When the Legends Die* (1972). In *Return of a Man Called Horse* (1972), the hero of the earlier film returns as a kind of counterinsurgency warrior to help his adopted people fend off White settlers and soldiers. An interesting variant of the formula is the small "cult" of films based on *Billy Jack* (1971). The hero is an American Indian and Vietnam veteran who comes to the aid of oppressed townsfolk and Indians in much the same way that the Magnificent Seven aid Mexican peasants—he is both an outlaw and a "professional" with soldier-like skills.

14. Matusow, *Unraveling*, pp. 277–80, 302–3 on N. O. Brown, and pp. 356–9, 363–73 on Fanon and H. Rap Brown; Judith Clavir Albert and Stewart Edward Albert, *The Sixties Papers: Documents of a Rebellious Decade*, pp. 38–46, 145–71, 247–70; and Gitlin, *The Sixties: Years of Hope, Days of Rage*, esp. ch. 17.

15. In the novel the woman survives the massacre and Crabbe abandons the Cheyenne life. Penn's film substitutes a movie convention for the novel's handling of this problem.

16. One film—*A Time for Killing*—portrays Black soldiers as marksmen so incompetent that they cannot make an effective firing squad; an execution in which they are involved degenerates into a cruel torture session for which their incompetence is responsible. The "Blaxploitation" Westerns include *The Legend of Nigger Charlie* (1972), *The Soul of Nigger Charlie* (1973), and *Adios Amigo* (1975). It is worth noting that *Buck* is an African-American production, produced and directed by Sidney Poitier and starring Poitier and Harry Belafonte—both of whom were prominent activists in the civil-rights movement. *The McMasters* (1969) has a similar theme.

17. However, not all Westerns in this period were pro-Indian or anti-war. Eastwood's *Two Mules for Sister Sarah* is a "Mexican Western" in the counterinsurgency tradition of *The Magnificent Seven* and *The Professionals*. Two Indian-war Westerns, made the year after *Little Big Man/Soldier Blue* and released in 1972, powerfully reassert the identification of Indians (and therefore of the Vietnamese enemy) as "savages." *The Revengers* reworks the vengeance theme of *The Searchers* without that film's anti-racist subtext. *Ulzana's Raid* (1972), directed by Robert Aldrich, was conceived as a direct refutation of the revisionist view of Indians in *Little Big Man/Soldier Blue* and of the anti-war subtext of those films. Aldrich emphasizes in graphic manner the sadism and cruelty of the raiding Apache and devotes crucial passages of dialogue to considering the

question of why certain peoples seem so passionately devoted to cruelty. But these films are exceptions, reactions against a revisionism that had become the new norm in the genre. Arnold and Miller, *Aldrich*, pp. 165–74, esp. 173; also pp. 197–9, 203–4. However, even Aldrich is critical of the way the war was fought after the counterinsurgency "scouts" were replaced by the brass hats and shavetails.

18. Though praised for its innovative approach to the subject, the latest work in this form, *Dances with Wolves* (1990), offers essentially the same reading of Native American history.

19. The casting of Chief Dan George as Josie's sidekick annexes to Eastwood's film the counterculture and anti-war mystique that attached to that Indian actor's role in *Little Big Man*. However, the latent racialism of the Western reasserts itself in classic form in a "rescue" scene in which Locke's virginal character is threatened with rape by a gang of *comancheros* of mixed but predominantly non-white racial composition.

20. Subsequent attempts to revive the historical Western (*Heaven's Gate* and *Tom Horn* in 1980) fared disastrously. Only the highly stylized rendering of the James Gang saga in *Long Riders* (1980) can be called a successful historical Western; and like *Josie Wales*, its success had no follow-on until the two *Young Riders* films (1988, 1990). *Rustler's Rhapsody* tried (and failed) to imitate *Silverado's* success by updating the "singing cowboy" Western.

21. For an overview, see Robin Wood, *Hollywood from Vietnam to Reagan*.

22. Among the more interesting variations on this theme are the *Billy Jack* series (1971*ff*.), and *The Exterminator* (1980), in which the converted Indian-hater is a returning Vietnam veteran (Billy Jack, an Indian) who vengefully exterminates a set of murderous youth gangs. As the "vigilante" designation suggests, these films clearly and explicitly invoke (and have reminded movie critics of) the formulas of the Western.

23. See for example J. Hoberman, "The Fascist Guns in the West," *American Film* (March 1986), pp. 42–8.

24. Tony Williams, "American Cinema in the '70s: The Texas Chainsaw Massacre," *Movie* 25 (1978), pp. 12–6. See the discussion of the Harpes and Murrell gang in Slotkin, *Fatal Environment*, pp. 132–6, and the discussions of witchcraft and of "white-Indians" in ———, *Regeneration*, ch. 5 and pp. 286–91.

25. *Aliens* is interesting for its combination of Western and combat-film conventions in its tale of a battle to rescue the last survivor of a massacred colony from the insectoid monstrosities that have devoured it. The protagonist-rescuer is a "woman who knows Indians," supported by an ethnic platoon. The struggle in the ruins of the colony and the hostility of the alien world are represented as a classic "Apache war," where a fate many times worse than death awaits those who lose and fail to save the last bullet for themselves (The aliens can rape both men and women; they bind their victims into their nests and impregnate them with crablike offspring who devour the victims from within.)

26. Herr, *Dispatches*, p. 49.

27. Lloyd B. Howard, *The Tainted War: Culture and Identity in Vietnam War Narratives*; Hellmann, *American Myth*, Pt. II; William Adams, "War Stories: Movies, Memory, and the Vietnam War," *Comparative Social Research* 11:1 (1989), pp.

165–83; Peter C. Rollins, "The Vietnam War: Perceptions Through Literature, Film, and Television, "*AQ* 36: 3 (1984), pp. 419–32. I am indebted to Gerald Burns for his suggestions that the heroes of much Vietnam War fiction are "inverted frontier heroes."

28. The concluding "rescue" section of Cimino's film echoes the ironic interdependence of search-and-rescue/search-and-destroy from *The Searchers*; the title of the film, and the continual paralleling of war with deer-hunting, echo Cooper's *Deerslayer*, and the deer-killing scene echoes a similar scene in *The Pioneers*, when Leatherstocking and his friends kill a deer in the lake.

29. Brian W. Dippie, "The Winning of the West Reconsidered," *Wilson Quarterly* (Summer, 1990), pp. 71–85; David M. Emmons, "Social Myth and Social Reality," *Montana: The Magazine of Western History* 39:4 (1989), pp. 2–9; W. Thomas White, "Race, Ethnicity, and Gender in the Railroad Work Force: The Case of the Far Northwest, 1883–1918," *WHQ* 16:3 (1985), pp. 265–84; Ralph Willett, "Nativism and Assimilation: The Hollywood Aspect," *JAS* 7:2 (1973), pp. 191–4. For African-Americans in the West, see Kenneth W. Porter, *The Negro on the American Frontier*.

30. See Werner Sollors, *Beyond Ethnicity: Consent and Descent in American Culture*, esp. chs. 1–3, 7. The most notable group of "historical" films of the last fifteen years has focused on the years between 1910 and 1940. These films deal with a variety of themes and include both recognizable genre films and odd variants that suggest the possibilities of a new genre map: the processes of immigrant assimilation (*The Godfather* series, *Hester Street, Once Upon a Time in America, Avalon, Mobsters, Bugsy*); the transformation of rural life (*Days of Heaven, Places in the Heart*); the Depression (*Bound for Glory, Hard Times*); the social milieu of the Second World War (*Yanks, Swing Shift*); the experience of Blacks before the civil-rights movement (the two *Roots* miniseries, *Leadbelly, Sounder, Bingo Long . . . , Autobiography of Miss Jane Pittman*); the Hispanic side of the Western (*Ballad of Gregorio Cortez*); and the conflict between labor and capital (*Mollie Maguires, Matewan*). Western imagery is prominent in Matewan, which brings its tale of labor conflict to a head in a classic shootout on the town's main street between railroad detectives and armed miners led by a tough-talking two-gun sheriff. Although these themes and settings may strike us as "modern" rather than "historical," they are separated from their audience in the 1980s by a chronological gap comparable to that which divided Fenimore Cooper from the heyday of Hawkeye's real-life equivalents, or that which divided the cattle-ranching frontier of the 1880s from John Ford's *Stagecoach* (1939). Cooper's three novels of 1823–27 nominally refer to events in 1757, 1794, and 1804, a difference of (roughly) 70, 30, and 23 years. Fifty-five years separate Geronimo's last outbreak from Ford's *Stagecoach*. The Depression-set movies of the 1970s and early 80s were some 40-plus years later than their subject. The *Godfather* films refer to the Great War era and the 1950s, between 60 and 25 years earlier. *The Untouchables* and *Matewan* appeared roughly 54 and 67 years after the events they relate. *Tucker* refers to events that occurred 40 years before.

31. See Elizabeth Traube and Moishe Postone, "The Return of the Repressed: Lucas/Spielberg's *Temple of Doom*," and Traube, "Redeeming Images: The Wild Man Comes Home," in Traube, *Dreaming Identities: Class, Gender and*

Generation in 1980s Hollywood Movies (forthcoming from Westview Press); and William Schneider, " 'Rambo' and Reality: Having It Both Ways," in Kenneth Oye, *et al.*, eds., *Eagle Resurgent? The Reagan Era in Foreign Policy*, ch. 3.

32. On the ideology of museum and theme-park restorations, see for example Michael Sorkin, ed., *Variations on a Theme Park: The New American City and the End of Public Space*, pp. 94–122, 205–32; Zelinsky, *Nation and State*, pt. 5; Warren Leon and Roy Rosenzweig, *History Museums in the United States: A Critical Assessment*; Michael Kammen, *Mystic Chords of Memory: The Transformation of Tradition in American Culture*, chs. 16, 18, 19; Jay Anderson, *Time Machines: The World of Living History*.

33. My thanks to Eric Greene, whose paper suggested this view of the film.

34. Michael Rogin and Garry Wills have noted the ways in which Reagan's own thought processes were characterized by a propensity for confounding things seen (or acted) in movies with actual events; they see this as a sign of the centrality of cinematic experience in Reagan's education and intellectual development. As a Hollywood actor it was his business to personify a range of figures, including historical personages like Wyatt Earp and George Armstrong Custer. And those impersonations engaged him more closely and for a longer time with the matter of American history than the book-learned history he may have acquired at Eureka College. It is therefore understandable that the line between history and movie should be somewhat blurred in his memory. However, what concerns us here is not Reagan's personal relation to movie-myth but the way in which his identification with the world of movies enabled him to address the crisis of public myth. Rogin, "Ronald Reagan," the Movie, ch. 1; Garry Wills, *Reagan's America*, chs. 16–22.

35. The same nostalgia for the mood of simple credulity associated with an (imaginary) past underlies the appeal of genre-genre films like *Indiana Jones* and *The Untouchables*, and "retro" TV series like *Happy Days*.

36. On the background of the "Reagan Revolution," see Sidney Blumenthal, *The Rise of the Counter-Establishment: From Conservative Ideology to Political Power*.

37. Hodgson, *America*, ch. 25, esp. pp. 493–5, describes the Turnerian basis of New Frontier economics and defines the ideological crisis of the 1970s as the product of disappointment with the apparent failure of the economic myth. I see the doctrines of "supply side" economics as a revised version of New Frontier macroeconomics, and Reagan's triumph as resulting in part from his appeal to the public's latent nostalgia for the mythic certainties of the Kennedy era. For a general analysis of the consequences of Reaganomics, see Benjamin M. Friedman, *Day of Reckoning: The Consequences of American Economic Policy*. The "jackpot" quotation is from Steven Waldman and Rich Thomas, "How Did It Happen?" *Newsweek* (May 21, 1990,), p. 27.

38. Some exemplary titles: Frank H. Tucker, *The Frontier Spirit and Progress* (1980); Gerard O'Neill, *The High Frontier: Human Colonies in Space* (1982); Daniel Graham, *High Frontier: A Strategy for National Survival* (1983); Robert M. Reich, *The New American Frontier* (1983); and National Research Council, Office of International Affairs, *The Race for the New Frontier: International Competition in Advanced Technology* (1983, 1984). On urban "frontiers," see Neil Smith, "New

City, New Frontier: The Lower East Side as Wild, Wild West," in Sorkin, ed., *Variations on a Theme Park*, pp. 61–93; and also pp. 94–122, 154–80.

39. Mark Twain, *Roughing It*, pp. 201–2, 277–8.

40. See Vernon Louis Parrington, *Main Currents in American Thought: An Interpretation of American Literature from the Beginnings to 1920*, vol. 2, pp. 178–9. Writing of Davy Crockett, Parrington says: "Wastefulness was in the frontier blood, and Davy was a true frontier wastrel . . . one of thousands who were wasting the resources of the Inland Empire, destroying forests, skinning the land, slaughtering the deer and bear, the swarms of pigeons and turkeys, the vast buffalo herds. Davy the politician is a huge western joke, but Davy the wastrel was a hard, unlovely fact."

41. Garry Wills, "The Politics of Grievance," *NYRB*, (July 19, 1990), pp. 3–4; Friedman, *Day of Reckoning*, esp. chs. 6, 9; Larry Martz, *et al.*, "The Bonfire of the S&Ls," *Newsweek* (May 21, 1990), pp. 20–5.

42. See for example Robert Heilbroner, "Lifting the Silent Depression," *NYRB* (October 24, 1991), pp. 6–8; Jerry Adler, *et al.*, "Down in the Dumps," *Newsweek* (January 13, 1992), pp. 18–22; Michel Crozier, *The Trouble with America: Why the System Is Breaking Down*; Kammen, *Mystic Chords of Memory*, esp. pp. 17–39, chs. 16–19.

43. Franklin, *MIA*, ch. 4; Traube, "Redeeming Images: The Wild Man Comes Home." See also similar "anti-terrorist" films set in the Middle East, like *Delta Force* and *Navy SEALS*.

44. On the "captivity" myth in the Iran hostage case, see fn. 2 above. On the Iran-*Contra* affair, see Inouye, *et al.*, *Iran–Contra Affair*; and Theodore Draper, "Reagan's Junta," *NYRB* (January 29, 1987), pp. 5–14; "American Hubris: From Truman to the Persian Gulf" (July 16, 1987), pp. 40–8; "The Rise of the American Junta," (October 8, 1987), pp. 47–58; "The Fall of an American Junta" (October 22, 1987), pp. 45–57; "An Autopsy" (December 17, 1987), pp. 67–77. These articles are updated and supplemented by additional research and argument in ———, *A Very Thin Line: The Iran–Contra Affairs*, esp. ch. 26.

45. On the Nicaraguan war, see Leslie Cockburn, *Out of Control: The Story of the Reagan Administration's Secret War in Nicaragua, the Illegal Arms Pipeline, and the Contra Drug Connection*; Joanne Omang and Aryeh Neier, eds., *Psychological Operations in Guerrilla Warfare*, a primary source for the "dirty war" doctrine in Nicaragua; Sam Dillon, *Commandos: The CIA and Nicaragua's Contra Rebels*; and fn. 47, below.

46. The career and public reputation of Oliver North are a case in point. North was praised by one of his colleagues, NSC Chairman Robert MacFarlane, for having maintained "a semblance of manhood" in administration policies vis-à-vis Nicaragua. On North's career and celebrity, see Peter Meyer, *Defiant Patriot: The Life and Exploits of Lt. Col. Oliver North*; "Ollie Takes the Hill," *Newsweek* (July 20, 1987), pp. 12–20. On "cowboy" metaphor and North, see Watson *et al.*, " 'Project Recovery,' " pp. 26–37; and for critical uses of the same metaphor, see for example M. R. Montgomery, "These Aren't Real Cowboys, Pardner," *The Boston Globe* (February 14, 1987), p. 11; and Draper, "The True History of the Gulf War," *NYRB* (January 30, 1992), p. 39.

47. Chris Lane, *et al.*, "The Newest War," *Newsweek* (January 6, 1992), pp. 18–23; Cockburn, *Out of Control*; Jonathan Kiwtney, *The Crimes of Patriots: A True Tale of Dope, Dirty Money, and the CIA.*

48. On the Gulf War, see Draper, "The True History of the Gulf War," *NYRB* (January 30, 1992), pp. 38–45; Micah L. Sifry and Christopher Cerf, *The Gulf War Reader: History, Documents, Opinions*, pp. 134–6, 172–99, 210–2, 228–9, 311–4, 334–6, 343–4, 355–93, 449–95. For "jobs," see Tom Mathews, Doug Waller, *et al.*, "The Road to War," *Newsweek* (January 28, 1991), pp. 54–65, esp. p. 64; for Bush's use of movie mythology, see Evan Thomas, "The One True Hawk in the Administration," *Newsweek* (January 7, 1991), p. 19, and fn. 49, below. It is worth noting that similar structures appear in recent debates over the potential for a "trade war" with Japan. The expansion of Japanese economic power is seen as a threat to both future "bonanza" growth, to national independence, and to our cultural (racial?) integrity. Japanese investment in American properties is seen as a form of "captivity" requiring rescue; and war—symbolic or actual—is imagined as a means of "rescue." Michael Crichton's novel, *Rising Sun*, plays this scenario as a detective thriller. See the discussion by Robert Reich, "Is Japan Really Out to Get Us?" *NYTBR* (February 9, 1992), pp. 1, 24–5; "The Pearl Harbor Metaphor," *Deadline* 6:3, pp. 4–5.

49. Thomas, "The One True Hawk," p. 19; ———, *et al.*, " 'No Vietnam,' " *Newsweek* (December 10, 1990), pp. 24–31; Mathews, *et al.*, "The Road to War," pp. 54–65; Draper, "The True History of the Gulf War," pp. 38–45.

50. For urban "savage war," see for example *The Warriors* (1979); *Escape from New York* (1981); *Fort Apache, the Bronx* (1981); and *Colors* (1988). On urban "frontiers," see Smith, "New City, New Frontier," in Sorkin, ed., *Variations on a Theme Park*, pp. 61–93, and pp. 94–122, 154–80. Ironically, during this same time period the boom in "gentrified" urban real estate produced a wave of promotions representing inner cities as a new "bonanza" frontier for enterprising "yuppies."

51. Friedman, *Day of Reckoning*, chs. 9–11; Larry Martz, et al., "Reagan's Failure," *Newsweek* (March 9, 1987), pp. 16–21; ———, "The Bonfire of the S&Ls," *Newsweek* (May 21, 1990), pp. 20–5; Adler, "Down in the Dumps."

52. On the divisiveness of political discourse in the 1980s, see Thomas Byrne Edsall, *Chain Reaction: The Impact of Race, Rights and Taxes on American Politics;* Kevin Phillips, *The Politics of Rich and Poor: Wealth and the American Electorate in the Reagan Aftermath*; Edward G. Carmines and James A. Atimson, *Issue Evolution: Race and the Transformation of American Politics*, ch. 2; Howard Schuman, Charlotte Steeh, and Robert Bobo, *Racial Attitudes in America: Trends and Interpretations*, chs. 1, 6.

53. Sacvan Bercovitch, "Investigations of an Americanist," *JAH* 78:3, 983–4.

54. Some of the possibilities for a revisionist approach to myth-making are suggested in Donald Lazere, ed., *American Media and Mass Culture: Left Perspectives*; and Brett Williams, ed., *The Politics of Culture*. Even a highly conventionalized form like the Western is susceptible of revision at the level of explicit ideology (as in *Dances with Wolves*) and even at the level of structure, as in the feminist Western *Heartland* (1979).

55. Robert Frost, "America Is Hard to See," *In the Clearing*, p. 21. The poem also contains the rather prophetic warning that, should a modern Columbus seek to complete the original quest by moving on to a new frontier in Asia, "He'll find that Asiatic state / Is about tired of being looted / While having its beliefs disputed. / His can be no such easy raid / As Cortez on the Aztecs made." (p. 23).

56. Adrienne Rich, "In the Wake of Home," *Your Native Land, Your Life*, pp. 59–60.

Bibliography

Archives

Buffalo Bill Historical Center, Cody, Wyoming

William F. Cody Papers, Denver Public Library: Cody Scrapbooks, vols, 1–8.

Buffalo Bill's Wild West. Programme. 1886, 1887, *Buffalo Bill's Wild West and Congress of the Rough Riders of the World.* Program. 1893, 1898, 1899, 1900, 1901, 1902, 1904, 1905, 1907, 1908, 1909.

Little Big Horn National Monument (formerly Custer Battlefield)

Newspapers and Magazines

Harper's Weekly, 1890–1903

Life, 1939–44, 1950–55, 1960–72

Nation, 1874–77

New York Herald, 1872–77

New York Times, 1960–75

New York World, 1872–77

Newsweek, 1960–76

Time, 1960–76

World's Work, 1900–7, 1909, 1916–17

Dime-Novel Series

New York Detective Library. New York: Frank Tousey, 1882–97. Library of Congress Microfilm.

Log Cabin Library. New York: Street and Smith, 1889–1898. Library of Congress Microfilm.

Deadwood Dick Library, New York: Beadle and Adams, 1877–1889; 1887–1894. Beinecke Library, Yale University.

Works Consulted

Adams, Brooks. *Law of Civilization and Decay: An Essay on History.* Edited by Charles A. Beard. New York: Alfred A. Knopf, Inc., 1943.

———. *The New Empire.* Cleveland: Frontier Press, 1967.

Adams, Charles Francis, Jr. "The Protection of the Ballot in National Elections," *Journal of Social Science* 1:1 (1869), pp. 91–111.

Adams, Charles Francis, Jr., and Henry Adams. *A Cycle of Adams Letters, 1861–1865.* Two Volumes. Edited by Worthington Chauncey Ford. Boston: Houghton Mifflin, 1920.

Adams, Hazard, and Leroy Searle. *Critical Theory Since 1965.* Tallahassee: Florida State University Press, 1986.

Adams, Les, and Buck Rainey. *Shoot-em-Ups: The Complete Reference Guide to Westerns of the Sound Era.* Metuchen, NJ: Scarecrow Press, 1985.

Adams, Ramon F. *Six-Guns and Saddle Leather: A Bibliography of Books and Pamphlets on Western Outlaws and Gunmen.* Norman: University of Oklahoma Press, 1954.

Adams, William. "War Stories, Movies, Memory, and the Vietnam War," *Comparative Social Research* 11 (1989), pp. 165–83.

Adelstein, Richard P. " 'The Nation as an Economic Unit': Keynes, Roosevelt, and the Managerial Ideal," *JAH* 78:1 (1991), pp. 160–87.

Adler, Jerry, *et al.* "Down in the Dumps," *Newsweek* (January 13, 1992), pp. 18–22.

Aikman, Duncan. *Calamity Jane and the Lady Wildcats.* Introduction by Watson Parker. Lincoln: University of Nebraska Press, 1987.

Albert, Judith Clavir, and Stewart Edward, editors. *The Sixties Papers: Documents of a Rebellious Decade.* New York: Praeger, 1984.

Alexander, Shana. *Anyone's Daughter.* New York: Bantam Books, 1979.

Allen, Robert L. *Reluctant Reformers: Racism and Social Reform Movements in the United States.* Garden City, NY: Doubleday Anchor Books, 1975.

Allombert, Guy, *et al. Le Western: Approches, Mythologies, Auteurs, Acteurs, Filmographies.* Paris: Le Mond en 10:18, Union Générale des Editions, 1966.

Altschuler, Glenn C. *Race, Ethnicity, and Class in American Social Thought.* Arlington Heights, IL: Harlan Davidson, 1982.

Ameringer, Oscar. *If You Don't Weaken: The Autobiography of Oscar Ameringer.* Foreword by Carl Sandburg. New York: Henry Holt and Company, 1940.

Anderson, Benedict. *Imagined Communities: Reflections on the Origin and Spread of Nationalism.* London: Verso, 1983.

Anderson, Jay. *Time Machines: The World of Living History.* Nashville: American Association for State and Local History, 1984.

Anderson, J. L. "Japanese Swordfighters and American Gunfighters," in Richard Dyer McCann and Jack C. Ellis, Editors, *Cinema Examined: Selections from* Cinema Journal. New York: E.P. Dutton, 1982, pp. 84–104.

Apter, David. *Ideology and Discontent.* New York: Free Press, 1964.

Ardrey, Robert. *The Territorial Imperative: A Personal Inquiry into the Animal Origins of Property and Nations.* New York: Laurel, 1966.

———. *The Social Contract: A Personal Enquiry into the Evolutionary Sources of Order and Disorder.* New York: Dell Publishing, 1970.

Armitage, Shelley. "Rawhide Heroines: The Evolution of the Cowgirl and the Myth of America," in Sam B. Girgus, editor, *The American Self: Myth, Ideology and Popular Cultures*, Chapter 11. Albuquerque: University of New Mexico Press, 1981.

Arnold, Edwin T., and Eugene L. Miller, Jr. *The Films and Career of Robert Aldrich.* Knoxville: The University of Tennessee Press, 1986.

Arpad, Joseph J. "Between Folklore and Literature: Popular Culture as Anomaly," *JPC* 9:2 (1975), pp. 403–23.

Ashby, LeRoy. " 'Straight from Youthful Hearts': *Lone Scout* and the Discovery of the Child, 1915–1924," *JPC* 9:4 (1976), pp. 775–93.

Atherton, Lewis. *The Cattle Kings.* Lincoln: University of Nebraska Press, 1961.

Atway, Robert, editor. *American Mass Media.* New York: Random House, 1982.

Austin, Bruce A. *The Film Audience: An International Bibliography of Research.* Metuchen, NJ: The Scarecrow Press, 1983.

Axeen, David. " 'Heroes of the Engine Room: American Civilization and the War with Spain," *AQ* 36:4 (1984), pp. 481–502.

Axtell, James. "Europeans, Indians, and the Age of Discovery in American History Textbooks," *AHR* 92:3 (1987), pp. 621–32.

Ayers, Edward L. *Vengeance and Justice: Crime and Punishment in the 19th Century American South.* New York: Oxford University Press, 1984.

Badger, R. Reid. *The Great American Fair: The World's Columbian Exposition and American Culture.* Chicago: Nelson-Hall, 1979.

Bain, David Haward. *Sitting in Darkness: Americans in the Phlippines.* Boston: Houghton Mifflin Company, 1986.

Baker, Mark. *Nam: The Vietnam War in the Words of the Men and Women Who Fought There.* New York: Quill, 1982.

Bakken, Gordon Morris. *The Development of Law on the Rocky Mountain Frontier, 1850–1912.* Westport, CT: Greenwood Press, 1983.

Bakker, J. "The Western: Can It Be Great?" *Dutch Quarterly Review of Anglo-American Letters* 14:2 (1984), pp. 138–63.

Balio, Tino, editor. *The American Film Industry.* Madison: University of Wisconsin Press, 1976.

Baltzell, E. Digby. *The Protestant Establishment: Aristocracy and Caste in America.* New Haven: Yale University Press, 1964.

Bancroft, Hubert Howe. *In These Latter Days.* Chicago: The Blakely-Oswald Company, 1918.

———. *Popular Tribunals. The Works of Hubert Howe Bancroft,* Volumes 36 and 37. San Francisco: The History Company, Publishers, 1887.

Banton, Michael. *The Idea of Race.* Boulder, CO: Westview Press, 1977.

Baritz, Loren. *Backfire: A History of How American Culture Led Us into Vietnam and Made Us Fight the Way We Did.* New York: Wm. Morrow & Co., 1985.

Barker-Benfield, G. J. *The Horrors of the Half-Known Life: Male Attitudes and Sexuality in Nineteenth-Century America.* New York: Harper & Row, 1976.

Barnet, Richard J. *Roots of War: The Men and Institutions Behind U.S. Foreign Policy.* New York and London: Penguin Books, 1972.

Barnett, Louise K. *The Ignoble Savage.* Westport, CT: Greenwood Press, 1975.

Barnett, Steve, and Martin G. Silberman. *Ideology and Everyday Life: Anthropology,*

Neo-Marxist Thought, and the Problem of Ideology and the Social Whole. Ann Arbor: University of Michigan Press, 1981.

Barnouw, Erik. *Tube of Plenty: The Evolution of American Television.* New York: Oxford University Press, 1975.

Barsness, John A. "Theodore Roosevelt as Cowboy: The Virginian as Jacksonian Man," *AQ* 21:3 (1969), pp. 609–19.

Barthes, Roland. *Mythologies.* Translated by Annette Lavers. New York: Hill & Wang, 1972.

Bascom, William. "The Forms of Folklore: Prose Narratives," *Journal of American Folklore* 78:1 (1965), pp. 3–20.

Basinger, Jeanine. *Anthony Mann.* Boston: Twayne Publishers, 1979.

———. "John Wayne, An Appreciation," *American Film* (June 1976), pp. 50–3.

———. *The World War II Combat Film: Anatomy of a Genre.* New York: Columbia University Press, 1986.

Bataille, Gretchen M., and Charles L. P. Silet, editors. *The Pretend Indians: Images of Native Americans in the Movies.* Ames: Iowa State University Press, 1980.

Baxter, John. *Hollywood in the Thirties.* London: A. Zwemmer, 1968.

Beard, Charles A., and George H. E. Smith. *The Future Comes: A Study of the New Deal.* New York: The Macmillan Company, 1933.

Beard, Charles A., and Mary Beard. *America in Midpassage. The Rise of American Civilization,* Volume III. New York: The Macmillan Company, 1939.

———. *The American Spirit: A Study of the Idea of Civilization in the United States. The Rise of American Civilization,* Volume IV. New York: The Macmillan Company, 1942.

———. *The Rise of American Civilization,* Volumes I and II. New York: The Macmillan Company, 1939.

Beard, Charles A., editor. *America Faces the Future.* Boston: Houghton Mifflin Company, 1932.

Becker, James F. "The Rise of Managerial Economics," *Marxist Perspectives* 2:2 (1979), pp. 34–55.

Behlmer, Rudy, editor. *Inside Warner Bros. (1935–1951).* New York: Simon & Schuster, 1985.

Beidler, John Xavier. *X. Beidler, Vigilante.* Edited by Helen Fitzgerald Sanders and William Bertsche, Jr. Norman: University of Oklahoma Press, 1957.

Beisner, Robert L. *Twelve Against Empire: The Anti-Imperialists, 1898–1900.* New York: McGraw-Hill Book Company, 1968.

Bell, Daniel. *The End of Ideology: On the Exhaustion of Political Ideas in the Fifties.* Glencoe, IL: Free Press, 1960.

Bell, Sidney. *Righteous Conquest: Woodrow Wilson and the Evolution of the New Diplomacy.* Port Washington, NY: Kennikat Press, 1972.

Bellamy, Edward. *Looking Backward, 2000–1887.* Boston: Ticknor and Company, 1888.

Bender, Thomas. *Toward an Urban Vision: Ideas and Institutions in Nineteenth Century America.* Lexington: University Press of Kentucky, 1975.

Bendix, Reinhard. *Work and Authority in Industry: Ideologies of Management in the Course of Industrialization.* Berkeley: University of California Press, 1956.

Bercovitch, Sacvan. *The American Jeremiad.* Madison: University of Wisconsin Press, 1978.

———. "The Typology of America's Mission," *AQ* 30:2 (1976), pp. 135–55.

Bercovitch, Sacvan, and Myra Jehlen, editors. *Ideology and Classic American Literature.* New York: Cambridge University Press, 1986.

Berger, Peter L., and Thomas Luckmann. *The Social Construction of Reality: A Treatise in the Sociology of Knowledge.* Garden City, NY: Anchor Books, 1967.

Berkhofer, Robert F., Jr. "A New Context for American Studies?" *AQ* 41:4 (1989), pp. 588–613.

———. *The White Man's Indian: Images of the American Indian from Columbus to the Present.* New York: Alfred A. Knopf, 1978.

Berman, Larry. *Planning a Tragedy: The Americanization of the War in Vietnam.* New York and London: W. W. Norton, 1984.

Betts, Raymond F. "Immense Dimensions: The Impact of the American West on Late Nineteenth-Century European Thought About Expansion," *WHQ* 10:2 (1979), pp. 149–66.

Betts, Richard K. *Soldiers, Statesmen, and Cold War Crises.* Cambridge: Harvard University Press, 1977.

Beveridge, Albert J. *The Meaning of the Times, and Other Speeches.* Freeport: Books for Libraries Press, 1968 [1906].

Biddiss, Michael D., editor. *Images of Race.* New York: Holmes & Meier Publishers, 1979.

Billington, Ray Allen. *America's Frontier Heritage.* Albuquerque: University of New Mexico Press, 1966.

———. *Frederick Jackson Turner: Historian, Scholar, Teacher.* New York: Oxford University Press, 1973.

———. *Land of Savagery, Land of Promise: The European Image of the American Frontier.* New York: W. W. Norton, 1981.

Bird, Robert Montgomery. *Nick of the Woods; or, The Jibbenainosay: A Tale of Kentucky.* Edited by Curtis Dahl. New Haven: College and University Press, 1967.

Birnbaum, Norman. *The Radical Renewal: The Politics of Ideas in Modern America.* New York: Pantheon Books, 1988.

Biskind, Peter. *Seeing Is Believing: How Hollywood Taught Us to Stop Worrying and Love the Fifties.* New York: Pantheon Books, 1983.

Blackstone, Sarah J. *Buckskins, Bullets, and Business.* Westport, CT: Greenwood Press, 1986.

Blair, John G. *Modular America: Cross-Cultural Perspectives on the Emergence of an American Way.* Westport, CT: Greenwood Press, 1988.

Blair, John M. *The Control of Oil.* New York: Vintage Books, 1978.

Blaufarb, Douglas S. *The Counterinsurgency Era: U.S. Doctrine and Performance.* New York: Free Press, 1977.

Bleiler, E. F., editor. *Eight Dime Novels.* New York: Dover Publications, 1974.

Blount, James H. *The American Occupation of the Philippines, 1898–1912.* New York: G. P. Putnam's Sons, 1912.

Blu, Karen I. *The Lumbee Problem: The Making of an American Indian People.* Cambridge: Cambridge University Press, 1980.

Blum, John Morton. *The Republican Roosevelt.* Cambridge: Harvard University Press, 1954.

———. *V Was for Victory: Politics and American Culture During World War II.* New York: Harcourt Brace Jovanovich, 1976.

Blumenthal, Sidney. *The Rise of the Counter-Establishment: From Conservative Ideology to Political Power.* New York: Harper & Row, 1988.

Blumin, Stuart M. *The Emergence of the Middle Class: Social Experience in the American City, 1760–1800.* Cambridge, England: Cambridge University Press, 1989.

———. "The Hypothesis of Middle-Class Formation in Nineteenth-Century America: A Critique and Some Proposals," *AHR* 90:2 (1985), pp. 299–338.

Bodnar, John. *Workers' World: Kinship, Community, and Protest in an Industrial Society, 1900–1940.* Baltimore: The Johns Hopkins University Press, 1982.

Bogdanovitch, Peter. *John Ford.* London, Studio Vista, 1968.

Bold, Christine. "The View from the Road: Katharine Kellock's New Deal Guidebooks," *American Studies* 29:2 (1988), pp. 5–30.

———. "The Voice of the Fiction Factory in Dime and Pulp Westerns," *JAS* 17:1 (1983), pp. 29–46.

———. *Selling the Wild West: Popular Western Fiction, 1860–1960.* Bloomington: Indiana University Press, 1991.

Boorstin, Daniel. *The Image: A Guide to Pseudo-Events in America.* New York: Harper Colophon Books, 1961.

———. *The Americans: The Democratic Experience.* New York: Random House, 1973.

———. *The Americans: The National Experience.* New York: Random House, 1975.

Booth, Ken, and Moorhead Wright. *American Thinking About Peace and War.* New York: Barnes & Noble, 1978.

Bordwell, David. *Narration in the Fiction Film.* Madison: University of Wisconsin Press, 1985.

Bordwell, David, Janet Staiger, and Kristin Thompson. *The Classical Hollywood Cinema: Film Style and Mode of Production to 1960.* New York: Columbia University Press, 1985.

Boston Publishing Company, editors. *The Vietnam Experience: War in the Shadows.* Boston: Boston Publishing Company, 1988.

Brace, Charles Loring. *The Dangerous Classes of New York, and Twenty Years Work Among Them.* New York: Wynkoop and Hallenbeck, 1872.

Braestrup, Peter, and Burns Roper. *Big Story: How the American Press and Television Reported and Interpreted the Crisis of Tet 1968 in Vietnam and Washington.* Two Volumes. Boulder, CO: Westview Press, 1976. Abridged edition. Garden City, NY: Anchor Books, 1978.

Branch, Taylor. *Parting the Waters: America in the King Years, 1954–63.* New York: Simon & Schuster, 1988.

Brands, H. W. "The Age of Vulnerability: Eisenhower and the National Insecurity State," *AHR* 94:4 (1989), pp. 963–989.

Brauer, Ralph, and Donna Brauer. *The Horse, the Gun and the Piece of Property: Changing Images of the TV Western.* Bowling Green: Bowling Green University Press, 1975.

Breitbart, Eric. "From Panorama to Docudrama: Notes on the Visualization of History," *RHR* 25 (1981), pp. 115–26.

Brenner, Anita. *The Wind That Swept Mexico.* Austin: University of Texas Press, 1971.

Brewer, Daniel Chauncey. *The Conquest of New England by the Immigrant.* New York: G.P. Putnam's Sons, 1926.

Brier, Stephen. "A History Film Without Much History," *RHR* 41 (1988), pp. 41–128.

Brinkley, Joel, and Stephen Engelberg, Editors. *Report of the Congressional Committee Investigating the Iran-Contra Affair, with the Minority View.* Abridged Edition. New York: Times Books, 1988.

Brodie, Bernard. *War and Politics.* New York: Macmillan, 1973.

Broehl, Wayne G., Jr. *The Molly Maguires.* New York: Vintage Books, 1964.

Brooks, Tim, and Earle Marsh, *The Complete Directory of Prime Time Network TV Shows, 1946–Present.* New York: Ballantine Books, 1979.

Brown, Dee. *Bury My Heart at Wounded Knee.* New York: Holt, Rinehart and Winston, 1973.

Brown, Richard D. *Modernization: The Transformation of American Life, 1600–1865.* New York: Hill & Wang, 1976.

Brown, Richard Maxwell. *No Duty To Retreat: An American Theme.* New York: Oxford University Press, 1991.

———. *Strain of Violence: Historical Studies of American Violence and Vigilantism.* New York: Oxford University Press, 1975.

Browne, Malcolm W. *The New Face of War.* Revised Edition. New York: Bantam Books, 1968.

Browne, Ray B., Sam Grogg, Jr., and Larry Landrum, editors. "Theories and Methodologies in Popular Culture," *JPC* 9:2 (1975), pp. 349–508.

Brownlow, Kevin. *The War, the West, and the Wilderness.* New York: Alfred A. Knopf, 1979.

Brownmiller, Susan. *Against Our Will: Men, Women and Rape.* New York: Simon & Schuster, 1975.

Brownstein, Ronald. *The Power and the Glitter: The Hollywood-Washington Connection.* New York: Pantheon, 1990.

Bruce, Robert V. *1877: The Year of Violence.* Indianapolis: Bobbs-Merrill, 1959.

Bryson, John. "Sam Peckinpah," *American Film* 10:6 (1985), pp. 21–6, 69.

Buckley, Peter G. "The Case Against Ned Buntline: The 'Words, Signs, and Gestures' of Popular Authorship," *Prospects 13* (1988), pp. 249–72.

Buel, James W. *The Border Outlaws* . . . St. Louis: Historical Publishing Co., 1881.

———. *Heroes of the Plains* . . . St. Louis: Historical Publishing Co., 1883.

———. *The Mysteries and Miseries of America's Great Cities.* St. Louis: Historical Publishing Co., 1883.

Burnette, Robert. *The Tortured Americans.* Englewood Cliffs, NJ: Prentice-Hall, 1971.

Burroughs, Edgar Rice. *At the Earth's Core.* New York: Ace Books, 1922.

———. *Beyond Thirty.* New York: Street & Smith, 1915. Reprinted as *The Lost Continent.* New York: Ace Books, 1973.

———. *Carson of Venus.* New York: Ace Books, 1939.

———. *Land of Terror.* New York: Ace Books, 1985.
———. *Lost on Venus.* New York: Ace Books, 1935.
———. *Pellucidar.* New York: Ace Books, 1972.
———. *Princess of Mars.* New York: Dover Publications, 1964.
———. *Tarzan of the Apes.* New York: Ballantine Books, 1974.
———. *The Eternal Savage.* New York: Ace Books, 1972.
———. *The Gods of Mars.* New York: Ballantine Books, 1973.
———. *The Land That Time Forgot.* New York: Grosset and Dunlap, 1925.
———. *The Mad King.* New York: Ace Books, 1914.
———. *The Moon Men.* New York: Ace Books, 1925.
———. *The Moon Maid.* New York: Ace Books, 1923.
———. *The Return of Tarzan.* New York: Ballantine Books, 1974.
———. *Warlord of Mars.* New York: Ballantine Books, 1973.

Burrows, Jack. *John Ringo, The Gunfighter Who Never Was.* Tucson: University of Arizona Press, 1987.

Buscombe, Edward, editor. *The BFI Companion to the Western.* London: Andre Deutsch/BFI Publishers, 1988.

Cable, Larry E. *Conflict of Myths: The Development of American Counterinsurgency Doctrine and the Vietnam War.* New York: New York University Press, 1986.

Calloway, Colin G. "Neither White nor Red: White Renegades on the American Indian Frontier," *WHQ* 17:1 (1986), pp. 43–66.

Campbell, Joseph. *The Hero with a Thousand Faces.* Cleveland, Meridian Books, 1965.

Canham, Kingsley. *The Hollywood Professionals: Michael Curtiz, Raoul Walsh, Henry Hathaway.* London: The Tantivy Press, 1973.

Capps, Walter, Editor. *The Vietnam Reader.* New York, Routledge, 1991.

Caputo, Philip. *A Rumor of War.* New York: Ballantine Books, 1977.

Carby, Hazel V. " 'On the Threshold of Woman's Era': Lynching, Empire, and Sexuality in Black Feminist Theory," *Critical Inquiry* 12:1 (1985), pp. 262–77.

Carmines, Edward G., and James A. Atimson. *Issue Evolution: Race and the Transformation of American Politics.* Princeton, NJ: Princeton University Press, 1989.

Carpozi, George. *The John Wayne Story.* New Rochelle: Arlington, 1972.

Carter, Everett. "Cultural History Written with Lightning: The Significance of *The Birth of a Nation,*" in Hennig Cohen, editor, *The American Culture: Approaches to the Study of the United States.* Boston: Houghton Mifflin Company, 1968, pp. 358–69.

Casey, Michael, Clark Dougan, Samuel Lipsman, Jack Sweetman, Stephen Weiss, and the Editors of the Boston Publishing Company. *The Vietnam Experience: Flags into Battle.* Boston: Boston Publishing Company, 1987.

Cassity, Michael J. *Chains of Fear: American Race Relations Since Reconstruction.* Westport, CT: Greenwood Press, 1984.

Castaneda, Carlos. *The Teachings of Don Juan: A Yaqui Way of Knowledge.* Berkeley: University of California Press, 1968.

Catlin, George. *Catalogue of Catlin's Indian Gallery of Portraits, Landscapes, Manners and Customs, Costumes, etc.* New York: Piercy and Reed, 1837.

———. *Letters and Notes on the Manners, Customs and Condition of the North American Indians.* Second Edition. New York: Wiley and Putnam, 1841.

Cawelti, John G. *Adventure, Mystery and Romance: Formula Stories as Art and Popular Culture*. Chicago: University of Chicago Press, 1976.

Cawelti, John G., editor. *Focus on* Bonnie and Clyde. Englewood Cliffs, NJ: Prentice-Hall, 1973.

Challener, Richard D. *Admirals, Generals, and American Foreign Policy, 1898–1914*. Princeton: Princeton University Press, 1973.

Chandler, Raymond. *Killer in the Rain*. New York: Ballantine Books, 1964.

———. *The Long Goodbye*. New York: Ballantine Books, 1971.

———. *The Simple Art of Murder*. New York: Ballantine Books, 1972.

Chandler, Alfred D. *The Visible Hand: The Managerial Revolution in American Business*. Cambridge, MA: Belknap Press of Harvard University Press, 1977.

Chase, Allan. *The Legacy of Malthus: The Social Costs of the New Scientific Racism*. New York: Alfred A. Knopf, 1977.

Chatman, Seymour. *Story and Discourse: Narrative Structure in Fiction and Film*. Ithaca, NY: Cornell University Press, 1978.

Chesnutt, Charles W. *The Marrow of Tradition*. Introduction by Robert M. Farnsworth. Ann Arbor: University of Michigan Press, 1973.

Chester, Lewis, Godfrey Hodgson, and Bruce Page. *American Melodrama: The Presidential Campaign of 1968*. New York: The Viking Press, 1968.

Child, Lydia Maria. *Hobomok and Other Writings*. Edited by Carolyn L. Karcher. New Brunswick, NJ: Rutgers University Press, 1986.

Chrisman, Harry E. *Fifty Years on the Owl Hoot Trail: Jim Herron, The First Sheriff of No Man's Land, Oklahoma Territory*. Chicago: Sage Books, 1969.

Clarens, Carlos. *Crime Movies, From Griffith to the Godfather and Beyond*. New York: W. W. Norton, 1980.

Clareson, Thomas D. "Lost Lands, Lost Races: A Pagan Princess of Their Very Own," *JPC* 8:4 (1975) pp. 714–23.

Clebsch, William A. "The American 'Mythique' as Redeemer Nation," *Prospects* 4 (1978), pp. 79–94.

Coan, Blair. *The Red Web*. Belmont, MA: Western Islands Press, 1925.

Coates, Paul. *The Lost Reflection: The Alienation of the Image in Polish and Western Cinema*. London: Verso, 1985.

Cochran, Thomas C. *Business in American Life: A History*. New York: McGraw-Hill Book Company, 1972.

Cochran, Thomas C., and William Miller. *The Age of Enterprise: A Social History of Industrial America*. New York: Harper & Row, 1961.

Cockburn, Leslie. *Out of Control: The Story of the Reagan Administration's Secret War in Nicaragua, the Illegal Arms Pipeline, and the Contra Drug Connection*. New York: Atlantic Monthly Press, 1987.

Cody, William F. *The Crimson Trail; or, Custer's Last Warpath, A Romance Founded Upon the Present Border Warfare as Witnessed by Hon. W. F. Cody. New York Weekly* 31 (1876).

———. *Kansas King; or, The Red Right Hand*. New York: Beadles Half-Dime Library, 1877.

———. *The Life of Hon. William F. Cody, Known as Buffalo Bill, the Famous Hunter, Scout and Guide: An Autobiography*. Hartford: [],1879.

Cohen, Bernard C. *The Public's Impact on Foreign Policy*. Lanham, MD: University Press of America, 1983.

Cohen, Bronwen, J. "Nativism and Western Myth: The Influence of Nativist Ideals Upon the American Self-Image," *JAS* 8:1 (1974), pp. 23–40.

Cohen, Hennig, editor. *The American Experience: Approaches to the Study of the United States*. Boston: Houghton Mifflin Company, 1968.

Cohen, Lizabeth. "Encountering Mass Culture at the Grassroots: The Experience of Chicago Workers in the 1920s," *AQ* 41:1 (1989), pp. 6–33.

Cohen, Stanley. *Visions of Social Control: Crime Punishment and Classification*. Cambridge, England: Polity Press, 1985.

Coleman, Peter. *The Liberal Conspiracy: The Congress for Cultural Freedom and the Struggle for the Mind of Postwar Europe*. New York: Free Press, 1989.

Commons, John R. *Races and Immigrants in America* (1907, revised and reissued 1920).

Commons, John R., and Associates. *The History of Labour in the United States*. Volume 1. New York: Macmillan Co., 1918.

Conk, Margo A. "Social Mobility in Historical Perspective," *Marxist Perspectives* 1:3 (1978), pp. 52–69.

Conkin, Paul K. *The New Deal*. Second Edition. Arlington Heights, IL: Harlan Davidson, 1975.

Conlin, Joseph R. *The American Radical Press, 1880–1961*. Volume 1. Westport, CT: Greenwood Press, 1974.

Conot, Robert. *Rivers of Blood, Years of Darkness: The Unforgettable Classic Account of the Watts Riot*. New York: William Morrow, 1968.

Cook, David A. *A History of Narrative Film*. New York: W. W. Norton & Company, 1981.

Cook, D. J. *Hands Up; or, Twenty Years of Detective Life in the Mountains and on the Plains*. Edited by Everett L. DeGolyer, Jr. Norman, OK: University of Oklahoma Press, 1958 [1882].

Cook, John L. *The Advisor*. New York: Dorrance, 1973.

Cooper, James Fenimore. *The Deerslayer; or, The First Warpath*. Philadelphia: Lea and Blanchard, 1841.

———. *The Last of the Mohicans: A Tale of 1757*. New York: Penguin Books, 1986 (1826).

———. *The Pathfinder; or, The Inland Sea*. Philadelphia: Lea and Blanchard, 1840.

———. *The Prairie; A Tale*. Introduction by Henry Nash Smith. New York: Holt, Rinehart and Winston, 1964.

———. *The Redskins; or, Indian and Injin*. New York: Townsend, 1860.

Cooper, Jerry M. *The Army and Civil Disorder: Federal Military Intervention in Labor Disputes, 1877–1900*. Westport, CT: Greenwood Press, 1980.

Cooper, John Milton, Jr. *The Warrior and the Priest: Woodrow Wilson and Theodore Roosevelt*. Cambridge, MA: Belknap Press of Harvard University Press, 1983.

Coppedge, Walter, *Henry King's America*. Metuchen, NJ, & London: The Scarecrow Press, 1986.

Cords, Nicholas, and Patrick Gerster. *Myth and the American Experience*. Two Volumes. Beverly Hills, CA: Glencoe Press, 1973.

Corliss, Richard. *Talking Pictures: Screenwriters in the American Cinema.* Woodstock, NY: The Overlook Press, 1985.

Corliss, Richard, editor. *The Hollywood Screenwriters: A Film Comment Book.* New York: Discus Books, 1972.

Corson, William R. *The Betrayal.* New York: W. W. Norton, 1968.

Cortner, Richard C. *A Mob Intent on Death: The NAACP and the Arkansas Riot Cases.* Middletown, CT: Wesleyan University Press, 1988.

Cott, Nancy F. "Two Beards: Coauthorship and the Concept of Civilization," *AQ* 42:2 (1990), pp. 274–300.

Cowan, Sam K. *Segeant York and His People.* New York: Funk & Wagnalls Company, 1922.

Coyle, Lee. "Kenneth Roberts and the American Historical Novel," in James C. Austin and Donald A. Koch, editors, *Popular Literature in America: A Symposium in Honor of Lyon N. Richardson.* Bowling Green, OH: Bowling Green University Popular Press, 1972, pp. 70–77.

Crane, Stephen. *Complete Short Stories and Sketches of Stephen Crane.* Edited by Thomas A. Gulleson. Garden City, NY: Doubleday, 1963.

———. *Reports of War. Works.* Volume 9. Charlottesville: University of Virginia Press, 1969–76.

Cremony, John C. *Life Among the Apaches.* Lincoln: University of Nebraska Press, 1983.

Cress, Lawrence Delbert. "An Armed Community: The Origins and Meaning of the Right to Bear Arms," *JAH* 71:1 (1984), pp. 22–43.

Cronon, William. "Revisiting the Vanishing Frontier: The Legacy of Frederick Jackson Turner," *WHQ* 18:2 (1987), pp. 157–76.

Crozier, Michel. *The Trouble with America: Why the System Is Breaking Down.* Translated by Peter Heinegg. Berkeley: The University of California Press, 1984.

Cuff, Robert, editor. "Samuel Gompers, Leonard Wood and Military Preparedness," *Labor History* 12:1, pp. 280–8.

Cunningham, Eugene. *Triggernometry: A Gallery of Gunfighters, with Technical Notes on Leather Slapping as a Fine Art . . .* New York: Press of the Pioneers, 1934.

Cunningham, Rodger. *Apples on the Flood: The Southern Mountain Experience.* Knoxville: University of Tennessee Press, 1987.

Custer, Elizabeth B. *Tenting on the Plains; or, General Custer in Kansas and Texas.* New York: Charles L. Webster and Company, 1887.

Custer, George Armstrong. *My Life on the Plains; or, Personal Experiences with Indians.* Edited by Edgar I. Stewart. Norman: University of Oklahoma Press, 1962.

Custer, George Armstrong, *et al. Wild Life on the Plains and Horrors of Indian Warfare, by a Corps of Competent Authors and Artists . . .* St. Louis: Continental Publishing Company, 1891. Reprinted, New York: Arno Press, 1969.

Cutler, James E. *Lynch Law: An Investigation into the History of Lynching in the United States.* New York: Negro Universities Press, 1969.

Dacus, Joseph A. *Annals of the Great Strikes in the United States.* New York: Burt Franklin, 1969.

———. *The Life and Adventures of Frank and Jesse James and the Younger Brothers.* St. Louis: N. D. Thompson and Co., 1882.

Daniel, Pete. "Commentary/The Metamorphosis of Slavery, 1865–1900," *JAH* 66:1 (1979), pp. 88–99.

Davie, Maurice R. *A Constructive Immigration Policy*. New Haven: Yale University Press, 1923.

Davies, Peter. *The Truth About Kent State: A Challenge to the American Conscience*. New York: Farrar Straus Giroux, 1973.

Davis, Britton. *The Truth About Geronimo*. Lincoln: University of Nebraska Press, 1976 [1929].

Davis, David Brion. "Ten Gallon Hero," *From Homicide to Slavery: Studies in American Culture*, chapter 5. New York: Oxford University Press, 1986.

Davis, Robert Edward. *Response to Innovation: A Study of Popular Argument About New Mass Media*. New York: Arno Press, 1976.

Dawley, Alan. *Class and Community: The Industrial Revolution in Lynn*. Cambridge, MA: Harvard University Press, 1976.

Dearborn, Mary V. *Pocahontas' Daughters: Gender and Ethnicity in American Culture*. New York: Oxford University Press, 1986.

Dearing, Charles L., Paul T. Homan, Lewis L. Lorwin, and Leverett S. Lyon. *The ABC of the NRA*. Washington: The Brookings Institution, 1934.

Debo, Angie. *And Still the Waters Run*. New York: Gordian Press, 1952.

DeLeon, Arnoldo. *They Called Them Greasers: Anglo Attitudes toward Mexicans in Texas, 1821–1900*. Austin: University of Texas Press, 1983.

———. *The American as Anarchist: Reflections on Indigenous Radicalism*. Baltimore: The Johns Hopkins University Press, 1978.

Denning, Michael. *Mechanic Accents: Dime Novels and Working-Class Culture in America*. London: Verso, 1987.

———. " 'The Special American Conditions': Marxism and American Studies," *AQ* 38:3 (1986), pp. 356–80.

Denton, Clive, Kingsley Canham, and Tony Thomas. *The Hollywood Professionals: Henry King, Lewis Milestone, Sam Wood*. London: The Tantivy Press, 1974.

Derber, Milton. *The American Idea of Industrial Democracy, 1865–1965*. Urbana: University of Illinois Press, 1970.

Destler, Chester McArthur. *American Radicalism, 1865–1901*. Chicago: Quadrangle Books, 1946.

Deverell, William F. "To Loose the Safety Valve: Eastern Workers and Western Lands," *WHQ* 19:3 (1988), pp. 269–86.

Diamond, Sigmund, editor. *The Nation Transformed: The Creation of an Industrial Society*. New York: George Braziller, 1963.

Dick, Everett. *The Lure of the Land: A Social History of the Public Lands from the Articles of Confederation to the New Deal*. Lincoln: University of Nebraska Press, 1970.

Diggins, John P. "Barbarism & Capitalism: The Strange Perspectives of Thorstein Veblen," *Marxist Perspectives* 1:2 (1978), pp. 138–56.

———. "Power and Authority in American History: The Case of Charles A. Beard," *AHR* 86:4 (1981), pp. 701–30.

———. "Republicanism and Progressivism," *AQ* 37:4 (1985), pp. 572–98.

Dillon, Sam. *Commandos: The CIA and Nicaragua's Contra Rebels*. New York: Holt, 1991.

Dimsdale, Thomas J. *The Vigilantes of Montana: or, Popular Justice in the Rocky Mountains* . . . Norman: University of Oklahoma Press, 1953.

Dipple, Brian W. *Custer's Last Stand: The Anatomy of an American Myth*. Missoula: University of Montana Press, 1976.

———. *The Vanishing American: White Attitudes and U.S. Indian Policy*. Middletown CT: Wesleyan University Press, 1982.

———. "The Winning of the West Reconsidered," *Wilson Quarterly* (Summer, 1990), pp. 71–85.

Dixon, Joseph K. *The Vanishing Race: The Last Great Indian Council* . . . Garden City, NY: Doubleday, Page and Co., 1913.

Dixon, Thomas, Jr. *The Black Hood*. New York: Grosset and Dunlap, 1924.

———. *The Clansman: An Historical Romance of the Ku Klux Klan*. Introduction by Thomas D. Clark. Lexington: University of Kentucky Press, 1970.

———. *The Fall of a Nation: A Sequel to the Birth of a Nation*. New York: D. Appleton, 1916.

———. *The Flaming Sword*. Atlanta: Monarch Publishing, 1939.

———. *The Leopard's Spots: A Romance of the White Man's Burden*. New York: Doubleday and Page, 1902.

Dodge, Richard Irving. *Our Wild Indians; Thirty-Three Years Experience Among the Red Men of the Great West* . . . Hartford, CT: A. D. Worthington, 1883.

Donnelle, A. J. editor. *Cyclorama of Custer's Last Battle* [1889]. New York: Argonaut Press, 1966.

Donnelly, Ignatius. *Caesar's Column: A Story of the Twentieth Century*. Edited by Walter B. Rideout. Cambridge, MA: Belknap Press of Harvard University Press, 1960.

Donovan, Timothy Paul. *Henry Adams and Brooks Adams: The Education of Two American Historians*. Norman: University of Oklahoma Press, 1961.

Doob, Leonard W. *Patriotism and Nationalism: Their Psychological Foundations*. New Haven: Yale University Press, 1964.

Dooley, Roger. *From Scarface to Scarlett: American Films in the 1930s*. New York: Harcourt Brace Jovanovich, 1981.

Dorson, Richard M. *America in Legend: Folklore from the Colonial Period to the Present*. New York: Pantheon Books, 1973.

———. *American Folklore and the Historian*. Chicago: University of Chicago Press, 1971.

Dougan, Clark, David Fulghum, and the Editors of the Boston Publishing Company. *The Vietnam Experience: The Fall of the South*. Boston: Boston Publishing Company, 1985.

Dougan, Clark, Samuel Lipsman, and the Editors of the Boston Publishing Company. *The Vietnam Experience: A Nation Divided*. Boston: Boston Publishing Company, 1984.

Dougan, Clark, Stephen Weiss, and the Editors of the Boston Publishing Company. *The Vietnam Experience: Nineteen Sixty-Eight*. Boston: Boston Publishing Company, 1983.

Douglas, Ann. *The Feminization of American Culture*. New York: Avon Books, 1977.

Dower, John W. *War Without Mercy: Race and Power in the Pacific War*. New York: Pantheon Books, 1986.

Doyle, Don Harrison. "Social Theory and New Communities in Nineteenth-Century America," *WHQ* 8:2 (1977), pp. 167–88.

Doyle, Edward, Samuel Lipsman, and the Editors of the Boston Publishing Company. *The Vietnam Experience: America Takes Over, 1965–67*. Boston: Boston Publishing Company, 1982.

Doyle, Edward, Samuel Lipsman, Terrence Maitland, and the Editors of the Boston Publishing Company. *The Vietnam Experience: The North*. Boston: Boston Publishing Company, 1986.

Doyle, Edward, Stephen Weiss, and the Editors of the Boston Publishing Company. *The Vietnam Experience: A Collision of Cultures*. Boston: Boston Publishing Company, 1984.

Drew, Bernard A., with Martin H. Greenberg and Charles G. Waugh. *Western Series and Sequels: A Reference Guide*. New York: Garland Publishing, Inc., 1986.

Draper, Theodore. "American Hubris: From Truman to the Persian Gulf," *NYRB* (July 16, 1987), pp. 40–8.

———. "An Autopsy," *NYRB* (December 17, 1987), pp. 67–77.

———. "Presidential Wars," *NYRB* (September 26, 1991), pp. 64–74.

———. "Reagan's Junta," *NYRB* (January 29, 1987), pp. 5–14.

———. "Rewriting the Iran-Contra Story," *NYRB* (January 19, 1989), pp. 38–45.

———. "The Fall of an American Junta," *NYRB* (October 22, 1987), pp. 45–57.

———. "The Rise of the American Junta," *NYRB* (October 8, 1987), pp. 47–58.

———. "The True History of the Gulf War," *NYRB* (January 30, 1992), pp. 38–45.

———. *A Very Thin Line: The Iran-Contra Affairs*. New York: Hill and Wang, 1991.

Drimmon, Richard M. *Facing West, The Metaphysics of Indian-Hating and Empire Building*. Minneapolis: University of Minnesota Press, 1981.

Dubofsky, Melvyn. *We Shall Be All: A History of the IWW*. New York: Quadrangle Books, 1969.

———. *Industrialism and the American Worker, 1865–1920*. New York: Thomas Y. Crowell Company, 1975.

Duffy, Christopher. *The Military Experience in the Age of Reason*. New York: Atheneum, 1988.

Dumezil, Georges. *From Myth to Fiction: The Saga of Hadingus*. Translated by Derek Coltman. Chicago: The University of Chicago Press, 1970.

Duncan, Donald. *The New Legions*. New York: Pocket Books, 1967.

Dundes, Alan. "Folk Ideas as Units of World View," *American Folklore* 84:1 (1971), pp. 93–103.

———. *Interpreting Folklore*. Bloomington: University of Indiana Press, 1980.

Dundes, Alan, and Carl Pagter. *Urban Folklore from the Paperwork Empire*. Austin, TX: American Folklore Society, 1975.

Dunn, H. H. *The Crimson Jester: Zapata of Mexico*. New York: National Travel Club, 1934.

[Dunne, Finley Peter]. *Mr. Dooley in Peace and in War.* Boston: Small, Maynard & Company, 1899.

———. *Mr. Dooley's Philosophy.* New York: R. H. Russell, 1900.

Dupuy, R. Ernest, and Trevor N. Dupuy, *The Military Heritage of America.* New York: McGraw-Hill, 1956.

Dyer, Thomas G. *Theodore Roosevelt and the Idea of Race.* Baton Rouge: Louisiana State University Press, 1980.

Easton, Robert. *Max Brand: The Big Westerner.* Norman: University of Oklahoma Press, 1970.

Edsall, Thomas Byrne. *Chain Reaction: The Impact of Race, Rights and Taxes on American Politics.* New York: W. W. Norton, 1991.

Edwards, John N. *Noted Guerrillas, or the Warfare of the Border* . . . St. Louis: Bryan, Brand & Company, 1877.

Elazar, Daniel J. "Land, Space, and Civil Society in America," *WHQ* 5:3 (1974), pp. 261–84.

Elley, Derek. *The Epic Film: Myth and History.* London: Routledge and Kegan Paul, 1984.

Ellis, Edward S., and Edward L. Wheeler. *Seth Jones and Deadwood Dick on Deck.* Edited by Philip Durham. New York: The Odyssey Press, 1966.

Ellis, John. *The Social History of the Machine Gun.* New York: Pantheon Books, 1975.

Ellsworth, Scott. *Death in a Promised Land: The Tulsa Race Riot of 1921.* Baton Rouge: Louisiana State University Press, 1982.

Elson, Ruth M. *The Guardians of Tradition: American Schoolbooks in the Nineteenth Century.* Lincoln: University of Nebraska Press, 1964.

———. *Myths and Mores in American Best Sellers, 1865–1965.* New York: Garland, 1985.

Emmons, David M. *Garden in the Grasslands: Boomer Literature of the Central Great Plains.* Lincoln: University of Nebraska Press, 1971.

———. "Social Myth and Social Reality," *Montana: The Magazine of Western History* 39:4 (1989), pp. 2–9.

Erickson, Paul D. *Reagan Speaks: The Making of an American Myth.* New York: New York University Press, 1985.

Estall, R. C. "Population Growth and Environment: Some Aspects of the Problem in the United States and the Response," *JAS* 6:1 (1972), pp. 55–68.

Etulain, Richard W., and Michael T. Marsden, editors. *The Popular Western.* Bowling Green, OH: Bowling Green University Press, 1974.

Everson, William K. *A Pictorial History of the Western Film.* Secaucus, NJ: The Citadel Press, 1973.

Ewen, Stuart. *Captains of Consciousness: Advertising and the Social Roots of the Consumer Culture.* New York: McGraw-Hill Book Company, 1976.

Eyles, Allen. *John Wayne and the Movies.* New York: Grosset & Dunlap, 1976.

Fairchild, Henry Pratt. *The Melting-Pot Mistake.* Boston: Little, Brown & Co, 1926.

Faulkner, William. *Absalom, Absalom!* New York: Modern Library, 1936.

———. *Go Down, Moses.* New York: Modern Library, 1942.

Federal Writers Program. Arizona. *Arizona: A State Guide. American Guide Series.* New York: Hastings House, 1940.

———. California. *California, A Guide to the Golden State. American Guide Series.* New York: Hastings House, 1939.

———. Colorado. *Colorado, A Guide to the Highest State. American Guide Series.* New York: Hastings House, 1941.

———. Oklahoma. *Oklahoma: A Guide to the Sooner State. American Guide Series* Norman: University of Oklahoma Press, 1941.

———. Texas. *Texas, A Guide to the Lone Star State. American Guide Series.* New York: Hastings House, 1940.

Feldstein, Stanley, editor. *The Poisoned Tongue: A Documentary History of American Racism and Prejudice.* New York: Morrow, 1972.

Fell, John L. *Film and the Narrative Tradition.* Berkeley: University of California Press, 1974.

Fellman, Michael. *Inside War: The Guerrilla Conflict in Missouri During the American Civil War.* New York: Oxford University Press, 1989.

Fender, Stephen. "The Western and the Contemporary," *JAS* 6:1 (1972), pp. 97–108.

Fenin, George, and William K. Everson, *The Western: From the Silents to the Seventies.* New York: Penguin, 1973.

Fiedler, Leslie. *Return of the Vanishing American.* New York: Stein and Day, 1968.

Fiedler, Leslie, *et al.*, *Buffalo Bill and the Wild West.* Pittsburgh: University of Pittsburgh, 1981.

Fink, Leon, *et al.*, "A Round Table: Labor, Historical Pessimism, and Hegemony," *JAH* 75:1 (1988), pp. 115–161.

Fite, Gilbert. *The Farmer's Frontier, 1865–1900.* New York: Holt, Rinehart and Winston, 1966.

Fitzgerald, F. Scott. *The Great Gatsby.* New York: Charles Scribner's Sons, 1925.

Fitzgerald, Frances. *Fire in the Lake: The Vietnamese and the Americans in Vietnam.* New York: Vintage Books, 1973.

———. *America Revised: History Schoolbooks in the Twentieth Century.* Boston: Little, Brown and Co., 1979.

Fitzhugh, George. *Cannibals All! or, Slaves Without Masters.* Edited by C. Vann Woodward. Cambridge, MA: Belknap Press of Harvard University Press, 1960.

———. *Sociology for the South; or, The Failure of Free Society.* Richmond, VA: A. Morris [1854].

———. *What Shall Be Done with Free Negroes?* Fredericksburg, VA: Recorder Job Office, 1851.

Flacks, Richard. *Making History: The American Left and the American Mind.* New York: Columbia University Press, 1988.

Fogelson, Robert. *The Los Angeles Riots.* New York: Arno Press and the *New York Times,* 1969.

Folsom, James K. *The Western: A Collection of Critical Essays.* Englewood Cliffs, NJ: Prentice-Hall, 1979.

Foner, Eric. *Free Soil, Free Labor, Free Men: The Ideology of the Republican Party Before the Civil War.* New York: Oxford University Press, 1970.

———. *Reconstruction: America's Unfinished Revolution, 1863–1877.* New York: Harper & Row, 1988.

———. "Why Is There No Socialism in the United States?" *History Workshop: A Journal of Socialist and Feminist Historians*, Number 17 (Spring, 1984), pp. 57–80.

Foote, Mary Hallock. *The Chosen Valley*. Boston: Houghton, Mifflin, 1893.

———. *Coeur d'Alene*. Boston: Houghton, Mifflin, 1895.

Ford, Paul Leicester. *The Great K & A Train Robbery*. New York: International Association of Newspapers and Authors, 1901.

Foster, Stephen William. *The Past Is Another Country: Representation, Historical Consciousness and Resistance in the Blue Ridge*. Berkeley: University of California Press, 1990.

Fox, Richard Wightman, and T. J. Jackson Lears, editors. *The Culture of Consumption: Critical Essays in American History 1880–1890*. New York: Pantheon Books, 1983.

Franklin, H. Bruce. *M.I.A.: Myth in America*. Brooklyn: Lawrence Hill Books, 1992.

———. *Robert A. Heinlein: America as Science Fiction*. New York: Oxford University Press, 1980.

Fraser, John. *America and the Patterns of Chivalry*. Cambridge, England: Cambridge University Press, 1982.

Frederickson, George M. *The Arrogance of Race: Historical Perspectives on Slavery, Racism, and Social Inequality*. Middletown, CT: Wesleyan University Press, 1988.

———. *The Black Image in the White Mind: The Debate on Afro-American Character and Destiny, 1817–1914*. New York: Harper Torchbooks, 1972.

———. *White Supremacy: A Comparative Study of American and South African History*. New York: Oxford University Press, 1981.

Freeman, Thomas. "The Cowboy and the Astronaut: The American Image in German Periodical Advertisements," *JPC* 6:1 (1972), pp. 83–103.

Freilich, Morris, editor. *The Relevance of Culture*. New York: Bergin & Garvey, 1989.

French, Philip. *Westerns: Aspects of a Movie Genre*. New York: Viking Press, 1974.

Friar, Ralph, and Natasha Friar. *The Only Good Indian: The Hollywood Gospel*. New York: Drama Book Specialists, 1972.

Fried, Albert, editor. *A Day of Dedication: The Essential Writings and Speeches of Woodrow Wilson*. New York: The Macmillan Company, 1965.

Friedman, Benjamin M. *Day of Reckoning: The Consequences of American Economic Policy:* New York: Vintage Books, 1988, 1989.

———. "A Deficit of Civic Courage," *NYRB* (June 1, 1989), pp. 23–6.

Friedman, Lawrence J. *The White Savage: Racial Fantasies in the Postbellum South*. Englewood Cliffs, NJ: Prentice-Hall, 1970.

Frisch, Michael. "American History and the Structures of Collective Memory: A Modest Exercise in Empirical Iconography," *JAH* 75:4 (1989), pp. 1130–55.

Frye, Northrop. *The Critical Path: An Essay on the Social Context of Literary Criticism*. Bloomington: Indiana University Press, 1973.

———. *The Secular Scripture: A Study of the Structure of Romance*. Cambridge, MA: Harvard University Press, 1976.

Fuller, Jack. *Fragments*. New York: Dell Books, 1984.

Fuller, R. Buckminster. *Operating Manual for Spaceship Earth*. Carbondale: Southern Illinois University Press, 1969.

Fussell, Edwin. *Frontier: American Literature and the American West*. Princeton: Princeton University Press, 1966.

Gaddy, Jerry J., editor. *Obituaries of the Gunfighters: Dust to Dust*. []: The Old Army Press, 1977.

Galbraith, John Kenneth. "Big Shots," *NYRB* (May 12, 1988), pp. 44–7.

Gallagher, Tag. *John Ford: The Man and His Films*. Berkeley: University of California Press, 1986.

Galperin, William H. "History Into Allegory: *The Wild Bunch* as Vietnam Movie," *Western Humanities Review* 35:2 (1981), pp. 165–72.

Gans, Herbert J. *Deciding What's News: A Study of* CBS Evening News, NBC Nightly News, Newsweek *and* Time. New York: Vintage Books, 1979.

———. *Popular Culture and High Culture: An Analysis and Evaluation of Taste*. New York: Basic Books, 1974.

Gard, Wayne. *Frontier Justice*. Norman: University of Oklahoma Press, 1949.

Gardner, Howard. *Art, Mind and Brain: A Cognitive Approach to Creativity*. New York: Basic Books, 1982.

Garland, Hamlin. *The Captain of the Gray Horse Troop*. Upper Saddle River, NJ: Literature House/Gregg Press, 1970.

———. *Hesper: A Novel*. New York: Harper & Row, 1903.

———. *The Eagle's Heart*. New York: Harper & Bros., 1900.

Gates, Paul Wallace. "The Homestead Law in an Incongruous Land System," *AHR* 41:3 (1936), pp. 652–81.

Gatewood, Willard B. *Black Americans and the White Man's Burden, 1898–1903*. Urbana: University of Illinois Press, 1975.

Geduld, Harry M., editor. *Focus on D. W. Griffith*. Englewood Cliffs, N.J.: Prentice-Hall, 1971.

Geertz, Clifford. *The Interpretation of Cultures: Selected Essays*. New York: Basic Books, 1973.

Gelb, Leslie H., and Richard K. Betts. *The Irony of Vietnam: The System Worked*. Washington, D.C.: The Brookings Institution, 1979.

George, Henry. *Progress and Poverty: An Inquiry into the Cause of Industrial Depressions and of the Increase of Want with Increase of Wealth . . . The Remedy*. New York: Robert Schalkenbach Foundation, 1981 [1880].

Gerzon, Mark. *A Choice of Heroes: The Changing Face of American Manhood*. Boston: Houghton Mifflin Company, 1982.

Gibbons, Floyd. *The Red Napoleon*. New York: Popular Library, 1977.

———. *The Perfect War: Technowar in Vietnam*. Boston: Atlantic Monthly Press, 1986.

Giddis, Anthony. *The Nation-State and Violence: Volume Two of a Contemporary Critique of Historical Materialism*. Berkeley: University of California Press, 1987.

Gidley, M. "Notes on F. Scott Fitzgerald and the Passing of the Great Race," *Journal of American Studies* 7:2 (1973), pp. 171–82.

Gidley, Mick. " 'The Vanishing Race' in Sight and Sound: Edward S. Curtis's Musicale of North American Indian Life," *Prospects 12* (1987), pp. 59–88.

Gilpin, William. *The Mission of the North American People: Geographical, Social, and Political.* Edited by William O. Clough. New York: Da Capo Press, 1974 [1874].

Ginger, Ray, editor. *William Jennings Bryan: Selections.* Indianapolis, IN: The Bobbs-Merrill Company, 1967.

Gitlin, Todd. *Inside Prime Time.* New York: Pantheon Books, 1983.

———. *The Sixties: Years of Hope, Days of Rage.* New York: Bantam Books, 1987.

———. *The Whole World Is Watching: Mass Media in the Making and Unmaking of the New Left.* Berkeley: University of California Press, 1980.

Glassberg, David. "History and the Public: Legacies of the Progressive Era," *JAH* 73:4 (1987), pp. 957–80.

Gleeck, Lewis E., Jr. *Americans on the Philippines Frontiers.* Manila: Carmelo and Bauermann, 1974.

Glennon, Michael J. *Constitutional Diplomacy.* Princeton: Princeton University Press, 1991.

Glover, David. "The Frontier of Genre: Further to John S. Whitley's 'Stirring Things Up: Dashiell Hammett's Continental Op,'" *JAS* 15:2 (1981), pp. 249–52.

Godkin, E[dwin] L[awrence]. *Problems of Modern Democracy: Political and Economic.* New York: Charles Scribner's Sons, 1898.

———. *Reflections and Comments, 1865–1895.* New York: Charles Scribner's Sons, 1895.

———. *Unforeseen Tendencies of Democracy.* Boston: Houghton, Mifflin, 1898.

Goldman, Peter, *et al.* "Ford's Rescue Operation," *Newsweek* (May 26, 1975), pp. 16–18.

Goldman, Peter, *et al.* "Rocky & Rambo," *Newsweek* (December 23, 1985), pp. 58–62.

Goldstein, Joseph, Burke Marshall, and Jack Schwartz, compilers. *The My-Lai Massacre and Its Cover-Up: Beyond the Reach of Law?* New York: Free Press, 1976.

Goodstone, Tony, editor. *The Pulps: Fifty Years of American Pop Culture.* New York: Bonanza Books, 1970.

Goodwyn, Lawrence. "The Cooperative Commonwealth & Other Abstractions: In Search of a Democratic Promise," *Marxist Perspectives* 3:2 (1980), pp. 8–43.

———. *Democratic Promise: The Populist Moment in America.* New York: Oxford University Press, 1976.

Gordon, David, Richard Edwards, and Michael Reich. *Segmented Work, Divided Workers: The Historical Transformation of Labor in the United States.* Cambridge: Cambridge University Press, 1982.

Gossett, Thomas F. *Race: The History of an Idea in America.* New York: Schocken Books, 1965.

Goulden, Joseph C. *Korea: The Untold Story of the War.* New York: McGraw-Hill, 1982.

Graebner, William. *The Engineering of Consent: Democracy and Authority in Twentieth-Century America.* Madison: University of Wisconsin Press, 1987.

Graham, Daniel. *High Frontier: A Strategy for National Survival.* New York: Tom Doherty Associates, 1983.

Graham, Otis. *Encore for Reform: The Old Progressives and the New Deal.* New York: Oxford University Press, 1967.

Grant, Madison. *The Conquest of a Continent.* New York: Charles Scribner's Sons, 1933.

———. *The Passing of the Great Race.* New York: Charles Scribner's Sons, 1916.

Gray, J. Glenn. *The Warriors.* New York: Harper and Row, Perennial Library, 1973.

Green, James R. *Grass-Roots Socialism: Radical Movements in the Southwest, 1895–1943.* Baton Rouge: Louisiana State University Press, 1978.

Green, Martin. *Dreams of Adventure and Deeds of Empire.* New York: Basic Books, 1979.

Greene, T. N., editor. *The Guerrilla and How to Fight Him.* New York: Frederick A. Praeger, 1967.

Greene, Theodore P. *America's Heroes: Changing Models of Success in American Magazines.* New York: Oxford University Press, 1970.

Greenleaf, William, editor. *American Economic Development Since 1860.* New York: Harper Torchbooks, 1968.

Gressley, Gene M. *Bankers and Cattlemen.* New York: Alfred A. Knopf, 1966.

Gressley, Gene M. *West by East.* Charles Redd Monographs in Western History, No. 1. Provo, UT: Brigham Young University Press, 1972.

Grey, Zane. *The Desert of Wheat.* New York: Harper and Bros., 1919.

———. *Heritage of the Desert.* New York: Harper and Bros., 1910.

———. *Riders of the Purple Sage.* New York: Grosset and Dunlap, 1912.

———. *Spirit of the Border.* New York: Grosset and Dunlap, 1906.

———. *The Vanishing American.* New York: Harper and Bros., 1925.

Griffith, Robert. "Dwight D. Eisenhower and the Corporate Commonwealth," *AHR* 87:2 (1982), pp. 87–122.

Griggs, Sutton. *Imperium in Imperio.* New York: Arno Press, 1969.

Grimshaw, Allen D., editor. *Racial Violence in the United States.* Chicago: Aldine Publishing Company, 1969.

Gruber, Frank. *Zane Grey, A Biography.* New York: World Publishers, 1970.

Guerif, François. *Clint Eastwood: The Man and His Movies.* Translated by Lissa Nesselson. New York: St. Martin's Press, 1984.

Gump, James. "The Subjugation of the Zulus and Sioux: A Comparative Study," *Western Historical Quarterly* 19:1 (1988), pp. 21–36.

Gunn, Giles. "Beyond Transcendence or Beyond Ideology: The New Problematics of Cultural Criticism in America," *ALH* 2:1 (1990), pp. 1–18.

———. *The Culture of Criticism and the Criticism of Culture.* New York: Oxford University Press, 1987.

Gustainus, J. Justin. "John F. Kennedy and the Green Berets: The Rhetorical Use of the Hero Myth," Paper presented at the Joint Convention of the Central States Speech Association and the Southern Speech Communication Association, 1987.

Guthrie, A. B. *The Big Sky.* New York: W. Sloane Associates, 1947.

Gutman, Herbert G. *Work, Culture, and Society in Industrializing America: Essays in American Working Class and Social History.* New York: Alfred A. Knopf, 1976.

Haber, Samuel. *Efficiency and Uplift: Scientific Management in the Progressive Era, 1890–1920.* Chicago: University of Chicago Press, 1964.

Hagedorn, Hermann. *The Boys' Life of Theodore Roosevelt.* New York: Harper and Brothers, 1918.

Haggard, H . Rider. *Allan Quatermain.* London: Macdonald, 1949.

———. *The People of the Mist.* London: Longmans, Green and Co., 1894.

Hair, William Ivy. *Carnival of Fury: Robert Charles and the New Orleans Race Riot of 1900.* Baton Rouge: Louisiana State University Press, 1976.

Halberstam, David. *The Best and the Brightest.* New York: Fawcett Books, 1972.

———. *The Making of a Quagmire.* New York: Ballantine Books, 1965.

Hall, James. *Legends of the West: Sketches Illustrative of the Habits, Occupations, Privations, Adventures and Spirits of the Pioneers of the West.* Cincinnati, OH: Robert Clarke, 1869.

———. *Letters from the West: Containing Sketches of the Scenery, Manners, and Customs; and Anecdotes Connected with the First Settlements of the Western Sections of the United States.* London: Henry Colburn, 1828.

———: *Sketches of History, Life, and Manners in the West.* Two volumes. Philadelphia: Harrison Hall [1835].

Hall, Kermit L. *The Magic Mirror: Law in American History.* New York: Oxford University Press, 1989.

Hammett, Dashiell. *The Novels of Dashiell Hammett.* New York: Alfred A. Knopf, 1966.

———. *Red Harvest.* New York: Vintage Books, 1972.

———. *The Big Knockover: Selected Stories and Short Novels.* Edited by Lillian Hellman. New York: Vintage Books, 1972.

Handel, Leo A. *Hollywood Looks at Its Audience: A Report of Film Audience Research.* Urbana: University of Illinois Press, 1950.

Handler, Richard. "Boasian Anthropology and the Critique of American Culture," *AQ* 42:2 (1990), pp. 252–73.

Hankins, *Racial Basis of Civilization: A Critique of the Nordic Doctrine.* New York: Alfred A. Knopf, 1926.

Hardy, Gordon, and the Editors of the Boston Publishing Company. *The Vietnam Experience: Words of War: An Anthology of Vietnam War Literature.* Boston: Boston Publishing Company, 1988.

Hardy, Phil. *The Western: The Film Encyclopedia.* New York: William Morrow and Company, 1983.

Harrington, Michael. *Toward a Democratic Left: A Radical Program for a New Majority.* New York: The Macmillan Company, 1968.

Harris, Neil, editor. *The Land of Contrasts, 1880–1901.* New York: George Braziller, 1970.

Harris, Trudier. *Exorcising Blackness: Historical and Literary Lynching and Burning Rituals.* Bloomington: Indiana University Press, 1984.

Hart, James D. *The Popular Book: A History of America's Literary Taste.* Berkeley: University of California Press, 1963.

Hart, John Mason. *Revolutionary Mexico: The Coming and Process of the Mexican Revolution.* Berkeley: University of California Press, 1987.

Hart, William S. *My Life East and West.* New York: Benjamin Blom, 1929.

Hartshorne, Thomas L. *The Distorted Image: Changing Conceptions of the American Character Since Turner.* Cleveland, OH: The Press of Case Western Reserve University, 1977.

Hauck, Richard Boyd. *Davy Crockett: A Handbook.* Lincoln: University of Nebraska Press, 1986.

Hauptmann, Laurence M. "Mythologizing Westward Expansion: Schoolbooks and the Image of the American Frontier Before Turner," *WHQ* 8:3 (1977), pp. 269–82.

Havig, Alan. "Presidential Images, History, and Homage: Memorializing Theodore Roosevelt," *AQ* 30:4 (1978), pp. 514–32.

Haywood, C. Robert. "No Less a Man: Blacks in Cow Town Dodge City, 1876–1886," *WHQ* 19:2 (1988), pp. 161–82.

Haywood, William D. *Bill Haywood's Book: The Autobiography of William D. Haywood.* New York: International Publishers, 1929.

Headley, J[oel] T. *Great Riots of New York, 1712–1873.* New York: E. B. Treat, 1873.

———. *Pen and Pencil Sketches of the Great Riots . . .* New York: E. B. Treat, 1882.

Healy, David. *U.S. Expansionism: The Imperialist Urge in the 1890s.* Madison: University of Wisconsin Press, 1970.

Heath, Jim F. *Decade of Disillusionment: The Kennedy–Johnson Years.* Bloomington: Indiana University Press, 1975.

Heidner, F. W. *The Laborer's Friend and Employer's Counselor: A Popular Treatise on the Labor Question.* Napersville, IL: By the author, 1895.

Heilbroner, Robert. "Lifting the Silent Depression," *NYRB* (October 24, 1991), pp. 6–8.

Hellmann, John. *American Myth and the Legacy of Vietnam.* New York: Columbia University Press, 1986.

Hemingway, Ernest. *Across the River and Into the Trees.* New York: Charles Scribner's Sons, 1950.

———. *For Whom the Bell Tolls.* New York: Charles Scribner's Sons, 1940.

———. *Islands in the Stream.* New York: Charles Scribner's Sons, 1970.

———, editor. *Men at War.* New York: Bramhall House, 1942.

———. *To Have and Have Not.* New York: Charles Scribner's Sons, 1953.

Hendrick, Burton J. *The Age of Big Business: A Chronicle of the Captains of Industry.* The Chronicles of America Series, Volume 39. New Haven: Yale University Press, 1921.

Henkin, Louis. *Constitutionalism, Democracy, and Foreign Affairs.* New York: Columbia University Press, 1991.

Henretta, James A. "Social History as Lived and Written," *AHR* 84:5 (1979), pp. 1293–1322.

Henry, William A. *Visions of America: How We Saw the 1984 Election.* Boston: Atlantic Monthly Press, 1985.

Herr, Michael. *Dispatches.* New York: Alfred A. Knopf, 1977.

Hersey, Harold Brainerd. *Pulpwood Editor: The Fabulous World of the Thriller Magazines Revealed by a Veteran Editor and Publisher.* New York: Frederick A. Stokes Company, 1957.

Hersey, John. *The Algiers Motel Incident.* New York: Bantam Books, 1968.

Higham, John. "Changing Paradigms: The Collapse of Consensus History," *JAH* 76:2 (1989, pp. 460–6).

Hijiya, James A. "Roots: Family and Ethnicity in the 1970s," *AQ* 30:4 (1978), pp. 548–58.

Hine, Robert V. *Community on the American Frontier: Separate But Not Alone.* Norman: University of Oklahoma Press, 1980.

Hirschhorn, Clyde. *The Warner Bros. Story.* New York: Crown Publishers, Inc., 1979.

Hoberman, J. "The Fascist Guns in the West," *American Film* (March, 1986), pp. 42–8.

Hobsbawm, Eric. *Bandits.* New York: Pantheon Books, 1981.

———. *The Age of Empire, 1875–1914.* New York: Vintage Books, 1989.

Hochman, Stanley, editor. *A Library of Film Criticism: American Film Directors.* New York: Frederick Ungar, 1974.

Hodgson, Godfrey. *America in Our Time: From World War II to Nixon, What Happened and Why.* New York: Vintage Books, 1978.

———. *The Colonel: The Life and Wars of Henry Stimson, 1867–1950.* New York: Alfred A. Knopf, 1990.

Hoffman, Frederick L. "Race Traits and Tendencies of the American Negro," *Publications of the American Economic Association* 11:1 (1896), pp. 1–329.

Hofstadter, Richard. *Social Darwinism in American Thought.* Boston: The Beacon Press, 1955.

———. *The Progressive Historians: Turner, Beard, Farrington.* New York: Alfred A. Knopf, 1968.

Hofstadter, Richard, and Michael Wallace, editors. *American Violence: A Documentary History.* New York: Vintage Books, 1971.

Holland, William E. *Let a Soldier Die.* New York: Dell Books, 1984.

Holloway, Jean. *Hamlin Garland: A Biography.* Austin: University of Texas Press, 1960.

Holman, Hugh C. "Detective Fiction as American Realism," in James C. Austin and Donald Koch, editors. *Popular Literature in America: A Symposium in Honor of Lyon Norman Richardson.* Bowling Green, OH: Popular Press, 1972.

Holmes, Oliver Wendell, Jr. *The Mind and Faith of Justice Holmes.* Edited by Max Lerner. Boston: Little, Brown and Co., 1945.

Holt, Robert T., and Robert W. van de Velde. *Strategic Psychological Operations and American Foreign Policy.* Chicago: The University of Chicago Press, 1960.

Holt, Thomas C. "The Political Uses of Alienation: W.E.B. Dubois on Politics, Race, and Culture, 1903–1940," *AQ* 42:2 (1990), pp. 301–23.

Holtsmark, Erling B. *Tarzan and Tradition: Classical Literature in Popular Myth.* Westport, CT: Greenwood Press, 1981.

Holtzman, Will. "Theory Number Three: Toward an Actor–Icon Theory," *Journal of Popular Film* 4:1 (1975), pp. 77–80.

Hoppenstand, Gary. "Pulp Vigilante Heroes, the Moral Majority and the Apocalypse," in Ray Browne and Marshall Fishwick, eds., *The Hero in Transition.* Bowling Green, OH: Bowling Green University Popular Press, 1983, pp. 141–4.

Horan, James D. *The Pinkertons: The Detective Dynasty That Made History.* New York: Crown Publishers, 1967.

Horn, Miriam. "How the West Was Really Won," *U.S. News and World Report* (May 21, 1990), pp. 56–65.

Horn, Tom. *Life of Tom Horn, Government Scout and Interpreter, Written by Himself.* Edited by Dean Krakel. Norman: University of Oklahoma Press, 1964.

Horne, A. D., editor. *The Wounded Generation: America After Vietnam.* Englewood Cliffs, NJ: Prentice-Hall, 1981.

Horsman, Reginald. *Race and Manifest Destiny: The Origins of American Racial Anglo-Saxonism.* Cambridge, MA: Harvard University Press, 1981.

———. "Scientific Racism and the American Indian in the Mid-Nineteenth Century," *AQ* 27:2 (1975), pp. 152–68.

Hough, Emerson. *The Covered Wagon.* New York: Washington Square Press, 1967.

———. *The Passing of the Frontier: A Chronicle of the Old West.* The Chronicles of America Series, Volume 26. New Haven: Yale University Press, 1921.

Howard, H. R. *The History of Virgil A. Stewart, and His Adventures in Capturing and Exposing the "Great Western Land Pirate" and His Gang, in Connexion with the Evidence* . . . New York: Harper and Brothers, 1836.

Howard, Robert E. *Worms of the Earth.* New York: Zebra Books, 1975.

Howells, William Dean, and Frank Norris. *Criticism and Fiction and the Responsibilities of the Novelist.* Cambridge, MA: Walker–de Berry, 1962.

Hudson, Robert V. *Mass Media: A Chronological Encyclopedia of Television, Radio, Motion Pictures, Magazines, Newspapers and Books in the United States.* New York: Garland Publishing, 1987.

Huggett, William Turner, *Body Count.* New York: Dell Books, 1973.

Humphrey, Seth K. *The Racial Prospect: A Re-Writing and Expansion of the Author's Book "Mankind."* New York: Charles Scribner's Sons, 1920.

Hunt, George T. *The Wars of the Iroquois: A Study in Inter-Tribal Relations.* Madison: University of Wisconsin Press, 1940.

Hunt, Michael H. *Ideology and U.S. Foreign Policy.* New Haven: Yale University Press, 1987.

Hurlbert, Archer Butler. *Frontiers: The Genius of American Nationality.* Boston: Little, Brown and Company, 1929.

Hutchinson, W. H. *A Bar Cross Man: The Life & Personal Writings of Eugene Manlove Rhodes.* Norman: University of Oklahoma Press, 1956.

Hutton, Paul Andrew. "From Little Big Horn to Little Big Man: The Changing Image of a Western Hero in Popular Culture," *WHQ* 7:1 (1976), pp. 19–46.

———. *Phil Sheridan and His Army.* Lincoln: University of Nebraska Press, 1985.

[Ince, Thomas.] *Custer's Last Fight,* in Custer Battlefield National Monument.

Ingham, John N. "Rags to Riches Revisited: The Effect of City Size and Related Factors on the Recruitment of Business Leaders," *JAH* 62:3 (1976), pp. 615–37.

Ingraham, Prentiss. *Adventures of Buffalo Bill from Boyhood to Manhood: Deeds of Daring and Romantic Incidents in the Life of Wm. F. Cody, the Monarch of the Bordermen.* Beadle's Boys' Library No. 1, 1881.

———. *Buffalo Bill and the Nihilists; or, A Dangerous Mission.* New York: Street & Smith, 1910.

———. *Buffalo Bill's Big Four; or, Custer's Shadow.* Beadle's Weekly, 1887.

———. *Buffalo Bill's Grip; or, Oath-Bound to Custer.* Beadle's Weekly, 1883.

Inouye, Daniel K., *et al. Report of the Congressional Committees Investigating the Iran-Contra Affair, with the Minority View.* Abridged Edition. New York: Times Books, 1988.

Jackson, Helen Hunt. *Century of Dishonor: A Sketch of the United States Government's Dealings with Some of the Indian Tribes.* New York: Harper and Bros., 1881.

Jacobs, Lewis. *The Rise of the American Film: A Critical History, with an Essay, Experimental Cinema in America, 1921–1947.* New York: Teachers College Press, 1967.

Jacoby, Tamar, with Robert Parry. "Casey's Domestic 'Covert Op,'" *Newsweek* (October 12, 1987), p. 36.

Jaffe, Julian F. *Crusade Against Radicalism: New York During the Red Scare, 1914–1924.* Port Washington, NY: Kennikat Press, 1972.

James, William. *William James, The Essential Writings.* Edited by Bruce W. Wilshire. Albany: State University of New York Press, 1984.

Jameson, Frederic. *The Political Unconscious: Narrative as a Socially Symbolic Act.* Ithaca, NY: Cornell University Press, 1981.

Jarvie, I. C. *Movies and Society.* New York: Basic Books, 1970.

Jay, Anthony. *Corporation Man.* New York: Pocket Books, 1973.

Jeffreys-Jones, Rhodri. "The Defictionalization of American Private Detection," *JAS* 17:1 (1983), pp. 265–74.

———. *Violence and Reform in American History.* New York: New Viewpoints, 1978.

Jeffries, John W. "The 'Quest for National Purpose' of 1960," *AQ* 30:4 (1978), pp. 451–70.

Jewett, Robert, and John Shelton Lawrence. *The American Monomyth.* Garden City, NY: Anchor Press, 1977.

Johannsen, Albert. *The House of Beadle and Adams, and Its Dime and Nickel Novels: The Study of a Vanished Literature.* Three Volumes. Norman, OK: University of Oklahoma Press, 1950–62.

Johannsen, Robert W. *To the Halls of the Montezumas: The Mexican War in the American Imagination.* New York: Oxford University Press, 1985.

Johnson, David A. "Vigilance and the Law: The Moral Authority of Popular Justice in the Far West," *AQ* 33:5 (1981), pp. 558–86.

Johnson, Diane. *Dashiell Hammett, A Life.* New York: Random House, 1983.

Johnson, Eric. *America Unlimited.* Garden City, NY: Doubleday, Doran and Company, 1944.

———. "Utopia Is Production," *The Screen Actor* (August, 1946), pp. 14–5.

Just, Ward. *Military Men.* New York: Alfred A. Knopf, 1970.

Kahin, George McT. *Intervention: How America Became Involved in Vietnam.* Garden City, NY: Anchor Books, 1987.

Kaminsky, Stuart M. *American Film Genres: Approaches to a Critical Theory of Popular Film.* New York: Laurel Books, 1974.

Kammen, Michael. *Mystic Chords of Memory: The Transformation of Tradition in American Culture.* New York: Alfred A. Knopf, 1992.

Kaplan, Amy. *The Social Construction of American Realism.* Chicago: University of Chicago Press, 1988.

Kaplan, Harold. *Power and Order: Henry Adams and the Naturalist Tradition in American Fiction.* Chicago: University of Chicago Press, 1981.

Karnow, Stanley. *Vietnam: A History.* New York: Penguin Books, 1984.

Karolides, Nicholas. *The Pioneer in the American Novel, 1900–50.* Norman: University of Oklahoma Press, 1967.

Karp, Walter. *The Politics of War: The Story of Two Wars Which Altered Forever the Political Life of the American Republic (1890–1920).* New York: Harper & Row, 1979.

Kass, Judith M. *The Hollywood Professionals: Don Siegel.* London: The Tantivy Press, 1975.

Keller, Morton. *Affairs of State: Public Life in Late Nineteenth Century America.* Cambridge, MA: The Belknap Press of Harvard University Press, 1977.

Kelley, Mary. *Private Woman, Public Stage: Literary Domesticity in Nineteenth Century America.* New York: Oxford University Press, 1984.

Kelly, Francis J. *Vietnam Studies: U.S. Army Special Forces, 1961–1971.* Washington, D.C.: Department of the Army, 1973.

Kelton, Elmer. *The Day the Cowboys Quit.* Fort Worth: Texas Christian University Press, 1986.

Kemble, C. Robert. *The Image of the Army Officer in America: Background to Current Views.* Westport, CT: Greenwood Press, 1973.

Kesselman, Stephen. "The Frontier Thesis and the Great Depression," *Journal of the History of Ideas* 29:2 (1968), pp. 253–68.

King, Charles. *An Apache Princess: A Tale of the Indian Frontier.* New York: The Hobart Company, 1903.

———. *Campaigning with Crook and Stories of Army Life.* New York: Harper and Bros., 1890.

———. *Foes in Ambush.* Philadelphia: J. B. Lippincott Co., 1893.

———. *A Tame Surrender: A Story of the Chicago Strike.* Philadelphia: J. B. Lippincott Co., 1896.

King, Margaret J. "The Recycled Hero: Walt Disney's Davy Crockett," in Michael J. Lofaro, editor, *Davy Crockett: The Man the Legend, the Legacy, 1786–1986.* Knoxville: University of Tennessee Press, 1985.

Kirkland, Edward Chase. *Dream and Thought in the Business Community, 1860–1900.* Chicago: Quadrangle Books, 1956.

Kirkman, Marshall M. *The Science of Railways,* Volume 1. New York: World Railway Publishing Co., 1896.

Kitses, Jim. *Horizons West: Anthony Mann, Budd Boetticher, Sam Peckinpah, Studies of Authorship in the Western.* Bloomington: Indiana University Press, 1969.

Klein, Joe. *Woody Guthrie: A Life.* New York: Alfred A. Knopf, 1980.

Kluge, P. F. "First and Last, a Cowboy / Half myth and half movie star, John Wayne rides a lost frontier." *Life,* 72:3 (January 28, 1972), pp. 42–6.

Kolodny, Annette. *The Land Before Her: Fantasy and Experience of the American Frontiers, 1630–1860.* Chapel Hill: University of North Carolina Press, 1984.

———. *The Lay of the Land: Metaphor as Experience and History in American Life and Letters.* Chapel Hill: University of North Carolina Press, 1975.

Konstan, David. "Comparative Methods in Mythology," *Arethusa* 19:1 (1986), pp. 87–99.

Koppes, Clayton R. "What to Show the World: The Office of War Information and Hollywood, 1942–1945," *JAH* 64:1 (1977), pp. 87–105.

Korman, Gerd. *Industrialization, Immigrants and Americanizers: The View from Milwaukee, 1866–1921.* Madison: State Historical Society of Wisconsin, 1967.

Koszarski, Diane Kaiser. *The Complete Films of William S. Hart: A Pictorial Record.* New York: Dover Publications, 1980.

Kovic, Ron. *Born on the Fourth of July.* New York: McGraw-Hill, 1976.

Kraut, Alan M. *The Huddled Masses: The Immigrant in American Society, 1880–1921.* Arlington Heights, IL: Harlan Davidson, 1982.

Kroeber, Clifton B., and Bernard L. Fontana. *Massacre on the Gila: An Account of the Last Major Battle between American Indians, with Reflections on the Origin of War.* Tucson: University of Arizona Press, 1986.

Krulak, V[ictor] H., editor. *Studies in Guerrilla Warfare.* Annapolis, MD: United States Naval Institute, 1963.

Kruse, Horst H. "Myth in the Making: The James Brothers, the Bank Robbery at Northfield, Minn., and the Dime Novel," *Journal of Popular Culture* 10:2 (1976), pp. 315–25.

Kuper, Leo. *Race, Class, and Power: Ideology and Change in Plural Societies.* London: Duckworth, 1974.

Kwitny, Jonathan. *The Crimes of Patriots: A True Tale of Dope, Dirty Money, and the CIA.* New York: Simon & Schuster, 1987.

LaCapra, Dominick. *History and Criticism.* Ithaca, NY: Cornell University Press, 1987.

LaFeber, Walter. *Inevitable Revolutions: The United States in Central America.* Expanded edition. New York: W. W. Norton, 1984.

———. *The New Empire: An Interpretation of American Expansion, 1860–1898.* Ithaca, NY: Cornell University Press, 1963.

Landor, A. Henry Savage. *China and the Allies.* Two Volumes. New York: Charles Scribner's Sons, 1901.

Lane, Charles, *et al.* "The Newest War," *Newsweek* (January 6, 1992), pp. 18–23.

Lane, Roger, and John J. Turner, Jr., editors. *Riot, Rout, and Tumult: Readings in American Social and Political Violence.* Westport, CT: Greenwood Press, 1978.

Lane, Winthrop D. *Civil War in West Virginia: A Story of the Industrial Conflict in the Coal Mines.* Introduction by John R. Commons. New York: B. W. Huebsch, 1921.

Langdon, Emma F. *The Cripple Creek Strike: A History of Industrial Wars in Colorado.* New York: Arno Press, 1969.

Langley, Lester D. *The Banana Wars: An Inner History of the American Empire, 1900–1934.* Lexington: University Press of Kentucky, 1983.

Laqueur, Walter. *Guerrilla: A Historical and Critical Study.* Boston: Little, Brown & Co, 1976.

Larralde, Carlos. *Mexican–American: Movements and Leaders.* Los Alamitos, CA: Hwong Publishing Co., 1976.

Larsen, Lawrence H. *The Urban West at the End of the Frontier.* Lawrence: Regents Press of Kansas, 1978.

Larson, T. A. *History of Wyoming.* Lincoln: University of Nebraska Press, 1965.

Lasch, Christopher. "Reagan's Victims," *NYRB* (July 21, 1988), pp. 7–8.

Lawrence, Elizabeth Atwood. *Rodeo: An Anthropologist Looks at the Wild and the Tame.* Chicago: University of Chicago Press, 1982.

Lawrence, John Shelton. "News and Mythic Selectivity: Mayaguez, Entebbe, Mogadishu," *JAC* 2:2 (1979), pp 321–30.

Lawrence, William. "The Relation of Wealth to Morals," *World's Work* 1 (1901), 286–92.

Layman, Richard. *Shadow Man: The Life of Dashiell Hammett.* New York: Harcourt Brace Jovanovich, 1981.

Lazere, Donald, editor. *American Media and Mass Culture: Left Perspectives.* Berkeley: University of California Press, 1987.

Lea, Tom. *The Wonderful Country.* Boston: Little, Brown and Company, 1952.

Leach, Douglas Edward. *Flintlock and Tomahawk: New England in King Philip's War.* New York: Macmillan, 1958.

Lears, T. J. Jackson. "The Concept of Cultural Hegemony: Problems and Possibilities," *AHR* 90:3 (1985), pp. 567–93.

———. *No Place of Grace: Antimodernism and the Transformation of American Culture 1880–1920.* New York: Pantheon Books, 1981.

Leary, William M., editor. *The Central Intelligence Agency: History and Documents.* Tuscaloosa: University of Alabama Press, 1984.

Leavitt, Scott. "The Far-Off War in Vietnam We Have Decided to Win," *Life* 52:11 (March 16, 1962), pp. 36–45.

Lebergott, Stanley. *The Americans: An Economic Record.* New York: W. W. Norton, 1984.

Lederer, William J., and Eugene Burdick, *The Ugly American.* New York: Fawcett Crest Books, 1958.

Lekachman, Robert. *Greed Is Not Enough: Reaganomics.* New York: Pantheon Books, 1982.

Lenihan, John H. *Showdown: Confronting Modern America in the Western Film.* Urbana: University of Illinois Press, 1980.

Leon, Warren, and Roy Rosenzweig. *History Museums in the United States: A Critical Assessment.* Urbana: University of Illinois Press, 1989.

Leonard, Elmore. *City Primeval: High Noon in Detroit.* New York: Avon, 1980.

Leonard, Thomas C. *Above the Battle: War-Making in America from Appomattox to Versailles.* New York: Oxford University Press, 1977.

Leuchtenberg, William E. *Franklin Delano Roosevelt and the New Deal.* New York: Harper Torchbooks, 1963.

———. "The New Deal and the Analogue of War," in John Braeman, Robert Bremner, and Everett Walters, editors, *Change and Continuity in Twentieth-Century America.* Columbus: Ohio University Press, pp. 81–143.

Levering, Ralph B. *The Cold War, 1945–1972.* Arlington Heights, IL: Harlan Davidson, 1982.

Levi, Steven C. *Committee of Vigilance: The San Francisco Chamber of Commerce Law and Order Committee, 1916–1919: A Case Study in Official Hysteria.* Jefferson, NC: McFarland, 1983.

Levin, David. *History as Romantic Art: Bancroft, Prescott, Motley and Parkman.* New York: Harcourt, Brace and World, 1959.

Levine, Lawrence W. *Black Culture and Black Consciousness: Afro-American Folk Thought from Slavery to Freedom.* New York: Oxford University Press, 1977.

Levine, Richard. "Indians, Conservation, and George Bird Grinnell," *American Studies* 28:2 (1987), pp 41–55.

Levi-Strauss, Claude. "From Mythical Possibility to Social Existence," ch. 11, *The View from Afar.* Translated by Joachim Neugroschel and Phoebe Hoss. New York: Basic Books, 1985.

———. *Structural Anthropology.* Two Volumes. Translated by Claire Jacobson and Brooke Grundfest Schoeph. New York: Basic Books, 1964–76.

Levy, Emanuel. *John Wayne: Prophet of the American Way of Life.* Metuchen, NJ: The Scarecrow Press, 1988.

Lewis, Lloyd B. *The Tainted War: Culture and Identity in Vietnam War Narratives.* Westport, CT: Greenwood Press, 1985.

Lewis, Sinclair, and Dore Schary, *Storm in the West.* New York: Stein and Day, 1963.

Lewy, Guenter. *America in Vietnam.* New York: Oxford University Press, 1978.

Lieberman, Robbie. "People's Songs: American Communism and the Politics of Culture, *Radical History Review* 36 (1986), pp. 63–79.

Lifton, Robert Jay. *Home From the War: Vietnam Veterans, Neither Victims Nor Executioners.* New York: Simon & Schuster, 1973.

Limerick, Patricia Nelson. *The Legacy of Conquest: The Unbroken Past of the American West.* New York: W. W. Norton, 1987.

Lincoln, Bruce. *Discourse and the Construction of Society: Comparative Studies of Myth, Ritual and Classification.* New York: Oxford University Press, 1989.

Linderman, Gerald F. *The Mirror of War: American Society and the Spanish American War.* Ann Arbor: University of Michigan Press, 1974.

Lindsay, Vachel. *The Art of the Moving Picture.* New York: The Macmillan Company, 1915.

Johnson, Fletcher. *The Red Record of the Sioux. Life of Sitting Bull and History of the Indian War of 1890–91 . . .* []: Edgewood Publishing Company, 1891.

Johnson, Lee Ann. *Mary Hallock Foote.* New York: Twayne Publishers, 1980.

Johnstone, Iain. *The Man with No Name: The Biography of Clint Eastwood.* New York: Morrow Quill Paperbacks, 1981.

Jones, Daryl. *The Dime Novel Western.* Bowling Green, OH: Popular Press, 1978.

Jones, Howard Mumford: "Patriotism–But How?" *Atlantic Monthly* 162 (November, 1938), 585–92.

———. *The Age of Energy: Varieties of American Experience,* 1865–1915. New York: The Viking Press, 1971.

Jordan, Philip D. *Frontier Law and Order: Ten Essays.* Lincoln: University of Nebraska Press, 1970.

Joseph, Paul. *Cracks in the Empire: State Politics in the Vietnam War.* New York: Columbia University Press, 1987.

Josey, Charles Conant. *Race and National Solidarity.* New York: Charles Scribner's Sons, 1923.

Jowett, Garth. *Film, the Democratic Art: A Social History of American Film.* Boston: Little, Brown & Co., 1976.

———. "The Emergence of the Mass Society: The Standardization of American Culture, 1830–1920," *Prospects* 7 (1983), pp. 207–28.

Lingenfelter, Richard E. *The Hardrock Miners: A History of the Mining Labor Movement in the American West, 1863–1893.* Berkeley: University of California Press, 1974.

Link, Arthur S. "That Cobb Interview," *JAH* 72:1 (1985), pp. 7–17.

Linn, Brian McAllister. *The U.S. Army and Counterinsurgency in the Philippine War, 1899–1902.* Chapel Hill: University of North Carolina Press, 1989.

Lipset, Seymour Martin, and Reinhard Bendix. *Society Mobility in Industrial Society.* Berkeley: University of California Press, 1967.

Lipsman, Samuel, Edward Doyle, and the Editors of the Boston Publishing Company. *The Vietnam Experience: Fighting for Time.* Boston: Boston Publishing Company, 1983.

Lipsman, Samuel, Stephen Weiss, and the Editors of the Boston Publishing Company. *The Vietnam Experience: The False Peace,* 1972–74. Boston: Boston Publishing Company, 1985.

Livingston, James. "The Social Analysis of Economic History and Theory: Conjectures on Late Nineteenth-Century American Development," *AHR,* 92:1 (1987), pp. 69–95.

Lodge, George C. *The New American Ideology.* New York: Alfred A. Knopf, 1975.

Logan, Rayford W. *The Betrayal of the Negro: From Rutherford B. Hayes to Woodrow Wilson.* New, enlarged edition. New York: Collier Books, 1965.

London, Jack. *The Call of the Wild.* New York: Macmillan Co., 1910.

———. *Children of the Frost.* New York: Macmillan Co., 1902.

———. *The God of His Fathers, and Other Stories.* New York: McClure, Phillips, 1901.

———. *The Iron Heel.* New York: Sagamore Press, 1957.

———. *The Sea Wolf.* New York: Macmillan Co., 1904.

———. *Smoke Bellew.* New York: The Century Co., 1912.

———. *Son of the Wolf.* Boston: Houghton, Mifflin Co., 1900.

———. *White Fang.* New York: Macmillan Co., 1914.

Lord, Glenn. *The Last Celt: Robert E. Howard, the Creator of Conan.* New York: Berkley Publishing Company, 1976.

MacCormac, Earl R. *A Cognitive Theory of Metaphor.* Cambridge, MA: MIT Press, 1985.

MacDougall, Hugh A. *Racial Myth in English History: Trojans, Teutons, and Anglo-Saxons.* Hanover, NH: University Press of New England, 1982.

"Machismo Diplomacy," *The Nation* (May 31, 1975), pp. 642–3.

MacPherson, Myra. *Long Time Passing: Vietnam and the Haunted Generation.* New York: Signet Books, 1984.

Maitland, Terrence, Peter McInerney, and the Editors of the Boston Publishing Company. *The Vietnam Experience: A Contagion of War.* Boston: Boston Publishing Company, 1983.

Maitland, Terrence, Stephen Weiss, and the Editors of the Boston Publishing

Company. *The Vietnam Experience: Raising the Stakes.* Boston: Boston Publishing Company, 1982.

Malone, Michael P., editor. *Historians and the American West.* Lincoln: University of Nebraska Press, 1983.

———. "Beyond the Last Frontier: Toward a New Approach to Western American History," *WHQ* 20:4 (1989) 409–28.

Manchester, William. *American Caesar: Douglas MacArthur 1880–1964.* Boston, Little, Brown, 1978.

———. *The Death of a President: November 20–November 25, 1963.* New York: Harper & Row, 1967.

Mangan, J. A., and James Walvin, editors. *Manliness and Morality: Middle-Class Masculinity in Britain and America, 1800–1940.* New York: St. Martin's Press, 1987.

Mangione, Jerre. *The Dream and the Deal: The Federal Writer's Project, 1935–43.* Boston: Little, Brown and Co., 1972.

Mardock, Robert Winston. *The Reformers and the American Indian.* Columbia: University of Missouri Press, 1971.

Marshall, James M. *Land Fever: Dispossession and the Frontier Myth.* Lexington: University Press of Kentucky, 1986.

Marshall, S. L. A. *Battles in the Monsoon: Campaigning in the Central Highlands, South Vietnam, Summer 1966.* New York: William Morrow & Company, 1967.

———. *Crimsoned Prairie: The Indian Wars of the Great Plains.* New York: Charles Scribner's Sons, 1972.

———. *Pork Chop Hill: The American Fighting Man in Action in Korea, Spring, 1953.* New York: William Morrow & Company, 1956.

———. *The River and the Gauntlet: Defeat of the Eighth Army by the Chinese Communist Forces, November,* 1950, *in the Battle of the Chongchon River, Korea.* New York: William Morrow & Company, 1953.

———. *West to Cambodia.* New York: Jove Books, 1986.

Martin, Arnold, and Edward Klein, editors. "America in Captivity: Points of Decision in the Hostage Crisis. An Inquiry by the *New York Times.*" *New York Times Magazine* Special Issue (1981).

Martin, Calvin, editor. *The American Indian and the Problem of History.* New York: Oxford University Press, 1987.

Martz, Larry, *et al.*, "Reagan's Failure," *Newsweek* (March 9, 1987), pp. 16–21.

Martz, Larry, *et al.*, "The Bonfire of the S & Ls," *Newsweek* (May 21, 1990), pp. 20–5.

Massa, Ann. "Black Women in the 'White City,'" *JAS* 8:3 (1974), pp. 319–38.

Massing, Michael. "The War on Cocaine," *NYRB* (December 22, 1988), pp. 61–7.

Mathy, Jean-Philippe. "Out of History: French Readings of Postmodern America." *ALH* 2:2 (1990), pp. 267–98.

Mathews, Tom. "The Sixties Complex," *Newsweek* (September 5, 1988), pp. 17–21.

Mathews, Tom, Doug Waller, *et al.*, "The Road to War," *Newsweek* (January 28, 1991), pp. 54–65.

Matthews, Fred. "'Hobbesian Populism': Interpretive Paradigms and Moral Vision in American Historiography," *JAH* 72:1 (1985), pp. 92–115.

Matusow, Allen J. *The Unraveling of America: A History of Liberalism in the 1960s.* New York: Harper Torchbooks, 1986.

May, Ernest R. *"Lessons" of the Past: The Use and Misuse of History in American Foreign Policy.* New York: Oxford University Press, 1973.

May, Lary, editor. *Recasting America: Culture and Politics in the Age of the Cold War.* Chicago: University of Chicago Press, 1989.

May, Lary (with Stephen Lassonde). "Making the American Way: Moderne Theatres, Audiences, and the Film Industry, *1929–1945,*" *Prospects* 12 (1987), pp. 89–124.

MacDonald, Ross [Kenneth Millar]. *The Zebra-Striped Hearse.* New York: Bantam Books, 1964.

McAdams, Dan P. *Power, Intimacy and the Life Story: Personological Inquiries into Identity.* New York: The Guilford Press, 1988.

McArthur, Colin, *Underworld USA.* New York: The Viking Press, 1972.

McCabe, James Dabney. "Edward Winslow Martin." *The History of the Great Riots . . . together with the Full History of the Mollie Maguires.* New York: Augustus M. Kelly, 1971.

McClintock, James L. *White Logic: Jack London's Short Stories.* Grand Rapids: Wolf House Books, 1975.

McCloskey, Robert Green. *American Conservatism in the Age of Enterprise, 1865–1910.* New York: Harper Torchbooks, 1951.

McCormick, Richard L. "The Discovery That 'Business Corrupts Politics': A Reappraisal of the Origins of Progressivism," *AHR* 86:2 (1981), pp. 247–74.

———. *The Party Period and Public Policy: American Politics from the Age of Jackson to the Progressive Era.* New York: Oxford University Press, 1986.

McCullough, Joseph B. *Hamlin Garland.* Boston: Twayne Publishers, 1978.

McDermott, John Francis. *The Frontier Re-examined.* Urbana: University of Illinois Press, 1967.

McDonald, J. Fred, Michael T. Marsden, and Christopher D. Geist. "Radio and Television Studies and American Culture," *AQ* 32:3 (1980), pp. 301–17.

McGrath, Roger D. *Gunfighters, Highwaymen and Vigilantes: Violence on the Frontier.* Berkeley: University of California Press, 1984.

McKinney, Doug. *Sam Peckinpah.* Boston: Twayne Publishers, 1979.

McMillen, Neil R. *Dark Journey: Black Mississippians in the Age of Jim Crow.* Urbana: University of Illinois Press, 1989.

McNeill, William H. "The Care and Repair of Public Myth," *Foreign Affairs* (Fall, 1982), pp. 1–13.

———. "Mythistory, or Truth, Myth, History, and Historians," *AHR* 91:1 (1986), pp. 1–10.

Mecklin, John Moffatt. *Democracy and Race Friction: A Study in Social Ethics.* New York: The Macmillan Company, 1914.

Melville, Herman. *Moby Dick.* Norton Critical Edition. Edited by Harrison Hayford and Hershel Parker. New York: W. W. Norton, 1967.

———. *The Confidence-Man, His Masquerade.* Norton Critical Edition. Edited by Hershel Parker. New York: W. W. Norton, 1971.

Mercer, Asa Shinn. *The Banditti of the Plains, or The Cattlemen's Invasion of Wyoming in 1892, the Crowning Infamy of the Ages.* Norman: University of Oklahoma Press, 1954 [1892].

Merritt, Russell. "Dixon, Griffith, and the Southern Legend: A Cultural Analysis of *Birth of a Nation,*" in Richard Dyer McCann and Jack C. Ellis, editors, *Cinema Examined: Selections from* Cinema Journal, pp. 165–184. New York: E. P. Dutton, 1982.

Meyer, Peter. *Defiant Patriot: The Life and Exploits of Lt. Col. Oliver L. North.* New York. St. Martin's Press, 1987.

Michener, James. *Kent State: What Happened and Why.* New York: Random House, 1971.

Miller, David, and Jerome O. Steffen, editors. *The Frontier: Comparative Studies.* Norman: University of Oklahoma Press, 1977.

Miller, Don. *"B" Movies: An Informal Survey of the American Low-Budget Film, 1933–1945.* New York: Curtis Books, 1973.

Miller, Nyle H., and Joseph W. Snell. *Great Gunfighters of the Kansas Cowtowns, 1867–1886.* Lincoln: University of Nebraska Press, 1970.

Miller, Stuart Creighton. *"Benevolent Assimilation": The American Conquest of the Philippines, 1899–1903.* New Haven: Yale University Press, 1982.

Mills, Nicolaus. *The Crowd in American Literature.* Baton Rouge: Louisiana State University Press, 1986.

Miner, Craig G. *The Corporation and the Indian: Tribal Sovereignty and Industrial Civilization in Indian Territory, 1865–1907.* Columbia: University of Missouri Press, 1976.

Miroff, Bruce. *Pragmatic Illusions: The Presidential Politics of John F. Kennedy.* New York: David McKay, 1976.

Mitchell, Lee Clark. "'When You Call Me That . . .': Tall Talk and Male Hegemony in *The Virginian,*" *PMLA* 102:1 (1987), pp. 66–77.

Mock, James R., and Cedric Larson. *Words That Won the War: The Story of the Committee on Public Information 1917–1919.* Princeton: Princeton University Press, 1939.

Mogen, David. *Wilderness Visions: Science Fiction Westerns, Volume One.* San Bernardino, CA: The Borgo Press, 1982.

Molnar, Andrew R., with William A. Lybrand, Lorna Hahn, James L. Kirkman, and Peter B. Riddleberger. *Undergrounds in Insurgent, Revolutionary, and Resistance Warfare.* Special Operations Research Office. Washington, DC: The American University. November, 1963.

Monaco, James. *How to Read a Film: The Art, Technology, Language, History, and Theory of Film and Media.* New York: Oxford University Press, 1981.

Monkkonen, Eric H. "A Disorderly People? Urban Order in the Nineteenth and Twentieth Centuries," *JAH* 68:3 (1981), pp. 539–59.

Montgomery, David. *The Fall of the House of Labor: The Workplace, the State, and American Labor Activism, 1865–1925.* New York: Cambridge University Press, 1987.

———. *Workers' Control in America: Studies in the History of Work, Technology, and Labor Struggles.* Cambridge: Cambridge University Press, 1979.

Montgomery, M. R. "These Aren't Real Cowboys, Pardner," *The Boston Globe* (February 13, 1987), p. 11.

Moore, Robin. *The Green Berets.* New York: Avon Books, 1965.

Morgan, Edmund S. *Inventing the People: The Rise of Popular Sovereignty in England and America.* New York. W.W. Norton, 1988.

Morgan, Lewis Henry. *Ancient Society: or, Researches in the Lines of Human Progress from Savagery Through Barbarism to Civilization.* Cleveland: Meridian Books, 1963.

———. *League of the Ho-De-No-Sau-Nee or Iroquois.* Volume 1. New York: Burt Franklin, 1901.

Morison, Samuel Eliot. *Oxford History of the American People.* New York: Oxford University Press, 1965.

Morison, Samuel Eliot, *et al. The Struggle for Guadalcanal, August 1942–February, 1943: History of United States Naval Operations in World War II.* Volume 5. Boston: Little, Brown, 1949.

Morn, Frank. *"The Eye That Never Sleeps": A History of the Pinkerton Detective Agency.* Bloomington: University of Indiana Press, 1982.

Morris, Edmund. *The Rise of Theodore Roosevelt.* New York: Coward, McCann & Geoghegan, 1979.

Morris, Ivan. *The Nobility of Failure: Tragic Heroes in the History of Japan.* New York: New American Library, 1975.

Morris, Jim. *War Story.* New York: Dell, 1979.

Morris, Richard B. *The American Worker.* Washington DC: U.S. Dept of Labor, 1976.

Moskin, Robert J. *The U.S. Marine Corps Story.* Revised Edition. New York: McGraw-Hill Book Company, 1982.

Most, Glenn W., and William E. Stowe. *The Poetics of Murder: Detective Fiction and Literary Theory.* San Diego: Harcourt Brace Jovanovich, 1983.

Mott, Frank Luther. *American Journalism: A History of Newspapers in the United States Through 250 Years, 1690–1940.* New York: The Macmillan Company, 1941.

———. *Golden Multitudes: A History of Best-Sellers in the United States.* New York: The Macmillan Company, 1947.

———. *A History of American Magazines.* Five Volumes. Cambridge, MA: Harvard University Press, 1930–68.

Mottram, Eric. "Living Mythically: The Thirties," *JAS* 6:3 (1972), pp. 267–88.

Mukerji, Chandra, and Michael Schudson, editors. *Rethinking Popular Culture: Contemporary Perspectives in Cultural Studies.* Berkeley: University of California Press, 1991.

Nachbar, Jack, editor. *Focus on the Western.* Englewood Cliffs, NJ: Prentice-Hall, 1974.

Nash, Roderick. *Wilderness and the American Mind.* New Haven: Yale University Press, 1967.

Nathan, Robert R. *Mobilizing for Abundance.* New York: McGraw-Hill Book Company, 1944.

National Association for the Advancement of Colored People. *Thirty Years of Lynching in the United States, 1889–1918.* New York: NAACP, 1919.

National Commission on the Causes and Prevention of Violence. Leon Friedman, General Editor. *Violence in America: Volume Two, Historical and Comparative Perspectives.* New York: Chelsea House, 1983.

National Research Council, Office of International Affairs. Panel on Advanced Technology Competition. *Decisions for America: The Race for the New Frontier: International Competition in Advanced Technology.* New York: Touchstone Books, 1983, 1984.

Nearing, Scott. *The American Empire.* New York: The Rand School of Social Science, 1921.

Neihardt, John G. *Black Elk Speaks: Being the Life Story of a Holy Man of the Oglala Sioux.* Lincoln: University of Nebraska Press, 1961.

Nelson, Keith L., and Spencer C. Olin. *Why War? Ideology, Theory and History.* Berkeley: University of California Press, 1979.

Newby, I. A. *Jim Crow's Defense: Anti-Negro Thought in America, 1900–1930.* Baton Rouge: Louisiana State University Press, 1965.

Nichols, Bill. *Ideology and Image: Social Representation in the Cinema and Other Media.* Bloomington: Indiana University Press, 1981.

———, editor. *Movies and Methods: An Anthology.* Volume 1. Berkeley: University of California Press, 1976.

———, editor. *Movies and Methods: An Anthology.* Volume 2. Berkeley: University of California Press, 1981.

Nichols, Roger L., editor. *American Frontier and Western Issues: A Historiographical Review.* Westport, CT: Greenwood Press, 1986.

Noah, Timothy, and Micky Kaus. "The Missing Witness," *Newsweek* (August 10, 1987), p. 15.

Noble, David W. *The End of American History: Democracy, Capitalism and the Metaphor of Two Worlds in Anglo-American Historical Writing, 1880–1980.* Minneapolis: University of Minnesota Press, 1985.

———. *Historians Against History: The Frontier Thesis and the National Covenant in American Historical Writing Since 1830.* Minneapolis: University of Minnesota Press, 1965.

Noel, Mary. *Villains Galore: The Hey-day of the Popular Story Weekly.* New York: Macmillan Co., 1954.

Nolan, Keith William. *Into Laos: The Story of Dewey Canyon II/ Lam Son 719, Vietnam 1971.* New York: Dell Books, 1986.

Nord, David Paul. "An Economic Perspective on Formula in Popular Culture," *JAC* 3:1 (1980), pp. 17–32.

Norris, Frank. *The Octopus.* New York: Ballantine Books, 1961.

———. *The Responsibilities of the Novelist. Works,* Volume 7. Garden City, NY: Doubleday, Doran & Company, 1928.

North, Oliver L. *Taking the Stand: The Testimony of Lieutenant Colonel Oliver L. North.* Edited by Daniel Schorr. New York: Pocket Books, 1987.

Novick, Peter. *That Noble Dream: The "Objectivity Question" and the American Historical Profession.* Cambridge, England: Cambridge University Press, 1988.

Nowlan, Philip Francis. *Armageddon 2419 A.D.* New York: Ace Books, 1962.

Nugent, Walter. "Frontiers and Empires in the Late Nineteenth Century," *WHQ* 20:4 (1989), pp. 393–408.

———. "The Shaping of a Canon: U.S. Fiction, 1960–1975," *Critical Inquiry* 10:1 (1983), pp. 199–223.

Oberdorfer, Don. *Tet!* Garden City, NY: Doubleday and Co., 1971.

O'Connor, John E., and Martin A. Jackson, editors. *American History/American Film: Interpreting the Hollywood Image*. New York: Frederick Ungar, 1979.

Odum, Howard W. *Race and Rumors of Race: Challenge to American Crisis*. New York: Negro University Press, 1969 [1943].

Oestreicher, Richard. "Urban Working-Class Political Behavior and Theories of American Electoral Politics, 1870–1940," *JAH* 74:4 (1988), pp. 1257–86.

Ohmann, Richard. *Politics of Letters*. Middletown, CT: Wesleyan University Press, [].

"Ollie Takes the Hill," *Newsweek* (July 20, 1987), pp. 12–20.

O'Malley, Ilene V. *The Myth of the Revolution: Hero Cults and the Institutionalization of the Mexican State, 1920–1940*. New York: Greenwood Press, 1986.

Omang, Joanne, and Aryeh Neier, editors. *Psychological Operations in Guerrilla Warfare: The CIA's Nicaragua Manual*. New York: Vintage Books, 1985.

Omi, Michael, and Howard Winant. *Racial Formation in the United States from the 1960s to the 1980s*. New York: Routledge and Kegan Paul, 1986.

O'Neal, Bill. *Encyclopedia of Western Gunfighters*. []

O'Neil, Paul, editor. *The Old West: The End and the Myth*. Alexandria, VA: Time-Life Books, 1979.

O'Neill, Gerard. *The High Frontier: Human Colonies in Space*. Garden City, NY: Anchor Books, 1982.

Oppel, Frank, editor. *Tales of the West*. Secaucus, NJ: Castle Books, 1984.

O'Reilly, Kenneth. "The FBI and the Politics of the Riots, 1964–1968," *JAH* 75:1 (1988), pp. 91–114.

Ornstein, Norman, Andrew Kohut, and Larry McCarthy, *The People, the Press, & Politics: The Times Mirror Study of the American Electorate*. Reading, MA: Addison-Wesley Publishing Company, 1988.

Orth, Samuel P. *The Armies of Labor: A Chronicle of the Organized Wage-Earners. The Chronicles of America Series*, Volume 40. New Haven: Yale University Press, 1921.

Osanka, Franklin Mark, editor. *Modern Guerrilla Warfare: Fighting Communist Guerrilla Movements*, 1941–1961. New York: The Free Press of Glencoe, 1962.

Osborn, George C. *Woodrow Wilson: The Early Years*. Baton Rouge: Lousiana State University Press, 1968.

Osterweis, Rollin G. *The Myth of the Lost Cause, 1865–1900*. Hamden, CT: Archeon Books, 1973.

Ostrander, Gilman M. *American Civilization in the First Machine Age, 1890–1940: A Cultural History of America's First Age of Technological Revolution and "Rule by the Young."* New York: Harper Torchbooks, 1972.

Page, Thomas Nelson. *The Negro: The Southerner's Problem*. New York: Charles Scribner's Sons, 1904.

———. *Red Rock: A Chronicle of Reconstruction*. New York: Charles Scribner's Sons, 1899.

Paine, Jeffrey Morton. *The Simplification of American Life: Hollywood Films of the 1930s*. New York: Arno Press, 1977.

Pakenham, Robert. *Liberal America and the Third World: Political Development Ideas in Foreign Aid and Social Science*. Princeton, NJ: Princeton University Press, 1973.

Palmer, Bruce. "American History's Hardy Perennial: Populism from the 1970s," *AQ* 30:4 (1978), pp. 557–66.

Palmer, Bruce, Jr. *The 25-Year War: America's Military Role in Vietnam.* New York: Touchstone Books, 1984.

Papanikolas, Zeese. *Buried Unsung: Louis Tikas and the Ludlow Massacre.* Salt Lake City: University of Utah Press, 1982.

Parker, Robert B. *The Judas Goat. Boston: Houghton, Mifflin,* 1978.

———. *Promised Land.* New York: Berkley Publishing Company, 1976.

Parker, Theodore. *The Rights of Man in America.* Edited by Franklin B. Sanborn. New York: Negro Universities Press, 1969.

Parkman, Francis. "Bancroft's Native Races," *North American Review* 120 (1875), pp. 34–47.

———. *Count Frontenac and New France Under Louis XIV.* Boston: Little, Brown, 1877.

———. *La Salle and the Discovery of the Great West.* Boston: Little, Brown and Company, 1922.

———. *Montcalm and Wolfe.* New York: Collier Books, 1962.

———. *The Jesuits in North America in the Seventeenth Century.* Volume II. Boston: Little, Brown and Company, 1922.

Parmet, Herbert S. *JFK: The Presidency of John F. Kennedy.* New York: Penguin Books, 1984.

Parrington, Vernon Louis. *Main Currents in American Thought: An Interpretation of American Literature from the Beginnings to 1920.* Three Volumes. New York: Harcourt, Brace & Company, 1927, 1930.

Pastor, Robert A. *Condemned to Repetition: The United States and Nicaragua.* Princeton: Princeton University Press, 1987.

Paterson, Thomas G. *Kennedy's Quest for Victory: American Foreign Policy, 1961–1963.* New York: Oxford University Press, 1989.

Paul, Rodman. *The Far West and the Great Plains in Transition, 1859–1900.* New York: Harper and Row, 1988.

Pauly, Thomas H. "Film: The Cold War Western," *Western Humanities Review* 33:3 (1979), pp. 257–73.

Paxson, Frederick L. *The Last American Frontier.* New York: Macmillan Co., 1910.

Pells, Richard H. *Radical Visions and American Dreams: Culture and Social Thought in the Depression Years.* Middletown, CT: Wesleyan University Press, 1973.

Perlman, Selig. *A Theory of the Labor Movement.* New York: Macmillan Co., 1928.

Person, Leland S., Jr. "The American Eve: Miscegenation and a Feminist Frontier Fiction," *AQ* 37:5 (1985), pp. 668–85.

Persons, Stow. *The Decline of American Gentility.* New York: Columbia University Press, 1973.

Pessen, Edward. *The Log Cabin Myth: The Social Background of the Presidents.* New Haven, CT: Yale University Press, 1984.

Peterson, Richard A. "Five Constraints on the Production of Culture: Law, Technology, Market, Organizational Structure and Occupational Careers," *JPC* 16:2 (1982), pp. 143–53.

Phelps, Glenn Alan. "The Populist Films of Frank Capra," *JAS* 13:3 (1979), pp. 377–92.

"Philippine Epic: General MacArthur and his Men Make a Thermopylae of Bataan," *Life*, April 13, 1942, pp. 25–26, 36.

Phillips, Kevin. *The Politics of Rich and Poor: Wealth and the American Electorate in the Reagan Aftermath.* New York, Random House, 1990.

Pickens, Donald K. "Westward Expansion and the End of American Exceptionalism: Sumner, Turner, and Webb," *WHQ* 12:4 (1981), pp. 409–18.

Pike, James Shepherd. *The Prostrate State: South Carolina Under Negro Government.* New York: Harper and Brothers, 1968 [1874].

Pilkington, William T., and Don Graham, editors. *Western Movies.* Albuquerque: University of New Mexico Press, 1979.

Pinchon, Edgcumb. *Viva Villa! A Recovery of the Real Pancho Villa, Peon . . . Bandit . . . Soldier . . . Patriot.* New York: Harcourt, Brace, 1933.

Pinkerton, Allan. *The Expressmen and the Detectives.* Chicago: W. B. Keen, Cooke and Co., 1874.

———. *The Mollie Maguires and the Detectives.* Edited by John M. Elliot. New York: Dover Publications, 1973.

———. *Strikers, Communists, Tramps and Detectives.* New York: G. W. Carleton and Co., 1878.

Place, J. A. *The Western Films of John Ford.* Secaucus, NJ: Citadel Press, 1974.

Poague, Leland. "'All I Can See Is the Flags': Fort Apache and the Visibility of History," *Cinema Journal* 27:2 (1988), pp. 8–26.

Polan, Dana. *Power and Paranoia: History, Narrative and the American Cinema, 1940–1950.* New York: Columbia University Press, 1986.

Pollack, Norman, editor. *The Populist Mind.* Indianapolis: The Bobbs-Merrill Company, Inc., 1967.

Porges, Irwin. *Edgar Rice Burroughs: The Man Who Created Tarzan.* Two Volumes. New York: Ballantine Books, 1975.

Porter, Glenn. *The Rise of Big Business, 1860–1910.* Arlington Heights, IL: Harlan Davidson, Inc., 1973.

Porter, Joseph C. "The End of the Trail: The American West of Dashiell Hammett and Raymond Chandler," *WHQ* 6:4 (1975), pp. 411–24.

Porter, Kenneth W. *The Negro on the American Frontier.* New York: Arno Press, 1971.

Post, Robert C. "A Theory of Genre: Romance, Realism, and Moral Reality," *AQ* 33:4 (1981), pp. 367–90.

Potter, David. *People of Plenty: Economic Abundance and the American Character.* New York: Harper Torchbooks, 1976 [1954].

Powers, Richard Gid. "J. Edgar Hoover and the Detective Hero," *JPC* 9:2 (1975), pp. 257–78.

———. "One G-Man's Family: Popular Entertainment Formulas and J. Edgar Hoover's F.B.I.," *AQ* 30:4 (1978), pp. 471–92.

Prados, John. *Presidents' Secret Wars: CIA and Pentagon Covert Operations from World War II Through Iranscam.* Newly revised and updated edition. New York: William Morrow, 1986.

Prassel, Frank Richard. *The Western Peace Officer: A Legacy of Law and Order.* Norman: University of Oklahoma Press, 1975.

Pratt, John Clark, editor. *Vietnam Voices: Perspectives on the War Years, 1941–1982.* New York: Penguin Books, 1984.

Pugh, David G. *Sons of Liberty: The Masculine Mind in Nineteenth Century America.* Westport, CT: Greenwood Press, 1983.

Pustay, John S. *Counterinsurgency Warfare.* New York: Free Press, 1965.

Putnam, Jackson K. "The Turner Thesis and the Westward Movement: A Reappraisal," *WHQ* 7:4 (1976), pp. 377–404.

Ramirez, Bruno. *When Workers Fight: The Politics of Industrial Relations in the Progressive Era, 1898–1916.* Westport, CT: Greenwood Press, 1978.

Ranelagh, John. *The Agency: The Rise and Decline of the CIA.* Revised edition. New York: Simon & Schuster, Touchstone Books, 1986.

Rankin, Hon. John A. "Speech of Hon. John A. Rankin, February 23 and March 10, 1942," *Congressional Record 1942,* Appendix A, 768–9, 931.

Rapping, Elaine. "The View from Hollywood: The American Family and the American Dream," *Socialist Review* 13:1 (1983), pp. 71–92.

Raskin, Marcus G., and Bernard B. Fall, editors. *The Viet-Nam Reader.* New York: Vintage Books, 1967.

Rastall, Benjamin McKie. *The Labor History of the Cripple Creek District: A Study in Industrial Evolution.* Madison: University of Wisconsin, 1908.

Ray, Robert. "Dialogue: Robert Ray Responds to Leland Poague's '"All I Can See Is The Flags": *Fort Apache* and the Visibility of History,'" *Cinema Journal* 27:3 (1988), pp. 45–50.

Real, Michael R. "Media Theory: Contributions to an Understanding of American Mass Communications," *AQ* 32:3 (1980), pp. 238–58.

Reed, Joseph W. *American Scenarios: The Use of Film Genre.* Middletown, CT: Wesleyan University Press, 1989.

Three American Originals: *John Ford, William Faulkner and Charles Ives.* Middletown, CT: Wesleyan University Press, 1984.

Reich, Robert B. "Is Japan Really Out to Get Us?" *New York Times Book Review* (Feb. 9, 1992), pp. 1, 24–5.

———*The New American Frontier.* New York: Times Books, 1983.

———"The Pearl Harbor Metaphor," *Deadline: A Bulletin from the Center for War, Peace and the News Media,* 6:3 (Fall, 1991), pp. 4–5.

Reinders, Robert. "Militia and Public Order in Nineteenth Century America," *JAS* 11:1 (1977), 81–102.

Remington, Frederic. *The Collected Writings of Frederic Remington.* Edited by Peggy and Harold Samuels. Garden City, NY: Doubleday and Company, 1979.

Rennert, Jack. *100 Posters of Buffalo Bill's Wild West.* New York: Darien House, 1976.

Reynolds, Quentin. *The Fiction Factory, or From Pulp Row to Quality Street:* New York: Random House, 1955.

Rhodes, Eugene M. *Paso Por Aqui.* Norman: University of Oklahoma Press, 1973.

———. *The Proud Sheriff.* Norman: University of Oklahoma Press, 1968.

Ribuffo, Leo P., editor. "The Burdens of Contemporary History," *AQ* 35: 1 and 2 (1983), *passim.*

Ricci, Mark, Boris and Steve Zmijewsky. *The Films of John Wayne.* New York: The Citadel Press, 1970.

Ridge, Martin. "Frederick Jackson Turner, Ray Allen Billington, and American Frontier History," *WHQ* 19: 1 (1988), pp. 5–20.
Rigg, Robert B. *Red China's Fighting Hordes*. Harrisburg, PA: Military Service Publishing Co., 1952.
Ringenbach, Paul T. *Tramps and Reformers, 1876–1916: The Discovery of Unemployment in New York*. Westport, CT: Greenwood Press, 1973.
Ringgold, Gene, and DeWitt Bodeen. *The Films of Cecil B. DeMille*. New York: The Citadel Press, 1969.
Roberts, Paul Craig. *The Supply-Side Revolution: An Insider's Account of Policymaking in Washington*. Cambridge, MA: Harvard University Press, 1984.
Robertson, James Oliver. *American Myth, American Reality*. New York: Hill & Wang, 1980.
Robinson, Donald, editor. *Dirty Wars: Guerrilla Actions and Other Forms of Unconventional Warfare*, introduction by General S.L.A. Marshall. New York: Delacorte, 1968.
Rockefeller, John D., Jr. *The Personal Relation in Industry*. New York: Boni and Liveright, 1923.
Roddick, Nick. *A New Deal in Entertainment: Warner Brothers in the 1930s*. London: British Film Institute, 1983.
Rodgers, Daniel T. *The Work Ethic in Industrial America, 1850–1920*. Chicago: University of Chicago Press, 1978.
Rogers, Robert. *Ponteach; or, The Savages of America*. London: J. Millam, 1766.
Rogin, Michael P. "'Make My Day!': Spectacle as Amnesia in Imperial Politics," *Representations* 29 (Winter, 1990), pp. 99–123.
———. Ronald Reagan, *The Movie and Other Episodes of Political Demonology*. Berkeley: University of California Press, 1987.
Rolle, Andrew F. *The Lost Cause: The Confederate Exodus to Mexico*. Norman: University of Oklahoma Press, 1965.
Rollins, Peter C. "The Vietnam War: Perceptions Through Literature, Film and Television," *AQ* 36:3 (1984), pp. 419–32.
Roosevelt, Franklin D. *On Our Way*. New York: The John Day Company, 1934.
Roosevelt, Theodore. "Francis Parkman's Histories," *Literary Essays. The Works of Theodore Roosevelt*, Volume 12. New York: Charles Scribner's Sons, 1926.
———. *An Autobiography*. New York: Macmillan, Co. 1913.
———. *Hunting Trips of a Ranchman. Works*, Volume 1. New York: Charles Scribner's Sons, 1926.
———. *Ranch Life and the Hunting Trail. Works*, Volume 1. New York: Charles Scribner's Sons, 1926.
———. *The Rough Riders*. New York: G. P. Putnam's Sons, 1900.
———. *The Wilderness Hunter. Works*, Volume 2. New York: Charles Scribner's Sons, 1926.
———. *The Winning of the West*. Seven volumes. New York: G. P. Putnam's Sons, 1907.
Roosevelt, Theodore, and Henry Cabot Lodge. *Hero Tales from American History. Works*, X, New York: Charles Scribner's Sons, 1926.
Roosevelt [II], Theodore. *Colonial Policies of the United States*. Garden City, NY: Doubleday, Doran & Company, 1937.

Rosa, Joseph G. *The Gunfighter: Man or Myth?* Norman: University of Oklahoma Press, 1969.

Rose, Edward J. *Henry George.* New York: Twayne Publishers, 1968.

Rosen, Philip, editor. *Narrative, Apparatus, Ideology: A Film Theory Reader.* New York: Columbia University Press, 1986.

Rosenbaum, H. Jon, and Peter C. Sederberg, editors. *Vigilante Poltics.* Philadelphia: University of Pennsylvania Press, 1976.

Rosenberg, Bernard, and David Manning White. *Mass Culture: The Popular Arts in America.* New York: Free Press, 1957.

Rosenberg, Charles E. "Sexuality, Class and Race in Nineteenth Century America," *AQ* 25:2 (1973), pp. 177–201.

Rosenberg, Emily S. *Spreading the American Dream: American Economic and Cultural Expansion, 1890–1945.* New York: Hill & Wang, 1982.

Rosencrance, Richard. *America as an Ordinary Country: Foreign Policy and the Future.* Ithaca: Cornell University Press, 1976.

Rosenstone, Robert A. "History in Images/History in Words: Reflections on the Possibility of Really Putting History onto Film," *AHR* 93:5 (1988), pp. 1173–85.

Rosenzweig, Roy. *Eight Hours for What We Will: Workers and Leisure in an Industrial City.* New York: Cambridge University Press, 1983.

———. *History Museums in the United States: A Critical Assessment.* Urbana: University of Illinois Press, 1989.

Rosenzweig, Sidney. "The Dark Night of the Screen: Messages and Melodrama in the American Movie," *AQ* 27:1 (1975), pp. 88–98.

Rostow, Walt Whitman. *The Stages of Economic Growth: A Non-Communist Manifesto.* Cambridge, England: Cambridge University Press, 1960.

Roth, John K., and Robert C. Whittemore, editors. *Ideology and the American Experience: Essays on Theory and Practice.* Washington, DC: Washington Institute Press, 1986.

Rothschild, Emma. "The Reagan Economic Legacy," *NYRB* (July 21, 1988), pp. 33–41.

Rourke, Constance M. *American Humor: A Study of the National Character.* New York: Harcourt, Brace and Company, 1931.

Ruehlmann, William. *Saint With a Gun: The Unlawful American Private Eye.* New York: New York University Press, 1974.

Ruhm, Herbert, editor. *The Hard-Boiled Detective: Stories from* Black Mask *Magazine, 1920–1951.* New York: Vintage Books, 1977.

Ruiz, George W. "The Ideological Convergence of Theodore Roosevelt and Woodrow Wilson," *Presidential Studies Quarterly* 19:1 (1989), pp. 159–78.

Rule, James B. *Theories of Civil Violence.* Berkeley: University of California Press, 1988.

Rundell, Walter, Jr. "W. P. Webb's *Divided We Stand:* A Publishing Crisis," *WHQ* 13:4 (1982), pp. 391–408.

Rusk, Dean, with Richard Rusk. *As I Saw It.* Edited by Daniel S. Papp. New York: W. W. Norton, 1990.

Russell, Don. *Custer's Last* . . . Fort Worth, TX: Amon Carter Museum of Western Art, 1968.

———. *The Lives and Legends of Buffalo Bill.* Norman: University of Oklahoma Press, 1960.

———. *The Wild West: A History of Wild West Shows.* Fort Worth, TX: Amon Carter Museum, 1961.

Russell, Henry B. *An Illustrated History of Our War with Spain and Our War with the Filipinos* . . . Hartford, CT: The Hartford Publishing Company, 1899.

Russett, Bruce M., and Alfred Stepan, editors. *Military Force and American Society.* New York: Harper & Row, 1973.

Ryan, Halford Ross, editor. *American Rhetoric from Roosevelt to Reagan.* Prospect Heights, IL: Waveland Press, 1987.

Ryan, Michael, and Douglas Kellner. *Camera Politica: The Politics and Ideology of Contemporary Hollywood Film.* Bloomington: Indiana University Press, 1988.

Rydell, Robert W. "The World's Columbian Exposition of 1893: Racist Underpinnings of a Utopian Artifact," *JAC* (Summer, 1978), pp. 253–75.

———. "The Trans-Mississippi and the International Exposition: 'To Work Out the Problem of Universal Civilization.' " *AQ* 33:5 (1981), pp. 587–607.

Sack, John. *M.* New York: Avon Books, 1985.

Sadler, Barry. *Phu Nam.* New York: Tom Doherty Associates, 1984.

Sahlins, Marshall. *Historical Metaphors and Mythical Realities: Structure in the Early History of the Sandwich Islands Kingdom.* Ann Arbor: University of Michigan Press, 1981.

Salvatore, Nick. *Eugene V. Debs: Citizen and Socialist.* Urbana: University of Illinois Press, 1982.

Samuels, Harold, and Peggy Samuels. *Frederic Remington: A Biography.* Garden City, NY: Doubleday & Company, 1982.

Santoli, Al. *Everything We Had: An Oral History of the Vietnam War by Thirty-Three American Soldiers Who Fought It.* New York: Ballantine Books, 1981.

Sarkesian, Sam C., editor. *Revolutionary Guerrilla Warfare.* Chicago: Precedent Publishing, 1975.

Sarris, Andrew. "Death of the Gunfighters," *Film Comment* 18:2 (1982), pp. 40–2.

———. *The John Ford Movie Mystery.* Bloomington: Indiana University Press, 1975.

Saum, Lewis O. "'Astonishing the Natives': Bringing the Wild West to Los Angeles," *Montana* 38:3 (1988), pp. 2–13.

Savage, William W., Jr. *The Cowboy Hero: His Image in American History and Culture.* Norman: University of Oklahoma Press, 1979.

Saxton, Alexander. "*Caesar's Column*: The Dialogue of Utopia and Catastrophe," *AQ* 19:2, Part 1 (1967), pp. 224–38.

———. *The Indispensible Enemy: Labor and the Anti-Chinese Movement in California.* Berkeley: University of California Press, 1971.

———. "Historical Explanations of Racial Inequality," *Marxist Perspectives* 2:2 (1979), pp. 145–68.

———. "Problems of Class and Race in the Origins of the Mass Circulation Press," *AQ* 36:2 (1984), pp. 211–34.

Schaefer, Jack. *Monte Walsh.* New York: Pocket Books, 1963.

———. *Shane: The Critical Edition*, edited by James C. Work. Lincoln: University of Nebraska Press, 1984.

Schank, Roger. *Dynamic Memory: A Theory of Reminding and Learning in Computers and People*. Cambridge, England: Cambridge University Press, 1982.

Schatz, Thomas. *The Genius of the System: Hollywood Filmmaking in the Studio Era*. New York: Pantheon Books, 1988.

———. *Hollywood Genres: Formulas, Filmmaking, and the Studio System*. Philadelphia: Temple University Press, 1981.

Scheick, William J. *The Half-Blood: A Cultural Symbol in 19th-Century American Fiction*. Lexington: The University Press of Kentucky, 1979.

Schell, Jonathan. *The Real War: The Classic Reporting on the Vietnam War*. New York: Pantheon Books, 1987.

———. *The Time of Illusion: An Historical and Reflective Account of the Nixon Era*. New York: Vintage Books, 1975.

Schemmer, Benjamin F. *The Raid*. New York: Avon Books, 1976.

Scherman, David E., editor. *Life Goes to War: A Picture History of World War II*. New York: Pocket Books, 1977.

Schickel, Richard. *D. W. Griffith: An American Life*. New York: Simon & Schuster, 1984.

Schiff, Stephen. "The Repeatable Experience," *Film Comment* 18:2 (1982), pp. 33–6.

Schlesinger, Arthur M., Jr. "On Heroic Leadership and the Dilemma of Strong Men and Weak Peoples," *Encounter* 15:6 (December 1960), pp. 3–11.

Schlesinger, Stephen, and Stephen Kinzer. *Bitter Fruit: The Untold Story of the American Coup in Guatemala*. Garden City, NY: Anchor Books, 1983.

Schlissel, Lillian,"Frontier Families: Crisis in Ideology," in Sam B. Girgus, editor, *The American Self: Myth, Ideology and Popular Culture*. Albuquerque: University of New Mexico Press, 1981, Chapter 10.

Schmidt, Dorey. "Magazines, Technology and American Culture," *JAC* 3:1 (1980), pp. 3–16.

Schmidt, Hans. *Maverick Marine: General Smedley D. Butler and the Contradictions of American Military History*. Lexington: University of Kentucky Press, 1987.

Schneider, William. " 'Rambo' and Reality: Having It Both Ways," in Kenneth Oye, Robert J. Lieber, and Donald Rothchild, editors. *Eagle Resurgent? The Reagan Era in Foreign Policy*. Boston: Little, Brown and Co., 1983.

Scholes, Robert. "Narration and Narrativity in Film," in Gerald Mast and Marshall Cohen, editors, *Film Theory and Criticism: Introductory Readings*. Third Edition, pp. 390–403. New York: Oxford University Press, 1985.

Schruers, Fred. " 'Young Guns,' " *Premiere* 1:12 (1988), pp. 40–50.

Schubert, Frank N. "The Suggs Affray: The Black Cavalry in the Johnson County War," *WHQ* 4:1, January 1973), pp. 57–68.

Schuman, Howard, Charlotte Steeh, and Robert Bobo. *Racial Attitudes in America: Trends and Interpretations*. Cambridge, MA: Harvard University Press, 1988.

Schwantes, Carolos A. "The Concept of the Wageworkers' Frontier: A Framework for Future Research," *WHQ* 18:1 (1987), pp. 39–56.

Schwartz, Norman B. "Villainous Cowboys and Backward Peasants: Popular Culture and Development Concepts," *JPC* 15:4 (1982), pp. 105–13.

Sebeok, Thomas, editor. *Myth: A Symposium*. Bloomington: Indiana University Press, 1965.

Segal, Ronald. *The Race War.* New York: Viking Press, 1967.

Seldes, Gilbert. *Mainstream.* New York: Charles Scribner's Sons, 1936.

Sennett, Ted. *Warner Brothers Presents: The Most Exciting Years—from "The Jazz Singer" to "White Heat."* []: Castle Books, Inc., 1971.

Seton, Ernest Thompson. *Two Little Savages: Being the Adventures of Two Boys Who Lived as Indians and What They Learned.* New York: Dover Publications, 1962 [1903].

Settle, William A., Jr. *Jesse James Was His Name: or, Fact and Fiction Concerning the Careers of the Notorious James Brothers of Missouri.* Lincoln: University of Nebraska Press, 1966.

Seydor, Paul. *Peckinpah: The Western Films.* Urbana: University of Illinois Press, 1979.

Shadoyan, Jack. *Dreams and Dead Ends: The American Gangster/Crime Film.* Cambridge, MA: MIT Press, 1979.

Shain, Russell Earl. *An Analysis of Motion Pictures about War Released by the American Film Industry, 1930–1970.* New York: Arno Press, 1976.

Shalom, Stephen Rosskam. "Death in The Philippines," Letter to the Editor, *NYRB* (March 4, 1982), p. 44.

Shapiro, Herbert. *White Violence and Black Response from Reconstruction to Montgomery.* Amherst: The University of Massachusetts Press, 1989.

Sheehan, Neil. *A Bright and Shining Lie: John Paul Vann and America in Vietnam.* New York: Random House, 1988.

Shibutani, Tamotsu. *The Derelicts of Company K: A Sociological Study of Demoralization.* Berkeley: University of California Press, 1978.

Shirley, Glenn. *The Last of the Real Bad Men, Henry Starr.* Lincoln: University of Nebraska Press, 1976.

Sifakis, Carl. *The Encyclopedia of American Crime: Abbandando to Zwillman.* New York: Facts on File, 1982.

Sifry, Micah L. and Christopher Cerf. *The Gulf War Reader: History, Documents, Opinions.* New York: Times Books, 1991.

Silk, Leonard and Mark. *The American Establishment.* New York: Basic Books, Inc., 1980.

Simmons, Garner. *Peckinpah: A Portrait in Montage.* Austin: University of Texas, 1976.

Simpson, Charles M. *Inside the Green Berets, The First Thirty Years: A History of the U.S. Army Special Forces.* New York: Berkley Books, 1983.

Sinclair, Andrew. *John Ford: A Biography.* New York: The Dial Press, 1979.

Sinclair, Upton. *The Coal War: A Sequel to King Coal.* Introduction by John Graham. Boulder: Colorado Associated University Press, 1976.

Singal, Daniel Joseph. "Ulrich B. Phillips: The Old South as the New," *JAH* 43:4 (1977), pp. 871–91.

Singer, Mark. *Funny Money.* New York: Laurel, 1985.

Sinkler, George. *The Racial Attitudes of American Presidents from Abraham Lincoln to Theodore Roosevelt.* Garden City, NY: Doubleday Anchor Books, 1972.

Siringo, Charles. *A Cowboy Detective: A True Story . . .* First Edition. Chicago: W. B. Conkey Co., 1912.

———. *Riata and Spurs: The Story of a Lifetime Spent in the Saddle as a Cowboy and Ranger.* New York: Houghton Mifflin and Co., 1927.

———. *A Texas Cowboy; or, Fifteen Years on the Hurricane Deck of a Spanish Pony.* New York: Signet, 1955 [1885].

———. *Two Evil Isms: Pinkertonism and Anarchism.* Edited by Charles D. Peavy. Austin, TX: Steck-Vaughn Co., 1968 [1915].

Skeyhill, Tom. *Sergeant York: Last of the Long Hunters.* Philadelphia: The John C. Winston Company, 1930.

Sklar, Robert. *Movie-Made America: How the Movies Changed American Life.* New York: Random House, 1975.

Slotkin, Richard. "Massacre," *Berkshire Review: Special Issue on Culture and Violence* (1979), pp. 112–32.

———. "Prologue to a Study of Myth and Genre in American Movies," *Prospects* 9 (1984).

———. "Narratives of Negro Crime In New England, 1675–1800," *AQ* 25:1 (1973), pp. 3–31.

———. *Regeneration Through Violence: The Mythology of the American Frontier, 1600–1860.* Middletown, CT: Wesleyan University Press, 1973.

——— and James K. Folsom. *So Dreadfull a Judgment: Puritan Responses to King Philip's War, 1675–77.* Middletown, CT: Wesleyan University Press, 1978.

———. *The Fatal Environment: The Myth of the Frontier in the Age of Industrialization, 1800–1890.* New York: Atheneum, 1985.

———. "Nostalgia and Progress: Theodore Roosevelt's Myth of the Frontier," *AQ* 33:5 (1981), pp. 608–38.

Smead, Howard. *Blood Justice: The Lynching of Mack Charles Parker.* New York: Oxford University Press, 1986.

Smith, Cornelius C. *Don't Settle for Second: The Life and Times of Cornelius C. Smith.* San Rafael, CA: Presidio Press, 1977.

Smith, Helena Huntington. *The War on Powder River: The History of an Insurrection.* Lincoln: University of Nebraska Press, 1966.

Smith, Henry Nash. *Virgin Land: The American West as Symbol and Myth.* New York: Vintage Books, 1950.

Smith, Robert Wayne. *The Coeur d'Alene Mining War of 1892: A Case Study of an Industrial Dispute.* Gloucester, MA: Peter Smith, 1968.

Smith, William, "provost" editor. *Historical Account of Bouquet's Expedition Against the Ohio Indians in 1764.* Edited by Francis Parkman. Cincinnati: Robert Clarke and Company, 1868.

Smith-Rosenberg, Carroll. *Disorderly Conduct: Visions of Gender in Victorian America.* New York: Oxford University Press, 1985.

Smythe, Donald. *Guerrilla Warrior: The Early Life of John J. Pershing.* New York: Charles Scribner's Sons, 1973.

Smythe, William E. *The Conquest of Arid America.* New York: Macmillan Company, 1905.

Snepp, Frank. *Decent Interval: An Insider's Account of Saigon's Indecent End Told by the CIA's Chief Strategy Analyst in Vietnam.* New York: Vintage Books, 1977.

Sobchak, Vivian C. "Beyond Visual Aids: American Film as American Culture," *AQ* 32:3 (1980), pp. 280–300.

Sollors, Werner. *Beyond Ethnicity: Consent and Descent in American Culture.* New York: Oxford University Press, 1986.

Sonnichsen, C. L. *From Hopalong to Hud: Thoughts on Western Fiction.* College Station, TX: Texas A & M University Press, 1978.

Sorensen, Theodore C. *Kennedy.* New York: Bantam Books, 1966.

Spence, Clark C. "The Landless Man and the Manless Land," *WHQ* 16:4 (1985), pp. 397–412.

Spencer, Herbert. *The Study of Sociology.* New York: D. Appleton & Company, 1874.

———. *On Social Evolution.* Edited by J. D. Y. Peel. Chicago: University of Chicago Press, 1972.

Spivey, Donald. *Schooling for the New Slavery: Black Industrial Education, 1868–1915.* Westport, CT: Greenwood Press, 1978.

Sprague, Marshall. *Money Mountain: The Story of Cripple Creek Gold.* Lincoln: University of Nebraska Press, 1955.

Springer, John. *The Fondas: The Films and Careers of Henry, Jane and Peter Fonda.* New York: The Citadel Press, 1970.

Stanley, John Mix. *Scenes and Incidents of Stanley's Western Wilds.* Washington, DC: Evening Star Office, 185[4].

Stanley, Peter W. *Reappraising an Empire: New Perspectives on Philippine-American History.* Cambridge, MA: Harvard University Press, 1984.

Stanton, Shelby L. *Green Berets at War.* New York: Dell Books, 1985.

Starr, Kevin. *Inventing the Dream: California Through the Progressive Era.* New York: Oxford University Press, 1985.

Stavins, Ralph, Richard J. Barnet, Marcus G. Raskin. *Washington Plans an Aggressive War.* New York: Random House, 1971.

Steckmesser, Kent Laird. *The Western Hero in History and Legend.* Norman: University of Oklahoma Press, 1965.

Stedman, Raymond William. *Shadows of the Indian: Stereotypes in American Culture.* Norman: University of Oklahoma Press, 1982.

Stein, Leon, editor. *The Pullman Strike.* New York: Arno Press, 1969.

Steinbeck, John. *The Grapes of Wrath.* New York: The Viking Press, 1939.

———. *Viva Zapata!: The Original Screenplay.* Edited by Robert E. Morsberger. New York: The Viking Press, 1975.

Steiner, Stan. *The New Indians.* New York: Harper and Row, 1967.

Stoddard, T[heodore] L[othrop]. *The French Revolution in Santo Domingo.* New York: Houghton, Mifflin Co., 1914.

———. *The Revolt Against Civilization: The Menace of the Under-Man.* New York: Charles Scribner's Sons, 1922.

———. *The Rising Tide of Color Against White World Supremacy.* New York: Scribner's Sons, 1920.

Stoessinger, John G. *Why Nations Go to War.* Third Edition. New York: St. Martin's Press, 1982.

Stohl, Michael. *War and Domestic Political Violence: The American Capacity for Repression and Reaction.* Beverly Hills: Sage Publications, 1976.

Storey, Moorfield, *et al. Secretary Root's Record: Marked Severities in Philippine Warfare. An Analysis of the Law and Facts Bearing on the Actions and Utterances of President Roosevelt and Secretary Root.* Boston: G.H. Ellis, 1902.

Stowe, William W. "Hard-Boiled Virgil: Early Nineteenth-Century Beginnings of a Popular Literary Formula," in Barbara A. Rader and Howard G. Zettler, editors, The Sleuth and the Scholar: Origins, Evolution, and Current Trends in Detective Fiction. Westport, CT: Greenwood Press, 1988.

"Strong But Risky Show of Force," *Time* (May 26, 1975), pp. 9–14.

Strong, Josiah. *Our Country.* Edited by Jurgen Herbst. Cambridge, MA: Belknap Press of Harvard University Press, 1963.

Summers, Harry G., Jr. *On Strategy: The Vietnam War in Context.* Carlisle Barracks, PA: Strategic Studies Institute, U.S. Army War College, 1981.

Sumner, William Graham. *Social Darwinism: Selected Essays of William Graham Sumner.* Englewood Cliffs, NJ: Prentice-Hall, 1963.

———. *The Conquest of the United States by Spain and Other Essays.* Chicago: Henry Regnery Co. [].

Susman, Warren I. *Culture as History: The Transformation of Society in the Twentieth Century.* New York: Pantheon Books, 1984.

Swierenga, Robert P. "Land Speculation and Its Impact on American Economic Growth and Welfare: A Historiographical Review," *WHQ* 8:3 (1977), pp. 283–301.

Symons, Julian. *Mortal Consequences: A History from the Detective Story to the Crime Novel.* New York: Schocken Books, 1972.

Tatum, Stephen. *Inventing Billy the Kid: Visions of the Outlaw in America, 1881–1981.* Albuquerque: University of New Mexico Press, 1982.

Taylor, George Rogers, editor. *The Turner Thesis Concerning the Role of the Frontier in American History.* Revised Edition. Boston: D.C. Heath and Company, 1956.

Taylor, Joshua C. *America as Art.* New York: Harper & Row, 1976.

Taylor, Philip. *The Distant Magnet: European Emigration to the U.S.A.* New York: Harper & Row, 1971.

Taylor, William R. *Cavalier and Yankee: The Old South and American National Character.* Garden City, NY: Anchor Books, 1963.

Tebbe, Jennifer. "Print and American Culture," *AQ* 32:3 (1980), pp. 259–79.

Tencotte, Paul A. "Kaleidoscopes of the World: International Exhibitions and the Concept of Culture–Place, 1851–1915," *American Studies* 28:1 (1987), pp. 5–30.

Terry, Wallace. *Bloods: An Oral History of the Vietnam War by Black Veterans.* New York: Ballantine Books, 1984.

"The Legacy of Vietnam: The War That Won't Go Away," *Newsweek* (April 15, 1985), pp. 32–71.

Thelen, David. "Memory and American History," *JAH* 75:4 (1989), pp. 1117–29.

Thomas, Evan. "The One True Hawk in the Administration," *Newsweek* (January 7, 1991), p. 19.

Thomas, Evan, *et al.* " 'No Vietnam,' " *Newsweek* (December 10, 1990), pp. 24–31.

Thomas, John L. "The Uses of Catastrophism: Lewis Mumford, Vernon L. Parrington, Van Wyck Brooks, and the End of American Regionalism," *AQ* 42:2 (1990), pp. 223–51.

Thompson, E. P. *The Making of the English Working Class.* New York: Vintage Books, 1966.

Thompson, John. *Closing the Frontier: Radical Response in Oklahoma, 1889–1923.* Norman: University of Oklahoma Press, 1986.

Thomson, David. *America in the Dark: The Impact of Hollywood Films on American Culture.* New York: William Morrow and Co., 1977.

———. "Better Best Westerns," *Film Comment* 26:2 (1990), pp. 7–13.

———. "The End of the American Hero," *Film Comment* 17:4 (1981), pp. 13–17.

Thurow, Lester C. *The Zero-Sum Society: Distribution and the Possibilities for Economic Change.* New York: Basic Books, 1983.

Tomkies, Mike. *Duke: The Story of John Wayne.* New York: Avon Books, 1971.

Tomkins, Sylvan S. "Script Theory: Differential Magnification of Affects," in H. E. Howe and R. A. Dienstbier, editors, *Nebraska Symposium on Motivation* 26 (1979).

Tompkins, E. Berkeley. *Anti-Imperialism in the United States: The Great Debate, 1890–1920.* Philadephia: University of Pennsylvania Press, 1970.

Tompkins, Jane. *Sensational Designs: The Cultural Work of American Fiction.* New York: Oxford University Press, 1985.

———. *Reader-Response Criticism: From Formalism to Post-Structuralism.* Baltimore: The Johns Hopkins University Press, 1980.

Tourgee, Albion W. *A Fool's Errand: A Novel of the South During Reconstruction.* Introduction by George M. Frederickson. New York: Harper Torchbooks, 1961 [1879].

Townsend, George Alfred. *The Swamp Outlaws: or, The North Carolina Bandits, Being a Complete History of the Modern Rob Roys and Robin Hoods.* New York: Robert M. De Witt, Publisher, 1873.

Townsend, Kim. "Francis Parkman and the Male Tradition," *AQ* 38:1 (1986), pp. 97–113.

Trachtenberg, Alan. *The Incorporation of America: Culture and Society in the Gilded Age.* New York: Hill & Wang, 1982.

———. Myth, History, and Literature in *Virgin Land,*" *Prospects* 3 (1977), pp. 125–34.

———. editor. *Democratic Vistas, 1860–1880.* New York: George Braziller, 1970.

Trachtman, Paul, editor. *The Old West: The Gunfighters.* Alexandria, VA: Time-Life Books, 1974.

Traub, Stuart H. "Rewards, Bounty Hunting, and Criminal Justice in the West: 1865–1900," *WHQ* 19:3 (1988), pp. 287–301.

Traube, Elizabeth. *Dreaming Identities: Class, Gender and Generation in 1980s Hollywood Movies.* Boulder, CO: Westview, 1992.

Triplett, Frank. *The Life, Times and Treacherous Death of Jesse James.* St. Louis: J. H. Chambers and Co., 1882.

Truettner, William H. *The Natural Man Observed: A Study of Catlin's Indian Gallery.* Washington, DC: Smithsonian Institution Press, 1979.

Tucker, Frank Hammond. *The Frontier Spirit and Progress*. Chicago: Nelson-Hall Publishers, 1980.

Turner, Frederick Jackson. *The Frontier in American History*. New York: Holt, Rinehart and Winston, 1962.

Turner, Jonathan H., and David Musick. *American Dilemmas: A Sociological Interpretation of Enduring Social Issues*. New York: Columbia University Press, 1985.

Turner, Victor L. *The Ritual Process: Structure and Anti-Structure*. Chicago: Aldine Publishing Company, 1969.

———. "Process, System, and Symbol: A New Anthropological Synthesis," *Daedalus* 1977, 1:61–80.

Tuveson, Ernest Lee. *Redeemer Nation: The Idea of America's Millennial Role*. Chicago: University of Chicago Press, 1971.

Twain, Mark. *A Connecticut Yankee in King Arthur's Court*. Norton Critical Edition. Edited by Allison R. Ensor. New York: W. W. Norton, 1982.

———. *Roughing It*. Berkeley: University of California Press, 1972.

Tyler, Robert L. "The I.W.W. and the West," in Hennig Cohen, editor, *The American Culture: Approaches to the Study of the United States*, pp. 30–42. Boston: Houghton Mifflin Company, 1968.

Tyler, Parker, "Hollywood as a Universal Church," in Hennig Cohen, editor, *The American Culture: Approaches to the Study of the United States*, pp. 283–95. Boston: Houghton Mifflin Company, 1968.

Underhill, Lonnie E., and Daniel F. Littlefield, Jr., editors. *Hamlin Garland's Observations on the American Indian*. Tucson: University of Arizona Press, 1976.

Ungar, Sanford J., editor. *Estrangement: America and the World*. New York: Oxford University Press, 1985.

Utley, Robert M. *Frontier Regulars: The United States Army and the Indian, 1866–1891*. New York: Macmillan Co., 1973.

———. *The Last Days of the Sioux Nation*. New Haven, CT: Yale University Press, 1963.

———. *High Noon in Lincoln County: Violence on the Western Frontier*. Albuquerque: University of New Mexico Press, 1987.

———. *The Contribution of the Frontier to the American Military Tradition*. Colorado Springs, CO: United States Air Force Academy, 1977.

———. *Custer and the Great Controversy: The Origin and Development of a Legend*. Los Angeles, CA: Western Lore Press, 1962.

Valeriano, Napoleon D., and Charles T. R. Bohannan. *Counterguerrilla Operations: The Philippine Experience*. New York: Fred Praeger, Inc., 1962.

Van Deburg, William L. *Slavery and Race in American Popular Culture*. Madison: University of Wisconsin Press, 1984.

Vanneman, Reeve, and Lynn Weber Cannon. *The American Perception of Class*. Philadelphia: Temple University Press, 1987.

Varenne, Herve, editor. *Symbolizing America*. Lincoln: University of Nebraska Press, 1986.

Vaughan, Alden T. *New England Frontier: Puritans and Indians, 1620–1675*. Boston: Little, Brown, 1965.

Veblen, Thorstein. "The Beginnings of Ownership," *The American Journal of Sociology* 4 (1898), pp. 352–65.

Vertzberger, Yaacov Y. I. *The World in Their Minds: Information Processing, Cognition, and Perception in Foreign Policy Decisionmaking.* Stanford, CA: Stanford University Press, 1990.

Vestal, Stanley. *Sitting Bull: Champion of the Sioux.* Norman: University of Oklahoma, 1957.

Veysey, Laurence. "The Autonomy of American History Reconsidered," *AQ* 31:4 (1979), pp. 455–77.

Vickery, John B., editor. *Myth and Literature: Contemporary Theory and Practice.* Lincoln: University of Nebraska Press, 1966.

Vietnam Veterans Against the War. *The Winter Soldier Investigation: An Inquiry into American War Crimes.* Boston: Beacon Press, 1972.

Vlastos, Stephen. "Television Wars: Representations of the Vietnam War in Television Documentaries," *RHR* 36 (1986), pp. 115–33.

Vorpahl, Ben Merchant. *Frederick Remington and the West: With the Eye of the Mind.* Austin: University of Texas Press, 1978.

———. *My Dear Wister: The Frederick Remington–Owen Wister Letters.* Palo Alto, CA: The American West Publishing Company, 1972.

Wade, Wyn Craig. *The Fiery Cross: The Ku Klux Klan in America.* New York: Touchstone Books, 1987.

Waldman, Steven, and Rich Thomas, "How Did It Happen?" *Newsweek* (May 21, 1990,), pp. 27–32.

Walker, Tom. *Fort Apache.* New York: Avon, 1976.

Walker, Francis A. "Restriction of Immigration," *Atlantic Monthly* (June, 1896), pp. 822–9.

Walker, William. *The War in Nicaragua.* Tucson: The University of Arizona Press, 1979.

Wallimann, Isidor, and Michael N. Dobkowski, *Genocide and the Modern Age: Etiology and Case Studies of Mass Death.* Westport, CT: Greenwood Press, 1987.

Walsh, Margaret. *The American Frontier Revisited.* Atlantic Highlands, NJ: Humanities Press, 1981.

Wambaugh, Joseph. *The Blue Knight.* New York: Dell Books, 1972.

———. *Lines and Shadows.* New York: Bantam Books, 1984.

Ward, George B. "Bloodbrothers in the Wilderness," Dissertation, University of Texas, Austin, 1981.

Warner, Sam Bass, Jr. *The Urban Wilderness: A History of the American City.* New York: Harper & Row, 1972.

Waters, Frank. *The Earp Brothers of Tombstone: The Story of Mrs. Virgil Earp.* Lincoln: University of Nebraska Press, 1960.

Watson, Russell, *et al.*, " 'Project Recovery': A handful of 'cowboys' leads Reagan into the biggest blunder of his presidency," *Newsweek* (December 1, 1986), pp. 26–37.

Weaver, John D. *The Brownsville Raid.* New York: W. W. Norton, 1970.

Webb, James. *Fields of Fire.* New York: Bantam Books, 1979.

Webb, Walter Prescott. *Divided We Stand: The Crisis of a Frontierless Democracy.* New York: Farrar & Rinehart, 1937.

———. *The Great Plains.* New York: Grosset & Dunlap, 1971.

Weigley, Russell F. *The American Way of War: A History of United States Military Strategy and Policy.* Bloomington: Indiana University Press, 1973.

———. *History of the United States Army.* New York: Macmillan, 1967.

Weinstein, James. *The Corporate Ideal in the Liberal State, 1900–1918.* Boston: Beacon Press, 1968.

Weiss, Richard. "Ethnicity and Reform: Minorities and the Ambience of the Depression Years," *JAH* 66:3 (1979), pp. 566–85.

Wells, David A. *Recent Economic Changes and Their Effect on the Production and Distribution of Wealth and the Well-Being of Society.* New York: D. Appleton and Co., 1889, 1891.

Wells-Barnett, Ida B. *On Lynchings: Southern Horrors, A Red Record, Mob Rule in New Orleans.* New York: Arno Press and New York Times, 1969.

Welter, Barbara Rush. "The Cult of True Womanhood, 1820–1860," *AQ* 18:2, Part 1 (1966), pp. 151–74.

West, George P. *Report on the Colorado Strike.* Washington, DC: Barnard and Miller, 1915.

Weston, Jack. *The Real American Cowboy.* New York: Schocken Books, 1985.

Weston, Rubin Francis. *Racism in U.S. Imperialism: The Influence of Racial Assumptions on American Foreign Policy, 1893–1946.* Columbia: University of South Carolina Press, 1972.

Wetmore, Helen Cody. *Last of the Great Scouts.* New York: Grosset and Dunlap, 1918.

Wheeler, Edward. *Deadwood Dick, The Prince of the Road; or, The Black Rider of the Black Hills.* New York: Beadle & Adams, 1877.

———. *Deadwood Dick on Deck; or, Calamity Jane, the Heroine of Whoop-Up. A Story of Dakota.* New York: Beadle & Adams, 1878.

Wheeler, John. *Touched with Fire: The Future of the Vietnam Generation.* New York: Avon Books, 1984.

Wheeler, John, Captain. "Rear Guard in Luzon," *Life* (March 2, 1942), pp. 51–2, 55.

White, G. Edward. *The Eastern Establishment and the Western Experience: The West of Frederic Remington, Theodore Roosevelt, and Owen Wister.* New Haven, CT: Yale University Press, 1968.

White, Grace Miller. *Custer's Last Fight: A Thrilling Story Founded Upon the Play of the Same Name.* New York: J. S. Ogilvie, 1905.

White, Hayden. "Historiography and Historiophoty," *AHR* 93:5 (1988), pp. 1193–9.

———. *Metahistory: The Historical Imagination in Nineteenth Century Europe.* Baltimore, MD: The Johns Hopkins University Press, 1973.

———. *Topics of Discourse: Essays in Cultural Criticism.* Baltimore, MD: The Johns Hopkins University Press, 1978.

White, John Kenneth. *The New Politics of Old Values.* Hanover, NH: University Press of New England, 1988.

White, Richard. "Outlaw Gangs of the Middle Border: American Social Bandits," *WHQ* 12:4 (1981), pp. 387–408.

———. "Race Relations in the American West," *AQ* 38:3 (1986), pp. 396–416.

White, Stewart Edward. *The Forty-Niners: A Chronicle of the California Trail and El Dorado. The Chronicles of America Series.* Volume 25. New Haven CT: Yale University Press, 1921.

———. *The Long Rifle.* New York: Doubleday, Doran and Co., 1932.

———. *The Westerners.* Garden City, NY: Doubleday, Page and Co., 1916.

White, Theodore H. "The Bell of Decision Rings Out in Vietnam." *Life* (September 1, 1967), pp. 54–8.

White, W. Thomas. "Race, Ethnicity, and Gender in the Railroad Work Force: The Case of the Far Northwest, 1883–1918," *WHQ* 16:3 (1985), pp. 265–84.

White, Walter. *Rope and Faggot.* New York: Arno Press, 1969.

Whiting, Cecilia. "American Heroes and Invading Barbarians: The Regionalist Response to Fascism," *Prospects 13* (1988), pp. 295–324.

Whittaker, Frederick C. *A Complete Life of General George A. Custer* . . . New York: Sheldon and Company, 1876.

———. *The Dashing Dragoon; or, The Story of General George A. Custer from West Point to the Big Horn.* New York: Beadle & Adams, 1882.

Wicke, Jennifer A. *Advertising Fictions: Literature, Advertisement and Social Reading.* New York: Columbia University Press, 1988.

Wicker, Tom. *A Time to Die.* New York: Ballantine Books, 1975.

Wiebe, Robert H. *The Search for Order, 1877–1920.* New York: Hill & Wang, 1967.

Wiener, Jonathan M. "Radical Historians and the Crisis in American History, 1959–1980," *JAH* 76:2 (1989), pp. 399–434.

Wilensky, Harold L. "Mass Society and Mass Culture: Interdependence or Dependence?" *American Sociological Review* 19:2 (1964), pp. 173–97.

Wilkinson, Rupert. *American Tough: The Tough-Guy Tradition and American Character.* Westport, CT: Greenwood Press, 1984.

———. "Connections with Toughness: The Novels of Eugene Burdick," *JAS* 11:2 (1977), pp. 223–40.

Will, George F. "How Reagan Changed America," *Newsweek,* January 9, 1989, pp. 13–7.

Willett, Ralph. "Nativism and Assimilation: The Hollywood Aspect," *JAS* 7:2 (1973), pp. 191–4.

Williams, Brett, editor. *The Politics of Culture.* Washington, DC: Smithsonian Press, 1991.

Williams, Raymond. *Keywords: A Vocabulary of Culture and Society.* Revised Edition. New York: Oxford University Press, 1983.

———. *Marxism and Literature.* New York: Oxford University Press, 1977.

———. *The Sociology of Culture.* New York: Schocken Books, 1982.

———. *Television: Technology and Cultural Form.* New York: Schocken Books, 1975.

Williams, Tony. "American Cinema in the '70s: The Texas Chainsaw Massacre," *Movie* 25 (1978), pp. 12–6.

Williams, W. Churchill. "Red Blood in Fiction," *World's Work* 6:1 (May, 1903), pp. 3694–700.

Williams, Walter L. "United States Indian Policy and the Debate Over Philippine Annexation: Implications for the Origins of American Imperialism," *JAH* 66:4 (1980), pp. 810–31.

Williams, William Appleman. *The Great Evasion: An Essay on the Contemporary Relevance of Karl Marx* . . . Chicago: Quadrangle Books, 1964.

———. *Roots of the Modern American Empire: A Study of the Growth and Shaping of Social Consciousness in a Marketplace Society.* New York: Vintage Books, 1969.

Williamson, Jeffrey G., and Peter Lindert. *American Inequality: A Macroeconomic History.* New York: Academic Press, 1980.

Williamson, Joel. *The Crucible of Race: Black-White Relations in the South Since Emancipation.* New York: Oxford University Press, 1984.

Wills, Garry. "The Politics of Grievance," *NYRB* (July 19, 1990), pp. 3–4.

———. *Reagan's America,* Second Edition. New York: Penguin Books, 1988.

Wilson, Charles R. "Racial Reservations: Indians and Blacks in American Magazines, 1865–1900," *JPC* 10:1 (1976), pp. 70–80.

Wilson, James C. *John Reed for the Masses.* Jefferson, NC: McFarland & Co., 1987.

Wilson, Woodrow. *A Crossroads of Freedom: The 1912 Campaign Speeches of Woodrow Wilson.* Edited by John Wells Davidson. New Haven, CT: Yale University Press, 1956.

———. *A History of the American People.* Five Volumes. New York: Harper and Brothers, 1902.

———. *Mere Literature and Other Essays.* Boston: Houghton Mifflin and Company, 1896.

Wingo, Hal, Joseph Eszterhas, Dale Wittner, John Saar, Tom Flaherty, and Reg Bragonier, with Kent Demaret and Jane Estes, photos by Ronald L. Haeberle, "The Massacre at Mylai," *Life* (December 5, 1969), pp. 36–45.

Wisan, Joseph E. *The Cuban Crisis as Reflected in the New York Press (1895–1898).* New York: Columbia University Press, 1934.

Wise, David. *The Politics of Lying: Government Deception, Secrecy and Power.* New York: Vintage Books, 1973.

Wise, Gene. "Paradigm Dramas in American Studies: A Cultural and Institutional History of the Movement," *AQ* 31:3 (1979), pp. 293–337.

Wister, Owen. *Roosevelt: The Story of a Friendship, 1880–1919.* New York: Macmillan Co. 1930.

———. *The Virginian: A Horseman of the Plains.* Edited by Philip Durham. Boston: Houghton Mifflin Company, 1968.

———. *The West of Owen Wister: Selected Short Stories.* Edited by Robert C. Hough. Lincoln: University of Nebraska, 1972.

Wolf, Eric R. *Peasant Wars of the Twentieth Century.* New York: Harper Torchbooks, 1969.

Wolff, Leon. *Lockout: The Story of the Homestead Strike of 1892.* New York: Harper & Row, 1965.

Woll, Allen L. *The Latin Image in American Film.* Revised Editon. Los Angeles: UCLA Latin American Center Publications, 1980.

Womack, John. *Zapata and the Mexican Revolution.* New York: Alfred A. Knopf, 1969.
Wood, Michael. *America in the Movies, or "Santa Maria It Had Slipped My Mind."* New York: Delta, 1975.
Wood, Robin. *Hollywood from Vietnam to Reagan.* New York: Columbia University Press, 1986.
Woodruff, Charles E. "Some Laws of Racial and Intellectual Development," *Journal of Race Development* 3:2 (1912), pp. 156–75.
Woodward, C. Vann. *Tom Watson: Agrarian Rebel.* London: Oxford University Press, 1963.
———. *The Strange Career of Jim Crow.* New York: Oxford University Press, 1957.
Worster, Donald. "New West, True West: Interpreting the Region's History," *WHQ* 18:2 (1987), pp. 141–56.
———. *Rivers of Empire: Water, Aridity and the Growth of the American West.* New York: Pantheon Books, 1985.
"Wounded Knee and My Lai," *Christian Century* 88, January 20, 1971. p. 59.
Wright, James Edward. *The Politics of Populism: Dissent in Colorado.* New Haven, CT: Yale University Press, 1974.
Wright, Will. *Six-Guns and Society: A Structural Study of the Western.* Berkeley: University of California Press, 1975.
Wu, William F. *The Yellow Peril: Chinese Americans in American Fiction, 1850–1940.* New York: Archon Books, 1982.
Wyman, Walker Demarquis, and Clifton B. Kroeber, editors. *The Frontier in Perspective.* Madison: University of Wisconsin Press, 1957.
Young, Marilyn Blatt. *American Expansionism: The Critical Issues.* Boston: Little, Brown and Company, 1973.
Young, Mary. "The Indian Question Revisited," *Marxist Perspectives* 1:1 (1978), pp. 34–49.
Zamora, Lois Parkinson. *The Apocalyptic Vision in America: Interdisciplinary Essays on Myth and Culture.* Bowling Green, OH: Bowling Green University Popular Press, 1982.
Zelinsky, Wilbur. *The Cultural Geography of the United States.* Englewood Cliffs, NJ: Prentice-Hall, 1973.
———. *Nation Into State: The Shifting Symbolic Foundations of American Nationalism.* Chapel Hill: University of North Carolina Press, 1988.
Zinn, Howard. *The Politics of History.* Boston: Beacon Press, 1970.

Selected Filmography

(Title. Studio, production company. Director. Year released.)

Al Jennings of Oklahoma. Columbia. Ray Nazarro. 1951.
Alamo, The. Batjac. John Wayne. 1960.
Aliens. 20th Century Fox. James Cameron. 1986.
All the Young Men. Columbia. Hall Bartlett. 1960.
American Empire. United Artists. William McGann. 1941.
An American Guerrilla in the Philippines. 20th Century Fox. Fritz Lang. 1950.
Angels with Dirty Faces. Warner Bros. Michael Curtiz. 1938.

Apache. Hecht-Lancaster. Robert Aldrich. 1952.
Apocalypse Now. Paramount. Francis Ford Coppola. 1979.
Appaloosa, The. Universal. Sidney J. Furie. 1966.
Aryan, The. Paramount. W. S. Hart. 1916.
Back to Bataan. RKO. Edward Dmytryk. 1945.
Bad Bascomb. MGM. S. Sylvan Simon. 1946.
Bad Company. Jaffilms. Robert Benton. 1972.
The Bad Man. MGM. Richard Thorpe. 1941.
Badman's Territory. RKO. Tim Whelan. 1946.
Bad Men of Missouri. Warner Bros. Ray Enright. 1941.
Bandido! United Artists. Richard Fleischer. 1956.
Bandolero! 20th Century Fox. Andrew V. McLaglen. 1968.
Baron of Arizona, The. Lippert. Sam Fuller, 1950.
Bataan. Paramount. Tay Garnett. 1943.
Battle Beyond the Stars. New World Pictures. Jimmy T. Murakami. 1980.
Battleground. MGM. William Wellman. 1949.
Beating Back. Thanhouser. Carroll Fleming. 1914.
Belle Starr. 20th Century Fox. Irving Cummings. 1941.
The Best of the Badmen. RKO. William D. Russell. 1951.
Big Trail, The. 20th Century Fox. Raoul Walsh. 1930.
Billy Jack. National Student Film Corp. "T. C. Frank" [Tom Laughlin]. 1971.
Billy the Kid. MGM. David Miller. 1941.
Billy the Kid. MGM. King Vidor. 1930.
Birth of a Nation, The. Epoch Producing Corp. David W. Griffith. 1915.
Bonnie and Clyde. Paramount. Arthur Penn. 1967.
Boss Nigger. Boss Productions. Jack Arnold, 1974.
Brigham Young. 20th Century Fox. Henry Hathaway. 1940.
Broken Arrow. 20th Century Fox. Delmer Daves. 1950.
Buchanan Rides Alone. Scott-Brown. Budd Boetticher. 1958.
Buck and the Preacher. E & R/ Belafonte. Sidney Poitier. 1971.
Bugle Sounds, The. MGM. S. Sylvan Simon. 1941.
Butch Cassidy and the Sundance Kid. TCF/Campanile. George Roy Hill. 1969.
Calamity Jane and Sam Bass. Universal-International. George Sherman. 1949.
Call the Mesquiteers. Republic. John English. 1938.
Cannon for Cordoba. Mirisch. Paul Wendkos. 1970.
Charge at Feather River. Warner Bros. Gordon Douglas. 1953.
Charge of the Light Brigade, The. Warner Bros. Michael Curtiz. 1936.
Cheyenne Autumn. Warner Bros. John Ford. 1964.
Cheyenne Social Club. National General. Gene Kelly. 1970.
Chief Crazy Horse. Universal. George Sherman. 1955.
Chisum. Batjac/Warner Bros. Andrew V. McLaglen. 1970.
Cimarron. RKO. Cecil B. deMille. 1930.
Clive of India. 20th Century Fox. Richard Boleslawski. 1935.
Colorado Territory. Warner Bros. Raoul Walsh. 1949.
Comanche Station. Ranown. Budd Boetticher. 1960.
Comancheros, The. 20th Century Fox. Michael Curtiz. 1961.
Command, The. Warner Bros. David Butler. 1954.

Conquest of Cochise. Columbia. William Castle. 1953.
Conquest of the Planet of the Apes. 20th Century Fox. J. Lee Thompson. 1972.
Coogan's Bluff. Universal. Don Siegel. 1969.
Covered Wagon Days. Republic. George Sherman. 1940.
Covered Wagon, The. Paramount. James Cruze. 1923.
Cowboy Commandos. Monogram. S. Roy Luby. 1943.
Culpeper Cattle Company. 20th Century Fox. Dick Richards. 1972.
Custer of the West. Security. Sidney Salkow. 1968.
Custer's Last Fight. Paramount. Thomas Ince. 1912.
Dances with Wolves. Paramount. Kevin Costner. 1990.
Dark Command, The. Republic. Raoul Walsh. 1940.
Dawn Rider, The. Monogram/Lone Star. Robert M. Bradbury. 1935.
Davy Crockett, King of the Wild Frontier. Buena Vista. Norman Foster. 1955.
Day of the Evil Gun. MGM. Jerry Thorpe. 1968.
Deadly Companions. Pathe-American-Carousel. Sam Peckinpah. 1961.
Death Wish. Paramount/Dino de Laurentiis. Michael Winner. 1974.
Deerhunter, The. Paramount. Michael Cimino. 1978.
Devil's Doorway. MGM. Anthony Mann. 1950.
Dirty Dozen, The. Paramount. Robert Aldrich. 1967.
Dirty Harry. Paramount. Don Siegel. 1971.
Distant Drums. US Pictures/Warner Bros. Raoul Walsh. 1951.
Distant Trumpet, A. Warner Bros. Raoul Walsh. 1964.
Dodge City. Warner Bros. Michael Curtiz. 1939.
Drums Along the Mohawk. 20th Century Fox. John Ford. 1939.
Drums. Paramount. Zoltan Korda. 1938.
Duel at Diablo. United Artists. Ralph Nelson. 1966.
Duel in the Sun. Selznick Releasing. King Vidor. 1946.
Eagle and the Hawk. Paramount. Lewis R. Foster. 1950.
El Cid. Paramount. Anthony Mann. 1961.
Enforcer, The. Warner Bros./Malpaso. James Fargo. 1976.
Exterminator, The. Interstar. James Glickenhaus. 1982.
Fall of the Roman Empire, The. Paramount. Anthony Mann. 1964.
Fastest Gun Alice, The. MGM. Russell Rouse. 1956.
Fifty-five Days at Peking. Paramount. Nicholas Ray. 1962.
First Blood. Carolco. Ted Kotcheff. 1982.
A Fistful of Dollars. Jolly/Constantin/Ocean. Sergio Leone. 1964.
A Fistful of Dynamite. Rafran/San Marco/Miura. Sergio Leone. 1971.
Flaming Star. 20th Century Fox. Don Siegel. 1960.
Fort Apache. RKO. John Ford. 1948.
The French Connection. 20th Century Fox. William Friedkin. 1971.
Fugitive, The. Paramount. John Ford. 1947.
Full Metal Jacket. Paramount. Stanley Kubrick. 1987.
Furies, The. Paramount. Anthony Mann. 1950.
Geronimo. United Artists. Arnold Laven. 1962.
Glory Brigade, The. 20th Century Fox. Robert D. Webb. 1953.
Glory Guys, The. Bristol. Arnold Laven. 1965.
Gone with the Wind. Selznick International. Victor Fleming. 1939.

Grapes of Wrath. Paramount. John Ford. 1940.
Great K & A Train Robbery, The. 20th Century Fox. Lewis Seiler. 1926.
Great Missouri Raid, The. Paramount. Gordon Douglas. 1951.
Great Northfield Minnesota Raid, The. Universal/Robertson Assoc. Philip Kaufman. 1971.
Great Sioux Massacre, The. Paramount. Sidney Salkow. 1965.
Great Train Robbery, The. Edison. Edwin S. Porter. 1903.
Green Berets, The. Batjac. John Wayne. 1968.
Gringo. Tecisa/Jolly. Riccardo Blasco. 1963.
Guadalcanal Diary. 20th Century Fox. Lewis Seiler. 1943.
Gun Glory. MGM. Roy Rowland. 1957.
Gunfight at the O.K. Corral. Paramount. John Sturges. 1957.
Gunfighter, The. 20th Century Fox. Henry King. 1950.
Gunfighters, The. Columbia. George Waggner. 1947.
Gung Ho. Paramount. Ray Enright. 1943.
Gunga Din. RKO. George Stevens. 1939.
Guns for San Sebastian. MGM/Cipra/Ernesto Enriques. Henri Verneuil. 1967.
Guns of the Magnificent Seven. Mirisch. Paul Wendkos. 1968.
Hanging Tree, The. Warner Bros. Delmer Daves. 1959.
Heaven's Gate. Partisan. Michael Cimino. 1980.
Hell's Hinges. Triangle. Charles Swickard. 1915.
High Noon. United Artists. Fred Zinneman. 1952.
High Plains Drifter. Malpaso/Universal. Clint Eastwood. 1972.
High Sierra. Warner Bros. Raoul Walsh. 1941.
Hombre. 20th Century Fox. Martin Ritt. 1966.
Home of the Brave. Stanley Kramer. Mark Robson. 1949.
Hondo. Wayne-Fellows/Warner Bros. John Farrow. 1953.
Hour of the Gun. Mirisch/Kappa. John Sturges. 1967.
How the West Was Won. MGM. Henry Hathaway, John Ford, George Marhsall. 1962.
I Shot Jesse James. Lippert. Samuel Fuller. 1949.
Intolerance. Wark. David W. Griffith. 1916.
Invitation to a Gunfighter. Kramer/Larcos/Hermes. Richard Wilson. 1964.
Iron Horse, The. 20th Century Fox. John Ford and Thomas Ince. 1924.
Jesse James. 20th Century Fox. Henry King. 1939.
Jesse James at Bay. Republic. Joseph Kane. 1941.
Joe Kidd. Malpaso/Universal. John Sturges. 1972.
Juarez. Warner Bros. William Dieterle. 1939.
Kansas Raiders. Universal-International. Ray Enright. 1950.
Kansas Terrors. Republic. George Sherman. 1939.
Khartoum. United Artists/Julian Blaustein. Basil Dearden. 1964.
Kid from Texas, The. Universal-International. Kurt Neumann. 1950.
Lady of the Dugout, The. Shipman. W. S. Van Dyke. 1918.
Lady from Cheyenne. Universal. Frank Lloyd. 1941.
Last Command, The. Republic. Frank Lloyd. 1955.
Last Hunt, The. MGM. Richard Brooks. 1955.

Last Outlaw, The. RKO. Christy Cabanne. 1936.
Last of the Fast Guns. Universal-International. George Sherman. 1958.
Last Outpost, The. Paramount. Lewis R. Foster. 1951.
Law and Order. Universal. Edward Kahn. 1932.
Law and Order. Universal. Nathan Juran. 1953.
Lawless Frontier. Monogram/Lone Star. Robert N. Bradbury. 1934.
Lawless Range, The. Republic. Robert N. Bradbury. 1935.
Left-Handed Gun, The. Warner Bros. Arthur Penn. 1958.
Life of General Villa. Mutual. Raoul Walsh. 1915.
Little Big Horn. Lippert. Charles Marquis Warren. 1951.
Little Big Man. Stockbridge/ Hiller. Arthur Penn. 1970.
Little Caeser. Paramount. Mervyn Leroy. 1930.
Lives of a Bengal Lancer, The. Paramount. Henry Hathaway. 1935.
Long Riders, The. Huka. Walter Hill. 1980.
Lost Patrol, The. Paramount. John Ford. 1934.
Magnificent Seven Ride, The. Mirisch. George McCowan. 1972.
Magnificent Seven, The. UA/Mirisch. John Sturges. 1960.
Magnum Force. Warner Bros./Malpaso. Ted Post. 1973.
Major Dundee. Columbia. Sam Peckinpah. 1965.
Man Called Horse, A. Sanford Howard. Elliot Silverstein. 1970.
Man from Colorado, The. Columbia. Henry Levin. 1948.
Man Who Shot Liberty Valance, The. Ford/Paramount. John Ford. 1962.
Man Without a Star. Universal. King Vidor. 1955.
Matewan. Paramount. John Sayles. 1987.
McLintock! UA/Batjac. Andrew V. McLaglen. 1963.
Meet John Doe. Paramount. Frank Capra. 1941.
Missouri Breaks, The. EK. Arthur Penn. 1976.
Mr. Smith Goes to Washington. Paramount. Frank Capra. 1939.
My Darling Clementine. Fox. John Ford. 1946.
Naked Spur, The. MGM. Anthony Mann. 1953.
New Frontier. Republic. Carl Pierson. 1935.
New Frontier. Republic. George Sherman. 1939.
Night Riders, The. Republic. George Sherman. 1939.
No Name on the Bullet. Universal. Jack Arnold. 1959.
North of 36. Paramount. James Cruze, 1926.
Northwest Passage. MGM. King Vidor. 1940.
Objective Burma. Warner Bros. Raoul Walsh. 1945.
Oklahoma Kid, The. Warner Bros. Lloyd Bacon. 1939.
One-Eyed Jacks. Paramount. Marlon Brando. 1961.
100 Rifles. Fox/Marvin Schwartz. Tom Gries. 1968.
One Minute to Zero. RKO. Tay Garnett. 1951.
Only the Valiant. Warner Bros. Gordon Douglas. 1951.
Orphans of the Storm. United Artists. D. W. Griffith. 1921.
Outland. Warner Bros./Ladd. Peter Hyams. 1981.
Outlaw, The. Howard Hughes. Howard Hughes. 1943.
Outlaw Josie Wales, The. Malpaso. Clint Eastwood. 1976.
Overland Stage Raiders. Republic. George Sherman. 1938.

Pale Rider. Malpaso. Clint Eastwood. 1985.
Pals of the Saddle. Republic. George Sherman. 1938.
Parson and the Outlaw. Charles B. Rogers. Oliver Drake. 1957.
Pat Garrett and Billy the Kid. MGM. Sam Peckinpah. 1973.
Patriot, The. W. S. Hart. 1916.
Phantom Empire, The. Mascot. Otto Brower, B. Reeves Eason. 1935.
Plainsman, The. Paramount. Cecil B. deMille. 1936.
Planet of the Apes. 20th Century Fox/Apjac. Franklin Schaeffer. 1968.
Platoon. Paramount. Oliver Stone. 1986.
Pork Chop Hill. United Artists/Melville/Milestone. Lewis Milestone. 1959.
Professionals, The. Columbia/Pax. Richard Brooks. 1966.
Public Enemy, The. Warner Bros. William Wellman. 1931.
Pursued. Warner Bros. Raoul Walsh. 1947.
Racketeers of the Range. RKO. Ross Lederman. 1939.
Rambo: First Blood, Part II. Anabasis. George P. Cosmatos. 1985.
Real Glory, The. United Artists. Henry Hathaway. 1939.
Rebellion. Crescent. Lynn Shores. 1936.
Red River. Monterey. Howard Hawks. 1948.
Red, White and Black (Soul Soldier). Hirschman-Northern. John Cardos. 1970.
Retreat, Hell! Warner Bros. Joseph S. Lewis. 1952.
Return of a Man Called Horse. Sandy Howard Productions. Irvin Kershner. 1976.
Return of Frank James, The. 20th Century Fox. Fritz Lang. 1940.
Return of the Badmen. RKO. Ray Enright. 1948.
Return of the Seven. UA/Mirisch. Burt Kennedy. 1966.
Ride the High Country. MGM. Sam Peckinpah. 1962.
Riders of the Whistling Skull. Republic. Mack V. Wright. 1937.
Rio Bravo. Armada. Howard Hawks. 1959.
Rio Conchos. 20th Century Fox. Gordon Douglas. 1964.
Rio Grande. Republic. John Ford. 1950.
Roaring Twenties, The. Warner Bros. Raoul Walsh. 1939.
Rocky Mountain. Warner Bros. Raoul Walsh. 1950.
Rovin' Tumbleweeds. Republic. George Sherman. 1939.
Run of the Arrow, The. Globe. Sam Fuller. 1957.
Saddlemates. Republic. Les Orlebeck. 1941.
Sahara. Columbia. Zoltan Korda. 1943.
San Antonio. Warner Bros. David Butler. 1945.
Sands of Iwo Jima. Republic. Allen Dwan. 1949.
Sante Fe Trail. Warner Bros. Michael Curtiz. 1940.
Santiago. Warner Bros. Gordon Douglas. 1956.
Savage, The. Paramount. George Marshall. 1952.
Savage Guns, The. Michael Carreras. 1962.
Sea of Grass, The. MGM. Elia Kazan. 1947.
Searchers, The. Warner Bros. John Ford. 1956.
Seminole. Universal. Budd Boetticher. 1953.
Sergeant Rutledge. Warner Bros. John Ford. 1960.
Sergeant York. Paramount. Howard Hawks. 1941.
Sergeants Three. E-C. John Sturges. 1962.

Seven Men from Now. Batjac/Warner Bros. Budd Boetticher. 1956.
Seven Samurai. Paramount. Akira Kurosawa. 1954.
Shane. Paramount. George Stevens. 1953.
She Wore a Yellow Ribbon. RKO. John Ford. 1949.
Shootist, The. Dino De Laurentiis. Don Siegel. 1976.
Silver River. Warner Bros. Raoul Walsh. 1948.
Silverado. Columbia. Lawrence Kasdan. 1985.
Sitting Bull. United Artists. Sidney Salkow. 1954.
Soldier Blue. Avco-Embassy. Ralph Nelson. 1970.
Soul of Nigger Charley. Paramount. Larry G. Spangler. 1973.
Squaw Man, The. Lasky. Cecil B. deMille. 1914.
Stagecoach. Walter Wanger Productions. John Ford. 1939.
Stalking Moon, The. National General, *et al*. Robert Mulligan. 1968.
Stand Up and Fight. MGM. W. S. Van Dyke. 1939.
Star Trek II: The Wrath of Khan. Paramount. Nicholas Meyer. 1982.
Star Wars. Paramount. George Lucas. 1977.
Steel Helmet, The. Paramount. Sam Fuller. 1951.
Tall T., The. Columbia. Budd Boetticher. 1957.
Taxi Driver. Paramount. Martin Scorsese. 1976.
Taza, Son of Cochise. Universal. Douglas Sirk. 1953.
Tell Them Willie Boy Is Here. Universal. Abraham Polonsky. 1969.
Texas. Columbia. George Marshall. 1941.
Texas Chainsaw Massacre. Vortex. Tobe Hooper. 1974.
Texans, The. Paramount. James Hogan. 1938.
Texas to Bataan. Monogram. Robert Tansey. 1942.
They Came to Cordura. Columbia. Robert Rossen. 1959.
They Died with Their Boots On. Warner Bros. Raoul Walsh. 1941.
They Were Expendable. Paramount. John Ford. 1945.
Three Bad Men. Paramount. John Ford. 1924.
Three Mesquiteers, The. Republic. Joseph Kane. 1936.
A Thunder of Drums. MGM. Joseph M. Newman. 1961.
A Time for Killing. Columbia/Sage Western. Phil Karlson. 1967.
Tin Star, The. Pearlberg-Seaton. Anthony Mann. 1957.
Tonka. Buena Vista. Lewis R. Foster. 1958.
Treasure of Pancho Villa. RKO. George Sherman. 1955.
Treasure of the Sierra Madre, The. Warner Bros. John Huston. 1948.
True Grit. Paramount. Henry Hathaway. 1969.
True Story of Jesse James, The. 20th Century Fox. Nicholas Ray. 1957.
Tumbleweeds. Hart/UA. King Baggot. 1925.
Two Flags West. 20th Century Fox. Robert Wise. 1950.
Two Mules for Sister Sara. Universal/Malpaso. Don Siegel. 1970.
Two Rode Together. Ford-Shpetner/Columbia. John Ford. 1961.
Ulzana's Raid. Universal. Robert Aldrich. 1972.
Undefeated, The. 20th Century Fox. Andrew V. McLaglen. 1969.
Under Western Stars. Republic. Joseph Kane. 1938.
Unforgiven, The. United Artists. John Huston. 1960.
Union Pacific. Paramount. Cecil B. deMille. 1939.

Untouchables, The. Paramount. Brian DePalma. 1968.
Vera Cruz. Hecht-Lancaster. Robert Aldrich. 1954.
Villa Rides. Paramount. Buzz Kulik. 1968.
Villa! 20th Century Fox. James B. Clark. 1958.
Virginia City. Warner Bros. Michael Curtiz. 1940.
Virginian, The. Paramount. Stuart Gilmore. 1946.
Virginian, The. Paramount. Victor Fleming. 1929.
Viva Villa! MGM. Jack Conway. 1935.
Viva Zapata! 20th Century Fox. Elia Kazan. 1952.
Wagonmaster. Argosy/RKO. John Ford. 1950.
Wake Island. Paramount. John Farrow. 1942.
A Walk in the Sun. Paramount. Lewis Milestone. *1946*.
Walk Like a Dragon. Paramount. James Clavell. 1960.
Walk the Proud Land. Universal-International. Jesse Hibbs. 1956.
Wall Street Cowboy. Republic. Joseph Kane. 1939.
Warlock. 20th Century Fox. Edward Dmytryk. 1959.
Wee Willie Winkie. Paramount. John Ford. 1937.
Western Union. 20th Century Fox. Fritz Lang. 1941.
Westerner, The. United Artists. William Wyler. 1940.
When the Daltons Rode. Universal. George Marshall. 1940.
Wild Bunch, The. Warner Bros.. Sam Peckinpah. 1969.
Wild Rovers. Geoffrey. Blake Edwards. 1971.
Winchester 73. Universal. Anthony Mann. 1950.
Wings of the Hawk. Universal-International. Budd Boetticher. 1953.
Wonderful Country, The. DRM. Robert Parrish. 1959.
Wyoming Outlaw. Republic. George Sherman. 1939.
Wyoming. MGM. Richard Thorpe. 1940.
Young Guns. Verston/Morgan Creek. Christopher Cain. 1988.
Young Guns II. 20th Century Fox/Morgan Creek. Geoff Murphy. 1990.
Young Mr. Lincoln. Paramount. John Ford. 1939.
Zulu. Paramount/Diamond. Cy Endfield. 1965.

TV Series

Big Valley, ABC, 1965–9.
Bonanza, NBC, 1959–73.
Branded, NBC, 1965–6.
Broken Arrow, ABC, 1956–60.
Cheyenne, ABC, 1955–63.
Cimarron Strip, CBS, 1967–71.
F Troop, ABC, 1965–7.
Gunsmoke, CBS, 1955–75.
Have Gun, Will Travel, CBS, 1957–63.
Kung Fu, ABC, 1972–75.
Laramie, NBC, 1959–63.
Laredo, NBC, 1965–7.
Law of the Plainsman, NBC, 1959–60, 1962.

Lawman, ABC, 1958–62.
Life and Legend of Wyatt Earp, ABC, 1955–61.
Lone Ranger, ABC, 1959–67.
Lonesome Dove, Miniseries. 1989.
Mackenzies's Raiders, 1958–59.
Maverick, ABC, 1957–62.
Rawhide, CBS, 1959–66.
Rebel, ABC, NBC, 1959–62.
Rifleman, ABC, 1958–63.
Sugarfoot, ABC, 1957–61.
Virginian, NBC, 1962–71.
Wagon Train, NBC-ABC, 1957–65.
Wanted, Dead or Alive, CBS, 1958–61.
Wild, Wild West, CBS, 1965–70.
Young Riders, ABC, 1989–

Index

About the Author

RICHARD SLOTKIN is the Olin Professor of English and Director of American Studies at Wesleyan University, where he has taught since 1966. His books include two novels, *The Return of Henry Starr* (1988) and *The Crater* (1980), as well as two previous books on the frontier to which *Gunfighter Nation* is a sequel—*The Fatal Environment: The Myth of the Frontier in the Age of Industrialization, 1800–1890* (1985) and *Regeneration Through Violence: The Mythology of the American Frontier 1600–1860* (1973), which won the American Historical Society's Albert J. Beveridge Award as the best book on American history in 1973 and was a finalist for the National Book Award. He lives in Middletown, Connecticut.